The Faber Companion
to
Samuel Beckett

The Faber Companion
to
Samuel Beckett

A Reader's Guide
to His Works, Life, and Thought

C. J. Ackerley
and
S. E. Gontarski

faber and faber

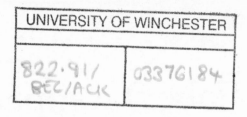
First published in the United States in 2004
by Grove Press, New York

Published in the United Kingdom in 2006
by Faber and Faber Limited
3 Queen Square London WC1N 3AU

Printed in England by Mackays of Chatham plc.

A CIP record for this book
is available from the British Library

ISBN 0–571–22738–4

2 4 6 8 10 9 7 5 3 1

For Marsha, who makes the wheels turn,
And for Wyn, with affection

Contents

Introduction:

Anywhere and Nowhere:
Mapping the Beckett Country

"What I am looking for is nowhere, as far as I can see."
—Belacqua Shuah, *More Pricks Than Kicks*

"Strictly speaking I believe I've never been anywhere."
—"The End"

"You and your landscapes! Tell me about the worms!"
—Estragon, *Waiting for Godot*

"to hell with all this fucking scenery."
—Malone

A paradox lies at the core of Samuel Beckett's creative enterprise. Arguably the pre-eminent avant-garde writing of the post–World War II era, a period we loosely call "postmodern," Beckett's work is equally the culmination of the Romantic agony; he is at once the emblematic deconstructive author and the heir to Kant and Schopenhauer (despite their emphasis on the phenomenal world), if not to Hume. In other words, his celebrated innovation and his assault on literary convention are themselves rooted in discernible literary and cultural traditions, as much pre- as postmodern, his sensibility reaching back to the classical—that classicism leavened by both late Romanticism and post-humanism. His celebrated aporia finally may be as rooted in pre-Socratic as in poststructuralist thought.

One useful starting point for reading Beckett, then, may be Beckett's own reading, particularly those works he read as he struggled to invent himself as a writer, among them: William Inge's *Christian Mysticism* (1899); John Burnet's *Early Greek Philosophy* (1892) and *Greek Philosophy* (1914); Robert Burton's *The Anatomy of Melancholy* (1621); Mario Praz's *The Romantic Agony* (1930); and Wilhelm Windelband's *A History of Philosophy* (1892 and 1900). The ghostly, disembodied, externalized voices of Beckett's late fiction and drama, arguably his most profound literary creations, derive initially if not primarily from the myth of Echo and Narcissus. (The electronic projection of the disembodied voice developed by Marconi and the internal discourse of fragmented Jungian or Lacanian ego thus are afterthoughts.) His ontology, a sense of discontinuous being or lack of fixity of any sort, owes as much to the contretemps between Heraclitus and Parmenides as it does to post-Freudian psychoanalysis. Heraclitus's emphasis on a world of becoming, a liminal world in perpetual transition, reverberates through Beckett's work where to utter "now" is always late, an afterthought, consciousness itself always belated. To utter "I," then, is inescapably retrospective, a corrupt distortion of memory, nostalgia for a present moment, as Kant suggested, always inaccessible to empirical consciousness. Moreover, while the cultural dislocation, alienation, and the dehumanization of the Shoah that blight the twentieth century dominate his art, it retains a remarkable if surprising coherence, his works forming part of a continuous series, if not a pattern.

As early as 14 May 1947, for example, in the midst of an explosive creative period he called "the siege in the room," Beckett detailed that continuity to friend and sometime literary agent George Reavey. Of *Watt* in particular he confessed, "It has its place in the series, as will perhaps appear in time"; and on 8 July 1948 he elaborated on that design: "I am now typing, for rejection by the publishers, *Malone meurt*, the last I hope of the series *Murphy, Watt, Mercier & Camier, Molloy,* not to mention the *4 Nouvelles & Eleutheria*" (Lake, 53). *Malone meurt* was, of course, not the end, the series (progressive or regressive) merely slowed by the author's corporeal demise in December of 1989, Beckett apparently still publishing from *au delà: Dream of Fair to Middling Women* in 1992, *Eleutheria* in 1995, as well as a series of notebooks and letters, all of which begin to constitute something like a gray canon of his work.

Throughout that series his creatures peopled what critics began to recognize as a distinct terrain, the Beckett country. It is a premodern world where bicycles outnumber motorcars, where theaters are lit by footlights, where clothes are fastened by buttonhooks, where parents still pass on family greatcoats and bowler hats to their offspring, hats tethered to coats[1]—a world of chamber pots, which put humanity in greater proximity to evacuation, and oil lamps. Beckett's roots reside firmly in turn-of-the-century turf, amid the Anglo-Irish bourgeoisie. It is a propertied world, where possession assured not only propriety but existence as well, a world whose dictum may have been, "I own, therefore I am." The residue of that tradition remains traceable in Beckett's work, the Ascendancy Big House having become Gothic in *Watt* and *Footfalls*. Beckett's creatures retain a curious, antibourgeois relationship to possessions or property, of course. They simultaneously seem obsessed by and strangely negligent of them or it.

Beckett's critique of that tradition includes the treatment of the body as possession, property about which his characters are often as careless as they are about their other chattels. As in much eighteenth- or nineteenth-century fiction, Beckett's characters are often expelled from a world of consequence, and thus become inconsequential. Beckett played with that materialist tradition, like Mr. Kelley and his kite, to the point of immateriality, his characters dispossessed of their property and the

---

[1] And so Beckett's characters are often "attached" to their hats.

ownership of their bodies, hence the emergence of ghostlike, neo-Gothic figures like May in *Footfalls* and her unnamed echo in *Ill Seen Ill Said*. The issues of property, of possession and dispossession, thus shift to the subjectivity of being. If one is de-fined by one's things, Beckett's characters slip or are pushed into a world of no thing, an immaterial world where even language, one's narrative voice, or its physical manifestation in writing, are beyond possession.

Beckett finally rejected bourgeois Dublin for bohemian Paris, there champion-ing the antifigurative painting of intimates like the brothers van Velde, Bram and Geer. His own art, however, reflects less such priestly moderns than figurative painters who might have been perfectly acceptable to Dublin's Anglo-Irish Ascendancy: Rembrandt, Caravaggio, and, perhaps most important, the German Romantic Caspar David Friedrich, one version of whose *Two Men Contemplating the Moon* (or its corollary *A Walk at Dusk*, with its megalithic stone tomb juxtaposed to the moon[2]) is echoed in the visual imagery of *Waiting for Godot*. *Krapp's Last Tape* may in turn take its visual cue from Rembrandt's *The Parable of the Rich Man* or *The Money Changer* of 1627, which Beckett saw, as noted in his Berlin diaries of 1936–37, in the Kaiser-Wilhelm-Friedrich Museum in Berlin in 1937.[3] He had been mulling such spotlight effects as dominate *Krapp's Last Tape* and the late plays as early as 1932 when he bought, on Thomas MacGreevy's advice, a copy of R. H. Wilenski's *An Introduction to Dutch Art* (1929). Of particular note for Beckett was Wilenski's discussion of "the Caravaggio-Honthorst tradition" of spotlight effects, particularly in the painting of Gerrit van Honthorst, dubbed "Gherardo delle notti," whose candlelight studies such as *Boy Singing by Candlelight* or *Girl Catching a Flea in Her Nightdress* are in the Doria Gallery in Rome.

In 1935 Beckett was discussing the technique with MacGreevy: "The Geertgen *Adoration* must be one of the earliest spotlight paintings. Surely it is only half the story to date them from Raphael's *Liberation of Saint Peter*. I never saw the Ox-ford Uccello mentioned in this connection either" (letter to MacGreevy, 20 Feb-ruary 1935). Beckett's spotlight theater, like the disembodied, suspended lips in *Not I*, owes less to radical surrealist iconography like Man Ray's dreamscape *A l'heure de l'observatoire—les amoureaux,* with its liberated flying lips, or the gro-tesque, divan-sized lips of Salvador Dali's *Mae West Lips Sofa* than to the Renais-sance imagery of Caravaggio's *Decollation of John the Baptist*. Beckett saw the paint-ing at La Valletta Cathedral while vacationing on Malta in October of 1971. "The

---

[2] In these haunting nocturnal landscapes, the moon elicits the promise of Christ's rebirth. In *Godot* the tramps' gazing at the rising moon is played against the moribund imagery of the tree associated as much with the crucifixion as with the Garden of Eden. But that finally is more Friedrich than it is Beckett.

[3] Beckett biographer James Knowlson offers the following entry from volume three of the German diaries, dated 5 January 1937: "Interesting very early *Geldwechster* (1627), apparently influenced by Honthorst. One aspect of Rembrandt is nothing but a development of Honthorst."

idea of having only a mouth on stage," notes Anne Atik, wife of painter Avigdor Arikha, in her memoir of Beckett's last years, "preceded his trip to Malta, but once there, Sam was deeply impressed by the dichotomy in the composition of the Caravaggio: the decapitated figure on the left and the curious but indifferent on-lookers on the right" (Atik, 4). James Knowlson has observed that the position of the ghostly May's arms in *Footfalls* may echo Antonello da Messina's *Virgin of the Annunciation*, which Beckett saw at the Alte Pinakothek in Munich (Knowlson, 552), and Arikha finds echoes of Gerard Terborch's *Four Spanish Monks*, with its black hat on a table, a painting that Beckett knew from the National Gallery of Ireland, in "Ohio Impromptu" (Atik, 6). Musically, while Murphy's heart may have been "Buttoned up and left to perform [. . .] like Petrouchka in his box," composers of note for Beckett were not the likes of Stravinsky but the German Romantics, Beethoven and Schubert. Maddy Rooney hears Schubert's String Quartet #14 in D minor, *Der Tod und das Mädchen* (*Death and the Maiden*), at the opening of his soundscape—a work that challenges the tyranny of the eye in art—the radio play *All That Fall*, and it was Schubert's final song cycle of 1828, *Winterreise*, that Beckett used to shape his own theatrical *Schwanengesang*, "What Where."

The humanist idea of authorship that Beckett both epitomized and felt impris-oned by was central to his creative makeup. He was among the last of the twentieth century's major authors thoroughly immersed in canonical European literature, and his memory was nearly eidetic. His was an elite, Ascendancy, Anglo-Irish education that even Joyce envied, and one that he continued as an autodidact. He had at his ready command, even in his later years, not only all of Shakespeare, Dante, Milton, Petrarch, the King James Bible (not to mention the *Book of Common Prayer*), and much of English and German Romantic poetry (Goethe, Heine, and Hölderlin, in particular), but Sterne, Defoe, Flaubert, and Yeats, as well as Dr. Johnson and his commentators (he owned *The Poetical Works of Samuel Johnson*, 1785, a 1799 edition of the *Dictionary*, and the six-volume Birbeck Hill edition of Boswell's *Life of Samuel Johnson*). He could quote easily from Burton's *The Anatomy of Melan-choly* (his a three-volume edition) and St Augustine's *Confessions*. He owned a com-pact OED, which he consulted regularly, and Anne Atik recalls his defense of arcane or obsolete language like "wearish" in *Krapp's Last Tape;* "feat" in *Footfalls;* "haught" in "What Where" and *Ill Seen Ill Said* (Atik, 25, 56); and "strangurie" in *Ill Seen Ill Said*. Such words, like his characters themselves, become cultural ghosts, the language rupturing the present to disclose the space of cultural memory. Beckett's allusions in general, fragmentary and submerged in the later work, function thus, as cultural traces. In 1960 he was "learning Matthias Claudius by heart! 'Friend Death'" (Atik, 65; her translation). Schubert had adapted Matthias Claudius for his lied *Der Tod und das Mädchen*, a song that features a young girl frightened by a ghost, the shadow of death. That ghost haunted Beckett's own 1969 (and so subse-quent) staging of *Krapp's Last Tape* as the wearish Krapp periodically senses the haunt-ing *Hain* behind him.

The richness of his education may finally have burdened Beckett as the European *eidos* permeated his being and haunted his consciousness to the point that much of his early work might be seen as pastiche. Beckett seemed to be working through what Roland Barthes in his seminal essay "The Death of the Author" described as "tissues of quotations drawn from the innumerable centers of culture." The more we know about those "centers of culture" on which Beckett drew, the more fully we understand Beckett's technique—much of which developed through what Knowlson has called a "grafting technique"—and, moreover, the more direct resemblance we find to methods of composition employed by Beckett's fellow Dubliner James Joyce.

> Joyce took particular care with his research, reading books primarily for what they could offer him for his own writing. (Indeed many people who knew him, including Beckett, have claimed he read almost exclusively for this purpose.) Though he was inspired more by disinterested intellectual and scholarly curiosity than Joyce was, Beckett's notebooks show that he too plundered the books he was reading or studying for material that he would then incorporate into his own writing. Beckett copied out striking, memorable or witty sentences or phrases into his notebooks. Such quotations or near quotations were then woven into the dense fabric of his early prose. It is what could be called a grafting technique, and at times it almost runs wild. He even checked off the quotations in his private notebooks once they had been incorporated into his own work. (Knowlson, 109)

One plausible explanation for Beckett's linguistic flight from English to French was his desire to evade those "centers of culture," to write, as he said only half jokingly about this change, without style.[4] His was an education with which he struggled during his early years in Paris, simultaneously admiring what Joyce did with his but uncomfortable about it for his own work, shunning the implications of mastery. After the Second World War Beckett would jettison the virtuosity of modernism (along with the English language, for a time), banish its blandishments, shun literariness for a linguistic literalness often confounding in its simplicity. Yet his work remained extraordinarily allusive and intertextual, his referentiality becoming less overt, less showy in the later work.[5] Even as he struggled to free himself from what he called, in his 1934 poem "Gnome," "the loutishness of learning," he could still in 1968 dictate to Anne Atik from memory long passages from Boccaccio's lectures on

---

[4] "They have no style, they write without style, do they not, they give you the phrase, the sparkle, the precious margaret. Perhaps only the French can do it. Perhaps only the French language can give you the thing you want" (*Dream of Fair to middling Women*, 48).

[5] In *Ill Seen Ill Said*, for instance, the allusions are mere hints as that to Malebranche's "L'imagination c'est la folle du logis" ("Imagination at wit's end spreads its sad wings," 56) or to Shakespeare's *King Lear*, "[Out,] vile jelly" (81).

Dante, particularly those on the allegory of the peacock (Atik, 79–81). Education for Beckett remained the sticky paper he could not quite shake from his boot. Yet too few critics have focused on the scope of Beckett's canonical immersion, his borrowings, his allusiveness, his *debt* to an intellectual tradition he was simultaneously struggling to dismantle. He retained a curious nostalgia for that tradition, his idea of authorship and the literary life shaped as much by Samuel Johnson as by his early mentor Joyce.

While a distinct Beckett country is discernible, its lineaments are not always discrete, and as a result few maps chart its terrain. A comprehensive cartography, its atlas, say, remains to be written—one that includes his life (since it impinged so dramatically, if obliquely, on his art), his reading (since it has informed his art incalculably), his thought, for want of a better word (since despite protests to the contrary his art is imbued with and informed by the philosophical, ontological, linguistic, and cognitive cruxes of his and earlier ages). Like Thomas Hardy and the southwest counties he called "Wessex," or like Graham Greene and his "Greeneland," or even William Faulkner and his Yoknapatawpha County (writers with whom he shares little else), Beckett has shaped a recognizable country. Hardy, Greene, and Faulkner provided their own atlases. Yoknapatawpha County, for instance, encompasses 2,400 square miles of territory with distinct boundaries and a frozen population: 6,298 whites and 9,313 "Negroes."

Moran associates the Beckett country with his shadow or alter ego, its boundaries, indistinct as they are, seemingly inviolable: "By the Molloy Country I mean that narrow region whose administrative limits he has never crossed and presumably never would" (*Three Novels,* 133). Such may be the territory finally of the self (so called), to which Moran and the host of omnidolent moribunds who inhabit the Beckett country are also bound. Beckett played the cartographer briefly with an exceptional novel, *The Lost Ones,* mapping a corner of that frozen world: 205 creatures inhabiting an issueless cylinder sixteen meters high, with a total surface area of 12 million square centimeters. But *The Lost Ones* charts its macrocosm, the phenomenal world; it is a mural image, finally, an outline for the late closed space fictions.

The Beckett landscape is finally more amorphous, more porous, more mutable, and considerably less populated than Wessex, Greeneland, or Yoknapatawpha County. It is, as he put it in his French poem of 1947, "bon bon il est un pays," "un pays sans traces," a pathless, borderless land associated more with mental than phenomenal terrain. It is a seeming land, never quite present to us—the land a specter, its population ghosts. As the French title for *The Lost Ones* suggests, this is a depopulated or de-peopled land. Even Beckett's celebrated Ireland is an impression, a dreamscape without presence, a land without soil, say, just as the book, the page, or the stage are always only images, as witness the late masterwork *Ill Seen Ill Said.* And so the Beckett country may finally be more simulated than geographically discrete, simultaneously anywhere and nowhere, marked by what Jean Baudrillard calls "hyperreality," where signifiers obliterate signifieds and language becomes less external than self-referential. This, then, is what we tend to call the postmodern Beckett, his world one in which models, codes, myths, words themselves float free, having lost touch with or broken from their origins, foundations, and points of reference. In Baudrillard's splendid inversion of causality, "It is the map which precedes the territory. [. . .] It is the map that engenders the territory."[6]

Eoin O'Brien has come as close as anyone to mapping the physical terrain of Beckett's Ireland, but the territorial, geographical limit is at once the strength and weakness of his monumental achievement, *The Beckett Country* (1986). It stops short of showing us how Ireland is absent or disappears from Beckett's work, how it exists as an afterthought, an aura, which is a specter with its subject gone. Despite his Irish roots and recent attempts of countrymen to recolonize him, Beckett was a consummate European, more comfortable in the intellectual milieu of Europe than that of his native "prosodoturfy." Much of the psychological landscape has been meticulously detailed by James Knowlson in his incomparable *Damned to Fame: The Life of Samuel Beckett* (1996), which fully takes the measure of the man and opened innumerable avenues of investigation for subsequent scholars. Most immediately, the biography has provided the impetus for books like John Pilling's edition of *Beckett's Dream Notebook* (1999) and his subsequent annotations to the novel in *A Companion to Dream of Fair to Middling Women* (2004), and for C. J. Ackerley's *Demented Particulars: The Annotated Murphy* (1998). J. D. O'Hara has obsessively detailed Beckett's own obsessive use of sources in *Samuel Beckett's Hidden Drives: Structural Uses of Depth Psychology* (1997). More recently Ruby Cohn has again taken us on a personal exploratory voyage through *A Beckett Canon* (2001), covering in detail the work in sequence, published and not, uncovering further interconnections and so the continuity of the whole. *The Grove Companion* builds on these works (among others) in its attempt to chart the spectral territory more fully, to plot the crossroads, byways, and lanes of Beckett's intellectual landscape. Much of that imagined terrain comprises canonical European literature and the discourse surrounding it. Dante, Shakespeare, Dr. Johnson are finally as integral to the Beckett country as are the Dublin mountains. The complexity of the Beckett country may doom all mapping expeditions to failure, a result Beckett himself flaunted in his work and taught us all to accept in our own enterprises. The best one can hope for is a rigorous attenuation, like that found in the fragmentary late works where completeness remains beyond possibility, absence of ending (hence of conclusion) evident in the works from *Godot* onward and signaled more directly in the radio plays "Embers," "Words and Music," and "Cascando"—each of which Beckett called a *piece* for radio—the Roughs for *Radio I* and *II* and for *Theatre I* and *II, From an Abandoned Work*, "A *Piece* of Monologue," and, of course, the *Fizzles*, among others.

---

[6] Jean Baudrillard, *The Infinite Conversation*, trans. by Susan Hanson (Minneapolis: University of Minnesota Press, 1993), 2.

The overall purpose of *The Grove Companion* is, nonetheless, to guide serious readers through the Beckett terrain. Its range of entries is designed to allow a reader to check on a word, allusion, or idea in the midst of reading, or to pause and contemplate in the longer, essay-length entries more complicated philosophical cruxes and historical oddities that Beckett cites and explores, or to wonder at the extent of his references to the Bible and Dante, to music and the visual arts. Many of the issues detailed herein extend far beyond Beckett's work per se. The aim is to situate it (and him) within a tradition that spans classical to modernist ages. More broadly and more boldly our aim is to alter the way Beckett is read, or reread, to suggest that Beckett's work is not the exclusive domain of students and scholars as we comment on, even as we often cannot completely resolve, some of the central cruxes, correspondences, and allusions that dominate his thought and so his art. These are often issues of broad intellectual, cultural resonance. Writing for Beckett was always a haunting echo of memory, personal and cultural. Learning to read Beckett, again, is to approach him as already a repetition, an echo of his reading, of his culture, and finally of himself. Reading, as we see in the late masterpiece *Ill Seen Ill Said,* is itself an aftereffect, a repetition that is never the same, a version of eternal return that Joyce called in *Finnegans Wake* "The seim anew" (215). We hope that the arrangement of material makes the volume browseable as well and that such browsing leads the reader continually back to Beckett in a series of loops that will always remain "The seim anew."

S.E.G.

C.J.A.

Acknowledgments

The list of scholarly debts the authors have incurred during this project is almost incalculable. To list them all would add sufficient weight to this volume to topple it. Those scholars on whose shoulders we stand are, for the most part, enumerated in the Bibliography, but a few in particular have read portions of the manuscript and offered suggestions and corrections and so merit individual mention. The indefatigable Ruby Cohn has read through the whole of an early draft, and her corrections and suggestions were, as always, pointed, useful, and sobering. J. D. O'Hara brought his razor-sharp eye and matching wit to bear on several key entries, and one is always the better for his scrutiny, painful as it often is. We have on occasion availed ourselves of a number of younger scholars with particular specialties to complement our own. Clare Beach wrote the piece on "law"; Dr. Julian Garforth contributed entries on "Germany," the "Schiller-Theater Werkstatt," "Elmar and Erika Tophoven," and "Suhrkamp." Damian Love has written the entries on "father," "Freud," "Jung," "psychoanalysis," "schizophrenia," and "symbolism"; Lisa Marr has been indefatigable in checking citations but also contributed two small notes; Paul Sheehan wrote on "existentialism," "humanism," and "zoomorphism"; and Paul Shields on "pseudocouples." Dr. Daniela Casselli provided essential material for entries on "Dante," "'Dante and the Lobster,'" and "'Dante . . . Bruno . Vico . . Joyce'"; and Michael Rodriguez has wittily drafted the first version of the Beckett chronology. These contributors are gratefully acknowledged here and by the citation of their initials at the end of their entries.

A Beckett Chronology

"And I am perhaps confusing several different occasions, and different times, deep down, and deep down is my dwelling, oh not deepest down, somewhere between the mud and the scum."

—Molloy

1902: Mary Roe "May" Beckett (1871–1950) gives birth to her first son, Frank Edward Beckett, in Cooldrinagh on July 26, some two months after the parents moved into their new Foxrock home.

1906: May gives birth to her second son, Samuel Barclay Beckett (SB), also at home in Cooldrinagh on April 13, Good Friday. The official birth certificate, however, lists May 13 as the date of birth, an error that has confused more than one of SB's early biographers.

1911–1915: SB attends a small, private kindergarten school run by two German sisters, Misses Ida and Pauline Elsner, in Leopardstown. Shortly thereafter the Beckett brothers leave the Misses Elsners' academy to attend a larger school called Earlsfort House in Dublin, not far from the Harcourt Street Station.

1916: Between April 24 and 29, the Easter Rising occurs in Dublin, an abortive (though profoundly momentous) attempt by the Irish Volunteers and the Irish Citizen Army to establish the Provisional Government of the Irish Republic. The Becketts are safely sequestered from any violence in the affluent, Protestant village of Foxrock, but the "Troubles" continue as the Anglo-Irish war (1919–21) is followed by the Irish civil war (1922–23). SB's father takes his sons, Frank and Samuel, to a hilltop where they can see the fires in neighboring Dublin. The image will stay with SB his entire life.

1920: Begins attending Portora Royal School, as did Oscar Wilde, in Enniskillen in the northern county of Fermanagh. For the 1921 school year SB discovered that he now attended school in a foreign country, Northern Ireland, U.K.

1923: Enters Trinity College, Dublin (TCD), as an undergraduate to study for an arts degree. Soon meets Thomas Rudmose-Brown, professor of modern languages, who is to have a lasting impact on SB, perhaps most notably developing SB's interest in contemporary French literature and by encouraging him to write creatively. SB would satirize his mentor as the Polar Bear in his first extended piece of fiction, *Dream of Fair to middling Women,* a novel he struggled with from 1931–32, offered to a series of publishers unsuccessfully, and then suppressed until his death. It was finally published in 1992. A second important lecturer is Bianca Esposito, who (along with Walter Starkie) teaches him Italian and inaugurates his lifelong passion for Dante. He would take private lessons from Signorina Esposito as well. Those lessons at 21 Ely Place were then caricatured in the short story "Dante and the Lobster." SB retained lifelong affection for Dante, however, evident by the fact that his student copy of *The Divine Comedy* would be at his bedside as he died in December of 1989. Soon after he arrives at TCD, SB falls in love, for the first time, with Ethna MacCarthy, a charming, experienced, mature young woman who inspires two of his poems, "Alba" and "Yoke of Liberty," appears as a fleeting reference in "Sanies I," and then more fully as the Alba in *Dream of Fair to middling Women.* The affection seems to have been one-sided, however, and she would eventually marry SB's friend A. J. "Con" Leventhal. Her death in 1959 increased the already close bond between SB and Leventhal.

1925–1926: Sees W. B. Yeats's versions of Sophocles's *Oedipus the King* and *Oedipus at Colonus* at the Abbey Theatre. Toward the end of 1926, insomnia, night sweats, and feelings of panic begin to afflict him. In August of 1926, he visits France for the first time, taking a bicycle tour of the châteaux of the Loire Valley, to improve his spoken French. On his return to Ireland he moves into rooms at 39 New Square in TCD. At the end of 1926, Alfred Péron arrives from Paris as the new exchange *lecteur.* Péron and SB's friendship lasts throughout the '30s and would have major significance during World War II.

1927: With an American friend, Charles Clarke, he tours Florence and Venice to improve his spoken Italian. While there he tours museums and galleries, studying artistic masterpieces that will resurface in much of his subsequent writing. At Trinity he completes his examinations, places first in his class, and receives his BA in modern languages (French and Italian).

1928: Wins a research prize (either £50 or £100) from TCD for his essay on "Unanimisme." Through the good offices of his mentor Rudmose-Brown he obtains a teaching post in French and English at Campbell College, Belfast, a residential public school, while he waits to take up his exchange lectureship as *Lecteur d'Anglais* at École Normale Supérieure in Paris. Teaches for two terms in Belfast and dislikes the experience, finding it difficult to teach elementary material and getting up in time for his first lesson. Returns to Dublin in the summer and meets his cousin Peggy Sinclair, who will appear as the Smeraldina-Rima in *Dream of Fair to middling Women.* Her fictional treatment is, to say the least, unsympathetic. In October, despite heated parental opposition, he visits Peggy in Kassel, Germany. Leaves Kassel at the end of October and arrives in Paris on the last day of the month to take up his teaching post at École Normale. Meets his predecessor Thomas MacGreevy, who becomes a lifelong confidant and who introduces him to influential writers and publishers living in Paris—James Joyce, Eugene Jolas, and Sylvia Beach, among them. Although he is not enthusiastic about a scholarly career, his immersion in the Parisian literary circle has profound artistic import. He returns to Kassel for the Christmas holiday, and much of that stay is parodied in *Dream of Fair to middling Women.*

1929: Meets Suzanne Deschevaux-Demesnil at a private tennis club; he will eventually marry her in 1961. SB publishes his first critical essay, "Dante . . . Bruno . Vico . . Joyce," in *transition* magazine, together with his first piece of fiction, "Assumption." Makes many trips to Kassel throughout the year to visit Peggy (and her family).

1930: Publishes his first separate work, the long poem *Whoroscope,* which he writes in several hours on June 15 for a contest, on the subject of time, sponsored by Richard Aldington and Nancy Cunard, which prize he wins. Begins to translate the "Anna Livia Plurabelle" section of Joyce's *Work in Progress* (later to become *Finnegans Wake*) with Alfred Péron. Under a commission arranged by Thomas MacGreevy, he begins to write the monograph *Proust,* which is heavily reliant on his deep reading of Schopenhauer; delivers completed monograph to Chatto and Windus toward the end of September on his way home to Dublin (via London) to take up his appointment as Lecturer in French at TCD. Meets Jack B. Yeats (in November), an artist who exercises considerable influence on him. SB eventually purchases a painting called *Morning,* which hangs over his Paris desk for most of his life.

1931: Reluctantly plays a part in three performances of *Le Kid* at the Peacock Theatre, February 19–21, SB's only known acting part. Has a falling out with his mother and grows increasingly dissatisfied with his teaching post at TCD. Visits France with his brother, Frank. Translates numerous pieces for the surrealist number of *This Quarter.* In September becomes engrossed in Victor Bérard's French translation of Homer's *Odyssey.* In late autumn writes "Enueg I." Regularly visits the National Gallery of Ireland. Decides to resign his post at TCD, though the execution of this decision comes the following year in a letter from Kassel, Germany.

1932: Moves to Paris, resumes friendship with Joyce in the first few weeks, and completes his first novel, *Dream of Fair to middling Women.* Writes "Serena I" after returning to Dublin at the end of August.

1933: Learns that Peggy Sinclair has died of tuberculosis on May 3. Father dies on June 26 of a heart attack, which death devastates (and haunts) SB. Finds out on September 25 that Charles Prentice accepted his collection of stories (several of which are recast versions of episodes from *Dream of Fair to middling Women*) called *More Pricks Than Kicks* (*MPTK*). Writes the story "Echo's Bones" as an end piece for the short story collection, but Chatto and Windus rejects it, and it remains unpublished. Commences intensive psychotherapy in London at the Tavistock Clinic after Christmas to manage his deepening depression. Translates numerous pieces for Nancy Cunard's *Negro Anthology*, which is published in 1934.

1934: Publishes "A Case in a Thousand" in the *Bookman* in August, which reflects his immersion in psychotherapy. *MPTK* is published in London on May 24. Writes the four-line poem "Gnome" and an enthusiastic review of MacGreevy's *Poems* for *Dublin Magazine*.

1935: Attends Carl G. Jung's third lecture at the Tavistock Clinic with his analyst, Wilfred Bion, in October, an experience that resurfaces most overtly in *All That Fall* (written twenty-one years later) and *Footfalls* (written more than forty years later). Begins writing *Murphy* on August 20, which makes extensive use of his detailed knowledge of London's geographical terrain. A collection of thirteen poems is published in December, *Echo's Bones and Other Precipitates*. He terminates psychotherapy.

1936-7: Returns to Dublin to complete *Murphy*. Briefly considers going to Moscow to the State Institute of Cinematography, writing to Sergy Eisenstein about the possibility of becoming his pupil, but this comes to nothing. Writes the poem "Cascando" in July. Leaves the family home, Cooldrinagh, on September 28 and travels around Germany, keeping a detailed diary of his excursions. Returns to Cooldrinagh. "Boss" Sinclair dies on May 4. SB's brother marries on August 24. SB leaves Dublin in the middle of October for Paris, which is to be his permanent home for the next fifty-three years.

1937: First significant attempt to write a play, which is based on the last years in the life of Dr. Samuel Johnson and is called *Human Wishes*. Returns to Dublin to give evidence at a trial against Oliver St. John Gogarty's book *As I Was Going Down Sackville Street*, the action brought by Harry "Boss" Sinclair, before his death, for accusations of slander. Following his testimony, during which he is thoroughly humiliated, SB returns to Paris.

1938: After dining with friends on January 7, SB is stabbed by a beggar and pimp named Prudent. Recovers in Hôpital Broussais, where he corrects proofs to *Murphy* and is visited by Suzanne, who not long thereafter begins to live with him. *Murphy* is finally published, after forty-two rejections, in March. SB starts to write poetry in French, which allows him to begin purging his writing of unnecessary superfluities.

1939: Hitler invades Poland on September 1; two days later Chamberlain announces that Britain is at war with Germany (as is France by this time). SB is caught in Dublin visiting his mother but immediately returns to Paris, famously declaring his preference for France at war to Ireland at peace. Joyce's *Finnegans Wake* is published.

1940: France crumbles under the Nazi assault in June.

1941: In February SB begins to write *Watt* in Paris. On September 1 joins the French Resistance cell called "Gloria SMH," primarily an information network, a decidedly dangerous enterprise despite SB's subsequently dismissive attitude regarding the experience. Joyce dies in Zürich in January.

1942: Alfred Péron is arrested. SB and Suzanne escape a close encounter with the Gestapo and find refuge on October 6 in the south of France in a small village called Roussillon.

1943: Continues on March 1 to write *Watt*, primarily to ward off ennui.

1944: Finishes manuscript of *Watt* on December 28.

1945: SB and Suzanne leave Roussillon for Paris early in the year, and SB immediately returns to Dublin to visit his mother only to learn that she suffers from Parkinson's disease. SB joins the Irish Red Cross as a translator and quartermaster in order to return to France and is posted at Saint-Lô, Normandy. Péron dies on May 1. SB returns to Paris toward the end of the year when his contract comes to an end. He is awarded the Croix de Guerre for his role in the Resistance.

1946: In Paris writes a short story titled "Suite," later called "La Fin," which is his first extended prose work in French. Begins writing his first novel in French, *Mercier et Camier,* on July 5, and completes it on October 3. In the final months of 1946, writes three more stories in French: "L'Expulsé," "Premier amour," and "Le Calmant."

1947: Writes first full-length play, in French, *Eleutheria*. Begins writing *Molloy* on May 2 at New Place in Foxrock. Between this date and January of 1950, completes *Molloy, Malone meurt* (begun on November 27), and *L'Innommable* (begun on March 29, 1949) in what amounts to SB's most creatively fertile period.

1948–1949: *En attendant Godot* is written between October of 1948 and January of 1949, between the writing of *Malone meurt* and *L'Innommable,* in order to break through an artistic impasse.

1950: May Beckett dies on August 25 and is buried with her husband in the Protestant cemetery at Redford. Signs an exclusive contract with Les Éditions de Minuit, which will be the publisher for his French work for the remainder of his life. Its publisher, Jérôme Lindon, will become a lifelong friend.

1951: *Molloy* is published in March, *Malone meurt* in October. The manuscript of *Textes pour rien* is completed in December.

1952: Builds a house, with money his mother left him, near the village of Ussy-sur-Marne, a place of refuge and solitude that soon facilitates SB's creative energies. *Godot* is published in October. *Eleutheria* is announced for publication and then withdrawn at the last moment.

1953: Roger Blin directs the premiere of *Godot* on January 3 at the Théâtre de Babylon. The show receives mixed but generally sympathetic reviews. *Watt* is finally published in English but in Paris. Fledgling American publishing house Grove Press becomes SB's exclusive American publisher, and its publisher, Barney Rosset, becomes a lifelong friend. SB begins to translate *Godot* into English for his American publisher. His international reputation is considerably advanced by his American publisher's willingness to promote so apparently uncommercial a writer.

1954: Learns that Frank is diagnosed with terminal lung cancer. SB, devastated, rushes to his aid in Killiney. Frank dies on September 13. SB writes first draft of what becomes *Fin de partie,* this early version with only two characters.

1955: The English edition of *Molloy* is published in March by Grove Press. *Waiting for Godot* opens in London and Dublin. Finishes first draft of *Fin de partie* in the summer. *Nouvelles et textes pour rien* is published in November. "Getting known."

1956: The American production of *Godot* opens on January 3 at the Coconut Grove Playhouse in Miami under the direction of Alan Schneider. The production is badly received. During the summer, SB writes *All That Fall* at the BBC's request; this radio play is clearly saturated with memories of his Foxrock upbringing.

1957: *All That Fall* airs on the BBC Third Programme on January 13; the broadcast delights SB who is busy rehearsing in Paris for *Fin de partie*. Jack B. Yeats dies in March. *Fin de partie* is produced in London on April 3 at the Royal Court Theatre in French. SB translates *Fin de partie* into English between May and August.

1958: Begins writing *Krapp's Last Tape,* a deeply personal play, in February. Also begins, in January, the laborious task of translating *L'Innommable* into English, published as *The Unnamable* by Grove Press. On July 8 SB and Suzanne set out for a three-week vacation to Yugoslavia. Begins writing *Comment c'est* in December.

1959: Sends "Embers" to BBC in February. Ethna MacCarthy dies on May 25. Receives an honorary D. Litt. from TCD on July 2, which he reluctantly accepts.

1960: Finishes *Comment c'est* in the summer. On October 8 begins to write what is to become *Happy Days,* working on it throughout the next three months. In the winter moves to a permanent apartment in Paris.

1961: Marries Suzanne on March 25 in a simple, private ceremony. Returns home after the wedding to revise *Happy Days.* Begins translation of *Happy Days* into French and *Comment c'est* into English, the latter published by Grove Press as *How It Is* in 1964. Donald McWhinnie's television production of *Godot* is broadcast on June 26 SB is not satisfied. In the autumn, SB befriends American academic Lawrence Harvey who is visiting Paris on a Guggenheim fellowship to write about SB's poetry and criticism. The work will be published as *Samuel Beckett: Poet and Critic,* the only important full-length study (even to date) of these facets of SB's oeuvre. "Words and Music" written between November and December and "Cascando" (his first radio play in French) in December.

1962: Begins "Play" in July and finishes translating *Happy Days* as *Oh les beaux jours* in November.

1963: Completes *Film* and "Play" and assists with the German production of the latter, thus establishing his continuous engagement with the production of his own plays. Meets Billie Whitelaw for the first time at the London production of "Play"; becomes captivated by her and commences a long working relationship and a close friendship with the actress.

1964: Travels to New York during the intensely hot summer to aid in the production of *Film,* starring legendary filmmaker and actor Buster Keaton (whose work SB greatly admires); this is to be SB's only visit to the United States.

1965: Writes *Imagination morte imaginez* and "Eh Joe" (his first television play) in the spring. Writes *Assez* and begins *Le Dépeupleur* in the autumn.

1966: Translates *Textes pour rien* into English and helps with the translation of *Watt* into French.

1967: SB is diagnosed with glaucoma. Thomas MacGreevy, one of his oldest friends, dies, which, consequently, devastates SB. Begins a directing career in Berlin at the Schiller-Theater Werkstatt with *Endspiel* (*Endgame*), which opens September 26.

1969: Writes *Sans* and translates it as *Lessness.* Awarded the Nobel Prize for Literature on October 23. A dark horse, SB beat out the favorite that year, Norman Mailer.

Rather than rejecting it like Jean-Paul Sartre, he sends his French publisher, Jérôme Lindon, to accept the prize in his absence and quickly disperses the prize money to needy friends.

1970: Finally consents to the long-delayed publications of *Mercier et Camier* and *Premier amour,* both of which were written in 1946. Undergoes eye surgery for cataracts.

1972: Writes *Not I* in the spring and translates *Premier amour* into English in April–May. During the summer, SB is inundated by friends, family, and visitors, among them Deirdre Bair, who is writing the first biography of SB. He famously tells her that he will neither help nor hinder her efforts.

1973: Despite an emotionally wrenching series of rehearsals, Billie Whitelaw leads a very successful production of *Not I* in London, thus deepening SB's respect for her talents. Writes "As the Story Was Told" in August.

1974: Experiences a creative explosion and is inspired to begin *That Time,* a companion piece to *Not I,* on June 8 in Paris; both of these highly experimental plays, as SB himself acknowledges, challenge the remotest limits of what is possible in a theater.

1975: Directs German *Godot* in Berlin in March and begins *Footfalls.* Also directs the French version of *Not I* (*Pas moi*) in Paris in April and writes "Pour finir encore" in December.

1976: Begins the television play . . . *but the clouds* . . . in the autumn. *Footfalls* and *That Time* are performed at the Royal Court Theatre on May 20 as part of a seventieth birthday celebration. Beckett himself directs Whitelaw in *Footfalls.*

1977: Begins to write *Company,* a profoundly personal piece saturated with memories from childhood. Filmed version of *Not I* is aired on BBC 2 in April. Directs *Krapp's Last Tape* in Berlin.

1979: SB's friend of more than fifty years, A. J. ("Con") Leventhal, dies on October 3. Begins writing *Mal vu mal dit* (*Ill Seen Ill Said*).

1980: On May 7, SB flies to London to direct *Endgame* with Rick Cluchey and the San Quentin Drama Workshop. At those rehearsals S. E. Gontarski asks SB for a new play for a symposium planned for May of 1981 in Columbus, Ohio, to honor his seventy-fifth birthday. He begins to write what will become "Ohio Impromptu."

1981: "Ohio Impromptu" has its world premiere in Ohio, directed by Alan Schneider, on May 9. Writes and translates *Rockaby* at the instigation of Danielle Labeille for another festival honoring his seventy-fifth birthday.

1982: Writes and translates "Catastrophe"; writes and directs "Nacht und Träume." SB's production of "Quad" is broadcast in Germany by Süddeutscher Rundfunk, and "Catastrophe" is performed at the Avignon Festival.

1984: Roger Blin dies on January 20. Visits London to oversee San Quentin Drama Workshop production of *Waiting for Godot,* prepared by Walter Asmus.

1986: SB's health starts to decline with the beginnings of emphysema.

1988: Writes "Fragment for Barney Rosset," which becomes *Stirrings Still,* published in a luxury edition with illustrations by Louis le Brocquy.

1989: Suzanne dies on July 17. On December 11, SB falls into a coma and dies at one P.M. on December 22. He is buried beside Suzanne in Montparnasse Cemetery.

1992: *Dream of Fair to middling Women* is published posthumously.

1995: *Eleutheria* is published posthumously.

The Faber Companion
to
Samuel Beckett

A

A: at the outset of *Molloy,* a figure walking toward **C** (in the **French** text, **B**). The two meet briefly, then each continues, A back to town and C on paths unknown. The encounter anticipates that of Molloy and **Moran**, one "transit" crossing another, or hunter meeting victim in *How It Is*. A and B are often paired ("**Act Without Words II**"); blind man and cripple ("**Rough for Theatre I**"); "**Bertrand**" and "**Morvan**" ("**Rough for Theatre II**"); the Dreamer and his dreamt self ("**Nacht und Träume**"). "A" denotes Animator in "**Rough for Radio II**" and a voice from "**That Time.**"

"Abandonné": a prose poem (1971), a *témoignage* to **art** (Paris: Georges Visat, 1972); twelve folio gatherings, boxed, illustrated by Geneviève Asse; seventy signed copies. The artist had asked for something to illustrate. SB offered this "piece of residua," untitled, asking that it be printed as on the monument on Boulevard Auguste Blanqui (passed en route to her studio) to Ernest Rousselle, president of the commission for **children:** a bronze statue of a shoeless child with "Abandonné!" cut into the base (Knowlson, 512–13). It became part of "**Pour finir encore**," the **skull** asserting human agency struggling into being, the piece "abandoned" before the two white dwarfs appear.

Abbey Theatre: the Irish Literary Theatre began in the Antient Concert Rooms with W. B. **Yeats**'s *Countess Cathleen* (8 May 1899). It found a permanent home in Abbey Street, opening with W. B. Yeats's *On Baile's Strand* and Lady Gregory's *Spreading the News* (27 December 1904). The Abbey's role in the Irish literary revival caused riots at **Synge**'s *Playboy of the Western World* (1907) and O'**Casey**'s *Plough and the Stars* (1926). **Murphy**'s will (that his ashes be flushed down its toilet during performance) recalls that the building was once a morgue, its necessary house notoriously noisy.

"à bout de songes un bouquin": an unrhymed quatrain, second of "**Deux poèmes**" (*Minuit* 33 [mars 1979]: 3): "at the end of dreams an old hare, compelled to say farewell to the den, tired of the chase deliberately forgets the candlestick" [to turn off the light]. SB puns on "bouquin," a book and (himself as) a male hare, leaving its "gîte," or form. Earlier he had noted from **Burton** "melancholy as a hare" (DN, 112); in the **Sottisier Notebook** he cited **La Fontaine**'s "Le Lièvre et les grenouilles": "Que faire en un gîte, à moins que l'on ne songe?" ["What can one do in a form but dream?"], the tone "un profond ennui."

Abraham's bosom: the rich man, Dives, cast to hell (Luke 16:22–26), looks up to see the beggar **Lazarus** carried into Abraham's bosom. Dives cries for mercy, begging Lazarus to dip his fingertip in water, but is told that Lazarus will be

1

comforted and he tormented, and of the great **gulf** fixed between them. The **Whoroscope Notebook** gives this in **French** and Italian. SB was intrigued by what he called in "**Denis Devlin**" (1938) "the Dives-Lazarus symbiosis," or a "conte cruel" (a phrase from Villiers de l'Isle-Adam). "Abraham's bosom" appears in *Dream* (3, 105, 183, 229); *Murphy* (5, 48); "**Human Wishes**" (*Disjecta*, 162); and "**Three Dialogues**" (122). **Hamm** is petitioned for bread by a starveling from **Kov**, "beyond the gulf"; his response is echoed in *How It Is* (38): "had I only the little finger to raise to be wafted straight to Abraham's bosom I'd tell him to stick it up"

"**L'Absent**": see *Malone meurt*.

absurdity: "In the beginning was the Word" (John 1:1), the NT antiphon to Genesis. The Logos expressed the Greek ideal, from **Socrates**, **Plato**, and **Aristotle** through **Augustine** and **Dante** to **Descartes** and beyond, affirming the existence of **God** and immortality of the soul. SB rejected both doctrines, preferring the **atomists** (qv), who asserted the soul's dissolution at **death**. Contemporary "atomists" revealed a quantum world where classical **physics** no longer pertains; and **psychoanalysis**, a darker world, where rational premises do not apply. Hence **Murphy's mind** (the light, half-light, and dark), and a human drama set in its shadows; not the **mystical** metaphor of ascent to the light, but an inverted journey, a regression into the darker self. **Irrationality**, mathematical, musical, or psychological, informs SB's distrust of the Christian-rationalist tradition that asserts reason as the highest form of **consciousness**, leading the mind to God. The dark zone of Murphy's mind is a "Matrix of surds," or womb of irrationality (112). **Arsene** offers the *risus purus*, the laugh that laughs at that which is unhappy (*Watt*, 48), a guffaw at the heart of *Three Novels*, and the absurd vigil of two tramps waiting for **Godot**. As Hesla notes (10), Western man has turned to **love**, courage, and God for the strength to endure, to go **on**; but there is a fourth way of coping with the fiasco, one lacking all dignity, heroism, and nobility: accepting the comic, the absurd. This, the **fundamental unheroic**, was SB's way.

Absurd, Theater of the: a study by Martin Esslin (1918–2002) of post–World War II drama, *The Theatre of the Absurd* (1961) grouped SB among dramatists and exiles writing in **French**, chiefly Eugene Ionesco, Jean Genet, and Arthur Adamov, and, later, Harold Pinter and Edward Albee. Esslin traced their intellectual roots to **Camus**'s musings during the Nazi occupation, particularly *The Myth of Sisyphus* (1942): "This divorce between man and his life, the actor and his setting, truly constitutes the feeling of Absurdity." For Esslin absurdity was "part of the 'anti-literary' movement of our time" (xxi), reflecting the breakdown of reason in western Europe. The chapter "Samuel Beckett: The Search for the Self" analyzes the plays to 1961; it influenced immeasurably the next two generations of critics. Esslin's emphasis on the disintegration of language and **irrationality** of existence, his linking SB with Ionesco and anti-literature, have fared less well. SB commented to Alan **Schneider** on a New York "Festival of the Absurd" (February 1962), that it was "about as vague as Cubism & Fauvism" (Harmon, 121). He told Charles Juliet that it implied value judgments, whereas "the kind of solution" an artist might find was "giving form to what has none" (*Conversations*, 149). Kenner suggested (190) that Esslin's "ad hoc category" was "not a useful bracketing" as it aligned SB with no literary tradition. Esslin wondered in his revised Preface (Penguin, 1968) whether he should feel pride, or hide his head in shame. His broad alignment of SB with philosophical absurdity remains useful. Alvarez calls SB an absurdist in the "strict, appalled sense" of Camus, life lived for its own sake in a universe no longer making sense because there is no **God**; that which Kierkegaard, more Christian, precise, and pessimistic, calls despair. In this narrower sense, linking SB to Camus *and* Kierkegaard is valid. See **existentialism**, **stoicism**, and **surrealism**.

"Accul": a poem (1947) published in *Cahiers des saisons* 2 (octobre 1955): 115; the title ("At Bay") later omitted (see "**bon bon il est un pays**"). The **Unnamable** reflects (346): "It's this hunt that is tiring, this unending being at bay."

"Acte sans paroles I" / "Act Without Words I": written in **French** (1956) for dancer Deryk **Mendel**, SB's first **mime** debuted at the Royal Court, **London** (3 April 1957), with **music** by his cousin John Beckett. First published with *Fin de partie* (Minuit, 1957); and, in English, with *Endgame* (Grove and Faber, 1958),

subtitled "A mime for one player." The title echoes Mendelssohn's "Songs Without Words." A film version with **puppets**, dir. Bruno and Guido Bettiol, produced by Cinéastes Associés, was shown at the Annecy festival of animated art (1965). By calling it a "codicil to *Endgame*," SB may have doomed it to minor status, for it is rarely performed. Among those few who have treated it, Ruby Cohn dismisses it as "almost too explicit," and Ihab Hassan as "too obvious and pat."

The piece seems a behaviorist experiment within a classical myth. The protagonist (Adam, **Tantalus**, Everyman?) is born into an environment where he cannot exist but cannot escape. **Nature** seems apart from and hostile to him. He is reflective, but not created to cope. He is less tragic than pathetic, born indeed designed to fail, a caged animal frustrated by an inept or malicious handler. He examines his hands, prehensile thumbs, his primary tools. Armed with mind and hands, features that separate him from lower orders, he tries to survive, to secure water. The mind works, partially. He learns—small cube on large. The plot derives from experiments on the learning abilities of apes by Wolfgang **Köhler** (qv). He invents—rather, inventions drop from the flies—scissors, cubes, ropes. But when he learns to use his tools, to exit the scene, so to speak, they are confiscated: scissors, to cut his throat; blocks and rope, to make a gallows. Thus, an obvious **allegory**: Tantalus punished, the offense uncertain.

The mime departs from SB's usual world. No words, for one. Or rather, one elemental word, "water," written not spoken. The protagonist is nameless and finally **unnamable**. As SB told Barney Rosset (1957), he is just "human meat—or bones." SB associated him with **Clov**, "gone from refuge." He remains active and healthy, not an avatar of **Belacqua**, **Murphy**, or **Watt**, not a paraplegic. He regresses toward immobility but suffers no further deterioration. His immobility seems willed. Whereas **Godot**'s existence remains uncertain, here an external force exists. Like Jacob, he wrestles with it to confront its materiality. Finally, the action is linear, apparently terminal, not SB's usual circle.

The superior force apparently defeats the inferior. Yet SB reacts against this obvious ending, for the real play begins with its terminus. The climax signifies not pathetic defeat but conscious rebellion, willful disobedience. **Lucky** has turned on **Pozzo** by refusing to validate him, as Clov does to **Hamm** in *Endgame*'s closing tableau. In this refusal, this cutting of the umbilical rope, a second **birth** occurs, that of Man. He has finally earned a name, Mankind or hu-Manity (another **M**). As he refuses the bidding of the outside force, to act predictably in self-interest, or to struggle for elemental needs, he breaks free of need as Murphy never could. Man, in a frenzy of (in)activity, is born—free. In his refusal to devote himself solely to physical existence, to survival and pleasure (shade, water, the offstage womb), he has created a separate self. He has said, with **Camus**, no further. Rebellion is dangerous, for the rebellious slave may be destroyed by his master, but the protagonist is most active when inert, and his life acquires meaning even as it closes.

"Acte sans paroles II" / "Act Without Words II": written in **French** (1958) and performed at the Institute of Contemporary Arts, **London** (25 January 1960). First English publication in *New Departures* 1 (Summer 1959): 89–90; rpt. in *Krapp's Last Tape and other Dramatic Pieces* (1960). The **French** text appeared in *Dramatische Dichtungen* 1 (1963), 330–37, with facing German translation; the first "French" printing was in *Comédie et actes divers* (1966). **Mimes** 1 and 2 were produced in Ulm-Donau (June 1963); Deryk **Mendel** directed "Spiel" and played in both mimes. Paul Joyce made a poignant film of the second (1976), titled *The Goad,* and it was published in *Nothing Doing in London* I (Anthony Barnett, 1966), an issue of 500.

SB's second mime seems less particularized than his first. Two burlap sacks sit stage left on an upstage platform, "violently lit," which runs the length of the stage, creating a "Frieze effect." Stage right of **B** is a small pile of clothes. A goad, "strictly horizontal," emerges stage left to prod **A** and awaken him to his daily ritual. A is the **Molloy** of this pairing, slovenly, disorganized. He gobbles pills, prays, dresses randomly, and nibbles a carrot, which he promptly spits out. His days are short; his principal activity, without apparent purpose, is to move the filled sack stage right and to resume his fetal position right of B so that they have changed positions and B is now vulnerable to the goad.

B is the **Moran** of this odd couple—precise, efficient, eager. He knows how to dress and brush his clothes. He takes better care of himself, but his days are no more meaningful. His **job** is to move A's sack farther right and the clothing right of both sacks. The drudgery is no less. The play is compelling only if the mechanical figures are somehow humanized. If comfort exists it is because the plight of humanity if futile or repetitive is at least shared, even if no intercourse exists. Meaning or purpose seems to be, almost instinctually, beyond the reach of the anthropomorphized goad, which counters by sporting wheels to reach the receding sacks. The repetition suggests that they will be some day beyond the goad's reach, but to what purpose? Without it to structure their days, will they remain immobile, comatose?

adaptations: SB largely resisted what Ruby Cohn has called "jumping genres." He refused permission to stage *All That Fall,* noting to Barney Rosset (27 August 1957): "If we can't keep our genres more or less distinct, or extricate them from the confusion that has them where they are, we might as well go home and lie down." Yet he often encouraged directors eager to stage his prose, and developed revealing stage adaptations of his short narratives. When Joseph **Chaikin** wanted to stage *Stories and Texts for Nothing,* SB invited him (26 April 1980) to mount a single *Text* with a precise staging: a figure, "Seated. Head in hands. Nothing else. Face invisible. Dim spot. Speech hesitant. Mike for audibility." SB wrote again (1 August 1980), developing his adaptation and revealing remarkable insights into his story; but Chaikin finally preferred his medley. SB conceded (5 September 1980) that his method was valid only for a single text. The idea was to caricature compositional labor, but

multiple texts required a different approach. Chaikin chose a more "theatrical" approach, but SB's adaptation was an astonishing dramatization of the mysterious **voice**, external to the perceiving self. It caricatures **Romantic** creativity, the artist's agonized communion with his uncorrupted inner being, **consciousness**, or imagination. SB's figure "A" has an unnamed collaborator, an external Other, as much audience to the emerging artwork as instigator, as he folds the voices of Others, origins unknown, into his own.

When Shivaun O'Casey, daughter of Sean, wanted to dramatize *From an Abandoned Work,* SB detailed a staging for her. O'Casey liked the analogy of "**Play**," but SB resisted, as it was not the kind of drama he visualized, and he thought the spotlight presentation wrong. He offered an alternative that separated speaker from spoken, as the **face** was irrelevant and monologue technique would not work; it should be presented as a document for which the speaker is not responsible. He urged "maximum of simplicity." In SB's adaptation the stage character is an accidental protagonist, a messenger. He "finds" the tattered manuscript in an ashcan, reads it ("Up bright and early . . ."), and puts it back. SB preferred this form of staging for his prose, a compromise between unadorned stage reading and full theatrical adaptation.

When **Mabou Mines** asked to stage *The Lost Ones,* SB approved a "straight reading." In rehearsal this developed into a complex adaptation with a naked actor "demonstrating" the text with a host of miniature figures. SB commented, "Sounds like a crooked straight reading to me." Again he resisted the resurrection of the monologue, a form he had developed in prose with the four *Nouvelles* (1947) and had adapted to the stage in *Krapp's Last Tape* (1958). The monologue embraced an ideology of concrete presence, a single coherent being (unified ego or **character**), an idea with which SB was increasingly uncomfortable, and which he had abandoned in his fiction.

Company's interlocutory nature has encouraged several dramatic readings and theatrical adaptations, beginning with Patrick **Magee**'s reading on BBC 3 (July 1980), and John Russell Brown's version for the National Theatre, **London**, that September, featuring Stephen Moore. Another London version was staged by Tim Piggot-Smith and Katherine Worth, with Julian Curry (1987); it appeared at the Edinburgh Festival and in New York (1988). There were two earlier American stagings. Frederick Neumann directed it for Mabou Mines, with Honora Ferguson (1983); and Stan Gontarski's production at the Los Angeles Actors' Theater with Alan Mandell (1985) was the English premiere of Pierre Chabert's adaptation (15 November 1984) at the Théâtre du Rond-Point, **Paris**, one with which SB (accentuating the "né" of *terminé* and "nie" of *Compagnie*) was associated. When Gontarski prepared *First Love*, SB offered possibilities like those for O'Casey. The question was how to break up an unrelieved reading of the text, again discovered in a rubbish heap. SB noted to Gontarski (2 September 1986): "The reading can be piecemealed by all kinds of business— such as returning it to bin (on which he sits to read)—exiting and returning to read to the end—looking feverishly for a

flea or other vermin—chewing a crust— getting up to piss in a corner with back modestly to audience—etc. etc. making the poor best of a hopeless job."

Despite his oft-cited resistance, SB not only approved adaptations of his prose work to stage but often collaborated in the process. While he gave full voice to the disintegration of character and fragmentation of monologue in *Not I*, and with the incorporeal, ghostly figure of **May** in *Footfalls,* he rejected adaptations that posited unity of character and narrative. Actors, then, have intuited what literary critics have often failed to articulate, that SB's experimental short fictions have an immediacy and emotional power, that of the spoken voice, which makes them accessible to a broad audience yet places them firmly within a tradition of Irish storytelling.

Adler, Alfred (1870–1937): Austrian psychiatrist in the **Freudian** tradition, who asserted the struggle to compensate for feelings of inferiority. SB found in *The Neurotic Condition* (1921) the "guiding fiction" of "masculine protest," the need to be a complete man. Thus, **Celia**'s determination to "make a man" of **Murphy**. SB noted to **MacGreevy** (8 February 1935) that he had finished with Adler: "Another one truth mind."

Adobard: mentioned in *Molloy* (166); perhaps Agobard of Lyons (779–840), prelate and reformer. **Augustine** contends (*De Naturâ et Gratiâ*, 36) that all have known sin except Mary, but nowhere does she conceive through the ear. As a conceit for the Annunciation, compare the **Unnamable**'s tympanum (383).

"à elle l'acte calme": a thirteen-line poem, second of the twelve *Poèmes 38–39*. Published in *Les Temps modernes* II.14 (novembre 1946), then *Minuit* 21 (novembre 1976): 13–14, and *Collected Poems* (1984), 42–43. A woman stands before the poet, attractive and confident in her sexuality, yet doubts arise as to his capacity for **love**. The rain ceasing before nightfall on an August night intimates a sense of grace vouchsafed, mingled gently with regret that it may have come too late.

Aeschylus (526–456 BC): Athenian dramatist. Informed by an oracle that he would die by a falling house he withdrew to the fields, but an eagle thought his bald head a stone and dropped a tortoise on him. Lord Gall threatens to drop **Belacqua** "like an oyster on the Aeschylus of **Wormwood**, pardon the reference" ("Echo's Bones," 10). The "reference" is Jeremy **Taylor**'s *Holy Dying* (1.i), where an eagle drops an *oyster* on Aeschylus's **skull**.

"Afar a bird": "**Fizzle 3**"; SB's translation (Paris, 28 March 1975) of *Foirade* 6, *Au loin un oiseau*. It features the familiar Cartesian **dualism**, an "I," a **consciousness** or mind within a moribund "he": "it was he, I was inside." "He" slowly treads a "ruinstrewn land," perhaps his last journey, stopping frequently to rest, hands weighing on the stick, head weighing on the hands. "I" evaluates their relationship: "it was he had a life, I didn't have a life, a life not worth having, because of me." An external reality is affirmed with "afar a bird" (compare Brahms's "In Waldeinsamkeit": "Ferne, ferne, ferne / Sang ein Nachtigall"); but complications within suggest interminable complexity: "someone divines me, divines us." "**Text 5**" (121) invokes "the bird the birdikin, with larvae she fetches from afar" in terms of Hamlet's divinity that shapes our ends and Providence in the fall of a sparrow. In *Company,* five years later, there is a "devised devisor." "I" feeds "he": "I'll put **faces** in his head, names, places, churn them all up together." Potentially sentimental, images of faces, remnants of **love** lost, drove much of SB's late work. In "Afar a Bird" the "I" supplies such images in an act of hostility, so that "he" may "love again, lose again."

"ainsi a-t-on beau": a fourteen-line poem, eighth of twelve *Poèmes 38–39*. Published in *Les Temps modernes* II.14 (novembre 1946); then *Minuit* 21 (novembre 1976): 16, and *Collected Poems* (1984). The opening line reads, awkwardly, "well, it's all right"; but the optimism of **happy days** ("le beau temps") gives way to pessimism ("le mauvais temps"). Lines 4–7 expand "temps" as both **time** and circumstance: the vision (as yesterday) sets off the age of mammoths and the dinotherium, and the ice ages that brought nothing new (only humanity). These are set against images from human time (the great heat of the thirteenth century, the **Lisbon** earthquake, the cold philosophy of **Kant**), and first kisses, as if to suggest that all are one in time. The sentiment is *tempus edax rerum,* the world devoured by time. Next, the **memory** of his **father**, in process of being forgotten (so what, he's dead), with the cynical view that one is not the less eaten if this happens without appetite. The poem concludes by recapitulating the opening lines, with the sentiment that "mauvais temps" lead to worse, so that "enfermé chez soi" no longer expresses the earlier acceptance but the deeper pessimism of one trapped in both his times and his self.

"Alba": a seventeen-line poem (August 1931), published in the *Dublin Magazine* 6.4 (October–December 1931): 4; revised for *Echo's Bones* (1934); and included in all later collections. Alfred **Péron**'s translation (which SB privately thought little of) appeared in *Soutes: Revue de culture révolutionnaire internationale* 9 (1938): 41. In a signed copy of *Echo's Bones* (HRHRC, #42), SB noted after "Alba": "39 **Trinity College,** Dublin"; his room the setting. In *Dream* (148) **Belacqua** murmurs the opening line. The poem was written with Ethna **MacCarthy** in mind, SB celebrating in ecstasy and despair (as **Dante** to **Beatrice**) the vision of her coming, and the leaden sense of self when she (or it) departs, the promise not "unveiled." The title refers to the **troubadour** dawn song: the night of **love** and elegiac regret as dawn signals day and the lover must depart. But things are not as they might be.

The poem is in three parts (Dante's number): the first anticipates her coming, in terms of "Dante and the Logos and all strata and mysteries," including "the white plane of **music.**" This echoes *Dream* (111, 182–83, 193), where the Eastern vision is integrated with music and the whiteness of dawn, damask silk and steel fused in the image of the silken blade. In the second part, the ecstasy of her presence is figured in celestial mu-

sic; for the singing silk (the lute), areca (its sounding board), and rain on the bamboos, see **k'în music.** The third part changes: her compassion and beauty, yes, but a bounty withheld, "so that there is no sun and no unveiling." The poem ends on a complex note, less bitterness (she is beyond such reproach) than a faded vision, perhaps masturbatory (no angels but a white winding sheet): "only I and then the sheet / and bulk dead."

the Alba: Alba Perdue, based on Ethna **MacCarthy**; the white vision of **Belacqua** in *Dream* and "**A Wet Night.**" *Dream* counterpoints the **Smeraldina**'s physicality against the Alba's ethereal presence, but resists any temptation to unite them in sonata form. She is, the **Polar Bear** says (151), "a wunnerful girl." Her red buttoned gown entices Belacqua to the **Frica**'s party, where, bedraggled, he is taken under her wing, and asked not only to see her home but into the Casa Alba, where there is a fire and a bottle, if not a bed. The ending as reworked for "A Wet Night" is more ambiguous (SB and Ethna never slept together). In "**What a Misfortune**" Alba Perdue is bridesmaid at Belacqua's wedding to Thelma **bboggs.** She dies "in the natural course of being seen home" ("Draff," 175), but resurfaces in a mysterious submarine in the postmortem world of "**Echo's Bones.**"

Aldington, Richard (1892–1962): Imagist poet whom SB met in **Paris** through Thomas **MacGreevy.** Aldington was judge of a poetry competition run by the **Hours Press** (1930), and his remark about the lamentable quality of submissions led to SB's dashing off an entry (*Whoroscope*). Aldington helped SB financially to stay on in Paris and complete *Proust*, a contract he had facilitated. He was the subject of MacGreevy's study, also in Dolphin Books (1931), which took its epigraph from *Proust*: "Yesterday is not a milestone . . . the calamity of yesterday" (13). Aldington's *Life for Life's Sake* (1942) recalls SB as a "splendidly mad Irishman who was James **Joyce**'s white boy," and who not only wanted to commit **suicide** but by playing his flute every night imposed the same fate on half the École (319). It was actually a tin whistle. Aldington fell from grace with his satire of **Eliot** (*Stepping Heavenward*, 1931), and by debunking Lawrence of Arabia. Yet SB remembered his kindness and, after Aldington's **death**, recalled with gratitude that he owed much to his good offices.

d'Alembert, Jean-le-Rond (1717–83): French philosopher, illegitimate son of the Marquise de Tencin and the Chevalier Destouches. Exposed on the steps of St. Jean-le-Rond, he was raised by a **glazier** named Rousseau. He contributed scientific and literary entries to **Diderot**'s *Dictionaire Encyclopédique* (1746–72), of which he was second editor. Diderot and d'Alembert favored the dialogue for philosophical and aesthetic discourse, a form SB later imitated in "**Three Dialogues**." SB admired Diderot's "Le Rêve de d'Alembert" (1769). A remarkable anticipation of evolutionary biology, it begins with a meditation on "First **nothing**, then a living point . . . To this living point is applied another, and yet another; and the result is a being that has

unity . . . But how did this unity come to be?" The paradox is exemplified by **bees** (291), a cluster forming one being, with a general sympathy and identity; sensible molecules losing "conscience de leur individualité pour acquérir une conscience collective," as the human individual is a composite of smaller units yet part of a greater whole. In *Dream* (167), the relationship of **Belacqua** and the **Alba** is that of a single bee in "the coagulum of continuous bees," each lacking a collective awareness so destined not to achieve greater unity of **consciousness**. That sentiment persists into *Molloy*, when **Moran** returns home to find that his bees have died, and he is no longer part of an integrated world.

Another element of d'Alembert's dream, intimating relative immortality (the whisky's grudge against the decanter, *Proust*, 21), appears in *Dream* (175; DN, 84), **Fontenelle**'s "storiette," that within the memory of the rose no gardener has been known to die. This is echoed in "**Draff**" (191): "No gardener has died, comma, within rosaceous memory"; repeated, commaless, in "**Echo's Bones**" (19). In "Draff" (179), where the gardener's stolen "rose" is the perforated nozzle of his hose. In the Addenda of *Watt*, Mr. **Knott**'s **serial** existence is suggested by the picture over the piano of his **father** (250), and by Arthur's encounter with an **old man** who worked for Knott's father (251–53). This might once have pleased Watt, but he is "an old rose now" and indifferent to the gardener.

Alesch, Robert (1906–48): Catholic priest who infiltrated **Gloria SMH**, the Resistance cell of which SB was part, and betrayed it to the Gestapo. Born in Luxembourg, he studied theology at Freiburg and was ordained in 1933. He saw the Occupation as an opportunity to enrich himself, contacted the Gestapo in 1941, and thereafter led an extraordinary double life (Knowlson, 285–87), taking Mass and visiting Resistance prisoners in jail, fornicating and drinking, and betraying the secrets of the confessional to the Abwehr. He seemed actively to enjoy his treachery. Members of the cell, including Alfred **Péron**, were picked up from 13 August 1942; some betrayed others under interrogation. SB and Suzanne escaped only because Mania Péron sent an open telegram warning them to flee. Alesch was tried and hanged (in the La Santé **prison** yard, visible later from SB's study) in May 1948.

allegory: in "**Dante**" (1929), SB commented: "Allegory implies a three-fold intellectual operation: the construction of a message of general significance, the preparation of a fabulous form, and an exercise of considerable technical difficulty in uniting the two" (*Disjecta*, 26). The danger is stated at the outset, the neatness of identifications (19) leading to a distrust of the allegorizing impulse in favor of "direct expression" (29). SB's distrust hardened into his statement that the Proustian equation is never simple (*Proust*, 11), in the recognition of separate dynamisms related by no system of synchronization (17) and in the affirmation of the "ideal real" (75). **Dante**, SB notes (79), drawing on de Sanctis, failed with his purely allegorical figures, as allegory must always fail, **Spenser**'s collapsing after a few cantos; for **Proust**, the

object is but the symbol of itself (80). "**An Imaginative Work**" (1936; *Disjecta*, 90) praises Jack **Yeats** for having no allegory, "that glorious double entry," or **symbols**, but rather details related as two values to a third (the echo of the "Dante" essay is odd), as stages of an image. **Watt** has troubles with surfaces, and the "fragility of the outer meaning" causes him to seek meaning elsewhere (see **pot**). The finale rejects the allegorical impulse: "No symbols where none intended." Many of SB's works *might* respond to allegorical readings. *Molloy* incorporates **Jungian** and **Freudian** elements, which constitute a tale of the disintegrated self; *Waiting for Godot* enacts the biblical story of salvation; and *How It Is* forms a miniature epic of a struggle toward the light. Yet allegorical comfort is denied. The **machinery** of *Molloy* proves a means to an end, the unaccommodated self; *WG*'s drama of hope deferred subverts its Christian narrative; and any incipient sense of purpose in *How It Is* is negated by the conviction that "this business of above" is "all balls." The rejection of allegory remains a constant in the Beckettian equation.

All Strange Away: a short prose text in English in 1964, "on the rocky road to *Imagination morte imagine*" (Lake, 135). Occasioned by Jack **MacGowran**'s **death** (1976), it was published in 200 numbered copies ("a beautiful edition," SB wrote) **illustrated** by Edward Gorey (1976); in *JOBS* 3 (Summer 1978): 1–9; then independently by **Calder** (1979) and by **Grove Press** in *Rockaby and Other Short Pieces* (1981). A facsimile typescript appeared in *Stereo Headphones* 8,

9, and 10 (1982): 3. A stage version, adapted and directed by Gerald Thomas with Ryan Cutron, opened at La Mama Experimental Theater Company, New York (1984). Thomas revived it later that year with Robert Langdon Lloyd. Adapted for the Edinburgh Festival (1998). The title echoes *Happy Days:* "here all is strange"; or Genesis 35:2: "Put away the strange gods that are among you." The piece begins with "Imagination dead imagine," a place ("that again"), the old **hat** and coat ("no, not that again"). It picks up the theme of "**Spring Song**," that only **death** can end desire, and responds to #4 of "**Faux Départs**." The setting is within bare walls, five feet square, six high, gradually becoming smaller as **memory** diminishes; the light on and off from no visible source; the protagonist talking to himself "in the last person" (169), responding as if to dramatic cues, with an impersonality at odds with the emotion to come. The story recalls love-making with "Emma," but memory is fading. The mind measures what it can, the dimensions of the cube, for instance. The final pages are entitled "Diagram," and language is further estranged as "past felicity" becomes fainter (the worst hell as the memory of past happiness, *Inferno* V.121–23). Finally, there is a "sop": a "tremor of sorrow at first memory of lying side by side and fancy murmured dead."

All That Fall: SB wrote to Nancy **Cunard** (4 July 1956): "Saw Barry of BBC TV who is interested in the **mime** (and why not?) and am told Gielgud wants a play for 3rd Programme. Never thought about radio play technique but

in the dead of t'other night got a nice gruesome idea full of cartwheels and dragging of feet and puffing and panting which may or may not lead to something." It did—to a one-act play in English ("**Ussy** September 1956"), translated by Robert **Pinget** as *Tous ceux qui tombent.* The autograph copy is titled "Lovely Day for the Races," a flippant greeting in a town like **Foxrock**, with the **Leopardstown** Racecourse nearby. BBC 3 liked the play, recorded it (dir. Donald **McWhinnie**, with Mary O'Farrell and J. G. Devlin), and broadcast it (Sunday, 13 January 1957; repeated 19 January). It was favorably reviewed, critics noting the affinity between SB's work and radio, and comparing it with Dylan **Thomas**'s *Under Milk Wood.* The BBC entered it, unavailingly, for the 1957 Italia Prize (later given to "**Embers**").

The American production, part of a Beckett Festival of Radio Plays, coproduced by Soundscape and RIAS, Berlin, dir. Everett Frost, was broadcast on National Public Radio (13 April 1986, SB's eightieth birthday), with Billie **Whitelaw** and David **Warrilow**. Despite qualms, SB authorized a **French** TV version adapted by Robert Pinget, shown by RTF (25 Janvier 1963). A German stage production was given at the **Schiller-Theater**, Berlin (January 1966); SB was not happy with either. First published, **Grove Press**, 1957; Grove issued a separate edition with a green cover and Christmas trees, "With Best Wishes for the Holiday Season from Grove Press." Reprinted in *Krapp's Last Tape and Other Pieces* (1965), 29–91. The first **Faber** edition, 1957, was subtitled "A Play for Radio." Small deletions were made after the first recording. A German translation (*Alle, die da fallen*) appeared in **Dramatische Dichtungen** 2 (Frankfurt: Suhrkamp, 1964), 6–81.

The action is simple but eventful. Maddy **Rooney**, minimally mobile after a protracted illness, shuffles to **Boghill** station to meet her blind husband, Dan, returning from his **Dublin** office on his birthday. The mood is set by **Schubert**'s "Death and the Maiden," which Maddy hears from "a ruinous old house" she passes. She meets the dung seller **Christy**; pines for "Little Minnie!," the **child** she lost fifty years earlier; and encounters Mr. **Tyler**, grandchildless because they "removed everything, you know, the whole . . . er . . . bag of tricks" from his daughter. She is greeted by Mr. **Slocum**, "her old admirer," now clerk of the racecourse. Dickensian comedy unfolds as he squeezes Maddy into his automobile: "I'm coming, Mrs. Rooney, I'm coming, give me time, I'm as stiff as yourself." They run over a **hen**. She encounters Miss Fitt, unfit for the corporeal world: "I am not there" (see *Footfalls*). Maddy asks for human kindness, reluctantly administered ("the Protestant thing to do"), to help her up to the platform.

Some mishap has delayed the train, and when it arrives blind Dan is last to alight. The tone changes, from light comedy to dark innuendo. Dan longs to sit before the fire, blinds drawn, and have Maddy read to him: "I think **Effie** is going to commit adultery with the Major." As they are jeered by the **Lynch** twins, Dan asks Maddy, "Did you ever wish to kill a child? (*Pause.*) Nip some young doom in the bud." They proceed, "Like **Dante**'s damned, with their faces

arsy-versy." Maddy tells of "attending a lecture by one of these new mind doctors" (**Jung**), who discussed a patient: "The trouble with her was," admits the doctor, "she had never really been born!" Noting the text of Sunday's sermon, "The Lord upholdeth all that fall and raiseth up all those that be bowed down" (Psalms 145:14), they burst into "wild laughter" (see **Hardy**). Young Jerry returns "a kind of **ball**" to Dan, and Maddy asks about the delay. "It was a little child fell out of the carriage," replies Jerry.

All That Fall has uncanny naturalistic qualities (precise locale with realistic ambient sounds), yet is replete with images of **death**, deterioration, and infertility, ranging from the Schubert *lied* that opens and closes the play to the dead hen and Dante's damned. The weather degenerates from a "Divine day" to the final "Tempest of wind and rain." Maddy and Dan live a **purgatorial** existence in a fallen world. Deteriorating like so many of SB's characters, they seem invidious of life. Does blind Dan fantasize about nipping "some young doom in the bud," or was he involved in the child's having "fallen" from the train? Was this an act of retribution for the loss of his own child? And what of little Minnie's demise (an abortion)? There are black secrets in the lives of the moribund Rooneys, about which they brood and which we glimpse only darkly. Everyone else, except the unseen person who replays "Death and the Maiden," seems preoccupied with race day.

Amiel, Henri-Frédéric (1821–81): professor of aesthetics and philosophy at

Geneva, his *Journal intime* (1883) a model of **Romantic** introspection. Linked with **Chateaubriand** as a "melancholy Pantheist" who cannot match **Proust**'s "pathological power" (*Proust,* 82).

Amy: daughter of old Mrs. **Winter** in *Footfalls* (qv), who may have responded "Amen" at evensong but insists she was not there. Her name is an anagram of "**May**," which links her to the speaker, and biographically to SB's **mother.**

an Ankou: in Breton mythology, death's henchman ("an" the definite article), a female spirit who travels down the lane in a cart, picking up souls. (*Dream* 85; "Yellow Love" may be yellow fever.) Compare *How It Is* (89): "wheels drawing near iron felly."

Andrea del Sarto (1486-1530): **Florentine** artist, honored with the epigraph "Andre senza errori." The "faultless painter" was famously critiqued in Robert Browning's dramatic monologue, which documents Andrea's problems with his wife Lucrezia. She is the subject of the painting *Madonna Lucrezia del Fede,* which **Belacqua** uses as an ambiguous touchstone of his feelings (*Dream,* 15 and 68).

"Anna Livia Plurabelle": part of *Work in Progress* (*Finnegans Wake*) translated by SB and others in collaboration with James **Joyce.** Published in the *Nouvelle revue française* 212 (mai 1931): 633–46; later (revised) in Philippe Soupault's *Souvenirs de James Joyce* (Éditions Charlot, 1943), 71–90; still later (unchanged) in *Finnegans Wake,* fragments adaptés par

André du Bouchet (Gallimard, 1962). The first draft was prepared by SB with the help of Alfred **Péron,** but with "Alfy" gone SB did not want to do the translation alone, nor sign a contract with "that bastard Soupault" (who was in charge of the project). He worried that Joyce might be disgusted "by the chasm of feeling and technique between his hieroglyphics and our bastard **French**" (SB to TM, 7 July 1930). His fears were realized. The translation got to the corrected proofs, when Joyce intervened. It was revised by others (Paul Léon, Eugene Jolas, Ivan Goll) under Joyce's supervision; then Joyce, Léon, and Soupault revised the revision, with further input from Jolas and Adrienne Monnier. The Péron/SB version at the Beinecke Library, Yale [Box 6F 3–8]. SB's contribution is indeterminable. At the "Séance consacrée à James Joyce" in Adrienne Monnier's bookshop (26 March 1931), Soupault described their translation as a "premier essai," needing to improve its rhythm and sense. SB resented the injustice, but made no protest. Published, with all extant versions and translations, as *Anna Livia Plurabelle,* traduzione francese di S. Beckett et al. (versione italiana di James Joyce e Nino Frank: *Anna Livia Plurabella* [Torino: Einaudi, 1996]).

ant: Democritus contended that if the vacuum surrounded us images from visible **objects** would reach the eye unblurred, and we might see an ant crawling on the sky. **Aristotle** (*De Anima,* 419.a.15) disagreed, and the image became contentious. Mr. **Endon**'s eyes are fixed on something remote, "perhaps the famous ant on the sky of an airless world" (*Murphy*, 248). The narrator of "**Text 6**" (123) tries to think of the infinite: "that ant, that ant, oh most excellent head that can't think." See also **formication**.

Antepurgatory: a region outside **Purgatory**, "beyond the frontiers of suffering" (*Murphy*, 78), where dwell the spirits of those who died impenitent, either in contumacy of the Church or having from indolence put off their repentance. **Belacqua** is of the latter, detained for a period equivalent to his natural life, unless that time is shortened by prayer. Hence **Murphy**'s hope (78), that no godly chandler shorten his time with a good prayer.

Anteros: in Neoplatonic tradition god of anti-**love**, son of Ares and Aphrodite, and brother to Eros, with whom he is in dispute; allegorically, overcoming **desire**. In *Dream* (68) the narrator admits to a note on Anteros, and a poem "cogged from the liquorish laypriest's Magic Ode" (see **Ronsard**). This is "**Return to the Vestry**," which addresses "Gentle Anteros" as "dark and dispassionate," and begs him come coil at the door; without wasting time in amorous regrets and poems of love. In *Dream* (121) the narrator retreats to the dark **gulf** of the mind, where "Eros was as null as Anteros."

Anthology of Mexican Poetry: compiled and edited by Otavio Paz, who contributed a foreword, with translations by SB (1950–51). First published, Bloomington (1958), SB's now-famous name prominent; rpt. **Calder** and Boyars (1970), and **Grove Press** (1985). SB thanks Gerald

Brenan for his assistance. It appeared by agreement between UNESCO and the Mexican government as part of a program of translations of works from 1521 to 1910 (Francisco de Terrazos to Alfonso Reyes). SB, who studied Spanish in 1933 but was never fully fluent, later dismissed it as "cette vieille foutaise alimentaire." To Kay Boyle (20 November 1961) he described it as "Without doubt I think my worst literary experience." He told Aidin Higgins that nine-tenths of the poems were shit; but the **Sam Francis Notebook** (RUL 2926) indicates the troubles taken with a thankless task, with glosses on difficult words and notes arranged poet by poet. It was SB's last commercial translation.

Antiochus: in **Racine**'s *Bérénice*, "roi de Camagène," who, in love with Bérénice, queen of Palestine, fears losing her to Titus, emperor of Rome, and, imagining her with him in Rome, laments (l.234): "Dans l'Orient désert quel devint mon ennui" ["In the bleak Orient what shall my boredom be?"]. The "quel devint" is approved by **Belacqua** in *Dream* (144). The name (Racine's addition to his source) denotes the Greek philosopher of Ascalon, who contended that happiness though based on virtue depends on outward circumstance.

"Antipepsis": SB's Hudibrastic satire of **Ireland** where biological existence has supplanted mental life: "Where before the ass the cart." The twenty-four-line English poem in tortured couplets (RUL 2906), inscribed by SB "1946 after **St Lô**," celebrates Ireland's "providential vacuum" of thought; it is an anti-peptic blast against those who "stroll amok / To eat, drink, piss, shit, fart and fuck." It ends in panic at the rumor that a thought has taken place in **Dublin**: "Purissima Virgo! We're undone! / Bitched, buggered and bewildered! / Bring forth your dead! Bring forth your dead!" First published in *Metre* 3 (Autumn 1997): 5, an issue devoted to "Irish Poetry and the Diaspora." **Malone** (242) names "peptic deficiency" among the furies and frenzies of the body.

antiquarian: a term of disparagement applied to the Twilighters in "**Recent Irish Poetry**" (1934), and to their visual-arts equivalents in "**Peintres de l'empéchement**" (1948), to denote artists working in the old ways, unaware of the disjunction between subject and **object**, of "the vacuum which exists between perceiver and the thing perceived."

Antonella da Messina (1430–79): Sicilian painter with a Flemish style, who brought the secret of oil painting to Italy. SB saw in Dresden (1937) a "stupendous" Saint Sebastian at the Zwinger Gallery, and in Munich a "Virgin of the Annunciation" at the Alte Pinakothek. This shaped later stage imagery, specifically **May**'s posture in *Footfalls* (Knowlson, 236).

Apelles (fourth century BC): greatest painter of antiquity. Alexander ordered him to portray Campaspe, one of his mistresses. When the painter fell in love with her, Alexander let them marry. The story (from Lemprière) is mentioned in *Dream* (78). Apelles's maxim "nulla dies sine lineâ" ("never a day without a line") is perverted by **Ticklepenny** (*Murphy*, 85).

Apmonia: with "Isonomy" and "Attunement" a term arising from SB's reading of the pre-Socratics, specifically **Burnet**'s *Early Greek Philosophy*. The joke turns on the witty Greek letter *rho* masquerading as a Roman "P"; "Apmonia" thus creates harmony, though its sense in Greek is akin to "octave." **Pythagoras** discovered that the concordant intervals of the **musical** scale could be expressed by simple ratios; such attunement was called *Apmonia*. Likewise, the "**strife of opposites**" is an attunement or harmony. Hot and cold, wet and dry, could be blended in a medical harmony associated with Alkmaion and termed the "isonomy," since the soul's attunement is intimately connected with the four elements and the human **body** as a **microcosm** of the greater harmony. For **Socrates**, the harmony of body and soul was like that of a lyre, but if the body is too tightly strung by ills, must the soul perish? SB found this an effective image for the **irrational heart**, from which **Murphy** suffers, and for which **Neary**'s sense of the closed circle and perfect attunement offers no relief. **Watt** lacks attunement, an element of discord preventing his hearing perfectly various **mixed choirs**.

apnoea: willed cessation of breathing, a "physiological impossibility" (*Murphy*, 185), as with loss of **consciousness** the involuntary nervous system takes over and the **body** breathes again. Mr. **Endon** is thought capable of **suicide** by apnoea, as in **Schopenhauer**'s contention (*WWI*, 1.2 #23) that we could voluntarily suffocate, were the will sufficiently strong. See **Rabelais**.

Apollinaire, Guillaume (1880–1918): pseudonym of Wilhelm-Apollinaris de Kostrowitski, French **symbolist** poet born of a Vatican nobleman and a Finnish-Polish mother; he died from a head wound sustained in World War I. Champion of innovation, cataloguer of the *Enfer* of the *Bibliothèque Nationale*, and lover of Marie **Laurencin**, his *Alcools* (1913) and *Calligrammes* (1918) represent the fractured self with startling lyricism. *Dream* invokes (171) his "ravaged zone" (see "**Zone**"). In "**Ex Cathezra**" (1934), SB praised "Chanson du mal-aimé" as worth as much as all the works of the late symbolists put together. He worked with Gabrielle Buffet-**Picabia** on her article "Apollinaire" (*Transition* 50.6 [October 1950]: 110–26). Pilling detects Apollinaire's presence ("Le Pont Mirabeau") in the refrain of *How It Is* (33): "**time** passes I remain" (*Frescoes*, 76).

aporia: an antinomy arising through the simultaneous existence of mutually exclusive entities, each irreducible to the terms of the other. This is the narrative mode from "**Assumption**": "He could have shouted and could not"; to *Texts for Nothing:* "I couldn't stay there and I couldn't go on" (100); and beyond. The **Unnamable** will proceed by aporia pure and simple, because the problem of finding the words to say must serve as both subject and **object** of investigation. He is soon back at what **Malone** called (181) his "old aporetics": "affirmations and negations invalidated as uttered" (291). The opening, "Keep going, going **on**, call that going, call that on," is echoed at the end: "I can't go on, I'll go on," to underline the final impasse, the failure to have

found "other shifts" (291). This is more emphatic in English, the original using first "aller" then "continuer."

Diogenes Laertius (IX.70) defined the **pre-Socratic** aporetics as "those in perplexity." Aporia is the poststructuralist trope par excellence; as Hill contends (65): "Aporia, in Beckett's writing, is a figure of indifference, of differences articulated then suspended." He sees indifference as the primary motivation behind the aporetic impulse in *Three Novels,* the goal not **nothing** but impasse. This rhetoric of contradiction typifies SB's writing, from his early love of words that embody a contradiction ("**asylum**") to the pursuit in later works of a form to "contain" the inexplicable, to "fail better." As Anna Smith argues in "Proceeding by Aporia," *Worstward Ho* progresses not to conclusion but by checks and contradictions that create an ambivalent textuality, subverting any conclusion about the nature of things.

apperception: for **Leibniz**, **Kant**, and **Schopenhauer** the active process of the mind reflecting on itself, its perception of itself as a conscious agent, the **consciousness** of being conscious. **Windelband** notes (463) that for Leibniz the term denotes the process by which unconscious, obscure, and confused representations are made "clear and distinct," *petites perceptions* transformed into self-awareness. This involves a logical paradox (Brett, 123): "If I do not perceive that I see in one indivisible act, there will be that which sees and that which perceives, and these will require a third faculty to unite them. To cut short this infinite process we assert that the sense perceives itself." Kant replaces **Plato**'s transcendence with the synthetic unity of consciousness. As used by SB in *Dream* and *Murphy,* apperception delineates the mental territory he would explore all his life, even as his distrust grew of the synthetic unity of the perceiving subject, the "I" (eye) to whom the field of immanence is ascribed. The endeavor culminates in *Film* with O's "flight from extraneous perception breaking down in inescapability of self-perception."

"Arènes de Lutèce": a twenty-three-line poem in **French**, eleventh of the twelve *Poèmes 38–39*. First published in *Les Temps modernes* II.14 (novembre 1946). The poem tells of an experience of *dédoublement,* the dilemma of the sundered self. Seated above the old Roman arena (the poem an "arène") in **Paris**, the poet watches himself and his companion as they enter(ed) earlier, and follows his path to the present point, ending with the shock of "returning" to himself in place and **time**, his companion beside him. Because it is felt not as vision but as event, the narrator's sense of his unreality is intensified, the self split into subject and **object**, an experience of *l'Autre.* It is a frequent theme in SB's writing, that of living "by proxy," a lost or **embryonic** self-adhering to the one that goes about mechanically and without conviction. That unreality is accentuated by the multiplex narrative framework, which creates a structure of infinite **apperception**, in which a **series** of selves observes past selves. The "nous" of the opening line dissolves into "je" and "elle," only ambivalently united at the end, an unnerving encounter with the misery ("triste visage") of the other, and so underlining the terrible isolation of the individual. The dualistic split is implicit in the woman watching "un petit chien vert" (wearing a cloth coat) and the narrator's naming of "his" left hand, a disjunction between the mind observing and the **body** observed. The contrast between ancient Rome and modern Paris accentuates the split, as do the street names (Arènes, Monge), the Roman name for Paris, Lutèce, and the plinth of the paleontologist Gabriel de Mortillet (1821–98), the fossil hunter fossilized. The vision is one of emptiness, the silent testimony of the past commenting mutely on the prospects before him. [Details from CB]

Aretino, Pietro (1492–1556): banished from his native Arezzo for writing a satirical sonnet against indulgences, he went to Rome and found favor with Pope Leo X until his obscene "Sonetti Lussuriosi" (1523). In **"Serena I,"** the poet has been reading **Thales** and Aretino. The scarlet beauty of the phlox and Thale's "all things full of **gods**" is qualified by the realities of a nasty world made manifest.

Arikha, Avigdor (b. 1929): Romanian-born artist who survived the concentration camps. He went to Israel, then **Paris**, where he was an abstract painter before turning to still life and portraiture. SB supported him financially from 1956. Arikha made many sketches and etchings of SB; see Ruby Cohn's *Back to Beckett* (76–77), and *Arikha* (1985). SB in turn made him generous offerings of books and manuscripts, including "Le **Petit sot**" (qv). SB spent long hours with Arikha in his studio (10 Villa d'Alésia) and, after his marriage, at their home (Square du Port Royal), discussing **art**, playing **chess**, or listening to **music**.

Arikha contributed six illustrations to a special 1958 edition of *Nouvelles et textes pour rien*. He used "**bon bon il est un pays**" for a **London** exhibition in the Matthiessen Gallery (6 April to 2 May 1959). *L'Issue* features six original engravings; and *The North* his etchings. A prospectus for a Samuel Beckett Theatre in Oxford (1965) reproduced the intended floor plan, announced an appeal for £140,000, and included a reproduced pencil portrait and Arikha's embossed silver-point portrait of SB as the front cover (the project was abandoned). A tribute from SB, in French then English, appeared in several books and exhibitions (see "**Pour Avigdor Arikha**"). *Arikha* (1985) offers this and two more: "**Ceiling**: *For Avigdor/September 1981*," and "Avigdor Arikha" (1982). On the first anniversary of SB's death Arikha produced a study entitled "Sam's Spoon" (1990), oil on canvas, the name "Sam" just visible on the handle of the small silver spoon that SB had given his daughter at her **birth**. Arikha's wife, Anne **Atik**, has written a touching and informative memoir of this period, illustrated with portraits and facsimiles of letters.

Aristotle (384–322 BC): Greek philosopher, born at Stageira, whose works form a huge compendium of learning, exercising an incalculable influence on subsequent ages. Following **Windelband** (133), who saw his epistemology as basically **Platonic**, SB associated him with an outmoded tradition of rationalism.

References are sardonic. These include: the Brothers **Boot** (*Whoroscope*); the **pun** on *catharsis* (*Murphy*, 89), from the *Poetics;* the **ant** in the sky (*Murphy*, 248), from *De Anima;* and his putative last words, *faede hunc mundum intravi* ("in filth I entered this world"), from Lemprière, in the *Watt* **Addenda**. "**Sendendo et quiescendo**" (qv) came courtesy of **Dante**; the citation in "**Text 8**" (134) of Aristotle, who "knew everything," via *Ulysses*. When **Winnie** asks if **Willie** would "concur with Aristotle," she refers to *omne animal post coitum triste est*, the "sad animal" of "**Fingal**," in conjunction with another Winnie.

Arschlochweh: *Improvisationslehrer* ("teacher of improvisation"), Swiss, melancholy, and highbrow, the **Smeraldina** stimulates in him "certain velleities of **desire**" (*Dream*, 14); later he has "married and gone to the Schweiz" (61). In life, one Dr. Gustav Guldenstein, who may not have deserved this name, crudely, "pain in the arsehole."

Arsene: servant of Mr. **Knott**. In his "short statement" (twenty-five pages) Arsene touches on several major inquiries. These include: the lonely road; **Lisbon**'s great day; the **Proust**-like change; the **Kant**-like encounter with Mr. Ash; the celebration of the seasons; the mirthless laugh; increeping and outbouncing house and parlor maids, **Mary and Ann**; the **coming and going** of Mr. Knott's servants; and his failure to eff the **ineffable**. The speech is a masterpiece of rhetorical compression, with delights within: a prose version of the poem "**Dieppe**"; a curious textual omission; embedded sonnets, one of iambic monometer; a parody of "The House-wife's Lament" ("In March it is mud, it is slush in December"); hymns ancient and modern; and plays on logical paradigms and truth tables. **Biblical** and literary echoes tease and provoke: Julien Sorel's servant in **Stendhal**'s *Le Rouge et le noir*, named Arsène; servants turning about Mr. Knott in tireless love, as in **Dante**'s *Paradiso;* the dream of **Descartes** (the little wind); the burning of Ridley and Cramner (a fire that "shall never be snuffed"); the epiphany in **Joyce**'s *Portrait* ("the seashore . . . hither and thither"); *Everyman* ("by your side, to be your guide"); St. Paul (what has been left undone); the Anglican Confession and *nunc dimittis;* the dying Lear ("bugger these buttons"). Another Arsene is a butler in "**Play**"; in the drafts he was **Erskine**.

art: SB's writing is characterized by a love of the visual arts, both classical and contemporary. This entry catalogues references in the early works (those in **bold** elaborated elsewhere) before looking at a letter of 1934 that intimates the need for a different aesthetic. The implications of this change of perspective appear in the picture of the circle and center in *Watt,* in the "**Three Dialogues**" with Georges **Duthuit** (1949), and in occasional reviews of artists whom SB admired. Finally, the influence of visual art on the plays and later prose is discussed. Grateful acknowledgment is made to James Knowlson's *Damned to Fame,* the best guide to the works that enchanted SB's imagination.

SB early cultivated the habit of visiting galleries and exhibitions. He regu-larly visited the National Gallery and Charlemont House, **Dublin**, developing a passion for the Dutch masters and cultivating the habit of close scrutiny. Years later he might recall tiny details of particular paintings. A 1927 visit to **Florence** proved a revelation, and **Kassel**, where his uncle was a dealer, opened his eyes. In **Paris** he met Thomas **MacGreevy**, whose knowledge of art was more sophisticated and with whom he spent countless hours in conversation and correspondence. **Surrealism** was exhilarating, if not persuasive, and Paris, in addition to museums like the Louvre, responded to movements like Die Brücke and Bauhaus.

Whoroscope invokes the portrait of **Descartes** by Franz Hals, **Mahaffy**'s frontispiece. *Proust* notes **Mantegna**'s *Assumption.* "**Dortmunder**" uses color provocatively: red spires, and black eyes reflected in the violet lamp like jade splinters. "**Alba**" is a portrait in white. "**Enueg 1**" sets "doomed **yellow**" against "the grey spew of the sewer." "**Serena III**" fixes a "pothook of beauty on this palette," as in **Hogarth**'s admiration of the sigmoidal form (Harvey, 151). In "**Malacoda**," SB's **imago** is a butterfly on a van **Huysum**; placing it on the coffin is a complex recognition in art of the inevitability of **death**. In "**Casket of Pralinen**" the poet stands before **Dülberg**'s *Abendmahl* (*Last Supper*). The scene is duplicated in *Dream* (76–77), where **Belacqua**, absorbed in **Vasari**, envisions himself as Judas in "Old Nick's bath." The "shrieking paullo-post-Expression" depicts his treatment of the **Smeraldina**, using "art" to avoid having to "promenade" her. *Dream* is saturated in allusions to artworks, their uneven presentation indicating an apprenticeship in progress, but testifying to a compositional mode that SB would develop, artwork framing the scene and defining it through the integrated effect of image and allusion.

Character portrayal is analyzed in *Dream* (161) in terms of the restoration of a work of art and the dubious deceptions of the artisan. The **Polar Bear** looks like "a starved **della Robbia**" (162). The Smeraldina is a problem in perspective, the "young Florentine" of **Franciabigio** invoked to define it (13). She is described as **Andrea del Sarto**'s *Madonna Lucrezia del Fede* (15 and 68), but with **Botticelli** thighs, Primavera buttocks (50), and a Rubensesque body. She flogs together eggs and tomatoes in a "Marie **Laurencin** polenta" (18), a misty composition in yellow and red. She appears like a Gozzi-Epstein (65, a Locomotive), blending the comedy of Carlo Gozzi with the sculpture of Jacob **Epstein**. Her father, the **Mandarin**, suggests George Chinnery's *A Portrait of a Mandarin* in the Dublin Gallery. The **Syra-Cusa** is a **Brancusi** bird with **Bilitis** breasts (33). The **Alba**'s eyes are black as sloes, as in El **Greco**'s *Burial of the Count of Orgaz*. Belacqua does not propose to **Blake** her, to Hieronymus **Bosch** her, that is, to play Adam and Eve or enter her Garden of Earthly Delights (193). The **Frica** is a "gem of ravished Quattrocento . . . of sweaty Big Tom" (215–16; see **Masaccio**). Belacqua imagines Nuremberg (71) by associating Albrecht **Dürer** with Adam **Kraft**, and the Smeraldina with both, an iron maiden; his rapture is like a **Zurbarán** Saint-Onan (72). He notes the "Giaconda smile" of the Pyrotechnist (96); sees **Lucien** "as in **Rembrandt**'s portrait of his brother" (116); then is displayed (133) like "the

dear little Buonarotti David in the Bargello," **Michelangelo**'s smaller bronze of his celebrated marble. It adds up to something like **Watteau** (159), a mannered elegance that is a departure point, if only for **Cythère**.

This continues into *MPTK*. A woman's face is like that by "the Master of Tired Eyes" ("Ding-Dong," 44). To visualize Ruby Tough the reader is directed to the Magdalene in the **Perugino** pietà in the National Gallery ("Love and Lethe," 87); she is compared (101) to the Infanta in **Velázquez**'s *Las Meninas* (Belacqua resembles something from Hogarth's *Harlot's Progress*). **Lucy**'s legs complement a **Signorelli** page ("Walking Out," 106), and her face suggests the Nobel **Yeats**, the portrait of W. B. by his brother, Jack. Thelma **bboggs**'s right hand is described ("What a Misfortune," 141) in terms of **Rodin** and Dürer; the postnuptial throng (151) as a **Benozzo** fresco. Belacqua in "**Yellow**" sees sunlight on "the grand old yaller wall," as in **Vermeer**'s *View of Delft*. His body is laid out "like the keys between nations" in Velázquez's *Lances* ("Draff," 180). The backdrop is likened to "swarthy **Uccello**" (182); and the mountains to a picture by Paul **Henry**.

Murphy handles art with wit. The linoleum suggests **Braque** (63); the walls "whine like Vermeer" (228), as in *View of Delft* or the yellow ivy in *Portrait* (178) that "whines upon the wall." Murphy on the jobpath is from Blake. Rosie **Dew**'s hot dog, Nelly, is "of such length and lowness" (100) that she might have been drawn by **Parmigianino**. Miss **Counihan** and **Wylie** share "**oyster kisses**" (117), in the Dutch tradition. Murphy's jest is likened to **Tintoretto**'s *Origin of the Milky Way* (140). Responding to **Bellini**'s *Circumcision* (251), his sympathies are entirely with the terrified child. SB refers to "Luke's portrait of Matthew" (215), but no such painting is known (see Rembrandt). **Claude**'s *Narcissus* expresses Murphy's **narcissism** (228). Murphy invokes "the **Phidias and Scopas** of fatigue" (238) as a meaningless distinction, as in the figures of "the Pergamene **Barlach**" or "**Puget**'s Caryatids of Strength and Weariness" (239).

A Hindu polyhistor trusts he will be granted Prana to finish a monograph entitled *The Pathetic Fallacy from Avercamp to Kampendonck,* but is unaware of the **Norwich school**. His thesis was anticipated in "**Lightning Calculation**." Central to SB's thinking is a rejection of landscape informed with feelings. A letter to MacGreevy (8 September 1934) offers a statement of his aesthetics, the important figure being **Cézanne** (qv), who rejected "landscapability" and "anthropomorphization" for nature as separate and alien, **atomistic**. SB rejects **Ruysdael**'s *Entrance to the Forest* as something loved that will no longer do, an emotion no longer authentic. As Knowlson concludes (188), it would be some years before SB learned to express this "incommensurabilty" of man with himself.

SB acquired in 1932 **Wilenski**'s *Introduction to Dutch Art*. This identified "the **Caravaggio**-Honthorst tradition" of spotlight effects, as in the painting of Gerrit van **Honthorst**, whose candlelit *Girl Catching a Flea in her Nightdress* suggested the Master of the **Leopardstown** Halflengths (see **Spiro**). SB had read **Schopenhauer** on artistic contemplation, on Dutch still lifes, which the beholder does not contemplate without emotion, for "they present to him the peaceful, still, frame of mind of the artist, free from will, which was needed to contemplate such insignificant things so objectively" (*WWI,* I.2 #38, 255). SB's dissatisfaction with this would grow, partly because artists like Cézanne and Jack **Yeats** had constructed an oeuvre on different principles, but also because he was moving away from unmediated expression toward relief and shade. The "**German Letter of 1937**" to Axel Kaun uses the visual arts to critique the subject-object dichotomy.

SB's 1936–37 visit to **Germany** had an indelible effect. The trip was a pilgrimage, partly to see old masters long admired but also to extend his knowledge of recent developments and see works before they were declared decadent by the Nazis. Knowlson records SB's daily activities and visits to major galleries. He notes how SB's perusal of guidebooks led him to items in galleries and churches in smaller towns. He records SB's growing appreciation of moderns such as **Ballmer**, **Munch**, and **Nolde**; his introduction to leading artists; his sense of poetry and painting as prayer (see "**Humanistic Quietism**"); and his growing distrust of rational attempts to impose order upon the straws and particulars of existence (228). He notes how certain images, such as **Giorgione**'s self-portrait, the Antonella *Virgin of the Annunciation,* and paintings by Caspar David **Friedrich** later became specific stage settings and dramatic images. The experience left SB exhausted and with a conviction of his dereliction

as opposed to the "authenticity of vocation" of others (Knowlson, 234); but it
had been a "**necessary journey**" (qv).

References to the visual arts in *Watt*
are both "facultatif" and essential. The
former is manifested in such details as the
racecourse (29), "so . . . ? . . . when
empty," the manuscripts reading "so (Indian artist)ish when empty," SB finally
preferring the lacuna. **Arsene**'s vision of
sun and wall derives from Vermeer, and
his final parting forms a tableau. Direct
allusions to painting, except for **Sam** likening Watt to the *Christ* by Bosch (159),
invoking **pity** for his slow **crucifixion**, are
restricted to the Addenda, **residua** of the
artistry that went into the book. These
include: **Art Conn** ("Black Velvet")
O'Connery; the Chinnery-Slattery tradition; and Master of the Leopardstown
Half-Lengths.

In **Erskine**'s room (128–30), Watt
looks at a picture: a circle, described with
a compass and broken at its lowest point,
black, and a point, in the eastern background, **blue**. As an "object of note" it
creates a problem of perception. An effect of perspective is obtained, but the
more Watt tries to understand the relationship between circumference and
point the less he knows. He wonders
what the artist intended to represent, but
"Watt knew nothing about painting";
the object of scorn is "represent." The
language of **physics** is used, in a parody
of Schopenhauer's discussion of the
thing-in-itself (*WWI*, I.2, #25, 168):
"true wisdom is not to be gained by
measuring out the boundless world, or,
what would be more to the purpose, by
actually traversing endless space. It is
rather to be attained by the thorough

investigation of any individual thing, for
thus we seek to arrive at a full knowledge
and understanding of its true and peculiar nature." But contemplation does not
lead to aesthetic understanding. Watt's
wish to know does not last. When he
leaves, the narrator comments that the
picture yielded nothing further: "On the
contrary, as **time** passed, its significance
diminished" (208).

SB's "frenzy of writing" after the **war**
included reviews of artists he admired:
"**MacGreevy on Yeats**"; Henri **Hayden**:
"La **Peinture des van Velde ou Le
Monde et le Pantalon**"; and "**Peintres de
l'empêchement**." These reflect SB's concern with the relation of subject and
object, as in *Texts for Nothing*, where he
moves uncertainly toward the "new
land" identified in the essays. The important statement is the "Three Dialogues"
(1949) with Georges Duthuit. These
espouse the conviction, no less powerful
for being now a cliché, that "art has nothing to express." Art is "defined" in terms
of impotence and failure, moving away
from "the plane of the **feasible**" (the artist yet remaining in the domain of the
particular). The breakdown of subject
and object means there is no longer any
valid mode of expression. Most artists
(**Tal Coat, Masson**) have but enlarged
the statement of compromise; only a few
(Bram **van Velde**) have tried to find a
form to accommodate the mess. That
attempt is doomed to fail, and so asked
why the obligation to express "**B**" can
only reply that he does not know. Out
of these "old **aporetics**" SB's greatest
writings arose.

SB saw painting as expressing what he
termed the "metaphysical concrete," a

quality he admired in Ballmer. Fleeting references in the later fiction have this immediacy. The poem "**bon bon il est un pays,**" arising from the need to appreciate another's art, suggests why they are so fleeting: the mind is a country, and the poet wishes to be left alone to explore it, without intrusion of images not his own. There are few direct references to the visual arts in 1940s novellas or *Texts for Nothing* (1950–52), and relatively few in *Three Novels.* Molloy apologizes for the "wealth of filthy circumstance" (63): "Homo mensura can't do without staffage" (small incidental details). He thinks of "flight and bivouac, in an Egypt without bounds" (66), as in *Rest on the Flight into Egypt* (Rembrandt). **Moran** is attached to his son with a long rope, "like a burgess of Calais" (129) (**Rodin**). Distant lights remind him of "Juno's milk" (159) (Tintoretto), but his life is otherwise devoid of art. Malone has not quite terminated his humanities, and makes specific allusions: Caspar David Friedrich (198); **Tiepolo** (235); Watteau (237); and the calm "repoussé" (raised in relief) sea. The **Unnamable**'s impotence is likened to Matthew and the angel (301), as in Rembrandt's painting of his son Titus. He calls his situation a "touching picture" (320), but his reduction to objet d'art is an incorporate head in a jar (340).

In his drama SB rendered setting as visual art. *Waiting for Godot,* as SB admitted, derives from *Zwei Männer betrachten den Mond* ("Two Men look at the Moon") of Caspar David Friedrich, which SB saw in Dresden in 1937 (but see Knowlson, 342). Other scenes derive from specific paintings or traditions: **Pozzo** and **Lucky** in act II re-create

Brueghel's *The Parable of the Blind* (in *All That Fall,* Dan **Rooney** comments, "We shall fall into the ditch"); Lucky is a grotesque from Brueghel's *The Land of Cockaigne;* and Pozzo raised from the ground between **Vladimir** and **Estragon** imitates the *Descent from the Cross.* Estragon's **boots** suggest van **Gogh**'s *Boot with Laces;* and the carrots, radishes, and turnips could be from the *The Potato Eaters.* More important is the sense of composition as tableau, down to the tiniest detail, recognizable iconography.

Hamm in his chair owes something to Velázquez's portrait of Pope Innocent X (1650) or Francis **Bacon**'s imitation thereof. *Krapp's Last Tape* is a nocturne in dark and light, spotlight painting evident, as in "**Play**" and in *Not I.* The latter was stimulated by SB's 1971 visit to Malta and his fascination with Caravaggio's *Decollation of St. John the Baptist. Krapp* may in turn take its visual cue from Rembrandt's *The Parable of the Rich Man* or *The Money Changer* of 1627, which SB saw, as noted in his Berlin diaries of 1936–37, in the Kaiser-Wilhelm-Friedrich Museum in Berlin in 1937. "**Berceuse**" ("**Rockaby**") draws on portraits of aging mothers (Rembrandt, Whistler, van Gogh). The Protagonist of "**Catastrophe**" suffers like countless martyrs, from St. Sebastian to **Christ**. "**Ohio Impromptu**" draws on the tradition of Dutch interiors; while *Footfalls,* according to Billie **Whitelaw**, is like an Edvard Munch painting. In his review of the 1999 Beckett Festival at the Barbican (*Guardian,* 1 September 1999: 10–11), criticizing *Not I,* Michael Billington claimed that SB wrote four imperishable masterpieces but that the rest will exist on the margins of repertory: "Architecture may, as Schiller said, be frozen music, but drama, if it is to survive down the ages, cannot simply be a petrified painting." The problem, he claimed, is that the later drama depends on the fixed image and is not capable of endless variation. Yet SB's experience with the paintings he loved was that they remained eternally new, and the image rather than the performance endured.

The image that most haunted SB was the head. As Knowlson notes (551), if SB's images were inspired by the old masters, they appear strikingly post-expressionist because he distorts them radically, isolating head or mouth from **body**, reducing corporality. From "**Eh Joe**" on, SB cultivated portraiture, accidentals stripped away, leaving the talking or listening head. Equally the **face**: in "**Words and Music**" Croak is moved by "The face in the ashes." The "dear face" is recalled in "Ohio Impromptu." In *That Time*, C (redrawn from Blake's "**Job**") recalls the National Portrait Gallery, London, sitting on a cold marble seat then looking up to see a vast oil, black with dirt and age, from which a face emerged, a turning point in his life. The face from the past, a woman loved, is a recurrent motif.

Past images sometimes return as photographs, constituting an identity that cannot be denied, as in the narrator's recollections in *How It Is* (15) of his past self as a child in prayer. Despite O's attempts to rip up his past, this photograph returns in *Film*. In *Company*, **memory** constitutes image and frames it accordingly. The minimalist works exemplify an artistry conscious of their own production, often expressed visually, as in *All Strange Away* and *Still*, where the text is pared down to small formal elements, movement reduced to frozen gesture, almost literally *still life*, the least that text can be yet retain narrative **motion**. "**One Evening**" is a *tableau vivant*, a nocturne first in black and white, then **green and yellow**. In "La **Falaise**" the observing "eye" views the cliff that separates him from and joins him to it in a process that blends perception and imagination; it might be described as a composition in words, evolving from the flux of impressions a rhythm and the crystallization of an image. Even in the smallest, most abstract compositions the humanities were never quite terminated.

"**Ascension**": an eighteen-line **French** poem, fourth of the twelve *Poèmes 38–39*. First published in *Les Temps modernes* II.14 (novembre 1946); rpt. in *Minuit* 21 (novembre 1976): 14–15, and *Collected Poems* (1984), 42. It comprises three sections, with a single-line comment after the first, and a cursory concluding couplet. On Ascension Thursday, forty days after Easter, **Christ** rose into heaven, but the invocation is ironic. The first section is mundane: through the thin partition the poet hears the child next door, "prodigue à sa façon," and a passionate voice "on the air" commenting on the World Cup, held in France in 1938, June 4–19; Ascension Day was May 12, so the overlap ("en même temps") is not exact. The line "toujours trop jeune," referring to the "enfant," is pivotal. Ascending to his open window is the "houle" (wave of sound) of a different crowd, the "foule" of the faithful. The third section is the emotional core, the ruthless suffering denying resurrection; the **memory** of one who died spurting blood all over the sheets, sweet peas, and her "mec" (her guy). This is the **death** from TB (in May) of Peggy **Sinclair** (the green eyes). The poem ends by mocking this involuntary ascension of memory: "elle rode légère / sur ma tombe d'air," horror intensified by the tinkling rhyme, the very lightness of tone.

Assez: original of "**Enough**," published in *Minuit* (19 février 1966), a limited edition of 662 numbered copies; then included in *Têtes-mortes* (1967), 31–47. A version published in *La Quinzaine littéraire* 1 (15 mars 1966): 4–5, described as "Un texte inédit de Samuel Beckett," did not in fact precede the first edition.

"**Assumption**": SB's first published story, in *transition* 16–17 (1929): 268–71; rpt. in Eugene Jolas's *Transition Workshop* (Vanguard Press, 1949), 41–44 ("Paramyth"). Like other early stories, "**A Case in a Thousand**" (**Freud**), "**Text**" (**Fletcher**), and "**Sedendo et Quiescendo**" (**Dante**), it retains the rhetorical ornament (**Baudelaire**'s translations of Poe?) and psychological probing of high modernism. That issue of *transition* also included his "Dante" essay, Jolas choosing to republish it.

The Feast of the Assumption (August 15) celebrates the entry of the Virgin Mary into heaven. **Malone** doubts he will pant on that far (179). *Proust* alludes to **Mantegna**'s *Assumption* (93), the fresco depicting in the archangel beauty and aspiration expressed as prayer. In the

story, an anguished young "artist" struggles to restrain "that wild rebellious surge that aspired violently towards realization in sound." "Assumption" opens with an **aporia** that would become SB's signature: "He could have shouted and could not." This is the reductio of *Proust* (64), **art** as "the apotheosis of **solitude**." The poet commands a "remarkable faculty of whispering the turmoil down." He can silence any "oblivious combatant" with a gesture, with "all but imperceptible twitches of impatience." His aesthetics separates Beauty from Prettiness. The latter proceeds up a staircase of sensation, and sits on the topmost stair "to digest our gratification." More powerful are sensations generated when we are pitched on the peak of a sheer crag, "which is the pain of Beauty."

"Assumption" develops an aesthetics of pain, the German **Romanticism** SB never purged from his art. As the artist struggles to restrain the animal voice that "tore at his throat," an unnamed Woman enters. She flatters and seduces the *artiste manqué,* and so, in contemplation and absorption, he loses "part of his essential animality." After he is seduced, "spent with extasy [*sic*]," the dammed "stream of whispers" explodes in "a great storm of sound" (compare *Not I*). The story ends in an ironic pietà: "They found her caressing his wild dead hair." "Assumption" works through (and against) the image of a **Promethean** artist: "Thus each night he died and was **God** [the Assumption?], each night revived and was torn, torn and battered." Whether the artist transcends the worldly to unite with the Idea, transcends **Schopenhauer**'s world of representation to achieve the pure will, or whether the title refers to the arrogance of such desire, may be the crux. The protagonist's romantic agony (in all senses of that phrase) may simply be postcoital depression, and so travesty the belabored agonies of a would-be artist.

"As the Story Was Told": a short prose work, composed between "4.8.73" and "13.8.73," according to the drafts, one inscribed "G. E. zum Gedächtnis." Wolfgang Hildesheimer's German translation was included in a memorial tribute, *Günter Eich zum Gedächtnis,* ed. Siegfried Unseld (Frankfurt: **Suhrkamp,** 1973), 10, 12; Ger. trans. 11, 13. Published in the *Chicago Review* 33.2 (1982): 76–77, then in *As the Story Was Told* (Calder, and Riverrun Press, 1990), 103–7, a gathering of previously uncollected prose. The short story invokes one waiting "in a hut," reminded of the **summerhouse** where as a child he used to sit for hours, in a small wicker chair, until a hand appeared in the doorway, holding a sheet of writing, which he read then tore into four pieces: "As the story was told me the man succumbed in the end to his ill-treatment." The story ends with an admission: he does not know what the **old man** would have to say to be pardoned, but he would have recognized it, had he seen it. The import is enigmatic, Kafkaesque. Affinities with the opening of *Molloy* and *The Unnamable*'s rotunda (317) are teasing, even after twenty-five years.

astronomy: many of SB's works create or exist within a cosmos, and references to the stars orient or confuse his characters. SB recorded details (DN, 145–50) from Sir James Jeans's *The Universe Around Us* (1929). At the **Frica**'s party (*Dream,* 221), the Ovoidologist booms that "the greatest triumph of human thought was the calculation of Neptune from the observed vagaries of the orbit of Uranus" (Jeans, 18; DN, 147). The sentiment (without the **Polar Bear**'s "And yours") is repeated in *Murphy* (280). Astronomers had noted that the orbit of Uranus did not conform to Newton's laws. In 1845 John Couch Adams calculated where the unknown planet must be. Urbain le Verrier in **Paris** reached the same conclusions, publishing his findings (30 August 1846); a squabble over precedence arose (French cartoons showed English astronomers with telescopes trained across the Channel, finding it in the papers of French scientists). SB switched loyalties in the **French** *Murphy,* praising le Verrier's "dix milles pages de calculs dont sortit Neptune."

Jeans gave SB the Vernier scale for measuring fractional subdivisions, as in a "vernier of appreciation" (*Dream,* 231) or the "vernier of appraisement" ("A Wet Night," 77); references to starfields (*Dream,* 16, 137), gravitational effects (222), spectral margins, ultraviolets and binary effects (28), and astral straws (119). **"At last I find in my confusèd soul"** likens two lovers to "syzygetic stars," astral bodies aligned in one conjunction; this is mocked in **"Love and Lethe"** (87–88) with Ruby's "itch for **syzygy**" (88), the gravitational urge of a binary star for its partner, or "a home-sick meteorite abounding in IT" (94). Murphy's "galactic **coalsack**" (188) finds mundane expression in *How It Is,* the protagonist "marked" by astronomy (41).

Molloy once took an interest in astronomy (39), but the best he can conclude is how difficult it is to speak of the moon and not lose one's head. Or that it is her arse she shows us always. Despite his studies he cannot read the stars (60). He is not alone. In *First Love* (45), as the narrator leaves **Lulu**, he looks in vain for the Wains. The protagonist of "The Calmative" (69) raises without hope his eyes to the sky for the Bears; the narrator of "**Text 1**" waits for them to guide him on his way (the **French** text [120] reads "les chariots," or Wains). In "**Assumption**" (6) and *Dream* (16 and 70) **Vega** is associated with mystical experience. "**Words and Music**" (132) refers to "Mira in the Whale"; this is Mira Ceti, a periodic star, one that undergoes an increase and diminution of luster, even extinction and revival, and so an emblem of **Croak**'s emotion. In "**Rough for Theatre II**," **A** and **B** irritably discuss the sky, A wondering if they can see Jupiter. B dismisses this: "No. It twinkles" (stars do, planets don't). A's "What is it then?" meets a typical negation: "No idea. Sirius." The dog star presides over the "divine dogday" of "**Malacoda**."

"**For to end yet again**" marks the appearance against the gray cloudless sky of two "white dwarfs": the **pun** on dying stars within the sepulchral **skull** implies that this is, indeed, the end. Compare the "dying dwarf" of "**Text 8**" (134). In *Mercier and Camier* (76) casual reference is made to the "transit" of Camier. *The Unnamable* is conceived in terms of Henri **Poincaré**'s paradox, atoms as infinitely small stars; the "transit of Malone" is explicitly noted (299), but others pass by, in fixed orbits or like comets. Unlike the lights (stars?) that are "unwavering and fixed" (294), the Unnamable is the Ptolemaic center, the nucleus about which others wheel, like planets about the sun, although he admits the possibility (295) of being in perpetual motion about another point, accompanied by **Malone** as the earth by its moon.

asylum: a word with **identified contraries** of sanctuary and insanity. SB treats the insane with sympathy, those in their **little world** retaining an integrity not obvious among the sane. Yet madness is not romanticized (saving **Murphy**'s view of the inmates); **schizophrenia** is recognized, and ironies are manifest. In "**Echo's Bones**" asylum is synonymous with the grave; and in *Dream* (44), with the mind at rest. "**Fingal**" unfolds near the **Portrane** asylum, and echoes of **Swift** question **Belacqua**'s state of mind. Murphy applies "asylum" to the "little shelter" near **Brewery Road** (73). At the **MMM**, Murphy imagines he might be a microcosmopolitan, self-sustained in his little world, only to realize that earthly asylum is attainable at the cost of sanity. O in *Film* tries to turn his **mother**'s room into a **monad**, but is finally unable to escape **apperception**. There is a myth that SB worked as an orderly at an asylum (see the **Calder** jacket of *Murphy*); rather, he visited Geoffrey **Thompson** at the **Bethlem Royal**, and took notes.

Watt pays the price that Murphy rejects, his quest leading him to the **mansions** of the madhouse (from the **Knott** house to the nuthouse?), based on the House of **St. John of God**, **Stillorgan**. That asylum is the setting of *Malone*

Dies and "The **End**." **Hamm** recalls a madman who thought the end of the world had come, and when dragged to the window he could see only ashes. The asylum is the abode of the unaccommodated self, that figure which pursues the *via negativa* of **Jung**'s quest for the integrated psyche. In the later texts "asylum" is often replaced by "home," with the same ambivalence. For details of SB's asylums, see O'Brien's *The Beckett Country*, chapter 7.

Atik, Anne: wife of Avigdor **Arikha**. Her tribute on SB's **death**, "The Uses of Poetry," is James Knowlson's frontispiece. As subject for her husband, she appears frequently in *Arikha* (1985). Her essay "Beckett as Reader" (1999) details SB's thirty-year **friendship** and documents the range of his reading, **musical** knowledge, and **memory**. A book version, with letters, photographs, and drawings by Avigdor, appeared as *How It Was: A Memoir of Samuel Beckett* (Faber, 2001). It includes a facsimile of "**Petit sot**" (10).

Atlas: son of the Titan Iapetus and ocean nymph Clymene, half brother of **Prometheus**; after the revolt of the Titans he supported the world on his shoulders. **Lucky** is mocked by **Pozzo** with the erroneous cry, "Atlas, son of Jupiter" (*WG*, 21.a). SB corrected the error to "Atlas, son of Japhetos" [Ruby Cohn to SG].

"**At last I find in my confusèd soul**": a sonnet, directed to Peggy **Sinclair**, written on the manuscript of *Whoroscope*. Published in "**Sedendo et Quiescendo**" (1932), then in *Dream* (70–71), with minor variants: "A strange exalted **death**" became "A rapturous strange death"; "two merged stars" became "syzygetic stars." SB rejected it, but it is a fine piece, the binary sonnet form striving against the single sentence that comprises the entire poem so as to be "whole." The "birdless, cloudless, colourless skies" echo the end of "**Assumption**" (1929) and the "starless inscrutable hour" of *Whoroscope*.

atomism: Gk. *atomos*, "that which cannot be divided." SB found in the atomists (**Democritus**, **Epicurus**, and **Lucretius**) a school at odds with prevailing Greek philosophy (**Socrates**, **Plato**, and **Aristotle**). Lesley **Daiken**'s 1930 notes indicate how the **pre-Socratics** (qv) were taught at **Trinity**, in one lecture, "The School of the Sophists": a definition of *to apeiron* was offered, and related to "infinite" and "indefinite" the better to dismiss it as "An ideology of negative attributes . . . Reactionary became Agnostic." Then followed a list of said negatives: infinitude, indefinable, indefinite, incomprehensible, inapprehensible, unattainable, unknowable; leading to a rejection of any system founded on the principle of *it is not,* and concluding, "The exponents of this school are on a low intellectual level."

SB found in the atomists a lasting fascination. His interest was rekindled at the **École Normale**, and enflamed in **London** (1932). Preparing for *Murphy* he read systematically commentaries like **Burnet**'s *Early Greek Philosophy* and *Greek Philosophy*, **Windelband**'s *History of Philosophy*, Beare's *Greek Theories of Elementary Cognition*, Bailey's *The Greek Atomists and Epicurus,* and whatever he could find on Democritus. SB was attracted to their attempt to explain the world without reference to purpose or first cause. *Murphy*'s end is not just an atomist joke, but a curious echo of the contemporary quantum **physics** shaking the foundations of Cartesian and Newtonian thought.

As Windelband indicates, the atomism of Leucippus develops from the Eleatic conception of being by asserting that that which is nonbeing must have a metaphysical reality; it thereby "shatters in pieces the world body of **Parmenides**, and scatters its parts through infinite space" (43). Such portions of being, however, like the absolute being of Parmenides, are eternal and indestructible, without beginning, indivisible, *atomoi,* in countless numbers infinitely varied in form. The things we perceive, Leucippus maintained, are combinations of such atoms, arising when they unite and dispersing when they part. Yet the mainstream of Greek thought affirmed the immortality of the soul after **death**, as in Plato's *Phaedra,* with Socrates's contention that death is but the separation of the soul from the **body**. Parmenides contended that death was not the end of sensibility, only the cessation of bodily sensation. Democritus, while not rejecting the soul, argued that as it was composed of atoms, albeit exceedingly fine ones, it follows that on death, when the atoms are dispersed, the soul must share the body's dissolution. The atomists thus directly denied the immortality of the soul. Hence the redistribution of Murphy's atoms; Ruby Tough's "almost atomic despair" ("Love and Lethe," 87); and Mrs. **Rooney**'s outburst: "oh to be

in atoms, in atoms! . . . ATOMS!" The cosmology of *The Unnamable* is a planetary system circling a sun, but also the electron circling its nucleus. "**Text 13**" invokes the despairing sense of individual existence as a flurry of dust, "where time passes and atoms assemble an instant, where the **voice** belongs perhaps." And where the mind, capable of little more, tries to assemble the fragmentary atoms of its existence by sensing periodic patterns of repetition.

Atropos: in Greek mythology, the black-veiled Fate whose scissors cut the thread of life, the "black old hag older than the world born of night" (*How It Is,* 106). Also invoked in "**jusque dans la caverne ciel et sol**" and the *mirlitonnade* "noire soeur."

Auber, Daniel François Esprit (1782–1871): composer who studied under Cherubini, his style marked by the lightness and grace of the French school. Associated with **Chopin** and the **Smeraldina** (*Dream,* 69), since operas feature tubercular heroines.

Aubervilliers: a town north of **Paris**, resort of pilgrims to Notre Dame des Vertus. The **Unnamable** (333) imagines himself, paralytic, dragged there or to the Bay of Naples to admire the celebrated view; then, uncured or with nothing to admire, jumping off a cliff ("See Naples and die"). In translation, SB left a hiatus then restored the **French** locale.

d'Aubigné, Théodore Agrippa (1552–1630): poet, historian, and satirist of the Protestant Reformation, author of *Les*

Tragiques, on the St. Bartholemew's Day massacre (24 August 1572). In "The **Calmative**" (28) the narrator leans against "the perishing oaks immortalized by d'Aubigné"; the "chesnes superbes" of *Ode* XIV, their beauty rotting as autumn advances.

Aucassin et Nicolette: a fifteenth-century romance of the illicit amour of Nicolette and her Saracen lover. Nicolette steals out before dawn to see her imprisoned lover, raising her silk dress because of the dew. The **Alba** comments, catching up her gown: "Nicolette in the dew" (*Dream,* 199). **Belacqua** refers to "gutter Nicolettes" (84) squatting in the stews. **Murphy**'s incandescent trailing through the grass at dawn (251) enacts the scene.

Auditor: in *Not I* adjunct to **Mouth**, a "tall standing figure, sex undeterminable, enveloped from head to foot in loose black djellaba, with hood." He stands on a podium invisible to the audience, "dead still" but for four brief movements, a simple sideways raising of the arms and their falling back, "a gesture of helpless compassion," each recurrence lessening till scarcely perceptible; the dramatization of "**Dante**'s rare movements of compassion in Hell" ("Dante and the Lobster," 19). The source of this gesture, Knowlson suggests (521), may be an old woman in **Caravaggio**'s *Decollation of St. John the Baptist* (but compare *Eleutheria,* 153). Auditor has proved problematic. Antoni Libera decided he should be visible only when performing his gesture, unreal and ghostlike. Having worked with Anthony Page on the Royal

Court *Not I* (1973), and having directed it at the Théâtre d'Orsay (1975), SB was ambivalent. He wrote David Hunsberger and Linda Kendall (16 November 1986) advising them to omit Auditor, since he is difficult to stage: "For me the play needs him but I can do without him. I have never seen him function effectively." With Madeleine **Renaud** (1978) he omitted Auditor, as did the BBC film with Billie **Whitelaw**, thereby raising the paradox of how one can speak if one is not heard.

Augustine, St. (354–430): greatest of the early Church fathers. He brought together Patristic and Hellenistic doctrine and laid the foundations of **scholasticism** for the next thousand years. Born in Numidia of a pagan **father**, he was brought up as a Christian by his devout **mother**, Monica. He studied in Carthage, where he had an illegitimate son, Adeodatus (mentioned in "**Echo's Bones**"). Attracted to **gnosticism**, he embraced skepticism, then Neo**platonism**, before a spiritual crisis led to his conversion and baptism (386), as related in *The Confessions.* As Bishop of Hippo from 396 until his **death** he became the champion of orthodoxy, his earlier assertions of the free will contradicted by the later conviction of original sin and grace. His *City of God* presents human history as the conflict between spiritual and temporal forces, ending in the triumph of the City of **God**, manifested on earth as the Church. As he died the Vandals were at the gates of Hippo.

Whoroscope represents the saint's dictum "si fallor, sum" (*De libro arbitrio,* II.iii.7) as "Fallor, ergo sum," linking it to **Descartes**. SB found in Augustine what **Windelband** (276) terms the absolute and immediate certainty of **consciousness**; and a philosophical statement of doubt similar to the Cartesian one: "For if I am deceived, I am. For he who is not, cannot be deceived." The phrase "He tolle'd and legge'd" refers to Augustine's conversion, SB explaining that "Saint Augustine has a revelation in the shrubbery and reads Saint Paul." The "redemptorist waistcoat" intimates Romans 13:13: "put ye on the Lord Jesus **Christ**; and make not provision for the flesh, to fulfil the lusts thereof."

John Pilling cites SB's "phrase-hunting" (DN, 11) in Pusey's Everyman translation of the *Confessions* and a Latin original. The Notebook lists a dozen pages of sequential entries, paradoxes and striking phrases, many ticked as having been used. Some went directly into *Dream,* contributing to **Belacqua**'s speculative thoughts. Several passages (73, 86) entirely derive from such phrases. Belacqua's "shadowy love" and the "boiling over of his neckings" (73) make little sense until recognized in the *Confessions* (2.i–ii). Belacqua's wish to be both continent and sustenant and the "non-eternal **voice**" derive directly from Augustine. Dozens of such details, from the **old man** (63) to the Greek baths (86), the gloom of carnal custom (166) and the will and nill (123), are identified here.

Material from *Dream* was recycled into *MPTK* and "**Echo's Bones**." Conversation between Belacqua and Lord Gall derives largely from Notebook entries. In "**Yellow**" (174) Belacqua repeats from *Dream* (122) Augustine's admonition to "Go back into your heart" (4.xii). The "nuts and balls and sparrows of the low stature of childhood" (1.ix), and the problems for astrology caused by Jacob and Esau being twins (7.vi), get into *Murphy* (38 and 23). **Malone**'s question "of a theological nature" (167) as to what God did before the creation is answered (11.x–xii): He was preparing Hell for pryers into such secrets. Augustine's metaphor "the glue of love" (4.x) is repeated from *Dream* (66, 70, 141), to *Malone Dies* (262): "love regarded as a kind of lethal glue, a conception frequently to be met within **mystic** texts"; and *How It Is* (82): "live together glued together **love** each other a little." The doctrine of the "sole elect" is finally rejected as "all balls." SB's best-known reference to Augustine is his comment to Harold Hobson about "the shape of ideas" in *Waiting for Godot.* This derives from Robert **Greene**'s "Repentance," which concludes with the sentiment about the **two thieves** (qv) that SB attributes to Augustine but cannot be found there. Even so, and in the theatrical mind certainly, the central dilemma of SB's best-known play is felt to arise directly from the greatest of Christian writers.

Au loin un oiseau: the seventh *Foirade,* translated as "**Afar a bird**" (qv). First published in a special limited edition of 120 copies (New York: Double Elephant Press, 1973), unbound folio gatherings, boxed, the text illustrated by Avigdor **Arikha**.

d'Aulnoy, Comtesse: Marie Catherine de la Motte, Baronne d'Aulnoy (1650–1705). Larousse comments: "Between a precocious marriage with a debauched husband whom she sought to have condemned to death, and an edifying end in a convent, she spent an 'adventurous' life in Europe." Known for her fairy tales, *Contes nouvelles ou les Fées à la mode* (1698), in the manner of Charles **Perrault**, others deriving from the *Pentamerone* of Giovanni Battista Basile (1637). Jack **Yeats** illustrated her "Beauty and the Beast." The Bluebird ("L'Oiseau bleu") features in "**Love and Lethe**" (98) and "**What a Misfortune**" (135); **Belacqua** echoes Florine at the window where she awaits her Prince Charmant, changed into a bluebird. The tale is mentioned in *Dream* (120); and the **Alba** appears as Florine at the high window, with, alas, not a "blue feather" in sight (154). The cypress covered with swords and daggers that gash the bird's wings, and the pie full of astrologers, doctors, and musicians are from the tale. Likewise the story of Mie-Souillon, the identity assumed by Florine to win back her prince by spending her nights in the Cabinet of Echoes, whence her sighs are wafted to her loved one. Belacqua in his wedding speech thanks the Maids, including "Belle-Belle their leader" (157). "**Sanies II**," like the "Circe" episode of *Ulysses,* is set in a brothel; "Gracieuse," "Belle-Belle," and "Percinet" appear, but in a sinister metamorphosis the Barfrau with the mighty bottom becomes Madame de la **Motte** (1756–91), infamous courtesan and poisoner, and enchantment turns to nightmare.

Auster: the South Wind, which in *Molloy* (16) "vents" the earthly paradise (omitted in the **French** text [20]). In *Murphy* (78), "the trembling of the austral sea" alludes to **Dante**'s ascent of Mt. Purgatory. "[A]ustral vento" (*Purg.* XXXI.71) is a notorious crux, the better reading being "nostral vento" ("our wind").

"**Authors Take Sides on the Spanish War**": answers to a loaded questionnaire organized by Nancy **Cunard** for the *Left Review* in June 1937, with the original broadside ("The Question") tipped in. Dated "**Paris**—June 1937," it was sent to various authors, asking: "Are you for, or against, the legal Government and People of Republican Spain?" Writers were asked for a statement in not more than six lines; SB's was the briefest and most ambiguous: "¡UPTHEREPUBLIC!" **Malone** echoes this, dubiously (236). The phrase retains a decidedly Irish edge as in the football cheer "Up Cork!" or the political chant for Eamon de Valera, "Up Dev!"

"**Avant** *Fin de partie*": the play that grew into *Fin de partie* (*Endgame*) went through many preliminaries. The first is a six-page fragment in a notebook (with part of *Malone Dies*) at **Trinity** (MS 4662), containing four pages of dialogue between F and X and two of notes. The **Sam Francis Notebook** (RUL 2926) has an early draft, and there is a twenty-one-leaf, lightly revised, undated typescript (RUL 1227/7/16/7), sans decor, called "Avant *Fin de partie*" (1953 or 1952). The dialogue is between X, an apparently blind **Hamm**-like character, whose name may be, according to his baptismal spoon, Jeannot (see **Baby Jack**), and F, his factotum, whose name changes from Donald to Lucien and Albert; he objects only to Arthur: "Tout sauf Arthur." There is no opening **mime**; it begins with X's monologue, in which he discusses his blindness and paralysis, both perhaps volitional.

Some themes are more overt than in the final play. X asserts that he means nothing: "Je ne représente rien, ne signifie rien." This is part of his quotidian routine, a ritual that maintains his present state: "Cela me conserve." X and F are trying to survive a day while awaiting an end. While waiting they **love**, amuse, and abuse each other. F does not kill X because F loves X, although he says so with disgust: "Si je pouvais aimer quelqu'un."

They fear they will have **nothing** to do: "Alors il n'y a rien à faire." X summons his factotum by beating on a drum, wanting him to enter on his knees. The master/slave relationship is present, but F insists on formalities. He wants to call X "sir," "boss," or "your honour," but X insists that F use "tu," as later he will demand that F call him "old fool." F expresses his need for harmony, for order. X shares this preoccupation, wanting to be in the center of the shelter with the maximum of air, space, emptiness, and solitude around him, to be at peace and hear the **music** of the spheres. This is *Godot* redux: two men countering a disintegrating world with a private, arbitrary order.

The fragment is set in Picardy, "plus precisement dans le Boulonnais . . . alentours de Wissant." The shelter, on a cliff, suggests former elegance. The protagonists are survivors of a World War I battle, their environment from 1914 to 1918 "Detruite progressivement . . . dans des circonstances mysterieuses." The house has a great bay window through which, before it was boarded up (blinded), they could see across the channel "les falaises d'Albion." In the earliest fragment X is called Albert, a town

in Picardy. Thereabouts is a town named Hamm, easily garnished with **Clov**.

X takes **painkillers**. He asks F to fill the syringe: "De morphine. De cocaine. De hachiche. De cyanure." X asks for a **Bible**, which once offered solace, and for F to read a psalm, then an unspecified passage from Jeremiah. Neither is effective, but the need persists: "Si on n'a pas la foi on est foutu. (*Un temps.*) Et si on l'a on est baisé." Syringe and Bible merge in a Marxist image: "(*Il jette la bible.*) Sale opium, va!" X wants a **dog**, a Pekingese, because he fears being alone. It will help him, he feels, serve some purpose before he dies. He wants independence but is thwarted by his blindness and because he cannot turn the wheels of his chair. He needs affection: "J'ai tant besoin . . . d'affection . . . beaucoup d'affection . . . beaucoup . . . beaucoup d'affection." So he invents a family, with F as **mother**. X wants a conventional structure with dog, wife, and mother. He creates a wild fantasy: a dutiful son within a matriarchal family, a mother and twelve daughters. The protagonist cares for his mother after a frightful accident. In X's narrative, she has been gone some eight days. Others thought that she had abandoned them and gone to **Paris** to "try her luck." X insists she is nearby, and rejects the possibility of her **suicide**. When she is eventually found, she has not one unbroken bone in her dear **body**. Her recovery is slow. She spends fifteen years in a cast, living on milk, attended by her dutiful son. When F appears as the mother, X rejects "her." But soon he asks for a kiss and wants his "mommy" to take him for a walk. When he asks if she loves him, she answers: "Non, mon pigeon, je ne veux pas te mentir." X ends the fantasy abruptly: "Enlève-moi cette putréfaction." Much of this burlesque suggests a dream, but the emphasis on play is more explicit than later, when the theme is carried by theatrical and **chess** terms. "Il joue de plus en plus mal," says X. "Moi aussi. Je dois jouer de plus en plus mal. Nous sommes trop vieux, le jeu est trop vieux."

The typescript returns to the epistemological theme, with much undercut, displaced, the fictionality emphasized. It is finally uncertain if X is blind, if the two are in Picardy, or if the story about the mother is real or imagined, actual or dreamed. The apparently blind X summons F, and says, "Tu es pâle." X laughs and asks F if he almost fell for the joke. SB seemed unsure how much disruption was necessary. He altered the way he dealt with this, finally settling on Hamm's chronicle, where the line between **memory** and imagination blurs, and he maintained this tale thereafter. The ending offers other uncertainties about the play's focus, a new element that is dropped. The last few lines of dialogue introduce "l'affaire **Bom**." X's response suggests the germ of the Mother **Pegg** story: "Bom . . . ah, oui,

cette pauvre vieille qui réclame une goutte d'eau." F corrects him; no, that is the **Bim** affair.

"Avant *Fin de partie*" contains much that survives into *Fin de partie*. There are no **Nagg and Nell**, but their roots are present in the mother. The **skull**-like shelter of "**Mime de rêveur, A**" is not yet incorporated, nor the handkerchief-covered face. But the essence of Hamm and Clov can be seen: F preparing to leave; X adjusting to being alone; both believing they are the last humans; X wanting to mean something. Much is a play within a play, staged to pass the time. In a routine that finds its way into *Happy Days,* F reads X's worn baptismal spoon: "longue . . . longue . . . horreur . . . non . . . heureuse . . . longue heureuse." The wordplay works only in French, as X confuses "l'ouïe" (hearing) with "Louis": "Ah, oui. Mon ouïe." X jests about the eternal order of things: to F's "everything has an end," he replies with the music-hall joke: "Except the sausage. . . . It has two." The vaudeville quality was evidently not enough to sustain SB's interest, or it may have been incompatible with X's struggle to order his life, for "Avant *Fin de partie*" ends, or rather stops, abruptly.

B

B: in the French *Molloy,* one of two "lar-rons" seen at the outset. For like pairings of A and B, see entry "**A.**" SB retains "B" for himself (to **Duthuit**'s "D") in "**Three Dialogues.**"

B. and I.: the British and Ireland Steam Packet, which left **Dublin**'s North Wall for Liverpool, an alternative to the **Dún Laoghaire** to Holyhead route. "**Che Sciagura**" mentions "the B & I boat threading the eye of the Liffey on Satur-day night." Miss **Counihan** leaves thus (*Murphy,* 129), her "fitting" less dress-making than to fit the plot. "Voice **A**" of *That Time* arrives off the B. and I. "night ferry" (232). His uncertainty about the route (O'Brien, 219–20) is curious: the "rise" to "the high street" may confuse the North Wall with Dún Laoghaire.

Babel: publication of the International Federation of Translators (volume 1, September 1955). *Babel* 3 (Spring 1984) contains "Correspondence on Translat-ing *Molloy*" (21–35), an exchange with SB's German translator, Erich Franzen (1954), suggestions for specific passages (24–25), and final versions (30–35). *Babel VI* (Schöndorf [1990]: 28–31) contains six poems by SB, five *mirlitonnades* ("en face," "rentrer," "écoute-les," "imagine si ceci," "fous qui disiez"), and "**le nain nonagénaire,**" with Kevin Perryman's facing English translations, these ac-knowledged as being without SB's authorization.

Baby Jack: the "woolly bear" of Jacques **Moran** Jr. (*Molloy,* 123), named after SB's childhood teddy bear (Knowlson, 36); compare **Lousse**'s dead **dog,** Teddy. In French (166), the bear is "Jeannot," the name engraved on X's baptismal spoon in "**Avant *Fin de partie.***"

babylan: an impotent lover and willing cuckold, like **Octave** in **Stendhal**'s *Armance.* The **Syra-Cusa** is besotted on "Belacqua babylan" (*Dream,* 50); and the plump **chess** champion (89) makes his move. In "**What a Misfortune,**" Belacqua asks Thelma if she has heard of a babylan, and offers a vision of impotence: a mule mired to its knees, a **beaver** ("castration") astride it, flogging it with a wooden sword ("spado").

Bacon, Francis (1561–1626): first Baron Verulam. He dreamed with **Descartes** of a new philosophy, based on experiment and induction, to replace **Aristotle,** yet resting on the metaphysics of **scholasti-cism.** **Murphy** (178) refers to "the beatific idols of his cave," those of the *Novum Organum* (1620), #39, the "four classes of Idols which beset men's minds"; illusions that to error. Category (2) is *idola specus,* each individual by his natural disposition shut into his cave (Windelband, 383, not-ing the echo of **Plato**). The others are (1) *idola tribus,* human nature; (3) *idola fari,* inadequacy of language; (4) *idola theatri,* fallacious philosophical constructs. Compare *Whoroscope* (66–67): "In the name of Bacon will you chicken me up that egg. / Shall I swallow cave-phantoms?" The **unnamable** quotes pigsty Latin (329), *de nobis ipsis silemus* ["Of myself I say nothing"], from Bacon's preface to the *Instauratio Magna.*

Bacon, Francis (1909–92): British painter, born in **Dublin**, whose twisted visceral forms speak of horror and loneliness. His studies after Velázquez's *Portrait of Pope Innocent X,* a scream of the atomic age, suggest **Hamm** in his chair.

Baillet, Adrien: author of *La Vie de Monsieur Des-cartes,* 2 volumes (Paris: Daniel Horthemels, 1691). SB absorbed incidental material, but his debt is less than often assumed. Baillet contributed little to **Whoroscope,** but offered a useful exposition of the *Méthode,* **Descartes**'s experience in the "poêle," and the three dreams of November 1619, where Descartes saw the path he would follow (compare **Krapp**'s epiphany). Dismissed by **Mahaffy** (6) as "a feeble and shallow, but earnest and diligent admirer."

Balfe: a **Foxrock** roadman who terrified SB as a child; recalled as "a little, ragged, wizened, crippled man" (Knowlson, 41). The narrator of *From an Abandoned Work* remembers with terror "the look I got from Balfe" (163). "**Afar a bird**" expresses latent fears: "he'll confuse his **mother** with whores, his **father** with a roadman named Balfe" (233).

ball: a motif of childhood grief. When **Krapp**'s **mother** died, he was throwing a ball for a little white **dog,** and will feel it forever: "But I gave it to the dog." In

Freud's "Beyond the Pleasure Principle" the child's reel ("fort . . . da") is a mechanism for coping with loss of the mother. Dan **Rooney** (*All That Fall,* 38) denies dropping "a kind of ball," then calls it a "thing" he carries; does it belong to the child who fell under the train? In *All Strange Away* a "small grey punctured rubber ball" (181) is the last **object** contemplated before Fancy is dead.

Ballmer, Karl (1891–1958): Swiss-born Jewish painter whom SB met in **Germany** (1936) and whose work he admired. Ballmer had been refused permission to exhibit since 1933, and his library had been seized. SB commented on the extraordinary stillness of his art and the "metaphysical concrete" (Knowlson, 224), in which the **object** is not exploited to illustrate an idea but remains primary, so that anything else in the optical experience is "by the way." He uses this to critique his earlier practice, as in "The **Vulture,**" which asserts an inescapable subjectivity. In "La **Peinture des van Velde**" Ballmer is called a "great unknown painter" (*Disjecta,* 118).

Bally: Gaelic *baile,* "a town." The **Molloy** country is a narrow region, a settlement and the surrounding countryside. **Dublin,** or "Baile Atha Cliath" ("Town of the Ford of the Hurdles") in *L'Innommable* Notebooks became "Bally je ne sais plus quoi" (18), or "Bally I forget what" (*The Unnamable,* 298). There is a system, "of singular beauty and simplicity," in saying Bally for Bally, Ballyba for Bally plus its domains, and Ballybaba for the domains exclusive of Bally (*Molloy,* 134). Thus, **Moran** lives in **Turdy,** hub of Turdyba, a semiotic that Derridada might admire. The principal beauty of Ballyba is a strangled creek, like that of "Blackpool"; this is "Dublin," from Gaelic *dubh,* "black," and *linn,* "pool." The **HRHRC** holds a curious typescript from the **Péron** accession: a chunk of *Molloy,* numbered 211 to 224, a commentary on "le pays de Molloy" and Ballyba. It offers other "facts": that the "nomenclature" (above) was created by a sixteenth-century Huguenot priest; its industry (bog oak amulets and scapulars); fertilization of poor pastures and lettuces from the excrements of its citizens; the **Obidil,** a tyrannical landlord in a Big House; their "poète metaphysique" named **Clarke;** one Colbert so prolific in the production of excrement that he was canonized; and their cloacal science (the study of odors). At its best bad **Swift,** the passage was discarded.

Balue, Jean (1421–91): cardinal and almoner to Louis XI, against whom he intrigued with Charles the Bold; he was put into a tiny iron cage for eleven years (1469–80), until Pope Sixtus IV freed him. Mentioned in *Proust* (24), and in *Mercier and Camier* (76).

Balzac, Honoré de (1799–1850): creator of *La Comédie humaine,* on which SB lectured at **Trinity. Belacqua** dismisses it (*Dream,* 119) as "a chloroformed world" planted with "clockwork cabbages," **characters** on whom a precise value may be placed. These are Balzac's "Old Curiosities," such as Birotteau, from the *Histoire de la grandeur et de la décadence de César Birotteau* (1837), and Chesnel, a "viel intendant de la famille," who appears in *Le Cabinet des antiques* (1833), SB's set text at Trinity, before making cameos in other novels. SB implies a like criticism of **Dickens.** Belacqua resents calling a distillation of Euclid and **Perrault** a human comedy, yet notes Balzac's "Jane the Pale" (125) as one to be relied on (*Wann-Chlore* [1825], or *Jane la pâle* [1836]). In **"Proust in Pieces"** (1934), SB rejected "the sweet reasonableness of plane psychology à la Balzac." He noted of *Cousine Bette:* "The bathos of thought is so enormous that I wonder is he writing seriously or in parody" (SB to TM, 8 February 1935). O'Hara suggests that **"Assumption"** embodies three of Balzac's Swedenborg-influenced tales, *Les Proscrits* (1831), *Louis Lambert* (1832), and *Séraphîta* (1834–45). **Molloy** refers (51) to "the famous fatal skin," Balzac's "peau de chagrin" (as in the French text, 69), the wild-ass skin that grants every wish but shrinks accordingly, until it is nothing and its owner is dead. Like Raphaël, Molloy attempts to wish for **nothing.** *Malone Dies* depicts the comedy of **Saposcat** among the peasants, a parody of *Les Paysans* (1844). Sapo's education is like that in *Louis Lambert,* which depicts one incapable of living in the outer world and so going mad (Big Lambert copes). *Three Novels* reflect Balzac's practice of characters and details reappearing from one text to another, but enact a human comedy of a very different order.

Bande et sarabande: Edith Fournier's translation of *More Pricks Than Kicks* (Minuit, 1994), sixty years after original publication and five years after SB's **death.** SB told Ludovic Janvier that his title was *Ni bouche ni éperon* ("Neither mouth nor spur"), or, foot in the mouth. Fournier's musical offering echoes *La Dernière bande* yet retains the irreverence (see **Bando**).

Bando: a remedy for impotence suggested to Mr. **Graves** (*Watt*, 170). Arthur is now vivacious, regular, almost a **father**, and a lover of boiled potatoes. Fr. *bander*, "to have an erection." SB toyed with "Bandvagita" (too obvious) and "Bandvita," warm milk suggesting "Bournvita." **Watt** and Mrs. **Gorman** suffer an "obstruction of some endocrinal Bandusia" (142); the "fons Bandusiae" was a spring near the birthplace of **Horace**.

"Bare Room": an unpublished dramatic fragment, three pages of the **Super Conquérant** Notebook (RUL 2934), undated, a dialogue between two speakers, **W** (on a bench) and **M** (at the window), in a bare room, dimly lit; immobile throughout. It is New Year's Eve, and snowing; the theme is **Shakespeare**'s Sonnet LXXI, "No longer mourn for me when I am dead." These words are deleted from a second draft.

Barlach, Ernst (1870–1938): German sculptor and carver, whose huddled figures in teak and stone express the horrors of his age in ways suggestive of SB's own. The Nazis branded him a degenerate. SB encountered his work in **Germany** (1937); he sent home Barlach's *Zeichner des Volkes*. *Murphy* (239) mentions "the Pergamene Barlach"; this is not in the typescript, a rare change between submission and publication. SB knew the Pergamene school of Hellenistic sculpture, and visited Berlin to see its greatest monument, the Altar of Zeus from Pergamon.

Mr. Barrell: stationmaster at **Boghill** in *All That Fall*, modeled on Thomas Farrell, **Foxrock**, whose station was also judged "the best kept of the entire network" (26). Mr. **Gorman** was named "Farrell" in the *Watt* notebooks.

Bartlett: in "A Wet Night" (50), but not in the parallel passage of *Dream* (202; but see 148, "Bartlett-in-the-box"), the would-be poet **Chas** is a "clockwork Bartlett," a cliché for every occasion. John Bartlett's *Familiar Quotations* provided many of the classical and biblical quotations that pepper the early texts. SB had his **father**'s copy of the 1885 (first) edition (Knowlson, 742). References to cats (*Murphy*, 202) and Miss **Carriage**'s various tags of *corajo*, from **Horace** and the **Bible** (230), derive from Bartlett.

Basil: a creature of the phenomenal world by whom the **Unnamable** has been lectured and who fills him with hatred (298). O'Brien suggests (116) one Tetley, SB's **mathematics** master at **Portora**; hence the **pensum**. Basil is rejected ("Inexistent") when the narrator turns to his true subject, the "I" of whom he knows **nothing** (304). He returns: "Basil is becoming important, I'll call him **Mahood**" (309). Keats's "Isabella" puts the head of her murdered lover inside a **pot** of basil watered with her tears; her murderous brothers find it and reveal their guilt.

Battersea Park: in **London**, opposite the Chelsea Embankment. Once frequented by cabbage and asparagus growers, it was opened to the public in 1858. **Murphy** proposes to **Celia** in the subtropical garden (created in 1863 as an emblem of Empire, with exotica such as palms, pineapples, and bananas). He recalls the owls in their artificial grotto (106), as does the **Unnamable** (393): "ah misery, will I never stop wanting a life for myself?" Earlier (293) he had likened himself to a great horned owl in an aviary. **Job** (30:29) is "a companion to owls."

Baudelaire, Charles (1821–67): French poet. In *Proust* (76), one who defines reality as "the adequate union of subject and **object**"; hence **allegorical**, unlike **Proust**, who pursues the Ideal by the concrete. *Proust* (68) refers to the "azur du ciel immense et ronde" ("La Chevelure"), and (31) the "gouffre interdit à nos sondes" ("Le Balcon"), the **gulf** whence involuntary **memory** might rise. In *Dream* (148), **Belacqua** hears "Ange plein," from "Réversibilité": "Ange plein de gaieté, connaissez-vous l'angoisse." SB cites Baudelaire from Praz, *The Romantic Agony*, including "Debauchery & **Death**," the two sisters of "**Echo's Bones**"; a chilling line from "Nymph macabre": "Ta carcasse a des agréments"; and "Kamchatka," Sainte-Beuve's notion that Baudelaire had gone "à l'extrémité du Kamchatka littéraire" to build a folly (DN, 57).

The "**German Letter of 1937**" invokes the "forest of symbols" ("Correspondences"), to reject the *Vöglein der Deutung*, the "little birds of meaning," that are never silent (*Disjecta*, 53). **Malone** feels better (237), he could "slip away as happy as if I were embarking for—I nearly said for **Cythera**, decidedly

it is time for this to stop." In "Un Voyage à Cythère" Baudelaire imagines a terrifying abode of the dead, where his likeness hangs from a gallows. He prays for the strength and courage "De contempler mon coeur et mon corps sans dégoût." In *Waiting for Godot* (11.b), **Estragon** says (voluptuously): "Calm . . . calm . . . The English say cawm"; this echoes "L'Invitation au voyage": "Là, tout n'est qu'ordre et beauté / Luxe, calme et volopté." Before writing *Endgame* SB read Baudelaire in a fine edition given to him by Pamela Mitchell (Knowlson, 366). **Hamm** quotes from "Recueillement": "Tu réclamais le soir; il descend; le voici"; in SB's translation (83): "You cried for night; it falls; now cry in darkness."

bboggs: the family into which **Belacqua** marries in "**What a Misfortune**," Thelma the fifth of his fair to middling women. The "bb" mocks the pretension of names like "ffowles" or "ffoulkes," Otto Olaf having risen from the depths of his profession (plumbing and toilet requisites). Thelma is not beautiful: unlike Helen of Troy she does not bring the elders running nor young men to a standstill (DN, 84); but, in the words of **Donne**'s second "Elegy," she has "the anagram of a good **face**" (128). The portents are not good. Belacqua dislikes her present (139); he wishes his love were in Australia (146); he speaks in a "white voice" (157); **Lucy** remains "atra cura" en route to Galway (160); and their future is clouded by the word "**babylan**" (160). Thelma is "a brave girl," but the marriage is fated; she perishes of "sunset and honeymoon" ("Draff," 175). Another bboggs is

Thelma's sister Una, for whom an ape has been set aside in hell (she will never marry). Her name and chastity echo **Spenser**'s heroine in book I of *The Faerie Queene,* sounding the minor chivalric chord that plays throughout the story.

Beatrice: in the *Vita nuova* **Dante** tells of his childhood meeting with Beatrice Portinari, daughter of an illustrious Florentine family (1274). His love for her, deeply **platonic**, was his inspiration, neither her marriage to Simone de' Bardi (1287) nor her **death** (8 June 1290) affecting its intensity (his daughter Antonia took the veil as Suora Beatrice). Dante's wife, Gemma, is not mentioned in the *Commedia,* but Beatrice is immortalized as the Lady. She appears at the end of the *Purgatorio,* guides the faltering Dante through the "canti in the moon" ("**Dante and the Lobster**," 9), and through the spheres of Heaven to the vision of the Godhead. She represents theology, or revealed **religion**. For SB she is the beatific vision, "blissful Beatrice" the usual tautology. She exemplifies the distinction between the sacred and profane, virgin and whore; hence the sardonic "little Miss **Florence**" (*Dream,* 73), metamorphosed into Florence Nightingale (80–81; compare *Purg.* VI.150–51). A picture of Beatrice (Rossetti's?) on the wall of Becky **Cooper**'s brothel features in "**Sanies II**," Dante and blissful Beatrice there, "prior to Vita Nuova." On the disastrous Silvester, **Belacqua** disputes with the **Mandarin** about the antinomy of love and **desire**. He is willing to admit Beatrice, or the brothel, but not Beatrice and the brothel; and he has no reply to the Mandarin's cynicism (*Dream,* 102). The

disjunction between **love** and sex is one that SB found less attractive than logically compelling; the disaster to follow reflects Belacqua's inability to cope with the dilemma.

Beaufret, Jean (1907–82): the "Bowsprit" (Fr. *beaupré*), SB's pupil from the **École Normale**, who appears in *Dream* as **Lucien**. He loved philosophy and introduced SB to **Parmenides**. SB commented to **MacGreevy** (July 1930): "The Bowsprit comes and talks abstractions," describing him as "charming, especially alone" but "an unhappy person." His devotion to SB was appreciated rather than reciprocated; SB recounts him arriving with a bottle of champagne "à la Charlus" (a homosexual advance): "il n'y a que cela, he said." He was unimpressed by SB's enthusiasm for **Schopenhauer**. Beaufret was an expert on Heidegger, and was for thirty years his advocate. Heidegger's "Letter on **Humanism**" (1946), refuting **Sartre**, **existentialism**, and structuralism, was addressed to Beaufret, who published their conversations. Cronin notes (87) that Beaufret's later career was darkened by a scandal with a pupil.

Beauty of Bath: a dessert apple, sharp but sweet. **Moran** sits peacefully beneath his, but his Eden is disturbed by **Gaber**'s advent. The **French** text (127) reads simply "pommier."

beaver: SB notes a "persuasive chapter of Natural History," where the beaver "bites his off" (*Dream,* 63; and *Murphy,* 217). Pliny tells how beavers when hunted *castoreum id vocant medici* ("for what the doctors call castor-oil") save their lives by biting off their testicles. This **allegory** of mankind casting aside temptation when pursued by Satan derives from L. *castor,* "beaver," with its scrotum-tightening sense of castration (see "**Che Sciagura**"). "**What a Misfortune**" ends with the impotent vision of a beaver astride a mule (see **babylan**).

Beckett country: SB's psychological landscape, not unlike "Greeneland," replete with **bicycles**, **dogs**, dustbins, and destitutes in **hats**, **greatcoats**, and ill-fitting **boots**. This is **Proust**'s "la patrie intérieure" (iii. 371), but to a degree unsuspected before Eoin O'Brien's *The Beckett Country* (1986), grounded in SB's boyhood **Dublin**, its mountains, forests, swamps, and coast. Poems like "**Enueg I**," "**Sanies I**," "**Serena I**" or "**Serena II**" can be traced upon a map, and details of *Dream* and *MPTK* located precisely. For example, "**Love and Lethe**" ends on the peak of Tibradden, from which **Dún Laoghaire** is visible, framed by Three Rock and Kilmashogue (O'Brien, 60). The 1940s **French** fictions use British currency and units of measurement. **Watt** journeys from the **Harcourt Street Station**, past the **Leopardstown** racecourse, to **Foxrock** (qv); Mr. **Knott**'s Big House, like **Moran**'s, resembles **Cooldrinagh**. Mr. **Hackett**'s accident occurred near **Prince William's Seat**. **Mercier** and **Camier** cycle over this area; their crags and quag (97) recognizably on the road to Glencree. "**Text 1**" invokes the mountains and loughs (the Irish translation of "lacs"), and the **father** who taught their names (*Dream,* 240): the Big Sugarloaf, Douce (Djouce), and Three Rock. **Molloy** sees from Nelson's Pillar the Dublin mountains and coast (10); **Moran** calls this "the Molloy country." *Malone Dies* ends on Dalkey Island. *En attendant Godot,* despite references to the Rhône and **Macon** country, is "set" on a lonely road crossing the high moorland near Glencree. Later works (except for *All That Fall*) are less specific in terms of locale, but such details as the anemometer (East Pier, Dún Laoghaire) in *Krapp's Last Tape,* **larches**, Graduation Day in *Film,* and St. Stephen's Green in "**Eh Joe**" testify to SB's childhood imagination, while *Company, That Time* and ". . . but the clouds . . ." nostalgically recall childhood backroads. Although SB left in the 1930s, **Ireland** is a presence in much of the later work.

This is not to suggest identification, for **Bally** is less Dublin than that city reduced to its **fundamental sound**; nor is "**Embers**" set unequivocally on **Killiney** Beach. Rather, the city, sea, swamp, forest, and ditch of the Molloy country are visualized minutely, yet are **Jungian** or **Freudian** in their provenance. Other features are created through language, as Molloy's "sorts" (19), a ditch so deep that he is rarely out of them; his refuge in an impasse; the **Unnamable** uses opinions (401) as the beaten track to get him over "the pretty pass." *Texts for Nothing* dispute the topography of figure and ground. The major disjunction in SB's work is less the consequence of his leaving Ireland than a change in his orientation. Narratives of **motion** gave way to stasis, settings became less specific. As the physical world was excluded from **summerhouse** or **skull**, the principles of representation and psychological **surrealism** that delineate the Beckett country changed to the poetry of the **closed space.**

Beckett, Frank (1902–54): SB's elder brother, born 26 July 1902. The two were close as boys, playing tennis and **chess,** collecting **stamps,** walking and swimming. Their interests diverged, Frank more like his **father** in his preference for the physical, and joining the firm as expected. After their father's **death** he supported SB through some difficult years. His marriage to Jean Wright (1937) widened the gap, but affection remained and SB was fond of their two children, Caroline and Edward. During the war and through their **mother**'s long illness Frank assumed responsibility, which accentuated SB's guilt. News of his terminal lung cancer further grieved SB, who spent three months at Frank's home, overlooking **Killiney Beach,** his brother dying on 13 September 1954. Frank features little in SB's writing, save the cameo of "John" in *Dream.*

Beckett, May (1871–1950): SB's **mother** (qv), whose relationship with her younger son was a trial for them both; SB's references to her lack the affection he had for his **father.** She ran **Cooldrinagh** with a ruthless efficiency, a strict mother to a son who did not respond well to rigidity. Like him, she had lasting moods of dark depression. SB's problems were affected by her dissatisfaction with his failure to get a **job.** She disapproved of his resignation from **Trinity,** and disliked his writing. SB complained to **MacGreevy** (27 December 1934) that she could not understand why he did not pull himself together, and prove to the

world he was a man: "Porca madonna . . . but what is the good of saying anything?" May Beckett appears most obviously in *Footfalls,* but her presence is felt elsewhere, and details such as her **donkey** cart and Pomeranian are mentioned. Following her husband's **death** she moved to **New Place.** She suffered from Parkinson's disease and dementia, and SB felt guilty that he could not be closer to her. She died 25 August 1950, in the Merrion Nursing Home, "the house on the canal" that **Krapp** associates with the **memory** of sitting by the weir in the biting wind, "wishing she were gone" (see "**je voudrais que mon amour meure**"). The neurotic relationship intensified SB's experience of her death, but from that matrix came some of his finest writing.

Beckett, Mr.: obscure narrator of *Dream* (69), not manifest until later (141). He appears in person (186) to behold a latter-day **Belacqua,** a dud mystic. His role is like that of **Sam** in *Watt,* or the unidentified "I" of the opening (only) of "**Ding-Dong,**" or the first sentence (only) of *Mercier and Camier,* complicating the perspective between the immediate subject and the narrative **voice.** A similar figure in *Eleutheria* (Beckett, Béquet) causes the "flop" (148).

Beckett, William (1871–1933): SB's **father** (qv), a successful quantity surveyor of Beckett & Medcalf, with offices at 6 Clare Street in the center of **Dublin.** SB sometimes wrote in the attic there. Good-natured and jovial, he won his younger son's lasting affection, and their moments together recur through SB's writing. He was a great walker, a fine swimmer and golfer, and liked bridge. He found more satisfaction in work than his marriage, never seriously under strain but based on **habit** as much as affection (Knowlson, 33). In *Dream* (53–54), he adopts the "old corduroy mode" of pipe and book (Edgar Wallace) and disappears into his study to read, precisely what the next morning he could not say. In *Company* (39), he retreats into the **summerhouse** to chuckle over *Punch*. A father leading a child by the hand (see *Worstward Ho*) is an obsessional image (see **diving board**). Although he did not understand his son's inclinations he did not discourage them. He died of a heart attack (26 June 1933), aged sixty-one, his last words being "Fight, fight, fight" and "What a morning." SB had difficulty accepting his **death**: "I can't write about him, I can only walk the fields and climb the ditches after him" (SB to TM, 2 July 1933). He was buried in Redford Cemetery, Greystones, a plot that his wife May would later share; this forms the setting of "**Draff**" and "**Echo's Bones.**" See "**Malacoda.**"

Beckettiana: a small journal of Beckett studies, in Spanish. It has appeared annually since 1991 from the *Seminario de Beckett* (Universidad de Buenos Aires), ed. Laura Cerrato.

"**Beckett on Film**": in 2000, an ambitious attempt began to film the **Gate Theatre** cycle of nineteen plays. Michael Colgan and Alan Mohoney (Blue Light Films) used top Irish and international directors and stars; the executive producer was Joe Mulholland, outgoing manager of television at RTÉ. The project had a budget of £4.5 million, raised from (Irish) RTÉ, (British) Channel 4, Section 481 investment, and some American backing. A weeklong screening in **Dublin**, January 2001, was followed by similar events in New York and **London**; and at film festivals (*Not I* featured at Cannes, 2000; *Endgame* and *Happy Days* at Venice), in the cinema, at Lincoln Center, and on TV channels worldwide, a boxed videocassette and DVD later available. Irish TV (RTF 1) featured the entire sequence (March 19 to April 2, 2001), preceded by *Check the Gate,* a documentary about putting SB on film (dir. Pearse Lehane). One early review noted how well the shorter pieces work, whereas the longer, better-known plays lack imagination. The sequence features (in approximate order of filming):

"**What Where**" (12 minutes); dir. Damien O'Donnell, with Sean McGinley, Gary Lewis; producer Tom Conroy.

Endgame (84 minutes); dir. Conor McPherson, with Michael Gambon, David Thewlis as **Hamm** and **Clov**, Charles Simon, Jean Anderson (both ninety-two years old) as **Nagg** and **Nell**.

"**Breath**" (45 seconds); dir. Damien Hirst, with Keith Allen, **voice**.

Not I (15 minutes); dir. Neil Jordan, with Julianne Moore, lighting-cameraman Roger Pratt.

Footfalls (27 minutes); dir. Walter Asmus, with Susan Fitzgerald, Joan O'Hara.

"**Act Without Words I**" (22 minutes); dir. Karel Reisz, with John Foley; music by Michael Nyman.

Krapp's Last Tape (55 minutes); dir. Atom Egoyan, with John Hurt.

"Catastrophe" (16 minutes); dir. David Mamet, with Harold Pinter, Rebecca Pigeon, John Geilgud (aged ninety-six, his last performance).

"Ohio Impromptu" (15 minutes); dir. Charles Sturridge, with Jeremy Irons.

That Time (15 minutes); dir. Charles Garrad, with Niall Buggy.

"A Piece of Monologue" (27 minutes); dir. Robin Lefevre, with Stephen Brennan.

"Play" (20 minutes); dir. Anthony Minghella, with Juliet Stevenson, Kirstin Scott Thomas, Alan Rickman.

Waiting for Godot (132 minutes); dir. Michael Lindsay-Hogg, with Barry McGovern, Johnny Murphy, Stephen Brennan, Alan Stanford. Filmed on location at Castlebaney.

"Rockaby" (16 minutes); dir. Richard Eyre, with Penelope Wilton.

"Act Without Words II" (9 minutes); dir. Enda Hughes, with Marcello Magni, Pat Kinevane.

"Rough for Theatre I" (18 minutes); dir. Kieron J. Walsh, with David Kelly, Milo O'Shea.

"Rough for Theatre II" (35 minutes); dir. Katie Mitchell, with Timothy Spall, Jim Norton, Hugh O'Brien.

Happy Days (102 minutes); dir. Patricia Rozema, with Rosaleen Linehan, Richard Johnson. Shot at a volcano in the Canary Islands.

Come and Go (6 minutes); dir. John Crowley, with Paola Dionisotti, Anna Massey, Sian Phillips.

Bécquer, Gustavo Aldolfo (1836–70): Spanish poet and romancier who died in poverty after eking out a living translat-ing novels. Listed among the melancholy writers in *Dream* (62).

Beeckman, Isaac (1588–1637): Dutch **mathematician** and rector of Dort; mentioned in *Whoroscope*. When **Descartes** was serving as a gentleman volunteer in Breda, several mathematicians there passed the time by posing and solving problems. Descartes was trying to understand one in Dutch, and asked a stranger to translate it into Latin. Beeckman obliged, and challenged Descartes to bring him the solution; the younger man did so, and they became lifelong friends. The story is recounted in **Baillet** (I.69) and **Mahaffy** (32).

bees: an image of the productive, ordered society, as in the **Moran** section of *Molloy;* but Moran returns home to find his bees have died. The image derives from **Diderot**'s "Le Rêve de d'**Alembert**" (qv). Moran's response is to rejoice in their dance, concluding with rapture that here is something he can study all his life and never understand. The bees thus accentuate how far he has come from his previous certainties. Compare **Windelband**'s comment (524) about man "stripped bare of all egotistical impulses," as in Mandeville's *Fable of the Bees* (1714), designed to illustrate the vileness of human nature.

Beethoven, Ludwig van (1770–1827): German composer. Thayer (1891) presented a noble passionate nature, a **Romantic** genius with the agonies of deafness, his later works attaining transcendental grandeur. In *Dream,* the narrator contemplates orchestral form, hoping for a symphonic rather than melodic composition (11), but finally rejecting harmonic composition for an involuntary unity (132). **Belacqua** imagines a tranquil Beethoven, eyes closed, smoking a long pipe, listening "to the Ferne, the unsterbliche Geliebte" (138) and unbuttoning himself to the nearer Teresa. This derives from Romain **Rolland**'s *Vie de Beethoven* (1903; DN, 157), and his song cycle *An die ferne Geliebte* ("To the distant beloved"). Rolland comments (4) that Beethoven sat thus "à mesure qu'il approche de la mort"; alludes (29) to Mariam Tenger's *Beethovens unsterbliche Geliebte* (Bonn, 1890); mentions Thérèse de Brunswick (33–34); and uses the word "déboutonné" ("aufgeknoepft") (41). The **Alba**'s scarlet dress, with the help of **God**, buttons down the back.

Beethoven is one who delimits "the **incoherent continuum**" (*Dream*, 102), a vertiginous path of sounds connecting unfathomable abysses of silence. The Seventh Symphony marks the pause before a storm, as articulated in the "**German Letter of 1937**" (*Disjecta*, 53): "die von grossen schwarzen gefressene Tonfläche in der siebten Symphonie von Beethoven" ("tonal surfaces eaten by great black pauses in Beethoven's Seventh Symphony"). This A major symphony was SB's favorite. The narrator rejects "dud Beethoven," saying that his sometime friend "lived a Beethoven pause" (40). In *Dream* (106), after the disastrous night, Belacqua rings at the studio of Herr Sauerwein for the **Smeraldina**, and comments cryptically: "From the **rosa mundi** . . . to the **rosa**

munda"; that is, from the carnal worldly rose to that which is pure, but suggesting **Schubert**'s "Rosamunde." The musical phrase that follows is from Beethoven's Seventh (as Yoshiki Tajiri discovered), bars 128–29 of the first movement, scored for cello. This is the pause before the "stürm," a moment of quiet passing into frenzy. Thinking back to the "calamitous Sylvester," there is a similar pause, then Belacqua rings hell out of the **Frica**'s door with this phrase moaning in his memory, "the ut [first note of the tritone, C#, C, B] sharpened, quantified and sustained to a degree that had never been intended by the Swan of Bonn" (229). This interlude is not in "A **Wet Night**," because the Smeraldina was eliminated. The emotion (compare Swann's "little phrase" in *A la recherche*) is intense. It carries over into "**What a Misfortune**," which for all its simulated casualness is marked by a moment in which Belacqua feels the presence of **Lucy**, and imagines her listening for the second incidence of the phrase "in the first movement of the Unbuttoned Symphony" (150).

In "**Malacoda**," the inevitability of **death** is articulated in "must it be it must be it must be," an echo of the *Muss es sein?* motif of Beethoven's last quartet, Opus 135 in F Major. Its coda is a musical joke that in popular tradition is his final word, his jesting acceptance of death. The coda inverts the phrase and answers it: *Es muss sein* ("It must be"). Knowlson (184) notes that SB went to concerts by the Busch Quartet (February 1934), and copied the words on the manuscript of Opus 135: *Der schwergefasste Entschluss* ("the difficult resolution"); he repeated "Es muss sein" at painful moments. Compare "Dante and the Lobster" (21), the "brute" about to go into the scalding water: "It had to." SB contemplated returning to this theme in "Play," telling Lawrence Harvey that the new work "Must speak . . . Must accept life" (Knowlson, 444).

SB's most elaborate use of Beethoven is of the fifth piano trio, "Der Geist" (Opus 70, #1) in "Ghost Trio" (qv), which derives its name thereby. The play uses the largo only, specific bars matched precisely to the text. The trio is named "The Ghost" after the mysterious slow movement, *largo assai espressivo;* and except for the coda of that movement, which brings the play to its end, uses passages from this "ghostly" second theme to foreshadow the climax, the appearance in III of the small boy who comes and goes as if in response to the music.

"Before Play": an undated manuscript (RUL 1227/7/16/6), thus entitled by SB. It anticipates "Play" with its spotlight moving on and off the faces of three characters (a woman, Nickie, and her lovers, Syke and Conk), each differentiated by facial features and hair color, enclosed up to the neck in three white boxes, "one yard high." Syke is a veteran who alludes to Horace's "Dolce et decorum," and lives happily with Nickie at a chicken farm in "the north" before Conk arrives. Both men blame Nickie for the disruption; Syke had felt loved for a time, wanted for the first time. The fragment is replete with bird imagery, from chickens to Grand Canary Island (this survives into *Play*), an injured sparrow, and a stuffed owl. The plot is altered dramatically in its next incarnation, but the machinery of desire, the source of emotional pain, drives the action as surely as in *Murphy*.

Beginning to End: A Television Exploration of the World of Samuel Beckett; a rewriting of "End of Day," broadcast on BBC 1 *Monitor* program, 23 February 1965; performed by Jack MacGowran, and introduced by Jonathan Miller with SB's cooperation. Rebroadcast 8 August 1967. A reedited version was broadcast under this title on Telefís Éireann (September 1965). The revised stage show was a hit in America, winning an Obie Award and a gold plaque from the Critics' Circle (1970); in Paris at the Théâtre Edouard VII (April 1970), where SB directed; and in the Berlin Festival at the Schiller-Theater (1971). Another American tour was cut short by MacGowran's untimely death (1973). A 1966 version from Claddagh records was called *MacGowran Speaking Beckett.* Despite SB's misgivings, a fifty-eight-minute TV version called *Samuel Beckett's Beginning to End* was filmed on location in California's high desert (4 November 1971), dir. Lewis Freedman for KCET television in LA and the PBS and distributed through Grove Press, Evergreen Films. Collected excerpts, illustrated by Edward Gorey, appeared as *Samuel Beckett's Beginning to End* in 1967 (actually, 1968) by Gotham Book Mart with Oliphant Press. The limited edition (300 numbered copies), misleadingly called "a previously unpublished work," was signed by SB and Gorey and sold for $150.

Belacqua [Shuah]: "hero" of the early fiction (his initials reversing SB's).

"Shuah" is the mother of **Onan** (Genesis 38:2). Belacqua was a **Florentine** lute maker, for indolence detained in **Ante-purgatory**. In *Purgatorio* IV, several figures rest in the shade of "un gran petrone" ("a great rock"). One, "che mi sembrava lasso, / sedeva ed abbracciava le ginocchia, / tenendo il viso giù tra esse basso" ("who seemed to me weary, was sitting and clasping his knees, holding his face down low between them"). This is the **embryonal** repose (adopted in the **closed space** fictions). Asked why he is sitting, Belacqua responds in the words SB much admired: "Frate, l'andare in su che porta?" ("Oh brother, what is the use of going up?"). An angel would only bar his entrance, so he will stay where he is. This inspired SB's response when, asked what he wanted out of life, he said, to do nothing but to sit on his arse and fart and read Dante.

"**Sedendo et Quiesc[i]endo**" calls Belacqua a lute maker, as in the Commentary of the Anonimo Fiorentino (1400), reproduced in Toynbee's *Dictionary* (74): "Ora l'Auttore fu molto suo dimestico: molto il riprendea di questa sua negligenzia; onde un dì, riprendendolo, Belacqua rispose colle parole d'Aristotile: Sedendo et quiescendo anima efficitur sapiens; di che l'Auttore gli rispose: Per certo, se per sedere si diventa savio, niuno fu mai più savio di te" ("Now, the Author was very intimate with him: he used to reproach him a lot for his negligence; so that one day, while he was reproaching him, Belacqua replied with **Aristotle**'s words: *Sedendo et quiescendo anima efficitur sapiens;* to which the Author replied: certainly, if to be seated is to be wise, then no man is wiser than thee"). This, and several other citations in the **Dream Notebook** (42–45) are annotated by Daniela Caselli, and indicates the range of SB's reading.

SB told Con **Leventhal** (21 April 1958) that he was "fascinated" by the character and "went to a lot of trouble to find out about him." From his first epiphany of a defecating **horse** to his final metamorphosis in "**Echo's Bones**," Belacqua is an unprepossessing figure, with his ruined feet, recurrent impetigo, capon belly, and habit of picking his nose. He neither warrants nor demands sympathy but occasionally compels **pity**, a complex emotion not to be registered as Aristotelian catharsis or moral dignity but as a flicker of **consciousness** in a ruthless universe. He emerges as a misogynist, until it is appreciated that the real target of the abuse is himself, guilt and self-loathing arising from a tragic relationship, from his inability to **love**. In this intense self-analysis SB depicts his own complexities, without excusing them; the third part of Belacqua's mind, the dark **gulf** of his being, details the deepest impulses that have made him (Belacqua, but also SB) what he is. The Belacqua of *MPTK* is less cerebral, and the satire is directed less against his inner self.

Belacqua is a prototype of many other figures. **Murphy** contemplates renouncing "Belacqua's rock and his embryonal repose" (78), and invokes the "Belacqua bliss" of the half-light (111). **Molloy** crouches behind a great rock like Belacqua or **Sordello**, he forgets which (10). **Estragon** "resumes his foetal posture" (*WG*, 45.a); and in *All Strange Away* (171) "he" "crouches down" with hands on knees. In *The Lost Ones* (205) "non-searchers" sit against the wall in the attitude, "which wrung from Dante one of his rare wan smiles." Dante's smile is recorded on a postcard (RUL 4123); "Dante smiles (at Belacqua) D's 1st smile?" In *How It Is* (24) Belacqua has "fallen over on his side tired of waiting forgotten of the hearts where grace abides asleep." But in *Company* (44) he is "the old lutist cause of Dante's first quarter-smile and now perhaps singing praises with some section of the blest at last." [Details from DC]

Belis, Andrew: SB's pseudonym in "**Recent Irish Poetry**"; in a copy given to John and Evelyn Kohler, SB wrote "c.f. pp. 235–244. AB was me." It was taken from his maternal grandfather, George Belas (Knowlson, 25).

Bellini, Giovanni (ca. 1430–1516): Venetian painter. **Murphy** sees in the sky "the Child in a Giovanni Bellini Circumcision" (251). The painting (National Galley, **London**) shows elders and rabbis gathered about a pudgy babe awaiting the knife. January 1, the eighth day, is the Feast of the Circumcision (Luke 2:21). The ritual signifies **Christ**'s acceptance of the Law, His descent through the flesh from Abraham; **Murphy** responds to the terror of Bellini's infant, poor little prick, facing the equally incomprehensible. The scene in *Godot* where **Pozzo** is raised then slumps may reflect Bellini's *The Dead Christ with Angels* (Knowlson, 539).

Benozzo: Walter Draffin likens a thronged drawing room to "a Benozzo fresco," and the **Alba** replies, "Ass and all" ("**What a**

Misfortune," 151). They refer to the frescoes of the Medici Palace, Florence (1459), the *Adoration of the Magi,* by Benozzo Gozzoli (ca. 1421–97).

Bérard, Victor (1876–1960): French translator of **Homer**'s *Odyssey,* an edition much admired by **Joyce**. SB read *L'Odyssée,* he told **MacGreevy** (September 1931), with the "childish absorption" of *Oliver Twist* and *Treasure Island.* Admiring its "fine phrases" he took notes (DN, 102–3) from the Circe and Nekyomanteia episodes (Bks. X and XI): "**moly**" ("molu"), the antidote to Circe's magic (X.304; *Dream,* 28; "Yoke of Liberty"; *Molloy,* 54); Homeric darkness (XI.11–13; *Dream,* 28; "Dortmunder"; "A Wet Night," 55; *Murphy,* 134, an Aegean nightfall); "the work of love over" (XI.246; *Dream,* 40, as "The usual over," and 54, "the work of prayer over"); "Kimmerean" (XI.14; *Dream,* 122); "jamais au grand jamais" (X.328; *Dream,* 143); "Green honey of Circe" (X.234; *Dream,* 155; "Echo's Bones," 14); and the "black cruiser of Ulysses" (X.244; "Draff," 184; "Text"; and *Molloy,* 51, where it is attributed to **Dante**).

"Berceuse": SB's translation of "**Rockaby**" (1982). Published by **Minuit** in *Berceuse suivi de Impromptu d'Ohio,* 99 numbered copies; then in *Catastrophe et autres dramaticules.* "Berceuse" means lullaby as well as **rocking chair**. Compare van **Gogh**'s *La Berceuse* (1889), a series of paintings of an elderly woman in a rocking chair.

Beresina: a river that Napoleon retreating from Moscow (October 1812) had to cross, after the Russians had destroyed the bridges; alluded to in *Dream* (203), "A **Wet Night**" (57), and SB's translation of **Éluard**'s "Confections."

Bergson, Henri (1859–1941): French philosopher, student of the **École Normale**, and winner of the **Nobel Prize** (1927), exponent of the life force. He substituted for **Descartes**'s "Je suis une chose qui pense" the sentiment "Je suis une chose qui dure," asserting the primacy within **consciousness** of duration. This would be central to SB's thought, and Hesla (57) rightly stresses the importance of "The Idea of **Nothing**" in *Creative Evolution* (1907). Bergson imagines extinguishing his sensations one by one to find that the "I" remains: what cannot be eliminated is consciousness itself. SB would seem to have a remarkable affinity with Bergson, and, indeed, the debt is real.

SB's lectures at **Trinity** made much of Bergson's distinction between "spatial time" and "duration," one that preoccupied **Proust** and persisted in his own writing, which unfolds in a world where duration entails endurance, and consciousness is all, where **time** would have passed but not so quickly. Yet attempts to associate SB with Bergson founder on one rocky reef: SB's total rejection of vitalism. SB asserted instead the fiasco, seeking not the Absolute but the Nothing, which Bergson denied. Direct references are dismissive. **Chas** defines the difference between Bergson and Einstein (*Dream,* 211–12). **Murphy**'s attempt (251–52) to picture those known to him parodies Bergson's metaphor of the cinematographical mind (reeling off a spool). In *Malone Dies* (243) **Macmann**

is not fledged for flights, preferring (like **Chamfort**) to sit or lie, to rise only "when the élan vital or struggle for life began to prod him in the arse again."

Berkeley, George (1685–1753): Bishop of Cloyne and Fellow at **Trinity College** (1707–24). His *New Theory of Vision* appeared in 1709, and his greatest work, *A Treatise Concerning the Principles of Human Knowledge,* followed in 1710. His major theme was the denial of matter, **Neary**'s "Immaterialise or bust" (*Murphy,* 58). Berkeley contended that perception was not causal but that the "proper objects" of vision are purely visual ideas "in the mind," the cause of these being the will of **God**. As **Boswell** observed to **Johnson** (*Life,* 6 August 1763), there is no way of refuting the sophistry that proves the nonexistence of matter and affirms everything as ideal. Johnson struck his foot against a large stone: "I refute it thus." Berkeley's inquiry *Concerning the Virtues of Tarwater* (1744), his nostrum for the material body, underlies "the idealist tar" in *Murphy* (108); and SB (whose middle name was Barclay) read Berkeley's *Commonplace Book,* finding it "full of sound things" (SB to TM, 23 December 1932).

Berkeley's argument is summarized in the dictum *esse est percipi,* "to be is to be perceived," the keystone to his work. This asserts that **objects** of sense perception (the tree in the Trinity square) have no knowable existence outside the mind that perceives them. From this he reasoned that all reality ultimately exists in the mind of God. Conversely, the sense of being is sustained by being perceived as an object by another: more fully, *esse* *est aut percipi aut percipere* ("to be is both to be perceived and to perceive"). Murphy's crisis is triggered when he perceives in Mr. **Endon**'s eyes himself unperceived, and knows that to Mr. Endon he does not exist. This raises the paradox of **apperception**: the escape from self is logically incompatible with the need to perceive that escape; the cost, therefore, of attaining self-sufficiency is the mind, at this moment of truth a price Murphy is unwilling to pay.

In *Watt* the paradox of perception is inverted—Mr. **Knott** cannot exist unless he is perceived, or **witnessed**; hence his need for servants. In *The Unnamable*, the existence of the entire cosmos is reduced to the **consciousness** of the solitary mind, the Unnamable himself, dependent on his "chief witness" (344), to validate his existence. In *Waiting for Godot* the essential Berkeley is rehearsed in such instances as the tree (the same as yesterday?), and **Estragon**'s **boots**, which fit today but not yesterday, and may not be the same color, "explained" by the supposition that someone with different-size feet has come in the night. This reduces to the **absurd** Berkeley's contention that no causal relationship in **time** can be proved between any two representations of the "same" thing. *Endgame* begins with the metaphor of awakening, of perceiving; those on stage exist only while observed by the audience. The tradition behind SB's "**Three Dialogues**" includes Berkeley's decidedly undramatic *Three Dialogues Between Hylas and Philonous*, echoes of which persist into *Fin de partie*.

SB's most elaborate demonstration of Berkeley is in *Film* (1964). SB gave it the motto "Esse est percipi," and defined his intention in accordance with Berkeley's credo. In summary:

1. all extraneous perception is suppressed.
2. flight from nonbeing breaks down in the inescapability of self-perception.
3. "No truth value attaches to above, regarded as of merely structural and dramatic convenience."
4. protagonist sundered into object (**O**) and eye (**E**), the former in flight, the latter in pursuit.
5. "It will not be clear until end of film that pursuing perceiver is not extraneous, but self."
6. until the end O is perceived by E from behind at an angle not exceeding 45°, and experiences "anguish of perceivedness" when this is exceeded.
7. E therefore keeps within the "angle of immunity," exceeding it only twice inadvertently (when he hastily reduces the angle), and deliberately at the end when O is cornered.

Those who become conscious of E (the genteel couple, the flower woman, and finally O) assume an expression "corresponding to an agony of perceivedness"; only the **monkey** is indifferent. The play finally asserts the identity of O and E, the inescapability of apperception, and thus the truth of Berkeley's paradox of perception, without requiring the mind of God to validate it.

Bethlem Royal Hospital: a mental hospital in South **London**, original of the fictional **MMM** in *Murphy*. SB visited it several times, toured the wards (23 September 1935), and took notes from his talks with Geoffrey **Thompson**, who worked there as a psychiatrist, and from a nurse; details in the **Whoroscope Notebook** help date composition of the novel. The Bethlem Royal dates from 1247, with a long history as a hospice (1329) and a hospital for the insane (1403), and the first State Criminal Lunatic **Asylum** was opened at Bethlem in 1816. In 1925 the governors of the Maudsley bought Monks Orchard Estate, south of London, and in 1930 the hospital moved there. As in the novel (156), it is "on the boundary of two counties," most wards in Surrey but one in Kent. SB's description matches the Bethlem Royal: the Tau-cross shape of **Skinner**'s House (Tyson's); the wards; the daily routine; the ingenious indicator, a model of a neurological stimulus-response system (238); the treatment of "uncooperative" patients; and the nightly procedure. The postmortem room and crematorium are added.

bêtise: a word meaning something between stupidity and animal existence; "folly" is perhaps the closest equivalent. It often has a religious overtone, as in "**Text 1**": "jamais une imprécation, pas si bête" (121). SB told Gabriel d'Aubarède (1961): "J'ai conçu **Molloy** et le suite le jour où j'ai pris conscience de ma bêtise"; only then did he begin to write the things he felt. This occurred in SB's **mother**'s house at **New Place**, the locale of *Molloy*, and marked a watershed for SB, ignorance and impotence affirmed in an uncompromising vision of human existence as folly.

Bibby: SB's childhood nanny, Bridget Bray, friendly, loquacious, and Catholic,

rich in folk tales and homespun wisdom; a big woman with a strawberry nose, fond of cloves and peppermints (*Watt*, 51), and an expression "the quality of ruined granite" (Knowlson, 36). "**Serena II**" ends with "fairy tales of Meath," the stories that Bridget, from County Meath, would tell Sam and Frank before bed. She was with the family for twelve years before leaving to marry a gardener named Cooney. Elsewhere she reflects the loss of the **mother** or substitute for a mother's love, as in "**A Case in a Thousand.**" In "**Text 3**" "her name will be Bibby, I'll call her Bibby, if only it could be like that." The narrator of "The **Calmative**" meets a boy holding a **goat** by the horn, and asks: "Where are you off to, my little man, with your nanny?" (66–67), only to blush with shame. In *Happy Days*, when the mouse runs up **Mildred**'s thigh, with obscure designs upon her virginity, Mildred screams and screams; among those who come running is Bibby.

Bible: SB's writings are full of biblical echoes, mostly from the King James Authorized version, but with occasional touches of the Vulgate and *La Sainte Bible*. He noted incongruities such as Deuteronomy 10:16: "Circoncisez donc la prépuce de votre coeur" ("Circumcise therefore the foreskin of your heart"; it continues magnificently, "and be no more stiffnecked"), blending the irreverent with intimate knowledge. SB's faith may have been agnostic, tinged with a reluctant atheism, with the conclusion (*How It Is*) that it is "all balls"; but the questioning is relentlessly theological, and Christianity more than a "convenient mythology." Religious echoes are more prevalent in English texts, SB often replacing demotic **French** with appropriate patches from **Shakespeare** or the Bible. They are abundant and often ostentatious in the early works, notably *Dream* and *Murphy*, where the intention is broadly literary, philosophical, and satiric. Most provocative of these is *More Pricks Than Kicks*, a title that mocks the Damascus experience of St. Paul (Acts 9:5); but the mockery continues in such little jabs as **Belacqua**'s "that was a true saying," with its echo of the Communion service and 1 Timothy 1:15: "This is a true saying, and worthy of all men to be received, That Christ Jesus came into the world to save sinners." The tone ranges from witty blasphemy (**Rahab** as the type of **Beatrice**; iniquity and whoredom in "**Hell Crane to Starling**") to bitterness and anger ("**Ooftish**" and "**To My Daughter**"). Numerous entries touch on biblical ironies that testify to SB's fascination with the faith he might ridicule and resent but could not ignore.

The five great mid-century texts, *Watt, Molloy, Malone Dies, The Unnamable,* and *Waiting for Godot* (a series extending to *Endgame* and *How It Is*), each replete with biblical allusion, constitute perhaps the important body of religious literature of the past century. *Watt* asks fundamental questions; *Three Novels* journey through a semiotic wilderness where phrases such as "at the beginning" or "nearly the end" suffuse the text with a pervasive biblical presence; *Godot* and *Endgame* are parables; the **voice** faintly heard by each protagonist of the *Three Novels* echoes in the *Texts for Nothing* and *How It Is*. The latter ends with a desperate "WHAT'S MY NAME" as a marked

interrogation of the words of God to Moses (Exodus 3:13–14): "I AM THAT I AM." Many titles, such as *First Love,* "The **Expelled**," "The **End**," *All That Fall, Come and Go,* and "**Enough**" (not to mention *Godot*) are markedly biblical; or, like "**Act Without Words I**" or "**Eh Joe**" ("Thou fool thy soul"), respond to biblical themes. These matters are discussed in the individual entries.

Like literary references and rhetorical effects, biblical echoes become fewer and fainter in the later writings, as **memory** replaces allusion and images of previous religious import fade to **residua**, ill said, ill heard. Yet time and again, like a **dog** chained to its vomit (*Proust,* 8), SB returns to the Bible for *Company* (Psalms 55:14: "We took sweet counsel together, and walked unto the house of God in company"). For a listing of SB's biblical allusions, text by text, chapter and verse, see Chris Ackerley's "Samuel Beckett and the Bible," *JOBS* 9.1 (1999): 53–125.

bibliography: Beckett studies has always attracted more critics than scholars, and the field still lacks standard research tools. SB began in the twilight of the twenties with two polemical essays and an arcane poem. His work garnered little critical attention until *Waiting for Godot* appeared in mid-century. By then he had completed six more prose works (three in English and a trilogy in French); a volume of poems (*Echo's Bones,* 1935); two full-length plays (one of which, *Eleutheria,* he withdrew); and several reviews. Publication lagged behind composition, and in 1951, aged forty-five, SB was largely unrecognized. Thus **Krapp**'s birthday memoir: "Seventeen copies sold, of which eleven at trade price to free circulating libraries beyond the seas. Getting known." At this midpoint SB's critical reputation turned. His **French** work appeared in *Minuit,* and gained notice from the likes of Bernard Pingaud, Maurice Nadeau, Jean Anouilh, Alain Robbe-Grillet, and Maurice Blanchot. The earliest serious assessment was a long review from Georges Bataille, in *Critique* (1951). Early enthusiasm for SB's French work is reflected in Maurice Blanchot's analysis of *L'Innommable,* "Où maintenant? Qui maintenant?"; in Richard Seaver's memoir "Beckett and *Merlin*" (excerpts from *Watt* and *Molloy*); and in Seaver's "Samuel Beckett: An Introduction" (1952).

Interest in the United States followed as translations of the French work appeared from **Grove Press.** Edith Kern published "Drama Stripped for Inaction: Beckett's *Godot*" (1954). Vivian Mercier produced essays and reviews of SB's work for *New Republic, Hudson Review, New Statesman,* and *The Nation* (1955). Ruby Cohn edited the first special Beckett issue of a journal, *Perspective* (1959), completed the first doctoral dissertation on SB at Washington University, St. Louis (1960), and published it as *Samuel Beckett: The Comic Gamut* (1962). The first book in English on SB's work was Hugh Kenner's *Samuel Beckett: A Critical Study* (1961 and 1962). In these early years SB commanded little academic respect; Cohn recalls an editorial rebuke: "We like your criticism, but we don't feel your author merits publishing space." In his "Introduction" to *Beckett at 60* (1967), John **Calder** claimed that more books had been written on **Christ,** Na-

poleon, and **Wagner** than anyone else, but by 2000 SB might rank fourth. Wildly extravagant, the hyperbole captures the growing interest in SB's art. Since the **Nobel Prize** (1969), the critical waters have substantially risen. Even so, the lack of foundational scholarship such as accurate texts and comprehensive bibliographies remains a hindrance.

By the mid-1960s several publishers were prompted to commission bibliographies, and attempts were made to compile checklists of both primary and secondary materials. James Tanner and J. Don Vann published an eighty-five-page checklist (Kent State, 1969). This was superseded by Raymond Federman and John Fletcher's monumental *Samuel Beckett, His Works and His Critics* (1970). This covered primary and critical material to 1966 (1968 for books), citing some 580 articles and thirty-one books; but it needed a supplement immediately. The University of California Press approached J. C. C. Mays to do so, but in 1976 Mays abandoned the project as unworkable, since the system of decimal numeration designed to allow expansion was already insufficient to accommodate the post-Nobel surge. In 1971 *Lettres modernes* published *Calepins de bibliographie* 2. It contained extensive "Essais de bibliographie" by Robin Davis (primary, 1929–66), and J. R. Bryer with M. J. Friedman (critical, 1931–66), supplemented at both ends (1929–69) and with "une esquisse . . . en autres langues" by P. C. Hoy (1953–69). Criticism outpaced the best efforts of bibliographers, however. When Tom Bishop and Raymond Federman edited the Beckett *Cahiers de L'Herne* (1976), they estimated that sixty-odd books and 5,000 articles were in print, a tenfold increase in one decade. Davis updated his "Essai" with a seventy-one-page *Checklist and Index* (1967–76), published by the library at Stirling (1979), but Breon Mitchell (*JOBS* 8 [1982]: 153) noted it was already five years out of date. Mitchell offered an update in "A Beckett Bibliography: New Texts 1976–1983," *Modern Fiction Studies,* 79 (Spring, 1983): 131–52. The problem may be relieved somewhat when St. Paul's Bibliographies with Oak Knoll Books publish Mitchell's descriptive bibliography of the primary works.

Peter Murphy et al. published a *Critique of Beckett: Criticism* (Camden House, 1994). This useful overview made the need for a comprehensive listing more urgent than ever. Their survey of German criticism was supplemented by Rolf Breuer and Werner Huber's *A Checklist of Beckett Criticism in German* (Paderborn, 1996). *JOBS* has published two bibliographical supplements: "Sam w Polsce / Sam in Poland" by Charles Krance in 11 and 12: 131–52, and "An Outline of Beckett Criticism in Italy" by Carla Locatelli in 3.1 (1993): 39–57.

To date, then, no comprehensive bibliography of even SB's primary work exists. Scholars instead have addressed parts of the problem. Richard Admussen's *The Samuel Beckett Manuscripts* (1979) is still useful, the early date indicative of the wider problem. Carlton Lake edited *No Symbols Where None Intended* (1984), an impressive catalogue of an impressive collection, the Beckett materials at the Humanities Research Center (see **HRHRC**), Austin. Washington University and Dartmouth College have catalogued their holdings, as has **Trinity College**. The **BIF**

(Reading) produced a first catalogue in 1978, issuing various supplements; then updated the work with *Beckett at Reading* (Whiteknights Press, 1998), ed. Mary Bryden et al. A team of scholars led by Martha Fehsenfeld and Lois Overbeck is working on SB's letters, authorized in 1985 but having a difficult birth for reasons ranging from copyright, funding, disorganization, and SB's impossible writing. Some 15,000 letters exist, widely scattered, of which about 2,500 will be included in full (some facsimiles) and some 3,500 to 5,000 in abridged form, in four volumes, with a *Calendar of Extant Correspondence.* SB's correspondence with Barney Rosset and Grove Press is in preparation. The value of these activities may be gauged by Maurice Harmon's *No Author Better Served* (1998), the correspondence of SB and Alan **Schneider**, which, despite deletions required by the estate and several mistranscriptions, offers unexpected insights into SB's life and creative thinking.

The ***Theatrical Notebooks*** of the dramatic texts reflect thorough bibliographical scholarship; but while Charles Krance's bilingual variorum editions of *Company/Compagnie* and *Mal vu mal dit/ Ill Seen Ill Said* (Garland, 1993 and 1996) set a fine precedent, others have been slow to follow. A collected poetry is overdue. Important materials remain in private hands, unavailable even for bibliographical description. Since SB's death much new material has become available, but despite the estate's generosity and its support of scholarship, legal and practical difficulties have made definitive bibliographical work as yet impossible, even as the gradual revelation of manuscripts and unexpected treasures (e.g., Pilling's edition of the **Dream Notebook**, 1999) whets the scholarly appetite for more. Isolated work has been done, some of it admirable, but much remains.

bicycles: a mode of **motion** through the Beckett country. "Sanies I" depicts the poet on his proud **Swift,** "pounding along in three ratios [gears] like a sonata," the verse imitating his freedom as he speeds north of **Dublin:** "all heaven in the sphincter"; then, at end of day, seeing her whom he has dismounted to love, the verse like the emotion becomes pedestrian. In "**Serena III**" he moves about the city, the frenetic pace and advice to "keep on the move" suggesting a bicycle (or a motorcycle; SB had owned an AJS). In **Paris,** on the "**Rue de Vaugirard,**" the cyclist stops for a moment to register on his mind a photographic image of the moment.

Belacqua debuts pedaling after **Findlater**'s van; he later reflects that should he ever drop a book, it will be "ramshackle, tumbledown, a boneshaker" (*Dream*, 139). In "**Fingal**" Belacqua "who could on no account resist a bicycle" (28) steals one and deserts **Winnie.** The parson who comes to bury him in "**Draff**" arrives on his "rustless all-steel" (193), and pedals away like a weaver's shuttle, that is, on a "**Swift**" (O'Brien's "**Raleigh**" misses the **pun**). **Murphy**'s hokey-pokey man has a cruel machine (14). Mr. Evans in *Watt* comes and goes by bicycle, and the train discharges one (245), for a Miss Walker. Hugh Kenner's "**Cartesian** centaur" of man and machine is observed in "The **Calmative**" (71), a cyclist reading his newspaper as he pedals slowly in

the street, mind in unison with machine. **Mercier**'s bicycle disintegrates (85), relieved of its wheels, saddle, bell, carrier, and taillight; the pump remains, inverted in dubious homage to the divine afflatus. **Molloy** has a green bicycle, with a red horn (like SB in his salad days). Apprehended by a **policeman,** he continues on foot, but takes the horn, which, in parody of Siegfried's **forest murmurs,** he toots in reply to the distant **gong** (89). **Moran** sends his son to purchase a bicycle, for £5, with a carrier, pump, lamp, and a bell; among **Malone**'s possessions is the top of a bell. In "**Text 12**" (150), the narrator, not the man he was, fears respectability, of "riding a bicycle" and joining the accountants' chorus, "opining like a single man." In *All That Fall* Mr. **Tyler** punctures his back wheel. **Hamm** asks **Clov** for two wheels, to help him round his world, but there are "no more bicycle wheels" (8). **Nagg and Nell** lost their legs in the Ardennes in a tandem accident, on the road to Sedan (16); the **allegory** is that of the Great War. After this there are no more bicycles.

BIF: a "Beckett Archive" was founded in 1971 at Reading University by Professor James Knowlson and Dr. James Edwards. It began as an exhibition, but the materials, including several donations from SB, became the nucleus of a collection that has grown immensely, thanks largely to SB's generosity and that of international scholars and admirers of his work. In 1988 it became the property of a charitable trust, the Beckett International Foundation, of which the University of Reading is trustee. The archive houses an extensive collection of manuscripts, books, papers, and ephemera; while not able to match the **HRHRC** in prose manuscripts, it is unsurpassed in its holdings of the drama. Judicious scholarly exchange (Washington University and Dartmouth College) has built up copies of many items not in its original possession. Among the gems are items from SB's personal library, notably his "abominable" Gallimard edition of **Proust**, with marginal annotations, the **German Diaries**, and the **Dream** and **Whoroscope Notebooks**. A catalogue was issued in 1978, and enlarged with various supplements. In 1989 Dr. Peter Mills was appointed to draw up a more inclusive volume; his work was completed by Mary Bryden and Julian Garforth. This resulted in *Beckett at Reading* (1998), a complete listing, with useful annotations, of SB's manuscripts at Reading, "a catalogue compiled by scholars for scholars," and itself an invaluable adjunct to Beckett studies. The collection continues to grow with donations (most recently the letters of Ruby Cohn and Jocelyn Herbert) and some few but judicious purchases.

Bilitis: the **Syra-Cusa** is described as a **Brancusi** bird with "Bilitis breasts" (*Dream*, 33); **Belacqua** refers to "the hard breastless Greek slave" and "the algor of Bilitis" (83–84); and the **Polar Bear** draws nigh with nary a trace of "of Bilitis or a chaste huntress" (162). "**Tristesse Janale**" describes beauty as "l'icone bilitique." These refer to an apocryphal poetess from *Les Chansons de Bilitis* (1894) by Pierre Louÿs (1870–1925), a popular hoax "translation" by an erudite Hellenist of 143 prose-poems that trace the life of Bilitis from her first **love** to Lesbos, then her life as a courtesan of Aphrodite on Kypros. Her small breasts are a recurrent motif.

billiards: SB played billiards at **Trinity** and in **Paris** cafés. The billiard table was an image of a Newtonian universe, mechanical worlds in collision (from Minchin's *Students' Dynamics* he traced the movement of billiard balls). In his Trinity lectures, Rachel **Dobbin** records, he described the naturalist writer as setting the billiard balls in **motion**. This defines Thelma **bboggs**'s attraction to **Belacqua** ("What a Misfortune," 118); Mr. bboggs sings about cannoning off the cush. SB calls snooker "slosh" in *Murphy* (168), a hypomanic teaching it to a Korsakow's syndrome. In *Watt* (14), **Cream**, setting himself for a long thin jenny, is put off his stroke by the wail of the newly born Larry (a "jenny" involves the object ball lying near the cushion and inside the line to the pocket; it is "long" if played from the far end of the table).

Billy in the bowl: a "character" from the "dim Georgian days" (O'Brien, 292), who, legless, propelled himself through **Dublin** in a wooden bowl shod with iron. Depicted by Jack **Yeats** (Ryle, 36). The **Unnamable** imagines his next "vice-exister" as "bowl on his head and his arse in the dust" (315); he refers to a "billybowl of thorns" (350). In "**Rough for Theatre I**" a blind fiddler with an alms bowl is called "Billy."

Bim and Bom: Russian clowns of the 1920s and '30s, permitted under the Soviet regime but who became for SB emblems of cruelty under a comic garb. They appear in "**Yellow**" (163); then (red and whiskered) in *Murphy,* as Thomas "**Bim**" **Clinch** and his relatives, Bom and Bum. They return in two draft passages deleted from *Waiting for Godot* and *Endgame;* remerge in *How It Is;* are heard faintly in "**Ping**"; and take a final bow in "**What Where.**"

Bing: a French prose text (1966); published by **Minuit** (1966) in a limited edition of 762; then included in *Têtes-mortes* (1967), 59–66. Fifty copies with eight blind-relief impressions by H. M. Ehrhardt appeared in 1970 (see **illustrations**). Six notebooks and several typescripts (sixteen versions) are held at Washington University, Saint Louis (20 July to 15 September 1966); photocopies are held at the **BIF** (RUL 1535/1–7), with facsimiles of nine untitled typescripts ("Préalables"). Of the sixteen versions ten are published in transcription (with variants), along with SB's English translation, *Ping,* in Federman and Fletcher (325–343). The remaining six facsimile manuscript drafts are published in Admussen (pp. 131–48) with a note on their relation to the ten transcriptions (325). Other bits appeared in the SB issue of *L'Herne* (1976). In a note with the manuscripts SB commented: "'Bing' may be regarded as the result or miniaturization of *Le Dépeupleur* abandoned because of its intractable complexities." The title "Bing" is a later addition, written on the first notebook beneath the caption "La Vita degli animali" (a picture of a **beaver**); it was earlier "Blanc." The text is composed in columns: corps, endroit, divers (the latter deleted), allowing SB to ar-

range his material in sequence and to place themes and variations, a technique he used elsewhere. Any slightness of the work is belied by the concentrated labor with intractable material, both the original composition and in translation. For analysis, see "**Ping.**"

biography: there was little public or scholarly interest in SB's life until the 1950s, when *Waiting for Godot* made him a figure of controversy. Even then curiosity was muted until the **Nobel Prize** (1969), when speculation ran rife. SB's determination to guard his privacy and a critical orthodoxy that affirmed the autonomous text meant that few readers knew much about the man. For years the only biographical detail was the occasional interview that SB permitted. The first such profile was an infamous "interview" with Israel Shenker in the *New York Times* (5 May 1956). Shenker took the stance of "this is what he would say" to present materials SB later called misleading. Hence the comment on **Joyce:** "He's tending toward omniscience and omnipotence as an artist. I'm working with impotence, ignorance. I don't think impotence has been exploited in the past." Authentic interviews took place with Tom Driver, "Beckett by the Madeleine" (1961); Gabriel d'Aubarède (1961); Lawrence Harvey (1961–62); John Gruen (1969); E. M. Cioran (1976); and Mira Avrech (1981). Some have been republished in Graver and Federman's *Critical Heritage* (1979), along with the impressionistic speculation that created a received idea of SB as a bleak and broody pessimist, hater of his kind. SB was interviewed three times (1953–56) by Richard Ellmann about Joyce, authenticating the **friendship** yet remaining guarded about himself. Compelling details were revealed by SB's friends in *Beckett at 60* (1967); but not until Lawrence Harvey's study of the poetry (1970) were scholars alerted to a body of work largely unknown and to teasing intimations of a life behind the texts. Harvey's insights, valuable as an expression of what SB had revealed, did not add up to a *life,* and were in vital respects misleading. And SB made him delete much of interest, saying that it was confidential.

Since 1970 many reminiscences and biographical surveys have appeared. These include: an interview with SB by Patrick Starnes, *Antigonish Review* 10 (summer 1972); Charles Juliet's *Rencontre avec Samuel Beckett* (1986); Eoin O'Brien's *The Beckett Country* (1986); Enoch Brater's *Why Beckett* (1989), reissued as *The Essential Samuel Beckett: An Illustrated Biography* (2003); John Gruen's *The Artist Observed* (1991); André Bernold's *L'Amitié de Beckett* (1992); and hundreds of feature articles and reviews in newspapers and magazines, more appearing with every new performance or publication. Web sites proliferate, offering huge amounts of detail, much inaccurate.

Deirdre Bair overcame enormous obstacles to her attempts to write a life of SB as a doctoral dissertation, then to publish it as *Samuel Beckett: A Biography* (1978). Its manifold errors were pointed out ruthlessly by her reviewers, but when the book was reissued after SB's death (Summit Books, 1990), in a new introduction to a sloppily corrected text Bair declared that she had made only one real error. That concerned her story that as

SB lay stabbed on the street he was come upon by his future wife, Suzanne, who promptly nursed him. Bair pleaded that she was duped by Maria Jolas, that she took too much on trust. The errors are depressing. Her self-congratulation, qualified only by the admission of occasional "glitches," astonishing under any circumstances, is the more so given the virulence of her reviewers and informants, many of whom (Martin Esslin, Con Leventhal, Ruby Cohn) dissociated themselves from the biography.

The errors were corrected in James Knowlson's authorized biography, *Damned to Fame: The Life of Samuel Beckett* (Bloomsbury, Simon and Schuster, 1996). With unprecedented access to the author and his archive, Knowlson wove a portrait of a life, fuller, and richer than anyone had suspected. Knowlson's record of the life is extraordinary. He drew on a stunning array of material—interviews with SB and his close friends, most of whom had refused cooperation with other biographers; journals, diaries, and letters previously unavailable, some wholly unknown—to create a three-dimensional portrait of an artist so committed to the art of failure that he became the century's major writer. Knowlson elucidated life and work with equal dexterity to belie SB's assertion that his life was of little significance; the work is richer, more subtle and complex, and more accessible when viewed through the prism of his life. *Damned to Fame,* SB's self-appraisal borrowed from Alexander Pope, is indispensable to anyone interested in SB, or in the literary pulse of the twentieth century.

Anthony Cronin's *Samuel Beckett: The Last Modernist* appeared contemporaneously with Knowlson's biography. September in **London** of 1996 was full of tantalizing hints of two Beckett biographies. The *Sunday Times* whetted appetites by publishing in August an extract from Knowlson's **Roussillon** years; a week later the *Observer* replied: "COFFEE WITHOUT BRANDY; that's how Samuel Beckett described sex without **love**." There followed a clutch of four features, ostensibly highlighting Cronin's book, but better suited to the *Sun*. "In Bed with Beckett" became a catch phrase, literary debate degraded to an undignified squabble as the Fourth Estate belatedly discovered that SB was not only a human being but had had the occasional affair. Equally shabby was the metaphor of confrontation: in one corner, the suave English academic, James Knowlson; in the other, the bluff Oirishman, Tony Crony, poet of the people. It proved no contest— Knowlson distancing himself from the nonsense, letting his book deliver the punches; and Cronin tripping over the canvas in the first round, with a pastiche of received ideas and opinions, a tendency, like Bair (on whom he often relied), to argue from the works to the life (an embarrassing account of Peggy **Sinclair**) and a contempt for intellectuals and "thesis writers," the more curious given SB's acute learning. Cronin was unaware of recent scholarship; he made little use of archival materials; and his readings of the primary texts are often strange (he omits the mockery of Austin **Clarke**, but has **Ticklepenny** meet **Murphy** in a **Dublin** pub, instead of a tearoom in **London**). In short, Cronin didn't do his homework. Five years later a major scandal threatened, when Bruce Arnold, literary editor of the

Irish *Independent,* was struck by a curious difference in the dating of SB's **birth** between proof and publication of Cronin's biography. He identified other changes, small but crucial, and concluded that these could have been made only if Cronin had had unauthorized access to an advance copy of Knowlson's biography, which he signally failed to acknowledge. Public reaction was muted, but Cronin's work was thus further discredited.

Lois Gordon's *The World of Samuel Beckett, 1906–1946* (1996) constructs a cinematic pan of Dublin and Ireland during the Rising and Civil War, London during the Depression, Paris during the Occupation, and Roussillon for the remainder of the war, focusing on the historical events through which SB lived (3). The book could not have been more untimely. Earlier it might have offered a few scattered insights, but within two months it was superseded by Knowlson. Equally recombinant is the SB volume in the *Overlook Illustrated Lives* series (Penguin, 2002) by Gerry Dukes. It adds nothing to existing knowledge of SB's life, and is stingy with acknowledgments. Profusely illustrated, but with only one new photograph, that of the Becketts at Roger **Blin**'s cremation, the book is devoid of serious scholarly interest.

Bion, Wilfred Ruprecht (1897–1979): SB's analyst for almost two years (1934–35) at the **Tavistock Clinic** (qv). He was born in India, educated privately, and read history at Queen's College and Poitiers. His studies were interrupted by wartime service in the Royal Tank Regiment, where he won the DSO. He qualified as a doctor in 1930 and without previous training in psychotherapy joined the Tavistock as an assistant in 1932, but was promoted to the senior staff in 1933. He served there many years, responsible for the theory and practice of group relations, before taking up private consultancy in Los Angeles.

Bion was deeply influenced by Melanie **Klein**. He offered private consultations, sometimes seeing SB three times a week. Despite "a background of Toc H and Tank Corps" (SB to TM, 8 October 1935), SB liked Bion, respected him as a therapist, and derived from him considerable information about the psychoanalytic world. While he presumably felt the sessions were doing some good, SB retained a detachment from the process, a reserve that meant that **psychoanalysis** would become a literary stratagem rather than a system of analysis or belief.

Baker sums up SB's difficulties (*Mythology*, 6): "He was in considerable distress, with 'somatization' (boils, tremors, an anal abscess) and night-terrors (*pavor nocturnus*, particularly associated with obsessionals). His psychiatrist friend Geoffrey **Thompson** persuaded him that his problems might be psychosomatic . . . Bion thought that his problems stemmed from his relationship with his **mother**, consolidating this as a theme in his life." One effect was crucial. SB wrote to **MacGreevy** (10 March 1935) about his **irrational heart**, noting that he had gone "to Geoffrey, then Bion" to learn of a diseased condition that began in his "prehistory," a "bubble in the puddle"; and that the "fatuous torments" that he had treasured as describing the superior man were part of the same pathology. He concluded that there was no way to re-

deem "a composition that was invalid from the word 'go' & has to be broken up altogether. If the heart still bubbles it is because the puddle has still not been drained." In short, he concluded, if the heart had not put the fear of death into him, he would still be "boozing & sneering & lounging around." Bion's therapy was a turning point.

The strength and weakness of the Tavistock approach was its eclecticism, ideas derived from **Freud** and **Jung** as well as Klein and (later) Laing. Bion employed with SB his "reductive analysis" (Knowlson, 170) to discover the dynamic links between symptom and etiology (often the trauma caused by an impossible relationship with the mother). He encouraged SB to write to help him understand the process, and to detail his dreams. Bion was intrigued by memories of the womb and prebirth psychology, and notions such as neurasthenia, **narcissic** regression, or the **embryonic** twin. SB shared this fascination, and borrowed books from Bion: **Rank**'s *The Trauma of Birth* (1929); Karin **Stephen**'s *The Wish to Fall Ill* (1933); Otto **Adler**'s *The Neurotic Constitution* (1921). Toward the end of his therapy (2 October 1935), Bion met SB for dinner (sole) at L'Étoile restaurant at 30 Charlotte Street, then took him to the Tavistock to hear a lecture by Jung, who spoke of how complexes may appear in visions and speak in voices, assuming identities of their own. Jung discussed the diagram depicting concentric and ever-darkening circles of **consciousness**, which SB made into the model of **Murphy's mind**; and he mentioned the **little girl** who had never really been born. The influence of this lecture on SB's subsequent writing cannot be overstated.

Didier Anzieu has argued that the impasse caused by SB's analysis was resolved in his writing, which thereby constitutes autoanalysis. He was not dissuaded when SB dismissed this as "a psychoanalyst's phantasms" (Baker, 177). Jean-Michel Rabaté explored the symbiotic relationship between Bion and SB, manifest in the way that Bion's later fictional "trilogy" derived from his analysis of the neurotic young Irishman. In "Beckett's Ghosts and Fluxions" (1994), part of *The Ghosts of Modernity* (1996), Rabaté cites **Berkeley**'s critique of Newton's attempt to transform "religious rubbish" into "opticks," affirming the importance of "ghosts" (impalpable traces) and "fluxions" (derivatives of **mathematical** functions) in the differential calculus of diminution ("Fluxions," 24). He suggests that "ghosts" for SB are encrypted words emerging from the deepest layers of the unconscious, "words that limn the dim contours of blurred yet luminous images" (33), a **voice** reiterating its insistent drone in the **skull** yet remaining invisible. The "impasse" of the **Unnamable** is explored in terms of the "ghosts" of the enunciating "I" in *Texts for Nothing*, a process that points toward "**Ghost Trio**" and beyond. Intriguingly, Rabaté finds Bion's analysis informing SB's later sense of a "**nothing**" out of which something comes, or a "something" diminishing *al niente*.

birth: in "**Sanies I**" the narrator recollects as he cycles along at Easter his being born "with a pop with the green of the **larches**," his **father** taking the day off and wandering in the hills, to return "to me a spanking boy." A drink for his father, and "sparkling beestings" (the first of his **mother**'s milk) for him. The date was Good Friday, 13 April 1906, magnificently appropriate. SB's birth certificate says "May 13"; but this was probably his father's error in registering the birth. The April date was his childhood birthday, and SB was unequivocal about it. He claimed to have memories of the **womb** and his birth, an experience burlesqued in *Watt*.

In **Nietzsche**'s *Birth of Tragedy,* asked what humanity most desires, Silenus replies: "not to be born, not to be, to be *nothing*. But the second best for you— is quickly to die." Nietzsche's source was **Schopenhauer** (*WWI,* I.3 #51, 328). The wisdom of Silenus offers a definition of modern tragedy. As SB put it (*Proust,* 49): "The tragic figure represents the expiation of original sin, of the original and eternal sin of him and all his 'socimalorum,' the sin of having been born." He then quotes **Calderón**'s *La vida es sueño:* "Pues el delito mayor / Del hombre es haber nacido" ("For the greatest crime of man is to have been born"). SB copied the tag "Optimum non nasci, aut cito mori" ("best is not to be born, or to die quickly") into the **Whoroscope Notebook**; it appears in **Geulincx**'s *Ethica* (54), **Burton**'s *Anatomy* (I.2.3.x, 184n), and as epigraph to **Rank**'s *The Trauma of Birth*. **Neary** evokes it as womb and **asylum**: "back to the cell, blood heat, next best thing to never being born" (*Murphy,* 44). The **Unnamable** improves on this: "some people are lucky, born of a wet dream and dead before morning" (379). In "**Text 5**," in an obscure assize, "to be is to be guilty" (117).

In *All That Fall* Mrs. **Rooney** emerges from Mr. **Slocum**'s car as a difficult birth: "Crouch down . . . At my time of life! She's coming . . . Am I out?" In "**Embers**," Henry recalls his father's last words, describing him as a washout: "Wish to **Christ** she had" (douched after sex). The protagonist of *From an Abandoned Work* notes, "all I regret is having been born." Birth is implicated with **death**. **Hamm** declares in *Endgame*, "The end is in the beginning"; and **Pozzo** states in *Waiting for Godot*, "They give birth astride of a grave." **Molloy** and **Malone** experience death as birth, or vice versa, one in a ditch (91), the other feeling the world's labia parting (189), then feet first from "the great cunt of existence" (283). "A **Piece of Monologue**" begins, "Birth was the death of him." "**I gave up before birth**" is an embryonic drama. In *First Love* the narrator's birthdate is "graven" on his memory (25). In *Watt* (104), "expelled" is the word used for giving birth. "The **Expelled**" offers an image of violent birth, forcible ejection from the comfort of the room/womb, into the glaring light of day: "I saw the door open and my feet come out" (49). "**Act Without Words I**" also opens with an image of forcible ejection, the protagonist flung onto the stage. In *How It Is* the protagonist feels "having been born octogenarian" (70); while *That Time* refers to an old Chinaman (Lao-tzu) born with long white hair and a beard. In *Footfalls*, V has M late in life, and begs: "Forgive me again"; and, after no response: "Forgive me again." The request is for the sin of having given birth.

Blake, William (1757–1827): poet and engraver; a maker of systems to whom SB was attracted while resisting that impulse himself. SB shared the growing respect for Blake as an original thinker and one whose imagination had resisted the orthodoxies of his age. Yet direct references are few. **Belacqua** does not propose to "Blake" the **Alba** (*Dream*, 193), despite the poet's advocacy of sexual liberation. **Murphy** on the jobpath is from an illustrated *Book of Job,* the master's conception of Bildad the Shuhite (one of Job's comforters) come to life. Bildad and Zophar are "fragments of Job" (70) in accordance with the notion that Blake's illustrations are best interpreted as a drama enacted in Job's soul. Murphy's **greatcoat**, the Blake League is informed, is aeruginous, not green; that is, not of the generative world. **Cooper**'s visions of gin palaces are described as Blake his angels. Figures in the later drama may be inspired by Blake; **Hamm** tells in *Endgame* of a "madman," an "engraver," with whom he associated himself; and Knowlson suggests (531) that the old man in *That Time* is like an engraving of **God**.

Blin, Roger (1907–84): SB's first director. When their paths first crossed Blin was a penniless director, and SB an unknown writer having difficulties placing his work. *Eleutheria* and *En attendant Godot* were circulated by Suzanne unsuccessfully until she saw Strindberg's *Ghost Sonata* at the Gaité Montparnasse (spring, 1950). Blin's production impressed her, and she dropped off both typescripts for him. Blin had heard of SB from Tristan Tzara, and although he did not understand *Godot* he liked it. But he decided to begin with *Eleutheria* because it was more traditional (Bair, 403). Economics affected the decision: "*Eleutheria* had seventeen characters, a divided stage, elaborate props and complicated lighting. I was poor . . . I thought I'd be better off with the *Godot* because there were only four actors and they were bums. They could wear their own clothes if it came to that, and I wouldn't need anything but a spotlight and a bare branch for a tree." With such reasoning was theater history shaped.

Blin's distinctive directorial style was his lack of any distinctive directorial style. His chief asset was his invisibility, his willingness to submerge himself totally within the text. Yet he would have been barely a footnote in the history of theater without six plays that saved him from oblivion, four by SB and two by Jean Genet. He staged world premieres of *En attendant Godot* (1953) and *Fin de partie* (1957), French premieres of *La Dernière bande* (1960) and *Oh les beaux jours* (1963), and two Genet plays, *The Blacks* (1959) and *The Screens* (1966). *La Dernière bande* altered the relationship between author and director. SB found the production hopeless and wrote to **Arikha** (31 March 1960): "it is as bad as ever and always will be. It's screwed up, better just to forget about it" (Atik, 65). He said he would not work with Blin again, but work again he did, at least once. After *Oh les beaux jours* Blin staged a revival of *Fin de partie* at Théâtre Chaptal 347 in 1968, and incorporated textual changes that SB had introduced into *Endspiel* at the **Schiller-Theater**, Berlin, a year earlier. But the rift over the 1960 *La Dernière bande* was irremediable, perhaps because SB had begun to direct

his own plays and with *Endspiel* went on to become his own best interpreter.

blue and white: Joyce's *Portrait* features the wading girl, her slate-blue skirts tucked into downy drawers in an emblem both sacred and profane. The next scene depicts the sordid Dedalus breakfast table, scattered with blue and white pawn tickets. Blue and white are called in "The **Calmative**" (75) "colours of the Virgin," but associated with the striped apron or curtains of the horse butcher. Compare **Macmann**'s cloak (*Malone Dies*, 276). *How It Is* invokes the blue and white of clouds and sky (27), then a **horse** stands in mute misery against the blue of the sky and white of the landscape, and the blue gives way to white dust. Saint Andrew's Cross, blue on white, is another emblem of cruelty (58, 88, 90). The narrator's eyes are blue, like those of Macmann, "Bluer scarcely than white of egg" (319). "**Ping**" accentuates the white body and blue eyes: "Head haught eyes light blue almost white silence within"; and invokes **memories** of a beautiful world "blue and white in the wind" (193). The colors are associated with **ineffable** longing, as in the picture in **Erskine**'s room (*Watt*, 128): "The point was blue, but blue! The rest was white." **Lucky**'s heaven is "so blue still and calm so calm" (*WG*, 28.b). This echoes Verlaine's "Si bleu, si calme" ("Le Ciel"), and Nell's "so white" (*Endgame*, 21). See **green and yellow** and **red and gray**.

blue flower: part of the timeless parenthesis of **Vega**, **God**, and the "birdless cloudless colourless skies"; as in "**As-**

sumption," *Dream* (70), or SB's review of **Rilke** (*Disjecta*, 66): "The mystic heart, geared to the *blaue Blume*, petrified." Plucked from Novalis's *Heinrich von Ofterdingen*, it became for **symbolism** an emblem of impossible longing, like the green carnation for decadence. In "**Calvary by Night**," the blue flower mingles with Bloom's languid floating flower in an image of **onanism**. **Watt** sees **Knott** looking at "a little blue flower and close by a fat **worm**" (146). They watch until the worm has gone, and only the flower remains; then Watt, looking up, sees Knott's eyes are closed, transcendence denied. See also Penelope Fitzgerald's novel *The Blue Flower* (1997).

Bocca: Bocca degli Abati, traitor during the battle of Montaperto (1260) between **Florence** and Siena; he cut off the hand of the Florentine standard-bearer, leading to panic and defeat of the Guelphs. **Dante** places him in the ninth circle of hell, encased in ice (*Inf.* XXXII.78ff). SB alludes to him in "**hors crâne seul dedans**": "tel Bocca dans la glace"; and in "**dread nay**": "in hellice eyes / stream till / frozen to / jaws rail / gnaw gnash / teeth with stork / clack chatter."

body: one point of departure is the Cartesian **dualism** of substances: "All things are either bodies or minds; substances are either spatial or conscious: *res extensae and res cogitantes*" (Windelband, 404). The relation is disjunctive, so that what is spatial is not conscious, and vice versa. The world thus falls into two separate realms, bodies and minds; the Cartesian split underlies the paradox of what SB called in his early writing "self-exten-

sion"; and the problem of being may be rephrased as that of spatio-temporal integration. A second premise is SB's acceptance of the **Occasionalist** conclusion: since we have knowledge of mental activity only, the mind is not master of the body nor cause of movement in it. The "I" is restricted to the act of thinking, but does not enter the *res externa*, or world of matter and extension, not even into its own body, with regard to which it is merely the **spectator**. Only in the **little word** of the mind can "I" be free; the body, accordingly, may be considered a **machine**, and "I" should set no value upon it (***Ubi nihil vales, ibi nihil velis***). Many of SB's characters are dyspraxic, metaphysically speaking, because of the failure of the body-mind synchronization. Yet another problem arises: the continued existence of **consciousness** is contingent upon that of the body, an increasingly frail machine, and of the heart, a notoriously **irrational** engine; indeed, without the body the word could not be articulated ("imagine . . . si ceci cessait").

Schopenhauer considers the **object** immediate to the subject, his own body. The body, for the pure knowing subject, is an idea like any other idea, an object among objects (*WWI*, I.2 #18, 129); yet that subject of knowledge becomes an individual only through his identity with the body, which thus becomes known in two different ways: as an object among objects and as immediately known, as *will*. Schopenhauer contends (130) that action of the body is the will objectified, or passed into perception; and that knowledge of the will cannot be separated from that of the body (132).

Knowledge of the body appears in consciousness in a special manner, and thus the knowing subject is an individual. This offers a mode of knowing other objects, by attributing to them the reality that our own body has. Thus, knowledge of the body is a first step toward knowledge of the material world.

As the **Unnamable** says (304), "It is well to establish the position of the body from the outset"; here, with respect to the Cartesian notion of the body as a machine, and Schopenhauer's relation of the perceiving subject to the object perceived. Otherwise "A man would wonder where his kingdom ended" (361), craving a **stick** as an extension of the body, or a stone as a missile, an extension of space. Recent theory has privileged the body with respect to what Blanchot calls "the space of literature"— the impenetrable relationship between material reality and the nonrepresentational aesthetics. This has led to some impenetrable prose. One response is to empathize with the Unnamable when he says (345): "I don't know where I end"; and even more so with his cry (313): "Ah for a neck"—less a plea for a body than an echo of Caligula's desire that the Roman populace had but one neck, that he might cut its head off.

Despite **Belacqua**'s contention that "bodies don't matter," he is meshed in the bosom of the **Smeraldina**. Her body is "all wrong" (*Dream*, 15), like the peacock's claws, that were **Dante**'s emblem of the earthbound spirit; but perched on top of her is "the loveliest little pale firm cameo of a birdface." This he contemplates with equanimity, until she rapes him (18), then all is "kaputt."

She wants (55–56) his "soft white body naked" (an unfortunate echo of *The Waste Land*), her body needs him "so terrible"; but like the poet of "**Assumption**" Belacqua is living the myth of the inviolate mind, into which the intrusion of the female is an impertinence. The somatic material enforces the split between body and mind: the **Syra-Cusa**'s body a dream but her head null (33); misogyny; **onanism**; **buttocks**; **Beatrice** and the brothel; Platonic adoration of the **Alba**—the trauma of an "inward man" (46) who cannot abolish the flesh.

Murphy's catastrophe ensues when his desire to retreat into the bodytight mind confronts the "reality" of Mr. **Endon**. His "deplorable susceptibility" (179) to **Celia** and ginger biscuits, the distractions of serenade, nocturne, and alba, keep him in the big world. Celia is body reduced to **fundamental sound**; statistics with a heavenly name (despite the echo of **Swift**) in marked contrast with her profession. Murphy's dilemma arises because she (and a **job**) intrudes upon his mind. His efforts to retreat into the hermetically sealed monadic mind (compare *Film*) confront the antinomy of **apperception**, and he realizes that the cost of inner freedom is awareness. That is, he probably realizes this, for during his last attempt to rock himself into the dark zone the gas is ignited and chaos ensues. Murphy's body is incinerated, for there must be no suggestion of its resurrection, but rather a **Democritan** guffaw as his "body, mind and soul" revert to the dust and **atoms** from whence they came.

As Thomas Cousineau notes ("Anti-Oedipal Tendencies," 73), the disappearance of the self means that the body is no longer subject to oedipal repression, no longer obligated to accept subordination to a unified coherent self. **Watt**'s "funambulistic stagger" (31) suggests that Occasionalist synchronization has broken down. His self is no longer an "id-entity" but a site of dislocation, an unstable self that establishes and abolishes itself with every utterance. Wrapping himself in the rags of rationalism (the Cartesian *methode*), Watt cannot adjust to the challenge, and he succumbs to the "little **voice**" (91) that is insistent when he reaches the end of the line. This theme is explored in the *Three Novels*, where the composite protagonist undergoes a process of disintegration that is also a liberation. Crudely: Molloy undergoes a **Jungian** quest, his goal not the expected integration of being but rather the discovery of unaccommodated man; **Moran** undertakes a **Freudian** task, and frees himself of the anal fixations that have constipated his being; **Malone** awaiting **death** divests himself of the extensions of self (clothes, food, sticks); and the Unnamable is at last able to speak of, as the **not-I**, without the "buffers" of characters and bodies (including his own) to distract him.

The endeavor ends in an impasse. *Texts for Nothing* attempt to go beyond the body, yet again. In "Text 1" the body is likened to "an old hack foundered in the street," urged to get up, to get "**on**." The body is distinguished from the "I" and the head: "I say to the body . . . I say to the head"; the motif "It's not me" is introduced. "Text 2" asserts "perhaps we're in a head"; again, the disjunction between the subject and its "ivory dungeon." "Text 3" urges action: "there must be a body, as of old, I don't deny

it." The "I" will *will* something for its self, a body, a head, a past, a fellow, but finally must confront the fact that "I'm here" and "it's still not me." "Text 4" presents a stranger to the self, "for whom alone accusative I exist." "I" am not in *his* head, or *his* old body, but for all that am there, with him, "hence all the confusion." The pun on "accusative" is embodied in "Text 5," where "I" finds itself on trial for the crime of having been born. In "Text 6" the metaphor of imprisonment continues, and in "Text 7" the disjunction between "I" and "me" (I in the accusative) becomes insistent, as in "that other who is me" of "Text 8." In "Text 9" the voice contemplates "a way out," the body a vehicle from womb to tomb, "to get there with." He (or "I") is tempted to "give up" in "Text 10," but in "Text 11" those vile words force "I" to believe that "I" has a head, and a voice (**Rimbaud**'s "je est un autre"), even if the "I" is reducible to *i*, "the square root of minus one." The disjunction between "I" and "me" is manifest in "Text 12," the problem of who's speaking unresolved. In "Text 13" the location of the voice is still in doubt, and the voice "that tried in vain to make me," to leave a trace of "my life," fades into the impersonal and incorporeal "it murmurs."

These delicate texts are reduced in *How It Is* to fundamental sounds: body as machine; self as constituted by **memory**; a somatic sense of pain as the condition of being; fellowship the jab of a can opener; dubious self-extension: "my sack my body all mine" (34). In "Les **Deux besoins**" (1938) SB had noted: "Préferer l'un des testicules à l'autre, ce serait aller sur les platebandes de la métaphysique"

(*Disjecta*, 55–56). The final conviction that it is "all balls yes" is a like leap into the metaphysical flower bed; in the ultimate deconstructionist jest, the body as the testicle's way of getting more testicles. In the late prose SB returned to earlier preoccupations (most deliberately in *Company*). Images of **closed space**, of bodies trapped within cubes or rotundas, revert to the Proustian **vase**, the body as container, as abode. The impulse toward stillness revisits **Geulincx**'s theme of the mind as spectator to the act of **motion**; and the **gulf** remains between the mind that thinks of motion, however minimal, and the body that stirs, however reluctantly.

In the drama SB's assault on the body continued along similar lines, particularly with the dispersion of character. Theater is a genre mediated by the body, and that "ineluctable modality of the visible" offers subversive possibilities. The paradox of the body, visible or invisible, on or off stage, corporeal or incorporeal, real or electronic, is explored from SB's first productions to his final teleplays. His most original character, **Godot**, is unembodied, yet omnipresent. The irony was not lost on SB who relished the physicality, the thereness of theater, even as he worked to erode it. He tried to sustain as much epistemological and phenomenal ambiguity as the semiotics of theater would allow; to subvert the senses that confirm theater's concreteness, the thereness of character; or to have the audience question what it thinks it sees. SB offers many figures or images that are not *there:* the **boy** in *Endgame,* the apparition in "**Ghost Trio**," **May** in *Footfalls,* the Voice in "**Eh Joe**," or Bam in "**What Where**." His most "fleshy" creation, the 200 pounds of fat that constitute Mrs. **Rooney** of *All That Fall,* is "seen" only in the mind's eye of the radio listener.

Alain Robbe-Grillet observed of *Waiting for Godot* that the two tramps do **nothing**, say virtually nothing, and have no other quality than to be present. For **Vladimir** and **Estragon** the basic problem is being there, in the empty space of the stage, in the empty space of the universe. Robbe-Grillet continues (111): "The human condition, Heidegger says, is *to be there.* Probably it is the theatre, more than any other mode of representing reality, which reproduced this situation most naturally. The dramatic character *is on stage,* that is his primary quality: he is *there.*" Easily overlooked is "the dramatic character" who is not "on stage," not phenomenally, but by reflection, as a spectral image. These two **witnesses** to **Godot**'s absence thus have doubts about their own presence and fear not being part of the phenomenal world, fear *not* being there. Gogo insists: "We weren't here"; Didi shouts at the boy, doubting his own corporeality: "You're sure you saw me, you won't come and tell me tomorrow that you never saw me!" (59.a).

Endgame covers familiar ground. **Hamm** is moribund; **Clov** has awkward movement; the two enact the Cartesian **conarium** within the auditorium of the skull. **Nagg and Nell** image the aged body, having procreated and now consigned to the ashbins of **time**. "**Play**" (1964) moves the incorporeal to center stage, motion is further restricted, and the monologues are orchestrated by the torturous light. M articulates the same dramatic and ontological problem when he asks, "Am I as much as being seen?"

However, the new theatrical problem that preoccupied SB was how to represent in language and stage imagery the incomplete being, the *être manqué*. He began a series of exploratory monologues, called, collectively, "**Kilcool**" (August 1963). These eventually developed into *Not I*, but are related to *Film* and "Eh Joe." The female narrator speaks of the joy of being unseen and introduces the theme of psychological duality: "Someone in me trying to get out, saying let me out." She seeks the sort of integration of personality that **Krapp** longs for, but which was becoming alien, other, to SB's sense of self.

With "Eh Joe" (1965) the disembodied "Voice" entered SB's theater. The woman's voice that assails Joe is an exteriorization of his internal conflict; her body exists only in the body of the text. Joe has an undeveloped or unborn opposite within him (like **Fox** of "**Rough for Radio II**"). He can still the voices in his head, but the Voice is not only that of **memory**, rearranged or juxtaposed, but of creative memory, leaching into imagination or creativity. This image of the creator creating himself, from the outside, is like a verbal Escher drawing, or an extension of Lacan's dictum that the subconscious is structured like a language so that self (each "self") is a verbal construct, not a substance, not a body. Compare *Company*.

In the 1970s SB continued this ontological exploration of being in narrative and being as narrative, producing in the body of the text the text as body. The thought-tormented body pacing in *Footfalls* is not "there," or exists only within the embedded narratives of the play. The subject of these late plays, as the late tales, is less the recesses of the repressed subconscious than the dispersed, post-Freudian ego, voice as alien other. May, who herself may be narrated, narrates a semblance of what we see on stage; she is, she insists, "not there." In the crucial short fourth act there is for ten seconds "No trace of May," a reminder that May was always "not there," or there only as a trace (compare "Text 13"). For further considerations, see **voice**.

In "What Where" the voice of Bam (V) controls the action (again, see **voice**). Recasting the play for television, SB altered the visual imagery, so that the speaking voice became a huge, distorted face. The effect is that of the ghost of Bam, of Bam imagining that he comes back to life, dreaming and seeing himself as a little **face** on the screen. Instead of players in long gray gowns, their corporeality suspect, the four figures of the revised "What Where" appear as floating faces dissolving in and out as the TV screen becomes the field of memory to replace the lighted rectangle of the stage. In this final statement the figures are even more disembodied, character ultimately reduced to a pattern of dots on a screen.

Boghill: setting of *All That Fall*, modeled on **Foxrock**. Ballyboghill is a village north of **Dublin**. In *Dream* (96) and "The **Possessed**," the epitome of all that is parochial.

"bois seul": a seven-line poem, not translated, seventh of twelve *Poèmes 38–39*. First published in *Les Temps modernes* 2.14 (novembre 1946); rpt. in *Minuit* 21 (novembre 1976), 16, and *Collected*

Poems, 47. A companion to "**musique de l'indifférence,**" it advocates being alone "comme devant": to drink, feed, desire, fornicate, and starve. Those absent are dead; those present stink; consider the reeds, or the ais (three-toed sloths): do they care? It's not worth the effort: the wind and simply being awake will suffice.

Bollitoes: thus in the Grove *Murphy* (37), but corrected in the Calder text to "Ballitoes": a brand of silk stockings, secured with suspenders to corset or belt.

Bom: in *Murphy* (156), Timothy Clinch, identical twin to Thomas "Bim" Clinch, sadistic head male nurse at the **MMM** (see **Bim and Bom**). In *How It Is* (60) Bom follows the narrator through the mud, cast in the role of tormenter, as the nameless one is torturer of his victim, **Pim.** Identified (112) with Bem, a figure from the past, "before Pim"; the mutation and permutation of the vowels "e," "i," and "o" corresponding to how it was, is, and will be.

"bon bon il est un pays": published as "**Accul**" in *Cahiers des saisons* 2 (octobre 1955): 115. Drafts are in the second *Eleutheria* Notebook. Included with "Six poèmes 1947–1949" in *Gedichte* (1959), and *Collected Poems* (1977), the original title omitted. Written (1947) at the request of Geer **van Velde** to accompany a painting, it appeared in *Avigdor Arikha: Paintings, Gouaches, Drawings* (London: Matthiessen Gallery, 8 April to 2 May 1959), Arikha asking to use it thus. The poem seeks the realm of the mind, but engages with an external **consciousness** ("bon bon": all right, all

right), that requesting the work: "vous voulez que j'aille d'**A** à **B** je ne peux pas." For a poem exploring "un pays sans traces" it is strangely regular, almost a sonnet with two sestets. Yes, he has **time,** but time is a **dog** devouring a bone. His grain of sky is fading fast, but a sunbeam arises from the dust of the dark past ("ocellé" having the sense of radiant maculation and the perceiving eye). He pleads (at bay) to be left in the world of his mind, to explore its traceless bounds, but is forced out: "oui oui c'est une belle chose que vous avez là une bien belle chose," the other's work acknowledged as a fine *thing,* but its tangibility an admission he is reluctant to make. The mind is "un pays," with its own reality; he wishes to explore it in **solitude,** away from the macrocosm that intrudes, asks questions, makes demands; he seeks its "calme." This is the realm sought by **Malone:** "beyond this tumult there is a great calm, and a great indifference, never really to be troubled by anything again" (198).

Bonnard, Pierre (1867–1947): **symbolist** painter who sought to integrate Impressionism with Japanese composition, and described painting as "the transcription of the adventures of the optic nerve." Mentioned in "**Three Dialogues**" (3) as one on the way to "impoverished painting."

Bonnelly: mentioned by **Vladimir** in *En attendant Godot* (86), but in the English version (40.a) a name he can't recall. His original was a farmer in **Roussillon,** whose red soil SB worked for potatoes and wine. The winery still produces a drinkable Côtes du Ventoux: "A Bonnelly Propriétaire-récoltant—Bâtiments neufs —Roussillon Vaucluse."

The Bookman: a **London** magazine that published a favorable review by Francis Watson of *MPTK* (July 1934: 219–20), and in which SB published "A **Case in a Thousand**" and "**Recent Irish Poetry**" (August 1934: 241–42, 235–44; a special number devoted to Irish writing). SB published three reviews in the 1934 Christmas edition: "**Ex Cathezra**"; "**Papini's Dante**"; and "The **Essential and the Incidental**" (10, 14, and 111). *The Bookman* commissioned "**Censorship in the Saorstat**," but this did not appear when it ceased publication to be incorporated with the *London Mercury* (January 1935). The reviews are collected in *Disjecta*.

Boot, the brothers: Gerard and Arnold, "explained" in SB's note to *Whoroscope:* "In 1640 the brothers Boot refuted **Aristotle** in **Dublin**." This was a Dublin detail **Joyce** did not know. SB derived it from **Mahaffy**, who recounts how the brothers Boot were encouraged by the learned Ussher to publish their refutations of Aristotle, "which they had long conceived and worked out in mutual conversation" (147). This was printed in 1642 [*sic*] in Dublin. See O'Brien (381).

boots: with **greatcoat** and **hat**, essential accessories of SB's protagonists. **Belacqua** tells of his ruined feet, ill-shaped from **birth**; then, in his youth, shod in exiguous patents (*Dream*, 128), like SB (in painful imitation of **Joyce**). Once in Italy Belacqua bought a pair of boots and set

out without breaking them in; the result was a sad hobbling home, "down the steep Calvary of cobbles" (130). In **Germany**, he buys another pair, to find that the right one pinches. His distress is relieved when the shopkeeper explains that the rare client whose feet are of equal size must pay for the asymmetry of an article addressed to the average client (132). In "**Dante and the Lobster**" Belacqua is afflicted with ruined feet and a spavined gait; in "**Yellow**" he asks that the **cat** might have his amputated toe. *First Love* lists pedal afflictions, fourteen "curiosities" (33).

Watt needed (seven years ago) five shillings to buy a boot. This singular circumstance is later "explained": the boot cost 8d, and Watt has 4/4 left; he needed one boot only because he had found a shoe, on the shore, "stiff with brine, but otherwise shipshape" (219). The boot is a 12, the shoe a 10, Watt's feet are 11; he tries to correct the asymmetry, but in vain. Such details confound the rationalist universe, but do not account for the shock felt by the moribund **Malone** (272) when he sees the undertaker's man in brown boots.

The name of *Godot*, SB told Roger **Blin**, was suggested by *godillots* and *godasses*, French slang for boots. **Estragon**'s boots suggest van **Gogh**'s various paintings of *souliers* (a similar pair, "lacerated and gaping," is among the "insignia" of "**Text 8**"). They encapsulate the dramatic eschatology, from the opening "**Nothing** to be done," through the pain of existence: "Hurts! He wants to know if it hurts!" (7.b), to moral culpability, man "blaming on his boots the faults of his feet" (8.a). Estragon's rejection of laces reflects his fear of being "tied" to

Godot. One boot fits, the other does not; one thief was saved, the other was not: the shape of ideas. The boots enact **Berkeley**'s epistemology: are they the same as yesterday? SB offered Colin Duckworth an alternative: "The second day boots are no doubt same as first and Estragon's feet wasted, pined, shrunk and dwindled in interval"; adding "there's exegesis for you!"

Bordas: Parisian publishers who acquired from Routledge the **French** translation rights to *Murphy* (1946), and the world rights to SB's other work, but after the novel's failure sold these for a pittance, with the remaining stock, to Jérôme **Lindon** of **Minuit**.

Borgia, Lucrezia (1480–1519): "niece" of Pope Alexander VI and an infamous poisoner (the "Borgian virtue" in *Proust*, 15). A prototype of the **Syra-Cusa** (*Dream*, 50).

Borstal Boehme: a *borstal* is a penitentiary for young delinquents, named after the first of its kind in Rochester, Kent. Jakob *Böhme* (1575–1624), author of *De Signatura Rerum*, German **mystic** and shoemaker. The **Polar Bear** dismisses **Plato** thus (*Dream*, 234). See **Inge**.

Bosch, Hieronymus (1450–ca. 1516): Catholic painter of the Spanish Netherlands, his works characterized by elements of fantasy and the grotesque; claimed by the **surrealists** as their forerunner. **Belacqua** does not propose to "Bosch" the **Alba**, to enter her garden of earthly delights (*Dream*, 193). **Sam** describes **Watt** in terms of "the **Christ** be-lieved by Bosch" (a deliberate ambiguity) "hanging in Trafalgar Square" (159); this is his *Christ Mocked (the Crowning with Thorns)*, in the National Gallery, **London**.

Bosquet, Alain (1919–98): French poet of Ukrainian background, for whom SB translated three poems: "In me, civil war," "Fresh sighs for sale," and "Knife." These appeared in *Selected Poems* (New Directions, 1963); rpt. for *Marginales* (Brussels) 24 (April 1969): 44–45. When brought out by Ohio University Press (1973), *Selected Poems* added: "Now that he has drained," "Why must the day," and "He can only live in shivers." SB's translation of "Fresh sighs for sale" was chosen by **London** Transport (1999) as one of its "European Poems on the Underground."

"Les Bosquets de Bondy": another title for *Mercier et Camier;* implying "a den of thieves."

Bossuet, Jacques-Bénigne (1627–1704): Bishop of Meaux, whose *Discours sur l'histoire universelle* (1681) affirmed that after the Fall **God** *providentially* ordained hereditary monarchy as the image of His sovereignty. In **"Dante"** (22), with an assist from **Croce**, SB makes a cavalier contrast of Bossuet with the "round-headed" **Vico**.

Boswell, James (1740–95): Scots lawyer and reprobate, whose *Life of Samuel Johnson* (1791) in the six-volume Birkbeck Hill edition (1887) SB kept till his **death**. SB described the *Life* to Mary **Manning** (11 July 1937) as "Boswell's wit and wisdom machine" (Knowlson, 250).

Botticelli, Sandro (1445–1510): **Floren-tine** painter famous for his *Primavera* (1477) and *Birth of Venus* (1488). **Belac-qua** regards the **Smeraldina**'s Botticelli thighs (*Dream*, 15) and Primavera **but-tocks** (50); in "**Sanies I**" Botticelli forks imply muscular legs. SB later discovered that Botticelli's drawings for **Dante's** *Commedia* depicted Belacqua in his own **embryonic** position (*Company*, 27); as such they contributed to the later **closed space** figures.

Bouvier, Bishop (Jean-Baptiste): author of the *Dissertatio in sextum decalogi prae-ceptum, et supplementum ad tractatum de matrimonio* (Le Mans, 1827), which kept **Murphy** awake as a theological student (72). After Bouvier's death several vol-umes were forged in his name by Maurice la Châtre, dealing with secrets of the con-fessional or marriage bed and other scurvy betrayals, as the *ciné bleu* scenario implies.

Bovril sign: a neon-lit sign at College Green, **Dublin**. In "**Ding-Dong**" and "A **Wet Night**" it goes "round and round," like paradise, moving from the jaundiced lemon of faith through seven theologi-cal phases. **Belacqua** adds (*Dream*, 200): "Of what avail is it to flog a dead cow." Bovril is a beef concentrate; a large bull sadly contemplates a small jar: "Alas, my poor brother."

Bowles, Patrick (b. 1927): SB published excerpts of *Watt* in a new English-language journal *Merlin* (1953), edited by Alexander Trocchi and Richard Seaver. The editors looked for a translator for *Molloy*. Bowles, a young South African, was writing a comparative literature the-sis at the Sorbonne, working as *assistant anglais* at the Lycée du Havre, and with Christopher Logue on *Points,* a magazine of new writing published by Sinbad Vail at 7 Rue Bernard-Palissey (home to *Les Éditions de Minuit*). He was encouraged to submit a few pages. SB selected them (25 July 1953), and over the next fifteen months Bowles, with SB, translated *Molloy* for **Olympia** and **Grove Press**. In 1962, he recalled his work: "A translator's task is to render another person's ideas into acceptable language, and his aim is to find some equivalent to the original unity of thought and speech." SB had stressed that it shouldn't merely be "trans-lated," but a new book in the new lan-guage, reflecting in the transposition of speech the transposition of thought.

boy: an unnamed character who appears at the end of each act of *Waiting for Godot*. He looks after the **goats**; his brother, he says, looks after the **sheep**. He appears just as the spectators may feel that **Godot** is an illusion. SB wished him to look as angelic as possible (Gk. *angelos,* "a messenger"). A breathless boy arrives at the end of *Watt* (243) and *All That Fall* (38), but closer to *Godot* is the spectral presence of the boy in "**Ghost Trio**." The boy sighted by **Clov** in *Endgame* is generated by his imagination and (perhaps) desire.

Bram van Velde: a book of essays by SB, Georges **Duthuit**, and Jacques Putman, with twelve color reproductions of Bram van Velde's work (one belonging to SB), first published in **French** (Paris: Georges Fall [*Musée de Poche*], 1958); then En-glish, trans. SB and Oliver Classe (Grove, 1960 [Evergreen Gallery 5, E-174]), with black and white photographs and twelve color tip-ins. Two of the four essays are by SB: an extract from "**Peintres de l'empèchement**" (1948); and part of "**Three Dialogues**" (1949, translated). SB added an epigraph (*Disjecta*, 151) to the deluxe *Edizioni d'arte* by Fratelli Pozzo (Torino), and Guy Le Plat (Paris), 1961; these add three illustrations by Bram to "Le **Calmant**," with a puzzling date of 1941. A New York edition of this (Harry N. Abrams, 1962) included an unauthorized translation of "Peintres." Extracts from "Three Dialogues" were included in Franz Meyer's catalogue for a 1968 exhibition "Bram van Velde: Paintings 1957–1967" (M. Knoedler, 1968), in New York (April 2–May 2) and Buffalo (May 6–June 2); and in the catalogue of a 1970 Exhibition (Paris: Zichieri), 83–84.

Brancusi, Constantin (1876–1957): Romanian sculptor and expressionist, attracted by formal simplicity and kinetic energy, as in his "Bird in Space" (1928), to which **Belacqua** likens the **Syra-Cusa**'s slender form (*Dream*, 33).

Braque, Georges (1882–1963): friend and contemporary of Picasso, with whom he created Cubism. SB described the linoleum in his room at Mrs. **Frost**'s as "Braque seen from a great distance" (SB to TM, 8 September 1934); it is laid in the room on **Brewery Road** (*Murphy*, 63).

Bray, Barbara: drama script editor at the BBC when she met SB through Donald **McWhinnie** in the mid-1950s. Their encounter was "highly significant" (Knowlson, 410), and she became a regular confidante thereafter, to the

end. Her correspondence with SB is at **Trinity College**, currently unavailable. Bray relocated to **Paris** as a translator, notably of Marguerite Duras, but also of Jean Genet, Michel Tournier, Julia Kristeva, and Robert **Pinget**.

"**Breath**": SB's most "popular" play is a twenty-five-second miniature, barely longer than a cycle of human respiration. Although SB called it a "farce in five acts" it is something less than an evening's theater. It was prelude to Jacques Levy and Kenneth Tynan's sextravaganza, *Oh Calcutta* ("O quel cul t'as"). John **Calder** claims that Tynan commissioned it; but Ruby Cohn disputes this, saying that SB had recited it to her years before, and that Calder published a fair copy but not the original, which SB had written on the paper tablecloth of a café (RC to SG). Tynan added to SB's opening tableau ("Faint light on stage littered with miscellaneous rubbish") "including naked people." After thirty-nine previews, it moved to Broadway (26 February 1971) and ran until 6 August 1989; 85 million people saw 1,314 performances, making it easily SB's most viewed SB play. These are records unlikely to be broken.

SB was appalled by the revisions, but his contract forbade interference. Worse, Barney Rosset included the excrescence in an illustrated book, attributing it to SB (Grove, 1969). The unaltered "Breath" premiered at the Close Theatre Club, Glasgow (October 1969), then played at the Oxford Playhouse (8 March 1970) as part of an unavailing plan to develop a Samuel Beckett Theatre. Tynan's review opened at the Round House (27 July

1970), without SB's contribution. The West End premiere of "Breath," by Edward Petherbridge and David Hunt, at the Arts Theatre, was much later (July 1998). The first British, indeed the first accurate publication, appeared in *Gambit* 4.16 (1969): 5–9, with a manuscript facsimile. The first trade edition was in *Breath and Other Shorts* (Faber, 1972); the first correct American publication appeared in *First Love and other Shorts* (Grove, 1974). The infamous association with *Oh Calcutta* is acknowledged only in *CSP* (1984) and *CDW* (1986).

The play is simplicity itself, an anonymous life cycle reduced to its **fundamental sound**. A debris-littered stage with "No verticals," a brief cry and inspiration as lights fade up for ten seconds and hold for five; then expiration and slow fade down of light and "immediately cry as before." The two recorded cries of **vagitus** are identical, as is the lighting on fade up and fade down. The simplicity is symmetrical, recalling **Pozzo**'s poignant comment: "They give **birth** astride of a grave, the light gleams an instant, then it's night once more." In the film version by Damian Hurst the debris features hospital and medical waste.

Breem, Joe: or Breen, a child's adventure story told by the narrator's **father** in "The **Calmative**" (64): "son of a lighthouse-keeper . . . who swam for miles in the night, a knife between his teeth, after a shark." In "**Text 1**," the story binds father and son, the narcotic comfort of a familiar tale well told.

Breton, André (1896–1966): "pope" of **surrealism**; SB was not an intimate but responded to his radical dislocations and "illuminist" thought. Breton's surrealist manifestos (1924, 1929) affect *Murphy*'s "short circuit" (5) and metaphysics of the kite (279). *Les Vases communicants* (1932) is suggestive. Breton edited the "Surrealist number" of *This Quarter* 5.1 (September 1932), SB contributing twenty translations, four by Breton and four (about mental debilitation) from Breton and Paul **Éluard**. He translated Breton's "Wolfgang Paalen" for Peggy **Guggenheim** (*London Bulletin* 10 [February 1939]: 16–17). **Moran**'s familiars include "le dragonnier de Ténériffe" (*Molloy*, 204; not in the ms.); this is Breton's dragon-tree, "L'abre immense qui plonge ses racines dans la préhistoire" (*L'Amour fou*, 82). Breton's "Dialogue créole" with André **Masson** (1941), poet and painter responding antiphonally, anticipates SB's "**Three Dialogues**."

Brewery Road: between the York and Caledonian Roads north of King's Cross; the location of Miss **Carriage**'s house. Set between the **Metropolitan Cattle Market** and Pentonville **Prison**, it delimits Murphy's "new life" with **Celia**. The little shelter in the Market Road Gardens, the Tripe Factory, **Milton** House, the Perseverance and Temperance Yards, the Vis Vitae Bread Co., and the improbable Marx Cork Bath Mat Manufactory are all taken from life.

"Brief Dream": a short poem (1987) in the **Super Conquérant** Notebook (RUL 2934), related to *Stirrings Still*. The theme is transitory life and acceptance of ending: "Go end there / One fine day." It appeared with "**Là**" in *JOBS* 1.1 and 2 (1992): 3.

Brignole-Sale, A. G.: as cited by SB from Praz, *The Romantic Agony* (49; DN, 36), a "17-century author of Erotica & Mystica," who alternated lascivious with pious writings. After his wife died he joined the Jesuits and practiced such severe flagellations that he was rebuked by his fellow priests. The **Frica**'s talons clutch "the *Anterotica* of Aliosha G. Brignole-Sale" in *Dream* (179) and "A Wet Night" (56); **Ronsard**'s **anteros** corrupting Aliosha, the saintly Brother Karamazov (Brignole-Sale was christened Antonio Guido).

Brueghel, Pieter (ca. 1525–69): elder of a family of Flemish painters, who shapes two images in *Waiting for Godot:* **Lucky** leading **Pozzo** as in "The Blind Leading the Blind," and the tableau of four fallen figures, as in "The Land of Cockaigne" (Knowlson, 539). In *All That Fall*, Dan Rooney says, "We shall fall into the ditch." "Black Velvet O'Connery" in the *Watt* "Addenda" (247) suggests Pieter's second son, Jan "Velvet" Brueghel (1568–1625).

Bruno, Giordano (1548–1600): "the Nolan"; Italian philosopher and Dominican friar who features in SB's "**Dante**" essay. SB's detail derives from J. Lewis McIntyre's *Giordano Bruno* (1903); **Joyce** thought this the weakest part of the essay. He is associated with the doctrine of **identified contraries**. Bruno's affirmation of Copernicus led him to the stake, where (in the words of Stephen Dedalus) he was horribly burnt.

Buridan's ass: a metaphysical paradox posed by Jean Buridan, rector of the University of **Paris** (1372): the ass that starved, unable to chose between two bales of hay. It reflects the debate between the will or intellect. In *Dream* (208), and in "**Ding-Dong**" (41) the **Alba** and **Belacqua** respectively consider their choices.

Burnet, John (1863–1928): Cambridge classicist, whose *Early Greek Philosophy* (1892) and *Greek Philosophy* (1914) are standard accounts of the **pre-Socratics**. Burnet traces the course of **atomism** from Eleaticism (**Parmenides**), and that of **Plato** from **Pythagoras**. Much in *Murphy* derives from *Greek Philosophy:* the **Apmonia** (3); the **tetrakyt** (5); Pythagoras, the dodecahedron and **death** of **Hippasos** (47); **Diogenes of Apollonia** (49); the **Doctrine of the Limit** (50); the figure of the three lives (90); forms without parallel (108); the etymology of gas (175); Miss **Counihan**'s step-ins (204); **Democritus** (246); and "the famous **ant**" (248).

Burton, Robert (1577–1640): scholar of Christ Church, Oxford, and author of *The Anatomy of Melancholy,* which first appeared in 1621 and then in augmented editions until the posthumous sixth (1651), eleven years after the **death** predicted by calculating his own nativity. The *Anatomy* is a medical treatise and a magnificent compendium of esoteria. It was written to escape melancholy, but **Democritus** Junior evokes the laughing philosopher. After a long preface, part I considers the causes of melancholy; part II, its cures; and part III (from which most of SB's allusions derive) **love** and religious melancholy. This entry cites the **Dream Notebook**, ed. John Pilling (some 300 entries). A typical reference (II.3.1.ii, 630) reflects Burton's Partition, Section, Member, and Subsection; plus a page number (London: Chatto and Windus, 1881).

SB read the *Anatomy* attentively (Pilling suggests September 1931), after having written "**Sedendo et Quiescendo**," "**Text**," the calamitous Silvester, and other episodes of *Dream,* including the ending, in which nothing of Burton appears. The Notebook was clearly at hand thereafter. Most citations are used, the novel assuming the *Anatomy*'s encyclopedic range. They defy easy iteration, but testify to SB's delight in demented detail, and show how he built up this work as a *cento,* as Burton described his book (7). A story lurks behind every allusion. When **Belacqua** in *Dream* (19) cites "that first assault on his privities" he alludes to Turkish eunuchs "deprived in their childhood of all their privities," penned in the seraglio ("left alone to their unchaste thoughts") with the wives who cannot have a cucumber or carrot sent in "but sliced" (III.3.2, 643). Exigencies of space preclude further examples, but the curious might begin with Pilling and continue in Burton.

Belacqua's portraits of his fair to middling women are deliberate *centi.* Often dismissed as misogyny, they inherit a literary tradition from **Juvenal**'s Sixth Satire, bits of the *Anatomy* laid together, the art of verbal marquetry. "**What a Misfortune**" blends Burton with **Swift**, the two curiously compatible, citing the *Anatomy* for some enigmatic phrases: see "**opopanax and assafoetida**"; "**Dum vivit aut bibit aut minxit**"; "**Mens mea Lucia lucescit luce tua**"; and "**whirligig.**" Earlier stories of *MPTK* ignore Burton, but "**Echo's Bones**" recycles details from

Dream (roaring-meg, looking babies, cold as January, column of quiet, Diana's well).

Murphy includes tags from Burton. Celia's yellow hair (29) links her to his Virgin Mary (III.2.2.ii, 520): "yellow-haired, of a wheat colour." **Ticklepenny** (87) is much changed ("quantum mutatus") from man's unfallen condition (I.1.1.i, 81); "gentle skimmer" (84), like "polyhistor" (196), derives from the preface (6). Mental patients as classified by "heads or bellies according to type" (167) reflect "the species or kinds of Melancholy" (I.1.3.iv, 112). "**Philautia**" (216), a key word in **Geulincx**, apears in Burton (I.2.3.xiv, 193). Other curiosities include: **Neary**'s "water from his mouth" (202), an "excellent remedy" for one who talks too much (III.3.4.ii, 658); Lucian's Goddess of **Gout** (220; II.1.4.i, 298); and Neary's "old flicker," an "old acherontic dizzard . . . shall flicker after a young wench " (III.3.4.ii, 655).

Direct echoes of Burton fade; but those perceptible express a delight in what **Johnson** called "hard words"; flecks of mica in different strata, the residua of reading. **Watt**'s impulse to drink only milk reflects Burton's sentiment (I.2.2.i, 142) that "Milk increaseth melancholy." **Malone**'s acquaintance, an Israelite named Jackson and his **parrot**, feature on his list of those who write of the postmortem existence of the soul (III.4.2.ii, 713): "Doctor Dove, Doctor Jackson." **Krapp** (55) is "a wearish old man," like Democritus or the forlorn figure of "**Enueg I**." And **Winnie**'s delight in seeing not an **ant** but "an emmet" (Burton's preference) is a mixed blessing or a great mercy, if only that in losing one's classics a part remains.

"... but the clouds ...": a "Play for Television," written (1976) to replace a film of "Play," which the BBC had sent to SB for approval (and which he rejected). First broadcast on BBC TV (17 April 1977), dir. Donald McWhinnie with Billie Whitelaw and Ronald Pickup, along with "Ghost Trio" and *Not I* (see "Shades"). Calling it "Poetry only love," SB said it had the same mood as "Ghost Trio" (Knowlson, 559). SB directed "Geistertrio" and "... nur noch Gewölk ..." (May 1977), at Süddeutscher Rundfunk, Stuttgart, with Klaus Herm and Kornelia Boje. Published in *Ends and Odds* (Faber, 1977), and in an enlarged edition of *Ends and Odds* subtitled *Nine Dramatic Pieces* (Grove, 1981). The title echoes the end of W. B. Yeats's "The Tower," the moving description as the poet "makes" his soul, when all that is left is intellect and feeling, the body fading but the mind aware. SB told Eoin O'Brien that these were Yeats's greatest lines.

The spirit of the play (of all SB's teleplays) is captured by Yeats's question: "Does the imagination dwell the most / Upon a woman won or woman lost?" "Clouds" examines this familiar theme, love lost, in a medium that concretizes the apparition, the face of a woman. There are two shots for the male figure: M hunched over, obscuring his desk, and M1, or M in the set, either dressed for the road, in dark "hat and greatcoat," or for bed, in light "robe and skullcap." M's voice, V, directs M, imagining, revising, and repeating his daily comings and goings and his conjuring or "begging" W, "woman's face reduced as far as possible to eyes and mouth," to appear in the dead of night. M details the possibilities: 1, she appears and instantly is gone; 2, she appears and lingers; and 3, she appears and utters the words of Yeats. A fourth possibility is that she does not appear at all, whereupon M busies himself with mathematics, cube roots, awaiting dawn and the resumption of his aimless wanderings. The closing image of the play features the poignant, even sentimental third possibility.

buttocks: the body as fundamental sound (no pun intended), and, like the Smeraldina's Primavera buttocks, ascream for a fusillade of chastisement (*Dream*, 50). SB recorded details from Cooper (qv) on flagellation; Pilling notes its use in *Dream*, "Sanies II" and "Echo's Bones" (DN, 47–57). Belacqua's fantasia on the human bottom (*Dream*, 97) wittily plays on Cooper: Horace on the defective bottom (*Satire* II; Cooper, 23); the Abbé Boileau's "faculty of assiduity" (the *Satires* of Nicolas Boileau-Despréaux, 1636–1711; 22); Rousseau's *penchant* for the rod (519); "Venus Callipyge" goddess of shapely buttocks (23); a monk with a flower in his rectum (24); the disrobing and submission of Caterina of Cardona (63); Adamites and Juniperus the Gymnosophist (47); the penance of St. Dominic Loricatus, who "filled both his hands with rods" (49). Cooper defines "fessade," "chiappata," and "claque" ("slaps" on the "seat of honour," "verberations" on the breech, 22–24). He reports Dr. Keate's reply to an old Etonian: "'E'en now,' says Keate, 'I cannot guess your name / Boys' b—s are so very much the same'" (438; DN, 52).

Neary does battle against the buttock of Cuchulain (*Murphy*, 42); that Red Branch bum being the camel's back.

Murphy's buttocks appreciate being lowered into his **rocking chair**; disappointed by the second "sit" in the tearooms (80), they find the oversprung seats of London buses "most insidious" (95). Rosie **Dew** (97) suffers from **panpygoptosis**, or ducks' disease. This initiates a fantasia on Steiss's nosonomy ("Steiss" crude German for "buttock"), and the frustrations this might cause Dr. Busby, whose rod "was the sieve which sifted the wheat of scholarship from the chaff" (Cooper, 430). Murphy's charred remains are identified by **Celia** (266) by the birthmark on the right buttock.

In "A **Case** in a **Thousand**," Dr. **Nye** is fascinated with buttocks (19). "**Malacoda**" intuits the surreptitious passing of air by an undertaker's assistant. Mr. Case has a memory for arses (*Watt*, 242). **Molloy** calculates that he rarely farts (30); he uses a digital thermometer, his finger up his arsehole (79). **Moran**, anally retentive, attends his son *à rebours*, first with a thermometer, then an enema (118). The **Unnamable** (333) concentrates on a **horse**'s rump. Maddy **Rooney** has a lifelong preoccupation with horses' buttocks. In *How It Is*, fellowship and pain are reduced to the bottom line: "Pim's though undersized were iso" (37); "right buttock then first contact" (53); "stab him simply in the arse" (71). Like Molloy, we must apologize for reverting to this lewd orifice, 'tis SB's muse will have it so. It is less an "eyesore" (80) than the symbol of the preterit, an enduring image of those "shat into grace."

Buxtehude, Dietrich (1637–1707): Swedish-born composer whose Abend-musik Bach once walked fifty miles to attend. Mr. **Knott**'s mantel supports his plaster bust (*Watt*, 71). He represents, Heath Lees suggests (177), composers turning from old vocal modes toward new tunings, the well-tempered scale overcoming the "**Pythagorean** comma," or discord arising from the **gulf** between acoustical realities and the **mathematical** ratios of musical scales.

Byrne, Deputy J. J.: well-named chairman of the Irish **Censorship** of Publications Board ("five fit and proper persons"), responsible for the Register of Prohibited Publications, which listed SB (see "**Censorship** in the **Saorstat**"). He has "burst his buttons" in defense of commonsense man, affirming it unnecessary to read all of a book before judging it. Hence in "To **Nelly**" (*Watt*, 11–12): "Burn, burn with Byrne."

Byron, Lord George Gordon (1788–1824): poet and rake. SB disliked the Byronic hero, as his account of Ravenna intimates (*Dream*, 220). "Lara" is mentioned in *Dream* (137). **Cain** appealed to both writers, but in different ways. **Molloy** (64) shares Childe Harold's rapture in the woods (IV.178; Byron was clubfooted). In the end, for all his wit, Byron to SB was a bore.

byssus: Egyptian linen to wrap mummies; Mr. **Endon** wears a dressing gown of scarlet byssus and "neo-Merovingian poulaines" of deepest purple (*Murphy*, 186). In Luke 16:19 (Greek), Dives is dressed in *porphyras* ("purple") and *byssus* ("fine linen") (see **Abraham's bosom**).

C

C: at the outset of *Molloy,* one walking toward **A, Cain** to Abel, hunter to victim? In the **French** text he is **B.** Molloy says he never saw A and C again, but he destroys the charcoal burner (84), and **Moran**'s circle intersects with C, or another like him (146). In "**Rough for Theatre II**" C (**Croker?**) stands near the window, being investigated by A and B.

"**Le Cadran**": a one-leaf typescript (RUL 2201), with a translation called "The Dial," being an extract from *Mal vu mal dit* (57); *Ill Seen Ill Said* (45–46). It displays minor variants from the published texts and notebooks (RUL 2200, f.15), which it precedes, since the manuscript includes autograph corrections from it.

Cain: one from whom **God**'s **pity** is withheld (Genesis 4:1–15). Cursed for having slain Abel, he was made fugitive and vagabond, a mark set upon him that none should kill him but rather he should live and suffer (see "**Dante and the Lobster**"). Cain was supposedly banished to the moon (see *Malone Dies,* 221), its spots representing thorns, tokens of his sin. **Belacqua** awakes to find Cain toiling up his firmament, shaking light from his brand: "that was what he was spared for" (*Dream,* 129). Compare the "branded moon" of "**Alba**." **Pozzo** responds to both "Abel" and "Cain" (he's "all humanity"); but **Vladimir** begins "to weary of this motif" (*WG,* 53.b).

Calder, John: British publisher of SB's fiction and poetry. Having left Zürich University in 1949 with "a useless degree," Calder in 1950 began a publishing firm, editing in the evenings and weekends. He published war memoirs and previously untranslated classics, then moved into contemporary politics. The firm was renamed Calder and Boyars (1964), until the earlier imprint was resumed (1975) before becoming the Calder Educational Trust. **Faber** had the drama, but Calder undertook to publish everything else, fiction, poetry, criticism, the first series of *JOBS,* and two Festschriften, *Beckett at 60* (1967) and *"As No Other Dare Fail"* (1986; for SB's eightieth birthday). He also edited *Gambit: An International Review* from 1963 through 1986. His commitment to SB was called "Calder's folly," but history has vindicated his belief, although the quality of the publications has often left much to be desired.

Calderón: Pedro Calderón de la Barca (1600–81), Spanish dramatist, whose *La Vida es sueño* ("Life Is a Dream") is the source of "Pues el delito mayor / Del hombre es haber nacido" ("For the greatest crime of man is to have been born"), cited by SB (*Proust,* 67), and evoked by **Neary** (*Murphy,* 44). SB's immediate source is **Schopenhauer** (*WWI,* I.3 #51, 328), for whom it was axiomatic that man needs the fiction of punishment for a crime uncommitted to sustain the burden of an otherwise intolerable isolation.

"Le Calmant" / "The Calmative": one of *Quatre nouvelles* (autograph ms. [HRHRC #179] signed 23 December 1946) withheld by **Bordas**. Published with "L'**Expulsé**," "La **Fin**," and *Textes pour rien* (Minuit, 1955), and included in *Cinq nouvelles nouvelles,* ed. Raymond Federman (1970), 14–35. "The Calmative" appeared in *Evergreen Review* 47 (June 1967): 46–49, 93–95, with two drawings by **Arikha**, then in *No's Knife* (Calder, 1967) and *Stories and Texts for Nothing* (Grove, 1967). SB considered calling it "The Sedative."

"The Calmative" is a central postwar text. An apparent postmortem tale, it features a narrator who tells of an "I" on his last journey. Whether the I narrating and the narrative I are identical, alive or dead, the journey physical or a dream, past or present, are questions that cannot be resolved. When he asks, "Into what nightmare thingness am I fallen" (69), the narrator may be summarizing what passes for plot, a physical fall. He admits, "we are needless to say in a skull." As a calmative he will tell himself another story, and perhaps thereby come back to life; at least he resumes a journey, stirring from his "refuge" on the outskirts of the "city of my childhood." He tells his story in the past, "as though it were a myth," to become "what I was." O'Brien sets it at "**Foley's Folly**" (qv). From this refuge the narrator or his figment journeys into the city and to the sea. His model is a childhood story, which, read by his **father**, calmed him (see **Breem, Joe**). He experiences picaresque encounters: a **boy** with a **goat**; a cathedral where he meets a potential **suicide**; a man riding a **bicycle**, reading a news-paper (compare *Un chien andalou*); another who fails to acknowledge his existence. He meets on a bench one who offers him a phial (a calmative?) in exchange for a kiss. There are few logical connections, and the action suggests dream or hallucination, qualities the narrator acknowledges. It may be that the fancied encounters are attributable to the fall, or he may have fallen after taking a calmative. Either way, the end returns to the beginning, where the narrator is "even older" than when he fell, calling for help. The opening **aporia**, the mutable action, the dispersion of **character**, the circularity of the story all suggest a cruder version of what will become *Molloy*.

"Calvary by Night": an early eighteen-line poem, included in *Dream* (213–14), then "A **Wet Night**" (65). Several lines intended seriously were changed for satiric effect (the "**blue flower**" of Novalis to the "blue bloom" of self-abuse). SB did not approve it for later collections. Autoerotic echoes of *Ulysses* ("rocket of bloom") merge Bloom's languid floating flower with "Nausicaa." Unwilling to consider an act of **onanism**, Harvey finds an unhappy balance between feeling and archaic diction. Yet the images of rocket, flower, and kingfisher, the sudden manifestation of blue against black, express the sublimated eroticism of "**At last I find in my confusèd soul**," also included (and mocked) in *Dream*.

Calvet, Mother: an old woman in "**Text 2**," with her **dog** and baby buggy, "creaming off the garbage before the nightmen come." She reappears in "**Still 3**" (269).

Camier: identified in *Mercier and Camier* as F. X. (Francis Xavier) Camier, Private Investigator and Soul of Discretion (54). In the **hardy laurel** tradition, he is short and fat. He features in "**Coups de gong.**"

camogie: a version of hurling, or shinty, played by women. Jem **Higgins** is not "a shinty or camogie man" (*Dream*, 152). **Lucky** includes it among "sports of all sorts" (*WG*, 29.a).

Campanella, Tommaso (1568–1639): Italian astrologer and visionary, who spent half his life in prison, frequently under torture (he was incarcerated with **Bruno**, and escaped the stake only by simulating madness). Known for his *Città del sole*, or *The City of the Sun* (1602), which proclaimed a Republican utopia based on laws of Reason and Theology, but governed by astrology. **Burton** calls it a witty fiction, but a mere chimera; **Windelband** (377) identifies the "inner contradiction." **Murphy** "rests" on this volume (17), using it to urge **Celia** to marry him; the point is Campanella's astrological determination of propitious times for intercourse. Omitted from the **French** translation.

Campbell House: before going to the **École Normale** (October 1928), SB spent nine "grim" months teaching French and English at Campbell House, a Protestant public school (rival to **Portora**) in Belfast. He did not enjoy the experience, nor did his pupils, described by the headmaster, William Duff Gibbon, as the cream of Ulster: "Yes, I know," SB replied dryly, "all rich and thick" (Bair, 56). At the end of his sentence he gladly decamped. The unhappy self-exposure anticipated the later more traumatic debacle at **Trinity.**

Camus, Albert (1913–60): French writer born in Algeria; active in the Resistance, friend of **Sartre**, and **Nobel** laureate (1957). SB considered *L'Etranger* (1942) important, but rejected the **existentialism** of "Le Mythe de **Sisyphus.**" In *Eleutheria*, Victor **Krap** dismisses his fiancée and notes his **father's death** with the indifference of Meursault.

cang: in Imperial China, a wooden yoke worn by criminals. "**Enueg I**" rejects "the cang of the wind"; and *Dream* (187) the "cang of emblem." **Cooper's** *Flagellation* (216; DN, 57) lists among Chinese instruments of correction: "a large block of wood, with a hole in the middle, through which the head of the criminal is passed." The **Unnamable** (332) is unable to move because a collar encircles his neck; this is his "cang."

"The Capital of the Ruins": SB's report on the Irish Hospital in **Saint-Lô** (1946) for Irish radio. The typescript was discovered in the archives of Radio Telefis Éireann (1983) and published (1986) by Eoin O'Brien in *The Beckett Country* (333–37); and in John **Calder's** Festschrift (1986) "*As No Other Dare Fail*" (71–76), also "published here for the first time." Dugald McMillan associates the quirky title with a booklet of photographs of the bombed-out city entitled *St. Lô, Capital des Ruines, 5 et 7 juin, 1944.* He says that it was read by SB on Radio Erin on 10 June 1946, SB's date on the final page of the typescript. Inquiries to Dairmuid Breathnach, chief librarian of RTÉ, contradict this; the piece was not broadcast.

SB's subject was the Irish Red Cross hospital in Saint-Lô, a city "bombed out of existence in one night." He noted, ironically, that the hospital's walls and ceiling were made of aeronautical aluminum, a "pleasant variation" on swords and plowshares. The picture was grim: scabies, diseases, falling masonry, detonators, and demining. SB uses "capital of the ruins" to MacGreevy (19 August 1945); it echoes Paul Éluard's *Capitale de la douleur* (1926), from which he had translated poems (1936). The prose is restrained, remarkable for details chosen "not quite at random" to image the devastation of the town and the work of the Irish Hospital. It is thus (to cite the end of the essay) equally a conception of humanity in ruins and "an inkling" of how the human condition is to be thought again.

Caravaggio, Michelangelo da (1573–1610): painter of the Venetian school noted for his masterly handling of light, works lit by their own sources of illumination, to create rich contrasts of shade and subtle variations of perspective. **Wilenski** discusses Caravaggio's development of spotlight effects; these had a lasting influence on SB's drama. SB visited Malta (November 1971) and saw *Decollation of St. John the Baptist* in the Oratory of St. John's Cathedral, Valletta; he sat an hour before it, letting it work on his imagination (Knowlson, 520–21). This was largely the inspiration for the **voice** and vision of *Not I*.

Carducci, Giosué (1836–1907): Tuscan poet and professor of Italian literature at Bologna, who wished to return to classical models. SB noted in a student essay that Carducci was "an excessively bad poet" (Knowlson, 630). His Pindar imitations are dismissed ("Dante and the Lobster," 17) as the clucking of an old **hen**, and his "Satan" described as one of the "great pharisee poems" ("Humanistic Quietism," 68).

Carlyle, Thomas (1795–1881): Scots historian, whose "beautiful bottle of soda-water" is dismissed in the foreword to *Dream;* the allusion is to Ruskin, **Proust** having translated *Sesame and Lilies* (1865). SB took notes from *On Heroes* (Everyman, 1908; DN, 39–43); these fed his incipient sense of the **fundamental unheroic**. **Hamm** embodies (as a ruined monster) something of Carlyle's sense of the hero as prophet, poet, or king.

Carmagnole: a Jacobin dress, which gave the name to a revolutionary song (1792), with the refrain: "Vive le son, vive le son, / Dansons la Carmagnole, / Vive le son / Du canon." Mentioned by the **Unnamable** (311); SB toyed in translation with the Highland Fling.

"Cascando": a thirty-seven-line poem published in the *Dublin Magazine* 11.3 (October–December 1936): 3–4; later collected in *Gedichte* (1959) and *Poems in English* (1961). A copy sent to MacGreevy (7 July 1936) begins: "Why were you not simply what I despaired for / an occasion of wordshed." It represented (SB felt) "that last echo of feeling," or **humanism**.

Later collected editions differ from the first printing, SB adding a three-line opening stanza. The title denotes diminishing volume and decreasing tempo. The poem emerged from unreciprocated feelings for Elizabeth Stockton, Mary **Manning**'s friend visiting her in **Dublin**. It concerns the pain of coming to terms with an old lost **love**, to open the possibility of the new; and marks a new mode of expression by forsaking indirection for a more direct and intense style, the organizing principle being the rhythm of the musical phase. It imitates MacGreevy's "Dechtire": "I do not love you as I have loved / The loves I have loved— / As I may love other." The poem is in three parts. It opens in bitterness, better to abort than be barren, using the metaphor of "grappling" the ocean bed, to bring up the bones of the past. The second part goes back to the past, the churning of stale words in the heart again, to the terror of loving, of not loving, but moving to an acceptance of such feeling, "if they love you." In the third part, a single line makes that affirmation unconditional: "unless they love you." **Cooper** sets out on his new life, but is distracted by a pub and the whisky in glass tanks, "a slow cascando of pellucid yellows," punning on "diminishing volume" (*Murphy*, 274).

"Cascando": a radio play, in **French**, subtitled "Invention radiophonique pour musique et voix," with **music** by Marcel **Mihalovici**; published in *L'VII* 13 and 14 (3 avril 1963). In response to a request from RTF, the composer turned to SB. First broadcast on "France culture" (13 octobre 1963), with Roger **Blin** (*L'Oeuverer*) and Jean **Martin** (*La Voix*).

SB's original title was "Calando," diminishing in tone, but RTF officials indicated that "calendos" was slang for "cheese" (F&F, #271.1). SB's translation appeared in *Evergreen Review* 30 (May–June 1963): 45–57, then *Cascando and Other Short Dramatic Pieces* (Grove, 1968). It was broadcast on BBC 3 (6 October 1964), dir. Donald **McWhinnie**, with Patrick **Magee** (**Voice**) and Denys Hawthorne (Opener). An opera was begun with SB's grudging permission (1972) by Charles Dodge. SB withheld public performance rights until Dodge sent him a tape of a 32' 15" private performance (1978), after which he recanted. The piece, a "Realization of Samuel Beckett's Radio Play," was performed, with John Nesci (Opener), the computer synthesized voice of Steven Gilborn (Voice), and computer synthesized music of Voice (Music); recorded on vinyl LP (1983) by CRI, #454. An American radio production (with "**Words and Music**") was produced by "Theatre for Your Mother," recorded (27 May 1979) and released on vinyl LP (TFYM 003). The 17' 20" recording was directed by Mark Lutwak with Frank Collison (Opener), Joseph J. Casalini (Voice), and Lesli Dalaba on trumpet (Music); experimental music by Wayne B. Horvitz. A new radio production was created (1988) as part of "The Beckett Festival of Radio Plays" and broadcast by National Public Radio with Alvin Epstein (Voice), Frederick Neumann (Opener), and an original score by William Kraft. Each American production has used new music although the general contract specifies that "Cascando" should not be performed without Mihalovici's music.

"Cascando" was part of a period of intense aesthetic experiment for SB. "**Words and Music**," its mirror image, was written in English (December 1961), and "Cascando" in French immediately after. The interplay of words and music is controlled by Opener, in whose head the performance may be happening. The opening theme articulated by Voice at Opener's behest is familiar: "story . . . if you could finish it . . . you could rest," provided, of course, "it's the right one." Having failed to tell the right one "thousands and one" times, Voice begins, resumes, the story of **Woburn**. Opener stops and turns to Music, first alone, then in concert with Words. Woburn, after waiting for night, goes into the "boreen." His going down to the sea may be in Opener's head; at least "they" say so. Opener is both source and audience as Woburn struggles through the stones to a boat, which he pushes out into the oblivion of the sea. Words struggles to tell the *complete* story that will bring this "obligation to express" to an end. But is it complete even on completion, Woburn having escaped either to an island or into oblivion? Despite the union of Words and Music in performance, to Opener, the play ends with them still urging the story on, "come **on** . . . come on—"; and the words die away in the musical decrescendo suggested by the title.

"**A Case in a Thousand**": SB's fourth published short story appeared in *The Bookman* 86 (August 1934): 241–42. It features Dr. **Nye** who "belonged to the sad men." Physician though he is, Dr. Nye "cannot save" himself (Mark 15:31: "He saved others, himself he cannot save"). He was called in to aid surgeon Bor who has operated on the tubercular glands of a **boy** named Bray, who then took a turn for the worse. He found "a rightsided empyema," then another on the left (a collection of pus in a cavity, needing to be drained; compare SB's description of **psychoanalysis** as "draining a puddle," and the final image of water flowing out of the shadow). He discovered that the boy's **mother** was maintaining a vigil on the edge of the canal, something told to SB by Geoffrey **Thompson**. In the story, she is his old nurse. As the boy worsens, the doctor regresses. The boy does not survive the operation, but after the funeral the mother resumes her vigil as if he were still alive—as in a sense he is. When Nye appears, "she related a matter connected with his earliest years, so trivial and intimate that it need not be enlarged on here." The undisclosed incident, at once a "trauma at the root of this attachment" and an incident "trivial and intimate," is at the root of his story as well. The matter is sexual, probably oedipal, and the unexpected disclosure may have left young Nye impotent, which would explain why he is now one of the "sad men."

"**Casket of Pralinen for a Daughter of a Dissipated Mandarin**": a seventy-five-line poem in *The **European Caravan*** (1931): 476–78; not collected later, but reprinted in Harvey (278–83), with a commentary based on his conversations with SB. A typescript among the **Leventhal** papers at the HRHRC differs in detail from Harvey. While "praline" is French slang for clitoris, the title refers to a box of chocolates (ground nuts and almonds, with a sugar coating and a German plural) bought for Peggy **Sinclair** (her **father** the **Mandarin**). The girl is (implicitly) writing him a letter, reminding him of the New Year's Eve spent together, and of standing before **Dülberg**'s painting *Das Abendmahl*. This becomes an excuse for an outpouring of literary wit and religious paradox, the point explicit: "Fool! do you hope to untangle / the knot of **God**'s pain?" The poem dramatizes the conflict between the attractions of his Irish fräulein, **art**, and **religion**, with reflections on the nature of evil, but becomes "rather too self-conscious." Yet the byplay has its moments, subtle sweets pulled from the literary casket to be savored, and the poem anticipates significant motifs of the later writing.

"Catastrophe": a one-act play written in **French** (1982) and translated under the same title later that year. First produced in the Avignon Festival (21 July 1982), dir. Stephan Meldegg with Pierre Arditi (Protagonist), Gerard Desarthe (Director), and Stephanie Loik (Assistant), as part of "Une Nuit pour Václav Havel"; SB considered it "massacred." Produced at the Harold Clurman Theater, New York (June 1983), dir. Alan **Schneider**, with Kevin O'Connor (Director), Margaret Reed (Assistant), and David **Warrilow** (Protagonist). Published in *Solo suivi de Catastrophe* (Minuit, 1982), 99 numbered copies; then in *Catastrophe et autres dramaticules* (Minuit, 1982). First U.S. printing in *The New Yorker* (10 January 1983): 26–27; then, with **"Rockaby"** and **"Ohio Impromptu,"** in

Evergreen Review 98 (1984): 43–46, and *Three Plays* (Grove, 1984). The play was written for and dedicated to Václav Havel (qv).

The play enacts a rehearsal, the final preparation of an icon of suffering designed to elicit maximum audience response. The silent human (**"P"**) is set on a plinth where the Assistant has prepared him for final viewing by the autocratic Director, who sits fur-clad in an armchair and rehearses her decisions. P's **face** is covered with a **hat**, hands in his pockets to create an all-black effect. Director wants the hands shown, "Crippled. Fibrous degeneration" (SB's condition), two claws, exposed (in Antoni Libera's 1986 Warsaw production the fingers formed an inverted "V" for Solidarity). Assistant takes notes and keeps Director's cigar lit. He wants more exposure, discarding gown and hat, baring the neck. When she suggests that they gag him, Director barks back, "For **God**'s sake! This craze for explicitation!" (The *Evergreen* text erroneously has "explication"; the error in stage directions, "*D in armchair downstairs*," remains uncorrected in all editions.) Director calls for a blackout with just the head lit to see the full effect of his mute image. He rejects Assistant's suggestion that they show his face: "For God's sake! What next? Raise his head? Where do you think we are? In Patagonia?" (another place of contemporary repression). At the final image, an audience roar is heard on tape in an empty theater as the Protagonist defiantly raises his head and "fixes the audience. The applause falters, dies." The play creates an image of the human spirit in the face of oppression, the prisoner exerting his will against directorial tyranny. It is thus a fitting tribute to the leader of the Velvet Revolution, at a "turning point" (the literal meaning of "catastrophe") in his own and his country's fortunes.

Caterina of Cordona: SB's mistranscription (DN, 51) of **Cooper**'s "Caterina of Cardona" (*Flagellation*, 63), a nun renowned for the severity of her self-chastisement. She enters a Callipygean rhapsody (*Dream*, 97–98); references to her "unmasking her charms" for a "lower discipline" (**Shakespeare** and Tertullian) are noted earlier (Cooper, 21; DN, 49).

Cathleen na Hennessey: a serving wench in *Murphy* (46), remarkable for her "lightning calculation" (62). She embodies Cathleen ni Houlihan, the "little old woman" who is the spirit of **Ireland**, as in W. B. **Yeats**'s play *The Countess Cathleen* or the old milk woman of *Ulysses*. As **Dublin** pubs closed between 2:30 and 3:30 ("holy hour"), **Wylie** orders "coffee," otherwise Hennessey's Three Star Brandy (the **Alba**'s favorite **painkiller**).

cats: with rare exceptions, like the cat that attacks the lobster in "**Dante and the Lobster**," or that evicted at the end of *Film*, cats feature little in SB's world, where they might have been emblems of cruelty. SB preferred **dogs** and **rats** to cats as basic animals, **goats** to **sheep** as religious emblems, **hens** to ducks as emblems of stupidity, **parrots** and **monkeys** to human bipeds, and **horses** to cows as emblems of man's brutality to beasts. See **zoomorphisim**.

cattleya: a genus of orchid native to Central America, bearing a profusion of violet, rose, or yellow flowers; named for the English botanist William Cattley. **Neary** arrives at the grave of Father **Prout** with a superb bunch for Miss **Counihan** (*Murphy*, 50), in imitation of **Proust**'s Swann, who pursues Odette thus, with occasional success, so that the phrase "faire cattleyas" signifies the act of possession. Neary, alas, is left with the sentiment of refusal: "Alors, pas de cattleyas ce soir" (*Swann*, II.26).

Caudine exit: the *furculae Caudinae*, or Caudine Forks, narrow passes in Compagnia, were the scene of a Roman defeat in the second Samnite war (321 BC). Alluded to by **Belacqua** ("What a Misfortune," 150) as marking the moment of his loss of interest in himself (in an echo of Aesop), "as in a grape beyond his grasp."

Cavendish: one of Mr. **Knott**'s solitary dactylic ejaculations (*Watt*, 209); in homage to Lord Charles Cavendish (1591–1654), eccentric **mathematician** and first to calculate the weight of the earth. Mentioned in **Baillet** (153). His library of rare mathematical manuscripts, collected in travel, was sold by his wife to the pasteboard makers. **Mahaffy** notes (86) that he petitioned Charles I to offer **Descartes** a post in England, to advance science there.

"Ceiling": an autograph manuscript at the **HRHRC**, originally called "On coming to"; eight sheets from a spiral-bound notebook, inscribed "Courtmayeur 10.7.81" and "**Paris** 26.7.81" (described by Carlton Lake, *No Symbols*, #431–33); six versions of a piece for Avigdor **Arikha**. It concerns one "coming to" who finds in white a stimulus for introspection as he emerges from the "dim **consciousness**" of sleep to awareness. The earliest drafts offer a plan: "One the coming to. Two the consciousness thereof. Three the eyes. Four the white." The final version focuses on consciousness alone, equated "With dread of being again." After each stanza an apparent obstacle ("Further one cannot") is surmounted, perception reactivated with a simple "**On.**" As consciousness is associated with being, first of mind, then of **body**, stimulated by the white, even dull white, the work concludes with the paradox of being (conscious), "Dread darling sight." Published in *Arikha* (12). In Arikha's typescript version the title is altered to "Somehow again" (Atik, 41), apparently SB's final choice.

Celestine V: called to the papacy in 1294 (5 July) aged eighty, reluctantly accepting election after living ascetically as a hermit. He abdicated (13 December) in favor of Boniface VIII. **Dante** called this *lo gran rifiuto* ["the great refusal" (*Inf.* III.61)]. Mrs. **bboggs** is "almost as non-partisan as Pope Celestine the fifth" ("What a Misfortune," 136). Victor **Krap** aspires to reach the "Grand refus. Le refus de l'être" (*Eleutheria*, 159). SB wrote to **Duthuit** (9 March 1949; RUL 2906), about the lack of "rapport" between subject and **object**: "Pour ma parte, c'est le gran rifiuto qui m'intéresse."

Celia: heroine of *Murphy*, who represents the Cartesian **body**, as Murphy does mind. She is celestial, so part of the astrological system outside Murphy's own; yet the **pun** on her name, sadly expanded by Mr. **Kelly** (115), throws the starry concave into doubt ("s'il y a"). There is a remote conjunction of a Celia and Murphy in **Fielding**'s *Amelia*, but Ben **Jonson**'s *Volpone* enters the bedroom tableau of chapter 2. Consider, too, **Swift**'s Caelia, whose name belies the physical necessities she must observe. Celia's externals are given with demented particularity. This parodies traditions in which the physical features of the heroine are carefully described (compare Pierre Louÿs, *King Pausole*, 4.5). The **Whoroscope Notebook** offers a catalogue headed by an enigmatic "Venus de Milo," presumably in jest, given that it includes measurements for upper arm, forearm, and wrist. Celia is thus part of a literary and comic tradition, one that Murphy *in sui* stands outside.

Céline, Louis-Ferdinand (1894–1961): pseudonym of Louis-Ferdinand Destouches; author of *Voyage à bout de la nuit* (1932). SB read his *Mort à crédit* (1936) en route to **Germany**, finding it "very **Rabelais** . . . superbly overwritten" (Knowlson, 217). He was attracted to its pessimism, lack of compromise, and calculated obscenity, and by its colloquial language and a narrator closely resembling the author. Cohn (*Comic Gamut*, 98ff) surmises a direct influence on SB's first fictions in **French**. Like **Molloy**, Céline was no enemy of the commonplace, and his ironic delight in deflating pompous idiom links him to SB as a stylist whose art is concealed beneath simulated casualness, layer on layer of literary and cultural reference, with **Proust** a major source. Céline later alienated his readership by his support of the Vichy government and anti-Semitic rhetoric, but his bleak vision and the sophisticated argot that expresses it binds him arsy-versy to SB in a way that neither might have wanted.

Cellini, Benvenuto (1500–71): **Floren-tine** goldsmith, his monument on the Ponte Vecchio mentioned in *Dream* (27). **Belacqua** imagines himself sitting in his store, carving the heads and necks of lutes and zithers, in a manner de-scribed as "Cellineggiava" (122). His technique differs from that of **Proust** by its emphasis on the external (*Proust*, 80).

"Cendres": translation of **"Embers"** by Robert **Pinget**, with SB; first printed in *Les Lettres nouvelles* 36 (30 décembre 1959): 3–14; then in *La Dernière bande, suivi de Cendres* (Minuit, 1960), which failed to note it as "un pièce radio-phonique." Reprinted from this in *L'Avant-scène* 313 (15 juin 1964): 21–25.

"Ce n'est au Pélican": a twelve-line poem (1931), unpublished but in-cluded in *Dream* (21). Listed among the **Leventhal** papers, and mentioned to George **Reavey** (7 January 1933). **Liebert** addresses his beloved **Lucie[n]**, neither piteous as the pelican nor pure as the phoenix, who might have cured him but has not. The alternative title "Text 2" relates it to **"Text"**: "My vari-cose veins take their kneeling thoughts / from the piteous pelican." The image is from de **Musset**'s "La Nuit de mai," the pelican an emblem of **Christ**, rend-

ing its breast to feed its young. As **Arsene** intimates (*Watt*, 42), "a pelican in her piety" is the correct heraldic phrase.

censorship: SB wrote to Barney Rosset (25 June 1953) stating that there were "certain obscenities of form" that he was not "disposed to mitigate." He was re-sponding, partly, to having had a piece of *L'Innommable* cut by the *Nouvelle revue française*. His position had been explicit since 1934 when *The Bookman* commissioned an essay on censorship in Ireland (see **"Censorship in the Saorstat"**). It did not appear, and SB's position did not prevail. Having sup-ported independence, the Church was rewarded for its fidelity, and a theocratic regime was set up that proved difficult to dismantle. Censorship of books and periodicals was instituted, and ignorance condoned as more conducive to godli-ness than was knowledge (Fletcher, "Modernism," 199). The first British production of *Waiting for Godot* clashed with the official licensor of productions, the Lord Chamberlain. SB informed Rosset (21 April 1954) that the incrimi-nations were so preposterous that the whole thing was off. Twelve passages were listed for omission, some of which SB (reluctantly) agreed to amend, but also passages vital to the play (the open-ing of **Lucky**'s tirade). The crisis was averted by performing the play privately, but, as **Faber**'s 1956 edition announced, "When *Waiting for Godot* was transferred from the Arts Theatre to the Criterion Theatre, a small number of textual dele-tions were [*sic*] made to satisfy the re-quirements of the Lord Chamberlain.

The text printed here is that used in the Criterion production."

In 1958 SB responded to Irish anti-intellectualism when an adaptation of *Ulysses* and O'Casey's new play, *The Drums of Father Ned,* were withdrawn from the **Dublin** International Theatre Festival because of objections by the Archbishop of Dublin. SB withdrew his contributions (two **mimes** and *All That Fall*). His London *Endgame* that year also fell afoul of the "Lord Chamberpot," who had earlier approved it, when it was performed in French. SB yielded slightly, replacing "clap" with "warts" and offering "swine" for "bastard" (he hoped that **God** was more pleased at being called a swine than a bastard). The play was finally licensed. SB's stand was personal as much as **political**. He wanted no external authority tampering with his work, censors, the Lord Chamberlain (whose powers remained until 1968), other playwrights, directors, or actors. He wrote Rosset (2 February 1956) to forestall "unauthorized deviations" in a forthcoming Broadway *Godot* with a new producer conscious of the play's Miami debacle, and who wanted it rewritten for an American audience (Thorton Wilder had begun a draft). SB said he was not intransigent about minor changes, but he refused to be improved by a professional rewriter.

In the 1970s the political clashed with the personal. The conflict concerned where the artwork was "created," in the study or the rehearsal hall; if the latter then those involved needed the freedom to create the performance. This forced SB deeper into his second career, as theatrical **director**, but it placed him in op-position to many productions of his work. He began to intervene in the theatrical process, objecting to an all-woman production of *WG* with the flippant comment, "women don't have prostates." Determined to protect the integrity of his work, he antagonized much of the theatrical community. SB tried to suppress JoAnne Akalaitis's controversial 1984 *Endgame,* then allowed it to proceed with a disclaimer in the program. Gildas Bourdet's pink *Fin de partie* (1988) was allowed to proceed only with the pink set covered at the Comédie Française and without Bourdet's decor on tour. Bourdet removed his name from the program. Robert Brustein, who produced the 1984 Akalaitis *Endgame,* in a review of Harmon for *The New York Times* (1999) suggested that SB's vigilance amounted to artistic censorship. A like controversy erupted at the "After Beckett" symposium in Sydney (2003), when Edward Beckett wished to close a *WG* afflicted with a loud musical score; Australian newspapers savaged the author's dead hand. In a considerable irony, SB, who liberated the theater in the mid-fifties, has been cast in the posthumous role of censor. See **adaptations** and **law**.

"Censorship in the Saorstat": a vitriolic essay, commissioned by *The Bookman* and "ground out" (August 1934); it did not appear, as the periodical ceased publication. The typescript, in the Baker Memorial Library, Dartmouth, was edited (1983) by Ruby Cohn (*Disjecta,* 84–88; misdated as 1935). "Saorstat" is the "Free State," behind which lurks the Zoar of Genesis 13:10, a city of the plain.

SB had made this connection in "**Hell Crane to Starling**" (qv). An act of 16 July 1929 had spawned the **Censorship** of Publications Board under the moral guidance of J. J. **Byrne**, SB's particular target. It provided for the prohibition of unwholesome literature, specifically that referring to sexuality or contraception. An attempt to throw a *cordon sanitaire* about the new state, threatened by writings contrary to Irish Catholicism, it remained a force for several decades. SB cites specific provisions, and mocks Byrne's advocacy of the "commonsense man." He commends the Register of Prohibited Publications for enacting a measure of which the Grand Academy of Balnibarbi might be proud, and for showing (30 September 1935) 618 books and eleven periodicals under ban, including works by Huxley, Faulkner, Lawrence, **O'Casey**, **Shaw**, and **Clarke**, foreign works, scientific "enchiridions," *Broadway and Hollywood Movies,* and *True Romances.* The delay allowed a personal touch: SB's number, if he might presume to say (*MPTK* was placed on the Register, 31 March 1935), is 465. The essay ends cynically: "We now feed our pigs on sugarbeet pulp. It is all the same to them."

Cette fois: SB's translation (1974–75) of *That Time* (Minuit, 1978), with a special edition of 100 numbered copies. The drafts (RUL 1657/1–3) indicate a mode of translation similar to original composition, the text divided into sections A, B, and C to facilitate ordering, and extensive revisions.

Cézanne, Paul (1839–1906): French painter, who moved from **Romanticism** through Impressionism toward the idea of **art** as the expression and emotional apprehension of color and pure form. SB's first comments are supercilious: the **Alba**'s tram is described as "a Cézanne monster" (*Dream,* 167); the narrator fancies himself as the Cézanne of the printed page. Seeing the Cézannes in the Tate profoundly impressed SB. Writing to **MacGreevy** (8 September 1934), he rejected "the impulse towards anthropomorphism." He contrasted Cézanne's **nature** (qv) with that of other artists, landscape "promoted to the emotions of the hiker"; whereas "Cézanne seems to have been the first to see landscape and state it as material of a strictly peculiar order, incommensurable with all human expressions whatsoever. **Atomistic** landscape with no velleities of vitalism, landscape with personality à la rigueur, but personality in its own terms." He stated (16 September 1934) that he felt in Cézanne the absence of a rapport that was all right for earlier artists "for whom the animising mode was valid," but which was as false for Cézanne as it would prove for himself. That sense of landscape as indifferent to man, as *atomistic, mineral,* and *inorganic* (see **geology**), would henceforth underlie SB's art.

Chaikin, Joseph (1935–2003): American actor and director, alumnus of the Living Theater, he founded (with Peter Feldman) the Open Theater in New York in 1963 where he played **Hamm** to Peter Maloney's **Clov** in the company's production of *Endgame* in 1969 (directed by Roberta Sklar, with James Barbosa as **Nagg** and Jayne Haynes as Nell). Chaikin staged it himself at the

Manhattan Theater Club in 1979. In 1980 he approached SB for permission to stage material not originally intended for the theater. SB cautioned him against staging the teleplays, especially "**Ghost Trio**," which could not "be transferred to the stage without severe loss." He suggested that Chaikin choose one of the *Texts for Nothing*, with a single figure (see **adaptations**); and proposed a title, Virgil's *Inania Verba*, "no doubt inacceptable." Chaikin called his program *Texts*, staging it at New York's Public Theater, then taking it on world tour. SB was not unhappy with the results. A stroke during open heart surgery left Chaikin aphasic in 1984, but he continued directing and acting and developed renewed interest in SB's work. He acted in what he now called *Texts for Nothing* (directed by Nancy Gabor in 1995 and Anders Cato in 1996) and staged new productions of it in 1992 with Bill Irwin (which won an Obie) and in 2000 at Seven Stages in Atlanta with Del Hamilton, the latter presented a "ditch at the top of a hill," allowing the actor to climb, fail, and finally end up in the ditch. He staged *Waiting for Godot* at the Taper, Too, in L.A. in 1990 and at Seven Stages in 1994, *That Time* at the Judith Anderson Theater in New York also in 1994, restaged *Endgame* with Del Hamilton at Seven Stages in 1995, and staged *Happy Days* at the Cherry Lane Theater in 2002 with Joyce Aaron.

Chamfort: Sébastien Roch Nicholas (1740–94). Of noble but disgraced birth, he determined to advance in the fashionable world, first as a libertine then as a writer and misanthropist. Master of the maxim, he acutely observed the follies of the *ancien régime* and the revolution until he was himself denounced. To avoid the guillotine he attempted **suicide**, shooting out an eye and inflicting twenty-two razor wounds, but survived only to die five months later from inept medical treatment. SB's *Huit maximes*, seven from Chamfort plus one from **Pascal**, appeared in *Collected Poems* (1977, 122–37). See "**Kottabista**" and "**Long after Chamfort**."

"Chanson de Toile": a sentimental "historiette" typically about sixty lines long, nine or ten stanzas with a brief refrain, simplicity of style contrasting with melodic ornamentation (Beck, 100–4). The theme is **love** that triumphs over all, service rewarded by tenderness. The **Polar Bear** notes Louise **Labbé**'s distrust of the tradition (*Dream*, 165), as in the twelfth-century *Doon de la Roche*, where Doon mistakenly rejects his wife, la belle Doette, for adultery before they are reconciled. SB recorded (DN, 73): "Chanson de toile (Belle Doette et son ami Doon: *E or en ai dol*)." Beck (103) gives *motz e son:* "Bele Doette as fenestres se siet, / Lit en un livre, mais au cuer ne l'en tient. / De son ami Doon li resovient, / Q'en autres terres est alez tornoier. / E or en ai dol" ("Belle Doette seated at the window reads a book, but her heart is not there. She remembers her lover, Doon, who is away fighting in other lands. And now of that must she have sorrow").

character: the idea of literary character as a representation of a self, a coherent and discrete entity, has become increasingly problematic. Influenced by **Freud**

and **psychoanalysis**, Modernism asserted a conception of human personality, character or self as interior, the core of human reality represented in the "stream of **consciousness**." Such assumptions informed literature from the great age of **humanism** (qv) to the postmodernist era. Experimenters like **Proust, Joyce, Woolf**, and Faulkner developed the "interior monologue" to capture that reality. Represented thus, literary character remained coherent, even if trifurcated by the Freudian paradigm of "id," "ego," and "superego." SB questioned this depiction of the human self. To him, character was not only unstable but finally unrepresentable, especially as what it is not, a coherent entity. The object of fiction may be to represent character or the self; the obligation of the writer to continue the pursuit; but such enterprise is doomed to failure. This does not mean that literature stops, only that the artificial expectations of unity and coherence cannot be met, and new forms must be created to acknowledge the resistance of the self to representation.

That resistance is central in *Dream*. SB considers how his "boys and girls" have been "doing their dope" (112); they have not been playing their parts like **lius** (116), predictable parts of a greater harmony (unlike **Balzac**'s "clockwork cabbages," 119). **Belacqua** *is simply not that kind of person* (124), and in his inability to conform to narrative demands he is the prototype of figures to come. The self for SB is both a "nothing to express" and the "**nothing** from which to express." It is inseparable from the Other, an inner world often indistinguishable from the outer. SB's associations with **surrealism**

were tentative and suspicious, but he accepted their assumptions that inner and outer "reality," self and other, observer and observed, bleed into each other. His first representations of character dichotomy are complementary pairs, **pseudocouples** (qv): **Neary** and **Wylie**; **Mercier** and **Camier**; **Vladimir** and **Estragon**; **Molloy** and **Moran**; **Hamm** and **Clov**, who are, SB said, tied to each other as two arms to a single human trunk. Dichotomy gave way to dispersal, the phenomenon best seen in SB's "late fiction," and accounting for much of its difficulty.

In the 1960s SB's fiction turned from stories of **motion** toward vignettes of stillness or barely perceptible movement, the breathing of a **body** or the trembling of a hand. These "**closed space**" stories entail little more than a figure in various postures, like exercises in human origami. The shift from journeys, movement from and return to "home" (**asylum**), to the later tales is announced in the fragments and *faux départs* that lead to *All Strange Away* (1964) and *Imagination Dead Imagine* (1965): "Out the door and down the road in the old **hat** and coat like after the war, no not that again." The *imaginative* alternative was now "A closed space five foot square by six high, try for him there." The change necessitated a new character, the nameless "him" who became SB's second major fictional innovation after the "**voice**" that had dominated the journey fictions from *Watt* to *From an Abandoned Work,* and which still makes occasional appearances in "closed" tales like *Company* and *Ill Seen Ill Said*. The "him" (occasionally "her," "one," or "it") is a narrator's creation, often "devised," an **object** to someone's imaginings.

The "closed space" tales often resulted in intractable creative difficulties, literary cul-de-sacs into which SB had written himself, and abandoned. As often they were unabandoned, resuscitated, revived, and revised as SB periodically returned to his "trunk manuscripts." That stuttering process of experiment and impasse, breakthrough and breakdown was folded into the narratives. These are tales designed to fail, continued until they failed, then continued further. They exist in multiple versions, most at some point published, like the abandoned *faux départ* called "**Fancy Dying**" (qv). The mid-1970s triplet, *Still,* "**Sounds**," and "**Still 3,**" features a narrative **consciousness** straining to apprehend images that may come from within or without, or both simultaneously, resulting in what the narrator of *Ill Seen Ill Said* calls, "the confusion now between real and—how say its contrary? No matter. That old tandem. Such now the confusion between them once so twain" (40). As SB's fiction developed beyond the pronominal unity of the four *nouvelles,* through the disembodied voices of *Texts for Nothing* toward the voiceless bodies of the later fictions, the body of the text became the text as body. If *Texts* suggest the dispersal of character and writing beyond the body, *All Strange Away* signaled a refiguration, the body's return, its textualization, the body as voiceless, static object, or the object of text, unnamed except for a series of geometric signifiers, being as **mathematical** formulae. The subject of these late tales is less the secret recesses of the repressed subconscious or the imagination valorized by **Romantic**

poets and painters than the dispersed post-Freudian ego, voice as alien Other.

Chas: a minor aesthete in *Dream,* modeled on Alfred **Péron**. He shares with **Belacqua** remarkable poetic comparisons and gloomy silences. The narrator agrees with the **Polar Bear** that Chas is a bore and a **morpion**. In "A **Wet Night**" he is called "a highbrow bromide of French nationality with a diabolical countenance compound of **Skeat**'s and Paganini's [a prominent, beaked nose] and a mind like a tattered concordance" (49)—a **Bartlett machine**, with the annoying habit of capping any quotation.

Chas, Jean du: a poet invented by SB; see "**Le Concentrisme**."

Chateaubriand, François-Auguste-René (1768–1848): **Romantic** writer. Cited in Praz as fascinated by the pleasures of melancholy (*Romantic Agony,* 30), and as "épicurien à l'imagination catholique" (321). His *Mémoires d'outre-tombe,* a posthumous meditation, inform **Malone**'s sensation of being beyond the grave (183); in French (15), "l'impression de l'outre-tombe." He is linked with **Amiel**, a "pair of melancholy Pantheists dancing a fandango of death in the twilight" (*Proust,* 82). **Belacqua** in "**Yellow**" calls the theater sister a "chateaubriant" (180).

Chaucer, Geoffrey (ca. 1342–1400): SB studied Chaucer's "Legend of Good Women" at **Trinity**, using it for *Dream,* which has as epigraph the opening lines: "A thousand sythes have I heard men telle / That there is joye in heven, & peyne in hell" (SB replaces "And I accorde wel that

hit be so" with "But—"). He used **Skeat's**
Chaucer (DN, 169–71) for prototypes
(Lucrezia, Clytemnestra, **Semiramide**) of
the **Syra-Cusa** (50). Other echoes are casual: in "**Sanies I**" sweet showers create an
illusory springtime; a guest at the **Frica's**
soiree is called the Man of Law; "The
Parlement of Foules" provides the "jealous swan" of "**Echo's Bones**" (11); and,
like Chaucer's Monk, **Watt** is not a man's
man (139). SB cites "Dan Chaucer the
first warbler" from **Tennyson's** "Dream
of Fair Women" (DN, 167); compare
Molloy's mother and Genesis 30:6:
"therefore called she his name Dan."

Chelsea: the **London** district where SB
lived in 1934. *Murphy* (chapter 2) describes the Embankment and Reach, the
bridges, the Old Church, the Chelsea
pensioner in his scarlet (lobster) tunic.
"A funnel vailed" refers to a boat dipping its funnel to get under the bridge,
as in "**Serena II.**" The **Whoroscope
Notebook** indicates: "**Purgatorial** atmosphere sustained throughout"; hence a
soulscape: "Hell roast this weather"
(15), the Eldorado man's "cruel **machine,**" and "devils" (printers' appren-
tices) among the lost.

"Che Sciagura": an anonymous satire in
TCD 36 (14 November 1929): 42, SB
mocking the Irish attitude toward the
importation of contraceptives. The
words ("**What a Misfortune**") derive
from **Voltaire's** *Candide,* continuing
"d'essere senza coglioni" ("to be without
balls"), a eunuch confronted with the
impenetrable beauty of Counégard. SB
used the motto "D.E.S.C." to mock the
Jesuitical "AMGD." The Editorial Sub-

Committee for Michaelmas Term 1929
commented: "*Che Sciagura,* by
D.E.S.C., was extremely clever, though
fortunately a trifle obscure for those who
do not know their **JOYCE** and their
VOLTAIRE" (F&F, 5). The motif is used
variously: in "**Echo's Bones**" (8), to golf-
ing Lord Gall ("'Then you have lost your
ball' said Belacqua. 'What a shame'"); in
the *Watt* manuscripts, sung by Erskine
and Watt as they prepare the poss; and of
Malone's misfortune when his pencil slips
from his fingers (222), the French text
reading (88) "**Quel malheur.**"

chess: SB learned chess from his brother,
Frank, and would play against his uncle
Howard, who once beat Capablanca in an
exhibition match (Knowlson, 30). The
Chess Club at **Trinity** was the only society in which SB took office, acting as trea-
surer in his final year. He might rehearse
on his **Staunton** chessboard (later stolen
from **Ussy**) moves of the masters, like
Evans the newsagent (*Watt,* 26). A favorite opponent was Henri **Hayden,** and he
had played with Marcel **Duchamp** during the **war.** SB built up a collection of
chess books, and studied the chess column
in *Le Monde.* SB claimed that chess and
music "had the same intellectual beauty"
(Bair, 397). Little wonder, then, that the
game entered his **art.**

Gerald Abrahams (*The Chess Mind,*
ix) states that chess is the closest the
human mind has come to creating a
game that is purely an act of imagination:
"a principle of activity in being which
cannot be explained away as a mere
epiphenomenon of material forces in collision." The narrator of "**Assumption**"
scorns those who can reply confidently

to P-K4, yet "are frozen into bewildered suspension by Pawn to Rook's third," those who prefer **habit** and routine. Yet chess is a confrontation in which one will meets another, with rational laws agreed to by both parties (the world reduced to intelligible rules), this restricting the free imagination; **Belacqua** records that the maneuvers required of him constitute a forced move (*Dream,* 43). References to chess illustrate this paradox of freedom and restriction.

Murphy's game with Mr. **Endon**, which SB refused to omit when potential publishers requested changes, is "an Endon affence" (243); "affence" derives not from Ger. *Affe,* "ape," despite the chess-playing chimps SB wanted on the cover (see **monkey**), but from *affidatus,* "immune from capture" (see **solipsism**). Alternatively, a *Zweispringerspott,* or "Two Knights Mockery," that variation of the "Two Knights Defence" beginning with Black's reply (Mr. Endon always plays Black), which should have been P-K4. White's K-P4 is the primary cause of his subsequent difficulties, as it initiates a movement toward disorder that cannot be reversed (see *Endgame*). Mr. Endon, to move his Bishops, is forced (moves 9 and 13) to make the smallest concessions to entropy compatible with the laws of chess. By then Murphy is in irreversible disarray. His early moves attempt to keep the faith, but when Black takes his Knight to K4 Murphy is confounded because the corresponding square is occupied. Hence the annotation (a parody of chess analysis): "Apparently nothing better, bad as this is." After White's ninth move, Black is perfectly composed, his Fabian outing

completed without loss, but White is poorly placed, then, at move 13, makes an ill-judged move. He is now two moves behind. Black places his Queen on K1, reversing the polarities of his own forces. White struggles on, then gives up ("The flag of distress"), at move 18 bringing out his Queen's Knight. After this further loss of tempo there is no catching up.

Move 20, Kt-QR4, is the first opportunity to take a piece without significant loss, for Black may win the Knight with either his Knight or his Queen. Instead, he moves his Bishop to Q2, and is attacking it three times. Move 22, K-QB1, earns the approbation "Exquisitely played" because White cannot duplicate it. He tries! By 23 Black has retained perfect symmetry and White's position is a disgrace. Move 27 is more despair than ingenuity: a Queen sacrifice with no return, to force Black to react. Mr. Endon calmly completes his perfectly symmetrical pattern; White can violate that integrity only by taking a piece. His efforts to force Black to do so are unsuccessful. At 30, Kt-QB5, White has three pieces *en prise*. His next move, Knight back to KR1, a *coup de repos,* however one might translate that, is totally futile; it is not even bad. Mr. Endon continues his wandering to find home.

As the note points out, at 34, Q-K1, Murphy is in check. This is adventitious, rather than advantageous; nevertheless, he moves out of check. His Kt-QR6 is "abject" because it threatens to force Mr. Endon to move his Rook back to its corner. But Black is immune to such threats. The moment of truth occurs at 42, following Murphy's Q-QB6. As Declan Kiely noted, in many editions move 42 is incorrect, K-Q2, an illegal move into check. The Routledge original, **Grove Press**, and the **French** translation correctly give K-K2; the error crept in when *Murphy* was reset for *Calder*'s 1963 Jupiter edition, and was replicated in the Picador reprint. Both sides may temporize, Black returning the minor pieces and White marking time with his King; but this move creates the crisis, for Black's move 44, returning the King home, will constitute an illegal move into check. Murphy has the options of doing nothing, removing his Queen, or moving into K8, to force Mr. Endon to respond. He resigns because the move to K8 would determine whether Mr. Endon perceives him, if he exists for Mr. Endon. Murphy knows the answer, but does not test it. His surrender acknowledges a fearful symmetry to which he has no other response; but it makes inevitable another to come. Murphy *could* force the issue by moving to K8 or insisting on the check, but Mr. Endon, without any trace of annoyance, would simply fade away. The game has been exquisitely comical, but the joke is on Murphy.

In *Eleutheria,* the **Spectator** comments on the dramatic (in)action (144), saying that something paralyzes him, players gaping at the chessboard, no move being made. **Hamm**'s opening line, "Me . . . to play," introduces a similar motif. SB explained the Berlin *Endspiel* in terms of the Spectator's complaint: "Hamm is king in this chess game lost from the start. He knows from the start that he is only making senseless moves . . . He's only trying to postpone the inevitable end . . . He is a poor player." SB noted the allusion to *Richard III*

(V.iv.7): "My kingdom for a nightman," to carry away **Nagg** and **Nell**, pieces removed from the board. Although he considered "knightman" unintended, SB drew it to the cast's attention, but warned of the limits of the chess imagery. Yet metaphors of attrition and entropy in the drama find their direct analogy in chess, where every move is an irreversible step toward an inevitable end: "Old endgame lost of old," Hamm concludes. The play is conceived on the model of chess, little left on the board, King and Pawn bound to each other, other pieces lost in play. Winning depends on the promotion of a pawn, but that possibility, if never quite negated, seems unlikely, and defeat by **death** is the only alternative to the stalemate of existence.

Chesterfield, Lord Philip (1694–1773), fourth earl: English statesman and writer. His posthumous *Letters to His Son* (1774) caused an outcry; in **Johnson**'s words, inculcating the morals of a whore and manners of a dancing master. *Murphy* (269) refers to a letter (11 December 1747) where Chesterfield describes a man who managed his **time** so well "that he would not even lose that small portion of it which the calls of **nature** obliged him to pass in the necessary-house, but gradually went through all the Latin poets." Mr. **Hackett**'s sense of **Watt** as "a native of the rocks" (21) is from this letter, which SB had memorized; he prepared for his 1936 trip by translating it into German.

children: to an impertinent question SB once replied that "Mr Beckett" was unsure if he was married, but was certain he did not have any children (see "**To My Daughter**"). This reflects the sentiment that the greatest crime is to have been born, a sin against innocence SB chose not to perpetuate. He projected an image of detestation mingled with **pity**, wrenching the biblical "Suffer the little children." Thus **Belacqua** comments (*Dream*, 127): "Children he abominated and feared"; and the **Expelled** is emphatic: "I loathe children" (51). **Molloy** is uncertain if he has a son, and the protagonist of *First Love* uses the **birth** of (presumably) his child as an excuse to be off. When **Mercier** is greeted by a little boy and girl who call him "Papa," he screams at them to "Fuck off out of here" (31). In *All That Fall* (31), Dan **Rooney** wishes to kill a child, to "Nip some young doom in the bud." He may have done so, and a mystery surrounds "Little Minnie"; **Schubert**'s "**Death** and the Maiden" hints at sorrow from the death of a child. SB was hugely affected by **Jung**'s tale of the **little girl** who had never really been born. Many later works, notably *Not I* and "**Rough for Radio II**," reflect an **embryonic** death, a life denied at **birth**. In "**Embers**," Henry wishes "to **God**" that he'd never had Addie, that his **mother** had douched herself of him. *Endgame* enacts the biblical Flood, but **Hamm** calls **Nagg** "cursed progenitor" and, whatever his relation to **Clov**, wants to break the cycle of generation. **Rat** and flea are "exterminated," and when a child is seen, "A potential procreator" (78), the impulse is to get the gaff, lest "humanity" begin again.

Chopin, Frédéric François (1810–49): Polish pianist and composer, cited (*Dream*, 69) less for his musical genius than for the TB from which (like Peggy **Sinclair**) he died. See **Auber** and **Field**. **Belacqua** dismisses Szopen's "Winkelmusik" (punning on chamber **music**) as that of "a sickroom talent"; "Mr **Beckett**" is thanked for "Kleinmeister's Leidenschaftsucherei," a small master's addiction to passion.

Christ: to **Vladimir**'s "What has Christ got to do with it?" **Estragon** replies: "All my life I've compared myself to him" (*WG*, 34.b). The comment has an uncertain validity, in the recognition of Christ not as son of **God** but as an emblem of human suffering, like **Cain**. Maria Jolas described SB as "a **Christ**-haunted man" (*Beckett at 60*, 16). Christ is often treated with irreverence. The **Polar Bear** mocks His "megalomaniacal impertinence" in interfering with **Lazarus**, but is bested by the Jesuit who asks him to wait until he is old enough to understand the humility that is beyond masochism (*Dream*, 209–10). This is the *humilitatis* of **Geulincx**, central to the ethos of **quietism** that SB made increasingly his own. In "**Dante and the Lobster**" (19–20), **Belacqua** calls the lobster a fish, and reflects: "Fish had been good enough for Jesus Christ, Son of God, Saviour"; this is the Greek ICHTHYS, an early symbol of Christ. Belacqua sees the lobster, exposed cruciform on the oilcloth, make a faint nervous act of life: "Christ!" he said "it's alive" (21). His aunt's reply has a fine irony: "Well" she said "it is to be hoped so, indeed." See also **crucifixion**.

Christina (1626–89): Queen of Sweden (1632–54). In *Whoroscope*, "Christina the ripper" for having required **Des-**

cartes, who preferred to remain in bed till midday, to rise at five in the winter to teach her **mathematics**, from which regimen he took chill and died.

Christy: he who looks after **Moran**'s garden (128); like Christy, the gardener at **Cooldrinagh** (O'Brien, 13, 20). He appears as a seller of dung in *All That Fall.*

cicisbeo: the recognized lover of a married woman, approved by a husband unwilling or unable to perform sexually. From **Nordau**'s *Degeneration* (5; DN, 89). **Belacqua**'s wish to found his marriage with **Lucy** on "this solid basis of a cuckoldry" is granted, but not quite as he anticipates ("Walking Out," 103, 113). See **babylan**.

Clarke, Austin [Augustine Joseph] (1896–1974): a leading Twilighter with whom SB clashed in "**Recent Irish Poetry**." SB called him "Austen Clerk," and one who had removed "the clapper from the bell of rhyme," alluding to his introduction to *Pilgrimage and Other Poems* about the assonance of Gaelic poetry. That phrase is applied to the **oyster kisses** **Wylie** shares with Miss **Counihan** (*Murphy*, 117). He is cast as the pot poet, Austin **Ticklepenny**. Clarke's marital, mental, and alcohol problems led to his confinement in St. Patrick's Hospital (1919), where he was placed in a padded cell and force-fed in the manner Ticklepenny finds distressing. On publication of *Murphy*, SB was told that Clarke was going through it "with his pubic comb"; but when **Gogarty** urged litigation Clarke declined. His retaliation was a brief re-view in the *Dublin Magazine:* "the whole thing is a bizarre fantasy, with a nasty twist about it that its self-evident cleverness and scholarship cannot redeem."

Claude Lorrain [Claude Gellée] (1600–82): French artist, apprenticed as a pastry cook; the leading landscape painter of his day, enriching the beauty of the Roman countryside with classical associations of antique grandeur to evoke a golden age. SB appreciated less the *paysage moralisé* than his subtle mastery of light, yet associated him with **Cézanne** as one not "humanised and romantic" (SB to TM, 14 August 1937). *Murphy* invokes his "**Narcissus**" in comic mode (228): high-class whores, their faces more the work of **art** than **nature**, breathe a malediction on the immunity of Narcissus from the ravages of **time**. Like Narcissus, Murphy is more absorbed in his own reflection than in the world of quid pro quo.

Clement: the chemist whose wife has fallen off the **ladder** and needs a **painkiller** (*Molloy*, 101). Compare *How It Is* (36): "in thy clemency now and then let the great damned sleep."

"The Cliff": translation of "La **Falaise**" (qv) by Edith Fournier for the *Complete Short Prose* (Grove, 1995), 257.

Clinch, Mr. Thomas: otherwise "Bim," head nurse at the **MMM** (*Murphy*, Ch. 9), with his relations Bom and Bum (see **Bim and Bom**). The name echoes **Swift**'s "Clever Tom Clinch, Going to be Hanged" (1727).

Clonmachnois: in 1936, with only three chapters of *Murphy* to write, SB went to Galway with his brother, Frank, and noted the indescribable beauty of Clonmachnois (SB to TM, 25 March 1936; *Murphy*, 267). The castle is a burial place at a crossing of the Shannon (Flann O'Brien's *At Swim-Two-Birds*), the mounds of many mighty chieftains resting there.

"Closed place": "Fizzle 5"; translation of "Foirade VI," in the **Minuit** periodical printing entitled "**Se voir.**" The **French** text is sometimes cited by its opening words as "**Endroit clos,**" translated variably as "Closed place" or "**Closed space.**" SB used both, but finally preferred "place," as in the **Grove Press** version. In *For to End Yet Again and Other Fizzles* (1976), John **Calder** cited "Closed place" in the list of contents, but "Closed space" within the text. The piece encapsulates the terrain explored in *All Strange Away*, "Ping," and *The Lost Ones:* a "closed space" in which the expiring **consciousness** struggles to retain a feeble grasp upon the mind or sensation, only to fall back hopelessly into oblivion and **solitude.** The "place" consists of an arena and a ditch, a track between the two, and beyond the ditch **nothing.** This may be **Dante**'s first circle of hell, a **limbo** of lost souls, but any literary echo is muted. There is room for "millions," the terrain divided into lots, rising as high into the arena as the surrounding ditch is deep. Many a visible **body,** but no two ever meet. The reflexive "Se voir" is reduced to the condition of **solipsism.**

closed space: in the mid-1960s SB's fiction turned from stories featuring **motion** toward stillness or barely perceptible movement. The "**necessary journey**" (the urge to **come and go**), a mainstay of his fiction from *Murphy* on, was replaced by the "closed space" stories, a change "announced" in the *faux departs,* which became *All Strange Away* and *Imagination Dead Imagine* and which received its fullest expression in *Nohow On* (qv). As settings change to small cubes or like constrictions (rotunda, **skull,** or **summerhouse**), **Voice** as protagonist gives way to a nameless "him," an **object** of the narrator's devising; and the homophones "seen" and "scene" become coeval (see **character**). Later works pursue an active "unwording of the world," as Carla Locatelli phrases it (see **unword**). There is consolation, even pleasure in so doing, for while the enterprise is doomed the imagination persists, even in the face of its **death.** Rather than reject language SB continued to explore its power as it is reduced, denuded, stripped bare. Images disappear or are discarded from the virtual space of **consciousness,** only to reappear through the imagination's ineluctable visualization and the tenacity of language to represent. Even when imagination is dead, or dying, a perverse consciousness struggles to imagine that death, and from that paradox the "closed space" fiction emerges.

Clov: servant/son to **Hamm** in *Endgame;* possible subject of Hamm's narrative. The name suggests a spice, clove to ham; or **clown** and ham actor; or one who wishes both to leave and to stay ("cleave"). For *clou,* see **crucifixion**. Bound to Hamm by physical needs (the key to the cupboard), emotional bonds (see **pseudocouples**), and metaphysical considerations (the need to **witness**, or to enact the Cartesian **dualism**), Clov yet intimates that on this extraordinary day, like yet unlike the others, something may have "slipped" (see **Zeno**).

clowns: the *reductio* of the **Occasionalist** disjunction of body and mind, arousing **pity** as much as laughter. **Grock**'s "nicht möglich" echoes through *Dream;* **Neary** and **Wylie** represent the **silent movie** (qv). SB's interest in comic routine persists into *Film,* notably Buster **Keaton**'s trials with the **cat** and **dog**. **Bim and Bom**, Stalinist clowns, appear early and remain late. **Watt**'s "funambulistic stagger" (31) derives from the circus, and **Molloy**'s testicles (36) are "decaying circus clowns." In *Waiting for Godot* the two central figures fill their days with "routines": actions generated by **habit** to pass the **time**. Roger **Blin** thought the play should be staged in a circus ring; Peter Hall immortalized the two as tramps. In *Endgame,* "Clov" suggests a clown (foil to a "ham"). **Nagg and Nell** once had the white **faces** of circus clowns, and **Hamm** a red face. **Krapp**'s red nose owed as much to his casting as clown as to his offstage drinking: his clothes were ill-fitting; his shoes white and large; his walk laborious (he nearly slips on a banana skin). SB reduced these details, minimizing the slapstick to accentuate the pathetic or the **gnostic**. Later works are divorced from these traditions, and it is a moot point whether SB's revisions of the "clonic" element lead to a more satisfactory theatrical experience.

coalsack: in the Milky Way, clouds of galactic dust and dark nebulae that reveal a blurred and dirty aspect to the naked eye. SB noted the term (DN, 147) from Sir James Jeans, *The Universe Around Us* (29). *Dream* (16) notes "interstellar coalsacks"; that dismal patch of sky matches **Murphy**'s condition (188); and **Watt** (224) feels similar desolation. The word reverts to its literal meaning (sacks of coal) in *How It Is,* but the sack into which the narrator imagines crawling (10) retains a sense of **asylum**, the **embryo**, the amniotic sac.

Cocteau, Jean (1889–1963): French poet, playwright, and filmmaker, *enfant terrible* of the *avant-garde*. SB dismisses his *Voix Humaine* as "an unnecessary banality" (*Proust,* 26). In 1938 he agreed to translate a preface by Cocteau for Peggy **Guggenheim**'s London show *Les Chevaliers de la table ronde* (Bair, 279). This "Cocteau Preface" is included in F&F (96).

coenaesthesis: the general feeling of existence arising from the sum of bodily feelings, rather than from the definite sensations of the special senses; thus, the vital sense, or, in **Kant**'s terms, the transcendental purpose embodied in the manifold, beneath the threshold of what constitutes **consciousness**. Thus **Belacqua**'s rueful reflection in "**Yellow**" (172), that his sufferings under the anaesthetic will be exquisite, but he would not remember them. SB took the word from **Nordau**'s *Degeneration* (249), and defines it (DN, 96): "general sensibility. Dimly perceived cellular organic Ego not involving cerebral consciousness." He distinguishes prenatal coenaesthesia from the exasperated coenaesthesia, the latter somatic, "monopolising consciousness of degenerate subject, distorting, excluding the **not-I**" (in Nordau's sense, the altruistic realm, as opposed to the egotistic). Casually used, it implies undirected feeling, as in "**Love and Lethe**": "the coenaesthesis of the consultant when he finds the surgeon out" (99); or "**Draff**" (175), when the **Smeraldina** experiences "a teary coenaesthesis." Belacqua dismisses the magic of dawn and dusk as "no more than the tumultuous coenaesthesis (bravo!) of the degenerate subject" (*Dream,* 32). He determines (123) to flog on his coenaesthesis, to expunge his consciousness. **Molloy** admits (54) that "coenaesthetically speaking" he feels more or less the same as usual; a state at odds with the "vigilant coenaesthesia" of the first Dialogue with Georges **Duthuit** (101). To Mary **Manning** (30 August 1937) SB described: "an end to the temptation of light, its polite scorching & considerations. It is food for children and insects. There is an end of making up one's mind, like a pound of tea. An end of putting the butter of consciousness into opinions. The real consciousness is the chaos, a grey commotion of mind." This is Kant's "Zweckmassigkeit ohne Zweck" ("purposiveness without purpose"), but denied its transcendental validation. SB describes the "coenaesthesic" as "a fullness of mental self-aesthesia that is entirely useless," the experience of the **monad** without conflict, lightless and darkless: "I used to dig about in the mental sand for the lugworms of likes and dislikes," but now (he says) he does

so no longer: "the lugworms of understanding." The passage offers a remarkable gloss on the third zone of **Murphy's mind**.

Coffey, Brian (1905–95): Dublin poet singled out for rare praise in "**Recent Irish Poetry**" (76); his rigor, Christian existentialism, and neo-Thomism distinguishing him from the **antiquarians**. SB approved his experiments with rhythm and syntax to dislocate perception and alienate language. He told **MacGreevy** that while Coffey was good on his subject, "the poetry is another pair of sleeves" (9 January 1935; Coughlan, 65). Coffey introduced SB to **Spinoza**, and in **Paris** (1937) they played **billiards** and avoided Peggy **Guggenheim**. Coffey later edited **Denis Devlin**'s *Collected Poems* (1964).

cogito: Descartes's *cogito, ergo sum* ("I think, therefore I am"), responding to **Augustine**'s *fallor, ergo sum* ("I err, therefore I am"), as in *Whoroscope*. This is the linchpin of Cartesian doubt, as outlined in the *Method* (1637) and *Meditations* (1642). To establish a firm base for his philosophy, Descartes resolved to doubt all that he could. What remained (he asserted), could not be doubted: the evidence of existence, not in the awareness of the **body** but in **consciousness** of being, a proposition so certain, so clear and distinct, that the most extravagant skepticism could not upset it. This is the Cartesian kernel, making mind more certain than matter, which is knowable, if at all, by inference from what is known of mind. For all its clarity, the formulation is problematic: if "I think" is the ultimate premise, does this assert an identity between "I am a *thing* which thinks" and "there are thoughts"? Descartes uses the categories of **scholasticism**, and nowhere proves that thoughts need a thinker. This disjunction would have profound consequences for SB's doubts concerning the origins of **memory, voice,** and **character,** as in l'**Innommable**'s refrain (177): "Ma voix. La voix"; or **Krapp** moving into the darkness, "then back here to . . . [*hesitates*] . . . me. [*Pause.*] Krapp."

Coleridge-Taylor, Samuel (1875–1912): English composer whose father was from Sierra Leone; best known for *Hiawatha's Wedding Feast* (1897). Popular in their day, his works became a byword for banality; hence the irony in *Murphy* (215) of "Coleridge-Taylor played with feeling." SB's French equivalent, rather unfairly, was Gounod.

Collected Poems: the first collection of SB's poems since *Echo's Bones, Poems in English* appeared (1961) from **Grove Press** and John **Calder** (rpt. Calder and Boyars, 1968 and 1971). It includes: *Whoroscope* (1930), *Echo's Bones* (1935), "**Cascando**" (1936) and "**Saint-Lô**" (1946), and "**Quatre poèmes**"—English and French versions of "**Dieppe**" (1937) and three poems (1948): "**my way is in the sand flowing,**" "**what would I do without this world,**" and "**I would like my love to die.**" The Calder and Boyars editions offer an alternative last line to "I would like my love to die" ("mourning she who sought to love me"). The Grove and all Calder editions contain an uncorrected anomaly, an abbreviated "Contents" page listing only one of the "Quatre poèmes," "Dieppe."

An expanded *Collected Poems in English and French* appeared from Grove and Calder (1977). It includes: three uncollected English poems, "**Gnome**" (1934), "**Ooftish**" (1938), and "**Home Olga**" (1934); later poems like "**dread nay**" (1974), "**Roundelay**" (1976), and "**thither**" (1976); more poems in French (1937–39; of these only "Dieppe" was in the 1961 collection); six untranslated French poems (1947–49), "**bon bon il est un pays,**" "**Mort de A.D.,**" "**vive morte ma seule saison,**" added to those of 1961; "Poème 1974," which contains "**hors crâne seul dedans**" and "**Something there**" (changed to "Poems 1974" in the following edition); translations of Paul **Éluard** from *This Quarter,* **Rimbaud**'s "Le Bateau ivre," and **Apollinaire**'s "**Zone**"; and *Huit maximes* called "Long after **Chamfort**." This edition included notes. Calder published a third edition, *Collected Poems 1930–1978* (1984). This adds: the *mirlitonnades* of 1976–78, in French only; "**Song,**" the first of two poems from "**Words and Music**"; and "**Tailpiece**" from the "Addenda" to *Watt.* This third edition is not available from Grove.

Calder had promised, and even advertised, a "Collected Poems 1930–1984," but when the 1984 edition was reissued (1999) nothing was added. This was partly due to permissions refused by Jérôme **Lindon,** but was far from complete. The juvenilia remained uncollected, as were early translations and late poems such as "**What Is the Word,**" "**Là,**" and "**Brief Dream.**" Items that have recently emerged, such as "**Antipepsis**" and "**One**

Dead of Night," are absent; the final two *mirlitonnades* are missing. The 1999 re-issuing underlined the need for a comprehensive edition. This condition was emphatically not met when *Poems 1930–1989* appeared in 2002 with the addition of "What Is the Word" and a few other previously uncollected items, for it includes such blunders as the attribution of the *Anthology of Mexican Poetry* to "Vittorio Paz," a mistranscription of the final "mue" as "mine" in "comme au / berceau," and the bizarre inclusion among the "Late Poems" of a stanza from Robert Browning's "Epilogue to Asolando." In the words of David Wheatley (*TLS*, 3 May 2002, 16), the "complete" edition is a "monumental screw-up."

Collected Shorter Plays: the first collection of SB's plays, excluding *Waiting for Godot, Endgame, Happy Days,* and *Eleutheria* but including "The Old Tune." *CSP* was published by Grove Press and Faber (1984) in both hardback and paperback. Although accepted as the best available, it contains unrevised texts of *Krapp's Last Tape*, "What Where," and "Quad," and an incomplete *Come and Go*. See *Theatrical Notebooks*.

Colossus of Memnon: having found his "little creature" Malone describes him (227) "stiff and set," like "the Colossus of Memnon, dearly loved son of Dawn." One of two sandstone statues, twenty meters high, guardians of ancient Thebes, sons of Eos, goddess of the Dawn, and the Nubian god Tithonus. It emits a strange musical sound: Dawn caresses her son, and he replies. Compare *Still* (241): "that old statue some old god twanged at sunrise and again at sunset." The old woman of *Ill Seen Ill Said* adopts (69): "the rigid Memnon pose." [LM]

Come and Go: a one-act "dramaticule" (SB's coinage) written in English (January 1965) and simultaneously translated into French as "**Va et vient**." First production in German, "Kommen und Gehen," at the **Schiller-Theater**, Berlin (14 January 1966), dir. Deryk **Mendel** with Lieselotte Rau as Lo (Flo), Charlotte Joeres as Mei (Vi), and Sybylle Gilles as Su (Ru). The first English production was at the Peacock Theatre, **Dublin** (28 February 1968), dir. Edward Golden with Deirdre Purcell, Aideen O'Kelly, and Kathleen Barrington. The first **London** production was at Royal Festival Hall (9 December 1968), dir. William Gaskill with Joan Plowright, Billie **Whitelaw**, and Peggy Ashcroft. It was later part of "a gala entertainment concerning depravity and corruption," a fund-raising event also at the Royal Festival Hall (23 March 1968), dir. Deryk Mendel with Adrienne Corri, Marie Kean, and Billie Whitelaw, the full text published in *The Arts and Censorship* for the National Council for Civil Liberties and the Defense of Literature and the Arts Society (London: Farlan Press, 1968). The first New York production was at the Theater for the New City (23 October 1975).

Written for and dedicated to John Calder, the play was published in the UK not by Faber but by Calder and Boyars (1967) in an edition of 2,000 copies, with a limited edition of 100 copies bound in buckram and signed by SB.

The opening lines were omitted from the first edition. SB's proofing did not result in their restoration, and although they appeared in the first American edition (1968), and in the French and German translations, subsequent English texts by Faber, as well as *CDW* and *CSP*, were based on the 1967 Calder and Boyars text, and lack the fugitive lines. However, they are in a text edited by Breon Mitchell for *Modern Drama* 19.3 (1976): 245–54. A trilingual edition, forty-five numbered copies illustrated by H. M. Erhardt (Stuttgart: Manus Press, 1968), includes a facsimile of SB's English text.

The play echoes **Eliot**'s "In the room the women come and go," but its situation the witches of *Macbeth:* "When did we three last meet?" It originates in SB's **memory** of his cousins, daughters of Rubina (Ru?) Roe, at Miss **Wade**'s. SB wrote to Jacoba **van Velde**, his Dutch translator: "I imagine a stone lion in the playground of the school. They used to sit on it together side by side" (Knowlson, 473). That image generated three florid characters, originally Viola, Poppy, and Rose, then Vi, Ru, and Flo. The drama is simple: three school friends now of indeterminable age sit huddled on an invisible bench, until one leaves temporarily. The visual patterning is strictly symmetrical: as each departs the remaining two close the gap, and one whispers a confidence to the other, unknown to the absent one and greeted with horror. In an early draft this is met with the **auditor**'s "Good Heavens," a title SB used for one draft. Each is finally moribund but mercifully ignorant. As SB wrote to van Velde: "They are 'condemned' all three" (Knowlson, 473). The apparent simplicity, the spare brush strokes of a Chinese painting or W. B. **Yeats**'s late drama, is the result of many rewrites, one showing two women exchanging sexual confidences to explain the health and vigor of one of them and the unhappy prognosis of the one absent. They read aloud from cheap romantic novels. Such sexual motifs are replaced by images of mortality. The closing image is enigmatic. As they cross hands Flo says, "I can feel the rings"; but in his comments on costume SB notes, "No rings apparent." They may be imagined, a symbol of the frustrated hopes of youth, of marriages that never occurred; or equally their eternal union, Vaughan's eternity, a ring of pure and endless light.

"Comédie": SB's translation of "**Play**," first published as "Comédie. Un acte de Samuel Beckett" in *Les Lettres nouvelles* 12 (juin-juillet-août 1964): 10–31; then in *Comédie et actes divers* (Minuit, 1966), with a special edition of eighty-seven numbered copies. Contents: "Comédie. Pièce en un acte"; "**Va et vient**," "**Cascando**," "**Paroles et musique**," "**Dis Joe**," and "**Acte sans paroles II**." This was the first commercial printing of each. "Comédie" also appeared in *Panorama du théâtre nouveau*, ed. Jacques Benay and Reihard Kuhn (New York: Appleton-Century-Crofts, 1967), I, 17–34. Another reprinting, not specified as a second edition, appeared in 1972, adding "**Acte sans paroles I**," *Film*, and "**Souffle**." The first **Paris** production was on 14 juin 1964 (ten days late), dir. Jean-Marie Serreau, with Eléonore Hirt (**W1**), Delphine Seyrig (**W2**), and Michael Lonsdale (**M**).

SB was involved in the rehearsals, his first sustained such venture. It laid the foundations for his later choreography of sound and silence, light and dark, **motion** and stillness, and was the basis of the 1966 film version, directed by Mariu **Karmitz**.

Comestor, Peter (d. 1178): theologian whose name "Comestor" acknowledged his prowess as a bookworm, his "digesting" of knowledge. Translated to **Paris**, he finished his *Historia scholastica,* a sacred narrative of the **Bible** and the source of **Moran**'s speculation (166) that the serpent walked upright: *tunc serpens erectus est ut homo* (*Liber Genesis,* c.xxi).

coming and going: if SB's writing illustrates a single biblical text, it would be Psalms 121:8: "The Lord shall preserve thy going out and thy coming in from this time forth, and even for evermore"; as in the *laetus exitus* theme of **Thomas à Kempis**, the glad going out and sad return. The motif underlines not so much the Lord's preservation as the transitory nature of the phenomenal world. Two statements best define the sentiment: the endless coming and going of the servants of Mr. **Knott**, who abides; and the **Unnamable**, who having asserted that you must come and go or else you are dead finds he must go **on**.

Comment c'est: a novel in three parts, called a "roman" on the cover but not the title page, and resembling a dramatic monologue. The original title *Pim* was bracketed until the **pun** on "Commencez" became irresistible. SB started writing ("17.12.58") at **Ussy** but two years later was still struggling with it. It was "horribly difficult," and the need to complete became obsessive. The first writing was finished in January 1960; and a substantial rewriting by "7.6.60"; revision continued until it went to **Minuit** at the end of summer. After some difficulties with the printer it appeared early in 1961, 3,000 copies, with a limited edition of 198; 3,000 more were reprinted (Mars 1961), and again (Janvier 1964). Extracts appeared as: "L'**Image**" in *X* (novembre 1959); "**Découverte de Pim**" in *L'VII* (décembre 1959); and "**From an Unabandoned Work**" in *Evergreen Review* (September–October 1960). The English translation, begun in 1960, proved equally arduous, and *How It Is* (qv) was not published until 1964.

The autograph manuscript (HRHRC #273) consists of six dense notebooks containing 477 pages of close writing, including 108 pages of revisions. These confirm the difficulty, with extensive deletions, doodles, diagrams, and calculations. The first drafts bear little resemblance to the final sparse prose, but the last two notebooks begin the process of revision. Yet that continued incessantly, for the **BIF** (Reading) also holds many pages of notes, drafts, and typescripts. The slow progress reflects the isolation of **fundamental sounds**: transition from the imperfect to the **mythological present**, deletion of punctuation, simplification of diction, and the evolution of final subdivisions, every movement through the mud meticulously planned. The **residua** of *Comment c'est* testify to the strenuous activity that went into what is finally a short text.

"Comment dire": a poem written in October 1988; SB's last original work, the "word" seeking utterance being "folie." Marginal notes to seven drafts (RUL 3316/1) reflect the care that went into this deceptively simple poem. See "**What Is the word.**"

Compagnie/ Company: a long prose-poem written in English, transposed into **French**, then retranslated into English. The French text appeared first (Minuit, 1980); followed by the English (Calder, 1980); then the American (Grove, 1982). *Company* is the first in a second series of **three novels** (*Ill Seen Ill Said* and *Worstward Ho*) with the collective title *Nohow On*. It has been frequently performed (see **adaptations** and **Mabou Mines**). The piece is dominated by scenes of SB's early life recurrent in his work that assailed him psychologically until the end. Many are painful. The **child** in these **memories** seems never to have been the boy his parents wanted. They suggest a loveless childhood where he was rebuked for his comment on the sun (11), or ridiculed for saying he could see the mountains of Wales from his "nook in the gorse" (25). There are loveless parents "stooping over cradle" (47), a lack of concern for a child who throws himself from "the top of a great fir" (21), the embarrassment of the child on exhibition at "the tip of a high board" (18; see **diving board**). And cruelty: "A small **boy** you come out of Connolly's store holding your mother by the hand" (10); his question about the distance of the moon from earth engenders "a cutting retort you have never forgotten" (11). The retort is sharper in "The **End**" (50): "Fuck off, she said";

and clinically cold in *Malone Dies* (268): "It is precisely as far away as it appears to be."

Voice recounts embarrassing incidents: the boy who played **God** by intervening in the life of a hedgehog; the child who looked out the **summerhouse** window to see that "all without is rosy" (39); the youth who believed his path was straight, "a beeline" (35), but one morning sees the helicoidal pattern in the fresh snow, "Withershins" (38). The incident is wryly comic even as it suggests the plight of one living the sinistral spiral of **Dante**'s hell. Even the sensual moments are painful. The young man's erotic feeling of the "fringe of her long black hair" (48) is intimately connected to the lover's pregnancy, with its **pun** about her being late, and the disastrous end, "All dead still" (42).

These scenes have tempted some to suggest that *Company* is coded autobiography: "You were born on an Easter Friday after long labour" (34). The mother-haunted *Ill Seen Ill Said* reflects the author's struggle with his own mother; the mystical union of father and son in *Worstward Ho* invokes SB's walks with his father (see "**Silence to Silence**"). This ignores the antiempiricism in these works. In SB's fictive world all is re-presentation, already repetition. The search for an originary model ignores the very nature of these late fictions where the narrator is a "Devised devisor devising it all for company." The narrator is, in *Company*'s persistent pun, "lying" from the first. If certain images parallel SB's life, this says little about their fictional function. Childhood experiences, like literary allusions, are "figments," "traces," "fables," or "shades," mixing memory and **desire** with imagination.

Company, like other "**closed space**" tales, is neither memoir nor autobiography, but a set of devised images of one devising images. It is an interplay of voices, a fugue between a hearer, "Himself," or "**W**," imagining himself into existence, and an external voice addressing him as "you" or "**M**." The voice's goal is "To have the hearer have a past and acknowledge it" (34). It is a pronominal *pas de deux*. Hearer is puzzled because the voice is not only sourceless but false, not his; the "life" it describes is not "his," the tale not autobiographical: "Only a small part of what is said can be verified" (7). Past images sound as in *Watt* (74): "an instant in the life of another, ill told, ill heard, and more than half forgotten." Memories are images ill seen and ill said. The voices of *Company* are fictions, figments of imagination whose function is aesthetic play, company for a narrator who is finally "as you always were. Alone" (63). The company of *Company*, then, is not nostalgic **Proustian** memory, the past recaptured, but the solitary solace of "conjuring of something out of **nothing**" (53).

Complete Dramatic Works (*CDW*): a tribute for SB's eightieth birthday, this case-bound edition became a textual farce. When **Faber** collected "all" SB's plays they inexplicably reprinted the bowdlerized 1956 *Waiting for Godot* (see **censorship**). The paperback corrected the blunder. Like *Collected Shorter Plays*, *CDW* includes unrevised texts of *Krapp's Last Tape*, "What

Where," and "**Quad**," an incomplete *Come and Go*, and it omits *Eleutheria*.

Complete Short Prose: SB's shorter fiction, 1929–89, ed. S. E. Gontarski (Grove, 1995); technically not complete, as permission was refused for "**Echo's Bones**." In "Notes on the Texts" Gontarski indicates the key issues: determination of "accurate" texts; corrections to "**Assumption**" and early works; British revisions not in American printings ("**First Love**"), and vice versa (*All Strange Away*); corrections to *The Lost Ones*, "**neither**," and *Stirrings Still;* clarification of the confusion about "The **Capital of the Ruins**"; and new translations by Edith Fournier of "L'**Image**" and "La **Falaise**" for this volume.

Conaire, Mr.: a minor character in *Mercier and Camier*, curiously brawny. He is to meet Camier but is finally told that he is not needed, that he is absent from Camier's thoughts as though he had ceased to be (63–64). Cohn suggests (*Comic Gamut*, 98) that Camier is performing a "conarectomy," removing any possibility of the meeting of **body** and mind.

conarium: the pineal gland, for **Descartes** the one organ with no correlative (single, not paired), and thus the place where **body** and soul have commerce, where animal spirits mingle with metaphysical essences. In **Baillet**'s words (153): "Son sentiment touchant la siège de l'Ame dans le cerveau, qu'il établissait dans la petite glande appellée conaire ou pinéale." Descartes accounted for changes of matter-in-**motion** by reference to extension, and psychic matters by the nature of the mind (see **dualism**). But this did not account for confused ideas (as opposed to "claire et distincte"), nor the passions and emotions they aroused. He proposed that **God** had arranged in man a coexistence of the two substances, so that a disturbance of the "animal spirits" (in the conarium) excited in the mind an unclear idea, whether sensation or emotion. At this point, "by special arrangement with the Deity, the mind is in contact with the nervous organism" (Mahaffy, 177). The **Occasionalists** (qv) disputed this. Even were it correct to identify the conarium as the place where the different spirits were infused, this did not explain the union, and it left unresolved the question of what felt passion, body or mind. **Murphy**'s conarium (5) has "shrunk to nothing" (he is unable to experience passion or any emotion); **Camier** fails to meet M. **Conaire**; and the characters of *Endgame* dubiously enact the vital union.

"**Le Concentrisme**": a literary parody, given in **French** by SB (November 1930) to the Modern Languages Society of **Trinity**; now at Reading (RUL 1396/4/15). Published in *Disjecta* (35–42), some lines overlooked; and translated by John Pilling (Menard Press, 1990). The piece identifies an invented poet by name of Jean du **Chas**, who shares SB's birthday, his affection for indolence and darkness, and knows his **Descartes**, **Racine**, and **Proust**. An unsigned letter purports to be from one who met "cet imbécile" in a Marseilles bar the night before he died, but cannot understand why anyone else

should wish to; nevertheless, du Chas has entrusted his manuscripts to him. The talk begins with du Chas's obsession with the institution of the concierge, the "pierre angulaire" of his "édifice entier." His major work is *Discours de la Sortie*, anticipating his **suicide** in Marseilles. His was a "vie horizontale," with no social dimension, but his journal records opinions, mostly dismissive, on his contemporaries. Du Chas has invented Concentrisme (compare **Unanimisme**), a movement tired of Proust (SB had finished his monograph) and at odds with all that is clear and distinct in Descartes. The essay culminates in the ringing conviction that this new school "est parfairement intelligible et parfaitement inexplicable." Was it intended to fool its audience? SB insisted otherwise, yet it is curiously compelling. No more is heard of Concentrisme, but Jean du Chas continued his virtual existence into *Dream*.

"**Conclusion of *How it is***": the finale of *How It Is*, in *Transatlantic Review* (London) 13 (summer 1963): 5–15, before full publication (1964).

Condom: a town in the department of Gers. It is, as **Moran** appreciates (141), on the Baïse, a tributary of the Gironde. The jest (Fr. *baiser*, "to screw") was added late to the French text ("Condom est arrosé par la Baise").

consciousness: "Why all this fuss and bother about the mystery of unconsciousness?" **Joyce** asked Frank Budgen. "What about the mystery of consciousness?" The topic is too vast for exhaustive treatment here. To trace SB's reading

(**Bergson**, **Descartes**, **Freud**, **Haeckel**, **Jung**, **Nordau**) is a curious journey into psychopathology and **coenaesthesis**. The clearest treatment of the topic, despite its reliance on **Hegel**, Husserl, Sartre, and Heidegger, to whom SB was indifferent, is David Hesla's chapter in *The Shape of Chaos:* "Reduction, Reflection, Negation: Some Versions of Consciousness." This offers a guide to the perplexed, a *vade mecum* to uncharted territory. Hesla's insights are cross-referenced to other entries.

Hesla takes Bergson's position that consciousness is not eliminated: "Consciousness is, and to be is to be conscious. To put it another way, consciousness 'goes **on**'" (58). He cites Descartes (*Method*, IV), in that there was something he could not doubt: "I could not for all that conceive that I was not" (Hesla, 114). **Windelband** (392) calls this a "fundamental rational truth." Hesla discusses in his sixth chapter (one thinks of *Murphy*) the phenomenology of consciousness, and contends that *Three Novels* represent the end (some might say, an *auberge* only) of a long road through territory explored in the earlier writings, beginning with what SB called in *Proust* "the only world that has reality and significance, the world of our own latent consciousness" (13). Hesla asserts (174) that in *The Unnamable* SB enters the transcendental ego and explores it as no other has done. One might note Roa Bastos, *I, the Supreme,* and its debt to the *Trilogy*, or prefer *A la recherche*, but the point holds.

Hesla's argument is simply stated: SB's dynamic oscillation between Cartesian **dualism** and Bergson's concept of mind as the continuously living process (177), summed up in William James's "fundamental fact" that consciousness "goes on" (178); the external world as vague and ambiguous (**Lousse** or Loy? **Edith** or **Ruth**?) when perceived or recalled by the subjective self (179); the splitting of the Ego from consciousness that it may observe its self, yet the rejection of an infinite regressus of perceiving selves in favor of the essential duality or dyad of subject and **object**, that which perceives and that which is perceived (183); **Sartre**'s insistence that consciousness is always consciousness of something (185); the Ego as nonsubstantive but rather constituted *from* states of consciousness (185); and the crucial distinction between consciousness and that of which consciousness is conscious (186). In his insistence that one cannot say "I am conscious," for this implies that consciousness is a thing that "I" can possess, Hesla anticipates later legions of SB's critics who have explored the bottomless abyss, the deconstruction (Hesla predates this term) of the Cartesian or Kantian transcendental subject to the "**Not I.**"

In summarizing Hesla's summary one might repeat his prayer: "God send I don't make a balls of it":

1. *Consciousness is nothing:* being is, and is all that is; consciousness stands outside being and interrogates it. See **nothing**.
2. *Consciousness is intentionality:* it exists as consciousness *of* something. See **object**.
3. *Consciousness is reflexivity:* for it may be conscious of itself. In Hesla's

example (189), while I suffer I must be conscious that I suffer. See **Schopenhauer**.

4. *Consciousness is freedom:* in virtue of its ability to oppose being it may stand outside the causal nexus that otherwise is the law of being. See **Geulincx**.

5. *Consciousness is not in-itself* (*en-soi*) but *for-itself* (*pour-soi*); it is separated from itself by virtue of its reflexivity. Consciousness is always and simultaneously consciousness *of* and consciousness of being conscious *of.* See **apperception**.

Hesla concludes: "When consciousness posits some transcendent object in the world, it is accompanied by the pre-reflective cogito, but when it posits itself it becomes the reflective cogito. When consciousness reflects upon itself, it structures itself as reflecting and reflected" (186). Hence the consciousness that says "I think" is not the consciousness that thinks (187). This reflexive structure of consciousness constitutes the "self" and so the term indicates a duality-within-unity: the self is itself as "the reflecting-reflected dyad" (188). But the fact that it is present to itself indicates that there is within the self a **gulf**, an impalpable fissure, and this fissure is Nothingness. This is the territory of the *Three Novels,* the littoral margin that the transcendental Ego may reach (**Molloy** beside the sea, *Malone Dies*). Hesla contends that this reflexive structure of consciousness he has laid out is the model of the self that SB comes to in the third volume, the culmination of all that has gone before, and the point of departure for later works. In a phrase, that is how it is.

Constance (1154–98): wife of the Holy Roman Emperor Henry VI. Once a nun, she was forced into a political marriage; in *Dream* (130), "one whose heart we are told was never loosed of its veil" (**Dante**, *Par.* III.117: "non fu dal vel del cor già mai disciolta").

contingency: **Murphy**'s wish to retreat into the **little world** is frustrated by his **desire** for **Celia** and ginger biscuits (168), by "contingencies of the contingent world." **Windelband** notes (398) that **Leibniz** distinguished between truths that are self-evident (the opposite unthinkable) and facts of experience (the opposite possible). In the former, intuitive certainty rests on the *Principle of Contradiction;* with the latter, on the *Principle of Sufficient Reasoning,* which asserts conditional necessity, contingency. This distinction underlies **Kant**'s analytic versus synthetic reasoning, and is fundamental to **Schopenhauer**, who explains (*WWI,* II.I.xvi, 354) why possessions and pleasures, which are goods, are nevertheless matters of indifference in a world independent of our will.

Cooldrinagh: SB's family home in **Foxrock**, at the junction of Brighton Road and Kerrymount Avenue; built by William **Beckett** in 1903, with dark mahogany paneling, a wide stairway, and a spacious garden. Phone: Foxrock 37 (O'Brien lists 87, a wrong number). SB was born in an upstairs room with a bow window looking west toward the **Dublin** mountains, probably that in which he was conceived (*Company,* 15). The Gaelic name means "back of the blackthorn hedge." The house serves as **Belacqua**'s home, and that of **Moran** and Mr. **Knott**, with such features as the wicket gate, **larches**, chimney stack with four flues, red-tiled kitchen, and **summerhouse**.

Cooper: in *Murphy*, **Neary**'s *âme damnée*, one-eyed and triorchous (three testicles). His one humane [*sic*] quality is a morbid craving for alcoholic depressant. He resembles "a destitute diabetic in a strange city" (this added to the typescript). His *acasthisia*, or inability to sit, is deep-seated and of long standing (see the OED). His name suggests the brew, half porter, half stout, of barrel makers (coopers). See also **Cooper, William** and "**orange peel.**"

Cooper, Becky: madame of a Dublin brothel that survived the 1926 closures and which SB visited, as recounted to **MacGreevy** (9 October 1931): "I looked into Becky Cooper's the other night and drank a 1/- bottle of stout." He saw on the wall of that "filthy **kip**" a reproduction of **Beatrice**, "sneered," and (he told Lawrence Harvey) was thrown out. In "Sanies II," these **memories** return as the atmosphere changes from enchantment to terror.

Cooper, Rev. William M., B.A.: identified by Pilling (DN, 47) as James Glass Bertram, a Victorian writer of books on fish and flowers, who compiled *Flagellation and the Flagellants* (1869; 544 pp.), "a true History of the Rod as an instrument for correctional purposes in the Church, the State and the Family." It is a curious compendium of learning and prurience; SB took extensive notes. Several details entered "Sanies II" (chastise-

ment), and *Dream* (fantasia on the human bottom). Other borrowings include: Dr. Keate of Eton ("Echo's Bones," 3), to whom all boys' backsides were alike; Dr. Busby of Westminster (*Murphy*, 97), who whipped them; the name "Caleken" for the **Frica**; a poem cited by **Chas** (*Dream*, 231); and "**cang.**" Mrs. **Nixon**'s strings are severed by one Professor Cooper (*Watt*, 15).

Coppée, François (1842–1908): French poet and dramatist who idealized the working class, the "ineffable gutter-snippets" dismissed in *Proust* (80).

Cork: Gaelic *corcaigh*, "marshy ground"; **Ireland**'s second city of ships and spires, and bumpkins from the Skerries. Contiguous with Gomorrha (*Watt*, 156). **Neary's Pythagorean** academy is there. Nearby Cobh was the ferry terminal to the continent (see the "Und" section of *Dream*). SB passed through en route to **Kassel** (1928 and 1936); the first entry in the **German Diaries** sketches the grave of Father **Prout** in Shandon Churchyard.

corncrake: in "**Walking Out**" (111) **Belacqua** hears the first corncrake (land rail) of the season, but fails to heed the **death** rattle implicit in the zoological name, *Crex crex*. His poem is dismissed as "corncrakes' Chinese chromatisms" (*Dream*, 70). **Murphy**'s telephone bursts into its "rail" and he is mocked by its "loud calm crake" (7). **Molloy** hears their awful cries (16), and associates them with the "rattle" of his **mother**.

Corneille, Pierre (1606–84): French classical dramatist, greatest of his day before a decline in his powers and rivalry with **Racine** diminished his reputation. SB preferred Racine's inward intensity of suffering to Corneille's outward action. SB's only stage appearance was in "Le **Kid**" (qv), a travesty of Corneille's *Le Cid.*

Costello, Nuala: an Irishwoman whom SB met in **Paris** through Lucia **Joyce**. He saw her in **Dublin**, becoming a little *amouraché* ("smitten") (Knowlson, 179); but his ardor soon cooled. He described her to **MacGreevy** (8 September 1935) as an "unclitoridian companion." In 1975 copies of "Le **Concentrisme**" and SB's translation of **Rimbaud**'s "**Drunken Boat**," both believed lost, turned up in her library. After her **death** (1984) they were left to the **BIF**.

Counihan, Miss: an Irish colleen, first name unknown, erstwhile beloved of **Murphy**, in **London**, she believes, to make her way in the Big World. The name intimates the cornice of **desire**, **Cathleen ni Houlihan**, Nancy **Cunard**, and **Voltaire**'s Counégonde. The subplot finds her launched in picaresque pursuit of Murphy. Her humiliation is complete when **Celia**, her rival, identifies Murphy's charred remnants by the nevus on the **buttock**.

"Coups de gong": an unpublished dramatic fragment from the 1950s (RUL 2931/2932), originally entitled "Espace souterrain," one character (*l'Englouti*) buried to the waist and sinking. The four names suggest an infinite series. *L'Englouti* disappears before a word is spoken, to the arhythmic strokes of a

gong; *l'Anonyme* counts the gong-strokes; a third, **Camier**, offers a continual murmur; a fourth, *l'Envoye,* appears on a rope from the flies. There are two holes, which Camier and *l'Anonyme* stand over; a rope is attached to *l'Anonyme*'s neck and to that of the sinking *l'Englouti,* but the former frees himself before being dragged into the hole. *L'Envoye* inspects the hole and nearly falls in, then he inspects the medals (gongs?) of Camier and *l'Anonyme,* before exiting to leave *l'Anonyme* to deliver a monologue on his loss and suffering, beating himself rhythmically as he does.

the Cox: second wife of **Neary**, first name "Ariadne" intimating her desertion (as Theseus at Naxos). Her surname, more pippin than orange, suggests dementia praecox, a form of **schizophrenia** (204). At the end of *Murphy,* she swallows 110 aspirins (compare *Ulysses,* "POST 110 PILLS"). A Mr. Cox, no relation, is among the Philistines at the end of *Watt.*

Craig, John (1663–1731): Scottish **mathematician** and friend of Newton, but one of the first to use **Leibniz**'s notation. In 1699 he published the *Theologiae Christianiae Principia Mathematica,* which applied probability to show that evidence of the truth of the gospels diminishes through time, reaching 0 in the year 3144, thus the limit of the Second Coming. **Moran** asks (167): "The algebraic theology of Craig. What is one to think of this?"

Cream: in *Watt* (15), there on the night that **Larry** was born; his potting is extraordinary, until the **vagitus** puts him off his stroke. He is, naturally, partnered with Berry. An older Cream, perhaps the father (for his son is Judge of the County Courts), appears in "The **Old Tune**"; **Gorman** mentions a Molly Berry.

Crécy: Arsene mentions (*Watt*, 44) the "void and bony concavity" that reminded his old tutor of the battle of Crécy (26 August 1346). SB first wrote "Agincourt" (25 October 1415); the change intimates **Proust**'s Odette.

Crémieux, Benjamin (1888–1944): critic of modern European literature, known for his translations of Pirandello, who died in Buchenwald. Disparaged in *Dream* (68), presumably for his studies of **Proust** (1924 and 1929).

cricket: a game SB played at **Portora** and **Trinity**. A left-hand batsman but a right-hand bowler of medium-paced off-breaks, and a good fieldsman, he made the first eleven in his first year at Portora and with Geoffrey **Thompson** became an established opening bat. He went on the University's two tours of England (1926 and 1927), each ending with a thrashing by Northamptonshire, losing by an innings and plenty. In the first match SB scored 18 and 12, and bowled 8 overs for 17 runs; in the second he made 4 and 1, then was 0 for 47 off 15 overs, but took two catches (Knowlson, 75–76; the note in the British edition [717] is omitted in the American). These were first-class fixtures, so SB is the only **Nobel Prize** winner mentioned in *Wisden,* the cricketers' bible (which has an error, as SB was bowled for 4 by Towell, not Powell). SB enjoyed watching cricket, spending the occasional day at Lords.

"Cri de Coeur": in the **Leventhal** collection at the **HRHRC**, an intermediate title for the three poems later named "**Serena**," each also listed by its original first line: "I Put Pen to This"; "This Seps of a World"; and "Gape at this Pothook of Beauty."

Croagh Patrick: a ridge (2,510 ft.) at Clew Bay, Mayo. St. Patrick reputedly fasted there for forty days, so pilgrims climb it before dawn on Garland Sunday (late July). In "**Serena II**" the Kerry Blue bitch dreams of that Western World, on a "Sabbath evening of garlands" ("Sabbath" has **Schopenhauer**'s sense of temporary respite from suffering).

Croak: the ancient Lord (compare Boss **Croker**) who calls for "**Words and Music**" to treat of **love**, then groans as the song invokes involuntary **memory**. Traditionally (compare Strauss's *Capriccio*), he is arbiter as the two **arts** contend for supremacy until reconciled in song; here Words set to **Music** invoke the pain of imperfect pitch and old age.

Croce, Benedetto (1866–1952): Italian philosopher, who defined abstract philosophy as the discovery and formulation of the immanent methodology of history. His views (expounded from 1903 in his journal, *La Critica*) led to a systematic exposition of the Philosophy of the Spirit. This manifests itself as **art** in the first form of knowledge; then, in the second or cognitive grade, it effects a synthesis between the individual and the universal. Such notions inform *La filosofia di Giambattista Vico* (1911), offering SB a point of departure and disagreement in his "**Dante**" essay, which draws heavily on it.

Croker's Acres: near **Cooldrinagh** on the Ballyogan Road; fields used by "Boss" Croker (1841–1922), who made his money at Tammany Hall. O'Brien (45–51) traces references to the Acres in "**Walking Out**" (101); *Company* (30–31); and *Not I* (220). He corrects the reference to the burial place of "Pretty Polly," the filly mentioned in "Walking Out," but oddly insists that SB has confused the sad nag Joss (*Watt*, 236) with Orby, winner of the Epsom Derby. In "**Rough for Theatre II**," testaments from "Mrs Aspasia Budd-Croker" and "Mrs Darcy-Croker," suggest that C may be named Croker. The protagonist of "**Words and Music**" is "Croak," a defunctive name in direct line of descent.

cromlech: a dolmen, part of a megalithic stone circle: two upright stones bearing a flat table stone. O'Brien identifies the one in *Watt* (49) as that at Glen Druid.

Crowder, Henry: friend and lover of Nancy **Cunard**, to whom she dedicated *Negro* (1934). SB wrote for him "**From the only Poet to a Shining Whore**" (qv). The poem appeared in *Henry-Music* (Paris: Hours Press, 1930, 12–14), the cover featuring a photomontage by Man Ray of Nancy's African sculptures and ivory bracelets, with Crowder part of the design.

crucifixion: SB was born on Friday the 13 in April 1906, Good Friday, as intimated in *Company:* "You first saw the light of day on the day **Christ** died" (20). Crucifixion refines the cruelty of being alive. Comparing himself to Christ, **Estragon** adds: "And they crucified quick" (*WG*, 34.b). As "**Ooftish**" testifies, SB could not accept any theological explanation of a **God**, certainly not a loving one, to account for the suffering of existence, and he rejected the notion that all must contribute to the "postgolgothian kitty" of senseless pain. Jack **Yeats** had said that he could work back from cruelty to original sin; this SB could not accept. His remains a world of inexplicable pain, which manifests itself in images of crucifixion.

"**Enueg I**" presents a dying barge, with "a cargo of nails and timber." Martin Esslin tells of this poem being read on the BBC, and SB asking for more stress on this detail, "which, after all, stood for the cross" (*Beckett at Sixty*, 56). **Molloy** sees (26): "a cargo of nails and timber, on its way to some carpenter I suppose." Compare Vonnegut's *Slaughterhouse-Five*, which SB later admired, Joseph and his son commissioned to make a cross. **Rank**'s *Trauma of Birth* (138) defines **crucifixion** as "the prevention of the **embryonal** position"; that is, constraining the desire to return to the womb, of curling in the fetal position. In "**Dante and the Lobster**" (14) the grocer flings out his arms "in a wild crucified gesture of supplication"; the lobster, "exposed cruciform on the oilcloth" (21), makes a faint nervous act of life. **Belacqua** imagines the **Alba**'s back as a cross-potent and "a bird crucified on a wall" (*Dream*, 205). In bed he spreads his arms like the transepts of a cross (52). **Murphy** is found in a "crucified position" (28); his toil from King's Cross is a Via Dolorosa (73); and his last night begins "at the foot of the cross" (236). **Watt**'s journey to Mr. **Knott**'s house intimates the Stations of the Cross. A **ravanastron** hangs from a nail, like a plover (71). Watt crumples "into his post-crucified position" (140). Mr. Ash has a watch with a crucifix (45); compare **Pozzo**'s sense of crucifixion by **time**. In "The **Calmative**," bats are "flying crucifixions" (64). Molloy's **mother** mingles with images of other women, which is "like being crucified" (59); his progress is "a veritable calvary" (78). **Moran**'s knee "excruciates" him (139). Mrs. **Lambert**'s crucifix hangs from a nail (213). SB added "lacrosse" to *Footfalls*, he said, because of its connotations. "**Dialogue between Ernest and Alice**" plays at the foot of a cross; *Endgame* begins with Christ's dying words and is replete with hammers and nails; and *How It Is* ends with the narrator, arms "spread like a cross," screaming that he will die. *Three Novels* feature such details as the **knife-rest** (63), two linked crosses; Malone's needle stuck into two corks (247); or **Moll**'s earrings (crosses), her one tooth carved as a crucifix, a Christ between **two thieves** (qv). In the **French** text she makes five ritual applications of oral hygiene, "une fois pour chaque blessure" (Bryden, *Idea of God*, 144). Crucifixion pervades *Waiting for Godot*, from the opening dialogue about the two thieves, to the various tableaux in which Pozzo sagging between the two tramps constitutes a visual emblem of the descent

from the Cross, a reminder if another were needed of retribution exacted for the crime of having been born.

Cunard, Nancy (1896–1965): born into wealth and privilege (the Cunard shipping line), Nancy in **Paris** flaunted a lifestyle that others found liberated or outrageous. She was committed to literary innovation, racial justice, and radical politics. In 1928 she founded the **Hours Press** (qv). SB read her *Parallax* (1929), but had "nothing to say." In 1931 she began her major work, *Negro: an Anthology*, inspired by her black lover, Henry **Crowder**. Motivated by her money (£25) or her passion, SB undertook nineteen translations, though he privately thought some of them "miserable rubbish." When Nancy promoted "**Authors Take Sides on the Spanish War**" (1937), SB contributed a brief entry. Her name ("Testew and Cunard") appears six times in **Lucky**'s speech. In 1955 Nancy wrote to SB praising *Godot*. She later asked permission to use *Whoroscope* in her memoir (*These Were the Hours*, 1969). SB agreed, assuring her that *Negro* was still "snug" on his shelves. Contact was maintained until Cunard, by then an anorexic alcoholic, died.

cupio dissolvi: Philippians 1:23: "desiderium habens dissolvi, et esse cum Christo" ("having a **desire** to depart, and to be with **Christ**"); the "Pauline" text (*Dream*, 138).

Cuq-Toulza: a town in the Tarn, in the south of France, mentioned by the curious figure of **Watt** in *Mercier and*

Camier (111), presumably for the oddity of its name.

Curtius, Ernst (1886–1950): German scholar who specialized in the impact of French literature on European culture. Author of *Marcel Proust* (1928). SB acknowledges a "little note" on **Anteros** (*Dream,* 68), and borrows his notion of **Proust**'s perspectivism (*Proust,* 85), notably, his identification of Proust's reading of **Schopenhauer** (Curtius, 70).

cylindrical ruler: the "rule of the father." The **Expelled** (54) visits a lawyer, Mr. **Nidder**: "He played with a cylindrical ruler, you could have felled an ox with it." A **policeman** threatens **Molloy** with one (22). The music master in "**Embers**" intimidates Addie, using it to "beat time," banging it on the piano. Animator in "**Rough for Radio II**" thumps the desk with his. SB's father was a quantity surveyor, and such a ruler, "a solid ebony cylindrical rod," Phil Baker discovered, was kept in the offices of Beckett & Medcalf.

Cythera: where Venus rose from the sea (*Malone,* 237). The phrasing suggests **Watteau**'s *L'Embarquement pour l'île de Cythère,* but see also **Baudelaire**'s "Un Voyage à Cythère."

D

Daiken, Leslie (1912–64): previously Yodaiken, or "Yod," SB's near contemporary at **Trinity**. In **"Recent Irish Poetry"** (75), one who writes verse "when his **politics** let him." His notebooks (**BIF**) record details from SB's lectures.

Dalton, John (1766–1864): English chemist who defined Daltonism, or color blindness; hence "Daltonic visualisations" (*Watt*, 51), handy in picking racing form.

Damals: German translation of *That Time* by Elmar and Erika **Tophoven**. SB delayed the **Suhrkamp** publication until he could revise it with them, and when he staged his production at the **Schiller-Theater Werkstatt** (1 October 1976), with Klaus Herm (whose **Lucky** had met with SB's approval), he revised it again. SB's rehearsal notebook (**RUL** 1976), and those for *Tritte* and *Spiel*, on the same bill, have been published in *The Theatrical Notebooks* IV. See Asmus, "Rehearsal Notes" (*JOBS* 2 [1977]: 92).

Dandieu, Arnaud (1897–1933): librarian and philosopher, whose *Marcel Proust* (1930) underwrites SB's *Proust*. McQueeny argues (107) that Dandieu makes psychology the key to **Proust's** work but SB looks to epistemology and aesthetics. Dandieu sees in Proust a neurotic pessimism, while SB sees it as metaphysical. Dandieu interprets Proust's seclusion as a kind of morbid **suicide**, but for SB it is the renunciation proper to the artistic vocation.

D'Annunzio, Gabriele (1863–1938): Italian poet of Dalmatian extraction, who led a dramatic raid on Fiume (1919) and held it for fifteen months, confounding those who had dismissed him as a decadent aesthete. *Il Fuoco* ("The Flame") (1901) is a lush glorification of Venice. SB, unimpressed, implicitly agreed with Praz (388) that he was the **Hugo** of Decadence. He condemns the misunderstanding of the Proustian stasis: "D'A seems to think they are merely pausing between fucks. Horrible. He has a dirty squelchy mind, bleeding and bursting like his celebrated pomegranates" (SB to TM, 7 July 1930). These return in the **memory** of Venice, "where the waters wither and rot and pomegranates bleed their sperm" (*Dream*, 188). Earlier, the rejection was more temperate: "You couldn't experience a margarita in d'Annunzio because he denies you the pebbles and flints that reveal it" (48). The "precious margaret" (pearl) is hidden, *abscondita* (see **Thomas à Kempis**); the flyblown style conceals its sparkle amidst the ashes.

"Dans le cylindre": a passage in *Livres de France* 18.1 (janvier 1967): 23–24, an issue dedicated to SB; with minor variants, the penultimate paragraph of *Le Dépeupleur* (1970) and *The North* (1972). The title echoes **Éluard's** "Dans le cylindre des tribulations."

117

Dante Alighieri (1265–1321): Italian poet, whose childhood **love** for **Beatrice** Portinari was his lifelong inspiration. Banned from **Florence** (1302), he resided in various places before retiring to Ravenna (his tomb is discussed in *Dream*, 220). Dante's masterpiece is the *Commedia* ("*divina*" was bestowed later); SB also read his *Vita nuova* (1293); *Convivio* (1304?); *De vulgari eloquentia* (1306?); and *Monarchia*, a political treatise (1310). The *Commedia* recounts Dante's journey from the "dark wood" of the world and self through Hell, **Purgatory**, and Paradise. He is guided by Virgil through the Inferno, a vast conical hollow with three divisions (incontinence, violence, and malice), reaching from the City of Dis through the Malebolge (abode of **Malacoda**) to the earth's center where Lucifer is fixed in ice. Dante and Virgil emerge at the foot of Mount Purgatory, as Easter Day is dawning. Purgatory has seven terraces, corresponding to the deadly sins; penance is borne willingly by waiting souls, including **Belacqua** and **Sordello**. On its summit is the Earthly Paradise, where Beatrice appears and Dante must bid farewell to his pagan guide. Beatrice leads him through the heavenly spheres to the Empyrean, where he is granted a vision of **God**, with whom his will is blended. There the poem ends.

Bianca **Esposito** nurtured SB's love for Dante's *Inferno* and *Purgatorio*. He found the *Paradiso* less compelling; as **Moran** comments: "Might not the beatific vision become a source of boredom, in the long run" (167); compare "unrelieved immaculation," in the "**Dante**" essay. There, SB asserts the "circumstantial similarity" between Dante and **Joyce**, using **Bruno** and **Vico** as intermediaries. He affirms Dante's creation of a new language, that of an ideal Italian who had assimilated the best dialect, citing him in Latin and Italian, mostly from the *Commedia* but also the *Convivio* and *Monarchia*. Boccaccio's image of Dante's language as the peacock's filthy feet is found in "**Text**": "a screechy flat-footed Tuscany peacock's / Strauss fandango and recitative / not forgetting he stinks eternal"; the Tuscan dialect, like the peacock's feet, seems ugly and mortal against the incorruptible Latin he might have used. SB compares their purgatories, Dante's conical and implying culmination, Joyce's spherical and excluding culmination.

Belacqua is drawn from *Purgatorio* IV, specifically Toynbee's "big Dante" *Dictionary* (1898). His **embryonic** posture pervades SB's works, including the late **closed space** tales. Belacqua gives the **Syra-Cusa** a beautiful copy of the *Commedia* (as in life SB did to Lucia **Joyce**), stolen at great personal risk (*Dream*, 51), but she leaves it in a bar, leaving him with a "beslubbered" Florentia edition in "the ignoble Salani collection." The "nice" book is Isidoro Del Lungo's edition (Florence: Le Monnier, 1926); the "ignoble" one the Salani edition (1921), edited by Enrico Bianchi. The **Whoroscope Notebook** copies from this the "Purgatorial distribution" facing the illustration of the Mount of Purgatory. These are the only editions SB mentions, but manuscripts indicate that he used others, notably Cary's translation (1869) and the Scartazzini-Vandelli edition (1922).

Belacqua's "amorosi sospiri" (19; identified by Pilling, *Dream Companion*, as from Guarini's *Il Pastorido*) echo the lost (*Inf.* III.22). The **Smeraldina**'s name derives from the "smeraldi" of *Purgatorio* XXXI.116; she is invoked (23–24) as Sordello, "Posta sola soletta" ("seated all alone"; *Purg.* VI.58–59); her palm a **Giudecca** (68). Belacqua's lack of volition parodies God's will (36): "Vuolsi così colà, dove si puote / ciò che si vuole, e più non dimandare" ("Thus it is willed there where that can be done which is willed; and ask no more" [*Inf.* III.95 & V.23]). His narrative impotence (43) echoes Dante's inability to proceed when faced by beauteous Beatrice: "Da questo passo vinti ci concediamo" ("At this pass we concede ourselves defeated" [*Par.* XXX.22]). He arrives at **Kassel** (64) like a dream-Dante in exile, and engages the **Mandarin** in a wild discussion about Beatrice in the brothel (41–42). "Little Miss Florence" (73) turning to ease her pain (*Purg.* VI.148–51) becomes Florence Nightingale (80); in **"What a Misfortune"** (136), Belacqua has "tossed and turned like the Florence of Sordello," finding all postures painful.

Belaqua imagines (113) the gay zephyrs of Purgatory, slithering in across the blue tremelo of the ocean with a pinnace of souls, as good as saved, to the landing stage, the reedy beach (*Purg.* I and II). His mind is defined (122–25) in terms of Dante's **Limbo** (the "Stygian speculum") and its purgatorial equivalent, the **sedendo et quiesc[i]endo** theme. The penultimate phrase of "UND" (141) is "L'andar su che porta," Belacqua's "What's the good of going up?" (*Purg.* IV.127). Likening himself (112) to the

mountaineer preparing for the final assault, he parodies Dante, who, starting his most difficult canticles after having climbed Mount Purgatory, asks Apollo for poetic power. Sprawled in the ditch with bloated feet (129–30), he invokes his pain and Dante's moon in terms of **Cain, Constance,** and **Piccarda.** Writing (168) is described as a Malebolge (in *Proust,* 56, Marcel's sufferings are a **Tolomea**). The reference in *Paradiso* III.1–10 to the almost invisible contrast created by a pearl on a white forehead is paraphrased in *Dream* (175), and referred to as "un caillou à peine visible contre une fronte exsangue" in "Le **Concentrisme**" (37). There is no "clot of moon" (the "spots" of *Paradiso* II) when the **Frica** mentions the **Alba** (181), for like Paolo and Francesca (*Inf.* V.138) Belacqua "heard [read] no more that day." On hearing of the **death** of **Nemo** (183) he sinks to his hands and knees "and with a good prayer truncates copiously the purgatorial villeggiatura," to shorten Nemo's "holiday" in Purgatory by praying for his soul, as a godly Chandler might do (*Purg.* IV.132–34; *Dream,* 24, *Murphy,* 78).

"Dante and the Lobster" is an inverted *Commedia,* beginning with Belacqua stuck in the canti of the moon and ending in the bowels of the earth, Purgatory between. **"Ding-Dong"** parodies the *Paradiso*'s peals of angelic joy that accompany the entry of a soul. In his early essay SB claimed that Dante "never ceased to be obsessed" by the number three. **"Echo's Bones"** has "three scenes," as does "Dante and the Lobster," **Murphy's mind,** the *Trilogy,* and *How It Is.* The undertaker's man in **"Malacoda"** measures, coffins, and covers in a poem structured by triads. "Home Olga," "Ding-Dong," and "A Wet Night" manifest the three colors (green, white, and red) of the Bovril sign, three theological virtues transformed to "Doubt, Despair, and Scrounging." Three women of *MPTK* (the Smeraldina, Alba, and Ruby) suggest the colors worn by Beatrice (*Purg.* XXX.28–33).

"Draff" refers to "the *bella menzogna*" (201). The "competent poet," as in "From the Only Poet to a Shining Whore," is Dante. In *Convivio* II.I.i, he comments on his *canzone* "Voi ch'intendendo. " The last line, "Ponete mente almen com'io son bella" ("Keep in mind, however, how beautiful I am") is quoted in *Proust* (76) to define allegory as "veritate ascosa sotto bella menzogna" ("truth hidden behind a beautiful lie"). This is Dante's discussion of the four modes: *litterale, allegorico, morale,* and *anagogico.* SB praises (77) Dante's description of the proud (*Purg.* X.138–39); his only poetic failure is with his allegorical figures, "whose significance is purely conventional and extrinsic" (79). This derives from Francesco de Sanctis's *Storia della letteratura italiana* (147). SB uses the Paolo and Francesca episode (*Inf.* V.70–138) in "Papini's Dante" (1934) of the critic's failure to appreciate the poetry, while the half line "ricordanosi del tempo felice" ("to recall happy times" [*Inf.* V.122]) is groaned in "A Wet Night" (74). In *How It Is* (37), Dante's "quel giorno più non vi leggemmo avante" ("that day we read no further" [*Inf.* V.138]), becomes "that day we prayed no further." "Hell Crane to Starling" takes its title from this episode (V.40), the birds as emblems of incontinence.

The title "Yoke of Liberty" derives from *De Monarchia* (II.i). In "Alba" the vision denied is cast in terms of Dante's lady. "Sanies II" varies "Beatrice and the brothel," Dante and Blissful Beatice there "prior to the Vita Nuova"; but "lo Alighieri" gets off "au revoir to all that" as the poem becomes a flagellation fantasia. The "superb pun" of "qui vive la pietà" (*Inf.* XX.28; *Dream,* 148; "Dante and the Lobster," 19), appears as "pity is quick with death" in "Text." In *All That Fall,* the Rooneys walk together, one forward one backward, "Like Dante's damned, with their faces arsy-versy" (*Inf.* XX.22–24). "Text" stages the "ingenious damnation" (*Inf.* III.60), mirrored in "What a Misfortune" (126), where Mrs. bboggs is "almost as non-partisan as Pope Celestine the fifth" (qv). "Malacoda" (qv) invokes the Malebolge of *Inferno* XXI, where Dante and Virgil meet devils called Malebranche; and Malacoda reappears in "Draff" as a "fat drab demon," neither sinister nor threatening.

The New Life is thwarted by Murphy's indolence (78). He dreams of Antepurgatory (*Purg.* IV), postmortem pleasure, the trembling of the austral sea (I.117), the sun obliquing to the north as the dayspring runs through its zodiac (IV.55ff), immunity from expiation (IV.133), the vision of Zion's antipodes (IV.68), and the outrageous gradient (IV.41–42). "Belacqua bliss" defines the second part of his mind, where he feels sovereign and free (see Murphy's mind). Such details shape SB's incidental orchestration: Murphy's ashes and the fires in *Watt* (38) both "greyen," in contrast with "il Zodiacal rubecchio" of *Purg.* IV.64; the link is the archaic word "dayspring." Dante's sensibility has become part of SB's own.

The Appendix of *Watt* notes (#35): *parole non ci appulcro* ("I will add no words to embellish it" [*Inf.* VII.60]), Virgil unable to speak of avaricious cardinals. His shade appears to Dante, "hoarse for long silence" (*Inf.* I.61–63). "The **Calmative**" (66) refers to this, the dark wood at the mouth of hell; it returns in *How It Is* (91) as "that voice ruined from such long silence." The "stars" close each part of the *Comedy*. If **Molloy** speaks of the stars it is "by mistake" (15), but in *Malone Dies* they promise guidance (220), as in "The Calmative" they are "assumed" to be there at the end. In "The **End**" (98), "There were stars in the sky, quite a few." "**Text 9**" suggests: "pass out, and see the beauties of the skies, and see the stars again." The **French** text (196) is closer to Dante: "et passer à travers, et voir les belles choses que porte le ciel, et revoir les étoiles." In *The Lost Ones* (205) non-searchers sit "in the attitude which wrung from Dante one of his rare wan smiles"; but Dante's stars imply a way out, an "**issue.**" One school "swears by a secret passage"; another dreams of a trapdoor in the ceiling and a flue "at the end of which the sun and other stars would still be shining" (206). Compare *Inferno* XXXIV.137–39: as Dante exits hell he and Virgil climb a "natural burella" (both "dungeon" and "tunnel") and by this "cammino ascoso" ("hidden road") reach a "pertugio tondo" ("round opening") (*Inf.* XXXIV.98, 133, 138), whence they "see again the stars." The "ascent" recalls the end of *Purgatorio:* Dante, having climbed the stairs, is "ready to ascend to the stars" (*Purg.* XXXIII.145: "puro e disposto a salire a le stelle").

"Text 6" discusses Dante's use of the past tense: "I was, I was, they say in Purgatory, in Hell too, admirable singulars, admirable assurance. Plunged in ice up to the nostrils, the eyelids caked with frozen tears, to fight all your battles o'er again, what tranquillity" (124–25). Allusion to the damned plunged in ice (*Inf.* XXXII.46–48) recurs in *Ill Seen Ill Said* (27): "The eye will return to the scene of its betrayals. On centennial leave from where tears freeze." Another image is quoted twice in the Whoroscope Notebook: "Cesare armato con gli *occhi grifagni* ("falcon-eyed Cesar armed," or "Cesar armed with ravening eyes" [*Inf.* IV.123]). This becomes in "**Vieille terre**" (45): "de mes yeux grifanes d'autrui, c'est trop tard"; and in "**Old Earth**" (238): "with my other's ravening eyes, too late" (238). A phrase from *Inferno* VII.121–22 is reproduced in Italian in "Vieille terre": "Tristi fummo ne l'aere dolce" ("We were sullen in the sweet air"); this is omitted in the English translation. The icy bed of "The Calmative" invokes this canto, and lines 35–36 appear in the fourth stanza of "**dread nay**" ("tel **Bocca** dans la glace"). M. **Krap** in *Eleutheria* (18) imagines himself there. *How It Is* (91) draws from this canto its image of two pressed so closely that the hairs of their heads intermix (*Inf.* XXXII.41–42). **Winnie** in *Happy Days* resembles Dante's traitors in the Caina, their heads protruding from frozen lake or livid stone. **May** in *Footfalls* walks like one of Dante's damned. In "**Rough for Radio II**," Animator asks if Stenographer has read the

Purgatory of the divine Florentine. She has only flipped through the *Inferno*, and does not know that in Purgatory "all sigh, I was, I was" (118). If SB's souls look back thus (*fui, fui*), they do not imagine that it constitutes the memory of happier times. [Details from DC].

"Dante and the Lobster": first published in *This Quarter* 5.2 (December 1932): 222–36; and, shortened and revised, as the opening story in *MPTK* (1934); rpt. in *Evergreen Review* 1.1 (1957): 24–36. The story, submitted for a competition run by *This Quarter,* did not win Heinemann's fifty-guinea prize (the winning entry was Leslie Reid's "Across the Heath"), but it was accepted for publication. It refers to the arrest and trial of Henry **McCabe** (qv), the "Malahide murderer"; O'Brien notes (361) that the *Evening Herald* did not feature a photograph of McCabe in 1926. Knowlson says (58) that the lobster incident occurred at SB's Aunt Cissie's house in Howth.

The inverted *Commedia* begins with a lesson in Paradise, and ends in the basement kitchen, "the bowels of the earth" (21); between these, a **purgatorial** process. **Belacqua** is "stuck in the first of the canti in the moon" (9), in the *Paradiso,* where **Beatrice** explains the celestial system. **Dante** draws attention (II.49–51) to the "dusky marks" on the moon's surface that remind earth dwellers of **Cain** (*Inf.* XX.126), banished there for the crime of fratricide. Blissful Beatrice explains that the moon, as farthest from the Empyrean, receives accordingly less of its excellence, and so reflects the sun's light unequally. This he can understand, but

her intricacies are beyond him. The exposition prepares Dante for the order of the universe, relations of grace, destiny and free will, the hierarchy of blessedness. Belacqua's incomprehension prefigures his later inability to understand the relationship of piety and **pity**. In Canto III, Dante turns (with relief) from Beatrice to **Piccarda**, who tells him that **love** reconciles us to **God**. The irony is pertinent.

A trinity of obligations awaits: lunch, lobster, and lesson (three types of "l"). Lunch enacts a comic torturing of toast, sawed from the round loaf; broiled, blackened, the kitchen an inferno of smoke and flame. The ritual is punctuated by references to the stigmata of God's pity, sacrifices, and burnt offerings. Belacqua's spavined gait identifies him as a figure of Cain, condemned to vagabond existence. He picks up the lobster, lepping fresh, a term he takes to mean freshly killed, puts the parcel on the hall table, and goes in for his lesson. The only difficulty is translating the "superb **pun**" (*Inf.* XX.28): "**qui vive** la pietà quando è ben morta," "pietà" meaning "piety" or "pity," the antinomy provoking the wretched Belacqua into pondering Dante's "rare movements of compassion in Hell" (19). Dante's pun persists into *Dream* (148) as a line to mumble in crisis; it is translated in "**Text**," as "pity is quick with **death**." Meanwhile, a **cat** has been attacking the parcel.

On the way home a **horse** is down, and a man sits on its head. A poor couple sag against the railings. Belacqua thinks of Jonah and the pity of a jealous God on Nineveh (the city spared, to the prophet's anger), and of McCabe, who will "get it in the neck" at dawn. Then the lobster, exposed **cruciform** on the oilcloth, makes a rare movement: "**Christ!**" says Belacqua, "it's alive." The faint nervous act of life is mediated through casual religious cliché. His aunt will "Boil the beast": lobsters must be boiled alive. The phrasing is that of "**Malacoda**," SB in revision invoking the pain of his father's death, and the "Es muss sein" theme from **Beethoven**'s Opus 135. Also present is **Keats**, "Take into the air my quiet breath," another bad jest: "Now more than ever seems it rich to die." Belacqua consoles himself piously: "it's a quick death, God help us all"; but that is contradicted by a violent breach of narrative decorum, an intruding **voice** with no authority save anguish: "It is not." When the book was reprinted (1966) SB was tempted to substitute "Like hell it is," but that would have diminished the searing negation of piety and pity entreated throughout the story, which, like McCabe's petition, is cruelly denied.

"**Dante . . . Bruno . Vico . . Joyce**": an essay in *transition* 16–17 (June 1929): 242–53; revised and reprinted as part of *Our Exagmination* (qv), 3–22. Technically, the book (May) appeared before the article (June). Included in *A Bash in the Tunnel,* ed. John Ryan (London: Clifton Books, 1969), 21–34; and *Disjecta* (19–33). SB explained the punctuation as the "jump" of centuries separating each writer (the *transition* proofreaders in the table of contents added a century between Vico and Joyce). The essay is erudite, compelling—and derivative, drawing on works

by McIntyre, **Croce**, **de Sanctis**, Michelet, and Symons, from the library of the **École Normale**. McQueeny sums it up as "a brilliant mosaic of secondary sources done by a rushed apprentice" (60), contrasting it with *Proust* where SB is more the master of his material.

The essay asserts the danger of the neatness of identifications. The first part is devoted to that "practical roundheaded Neapolitan" **Vico**, to challenge Croce's interpretation of him as "mystic, essentially speculative." SB condenses Vico's thesis of cyclical history, showing that the *Scienza nuova* is yet rooted in the **identified contraries** of **Bruno**. Having argued for a "structural" adaptation of Vico by Joyce, SB states that Vico is substantially present in *Work in Progress.* Vico's "dynamic treatment of Language, Poetry, and Myth" (24) is linked to Joyce's "direct expression" (24), where "form *is* content, content *is* form" (25). Those unable to understand this are declared "too decadent to receive it" (26). This writing, which "is not *about* something; *it is that something itself,*" (27) is defined as "desophisticated" (28).

SB introduces **Dante** through **Leopardi**'s "Sopra il monumento di Dante che si prepare in Firenze," and through Dante's reply to Catalano dei Malvolti and Loderingo degli Andalò in section six of the Malebolge (*Inf.* XXIII.94–95). Dante's work is said to possess "considerable circumstantial similarity" to that of Joyce. This is based on linguistic innovation, an assemblage of "the purest elements from each dialect," and a "synthetic language" (30). Two "caps" from the *Convivio* illustate this point. The first is a quotation (I.xi) from Boethius used to define people who lack *discrezione* ("discretion"), and therefore go "contra nostro volgare" ("against our vernacular"). The second (book I), reproduces Dante's claim that his vernacular will be like "new light" and a "new sun," and compares it to Joyce's linguistic project. The prophetic dimension of Dante's claim is translated into contemporary "ennui," the premise of a "formal innovation." Just as Dante's audience was used to the "suave elegance" of Latin, so Joyce's readers are used to English. SB asserts that "Boccaccio never jeered at the 'piedi sozzi' of the peacock that Signora Alighieri dreamed about." The "peacock" is Dante; its "filthy feet" the vernacular. This episode is narrated by Boccaccio in his *Trattatello in laude di Dante* (#16–18, 423–538): Dante's mother while pregnant dreamt that she was giving birth to a child who, feeding himself on laurel berries, became a shepherd and then a peacock. Boccaccio explains that Dante's *Commedia* has four important characteristics of the peacock: "penna angelica; . . . sozzi piedi; voce molto orribile ad udir . . . la sua carne è odorifera e incorruttibile" ("angelic feather; . . . filthy feet; a voice horrible to hear; . . . odorous and incorruptible flesh" [#221]). The *Commedia* is like the flesh of the peacock because it tells the "simple and immutable truth"; it is incorruptible. As the feet sustain the body, so language sustains literature. The favorable reception of Dante's works by his near contemporary is misconstrued by SB as an example of an illustrious author who could appreciate Dante's vernacular while still defining it as "piedi sozzi."

The "ultima regna canam, fluido contermina mundo," opposed in the text to the opening of the *Commedia,* is also taken from the *Trattatello.* Boccaccio states that Dante began with Latin, but was forced to use the vernacular to be better understood by a society that despised Virgil and the classic authors (#192); SB reverses the point. The quotations (*Purg.* VI.118 and XXXII.149) exemplify Dante's explicit attacks against the Church of his time. Its rage against Dante is illustrated by the references to Cardinal Bertrando and Pino della Tosa, an almost verbatim quotation from Boccaccio's *Trattatello* (#196–97).

The essay ends with a distinction between Dante's **purgatory** (conical, implying culmination) and that of Joyce (spherical, excluding culmination). The two purgatories are constructed as similar because both are moving; in Joyce, however, **motion** has lost its redemptive guarantee. SB contends that Joyce's vision is purgatorial in its "absolute absence of the Absolute." In this precious paradox lies the aspect of "self-extension" that SB had noted at the outset, the essay having moved erratically toward this one moment of "direct expression" concerning his own position (his a fifth name implicit in the title, perhaps). Taken as a whole, the essay anticipates that purgatorial function in SB's work-not-yet-in-progress, but the tone is arrogant. The reader is made to feel "too decadent to understand" should s/he not comprehend its direct expression, and stands accused of skimming the "scant cream" of sense if unable to appreciate that its form and content are one. This is willful, but if the purgatorial process as an incipient reaction against the Joycean mode may be detected only retrospectively, hints of SB's later genius are present, however recondite (and annoying) they might at present be. [Details from DC]

Darwin, Charles (1809–82): pioneer of experimental biology, who spent twenty years accumulating evidence of his theory of evolution before publishing it, somewhat reluctantly, as *On the Origin of Species* (1859). Its thesis is that present morphology is the outcome of an evolutionary process arising from the gradual and opportunistic mechanism of natural selection, summed up as the survival of the fittest (Darwin's "missing link" the laws of genetics). The theory aroused bitter controversy, combatants aligning themselves with the apes or the angels. Like the works of **Descartes**, it unleashed a spirit of scientific inquiry that went far beyond and ultimately threatened the Christian tenets of its author. SB bought a copy of the *Origin* in **London** for 6d. He described it to **MacGreevy** (4 August 1932) as "badly written cats-lap," preferring, he said, *Moby-Dick,* which he got at the same time and price: "that's more like the real stuff, white whales and natural piety." He said that he could remember only one thing, that blue-eyed cats are always deaf ("**What a Misfortune**," 133). Touches of Darwin appear at odd moments, such as the burrowing **tucutucu** mentioned there, **Darwin's caterpillar** in *Murphy* and *Watt,* the **hinny** in *All That Fall,* or **Estragon**'s comment in *Waiting for*

Godot (English only): "People are bloody ignorant apes" (9.b). The landscape of *How It Is* is a Darwinian "warmth of primeval mud impenetrable dark" (11), the nameless narrator's life following "not all a selection natural order vast tracts of **time**" (7) as he experiences the inevitable "loss of species" (27). The phrase was used in *Watt* (85), and of caged beasts born of caged beasts born and dead in a cage, in *The Unnamable* (387). "**B**" in "**Rough for Theatre I**" (71) hopes he might find a few rags of **love** in his heart, and die reconciled with his species. In "**Rough for Theatre II**" (82), C's "bits and scraps" include an unfinished **chess** game with a correspondent in Tasmania, and the "hope not dead of living to see the extermination of the species." The genocide of the Tasmanian Aborigines images the wider human condition.

Darwin's caterpillar: a parable from **Darwin**'s *Origin of Species* (VII, 208) about instinct, which is likened to **habit** and repetition. A caterpillar, interrupted in building its complicated hammock and returned to that **job** or to another at a similar point, would normally complete the work; but if taken to one at a further state of completion it would attempt to start not from the point given but from where it had left off. **Belacqua** tells the story in "**Echo's Bones**" (23): "'He was working away at his hammock' said Belacqua, 'and not doing a damn bit of harm to man or beast, when up comes old Monkeybrand bursting with labour-saving devices. The caterpillar was far from feeling any benefit.'" Miss **Counihan** stops in mid-flow, and seems likely to go back to the beginning, "like Darwin's caterpillar" (*Murphy*, 218); in *Watt* (194), Mr. Magershon spins the original yarn but, appropriately, is disturbed as he does.

"Da tagte es": a four-line poem, rhyming *abba*, presenting as epigram the sense of parting in an image whose tenor is **death**, the final farewell. The title is taken from a poem, "Nemt, frowe, disen kranz" ("Take, lady, this wreath") by **Walther** von der Vogelweide, in which, after a vision of idyllic **love**, the illusion is dispelled: "dô taget ez und muos ich wachen" ("then dawn came and I had to waken"). This is no temporary parting of lovers; like "**Malacoda**" it was written after the death of SB's **father** and features a death ship. The line "the glass unmisted above your eyes" reflects **Joyce**'s "Ecce Puer" of February 1932, also written after a father's death.

Davus complex: as recorded in the **Whoroscope Notebook** and used in "**Denis Devlin**," a criticism of those wanting tidy solutions: "the go-getters the gerrymandlers, Davus and the morbid dread of sphinxes, solution capped on problem like a snuffer on a candle, the great crossword public in all its planes" (*Disjecta*, 92). SB notes: "**Watt**'s Davus complex (morbid dread of sphinxes)" (251). In his copy and so the **Calder** text (252) this becomes "sphinges." In Terence's *Andria* (194), a slave says, "Davos sum, non Oedipus" ("I am Davus, not Oedipus"), i.e., how would I know? Watt suffers from the insatiable

need to know, to resolve what **Schopenhauer** called "the riddle of the world" and **Haeckel** "the riddle of the universe"; the protagonist of *Three Novels,* on the other hand, finds increasing comfort in the insoluble nature of the enigma.

death: with **birth**, existence, and the **irrational** urge to express, one of SB's inescapable imperatives. Deep pessimism arises from the lasting conviction that it were better never to have been born. Yet for SB death, though inevitable, does not come quickly. **Estragon** comments that at least in **Christ**'s day "they crucified quick" (*WG*, 34.b), as in the quick and the dead. **Molloy** (68) has always preferred slavery to death, that is, being put to death: "For death is a condition I have never been able to conceive to my satisfaction." He wonders if it is not a state worse than life, if, say, **consciousness** persists, so finds it "**natural**" not to rush into it; but the interval is long, and existence manifests itself as a lingering **crucifixion**.

In *Whoroscope,* the life of **Descartes** is set against its inevitable cessation. The **embryonic** chicken, devoured with gusto, is an image of pitiless existence (an adder "broaches" her **rat** in "**Serena I**"). His death is an emblem of the ultimate separation of mind and **body**, the end of consciousness (perhaps). The "death" of the would-be poet of "**Assumption**," even if interpreted as coition, is a **roman**tic gesture such as SB would not permit himself again. "A **Case in a Thousand**" and "**Dante and the Lobster**" reject **pity**. Death may be treated with irony and derision, as in the finale of "**Love and Lethe**," the casual dismissal of **Lucy** and

Thelma **bboggs**, or the departure of **Belacqua**, victim of the bad joke in "Yellow." His death offers in "**Draff**" a mockery of institutionalized religion, as in the burial service. His "post-obit" existence in "**Echo's Bones**" permits a skeptical scrutiny of the futile optimism that seeks consolation beyond the grave.

Murphy adopts a similar tone. SB aligns himself with **Democritus** in opposition to the tradition, philosophical and religious, which has permeated Western culture even unto SB's day, that would remove death's sting and find pious consolation in an ultimate indignity. If the death of the "Old Boy" gives **Celia** an existential shock, that of Murphy is grotesque. The impulse to flush his ashes down the toilet of the **Abbey Theatre** is frustrated when the remains of his "**body, mind and soul**" are swept into the gutter, affirming in jest the **atomist** contention that the soul must share the dissolution of the body. Murphy's death challenges the reasonable reader who cannot determine if it is an accident (see **suicide**). Through the postmortem tales, however, especially *Malone Dies* and *The Unnamable,* is the suggestion that mind or soul, and hence consciousness, may persist beyond the grave, as Christianity would have it. If so, the death of the body, however natural, may offer little relief.

Two deaths left a lasting imprint. Peggy **Sinclair**, SB's first **love**, died of TB (May 1933), on the day of SB's operation (see "Yellow"). The green eyes and/ or shabby green coat of the **Smeraldina** appear in "Assumption" ("consumption"?); "**Enueg 1**"; "**What a Misfortune**" ("sage-green"); "**Ascension**" ("les grands yeux verts"); the girl in "**Eh Joe**" ("the green one"); and **Krapp**'s recollection (58) of "A girl in a shabby green coat," of whom his rereading of *Effie* reminds him. The death of SB's **father** (June 1933) is poignantly dramatized in "**Malacoda**." It determines the "obsessional image" of a father and son, as in the "Joe **Breem**" readings in "The **Calmative**" and "**Text 1**"; or in *Company, Worstward Ho,* and other late writings. In *First Love* the narrator cannot remember his birth, but his "marriage" is imbricated with his father's death. The casual opening, with its account of gravestones and the narrator's preference for the sweet smell of death over the stink of the living, for all its humor (he has "no bone to pick with graveyards") constitutes a complex emotional image intricately and destructively bound into the end of the story. His inability to come to terms with that death defines his inability to love. The other *Quatre nouvelles* enact the consequences of this. "The **Expelled**" culminates in a process of birth that is equally one of death; "The Calmative" (like "Echo's Bones") is a postmortem text ("I don't know when I died"), in that the distinction between death and life is blurred; while "The **End**" relates the narrative the author "might have told" (99), a **psychoanalytical** setting out to sea, a "voyage" again associated with **memories** of his father.

Molloy begins (and ends, since the first paragraph is equally the last) with the distinction, applied to his **mother**, between being dead and dead enough to bury (7). *Three Novels* were written as SB's mother was dying. The shadow of the **shambles** is ever present, but the deaths in the dark wood are part of the process whereby the complex Molloy-Moran figure attains the state of unaccommodated man by destroying the Shadow (the "old man") within. *Malone Dies* constitutes an "interlude" between *Molloy* and *The Unnamable,* Malone filling the time by telling stories until he feels "it" coming; one of the more grotesque sequences concerns the "vivifying" spectacle (212) of the mule's death and Big Lambert's killing of pigs and rabbits. The narrative reflects the process of "decomposition" (the pencil becomes shorter, the prose more fragmentary), until in another monstrous parody of a birth (compare "The Expelled" and "All That Fall"), the narrator feels his feet already clear "of the great cunt of existence." It is a breech death, his head "the last to die"; but the Unnamable is born, to exist in a mythological present determined less by the limits of birth and death than by the other two imperatives, consciousness of being and the need to express, to go on.

Texts for Nothing attempt to go beyond this impasse by offering compelling images of what it is to be within a skull, or of the terrors of age (the Père Lachaise in "Text 8," the *pissoir* of "Text 11"). They are not without black humor, as in "Text 4" (116): "make no bones about it"; but the final *Text* ends with the voice weaker still, with the futility of the wish to leave a trace in the dust, and with the uncompromising recognition of "the extinction of this black nothing," of the silence, empty and dark, embracing the faint murmur. This is the terminus for *How It Is,* perhaps the most ruthless consideration of the issueless issue. It

culminates in the emphatic assertion that the panting, the sacks, "all this business of above" is "all balls, yes"; that even the murmur will cease; and that the hypothetical imperative I MAY DIE becomes the categorical one, I SHALL DIE. These sentiments are repeated in *Fizzles,* where the narrator's hope implicit in "Afar a bird" gives way to first the despair of "Closed Place," then the quiet meditation of "Old Earth," in which he experiences a rare sense of contentment at seeing himself as part of the process. In Ezra Pound's *Pisan Cantos* (83), the sense of the Tao, the process, gives way to the chthonic terror of imagining one's own death; in George Eliot's *Middlemarch* Casaubon's abstract sentiment that all men must die translates into the immediate awareness that he must die, and soon: so does this moment pass. In "For to End Yet Again" the dust from whence he came is that to which he must return (Genesis 3:19), with the uncanny apparition of the two white dwarfs, the astronomical pun incorporating the sepulchral vision of personal dissolution with the cosmic vision of ultimate white oblivion.

In *Waiting for Godot* the two tramps are equally waiting for death, passing the time with pointless routines that constitute what Schopenhauer calls distractions, "pastimes" to deflect the mind from futility. Suggestions of suicide and images of crucifixion pervade the play, but the final reality is that of waiting, the bleakness enforced by Pozzo's speech about giving birth astride of a grave (57.b), and Vladimir's sense of the grave and a difficult birth (58.a). *Endgame* is bleaker, a universe running down, the sense of death (personal, social, and cosmic) more immediate and the conviction that life is a mistake not to be repeated. *Happy Days,* for all its cheerfulness, is equally chilling in its inevitability. The shorter plays return to the personal. **Krapp** looks over his shoulder into the surrounding dark for "Freund Hain." SB had been memorizing Matthias Claudius's "Der Tod," and commented, "'Friend death.' To get to such a point! I often think of the sea" (Atik, 65). This image echoes **Schubert**'s "Death and the Maiden" ("Bin Freund, und komme nicht zu strafen"). That theme is present in *All That Fall,* where the "divine day" is underscored by various deaths, ranging from that of the **hen** in the middle of the road to that of the **Rooneys**' daughter, the child who falls under the train, and the unspoken tragedy of the unseen woman who replays Schubert's quartet. "**Rough for Theatre II**" offers a lovebird or finch singing, like **Hardy**'s "Darkling Thrush," after its mate has died, as **C** awaits confirmation that his life is without prospects so he can jump from the window. "**Cascando**" presents one "petering out" among the stones; and "**Words and Music**" captures **Croak**'s agony as he remembers the **face** in the ashes. "Eh Joe" and "**Embers**" offer a protagonist conscious of the end. Billie **Whitelaw** asked SB about the woman in *Footfalls,* whether she was dead or alive at the end, only to receive the enigmatic answer: "Let's just say you're not quite there" (Kalb, 235). *Footfalls* depicts a **mother** near the end of her life ("Eighty-nine, ninety"), "not quite there" but endlessly "rehearsing" it all again, while the pacing daughter is "not

quite there" physically, in church or on stage. The relationship is reprised in "**Rockaby**." There is a tonal shift toward the end of SB's career, "**Ghost Trio**," "**Ohio Impromptu**," and "**Nacht und Träume**" each offering an intimation of something beyond the mystery of death. Even more poignant is "**. . . but the clouds . . .**" with its echo of W. B. **Yeats**, his making of the soul, and the sense of imminent departure from this life, while "**What Where**" features, according to SB, **voices** from beyond the grave.

SB was born on 13 April 1906, Good Friday, and completed an ironic pattern when he was buried on Boxing Day, having died just short of Christmas, 22 December 1989, of what was officially described as respiratory failure. Momentous events were happening on the world stage: the fall of the Berlin Wall; the American invasion of Panama; the execution of the Ceauşescus in Romania; but for many the haunting moment was the death of one man who, more than any other, had captured in his writings the sense of what it means to be alive, and whose death therefore had an immediacy beyond the historical. He was buried (not "laid to rest") with his wife, Suzanne, in the Cimetière de Montparnasse, with a private ceremony as he would have wished. His last piece of work, the English translation of "**What Is the Word**," featured in many obituaries; but a more poignant tribute might be the *mirlitonnade* (cited in Christopher Ricks, *Beckett's Dying Words*): "imagine si ceci / un jour ceci / un beau jour / imagine / si un jour / un beau jour ceci / cessait / imagine." One day it did.

"Découverte de Pim": an early version of part 2 of *Comment c'est*, in *L'VII* ("Le Sept") (Brussells) 1 (décembre 1959): 9–13; divided into thirteen paragraphs, syntax and punctuation more normal than in the final version.

Defoe, Daniel (1660–1731): English dissenter, pamphleteer, essayist, and novelist. In "**Serena I**," having mounted to the platform of the Monument ("Wren's giant bully"), the poet looks out on **London** and laments that he was not born Defoe, to excoriate the city. In *Murphy* (220), **Wylie** denies that he is "a true-born jackeen," a variant of *The True-Born Englishman* (1701). *Robinson Crusoe* (1719) is referred to several times. In "**What a Misfortune**" (125) **Belacqua** imagines kneeling in the Church of **Saint Nicolas** in Galway, like Crusoe before him. In "**Yellow**" (161), he hears the asthmatic overhead coughing, "as Crusoe laboured to bring his gear ashore, the snugger to be." **Malone** making his inventory continues the metaphor of isolation; and **Winnie** in the early drafts of *Happy Days* records the passing days by notches on a tally stick, in precisely the manner of Crusoe.

defunge: used by **Malone** (236), as he considers the characters he has killed: "let us first defunge." **Geulincx** uses *defungo* in the sense of "I dis-create." The phrase "défongeons d'abord" was added to the manuscript (NB7, 90).

Dekker, Thomas (ca. 1572–1632): English playwright and pamphleteer. **Celia** in *Murphy* was partly inspired by Bellafront in *The Honest Whore* (1604).

SB entered several details from *Old Fortunatus* (1599) into the **Whoroscope Notebook**, and commented: "Dilemma in Old Fortunatus—Give to **Neary**: Whether more torment to **love** a lady & never enjoy her, or always to enjoy a lady whom you cannot choose but hate." This paradox of **desire** was finally given to Miss **Counihan** (131) but underlies much of the action of the novel. Murphy's "wandering to find home" (4), from *The Witch of Edmonton* (IV.ii.31), by Dekker, Rowley, and **Ford**. Dekker, Webster, and perhaps **Marston** wrote *Westward Hoe* (1604), the departure point for SB's *Worstward Ho* (1983).

Della Robbia, Luca (ca. 1400–82): first of a family of Florentine sculptors, best known for a Singing Gallery in **Florence** Cathedral. His nephew Andrea (1435–1525) was responsible for the roundels of infants on the facade of the Foundling Hospital; hence the reference (*Dream*, 162) to the "starved della Robbia."

"Delta": a twenty-four-line poem, translated from the Italian of Eugenio Montale (1896–1981) and published in *This Quarter* 2.4 (April–May–June 1930): 630. The poet wills "to thee" the life "drained" from the river of his life as he sets forth, "into the bright **gulf**." SB did not authorize its republication, but it appeared in the Irish poetry magazine *Metre* (1999). Montale, who won the **Nobel Prize** (1975), was best known for his 1925 collection (from which "Delta" is taken) *Ossi di seppia* ("cuttlefish bones"), a title not unlike *Echo's Bones*. "Cuttle Bones," subtitled "A Poem for a Friend" (trans. Samuel Putnam), appeared in the same issue (654). Montale was an ironist with the difficult vocabulary and metrics of the **Provençal** songsters of *trobar clus* whom he admired; SB's translation, compared with the recent one by Jonathan Galassi, is more idiosyncratic than literal yet retains the archaic touch.

Democritus (ca. 460–370 BC): called by **Horace** the laughing philosopher, in contrast with **Heraclitus**, the weeping one. Little is known about his long life: he reputedly traveled much, then founded his school in Abdera where he wrote much that has not survived. Abdera was a city of Thrace, known (says Lemprière) for its unwholesome air and the stupidity of its inhabitants. Weiland's *Geschichte der Abderiten* (1780) tells how the Abderites, doubting the sanity of Democritus, called in Hippocrates, who pronounced Democritus sane and the citizens mad. "Democritus Junior" is the putative narrator of **Burton**'s Preface to the *Anatomy:* "a little wearish old man, very melancholy by nature, averse from company in his later days, and much given to solitariness." Such a figure appears in **"Enueg I,"** and "wearish" is used of **Krapp**. Democritus valued **friendship**, but thought ill of women and **children** because they interfered with philosophy. A materialist, he rejected the ethics of **Socrates**, the idealism of **Plato**, and the organon of **Aristotle**. Hence his relegation to a minor tradition, that inherited by **Lucretius** and **Epicurus** but dismissed by Christian rationalism. Democritus derived his theories of **atomism** (qv) and the void from Leucippus, of whom little is known. Both were strict determinists, who believed that nothing happened by

chance, and that what *is not* is as real as what *is;* in SB's encapsulation of that central doctrine, uttered by **Murphy** (246) and **Malone** (192), *Nothing is more real than nothing.* The "guffaw of the Abderite" (*Murphy,* 246) was directed finally at the doctrine of the immortality of the soul. It is the progenitor of that mirthless laugh, the dianoetic laugh of **Arsene,** "the *risus purus,* the laugh that laughs at that which is unhappy" (*Watt,* 48), and the guffaw of the "knowing non-exister" in **"Text 12."**

"Denis Devlin": a review of Denis Devlin's *Intercessions* (London: Europa Press, 1938) in *transition* 27 (April–May 1938): 289–94; reprinted as "Intercessions by Denis Devlin" in *Disjecta* (91–95), and *Lace Curtain* (Dublin) 3 (Summer 1970): 41–44. SB was responding to a *TLS* review of *Intercessions* (25 October 1937) that had called it "more intoxicated than intelligible" and "a gulf of tangid [*sic*] incoherence" (F&F, #27). SB approved of Devlin as a "non-**antiquarian**," his verse constituting "the nucleus of a living poetic in **Ireland**" ("Recent Irish Poetry," 76). Much of the essay is generalized, with several sentiments uttered elsewhere: "severed the connection"; "the need to need" ("Les **Deux besoins**"); **Davus** and the "morbid dread of sphinxes" (see *Watt,* "**Addenda**"); or the "Dives-**Lazarus** symbiosis" (*Dream* and *Murphy*). The essay ends in unequivocal praise: Devlin's mastery of the image whence **consciousness** emerges with the least loss of integrity; his recognition of the principle that **art** has nothing to do with clarity; and so "a mind aware of its own luminaries." If he knew of any recent writing to compare with this, SB states, he would not do so.

Le Dépeupleur: a longish prose text ("13.10.65" to "28.11.65"), published 1970 (Minuit), 10,000 copies, with special numbered editions, 399 in all (Davis, #70–7). Translated as *The Lost Ones* (qv). The title alludes to **Lamartine**'s "L'Isolement," the first *Méditation* (28): "Un seul être vous manqué et tout est dépeuplé," reflecting the poet's feelings after the **death** of his beloved Mme. Charles.

La Dernière bande: translation by SB and Pierre Leyris of *Krapp's Last Tape* (1958); first published in *Les Lettres nouvelles* 1 (4 mars 1959): 5–13; then in *La Dernière bande, suivi de Cendres* (Minuit, 1960). Republished 1960 by the Théâtre National Populaire (Collection du répertoire, 42), with Robert **Pinget**'s *Lettre morte;* these, plus Simone Dubreuilh's *Une demande de marriage,* were printed in *L'Avant-scène* (Paris) 222 (15 juin 1960). First **Paris** production at the Théâtre Récamier (22 mars 1960), dir. Roger **Blin**, with R.-J. Chauffard as Krapp, a role SB would have preferred for Blin. SB directed four productions of *Krapp* in three languages (Berlin 1969, with Martin Held; Paris 1970, with Jean Martin; Paris 1975, with Pierre Chabert; and Berlin 1977, in English, with Rick Cluchey).

Derrière le miroir: a small *cahier d'art* from the Galerie Maeght (Paris: Éditions Pierre à Feu) published in its issue devoted to Bram et Geer **van Velde** (11–12 [juin 1948]) SB's "**Peintres de l'empêchement**" (3, 4, 7). The first En-glish translation, by someone unknown, appeared in *Bram van Velde* (Harry N. Abrams, 1962), 16.

de Sanctis, Francesco (1817–83): revolutionist and exile, and Professor of Comparative Literature (1871–79) at the University of Naples. His *Storia della letteratura italiana* (Turin: Contini, 1869) challenged the traditional sense of **Dante** as more a philosopher than a poet, the poetry asserted in what de Sanctis called the *bella menzogna,* or "beautiful lie." The discussion of **allegory** (*Proust,* 79) and the sentiment "Chi non ha la forza di uccidere la realtà non ha la forza di crearla" ("he who has not the strength to kill reality has not the strength to create it") derive from de Sanctis (147).

Descartes, René (1596–1650): SB worked on Descartes at the **École Normale**, from November 1928 to September 1930, taking extensive notes from many sources and immersing himself in the life and works of a philosopher to whom he would owe an enduring debt. Although he could not accept all, if indeed any, of the Cartesian premises and conclusions, the rationalist tradition from **Spinoza** through **Geulincx**, **Leibniz**, and **Kant** to **Schopenhauer** became his intellectual milieu, and he remained one for whom the logical impasses of post-Cartesian thought held a lasting attraction. One aspect of Descartes he made particularly his own: "Plus il avançait, plus il découvrait son ignorance" (Baillet, 14).

René Descartes, Seigneur du Perron, is a pivotal figure in the history of Western philosophy. His work, though retaining much of **scholasticism**, was affected by the new **mathematics** and marks the emergence of modern philosophical and scientific thinking. Born at La Haye, near Tours, he objected to his birthdate (March 31) being known "because it exercised idle people in superstitions about his horoscope" (Mahaffy, 9). **Mahaffy** notes (10) that he had as a playmate a little girl with a squint, which made him regard that defect with favor. He was educated (1604–12) at the Jesuit College of La Flèche, to which the heart of Henri IV was brought while he was a student there. He went to **Paris** (1612) to work at geometry, but to secure complete quiet he enlisted in the Dutch army (1617) and enjoyed two years of undisturbed meditation. His facility in mathematics and disputation impressed the likes of **Beeckman**, Faulhaber, and Pierre Roton (see **Whoroscope**). In October 1619 Descartes went into winter quarters at Ulm, where he remained all day in the celebrated "poêle," a small room heated by a central stove (in **Dream**, 76, **Belacqua** prefers to hatch a great thought over the stove). There the germ of his great enterprise developed: to demolish the edifice of traditional knowledge and construct a new system on different foundations, a universal mathematics. This endeavor caused him violent mental agitation, and, his brain on fire, he fell into a rapture. On the night of November 10, having conceived that the method of analytical geometry might be extended to other studies, he had three curious dreams, one including a strange wind. These confirmed his sense of the way he would follow, and the fundamental synthesis of mathematics and methodology.

Descartes moved to Holland (1628) to escape the risk of persecution for sharing two of **Galileo's** heresies, the earth's rotation and the infinity of the universe. He had a natural daughter, Francine, who died of scarlatina in 1640; this was, he said, his greatest sorrow. He was not industrious, preferring to sleep all morning, yet worked prodigiously in concentrated bursts. He disputed with "**Grassendi**" (1629) on the nature of thunder and parhelia; and with Voët, "the son of a sutler, brought up among harlots and camp-followers" (Mahaffy, 105). His views were said to lead to atheism, but he published his *Geometry* (1637); *Philosophical Essays* (1637); treatises on optics, geometry, **motion**, the circulation of the blood and formation of the fetus; *Discourse on Method* (1637); *Meditations upon the First Philosophy* (1641); and *Principles of Philosophy* (1644). Queen **Christina** of Sweden ("Christina the ripper") sent a warship to bring him to her court. She wanted daily lessons at 5 A.M., but Descartes, unaccustomed to early rising, caught a chill and died. His last words urged the physician, **Weulles**, wishing to bleed him, to spare the blood of a Frenchman.

One Cartesian curiosity is that the theory of the mind is a striking exception to the universal insistence on mechanical and mathematical explanations of motion. Descartes distinguished between physical substance (*res extensa*) and thinking substance (*res cogitans*): the human **body** belongs in the first category, but the mind, including thought, **desire,** and volition, in the second. Descartes regarded bodies of men and animals as **machines**, but humans differentiated by souls, which reside in the **conarium**, or pineal gland, where they engage with the "vital spirits," through which contact there is interaction between body and mind. This relationship of the mental and physical was questioned by the next generation of Cartesians (see **Occasionalism**). *Murphy* has been aptly described as a "Cartesian catastrophe," the protagonist unable to reconcile this **dualism**.

In his *Meditations* and *Discourse on Method* Descartes expounded his philosophy of doubt, whereby he rejected all evidence of the senses, hallucinations, and dreams, there remaining one thing that cannot be doubted, the **consciousness** of thought, and thus of the self that thinks. This led to the famous *cogito, ergo sum* ("I think, therefore I am"), the Archimedean point from which Descartes extended his foundation of knowledge and on which he raised the edifice of thought, adopting as his method the principle that all things conceived as clear and distinct are true. **Molloy** (82) finds that all that is false may be reduced to "notions clear and distinct." **Baillet** outlines (12ff) Descartes's Four Rules: (1) to accept as true only that which was presented to his mind so clearly and distinctly as to exclude all ground of doubt; (2) to divide difficulties into as many parts as possible, the better to understand them; (3) to order his thoughts beginning with the most simple and rising by degrees to the knowledge of the more complex; and (4) to make enumerations so complete that he might be assured that nothing was omitted. From this arose the *Méthode,* the clear and distinct outline of rational thought that ultimately,

Descartes reasoned, might lead to the knowledge of **God**. **Watt** tries to live by this code, but his attempts to eff the **ineffable** lead to disaster and, instead of to God, to the **asylum**. In *Three Novels* the *cogito* is the first principle of thought: having examined himself, Descartes concludes in part IV of the *Méthode* that while he might suppose that he had no body, or that there was no place in which he might be, he could not suppose that he was not. This suggests the disembodied and deracinated figure of the **Unnamable** and the incipient theme of "**Not I**"; but, unlike Descartes, SB could not move beyond the *cogito,* the novel beginning and ending with the "I" as the limit of what can be known, and that dubiously ("I, of whom I know **nothing**").

An initial academic theme was the Cartesian dimensions of SB's early works. Samuel Mintz (1959) drew attention to the Cartesian and Occasionalist elements in *Murphy;* and Hugh Kenner (1961) proposed the image of the "Cartesian centaur," man on a **bicycle**, to represent the dualism of body and mind. Critical fashion changed, readers questioning the simple statement of SB as a Cartesian and pointing to the ironies present in even such works as *Whoroscope,* where the debt to Descartes is explicit though not unequivocal. Because *Endgame* is set within the skull, it does not follow that the relationship of **Hamm** and **Clov** is a Cartesian dualism; **Lucky**'s speech may not parody the *cogito.* It was argued that Schopenhauer's pessimism more accurately defines the tone of the early works; or that the theory of perception in *Murphy* or *Film* owes more to **Berkeley**. Some formulations

went too far in throwing out the Cartesian devil with the dubious ditch water,
as the major novels are based clearly and
distinctly on a Cartesian entelechy,
however qualified by irony. They are
Cartesian in their premises, but ironic
in their method. *Murphy* implies a questioning, and thus a subversion of dualism; *Watt,* the rigorous application of a
method that leads not to God but to **irrationality**; while *The Unnamable*
circles about the *cogito,* only to find the
impossibility of extension beyond that
point which is the self. As often with SB,
that which he loved was not that which
he could accept, and the premises of
Cartesianism, followed into their logical impasses, remain a significant element in his private theater of the **absurd**
and his comic subversion of the rationalist universe.

**Deschevaux-Dumesnil, Suzanne Georg-
ette Anna** (1899–1989): SB's live-in companion (and later wife) of fifty years, an
intimacy often troubled but intensely private. Suzanne shared many of the experiences that went into the greatest writing,
yet avoided the limelight that increasingly
intruded during the years of fame. The
two met in 1929, when SB accompanied
Alfred **Péron** to a private tennis club outside **Paris**, where he played against her
with no intimation that this handsome
older woman (then twenty-eight to his
twenty-three) would feature in his life.
Deirdre Bair propagated the story that
they met when SB was stabbed in
the street (7 January 1938), Suzanne
happening on the scene and calling an
ambulance. More mundanely, she read
about the stabbing, remembered SB, and

visited him at the Hôpital Broussais. She
came into his life, took over the role that
his **mother** had played, and SB accepted
her presence dispassionately, without any
expectation that it would or would not
endure.

Knowlson describes Suzanne as attractive in a slightly masculine kind of way
(Bair says "rawboned and plain"), a smart
but sober dresser, a strong, mature, and
independent woman of left-wing opinions whose family came from Troyes.
She had chestnut hair and striking gray
eyes. Much of her girlhood had been
spent in Tunisia. An accomplished pianist with perfect pitch, she had an interest in literature and the theater. She had
published a pedagogic work, *Musique
Jeux* (Paris: Henry Lemoine, 1935; see
"F—"). She was a first-rate dressmaker
but a poor cook, practical yet with a belief in homeopathy (this later did SB little
good), generous and tolerant of SB's
often difficult ways (she had early a total
belief in his genius) but inclined to be
sharp and dismissive of those she did not
like. She understood and shared SB's
need for silence, and helped erect a wall
of privacy about them that others found
impossible to penetrate. Later, when they
were financially well-off and in the public eye, many differences manifested
themselves, yet she retained that sense of
total privacy to protect herself and him.
Like SB, she was not spoiled by sudden
wealth or fame, but a certain resentment
sometimes found mute expression.

Suzanne shared SB's exile in **Roussillon** and supported him through those
difficult years; if the tension of two
people in forced proximity to each other
manifests itself in *Waiting for Godot,* so

does the bond of loyalty and necessity that unites them. After the **war** her dress-making skills earned them something to live on. She was indefatigable in circulating his manuscripts, contacting publishers and directors, and promoting his work but otherwise kept a low profile; SB commented to Georges **Pelorson** (28 January 1951): "Quant à Suzanne, nous avons la quasi-certitude qu'elle existe . . . Mais pour la faire sortir, macache [*sic*]." She disapproved of SB's drinking and some of his friends (she spoke little English), and the couple evolved separate lifestyles (beds and rooms) beneath the same roof, still closely bonded and taking holidays together. When they acquired the house at Ussy, SB began to spend more time there on his own.

In 1961 SB and Suzanne moved into a larger apartment at 38 Boulevard Saint-Jacques, giving each a larger measure of independence, with a shared sitting room and kitchen but independent quarters, less separate lives than private ones. Suzanne was not unaware of SB's liaisons; they were probably not having sexual relations (Knowlson, 422). Knowlson notes that Suzanne resented being no longer necessary for SB's work, and tended to be intolerant of some of his activities. Tensions found expression in "**Play**" (1962–63); but before that appeared SB made a surprising decision to marry Suzanne, partly to protect her legal rights but also to affirm, in the face of a growing commitment to Barbara **Bray**, a lasting loyalty. The ceremony was performed in privacy, in haste, in England (just as **Joyce** had married Nora thirty years earlier), in a Folkestone Reg-

istry Office (25 March 1961), SB commenting "Thank God it's done at last" (Knowlson, 432). After an international flurry of interest it made little difference to either his relationship with Suzanne or that with Barbara Bray.

Suzanne's response to the **Nobel Prize** in 1969 was "Quel catastrophe," a genuine response to the invasion of privacy that the award entailed. She deflected the attention from SB, and organized vacations (Malta, Madeira, North Africa) away from the crowds to where the sun could mitigate the pains of lumbago (hers) and bronchitis (his). Suzanne later suffered from respiratory problems and other ailments but trusted her homeopathic advisers to deal with these. SB worried about her health, but his own "respiratory troubles" (emphysema) became more precarious, and he was finally unable to cope with her frailty, which later manifested itself in terms of egotism and hostility toward him. She died on 17 July 1989, SB attending the funeral at the Cimetière de Montparnasse. He did not outlive her for long.

desire: the word that, rather than "**love**" (qv), defines SB's early writings, above all in the identification of the subject with his desire, only to discover the nullity of attainment. In the terms set forth in *Proust* (13), the aspirations of yesterday were valid for yesterday's ego but not today's. An epigraph from **Leopardi** asserts (18): "non che la speme, il desiderio è spento" ("Not the hope, but the desire is extinguished"). This refers to the wisdom in not the satisfaction but the ablation of desire. SB announces his sense of the subject as "mobile" (17), and the object as "ideal," or exempt from the vulgar flux. When that object is another person, "whose mobility is not merely a function of the subject's," we find "two separate and immanent dynamisms related by no system of synchronisation." Thus an impasse: a thirst for possession, defined (57) as "the complete identification of object and subject," which is, by definition, insatiable. SB considers the Marcel-Albertine relationship as "the type-tragedy" of the human relationship whose failure is inevitable: "One only loves that which one does not possess entirely."

Windelband (149) offers the curious conjecture that the purposive **motion** of the animal **body** proceeds from desire, feelings of pleasure or pain that are bound up with and presuppose the *idea of their object*. **Schopenhauer** develops the implications of this (*WWI*, I.3 #52, 336): "Now the **nature** of man consists in this, that his will strives, is satisfied and strives anew, and so on for ever. Indeed his happiness and well-being consist simply in the quick transition from wish to satisfaction, and from satisfaction to a new wish. For the absence of satisfaction is suffering, the empty longing for a new wish, languor, *ennui*." The inner being of **consciousness** is a constant striving without end and without rest; but if it lacks objects of desire, or is deprived of them by a too easy satisfaction, then a terrible void ensues, and existence becomes unbearable: "Thus life swings like a pendulum backwards and forwards between pain and ennui" (402). In *Proust* (28), SB's pendulum oscillates between Suffering (the window opened upon the real) and Boredom (**habit**).

Windelband (191) underlines the assumption, from **Socrates** to **Descartes**, that wrong action proceeds from a view clouded by desires (one that is not "clear and distinct"), the ethical conception of freedom contingent on this premise. **Neary** represents this process, his rationalist convictions (and with them the Cartesian framework of *Murphy*) inconstantly subverted by desire. It is a lesson he never learns, and he suffers accordingly, in keeping with the principles that as consciousness ascends pain increases (*WWI*, I.4 #56, 400), the rarer the talent, the greater the suffering (405). SB redefines the dilemma in terms of **Gestalt** notions of figure and ground. **Neary** wants to know why the object of his affections, once attained, becomes one with the ground against which she had figured so prettily; constant change in the object of his affections, even at the end of the novel, chains him to a future of unsatiated desire. To continue this critique, see **love**.

"Les Deux besoins": an untranslated essay (1938), now in the Baker Memorial Library, Dartmouth College, unpublished until 1983 when Ruby Cohn gathered it for *Disjecta* (55–57). It addresses the "monotone centralité" of individual existence, yet the need to cultivate that state, the two needs being "Besoin d'avoir besoin" and "besoin dont on a besoin," or, crudely, necessity and the need to respond to it. In **"Denis Devlin,"** SB noted "the need to need." Cohn (173) articulates SB's plea "for an **irrational** interrogative art," and sees the "disjunctive" paragraphs of the essay as illustrating this process. The imagery is precisely that used in *Murphy:* the **monad**, the dode-cahedron of **Pythagoras**, the incom-mensurability of side and diagonal, and the story of **Hippasos**, each with a com-mon element of the irrational. The two needs are incommensurable, but **art** (the hexagon formed by the intersection of two triangles of necessity) is their prod-uct; to chose either is to prefer one tes-ticle to the other. The apparently irrel-evant wit of SB's examples (the movement of **Galileo**'s cradle, the clouding of **Stendhal**'s **mirror**, Hippasos as neither fascist nor communist) is in keeping with the theme. These are the "enthymèmes de l'art," syllogisms based on premises at best only probable, with uncertain con-clusions (the diagram is presented with the flourish: "Falsifions davantage"). The essay is thus an early intimation of the irrational need to express despite the antinomies that make expression impos-sible. Yet while anticipating the needs of the works to follow it by no means breaks with those of the past.

"Deux poèmes": "le nain nonagénaire" and "**à bout de songes un bouquin**" (*Minuit* 33 [mars 1979]: 2–3). The first edition of *Poèmes suivi de mirlitonnades* (1978) wrongly included them among the *Poèmes,* but in later printings they conclude the *mirlitonnades.* Omitted from *Collected Poems* (1984 and 1999).

"Deux textes pour rien": two pieces from "**Nouvelles et textes pour rien**," published in *Monde nouveau—Paru* [Paris] 89–90 (mai–juin 1955): 144–49; "Texte I" slightly revised, but "Texte XII" unaltered.

Dew, Rosie: a middle-aged woman, with a distressing case of duck's disease, or **panpygoptosis**. She asks **Murphy** to hold her little **doggy** while she feeds lettuce to the **sheep**. Her name suggests **Homer**-dusk and pastoral tranquility, as in Pope's "Summer": "bees from Blossoms sip the rosie Dew"; yet also menstrua-tion. She is based on Hester Dowden, "medium and psychic investigator," **MacGreevy**'s landlady in Cheyne Walk, **London** (Knowlson, 201), and/or a pa-tient of Geoffrey **Thompson's** at the Ro-tunda Hospital, **Dublin** (Bair, 170).

"Dialogue between Ernest and Alice": a forerunner of *Endgame;* nine leaves of an untitled and unpublished play in French (RUL 1227/7/16/2), dating from early 1955, with a dialogue between a **Hamm**-like Ernest, not in a wheelchair but on a cross, and his wife, Alice, who ministers to his needs (the aperitif is ex-hausted). The **crucifixion** imagery is striking: Ernest on the cross, a **veronica**-like handkerchief over his **face**; Alice at the foot, like Mary; and a ritual washing of Ernest's body. But the **allegory** was too obvious and the piece was aban-doned accordingly.

"Dialogue Samuel Beckett—Georges Duthuit": SB's translation of the third of "**Three Dialogues**" with Georges **Duthuit** concerning Bram **van Velde**. Published as a folio broadsheet associated with an exhibition of Bram's work at the Galerie Michel Warren, **Paris** (7 mai to 1 juin 1957); a large brochure on one sheet of stiff paper folded down the middle, white and dark green. The outside offers brief details about Bram; the inside discusses the composition and translation of the text, set out in two columns, SB's contributions in Roman intercalated with Duthuit's in italics (F&F, #31.01). A summary appeared as "Samuel Beckett et la peinture" in *La Nouvelle revue française* 54 (juin 1957): 1125–26.

Dick Deadeye: a walleyed ex-serviceman (*Dream,* 158), who impedes the passage of the **Polar Bear**. The name, punning on "Deadeye Dick" of the Wild West, derives from a sailor in Gilbert and Sullivan's *H.M.S. Pinafore,* "whose noblest sentiments sound like the black utterances of a depraved imagination."

Dickens, Charles (1812–70): English novelist, master of the quizzical and grotesque. SB did not admire him, much as he disliked **Hardy** (overreliance on coincidence) or **Balzac** (suspect realism). He praised *Great Expectations* in his "Exagmination" essay (*Disjecta,* 28): "the ooze squelching through Dickens's description of the Thames." The phrase *"flaws* of wind (Little Dorrit)" (chapter 9; DN, 145) is varied as "little flaws of saliva" (*Dream,* 187), "little flaws of dawn" ("Yellow," 176) and "grey flaws of tramontane" ("Echo's Bones," 27). The Ungeküsste Eva has lost her looks, "suppositiously, in Dickens's striking adverb" (*Dream,* 95), as of Mrs. Gamp's imaginary friend, Mrs. Harris. Dickens is implicated with Balzac in the "Old Curiosities" (118); the well-fed German salesgirl in the boot-shop is "an hypertrophied Dorrit" (131). A final curtain

may come down "like Pecksniff's palpebra" (149), his eyebrow, as the hypocrite gets his due; the sentiment that "we are all **dogs** together in the dogocracy of unanimous scurrility" (159) is dismissed as "Overstatement. Dickens"; and Dickens, with **D'Annunzio,** is finally "forgotten" (188). Or almost: "This may be premature. We have set it down too soon, perhaps. Still, let it stand" (216; *David Copperfield,* Ch. 3). Finally, the **Alba** in *Dream* (235) and "A **Wet Night**" (84) warns **Belacqua** not to "put across the Mrs Gummidge"; she refers to a "lone lorn creetur" in *David Copperfield,* who peevishly laments her condition, as Belacqua is not inclined to do.

Diderot, Denis (1713–84): French encyclopedist, whose *Pensées philosophiques* (1748) were burned publicly. His freethinking troubled the ecclesiastical authorities and led to imprisonment. His *Dictionaire Encyclopédie raisonnée des sciences,* which began as a translation and adaptation of Chambers's *Cyclopaedia* but soon assumed its own shape, was published clandestinely (1746 and 1772) with the aid of many prominent scholars (d'**Alembert, Rousseau, Voltaire**). His work came to the attention of Catherine of Russia, who rescued him financially and invited him to her court to engage in philosophical dispute (as **Christina** of Sweden had **Descartes**). Diderot's major fictional work was *Jacques le fataliste* (1773, but suppressed until 1796), a skeptical picaresque work that SB admired. He likened it to *Joseph Andrews* (SB to TM, 8 October 1932) and borrowed a handful of details (DN,

135–36 and 153), including the paraphrased "abrégé" of *Dream* (117) and the "quiproquo [*sic*] of living," which detains **Murphy** (2). *Jacques* is the prototype of *Mercier et Camier*, and of the manservant in *Eleutheria*. SB admired the philosophical dialogue *Le Neveu de Rameau* (1760 but first published in German by **Goethe** in 1804); set in a **Paris** café, with two interlocutors, "Moi" and "Lui," it offered a model for *Three Dialogues*, the "Exit weeping" of the second echoing Diderot's final "Rira bien qui rira le dernier." **Belacqua**'s "belle face carrée" (*Dream*, 124) resembles that of "Lui." "Le Rêve de d'Alembert" offered SB images of **bees** and a rose. The example of Diderot, an atheist in a bigoted world, was a fine one, and SB found in him another who preferred the **atomist** tradition of **Epicurus** and **Lucretius** to the conventional pieties of his age.

"**Dieppe**": a short, imagist verse of five lines published in the *Irish Times* (9 June 1945): 2; then, the first two lines run together and dated 1937, as ninth of the twelve *Poèmes 38–39*; later collected in *Gedichte* (1959). SB included a translation in *Poems in English* (1961) and *Collected Poems* (1977), in the latter changing the final line from "the lighted town" to "the lights of old." The poem depicts a moment of choice, as the poet stands on the dead shingle at the last ebb of the tide, looking seaward then turning toward those lights. The sentiment is poised between the impulse to go into the dark or return to the world of others. Harvey (218) senses its origins in **Hölderlin**'s "Der Spaziergang," where the four lines beginning "Ihr lieblichen Bilder im Tale" show the poet turning toward a scarcely visible path by a brook. SB refers to this passage in "**Denis Devlin**" (1938), accentuating its "extraordinary evocation of the unsaid by the said." A version of the poem is insinuated into **Arsene**'s short statement (*Watt*, 40) as he acknowledges the pull of the old ways, the old windings.

"**Ding-Dong**": third story of *MPTK*, written in late 1932, the title resonating between Ariel's "Ding dong bell" in *The Tempest* and the carol, "Ding Dong Merrily on High." This is neatly inapposite, given that the story forms an ironic parody of **Dante**'s *Paradiso*, specifically, the end of Canto X, which describes the "glorious wheel" going round and round in harmony and sweetness making a "tin tin" sound as it moves (X.142). Here Dante addresses the "lettore" in his own **voice**, which fades into that of his character. "Ding-Dong" assumes a like narrative voice, that of **Belacqua**'s "sometime friend," who fades imperceptibly into the story until his **voice** is indistinguishable.

The story tells how Belacqua "enlivened the last phase of his **solipsism**" (36) by moving constantly. One day, having emerged from the underground toilet near the statue of Thomas **Moore**, he finds himself unable to move, seeking a sign. The big **Bovril** sign offers neither Faith, Hope, nor Charity, but there is a "futile emblem" of the latter in the blind paralytic from the **Coombe**. Belacqua, responding to this, makes off in the opposite direction. He sees a little girl who has been run over, the queue for the Palace Cinema torn between seeing the excitement or losing their places; but one debauched girl risks the latter to steal the little girl's loaf of bread. This is a world without **pity**, the narrative assuming an indifference to the suffering it describes so that the ending will have the requisite bleak irony of a tale saturated in religious emblems but devoid of charity. The climax arises as, staring at his dying porter in a pub, Belacqua looks up to see a hatless woman advancing on him, a shabby **Beatrice** ("serene, serenissime") who offers him "Seats in heaven," that is, in the "**Gods**" at the theater. She tells him that Heaven goes "rowan an' rowan"; but he, like Dante at the end of the *Purgatorio,* is unable to look to his salvation, drinking his "dead porter" as Dante and Beatrice the sweet waters. Phrases like "petrified in radiance" (Dante's *rime petrosa*), "deplorable" feet (as the peacock), and "sweet style" (his *dolce stil nuovo*) enforce the analogy. Belacqua buys the tickets, why he knows not. She leaves "lighted" by her countenance, but he departs for the **kips** of Railway Street, beyond the Liffey, more like the dismal stream of Acheron at the first circle of Hell than the fair stream over which Dante must pass to enter Heaven.

Diogenes of Apollonia (ca. 435 BC): a pre-Socratic philosopher whose work is preserved in fragments only. **Neary** calls **Murphy** a "long hank of Apollonian asthenia" (49); for Diogenes the primary substrate was air ("a small portion of the **God**"), from which by condensation and change of state all else arises (Burnet, *Early Greek Philosophy,* 352–58).

Dionysius the Areopagite: in Acts 17:34 a follower of Paul. A Syrian monk at-tached that name in pious fraud, 400 years later, to theological tracts that form a remarkable synthesis of Christian, Greek, Jewish, and Oriental teaching. Inge's *Christian Mysticsm* (1899) defines his object as "to present Christianity in the guise of a Platonic mysteriosophy," using technical terms for the Mysteries whenever possible; SB mocks his "all-transcending superessentially super-existing super-Deity" (*Dream,* 17; Inge, 106). The thrust of his teaching, as summed up in *Dream* (17), is the sense of life ascending from its lower forms unto the divine source by the circular movement of the mind (Inge, 108; DN, 98–99).

directing: SB's transformation from playwright to theatrical artist is a seminal development of late modernist theater and yet one slighted in the critical and historical discourse that privileges print over performance, the apparent stability of literature over the vicissitudes of theater. The neglect of SB's work on the boards distorts the arc of his creative evolution, his emergence as an artist committed to the performance of his drama as its full realization. He would embrace theater not just as a medium where a preconceived work was given its accurate expression, but as *the* means through which his drama was created. As SB evolved from being an adviser to taking full charge of staging his plays, practical theater offered him a unique opportunity for self-collaboration through which he reinvented himself as an artist.

The transformational year was 1966. SB was preparing (with Mariu **Karmitz** and Jean Ravel) a film version of Jean-

Marie Serreau's June 1964 version of "Comédie." He rushed off to **London** to oversee "**Eh Joe**," with Jack **MacGowran** and Siân Phillips, nominally directed by Alan Gibson (BBC 2, 4 July 1966): "Really pleased with result." He oversaw two vinyl recordings for Claddagh records: *MacGowran Speaking Beckett* (CCT-3); and *MacGowran Reading Beckett's Poetry.* He then rushed back to **Paris** to oversee Serreau's series of one-acts at the Odéon, Théâtre de France, including a reprise of "Comédie," "**Va et vient**," and SB's staging of Robert **Pinget**'s *Hypothèse* with Pierre Chabert, originally presented at the Musée d'Art Moderne (18 octobre 1965). These opened 14 March 1966. The first of his works for which SB received full directorial credit, however, was the 1966 Stuttgart telecast of "Eh Joe" (broadcast by SDR on SB's sixtieth birthday, 13 April 1966).

In 1967, after almost a full year of nonstop theater ("Forget what writing is about"), SB accepted an invitation from the **Schiller-Theater** to direct a play; he chose *Endspiel,* the "favourite of my plays" (*Berlin Diary*). The monumental decision would result in the transformation of nearly all of his works for theater over the next two decades. He prepared a *Regiebuch,* a director's notebook; such notebooks would thereafter characterize his meticulous approach to directing (see *Theatrical Notebooks*). In his directorial appearances SB approached his work as another; that is, the SB who authored *Waiting for Godot* and the one who staged it at the Schiller-Theater were not the same artist. The conjunction of the two, the writing self of 1948 and the directing "other" of 1978, is one of the

defining moments of late modernist theater, such conjunction occurring sixteen times on the stage and six times in the television studio. Each time, SB seized directing opportunities to refine and redefine his creative vision, to discover latent possibilities in his texts, to reaffirm a fundamentally modernist aesthetics by expunging anything he deemed extraneous, and to demonstrate afresh his commitment to, his preoccupation with, the aesthetic shape of his work. His theatrical notebooks for "**Spiel**," for example, contain twenty-five separate outlines as he combed his text for visual and aural parallels, reverberations, echoes, in preparation for his own staging. SB developed into a major theoretician of the theater in the process of staging his plays.

SB's attraction to working in theater went beyond correcting errors of others or simplifying and shaping his text. An accomplished musician and a writer with a deep interest in the visual arts, he discovered that theater allowed him to paint (or sculpt), to work directly with form as a visual artist. For theater is not language alone but a spatial as well as a temporal genre. Staging offered him the opportunity to deal with form—with shape, relation, balance, but only occasionally color—in a way that language alone never could. To the **music** and poetry of words he could add the arrangement of forms in a controlled, framed space (hence his abiding interest in the proscenium stage and in television, both frame-dominated).

As a director SB remained a generic purist, treating the systems of theatrical communication separately, keeping, for instance, music and **motion** distinct.

Such separation reaffirms a **Gnostic** or Manichaen reluctance to mingle opposites. Practically, it maintains balance of action and language, of the theatrical and the linguistic. SB admonished his actors: "Never let your changes of position and voice come together. First comes (a) the altered bodily stance; after it, following a slight pause, comes (b) the corresponding utterance" (*Berlin Diary*). Such phrasing suggests a series of still pictures or photographs more than continuous action or movement. SB even asked his actors to forgo curtain calls. When they agreed he seemed relieved and confessed that it would have hurt to break up the still picture at the end. The phrase used in the Riverside Notebook is "frozen postures." The whole of *Endgame* drives to that final "frozen posture," outside, beyond language, yet as tied to and dependent on it as **Lucky** to **Pozzo**, as light to dark, as music to rest, as being to **nothing**: Clov dressed to leave, yet hesitating; Hamm resigned to an inevitable end, yet resisting. SB had visualized the resolution of *Godot* this way; fourteen years earlier to Roger **Blin** he had invoked "ce touchant tableau final."

Pattern was as crucial to SB's eye as to his ear, dominating his theatrical notes: motion to echo motion, posture to echo posture, gestures to echo gestures, sounds to echo sounds. The action of *Endgame* is filled with circles, arcs, and crosses, from Hamm's rounds to Clov's thinking walk. Even when the phrasing was not parallel, SB established an echo, as in his Schiller Notebook where he suggests that "Why this farce" should have the "same quality as 'Let's stop playing.'" His direction of *Endgame* fulfilled the struc-

ture he had outlined for Blin's *Fin de partie* (1957). He looked on it as a kind of musical score, Blin noted. When a word occurred or was repeated, when Hamm called Clov, the effect was like a musical phrase coming from the same instrument with the same volume. Ten years later SB realized this musical conception of the play. "The play is full of echoes," he told his German cast, "they all answer each other." SB's direction was also marked by a surprising realistic subtext, precise motivations for almost imperceptible action. He insisted on not intellectualizing his text in rehearsals, wanting the play to take shape on stage as dramatic material. In the final analysis, SB's directing was his theatrical realization of the shape of ideas.

SB's productions:

In Paris:
Robert Pinget's *L'Hypothèse,* with Pierre Chabert, Musée d'Art Moderne, 18 Octobre 1965
"Va et vient" and Robert Pinget's *L'Hypothèse,* Odéon Théâtre de France, 28 Février 1966 (SB uncredited for his own play but credited for the Pinget)
La Dernière bande, Théâtre Récamier, 29 Avril 1970
La Dernière band with *Pas moi,* Théâtre d'Orsay (Petite Salle), Avril 1975
Pas with *Pas moi,* Théâtre d'Orsay, Avril 1978

In Berlin at the *Schiller-Theater Werkstatt:*
Endspiel, 26 September 1967

Das letzte Band, 5 October 1969
Glückliche Tage, 17 September 1971
Warten auf Godot, 8 March 1975
Damals and *Tritte,* 1 October 1976
Krapp's Last Tape (English), *Akademie der Künste* with the **San Quentin Drama Workshop**, rehearsals 10–27 September 1977
"Spiel," 6 October 1978

In London:
Footfalls, Royal Court Theatre, May 1976
Happy Days, Royal Court Theatre, June 1979
Endgame, with the San Quentin Drama Workshop, Riverside Studios, May 1980
Waiting for Godot, with the San Quentin Drama Workshop; rehearsals at the Goodman Theater, Chicago (Nov. 1983 to January 1984), dir. Walter Asmus; SB joined the group at the Riverside Studios, London (2 February 1984), and rehearsed the actors for ten days. Premiered at the Adelaide Arts Festival (13 March 1984).

Teleplays:
(all at Süddeutscher Rundfunk, Stuttgart; with date of broadcast):
"He, Joe," dir. March 1966 (with Deryk **Mendel** and Nancy Illig), 13 April 1966
"Geistertrio," dir. May–June 1977 (with Klaus Herm and Irmgard Foerst), 1 November 1977
"Nur noch Gewolk," dir. May–June 1977 (with Klaus Herm and Kornelia Bose), 1 November 1977
"He, Joe," dir. Jan. 1979 (with Heinz

Bennent and Irmgard Först), September 1979
"Quadrat," dir. June 1981 (with Helfrid Foron, Juerg Hummel, Claudia Knupfer, and Suzanne Rehe), 8 October 1981
"Nacht und Traüme," dir. October 1982, 19 May 1983
"Was Wo," dir. June 1985, 13 April 1986

Disjecta: subtitled "Miscellaneous Writings and a Dramatic Fragment by Samuel Beckett," edited and with a foreword by Ruby Cohn; a handy collection of SB's early and minor writings. Published (1983) with SB's reluctant agreement for the sake of scholars, fragments in **French** and German at his insistence in the language of composition. The title was SB's own, from **Ovid**'s *Metamorphoses* (book VI), the *disjecta membra* or "scattered limbs" representing his sense that the pieces are of little value. Cohn takes issue with this dismissal, arguing that while the miscellany resists coherence it yet "harbors an esthetic." Her grouping is by subject, ranging from "more or less formal esthetics" through literary criticism to art criticism, then a few excerpts from letters and a fragment of "**Human Wishes**." A useful set of notes, not without errors, identifies for each piece the place and date of original publication (but curiously omitting volume numbers and pagination), the location of pertinent manuscripts or documents, and (occasionally) the sense of obscure references.

"**Dis Joe**": SB's translation (June 1965) of "**Eh Joe**" (qv). First appearing in *Arts:*

l'hebodomadaire complet de la vie culturel 15 (janvier 5–11 1966): 3; subtitled "un inédit de Beckett" but anticipating its publication in *Comédie et actes divers* (Minuit, 1966), 79–91. "Dis Joe," with Jean-Louis Barrault and Madeleine **Renaud**, dir. Michael Mitrani, was broadcast on RTF (2 février 1968). A multimedia stage version mounted (with SB's reluctant consent) by Jean-Claude Fall, who played Joe, opened at the Théâtre de la Bastille (1984).

diving board: a recurrent **Freudian** motif in which the **father** urges the son to plunge from a high board into the water full of large rocks. This is the **memory** of the Victorian seawater baths near the "Forty Foot" swimming hole, **Dún Laoghaire**. It appears in "**For Future Reference**," *Dream* (34), and *Eleutheria* (125). It is explicit in **Watt**'s "uneasy sleep, lacerated by dreams, by dives from dreadful heights into rocky waters" (222). In *Company* (18) the narrator's imagination is still haunted by the memory: "You stand at the tip of a high board. High above the sea." The embarrassment of the child on exhibition, urged to "Be a brave boy" (18) and dive into the frigid Irish Sea, is something SB brought up frequently enough to receive mention in Anne **Atik**'s memoir (33). He was wrestling with this image shortly before his **death**, for he asked Herbert Blau about recurring dreams: "I am up on a high board, over a water full of large rocks . . . I have to dive through a hole in the rocks."

Dobbin, Rachel: née Burrows; a student at **Trinity** (1930), whose notes from SB's lectures (TCD, MIC 60) are a valuable record of his teaching. See *JOBS* 11 and 12 (1989): 5–15.

Doctrine of the Limit: a tractate attributed to **Neary** (*Murphy*, 50), which alludes to this central **pre-Socratic** concern. The Pythagoreans had regarded the limit (*peran*) and the unlimited (*apeiron*) as the elements of number, and therefore the elements of things. From this simple paradox all flows: the association of odd and even numbers with the limit and the unlimited; the spatial character of geometry as opposed to the linear nature of arithmetic; aspects of the musical scale; the relation of the doctrine to the theory of **Apmonia** or Attunement; the distinction of Being and Becoming; the problems of the One and the Many; the identification by **Pythagoras** of the Limit with Fire and the Unlimited with Darkness; the debate as to how the limit gave form to the unlimited, or boundless (a central problem of Greek thought). For **Democritus** the Doctrine was the basis of **atomism**, for without a limit things would pass out of existence. **Malone**, about to do so, has sought, he says (197), the forms in which the unchanging seeks relief from its formlessness. Neary's tractate, were it recovered from Miss **Counihan**, might have helped him with that quest.

dogs: although **Belacqua** despises dogs, for their obviousness (*Dream,* 127), SB was fond of the family's Kerry Blue terriers, one of which, Wolf, pants his pleasure in "**Sanies I**." Years later, fat and half-dead, the other dreams in "**Serena II**" of the dark old days, of dropping her young in a distant hag (a firm bit in a bog). She accompanies Belacqua in "**Walking Out**," so old that she cannot run. SB was distressed when his **mother** had her chloroformed in his absence. **Nelly**, the **panpygoptic** canine, eats **Murphy**'s biscuits, puts him out by twopence and a critique of pure **love** (103), i.e., negates any sympathy for the misfortunate. Although Mother **Calvet** in "**Text 2**" has her dog, the only suggestion of man's best friend is in *Watt* (172), where the faithful **O'Connor** is drowned in a bog then roasted over a fire of flags (reeds) and cotton blossoms (*Eriophorum,* a bog grass with cottonlike fiber balls). Watt has no love for dogs, "greatly preferring **rats**" (115).

Watt offers the famished dog as a satire of **preestablished harmony**. His mode of reasoning explodes exponentially, each assertion raising further needs and objections, and to cater for these, more contingent reasons are required so that within a few pages the conditional existence of the dog has become a declarative statement: "The name of this dog . . . was Kate" (112). Complex as the passage is in the "finished" novel, in the Notebooks it is more so, the logic of explanation demanding that such things as the breed be known (Irish Setter and Palestine Retriever), as well as the intricacies of the breeding program.

The dog is the animal kingdom reduced to its **fundamental sound**: "head sunk tail on balls" (*How It Is,* 30), pink and black penis (repeated in "The **Image**," 167); and "my spinal dog it licked my genitals Skom Skum run over by a dray" (85), so that a "column of quiet" (**Burton**'s epithet for a faithful wife) becomes

a "broken column." **Mercier and Camier** witness a gross spectacle (9–16): in each other's arms, they feel awkward, but two dogs "were already copulating, with the utmost naturalness." The dogs become locked together (12): "they yearn to part, to go and piss against a post or eat a morsel of shit, but cannot"; instead, they are attacked and "buggered" by the ranger, for locked together they cannot escape, and unable to pull apart they can be kicked. **A** or C in *Molloy* (11) is followed by a wretched Pomeranian, the kind owned by SB's **mother**. Molloy (32) runs over a dog, Teddy, a mongrel or a pedigree, he cannot tell the difference, but he may have done it a favor as **Lousse** was taking it to be put out of its misery. Teddy is buried beneath a **larch**, and Molloy notices (37) in his ears the little ticks to be buried with him.

SB recorded in the **German Diaries** the little round song the **Unnamable** uses (379) to call up a multitude of living bastards, and which in *Waiting for Godot* (37) is an image of infinite regression, like the play itself. The French dog steals an "andouillette," or horsemeat sausage; in the German original, an egg. In *Endgame,* **Clov** is described as not raised but whelped (14). He attacks the flea "laying doggo" (34), a solecism corrected by **Hamm**: "If he was laying we'd be bitched." Hamm demands his dog, "a kind of Pomeranian," but it is not "ready," for it lacks a leg, falls on its side, and the "sex" (and ribbon) hasn't gone on yet. Hamm angrily orders his invisible audience to **love** one another: "Lick your neighbour as yourself!" (68), before admitting "Not even a real dog" (69). There is a "real dog" in the room at the end of *Film*, until it and the **cat** are evicted. Aware of "**O**" but not of "**E**" the animals lack the capacity of **apperception**, and cannot therefore reflect upon their impossible predicament in a **body**-bound world, finished or otherwise.

Donaghy, John Lyle (1902–47): born in Ulster and educated at **Trinity**. Described by O'Brien (377) as one who published several volumes of poetry yet never fulfilled his promise. "**Recent Irish Poetry**" (75) mocks his "Primordia Caeca" (1927) and "objectless" poetry, but acknowledges a fine poem about a steamroller.

donkey: SB's **mother** had a small donkey cart (see Bair,114–15, and O'Brien, 13) and a succession of donkeys to draw it. SB was fond of them, and invited Jack **Yeats** to **Cooldrinagh** to see one that Yeats wanted to paint. **Belacqua** claims to dislike domestic animals of all kinds, "save the extraordinary countenance of the donkey seen full-face" (*Dream,* 127). A photograph approximating that description is recalled by **Malone** (251). Earlier, **Molloy** as he leaves the town hears angry cries and dull blows (26), then sees a team of little gray donkeys pulling a barge with a cargo of nails and timber, the boatman having a long white beard (not in the **French** text). In *Mercier and Camier* (77–78), Mercier experiences a kind of epiphany as he sees the old ragged man with his donkey. See **hinny.**

Donne, John (1572–1631): English metaphysical poet and divine, whose **love** poetry is matched in passion and wit by his devotional verse. In "**What a Misfortune**" (128), Thelma has "at least the anagram of a good **face**" (*Elegy,* 2). **God** comes to the aid of **Belacqua** with one of Donne's *Paradoxes,* offering him **Democritus** or **Heraclitus** ("Yellow," 162). Donne's *Problems* ask why women have souls (VI), answer, that they might be damned, a jest **Moran** appreciates (*Molloy,* 137). **Murphy**'s anguish over his biscuits (103) may be gauged by the hyperbole of his "Oh, my America" ("To his Mistress on Going to Bed"); and his heart's desire reflects Donne's *Holy Sonnet* (V.1): "I am a **little world** made cunningly." Donne's last sermon (25 February1630), in conscious anticipation of his own death, may have influenced SB (see **issueless**). In 1983 SB sent to Jim Lewis, cameraman of "**What Where**," a postcard of a cowled figure of Donne, the 1631 statue by Nicholas Stone in the east end of the Chancel of St. Paul's where Donne is buried, suggesting that the costumes for his last play might be modeled accordingly. The shrouded spectral Dean in this sculptured rendering makes a fitting death mask for the image of Bam beyond the grave.

"**Dortmunder**": a fourteen-line poem, vaguely sonnetlike (January 1932), published in *Echo's Bones* (1934); rpt. in *transition* 24 (June 1936). On a signed copy, now in the **HRHRC** (#42), SB noted "Cassel revisited." The setting is a brothel and the central tension is between obligation (the "spire of sanctuary") and shame (the bawd), the world of the violet lamp and thin k'în music resolved in the "long night phrase" between dusk and day, the black eyes of the bawd different from the green ones (Peggy **Sinclair**) he has known. SB admitted to **MacGreevy** (21 November 1932) that he was susceptible to "the German fever" (recollections of Peggy) close to Christmas. The title refers to a brand of German beer, the poem (SB told John Fletcher) the outcome of consuming too much of it, but the vignette invokes the magic of the night world before the **music** ends and the bawd puts her lute away. Much of the detail is also in *Dream*. **Schopenhauer** "dead" means the end of will, or **desire**. A reference to **Habakkuk** 2:10 forms a subtext: "Thou has consulted shame to thy house by cutting off many people, and hast sinned against thy soul." Hence the self as "mard" of all sinners, from **Burton**'s *Anatomy*, meaning excrescence, or turd. For a reading asserting the poet's undeviating allegiance to the night world, see Harvey (73–78).

Dostoyevsky, Fyodor Mikhailovich (1821–81): Russian novelist. SB told **MacGreevy** (25 May 1931) that he had been reading *The Possessed* in a foul translation, but no one caught the insanity of dialogue as "Dostoievski" [*sic*] did. SB's "The **Possessed**" reflects this quality. SB proposed to Charles **Prentice** that he extend his *Proust* essay to develop the parallel with Dostoyevsky. He offered a similar essay on Dostoyevsky, but told MacGreevy that this was for the sake of something to say. Casual details only appear in SB's writing, such as the "fine Dostoievskian contempt for the vulgarity of a plausible concatenation" (*Proust*, 82), probably the ramshackle structure of *Crime and Punishment* (1866). Dostoyev-

sky's characters, SB asserts, are stated without being explained (*Proust*, 87). SB calls Nastasia Filippovna, from *The Idiot* (1868; *Dream*, 105), the true **Shekinah**, and alludes (179) to Aliosha, the saintliest of *The Brothers Karamazov* (1880). To MacGreevy (7 July 1936), he cited Aliosha with respect to **Murphy** and the danger of an author identifying too closely with his character.

"The Downs": a fifty-five-line poem in English, undated, in typescript (RUL 911/1–2), seven stanzas of short lines, all but the first of eight lines. The poem invokes walking hand in hand with the loved one, long summer days over the downs, to the edge of the cliff, then speechless, winter nights, gazing down at the foaming flood, no meaning but the light, faintly light, the foam, the snow. The holograph manuscript, 183 lines of extensive autograph revisions and deletions, signed and dated "**Paris**, 1981," was offered by SB for sale in aid of Oxfam. SB described it as a "quick miscarriage"; Sotheby's aborted it further by a mistranscription: "The worms . . . long summer days over the worms / Hand in hand with the loved one."

Doyle, Mick: groundsman of "**Draff**," left to finish **Belacqua**'s burial. He is named in "**Echo's Bones**," where, naked save for a truss and his **boots**, and with the words "Stultum propter Christum" (see **Thomas à Kempis**) tattooed across his tum-tum, he comes as a resurrection man to excavate Belacqua's grave. After an obscure conversation, a bet is made as to what will be found when the coffin is opened (answer, a handful of stones).

Draeger: Dr. A. Draeger, *Historische Syntax der lateinischen Sprache* (2 Bde., Leipzig, 1874–78); as in the "Lexiques" and "tattered Syntaxes" of "Jolly and Draeger" of "**Faux départs**" (271–72) and *All Strange Away* (169–73).

"**Draff**": tenth and final story of *MPTK*. SB wanted this as the title of the whole, but Charles **Prentice** demurred, considering it too obscure. The word refers to lees of grain left over after brewing, husks fed to swine, as in *Dream* (46): **Belacqua** is one who delights "in swine's draff." SB found the word in the archaic EETS translation of *De Imitatione Christi* of **Thomas à Kempis** (III.xv; Ingram, 83): "I saw them delight in swine's draff" (DN, 85). The story was written after the **death** of SB's **father**, as indicated by echoes of "**Malacoda**," and by the setting in the graveyard of Redford, where Bill **Beckett** had been interred.

The story is "draff" in that it mashes the lees and husks of SB's other writing with a coarse disregard for tonal unity. The narrative is an adequate slops bucket, but finer points are mangled. "Mrs Shuah" is the **Smeraldina**, other wives having literally or figuratively "gone west." Her description (176) is rehashed from *Dream* (15 and 68–69), and the disregard of narrative niceties continues with the arrival of "Mr **Malacoda**" ("Nick"), who has come to measure, and to coffin. There is no intense suffering or anguished farce, but an imbalance between casual realism and misplaced **allegory**. The undertaker is invested with perfunctory demonic qualities ("black claws"); the driver is named "Scarmiglione" (185)

without irony; and the anguished ending of the poem carelessly drops into the prosaic: "All aboard. All souls at half-mast. Aye-aye" (185). An echo of *Romeo and Juliet* (185) is bathetic. This is a mixture for swine, pearls of paste casually strung together.

The ending offers a casual disregard for the consolations of piety but equally for Belacqua's rejection of them. They return home to find the place on fire, a contrived retelling of the **McCabe** murders that locks the last story into the first with a conscious click of the jigsaw. Capper **Quin**'s proposal has a glorious ambiguity, the Smeraldina being "more than ever at a loose end now" (190), that she come with him and be his love. The story ends happily after all, if not ever after, this undoubtedly being what her darling Bel would have wished; but that is not the last word even though what might have been inscribed upon his tombstone ("vox es praetera nihil?") has been blotted from **memory**. In a final extravagance, the groundsman has the last word, a meditation on mortality, d'**Alembert**'s rose to the rose: "No gardener has died, comma, within rosaceous memory." This is not princely art, nor was meant to be but, taken for what it is, most satisfying swill.

Dramatische Dichtungen: a collection of SB's dramatic works (Frankfurt: Suhrkamp). Volume I (1963; 535 pp.), French originals and German translations, with SB's English translations at the end: *Waiting for Godot, Endgame,* "**Act Without Words**" (I and II)," and "**Cascando**" (its first appearance in book form). Volume II (1964; 429 pp.), English originals and German translations, with SB's French translations at the end: *All That Fall, Krapp's Last Tape,* "Embers," *Happy Days,* and "Play." "Words and Music" appeared with the German translation only ("Worte und Musik"). A one-volume edition appeared in 1981.

"dread nay": a poem of eight stanzas (1974), included in *Collected Poems* (1984). The figure encased in ice is Bocca degli Abati. See "hors crâne seul dedans."

Dream Notebook: one of SB's private notebooks of the early 1930s, donated by Edward Beckett to the BIF at Reading, and edited (1999) by John Pilling, who has identified most of the sources. Its content largely determines the texture of *Dream,* and was primarily compiled for that purpose, but other details made their way into other works. As usual, SB wrote on the rectos, leaving the versos blank for later additions. The Dream Notebook is an invaluable guide to SB's early reading and offers fascinating insights into his creative method, testifying to his conscious "notesnatching," and to the centolike nature of his early works.

Dream of Fair to middling Women: SB's first novel covers the period (1928–30) when he was in Paris at the École Normale. Begun in 1931, but mostly written over the summer of 1932, at the Trianon Hotel on the Rue de Vaugirard. Two extracts, "Text" and "Sedendo et Quiesciendo" [*sic*] appeared in small magazines, but there was no wider interest. *Dream* was submitted to several publishers, and rejected among others by Chatto and Windus, who had accepted

Proust. Charles Prentice was firm: it would not do. SB was reluctant to accept this verdict. He later refused to release it, partly because of this disappointment, partly because of its immaturity, and because much had been cannibalized for *MPTK* and *Murphy.*

SB gave the typescript to Lawrence Harvey (1961) for his study of the poetry. Harvey gave it to Dartmouth College, and a typed transcription (with minor variants) was later made for the BIF. Copies circulated, and while scholars accessed these the text retained the fascination of forbidden fruit. SB resisted entreaties to have it published until 1986, when he allowed Eoin O'Brien and Edith Fournier to edit it and to bring it out after he had died. The novel was published in 1992, amidst controversy. O'Brien had intended publication by John Calder, but unseemly arguments arose about setting the text, leading O'Brien to go it alone through his Black Cat Press (Dublin, 1992). Calder produced his more "economical" edition with the identical text, even to the choice of ending (the manuscript offering two versions but the published versions only one), bringing out an injunction to prevent O'Brien's distributing it within the UK. Calder sold the American rights to Arcade Books, where Richard Seaver made minor corrections but (according to O'Brien, in a deposition after the squabble) retained most of Calder's errors (misspellings and "correction" of deliberate errors; random hyphens) that had caused the disagreement. O'Brien and Fournier disassociated themselves from these editions, which, nonetheless, retain their introduction.

SB called it "the German comedy," commenting to Prentice (12 July 1931): "Of course it stinks of **Joyce** in spite of most earnest endeavours to endow it with my own odours. Unfortunately for myself that's the only way I'm interested in writing." The impulse toward complexity lasted until *Murphy* (1936). *Dream* is not entirely successful, but it is innovative, and SB displayed his talent, ingenuity, erudition, and arrogance. The work is less a novel than scenes within a dream structure, like **Chaucer**'s "Legend of Good Women," which is the primary model (though the influence of *Finnegans Wake* might be discerned, as well as that of **Freud**). It is loosely orchestrated according to **musical** principles (sonata form, the twelve **liù-liú**) that are themselves subverted. Much of the detail, and particularly the portraits of the fair women, is taken directly from **Burton** and other sources (see the **Dream Notebook** and John Pilling's later *Dream Companion*). It was an attempt to free fiction from constraint: "ramshackle, tumbledown, a boneshaker" (139), debunking "narrative recta," its only unity "an involuntary unity" (132). A story of sorts moves from a glimpse of **Belacqua**'s childhood ("One"); to his relationships with the **Smeraldina** and the **Syra-Cusa** ("Two"); a brief return to **Dublin** ("Und"), where he pursues the **Alba** ("Three"), before coming out in the rain ("And"), to be told, as at the outset (for the novel is full of such symmetries), to "move on," with no particular place to go. This is conceived not as leading to any climax, but as a challenge to conventional narrative form.

Title and epigraph associate **Tennyson** and Chaucer in a dream of fair women, with one emendation, whereby Chaucer's affirmation of the joys in heaven and torment in hell loses its third line, "And I accorde wel that it ys so," leaving the first word of the fourth: "But—." SB (through Belacqua) vents his feelings about the various women in his life: the tragic affair with Peggy **Sinclair** (the Smeraldina), culminating in the dreadful New Year's Eve (1929); the uncertain involvement with Lucia **Joyce** (the Syra-Cusa); and the impossible adoration of Ethna **MacCarthy** (the Alba). The novel is not quite a roman à clef, but the characters are close to those in SB's life: Belacqua (SB); John (his brother, Frank); "**Mammy**" (Aunt Cissie); the **Mandarin** ("Boss" Sinclair); **Lucien** (Jean **Beaufret**); **Liebert** (Georges **Pelorson**); the **Polar Bear** (Thomas **Rudmose-Brown**); Jean du **Chas** (Alfred **Péron**); and the **Fricas** (Susan and Mary **Manning**).

The novel proper begins in Dublin, Belacqua farewelling "a slob of a girl called Smeraldina-Rima," an unkind portrait yet testifying to feelings intense enough to indicate that the spleen derives from genuine emotion, in which affection as well as resentment may be discerned. Belacqua follows her to "Schule Dunkelbrau," the Hellerau-Laxenburg school near Vienna, which Peggy attended (Knowlson, 152), and visits the family in **Kassel**, where he treats her with enchantment and contempt. The poem "**At last I find in my confusèd soul**" (70–71) testifies to his intensity of feeling, but is scorned as a May-night "hiccupsob." His adoration of her **face** is undercut by her **body**; loving her, rejecting her, he

strives to retain her in his mind inviolate. Until she rapes him. Thereafter the
relation deteriorates. The climax occurs
on New Year's Eve, when an evening of
misunderstanding and sexual betrayal
leads to a final parting, the description
arrogant but the pain present beneath
that façade. The victim of the scorn, finally, is Belacqua, who neither asks for
sympathy nor makes it easy for the reader
to grant it. The Syra-Cusa is dealt with
more sketchily: "her body more perfect
than dream creek, amaranth lagoon"
(33). She has a "lech" on him, as Lucia
Joyce had on SB. She remains hors
d'oeuvre (49), and yet he gives her his
lovely book (a copy of **Dante**), which
she promptly leaves in a bar. That leads
to a final rejection (51): "Be off,
puttanina, and joy be with you and a
bottle of moss" (the roles of Titania
and Bottom reversed).

The novel tells a "little story about
China" (10), about how Ling-Liûn went
to the Bamboo Valley and cut there a
stem on which he could play the twelve
notes, or liù-liú (see **music**). The characters (it is devoutly to be hoped) will
"do their dope" like well-minded liu. But
they will not; they will not let themselves
be orchestrated, nor will "our principal
boy" (11). Nor will the other musical
form suffice, that of the sonata, with the
Smeraldina as one theme and the Alba
as the other. The novel will not easily
find its melodic form. The theme is revisited in the interlude, "Und," SB
invoking the difficulty of making his
characters perform when he, as author,
is neither Deus enough nor ex machina
enough to do so. A key part of the interlude (120–25) concerns Belacqua's es-

sential being, a structure like **Murphy's
mind** (qv). The third part is the dark
gulf, where the glare of will is switched
off, the mind having gone into its inner
dark; this condition he cannot readily
attain, it being impossible to switch off
the inward glare.

In the final section, Belacqua is back
in Dublin. Much is social satire (another
reason SB did not wish it in print). The
portraits are witty and cruel, but they are
incidental to the adoration of the Alba
by Belacqua, an unlikely suitor with his
dirty clothes and spavined gait. Yet at the
Frica's party (recycled in "A **Wet
Night**"), where the vacuity of everyone
else is exposed, the Alba takes **pity** on the
bedraggled Belacqua and takes him
home. No, he does not stay the night,
but there is a fire and a bottle and brief
respite before he comes out into the dark
and the rain (a parody of "The Dead"),
forced to sit down on the streaming
pavement to ease his pain, before the
voice of authority, more in sorrow than
in anger, enjoins him to move on. In
the **Whoroscope Notebook**, SB had
noted the Dynamist ethic: "Keep moving the only virtue." There is no climax, no epiphany, simply the need to
go **on**, however he can.

Drinker machine: after Philip Drinker,
American health engineer (1894–
1972); a respirator, or iron lung, for
polio. *Murphy* (49).

"Drunken Boat": SB's most ambitious
early translation was **Rimbaud**'s *Le
Bateau ivre*, a poem in twenty-five quatrains. He imitated it faithfully, but ignored the ABAB rhyme scheme for a

freer verse. The sustained metaphor is that of the poet as a drunken boat making its way through the reefs and tempests of the world, beset by and reeling from the blasts. SB offered it to Edward Titus, editor of *This Quarter*, for Fr. 1000, and was given 700, but the periodical ceased before the poem could be printed. It was thought lost, but a copy given to Nuala **Costello** turned up (1975) inside her *Oxford Book of French Verse* and is now at the **BIF** (RUL 1396/ 4/1). Published in a deluxe edition (100 copies) by Whiteknights Press in 1976, ed. James Knowlson and Felix Leakey; included in *Collected Poems* (1977), with an account of its genesis and history; and read by Ronald Pickup on BBC 3 (12 March 1977).

dualism: the expression of an inner discord running through the entire Greek and Roman worlds (and beyond), in the opposition of the sensuous world of the perishable to a supersensuous world of the divine (Windelband, 211). Accordingly, **Augustine** regarded the soul as immaterial substance, man as the union of **body** and soul, that union as an incomprehensible enigma, and the psychomachia or battle between good and evil (light and dark, **God** and Satan) its expression (the **gnostic** elements a lasting Christian legacy). More simply, dualism denotes the body-mind problem, the Cartesian crux. According to **Descartes**, the mind is a thinking thing (*res cogitans*), while matter is an extended thing (*res extensae*); each is sui generis with respect to the other, so what is spatial is not conscious, and what is conscious is not spatial. Hence a dilemma: how can two incommensurates, body and mind, interact? Faced with a paradox, he answered with a paradox: animal spirits, he asserted, mingle in the pineal gland, or **conarium**, it being the nature of such entities that they can affect both kinds of substance. The **Occasionalists** were quick to point out that this was an inadequate explanation, if only because substances that are sui generis cannot (ipso facto) interact. **Murphy**'s attitude toward the conundrum is a supreme irony in a novel predicated on the very question: "The problem was of little interest." For SB the problem was of lasting interest, and dualism is a concern in works as various as *Three Novels, Krapp's Last Tape,* and "**Ohio Impromptu**," as well as later prose texts like *Still,* where the Cartesian divide between mind and body is recentered (see **Mauthner**) as a schism in language.

Dublin: the publication of Eoin O'Brien's *The Beckett Country* (1986), with its superb photographs by David Davison, met an ungrateful response from some academics of a formalist persuasion. Such close attention to Dublin specifics, it was argued, encouraged train-spotting and overreading. Yet James Knowlson's Preface affirms that the early works are illuminated by the identification of people and places; that the recognition of these helps define SB's "Irishness" (including much **French** writing); and that even as the later works become less localized and explore the inner landscape they yet incorporate "shards of observed reality" (xvi) that pin "the fragility and ephemerality of the human experience" (xvii) to SB's experience and a precise locale. As the narrator of "The **Calmative**" comments

(62), "I only know the city of my child-hood." The image of "dear old indelible Dublin" (*Murphy*, 267) is seared into the psyche of SB's writings as deeply as it was in **Joyce**'s. This entry offers a brief guide to matters in other entries (in **bold**). See also **Foxrock** and **Ireland**.

"**Enueg I**" traces a peregrination about the city, noting its stench and decay. The poet exits from the **Portobello Nursing Home** near Lock Bridge and the Grand Canal, backdrop of the final scene of *Mercier and Camier*, a "grim pile" for "Diseases of the skin" (121). He follows the canal inland past Parnell Bridge to the Fox and Geese near Chapelizod (chapel of Iseult), where he cuts north and sees a "perturbation" of sweaty heroes from Kilmainham (site of the jail, where the heroes of the Easter Rising were executed). There (Island Bridge, opposite Phoenix Park) he sees in the filth of the Liffey the antithesis of **Rimbaud**'s "Illuminations," on which the poem ends. The canal sets the scene in "A **Case in a Thousand**," *First Love, Molloy* (26), *Mercier and Camier* (22) and *Krapp's Last Tape*. In "*Enueg II*" the final stasis occurs on O'Connell Bridge, with the light, the **tulips** of the evening, "like an anthrax / shining on Guinness's barges."

"**Serena I**" on return to Dublin has the sense of being trapped like a **fly**. "**Serena II**" is set in the Dublin Mountains south of the city, which Molloy imagines from the top of Nelson's Pillar (9), with its view of the city, and the harbor and steeples of **Dún Laoghaire**. One peak, Tibradden, is the setting of "**Love and Lethe**." Krapp recalls (63) being on the **Croghan**; and **Malone**

(206) remembers the bells and clink of hammers of the quarries there. "**Serena III**" begins in the city, moving south from **Butt Bridge** past Misery Hill (once a lazaretto), the gasometer on Sir John Rogerson's Quay, the Church of the Immaculate Heart of Mary, the Bull (harbor wall) and Pool Beg (lighthouse), over Victoria Bridge, down Ringsend Road, past Irishtown (a glimpse of the ruined Hellfire Club in the hills), Sandymount (Joyce's tower), the Merrion flats, and Booterstown ("Bootersgrad"), ever on the move. Molloy will find shelter in a cave at Whiterock, near **Killiney Beach**.

Like *Dubliners*, the stories of *MPTK* are precisely located. The central action of "**Dante and the Lobster**" unfolds at the little school at 21 Ely Place, where SB took Italian lessons. **Belacqua**'s residence is not specified, nor that of his aunt, but O'Brien (174) identifies "the little family grocery" as Kennedy's of Westland Row. "**Fingal**" identifies the Hill of Feltrim, the Castle woods, the Hill of Wolves, Ireland's Eye and Lambay (islands off the coast), the Naul to the north, the **Portrane** Asylum, and Taylor's public house (The Star) in the village of Swords. The history of these places is outlined in O'Brien (227–39). The terrain is not simply descriptive but sets a rhythm of ruin and madness, most poignantly in the story of Dean **Swift** and his "motte" (**Winnie** is the mute sufferer here). In "**Ding-Dong**" the big **Bovril** sign (north of College Green) rings the changes on the theological graces that counterpoint the action. The city is invoked in its particularity, from the **Coombe** to the Bank of Ireland, and in the conceit of Dublin as **Florence**. The "triturated" girl has come from the Mark Street tenements, nearby; the "Monumental Showroom" (55) is that of C. W. Harrison & Sons, Architectural and Monumental Sculptors, 178 Pearse Street (O'Brien, 173–77). Having gone along Pearse Street, Belacqua turns in "Ding-Dong" into Lombard Street, "the street of the sanitary engineers" (compare the Florentine bankers). The ending plays off **Dante**'s *Paradiso* against the sordid necessity of Railway Street, the **kips** recalled in "**Sanies II**" and smelled in *Mercier and Camier*. The blind beggar assumes his position in "A **Wet Night**" and in *Dream,* near the statue of Thomas **Moore**, and the Florentine conceit is elaborated in both. A similar route is traced in "A Wet Night," but here Belacqua staggers down Westland Row. He looks at "Johnston, Mooney and O'Brien's clocks" (70), those of a popular bakery on Leinster Street (O'Brien, 181), and the names of three pigs in J. G. Farrell's *Troubles.* He walks along Leinster and Kildare Streets toward the Baggot Street bridge and the "Casa Frica," somewhere near the canal. His final encounter with the **policeman** takes place on the Huband Bridge, over the Grand Canal closest to the Basin. This is the setting of "the house on the canal" where Krapp's **mother** lay dying, as SB's had, in the Merrion Nursing Home overlooking that bridge.

Fittingly, the Toughs of "**Love and Lethe**" live in Irishtown, near but socially remote from affluent Foxrock. Belacqua is "**Walking Out**" in **Croker**'s Gallops, his lovely **Lucy** mounted on her fair jennet. The **bboggs** of "**What a Misfortune**" live at 55 North Great George's Street,

a "lousy locality" north of the Liffey, a detail fictitious but robust; Mr. bboggs frustrates his wife's and daughters' wish to move to Foxrock. Capper **Quin** visits a florist in Mary Street; **Sproule** receives his commission in the Oval Bar (Abbey Street); Hairy meets Walter on the Metal Bridge; a funeral passes in Parliament Street; the Morgan is collected from Molesworth Street and left in Denmark Lane, which runs behind North Great George's Street; only the Church of St. **Tamar** is fictional. "**Yellow**" unfolds, SB informed O'Brien (364), in the Elpis Nursing Home, 17–21 Lower Mount St., where **Synge** had died; Belacqua can see the clouds in the east beyond the Land Commission (165), in Merrion Street. *Dream* opens with a scene from Belacqua's childhood in Foxrock, followed by another set on the Carlyle Pier, Dún Laoghaire. In the second half of the novel Belacqua peregrinates through Dublin. Most of the Dublin detail is recycled in *MPTK,* but the figure of **Nemo** on various bridges is more intrusive, until his last leap at **Leixlip** (182).

In *Murphy,* London comedy is diverted by Dublin byplay. The subplot begins when **Wylie** sees **Neary** in the **General Post Office** dashing his head against the **buttocks** of Cuchulain. Dublin detail is specific: the Dalkey tram; Nelson's Pillar; Railway Street dosses; Mooney's and **Wynn**'s Hotels; the Saturday **B. and I.**; and the toilet of the **Abbey Theatre**. From Charlemont Street Bridge **Watt** goes to **Harcourt Street Station**, to catch the **Slow and Easy** to Foxrock. **Cooldrinagh** is the model for Mr. **Knott**'s house (and that of **Moran**); many minor characters, from the postman (see **Shannon**) to various workers and passengers at the station, are drawn from SB's childhood recollections. Malone's "beloved church" is the Tullow Parish Church, where SB's family worshiped (O'Brien, 23); here **Krapp** "fell off the pew" (63). Moran has his "plot in perpetuity" (135) at Tully. Foxrock is imaged in *Mercier and Camier,* as the characters come and go from a city that is a composite of Dublin and Gomorrah. *All That Fall* is located there, **Leopardstown** race track visible from the station platform.

The great fiction from *Quatre nouvelles* to the *Texts pour rien,* and perhaps beyond, is set in the Molloy Country, in which Dublin ("Blackpool") forms the archetypal city of the plain in a soulscape of coast and swamp, near a dark wood, in a forest of symbols (see the **Beckett country**). Molloy begins and ends his quest in the city, the "ramparts" of which suggest the old walls of Dublin, about the Liberties and Castle (consider his brush with authority). Malone spends his last days in an **asylum** recognizably that in **Stillorgan**, imagining a final journey through southeast Dublin to Dalkey Island. He refers to the "nearest cemetery" (262); the French text states "Glasnevin" (148), with an ironic footnote: "Nom d'un cimetière local très estimé." The French "Hôtel Bellevue" (229) was originally "Hôtel Wynne." The "beautiful view" of gulls about the sewer outlet (compare "Enueg I") is relocated to Capel Street Bridge, where the Poddle discharges its waste into the Liffey.

Later writings invoke the "obsessional images" of childhood (notably *Company*) rather than the city, but there are exceptions. "**Eh Joe**" and "Text 6" (English only) mention St. Stephen's Green. SB's translation of **Pinget**'s "The **Old Tune**" transposes the Parisian street scene into its Dublin equivalent; and "**Rough for Theatre I**" combines W. B. **Yeats**'s archetypes of blind man and fiddler with SB's blind beggar from the Coombe. The most poignant return in **memory** to Dublin is *That Time,* sketched from SB's own return in the 1950s. An old man arrives off the B. and I. to revisit the folly (**Foley's Folly**) of his youth, only to find everything changed: tramlines rusted, trams no longer running, and the familiar train line from Harcourt Street to Foxrock closed forever, a haunting image of the ravages of **time**.

Dublin Magazine: "A Quarterly Review of Literature, Science and **Art**," the price 2/6, ed. Seamus O'Sullivan ("Seamus O'Solomon"), pseudonym of James Sullivan Starkey (1879–1958). First a monthly then a quarterly; hence a sneer in "**Echo's Bones**" (5) at the Editor "of a Monthly masquerading as a Quarterly." The foremost Irish literary periodical of the 1930s, it appeared in two series, 1923–25 and 1926–58. SB contributed: "**Alba**" (1931); "**Gnome**" (1934); "**Humanistic Quietism**" (1934); "An **Imaginative Work!**" (1936); and "**Cascando**" (1936). *Dublin Magazine* (XIV. 2 [1939]:98) published Austin **Clarke**'s anonymous review of *Murphy,* the only Irish critique it received. Letters from SB to O'Sullivan are held in the Starkey Papers at Indiana University.

Duchamp, Marcel (1887–1968): French artist and sculptor, who originated the objet trouvé and whose innovations caused scandal (a mustache on the *Mona Lisa*, a urinal proffered as art). Basing his early style on **Cézanne**, Duchamp initiated a dynamic version of Analytic Cubism, similar to Futurism, superimposing successive phases of movement, as in multiple-exposure photography; see *Nude Descending a Staircase* (1912). He wrote an occasional **chess** column in *Ce Soir*, and coauthored a book (1932), which SB knew, on the **endgame** and making contributions to the theory of *Zugzwang*, or Opposition. SB met him through Peggy **Guggenheim**, with whom both had an affair, and in 1940 spent three months with him in Arcachon, playing chess to pass the time, Duchamp proving the stronger (Knowlson, 276).

Ducroix: in *The Unnamable* (340), a memorial on the corner of Rues Castagnary and Brançion near the **shambles**, identified in SB's marginal note (I.115) as Émile D[e]croix, "propagateur de la viande de cheval" (1821–1906); in English, "apostle of **horse** meat" (327). His medals and "hippophagist" ("horse eater") suggest the Commune during the 1870 siege of **Paris**, when the populace ate not only horses but hippos in the zoo (and even, according to urban myth, the poet Lautréamont).

Dülberg, Ewald (1888–1933): misidentified in Harvey (277) as Dahlberg. Expressionist painter and theater designer whose *Das Abendmahl* (*The Last Supper*) was once owned by and hung in the *Kassel* apartment of SB's uncle, William Abraham "Boss" **Sinclair**, where SB certainly studied it. Presumed lost and destroyed in the Nazi purges of decadent art, its sole record is a lone photograph. Featured in the poem "**Casket of Pralinen**," where the poet stands before the picture. The scene is reprised in *Dream* (76–77).

Dum vivit aut bibit aut minxit: cited in "**What a Misfortune**" (147), from **Burton**'s *Anatomy of Melancholy* (I.2.2.ii): "born to no other end but to eat and drink, like Offellius Bibulus, that famous Roman parasite, *Qui dum vixit, aut bibit aut minxit*" ("Whoever has lived has either drunk or pissed"); a cask that mars wine.

Dún Laoghaire: the ferry terminal for Holyhead and thence by train to **London**. "**Serena II**" mentions the "kindergarten of steeples" visible from the **Dublin** Hills, as in "**Love and Lethe**" (100): "the long arms of the harbour like an entreaty in the blue sea." The harbor is likened to "a woman making to cover her breasts." These refer to the two massive granite piers, the "disappointed bridge" of *Ulysses*. Compare the "hopeless harbour look" of the mortuary in *Murphy* (259). *How It Is* (30) invokes the "silent location of steeples and towers." The Carlyle Pier (*Dream*, 3) is a smaller wooden structure within the arms, from which the mail-boat leaves. The East Pier, with its anemometer, is where **Krapp** sees the whole thing. Lord Gall wears "dundraoghaires" ("**Echo's Bones**," 12).

D'un ouvrage abandonné: translation (1957) of *From an Abandoned Work* by Ludovic and Agnès Janvier in collaboration with SB. Published (Minuit, 1967) in a special issue of 222 numbered copies. Included in *Têtes-mortes* (1967), 7–30; and in a special edition of fifty-five (Stuttgart: Manus Presse, 1967), English original and a German translation ("Aus einem aufgegeben Werk") by Erika and Elmar **Tophoven**, lithographs by Max Ernst.

Dürer, Albrecht (1471–1528): German painter and engraver. In *Dream* (35), **Belacqua** contemplates the beauty of drypoint, then imagines visiting Nuremberg (71). SB had in his room at **Cooldrinagh** Dürer's etching of two praying hands, alluded to in "**What a Misfortune**" (141), recalled in *Company* (26), and shaping "**Nacht und Träume**" and "**Ohio Impromptu**" (Knowlson, 600).

Duthuit, Georges (1891–1968): author of a book on **mysticism** and modern **art** (1936). Eager to establish a literary journal, Duthuit was thwarted by rationing of paper, the **French** government prioritizing pre**war** publications. Eugene Jolas, editor of *transition* (1927–1938), offered Duthuit (1947) the name, remaining as advisory editor to satisfy the authorities. Duthuit repositioned the periodical exclu-

sively toward the visual arts and French literature. In his words, *Transition Forty-Eight* became "the only English-language review entirely devoted to CONTEMPORARY FRENCH WRITING." It was financed by his wife, Marguerite, whose father, Henri Matisse, donated several cover illustrations and graphics. SB was a frequent translator, responsible for some of Duthuit's essays, "**Sam Francis** ou l'animateur du silence," for one. SB wrote up their conversations on art for *Transition Forty-Nine* 5 (97–103), as "Three Dialogues: **Masson—Tal Coat—Bram van Velde**" (see "**Dialogue Samuel Beckett—Georges Duthuit**" and "Three Dialogues"). These were usually credited to both until *Trois dialogues*, trans. Edith Fournier (Minuit, 1998), attributed them solely to SB, Fournier arguing in her preface that although SB adopts the dialogue form it was not a verbatim transcription, and that Georges Duthuit did not collaborate in the writing. A substantial correspondence belies this. Duthuit and SB debated issues and artists extensively, and the final "dialogues" contain near exact excerpts from their letters, even if SB alone put pen to paper. Fournier is technically correct, but her position that authorship is the act of transcription is dubious.

E

E: the Eye, or camera, in *Film* (1964), as opposed to "**O**," the **object** of perception. The film is predicated upon **Berkeley**'s *esse est percipi* (E = Esse), but accepts **Schopenhauer**'s insistence (*WWI*, I.1 #7, 38): "no object without a subject." Schopenhauer intimates the existence of the world as dependent on the perceiving eye: "For such an eye is a necessary condition of the possibility of knowledge." For SB the eye is often coeval with the "I," the eye of perception confirming the "I" of being, but the eye can also be unblinking, tyrannical, devouring, which, along with the voice, needs to be suppressed: "for the eye of prey the infinitesimal shudder instantaneously suppressed" (*Imagination Dead Imagine* 185).

Earlsfort House: a preparatory school; then at 3–4 Earlsford Place (now 63 Adelaide Road), **Dublin**, near the **Harcourt Street Station**. SB spent four years there, from age nine, with M. Alfred le Peton and William Exshaw. He "took an interest" in his studies, composition, conation, and "sports of all sorts."

ecce homo: L. "behold the man": the words of Pilate displaying the scourged **Christ** to the populace below (or this tradition in **art**). To Brother **Juniperus** (*Dream*, 98), it refers to an extraordinary Carmelite penance, singing the *Misère* followed by a penitent stripping to the waist, covering his face with ashes, wearing a crown of thorns, placing a cross beneath his left arm, and scourging himself (Cooper, *Flágellation*, 60–61).

"Echo's Bones": twenty-eight closely typed pages, intended as the "recessional" story in *MPTK*. SB gave the typescript to Lawrence Harvey, who left it to the Baker Memorial Library, Dartmouth College. A carbon copy is among the **Leventhal** papers at the **HRHRC**. Charles **Prentice** of Chatto and Windus suggested (29 September 1933) "Another 10,000 words, or even 5,000"; SB obliged. Prentice received the story (November 10), but decided to publish the volume in the original form. SB told MacGreevy (December 6) that he had put his all into the last story and was discouraged by its rejection. He subsequently refused permission for its later publication. The story is difficult, and full of enigmatic echoes, yet is a vital missing link in the reconstruction of the early SB. Its lack of easy access is to be regretted. The legal problems of Lord Gall were worked into *Murphy* (chapter 5), but without the original they remain opaque.

The story is a triptych, the first panel revealing a "post-obit" **Belacqua**, restored to the low stature of animation. He explains this to **Zaborovna**, who laments his lack of shadow. Returned to the familiar attitude (**embryonic**, on the fence), he receives a stunning crack on the eminent coccyx from a golf ball hit by Lord Gall, a colossus with a like problem. Childless and impotent ("aspermatic"), he fears his Eden of **Wormwood** will fall into the hands of his enemy, Baron **Extravas**, "reversioner of Wormwood and fiend in human disguise," who, moreover, has inflicted his wife, **Moll**, with syphilis. The estate can be saved only if a male heir is produced, and Belacqua ("fit as a flea") agrees to act. Moll becomes pregnant, and a life is dropped. Lord Gall is downstairs, counting his golf balls (sperm). His medical advisers file in: "It was a dramatic moment. 'May it please your lordship,' said the foreman, 'it is essentially a girl.'" An extended coda ensues, Belacqua sitting on his tombstone. He has a vision of the **Alba**, then chats with **Doyle**, groundsman of "**Draff**," who excavates his grave, a scene "Worthy of Mark Disney." Belacqua expects **nothing**, but in fulfillment of the myth an Ovidian metamorphosis occurs, and Belacqua (like Echo) turns into the handful of stones found there: "So it goes in the world."

"**Echo's Bones**": last poem of *Echo's Bones* (November 1933), a five-line precipitate. It invokes the "**asylum**" of the grave after the "**gantelope**" of life is run, and the muffled revels of the flesh (compare Prospero's "Our revels now are ended" in *Endgame*) have been "taken by the maggots for what they are." The poem is an epigraph, a memento mori, for the **father** and a requiem for the entire collection.

Echo's Bones and Other Precipitates: thirteen poems: "The **Vulture**"; "**Enueg I**"; "**Enueg II**"; "**Alba**"; "**Dortmunder**"; "**Sanies I**"; "**Sanies II**"; "**Serena I**"; "**Serena

II**"; "**Serena III**"; "**Malacoda**"; "**Da tagte es**"; and "**Echo's Bones**"; published by George **Reavey** (Paris: Europa Press, 1935), #3 in their Europa Poets series; 327 copies, twenty-five signed by SB. The title echoes **Eliot**'s *Prufrock and Other Observations*. The death of SB's **father** (June 1933) shaped the last six poems. The subscription list included Brian **Coffey**, Denis **Devlin**, **Rudmose-Brown**, Charles **Prentice**, Rev. E. G. Seale (Headmaster at **Portora**), SB's mother, and Sylvia Beach; review copies were sent (unavailingly) to T. S. Eliot, Robert Graves, Laura Riding, I. A. Richards, and W. H. Auden. The collection met with gloomy silence, but SB (unusually) allowed it to be reprinted, in *Gedichte* (1959), in *Poems in English* (1961), and in *Collected Poems* (1977 and 1984). It appeared in the inaugural issue of *Evergreen Review* 1.1 (1957): 179–92, omitting "Alba," "Dortmunder," and "Malacoda."

The title derives from **Ovid**'s *Metamorphoses* III.395ff, telling of the nymph, Echo, whose loquacity displeased Jupiter. He deprived her of speech, other than to answer questions. She fell in **love** with **Narcissus**, enamored of his own reflection; rejected, she pined away and was changed into a stone, which was permitted the power of **voice**: "her body dries and shrivels, until only voice and bones remain, then she is voice only, the bones are turned to stone." The poems are the calcified and petrified remnants of what once was, arranged by a voice that is now no more, but whose echoes will be heard in SB's later writing.

Eckehart, Johannes (ca. 1260–1327): Meister Eckehart, German, first of the great speculative Western mystics. His roots were **scholastic**, Aristotelian elements in Aquinas colored by the **mysticism** of the pseudo-**Dionysius**. His doctrine concerns the divine nature and the human soul, whose end is union with **God**. To accomplish that union the soul must understand that creatures are themselves **nothing**; then, having perceived the continuity of being with the divine, the soul may dispense with external means of salvation and abandon itself to God. SB recorded from **Inge**'s *Christian Mysticism* (1899): "Eckhart's '<u>Fünkelein</u>': organ by which the personality communicates with God & knows him" (DN, 100); the word ("little spark") is twice used in *Dream* (17, 160), and once in "**Walking Out**" (106). This doctrine of the divine spark is known as *synteresis* (Inge, 282). SB does not refer again to Eckehart, but Gottfried Büttner has testified that SB later read him closely. In applications of **negative theology**, SB's rhetoric of negativity is related to the *via negativa* and the neo-**Augustinian** contention that one cannot know what God is but only what he is not.

École Normale Supérieure: Rue d'Ulm, **Paris.** Founded (1794) to train teachers for higher education, it attracted an intellectual elite. Pupils have included **Bergson**, Merleau-Ponty, **Rolland**, **Romains**, and **Sartre**. As the exchange scholar from **Trinity** SB attended the École (November 1928 until 1930), intending to work on **Jouve** and **Unanimisme**. The École was largely residential, with most classes taken at the Sorbonne. SB's responsibilities were light, with only one "conscrit," Georges **Pelorson**. He met Thomas **MacGreevey**

and Jean **Beaufret**, and renewed his **friendship** with Alfred **Péron**, a recent exchange scholar to Trinity (Beaufret would soon be one). SB loved its fine old library and magnificent books, and cultivated there the habit of working closely with commentaries, dictionaries, and reference texts. Two early essays ("**Dante**" and *Proust*) were largely written from books at the École.

eels of Como: a curiosity in *Watt* (27–28). SB's source, as Mary Bryden discovered (*Idea of God*, 78), is E. P. Evans, *The Criminal Prosecution and Capital Punishment of Animals* (1906). Evans tells of Bartholomew Chassenée (b. 1480), counsel for some **rats** on trial for having feloniously eaten and wantonly destroyed the barley crop. His treatise originated "in an application of the inhabitants of Beaune to the ecclesiastical tribune of Autun for a decree of excommunication against certain noxious insects called huberes or hurebers, a kind of locust or harvest-fly. The request was granted, and the pernicious creatures were duly accursed" (Evans, 22). Of the pestilent creatures in *Watt,* only the hurebers of Beaune exactly echo Evans, though the "bloodsuckers" of Lausanne (25) are kin to the leeches.

Effi Briest: a novel by Theodore Fontane (1819–99), published 1895, telling of a young woman trapped in a loveless marriage. Effi has an affair, and when her husband later discovers this, the code of honor demands that he banish his wife and kill her lover. Effi is forced to live alone, and when a visit from her daughter proves an emotional disaster incipient consumption sets in, and she soon dies, her parents belatedly realizing their culpability. SB read it with Peggy **Sinclair**, who also died of TB. **Krapp** recalls the novel: "Scalded the eyes out of me reading *Effie* again, a page a day, with tears again. Effie . . . Could have been happy with her, up there on the Baltic, and the pines, and the dunes." Bair notes (654) that Krapp remembers the gooseberries from the opening scene of the novel; Knowlson, however, traces the allusion to T. F. Powys's 1925 novel, *Mr. Tasker's Gods (JOBS* 9.2 [2000]: 81). In *All That Fall*, Mr. **Rooney** asks his wife to read to him: "I think Effie is going to commit adultery with the Major" (29).

"Eh Joe": SB's first teleplay, a "spoken **mime**," written at his **Ussy** retreat (13 April to 1 May 1965). Begun on his fifty-ninth birthday, the teleplay was broadcast in German as "He, Joe" on his sixtieth with Deryk **Mendel** as Joe and Nancy Illig as **Voice**. Filmed at Süddeutscher Rundfunk, it was SB's first acknowledged **directing** effort. The first English version was produced for BBC 2 (4 July 1966), dir. Alan Gibson (SB in attendance), with Jack **MacGowran** (for whom the play was written) as Joe and Sian Phillips as Voice. SB redirected it (January 1970), again at SDR, with Heinz Bennet and Irmgard Först. A third version from SDR (1988), dir. Walter Asmus, with Klaus Herm and Christine Collins, was shot for academic distribution and is available as *Three Plays by Beckett* from Films for the Humanities and Sciences. First published in English, with "**Act Without Words** II" and *Film*, in *Eh Joe and Other Writings* (Faber 1967); and in the United States

in *Cascando and Other Short Dramatic Pieces* (Grove, 1968) and *Evergreen Review* 62 (January 1969): 43–46. The latter was accompanied by stills from the 1966 WNDT-TV production dir. Alan **Schneider**, with George Rose and Rosemary Harris. The French version appeared in *Comédie et actes divers* (Minuit, 1966) and in *Paroles et musique; Comédie; Dis Joe*, Introduction by Jean Jacques Mayoux (Aubier-Flammarion, 1972). "**Dis Joe**," with Jean-Louis Barrault and Madeleine Renaud, dir. Michael Mitrani, was broadcast on RTF 2 (Février 1968). A German parallel text, by Erika and Elmar **Tophoven**, appeared in 1979. First staged at New York University and at the Festival d'Automne in **Paris** (1981), with David **Warrilow** and Helen Bishop directed by Schneider.

The monologue features a man in his fifties, alone in a room, assailed by a recurrent voice in his head. As in *Film*, the protagonist tries to avoid the pains of being by avoiding perception (see **Berkeley**). The opening mime virtually reenacts the early room sequence of *Film* (in a note to the first holograph, Joe spent the night in a chair). The plot is "simple," SB noting "a passion to kill the voices which he cannot kill." Joe has apparently stilled the voices of his **mother** and **father**, and is on his way to stifling this Voice, which may be as "Unstillable," SB notes in his 1976 production notebook, as the voice of **God**. According to Voice, Joe is safe in his room: "No one can see you now . . . No one can get at you now" (202). The utterance belies the message, since the threat is internal. As SB suggested to

Schneider, "The feeling is of camera sneaking behind him hugging walls" (Harmon, 201). Joe is unaware of it and should never stare directly into it. In the earliest holograph Voice tempts "Jack" (MacGowran) to shut off the light, "In case there's an eye you've forgotten." In the dark Joe may be safe from perception, but Joe, as Voice well knows, fears the dark.

SB sketched the thematic and theatrical conflicts, emphasizing God as that voice impossible to quell (*Theatrical Notebooks* IV, 259):

1. Out of sight, reach. Fear of dark.
2. Rupture formula—'Best to come' (1).
3. Voices in head—behind the eyes. Mental thuggee.
4. Present voice last, then his own to still, then silence till God's, unstillable.
5. Clues for voice and hearer. Worse when nearly home. What if final whisper unstillable?
6. God to him 1.
7. Deficient in kindness, strength, intelligence, looks, cleanliness, normality.
8. Green one. 'Best to come' 2. Duly laid.
9. Same as 4.
10. Voice falling to whisper.

A year after *Film*, SB was still thinking through its imagery, reducing the camera's role (but maintaining its conspicuous presence), and constricting the action to a room. "Eh Joe" returns to that adroit fusion of mime and monologue as in *Krapp's Last Tape*, to which it bears striking affinities in content, form, and genesis. Krapp and Joe are obsessed with the past, with a girl in green whom they have "Duly laid," then deserted. Both have abandoned **love** to pursue something other, but Joe is assailed by a vision of one who committed **suicide**. He struggles to be rid of this, but given conscience (or God) he cannot. His protagonist represents an aspect of psychological duality, akin to **Jung**'s Anima or Shadow. Voice in "Eh Joe" is less Joe's dark or evil side than his opposite: feminine, constant, secure, and irreligious, to Joe's masculine, lecherous, dishonest, but (surprisingly) religious self (or selves). Voice suggests that what Joe deserted was genuine and eternal love, unlike hers or even God's. Of the green girl's suicide, an act that has permanently fixed her love for Joe, defeating **time**, Voice notes, "There's love for you . . . Isn't it Joe? . . . Compared to us . . . Compared to Him" (206–7). Voice is not disinterested, however. She is mounting the strongest attack possible; and since she is an extension of Joe, he finds that hell is not only other people but himself. SB noted to Schneider, "Voice should be whispered. A dead voice in his head. Minimum of colour. Attacking. Each sentence a knife going in, pause for withdrawal, then in again" (Harmon, 201).

Except for one break in composition the monologue came easily to SB. After a holograph outline, SB laid out the play like verse in the earliest typescript, short sentences, one to a line, with no stage or camera directions. He used this "continuity" version to divide the monologue into eleven units, punctuated by ten camera moves (finally ten sections and nine camera moves). The relationship between camera and monologue was established in the first typescript (TS0). An early draft of stage directions and three typescripts then followed the continuity version. SB's revisions suggest that the work is a complex technical and structural achievement of a writer as yet wholly inexperienced with the medium. The original of TS3 was evidently sent to the printer, but he edited the carbon for the BBC production. Voice's last speech was heavily revised, with the repetition of key words, "Imagine," "the stones," and "the lips," absent from the published versions. Two subsequent typescripts exist, one marked by SB (TS4) and a "Final version typescript." This (TS5) is only lightly revised but includes notes on shooting and deletes some repetitions of TS3. It retains, however, the recurrent "Imagine." The textual history of "Eh Joe" is thus as complicated as any other production with which SB was involved, but printed texts do not include his final performance revisions. For the 1966 BBC production, SB "simplified" Voice's penultimate utterance, and he asked Schneider to ignore the direction "Image fades, voice as before," and instead introduced a smile when Voice stops to suggest "having done it again" (Harmon, 198, 202). That is, while Joe may not stop Voice permanently, he succeeds at least in stifling it a while, hence the smile. Here for the first time Joe looks at the camera.

The drafts reveal SB's compositional difficulty. At one point he wrote a holograph in a notebook, typed that out, then waited two weeks before returning with a new religious emphasis. At this break in composition SB's principal formal change occurred. His conception of the play heretofore was to have Voice tell *her* story. Had this continued, the result would have been a maudlin account of guilt. When SB returned to his composition he had two versions of deserted women, Voice, who apparently rebounded successfully (although she doth protest a bit much), and the suicide. After the break Voice was clearly telling the story of another: "*She* went young . . . Ever know what happened?" This change raises mediocre monologue to high levels of complexity and formal interest. The revision creates a voice within a voice within Joe, a Chinese-box regression. SB devised Joe, who devised Voice, who devised the girl in green on the strand. The second story raised the level of antagonism between Voice and Joe. While Joe was trying to stifle her, she assailed him with her most potent weapon, potent because Joe as a Catholic (as the prayer to Mary suggests) is responsible for the suicide's eternal damnation.

Joe is an incomplete creative personality, the *être manqué*. The Voice that assails him is neither external, nor memory, nor the subconscious, but imagination, or creativity. The narrative is characterized by literariness (echoes of Poe, say): "Faint lap of sea through open window" and "Unconscionable hour by now"; it is an imaginative construct, a devised tale, a fiction, created by the Voice created by Joe. This structure runs parallel to the audience's experience: viewers must exercise their imagination as the words grow inaudible. Joe's struggle is not simply with his past but with his creative impulses, so that the artful climactic account is very much *a story* of the lover's suicide. Note the similarity of the two women's experiences. Joe leaves each with the same Browning quotation from "Rabbi Ben Ezra": "the best is yet to come"; helping each on with her coat accents the formal ties. In both instances the attempt to reconstruct memory is necessarily fictive. When SB wanted to increase the conflict and dramatic tension near the end of the holograph, he outlined which thematic words would be audible amid Voice's last mumble of speech: "more imagines," he noted. Imagination is an assailant. But assault, or devising an assault, is **company** as well, "Up to a point." Despite the assault of Voice, Joe strains to hear the whispered words that assail him, for these are the creative fountainhead.

At the hiatus in composition another significant change occurred. At first the suicide was followed by a treacly, doggerel prayer, the sort Irish schoolchildren might learn: "Guard her, Oh Mary, don't leave her alone, Love her dear Jesus as we did at home." This became: "On Mary's beads we plead her needs, And in the holy Mass." Voice uses the prayer to attack Joe's piety, which piety becomes a backdrop against which the love of the "green girl" is projected. In a holograph note, SB reminded himself, "God story-prepare." He listed three allusions: "Dust thou art" (Genesis 3:19); "Whence comest thou" (Genesis 16:8); and "Thou fool this night thy soul" (Luke 12:20). Two were finally used, the first derisively changed to "Mud thou art" and the last abbreviated to "Thou fool thy soul," to suggest Joe's imminent death. Luke's parable of the foolish rich man who stores up earthly treasures underlines Joe's spiritual dearth. Voice's mockery of Joe's faith led to another change. She referred to Joe's plight as "Joe's woe," but in an autograph revision SB broke the rhyme, changing the woe to "The passion of our Joe" (SB wanted a capital "O," but this is missed in all printed versions), juxtaposing Joe's minor suffering against that of **Christ**.

Eleutheria: a three-act play in **French**, written (as a ms. note indicates) "Prior to *Godot*," then "jettisoned." Two soft-cover exercise books at the **HRHRC** contain the original, and a revised typescript is held at Dartmouth College. It was begun (18 January 1947) as SB's retreat from "the awful depression the prose led me into" (Bair, 361). He completed a draft of the play (24 February), and by late March turned over a typescript to Toni Clerkx, who interested Jean Vilar at the Théâtre Nationale Populaire. Vilar wanted SB to cut it to one long act, and when SB refused he dropped his interest. Suzanne **Deschevaux** began to circulate his work and in early 1950 left a copy with Roger **Blin** (qv), who wanted to produce it but elected instead the more economical *Waiting for Godot*. Jérôme **Lindon** accepted *Eleutheria* for publication, but SB withdrew it. Part of the play was published (1986) in a special issue of the *Revue d'Esthétique* (Paris: Éditions Privat): 11–32; and the dialogue between the **Glazier** and his son appeared in *Beckett in the Theatre* (1988). Two translations were published after SB's death: *Eleutheria*, trans. Michael Brodsky (Foxrock, 1995); and *Eleutheria*, trans. Barbara Wright (Faber, 1996). These were controversial, as SB to the end wished the play withheld. The imminent publication of the first English translation forced Lindon to rush the French original into print; for details of this messy affair, see **Grove Press**.

The setting is contemporary **Paris**, in a cul-de-sac named L'**Impasse de l'Enfant-Jésus**. The title implies the Greek word for "freedom" (or "self-reliance"); Miss **Counihan** in *Murphy* (131) suffers from *eleutheromania*. Hölderlin's "Mnemosyne," quoted in *Dream,* invokes "Elevtherä" as **Memory**'s town. The play depicts Mme. **Krap** trying to make a man of her son, ironically named Victor, by provoking him into rising, getting a **job**, finding **love** and marriage, that is, by doing and being. To little effect: Victor has espoused **Schopenhauer** and renounced all **desire**, preferring to lie in his bed ("sordid inertia"), doing **nothing** as the assertion of his freedom, his choice. The inaction unfolds on three successive winter days, a split set implying different angles of vision, Act I in the Krap drawing room and Act II in Victor's bedroom, which in Act III expands to fill the entire stage. Victor's room thus moves imperceptibly into the Kraps', "as the sullied into the clean, the sordid into the decent." Characters **come and go**, or are simply mentioned: Victor's **father** Henri (who dies in the second act), the servants **Jacques** and Marie, Madame Meck (Fr. *mec,* "a pimp"), Dr. and Mme. Piouk, a Romanian patient named Verolescu, Olga Skunk, **Tchoutchi** the Chinese torturer, Joseph the wrestler, a Glazier and his son Michel, and a Pirandello-like creature named "le commissaire du peuple," or **Spectator** (Audience Member), who intrudes in Act III to comment on the action as a game of **chess** between two tenth-rate players. Finally, rejecting both return and **suicide**, Victor declares his independence, looks at the audience, and turns his back on it. There is something of the vaudeville or **silent movie** tradition about it, but because the protagonist is so static SB has not resolved the major dramatic difficulty of imposing his presence through his nonexistent characteristics; Victor thus eludes sympathy and understanding.

To Jérôme Lindon, *Eleutheria* was an absolute failure, "une pièce ratée." Ruby Cohn agreed, but Carlton Lake (*No Symbols,* 51) emphasizes its historical significance as a bridge between the English SB and the French SB. *Molloy* evolves from Victor's futile struggles to explain himself. Knowlson and Pilling suggest that *Eleutheria* fails because it cannot adapt the parody of bourgeois comedy to the vaudeville tradition, but they note as well how its idiom and wit inform later works: the name **Krap(p)**; women named after flowers, as in *Come and Go;* Michel anticipating the boy in *Godot;* the father and son of "**Embers**"; the gesture of arms helplessly falling, later used in *Not I;* the cruel banter of *Endgame* (*Frescoes,* 25). For Dougald McMillan, *Eleutheria* was the culmination of SB's examination of his received theatrical tradition, a statement on dramatic method that clearly influenced his later plays.

SB was not happy with the play (but that was so with most of his work). *Eleutheria* is by design a drama in the throes of resisting becoming a drama, a play in which the main character refuses to or cannot explain his action. SB was learning to risk absence, to empty the theatrical space, first of motive, then of character. It would take another play to solve this dramatic problem of presenting "nothing" by removing a central character (**Godot**) from the stage. *Eleutheria* is not yet there, but it is the beginning of "it all," anticipating much of the later work. Yet it has its own qualities, and it is up to a broader public to determine its success. If its availability finally does little to enhance SB's record as a dramatist, it indicates how far from that earliest venture the later drama would move.

Eliot, T. S. (1888–1965): the celebrated poet of his age, but as such for SB a point of witty irreverence; Eliot in return intensely disliked SB's work. The two might seem to have much in common: complex allusion, discontinuous form, **musical** paradigms and rhythms, **time** and **memory**, and a love of **Dante**; but Eliot's establishment values, right-wing pontifications, and sanctimonious **religion** precluded deep rapport. The notes for *Whoroscope* imitate *The Waste Land,* and *Echo's Bones and Other Precipitates* echoes *Prufrock and Other Observations.* Seamus O'Sullivan sent SB Eliot's translation of St. John Perse's *Anabase* to review for the *Dublin Magazine* (1931), but SB did not like it ("bad Claudel"). The review was not written, but SB expressed a reluctant admiration for Eliot's "phrase-bombs" (SB to TM, 3 February 1931). He pointed out that "T. Eliot" spelled backward was "toilet" (9 January 1937), and professed his distaste of the

methods of Eliot and Pound, calling them "jewel thieves" (Bair, 95)—somewhat inappropriately, given his own early practice.

Thomas **MacGreevy**, whose book on Eliot generated *Proust* (qv), initiated a meeting between SB and Eliot, which led to SB's review of **Rilke** for *The Criterion* (July 1934); but SB's vitriolic disparagement of Rilke's relation to **God** did not lead to further commissions. In "**Recent Irish Poetry**," SB linked *The Waste Land* with the art of Jack **Yeats** as notable statements of the no-man's-land between the artist and the world of **objects** (*Disjecta,* 70). When Eliot visited **Dublin** in 1935, SB attended one lecture only because he resented Eliot's flippant remark that **Joyce** was "an unconscious tribute to a Catholic education acquired at a time when few people were educated at all," describing it to MacGreevy (29 January 1936) as "The old fall back on pedagogics."

Nevertheless, echoes of Eliot infiltrated SB's work. In "**Echo's Bones**" (5) a nest of rank outsiders mend "in perfect amity a hard place in Eliot." In *Dream* (14), the **Smeraldina** stimulates in Herr **Arschlochweh** "certain velleities of desire," echoing "Portrait of a Lady." The narrator's sad spaniels (111) make "a sudden leap," like Prufrock's alley cat. **Belacqua** affirms that "The bang is better than the whimper" (177); in "**Love and Lethe**" Ruby Tough anticipates a "fairly beautiful bang" (90), but ends with a whimper. In the Dublin mountains, young priests sing in a wood (95), like "Sweeny Among the Nightingales." Belacqua in "**What a Misfortune**" is throttling snapdragons at the "indigo hour" (Eliot's "violet hour"), to sounds from distant mountains (115); this is echoed in *Molloy* (9). **Murphy** ends not with a whimper but a bang. Miss **Counihan**'s "belladonna" suggests the "lady of situations" in *The Waste Land*, and her "dying fall" invokes "Portrait of a Lady."

When **Watt** appears in the distance (16), Tetty is not sure "whether it was a man or a woman." This echoes the Divine Providence theme of *The Waste Land*, with its sense of the Third who walks beside, and who perhaps reappears as Watt walks to the station. *Waiting for Godot* shares with part V of *The Waste Land* the **mythological present** of a perpetual Easter Saturday. In *Endgame*, echoing Eliot's corpse buried in the garden, **Nagg**'s seeds fail to sprout (13); and **Hamm** senses that the end is in the beginning (69), as in "East Coker." *Come and Go* sounds the futile refrain of "Prufrock"; *Footfalls* "echo in the memory," as in "Burnt Norton"; and the axletree of *That Time* (231) could derive from that poem. *First Love* (44) offers a deliberate parody of the hyacinth garden: "She gazed at me with her big eyes whose colour I forget, with one big eye rather, for the other seemed riveted on the remains of the hyacinth." There follows the sentiment that one should not dread the winter, the snow which gives warmth and deadens the tumult ("Winter kept us warm"), and offers an objective correlative for the numbed emotions of SB's protagonist. Such sustained parallelism is rare in SB's writings, but it testifies to Eliot's significance as one who had once inhabited the waste land, even if he later set his lands in order in a way that SB could not.

"**elles viennent**": a five-line lyric, first of twelve *Poèmes 38–39*, published in *Les Temps modernes* (novembre 1946). An English translation features in Peggy **Guggenheim**'s *Out of This Century* (1946), 205n, as "a poem written by **Oblomov**" (1937), and in SB's recollection originally in English. The poem notes of various unspecified lovers that with each love and its absence it is both different and the same. The words "amour," "absence," "autre," and "pareil" are varied and repeated until the poem seems less concerned with the referents of "elles" than a meditation about these words.

Ellis, Havelock (1859–1939): English psychologist, whose *Studies in the Psychology of Sex* (6 vols., 1898–1910) were notorious. His presence (*Dream*, 179, and "A Wet Night," 56) suggests the **Frica**'s rampant sexuality. He edited the Mermaid "Old Dramatists," specifically the **Ford** that SB used.

Elsner sisters: Misses Ida and Pauline Elsner, German-born but naturalized neighbors of SB, who attended their kindergarten from ages five to nine. The sisters taught **music** as well as general subjects. SB commented that **Chopin**'s piano teacher in Poland was named Elsner (Knowlson, 43). SB first learned French from Miss Ida. They had a cook named Hannah and an Aberdeen terrier called **Zulu**; all four appear in *Molloy* as neighbors of **Moran**. The draft of *Molloy* toys with their German origins in conjunction with the Jewish name "Hanna," then drops the idea. In *Murphy* (228), Miss **Counihan** refers to "the **Engels** sisters." The sisters were local characters.

Pauline, a Mrs. Stewart "of whom no Mr Stewart is recalled" (O'Brien, 17), was quiet and reserved; Miss Ida, known as "Jack" because of her eccentric mannish manner, rode a bicycle, erratically. Her tendency to fall and sprawl in the road may underlie Maddy Rooney's wish in *All That Fall* to flop like a jelly (Knowlson, 44).

Éluard, Paul (1895–1952): pseudonym of Eugène Grindel, surrealist poet, whose trenchant experiences in World War I turned him into a lifelong pacifist and communist. He was a friend of André Breton, with whom he collaborated. *L'Immaculée conception* (1930) simulated the verbal symptoms of various mental disorders. SB translated a dozen of his poems and prose pieces for the surrealist number of *This Quarter* (1932). Some were reprinted in Éluard's *Thorns of Thunder*, ed. George Reavey (1936): "Lady love," 1; "The invention," 8; "Second nature," 23; "Scarcely disfigured," 36; "Scene," 37–38; "Universal solitude," 40–41; and "Out of sight in the direction of my body," 42. "Universsolitude," with SB's translation, appeared in Cecily Mackworth's anthology, *A Mirror for French Poetry 1840–1940* (Routledge, 1947), 200–3. John Calder reprinted most of these in *Poems in English* (1961) and *Collected Poems* (1977).

"Embers": a one-act radio play, forty-five minutes (written 1957); translated by Robert Pinget, as "Cendres." SB did not send it to the BBC until February 1959. Other titles contemplated were "The Water's Edge"; "Why Life, Henry?"; "Not a Soul"; and "All Day All Night." First produced on BBC 3 (24 June 1959), dir. Donald McWhinnie, with Jack MacGowran as Henry, Kathleen Michael as Ada, and Patrick Magee as Riding Master and Music Master. The play won the RAI prize in the 1959 Prix Italia contest, discreetly bowdlerized. Holloway on the hearth rug is not "trying to toast his arse," nor is young Henry a "sulky little bastard." Four religious expletives are also deleted, although two "Christ"s remain. More reliable is the American version, dir. Everett Frost with Barry McGovern as Henry, Billie Whitelaw as Ada, Michael Deacon as Riding Master and Music Master; broadcast on National Public Radio (1989) as part of the Beckett Festival of Radio Plays. The first stage production was by the French Graduate Circle of Edinburgh, Edinburgh Festival, 1977. Published in *Evergreen Review* 3.10 (November–December 1959): 28–41; in *Krapp's Last Tape and Embers* (Faber, 1959), and in *Krapp's Last Tape and Other Dramatic Pieces* (Grove, 1960). There is a bilingual German text, *Embers/Aschenglut*, trans. Erika and Elmar Tophoven (Stuttgart: Reclam, 1970).

SB had reservations, calling it "not very satisfactory, but I think just worth doing . . . I think it just gets by for radio" (Zilliacus, 76). He noted that it rests "sur une ambiguité: le personnage a-t-il une hallucination ou est-il en présence de la réalité?" (83). The play is set, like *Endgame,* on the margins of land and sea; Henry alone speaking at first to his drowned father, who took his evening sea bath "once too often" and whose death has haunted Henry since; then to his wife Ada about educating (or disciplining) their daughter Addie. The incessant sounds of the sea, agitating the shingle of the **Killiney** strand, are a continuo to the tumult in Henry's mind. Conveyed in the BBC performance by an organ drone, they merely produced the effect of a scratchy recording. The effect is achieved more cleanly (Dolby B Noise Reduction) in the American remake. Henry is haunted by the sound of the sea, but he has deadened its drone by talking to himself (as his father did), telling himself stories, particularly the ongoing tale of two old men, Bolton and Holloway (the latter Henry's doctor), on a freezing night standing before a fire, whose flames, like their lives, have been reduced to embers. Bolton/Henry has summoned Holloway at midnight for relief, a **painkiller**. A failed writer, Henry admits of his story, "I never finished it. I never finished any of them" (94). The story itself is not enough to still the haunting sea, and Henry needs to conjure up people, his father then Ada. That is, he needs an audience. Henry and Ada review two scenes in the life of Addie, her subjugation to a Music Master and a Riding Master. Both end in tears (see **cylindrical ruler**). SB suggested that Addie play **Chopin**'s fifth waltz in A flat major, but neither production specifies the music. Instead, Addie runs through some scales, playing E for F, to the impatience of the Music Master. With the Riding Master her failure is posture. Again she falls short of Ada's expectations. Henry's conversation with Ada (like his ardor, perhaps) dwindles to embers, Ada warning that in time "there will be no other **voice** in the world but yours" (102). The play ends with Henry's talking to himself, as he always has, recalling the pain of a dying man, his and Bolton's, the waste of words and days.

Written shortly after *Endgame,* the radio drama could be a monodrama, the action taking place in a **skull**. Paul Lawley has suggested that the enigmatic scene with Bolton's opening and shutting the heavy drapes enacts the blinking of an eye, the room thus becoming a skull and the images increasingly desperate correlatives for Henry's failing creativity. The play invokes a frequent trope, the play on eye/I. Discussion between Bolton and Holloway parallels that between Henry and Ada about Henry's sickness, and how to end his torment, as perhaps his father has done (but his mother did not), letting him be "washed out" to sea. The end Henry desires for his story and his self may simply be the family solution (or curse), but each time he approaches the sea he demurs.

embryo: SB claimed an awareness of the prenatal experience, his memories beginning on the eve of his **birth**, under the table, when his **father** gave a dinner party at which his **mother** presided (Bair, 328). This scenario is outlined only partly in parody in *Watt.* Frequent images of the embryo testify to SB's fascination with birth and the **desire** to return to the womb; as **Belacqua** puts it in "**Fingal**" (29): "back in the caul, on my back in the dark for ever." SB had read **Rank**'s *The Trauma of Birth,* which identified the "intrauterine primal pleasure" (17) and saw it as interrupted by birth, so that life consists in uterine regression; this offered a libidinal explanation of the difficulties with his mother. An embryonal Paradise Lost is a recurrent image, and he told

Peggy **Guggenheim** that he retained a terrible **memory** of his mother's womb. As Baker notes (69–73), Rank's definition of the pre-oedipal relationship offered SB a dramatic structure to explore his relationship with his mother, and of all the psychoanalytical myths he had the least critical distance from this one.

Belacqua desires to go "wombtomb" (*Dream,* 121), and **Murphy**'s third zone of his mind is conceived as a "Matrix of surds" (112), or womb of **irrationality**, defined in terms of the primal pleasure. Ernst **Haeckel**'s *The Riddle of the Universe* likens the development of the soul to that of an insect, which, in the womb, surrounded by placenta and amnion, exists in a state of embryonic slumber similar to the chrysalis. Thus **Celia**, sitting in the chair (67), feels embedded in a jelly of light, and Murphy imagines his projection, "**larval** and dark" (183), into the world. Watt assumes at various places (ditches, the waiting room) the sigmoidal form of embryonic repose, and twice (expelled from the tram at the outset, and covered in slops at the end) symbolically undergoes a kind of birth. The fetal position "doubles up" as an image of **death**. The various stages of embryonic development apply to **Molloy**'s passage through the dark wood, until he finds himself "reborn" in the ditch at the edge of the forest. Fetal images underlie the title and finale of "The **Expelled**."

Knowlson comments that SB "felt his **solitude**, sometimes very acutely, but it was a solitude that he also cultivated deliberately, "obscurely aware that something was happening within him as, eclectically, he accumulated knowledge" (191). That "something" was conceived throughout his writings in terms of a self that had never properly been born. SB was intrigued at **Jung**'s third **Tavistock** lecture by the **little girl** who had never really properly been born. This is very much the state of **Quin**'s soul in the early drafts of *Watt,* as indicated by the placental remains in the Addenda, where the phrase "the foetal soul is full grown" is glossed with a reference to Cangiamilla's teachings on the salvation of the fetal soul in difficult births. Embryonic images "lepp" in the later works. **Estragon** resumes his fetal position, head between knees, when trying to sleep (*WG,* 45.a). In *How It Is* (24), the figure in mud assumes the standard position ("it's preferable") of "knees drawn up the back bent in a hoop the tiny head near the knees curled round the sack." *All That Fall* tells again of the little girl not quite born. **Fox** in "**Rough for Radio II**" has an embryonic twin, a self never entirely born, SB having read about the medical rarity of an undeveloped twin trapped in fetal form within the **body** of the other. The persistence of such images testifies to his enduring fascination with the mysteries of birth and being.

Empedocles (ca. 490–430 BC): **pre-Socratic** philosopher, a younger contemporary of **Parmenides** with affinities to **Hercalitus**. His "**strife of opposites**" asserted a universal dynamic of strife and love, as in *Murphy*'s "love and hate" (112). Empedocles leapt into Mt. Etna that he might be remembered ("Love and Lethe," 95).

En attendant Godot: a play in two acts for five male actors (Minuit, 1952 [17

October]), published before first performed; 2,500 copies of the first issue sold at Fr. 3.60, and some 45,000 copies were reprinted over the next twelve years. SB copied out an autograph manuscript for Jake Schwartz (**HRHRC** #124), but refused to part with the original, written into a small exercise book, which he sometimes made available to scholars. He wrote the play between 9 October 1948 and 29 January 1949, after *Molloy* and *Malone meurt* but before *L'Innommable,* as an interlude of sorts. It did not find an immediate taker. Early in 1950 Roger **Blin** (qv) was shown the play, found something that appealed, and decided to stage it. It took two years to find sufficient money and a suitable theater. Blin did not fully appreciate *Godot,* but as they rehearsed, with SB following the process closely, its richness emerged for him and the other actors. First performed 5 January 1953, in the Théâtre Babylone, 38 Boulevard Raspail, Paris; theatre manager Jean-Marie Serreau, with decor by Sergio Gerstein. The cast comprised Pierre Latour (**Estragon**), Lucien Raimbourg (**Vladimir**), Jean Martin (**Lucky**), Roger Blin (**Pozzo**), and Serge Lecointe (*un jeune garçon*). First reactions were mixed, and the audience sparse; but the word spread. Jean Anouilh compared its premiere to the opening of Pirandello's *Six Characters in Search of an Author* (1923), and described it as "a music-hall sketch of **Pascal**'s *Pensées* as played by the Fratellini clowns." People were soon being turned away; it ran for some 400 performances and made its way to the world. A watershed in theatrical history, *Godot* brought SB financial success, established his reputation as the most original dramatist of his time, and vindicated the integrity with which he had remained true to his vision, even when no audience had seemed willing to share it. See also *Waiting for Godot.*

"Encore un pour rien": eleventh of the *Textes pour rien,* subtitled "Texte inédit de Samuel Beckett"; published in *Arts-Spectacles* 418 (3–9 juillet, 1953): 5; with many variants.

"The End": English translation of "La Fin" (1946), SB's first extended piece of fiction in **French**. "Translated from the French by Richard Seaver in collaboration with the author," it first appeared in *Merlin* 2.3 (1954): 144–59, with a line drawing by Stanley William Hayter; then in *Evergreen Review* 4.15 (November–December 1960): 22–41 (a revised edition, closer to the original French); *Writers in Revolt,* ed. Richard Seaver, Terry Southern, and Alexander Trocchi (Frederick Fell, 1963), 350–66; *No's Knife* (Calder, 1967); *Stories and Texts for Nothing* (Grove, 1967); and *Four Novellas* (Calder, 1977). The **Unnamable** cites the opening line (312), in a bid for sympathy.

While "in the likeness" of SB's life, filled with childhood reminiscences, the story is set in a strange **Dublin**, the narrator returning after an extended confinement (in SB's case, after the **war**). The city is simultaneously familiar and strange. As it is estranged so is narrative; distinctions between what occurs and what is imagined become impossible to determine. Thus the four postwar French stories, and "The End" in particular, anticipate narrative strategies and inno-

vations of the forthcoming *Three Novels.*
Like all the *Quatre nouvelles,* it is a story
of expulsion, from some sort of asylum
where the narrator resided naked; presumably the House of St. John of God,
as in *Malone Dies.* He is given clothing,
his having been burned on admission,
and some money, and told to leave since
he is now "well enough." Waiting in the
cloister for the rain to stop he has a childhood memory, one of SB's recurrent
images, of asking his mother a question:
how the earth could make a sound as if
it sighed, or rain fall from a cloudless sky.
She retorts sharply: "Fuck off." Wandering in search of lodgings, without success
because of his oddities, the narrator
stumbles on quarters where from his bed
he can watch the feet of Dublin through
the basement window. But the landlady
extorts his remaining funds, and he is
expelled again, replaced by a pig. Wandering, he claims to see his "son," then
meets a man he once knew, who offers
him shelter in his seaside cave, which he
rejects in favor of a mountain cabin his
friend had abandoned. He tries begging
and becomes the object lesson for a zeal-
ous Marxist, who argues that "charity is
a crime." He takes refuge in a shed,
which O'Brien locates at Collins' Barracks on Benburb Street near Wolf Tone
Quay. There he finds a boat into which
he seals himself as if in a coffin, and has
"visions" of sailing down the Liffey, out
to sea. He sees or imagines the lights and
lightships of Dublin harbor, having
viewed them from the mountains with
his father (another recurrent image). He
re-creates childhood memories of the
summer, of the burning gorse. Finally,
the narrator chains himself to the boat

and scuttles it. As he swallows a "calmative" he prepares for "the end." But this
is a story, one (or another) the narrator
"might have told, a story in the likeness
of my life, I mean without the courage
to end or the strength to go on."

Endgame: English version of *Fin de
partie,* translated by SB (7 May to 5 June
1957). He found the process difficult
and professed dissatisfaction with the
outcome, describing it to Nancy Cunard
as "the one-act horror." When the final
version reached the Lord Chamberlain
(December 1957) several phrases were
found objectionable. SB agreed to
changes but refused to remove the line
about God: "The bastard! He doesn't
exist!" The license was refused, and after
a series of comic negotiations "swine"
was accepted instead. *Endgame* was first
produced at the Cherry Lane Theatre,
New York (28 January 1958), dir. Alan
Schneider, with Lester Rawlins (Hamm),
Alvin Epstein (Clov), P. J. Kelly (Nagg),
and Nydia Westman (Nell). It featured
windows painted on the brick back wall
and Clov carrying snow skis for his final
departure. Before the first performance
a stagehand turned off the central heat-
ing, which caused the radiators and pipes
to clang as they cooled. Critics praised
the effect, so the accidental entropic
touch was retained. The production was
published as a high-fidelity recording by
Grove Press in its Evergreen Records
series, EV 003. The first London performance (28 October 1958) was at the
Royal Court, with *Krapp's Last Tape;*
George Devine directed and played
Hamm, with Jack MacGowran (Clov),
Richard Goolden (Nagg), and Frances

Cuka (Nell). The first radio production (recorded) was by Michael Bakewell for BBC 3 (22 May 1962), with Hadyn Jones (Narrator), Donald Wolfit (Hamm), Maurice Denham (Clov), Richard Goolden (Nagg), and Mary O'Farrell (Nell). *Endgame* appeared with **Act Without Words** I (Grove [Evergreen], 1958), in cloth and paperback, with a limited edition of 100 numbered copies. The **Faber** edition followed in 1958, but the Faber paperback did not appear until 1964.

What passes for action in *Endgame* is simple if not slight. A male couple, master and servant, Hamm and Clov, reside in a shelter or bunker of some sort. The imagery is apocalyptic, as if they were survivors of an unspecified cataclysm. Both are moribund if not already dead since there is "no more **nature**." The shelter exists on a cliff, on the margin of two worlds. Audience left is a window facing the sea; right, facing the earth (SB's stage directions are given from the audience perspective). The windows are too high for Clov to peer through without the aid of a **ladder**. The set creates the sense of the inside of a human **skull**. Outside is a physical wasteland; inside, a divided **consciousness**. Although the play was written in the aftermath of World War II, early drafts locate the action during and immediately after World War I, specifically in Picardy (see "**Avant** *Fin de partie*").

In this cliffside domicile, on the margin of land and sea, sheltered against a devastated world, the couple lives out a life dominated by rituals and repetitions. The play opens with a dumb show, a **mime** that suggests a morning routine.

SB called the opening an "unveiling," that is, Clov's action echoes the curtain raising as the stage is unveiled. Clov makes no opening entrance, as he will make no final exit. He is always already present in this space, uncovered, unveiled by the proscenium curtain. The only mobile member of this group, he unveils every "day" the windows, the two trash bins, and finally the armchair with the seated figure. His opening monologue anticipates the play's conclusion: "Finished, it's finished, nearly finished, it must be nearly finished." This is **Christ**'s Parthian shaft, his final words on the cross (John 19:30): "When Jesus therefore had received the vinegar, he said, It is finished: and he bowed his head, and gave up the ghost." Hamm will echo these words near play's end to announce his own demise, his giving up the ghost, but his echo of Christ will return to Clov's opening words, which suggest that dialogue throughout is already an echo. His repetition suggests that Clov's opening is a recital, an echo of Hamm's set piece, for Clov can only respond: "I use the words you taught me. If they don't mean anything any more, teach me others. Or let me be silent" (44). This echoes Caliban's malediction to Prospero in *The Tempest* (I.ii.365–67): "You taught me language; and my profit on't / Is, I know how to curse. The red plague rid you / For learning me your language!"

Clov might offer some exposition of what is finished: the morning ritual, "day after day," or, apocalyptically, their existence? Instead, he launches into an extended, arcane metaphor: "Grain upon grain, one by one, and one day, suddenly, there's a heap, a little heap, the impossible heap." In his inspection of the room, Clov senses the impossible, an almost imperceptible change to this day, the single extra grain "needed to make the heap—the last straw," according to SB (see **Zeno**), and that sense of change, the almost imperceptible alteration, provides the dramatic impetus for the rest of the day and play. Hamm reiterates it in human terms: at what point do separate moments of existence add up to something: "all life long you wait for that to mount up to a life" (70).

In the play's third unveiling, Hamm removes his "Old stancher," the handkerchief he uses to stop his bleeding—from a cerebral hemorrhage or an aneurysm. His first line invokes a game of **chess**: "Me . . . to play." Hamm is King in a game lost from the start, making senseless moves that only postpone the inevitable. He is resisting defeat in an endgame, trying to salvage tragic dignity in a futile position. "Can there be misery [. . .] loftier than mine?" he intones, and answers his question: "No doubt. Formerly." During an age of tragic heroes, perhaps, but not for this fallen king or **clown**. Hamm's oratory, his set pieces, which he repeats, revises, and rehearses daily, begins to sound more like those of a "ham" actor than that of a tragic figure. His pains are rehearsed, theatricalized misery. His resistance to an inevitable end, or action of any sort, echoes the English theater's great procrastinator, Hamlet: *resolve:* "Enough, it's time it ended"; *recantation:* "And yet I hesitate, I hesitate to . . . to end"; then *recapitulation:* "Yes, there it is, it's time it ended and yet I hesitate to . . . to end."

With the introductory themes established, by the dumb show and symmetrical opening monologues, the play moves into its dramatic conflict. SB described the tempo: "There must be maximum aggression between them from the first exchange of words onward. Their war is the nucleus of the play." One trope to express this aggression is a hammer (Hamm) driving three nails: Clov (Fr. *clou*), Nagg (Ger. *Nagel*), and Nell (Eng. *nail*). Mother **Pegg** may constitute a fourth. Hammer and nails, Hamm's tapping on the wall, Nagg's tapping on Nell's bin lid, Clov's tramping his booted feet all suggest the **crucifixion**. Another time SB explained the Hamm-Clov tension as fire and ashes, one character agitating the other, and from that stirring the fire flares. Clov's goal is escape, to the kitchen at least, or perhaps beyond, for grains of millet may have reached a critical mass. But Hamm warns him, "Outside of here it's **death**." His goal is to detain and thereby retain his lackey. Like the characters waiting for **Godot**, Hamm and Clov are tied to this spot and to each other, and to pass the **time** they abuse each other. Hamm and Clov are, after all, Didi and Gogo at a later stage in their lives.

Hamm has another means of filling time: "story time." His chronicle is a set piece, a performance with four distinct **voices**, each corresponding to a distinct attitude. As Hamm changes his posture to address the beggar lying at his feet, for instance, a sacral tenet of SB's direction is evident: movement and dialogue remain separate. First the change of posture, then an ordering pause, then the voice. Hamm's movements are painful.

"Hamm is fenced in," SB told his German cast. Like SB's Aunt Cissie (**Sinclair**), he is "crippled; it is an effort to bend forward, to reach out his arm." The atmospheric reports sprinkled amid his monologue are spoken, according to SB, as if "filler" while Hamm is inventing or remembering the next episode. The meteorological statistics suggest a formal, circular structure, 0–50–100, then back to 0. The return to zero foretells the play's end, and so the end of humanity, from nothing to nothing, but the pattern also suggests a possible new cycle. "The end is in the beginning," Hamm warns, "and yet you go **on**." Dramatically the theme is developed with Clov's sighting (or feigning sight) of a small **boy**, who may potentially replace Clov, who may replace Hamm, who may replace Nagg.

The theatrical nature of Hamm's chronicle, his need for an audience to **witness** his performance and so validate his story (and thereby his being), asserts the theatrical metaphor for the entire play. *Endgame* is, after all, a play about a play. The repetitions (**French** for "rehearsals") of dialogue and action suggest that the characters are caught in a play, a Möbius strip of narrative, in a chamber where there are only echoes. Clov threatens departure with the phrase "What is there to keep me here?" Hamm answers, "The dialogue"; he then entices Clov to play audience: "I've got on with my story." Nagg and Nell, an aged couple living without their "shanks" in separate dustbins, Hamm's "accursed progenitors" evidently, no longer function in life (hence their relegation to dustbins) *except* as an audience for

Hamm's performances and so they witnesses his existence. Nagg's music-hall story of the tailor, complete with multiple voices, parallels Hamm's narrative.

On this extraordinary day in a world where nothing is left to change, where everything has run out, especially **painkiller** (a palliative mentioned seventeen times in the play), something *has* changed, as Clov observed from, or before, the raising of the curtain: Nell dies and a flea appears; one life replaces another. The lowly flea terrifies Hamm and he shouts: "But humanity might start from there all over again!" Hamm has a fear of not ending, of a cyclical, recurrent, repetitious existence. There is an anti-creation theme in *Endgame;* Hamm, as Ham, the cursed son of Noah, fears that the whole cycle of humanity might restart from the flea, and so all this suffering—his own and humanity's—may have come to naught. The setting, the shelter, assumes the qualities of Noah's ark, from which, according to Genesis, all earthly life began again (in the discarded two-act version of the play, a Clov-like **B** reads aloud the story of Noah). In the theater, action assumes exact repetition the next day. The final irony of the *play* (in both senses of that term) is that while Hamm has been resisting the end, he is finally coming to terms with it, ready to say "yes" to the **nothing** as he prepares his own reveiling. The gesture is belied, betrayed, by Clov's silent, unresponsive presence, a persistence that suggests that there may be one more turn to the wheel. If Hamm finally accepts that "All's Well that Ends," well or ill, he may be deceived yet again. Clov may have outplayed Hamm in this "endgame" again. It is Clov's best joke, one that can and must be shared with an audience and at Hamm's expense.

Or is the joke on Clov? As many have observed, the setting of *Endgame* suggests the human skull, the action a mono-drama, the discrete characters merely aspects of a single **consciousness**, vital spirits mingling within the **conarium** (qv). In this paradigm Hamm may represent the reasoning function of mind, Clov its senses, and Nagg and Nell memories or dreams. As such, Clov could not leave, as Hamm well knows, no matter how often he threatens. The retreat from the physical world into the shelter echoes the **solipsistic** retreat (perhaps of an artist) into the recesses of the mind, only to find that it proves no retreat since consciousness itself is a conflicted, warring entity rather than a coherent unity; and so no refuge, no **asylum**. Such a reading suggests that in *Endgame* SB continues to explore creative possibilities that follow from the dissolution of **character** and personality that began with the doppelgänger imagery of "**Arènes de Lutèce**," the themes of which dominate his late theater and fiction, and anticipate the ghost plays to come.

"End of Day": "An entertainment from the works of Samuel Beckett," based on an idea of Donald **McWhinnie**, performed by Jack **MacGowran** at the Gaiety Theatre as part of the **Dublin** Theatre festival or *Tóstal* (5 October 1962); reprised at the New Arts Theatre, **London** (October 16). It comprises selections from various dramatic writings read and performed to a "continuo" provided by "**Act Without Words I**" but featuring a character in **greatcoat** and tattered **boots** against a great gray rock (designed by Ming Cho Lee). Devised by MacGowran but reshaped in consultation with SB, it is predicated upon **Molloy**'s "I shall soon be quite dead at last," and the twin certainties that he was born and will die, absurdity mitigating despair. The text was revised to become *Beginning to End*.

Endon, Mr.: an amiable inmate of the **MMM**, in his scarlet **byssus** and purple poulaines. **Murphy**'s opponent in a curious game of **chess** (his "one frivolity"), his victory precipitates the final catastrophe as Murphy is made to realize he cannot be a true microcosmopolitan, a denizen of that **little world** of the mind. The Greek preposition *endon* means "within," and the character is based on SB's friend Thomas **MacGreevy**. There may also be a touch of Paul **Morphy** in his makeup, the master being small and delicate of feature.

Mr. Endon exemplifies yet parodies **Schopenhauer**'s notion that by aesthetic contemplation one might escape the Will. His is a special madness, the ability to remain truly indifferent—a condition Murphy envies but cannot attain: Schopenhauer, describing how aesthetic contemplation counters the Will, says that complete indifference to volition can be achieved only by geniuses. But these geniuses, he adds, "may exhibit certain weaknesses which are akin to madness"; the outward behavior of those who perceive the ultimate nature of reality is what most would label madness. SB was acquainted with this passage (*WWI*, I.3 #36, 246), having alluded to it when claiming that the **Proustian** stasis is contemplative, "a pure act of understanding, will-less, the 'amabilis insania' and the 'holder Wahnsinn'" (*Proust*, 91). The climax comes when, having tried in vain to force Mr. Endon to acknowledge his presence, Murphy looks into Mr. Endon's eyes, only to see there the image of himself unseen: "a speck in Mr. Endon's unseen" (250). As he is not perceived by Mr. Endon he therefore does not exist for him; however, Mr. Endon may see, but he does not *apperceive* his own existence (see **apperception**). The cost, in other words, of attaining the freedom of the mind is the abnegation of awareness, and that is a price, Murphy suddenly understands, that he is unwilling to pay.

"Endroit clos": see **"Se voir."**

Ends and Odds: four plays ("Ends") and four "roughs" or sketches ("Odds"), categories and title offered by SB. The 1976 **Grove Press** first edition was subtitled "Eight New Dramatic Pieces": *Not I, That Time, Footfalls,* and "**Ghost Trio**" (first book publication), "**Rough for Theatre I** and **II**," and "**Rough for Radio I** and **II**." The 1977 **Faber** edition was subtitled "Plays and Sketches," adding a second teleplay "**. . . but the clouds . . .**" (first printing). Grove's "enlarged edition" (1981) became "Nine Dramatic Pieces."

Engels sisters: a common confusion of Marx with Engels (*Murphy*, 228). Friedrich Engels (1820–95) came to England in 1848 but did not marry until 1864; whereas Jenny, Laura, and Eleanor, daughters of Karl Marx (1818–83), shared their **father's** exile. There is a hint of the **Elsner sisters**, German-born neighbors of SB and **Moran**.

"Enough": SB's translation of **Assez** (Minuit, 1966); first English publication in *Books and Bookmen* 13.7 (April 1967): 62–63; then in *No's Knife* (**Calder,** 1967); first American publication in *First Love and Other Shorts* (Grove, 1977). Compare 1 Kings 19:4: "But he himself went a day's journey into the wilderness . . . and said, It is enough; now, O Lord, take away my life"; or Proverbs 30:15–16, the **horse leech's daughter** and four things that say not, It is enough: "The grave; and the barren womb; the earth that is not filled with water; and the fire that saith not, It is enough." This implies an **allegory** of desire.

"Enough" announces a bold change: "All that goes before forget"; yet it echoes the past. Like *First Love,* the unnamed narrator outlines a life after the separation from a **father** figure, with whom s/he tramped the hills hand in hand and learned the constellations. The phrases "lick his penis" (186), "mucous membrane" (187), and "my old breasts" (192) imply a female companion. Both narrators comment on the narrative, particularly the meta-narratological first paragraph of "Enough." In *First Love* the narrator divellicates the urtica (tears asunder the nettle) in a prickly version of love me, love me not; in "Enough" flowers are of the stemless variety that the narrator's companion trod and ate. Both are pursued by **voices**. The tale of a youngster taken into the service of a nearly blind, failing fatherlike figure echoes both *Endgame* and *King Lear*. In "Enough" the Clov-like narrator takes up the chronicle of a voice, which like the silence is often too much. The younger one is preoccupied with having been summarily dismissed; "my disgrace," s/he calls it, suggesting the Fall. One whose only desires were those of the elder has tramped hand in hand with him for decades. Alone now s/he records the voice or "kinds of gleams in my skull" (187), remembering the flowers they trod (and ate). Psalms 103:15–16 reads: "As for man, his days are as grass: as a flower in the field, so he flourisheth. For the wind passeth over it, and it is gone." The narrator records their meeting, their tramping, some three miles per day and night for some seven thousand miles, the endless mathematics, a syzygy finally adding to nothing. The gradient of one in one (190) is that of *Purgatory*. Their posture asleep, two right-angled triangles (like the "sacrum" twice mentioned), anticipates later sepulchral tales such as "Ping" and "Lessness."

"Enough" was adapted for performance as a showpiece for Billie Whitelaw to follow "Rockaby," which opened at the Center for Theater Research, SUNY at Buffalo (8 April 1981). The show then moved to La Mama ETC, New York (13 April), then to SUNY at Purchase (16 April). The production opened in London at the Cottesloe theater (9 December 1982). With *Footfalls* added, "Enough" and "Rockaby" were reprised by Whitelaw as part of festivities (16 February 1984) that included renaming the "Writers and Directors Theatre" (West 42nd Street) as the "Samuel Beckett The-

atre." In London, Alan Schneider wrote to SB of the show's success (2 March): "We are selling out the Samuel Beckett Theatre (!), turning away hundreds on weekends. We are the talk of the town." Immediately after posting the letter, Schneider was struck by a motorcycle and never regained consciousness.

"Enueg I": the *enueg* is a poetic form cultivated by the troubadours during the twelfth and thirteenth centuries. It derives, Beck suggests (90), from "l'ennui," and the poems are complaints, treating life's frustrations in a shrill tone, subverted by wit. The form is flexible, depending less on epigram and desolate vision, often just a string of improvisations. SB invoked Rimbaud, who composed while walking, adding, "I underestimated this terrible Dublin" (SB to TM, 8 November 1931). In the first Enueg (late 1931?), SB imagines exiting in a spasm from Portobello House (qv), where his loved one is dying of tuberculosis. Peggy Sinclair would die in Kassel on 3 May 1933, but the gray morbid setting expresses his sickness of heart. The poem was rejected by Seamus O'Sullivan for the *Dublin Magazine*, SB told MacGreevy (20 December 1931), because of the "red sputum."

The Nursing Home has its "secret things"; as the Dantean echo suggests (*Inferno* III.21), these are gates that open to Hell. Yet the world outside seems equally hopeless. In sullen mood the poet toils to the perilous footbridge that crosses the canal (5), stares at the obscene hoardings and into a sky "throttled with clouds" (9), then walks westward to Parnell Bridge, where he sees a "dying barge" with its cargo of nails and timber (19), unwitting emblems of **crucifixion** (compare *Molloy,* 26). The landscape is ugly, the stillborn evening a filthy green. He splashes past "a little wearish old man" (30; see **Democritus**); passes by a sudden blaze of scarlet and blue of a football match; and **on**, "derelict" (43), his melancholy unrelieved by the hint of "flagrant **rafflesia**." Next, a family of "grey verminous **hens**"; then, into Chapelizod, bereft of any romantic suggestion of *Tristan und Isolde.* The poem ends with the desolation unrelieved: blotches of doomed yellow in the pit of the Liffey, where the Poddle spews sewage into the dark waters, to be picked at by the vigilant gulls, and the self-mockery of a poem (a banner) made not of the silk of the seas nor of Rimbaud's impossible arctic flowers (the *Illuminations*) but of bleeding meat and his darling's red sputum.

"Enueg II": the second such lament in *Echo's Bones,* more succinct than the first; written in the summer of 1931, probably before "**Enueg I**." SB told **MacGreevy** (#13, n.d. [1931]; the microfiche is wrongly sequenced) that Seamus O'Sullivan (of the *Dublin Review*) wouldn't touch "give us a wipe" and didn't like the Anthrax. It pictures the poet's misery in **Dublin**, feeling like Judas for having betrayed a trust. Harvey suggests (120) that it anticipates SB's resignation from **Trinity**, but better is his alternative suggestion (123) of the face of the **Smeraldina** behind the decaying images of green. The final "doch doch" confirms the diagnosis of the "German fever," SB's lost love for Peggy **Sinclair**.

The poem is a complaint against the "world world world world" (the original title). A **face** (qv) appears in the evening sky, only to be dismissed as a gaffe, an accident rather than a "true icon." The sentiment is of those about to die (*de morituris,* as those saluting Caesar), of whom nothing (not *nihil nisi bonum*) need be said. The middle section invokes the *via dolorosa,* the poet's progression tired and painful, and without one wipe ("for the love of Jesus") from the *veronica mundi* (the **Veronica** "of the world"), let alone the *veronica munda* ("splendid" or "pure"); Saint Veronica wiped **Christ**'s face on His way to Calvary. Tired and perspiring, feet in **marmalade**, the old heart breaking, he lies on O'Connell Bridge and sees the "green **tulips**" of evening, the baleful half-light, shining like an anthrax on the barges laden with Guinness, images echoed in *Dream* (28); a vision without redemption, and as final as a **crucifixion**: "doch doch I assure thee."

Epicurus (341–270 BC): native of Samos and founder of the school of Epicureanism, first in Mitylene and later in Athens, where he died, from the "stone" or calculus of the bladder. His philosophy derives from the **atomism** of **Democritus** but emphasizes tranquility: post-atomist Epicureanism asserted pleasure as the end of life but denied immaterial reality, final causes, immortality of the soul, and universal ideas. His writings survive only in fragments, but they were absorbed by **Lucretius**. Epicureanism accepted the duality of **body** and soul, and with that (rejecting the **stoic** doctrine of fate, but sharing its principle of *ataraxy,* or imperturbability) the choice of freedom in the soul's activity. Yet the view of pleasure as a good was pessimistic, Epicurus seeing it as freedom from pain. **Murphy** in his **rocking chair** seeks such pleasure that pleasure is not the word, having accepted the principle that pain is a **motion** and pleasure is a motion, but not to move is best. The resolution proposed is Epicurean: **equilibrium**, with the rocking chair (motion) as the means of attaining that state of rest; in **Windelband**'s words (165), "To rest unmoved within one's self." **Spinoza** suggests (*Ethica* III.xl, n) that pleasure signifies a state wherein the mind passes to a greater perfection, and pain wherein it passes to a lesser. In the French *Murphy* SB was more explicit: "un tel plaisir que c'était presque une absence de douleur." Here **Schopenhauer** is marked, more than in the original, but what SB discovered in the Greek atomists was ratified in the German pessimist, and vice versa.

Epimetheus: a Titan, brother of **Prometheus** and husband to Pandora, charged with making man and the animals; having given all qualities to the animals, however, there was none left for man, until Prometheus found fire. His followers are among the melancholy writers of *Dream* (62), the "afterthinkers." SB recorded (DN, 107) from **Burton**: "pauci Promethei, multi Epitmethei (*sic*) / multi thyrsdigeri, pauci Bacchi" ("there are few Promethei, many Epimethei / many who carry the thyrsis, but few Bacchi").

Epstein, Jacob (1880–1959): British sculptor of Russian-Polish descent who lived in **Paris**, where he carved the sphinx for the Oscar Wilde memorial in the **Père Lachaise**, then **London**, where he created the bas-relief of **Rima** (qv). The **Smeraldina** advances up the platform "like a Gozzi-Epstein" (*Dream*, 65), a type of German railway locomotive (Pilling, *Dream Companion*).

equilibrium: SB commented in his **Trinity** lectures on **Racine**: "Comic resolution is establishment of equilibrium. Tragic resolution is the abolition of any need for equilibrium" (**Dobbin**, 8). Equilibrium is manifested in the image of humanity as a well with two buckets (*Murphy*, 58), attributed in the **Whoroscope Notebook** to **Marston**. In *The Malcontent* (III.iii.60–62), Malevole describes the buffets of Fortune: "Did you e'er see a well with two buckets, whilst one comes up full to be emptied, another goes down empty to be filled? Such is the state of all humanity." This defines the principle of equilibrium in the Newtonian universe, or its equivalent of the closed system of **desire** in *Proust*. In *Watt* (55), Mary's one hand on its way down to be filled meets the other on its way up to be emptied. **Malone** (185) has two **pots**, one for soup and the other for bodily needs, the second filling as the first is emptied; his decline is signaled when one remains full even as the other is filling (252).

The principle appears in such doctrines as the **Apmonia** (qv); the tranquility of **Epicurus**; or the **Gestalt** impulse toward closure and completion. It sometimes appears as comic **absurdity**. Hairy "Capper" **Quin** sustains a new lease on life after **Belacqua**'s death in "**Draff**"; Murphy's **death** is balanced by **Cooper**'s gains, as he sits on his **hat**; **Molloy** cannot distribute his sucking stones without imbalance, according to which pocket is weighted most (74); and the **Expelled** experiences "a loss of equilibrium, followed by a fall" (50), as he enacts the aboriginal calamity. **Pozzo** insists (*WG*, 22.a) that the tears of the world are a constant quantity, and that "our generation" is not unhappier than its predecessors. **Wylie** comments (*Murphy*, 57) that "the syndrome known as life is too diffuse to admit of palliation. For every symptom that is eased, another is made worse. The **horse leech's daughter** is a closed system. Her quantum of wantum cannot vary." The phrasing derives from **Windelband** (546), who argues that in **nature** substance is permanent, "its quantum can neither be increased nor diminished." **Atomists** like **Epicurus** and **Lucretius** emphasized the change but not cessation of the universe. **Winnie** in *Happy Days* insists that everything is "no better, no worse . . . no change," her sense of a world where things get neither worse nor better, in keeping with the First Law of Thermodynamics (conservation of energy). Yet there is attrition between the first and second acts, as **Winnie** is embedded more deeply in the sand. In *Godot*, similarly, Pozzo becomes blind, his deterioration a reminder that we are all one day closer to the final equilibrium of death. In *Endgame*, the universe is running down, reflecting the Second Law of Thermodynamics, which insists on inevitable heat loss until homeostasis is reached, when no further **motion** is possible. The Newtonian universe was challenged by such scientific discoveries (see **physics**) as entropy, which asserts that while pockets of order may lie in local systems the universal principle is that of disorder. If human existence in the lucid intervals is neither better nor worse than it was, or will be, the ruthless equilibrium of the Second Law negates even that dubious consolation.

Esposito, Bianca: SB's Italian tutor, who held private classes at a little school of languages, 21 Ely Place. Signorina Ottolenghi in "**Dante and the Lobster**" is based on her, the name taken from SB's landlady in **Florence** (via Campanella 14, 30 lire per day with three meals) during his 1927 visit. Her charm and intelligence are recalled in *Krapp's Last Tape* (58), as the older man listens to his younger self: "I was still living on and off with Bianca in Kedar Street" ("Kedar" is an anagram of "darke," or Hebrew for "black"). SB had at the end the little *Divine Comedy* he had studied in her classes, with her card that he had used as a bookmark for sixty-three years (Knowlson, 67–68, 83–84).

Espronceda, José de (1808–42): Spanish poet known for *El Estudiante de Salamanca,* which is heavily indebted to **Byron**'s *Don Juan.* Included (*Dream,* 62) among the melancholic writers whose darkest passages **Belacqua** declines.

"**Esquisse radiophonique**": "sketch" of a radio play (translated 1975 as "**Rough for Radio** I") published in *Minuit* 5 (septembre 1973): 31–35; then as the fourth of *Quatre esquisses* in *Pas suivi de quatre esquisses* (Minuit, 1978). The text suggests "vers 1962–63," but the manuscript is dated 29–30 November 1961, thus preceding "**Cascando**," to which it is closely related. SB gave the manuscript to a **London** group planning a charity sale (Admussen, 47).

"The Essential and the Incidental": review of Sean **O'Casey**'s *Windfalls* (Macmillan, 1934) in *The Bookman* 87 (Christmas 1934): 111; rpt. in *Disjecta* (82–83). SB praises O'Casey for his "dramatic dehiscence." His destructive intelligence exacts "the tumult from the unity," but SB is willing to give him credit of **allegorical** intention in "I Wanna Woman." SB's lasting concern is reflected in O'Casey's recognition that the essential and the incidental are not inimical to each other, since the latter facilitates "a definition of the former."

Estragon: in *Waiting for Godot*, one of the two keeping his appointment, **Hardy** to **Vladimir**'s Laurel. The name suggests tarragon, a bitter herb. Estragon tends to be the more direct, intuitive rather than intellectual, given to single pained perceptions rather than agonizing about them. He has troubles with his **boots**, whereas Vladimir has problems with his **hat**. First named Lévy, a postholocaust touch, but when questioned by **Pozzo** gave his name unhesitatingly as "Magrégor, André", thus making himself "one of the great family of Beckett's **M**'s" (Duckworth, lxiii). He responds to "Catulle" in **French** and "Catullus" in the first Faber edition. This became "Adam" in the American edition; SB's only explanation was that he was "fed up with Catullus" (Duckworth, lxiv).

"être là sans mâchoires sans dents": a twenty-line poem, third of twelve *Poèmes*

38–39; published in *Les Temps modernes* (novembre 1946); rpt. in *Minuit* 21 (novembre 1976): 14. The poet imagines himself lying in bed awaiting his lover who is readying herself. His thoughts are discouraging: **bodily** decrepitude; empty abstractions of thought (see **Roscelin**); vanity of language ("on attend / adverbe"); the insufficiency of song; the obscenity of the act ("qu'elle mouille"); the anticipated **alba** of carts in the market and water in the pipes; and the essential **nothing** should she come to his idiot mouth, his **formicating** [*sic*] hand, and the dark cave of his senses wherein he hears the distant scissors of the Fates.

eudemonism: the ethical system, associated with **Socrates**, premised on the contention that rectitude and reason contribute to happiness. **Kant** rejected the doctrine on the grounds that it leads to merely **hypothetical imperatives** (Windelband, 552). **Molloy** considers the "eudemonistic slop" (55), but his rejection is constrained by the **voice**, which like the "daimon" of Socrates must be obeyed.

The European Caravan: ed. Samuel Putnam (New York: Brewer, Warren and Putnam, 1931 [13 November]), "an anthology of the new spirit in European literature," Part I: France, Spain, England, and Ireland ("Part I" was the only issue). Jacob Bronowski's introduction stated that "S. B. Beckett is the most interesting of the younger Irish writers," adding that he "has adapted the **Joyce** method to his poetry with original results," his lyric impulse deepened through this influence and that of **Proust**. SB had a hand in this overt self-promotion. In evidence four poems were published: "**Hell Crane to Starling**" (475–76); "**Casket of Pralinen**" (476–78); "**Text**" (478–80); and "**Yoke of Liberty**" (480).

evacuation, truly military: experienced by Belacqua in "**Yellow**" (183), its perfect exemplum said to be (in ASC tradition) once and a half around the bowl, neatly pointed at both ends. SB's earliest extant verse, "lavatorial lines," celebrates the expert who does better, encircling twice the glittering pan (Knowlson, 59).

Evergreen Review: in the tradition of the quarterlies that sparked and fueled Modernism, *ER* fostered the turbulence of the sixties. Like the "little magazines" it became an outlet for artists whose work had been ignored or repressed. Supported by **Grove Press**, *ER* could operate on an unprecedented scale, selling thousands of copies, first quarterly, then monthly. Named after Grove's line of trade paperbacks, the first *ER* carried its own number, E-59. Barney Rosset steered the magazine toward political topics, and his interest in photography was reflected throughout Evergreen's history. He had been publishing avant-garde writers since 1953, and *ER* 1 contained SB's "**Dante and the Lobster**" (24–36), which revived interest in *MPTK*. The first issue also contained ten poems reprinted photographically from *Echo's Bones,* omitting "Alba," "Dortmunder," and "Malacoda." SB appeared regularly in *ER,* from its first to its final issues. *From an Abandoned Work,* 3 (March 1957): 83–91; *Krapp's Last Tape,* 5 (summer 1958): 13–24; "**Text for Nothing I**," 9 (summer

1959): 21–24; "**Embers**," 10 (November–December 1959): 28–41; "**From an Unabandoned Work**," 14 (September–October 1960): 58–65; "**The End**," 15 (November–December 1960): 22–41; "The **Old Tune**," 17 (March–April 1961): 47–60; "The **Expelled**," 22 (January–February 1962): 8–20; "**Words and Music**," 27 (November–December 1962): 34–43; "**Cascando**." 30 (May–June 1963): 47–57. With issue 32 (April–May 1964) *Evergreen* abandoned its quarto format for a glossier image. SB remained integral: "**Play**," 34 (December 1964): 42–7; "**Imagination Dead Imagine**," 39 (February 1966): 48–49; "The **Calmative**," 47 (June 1967): 47–49, 93–95; "**Eh Joe**," 62 (January 1969): 43–46; and *Lessness,* 80 (July 1970): 35–36. The *Evergreen Review Reader, 1957–1967* (1968) reprinted "Dante and the Lobster" (3–8) and "The Expelled" (448–54).

Evergreen roused the ire of the emerging feminist movement. In April 1970 a group of women took over its offices. *ER's* New Left constituency split over the issue, and Grove published the last *ER,* 94 (December 1971). Grove tried to revive its now infamous magazine, publishing a Dell paperback, 95 (fall 1972), and another, 96 (spring 1973), with the "Complete Text of Samuel Beckett's *The Lost Ones.*" Grove tried a tabloid edition devoted to *Last Tango in Paris,* 97; rpt. (Dell) as an Evergreen Review Special, but by 1973 the magazine had lost its audience. Rosset attempted again to revive *Evergreen* with 98 (1984), which contained "**Ohio Impromptu**," "**Catastrophe**," and "**What Where**"; but the publication could not attract a readership.

In all, SB appeared in eighteen issues over a twenty-seven-year period. Some of the most important (and most accurate) printings of his work appeared in *ER*, notably "Play," 34, and *The Lost Ones*, 96. By 1984 the principal appeal for *Evergreen* was nostalgia, and its era had passed.

"**Ex Cathezra**": SB's review of Ezra Pound's *Make it New* (Faber, 1934), in *The Bookman* 87 (Christmas 1934), 10; rpt. in *Disjecta* (77–79). The title rejects the tendency to evaluate a work in categories foreign to its *virtù*. SB was not unaware of the lapses of taste and judgment to which Pound was disposed. Yet he appreciated Pound's account of the deterioration of **Provençal** poetry, his insights into the French poets, and his discussion of Calvacanti, a "terrific organon." Sympathetic to the notion of "education by provocation," SB concludes that this is "a galvanic belt of essays," a sentiment at odds with the tenor of most of his other reviews, and perhaps with his personal feelings about Pound.

"**Excerpt: The Unnamable**": a prepublication passage, in *Chicago Review* 12.2 (summer 1958): 82–86; translated by SB but varying slightly from the **Grove Press** first edition.

Exelmans, René Joseph Isidore (1775–1852): Marshal of France, who distinguished himself during the retreat from Moscow. His name forms a dactylic expletive favored by Mr. **Knott** (209) and used by the protagonist of "The **End**" (80).

existentialism: founded conceptually by Søren Kierkegaard (1813–55) in reaction to **Hegel**'s abstractions and inflated affirmation of rationality, but not named as such until adopted by various twentieth-century German and French writers. Immediate influences were German phenomenologists Edmund Husserl and (especially) Martin Heidegger. Though Heidegger strenuously resisted the role he was to play, his religious background, which he later abandoned (he once aspired to be "a new Luther"), is emblematic of the division in later existentialism. Christian solutions to problems of existence were sought by Karl Jaspers, Gabriel Marcel, and Paul Tillich, while atheists such as Jean-Paul **Sartre**, Maurice Merleau-Ponty, and Albert **Camus** inhabited a world recovering from the "death of **God**."

In the classic existentialist apothegm, "existence precedes essence." The primary fact of the human being is not some abstract notion of intrinsic properties, but the experience of finding oneself alone in a godless cosmos. Out of chaos and meaninglessness man must wrench free authentic existence, to find relief from **contingency** and **absurdity**. Because he is free of all determinations, natural and supernatural, man must assume responsibility for his being; evading this cardinal responsibility is *mauvaise foi*. Existentialism is inseparable from the heroic vocabulary of *authenticity, commitment, engagement,* and *responsibility*.

Sartre is associated with secular existentialism (declaring, 1946, that "L'Existentialisme est un humanisme," despite ridiculing humanists eight years earlier in *La Nauseé*). From phenomenology (and, indistinctly, **Kant**) he made the distinction between *pour-soi,* or purposive possessors of will and **consciousness** who make up human existence, and *en-soi,* the self-sufficient world of inert matter. The freedom granted the *pour-soi* is sometimes caricatured as easily won, because of its denial of the outside determinants (in *Being and Nothingness,* Sartre characterized appeals to the unconscious as *mauvaise foi*). This is to overlook the agonistic element of freedom, as burdensome as it is liberating. In being free to choose, human beings are condemned to make choices; that is, condemned to be free.

Waiting for Godot with its dramatic irregularities appeared to present its two attrited principals as kin to the existentialist hero, poised for self-invention. Abandoning not just theatrical artifice but, it seemed, scripted dialogue, they were seen as stark exemplars of the *pour-soi.* Theirs was a limited autonomy, however, as Robbe-Grillet pointed out ("Presence," 113): "Just as there is nothing for them to recite, so there is **nothing** for them to invent, either, and their conversation, which has no continuous thread to sustain it, is reduced to absurd fragments." Rather than be free, Didi and Gogo are "tied" to their man, Godot. The works that followed *WG,* in their vagueness of **time** and locale, their sketchy backgrounds, and their absence of conventional dramatic and narrative devices, invited explication based on **allegory**, and the conviction that their concern was the "human condition." That work so profoundly suspicious of order, belief, and systematic thought should have a generalized, all-purpose label assigned it is intensely problematic, and not easily resolved.

It is difficult to ascertain when SB engaged with existentialism. In **Dream** (198) the **Silver Strand** episode confirms Belacqua's choice of "the marginal part." In "**Recent Irish Poetry**" (74) SB called MacGreevy an existentialist; Cronin notes (194) that the word was creeping into English, and suggests Jean **Beaufret**'s reading of Heidegger. After the war SB read **Camus**, referring to *L'Étranger* as important, but mocking "Le Mythe de Sisyphe": "But I do not think even **Sisyphus** is required to scratch himself, or to groan, or to rejoice, as the fashion is now" (*Molloy,* 133). Richard Coe argued (*Beckett,* 73–74) that with *Murphy,* SB "revealed himself as an *existentialiste avant la lettre,*" and characterized the vice-existers of the *Trilogy* as "Existentialists who have failed." Edith Kern advanced the encounter (*Existential Thought,* 184): "Beginning with *Watt,* Beckett's fiction, not unlike Kierkegaard's is expressive of the individual's essential isolation and the incommunicability of his most crucial experience." In "Philosophical Fragments," Ruby Cohn recognized in SB's turning from English to French a parallel turn (175): "The French work is Existentialist in conveying human dread and despair, at a world of unreconstructed absurdity."

A much-quoted incident supports the earlier speculation. On a Parisian street (January 1938), SB was stabbed in the chest. Confronting his assailant outside court, SB asked why he did it: "Je ne sais pas, Monsieur," came the reply (Knowlson, 261). The incident has been depicted as an *acte gratuit,* often regarded (despite Sartre's repudiation) as the existentialist trope par excellence, but more apposite to **surrealist** provocation. Popularized by André **Gide** in *Les Caves du Vatican* (1914), it is a self-defining action performed with neither motive nor moral regard, merely because one does not refrain from doing it. Yet in *Proust* (19–20), long before "existentialism" was current, SB scorned the "analogivorous" who would interpret "Live dangerously" (*Les Caves du Vatican*), that "victorious hiccough in vacuo," as "the national anthem of the true ego exiled in **habit**."

Martin Esslin proposed a different kinship. In his essay in *The Novelist as Philosopher* (131), Esslin saw in SB's recurrent anxiety of antenatal helplessness "a summing-up of the entire human condition. For, once born into our world, man ultimately remains as unable to grasp the why and wherefore of his situation, the nature of his own identity, as the foetus in the womb." Yet such existentialist affiliations are at best speculative. This is due, largely, to the unavailability of the capacity for agency, purposive self-determination that defines the *pour-soi*. It becomes snagged on the Cartesian coordinates of *res cogitans* and *res extensa*, as when Murphy's **rocking chair** (2) "set him free in his mind. For it was not until his **body** was appeased that he could come alive in his mind." For **Molloy** "freedom" is as unsettling epistemologically as anything else (13): "free, yes, I don't know what that means but it's the word I mean to use, free to do what, to do nothing, to know, but what . . ." That freedom to do nothing was the focal point of *Eleutheria*, whose title proclaims the play's subject, freedom, even as its pursuit constitutes a farce of frustration. Such examples seem overoptimistic in comparison with such

later narrators as the frustrated protagonist of "**Act Without Words** I" or the mired inhabitant of *How It Is*, compelled to participate in an elaborate choreography of torture and suffering. Recent critical approaches to SB have specifically targeted the precepts of humanist existentialism (compare his rejection in **art** of the "anthropomorphic" impulse). Various branches of poststructuralist inquiry have challenged a presumptuous anthropocentrism that glorifies human autonomy, focusing instead on inhuman forces of heteronomy complicating *authenticity*, clouding *commitment*, distrusting *engagement*, and dissolving *responsibility*. See **humanism**. [PS]

"The Expelled": English version of "L'**Expulsé**" (1946), trans. by Richard Seaver in collaboration with SB and published in *Evergreen Review* 6.22 (January–February 1962): 8–20. First published in book form in *Stories and Texts for Nothing* (Grove, 1967), and in *No's Knife* (Calder and Boyars, 1967); reprinted in *Four Novellas* (Calder, 1977), *Collected Shorter Prose* (Calder, 1984), and, slightly altered, in the *Complete Short Prose* (Grove, 1996). It appeared in *The Existential Imagination*, ed. Frederick J. Karl and Leo Hamalian (Fawcett, 1963), 217–29.

After World War II SB turned to short fiction for "the French venture," with four *nouvelles: Premier amour*, "L'Expulsé," "Le **Calmant**," and "La Fin" ("**Suite**"). These stories, "the very first writing in French," tapped a creative reservoir, for a burst of writing followed: two full-length plays, *Eleutheria* and *En attendant Godot*, and three novels,

Molloy, Malone meurt, and *L'Innommable.* "L'Expulsé" was the second story, but as the narrator concludes, "I don't know why I told this story. I could just as well have told another. Perhaps some other time I'll be able to tell another." He tells of rejection and the fear of abandonment. The opening conjures up images of **birth**: "In a sort of vision I saw the door open and my feet come out" (49); and of the Fall: "The fall was therefore not serious" (47). The unnamed narrator of this four-story sequence is invariably, suddenly and inexplicably, expelled from the security of a shelter, an ejection that mimics the birth trauma, anticipates Molloy, and remains a theme in "**For to end yet again**," where the expelled one "falls headlong down." One of SB's preoccupations is developed in full complexity: the psychological, ontological, narratological bewilderment at the inconsistency, the duality of the human predicament, the experience of existence. On one side is the tradition of **humanism**, through the Renaissance into the rationality of the Enlightenment. This is the world of school room and laboratory, **mathematics** and proportion, classical symmetry, the **pensum**. For SB's narrators, the sentient experience of existence, being in the world, punctures that humanistic promise, the empiricism of the classroom, but the latter never loses its appeal and is potentially a source of comfort (although it destroys **Watt**). At the opening of "The Expelled" the narrator focuses not on the trauma of rejection and ejection but on the difficulty of counting the stairs down which he has been dispatched. There is little resentment having been ejected from one place

and having now to find another. SB's focus on injustice is seldom local, civil, or social but cosmic, the injustice of having been born, after which one finds consolation where one may—in **mathematics**, say. The Expelled finds what comfort he can in calculations.

"The Expelled" is "a wandering to find home." With cash from a second windfall, a bequest that parallels that from his deceased **father**, the narrator hires a cab, and instead of finding a furnished room returns at close of day to the cabbie's home where he elects to sleep with the **horse** in the barn, and then inside the cab again. Finally he flees through a window, resisting the temptation of setting the barn ablaze, expelling himself instead headfirst, as dawn approaches. Symmetries are pronounced. Although the narrator calls attention both to the narrative as narrative and to its apparent pointlessness ("No reason for this to end or go on. Then let it end"), the parallel with the opening ejection is unmistakable.

"**L'Expulsé**": original of "The **Expelled**," with "the same old deadbeat as in '**Suite**'," as SB told George **Reavey**, so accentuating the continuity of the protagonist in a sequence of texts. The autograph manuscript is dated 6 to 14 October 1946, 51 pp. First published in *Fontaine: Revue mensuelle de la poésie et des lettres françaises,* ed. Max-Pol Fouchet, 10.57 (décembre 1946–janvier 1947): 685–708, then included in *Nouvelles et textes pour rien* (1955). The short story differs slightly from the book, one elision being the narrator's thought of using his bad breath against **policemen**.

"Extract from *Molloy*": in *Merlin* 2.2 (autumn 1953): 88–103, trans. Patrick Bowles; from the opening until **Molloy**'s encounter with the **donkey**. Another "Extract from *Molloy*," the sucking stones, appeared in the *Paris Review* 2.1 (spring 1954): 124–35 (see "**Stones**"). Yet another, translated by SB, appeared in *Transition Fifty* 6 (octobre 1950): 103–5, plus an extract from *Malone meurt*, 105–6 (pp. 97–100 and 7–9 of the respective originals, the publication of which they anticipated). An extract from the end of part 1 (English) appeared in *French Writing Today*, ed. Simon Watson Taylor (Penguin, 1968), 50–57.

"Extract from *Watt*": in *Envoy* 1.2 (January 1950): 11–19; pp. 16–24 of the first edition, plus a bad joke: when Mr. **Nixon** asks **Watt**'s name, Mr. **Hackett** says, "What?" *Envoy* was a short-lived (1949–50) **Dublin** monthly, ed. John Ryan. Like pieces were published in **Cork**, in *Irish Writing* 17 (December 1951): 11–16, the beginning and the final paragraph of part 3; in **Paris**, in *Merlin* 1.3 (winter 1952–53): 118–26, the close of Watt's stay with Mr. **Knott**; and again in *Irish Writing* 22 (March 1953): 16–24, the **Galls**, father and son. Each varies slightly from the published text.

Extravas, Baron: in "**Echo's Bones**" (11) and *Murphy* (99, 104), enemy of Lord Gall, who, as reversioner and protector, will inherit **Wormwood** of Eden if Lord Gall cannot produce an heir and will cut off the cruel entail. The name, from **Garnier**'s *Onanisme* (DN, 68), means "outside the vessel," rather than "within the natural female organ." See **onanism**.

F

"F—": a short story by Suzanne **Deschevaux-Dumesnil**, in an unsigned translation by SB, in *Transition Forty-Eight*, 4 (January 1949): 19–2; reprinted, with a commentary, by Ruby Cohn in *Samuel Beckett Today* (7 [1998]: 41–45). The narrator, en route to F— on a cold windy night, is struck from behind by a "fellow" traveler. Communication is uncertain. The other has "lost something very important, I don't know what." He is distressed. Close together, they have difficulty perceiving each other. They move on, side by side, beside the sea, but question: "Was this road the right road?" The narrator has a vision: "I saw us turn back. I saw us go on. I. Us." The other proposes to go somewhere and return; s/he will rest in a ditch, "a kind of shelter." Then, apparently abandoned, "In the sorry light of dawn I rose" to continue the journey to F— alone: "So. There I was. Or nearly." The motif of two travelers on the road to an uncertain destination, prose and syntax replete with uncertainties, ellipses, absence of motive, all suggest a Beckettian pattern. Any doubt about SB's involvement is dispelled in the "Note about Contributors": his future wife is "Forgotten in musical, unknown in literary circles."

Faber: the publishers began as The Scientific Press, owned by Sir Maurice and Lady Gwyer, who joined with Geoffrey Faber to found Faber and Gwyer (1925), 24 Russell Square, Bloomsbury. Geoffrey soon replicated himself as Faber and Faber. T. S. **Eliot** became their literary adviser. Their authors have constituted a veritable Who's Who of contemporary writing. SB's first work to appear with Faber was his "**Dante**" essay in *Our Exagmination* (1929). His vitriolic review of **Rilke**'s translated poetry appeared in Faber's *The Criterion*. SB was invited (1936) to translate for Faber the poems of Joachim **Ringelnatz**, but this did not eventuate. Faber was one of many to turn down *Murphy* and later *Molloy*. Faber contracted the rights to SB's work with *Waiting for Godot*, purchasing them from **Grove Press** through Rosica Colin (September 1955) for £50. They chose not to take his fiction and poetry, which gave John **Calder** the opportunity. They continue to publish the drama, available in slim volumes and in the *Collected Shorter Plays* (1984) or *Complete Dramatic Works* (1986; lacking *Eleutheria*, which Faber published separately in 1996). Commercial realities and scholarly imperatives have not always coincided. Faber long retained a bowdlerized *Godot* (see **censorship**), and later imprints have failed to correct obvious errors, or consider changes made in performance, even when sanctioned by SB. Many standard editions of SB's dramatic texts are still unreliable.

faces: recurrent images in SB's writings, forgotten, seen suddenly in the clouds or sky or ashes. This motif anticipates findings in psychology concerning the selective mechanisms of the brain that identify faces as distinct from other features, and contends that this is as much constituted by **memory** as by perception, "seeing" a mode of "dreaming." "**Enueg II**" sets the despair of the "world world world world" against a face in the sky; but the image crumbles and no **veronica** retains its imprint. In *Murphy* (4), **Neary** isolates the face as a figure against the "big blooming buzzing confusion," William James's dictum is cited by **Woodworth** (107) as a first principle of **Gestalt** perception (Ger. *Gestalt*, "figure"; Fr. *figure*, "face"), a baby learning to distinguish the meaningful configuration of a face from the "blotch." **Celia**'s features (29) emerge from an identical confusion, but Murphy later fails to "get a picture" of Celia, his **mother**, or his **father** (251). **Watt** is not successful in eliciting the image of his father (77). In "**Old Earth**," the narrator, standing at gaze, recalls memories seen on the screen of the sky, and fails differently: "For an instant I see the sky, the different skies, then they turn to faces." **Molloy** and **Moran** seek their images in the water. The **Unnamable** (307) imagines a face in the embers, doomed to crumble; its appearance would be "encouraging" (362). In *How It Is* the narrator recalls his mother's face (15). The vigil in "**Still 3**" leads to the apparition of faces of the long dead emerging from the dark, "on off" (as in "**What Where**"). In "La Falaise" a skull emerges from the rocky face. In "**Words and Music**," after many false starts, Words invokes **Croak**'s theme of the face on the stairs, the memory in age of the woman "Who loved could not be won,"

but whose face in the ashes reflects old starlight on earth again. SB added this verse to *Collected Poems*.

"**La Falaise**": the prose poem "**Pour Bram [van Velde]**," published in *Celui qui ne peut se servir de mots* (Montpellier: Fata Morgana, 1975); translated as "The Cliff" by Edith Fournier for the *Complete Short Prose* (1995), 257. Admussen calls it (83–84) "Texte pour Bram van Velde." It is a still-life picture, a composition in words, rhythm evolved from the flux of impressions and crystallizing an image. Numerous drafts (RUL 1396/4/34–40, janvier 6 to mars 26, 1975) shape a lengthy piece into an abstract minimalist composition. SB returns to the subject-**object** dichotomy of earlier pieces about Bram ("La **Peinture des van Velde**," "**Peintres de l'empêchement**," and "**Three Dialogues**"). The window (the frame) through which the observing "eye" views the cliff separates him from and joins him to it in a process that blends perception and imagination, the rocky **face** gradually assuming the proportions of a **skull**, before vanishing into the whiteness of nonperception.

"**Fancy Dying**": an abandoned text that developed into *All Strange Away* and *Imagination Dead Imagine*, other bits reshaped for "**Faux départs**." It anticipates the "**closed place**" texts and the "**Still**" stories. The title echoes Jeremy Taylor's *Holy Dying*.

father: a figure constituted by **memories** of SB's father and **Freud**'s father **imago**. SB's relationship with his father was affectionate and nonthreatening, not the inimical triangle of the oedipal drama. William **Beckett** was an affable and re-laxed parent, the more so by contrast with May **Beckett**, whose **mother** love was aggressive. In *Dream* (53–54), and later in *Company,* SB fondly recalls the father who would settle down to read, absorbed and motionless. Such memo-ries suggest a happy childhood. His **death** grieved SB, at a time when he had nothing to justify himself to his father; should he not grow up, acknowledge the demands of society and become the model citizen his father exemplified?

"**Malacoda**" records SB's anguish at his father's death. In "**ainsi a-t-on beau**" that is seen in the context of universal horror: "oublier son père / ses yeux s'il portait la moustache / s'il était bon de quoi il est mort. " **Watt** has **Proustian** memories of his father, associated with **flowering currant**. The narrator of *First Love* associates his marriage with his father's death. "**Afar a bird**" (233) reveals latent fears: "he'll confuse his mother with whores, his father with a roadman named **Balfe**." Such fears shape *From an Abandoned Work:* "Did I kill my fa-ther?" (160). Henry in "**Embers**" expe-riences his father with him, "back from the dead," and Bolton acts as a father fig-ure, a testament to his need, his loss.

SB eventually "got over it," but his ex-perience determined the father as a fig-ure representing the imperative of matu-ration and society. This is **Freudian** territory: transition from natural to civi-lized existence is echoed by the child's maturation for both depend on an alli-ance with the paternal figure. The primi-tive mother-son dyad threatens to engulf the child in an **irrational** emotional world; alliance with the father permits passage into a rational world where plea-sures and dangers are moderated. The paternal figure reinforces society's de-mands on behavior, as does the **police-man** in *Molloy,* or **Moran** with his son. The "**stamp** of the father" is reflected in the Timor 5 reis orange of 1895 and the mustachioed authority figure depicted thereon (Baker, 37–47). SB depicts the process with a comic absurdity, suggest-ing that he does not take the oedipal rhetoric altogether seriously. But the fa-ther as an internalized principle institut-ing a moral obligation to grow up and comply is something he felt deeply, hence the **cylindrical ruler** as a phallic reminiscence of his father's profession. SB's defiance of his parents' expectations consisted precisely of a literary urge that he could not justify to them. Thus he recasts the oedipal drama as a tortured suspension of **consciousness** between the need to express in the hope of achieving (**embryonic**) quietude, and language (or the rational/paternal principle), which entails a paradoxical inability to satisfy the need it is supposed to meet because it inherently and perpetually divides con-sciousness into the problematics of self and Other. [DL]

"**Faux départs**": a work in four sections, three in **French** and one in English, in *Kursbuch* I (June 1965): 1–5, with Elmar **Tophoven**'s German translation; in-cluded in *Collected Shorter Prose* (271–73). The French sections resemble pas-sages in *Imagination morte imaginez;* the English piece corresponds to the opening of *All Strange Away.* They represent an attempt to reshape the remains of an aborted longer fiction, tentatively entitled "**Fancy Dying**." They signal less a false start than a major aesthetic shift, a rejection of the "journey and return" structure in favor of the "**closed space**" terrain.

feasible: in "**Three Dialogues**" (103), the "plane of the feasible" implies that mode of existence that in **art** might be rendered, even extended, through representation, as in the works of **Matisse** and **Tal Coat** but rejected by Bram **van Velde**. Charles Juliet tells of Bram finding and wearing a useless pair of spectacles; asked by an optician what he did, he replied, "I paint my inner life." Previous painting (he said) was on the side of the positive, the feasible; he had to go toward what was not feasible (*Conversations*, 5, 96). In "**Text 4**" the "I" experiences a rare absence of the "he" (**voice**) and is "almost restored to the feasible."

"**Fenêtre entre ciel et terre**": an untitled prose text beginning thus, SB's contribution to a tribute to Bram **van Velde**, *Celui qui ne peut se servir des mots: à Bram van Velde par Alechinsky, Asse, Beckett* [et al.] (Montpellier: Fata Morgana), 1975, 17; a limited edition of 100, including "une suite de lithographies de Bram van Velde."

Field, John (1782–1837): **Dublin**-born composer who resided in Moscow. His nocturnes were the model for **Chopin**'s; hence the "sickroom talent" of *Dream* (69).

Fielding, Henry (1707–54): English novelist. SB made a late discovery of Fielding,

reporting to **MacGreevy** (8 October 1932): "I'm enchanted with *Joseph Andrews,* Jacques and the Vicar of W. in one." He appreciated the reminiscences of **Diderot**, the ironical replis giving away the show pari passu with the show: "Such a thing never to have read!" He thought the short chapters "an idea," one he would weave into *Murphy.* By November he was reading *Tom Jones* ("a great book, pitted with faults"), but felt he expected more, that the burlesque was clumsy, and the ending the best part. In 1933 he read *Amelia,* which has a Murphy and a **Celia**, and *A Voyage to Lisbon,* with its graphic descriptions of **tarwater** and dropsy. SB found in the dying Fielding a grotesque emblem. "**Love and Lethe**" finds Ruby Tough "in the posture of Philosopher Square behind Molly Seagrim's arras" (90); in "**Walking Out**" (103), **Belacqua** seems "a kind of cretinous Tom Jones." Fielding offered an apprenticeship from a master of the craft; *Murphy,* SB's picaresque novel, showed the lessons had been learned.

Fifty Shilling lapels: the Fifty Shilling tailors, a ready-to-wear company known for cutting corners as well as prices. *Murphy* (271).

Film: SB's only screenplay, *Film* was commissioned by Barney Rosset of **Grove Press** for a series to include short films by Harold Pinter, Marguerite Duras, and Alain Robbe-Grillet. The SB project consumed the entire production budget. SB began work on 5 April 1963 and a first draft, called both "Notes for Film" and "*Percipi* Notes," was completed four days later. A second draft, "Outline Sent to

Grove" (22 May 1963), was succeeded by a forty-leaf "Shooting Script," which scheduled 20 July 1964 as the shooting date. It was shot in New York, dir. Alan **Schneider**, with Buster **Keaton** as **O** (Zero Mostel and Jack **MacGowran**, of whom SB was "enthusiastically in favour," were unavailable). This occasioned SB's only visit to the United States. The film was shown at the Venice Film Festival (October 1965), the New York Film Festival (1965), and periodically at Grove's **Evergreen** Theater. It was remade by the British Film Institute (1979), in monochrome and without SB's supervision, as *Film: a screenplay by Samuel Beckett,* dir. David Rayner Clark with Max Wall (16mm, twenty-six minutes), a transformation far from SB's intentions. *Film* was first published in *Eh Joe and Other Writings* (Faber, 1967); in *Cascando and Other Short Dramatic Pieces* (Grove, 1969); and as *Film: Complete Scenario / Illustrations / Production Shots* (Grove, 1969; Faber, 1972), with textual notes, illustrations, production shots, and an essay, "On Directing *Film*," by Alan Schneider. A German translation by Erika and Elmar **Tophoven** (Suhrkamp, 1968) preceded SB's **French**, which appeared first in *Film, suivi de Souffle* (Minuit, 1972), in a special edition of 342 copies, before being included in *Comédie et actes divers* (1972).

Film explores the dual nature of being and **consciousness**, through the perceiver, E, and the perceived, O. In SB's notes: "In order to be figured in this situation the protagonist is sundered into object (O) and eye (E), the former in flight, the latter in pursuit." The character is the object of perception and the camera the perceiver, the **machine** drawn into the perceptual frame. Like **Godot** the camera never appears, but as a metaphor of self-perception, the camera photographing itself photographing itself becomes a trope for the paradox of **apperception**. Like the human eye with which *Film* begins, a substitution after the planned original shot was lost, the camera is never neutral. It records and participates, intruding on, affecting what it records. As it enters the field of perception, that is, as the roles of E and O are temporarily reversed, each is appalled by the notion of being watched. O, emblematic of humanity, attempts to flee perception, to attain sanctuary (**asylum**), repose, nonbeing. O is at ease only when E is within the angle of immunity, 45° on either side, where an observer standing by a **mirror** can no longer see his own reflection. The theme is summed up in SB's notes: "*esse est percipe.* All extraneous perception suppressed, animal, human, divine, self-perception maintains in being. Search of non-being in flight from extraneous perception breaking down in inescapability of self-perception." Even as O symbolically destroys a print of **God** the **father** (Abu), E will replace the deity, self-perception replacing divine observation and maintaining O in being. The final epiphany suggests the impossibility of escape; that is, the pursuing perceiver is "not extraneous but self." Such an exploration of the duality of being or consciousness returns to *Murphy*. Both works imply that the impossibility of avoiding apperception is a condition of sanity.

In conception and in production the film was plagued with problems, many never satisfactorily solved. One problem was establishing the difference in vision between E and O. SB was concerned "that the two visions are to be distinguished," E's clear and normal, O's occluded, as if he suffered from cataracts, the effect achieved with a gauze over the camera lens. So O's perceptions of the couple in the street, and of the flower woman on the stairs of the building, are in this occluded mode, instances of O's view used to establish the convention in preparation for the room sequences. With such preparation SB deviated from his initial conception ("Throughout the first two parts all perception is E's"). In this earlier conception a broader populace would be shown somehow perceiving, "all content in *percipere* and *percipi*." O, on the other hand, would be plagued by the "*agony of perceivedness.*"

Once in what SB's notes identify as his **mother**'s room (compare *Molloy*), O suppresses all possible perception (human, animal, divine), after which he sits in a **rocking chair** and peruses his photographs: "O at different ages from his infancy to his present age or thereabouts (the last photo permitting identification)" (Harmon, 159). The photographs reinforce O as *percipi*, both observed by figures within the photographs (by mother, by **dog**, by infant daughter, for example) and the object of the camera in the stills he is observing, just as he is simultaneously being observed by the camera, E. Even within the angle of immunity—an illusion since the audience observes him—O's sense of being perceived is intensified by his viewing the photographs, and he responds by obliterating them. Apparently at rest, he is finally confronted by E full front.

SB was dissatisfied as he struggled with the compromises his film demanded. He found portions of it powerful if "Not quite the way intended"; he told Rosset that it was an "interesting failure," an opinion many share. The Berkelean framework, SB admitted to Schneider, is something "you and I and a few others can discern." Despite his reservations it retains a power and mystery. Though not a commercial success it won festival awards in Venice, New York, and **London** (1965), and at Oberhausen, Tours, Sydney, and Kraków (1966).

"La fin": a short story, one of *Quatre nouvelles*, earlier called "**Suite**" (qv), trans. Richard Seaver in collaboration with SB as "The **End**." Finished in May 1946, the first half published immediately in *Les Tempes modernes* 10 (juillet 1946): 107–19. SB expected the second to follow, but Simone de Beauvoir refused to publish the rest. SB argued that printing half the story was a "mutilation," but she remained adamant. It was nine years before the whole appeared in *Nouvelles et textes pour rien*.

Fin de partie: French original of *Endgame*, written for Roger **Blin** and dedicated to him. First published by **Minuit** (1957) as *Fin de partie suivi de Acte sans paroles*, 3,000 copies, 65 deluxe, with another 4,500 a few months later and frequent photographic reprintings thereafter. Reprinted in *L'Avant-scène / Fémina-théâtre* 156 (août, 1957): 7–22; and in *Vingt pièces et un acte choisies dans le théâtre contemporain*, ed. Odette Aslan (Paris: Éditions Seghers, 1959), 67–104. First performed, in **French** but in **London**, at the Royal Court Theatre, 3 April 1957, when the Théâtre de l'Oeuvre in **Paris** backed out, with Roger Blin as **Hamm**, Jean **Martin** as **Clov**, Georges Adet as **Nagg**, and Christine Tsingos as Nell. There were problems with "the Lord Chamberpot" (see **censorship**), but permission was finally granted. After six performances the play moved to the Studio des Champs-Élysées, Paris (26 April 1957), with the same cast, save Germaine de France as Nell. A recorded studio performance in French appeared on BBC 3 (2 May 1957). The text was edited by John and Beryl Fletcher (London: Methuen, 1970).

Fin de partie had a difficult birth, emerging only after a turbulent creative process beginning before 1954 and not completed until 1957. It presented SB with extraordinary problems, and no other theatrical work testifies to such groping for form and matter. SB tried a two-act structure with less than symmetrical halves. In a letter to Alan **Schneider** (11 January 1956), he still referred to a two-act version. This structure did not fit the new material, or was the sort of mechanical solution he abominated, a self-imitation or self-parody. The long first and short second acts were combined into one, and SB wrote Schneider (21 June 1956): "Have at last written another, one act, longish, hour and a half, I fancy. Rather difficult and elliptical, mostly depending on the power of the text to claw, more inhuman than *Godot*" (Harmon, 11).

SB responded to the difficulties of composition by returning to English and by a change of medium, with the radio play *All That Fall* (1956), then an adaptation of that voice to stage in *Krapp's Last Tape* (1958). These came almost whole, and substantial portions of the earliest drafts remain intact, whereas *Fin de partie* groped toward a form that allowed the inclusion of many disparate, sometimes intensely personal elements that SB struggled to rearrange. These included bits of dialogue, the **war**, family **deaths**, sexual frustrations, and failures of **religion**. The **memories** driving *Fin de partie* were deeply and painfully personal. Much can be traced to his experience working for the Irish Red Cross in **Saint-Lô** (see "The **Capital of the Ruins**"). Images of devastation were exacerbated by the unexpected death of his brother, Frank (13 September 1954) and the incapacitation of his aunt Cissie, confined to a wheelchair with a telescope to amuse herself watching the ships in Dublin Bay. SB's solution to his impasse was to center the play around parallels and reverberations so the dramatic structure became that of an echo chamber; then to develop its darkly comic mood. If, as the moribund Nell asserts, "Nothing is funnier than unhappiness," then *Fin de partie* is one of SB's most richly comic works. See also "**Avant** *Fin de partie*"; "**Mime de rêveur, A**"; and *Endgame*.

"**Fingal**": the second story of *MPTK*, begun early in 1933. The title refers to a district north of **Dublin**, but names the hero of James Macpherson's **Ossian** (1762), as in the pseudo-heroic. **Belacqua** takes the middling **Winnie** to the Hill of Feltrim, or Hill of Wolves, where, appropriately, he soon feels a very sad animal (the classical tag, *post coitum omne animal triste est*). Visible is the Portrane **Asylum**, which Belacqua and Winnie head for, rounding the estuary with its "theories" of swans and coots (Gk. *theorein*, "to look at"), passing by the Martello tower. This is the landscape of "**Sanies I.**"

Attracted by her "sincerities" (the legs of **Herrick**'s Julia), Belacqua is as wax in her hands. Their goal is another hill, marked by a Round Tower commanding a view of the asylum. He again becomes a sad animal, but he is distracted by the scenery, which he finds curiously moving, and by thoughts of a **bicycle**. Dr. **Sholto** appears, and Belacqua takes the opportunity to dump Winnie for the bicycle, which he steals first to visit another tower, one that gives him "sursum corda" (29), an uplifting of the heart. This is the tower, as the old man from Lambray explains to Winnie, in which "Dane **Swift**" kept his "motte" (33). The incident reflected SB's experience, as told to **MacGreevy** (5 June 1933), Winnie's confusion being SB's own. The landscape of Fingal accentuates the **fundamental unheroic**, and its history of suffering and madness implies a critique of Belacqua. The final image of him strangely laughing (an escaped patient?) in Taylor's public house in the village of Swords is not a wholesome one. In the Grove text this effect is muted, for he is drinking only.

First Love: written in French in 1946 as *Premier amour,* the first of *Quatre nouvelles* (qv), for which SB had expectations. However, he withdrew it, and it languished among his trunk manuscripts, unpublished until 1970 and not translated until 1973. It appeared in English as a separate volume (Calder and Boyars, 1973), 100 signed copies, specially bound; then in *First Love and Other Shorts* (Grove, 1974). The third paragraph of *First Love* originally began,

"Personally I have nothing against graveyards." SB introduced a last-minute **pun** to the British edition: "Personally I have no bone to pick with graveyards"; this was not adopted in any American edition prior to the *Complete Short Prose*.

Much of the material withheld from publication contained incidents SB deemed too personal for publication. *First Love* was among these. The title defines **love** in psychoanalytical terms deriving from Melanie **Klein**, that between the child and the breast, as conducive to the first awareness of otherness; this is underlined by an echo of Revelation 2:4: "Nevertheless I am somewhat against thee, because thou hast left thy first love." *First Love* details a love, of sorts, and the unexpected **birth** of a **child**, followed by the departure of the alleged **father**. This desertion is framed by **memories** of a faithful father, suggesting that the narrator cannot accept and assume his responsibilities because of his psychological dependence on not the **mother** but the father. After his father's **death** he is expelled from his home with only a small inheritance. His father's grave he finds wanting; he has traveled in **Germany**, preferring the lion headstone of **Hagenbeck** in the Ohlsdorf cemetery to that of his father. In his wanderings in a city very like **Dublin**, along the canal, he meets **Lulu** (qv), whose name he changes to Anna midway through the story. Like **Murphy**, he seeks the supine mind, but the relationship with Lulu forces him into erection, so to speak. Despite sending her away, he longs for her and finds himself inscribing her name "in old cowshit." Freedom from **desire** comes only in her presence.

The narrator moves in, removing all the parlor furniture to the corridor save the sofa on which, having faced it to the wall, he sleeps undisturbed except for the clients she entertains. One night he awakes with her beside him naked: "It was my night of love." He applies the word "marriage" to his relationship, for "it was a kind of union in spite of all." She is soon pregnant, as evidenced by the darkening haloes of her breasts: "Abort, abort, and they'll blush like new," is all he can offer. With the birth of the child he leaves without being put out. The final image is of his father, who taught him the constellations as he had the names of the lighthouses and lightships of Dublin harbor. But his head is full of the **vagitus**; his only defense is to keep moving: "As long as I kept walking I didn't hear them, because of the footsteps." With its obsessive themes of birth and death, **coming and going** as the only solace, the breakdown of literary **character**, and its epistemological crisis, *First Love* anticipates many later themes. Its relative neglect is difficult to account for, one exception being John Banville who described it (*Irish Times,* 11 March 1975) as "the most nearly perfect short story ever written."

Fizzles: translations of the ***Foirades,*** the English word implying a failure, a sputter or hiss, or the act of breaking wind quietly (SB's preferred sense). A group of six (or seven, or eight) short prose texts, all but one first written in **French**, five translated into English (1974) for a special edition (see ***Foirades/Fizzles***). ***Immobile*** might technically be excluded on the grounds of its English origin; "**Pour finir encore**" was added later.

The order of composition does not match that of any publication. First published in *For to End Yet Again, and Other Fizzles* (**Calder**, 1976), each entitled by its opening words. They appeared in *Fizzles* (**Grove**, 1976), the segments in a different order from the French or British texts, and (except for 3, 7, and 8) numbered from "Fizzle 1." They appear thus in the ***Complete Short Prose,*** 224–46. Here, 1–8 represent the Grove text (reportedly the sequence SB approved); a–h the Calder edition; A–F the manuscript sequence (*Still* and "Pour finir encore" were composed later). The French order is complicated because some pieces are titled but others numbered; "I" to "IV" reflect the numbers given in the text but follow and are followed by two with titles. See ***Foirades*** and the individual entries:

1.	c	A	I	Il est tête nue	He is barehead
2.	d	C	III	Horn venait la nuit	Horn came always
3.	e	D	[7th]	Au loin un oiseau	Afar a bird
4.	f	B	II	J'ai renoncé avant de naître	I gave up before birth
5.	g	F	[8th]	Se voir [Endroit clos]	Closed space [Closed place]
6.	h	E	IV	Vieille terre	Old earth
7.	b		[2nd]	Immobile	Still
8.	a		[1st]	Pour finir encore	For to end yet again

Flaubert, Gustave (1821–80): French novelist whose mastery of style and sense of human folly (see **bêtise**) link him with SB. **Belacqua**'s affair with the **Smeraldina** (*Dream*, 109) leaves "a sentimental eructation" (Flaubert's *L'Éducation sentimentale*, 1869; an epigraph from which heads "Les **Deux besoins**"). **Moran** mentions how the great Gustave heard benches crackling in the assizes (*Molloy*, 126); and **Malone**'s sense of "the paraclete perhaps, psittaceously named" (249) links his **death** to that of Félicité in "Un Coeur simple." In the French text (145), **Moll** calls **Macmann** "mon loulou"; the English reads (261) "sweet pet." The narrator's speculation in *First Love* that death for **Hagenbeck** must have had the countenance of a lion echoes the ending of "Un Coeur simple." SB's sustained tribute to Flaubert is *Mercier et Camier*, which in form and tone imitates *Bouvard et Pécuchet*, Flaubert's last and unfinished novel.

Fletcher, John (1579–1625): Jacobean dramatist and author of *The Faithfull Shepherdesse* (1610). **Murphy** conducted his amours (49) like the Sullen Shepherd, to whom all shepherdesses, virgin or careless wanton, are alike. SB picked up "goatish Latin" (*Murphy*, 72) from *Philaster* (V.iii.153), and "Gazed on unto my setting" from Cynthia's masque in *The Maid's Tragedy* (a late addition to the *Murphy* typescript, 106).

flies: existence reduced to its **fundamental sound**: "crawling and fluttering in the warm corners, puny, sluggish, torpid, mute . . . That is a strange race of flies" (*Molloy*, 166). Earlier (27) **Molloy** concluded he must be alive, because the "famous flies" are not in evidence. The image of flies trapped against a pane, dead or barely alive, like the butterflies of W. B. Yeats's "Blood and the Moon," recurs in: "La **Mouche**," "**Serena I**," *Watt* (236–37), and "**Text 6**." The **Unnamable**, near the **shambles**, is beset with bluebottles (328); compare *Othello* (IV.ii.67–70): "as summer flies are in the **shambles** . . . would thou hadst ne'er been born."

Florence: Tuscan city, home of **Dante**, which SB visited in 1927, when he stayed in a *pensione* run by Signora Ottolenghi, whose name appears in "**Dante and the Lobster**." SB identifies **Dublin** and Florence. As **Belacqua** goes up Pearse Street (*Dream*, 201–2), he imagines walking through Florence, from the Piazza della Signoria past the "sinister Uffizi" to the parapets of the Arno. The fire station at the corner of Pearse and Tara Streets has a lookout tower copied from the Florentine original, "In homage to **Savonarola**? Hee! Hee!" Belacqua earlier imagined as he crossed the Liffey (27) the monument to **Cellini** on the Ponte Vecchio across the Arno. For the "Florence of Sordello," who tosses and turns into Florence Nightingale (*Dream*, 73 and 80), see **Dante** (*Purg.* VI.148–51).

flowering currant: Marcel, his autoerotic passion spent (*Swann*, 1.207), sees the trace of a snail among the sprays of "cassis sauvage," and senses he is alone, night falling on a sterile land. **Watt** recalls a similar moment, "when alone in a rowing-boat, far from land, he suddenly smelt flowering currant" (73–74, 80); the draft reads "violets" (NB5, 17). **Molloy** encounters spike lavender (48); and the **Unnamable** invents "the smell of flowering currant" (305) to escape from himself. See also **hawthorn** and **verbena**.

Foirades: meaning "squitters" or "jitters," a disaster or flop; in SB's understanding "a wet fart"; the originals of *Fizzles*. Related to *Comment c'est* as attempts to "go on" beyond the point of closure, intimations of minimalism. Their date is uncertain, but SB thought the early 1960s. *Foirade I,* "**Il est tête nue**," was published in *Minuit* 1 (novembre 1972): 22–26; *Foirade II,* "**J'ai renoncé avant de naître**," in *Minuit* 2 (janvier 1973): 40–41; *Foirade III,* "**Horn venait la nuit**," in *Minuit* 2 (janvier 1973): 41–42; *Foirade IV,* "**Vieille terre**," in *Minuit* 4 (mai 1973): 71; *Foirade V,* entitled "**Se voir**," in *Minuit* 4 (mai 1973): 72. I to IV are inscribed "années 50"; V, "années 60." There were limited editions of fifty numbered copies, and sets with original etchings of *Au loin un oiseau* by **Arikha** and *Still* by Stanley William Hayter. The first trade edition was *Pour finir encore et autres foirades* (Minuit, 1976).

Foirades/Fizzles: a deluxe edition ($75), with thirty-three original etchings by Jasper Johns, ed. Véra Lindsay; 300 numbered copies signed by author and artist (London and New York: Petersburg Press, 1975). There are five texts, translated into English for this edition: "**I gave up before birth**"; "**He is barehead**"; "**Old earth**"; "**Closed place**"; and "**Horn came always**." The etchings were printed on the handpress of the Atelier Crommelynck in **Paris**, on handmade paper watermarked with SB's initials and Johns's signature, the text handprinted by Paris typographers Fequet et Baudier. See **illustrations**. SB suggested, when a collaboration was proposed, that Johns work with *Waiting for Godot,* but the artist preferred an unpublished text, basing his etchings on a four-panel painting from 1972, called *Untitled.* The counterpoint of text and illustrations is "very subjective" (Lake, *No Symbols,* 162).

Foley's Folly: identified by O'Brien as Barrington's Tower, in the **Dublin** mountains about a mile from **Cooldrinagh**; recalled in "The **Calmative**" ("a ruined folly," 61), *Company,* and *That Time* as a childhood refuge with a view of the Wicklow mountains, the coast of **Killiney**, and perhaps the mountains of Wales. Nearby is the **cromlech** of Glen Druid (*Watt,* 49). "Barrington's Tower" is erased on the first manuscript of *That Time* (RUL 1477/1; O'Brien, 350). **A**, an old man, returns. He hoped to take the 11 bus to Clonskeagh, and go "**on** from there"; but there is "no getting out to it that way." The **trams** are no longer running and the "old rails" have been left to rust. The story alludes to Proverbs 26:11: "As a **dog** returneth to its vomit, so a fool returneth to his folly."

Fontenelle, Bernard le Bovier de (1657–1757): French polymath associated with **Diderot** (qv) and the *Encyclopédie.* SB's rendering (14 September 1977) of his "De mémoire de rose on n'a vu que le même jardinier" from *Entretiens sur la pluralité des mondes* (1686) was reproduced by Anne **Atik** in facsimile in her

memoir, with "his own beautiful translation" (Atik, 87). SB's immediate source
was Diderot's *Le Rêve de d'Alembert* (qv).

Footfalls: SB announced to Alan **Schnei-
der** (23 November 1975): "have nearly
completed a short piece (15 min.) for
Billie **Whitelaw**"; written to accompany
That Time. He agreed to direct her to
celebrate his seventieth birthday at the
Royal Court Theatre. The production (20
May 1976) was designed by Jocelyn
Herbert with Rose Hill as the Woman's
voice. SB staged it as *Tritte* at the **Schiller-
Theater Werkstatt** (1 October 1976),
with Hildegard Schmahl as **May** and
Charlotte Joeres as *Stimme der Mutte*. He
translated the play (May 1977) as *Pas*,
directing it at the Théâtre d'Orsay, Paris
(11 avril 1978), with Delphine Seyrig as
May and Madeleine **Renaud** as *la voix de
maman*. Schneider considered using the
same voice for May and her **mother**, a
plan SB thought "dubious." Irene Worth
"Intends to make it funny," SB noted,
adding "I hope she doesn't succeed." The
American premiere opened at the Arena
Stage's Kreeger Theater, Washington,
DC (3 December 1976), with Dianne
Wiest as May and Sloane Sheldon as
Mother's Voice. A one-act opera version
by Earl Kim was presented at the Second
International Samuel Beckett Festival,
The Hague (1992).

    Footfalls, featuring an aged pacing
woman in tattered nightwear, is divided
into four parts, each separated by chimes,
which grow fainter in each sounding. SB
intended a **musical** conception, and his
opening to the Royal Court production
featured the sound of footfalls in the
aftermath of the chimes (the title suggests

Eliot's "Burnt Norton": "Footfalls echo
in the **memory**"). SB's intention was to
dramatize deterioration with visual and
aural diminuendo. In part I the pacing
May addresses the voice of her dying
mother, whom she is apparently attending at her last, the mother in her nineties, May in her forties. In part II the
Mother's Voice observes and narrates her
daughter's obsessive pacing as the daughter tries to confirm her existence with the
material sounds of her footsteps and the
dragging of her tattered night wear. The
"Sequel" (SB suggested to Billie Whitelaw "Seek well") begins part III, May's
story, and the voice here is a little more
alive, he said. "One can suppose," he
noted, "that she has written down everything which she has invented up to this,
that she will one day find a reader for her
story—therefore the address to the
reader" (Asmus, 339). In Germany SB
complained that his actress was using too
much color in her voice: "Monotone.
Without colour, very distant. You are
composing. It is not a story, but an improvisation" (340). The improvisation is
precisely orchestrated. Part of the reason,
SB explained, is that May's story should
parallel the Mother's: "The daughter
only knows the voice of the mother,"
having been secluded all her life. The
Mother's "Not enough" should sound
exactly like the "Not there?" of Mrs.
Winter in Amy's story.

    Part IV of *Footfalls* has proven difficult
in production, given the brief fourth
chime and the empty stage. SB was aware
of the difficulty: "How avoid end of play
audience reaction after 3rd fade-out before last chime, fade up & final fade-out?
By reducing to minimum (in all 3 cases)

pause after fade-out" (*Theatrical Notebook,* 297). Concerned that the audience might think the play ended if the pause was prolonged, in rehearsals for the German production SB proposed a solution, shortening the two previous fade-outs then adding a vertical strip of light visible in the background, to give the impression that the light was falling through the crack of a door, and that light slowly fading.

The coda asserts its thematic significance, emphasizing that the thought-tormented **body** pacing before the audience is not there, or rather exists only within the embedded narratives of the play. In part III May, who herself may be narrated, narrates a semblance of what is on stage. May's anagrammatic other, **Amy**, replies to her mother, Mrs. Winter, about her attendance at Evensong: "I observed nothing of any kind, strange or otherwise. I saw nothing, heard nothing, of any kind. I was not there" (243). The short fourth act of *Footfalls,* the final ten seconds with "No trace of May," is a crucial reminder that May was always "not there," or there only as a "trace." In 1976, in Berlin, SB told Hildegard Schmahl about the **little girl** who didn't really exist (see **Jung**). This was in part his explanation for the incompletely developed May, who hears (or creates) her mother's voice, or is created by her mother's narrative. The theatrical problem that would preoccupy SB thereafter was how to represent in language and stage iconography the incomplete being, the *être manqué.* *Footfalls* may be his most thorough realization of the theme.

Footfalls marked an unprecedented level of SB's involvement in theatrical productions, and his acceptance of the principle that theater is created on stage, not exclusively in the study. His working in performance added a crucial component to his creative process. Early publications are often incomplete. Faber, eager to make *Footfalls* available on opening night, set its first edition from a typescript not fully tested on stage. SB made fundamental changes in both the British and the German productions (1976), increasing May's steps from seven to nine. No English text, save that in the *Theatrical Notebooks* (IV), is consistent on this revision. This was no minor adjustment since (as SB's notebooks confirm) the number of steps and points of turning and pause are minutely detailed and effect the tempo of this very musical composition. SB was obsessive about timing. He told his technical directors in Berlin that the unit of time should be seven seconds: "The bell at the beginning of *Footfalls* dies away in seven seconds; then the light comes up during seven seconds and one can see May walking. At the end of the three parts, the light fades out each time inside seven seconds, the bell dies away in seven seconds, and the light comes on again in seven seconds" (Asmus, 336). Pacing nine rather than seven steps effects the rhythm and impact of the entire play.

SB made changes to the play's lighting, which he never incorporated into any English text, changes consistent in his three productions. He introduced a "Dim spot on face during halts at R and L" (*Theatrical Notebook,* 275), so that May's **face** could be seen during her monologues. He brought into his German staging a vertical ray of light to create the effect of its coming through a partially opened door, to counterpoint the horizontal beam on the floor. These were incorporated into the **French** translation written after the English and German productions, and are thus developments of a performance text. He revised an English text, but published texts remain incompletely revised or contain inconsistencies that editors failed to query or SB failed to detect. Any production based on current English texts of *Footfalls* will inevitably introduce confusion into this most delicate play.

Ford, John (ca. 1586–1639): English dramatist. SB read Ford as preparation for his writing. **"Text"** (qv), an early prose piece, weaves words from five of Ford's plays into a new design; this became part of the **Kassel** sequence in *Dream* (83). "Girds" (sarcasms) (*Dream*, 121) is from *Love's Sacrifice* (III.ii). Quotations from the Mermaid edition of Ford (ed. Havelock **Ellis**) enter the **Whoroscope Notebook**, often ticked to show they have been used (mostly in *Murphy*). These include "the ruins of the ruins of a fine man," from *The Broken Heart* (II.iii), rephrased by **Wylie** as "the ruins of the ruins of the broth of a boy" (226); and "not a rag of love about me," from *The Lover's Melancholy* (III.i), implicit in Neary's undress (212), and used in **"Rough for Theatre I"** (71). A phrase recorded but not used until 1956 was "Sigh out a lamentation of things / done long ago and ill done," from *The Lover's Melancholy* (IV.ii), imperfectly recalled by Maddy **Rooney** in *All That Fall* (14).

forest murmurs: unheard by **Molloy** (89) as he listens in vain and hears instead a distant **gong**, to which he replies not with a hunter's horn but that taken earlier from his **bicycle**. This echoes Act II of **Wagner**'s *Siegfried,* in the depths of the forest, where the hero, about to fight the dragon Fafner, lies on his back and hears the beautiful forest murmurs: "Aber—wie sah mein Mutter wohl aus? Das—kann ich nun gar nicht mir denken" ("But—just what did my **mother** look like? I simply cannot imagine that now"). He responds to distant hunting horns. Despite not hearing the forest murmurs, Molloy is on his way to mother (90). The *Siegfried* episode is alluded to in **Joyce**'s *Portrait* (237), and echoed in SB's 1937 **"German Letter of 1937"** (*Disjecta,* 53): "Denn im Walde der Symbole, die keine sind, schweigen die Vöglein der Deutung, die kein ist, nie" ("For in the forest of symbols, which do not exist, the little birds of meaning, which does not exist, are never silent"). Esslin's translation (*Disjecta,* 173) is imprecise. For "forest of symbols," see **Baudelaire**'s "Correspondances."

"For Future Reference": a seventy-four-line poem, published in *transition* 19/20 (June 1930): 342–43; reprinted in Harvey (299–301). The **Leventhal** papers (**HRHRC**) include a carbon copy. SB did not permit it in later collections of his poetry. Despite the title (from Eugene Jolas's notes on contributors in *transition* 16/17), the poem looks backward to the days of childhood, at **Portrane** and **Trinity** (see **diving board**). The dreams that emerged from the experiences have shaped the present and, by future reference, what is to come. The final reference to the snowy floor of the **parrot**'s cage and the "palaiate" of the poet's strange mouth (the typescript reads "palate") encapsulates the horror of **memory**. Pilling notes ("Itch to Make," 23), that this echoes Verlaine's "Chant d'amour brutal": "ma bouche est aride, altérée."

Formentor Prize: the *Prix Formentor,* named for the Hôtel Formentor on Cape Formentor (Majorca) where international publishers met (before Franco barred them), consisted of two prizes. The first was for new fiction; the second, the *Prix International de Littérature,* for a single work from that year. This was awarded to SB and to Jorge Luis Borges (1961). The work that made SB eligible was *Comment c'est,* but when *How It Is* appeared (1964) no mention was made of the award. The prize was worth $10,000, which SB distributed to friends. His first international award, it fueled speculation about the **Nobel Prize** (qv).

formication: a psychological term to describe the feeling of something moving over the skin, as of ants. SB used it in "être là sans machoires sans dents," the waiting lover conscious of "la main formicante." The protagonist of "The **End**" (89) lacks the right word: "My hands and feet felt as though they were full of ants." That is, pins and needles (in **French**, "J'ai les fourmis"). In *Happy Days,* as **Winnie** watches through her magnifying glass an emmet carrying its egg, **Willie** remarks, "Formication." Winnie relishes this: "How can one better magnify the Almighty than by sniggering with him at his little jokes." The joke is at least fourfold: visual (magnifying glass), linguistic (fornication), ontological (reproduction as a cosmic joke), and **religious** (the Magnificat, "My soul doth magnify the Lord").

"For to end yet again": *Fizzle* 8 (Grove) or 1 (Calder, Minuit); SB's translation of **"Pour finir encore,"** first published in *New Writing and Writers* 13 (Calder, 1976 [1975]): 9–14; rpt. in *For to End Yet Again and Other Fizzles* (Calder, 1976) and *Fizzles* (Grove, 1976). In the French and British editions it is the first and title story, while it concludes the American volume. Among the last of the *Fizzles* to be written and posing a set of permutations on the theme of ending, yet again, the American placement, overseen by SB, seems apposite. It explores eschatological images: a world turned to dust, a crumbling refuge, and a **skull** in "the box last place of all," which may "glimmer again in lieu of going out" (243), like dying stars (white dwarfs). The story is tentative, images appearing "all at once or by degrees," the alternatives, from a "bird's-eye view," lead to the same gray end. Amid the gray dawn the eye perceives the **expelled**, gray save for some brightness of the eye. The one variation is a pair of white dwarfs facing each other carrying a litter, the backward-facing leading the way, the forward guiding. These white creatures appear for a "he," the last expelled, to decipher. The tale loops back on itself as "he" observes the refuge collapse, yet again. For the last change the expelled falls like a statue, a piece of the ruin itself. The scene is like a dreamscape where all footsteps bring one no closer to nor farther from anywhere, an image to which SB returns in *Company.* It echoes **Clov**'s dream: "A world where all would be silent and still and each thing in its last place, under the last dust" (120). The narrator poses a variation on this: "Sepulchral skull is this then its last state all set for always." The one certain response is that darkness falls, yet again, like a theater curtain, perhaps, but intimating a recurrent text (Genesis 3:19): "dust thou art, and unto dust shalt thou return."

Four Novellas: the first selection (Calder, 1976) in which *First Love* was finally grouped with "The **Expelled**"; "The **Calmative**"; and "The **End**" to form one "bookend" (*How It Is* the other) of SB's great creative period.

Fox: subject of interrogation in "**Rough for Radio II**." The Animator forces him to speak by thumping the desk with his **cylindrical ruler** and ordering the mute Dick (a curious concept in a radio play) to whip him with the bull's pizzle. "Fox," the unvoiced form of "Vox," implies that the truth is evasive. His utterance remains enigmatic, but his tale of the mole intimates a **pity** beyond words. In contrast to **Dante**'s *fui* ("I was"), he is concerned about his **embryonic** twin, the self that never was, or that was never properly born.

Foxrock: a fashionable south **Dublin** suburb, location of **Cooldrinagh**, SB's family home, ten miles from the central city, and near the Dublin Mountains, **Killiney** coast, **Dún Laoghaire**, the **Leopardstown** racecourse, and **Croker's Acres**. It consists of a main street, extending from a central nucleus of shops, houses, hotel, church, and the railway station that once linked suburb to city by the "**Slow and Easy**." Mrs. **bboggs** and Una long for a home there ("What a Misfortune," 117). *Dream* opens with an overfed **Belacqua** pedaling after Findlater's van, that of a Dublin victualler with a Foxrock branch (O'Brien, 376). "**Walking Out**" is set near Foxrock; the **Smeraldina**'s house in "**Draff**" is presumably there. **Mercier** and **Camier** visit the town. **Memories** of Foxrock recur in texts as diverse as "**Serena II**"; "**The End**"; *Texts for Nothing* (1, 2, 3, 7); *That Time* ("**Foley's Folly**"); and *Krapp's Last Tape* (63). **Moran**'s house, church, and neighbors in *Molloy* draw on Foxrock memories, which in turn contribute to the mythological **Beckett country**. Moran on leaving the house goes by what is recognizably the graveyard at nearby Tully. Foxrock is backdrop for the childhood memories of *Company* (qv).

Watt, the most "universal" of SB's works and written in France, is grounded firmly in this locale. The station is not named ("Watt named the place," 28), but the train trip is precisely that from **Harcourt Street** to Foxrock, the dimensions and features of its waiting room are identical to Foxrock's, and Watt walks the distance from the station to Cooldrinagh, model for Mr. **Knott**'s house. References to **Glencullen** (15), **Prince William's Seat** (16), stonecutters in the hills (16), and the **cromlech** (49) define the setting. Minor characters are based on individuals SB had known: Severn (**Shannon**), the consumptive postman; the milkboy from Tully's dairy; and Cack-faced (Ivan) Miller, son of a local wine merchant (O'Brien, 350). *All That Fall* is even more localized, some details carried over from *Watt* to **Boghill** but others added: Mr. **Barrell** (Farrell), the Station-master; **Christy**, the gardener; the nearby church (Tullow Parish Church); the Reverend **Hardy**; Mr. **Slocum** (Clarke); and **Tyler**, not yet the sinister figure of *Malone Dies* or *Company.*

Foxrock, Inc.: the firm (61 Fourth Avenue, New York), named after SB's birthplace, created by Barney Rosset, with John Oakes and Dan Simon of Four Walls Eight Windows, Inc., to publish *Eleutheria* after SB's death. See **Grove Press.**

"Fragment de théâtre I": a sketch from the late 1950s, in *Minuit* 8 (mars 1974): 65–72; then as the first of *Quatre esquisses* (Minuit, 1978); translated as "**Rough for Theatre I.**"

"Fragment de théâtre II": a sketch from the late 1950s, originally called "Théâtre." First published in *L'Herne* (1976), 15–23, then as the second of *Quatre esquisses* (Minuit, 1978); translated as "**Rough for Theatre II.**"

"Fragments Prose (Début 1968)": title of a notebook at Reading (RUL 2928), in which SB recorded two outlines. One ("25.3.68") relates to "**Endroit clos,**" fifth of the *Foirades;* the second is an unidentified film or TV outline, four pages headed "Film video-cassette projet" (November 1972), with subheadings "Film 1" and "Film 2." These anticipate "**Ghost Trio.**" It involves a man in a room, bare apart from a chair, a window, and a door, watching a videocassette of another man, perhaps himself in perhaps the same room. He goes through an elaborate ritual before plugging in the **machine.** There are suggestions of external interference, such as hands at the window or door, and of a "confrontation" between the gazes of F1 (dressed for summer) and F2 (winter), each confronting his reflected image.

Franciabigio (ca. 1482–1525): Francesco di Cristofano, **Florentine** portaitist who worked with **Andrea del Sarto**; SB alludes to his "young Florentine in the Louvre" (*Dream,* 13).

French: asked in 1956 why he began to write in French, SB replied, "Parce qu'en français c'est plus facile d'écrire sans style." By 1953 Roland Barthes would elevate such café chatter to an aesthetics, and call it "writing degree zero." But SB's comment (to Nicholas Gessner) was a recasting of an aesthetics-in-progress developed in his first sustained piece of fiction, *Dream of Fair to middling Women.* **Belacqua** rejects the man with a style: "Perhaps only the French can do it. Perhaps only the French language can give you the thing you want" (48). As SB later told Charles Juliet (*Conversations,* 143), it was a new language for him, "still with an aura of unfamiliarity about it," which "allowed him to escape the **habits** inherent in the use of a native language." Having come of age amid the excesses of Modernism, SB was lured to the prison house of style. *Ulysses* had been the forbidden fruit of his formative years, and, in an act as much of literary masochism as reverence, he translated "**Anna Livia Plurabelle**" into French. He read **Proust** closely enough to write a monograph on the obsessive stylist

("Don't be too hard on him," pleads *Dream*'s narrator, "he was studying to be a professor"). And he translated the excesses of **Rimbaud**'s *Bateau ivre* into rhetorically equivalent English (see "**Drunken Boat**").

Asked if he were English, SB famously replied, "au contraire." His embrace of French was equally an avoidance of English "because you couldn't help writing poetry in [English]." To Herbert Blau he suggested that French had the right "weakening effect," and in the desire to "impoverish" himself still further it was a liberation from Joycean allusion, complexity, and compression, of being enclosed in a tradition. Linguistic expatriation enabled SB to recast his literary lineage, to **father** himself, as it were, by sloughing the heritage of English style. In "**Casket of Pralinen**," SB was already repenting the Joycean aesthetics of mastery: "Oh I am ashamed / of all the clumsy artistry / I am ashamed of presuming / to arrange words / of everything but the ingenuous fibres / that suffer honestly."

What continues to claw in SB's work is not solely the sparseness of narration and dialogue, textual indeterminacy, but the rejection of the grandiloquence of Modernism, of the rhetoric and figuration that SB associated with English. French as an "other" language better suited his recurrent sense of living by proxy. He became adept at writing without or beyond style, in the style of stylelessness, as the **surrealists** wrote in the style of the insane. Much of his early work, written under the temporary delusion that he could be **Joyce**, charts disillusionment—with Joyce, with Mod-

ernism, with literature and **art**. He would chart the void art refused to fill, failing at each attempt, but each time failing better. After World War II SB jettisoned the virtuosity of Modernism (and with it the English language), its bravado, its literariness, for a literalness confounding in its simplicity ("Alas **cang** of emblem"), as in the "no symbols where none intended" of *Watt*. The shelter of *Endgame* resists **allegory**; likewise the road of *Waiting for Godot*, the cylinder of *The Lost Ones*, the mud of *How It Is*. Sometimes a shelter is just a shelter, a road a road, and mud mud. These are **fundamental sounds** (qv), ruthless, unrelieved abandonment of the literary, embracing "the ingenuous fibers that suffer honestly."

The publication of *Dream*, sixty years after its incubation, returned SB's readers to that aesthetic **vagitus**. Most come to SB through the desiccated symmetries and astringent syntax of the late works where he had become if not the **Cézanne** then the **Giacometti** of the printed word. *Dream*'s atonality grates. It speaks of an "aesthetic of inaudibilities" (after **Beethoven**), but the novel is a yawp (after Whitman). Belacqua plans to write the anti-*Ulysses*: "where the phrase is self-consciously smart and slick," where the blown roses of a phrase catapult the reader into the **tulips** of what follows. The reader's experience would be between the phrases, in the silences, communicated by the intervals, between the flowers that cannot coexist, the antithetical seasons of words (137).

After *Watt* SB exiled such "smartness and slickness." *Watt* is "remarkable" for the number of French words and phrases in implicit translation, which constitute resistance to the English reader. *Quatre nouvelles* and *Three Novels*, the first major manifestations of the turn to French, incorporate similar resistance, notably the use of English terms of currency and measurement (pounds, miles) in the French texts, and in the creation of the **Beckett country**, which delineates in French the landscape south of **Dublin**. There are many instances in the early French writing, and notably with respect to **puns**, jokes, and allusions, where the resistance is too much and translation is not possible. *Eleutheria* offers this exchange: "M. **Krap**: 'je sense que ma femme approche.' / Mlle Skunk: 'ta fin?' / M. Krap: 'ma FEMME. Cette catastrophe.'" The French *Molloy* makes a curious connection between his "bequilles" (crutches) and the "lourdes dettes" (238) that follow. Conversely, the (Irish) protagonist of "The **Calmative**" finds himself blushing over the word "nanny" (67), a **Bibby** goat perhaps, as his counterpart in "Le **Calmant**" cannot. The French **Moran** goes into the kitchen "à la recherche des oignons" (139); SB does not even try to capture the **Proustian** nuance in the English text, which, however, incorporates many other echoes of the English literary tradition and (more curiously, for this could have been possible in French) the **Bible**. Patrick Bowles has recorded SB's insistence that the text should not be "translated," but that a new book should be written: "For with the transposition of speech occurs a transposition of thought, and even at times, of action" (Bair, 439). Consider verbal tense, the French imperfect (neither past nor present) forcing SB to compose much

of his English text in what Molloy felicitously calls the **mythological present** (qv). The texts of this middle period exist in two languages and two forms, the French being the original but the English less a translation than a reinvention in a different linguistic mode, something quite different from even the genius of **Nabokov**'s self-translations.

The later writings differ again. From *Textes pour rien* on, with few exceptions (*Worstward Ho* the most notable), they constitute "sibling texts," sometimes written first in one language and sometimes the other (sometimes together), **neither** taking precedence over the other. Charles Krance, Brian Fitch, Leslie Hill, and others have written on SB's bilingualism and self-translation (a topic too vast to be more than briefly entertained here). They have noted the special status of the bilingual text, written with its other-language counterpart, a mode of composition SB utilized more frequently toward the end. Texts like *Company* and/or *Compagnie* cry out their mutual insufficiency (to choose either is to prefer one testicle to the other), but the imaginative blending produces something that is more than either. To read SB bilingually (some would contend) is essential, for only by so doing does one gain an intimate glimpse of the inner drama that went into the shaping of the texts. As SB might say, *peut-être,* but he remains the outstanding, perhaps unique instance of one whose most important work manifests itself equally in two languages, neither a "translation" of the other, in the usual sense of a composition in one tongue rendered (with inevitable loss and failure) into another.

Freud, Sigmund (1856–1939): father of psychology and **psychoanalysis**. From 1873 he studied medicine at the University of Vienna, contemplating a career in biological research. Medical practice became a financial necessity, and psychiatry offered virgin territory for his ambition. He worked at the Salpêtrière under Charcot, who showed him the possibilities of hypnotism, and he set up a practice for nervous diseases in Vienna (1886). His dynamic theory of mind emerged from his clinical practice, despite various false starts, and *The Interpretation of Dreams* (1900) launched his fully fledged system, which over the next thirty years he submitted to an exhaustive process of revision and elaboration. He abandoned case histories in favor of "metapsychology" and produced a succession of classics, the most celebrated being: "On **Narcissism**" (1914), *Beyond the Pleasure Principle* (1920), *The Ego and the Id* (1923), *Civilization and its Discontents* (1930), and *New Introductory Lectures on Psychoanalysis* (1932). Disciples gathered and Freud became the elder statesman of a dedicated, albeit controversial, movement with a profound impact on psychiatric treatment and the intellectual currents of the age. In 1913 his heir apparent, C. G. **Jung**, broke with Freudian orthodoxy to establish the principal competing variant of psychoanalysis. Cancer necessitated two drastic operations on Freud's jaw and palate (1923), a condition that caused him constant pain and proved terminal. He died in **London**, where he sought refuge (in 1938) from Nazism. The cataclysmic course of German history combined with his private suffering to influence his pessimistic assessment of human **nature**.

Freudian material is ubiquitous in SB's writing. Phil Baker's *Beckett and the Mythology of Psychoanalysis* offers a comprehensive analysis of this theme, while O'Hara's *Hidden Drives* is a more provocative study of SB's use of Freud and Jung (and their predecessor **Schopenhauer**) as the "structures of thought that uphold SB's literary works." The life of the ego is for Freud a perpetual battleground where the blind instinctive drives of the id, or, as **Neary** puts it, the pudenda of his psyche (*Murphy*, 47), fight for expression against the demands of the physical world and the repressive conformity of civilization imposed by the internalized superego. One's life narrative is a continually renegotiated compromise between three forces making conflicting demands, and suffering is thus an intrinsic feature of human life. The degree of suffering depends on the relative neatness with which the ego can negotiate the compromise, and maladroit negotiation is played out in the symptoms of hysteria and neurosis. Freud thus grounds psychopathology firmly in the context of general mental functioning, and SB endorsed his collapsing of false distinctions between pathology and normality. Neurosis is not some sort of alien infection but the mind resorting to extreme and painful measures to sustain the process of negotiation that *is* life and that ends only with **death**. On this view the redeeming values of humanity—faith, charity, **love**—are ultimately no more than slickness of negotiation. Not to be despised for all that, said Freud, but ultimately disposable.

Freud's theories culminated in his hypothesis of the conflict of the life and death instincts. Libidinous energy directed at sex specifically and participation in life generally is counteracted by the organism's yearning for the cessation of tension that comes with fulfillment or renunciation and is perfected only in death. Affinities with Schopenhauer's ideal Sabbath of the will are obvious, and Freud is but one of many sources running into the confluence of SB's thought. Suffice it to say that the death instinct is as sure an underlay as any for the systematic process of renunciation in the *Three Novels,* of **Malone**'s longing for the great calm as he applies himself to the business of dying. The life instinct is a biological imposition, the recoil of a spring that kicks in whether we like it or not and holds us in the breathless suspension of the **unnamable**, unsure whether we are waiting to be born or to die, and wanting to be alive to appreciate the peace of our own death. Even at this core of existence the irrepressible detritus of life has a way of creeping in; what are the life and death instincts but Sucky **Moll** and **sausage poisoning**?

One of the deepest consonances between Freud and SB is a flair for the particular, the psychoanalyst a detective who seizes on seemingly incidental or trivial details and interprets them in contexts that amplify their significance. Freud's case histories are often inaccurate or fraudulent, but they are literary masterpieces; vivid and intriguing characters people his narratives, and however perverse his conclusions there is exhilaration in the sheer ingenuity with which he unlocks word or image and opens up a complex of meanings. For SB, seeking to escape the influence of **Joyce**, Freud represented a narrative method he was tuned to appreciate but that he could trace back, in a process of narrative deconstruction that, by the time of his late prose, becomes as precise and clinical as anything Freud ever wrote. Freud not infrequently piled more weight onto details than they could sensibly bear, sometimes to the point of absurdity (consider the wolves in his history of the wolf-man); but in so doing he was acting out a psychological tendency that in SB's characters as they unfold their narratives becomes part of the drama, an insinuation of arbitrariness that may have an edge of comic **absurdity** (Mrs. **Rooney**'s "lifelong preoccupation with horses' **buttocks**"). In this respect SB's sense of irony and the absurd allows him to convey a vital psychological aspect of life in almost a critique of Freud. There is a never-ending need to ascribe meaning to things, which has more to do with the symbolic language instinct of **consciousness** than with the visceral instincts of the id. This goes to the heart of SB's dramatization of psychoanalytic process; particulars sometimes employ psychoanalytic scaffolding and sometimes not, but they invariably bear witness to the aesthetic legacy that was perhaps Freud's enduring contribution to modern culture.

SB's digestion of Freud was gradual. "A **Case in a Thousand**" recapitulates the oedipal complex without developing the possibilities of language as the protagonists use it; a generation later **Moran** yet refrains from speaking of the **Odibil**. *From an Abandoned Work* shows the mature writer's virtuosic synthesis of language, phenomena, and **memory** in the direct voice of the talking cure. O'Hara contends this is the most deliberately Freudian of all SB's works, functioning as a kind of anamnesis (*Hidden Drives,* 90). It dispenses with Freudian jargon but acknowledges crucial matters. A major unifying theme is the emphasis on traumatic childhood and the ghosts of memory haunting the maladjusted adult, as with **Watt**'s partial recollections of his **father**, or in *Not I,* with **Mouth**'s recollections of her past, or in *Happy Days,* the story of **Mildred** and the mouse. Unassimilated past recurs in such works as *That Time, Krapp's Last Tape,* with its anal "spool"/stool punning, and "**Eh Joe**," with its residua of guilt. Freud got much wrong on the subject, but he provided a potent means of dramatizing such matters, structures that might be used as literary strategies, of which SB availed himself (see also **psychoanalysis** and **Jung**).

Freud, with characteristic modesty, announced the third great blow to human vanity: Copernicus dethroned man from the center of the universe; **Darwin** banished him from the center of nature; and psychoanalysis showed that the ego is not even master in its own house. **Wylie** sums up the implication: "the little ego and the big id" (*Murphy,* 218). The older SB by no means did away with the id, and certainly would not have wished to argue that the ego *is* master in its own house; he implies, though, that Wylie's summary is inaccurate, that the ego is rather larger, relatively, than some would believe. [DL]

Fricas: mother and daughter, hostesses in "A **Wet Night**" and in the correspond-

ing part of *Dream.* The satire is based on Mary **Manning** (qv) and her mother Susan, the person and soirees of the latter forming the chief target. SB makes this explicit in a letter to **MacGreevy** (18 August 1934). In the short story the distinction between mother and daughter is blurred, and the satire is less specific, so the effect is more of an exercise in **Swiftian** caricature, "Not saeva, fabricated" (*Dream,* 216), than a roman à clef. The Mannings also appear among the rabble in "**Echo's Bones**" (5). "Frica" derives from "fricatrice," as in **Jonson**'s *Volpone* IV.ii, "A base harlot, a lewd fricatrice"; but SB's source was **Garnier** (448). "Caleken" refers to Caleken Peters, a young woman who was a victim of Cornelius Hadrien's whipping institution, as in **Cooper** (*Flagellation,* 122–33; DN 53). Hadrien, a Franciscan priest, disciplined his naked female penitents and instructed Caleken in "holy obedience"; for questioning his need for private discipline she was denounced and excommunicated by him (1558). The Frica clutches such depraved volumes as **Portigliotti**'s *Penumbre Claustrali,* **Sade**'s *Hundred Days,* and **Brignole-Sale**'s *Anterotica* (*Dream,* 179), details deriving from Praz, *The Romantic Agony* (DN, 36–38). The younger Frica creates an effect of "throttled gazelle" (*Dream,* 214); she has a crone-mother, "a bald caterwauling bedlam [*sic* for "beldam"] of a ma with more toes than teeth" (180). The abuse derives from **Burton** (DN, 118, 124), and is compiled as a deliberate cento. For the ironic aftermath, see **Manning, Mary**.

Friedrich, Caspar David (1774–1840): German Romantic painter who broke new ground in his rendition of **nature**, in terms of the effect of light to create unity of mood. His **Romanticism** was intensely contemplative, focused inwardly by melancholy but created through a strict formalism; SB responded to both qualities. **Malone**, gazing at the night sky, reflects that "It is such a night as Kasper David Friedrich loved, tempestuous and bright" (198). "**Macmann** pygmy beneath the black gesticulating pines gazes at the distant raging sea" (274) surely refers to *Monk by the Sea,* Friedrich's statement of cosmic loneliness, in which a tiny figure is hemmed in by a narrow bare foreground cut off from a vast waste of sea and sky, unbreachable **solitude** confronting the infinite abyss. SB became intimate with Friedrich's work during his 1937 visit to Dresden, confessing in his **German Notebook** 5 (14 February 1937) to having a "pleasant predilection for 2 tiny languid men in his landscapes, as in the little moon landscape," this being "the only kind of romantic still tolerable." Knowlson indicates (342) how *Waiting for Godot,* and particularly the final scenes where the two figures by the tree watch the moon rise, was inspired by Friedrich's *Zwei Männer betrachten den Mond (Two Men Watch the Moon)* in Dresden's Gemäldegalerie Neue Meister. SB told Ruby Cohn that the source was a similar work, in Berlin, *Mann und Frau den Mond betrachtend (Man and Woman Watching the moon)*, having confused or blended the two paintings. SB as director of *Godot,* and the film version based on the **Schiller-Theater** production, accentuated this image. Despite their artificiality, Friedrich's paintings do not degenerate into **allegory**, as form and symbol are subordinated to an intense Christian mood in which precision and symmetry contribute to awe and mystery. Leafless oak trees are symbols of suffering and despair, and the moon is an emblem of renewal, a token of **Christ**'s promise that He will come again, offering consolation to those who regard it. The presence of moon and tree in each act of *Godot* comments (ironically) on that. [Details from DL]

friendship: SB commented to **MacGreevy** (24 February 1931): "In 20 years I may be fit to have friends." Despite many lasting friendships, SB's writings reflect that intellectual distrust outlined in *Proust,* where the "**habit** of friendship" is invoked (22) as insulation against the terror of isolation, then (63–67) defined as a function of man's cowardice, "the negation of that irremediable **solitude** to which every human being is condemned" (in SB's copy of **Proust**, *Jeunes filles* II.196, "irrémediablement seuls" is underlined). Friendship is a social expedient, "like upholstery or the distribution of garbage buckets" (63); the artist must reject it, because "**art** is the apotheosis of solitude" (64); and "We are alone" (66). Proust situated friendship "somewhere between fatigue and ennui"; the sentiment is **Schopenhauer**'s, but the rejection of it as having not the least "intellectual significance" (65) will echo through SB's oeuvre. Compare **Windelband** (174–75), who sets the Epicurean view of friendship, arising from the **atomist** assumption that individuals first exist for and by themselves, against the **stoic** sense of the world constituted by **nature** for society, and thus rational.

Yet the tragic inevitability of these conclusions does not make "the craving for a fellow" (*Molloy,* 15) the less real. **Neary**'s concept of friendship is "curious," for he seeks a friend, perhaps the Friend (202); but **Murphy**'s need for brotherhood (176) assumes a terrible irony in the light of what follows. **Watt** gives no outward indication of such need, but he pays a high price for his loneliness. Molloy resists the impulse to follow **A** or **C** (11). The protagonist of *Three Novels* separates his self from the various "**puppets**" and "**buffers**" he has created to play with (*Malone Dies,* 180), "company" to be scattered to the winds (*The Unnamable,* 292) before he can be alone. Despite the "long imploring gaze" (298), like that of **Lucky**, they do not fool him, all these Murphys, **Molloy**s and **Malones**; they have made him waste his time, to speak of them when he should have been speaking of himself "alone" (303).

If **Saposcat** has his "little friends" (189), they are not much in evidence. In "**Text 3**" the narrator says that he will have a "crony," with whom he can relive campaigns and compare scratches. **Pim** in *How It Is* represents a possibility of "a fellow creature" (54), but even if transcendence is rejected the craving remains. In *Waiting for Godot* (54.b) **Pozzo** wants to know if the tramps are friends; **Estragon** laughs noisily until **Vladimir** corrects him: "No, he means friends of his." By *Endgame* affection has degenerated to mutual dependence. And the problem of the **voice** remains. A poem written in 1948, part of the frenzied activity of that time, offers a blueprint for the writing to come. The dilemma articulated by the **Unnamable** and pursued through *Texts for Nothing* and into *How*

It Is finds expression in "**que ferais-je sans ce monde**," where the irremediable solitude is invoked, and the need to look for another "without" must be rejected; instead there may be the possibility of finding that other "within" the head, an intimation of a process that will lead to *Company,* and the dubious comfort of the voice that comes to one in the dark.

From an Abandoned Work: a short prose piece, written about 1954–55, a step toward a novel soon abandoned; the first text written in English since *Watt.* First printed in *Trinity News* 3.17 (7 June 1956): 4, the student editors "improving" SB's punctuation and tidying the text. A truer version appeared in *Evergreen Review* 1.3 (1957): 83–91; rpt. in *From an Abandoned Work* (Faber, 1958); in *Breath and Other Shorts* (Faber, 1971), 39–48; and in *First Love and Other Shorts* (Grove, 1974). Translated by Ludovic and Agnès Janvier with SB as *D'un ouvrage abandonné* (Minuit, 1967). A German translation appeared in a trilingual text (Stuttgart: Manus Presse, 1967), with original lithographs (Paris: Visat) by Max Ernst. Recorded and produced as "a meditation for radio" on BBC 3 (Saturday, 14 December and Thursday, 19 December 1957), producer Donald **McWhinnie**, speaker Patrick **Magee**; and given in a concert in *Music Today* at the Royal Festival Hall, 5 April 1960, also with Patrick Magee.

The story inhabits margins that in SB's future works were to become more blurred, between prose and poetry, narrative and drama, completion and incompletion. It deals with three days in the life of an **old man** recalling his childhood, as uneventful as it was loveless. The **father** died when he was young; he lived with his **mother** until she died. His life is ordered by the daily journey and return (159; see **Thomas à Kempis**). He has taken long walks with his father, and these have continued after his **death**, though the **motion** is directionless and his recollections are marked by hostility.

O'Hara questions the assumption that the piece is incomplete and argues that the title is a **pun**, the protagonist abandoning his therapy, "for which the story functions as a kind of anamnesis" (*Hidden Drives*, 90), the recollection of a medical history. This accounts for the narrative incoherence, the way that the narrator sets out as a child and ends three days later in old age, **memories** of his parents, and inhibitions such as the trauma of **birth** and oedipal repression acted out along the way. The journey is unfinished because the therapy is not completed, that is, was not successful. His repressed anger is expressed variously: his love of things rooted (his dead father?) but hostility to living creatures (155); libidinal release ("vent the pent," 158); his sore throat and blinding rages (157); inability to accept his father's death (158); regret that he was born (158); a voice on his shoulder "like a marmoset" (159); memories of his mother (162); the sense of having killed his parents (159); his childhood terror of **Balfe** (163); the incessant vision of whiteness: the Schimmel, or white **horse** (157); and the way he was set on and pursued by a family of stoats (161). These images, O'Hara indicates, reflect the relationship between the narrator and his family, rage and guilt displaced in the psychotherapeutic process for one unable to **love**, and whose wish for

oblivion is expressed in the desire to sink down and disappear among the ferns.

"From an Unabandoned Work": an earlier version of the opening pages (1–17) of SB's translation of *How It Is*, in *Evergreen Review* 4.14 (September–October 1960): 58–65, before the **French** text was published, with several variants from the English text (1964).

"From *How It Is*": an extract from part III of *How It Is*, published by Patrick **Bowles**, in *The Paris Review* 7.28 (summer-fall 1962): 112–16.

"From the Only Poet to a Shining Whore": a poem of seventeen lines in four verses "For Henry **Crowder** to sing" (tempo slow), written in the Dôme Café, Montparnasse, for Nancy **Cunard**'s *Henry-Music:* six poems by various authors set to music for her Afro-American lover, published by the **Hours Press** in 1930 (12–14). Sometimes sung to mime by Crowder in cafés; a recording was made by Sonabel. The "only poet" is **Dante**, here addressing **Rahab**, the Old Testament harlot (Joshua 2:1–24) who concealed the spies in Jericho, hiding them among the flax on the rooftop and lowering them with a line of scarlet thread from the wall; for this Dante put her into heaven. The contrast is between her sensuality and the "fierce pale flame" of **Beatrice**'s anger at such a woman being saved. See **"To Be Sung Loud."**

Frost, Mrs. Queenie: 34 Gertrude Street, **London** SW 10, originally from Athlone; "a kind of **mother** on draught" (SB to TM, 8 September 1934). She offered SB a home for a year from September 1934. There was a "larval piano" in the drawing room; the linoleum was "like **Braque** seen from a great distance," and Mrs. Frost did not flinch when SB preferred his Lapsang to her Lipton's. These details entered *Murphy*.

fundamental sounds: in a letter to Alan **Schneider** (29 December 1957; Harmon, 24; *Village Voice*, 19 March 1959), SB rejected exegesis: "That's for those bastards of critics . . . My work is a matter of fundamental sounds (no joke intended) made as fully as possible, and I accept responsibility for nothing else. If people want to have headaches among the overtones, let them. And provide their own aspirin." Critical bastards might deconstruct this as the paradox of simplicity, Occam's razor applied to assert that the obvious meaning is invariably the right one. In SB's later work stark simplicity creates the effect, not allusive complexity. Yet "simplicity" is not easily defined; it remains a moot point whether it is more foolish to ignore "**God**" in "**Godot**" than to insist upon it. Resolution is by further paradox: the simple truths of existence (God, **birth**, **death**, belief, **consciousness**) are so complex that they can be grasped only through basic images, but these are in turn a distillation of the best and most strenuous endeavors of the most assiduous thinkers, so that the simple image of God(ot) draws on centuries of cultural history. The simplicity of fundamental sounds is inextricably tied to the insistence of words and allusions, ill heard and more than half forgotten.

The stage directions of *Godot* specify "A country road" (direction, purpose, progress); "A tree" (**nature, Berkeley, crucifixion**); "Evening" (darkness, death, extinction). An impulse toward minimalism defines the drama and shorter prose. Narrative and movement give way to still life and stasis; entropy and attrition set in. Two texts suffice, as emblems of the others: in "**Act Without Words II**" the world is reduced to its essentials: carrot (food); watch (**time**); compass (space); sack (possessions, **preestablished harmony**). Life and action are reduced to the rituals of brushing teeth, combing hair, eating, waking, and sleeping. *How It Is* is even more reductive, existence reduced to **atomist** principles: mud, dark, silence, sack, tins, **dog**: "these details in preference to **nothing**" (34); with the use of small Roman CAPITALS to render these to even more elemental particles: YOUR LIFE ABOVE IN THE LIGHT . . . HERE . . . YOUR LIFE CUNT ABOVE CUNT . . . YES OR NO . . . ATE . . . DIE ONE DAY . . . DIE . . . I MAY DIE . . . I SHALL DIE . . .

fundamental unheroic: SB's evolution may be seen as a reaction against **Joyce**, in terms of a recurrent theme, the *fundamental unheroic*. Even in 1989, SB admired Joyce's heroism: "That's what it was, epic, heroic, what he achieved. But I realised that I couldn't go down that same road" (Knowlson, 111). In the **German Diaries** 4 (18 January 1937), SB noted that the "**necessary journey**" was an illusion, and that **Murphy**, tied to his **rocking chair**, was a manifestation of self-bondage, "acceptance of which is the fundamental unheroic." This is a first expression of the realm of ignorance and impotence that SB would make his own.

G

Gaber: the go-between who brings **Moran** instructions from **Youdi** (the "queer one" who visits **Molloy** every Sunday?). An agent of the **Freudian** preconscious, the mechanism that delivers material to **consciousness**, he curiously cannot remember messages or justify his instructions. In his somber Sunday best, with a chestnut walrus mustache and a liking for beer, he seems more a figure from a 1930s American detective story than the angel Gabriel from whom his name derives. His best-known mission is implicit in his complaint that their employer made him get up in the night, just as he was getting into position to make **love** to his wife (94). As a messenger (Gk. *angelos*), he has a notebook and a weekly wage of £8, compared with an agent's £6.10. The Molloy business is not their first such case; Moran recollects the **Yerk** affair. Gaber reappears (163), with the instruction: "Moran, Jacques, home, **instanter.**" He tells Moran that the chief has not changed but is getting older, like the world, and had said the other day that life is a thing of beauty and a joy forever. Moran wonders if Youdi meant human life but opens his eyes to find himself alone.

Galileo (1564–1642): Italian astronomer and philosopher who discovered the laws of the pendulum, the acceleration of falling objects (the "little adjustments" of *Molloy,* 88), and, with his improved telescope, Jupiter's satellites (1609). The Church admonished him in 1616 not to "hold, teach or defend" Copernicanism, but when his *Dialogo dei due massimi sistemi del mondo* appeared in 1632 he was summoned to Rome and examined by the Inquisition. His recantation and the apocryphal Jesuitical qualification, *eppur si muove* ("yet it moves") is quoted by **Chas** (*Dream,* 203). In *Watt* (131), a jest about Galileo's cradle is repeated from "Les **Deux besoins**" (*Disjecta,* 55); it underlies the paradox of **motion** in *Whoroscope* (10): "That's not moving, that's *moving.*" The poem dismisses Galileo as a "vile old Copernican leadswinging son of a sutler," a reference to both his pendulum experiments and "swinging the lead," or expedient sophistry (SB's note; equally, **Descartes**'s habit of staying in bed). The confusion over "Galileo Jr." derives from **Mahaffy** (35): "He thinks Galileo the author of a work on **music** really written by his father." "[S]on of a sutler" does not imply, as Harvey suggests (14), Galileo's inferior birth; in Mahaffy (105) it disparages his rival Voët: "the son of a sutler, brought up among harlots and campfollowers."

Gall, Lord: see **Wormwood.**

the Galls: the first "incident of note" during **Watt**'s time with Mr. **Knott** is the visit of the Galls **father** and son (the appositional phrase is invariable) come to "choon" the piano, of which nine damp-

216

ers and nine hammers remain, in one case corresponding. They conclude that the piano is doomed, the piano tuner and pianist too. The event is of diminishing significance to Watt as the "fragility of outer meaning" fades to an incident in the life of another, "ill told, ill heard, and more than half forgotten" (74). Culik suggests Franz Josef Gall, founder of phrenology ("Entropic Order," 101). They may be poor relatives of Lord Gall of Wormwood; or Mr. Gall (Gast), mine host of *Mercier and Camier*. This incident first appeared in *Irish Writing* 22 (March 1953): 16–24.

Garnier, Pierre (1819–91): a doctor at the Asile de Bon-Secours, Paris. His *Onanisme seul et à deux sous toutes ses formes et leurs conséquences* was published in the 1880s by Libraire Garnier Frères, in their *Hygiène de la Génération* series. SB consulted the rare tenth edition at **Trinity** in 1931, making extensive notes (DN, 59–69). Garnier provided facts about **onanism**, contributing to **Belacqua**'s autodidacticism, and was SB's source of many "hard words": "glabrosity," applied to Capper "Hairy" **Quin** and the bald Lord Gall of **Wormwood**; "dehiscence," the "opening of pod at maturity," a sexual metaphor in *Dream* (116), "**What a Misfortune**" (139), and "The **Essential and the Incidental**" (*Disjecta*, 82); "clitoridian" (*Dream*, 111; "**Echo's Bones**," 19); "marasmus" (*Dream*, 208; "What a Misfortune," 140; *Murphy*, 138); "aspermatic" ("Echo's Bones," 11); "prurit," the urge to scratch the spot that itches (*Murphy*, 193); and "infundibuliforme" (*The Unnamable*, 323), where Garnier's reference to excessive sodomy is feminized. Garnier provided the names

"**Frica**" and "**Extravas**," and the image that begins *Dream,* of a boy in the country climbing trees and in the town sliding down a rope. See **Jalade-Lafont**.

Gassendi, Pierre (1592–1655): French philosopher who contended with **Descartes**. *Whoroscope* (18) invokes a "sunred crystally cloud," from his dissertation on parhelia (1631), which Descartes discussed in a treatise on meteors (1636); **Mahaffy** (53) reports the remarkable parhelia seen at Rome (20 March 1629), "discussed by various *savants,* and not least Gassendi." Descartes was dismissive: Gassendi's problems are likened to "hen-and-a-half-ones," as easily resolved as that conundrum.

Gate Theatre: founded by Micheáll mac Liammóir and Hilton Edwards in 1928, to promote European drama, as opposed to the nationalist **Abbey**, which it overtook as the preeminent **Dublin** theater. It began as the Dublin Gate Theatre Studios, working from the Peacock Theatre in the Abbey annex, the first production (14 October 1928) being Ibsen's *Peer Gynt*. In 1930 it moved to the Assembly Rooms of the Rotunda Building on Parnell Square where it has been since; the first production (February 1930) was **Goethe**'s *Faust*. As well as classics, the Gate encouraged younger Irish playwrights such as Denis Johnston and Brian Friel. SB saw there in 1932 a disappointing *Romeo and Juliet* (*Murphy*, 86), and in 1933 W. B. **Yeats**'s *Resurrection* and *King of the Old Clock Tower*. A 1935 London season enhanced its reputation, but financial pressures meant sharing the venue with Longford Productions, one company "touring" while the other was "at home." In 1945 the Gate had a season in the Dublin Gaiety Theatre and further international tours. SB's restrictions on Irish productions limited possibilities, but in 1989 the Gate staged a fine *Waiting for Godot,* with designs by Louis le Brocquy; then, objecting to an obituary that mourned SB as a great loss to France, Michael Colgan, the artistic director, followed this in October 1991 with a triumphant Beckett festival, the prodigal reclaimed. Colgan's idea, earlier discussed with SB, was to have a single set serve all the plays, "one great show in nineteen scenes," four single and five combined bills unified by a core design (Robert Ballagh) and lighting (Alan Burrett). Respecting SB's wish he staged *Endgame* (dir. Antoni Libera) separately, but ensured continuity with *Godot* (dir. Walter Asmus) by retaining the "same" characters: Alan Stanford as **Pozzo** and **Hamm**; Barry **McGovern** as **Vladimir** and **Clov**. The Gate has since repeated almost a full cycle of SB's plays, taking them to New York (Lincoln Center, 1996) and London (Barbican, 1999) to acclaim, bringing them to new audiences, and underlining their Irish intonation. These productions, some with different casts and directors, have been filmed (see "**Beckett on Film**").

Gaultier, Jules de: author of *De Kant à Nietzsche* (Paris, n.d.), from which SB drew some tenets and images for his early work (DN, 164–66): "divulgation" ("A Wet Night," 58; "Love and Lethe," 94); or Titania pressing to her bosom the head of an ass (*Dream,* 160; "Echo's Bones," 4; *Murphy,* 49), reason undone

by **desire**. Others concern decline, darkness, the strife of knowledge and life, the violated matrix of reason, and, most important, the relation between "the **object** & its representation, between the stimulus & molecular disturbance, between percipi and percipere"; this defines the "nice distinction" that **Murphy** abuses (246), and anticipates "**Three Dialogues**," fifteen years later.

Gedichte: SB's poems in English and **French**, with facing German translations by Eva Hesse (English) and Elmar **Tophoven** (French), published by Limes Verlag, Wiesbaden, 1959, in an edition of 2,000 copies; the first attempt to collect SB's scattered works. It includes *Echo's Bones* (*Echos Gebein;* 8–47); "Cascando" (48–51); several French poems, 1937–39 (54–77); and *Six poèmes,* 1947–49 (80–91). "Der Geier" ("The **Vulture**") was reprinted from this in *Lyrik im Limes Verlag* (1961), a publicity booklet for the press.

"**Geer van Velde**": SB's appreciation of the Dutch painter at Peggy **Guggenheim**'s London gallery. Published in *London Bulletin* 2 (May 1938): 15, ed. E. L. T. Mesens and devoted to **surrealism**; rpt. in *Disjecta* (117). SB outlines Geer's life (**tulips** and **Rembrandt**), and says painting should "mind its own business," that color should not try to be or do anything else. SB contributed to the *Bulletin* a translation of "Wolfgang Paalen" by André **Breton**, and (perhaps) "Abstract and Concrete Art," a preface by **Kandinsky**, both unsigned.

General Post Office: an imposing granite building in Sackville Street (now

O'Connell Street), **Dublin**, built in the Ionic mode with "a noble hexastyle portico of Portland stone," with impressive columns and, above the pediment, sizable statues of Hibernia flanked by Mercury and Fidelity; designed by Francis Johnston and completed in 1817 at a cost of more than £50,000 (O'Brien, 184–85, 367). Associated with Easter 1916, when resentment of English rule erupted into rebellion. Led by Padraic Pearse and James Connolly, the Irish Volunteers and Citizens' Army seized fourteen key buildings, notably the Post Office. On its steps, Pearse proclaimed the independence of Eire and called on his countrymen to fight for that freedom. Six days of bitter fighting ensued, 64 rebels, 134 police and soldiers, and some 200 civilians dying. It was not a popular cause until the British, in a display of military intelligence, executed fifteen rebel leaders in Kilmainham Jail, a dying Connolly wheeled in to be shot in his chair. The uprising could not have succeeded, but it created the martyrs the rebels had sought and made eventual independence inevitable. SB recalled being taken by his **father** into the Dublin mountains to see the city burning by night, but his response was irreverent: the "sacrifice" is mocked in *Murphy* (42); while in "**Ding-Dong**" (40) **Belacqua** makes off down Pearse Street, a most pleasant street, "despite its name."

The number who claimed to be inside the GPO outmatches its capacity to hold them; hence in "**Text 3**," "potting at the invader from behind a barrel of Guinness" (111). **O'Casey** gave offense with his irreverent treatment of the uprising in *The Plough and the Stars* (1926).

Within the GPO is the bronze statue of Cuchulain, whose deeds were celebrated by W. B. **Yeats**. Carved by Oliver Sheppard, RHA, and unveiled 21 April 1935 as a memorial to those who died in the Easter uprising, it depicts the Red Branch hero defiantly meeting his end and is inscribed with the names of the seven signatories to the Proclamation of the Irish Republic. Now in the window, the statue was previously in the lobby, where, like that of St. Peter in the Vatican, the hero's foot was polished by pilgrims touching it as a talisman. **Neary** offers an indignity on "holy ground" as he bares his head, the better to engage with Cuchulain's **buttock**. Con **Leventhal** recalled an unusual request: "Would I betake me to the Dublin Post Office and measure the height from the ground to Cuchulain's arse?" (*Beckett at 60*, xx). SB had to know "whether this violent gesture was in fact possible." SB disliked the "Cuchulainoid clichés" of the literary revival, and disparages their adulation ("**Recent Irish Poetry**," 71). A post office (in **London**, near the National Gallery) is recalled more warmly in *That Time* as one of the places, when it was cold and wet, that "you hadn't to pay to get in."

geology: a geological table appears in SB's **Whoroscope Notebook**, apparently copied from an encyclopedia. This became a metaphor for the prehistoric landscape of **consciousness**, or, in **French**, *conscience*, suggesting the strata of guilt and repression, and poetically conceived as a landscape of the mind where great saurians yet abound, as in "**ainsi a-t-on beau**," where human consciousness is set against past eras. Knowlson testifies (46) to SB's love of stones. As a child he might bring them home to protect them from the waves and later came to rationalize this impulse as an early fascination with the mineral, with things dying and decaying, with petrification, linking this to **Freud**'s prebirth nostalgia of return to the mineral state. To **MacGreevy** (14 August 1937), SB praised **Watteau**'s painting, as that of Jack **Yeats**, for its *inorganism,* his people finally "mineral." Hence, perhaps, **Molloy**'s sucking stones, or **Malone**'s intention to tell a story about a stone, "probably." The **Expelled** gains the cabman's attention by knocking with a stone (55), perhaps that carried by the narrator of "The **Calmative**" (67). In "**Eh Joe**," the woman's **death** enacts the return to the mineral, her lips, breasts, and hands clutching the stones.

Diderot in "Le Rêve de d'**Alembert**" articulates the paradox of life generated from the plane of inert sediment, and returning to that state, his literal interpretation (283) of the biblical injunction *momento quia pulvis es, et in pulverem reverteris* (Genesis 3:19: "for dust thou art, and unto dust shalt thou return"). In his *Méthode* part III, **Descartes** was determined to find ground of assurance, casting aside loose earth and sand, that he might reach the rock and clay. In *Proust* (65), the only fertile research is said to be "excavatory." The stated intent in early drafts of *Watt* is "auto-speliology" [*sic*], the desire to go "deep down in those palaeozoic profounds, midst mammoth Old Red Sandstone phalli and Carboniferous pudenda . . . into the pre-uterine . . . the agar-agar . . . impossible to describe . . . anguish . . . close eyes, all close,

great improvement, pronounced improvement." Harvey records (247) SB's attempt to find his lost self by getting down, "getting below the surface . . . the infinitesimal murmur . . . a gray struggle, a groping in the dark for a shadow." In "**Rough for Radio II**," **Fox** returns to those depths, "all stones all sides," with little lichens, tunnels, and a **voice** (his own, or that of his fetal twin) yelling, "Let me out! Peter out in the stones!" **Lucky**'s diatribe evokes the light, the grave, the lost labors of Steinweg and Peterman (Ger. *stein* and Gk. *petros,* "a stone"), the world an abode of stones, the **skull** in Connemara. The **Unnamable**, despite his stupid "obsession with depth" (293), must utter, lest he "peter out" (307).

In *How It Is* the mud is an amorphous plane between the rock below and air above: "a sky an earth an under-earth where I am inconceivable" (37). The question arises of life being "ordered" from above (hierarchy and command), or how it was before the others, "sedentary" (39), between strata. Molloy lives deep down, "oh not deepest down, somewhere between the mud and the scum" (14). **Moran** finds in **nature** a **superfoetatory** proof of the existence of **God** (99), but as he regresses to the state of unaccommodated man that conviction is lost. The Unnamable is trapped in his head, like a fossil in a rock (393). **Worm** and the poor creature crawling through the mud of *How It Is* try to move to a higher synthesis, a life in the light, to salvage a transcendence that might justify the **larval** stage of limited consciousness. The narrator's hope, that he might have his life there, is doomed. He is forced to conclude that it is all "balls," this talk of voices, of the life above, journeys and **company**, "the whole story from beginning to end yes completely false" (144). There remains "the primeval impenetrable dark," in which all is ill seen, ill heard, the individual little better placed than the dark figure of **Woburn** in "**Cascando**," face in the stones, in the sand, in the mud, in the bilge, crashing his way to the sea, that littoral threshold of a consciousness ultimately denied its metamorphosis and so returned to the mineral from which it somehow arose.

German Diaries: six notebooks, discovered after SB's **death** in a trunk in the cellar of 38 Boulevard Saint-Jacques by Edward Beckett, and described in Knowlson's biography (Chapter 10, "**Germany:** The Unknown Diaries 1936–37"), a definitive account of SB's obsessive attention to the **art** he saw and commented on for six months, a deliberate program of study. The diaries, now at the **BIF** (Reading), record SB's daily movements, galleries visited, people met, and his awareness of the cultural, political, and economic circumstances. They testify to the rich impact of that visit on his writing, confirming his deep appreciation of visual culture, both traditional and contemporary. They provide valuable indications of his reading, and of the philosophical and literary speculations that underpin his thought, sometimes predictably (rationalism as the last form of animism) but often surprisingly (authentic art as prayer).

"German Letter of 1937": a letter in German dated 9 July 1937, three months after SB's return from **Germany**, to Axel Kaun, met during his visit to Berlin, who had suggested that SB might translate some poems by Joachim **Ringelnatz**; the idea did not finally appeal. The offer had been made earlier, and SB had agreed "en principe" (SB to TM, 5 June 1936). The "German Letter" survives in the Baker Memorial Library (Dartmouth College), and was included (with a translation by Martin Esslin) in *Disjecta* (51–54; trans. 170–73). It offers invaluable insights into SB's growing alienation from public opinion, and his intuition (see **Mauthner**) that language seemed increasingly a "veil that must be torn apart to get at the things (or the Nothingness) behind it." He yearns for silence to bore holes in language, until that **Nothing** seeps through, waiting to hear a whisper of "that final **music** or that silence that underlies All." The latest work of **Joyce** or the logographs of Gertrude Stein, he asserts, have nothing to do with this, the one being an apotheosis of the word and the other in love with her vehicle, whereas he seeks "the literature of the **unword**" and a form of "Nominalist irony."

Germany: SB's attraction to Germany has no obvious roots. Apart from attending a private school run by two elderly German spinsters, the **Elsner sisters**, where he may have heard his first phrases, he did not learn German formally at any level. Entering **Trinity College** SB took French and Italian, winning in his third year a Foundation scholarship in modern languages. Bair claims that by this stage SB showed an interest in "the regularity, precision and rigid structure of the German language" (54), but the challenge of a different medium probably appealed more than the language itself. Only later did he master German, but despite the lack of formal instruction he was early drawn toward the country. In September 1928 he visited his Aunt Cissie in **Kassel**, the main attraction his cousin Peggy **Sinclair**. Germany had a reputation for sexual liberation and SB's parents feared for their son's moral welfare. Their fears were well founded, as he returned to Kassel at Christmas, cementing a relationship with Germany that grew during the 1930s.

In September 1936 SB traveled through Germany to visit **art** galleries, disappointed that the Nazis had removed many works as degenerate. He was introduced to the work of the most innovative German artists and writers. While the time was unproductive in terms of creative writing, SB's **German Diaries** (qv) outline his attraction to German philosophy and his growing interest in contemporary art and literature. Entries in German in the **Whoroscope Notebook** from **Mauthner** and **Kant** probably date from this time.

Germany represented three things for SB: **love**, art, and philosophy. Its language enabled him to travel and to read literature. Returning to **Dublin**, he wrote to Axel Kaun (see "**German Letter of 1937**"), describing his pleasure in "sinning willy nilly against a foreign language, as I should love to do with full knowledge and intent against my own." In his early prose, elements of German were inserted randomly: "sonst, in the words of the song, gar nix" (*Dream*, 11; the "song" by Marlene Dietrich from her 1928 film *The Blue Angel*). Of SB as

Belacqua: "Scraps of German played in his mind in the silence that ensued, grand, old, plastic words" (191). The appeal was sonority and the shape of words: "Himmisacrakrüzidirkenjesusmariaundjosefundblütigeskreuz" (239). The scholarly approach came later, with his reading of **Goethe** (*Faust* and *Werther*) and **Hölderlin**. Siegfried Unseld, SB's German publisher, confirmed that SB read German classics in the original.

Warten auf Godot was an immediate success in Berlin with audiences and critics alike. In 1953 it appeared simultaneously in eight German cities. Although SB declined to attend his German premieres, he forged a strong bond with Albert Bessler and Boleslaw Barlog of the **Schiller-Theater** (qv) and maintained an involvement with productions of his drama in Germany. If critical reaction to his plays varied, the initial popularity of *Godot* in Germany affirmed his reputation beyond the avant-garde French theater. SB's appreciation of this acceptance was reflected in his dedication to the Schiller-Theater thereafter.

Not entirely satisfied with the German productions, SB was impressed by the patience and meticulousness of the German actors he encountered at rehearsals for the world premiere of "**Spiel**" in Ulm (1963) and while assisting Deryk **Mendel** with *Godot* in Berlin (1965). The next year he became involved with "**Eh Joe**" at Süddeutscher Rundfunk, Stuttgart. By now SB had sufficient confidence in his German to direct in that language. Between 1967 and 1978 SB directed seven stage plays in German in Berlin: *Endgame* (1967), *Krapp's Last Tape* (1969), *Happy Days* (1971), *Wait-*

ing for Godot (1975), **That Time** and *Footfalls* (1976), and "**Play**" (1978). As he assisted Elmar **Tophoven** with textual revision for these productions his command of the intricacies of German increased, as subtle revisions testify. His growing confidence as a **director** is reflected in attention to detail, as recorded in the *Theatrical Notebooks*. His productions, regarded as authoritative, have been re-created subsequently worldwide. For his German television productions, SB restricted his activities to the SDR in Stuttgart, directing versions of *Eh Joe* (1966), "**Ghost Trio**" and "**. . . but the clouds . . .**" (1977), "**Quad**" (1981), and "**Nacht und Träume**" (1983), and adapting "**What Where**" for TV in 1986. This opened the way for productions by other directors, varying greatly in standard and success.

SB's influence on contemporary German directors is considerable. Equally, he influenced several dramatists writing in German. Peter Handke's *Hörspiel Nr. 2* mixes sections of the English version of "Eh Joe" with the Jimi Hendrix song of the same name, to create a bizarre mélange of languages and styles. Volker Braun, originally from East Germany, incorporated elements of SB's drama into his own; part of *Simplex Deutsch*, written when SB's drama was officially banned in the East, is subtitled "Auftritt Godot." Thomas Bernhard is often described as the Austrian Beckett; *Der Schein trügt* relates the ritualistic existence of two elderly brothers who meet regularly to revel in reminiscences of their respective professions and experiences. These pieces with their roots in SB's drama are his most obvious descendants, but they represent merely a few instances of his far-reaching influence on contemporary German drama. [JG]

Gestalt psychology: a reaction against associationism, noted for its insistence on pattern and form, figure and ground, elements largely ignored by other schools and particularly by behaviorism. In the 1930s Gestalt psychology was one of the more vigorous emerging schools. To SB it remained attractive, the triumph of the **rats** over the configurationists a sad regret. He had read **Köhler** and **Koffka**, but Gestalt detail in *Murphy* derives from Robert **Woodworth**'s *Contemporary Schools of Psychology* (1931), which accentuated fundamental aspects of the organized whole, closure, and the opposition of figure and ground. **Neary**'s "blotch" derives from Woodworth's description (106) of how a figure (Fr. *figure*, "**face**") emerges from an indistinct background; his "heterogeneous stimulation" wittily varies Woodworth's "homogeneous stimulation" (107). Neary uses these terms to define his changing feelings for various objects of **desire**, and his fate reflects a Gestalt conception of desire as a condition requiring completeness and **equilibrium**. Gestalt principles underlie **Belacqua**'s paradox of the **object** that becomes invisible being brightest and best (*Dream*, 12), and **Watt**'s puzzlement over the changing relations between circle and point. The wider problem is mocked in "**Text 6**" (123), where all that is needed is "a little resolution."

"Getting One's Money's Worth": an extract from the French translation of *Murphy* reprinted in *Advanced Level*

French Course, Book I, by W. T. John and M. A. Crowther (London: Thomas Nelson and Sons, 1962), a shortened, slightly adapted version of the tearoom scene from "Apportez-moi une tasse de thé" to "1,83 tasse approximativement"; #21 among "Prose Passages for Translation" (F&F, #145.001). See "A **Seaside Reminiscence**."

Geulincx, Arnoldus (1624–69): Flemish metaphysician and philosopher whose *Ethica* were of lasting fascination to SB. Born in Antwerp, he studied philosophy and theology at Louvain, where he became professor in 1646. In 1658, following charges prompted by his attacks on **scholasticism** and accepted **religion** (he forsook Catholicism for Calvinism), he was deprived of his position and left for Leiden. After some poverty he was appointed Professor of Philosophy, and he remained there until his **death**. Deeply influenced by **Descartes** and the Cartesian Guillaume Phillipi, his later works are rooted firmly in the rationalist tradition and include commentaries on **Descartes**'s *Principles of Philosophy.* He published in 1662 and 1663 respectively the *Logica* and *Methodus Inveniendi Argumenta,* which provided the framework for his more significant works, the *Physica, Metaphysica,* and *Ethica.* These were published after his death, the texts taken from manuscripts used in his classes.

SB encountered Geulincx at the **École Normale**, but read him closely early in 1936, well into the writing of *Murphy.* For some weeks he went from **Foxrock** to **Trinity** to sit in the Long Room and read Geulincx in the original (the three-volume *Opera Philosophica,* ed. J. P. Land). He took fifty closely typed pages of notes, mostly from the *Ethica,* fascinated, he told **MacGreevy**, by its conviction that the sub specie aeternitatis vision is the only excuse for remaining alive. He would later tell scholars of his work that Geulincx's ***Ubi nihil vales, ibi nihil velis*** (qv) ("Where you are worth nothing, there you should want nothing") was one place to begin. That ethical axiom became for SB the foundation of doubt and humility, the **bêtise** that underpins his life's work. Aspects of the *Ethica* appear in the fiction. *Murphy* refers (178) to the "beautiful Belgo-Latin" of the *Ubi nihil,* and **Occasionalist** principles structure **Murphy's mind.** In "The **End**" (91), a teacher named Ward once introduced the protagonist to the *Ethics.* About to leave **Lousse, Molloy** invokes the dubious freedom of "old Geulincx" (51), crawling to the East along the deck of a westward-moving ship, the black boat of **Dante**'s Ulysses (*Ethica,* 167 n7); likewise in *The **Unnamable*** (336), as the galleyman "bound" for the Pillars of Hercules crawls toward the rising sun.

"Ghost Trio": a television play written in English (1975); taped October 1976 and first broadcast on BBC 2 (17 April 1977), dir. Donald **McWhinnie** (supervised by SB) with Ronald Pickup and Billie **Whitelaw.** "Geistertrio," directed by SB, was broadcast by Süddeutscher Rundfunk, Stuttgart, in May 1977, with Klaus Herm and Irmgard Först. SB's **French** translation, "Trio du fantôme," has never been performed. Originally called "**Tryst**," the play's final title and its three scenes reflect **Beethoven**'s Fifth

Piano Trio, "Der Geist" (Opus 70, #1). First published in *JOBS* 1 (winter 1976): 1–7, then collected in **Ends and Odds** (Grove Press, 1976; Faber, 1977), "Ghost Trio" is among SB's "unreadable" late works, part of a postliterary phenomenon that began with **"Play"** in 1963, the beginning of a new approach, closer to total theater or the Wagnerian *Gesamptkunstwerk.*

This change is immediately evident to readers without access to productions of "Play," **"Breath,"** *Come and Go,* "Ghost Trio," *". . . but the clouds . . . ,"* **"Nacht und Träume,"** or **"Quad."** On the page, without iconic, gestural, and musical complements, the works are unreadable in any traditional sense; their primary effect is extraliterary, postliterary, perhaps. "Ghost Trio" may be SB's most fully realized theater work, with **music**, gesture, sculptural iconography, and poetry perfectly integrated and balanced, yet unassimilable on the page. It represents SB's one attempt to write something approaching opera (as "Quad" was his one attempt to write something like ballet, complete with music and choreography). On the typescript of "Tryst" (the first draft), SB penned "Macbeth" (Knowlson, 549). Asked why, he said that in his version of the trio, by Daniel Barenboim, Beethoven's music was linked to a planned opera on **Shakespeare**'s *Macbeth.* According to the liner notes for that recording, the D-minor largo (the key proposed for the witches' chorus) plunges the piece into the spirit world of the night, with flickering expanses of sound, piano tremolos, and descending chromatic scales conjuring up an uncanny, oppressively deathly mood. The trio is named "The Ghost" because of the mysterious slow movement, *largo assai espressivo;* except for the coda of that movement, used to bring the play to its end, the passages selected by SB are from the "ghostly" second theme, to foreshadow the climax of the play, the appearance of the small **boy** whose presence **comes and goes** as if in response to the music.

With "Ghost Trio" SB undertook an elaborate integration of music and theater. His script details, as precisely as any composer, which bars of music are to accompany which gestures. Here are SB's designations, corresponding to act (Roman) and scene (Arabic), as elaborated in Fletcher, *Student's Guide* (214–16):

a. I.13: *beginning bar 47:* faint music, for five seconds, the recapitulation of the second motif of the opening subject, the ghostly haunting theme. Music linked to the camera's focus upon the door.

b. I.23: *beginning bar 49:* "a more dissonant and highly charged version of the motif, with the main rising interval of the melodic line being greater, thus producing greater tension." Again, the music is linked to the door.

c. I.31–34: *beginning bar 19:* as at I.13, but with piano accompaniment, with crescendo, increasing harmonic tension, rising pitch, and a *stretto* effect as motifs overlap.

d. II.26–29: *beginning bar 64:* a paralleled passage, a recapitulation of that used in I.31–34, but with the *stretto* effect beginning earlier, and so greater tension.

e. II.35–36: *beginning bar 71:* like the previous passage, but with the "ghostly" theme overlapping itself, with more movement in the piano part.

f. III.1–2, 4–5: *beginning bar 26:* again a recapitulation, the equivalent passage to bar 71; marginally more restful since the rising intervals are all octaves.

g. III.29: *beginning bar 64:* the same music as II.26, but this time the footsteps are heard and the boy appears.

h. III.36 to end: *beginning bar 82:* the music grows as the camera moves in; this is the coda, the end of the movement.

For Fletcher, the teleplay takes up the metaphor of the artist as musician, playing on the Beethoven trio, the tripartite structure of the teleplay, and the three "ghostly" characters, voice, figure ("Sole sign of life"), and boy (exception to former). More important is the asynchronous relationship between the cassette the seated figure holds and the music, which, like the **Voice** in SB's late drama, seems to originate from an inexplicable beyond as much as an individual **consciousness**. Despite the primary visual icon, a frozen figure hunched over a cassette recorder, the music exists outside human control, beyond words, outside **time**, space, and the human dimension. It offers a profound reflection upon one particular motif from the second movement of the trio, employing the music to counterpoint dramatic action that culminates in disappointment, impotence, and loneliness.

As inexplicable as the music is Voice, who guides the viewer or controls camera or point of view [p.o.v.]. In Act I she addresses viewers directly, urging them to adjust the volume of their televisions, conducts a tour of the colorless, shadowless scene, and redirects attention: "Look again" (248). In Act II she comments on Figure's behavior. He believes he hears "her," Voice says; he moves to the door, opens it, ditto window, inspects pallet, all in apparent response to some unheard sound or the commands of Voice. But Figure is not controlled by Voice's narrative, and his move to the **mirror** surprises Voice. When her narration calls for his return to the door, he instead returns to stool. Act III is embedded in Act II, the "Repeat" Voice called for at the end of II, this time as **mime**, without narration, but with camera adopting Figure's p.o.v. on occasion. Figure opens door, to "corridor seen from door," ditto window, with added sound and sight of rain, ditto pallet, ditto mirror ("reflecting **nothing**" at first, then his reflection from his p.o.v.), each inspection interspersed with a **God**-like view from above. The "Repeat" is an augmentation of Act II and culminates in the sound of steps and the appearance not of "her" but of "him," a small boy whose only gesture is to shake his head. "She" will not come today, the boy seems to suggest, but surely tomorrow. After Figure's disappointment, the final image is of his embracing the cassette, like **Krapp** his tape recorder, till the crescendo of the largo. In this image of a haunting, by the image of a woman loved and lost, the first two scenes are rehearsals for the drama of isolation punctuated by Beethoven's ghosts. The combination of the music and ghosts of **love** suggests the German **Romanticism** that SB never relinquished. His SDR production departed from the textual ending by having Figure raise his head, stare into the camera, and offer a slight, enigmatic smile. This performance revision, not in any published text, links "Ghost Trio" with *That Time,* the BBC and SDR productions of "**Eh Joe,**" and potentially "**Catastrophe.**" It is one of SB's miniature masterpieces.

Giacometti, Alberto (1901–66): Swiss sculptor and painter who lived in **Paris** and was heir to Cubism and **surrealism.** His attenuated figures express a painful vulnerability, an isolated individuality; **Sartre** defined him as the preeminent **existential** artist. He often met SB "in late bars during their mutually insomniac early-morning hours" (Knowlson, 335). For the 1961 Odéon Théâtre production of *En attendant Godot* he sculpted a magnificent tree, which has since disappeared. Affixing its plaster leaves in Act II created a problem. Giacometti's *Skull 1923* is reproduced on the cover of the 1962 Penguin *Malone Dies.*

Gide, André (1869–1951): French novelist whom SB studied at **Trinity** and later taught (his comments recorded by his student Rachel **Dobbin**). SB considered following *Proust* with another volume on Gide, subtitled "paralysed in ubiquity" (Knowlson, 161), but Charles **Prentice** demurred. Gide's novels are intensely patterned, their complex formal symmetries intimating the conflict between the world and its representation. They offered a model, but SB mentions Gide only in *Proust* (20), where he mocks his "Live dangerously" as the "hiccough in vacuo" of the "analogivorous." SB rejected Gide's public persona of the committed intellectual, but he published twice in Gide's *Nouvelle revue française.*

gigerl: a word gleaned from **Nordau**'s *Degeneracy* (33; DN, 90), and used in *Dream* (89). To **MacGreevy** (1 November 1933), SB defined it as "Viennese for negligent fop," and applied it to **Denis Devlin:** an exquisite imagist but "a jazz Jesus, a Jiggle . . . a giggler and a gigerl."

Gilles de Rais (1404–40): Marshal of France, associate of Joan of Arc, but infamous for his practices of alchemy and necromancy, for which he kidnapped and tortured small boys and drank their blood. His "orbs" (eyes) are invoked in *Dream* (79). Called by Praz (127) a "genuine Bluebeard," as compared to **Sade,** a "mental Bluebeard." See **Rio Santo.**

Gillot, Jean: Huguenot valet of **Descartes,** barely mentioned by **Baillet** (I.68) save to note that he was asked to resolve **mathematical** problems deemed too trivial for his master. **Mahaffy** confirms this (77), citing "Give that to Gillot," which SB used in *Whoroscope.*

Gilmigrim jokes: favored by **Murphy** (139), in error for "glimigrim," as in *Gulliver's Travels* (I.5), where Gulliver, having drunk plenty of that Lilliputian wine, recycles it to good effect and puts out the palace fire.

Giorgione, Giorgio Barbarelli (1477–1511): Italian painter of the Venetian school, whose landscapes such as the *Tempesta* (Accademia, Venice), the *Concert champêtre* (Louvre), and *Sleeping*

Venus (Dresden) contributed a new unity of figure and setting through their use of color, atmosphere, and proportion. The first two are cited in **Proust.** SB took angry exception to **D'Annunzio**'s dismissal of Proust's "floral obsessions" and his vulgar misreading of Giorgione's rapt figures (SB to TM, 7 July 1930). In 1936 SB saw in the Herzog-Anton-Ulrich Museum in Brunswick Giorgione's brooding self-portrait, which so obsessed him that he returned three times, buying a large reproduction of it. Knowlson suggests (225, 583, 665) that the head with its knitted brows and anguished eyes (SB's terms) emerging from the dark background resembles SB's late dramatic images in *That Time, Footfalls,* "What Where," and perhaps "**Rockaby.**"

Girodias, Maurice: see **Olympia Press.**

Giudecca: innermost zone of Cocytus, named for Judas Iscariot ("Giuda Scaṙiotto") who dangles there from Satan's mouth (*Inf.* XXXIV). Used, in **Dante**'s time as later, for the ghettos. In *Dream* (68) **Belacqua** squeezes the Giudecca of the **Smeraldina**'s palm; in *First Love* (43) the narrator feels closer to Giudecca "in the hell of unknowing" than to **God.**

Glass, Philip (b. 1937): electronic composer. His opera *Einstein on the Beach* (1972) derived from his experience in **Paris** of SB, whom he cited as inspiration for his minimalist style. He produced for **Mabou Mines** scores for *Play* (1979, for two soprano saxophones); *The Lost Ones* (1975); "**Cascando**" (1975); an adaption of *Mercier and Camier* (1979); *Com-*

pany (1983; his String Quartet #2); and *Worstward Ho* (1986). Excepting *Music for Company* (Kronos Quartet, 1987), these are currently unreleased.

Glazier: a character in *Eleutheria,* who appears instantly to mend the window broken by Victor **Krap**, Mephistopheles to an unaspiring Faust. His "taylorizing sentimentality" (147) refers to Frederick Winslow Taylor (1856–1915), father of time and motion studies, implying that he regulates the performance of other characters. SB confirmed that Glazier's dialogue with his son, Michel, underlies that with the **boy** in *En attendant Godot.*

Glencullen: near **Foxrock,** at the end of the Glencullen Road leading to the Dublin Mountains. The valley had several quarries, Glencullen granite used in the police barracks on Pearse Street ("**Ding-Dong,**" 40). Stonecutters are heard in *Watt* (16) and *Malone Dies* (206). Mr. **Hackett,** asked if he is of the Glencullen Hacketts, says it was there that he fell off the **ladder** (*Watt,* 15). The manuscript (NB1, 41) reads "Rathcullen."

"The Gloaming": an unpublished dramatic fragment (RUL 1396/4/6), dated December 1956, sixteen pages torn from a squared notebook, a first draft of "**Rough for Theatre I.**" The original title, "The Beggar and the Cripple," is deleted and "The Gloaming" placed below, as in the song "Roaming in the Gloaming." It features a fiddle-playing beggar, **B** (Blind), his colocutor **C** (Cripple), but breaks off during C's telling of his childhood sorrows.

Gloria SMH: the Resistance cell into which SB was recruited (September 1941) by Alfred **Péron**; part of British Special Operations. "Gloria" was the alias of its leader, Jeannine **Picabia** (qv); "SMH" reverses "His Majesty's Service." SB collated information and typed it up, the sheets taken to one "Jimmy the Greek" for microfilming and dispatch to London. The work was dangerous as it meant clandestine documents in his flat and incriminating material to be carried. The cell (about eighty members) was infiltrated by a renegade priest, Robert **Alesch** (qv), who betrayed it. Péron was arrested, but his wife Mania sent SB a telegram warning him and Suzanne to escape. They took refuge in **Roussillon** (qv). SB's Resistance activities, for which he received the Croix de Guerre and the Médaille de la Reconnaissance, are not obvious in his writing, but consider the "Organization" to which **Moran** belongs and the messengers in *Molloy* and *Waiting for Godot.*

Glückliche Tage: the German *Happy Days* or *Oh les beaux jours,* trans. by Erika and Elmar **Tophoven** with the help of SB, who directed it at the **Schiller-Theater**, Berlin, 17 September 1971. The manuscript notebook (RUL 1396/4/10), in the words of the Reading catalogue, "An extraordinary detailed and revealing document" (47), contains SB's notes of actions, props, and movements. It displays "the meticulousness and fine precision with which Beckett approached the direction of his own work" (48). Another notebook (RUL 1227/7/8/1), inscribed by SB "Notes for *Glückliche Tage* **Regiebüch**, 1970/71," precedes the former, with detailed notes on the physical actions of the players and dynamics of the play; this is the "quarry" from which production details were mined. See *Happy Days: Samuel Beckett's Production Notebooks,* ed. James Knowlson (Faber, and Grove Press, 1986), which anticipated the **Theatrical Notebooks.** A trilingual edition appeared as *Glückliche Tage: Happy Days: Oh les beaux jours* (Frankfurt: Suhrkamp, 1975).

"Gnome": a quatrain written after SB's resignation from **Trinity**; published in the *Dublin Magazine* 9.3 (July–September 1934): 8; signed "Sam Beckett." The title insinuates "gnomic," as in short and enigmatic, but also **gnosticism,** knowing: traditional wisdom in pithy, proverbial form (an Old Irish mode). It expresses SB's despair at "the loutishness of learning," yet stands in contrast to that, being an imitation of **Goethe**'s "**Xenien.**" With its "Hiawatha" rhythm, pentameter and tetrameter couplets, patterned participles, and feminine rhymes, its form subverts the sentiment without quite denying it.

gnosticism: a **religion** that arose in the third century, Neoplatonic systems of Alexandria combined with Manichaeism (from its Persian founder, Manes, ca. 240–80 AD, **crucified** for his faith). It accentuates the **strife of opposites** (good and evil, light and dark, soul and **body**). **Augustine** was briefly an adherent. SB's attraction to gnosticism is revealed in his reading of the *Confessions,* his delight in **troubadour** verse (steeped in the Cathar heresy), and his fascination with **dualism** (the "**panpygoptic** Manichee" of *Murphy*, 104). *Krapp's Last Tape* follows gnostic tradition, the play exemplifying the conflict of light and dark, the rift between **God** and the world (spirit and flesh), even abstention from intercourse and marriage. The setting, a pool of light surrounded by the dark, indicates a cosmic conflict, with images of the woman (Bianca) in black and white, the nurse in white with the black pram, the black **ball** given to the white **dog**, and Krapp's black waistcoat offsetting his soiled white shirt. SB noted of *Das letzte Band* (1969): "Krapp decrees physical (ethical) incompatibility of light (spiritual) and dark (sensual) only when he intuits possibility of their reconciliation as rational-irrational." Knowlson (*Frescoes*, 88) identifies the warring elements as spiritual versus sensual, independent and incompatible unless reconciled at the intellectual level. He reports SB's comment that Krapp is guilty of transgression, as the duty of the intellect is to separate light from dark, not to seek their reconciliation. SB's 1969 production accentuated this dualism, which seems not to have been a lasting element of his thought.

goat: an image of the preterit, those passed over, as in the "small malevolent goat" of "**Enueg I**," "pucking" the gate, "exiled" from its Eden. Consider Matthew 25:32, **Christ**'s separation of the **sheep** from the goats (**Godot**'s **boy** looks after the goats, his brother the sheep); and Leviticus 16, the scapegoat (*pharmarkos*) as a figure of atonement. **Molloy** in the wilderness (85) eats carobs, "so dear to goats." In "The **Calmative**" (66–

67) the narrator meets a boy with a goat, and asks, "Where are you off to, my little man, with your nanny?" only to blush with shame. SB preferred goats to sheep (**Cain** to Abel). **Murphy**'s **horoscope** intimates the irony of a Good Shepherd born under Capricorn; his fate is "capricious" (32); Miss **Carriage** "capers" (134) with a goatish smell, and in the "tragic" mode (L. *caper*, and Gk. *tragos*, "goat"). **Celia**'s eye (137) is everted "like an aborting goat's," a postern to **Nothing**; and **Wylie** wonders if "a real goat" has been in the house (235). A goat was present when Mr. **Hackett** fell off the **ladder** (*Watt*, 16); and **Watt**'s meal (36), vaguely theological, is goat's milk and uncooked cod. "Reilly's puckaun" (an Irish billy goat) finally bears **witness** to what Doherty calls (20) a metaphysical farce of cruelty in a self-satisfied world: "And they say there is no **God**."

God: SB was fascinated by the variety of verbal and symbolic systems by which believers expressed their sense of a superior being. He contrasted **Dante** with **Joyce** in respect of "the Absolute"; his insistence that the latter's work was "**purgatorial**" implies his own position: "the absolute absence of the Absolute" ("Dante, " *Disjecta*, 33). This is a given, but God as the major paradox and impasse of **religion** would remain "a teaser," intellectually rejected but emotionally necessary. This entry has two concerns: philosophical and intellectual notions of God in the post-Cartesian tradition; and the Old Testament patriarch as a literary image.

The Western Christian tradition conceives the world as theomorphous, with

God as the efficient first cause; mankind created in His image and thus deiform; and God, the world, and mankind mutually congruent, as in the concept of the **microcosm**. This was the inheritance of seventeenth-century rationalism, arguably SB's philosophical and theological point of departure. **Descartes** inserted the wedge that eventually split man from God, and **Pascal** was unable to forgive him for doing so. God was no longer necessary to set the **whirligig** world in **motion**, and the problem of **body** and mind became paramount. As Hesla notes (78): "What is common to Descartes's successors is that each solved the problem by recourse to God. For the **Occasionalists** God is the worker of miracles; for **Leibniz** he is the supreme architect, the clockmaker who built such a perfect mechanism that the spiritual and hyletic dimensions of the **monad** are always in perfect synchronization; for **Spinoza** he is the one substance, whose intellectual **love** for himself is identical with the intellectual love wherewith he loves man and wherewith man loves God; and for **Berkeley**, God is the Mind in which the ideas of things subsist." Add **Kant**'s sense of the transcendent self, **Schopenhauer**'s critique of that, retain **apperception**, and this gives a crude summary of SB's sense of the world, the universe, and everything in it.

In short, SB offers a **Proustian** critique of a rationalist universe, in which God is an **irrational** proposition; this renders His role imperative, in every sense. The **Unnamable** insists (305) that he never believed, not a second, in the "fomentor of calm" (one might expect "fiasco"), but he is terrified by the Master, who imposes the **pensum**. God assumes a patriarchal guise throughout SB's writings, less a belief than a literary trope. **Moran**'s authority is that of the Old Testament Freudian **father**, but is in turn subject to **Youdi**. **Godot** reputedly has a white beard and punishes those who abandon their vigil. **Mercier** and **Camier** scorn the "Omni-omni" and castigate God as one who has "emmerded" them; **Clov** tries to kill a flea "for the love of God." **Watt** seeks **Knott**. God is beginning to disgust **Hamm**. **Winnie** magnifies the Almighty by "sniggering with him at his little jokes, particularly the poorer ones." The terror returns in *How It Is* (74), with despair at the impossibility of either belief or disbelief: "God on God desperation utter confusion did he believe he believed then not couldn't any more his reasons both cases my God."

Godot: the deus ex machina of *Waiting for Godot,* a significant nonsignifier, his very name implying infinite deferral. In *En attendant Godot* he is of alien English stock; but the French diminutive subverts this identity, as does the prolonged farewell between **Pozzo** and the tramps: "Adieu . . . adieu." SB told Roger **Blin** that the name was suggested by *godillots* and *godasses,* French slang for **boots**. Other suggestions include spectators at the Tour de France waiting after the bunch had passed ("Nous attendons Godot"); a prostitute in the Rue Godot de Mauroy who asked if SB was saving himself for Godot; or **Balzac**'s *Le Faiseur,* in which Mercadet awaits "Monsieur Godeau" to come and save him from ruin, before crying in despair, "Mais Godeau est un mythe! est une fable! Godeau, c'est un fantôme!" There are post hoc anecdotes as well: SB's flying to London: "Le capitaine Godot vous accorde des bienvenues" (Bair, 390); and a card from one Georges Godot, of Paris, who apologized for keeping SB waiting (Knowlson, 506). As John **Calder** remarked, the more such stories the better.

SB's standard answer to the question "Who is Godot?" was, "If I knew I wouldn't have written the play." To SIR Ralph Richardson (SB's capitals) he was emphatic: "if by Godot I had meant God I would say God, and not Godot. This seemed to disappoint him greatly." Of the celebrated **San Quentin** performance (1957) he commented: "They knew what is meant by waiting—and they knew if Godot finally came, he would only be a disappointment." Godot's manuscript existence is more definite: **Vladimir** and **Estragon** have a written assignment for "Saturday evening and subsequent evenings." SB toyed with the idea of Pozzo as Godot, failing to recognize Vladimir and Estragon.

Alexei Sayle has devised a neat little parody. Two men stalk the stage, looking at their watches and wondering where Godot is, their pointless routines cut by flashes of figures in a **greatcoat**, lank hair and a long white beard, rushing through the London traffic, trying frantically to catch buses; then back to the stage, more waiting and muttering, until finally the actors give up and prepare to go—whereupon three Godots enter: "Bloody typical—wait all day for one, then three turn up at once."

Goethe, Johann Wolfgang von (1749–1832): German poet, dramatist, and literary giant whose presence, like **Shake-**speare's, SB assumed as a given. References in *Dream* are facetious. The **Smeraldina** embellishes her angst with Gretchen's song: "Mein Ruh ist hin" (59), attributed to "Herr Geheimrat Johann Wolfgang Goethes Faust" (echoing Praz's mockery, *Romantic Agony*, 111). **Belacqua**'s "Bitchlein" ("little bitches") that "schweigen niemals im Wald" ("are never silent in the wood") is adapted (80) from "Wanderers Nachtlied II" (DN, 154), with the change to "sweifen" (Swabian for "fuck"). The narrator wishes to "honour our **Father**, our **Mother**, and Goethe" (178); this advice is given by **Doyle** in "**Echo's Bones**" (24) and derives from **Renard**'s *Journal*, but with Virgil (DN, 31).

Yet SB took Goethe seriously. "**Gnome**," his farewell to learning, imitates the **Xenien**; "The **Vulture**" is indebted to "Harzreise im Winter." He read *Dichtung und Wahrheit* (1935), finding it absorbing, especially the Leipzig years, and took forty-one pages of notes. He copied out "**Prometheus**," and read *Tasso* and *Iphigenia* (Knowlson, 213), but told **MacGreevy** (25 March 1936) he needed **Racine** to remove the taste. By August 1936 he had finished part I of *Faust* (Knowlson, 662), finding it "fragmentary" and the "on and up" (Goethe's "Wer immer strebend sich bemüht") rather tiresome, but was looking forward to part II. *Wilhelm Meister* followed. **Murphy**'s sense of the **little world** owes an indefinable *etwas* to *Die Leiden des jungen Werthers* (1774), which SB was then reading (apparently in French): "Ich kehre in mich selbst zurück und finde eine Welte!" ("I turn back into myself and find a world" [22 Mai]), with the implication that such a world may be unsustainable: "Wenn wir uns selbst fehlen, fehlt uns doch alles" ("When we fail our selves, then everything fails us" [22 August]). Faust's cry "Die Erde hat mich wieder" (I.784), cited in the **Whoroscope Notebook** (2/10/36), is among the addenda to *Watt,* invoking the **mixed choirs** of angels who dissuade Faust from **suicide**. **Lulu** sings Goethe's "Kennst du das Land, wo die Zitronen blühn?" (*First Love,* 37). **Molloy**'s vision of draining the swamp (76) combines Faust in part 2 draining the Zuider Zee with the **psychoanalytical** experience of "draining the puddle." Summing up his bourgeois existence, **Moran** invokes the imperative, "**Sollst entbehren**" ("You must renounce," *Molloy,* 110), the precept that incited Faust to rebellion (I.1549). **Malone** calls out for "light, light" (288), like Goethe on his deathbed (he wanted the curtains opened); the **Unnamable** is attended by **Marguerite**. SB copied bits of Goethe into his later notebooks, particularly the poems **Schubert** had immortalized (Goethe was unappreciative). The upright figure of "**Lessness**," Knowlson suggests (504), has the shabby grandeur of Goethe's Prometheus as he curses his maker.

Gogarty, Oliver St. John (1878–1957): wit, raconteur, and physician, known (to his lasting irritation) as the original of Buck Mulligan in *Ulysses.* Educated at the Royal University, **Trinity College**, and Oxford, his medical practice flourished like his bawdy wit and verse. In "**Recent Irish Poetry**" (*Disjecta,* 57), SB called him a prize canary. SB appeared for his uncle Harry in a libel case (23–27 November 1937). Harry Sinclair won

the case, which cost Gogarty £2,000, but SB found the humiliation unsavory. He was pilloried as a writer of filth, a bawd and a blasphemer, not a **witness** in whom Justice O'Byrne would place much reliance (Knowlson, 254–59). The trial worsened things between SB and his **mother**, and reinforced his decision to remove himself permanently from narrow, bigoted **Dublin**.

Goncourts: two brothers, Edmond (1822–96) and Jules (1830–70), aesthetes devoted to **art** and literature, whose *Journal* offers a fascinating portrait of their age, but whose "notes d'après **nature**" SB casually dismisses (*Proust,* 80). The Prix Goncourt (*L'Innommable,* 154) becomes in translation the Pulitzer Prize (*The Unnamable,* 379).

gong: with its variant the bell or whistle, the gong has the force of a theological imperative. It reminded SB of his **mother**, for it was struck at **Cooldrinagh** to summon the family to dinner. To **MacGreevy** (19 October 1930), SB said he was doing nothing but sitting in an armchair listening for the gong. **Molloy** hears the bell for the last lap (81), and, about to "lapse" into the ditch (91), hears a distant gong (see **forest murmurs**), to which he replies with his **bicycle** horn. In "**Coups de gong**" characters sink to the arrhythmic strokes of a gong. Related sounds include: **Quin** ringing bells in the drafts of *Watt,* "as a sign to Watt that he could clear away"; **Clov**'s reliance on **Hamm**'s whistle in *Endgame;* the whistle in "**Act Without Words I**"; the "Faint single chime" of *Footfalls;* and the piercing bell of *Happy Days,* awakening

Winnie and assuring her that someone is looking, caring for her still. SB participated in a London recording of his works by Jack **MacGowran** and Denys Hawthorne (February 1966), made for Claddagh Records and broadcast by the BBC (March 8), striking a simple dinner gong to separate one extract from another (Knowlson, 479).

"Good Heavens": an early manuscript (RUL 1227/7/16/4) of part of a play in English, a forerunner of *Come and Go*, the titular phrase whispered in the characters' ears, an indictment of **God**'s mercy. It features three characters (**A**, **B**, and **C**), secrets exchanged between two in the absence of the third, and how each is "looking." This version is longer and more explicit, the terminal nature and likely duration of the absent one's ailment spelled out more fully.

Gorgias (483–375 BC): of Leontini; a Sophist who took the Void to its epistemological conclusion. **Burnet** outlines his reasoning (*Greek Philosophy*, 120): "he sought to prove (1) that there is **nothing**, (2) that even if there is anything, we cannot know it, and (3) that, even if we could know it, we could not communicate our knowledge to anyone else." Gorgias, says Burnet, first contended that "What is not" *is* not, that is to say, it *is* just as much as "what is."

Gorman, Mrs.: the fishwoman who pleases **Watt** greatly (in the absence of other qualities) with her distinguished carriage, acquired from carrying her basket of fish (139); in the manuscripts she was called "Mrs Piscoe." Presumably the

wife of the stationmaster, Mr. Gorman, she has had other admirers before, after, and during him. An older Gorman appears in "The **Old Tune**," reduced to playing a barrel organ in the street. He refers to his wife's hospitalization: "Still in it, still in it, but for how long."

Gottesfreund: *der grosse Gottesfreund von Oberlande*, imputed author of many texts from the mystical Gottesfreunde, a literary deception perpetuated by Ruland Merswin (1307–82), patrician of the Order of St. John in Strasbourg. **Inge** notes (*Christian Mysticism*, 180) that the society was based in Basel but he does not use the German name; Pilling suggests (DN, 88) that SB derived it from the *Britannica* article on "**Mysticism**." *Dream* (185).

Gout, Goddess of: see **Burton** (II.1.3, 298): "Lucian makes Podagra (the gout) a goddess, and assigns her priests and minister." The Alexandrian satirist's *Podagra* depicts the triumph of the gouty (*podagros*) over the doughty (*podargos*). The Goddess calls on her Pains to assail every joint; her opponents venture an ineffective ointment. A Doan's Pill was a popular patent remedy for backache. *Murphy* (220).

Graves, Mr.: the gardener in *Watt*, who comes to the back door four times a day (in the **Olympia** and first **Grove** editions [142] three times, an error silently corrected). Watt likes him because he pronounces "th" so charmingly: "Turd and fart, he said, for third and fourth" (143). All his married life he has got on with his wife "like a house on fire" (compare

"**Draff**") but lately has been unable to do so. He is willing on Arthur's advice to give **Bando** a try. The name "Graves" was a late addition. In *Mercier and Camier* (47) a Mr. Graves enters the pub, and in "**Text 2**" (107) the narrator passes the farm of the Graves brothers.

greatcoat: the distinguishing (if undistinguished) outer garb of many of SB's characters. During his *Wanderjahre* SB owned such a coat, inherited from his **father**, who had bought it for motoring; SB in turn donated it to his characters, though not those of *Dream* or *MPTK*. **Murphy's mind** pictures itself as hermetically closed (107), and his body self-contained, sealed in its nonporous greatcoat of aeruginous green, into the composition of which much *felt* (sensation) and *size* (extension) has entered (72). Murphy in **motion** embodies the atom (**Democritus**), or the monad (**Leibniz**); he is a **microcosm**. Or, better, as in **Swift**'s *Tale of a Tub,* its puff of clothes and appearances over essences, a "microcoat." Murphy's greatcoat is not quite vapor tight, for when **Celia** gives it "a bit of a dinge" it fills out, "as a punctured ball will not retain an impression" (141). The boys in the road are playing football; a football is the everyday embodiment of the mystical **Pythagorean** dodecahedron; Murphy hisses as he sets off to work. A strange image suggests itself: a thorn in the side of the hermetic sphere, the monad spiked by the exigencies of a **Job**, and a hiss as the vital element of air escapes.

Watt wears the "same" greatcoat. When first seen (16), he looks like a parcel, a carpet, a roll of tarpaulin tied about the middle. The coat is not mentioned again until page 217, where it is described as still green here and there, and of a length as to hide his trousers. It was bought secondhand, from a meritorious widow, by Watt's father, and has since remained unwashed, "except imperfectly by the rain, and the snow, and the sleet, and of course occasional fleeting immersion in canal water." The material is thick and strong; it buttons up the front; patches of velvet cling to the collar; the skirts are not divided. In *First Love* (29), this coat is part of the narrator's "travelling costume"; in "The **Expelled**" (59) it impedes his efforts to leave by the window; in "The **Calmative**" (65) it is green with a velvet collar, "such as motorists wore about 1900, my father's"; but in "The **End**" (78) it is burned with his other clothes. **Mercier and Camier** share the one coat, and the handkerchief in its pocket. When **Molloy** sees **A** and **C** (9), they are wearing greatcoats, as is he (14), his **hat** fastened to its buttonhole. It is recalled by the **Unnamable** (305). **Malone** includes his coat in his inventory (227–28), much deteriorated: the thread of its sleeves bare and frayed but the collar intact, being of velvet or shag; green "predominates," cab or bottle green. The buttons are now cylindrical pegs but, like Murphy's coat, the material looks like felt and retains dints and dinges: "So much for this coat."

Woburn in "**Cascando**" wears "the same old coat"; the narrator in "**Heard in the Dark I**" describes "The skirts of the greatcoat resting on the snow" (248); and in *Film* (164) "**O**" is wrapped in the "Long dark overcoat," which seals him from the world. In *That Time* (232) C recalls "the old green holeproof coat your father left you," and A "the old green greatcoat." The garment links diverse memories to one center of **consciousness**. The protagonist of *From an Abandoned Work* (161) rejects his "long coat" and cannot bear its flapping about his legs; his "sudden violent dislike" is explicable in terms of an unhappy homelife and the coat having been his father's. *All Strange Away* (169) is ambivalent: "the old hat and coat like after the war, no, not that again." Yet *Stirrings Still* features the "Same hat and coat as of old" (260); in "**Ghost Trio**" F is dressed in the familiar old coat; and in ". . . **but the clouds . . .**" M1 emerges from the shadow in his greatcoat and hat. The coat thus asserts "identity" even as **character** and **memory** fade.

Greco, El: Doménikos Theotokópoulos (1541–1614). Born in Crete, he studied under Titian and worked in Toledo. His tortured spirituality found expression in cold bluish tones and exaggerated figures. The **Alba**'s eyes are as "big and black as El Greco painted" in his *Burial of the Count of Orgaz* (1586); the "debauched" eyes are those of the young person looking at the painter while Saints Stephen and **Augustine** lower the coffin into its grave (*Dream*, 174).

green and yellow: the decay of **nature**, the emerald in its sere, as in *Mercier and Camier* (109): "the pretty colours, expiring greens and yellows vaguely speaking; they grow paler and paler still but only the better to pierce you, will they ever die, yes, they will." The vegetative world of decay and **death** is set against patterns of **blue and white** and **red and gray**, with

their suggestions, however ironic, of religious aspiration and life and death. The green eyes of the **Smeraldina**, those of the doomed Peggy **Sinclair**, pervade the "green **tulips**" of "**Enueg II**" and *Dream* (28), shining like an anthrax. *Murphy* in the **Whoroscope Notebook** was to have assumed the colors of the rainbow, but only a faint iridescence (2) is left as these gave way to **Braque**-like shades. The "green and yellow melancholy" (*Twelfth Night,* II.iv.116) is present in **Neary**'s "salts of lemon" (**suicide**) and a vision of green and yellow in a puddle (229). **Celia** has green eyes and yellow hair, but shaken by the **Old Boy**'s death the clear green of her eyes is "silted with yellow" (137). Murphy forces back his lids (106) so that the yellow oozes into his skull and a belch comes wet and foul from the green old days ("salad days"). The sky is "aerugo" in "**Ding-Dong**" (38), and "viridescent" in *Murphy* (152). **Watt**'s moon (30) is "an unpleasant yellow colour," not unlike the incessant yellow light in *The Lost Ones*. Mr. **Hackett** watches the "long greens and yellows" of the evening, the dying day (9). Murphy's **greatcoat** is aeruginous (71). Watt's was once green and his **hat** yellow (218); now the coat is yellow, and the hat green. The hat of his hallucinatory double is like an inverted chamber pot, "yellow with age, to put it politely" (226). The **Polar Bear** ("A Wet Night," 80; *Dream,* 235) and Murphy (31) turn yellow, SB having noted from **Burton** (III.3.1.ii, 634): "He turned a little yellow—as well he might." The title "**Yellow**" may reflect that phrase. The impulse to "paint" thus did not persist after the early fiction, except in "The **Image**" (167), where the narrator is in the morn of life, with "green tweeds yellow boots cowslip or such like in the buttonhole," set against his red hair, the "black and pink" penis of the **dog**, and the "blue and white" sky above the **horse** and mud. The "colors" of rhetoric help create the "Image."

Greene, Robert (1560–92): Elizabethan dramatist and poet, known for his learned wit and dissipated life; he fed his muse (said **Dekker**) on fat capon, burnt sack and sugar, and shortened his days by keeping company with pickled herrings (a surfeit of which caused his final illness). Reviled by his fellows for attacking other dramatists (he decried **Shakespeare** as "an upstart crow beautified with our feathers"). SB read widely in Greene's works and "Catch-cony life" (*First Love*, 32), and when "Londonizing" *Murphy* included three of Greene's fine feathers: the miasma of legal terms (79) at Lincoln's Inn Fields (cross-biting, conycatching, sacking, and figging); the song "Weep not, my wanton," from *Menephon* (235); and the motif "one thief was saved" (213) from Greene's "Repentance." His recantation concludes with an allusion to **Augustine** and the **two thieves**, which so appealed to SB that he made it henceforth his own.

Grock: Charles Adrien Wettach (1880–1959), Swiss **clown** famous for his wit and musical virtuosity; SB may have known his early biography, translated as *Life's a Lark* (London: Heinemann, 1931). His cry of "Nicht möglich" ("Not possible"), with agonized variations, winds in comic despair through *Dream* and "A **Wet Night**." In "**Yellow**" (163),

Belacqua decides in favor of "**Bim and Bom**, Grock, **Democritus**," but the joke is on him.

Grove Press: on 18 June 1953, Barney Rosset, new owner and sole editor of a fledgling press, wrote to a new author, promising to make his work known in America. That letter from an obscure American publisher to a little-known author began one of the most extraordinary relationships in publishing history, as Rosset guided a small reprint house, which he bought in 1951 for $3,000, into the most aggressive, innovative, audacious, politically active, and often reckless publishing concern in the United States. Throughout SB remained a featured author, and their relationship grew from *Waiting for Godot* until SB's death.

It seemed an unlikely association: a classically educated taciturn Irish artist and a scrappy, street-smart American entrepreneur (with some Irish on his mother's side). They were nearly a generation apart in age (Barnett T. Rosset, Jr., born in Chicago May 28, 1922), but over thirty-five years a bond developed between the upstart American bent on challenging restrictions in publishing and the upstart Irishman bent on challenging the traditions of Western literature. The relationship was mutually influential. Rosset urged his author to translate his own novels, and encouraged SB to return to writing in English. SB soon produced *All That Fall* and *Krapp's Last Tape*, and thereafter wrote in both languages. In 1963 Rosset commissioned a film script; the result was *Film*, SB's one true film. Two years before his death, SB dedicated

Stirrings Still to Rosset. SB in turn steeled Rosset for his crusade against **censorship** (qv), stating that certain matters he was not prepared to mitigate. Duly warned, indeed exhilarated, Rosset persevered not only with SB's "obscenities of form" but to publish in 1959 the unexpurgated *Lady Chatterley's Lover* (which Sylvia Beach had rejected in 1928) and Miller's *Tropic of Cancer.* Over the next three decades he would publish virtually all of SB's works under the Grove imprint or in *Evergreen Review* (qv).

The *Eleutheria* affair

In 1986 Parisians honored the eightieth birthday of their adopted son. The Center Pompidou sponsored a weeklong celebration of SB's work, with lectures, exhibits, performances, and a special issue of the *Revue D'Esthétique.* SB absented himself, as usual. He met friends quietly, but spent most of the time at Ussy. On his birthday, back in Paris, he attended a small reception at La Coupole, which he had avoided for two decades, preferring the Falstaff around the corner or the hygienic anonymity of the Hôtel PLM, near his Boulevard St. Jacques apartment. As a group sipped drinks at the Bar Américain, Rosset entered in a flurry announcing that he had been discharged from Grove, the company he had built, brought to international prominence, and run for thirty-three years. The mood shifted. It seemed impossible that Rosset could be separated from Grove; he *was* Grove Press. But he had sold it a year earlier in an ef-

fort to recapitalize. The new owners, Ann Getty and Lord Weidenfeld, had pledged to keep Rosset on for five years as editor in chief, but his contract stipulated that he served at their pleasure, and they were displeased at his inability to adapt to the new corporate structure.

When SB arrived at eight he asked what could be done. Rosset shrugged and muttered, "Start over, I guess." Perhaps he might find something in the trunk to help Rosset begin yet again? They met several times to work out details. The obvious choice was *Dream,* but this remained sensitive. Something of a roman à clef, it featured a transparent alter ego of the author, and some still alive would be embarrassed by its publication. SB settled on *Eleutheria,* inscribing a copy to BR to seal the agreement, then withdrew to Ussy to translate it. This proved difficult. SB soon abandoned it, as it meant re-creating a play written four decades earlier. Rosset was disappointed, but SB offered instead three short prose works called *Stirrings Still,* dedicated to Rosset and published in a collector's edition under his Blue Moon imprint (1988) and as a trade paperback in his North Star Line (1993).

Rosset never abandoned *Eleutheria.* After Grove changed hands again he considered his agreement null. He wrote to Jérôme **Lindon** (3 March 1993), suggesting that they publish *Eleutheria* in cooperation, without the confusion and legal battles that had surrounded *Dream.* Lindon (5 March 1993) was equivocal, suggesting negotiation, but stressing SB's *interdictum.* Rosset commissioned a second translation from Albert Bremel and took a copublisher, John Oakes and Dan Simon's Four Walls Eight Windows, forming **Foxrock**, Inc., to publish the play. Negotiations grew acrimonious, both publishers convinced that they had SB's best interests at heart. Lindon was trying to fulfill SB's wishes to the letter; BR was acting through the imperative that had driven his thirty-three years at Grove, that major work by major writers should not be suppressed. And SB *had* offered the play to him in 1986.

In September 1994 Rosset decided to bring the play to broad attention with a public reading in New York. Edward Beckett denounced this to the *New York Times,* threatening legal proceedings. That scared off the New York Theater Workshop, where the reading had been scheduled; they asked Rosset to post a $25,000 bond, which he could not do. Undeterred, Rosset gathered the audience outside the workshop and led them through the streets, to his apartment building where space was found for thirteen actors and a hundred guests. By November the acrimony had increased. The Estate discharged Rosset as SB's theatrical agent, and Lindon wrote to Oakes and Simon, warning that they would prosecute all accessories to the illicit action.

Just as a protracted court battle seemed inevitable the issues were resolved. A third translation was commissioned from Michael Brodsky, and Lindon published the play in French before its English appearance. His "Avertissment" states that he was doing so against his better judgment, since "tous les vrais connaisseurs de son travail que j'ai connus considéraient comme une piéce ratée." Rosset thought such judgments best left to history, given that SB was often overcritical of his own work and that Lindon himself had pressured SB to publish another *oeuvre inachevé, Mercier et Camier* (Minuit, 1970; Grove, 1974). Fortunately, an agreement was negotiated. Grove has never published *Eleutheria* but included *Stirrings Still* in *The Complete Short Prose* (1995).

Guggenheim, Peggy (1898–1979): art collector and patron. Leaving the Jacobi School she became a radical bohemian in **Paris**, where in 1941, after and during a promiscuous life, she married Max Ernst. Peggy was sexually liberated, with an original mind. She began an affair with SB on Boxing Day 1937; the details, mostly amusing, are recounted in Bair (273–91), Cronin (281–83), and Knowlson (262–65). The relationship was short but intense, Peggy "obsessed" but SB less so. About then (he was involved with Adrienne Bethell and had met Suzanne) he commented that sex without **love** was like "taking coffee without brandy," which Peggy interpreted as being herself the brandy. The relationship survived as an unusual friendship, a passion for **art** (Peggy opened avant-garde art galleries in **London**, New York, and Venice) the common bond. She asked his advice about collecting, and offered him work translating for her gallery or writing for Mesen's *London Bulletin.* In her memoir, *Out of This Century* (1946), Peggy discusses SB, whom she calls "**Oblomov**." The book contains "They Come," the French version of which ("**elles viennent**") was published that year in *Poèmes 38–39.* See also her *Confessions of an Art Addict* (1960).

gulf: a metaphor for the incommensurability of finite and infinite, the **scholastic** disjunction between *esse in intellectu* and *esse in re,* or the gap between subject and **object**, as in *Proust* (31): that "gouffre interdit à nos sondes," from **Baudelaire**'s "Le Balcon." SB was fascinated by "the great gulf that separates Lazarus and Dives" (see **Abraham's bosom**), that between the preterit and the saved (**goats and sheep**), or the self and world ("**Text 5**," 118–19). **Schopenhauer** notes (*WWI,* II.2.xix, 450) the "impassable gulf" between a great man and a fool. **Psychoanalysis** should "bridge the gulf" (*Murphy,* 177), but **Murphy** dreads that between himself and the inmates (236). It is finally one over which he cannot pass.

"Günter Eich zum Gedächtnis": "In Memory of Günter Eich." Eich was an Austrian poet (1907–72) who served in World War II and as an American POW. He joined Gruppe 47, advocating a literature of **political** engagement but trying to decontaminate it of its Nazi past. SB dedicated to Eich a prose work (see **"As the Story Was Told"**) for the tribute, *Günter Eich zum Gedächtnis,* hrsg. von Siegfried Unseld (Frankfurt: Suhrkamp, 1975), 10 and 12, Ger. trans. (by Wolfgang Hildesheimer) 11 and 13.

H

Habakkuk: Old Testament prophet who asks **God** to account for the burden of sin and the iniquities about him. Invoked in "**Dortmunder**" ("mard of all sinners"), and by Mr. **Knott** (*Watt,* 209), with reference to God knows what. A poem in the **Olympia** *Watt* (49), deleted from the **Grove** (45), rhymes "East India Runner Duck" with "Habbakuk" (*sic*).

habit: SB's *Proust* articulates the thesis (18–23) that the laws of **memory** are subject to habit, defined as the compromise between the individual and his environment, "the ballast that chains the **dog** to his vomit" (Proverbs 26:11: "As a dog returneth to his vomit, so a fool returneth to his folly"). In sum: "Breathing is habit. Life is habit." Habit protects us from the suffering of being. Only when the **object** is seen as particular and unique may it be a source of enchantment; habit lays a veto on such perception. It is an infliction, as it opposes the exaltation of the real, but a blessing, in that it palliates the cruelty (35). Life is a pendulum oscillating between two extremes: suffering, which opens a window on the real (the condition of artistic experience), and boredom, which insulates. Changes of routine or the advent of **desire** may set it aside, but otherwise there is boredom, ennui. Even **friendship** is somewhere between fatigue and ennui (65), a function of habit.

Voluntary memory is related to habit. **Proust** asserts that we are creatures of habit, but a germ of salvation is offered by involuntary memory, or apprehension in the absence of habit, awareness of the unfamiliar. Although largely motivated by will, Marcel has a will-less aspect, which works on data unused by habit and stores them in metaphoric **vases** (*Proust,* 73), preserved from the scrutiny of voluntary memory. If habit is relaxed, involuntary memory may enter, the experience of the past restored through imagination. This constitutes the Proustian moment, the **madeleine** experience of the will-less self, memory independent of will. Such moments are valuable, for they break the chains of habit, but in SB's writing they are underpinned by a ruthless cynicism. He does not deny the experience but, unlike **Joyce**, who affirmed life through the epiphany, he distrusts its ultimate significance.

In *Dream* (75) the **Mandarin** proclaims that "Der Men[s]ch ist ein Gewohnheitstier" ("Man is a creature of habit"). Likewise his universe: in "**Yellow**" (166) the sun is "that creature of habit," shining, as in *Murphy,* "on the nothing new" (Ecclesiastes 1:9). Charles Juliet noted Bram **van Velde**'s conviction that to paint the inner life the artist must forgo the human urge to create superficial certainties: "He must keep the deadening force of habit at bay" (*Conversations,* 5). **Malone** tells stories to do so, something the **Unnamable** calls "the grace of inurement" (350). He notes the "dulling effect of habit" (367), a phrase echoed in **Vladimir**'s "habit is a great deadener" (*WG*, 58.b). Vladimir and **Estragon** enact familiar encounters ("You again") and play out social rituals, meaningless activities that pass the **time**. They are like two actors unsure of their roles, their routine, a **pun** picked up in *Endgame* (32), when **Clov** asks, "Why this farce, day after day?" Hamm replies: "Routine. One never knows." But one does know: patterns will be repeated, lines rehearsed, action replayed. Something is taking its course, but as for its meaning something, "Ah that's a good one."

Hackett: Hunchy Hackett, a minor character who initiates the inaction of *Watt*. Watching the evening fade he is approached by the **Nixons**, to whom he reads "To Nelly" (12) and tells how he fell off the **ladder** (15–16), anticipating **Arsene**'s metaphysical sense of "existence off the ladder" (44). All three observe the arrival of **Watt**, and Mr. Hackett demands an explanation of this strange figure. None is forthcoming, and the Nixons depart, leaving him alone, in the dark. The episode foreshadows the story to come, in terms of what can be known, which is not much. Mr. Hackett does not reappear, which constitutes an affront to narrative structure. Looking back on the games he used to play, **Malone** recalls that if he needed a hunchback one would come running, "proud as punch" (not in the **French**). The name suggests Francis Hackett (1883–1962), a minor **Dublin** author of historical fiction.

Haeckel, Ernst (1834–1919): German philosopher and natural historian; au-

thor of *The Riddle of the Universe* (trans. 1900), in which SB found the amniotic or **embryonic** soul. Known for his dictum that "ontogeny recapitulates phylogeny," Haeckel links man's psychic activity to the development of the insect and discusses the "**larval stage**" of embryonic formation, emphasizing its complex psychic nature. This accounts for the "Imago" of "**Malacoda**," and underlies **Celia**'s experience in *Murphy* (chapter 5) of being embedded in a jelly of light. The image enters *The Unnamable* as **Worm**, and determines the phylogeny of "larval man" in *How It Is,* imagined as "mad or worse transformed à la Haeckel" (42).

Hafiz: Shams-ud-din Mohammed (1300–88); Sufi poet whose *ghazals* celebrate wine and song. His sobriquet applies to one who has learned the Koran by heart. Cited with **Saadi** (DN, 88), SB misspelling his name as "Hatiz" there as in *Dream* (62), where he is listed among the melancholy writers.

Hagenbeck, Carl (1844–1913): wild-animal dealer, born in Hamburg. He inherited his **father**'s collection in 1865, built it up, and exhibited it through Europe. The narrator of *First Love* (27) recalls visiting the Ohlsdorf cemetery and finding his grave there, with a lion carved on it.

Hamm: protagonist of *Endgame,* the "ruins of a monster," whose name intrigues: ham, garnished with a clove; a ham actor with a clown; or a variant of "Hamlet," given the theatrical imagery and Hamm's desire to finish his piece. There is a town called Hamm in Picardy, where early drafts of *Fin de partie* are set. SB said during the rehearsals of *Endspiel,* "There must be maximum aggression between them from the first exchange of words onward. Their war is the nucleus of the play" (*Theatrical Notebooks* II). Thus, Hamm as hammer, **Nagg, Clov,** and Nell (*nagel, clou,* and *nail*) as his nails (see **crucifixion**). Mother **Pegg** is a fourth nail. In the **Bible** Ham, the youngest son of Noah, survives the catastrophe to become the "accursed progenitor" of the dark races; for viewing his drunken father he brought a curse on Canaan (Genesis 9 and 10). Clov's line, "But humanity might start from there all over again," asserts the anti-creation theme.

Hapak: in *Dream* (140), as in the typescript, SB's error for the Hamburg-America line *Hapag* (Pilling, *Dream Companion*).

Happy Days: a play in two acts, written in English (1960), and translated as *Oh, les beaux jours.* First published by **Grove Press** (1961; **Evergreen** Books, E-318) and **Faber** (1962). An offprint of page 35 appeared in *Sample* 1 (spring 1962): 6, Faber's publicity brochure. First production at the Cherry Lane Theatre, New York (17 September 1961), dir. Alan **Schneider** with Ruth White as **Winnie** (for which she won an Obie) and John C. Becher as **Willie.** The first **London** production was at the Royal Court Theatre (1 November 1962), dir. George Devine and Tony Richardson, with Brenda Bruce as Winnie (replacing a pregnant Joan Plowright) and Peter Duguid as Willie. SB directed *Glückliche Tage* (in Erika and Elmar **Tophoven's**

translation, revised in production) at the **Schiller-Theater Werkstatt,** Berlin (17 September 1971), with Katharina Schultz (whom SB thought too young) as Winnie and Rudi Schmitt as Willie. Two celebrated revivals opened in London, the first a National Theater production at the Old Vic (April 1975), dir. Peter Hall with Peggy Ashcroft; the second at the Royal Court (June 1979), dir. SB with Billie **Whitelaw,** the latter shown on BBC TV (October 1979) and BBC 2 (12 November 1982). *Oh, les beaux jours* opened at the Teatro del Ridotto for the Venice Theatre Festival (28 septembre 1963) and moved to **Paris** at the Odéon-Théâtre de France (21 octobre), dir. Roger **Blin,** with Madeleine **Renaud** as Winnie and Jean-Louis Barrault as Willie.

The startling opening image, a woman buried to her waist in a scorching desert, retakes the closing image of the Buñuel/ Dalí *Un chien andalou. Happy Days* is less a celebration of **surrealism,** however, than a critique of **humanism.** Winnie's physical world is in ruins, and her mental landscape is catching up. SB wanted the set "to suggest scorched grass—but smooth, i.e. no stones sticking up or such like, nothing to break the monotony of symmetry. What should characterize whole scene, sky and earth, is a pathetic unsuccessful realism, the kind of tawdriness you get in 3rd rate musical or pantomime, that quality of *pompier,* laughably earnest bad imitation" (Harmon, 94). This metatheatrical emphasis is built into the play as SB develops an audience for Winnie's plight: "There floats up— into my thought—a Mr Shower" (41). As SB explained to Schneider, "Shower

& Cooker are derived from German 'schauen' & 'kuchen' (to look). They represent the onlookers (audience) wanting to know the meaning of things" (Harmon, 95). Shower thus voices their questions: "What's she doing? . . . What's it meant to mean? . . . Why doesn't he dig her out?" Winnie files her nails as she narrates, and then, in SB's words, "raises head & let's 'em have it."

Shower's questions remain unanswered, the emphasis shifting to an exhausted couple, an exhausted theatrical tradition, an exhausted culture, an **old earth**. SB wrote to Schneider (9 December 1960): "Two acts, the second considerably shorter than the first. Same set for both. The first problem was how to have her speak alone on stage all the time without speaking to herself or to the audience. Solved that after a fashion." No movement would be possible in the first act except of the upper **body**, none of any kind possible in the second. No help except from the bag, "pockets if it had been a man as was originally the case." In the first act she is embedded up to her waist in a mound, in the second up to her neck, an empty plain, a burning sun: "Scene extended to maximum by painted backcloth in *trompe-l'oeil* as *pompier* as possible. This to give you some idea. Too difficult and depressing to write about . . . Opulent blonde, fiftyish, all glowing shoulders and *décolleté*. Enough, *Gott hilfe mir, amen*" (Harmon, 77).

For SB the play represented profounds best not examined too rationally. As he wrote to George **Reavey** (22 September 1961): "I'm afraid for me it is no more than another dramatic **object**. I am aware vaguely of the hidden impetuses

that are behind its making but their elucidation would prevent the making." The visual image of immobility, Winnie buried up to above her waist, was present in SB's earliest available notes for the play (in a notebook at **Trinity** called *ÉTÉ 56* [summer 1956]). Willie (then Tom) was part of the opening tableau. An early revision eliminated him from the opening, in keeping with the working title, "female solo." SB wanted the audience's attention on Winnie. Her opening lines establish the dramatic conflict between circumstance and attitude with "Another glorious day" and two "Amens" after her silent prayer. Revision of a single word altered the direction of the entire opening, from "glorious" the day became "heavenly." Winnie's plight thus played heavenly bliss against its potential horror, changeless, bland eternity. The contrast was echoed by a quotation from **Milton**'s *Paradise Lost*, the "Holy Light" juxtaposed against Winnie's "blaze of hellish light" (11). In revision SB increased the hostile environment, altering "grassy expanse rising gently" to the final "expanse of scorched grass rising center." The lighting likewise changed from "Strong sunlight" to "Blazing Light."

The horror of heavenly stasis was reinforced by two more changes to Winnie's opening speech. Rather than her morning prayers being inaudible, as first conceived, SB gave her two fragments: "For Jesus **Christ** sake" and "World without end." Horror emerges from these innocent prayers when we realize, as Winnie never does, that the Christian concept of an eternal heaven is the opposite of what SB's characters desire. Winnie wants an end, if only to the day, but heaven is endlessness, the perpetuation of that something that always remains, **consciousness** or the soul. She never explores the implications of her prayers. They remain simply routine, her morning ritual. She thus becomes an ironic victim by her innocent unawareness. Brushing her teeth, she inspects them with (the phrases added to the first typescript): "Good Lord . . . Good **God**." Winnie is not bothered by such incongruities because words have become **habit**. The second act is "as before," even as Winnie is now buried up to her neck. Such change is, however, as superficial as that described in Ecclesiastes: "there is no new thing under the sun. Is there anything whereof it may be said, See, this is new?" Winnie echoes these lines: "Something has seemed to occur, and **nothing** has occurred, nothing at all" (39). The stasis was accented when SB added "no change" twice to Winnie's opening monologue.

Winnie is a creature of the air (like Vladimir), Willie of the earth (like Estragon), wallowing on all fours, often naked. Winnie is mind or spirit, albeit limited and defective, Willie nature or earth. So neat a dichotomy may oversimplify, but it relates **character** to a central premise. Like **Words and Music** and **Voice** and Music in "**Cascando**," Willie and Winnie are cacophonous, aspects of an unharmonious entity. The theme is voiced by Winnie with little understanding: "I know it does not follow when two are gathered together . . . in this way . . . that because one sees the other the other sees the one" (28) (see Matthew 18:20).

As the play ends Willie comes to the fore. Until then awareness of him has been filtered through Winnie, through a consciousness that has failed to see or understand its own plight. Winnie then misreads Willie as one content. He sleeps, unaffected by the bell, enjoys a pornographic postcard, is the brute beast she on occasion envies. But in the final scene Willie, "dressed to kill" (a **pun** reserved for readers), emerges desperate, struggling to attain the one symbol of ending that has been present throughout the play, one that Winnie fails to recognize—the revolver. The audience perceives for the first time a Willie in torment, trying to end his own life, Winnie's, or both. Winnie's response is another misprision. Her attitude toward the gun has been **romantic** and empirical. When first she pulls it from her bag, she gives it a kiss and wonders why natural law has not pulled it to the depths of the bag. But natural laws no longer apply. The decaying gun sits atop the mound throughout the play, a possible means of ending the agony of living, if indeed it functions. The Browning may be more efficacious than poetry for relieving stress. Winnie misreads its potential, however, as she misreads Willie's struggle toward her. His quest only rekindles girlish romance in her. She sings a sentimental waltz duet from *The Merry Widow*, while Willie musters all his strength to end, something that Winnie is incapable of. Willie struggles to end, to "Win," and Winnie sings: "It's true, it's true, you **love** me so!" The two have not united. The day has not ended. All has moved in a symmetrical circle. Tomorrow, to speak in the old style

(**Dante**'s "*dolce stile nuovo*"), and like the theater it may all begin again.

Harcourt Street Station: city terminus of the **Dublin** and South Eastern Railway, the departure point of the **Slow and Easy** to **Foxrock** and **Bray**; the round end rather than the square one (*Watt,* 244), the station having one platform and a turntable. Its "pretty neo-Doric colonnade" is recalled in "**Text 7**" (128–29) as the narrator sits dreaming in the third-class waiting room, the last train going at "twenty-three thirty," then the station closed for the night. On its platform **Watt** bumps into a porter wheeling milk cans, like **Sisyphus**. In *That Time,* the speaker, an old man, returning to the Folly of his youth, finds the terminus "all closed down and boarded up" (231), the colonnade crumbling. The last train departed 31 December 1958, after which the line was closed and the tracks removed.

Hardy, Thomas (1840–1928): Wessex novelist not much admired by SB, who thought his reliance on coincidence excessive. Hence the "vulgarity of a plausible concatenation" (*Proust,* 82). In "**Yellow**" (158) **Belacqua** underlines "a phrase in Hardy's *Tess*"; this is the comment (Chapter 35): "When sorrow ceases to be speculative sleep sees her opportunity" (Tess on her wedding night). SB's **father** had "brought in Tess" when SB was in the Merrion Nursing Home after the operation on his "blasted neck" (SB to TM, 12 December 1932). **Moran** succeeds in dozing off, "which is not so easy, when pain is speculative" (*Molloy,* 102). In the drafts of *Watt* the pedigree

of the famished **dog** is described with speculation as to where it might originate: "Eire? Pelasgia? the Hardy country?" "**Old Earth**," its speaker over the loved one's grave, desiring his **death** that he may be with her, has affinities to Hardy's poems; the lovebird in "**Rough for Theatre II**" sings like the darkling thrush. Dan **Rooney** in *All That Fall,* told that the preacher will be Hardy, asks, "'How to be Happy though Married?'" There was in **Foxrock**, in Kerrymount Avenue, a Rev. E. Hardy (Knowlson, 386), not to be confused with Edward John Hardy, author of *How to be Happy though Married, Being a Handbook to Marriage* (1885) and *Still Happy though Married* (1914). Mrs. Rooney's reply is finely ambiguous: "No no, he died, you remember. No connexion."

hardy laurel: a favorite **pun**. **Wylie** and **Neary** enact Stan Laurel and Oliver Hardy; **Mercier** and **Camier** are respectively a "long hank" and a "little fat one" (48); **A** and **C** appear at the outset of *Molloy,* "one small and one tall." Although nothing requires it, **Estragon** is often played as fat (Hardy), and **Vladimir** as thin (Laurel). Mr. **Knott**'s servants are of these two types. In the *Watt* "**Addenda**" (252), Arthur laughs so much that he has to lean for support "against a passing shrub, or bush, which joined heartily in the joke." He asks an old man the name of this extraordinary growth and is told, "That's what we calls a hardy laurel." The episode appears in all early drafts, anticipating Watt's encounter with Knott in the garden (145–46). *How It Is* invokes (35) "distant perfume of laurel felicity."

Harvey, William (1578–1657): English physician and discoverer of the circulation of the blood (1628). Invoked with affection ("Harvey belovèd") in *Whoroscope* (37–40).

hats: "insignia" that like the "scutal" bowler of "**Malacoda**" or the blue cloth cap of the newsagent (*Watt*, 26) define one's social position. In "**What a Misfortune**" (144), **Belacqua** since the "commitment" of his **Lucy** wears a hat, on the off chance of meeting a cortege. To **MacGreevy** (October 1930), SB complained of his **mother**'s wish to "make a man" of him, that he get a **job**: "They want me to wear a bowler"—anticipating the shabby respectability later vouchsafed the tramps of *Waiting for Godot*, and the rejection in "**Text 8**" (134) of a bowler hat as the "sardonic synthesis of all those that never fitted me." **Murphy** never wears a hat, as it awakes poignant memories of the caul (73); in Otto **Rank**'s *The Trauma of Birth* (91), the loss signifies separation from one's ego. **Cooper** never takes his off until Murphy's death, when he sits on it spectacularly; compare Baron Charlus (Proust, *Guermantes* II.219). **Watt**'s "hard hat" (31) protects him from Lady MacCann. When **Arsene** leaves the house (39) he wears no hat (compare "**He is barehead**"), but Watt retains his grandfather's block hat, then mustard but now pepper in color. The undertaker's man in *Malone Dies* (271) also wears a block hat. These intimations of **birth**, trauma, and **death** suggest that the hat, like the **greatcoat** and **boots**, is more than a trapping of being.

The hat suggests an identity, an entelechy that persists despite the changing self. The protagonist of *First Love* thinks about kepis (joining *La Légion étrangère*), then of the hat his **father** gave him (35). He is reluctant to remove it inside **Lulu**'s house ("I'll treat of my hat some other time perhaps"), but puts it on when he leaves. The narrator of "The **Expelled**" has his thrown after him as he "falls" down the steps. He was given it by his father when his head had attained "its maximum dimensions" (48); it was "as though it had **pre-existed** from time immemorial." In "The **Calmative**," the hat is laced to a buttonhole; the "Other" requests it in exchange for a mysterious phial but is refused vehemently (74). As the narrator of "Text 1" **puns** when his hat is lost (103), he was attached to it. The narrator of "The **End**" inherits the garments of a dead man, his having been burnt; the hat is too small, "then it got used to me" (79). He learns to doff it courteously, says he has resolved the problem by wearing a kepi (echoing *First Love*), then denies that (83). The hat proves useful as a **pot** when he milks a cow (90).

The divesting of hat from self in *Three Novels* leads to the state of unaccommodated man. **Molloy**'s hat is fastened to the buttonhole of his greatcoat by a long lace (as Gulliver in Lilliput). He notices (10) that **C** wears a cocked hat, but **A** is bareheaded. His "craving for a fellow" (15) is expressed as his soul's leap, at the end of its elastic (11), a conceit that aligns the hat with Cartesian images like the kite. Molly panics when he thinks **Lousse** has burned his hat (44); he tries to throw it away, but it comes back with the lace (61). He fears losing his hat (90) for, lost in the dark wood, how might he salute a lady? **Moran**'s boater (126), fastened on his head with an elastic fixed to two holes in the brim, suggests his dubious identity with Molloy. Malone is visited (146) by a stranger who takes off his hat ("I shall not attempt to describe it") to reveal a shock of dirty snow-white hair. **Macmann**'s hat should have followed him as he rolls on the ground but it does not, remaining behind like a thing forsaken (246); how it returns is a mystery, but he will not stir a step without it (284). The **Unnamable** recognizes Malone's brimless hat but wonders if it is Molloy wearing Malone's hat (293). His confusion testifies to a sustained identity among all three.

As the action moves within the head, the hat loses its signifying power, save in pieces such as *That Time* and "**Ohio Impromptu**" (**Joyce**'s Latin Quarter hat), or in set scenes, such as **Clov**'s possible exit from *Endgame* ("Panama hat, tweed coat") or **Willie** "dressed to kill" in his top hat at the end of *Happy Days*. The bowlers worn by **Vladimir**, **Estragon**, and **Pozzo** make a complex semiotic statement. One comic highlight of *Godot* is the parody of the hat-swapping routine from the Marx brothers' *Duck Soup*, culminating in **Lucky**'s torrent of words that comes to an end only when his hat is seized and thrown to the ground. It is his thinking cap, and in that casual quip and brutal denouement resides the entire paradigm of **absurdity**.

Havel, Václav (b. 1936): Czech playwright who studied at the Prague Academy for Dramatic Art, worked as a theater stagehand, and became resident writer for the Theatre on the Balustrade

(1960–69). He was imprisoned in 1979 for four years for support of human rights and his part in the "Velvet Revolution," including his membership in the Committee for the Defense of the Unjustly Persecuted (VONS) and his signing of the Charter 77 manifesto. SB's "**Catastrophe**" (1982) was dedicated to Havel, its silent Protagonist a tribute to one whose defense of human rights led to his own **voice** being banned. Havel wrote to SB after his release, to speak of the impact SB's work had on his own and to tell him how much the gesture had meant. His later play *Mistake* was dedicated to SB and written in homage to "Catastrophe," sharing with it a central character who says nothing ("a bloody foreigner . . . Well, that's his bloody funeral") throughout brutal interrogation. English translations of both works were printed together in the *Index on Censorship* 13 (February 1984): 11–15, with Havel's letter to SB. "Catastrophe" and *Mistake* were produced as a double bill at the Stockholm Stadsteater (29 November 1983) as part of an evening of solidarity with Havel and his fellow Czech dissidents (Brater, 140).

hawthorn: associated with **Proust**'s pre-**madeleine** experience in the "Combray" section of *Du côté de chez Swann,* as Marcel and his father return home along a path throbbing with the fragrance of hawthorn. Marcel is overcome by a mysterious longing and attracted by one whose flowers are pink. At this moment he has his first vision of Gilberte, associated thereafter for him with the budding of blossom. Hence the enormity of the opening of *Dream:* an overfed **Belacqua**

pedaling frenziedly down "a frieze of hawthorn" until halted by the prospect of a defecating **horse** (less a critique of the Proustian moment than a deliberate affront to it). The **Expelled** lies in the gutter until roused from the reverie of a landscape "charming with hawthorn and wild roses" (47); **Molloy** lies in the ditch beside his bicycle (27), the hawthorn stooping toward him. See **flowering currant** and **verbena**.

Hayden, Henri (1883–1970): French painter of Polish-Jewish ancestry whom SB met in **Roussillon**. A member of the late Cubist movement, he later painted landscapes and still lifes. SB contributed a few brief introductions to his work: "Henri Hayden, homme-peintre," a short article (janvier 1952), for a special number of *Arts-documents* (Geneva) 22 (novembre 1955), 2 (*Disjecta*, 146–47). This appeared in *Henri Hayden: Recent Paintings* (London: Waddington Galleries, 1959), and in Jean Selz's *Hayden* (Genève: Éditions Pierre Callier, 1962), 40–41, which contains two Roussillon landscapes. SB acknowledged *Cinquante annés de peinture* for the catalogue of the Hayden retrospective exhibition, Musée des Beaux-Arts de Lyon, 1960, and wrote an anonymous note (Juin 1960) for an exhibition at the Galerie Suillerot, Paris (*Disjecta*, 150). The two tributes were reprinted in *Hayden: Soixante ans de peinture* (Paris: Musée National d'Art Moderne, 1968), with a third "text" (complete): "Plus il va, plus c'est beau." The common theme is SB's admiration for this solitary painter and his works that reflect a patient silence. SB donated three Hayden works to the **BIF**: a black-and-white ink drawing of Roussillon (presented January 1973 [RUL 1227/3/11]) and two framed and glazed color-wash sketches of trees (RUL 1227/3/15), and of Roussillon (RUL 1227/3/16) (presented April 1973). A fourth work, a glazed still life in oils (RUL 1227/3/14), was presented to the archive by Mme. Josette Hayden (1972).

Haydn, Josef (1732–1809): Austrian composer, mentor of **Mozart**. SB's first published work may have been a sonnet titled "To the Toy Symphony," when he was at **Portora**. *Murphy* cites (195) the opinion of the "decaying Haydn" on cohabitation as "Parallel thirds." Haydn married in 1760 Maria Anna Keller, daughter of a wig maker, preferring her younger sister Josepha, who entered a convent. The marriage was not a success, and the couple spent most of their lives apart. "Parallel fifths" imply harmony, "parallel thirds" discord. SB had used "consecutive thirds" in *Whoroscope* (6). Haydn was a composer of whom SB was fond; several Haydn scores were found at **Ussy** after his **death** (Knowlson, 722).

"Heard in the Dark I" and "II": two consecutive extracts from a work then in progress, *Company* (1980). The former was sent to John **Calder** for publication in *New Writing and Writers* 17 (1980): 11–12; the latter was drawn from sections 58 and 59 of the notebook and sent for publication in *JOBS* 5 (1979): 7–8. Both were reprinted in *Collected Shorter Prose* (1984), 203–7 and again in *As the Story Was Told* (1990), 83–96, the latter appearing jointly from Calder's short-lived American imprint, Riverrun Press. **Grove** published both in *Complete Short*

Prose (1995), 247–52. "**Heard in the Dark I**" (¶ 39 of *Company*) depicts one walking on a snowy spring morning "across the white pasture afrolic with lambs in spring and strewn with red placentae." This is a walk made alone since his **father** (or father's shade) no longer accompanies him. Rather than the "beeline" he thought he was making, he sees in the snow the counterclockwise pattern of **Dante**'s inferno: "Withershins." This springtime episode with its anti-pastoral imagery is heard as from another and of another, or re-created by one, a **consciousness** lying in the dark, hence the title. "**Heard in the Dark II**" (¶40) offers the **memory** of a **summerhouse**, where he recalls meeting a lover during his "Bloom of adulthood," the bloom apparently a fetus in the partner whose breasts and belly have swelled. It will be nipped in the bud, as the closing image suggests "That dead still."

Hegel, Georg (1770–1831): German philosopher in the Kantian tradition. His influence during the nineteenth century was considerable, in **politics** through Marx, but many Protestant theologians adopted his doctrines, attracted by his sense of the absolute, his doctrine of the state, and his dialectical reasoning. SB, unimpressed, preferred Hegel's rival **Schopenhauer**. In *Murphy* he parodies Hegel as **Neary** (based on the Hegelian scholar H. S. Macran), who achieves an unsatisfactory "sublation," failing to reach (by negativity or antithesis) the higher category of thought. The tripartite structure of *How It Is* implies the dialectical model (before **Pim**, with Pim, after Pim), but there is no synthesis, no

transcendence, only a denial of the absolute in favor of the conclusion earlier reached by **Molloy** (13), that the whole ghastly business looks like what is: "senseless, speechless, **issueless** misery."

"**He is barehead**": "**Fizzle 1**," translation of "**Foirade I**": "**Il est tête nue.**" First published in *Foirades/Fizzles,* a deluxe edition ($75), with thirty-three original etchings by Jasper Johns; then separately in *Tri-quarterly* 38 (winter 1977): 163–67. The title echoes **Molloy**'s recollection of **A** or **C**: "He was bare-headed" (11). "He is barehead" (1973) opens the American *Fizzles* (Grove, 1976) and French *Pour finir encore et autres foirades* (Minuit, 1976); it is third in *For to End Yet Again, and Other Fizzles* (Calder, 1976). The protagonist, dressed in "vaguely prison garb," journeys through a lightless, damp, unfathomable, **issueless** labyrinth. His experiences are tactile; that he is bareheaded and barefoot he knows by sensory experience. His choices of direction seem random, impulsive, constrained by physical impediments. He knows to stop when he crashes into a wall. He has a vague association with **Murphy**, both having good legs, but that seems as tenuous as the life described by a disinterested narrator seems purely biological. The dark seems impenetrable, but he is observed by a narrator who guides the reader, **motion** reduced to its **fundamental sound**. Unforgettable experiences are said to be sensory—*maxima* (steepest incline, loudest sound) and *minima* (least steep, least loud)—and transitory, temporarily glorified as they are replaced by others, greater and lesser. The narrator draws what inferences he can: "little by little his history takes shape" (227). In the final sentence a lengthy new motif, bones, is promised, but the narrative, well, fizzles.

"Hell Crane to Starling": a twenty-five-line poem published in *The European Caravan* (1931): 475–76, but not permitted by SB to be reprinted (except in Harvey, 303–4). He had this piece particularly in mind when condemning his early work as "showing off," dismissing its display of erudition as "the work of a very young man with nothing to say and the itch to make." The poem is ostentatious, but, that overcome, it is hilarious, an irreverent variation on "Come live with me and be my **love**." The title alludes to **Dante**'s *Inferno* (V.40–51), the story of Paolo and Francesca, of whose infidelity the starling and crane are emblems, but the **voice** is that of one wooing "Oholiba" (*Aholibah,* whore of Egypt, Ezekiel 23:1–4). His petition embraces whoredom and adultery in various Old Testament stories, with the enticement of an ass in a cave above Tsoar, and stout and potatoes *impurées,* fine fodder in the "Saorstat," or Irish Free State. Hippolytus, son of Theseus, refused to pollute his **father**'s bed when his stepmother Phaedra fell in love with him; hence "Hippolitus-in-hell." Harvey comments parenthetically (273) that the poem is "more a lecherous leer than the recalled emotion of authentic experience," but he fails to appreciate the witty lepp into Oirish as Old Testament stories are retold in the peasant idiom of **Synge**. For a bitter variation, linking the poem to SB's affair with Mary **Manning**, see **"To My Daughter."**

Henry, Paul: Irish landscape artist (1877–1958) renowned for his effects of light (O'Brien, 100). His Wicklow Mountains are seen through an anti-dazzle windscreen ("Draff," 203).

hens: recurrent emblems in SB's world of the futility of existence, culminating in foolish **death**. In *Dream* (190), the **Alba** accuses **Belacqua** of brooding like a sick hen, which he resents, saying he is not brooding but reflecting, and that there is a long poem to be written about hens and eggs. *Whoroscope* is that poem, using the **embryonic** development of the chicken (the shuttle of the ripening egg combing the warp of **Descartes**'s days) to parallel the "hatching" of man into death. There is something ghoulish in the gusto with which Descartes faces his "abortion of a fledgling" (87), a twinge of **pity** for the life denied. Other instances may be cited: the "grey verminous hens" of "**Enueg I**"; those of **Moran**, and particularly the gray (*Molloy,* 101), which neither brood nor lay but are dead on his return (174); a gray hen, perhaps *the* gray hen, that enters the kitchen in *Malone Dies* (203); and that run over by Mr. **Slocum** in *All That Fall,* like the child on the train, that fate awaiting all. The miracle of life, wondrous in the egg, culminates in the image of a sick hen sitting (like **Job**) in the dust.

Heraclitus (ca. 540–480 BC): citizen of Ephesus, misanthrope and mystic, whose sense of cosmic unity arose from the harmony of opposites, from diversity, the many less real than the one. He believed fire to be the primordial element. SB read the existing fragments closely in the early 1930s, noting such assertions as *all things* *are flowing;* or, *you cannot step twice into the same river.* These are implicit in the gutter of "The **Expelled**" (52) and in **Estragon**'s contention (*WG,* 39.a) that "everything oozes," it's "never the same pus from one second to the next." His sentiment that the sun is new every day is parodied in the opening sentence of *Murphy,* and the "short circuit" of love requited (5) confutes the Heraclitean principle of "the circuit completed by matter in its successive changes in the universe" (Windelband, 49–50). Heraclitus was the "weeping philosopher" of Greek tradition, as opposed to **Democritus**, the laughing one. In "**Yellow**," **Belacqua**, fearing the operation, elects the latter. **Hamm**'s end that is in the beginning is Heraclitean (*Endgame,* 69); "Heraclitus the Obscure" (*How It Is,* 34) is recalled from **Windelband** (30). Little is known of his life, but SB recorded from **Burnet** (131) the account of Heraclitus trying to cure himself of dropsy by wrapping himself in dung. His lasting influence on SB lies in the sense of all existence as flux, a process of continuous becoming, without the **Platonic** assurance of its being somehow immanent to *something.* **Parmenides** held that only what has being is real and regarded all coming to be and passing away as illusion or semblance, but for Heraclitus nothing was permanent. Thus, the impossibility of stating the "I," or of seeing it as coeval with being in *Three Novels,* particularly *The Unnamable.* Much of what is (often glibly) deemed SB's postmodern view of being, ego, and literary **character** is traceable to such **pre-Socratic** contrasts.

Herculaneum: the eruption of Vesuvius (AD 79) destroyed Pompeii and devastated nearby Herculaneum, which was covered by a shower of ashes and cinders and drenched with water, so that the effluvia hardened into a kind of tufa, in places sixty-five feet deep. The deluge acted like clay or plaster of paris, making it possible later to take molds of artifacts and dead bodies "frozen" in the precise positions of the calamity. SB uses the event in *Murphy* (239) of the posture of those asleep in the **asylum**, associating it with the **Lisbon** earthquake as an "act of **God**" that cynically questions that received idea.

Herrick, Robert (1591–1674): Cavalier poet whose *Hesperides* (1647) contain some 1,200 short poems that reveal a subtle lyrical talent. In "**Fingal**" (25) and "**Love and Lethe**" (94) **Belacqua** is attracted by the "sincerities" of his companion, an allusion to Herrick's Julia, a sweet disorder in the dress revealing the fairness of her legs. In *Murphy* (263) the coroner quotes from bitter memory from "The Rose": "But ne're the Rose without the thorn." Herrick's "fair daffodils" are invoked in "**thither**." **Winnie** alludes to Herrick's "To the Virgins, to Make Much of Time"; as **Willie** reappears she asks, "Where are the flowers?" (166), the allusion muted in revision from "Gather ye rosebuds while ye may." Other images from Herrick, such as "Delight in Disorder," time "a-flying," and "The glorious lamp of heaven, the sun," serve as ironic counterpoints to Winnie's plight. Compare the **unnamable**: "For me to gather while I may" (350).

Higgins, Frederick (1896–1941): pioneer of the labor movement then a literary yeoman; friend of Austin **Clarke**. In "**Recent Irish Poetry**" SB mocked "Island Blood" (1925) for accumulating more "By Gods" than all the other **antiquarians** put together, and "Arable Holdings" (1933) for its blackthorn stick and "good smell of dung" (*Disjecta*, 73). He is mocked in *Dream* as Jem Higgins, weight lifter and rugby man but not a literary cove in any sense of the word, who has fallen for the **Alba** "like an angel come down from Heaven in the middle of all those little tarts" (153). SB mentions him to **MacGreevy** (9 April 1936) as "breaking out of the Fire Insurance Co., looking like a fair-isle **Yeats**," adding that he was twice "cut" by Higgins at the National Gallery. He retaliated in *Murphy* by putting Higgins in the **asylum**, the threat of hara-kiri (Higgins admired Japanese poetry) avenging the cuts.

hinny: according to **Darwin** (*Origin of Species,* VIII), "the off-spring of the female ass and stallion." The wider discussion concerns sterility in such crosses. In "**Echo's Bones**" (9), Lord Gall praises the ass above the horse and mule and "ginnet" (Gk. *ginnos*), these last refusing to carry "our Lord," who therefore laid the curse of sterility upon them. Maddy **Rooney** in *All That Fall* (37) speculates that **Christ** rode into Jerusalem on a hinny.

Hippasos (ca. 500 BC): follower of **Pythagoras** and scapegoat expelled from the order for betraying its mysteries, such as the nature of pi or the existence of **irrational** numbers. His drowning was seen as divine retribution for his perfidy. SB cited this detail in *Murphy* (47) and

in "Les **Deux besoins**" (*Disjecta,* 56) from **Burnet**'s *Greek Philosophy.*

"**L'Histoire de Watt**": an extract from part IV of *Watt* published in *Les Lettres nouvelles* (septembre–octobre 1968): 11–16; the full **French** translation appeared early in 1969.

Hogarth, William (1697–1764): English painter and engraver, known for his moral satires *A Harlot's Progress* (1732) and *A Rake's Progress* (1735); in "**Love and Lethe**" (95) **Belacqua** is said to resemble one of his ancient degenerates. Hogarth's treatise *The Analysis of Beauty* (1753) offers the painter's admiration for the sigmoidal form, as in "**Serena III**": "fix this pothook of beauty on this palette."

Hölderlin, Johann Christian Friedrich (1770–1843): Swabian poet whom SB read intently, and whose fusion of the **Romantic** and Classical, pathos and precision, intrigued him. Hölderlin's moody hypersensitivity and **schizophrenia**, lit with brilliant touches, made him a compelling emblem. He is cited in *Dream* (138): "alles hineingeht Schlangen gleich" ("Everything enters like a snake"), the narrator repeating "Schlangen gleich." A fragment of *Hyperions Schicksalsleid* inadequately recalled at the end of *Watt* (239) foreshadows Watt's mental breakdown: "Doch uns ist gegeben / auf keiner Stätte zu ruhn / es geschwinden, es fallen / die leidenden Menschen / blindings von einer / Stunde zur andern, / wie Wasser von Klippe / zu Klippe geworfen / jahrlang ins Ungewisse hinab" ("But it is not given to us to rest in any place; suffering humanity perishes and falls blindly from one hour to another, like water dashed from crag to crag year after year, down into the unknown"). Years later, SB visited the tower in Tübingen where Hölderlin had spent the last years of his life. He glossed *Damals* with a bit from the *Hyperion-Fragment:* "Alles war nun Stille. Wir sprachen kein Wort, / Wir beruehrten uns nicht, wir sahen uns nicht an." Hölderlin's sense of the terror that strikes when we are so close to **nature** that we fear we shall become one with her, devoured by her, deprived of speech and identity by her, yet terrified by our expulsion from her (our silence within, our **solitude** without), equally haunted SB's imagination.

Hole: a town in the **Molloy** Country, whence Jacques Jr. is sent to buy a **bicycle**; in the French text the distance is "quinze milles." The manuscript originally read "Carrick." The cliché ("this hole") is made literal in *The Unnamable* (358), when **Worm** must be dragged out by a hooked pole. In *Not I* (216), the **little girl** is born before her time, into (out of?) this "godforsaken hole called . . . called . . . no matter."

"Homage to James Joyce": SB's brief tribute to **Joyce** ("29.9.80"), in *James Joyce: An International Perspective. Centenary Essays in Honour of the Late Sir Desmond Cochrane. With a Message from Samuel Beckett and a Foreword by Richard Ellmann,* ed. Suheil Badi Bashriu and Bernard Benstock (Colin Smythe, 1982), vii: "I welcome the occasion to bow once again, before I go, deep down, before his heroic work, heroic being."

"The Home-coming": a short story translated by SB from the Italian of Giovanni Comisso, published in *This Quarter* 2.4 (April–May–June 1930): 675–83. It tells of a soldier, lying in camp during a cholera outbreak, dreaming that he had gone back to his native town, where his humble treasures were sealed up to prevent the Austrians looting them. A few days later, visiting his CO, he finds things that had belonged to his mother and him, looted by his fellows. Deciding not to report the matter, he instead enjoys seeing his CO's fear.

"Home Olga": a ten-line acrostic, published in *Contempo* (Chapel Hill, NC) 3.13 (15 February 1934): 3; a special **Joyce** issue, edited by Stuart Gilbert. Based on the letters of James Joyce's name, it was composed for his birthday or (probably) Bloomsday, 1932. SB claimed to have forgotten about it, but it was quoted in Ellmann's biography (1959), misdated, and in Ruby Cohn's *Comic Gamut* (1962). Published in *Collected Poems* (1977). The title is a private joke: members of the inner Joyce circle present at some boring occasion would call "Home Olga" as a signal to abscond and regroup. As SB wrote John **Calder** (6 November 1976): "Euphemism for 'foutons le camp d'ici.' Obscure **Dublin** origin. Freely used by Tom **MacGreevy** and his friends." The recondite allusions are in the Joycean vein of curious learning (the "haemorrhoidal isle" **puns** on **Ireland**, St. Patrick, and snakes, the haemorrhoid a snake whose bite could not be stanched). The title plays on *Homo Logos,* wordman, and suggests "homologous" and "homage." It builds to an epiphany, where Joyce and **Christ** are homologous, "counterparts." The poem is filled with arcane allusions and word-play and structured around emblematic patterns, the author a counterpart.

As well as being an acrostic, the poem is structured around the three theological virtues, hope, charity, and faith, each with its corresponding color: green ("jade of hope"), red ("erythrite of **love**"), and white ("opal of faith"). The poem develops Stephen Dedalus's three defenses (*Portrait*, 246–47), "silence, exile, and cunning," a strategy perhaps indebted to **Balzac**, whose Lucien de Rubempré says in *Splendeurs et misères des courtisanes:* "J'ai mis en pratique un axiome avec lequel on est sûr de vivre tranquille: Fuge . . . Late . . . Tace." The poem is filled with Joycean wordplay: "in stomacho" plays on *in petto;* Dante's *dolce stile nuovo* is "sweet noo style." The epiphany in the last line reveals how SB saw the relationship: "Exempli gratia: ecce himself and the pickthank agnus." Joyce is the Man, ecce homo, the Christ rejected by his people; SB the "pickthank agnus," the peccable, thankless lamb. "Home Olga" shows the poet making words do their maximum. A modest touch appears in the closing cryptogram, "e.o.o.e.," errors or omissions excepted. Compare the analysis of **friendship** Joyce offered in *Exiles:* "There is a faith still stranger than the faith of a disciple in his master . . . The faith of a master in the disciple who will betray him." Eugene Jolas thought it "acid and not funny," but to Joyce it was "all right" (F&F, #212).

"Hommage à Jack B. Yeats": a brief appreciation of an exhibition by the eighty-four-year-old Jack **Yeats** at the Galerie Beaux-Arts, **Paris** (March 1954); in *Les Lettres nouvelles* 14 (avril 1954): 619–20; rpt. in *Disjecta*, (148–49), with what Ruby Cohn calls an "extraordinary" translation, from a catalogue of Yeats's paintings edited by James White. "Hommage" is appropriate, SB offering an uncritical affirmation of "cette grande oeuvre solitaire."

Honthorst, Gerrit van (1590–1656): Dutch painter of Utrecht, whose life as recounted by **Wilenski** (51–54) shaped that of Matthew David McGilligan (see **Spiro**). He trained under Bloemaert, but at twenty went to Rome, where he saw Raphael's *Liberation of St. Peter* in the Vatican, as well as works of **Caravaggio**, and began to exploit the effects of artificial light. Wilenski (xiii) describes what he calls "the Caravaggio-Honthorst tradition . . . whose candlelit effects influenced one aspect of **Rembrandt**'s work" —his use of torchlight scenes as the source of illumination within the work, the technique of "spotlight" painting. Honthorst made a sensation in Rome with such pictures, and was dubbed "Gherardo delle notti." Larger works include *The Beheading of St. John the Baptist,* illuminated by torchlight, and *Christ before Caiaphas,"* a candlelit piece. Wilenski adds (52) that he found enthusiastic purchasers for small candlelight studies like *Boy Singing by Candlelight* and *Girl Catching a Flea in her Nightdress,* both now in the Doria Gallery in Rome. Indeed they are, but the Doria now attributes them to the "Maestro della Candella," one Trophime Bigot il Giovane, a follower of Gerrit, rather than to Gerrit himself. SB's fascination with the history of spotlight painting is evidenced by the spotlight effects in his later plays.

Horace: Quintus Horatius Flaccus (65–8 BC); son of a freed slave and great lyric poet of the Augustan age. He sought military glory, but timidity at Philippi turned him from arms to odes; he described himself on his Sabine farm as "A fat sleek porker from **Epicurus**'s herd" (*Epistle*, IV.20). SB was attracted by what Lemprière regrets, licentious expressions and indelicate thoughts, as much as by what he commends, elegance and sweetness. SB uses casual tags, as in the "ridiculus mus" (*Dream*, 165; *Ars Poetica*, 139); or Miss **Carriage**'s "Nil desperandum" (*Murphy*, 230; *Odes*, I.7). He takes Horace's advice to be brief and risk obscurity (*Ars Poetica*, 25), as when **Lucy** is described as "atra cura" on the way to Galway ("What a Misfortune," 151); the allusion is to Horace's "Post equitem sedet atra cura" ("Behind the horseman sits black care"; *Odes*, III.1), as used in "**Sanies I**," the "Ritter" on his **bicycle**, a witty variation rather than a commonplace. **Belacqua** makes a covenant that should **Chas** (a "clockwork Bartlett") come out with "ars longa" ("A Wet Night," 50) he will regret it; instead, Chas offers "limae labor" (*Ars poetica*, 292), the tedium of the poet's craft. Walter Draffin's book is held up in the *limae labor* stages ("What a Misfortune," 143); the phrase is used of the adder broaching her rat in "**Serena I**." A dubious **pun** on *ars longa* emerges in *Dream* (97), when, ignoring the **Mandarin**'s "Carpe diem" (*Odes*, I.11),

Belacqua expounds his theory of the defective bottom, flat nose, and long foot being worthy of esteem (from *Satire* II, how **love** makes one blind to a woman's defects). SB derives this from **Cooper** on flagellation (DN, 50) and linking it to the Abbé Boileau's praise of the posterior (DN, 49). This contributes to the jest in "**Yellow**" (169) about the "lang tootsy," soon to be syne (as in "Auld lang syne").

In *Proust* (91) SB mentions Horace's *amabilis insania*, his "amiable madness" (*Odes*, III.4), cited by **Schopenhauer** (*WWI*, I.3 #36, 246) to define the pure act of understanding; Mr. **Endon** is described as "amiable" (*Murphy*, 186). *Dream* invokes (138) the corrosive groundswell of **art** by Horace's "solvitur acris hiems" (*Odes*, I.iv). Mr. **Quigley**'s residence in Holland as a "Dutch uncle," an excessively stern mentor, is from Horace's "mentuentes petruae verbera linguae" ("dreading the castigations of an uncle's tongue"; *Odes*, III.12). The citation "Non me rebus sed mihi res" ("Not me to the world [thing], but the world to me"; *Epistles*, 1.1, 18–19), Horace's advocacy of public affairs, becomes in *Murphy* (98) a statement of neurosis. The affection between **Watt** and Mrs. **Gorman** is impeded by a "tractable obstruction of some endocrinal Bandusia" (142); the allusion is to Horace's *fons Bandusiae* (*Odes*, III.13), a spring near his birthplace, here associated with **Bando**. SB takes the cliché and creates from its possibilities the verbal equivalent of Horace's dictum (*Ars Poetica*, 361) "ut pictura poesis." For the impossible heap ("Ratio ruentis acetvi") and the *sorites* paradox of *Endgame*, see **Zeno**.

"**Horn came always**": "**Fizzle 2**"; SB's translation of "**Foirade III**": "**Horn venait la nuit**"; the manuscript is dated "12.12.73." In this enigmatic *Fizzle* the unnamed narrator describes the visits of an alter ego called Horn. The name suggests sexual tension, the narrator perhaps a cuckold, still "horny," or that the story deals with his being able to "get out of bed again." When he thinks of asking ("Were I to ask . . .") a question of Horn, it would focus on the gown "she" wore "that day." Horn's response adds color to this night tale: "The yellow." His activity with the notes, torch, and matches imitates **Gaber** and **Moran** (*Molloy*, 163). Could the narrator be **Youdi**, growing old like the world? The core of the story is his spectral relationship with Horn, the latter an external entity acting as **mirror** to one who resists seeing his own **face** in Horn, hence Horn's always coming at night. The time scheme is unstable, the "then" of the past discussed as the historical present: "For I was now beginning, then if you prefer, to get out of bed again." But as he now, or then, can rise again, he asks Horn to light his **face**, suggesting the myth of Psyche and Eros. The result is that "I still see, sometimes, that waning face disclosing, more and more clearly the more it entered shadow, the one I remembered." The object of **memory** is calculatedly ambiguous, the image that of "outer space, not to be confused with the other [inner]." This he knows because he can block that image were he to "interpose my hand, or close my eyes." Apparently "elucidating" his last journey of "five or six years ago," the illumination of Horn's face (an epiphany?) suggests that he "must undertake another" (like Psyche, seeking her lost lover?), but this is difficult now, because (in an anticlimactic non sequitur) his body has been ruined by athletics ("throwing the javelin" may imply **onanism**, but the tale lacks definition).

"**Horn venait la nuit**": "**Foirade III**"; published in *Minuit* 2 (janvier 1973): 41–42, and translated as "**Horn came always**" (qv).

horoscope: SB's early interest in horoscopes is unexpected. *Whoroscope* is predicated on the curious detail, given in **Baillet** and **Mahaffy**, that **Descartes** would not let his birthday be known, lest his enemies publish a malicious horoscope. **Jung** insisted on his patients having their horoscopes cast; **Bion**, SB's analyst, took a keen interest in them, and SB may have had his done at Bion's request (Knowlson, 197). In *Murphy* (31), **Celia** cannot utter the word. As the **Whoroscope Notebook** reveals, the novel began with "H" (the horoscope) and "X" (the protagonist), the impetus given by H (a "1/- corpus of motives") to X (no motive at all). H was to direct the action, gradually acquiring a fatality until "No longer a guide to be consulted but a force to be obeyed"; whereby H and X were to be "clarified" side by side, as "**monads** in the arcanum of circumstance" (see **Leibniz**) until they perished together, "fire *oder was*." Above all (as it were), there is the enormous jest of a Big World constructed according to Cartesian **dualism**, with astrology taking the place of **God**.

The horoscope in *Murphy* is eclectic. The *British Journal of Astrology* then sold at 6d, the price of Suk's nativity, but details are drawn from various sources. Mercury as "the planet *par excellence*" (31) derives from an enigmatic phrase in the *Britannica;* "Suk" implies a marketplace or bazaar. Murphy responds to "Then I defy you, Stars" with the previous words from *Romeo and Juliet* (V.i.24): "Is it even so." Other details, such as this Native's intense **Love**, his inclination to Purity, and the wish to be in two places at once, assume irony when it is appreciated that Murphy's birthday is Christmas Day. The "sudden **syzygy**" (93) of lunatic and custodian make Murphy accept a **job**, and what began as an attempt to structure a novel upon a *Thema Coeli* ends as a different kettle of red herrings.

"**hors crâne seul dedans**": a twelve-line poem translated as "**Something there**"; published in *Collected Poems* (1977) as "Poème 1974," then included in the 1976 **Minuit** *Poèmes* (25).

horse: Flann O'Brien pondered the paradox of why the horse, with a round orifice, should produce a square excrement. *Dream* opens unromantically with the image of a defecating horse. Its fair to middling women, notably the **Frica** (179–80), are described in equine terms, largely drawn from **Burton**, as rhetorical abuse. **Belacqua** rejects the "Lex stallionis" (101). Dr. **Nye** and Maddy **Rooney** have had a lifelong preoccupation with horses' **buttocks**. The **unnamable** tries in vain (332–33) to raise a "flutter" out of his penis by concentrating on a horse's rump: "A Clydesdale. A Suffolk stallion." In *Embers,* Henry hears hooves beating in his head.

From an Abandoned Work (157) offers a completely white horse, a Schimmel, a Freudian image of white rage.

The horse is a mute emblem of suffering. At the end of "**Dante and the Lobster**" a horse is down, a man sitting on its head; **Belacqua** reflects (20) that this is considered the right thing to do: "But why?" **Malone** considers (230–31) "the last stage of the horse," in the traces before the **shambles**, standing in dejection then rearing its head, like **Job**'s warhorse (39:25), scenting battle. The unnamable outside the horse-meat café near the shambles likens himself to "an old broken-down cart or bat-horse" (320). In "**Text 1**," the "old hack" again represents the **body**. In *All That Fall* (13) the **hinny** refuses to advance, but instead looks at Mrs. Rooney in dumb reproach "with her great moist cleg-tormented eyes." In "**Walking Out**" (101) the evocation of spring in **Croker's Acres** includes the death of Pretty Polly, Belacqua regretting the horses of yesteryear. **Lucy**'s "jennet" (110) is struck by a superb silent limousine, the wheels jolting over what is left; it expires in the twilight, "sans jeter un cri." Lucy is not so fortunate, being crippled for life.

In "The **Expelled**" man's cruelty to beast is imaged in the cabman's horse, given no food or drink until back in the stable, its jaws tied so as "not have to suffer from the kind hearts of the passersby" (58). Earlier (51) the narrator had almost crushed a child, wearing a little harness: "he must have taken himself for a pony, or a Clydesdale." In "The **Calmative**" (74–75), the narrator finds himself opposite a horse butcher's, rough canvas curtains striped **blue and white**, "colours of the Virgin," and stained with pink, through which he sees "dim carcasses of the gutted horses hanging from hooks head downwards." **Watt**'s exhaustion is depicted in the print of the horse Joss, with its "inscription of great ?" (the word implied [NB6, 91] is "clarity"). *Malone Dies* (211–13) describes the grotesque burial of Big **Lambert**'s mule, its features as contorted in the final rictus, a striking death's-head. It was rescued from the slaughterhouse because Big **Lambert** could "screw" two more years out of it; this reflects the "bêtise" informing the *Three Novels*. All these elements come together in *How It Is* with the horse "motionless back bent head sunk" outlined against the "blue and white of sky" (31), an image of exhaustion in a world where grace and **pity** are denied.

horse leech's daughter: Proverbs 30:15: "The horseleach hath two daughters, crying, Give, give. There are three things that are never satisfied, yea, four things say not, It is **enough**." This image of insatiable **desire**, prettily put by **Wylie** (*Murphy*, 57), affirms the universe as a closed system (see **equilibrium**); for every symptom palliated another is made worse. For "quantum of wantum," see **Windelband** (416): **God** has given the corporeal world "a *quantum* of **motion** which changes only in its distribution among the individual corpuscles."

Hours Press: a small **Paris** press founded in 1928 by Nancy **Cunard** (15 Rue Guénégaud). In 1930 it offered £10 plus publication for a poem of not more than 100 lines on **time**; this was won by SB's *Whoroscope* (qv). The press published

Henry **Crowder**'s *Henry-Music,* which included SB's "**From the Only Poet to a Shining Whore**." Cunard closed the press in 1932 to devote herself to a major project it could not handle, the editing of *Negro* (qv).

How It Is: SB's translation of *Comment c'est,* begun in the early 1960s and completed with difficulty. First published in 1964 (Grove, and Calder and Boyars). The American text was reasonable ($3.95) but the British reflected the commercialism that would bedevil SB's texts: 4,000 copies at 30/-, with 200 more on handmade paper, numbered and signed by the author, bound in vellum (A1 to A100, 12 guineas) or morocco (B1 to B100, 10 guineas); this was announced "in advance of the first edition," but in practice followed it. The standard edition was reprinted in 1972. All fail to set each block of text entire on a page. Parts had been published, with variants: "**From an Unabandoned Work**" (*Evergreen Review,* September 1960): 58–65 (the opening pages); "**From *How It Is***" (*Paris Review,* summer–fall 1962): 113–16 (beginning of part 3); "**How It Is**" (*ARNA* [Sydney], July 1962): 32–35 (the same episode); and "**Conclusion of *How it is***" (*Transatlantic Review,* summer 1963): 5–15 (end of part 3).

The theme of the "novel" (so-called in **French** but not in English) may be the struggle of incipient form to emerge from existential formlessness; an exegesis of **Dante**'s *Inferno* VII.121–26 (in Cary's translation): "Fix'd in the slime . . . but word distinct can utter none"; or a return to **Leopardi**'s "E fango è il mondo," the world as mud. SB described to Donald **McWhinnie** (6 April 1960) a man lying panting in the dark, murmuring his "life" as he hears it, obscurely uttered by a **voice** ("within"). This utterance is a fragmentary recollection of a voice ("without") once heard "**quaqua** on all sides"; only when it abates can he catch a fragment of what is being stated within. The work is in three parts: the first ("before **Pim**") a solitary journey in the dark culminating in the discovery of another creature ("couple"); the second ("with Pim") motionless in the dark and mud, and culminating in the departure of Pim ("abandon"); the third ("after Pim") **solitude** without **motion** in the dark and mud. The voice and thus the "I" is from the outset in the third part, and so the first and second although stated in the **mythological present** are "already over." This suggests neither the bleak poetry of the bare narrative nor the difficulty of reading SB's most intimate and passionate reduction of all things to their **fundamental sounds**, a last impossible attempt to break from the impasse stated at the end of *The Unnamable* and further explored in *Texts for Nothing*, the imagery of which (notably "Text 5") constitutes the groundwork of failure for *How It Is*.

The first six "paragraphs" form an invocation, with four motifs. The first is implicit in "before Pim with Pim after Pim," which aligns each part with SB's three certainties, **birth**, existence, and **death**. The second is the voice, once without, now within: "an ancient voice in me not mine." The third is **memory**, "old dreams," which come back as images "illrecaptured" although "nearly all" are lost. The last is SB's fourth tempter, the inex-

plicable need to express, which drives the rest, even if reduced to the bare statement: "recorded none the less it's preferable," in the dubious hope, not even that, of "someone listening." Somehow these "bits and scraps" strike out a life, "my life natural order more or less"; the arrangement is **musical**, as themes and motifs couple and abandon in a complex orchestration.

The first motif is expressed in terms of basic being: "how I got here" and "whence the sack"; such questions are "not known" and of "no importance" (7). Given is the sack, the tins (SB had a stockpile of Heinz minestrone at **Ussy**), the "warmth of primeval mud impenetrable dark" (11), basic conditions of existence. The second motif, the voice, is not yet formulated, but the text hints at its presence, "**nothing** then suddenly something," the voice and then the silence. Memory **comes and goes**: "first image some creature or other"; "I scissored into slender strips" (9); "another image so soon again a woman" (10); "my **mother**'s **face** . . . a veranda smothered in **verbena** . . . in a nightshirt I pray" (15). This last image recurs at the end of *Film*, and an extant photograph further testifies to it. From such "moments" arise the "formulations" he must make, about the dark and silence and **solitude**; or life "above in the light" (8); his "life"; and the "question" (13) whether "others" are there ("important most important") or whether he is "sole elect." The latter prevails.

With such formulations he begins his journey, his movement through the mud. The first gesture is that of the hand (15), anticipating the "**Still**" prose poems; then "left leg left arm push pull" (19), "right leg right arm push pull" (47), chevrons **mathematically** defined ("dear figures") until finally (48) the hand reaching out claws not slime but the arse of Pim. During that "vast stretch of **time**" other moments are recorded, formulations made. He murmurs to the sack "thou thou" (17), acknowledging the disjunction between self and object. He invokes **witness** and scribe (18); establishes the paradigm of journey, couple, abandon; remembers "moments" that passed the time, pearls amidst the mute mud (26); "awful" syllables such as "asparagus" (the longest English morpheme) or "burst abscess" (25); and further images, such as the yellow crocus (21) from "The **Expelled**," or the time in the **Dublin** mountains with "a little girl friend" and **dog** (28–31), independently published as "The **Image**." He considers the "loss of species" (27), in accordance with **Windelband**'s contention (126) that the ethical ideal of Platonic philosophy lies not in the ability and happiness of the individual "but in the ethical perfection of the species"; thus, loss of species constitutes loss of form, of what makes one One with others.

Part 2 ("with Pim") continues the tale. Contact has been made, and so the paradox of the other, the fellow: if two, why not billions? The first thing (awaiting the arrival of **Bom**) is to establish the entity of the other, and by rummaging in the mud (54) he brings up a testicle or two ("the anatomy I had"). Pim sings a little tune (55), and they learn the rudiments of communication (like **Molloy** with his mother): thump on **skull**, stop; stab in the arse, speak; nails in armpit, sing; bang on kidney, cry. Larger questions are not ignored: grace in the cellar (61); YOUR LIFE ABOVE IN THE LIGHT (72), or YOUR LIFE HERE, in the mud (98); the

"utter" confusion of the voice (74 and 87); memories of **love** and Pam Prim (77); **Kram** and Krim, as **witness** and scribe (80); and the incipient sense (96) that he will DIE ONE DAY. Inevitably, he must leave Pim, "why not known not said" (99), to find himself alone in the mud, in the dark, and "that's how it was with Pim."

"[H]ere then at last" (I quote), part 3, "after Pim," the interrogation of "how," for this, "after all," is the given situation. The "passing moment" is like a hummingbird, as nothing against "vast tracts of time" (103), leaving "indelible traces" that are "only sithence" (104) measured against the vast scale of eternity. He takes stock: "breath in the head"; "a sack bravo colour of mud"; and "a **body** what matter" (105). The need to "make an end" is asserted (106) but the voice returns; but "a voice," "the voice," a choir or even megaphones (107): the voice of "us all," tormenter and victim, those alone or "glued together" (108; **Augustine**'s glue of **love**). A new theme enters: "something wrong there."

This manifests itself in the sudden intrusion of "Bem" into the Bom-I-Pim series (109) and, dramatically (111), in the problem of the sack. If Pim has left without a sack, thereby confounding the ratio of sacks and "souls" (112), then the foundation of **preestablished harmony** is undermined. The differentiation between Bem (how it was) and Bom (how it will be) is also threatened, for they "could only be one and the same" (113). It follows, then, and over the next fifteen pages is relentlessly, mathematically proven "correct", that the possibility of millions thus coupling and abandoning must reduce itself inexorably "in simple words" (124) to "I am alone" (**Proust**'s "irrémediablement seul"). Likewise, "the voice quaqua on all sides" must be "within in the little vault empty closed eight planes bone-white" of the skull (128). That is how it is, present formulation (129).

This is qualified (132): "on condition that by an effort of the imagination the still central episode of the couple be duly adjusted"; but when the panting stops it is his life, and his alone (in both senses), however ill spoken, ill heard, or ill remembered (135). By "last reasonings" (136), the problem of the "acervation of sacks" is reduced to a little room (137) and a rejection of a love that lays them along the track where needed. Likewise, the "principle of parsimony" by which that love might also act as witness is rejected in favor of "desert flower" (138), that is, blooming (withering) unperceived. These are the processes (rations, rationality) that, in a ruthless **pun**, "inable us to advance" (139).

The text ends in a powerful crescendo as its fundamental elements and sounds are rehearsed and restated, but the conclusion is finally unmistakable (144–45): "no all balls from start to finish yes this voice quaqua yes all balls yes only one voice here yes mine yes when the panting stops yes." All this "business" (in **Pascal**'s sense of "distractions") of voices, sacks, and the light above is similarly dismissed as "yes all balls yes" (145). No reply to the scream of "WHAT'S MY NAME" (with its implied biblical text, "I am that I am"), and to all the panting, the murmuring, the questioning, only the final screams: "DIE . . . I MAY DIE . . . I SHALL DIE." That is how it was, is, and ever shall be.

HRHRC: the Harry Ransom Humanities Research Center at the University of Texas at Austin; repository of many of SB's manuscripts and editions, with impressive holdings from the early years. Much arrived via Jake Schwartz, a dentist turned bookseller to whom SB in the late 1950s gave or sold for a pittance many invaluable manuscripts, inscribing them affectionately to his "good friend" before belatedly appreciating how that **friendship** was being exploited. SB later referred to him as "the Great Extractor" (Bair, 534). Most were sold to T. E. Hanley of Bradford, Pennsylvania, a major collector of twentieth-century rare books, whose library was purchased by the University of Texas in 1957. Many significant items, including first editions, correspondence (George **Reavey**, Mary **Manning**, Con **Leventhal**), and scholarly editions, have since been acquired. These are listed in *No Symbols Where None Intended,* a catalogue of books, manuscripts, and other materials relating to SB in the collection, ed. Carlton Lake (1984), an invaluable description of the Center's holdings. The HRHRC holdings were recatalogued in 1999 by Chelsea Jones (TXRC00-A1) and organized into three series, arranged alphabetically and chronologically: Works 1930–87 (seven boxes); Correspondence 1935–89 (one and a half boxes); Works and Correspondence by Other Authors 1959–90 (one and a half boxes). Other materials may be found in related collections. More recent materials are in the [Carlton] Lake Collection (TXRC00-A2). The gem of the collection is, indisputably, the autograph manuscript of *Watt*, but equally precious are the notebooks into which the originals of *Molloy, Malone meurt,* and *L'Innommable* were poured. As well as items relating to the early poetry (*Whoroscope*) and fiction ("Le Calmant," *Comment c'est,* "L'Expulsé," *From an Abandoned Work, Mercier et Camier, Murphy, Premier Amour, Textes pour rien*), there are autograph manuscripts (fair copies) of *Waiting for Godot,* in both French and English, and manuscripts, typescripts, drafts, and notes of some of the early drama ("Act Without Words," *All That Fall,* "Cendres," *Eleuthéria, Fin de partie* and *Endgame,* and *Krapp's Last Tape*).

Hugo, Victor (1802–85): the great poet, novelist, and dramatist of his age (*hélas*), brilliant, erratic, conceited, and egotistical; the *massif central* of **Romanticism.** His work has lyricism, beauty, and strength, but also bombast and vulgarity; thus SB to **MacGreevy** (25 March 1936): "Poe says bright or white, **Goethe** golden, and Hugo vermeil." **Belacqua** denies in *Dream* (68) all knowledge of *Hernani* (1830), a melodrama depicting a conflict of honor in sixteenth-century Spain. In *Proust* (80) Hugo is said to be one receding rather than proceeding, returning to an outmoded romanticism. **Neary** has something of Hugo about him (*Murphy,* 201): egotism with hope unending, the attribution of lasting value to his sufferings.

humanism: debates about the merits of humanism and antihumanism, or rather posthumanism, have proliferated over the past twenty years, and SB's work is often invoked in these skirmishes. If the work is an ongoing area of contestation, still fiercely fought over, it is because the questions it raises are so fundamental. In peopling his worlds almost exclusively with old, infirm, and/or indigent characters, SB has been accused, from different quarters, of both wallowing in human frailty and exonerating it. Like **Joyce,** SB is a barometer of critical taste, registering hermeneutical changes in the literary climate. The critical reception of SB's work forms two distinct phases, the first when it came to public attention in the 1950s. The focus then was on the value accorded human beings, voices of doubt reproaching SB for nihilism and inhumanity. Philip Toynbee wrote of *Molloy,* in 1955 ("Review," 75): "As for the excrement, the blasphemy, the cruelty, the reiterated indifferentism, it seems to me that this is an attitude to life which cries out for at least some hint of an opposing one." Kenneth Tynan expressed similar reservations about *Endgame,* in 1957 ("Review," 166): "Last weekend's production, portentously stylised, piled on the agony until I thought my **skull** would split . . . I am prepared to listen in any theatre to any message, however antipathetic. But when it is not only disagreeable but forced down my throat, I demur." These objections were reflected in Esslin's remark ("Dianoetic Laughter," 19) that "the view widespread in the popular consciousness which sums up Beckett's work [is] the image of the heads protruding from dustbins in *Endgame*. Humankind as rubbish."

Champions of the work during this period followed a line echoed by the Swedish Academy, when SB was awarded the **Nobel Prize** (1969). SB's oeuvre, declared the academy, "had transmuted the destitution of modern man into his exaltation." The singular combination of humor and horror was seen as courageous and cathartic, a therapeutic union bestowing a kind of redemption on the characters and their terrible plights. The vogue in philosophical and literary circles for **existentialism** enhanced this reading, seeing it as a sustained **allegory** for the isolation, absurdity, and contingency that delineates the human condition. In January 1938, fending off an *apache*, SB was stabbed in the chest. Later confronting his assailant outside court, SB asked why he did it: "Je ne sais pas, Monsieur," came the nonchalant reply (Knowlson, 261). The incident has been depicted as an *acte gratuit*, the existentialist trope par excellence. Popularized by André **Gide**, in *Les Caves du Vatican* (1914), it is a self-defining action whose chief characteristic is that it is performed without moral regard, merely because one does not refrain from doing it.

This disputation endured until the early 1980s. French thought had moved away from **Sartre** toward other figures, and a similar shift belatedly occurred in Beckett studies. Reflecting on this (*Meaning of Being* [1990], x), Butler and Davis referred to SB as "the poet of the post-structuralist age." The assimilation of his work to the various branches of literary and cultural theory has taken the debate onto a more rarefied level. The question of value ("humankind as rubbish" versus humankind as exalted) is now less important than that of autonomy. Instead of SB being admonished for his "antihuman" tendencies, inflicting wanton cruelty and torment on destitute mankind, he is acknowledged as a forerunner of theoretical posthumanism, acutely recognizing the forces of human heteronomy putatively determining who and what we are (language, discourse, technology, **desire**, ideology, the unconscious, and social formation). The pitiless permutations of *Watt*, the relentless self-undercutting of *The Unnamable*, and the compulsive incantations of *How It Is* and *Not I* all offer evidence of language as an inhuman archive of alterity with its own impersonal agency.

The indeterminacy of the humanist/posthumanist question persists largely because of SB's unresolved treatment of Cartesian **dualism**. Humanism based on the transcendental power of the **cogito**, on the mind's ability to think its way through falsehood and illogicality to foundational self-grounding, is both confirmed and quashed. The **body** is not subordinated to the mind; "it wasn't their fault I couldn't dig, but my leg's," complains **Molloy** (36). Yet the mind cannot claim sovereignty over itself. It is ever alert and active, sifting possibilities, weighing alternatives, and generally manifesting the powers of rational analysis ascribed to the cogito. But its meticulous attempts at staging logical argument invariably end in confusion. In the drama, the mere fact of the live actor secures the "presence" that the prose so remorselessly challenges. Humanist critics have generally tended to be more attentive to the dramatic works, and posthumanist critics to the prose (especially *Three Novels*). Individual pathos is more vividly brought to life in performance than on the page, particularly when the latter is couched as monologues congested with expostulations of self-doubt. SB told Michael Haerdter, his directorial assistant at the **Schiller-Theater** *Endspiel* (1967), that "Theater for me is first of all recreation from work on fiction. We are dealing with a given space and with people in that space. That is relaxing." The phrase, "people in that space," is disingenuous, for part of SB's fascination with theater was to undermine or play against that very solidity and presence, to sustain as much epistemological and phenomenal ambiguity as the semiotics of theater would allow. He often subverted the senses with which an audience confirms theater's concreteness, the thereness of characters, by having the audience question what it thinks it sees, by offering figures who are not "there," like the boy **Clov** sights in *Endgame*, the pacing **May** of *Footfalls*, the **Voice** in "Eh Joe," **Bam** in "What Where," and **Godot** himself.

Michel Foucault, in "What Is an Author?" (210), concluded with a (mis)quotation from "**Text 3**": "What difference does it make who is speaking?" Georges Bataille and Maurice Blanchot were early enthusiasts of *Molloy* and *The Unnamable*, respectively. The most sustained early application came from Theodor Adorno. In "Trying to Understand *Endgame*" (1961), he regarded SB's work as the only fitting artistic response to the moral depravity of the death camps, a testament to the destitution of

"post-Auschwitz culture" (Adorno abjured links between SB and existentialism). In the mid-1980s systematic theoretical studies of SB's works began to appear. Steven Connor's *Samuel Beckett: Repetition, Theory, and Text* conducted a rapprochement with Deleuze and Derrida, and Leslie Hill, in *Beckett's Fiction: In Different Words,* attempted something similar with Derrida and **psychoanalysis**. These forays suggest rough groupings of followers. Degrees of indebtedness to Deleuze, Blanchot, and Derrida can be seen in works by Thomas Trezise, Carla Locatelli, Richard Begam, and Anthony Uhlmann. Commentaries drawing on Lacan and psychoanalysis include those by David Watson, Catharina Wulf, and Phil Baker. The dynamics of textuality inform Bersani and Dutoit, and Simon Critchley has engaged in critical dialogue with Adorno. Lance St. John Butler and Paul Davies have addressed philosophical (rather than theoretical) antihumanism. A double issue of *JOBS* (10.1 and 2 [2000/2001]) introduced *Other Becketts* (ed. Daniela Caselli, Steven Connor, and Laura Salisbury). To Derek Attridge (1989), Jacques Derrida explained why he had not attempted any sustained critical analysis of SB (*Acts of Literature*, 61): "This is an author to whom I feel very close, or to whom I would like to feel myself very close; but also too close ... I have perhaps avoided him because of this identification." This "avoidance" validates the work of his followers more effectively than any theoretical commentary could do.

Andrew Gibson has remarked (*Reading Narrative Discourse*, 150) that

"Beckett's principal targets have always been manifestations of traditional humanism." This does not preclude the possibility of a more heterodox humanism asserting itself. In *Three Novels*, the figure of the "human" remains elusive, though its pursuit remains paramount. This is not the humanist convention of a quest for stable selfhood (the "human" as a goal or a destination), nor something to be achieved or to become. The "human" is only ever hypothetical, a permanent possibility. Its pursuit is enabled by the minimal, provisional conditions of being that SB admits: the impetus to produce narrative, the need for self-scrutiny, the obligation to express. Since the sui generis "humanism" that can be glimpsed from this pursuit involves a dehumanization of orthodox notions (the human as a knowable entity possessing certain essential attributes), it shares as little with those doctrines as it does with the expropriating forces of theoretical posthumanism. See **existentialism** and **zoomorphism**. [PS]

"Humanistic Quietism": SB's review of the *Poems* of Thomas **MacGreevy** (Heinemann, 1934), *Dublin Review* 9.3 (July–September 1934): 79–80; rpt. in *Disjecta* (68–69). Later used as the foreword to Thomas Dillon Redshaw's *Thomas MacGreevy: Collected Poems* (1971). SB praises MacGreevy for writing poetry like prayer, the poems evolving from a "nucleus of endopsychic clarity," creating its object, a radiance without counterpart in contemporary poetry. Little cited justifies the extravagant praise; even allowing for SB's European values the review is more an expression of **friendship** than

a critical evaluation. Yet the sense of poetry as prayer enters *Murphy* in the encounter with Mr. **Endon**, the language quietly imitating that of MacGreevy.

"Human Wishes": a fragment of an unfinished full-length play, for which SB had read and taken notes extensively, filling three notebooks (now at the **BIF**) with materials from or relating to the life of Samuel **Johnson**, particularly his relationship with Mrs. Thrale. The title derives from Johnson's **Juvenalian** satire, "The Vanity of Human Wishes." The notebooks were compiled in 1936–37, but the piece may have been composed early in 1940. First published in Ruby Cohn's *Just Play* (1980), and reprinted in *Disjecta* (153–66), it consists of part of a first act: "A room in Bolt Court. Wednesday, April 14, 1781. Evening." The date is that of Thrale's **death**, but this is not explicit. The characters (Johnson's "seraglio" in his **London** house) are: Mrs. Williams (*meditating*); Mrs. Desmoulins (*knitting*); Miss Carmichael (*reading*); and the **cat** Hodge (*sleeping—if possible*). Inconsequential conversation follows, in Johnson's authentic mode. Although the Grand Cham makes no appearance, the fragment reflects his manner: elegant diction, sesquipedalia, humorous touches, testiness, aversion to merriment, and scathing cynicism: "You wish to provoke me, Madam, but I am not provoked. The peevishness of decay is not provoking." Too little exists to allow definite judgment, SB losing interest in the project, despite his extensive reading, as the "Johnson fantasy" of the great man's impotence became less compelling (Knowlson), or as he was unable to cope with the problems of accent (Bair). The fragment remains a tantalizing touch of what might have been, an elegant anticipation of the formality of some of SB's later writing.

Hume, David (1711–76): Scotland's greatest philosopher, whose masterpiece is the *Inquiry Concerning Human Understanding* (1748). He refined Locke, to the effect that a content of **consciousness** is either original or the copy of an original, either an "impression" or an "idea"; all ideas, therefore, are representations of impressions. Denying causation, he affirmed rather relations between ideas. Thus, a curiosity: as Librarian of the Advocate's Library in Edinburgh he wrote his *History of England*. Ellmann (648) tells of **Joyce** asking, "How could the idealist Hume write a history?" SB replied, "A history of representation."

Huysmans, Joris Karl (1848–1907): French novelist, author of *A rebours* (1884) and *Là-bas* (1891), which promoted an aestheticism expressing itself in luxuriant symbolism, paradox, and perverse eroticism, as in the paintings of Gustave Moreau, which he admired and imitated. Praz likens him to a Dutch still-life painter (*Romantic Agony*, 309). In *Proust* (80), SB senses within Huysmans something of the "retrogressive tendency" he detects in **Proust**, but loathed and repressed, so that while speaking of the "ineluctable gangrene of **Romanticism**" he can yet create Des Esseintes (the aesthete and hero of *A rebours*) as "a fabulous creature" who wages war on

nature by re-creating artificially his pleasures. Patients are fed in a manner "highly irregular" (*Murphy,* 182); this is in translation "alimentation par l'autre bout," such ends and means (an enema) one of the scandals of *A rebours.*

Huysum, Jan van (1682–1749): Dutch flower painter. In **"Malacoda,"** the son lays "this Huysum" on the coffin as an act of devotion in **art** to the **father**. The **imago,** or butterfly, suggests that the specific painting is that in the National Gallery, **London,** rather than the one in **Dublin** (O'Brien, 145), which has no such figure on it.

Hy-Brasil: a mythical utopia, somewhere west of **Ireland.** SB likens landing in **Cobh** (*Dream,* 140) to arrival there, the harbor lights as fireflies, the hills alive with priests with bludgeons (seeking courting couples). Walter Draffin mentions the island of Ui Breasail ("What a Misfortune," 147). SB likened Jack **Yeats**'s *A Race in Hy Brazil* (1937) to **Watteau**'s *L'Embarquement pour Cythère* (Pyle, 136).

Hyde, Douglas (1860–1949): scholar and politician; founder of the Young Ireland Society (1891) and Gaelic League (1893); author of *Love Songs of Connacht* (1893); first professor of Irish at UCD (1905); Free State Senator (1923–26); and first President of **Ireland** (1938–45). The Jekyll behind Hyde (*Watt,* 11).

hypothetical imperatives: with reference to the "**nimis sero**" ("too late") of **Molloy** (87). These arise from what **Kant** terms the synthetic relation of ends and means, as defined by **Windelband** (552): "They all assert, 'If you will this or that, then you must proceed thus or so.' They are on this account *hypothetical imperatives*. They presuppose a volition as actually present already, and demand on the ground of this the further act of will which is required to satisfy the first." For the composite protagonist of the *Trilogy*, the hypothetical imperative of the **voice** soon becomes categorical, a *command absolute*, to be fulfilled *solely for its own sake*.

I

identified contraries: attributed by SB to Giordano **Bruno** (qv), to whom **God** was the meeting of opposites, the *coincidentia oppositorum,* in such maxims as "minimal heat equals minimal cold," or "maximal speed is a state of rest" ("**Dante**," *Disjecta,* 21). These go back to Nicolaus Cusanus (1401–64), whom SB had not then read. SB became fascinated with the doctrine of learned ignorance and **negative theology**: God as **Nothing**, yet infinite; God as greatest (*maximum*) yet smallest (*minimum*); and words like "**asylum**" or "cleave" that contain their antitheses. These he parodied, as in "**Che Sciagura**" (of the Church): "Maximal negation is minimal affirmation." The **diving board** in "**For Future Reference**" vibrates so rapidly that the highest and lowest points coincide. **Murphy** in his **rocking chair** enacts the paradox of **motion**, whereby maximal speed attains maximal rest, or *ataraxy,* Epicurean freedom from disturbance in the absence of motion (see **Murphy's mind**).

"**I gave up before birth**": "**Fizzle 4**" in **Grove** (5 in **Calder**), SB's translation of "**Foirade II**," "**J'ai renoncé avant de naître.**" The manuscript is dated "15.12.73"; and a fair copy "**Paris** Aug. 74." It explores dual nature: the "I" who gave up before birth and the "he" (the fetal twin?) whom the "I" inhabits, who is physically born. Impossibly, "I" has a **voice** to tell of "he," whose life it tormented, and so will persist beyond the death of "he." The tale is of torment, **desire** for **death**, drowning (see Matthew 18:6, for the "millstone" about his neck). That urge spent, death remains a mystery, the result of a sinister turn, to the left (as in **Dante**), about which "I" has nothing to say. Any resolution to the ontological paradox or enigma of **consciousness** resides in the creative act, that of voice. The impossible "I," then, is performative, that which acts to tell a story and hence goes **on**.

"**Il est tête nue**": "**Foirade I**," in *Minuit* 1 (novembre 1972): 22–26; see "**He is barehead.**"

Ill Seen Ill Said: English version of *Mal vu mal dit,* translated (December 1980 to January 1981) even as the **French** was written (24 octobre 1979 to 21 janvier 1981), with fifteen months between the original opening and the remainder (see the bilingual edition, ed. Charles Krance [New York: Garland, 1996]). Early versions of the opening appeared as "**One Evening**" and "**Un soir.**" Published complete in *The New Yorker* (5 October 1981: 48–58), then by **Grove** (1981); collected with *Company* and *Worstward Ho* in *Nohow On,* the only one written first in French. The first English trade edition (Calder, 1982) was anticipated by a special edition of 299 numbered copies (Northridge: Lord John Press, 1982). Performed on BBC 3 (September 1982) by Patrick **Magee**. The holograph manuscript (RUL 2200) arranges the text as in the final version in sixty-one unnumbered sections separated by a dash, headed "The Evening or the Night" (partially deleted), varying the motif "When not night evening"; paragraphs #29 and #30 were later reversed.

The novel explores the mysteries of perception and **consciousness** and so being itself. Seeing is always ill seeing, saying is always ill saying. Since "Ill" and "Mal" are nouns as well as adjectives, the tale is equally of one seeing ill in the world and saying ill of it. The elusive, ghostly tale opens with a reclining woman watching first Venus then the sun rise, that image immediately adjusted by a reporting narrator urging himself **"On"** and thence "Careful." The black-clad, white-haired, unnamed "she" moves about her space "as though by enchantment" (54): a cabin (or hovel) in a lifeless "zone of stones" about a furlong in diameter, ringed by twelve (megalithic?) stones that recede or approach, maintaining the same distance from her as she moves. Beyond the stones is verdant pasture, once moor where **sheep** grazed, on which the stones encroach. She appears, within or without, fleetingly, the imagination desiring to seize her as she wanders, "drawn to a certain spot," either a tomb or one of the twelve stone guardians that ring the cabin. The observer might renounce the vigil, so sporadically does she appear. His personified eye, the devouring eye of prey, *King Lear*'s "vile jelly," strains on the details from which she is absent to the point of tears. Whether the tears are those of the narrator or the narrated remains inconclusive. "The eye of flesh" (Job 10:4) is among the novel's synesthesia (65); it

"breathes" (59), "devours" (60), "digests" (61), and narrates. The ill seer can also ill say (or say ill). The eye is also inner eye, with no need of light to see. Things observed and imaginings (Fr. *chimère*) are thus confused, this dead or dying woman "in the madhouse of the **skull** and nowhere else" (58)—perhaps. In moments of panic the narrating eye (I) declares all to be figment save the void: "Nothing else. Contemplate that. Not another word. Home at last" (66). Would that perception could be so dismissed, as mere images, imaginings, beyond the control of volition and inextricably commingled with things. With the passing of panic, imaging resumes. Views are often cinematic: "Seated on the stones she is seen from behind" (64); "The hands. Seen from above" (66); or the zoom in, "The curtain. Seen closer thanks to this hiatus it reveals itself finally for what it is. A black **greatcoat**" (77). Other images are explored: the cabin's interior, wall, coffer, trapdoor, clock; without all is enshrouded, "Haze sole certitude" (78). At the heart of the chimeric story are mysteries of life and death. She has returned "after many winters" to the place whence she fled. To whose tomb is she drawn? How came the ring finger once adorned with a "keeper" to be missing? The absent digit suggests passion (even panic) belied by the narrative's calm. This narrative of "The Evening or the Night," of the enchanted woman in black mourning a lost **love**, has associations with SB's **mother**, May, but to see the tale as veiled autobiography is as much oversimplification as to see the images as purely fictive without reference to an outer world or narrator's **memory**; the narrator cautions against this. A desiring eye, "having no need of light to see" (50), pursues a ghostly old woman (perhaps from his past) who herself pursues a mystery in attempting to recover a lost past; she too is evidently subject to visions. These ghostly images are ill seen and ill said because the right word is always the wrong word: "as from an evil core the what is the wrong word the evil spreads" (50). There are two sets of eyes: "[She] No longer anywhere to be seen. Nor by the eye of flesh nor by the other" (56). An "imaginary stranger, another searcher, appears" (53). As she walks from cabin to stone she is **witnessed**: "On the snow her long shadow keeps her company. The others are there. All about. The twelve. Afar. Still or receding" (55). These "guardians" move as she moves, to "keep her in the centre" (60). As the ill seen ill said images degrade with the occlusion of the "vile jelly," as images lessen or worsen in the haze into "collapse" (78), the narrative anticipates *Worstward Ho*. Little wonder that Ruby Cohn calls this, unqualifiedly, "The Beckett Masterwork" (*Canon*, 363). See also "**Long Observation of the Ray.**"

illustrations: SB resisted George **Reavey**'s suggestion (1934) that *Echo's Bones* be illustrated by Stanley William Hayter, because the poems should stand alone. While SB has inspired many visual artists, illustrations of his texts were always independent responses. Avigdor **Arikha** supplied engravings for the second edition of *Nouvelles et textes pour rien* (1958). These remained part of *Stories and Texts for Nothing* (Grove, 1967), but not *No's Knife* (1967) nor *Texts for Nothing* (Calder, 1974). Arikha illustrated *L'Issue,* with six original en-

gravings (Paris: Georges Visat, 1968); *The North,* with etchings (London: Enitharmon, 1972); and *Au loin un oiseau* with etchings (New York: Double Elephant, 1973). Max Ernst illustrated a trilingual edition of *From an Abandoned Work* (Stuttgart: Manus Presse, 1969). H. M. Erhardt illustrated for Manus Presse *Bing* (1970), eight blind-relief impressions in an edition of fifty numbered copies; and also *Act Without Words I* and *II* (1965), *Come and Go* (1968), and *Watt* (1971). Hayter made etchings for *Still,* ed. Luigi M. Majno (Milan: M'Arte Edizione, 1974). Jasper Johns created a series of etchings for *Foirades/Fizzles* (qv), ed. Véra Lindsay (New York: Petersburg, 1976); seventy-four plates of proofs appeared in *Foirades/Fizzles: Echo and Allusion in The Art of Jasper Johns* (Los Angeles: Grunwald Center, 1987), 235–310. The Whitney Museum of American Art catalogue, for the *Foirades/Fizzles* exhibit (October 11–November 20, 1977), includes "**I gave up before birth**" and "**J'ai renoncé avant de naître.**"

After Jack **MacGowran** died SB authorized an edition of *All Strange Away* illustrated by Edward Gorey (New York: Gotham Book Mart, 1976). *Imagination Dead Imagine* was illustrated by Sorel Etrog (Calder, 1977). A passage from *Le Dépeupleur, Séjour,* featured engravings by Louis Maccard from original drawings by Jean Deyrolle (Paris: Georges Richar, 1970); these Maccard completed when Deyrolle died in mid-project. *The Lost Ones* was illustrated by Philippe Weisbecker for *Evergreen Review* 96 (1973): 41–64, and by Charles Klabunde (Stamford, CT: New Overlook, 1984). *Stirrings Still,* dedicated to Barney Rosset, was illustrated by Louis le Brocquy (Blue Moon, and Calder, 1988) for a collector's edition of 226 copies. These comprise one two-tone lithographic image of SB, eight lithographs in black ink, and a motif stamped in eighteen-carat gold on the parchment cover. A trade edition with black-and-white illustrations appeared from North Star Line (1993). Dellas Henke's oversized edition (forty copies) of *Waiting for Godot* (1979) was followed by *Company* (1983), fifty-two copies signed by Henke and SB. Both were printed privately by the Iowa Center for the Book. A Limited Editions Club *Nohow On* appeared in 1989, 550 quarto copies, bound in gilt-lettered black Nigerian Oasis goatskin, in suede-lined cotton clamshell box, containing six etchings by American artist Robert Ryman, signed by SB and Ryman. The text was printed on Magnani paper at the Shagbark Press; etchings on Arches at Wingate Studio and Renaissance Press; design by Benjamin Shiff. The LEC brochure contained an essay by John **Calder** on SB's late texts.

"**Illustrations for the Bible**": 105 etchings by Marc Chagall, facsimile reproductions of watercolors painted 1930–55, from Genesis to Ezekiel, heliogravures by **Draeger** Frères; plus sixteen original color lithographs and twelve in black and white, cover and title page, lithography by Mourlot Frères; composed specially for a double edition of the deluxe art review *Verve* (Paris) 8.33/34 (1956). Introduced by Meyer Schapiro, with text by Jean Wahl: 200 lines of poetry entitled "L'Écriture est gravure," translated by the author "with the kind assistance of Samuel Becket" [*sic*]. An English edition appeared as *Verve* 9, similar format, but seven pages of poetry, compared with the original six (New York: Harcourt, Brace, 1956).

"**L'Image**": an excerpt from *Comment c'est* (33–38), its first appearance in any form, in *X: A Quarterly Review* [London] 1.1 (November 1959): 35–37. A muddy encounter is made between "La langue se charge de boue" and "C'est fait j'ai fait l'image." It was published as a very slim volume (Minuit, 1988). An English version in *As the Story Was Told* (31–40; Calder, 1990) aroused suspicion from readers and scholars, who argued that the unattributed translation could not have been SB's, but had been cobbled together with scraps from *How It Is,* and idiosyncratic additions even where SB's renderings were available. For Gontarski's *Complete Short Prose* (1995) Edith Fournier made a new translation, respecting SB's phrasing; this first appeared in *JOBS* 4.2 (1995): 1–3, followed by John Crombie's "The Well-Made Image" (15–27), which demolished **Calder**'s concocted translation. See **MAC.**

Imagination Dead Imagine / Imagination mort imaginez: written in **French** in the 1960s; published in *Les Lettres nouvelles* 13 (octobre–novembre 1965): 13–16; and translated for *The Sunday Times* (7 November 1965): 48. Published (Minuit, 1965) in a special edition of 612 numbered copies, then in *Têtes-mortes* (1967), 49–57. An English text appeared *hors commerce* from **Calder** and Boyars (1965), 100 copies on handmade paper, numbered and signed, before the trade edition (1966). The first American printing was in *Evergreen Review* 10.39 (February 1966): 48–49. The text is the "residual precipitate" of *All Strange Away*, re-created as an independent work. It explores the theme of the dying imagination yet conscious of its own activity, within the closed space of the later fiction, with "two white bodies" (alive, for the mirror mists) in the rotunda, positions mathematically defined but their gazes (the "eye of prey") rarely meeting, and the identity of each finally a "white speck lost in whiteness"; a whited sepulchre (Matthew 23:27), perhaps.

"An Imaginative Work!": SB's review of Jack Yeats's *Aramanthers* (Heinemann, 1936), published in the *Dublin Magazine* 11.3 (July–Sept. 1936): 80–81; rpt. in *Disjecta* (89–90). The title was not SB's. The unsolicited article was cut to 500 words. SB distinguishes between critic and artist, rejecting the "chartered recountants" (from Yeats's *Sligo*, an earlier book) who take the thing to pieces and put it together again. SB praises Jack Yeats's "analytical imagination," his Ariostesque irony and refusal to use allegory (that "glorious double-entry" of the chartered recountants) or symbols: details are related, "not by rule of three, as two values to a third, but directly, as stages of an image." Privately SB was reserved, telling MacGreevy (9 June 1936): "I was kind and it was bad. I compared him with Ariosto."

imago: the adult stage of an insect; in psychoanalysis, the son's idealized image of the father. See Haeckel and "Malacoda."

Immobile: SB's translation of "Fizzle 7," *Still*, the only "Fizzle" written first in English. Published in a special edition of 125 copies (Minuit, 1976), then included in *Pour finir encore et autres foirades* (1976).

l'Impasse de l'Enfant-Jésus: a cul-de-sac off the Rue de Vaugirard between the Boulevards du Montparnasse and Pasteur, near Rue des Favorites; location of Murphy's mew in the French translation and Victor's room in *Eleutheria*. Molloy (62) takes refuge in an impasse.

"Impromptu d'Ohio": SB's translation of "Ohio Impromptu"; published in *Berceuse suivi de impromptu d'Ohio* and in *Catastrophe et autres dramaticules* (Minuit, 1982). First staged by Pierre Chabert, with "Catastrophe" and "Berceuse," at the Théâtre du Rond-Point (15 décembre 1983), with Michaël Lonsdale (*Lecteur*) and Jean-Louis Barrault (*Entendeur*).

incoherent continuum: expressing in *Dream* (102) the nothing behind the veils of language, the gulf or ström of incoherence that destroys the postulated existence of such notions as the "I am." This, Belacqua asserts, is exlored by Rimbaud, Hölderlin, and especially Beethoven, whose art is a "punctuation of dehiscence" (no way to get from point to point), a "continuity bitched to hell," a "blizzard of electrons; then vespertine compositions eaten away with terrible silences," pitted with "dire stroms of silence" (138–39). SB mocks this "aesthetic of inaudibilities," yet his fiction attempts a similar music of silence, at the cost of "as bloody a labour" as that of the later Beethoven.

ineffable: the incapacity of human understanding to comprehend **God.** Geulincx uses "ineffabile" in his *Ethica* of the conjunction of mind and body, then glosses it in the "Annotata" (242–43) as the hypostasis, or dual nature of God in **Christ. Arsene** attempts to eff the ineffable (*Watt,* 62); **Malone** contemplates conating and ineffing (218).

Inge, William Ralph (1860–1954): the "gloomy dean"; English divine and Dean of St. Paul's; listed in *Dream* (62) among other pessimists. Despite Inge's conviction that where **Christ** is, there is heaven, and that to believe otherwise is to suppose an **irrational** universe (9), SB read his *Christian Mysticism* (1899), using several details in *Dream* (DN, 97–102):

"Great Dereliction" (6, 185): St. Teresa's **ineffable** loneliness after being abandoned by **God** (Inge, 221), yet the path to incomparable happiness.

"all manner of thing shall be well" (9): the sentiment of **Juliana** of Norwich (Inge, 26, 208). "**What a Misfortune**" (121).

"an apex" (17): St. Bonaventura's *apex mentis* (Inge, 7, 360), the mystical doctrine of the spark within the mind consubstantial with the uncreated ground of the deity. Applied to **Dionysius the Areopagite** in *Dream* (17, 185).

"circular movement" (17): Dionysius distinguishes three movements of the human mind, the first (*circular*) wherein the soul returns in upon itself (Inge, 108).

"Fünkelein" (17, 93, 160): the "little spark" at the *apex mentis,* from Meister **Eckehart** (Inge, 156, 184), the "organ by which the personality communicates with God & knows him" (DN, 100). "**Walking Out**" (106).

"all-transcending superessentially superexisting super-Deity" (17): the "barbarous jargon" of Dionysius (Inge, 106).

"his time of the lilies" (18): Jakob Böhme's phrase for the time of redemption when all **nature** shall be delivered from bondage (DN, 102; Inge, 285).

"transelemented" (35): misquoted from Inge (257; DN, 101), where the Church father Theophylact says that we are *"transelementated* into Christ."

"totum intra omnia . . . et totum extra" (35): "immanent and transcendent" (DN, 99); St. Bonaventura's definition of God as "sphaera intellibibilis, cuius centrum est ubique, et circumferentia nusquam" (Inge, 35), an intelligible sphere with "centre everywhere, and circumference nowhere." *Murphy* (60).

"bride of his soul" (40, 183): "Bridegroom of the soul," John of Ruysbroek's motto of the active life or sensitive (sensual) soul (Inge, 169; DN, 99).

"pleroma" (42): "totality of divine attributes" (DN, 198; Inge, 81). SB said he had replaced the plenitude that **Thomas à Kempis** calls God by a pleroma to be sought among his own feathers and entrails; hence the "fine feathers" (SB to TM, 10 March 1935).

"the gift and the giver" (42): the gift of love in God's **mansions** or the brothel, a "horrible confusion" of Walter Hilton's *The Scale of Perfection* (Inge, 201).

"Philippus Bombastus von Hohenheim" (48): **Paracelsus** (DN, 101; Inge, 273).

"aliter sic" (135): "otherwise thus"; Gerson, Rector of Paris, offers alternative definitions of mysticism (DN, 102; Inge, 335).

"*te praesente nil impurum*" (183): from "Amor Patris Filique" by Adam of St. Victor (1130–80), medieval hymnist described in *Dream* (182–83) as a notorious poacher and associated (by tenuous connection with Adam **Kraft**) with the Iron Maiden of Nuremberg (DN, 98; Inge, 38).

"Dark Night of the Soul" (185): **St. John of the Cross** (Inge, 224) "consonantally adjusted" to "Dark Shite of the Hole" (DN, 101), or the hypostatical enema, cause of St. Teresa's postevacuative depression.

"dearworthy" (192): Juliana of Norwich on Christ's death (DN, 100; Inge, 203). "What a Misfortune" (115).

"undaunted daughter of desires" (222): from Crashaw's "On St. Teresa" (DN, 100; Inge, 212). Adapted in "A **Wet Night**" (68) and "**Sanies I**."

"**Plato** . . . **Borstal Boehme**" (234): Böhme lacking only learning and the gift of clear expression to be a German Plato (Inge, 278; DN, 101).

L'Innommable: last of the *Three Novels* (Minuit, 18 juillet 1953), 3,000 copies with fifty deluxe. A facsimile page appeared in *Arts-Spectacles* 418 (juillet 3–9, 1953): 5; and an extract (with another from *Molloy*) in *Écrivains aujourd'hui, 1940–1960: Dictionnaire anthologique et critique,* ed. Bernard Pingaud (Paris: Grasset, 1960), 93–100. After finishing *Malone Dies,* SB could not face writing the final text. This began after the "interlude" of *Waiting for Godot,* with which it shares much. The first page of the two clothbound autograph notebooks (HRHRC #109) is dated "29.3.49"; the final entry, on the last page of the second (the "end" determined by the pages available?) states "Fin. Cinq janvier 1950," the last words being "il faut continuer, je vais continuer." The opening reflects the difficulty SB had starting, much crossed out and rewritten, save the emphatic statement: "Je ne me tairais jamais. Jamais." Several pages are left blank before the story resumes with "Je me serai donc plaint" (14), after which it pours forth with few alterations. Contrary to his usual habit of writing on the rectos and leaving the verso free for revision, SB wrote *L'Innommable* entirely on the versos. Another oddity is the omission from Notebook 2 (106) of the passage from "Ma voix. La voix," to "Maintentant il n'y a personne" (177–79; English, 393–94). Two sheets pasted into the end of Notebook 1 contain this. Internal evidence confirms that this interlude, dealing with the loss and recovery of the **voice** (qv), antedates the rest. This is literally the Unnamable's first voice, a major theme, the search to locate the mysterious voice, and doomed to frustration. For commentary, see *The Unnamable* (1958).

instanter: a legal term, meaning "forthwith"; used as a categorical imperative, authority insisting on immediate action, as in *Dream* (5), where the **body** must obey the mind. In "**Dante and the Lobster**" (17), the fishman hands over the lobster "instanter." **Moran** receives **Gaber**'s instructions from **Youdi**: "Moran, Jacques, home, instanter" (163). The theological component is marked in *How It Is* (63): "I am punished instanter."

"In the Train with Madden": early translation of an extract (the opening of III, 37–40) from *Mercier et Camier* offered to David Hayman (April 1973) for the *Iowa Review*. The three-page draft, with autograph corrections, is in the Barney Rosset / Samuel Beckett Collection at the John J. Burns Library, Boston College.

Ireland: an exile, émigré, refugee from his native rock who preferred France at war to Ireland at peace, SB maintained an ambivalent relationship with his homeland. The witticism serves as a **political** comment on Ireland's neutrality during World War II; while the twenty-six counties stood idly by, SB could not. His rejection centered on the Irish political control of the arts and such personal matters as sexuality. As a student his "**Che Sciagura**" attacked the Irish attitude toward contraception. An early poem, "**Hell Crane to Starling**," mocks in brogue Ireland's hypocrisies, iniquities, and clichés. SB was sensitive to **cen-**sorship, his position made explicit (1934) when *The Bookman* commissioned an essay, dealing with the Act of 16 July 1929 that listed *MPTK* on its Index. "**Censorship in the Saorstat**" did not appear until 1983 (*Disjecta*, 71), but it outlined SB's discomfort with Irish theocracy. In an earlier *Bookman* essay, "**Recent Irish Poetry**," SB had sneered at Irish mythology's "iridescence of themes —Oisin, Cuchulain, Maeve, Tir-nanog, the Táin Bo Cuailgne, Yoga, the Crone of Beare—segment after segment of cut-and-dried sanctity and loveliness." He castigated George **Russell**, who entered his heart's **desire** "with such precipitation as positively to protrude into the void" (71); Frederick **Higgins**, whose poetry has "a good smell of dung, most refreshing after all the attar of far off, most secret and inviolate rose" (73); and Austin **Clarke**, the "Pot Poet" **Ticklepenny** in *Murphy,* for "the deeper need that must not be avowed" (73). Ticklepenny sucks his "gaelic prosodoturfy" from mugs of Beamish porter. *First Love* (1946) resumes the cause: "What constitutes the charm of our country, apart of course from its scant population, and this without help of the meanest contraceptive, is that all is derelict, with the sole exception of history's ancient faeces . . . Wherever nauseated time has dropped a nice fat turd you will find our patriots, sniffing it up on all fours, their faces on fire" (34). SB lamented to **MacGreevy** (1 January 1935): "ask for a fish & they give you a bit of bog-oak."

SB's Anglo-Irish origins, his voluntary exile, his writings in **French** (at variance with Irish pieties), and his internationalist perspective might suggest that his work is instilled less with Irish pro-sodoturfy than with the *goût de terroir* of **Bonnelly**. But to dismiss SB's Irishness is as reductive as seeing him solely through Irish eyes, smiling or frowning. His nationalism reflects that version of home(land) expressed "between two lit refuges" and so *neither,* or the failed **syncretism** of *First Love. Three Novels, Waiting for Godot,* and *Texts for Nothing* are located *feelingly* among the glens, loughs, and quags of the Wicklow hills, his boyhood haunts. Translations of these into "English" are steeped in the syntax, cadences, and commonplaces of **Dublin** ("Faith, there's an idea"). "The **Old Tune**" and *That Time* return to this locale. SB surrendered neither his Irish citizenship nor his Irish passport. He softened as Ireland matured. Following an honorary D. Litt. (2 July 1959), he donated several manuscripts to the **Trinity** Library. After his **Nobel Prize** (1969) the Irish made numerous attempts to colonize him. Consider Harrington's *The Irish Beckett* (1991), which seeks to "legitimize" that notion (146) via the sense of "place"; or O'Brien's *The Beckett Country* (1986), which shows how SB's works are saturated with the auld sod. That feeling persisted through the years abroad. As **Quin** might say, "for all the good it did him, he might as well have remained in Ireland." Or as the **Unnamable** says (326): "The island, I'm on the island, I've never left the island, God help me."

Critics like Anthony Roche have struggled to situate SB's theater within an Irish tradition. Roche constructs a line of descent from **Synge** and **O'Casey**, but also W. B. **Yeats** (the theater of failure), and asserts SB's importance as the "pre-siding genius of contemporary Irish drama, the ghostly founding **father**" (5), an influence emerging from his self-imposed isolationism. Although Roche seems intent on imaging SB as the **Godot** of Irish drama, his deeper significance for Irish writers may be as an exemplary figure who raises such issues as translation, exile, estrangement, and dispossession, themes at the heart of plays that occupy a recognizably Irish setting. This is not to posit direct influence (though playwrights like Frank McGuinness and Marina Carr, and novelists like John Banville have acknowledged such), but placing SB within contemporary Irish drama reveals preoccupations shared with more "rooted" Irish playwrights: "a rejection of naturalism and the linear plot of the well-made play as inappropriate to a post-colonial society like Ireland; a favoring dramatically of an imposed situation in which the characters find themselves and which they either disguise or subvert through rituals of language, gesture and play." Situating SB's work thus reveals features more culturally grounded than is usually recognized, yet facilitates the emergence of a more international and purely theatrical dimension of "Irish" plays.

Fintan O'Toole sees continuities between austere forms of Irish naturalism and SB's minimalism. *Godot,* he says, "bears an uncanny relationship to the kind of jokes that people in Ireland were making about the rather bleak nature of the place in the 1950s, when isolation and emptiness had a literal resonance in the depopulation of the countryside." He adds: "Before Samuel Beckett shocked European culture with theatrical images of things that were not happening, there were people in Ireland who had images in their heads of a theater like his, not as an exercise in the avant-garde, but as a description of reality. Irish reality itself had a surreal quality." Indeed; but O'Brien rightly cautions that SB's Irishness "should not be seized upon by the patriotic purveyors of national character and genius for public display." See also: **Beckett country**; **Cork**; **Dublin**; **Foxrock**; and **politics**.

Irish Writing: a literary quarterly based in **Cork**, ed. David Marcus and Terence Smith (1946–54), and Seán J. White (1954–57). It published two extracts from *Watt* (17 [December 1951], 11–16; and 22 [March 1953], 16–24), and one from *Malone Dies* (34 [spring 1956], 29–35). To Mania **Péron** (4 août 1951), SB noted that this "mauvaise revue" had requested a contribution, and that "dans ma grande bonté" he had agreed, choosing the pieces because he could not find anything "moins scandalisant."

irrational heart: a condition affecting many of SB's characters, so part of the **fundamental unheroic**. Medical and **mathematical** extensions of **Pythagoras** (see **apmonia**) assert the **irrationality** that is a central concern in the early works. Murphy has such an irrational heart that no physician could get to the root of it (3); **Neary**'s hair turns white as he experiences the syndrome (224). **Quigley** and **Dr. Nye** suffer thus, the latter given a heart "that knocked and misfired for no reason known to the medical profession." In 1926 SB first experienced "the old internal combustion heart"; attacks be-

came more frequent and distressing. He told **MacGreevy** (24 February 1931): "I went to my doctor because my bitch of a heart was keeping me awake. He smoothed my sense of importance with a contemptuous 'Smoke less.' So I try to smoke less." **Pozzo** cannot smoke two pipes, lest his heart go pit-a-pat (*WG*, 19.a). Tremors continued long after SB's **father** died from cardiac complications (1933). To Mary **Manning** (1937), SB described the "stone" in his heart, the "cardiac calculus" he had earlier reported as symptomatic of a diseased condition in his prehistory, "a bubble in the puddle . . . If the heart still bubbles it is because the puddle has not been drained" (SB to TM, 10 March 1935). See **Bion** and **psychoanalysis**.

irrationality: SB's early writings dispute with **Descartes**, whose cosmos is governed by laws that are clear and distinct. Accordingly, its inhabitants recognize the rationalist tradition, in which the right pursuit of Reason is the highest activity of the immortal soul, leading to the love and understanding of **God**; in **Windelband**'s terms (209), Reason is both *nous* (mind) and *physis* (nature). SB's gospel was **Geulincx**'s *Ethica,* the opening sentence of which affirms that virtue is uniquely the love of right reason, with its consequence, *Ubi nihil vales, ibi nihil velis,* which (he told Sighle Kennedy) was one point of departure for his work. **Mahaffy** (96) identifies the chief difficulty of Cartesianism, as summed up by Hobbes: that what Descartes conceived as clear and distinct may have seemed to him to be so and thus provide a foundation for thought.

But such clarity is at best metaphorical, which may be why a man holds some opinion, "but it cannot tell him with certainty that the opinion is true." This principle constitutes SB's foundation of doubt. If *Murphy* is a Cartesian **machine**, its entelechy is dubious, and Murphy's attempt (by agency of Geulincx) to live in the **little world** ends in chaos. The impossible seven scarves binding him to his **rocking chair** (where is the seventh and who tied it?) are the first of many affronts to reason, the process culminating in his **death** (accident, **suicide**, or murder?). **Neary**'s rationalism is subverted by **desire**. Other microbes in the ointment are the **atomists** (qv), classical and contemporary, whose quantum world subverts the rationalist universe (see **absurdity, physics,** and **Poincaré**). Hence SB's second point of departure, the **Democritean** dictum that *Nothing is more real than nothing*. The cosmos of *Murphy* is a would-be **Occasionalist** universe shattered by the guffaw of the Abderite.

Windelband notes, #43, "The Metaphysics of the Irrational," that the attempt to deduce all phenomena from one fundamental principle gives rise to other theories, which are forced to maintain "the unreason of the Word-ground" (615): that which cannot be comprehended by reason constitutes the irrational. He notes the influence of Schelling, who transferred the irrational to the Absolute (618), and the manifestation of that impulse in **Schopenhauer**, who asserted "the absolute unreason of an objectless will" (620), grounding pessimism in the unhappy will within a world of suffering. SB's argument, articulated in *Proust* and repeated in *Murphy*, that

pleasure is but the removal of pain and man's best lot is never to have been born, is contingent on this metaphysics, as stated precisely by Windelband.

This pessimistic critique of Cartesianism remained a central tension in SB's work, accompanied by the growing distrust of the rationality (see **Cézanne**) implicit in the Greco-Christian philosophy of history, which was essentially anthropocentric, man the measure of all things, the end of creation. As SB noted in his **German Diaries** 4 (15 January 1937), all he can know is the straws and flotsam of existence, and not the inhuman and incomprehensible machinery of causes and effects that underlie them. He wonders at the kind of appetite that can be appeased by rationalizing them: "Rationalism is the last form of animism. Whereas the pure incoherence of times and men and places is at least amusing."

Watt, with its critique of the *méthode*, and *Three Novels*, with their subversion of the **cogito**, realize in fiction principles that SB expressed in the "**German Letter of 1937**," in the postwar criticism, and in correspondence with Mary **Manning** and Thomas **MacGreevy**. *Watt* enacts the tragedy of one who tries to live by rationalist principles and finds that the world cannot accommodate them. The Unnamable admits (298) that "They" taught him to count, and to reason: "Some of this rubbish has come in handy on occasions, I don't deny it." He uses it to scratch his arse: this is the "rational prurit" (*Murphy*, 193), reflecting SB's attraction to rationalist impasses, the urge to scratch the spot that itches. **Molloy** deploys Descartes's second maxim: to be firm and resolute, as one lost in the forest proceeds in a straight line; that way (he affirms) if the traveler does not reach the point desired he at least comes to somewhere preferable. But one so lost goes round in a circle, as Molloy does. **Moran** deplores "the falsetto of reason" (107). As the narrator says in "The **Expelled**" (51), "we may reason on to our heart's content, the fog won't lift." Compare the sublime stage direction (*WG,* 12.b): "Vladimir uses his intelligence"; only to remain in the dark. Rationality remains entropic: order a tiny subset of universal disorder; meaning a fragment of the absurd; figure in dubious relationship to ground; the **face** against the blooming buzzing confusion (from *Murphy* to "La **Falaise**"); **consciousness** the tip of an iceberg in a sea of the unconscious; the audible an uncertain distillation of sound. Human receptivity is an unreliable radio tuning in to the void, a small significant band within the wider spectra of the **incoherent continuum** (qv), the word ill heard in a world ill seen, and finally fading.

L'Issue: a passage from *Le Dépeupleur* (third and fourth paragraphs, with variants), and six original engravings ("eaux-fortes") by **Arikha** (Paris: Georges Visat, 1968); a limited edition of 154 numbered copies, loose sheets within embossed wrappers, uncut.

issueless: consider "MacGreevy on Yeats" (*Disjecta,* 97): "the issueless predicament of existence." **Molloy** sees writing as blackening margins and filling the holes of words, till "the whole ghastly business looks like what is, senseless, speechless, issueless misery" (13). The

word is contradictory, "no way out" and "without progeny"; the only way out is never to have been born. Lord Gall proclaims ("Echo's Bones," 8): "Possibility of issue is extinct." John **Donne**'s last sermon (25 February 1630), preached in anticipation of his **death**, took for text Psalms 68:20: "And unto God the Lord belong the issues from death." As **birth** is deliverance from death in the **womb**, an issue from death, so might the *exitus mortis* be deliverance from death. "**Text 9**" (137) implies that there is no way out (**French,** "issue") of such misery. "Le **Calmant**" (39) captures the sense of being trapped in the **body** "sans issue." The word is a motif in *Lessness.* The minimalist texts visualize a **closed space,** a cube, a rotunda, a figure forced into an **embryonic** posture, with no exit.

"**It is high time lover**": an unpublished thirty-one-line poem among the **Leventhal** papers at the **HRHRC**. It invests "hochzeit" ("wedding") with the imperative that it is "high time" to lay "belted livery all adown," to marry. This is drawn from "**Return to the Vestry**"; **Ronsard** did not marry Hélène and is now dirt in a stable. The tone is ambivalent, but **Anteros** lays the moon, and **desire** is undone.

"**I would like my love to die**": SB's translation of his 1948 quatrain "**je voudrais que mon amour meure,**" published beside the original in *Poems in English* (Calder, 1961), unpublished by **Grove**. The sentiment originates in **Ovid** (*Metamorphoses,* III.468): "vellem, quod amamus, abesset" (DN, 158). The poet imagines the rain on the graveyard, on himself, walking the street and "mourning the first and last to love me." SB sent a presentation copy to Kay Boyle in April of 1963, and she promptly objected to the author's translation of the last French line, "pleurant celle qui crut m'aimer," itself revised from the earlier "pleurant la seule qui m'ait aimé." At her instigation SB revised the line to "mourning her who sought to love me," which appeared in the 1968 reissue of the *Poems in English* as an "Alternative last line;" the alternative finally became the accepted as "mourning her who thought she loved me" in the Calder *Collected Poems 1930–1978* (1984). Calder claims the poem concerns Lucia **Joyce**, but Harvey (229) cites **Racine**'s *Phèdre* (I.iii.253–54) and associates it to the long illness of SB's **mother**, who died a year later. **Krapp** looks at the window where his mother is dying (59): "There I sat, in the biting wind, wishing she were gone."

J

Jacques: in *Eleutheria,* manservant in the **Krap** home, his name derived from **Diderot**'s *Jacques le fataliste* (he calls M. Krap "Master").

"J'ai renoncé avant de naître": "Foirade II"; in *Minuit* 2 (janvier 1973): 40–41. See **"I gave up before birth."**

Jalade-Lafont: in **"Draff"** (198), the **Smeraldina** considers a husband a "prophylactic, a wire bandage of Jalade-Lafont." SB noted the phrase (DN, 66) from **Garnier**'s *Onanisme* (248), "Prophylaxie," which discourages "cette funeste habitude." Should exercise and Christian instruction not prevail, or stringent measures, such as sponging the genitals with vinegar or camphor, not prove efficacious, then Jalade-Lafont may be required. This is a "ceinture" like a chastity belt, with metallic "bandages" laced behind, "Triangulaire pour les filles" but "pour les garçons une sorte de moule dont la capacité est double de celle des organes à contenir," permitting "l'issue d'urine par une ouverture." Garnier gives it his blessing, which modesty forbids us to translate: "Tel est le bandage de Jalade-Lafont contre l'onanisme dont il retira les bons effets. Tous les bandages en peuvent fabriquer sur mesure, afin de ne pas blesser les organes ni gêner les mouvements. Perfectionnes en tissus élastiques, ils sont à peine apparents sous le pantalon. On les conserve en place la nuit et il est même nécessaire, chez certains enfants, de ne les enlever momentanement que pour les nettoyer et entrenir la propreté indispensable des parties génitales."

Jeffreys, George (1648–89): Judge Jeffreys, Baron of Wem, infamous persecutor of the Popish Plot who headed the "bloody assizes" after Monmouth's insurrection (1685). A pupil of "the celebrated Busby," his excesses are outlined in **Cooper** (*Flagellation,* 156–60). Mentioned in *Watt* (144) as presiding over the Ecclesiastical Commission, responsible for the revenues of the Established Church, but this was not instituted until 1835.

"Jem Higgins' Love-Letter to the Alba": a fragment from *Dream,* first published in *New Durham* (June 1965): 10–11, ed. Peter Mew, with an essay by John Fletcher.

Jerome: Eusebius Hieronymus (ca. 347–419), Church Father and translator of the Vulgate. *Murphy* (104) compresses three parts of his life: *Calchis* (373–79), where he retired after **Christ** in a dream reproached him for being more Ciceronian than Christian; *Rome* (382–85), where he began his Vulgate translation, amid a circle of Roman widows and maidens to whom he taught Hebrew and the virtues of celibacy (no mention of a [Magda]Lena, let alone a **panpygoptic** Manichee); and *Bethlehem* (from 385), where he settled after falling from favor with the new Pope.

"**je suis ce cours de sable qui glisse**": first of *Trois poèmes: Three poems* (1948), translated in *Transition Forty-Eight*, as "**My way is in the sand flowing.**" The poet acknowledges that his way is between shingle and dune (the setting is **Killiney** beach), his peace in the receding mist: a littoral then liminal existence, as a door "that opens and shuts." Ambiguity arises from "je suis," both identity and following. In *Watt* (43), "glissant" is used of sand slipping at an almost significant moment.

Jetzer, Johannes (1483–1514): an unlettered Dominican lay brother who claimed visions of Mary, who afflicted him with the stigmata. Exposed as deceit, this was investigated by the Inquisition (1508–9). The "Jetzerhandel" became an index of misunderstanding between the monasteries and the Church. SB recorded from **Cooper**'s *Flagellation* (95; DN, 52): "Brother Jetzer vomited up the poisoned host." In "**Echo's Bones**" (7), Lord **Gall** is likened to "Jetzer or **Juniperus**."

"**je voudrais que mon amour meure**": third of *Trois poèmes: Three poems* (1948), a four-line verse, translated in *Transition Forty-Eight* as "**I would like my love to die**" (qv).

"**J. M. Mime**": begun for Jack **Mac-Gowran** (1963) but abandoned, "in the absence of all inner need" (Knowlson, 451). Sketched on two pages in a "Herakles" notebook, now at **Trinity**. Two players begin their "progression" at the center of a **quincunx** ("quink"), their **motion** conditioned by the structure, as in "**Quad**" (qv). Published in facsimile in Gontarski, *Intent of Undoing*.

Job: for **Murphy**, the agonies of Job as the need to work; SB's **mother**, like **Celia**, wanted to "make a man" of one who rejected this goal, "fictitious" as it sacrifices inner freedom to bodily contingencies. The book of Job was SB's touchstone of **absurdity** (see the "hippopot" and "airtight alligator" of "**Text**") and a source of such maieutic saws as "What is man that he should be clean?" (15:14). **Moran**'s gray **hen** sits with her arse in the dust, "like Job, haha" (101). **Swift** on his birthdays read Job 3, where Job curses the day he was born; compare **Neary** (*Murphy*, 46) and Mr. **Tyler** (*All That Fall*, 15). Ionesco thought SB a Job figure, and perhaps he was not wrong.

Johnson, Dr. Samuel (1709–84): English author and lexicographer whose consummate achievement was the *Dictionary* (1755). SB owned a 1799 edition, the source of such words as "tardigrade" and "equipendency" (*Watt*, 30–31). He also owned **Boswell**'s *Life* in the 1887 Birkbeck Hill edition, the *Johnson Miscellanies,* and *Rasselas.* SB read Johnson through the 1930s and (July 1935) visited his house at Lichfield. He recognized in Johnson not merely a great and fascinating writer but a soul mate, another **Sam**: "They can put me wherever they want, but it's Johnson, always Johnson, who is with me. And if I follow any tradition, it is his" (Bair, 257).

SB's "Johnson fantasy" was a play that would center on the relationship between Johnson and Hester Thrale, thirty-one years younger, covering the period from Thrale's death (1781) until Mrs. Thrale's remarriage, to Johnson's fury, to an Italian **music** teacher, Gabriel Piozzi (1784).

SB believed that Johnson was in **love** with Mrs. Thrale for fifteen years while living with them, and was impotent, not while Thrale was alive and commerce was impossible but when he died and the possibility arose. He filled three note-books about Johnson after returning from **Germany** (1937). Smith notes SB's reading (*Eighteenth Century*, 112–13): Boswell's *Life*, Hester Thrale's *Anecdotes of the Late Samuel Johnson, LL.D* (1786), Leslie Stephen's biography (1878), Thomas Secombe's "Essay Introductory" to Broadley's *Doctor Johnson and Mrs Thrale* (1910), the *DNB*, and Vulliamy's *Mrs Thrale of Streatham* (Cape, 1936), a "scholarly romance" SB owned. Smith notes (114) the 1937 discovery of Johnson's medical journal, recording his final illness, and he details SB's fascina-tion with Johnson's condition (124–27). SB gave his notebooks to Ruby Cohn, who passed them to the **BIF** (Reading). He tried to "whittle the material down" but only part of one act was written (see "**Human Wishes**"). He lost enthusiasm as the impotence theory eroded. What took its place (but was unsuited to dra-matic expression) was the image of the melancholy hypochondriac in physical decline, the horror of annihilation and fear of going mad, yet self-consciously intrigued by the shabby spectacle of his own deterioration, the "necessity of suf-fering" (Smith, 115). SB's reading and personal sense of Johnson were thus sub-limated into *Watt* and *Three Novels*.

John the Baptist: prophet who baptized Jesus and was beheaded by Herod Anti-pas. As patron saint of **Florence** he is invoked by **Belacqua** ("A Wet Night," 49). His feast is June 24, Midsummer Day, when **Murphy** meets **Celia** and loses his head. **Malone** hopes to survive that fes-tival and Bastille Day (179). **Caravaggio**'s decollation of John the Baptist was a for-mative image for *Not I*. Pears that ripen in December (*Malone Dies*, 261) are St. John's pears (but after the Evangelist, whose feast is December 27).

John of the Cross, St.: Juan de Yepes y Alvarez (1542–91); Spanish mystic (Inge, 223–31). His *Dark Night of the Soul* treats the divine union; compare **Moran**'s "It is midnight." SB summa-rized his three divisions of the Night of Sense (mind, will, and **memory**), another tripartite analogue to **Murphy's mind**. **Belacqua** is "a dud mystic" (*Dream*, 186), a John of the Crossroads who comes too late into a little knowledge of himself.

Joly, Verger: verger at Father **Ambrose**'s church (*Molloy*, 96), who ticks off the faithful at absolution. In "**Text 2**" (107), with but one leg and a half, he climbs to the belfry. A "Lise Joly" (*Mercier et Camier*, 88) does not survive into English.

Jones, Ernest (1879–1958): Welsh-born psychoanalyst who compared Hamlet and Oedipus (1910), and wrote the de-finitive *Life* of Freud (1953–57). The **Unnamable**, considering various forms he might take (339), includes Jones. The **French** equivalent is "Tartempion" used in gentle mockery. SB was fond of the **pun**, "erogenous Jones."

Jonson, Ben (1572–1637): English clas-sical poet and dramatist whom SB studied during his "crash course" in Jacobean drama, 1934-36. *Volpone*'s "fricatrice" gave the **Frica** of *Dream* and "A Wet Night"; *Murphy*'s subplot is modeled on *Volpone*, and Chapter 2 imitates its opening. *The Poetaster* offered "pot-poet" (pentameters for pints), which SB applied to **Ticklepenny** (84).

"les joues rouges": a twenty-four-line unpublished poem (RUL 2912), written 1938–39. The poet invokes the red cheeks and the hate he loves more than beautiful things and fine people. These sustain him through the white hours, the golden hours, and the gray, until swallowed in the greater hate of the black night. In this mood the "**petit sot**" (qv) walks in the woods, along a ditch, where others, without **love**, without hate, "étaient ce qu'ils devraient être."

Journal of Beckett Studies: founded (1976) by James Knowlson, who founded the Samuel Beckett Archive (**BIF**) at Reading University (1971). *JOBS* was published until 1989 by John **Calder**, 18 Brewer Street, **London**. The editorial board included John Fletcher, Ruby Cohn, Enoch Brater, A. J. Leventhal, Martin Esslin, John Pilling, and Claus Zilliacus; Calvin Israel, Richard Admussen, and S. E. Gontarski were soon added. Some have served to this day. *JOBS* featured unpublished works and a commissioned tribute from SB in its first six issues. Run as an unsubsidized commercial enterprise, with the intention of appearing twice yearly, *JOBS* emerged irregularly, only eleven times in its first fifteen years. While Calder remained committed to keeping SB in

print, economic realities restricted publication, particularly with the demise of his press (1991). Florida State University began a new series (1992), S. E. Gontarski assuming the editorship. Special issues have featured Irish writers or the French Beckett. Chris Ackerley's *Demented Particulars* (1998) was the first *JOBS* Book; the second was *Other Becketts*, ed. Daniella Caselli, Steven Connor, and Laura Salisbury (2001); the third is John Pilling's *A Companion To Dream Of Fair To Middling Women* (2004). The Calder issues, collectors' items long out of print, are available on the *JOBS* Web site. *JOBS* has remained a force because of its ability to attract prominent as well as the best younger scholars. Many essays have subsequently reappeared in book form. *The Beckett Studies Reader* (1993) closed the first phase of the journal's history by reissuing others that had not received the distribution they deserved. Into the new century *JOBS* continues to publish biannually, with the occasional double and special issues. It remains the journal of record for Beckett studies.

Jouve, Pierre-Jean (1887–1976): French writer whose early work was influenced by the late **symbolists**, then Jules **Romains** and **Unanimisme** (qv). SB admired Jouve's prewar poems, which despite their emphasis on communal feeling accentuated the individual's sensations and reactions. He went to **Paris** (1928) intending to work on Unanimisme, but found neither the man nor his religious verse sympathetic, Jouve having rejected his earlier work in favor of mystical and psychoanalytical writing. SB probably wrote an essay on "Jouve and Unanimisme" that summer, but no copy has survived. Fletcher suggests (24) that Jouve's "desperate ethics" fed SB's own, and that SB's **French** verse resembles Jouve's.

Joyce, James (1882–1941): shortly after arriving in **Paris**, having read *Dubliners* and *Portrait* but not yet *Ulysses,* SB was introduced to Joyce by Thomas **MacGreevy.** He became one of the inner circle, visiting the flat in the Place Robiac, assisting Joyce with literary tasks, and helping translate "**Anna Livia Plurabelle.**" SB attended the *Déjeuner "Ulysse"* given by Adrienne Monnier (27 juin 1929) at the Hotel Leopold, Les Vaux, to celebrate the French *Ulysses* and silver anniversary of Bloomsday. *En retour,* he disgraced himself sufficiently, Joyce told Valery Larbaud, to be abandoned in a palace "inseparably associated with the memory of the Emperor Vespasian" (a *pissoir).* The **friendship** was complicated by Lucia's "lech" for SB (see **Joyce, Lucia**), but "**Home Olga**" (qv) testifies to renewed intimacy.

Despite different social backgrounds, SB and Joyce had much in common: a keen intellect; degrees in French and Italian; curiosity about the rhythms, subtleties, and shapes of words; a fascination with **religion** deeply undercut by skepticism; a love of **music, Dante, Synge, art,** and Charlie Chaplin; respect for silence; and total commitment to writing. A mark of intimacy was Joyce's dropping of "Mister" to refer to SB as "Beckett" (never "**Sam**"). SB was sycophantic, imitating Joyce's posture, drinking white wine, holding his cigarette affectedly,

and wearing tight shoes (Joyce was proud of his small feet) to the detriment of his walking. He resented being told (by Henry Miller) that he had too much talent to waste it imitating Joyce (Bair, 144), or being asked (by Ezra Pound) whether he was writing the next *Iliad* or *Divine Comedy* (Bair, 85). Despite the lasting admiration for Joyce, during his *Lehrjahre* SB was forging his own aesthetics, shaped as much by resistance to as emulation of the most enduring influence on his career. But it took many years to emerge from the "cotton-wool" into which members of the Joyce circle invariably sank.

SB's contributions to *Finnegans Wake* are impossible to measure. He was not Joyce's "secretary," but he read aloud, ran errands, and found for "the Penman" significant details. SB's papers include notes for Joyce on mythology, Irish history, and "The Cow" (Knowlson, 106). Ellmann tells (398) how SB's comment on the story of Buckley and the Russian General *(FW,* 353), "Another insult to **Ireland,**" became part of the text. SB apparently told Ellmann that as Joyce was dictating *FW* there was a knock on the door that SB didn't hear; Joyce said, "Come in," and SB wrote that down. The phrase was queried, but Joyce decided to "let it stand" (Ellmann, 649). The detail has proved notoriously impossible to find; perhaps, like the inaccurate dating of **Mauthner** (Ellmann, 649) or the "Illstarred punster" *(FW,* 467), SB's **memory** was at fault, or the biographer's leg was pulled.

"**Dante**" acknowledges Joyce as heir to the Italian tradition. SB emphasizes that literary criticism is not bookkeeping;

that far from being among the "analogy-mongers" Joyce is an artist who creates systems, notably Viconian ones, only to smash them; and that his vision, unlike Dante's, is ultimately **purgatorial**. Like much in the essay, this says more about SB's intention than Joyce's achievement; few would concede that *Work in Progress* exemplifies "direct expression" (26) or "statement of the particular" (29). More important is the foreshadowing of SB's aesthetics, "savage economy" rather than "hieroglyphics."

As a young man with "nothing to say and an itch to make" (SB's dismissal of his early works), SB, according to the contributors' notes of *The European Caravan* (1931), "adapted the Joyce method to his poetry with original results" (his description). He adopted Joyce's technique of reading for the sake of writing, copying phrases and ticking them off in notebooks to show they had been grafted into his work, less plagiary than a private dialogue. *Dream,* the early poems, and *Murphy* are shaped by this accretive and often pretentious method (SB called such **xenia** "helps"). SB admitted to Charles **Prentice** of *Dream* that "of course it stinks of Joyce," noticeably in the "**Sedendo et Quiesc[i]endo**" episode (64–74), despite endeavors to endow it with his own odors. Yet SB had not entirely "gone Joyce." Other than this section and a parody of "The Dead" in "A **Wet Night**," specific borrowings are few and usually oblique, obscure kips rather than smooth taut beds of intertextual pleasure (see *Ulysses*). Rewriting *Dream,* he toned down the obscurities of "TWO." The "Joyce method" is as much exorcism as imitation. While *Murphy* imitates in

London Joyce's observation of **Dublin** (**Brewery Road** as the type of Eccles Street), the treatment is ironic. Little derives from *Finnegans Wake;* the **Alba**'s reference to the Egyptian Book of the Dead (*Dream,* 164) is one exception, and the thunder of *Finnegans Wake* (239) another.

More lasting was an understanding of what words could do, in echoes and implications. SB's "Joyce" is the Stephen of *Portrait* taken at his own evaluation, the impersonal Artist-as-**God**, not today's young man who may become an artist but whose every act is tempered with irony. For Joyce, art was the human disposition of intelligible or sensible matter for an aesthetic end; for SB, it was the arrangement of the inexplicable: "It never explains." SB reacted against the classical Joyce, the master of omniscience and omnipotence identified in the "interview" with Israel Shenker (1956) where SB was described as working with "impotence, ignorance," and stated that the "other type of artist—the Apollonian—is absolutely foreign to me." This expresses the **fundamental unheroic**. SB's admiration for Joyce's heroism remained, but Joyce's way was not for him. Bloom's homecoming is a triumph of abnegation, not unlike **Christ**'s paradox of humility, the greater victory through suffering. For SB that was no triumph. The "post-Golgothian kitty" of "**Ooftish**" is a senseless accumulation of pain, and SB's assertion of his artistic terrain ("I don't think impotence has been exploited") reflects that awareness.

Both writers loved the trivial, but in different ways. For Joyce (Richard Ellmann noted), the commonplace was uncommon, the ordinary extraordinary;

for SB, demented particulars were the flotsam and jetsam of existence, straws at which a desperate mind might grasp, but any bricks built from them an imponderability. SB's decision to write in **French** was largely a reaction against Joyce, whose proud boast that he could make words do anything met SB's growing distrust of words and meaning. French allowed greater resistance to the insistent interconnectivity of metaphor and ubiquitous allusion. SB could hear the universal music of *Finnegans Wake* but cultivated instead an equal but opposite technique of distant echo and semi-allusion, a mode he made increasingly his own.

SB never wavered in his loyalty to Joyce, whom he last saw at Easter 1939. Joyce's **death** moved him greatly, but he preferred not to talk about it. From 1953–56 he met with Richard Ellmann, whom he liked at first, despite too many questions and "incessant note-snatching" (SB to AJL, 6 August 1953). He was offended by Ellmann's publication of Joyce's intimate ("my little fuckbird") letters to Nora. When Ellmann suggested writing SB's **biography**, SB was discouraging; this probably fueled Ellmann's vitriolic *NYRB* review of Deirdre Bair. One theme was consistent: Joyce, SB insisted, had made him realize artistic integrity. From one uncompromising in such matters, this is the supreme accolade.

Joyce, Lucia (1905–1982): daughter of James and Nora **Joyce**, born in the pauper's ward of Trieste hospital, a disturbing influence in SB's early life and model for the **Syra-Cusa** of *Dream* (33): "dream creek, amaranth lagoon." SB met her at Joyce's flat (1928) and was attracted by her vivacity, dark hair, and bright blue eyes, although her looks were marred by a scar on her chin and a slight squint (strabismus). She was studying dance, and SB saw her at the *Bal Bullier* (28 mai 1929) in a striking silver and green fish costume. SB became attuned to her unpredictability, the product of an irregular family life and (ironically) the lack of a stable language, but he perceived signs of mental instability. One irony is that Joyce, intensely superstitious, named his daughter Lucia (as in *Lucia di Lammermoor*), yet remained oblivious to her condition. This was not helped by her "lech" for SB. She would call at the **École Normale**, and they might go out together, or join Joyce's entourage. She would lie in wait for him, gaze at him passionately, and monopolize his attention. As she became more hyperactive, SB would watch, fascinated by aspects of the **father**'s mind running rampant in the daughter (Bair, 84). An undated letter to **MacGreevy** comments: "as usual impossible to see Joyce for Nora and Lucia. Usual fucking complications & flight." Lucia, he noted, looked "foutue." He evaded her, but in May 1930 he had to say that he had come to visit her father, and was not interested in her amorously. After an emotional scene, Mr. Joyce icily informed Mr. Beckett that his presence was no longer welcome.

SB was devastated, and the rift was not repaired until Joyce, reluctantly, accepted that his daughter was ill. The friendship resumed in 1932 (see "**Home Olga**"), but SB avoided the flat when Lucia was there. Much remains uncertain. Biographers agree that SB's involvement was reluctant and imply that Joyce was unfair. Yet Lucia was not unattractive; there was more to the relationship than is usually admitted, and Joyce's response as outraged father may not have been totally unwarranted. Knowlson comments (111) that SB was "unlikely" to have let things become sexual, since he was involved with Peggy **Sinclair**; and he cites Albert Hubbell, with whom Lucia later had a physical relationship, as saying that she was still a virgin. In *Dream* (34) the narrator asks of the Syra-Cusa: "Would she sink or swim in Diana's well? That depends what we mean by a maiden." This fictional suggestion of dalliance is endorsed by a letter to MacGreevy (10 March 1935), where SB admits to "the Lucia ember" again flaring up and fizzling out.

Although briefly engaged to Alex Ponisovsky in March 1932 (Knowlson, 153, calls it "an attempt at a more or less arranged marriage"), Lucia deteriorated. So began endless consultations (some with **Jung**), occupational therapy, clinics, injections, and operations. She pursued SB intermittently, SB receiving an "utterly insane" letter ("It is really disturbing. I suppose that I can only do nothing" [SB to MacGreevy, 29 January 1935]). Much of Lucia's later life was spent in *maisons de sanité*, at Ivry, or St. Andrew's Hospital, Northampton, where she passed her final years. SB kept contact, writing to her and directing the royalties from *Our Exagmination* (reprinted 1962) toward her upkeep (Bair, 535). He received letters, and dutifully replied, a loyalty that caused an academic scandal when Stephen Joyce informed a

stunned Joyce symposium in Venice (1988) that he had, with SB's tacit agreement, burned some of that correspondence and threatened to destroy the rest, because of prurient biographers. The ramifications of this, even now, are uncertain.

Jude, St.: patron of desperate and dangerous causes. Invoked by **Lucien** in "Ce n'est au Pélican" (*Dream*, 21), the **Unnamable** (362), and **Hamm**. His emblem is the boat hook; compare the **stick** used to dislodge **Worm** (358) and **Hamm**'s gaff (82).

Julian[a] of Norwich (1342–1413): an anchorite who dwelt in the churchyard of St. Julian at Norwich. Discussed by **Inge** (*Mysticism*, 201–9), whence SB took her sentiment that "all shall be well" (*Dream*, 9; DN, 98), contrasting it with **Grock's** "Nicht möglich." Una **bboggs** is a sourer and fatter version of Juliana, without charity and prayers ("What a Misfortune," 121).

Jung, Carl Gustav (1875–1961): Swiss psychologist. He discovered psychiatry as a discipline with the potential to accommodate both biology and religious, spiritual, and occult phenomena. In 1906 he met **Freud**, whose system was congenial to his developing ideas, although as a disciple he had to subordinate his interest in mythology to theories of sexuality that he distrusted. As Freud's intellectual heir he was appointed Permanent President of the International Congress of **Psychoanalysis** (1910). Tension with Freud resulted in a decisive break and his resignation of the presidency (1914). He pursued a high-profile career until his retirement to Bollingen Tower (1947). His output was profuse, centering on the role of mythology in the human psyche. His explorations of occult and archetypal psychic material were conducted so obsessively that his **equilibrium** was often precarious. At his death he was a revered figure with an international following.

SB told **MacGreevy** (8 October 1935) that Jung struck him as a safer AE [George **Russell**], the mind (like a Swiss watch) more ample, informative, and penetrating, but the same "cuttlefish's discharge," the impulse to escape the issue. A definitive moment came when SB and **Bion** attended the third of Jung's five lectures at the **Tavistock Clinic** (1935). Jung showed a diagram he had used earlier, which became for SB a virtual archetype of the mind. It is strikingly simple: a series of concentric spheres representing gradations of the mind from the outer light of ego **consciousness** to the dark center of the collective unconscious. SB records Jung's commentary: "The closer you approach that centre, the more you experience what Janet calls an *abaisement du niveau mental:* your conscious autonomy begins to disappear, and you get more and more under the fascination of unconscious contents" (Knowlson, 206). This reaches its extreme in cases of insanity. Jung's diagram structured **Murphy's mind** with its "three zones, light, half light, dark" (111). SB shows little interest in Jung's archetypes; instead, he responds to the *fascination* of the inner dark. In Murphy's case, a willful retreat into the inner sanctum, the disturbing aspects of this process are alleviated by Cartesian farce, and any weakening

"conscious autonomy" is overcome by Murphy's regrettably fundamental sanity.

Jung mentioned the **little girl** who had never really been born, and who by age ten had still not emerged from the archetypal dreams in which children's dawning consciousness is immersed. This haunted SB. Many of his protagonists have never really been born; even as old men they are troubled by an unresolved desire for quietude symbolized by a return to the womb; psychic birth, the most fundamental transition, has not been realized, as (SB felt) in his own case. In contrast to Freud's prosaic assessment of human potential ("lieben und arbeiten"), Jung envisaged psychic life as a lifelong process of spiritual enrichment. A developing personality, having established in childhood a lucid ego consciousness, must assimilate the archetypal forms of its collective unconscious, through the mediation of dream symbolism or mythology, into its ego consciousness. The key to psychic health is to "know thyself"; those who subsume the various archetypes within a unified conscious identity will be well adjusted to meet life's demands and spiritually enriched by their contact with mankind's psychic heritage. But if one's ego consciousness is weak, the archetypes are not integrated but thrust indiscriminately into consciousness and dominate it. Jung continued in his Tavistock lecture: "The fascination of unconscious contents gradually grows stronger and conscious control vanishes in proportion until finally the patient sinks into the unconscious altogether and becomes completely victimised by it. He is the victim of a new autonomous activity that does not start from the ego but starts from the dark sphere" (*Symbolic Life,* 74). Worse, he is the victim of separate, autonomous activities, corresponding to the various archetypes without a dominant ego to coordinate them: "In hysteria the dissociated personalities are still in a sort of interrelation, so that you always get the impression of a total person . . . In the case of **schizophrenia** that is not so. There you encounter only fragments, there is nowhere a whole" (100).

Jung's principal archetypes are the *shadow,* the *anima,* and the *animus.* The shadow is a projection of the personal unconscious onto a fellow; it consists of the individual's dark aspects, qualities he does not acknowledge as his own. To make that acknowledgment, to realize that the projection *is* a projection, requires considerable moral effort. The anima is man's projection of the archetypal form of Woman onto specific women. Subsuming the role of Freud's mother **imago**, the anima first appears as the **mother** and her all-absorbing world of maternal nurture, the archetypal marriage of mother and son from which the male can tear himself away only by a traumatic effort. The anima reprojects itself onto subsequent female partners in relationships that maladaptively reproduce the mother-son, unless the source of the projection is recognized in one's own psyche, thus making space for the full range of female imagos (sister, daughter, beloved). If this is achieved, the fortunate male can dominate the feminine qualities of the anima and integrate them into his overall masculine personality. The animus is a woman's equivalent archetype of man (of little concern to SB).

Jung conceives of psychic life as a drama acted out on the stage of consciousness by these and other archetypes. **Molloy** is a Jungian ego consciousness on a quest to reconcile his anima and thus be born into a state of integrated selfhood. His dilapidated mother is an absent figure whom he must metaphorically find: he must recognize her as a projection and reject her dominating influence as a first step toward integration. Sophie **Lousse** is another projection of the anima. Her numinous sphere of maternal nurture demonstrates Molloy's subjection to the anima's feminine nature; his relationship with her merely apes the mother-son relationship and represents no progress, so he must pursue his quest elsewhere. Nor has his sterile encounter with **Ruth/**Edith improved his understanding of the fair sex.

Molloy's bludgeoning of the charcoal burner represents a confrontation with his shadow wherein he fails to assimilate it. The drama is set in a landscape of archetypal spareness: town (society), sea (unfathomable unconscious), forest (dark unconscious), swamp (the unconscious bubbling into consciousness). The ditch in which he ends his narrative is the uterine canal, a place of transition where he awaits his **birth** into integrated selfhood, but experiences instead an anti-birth into a pathological disintegration of personality. His return to his mother's room is not an integration of his anima but a capitulation to the quietude of the womb. **Moran** is a Freudian ego engaged with a Freudian psyche; his relationship to Molloy is that of an ego to its Jungian shadow. Moran is afraid of the psychic unknown and tries to suppress the

Molloy within himself and any form of female imago or anima. Such behavior will fail: suppressed archetypes will force themselves into consciousness with a traumatic effect proportionate to the strength of the repressive ego mechanisms they must shatter to do so. Thus Moran is overwhelmed by the Molloy-like unconscious personalities arising within, and his consciousness disintegrates.

SB's structural use of Jung is controversial. Jungians may hold that his primary artistic concern is the dramatization of Jung's psychological insights. There are problems with this. SB also presents a set of Freudian paraphernalia, much bleaker than Jung's. The Freudian unconscious is reducible to mere animal appetites, the glories of civilization ultimately no more than an elaborate channeling of those urges; from libido they came, to libido they return. There are no irreducible mythic archetypes to offer possibilities of spiritual fulfillment; psychic life is at best a compromise between the world and the id, with an inherent element of suffering. SB's sympathies lay with Freud; he showed no interest in Jung's mythological peregrinations through alchemy and mandala symbolism. Freudians will hold that SB draws on the best of Freud and Jung in the belief that both offer genuine insights, but that the dramatic structure squeezed from Jung is subordinated to Freud's biological insistence. There is some truth in this, but it does not follow that SB's primary artistic concern is the dramatization of Freud's psychological insights supplemented by Jung; his use of Freud is equally a dramatic process.

Opinion will divide over how much credence SB gave to the psychoanalytic material he used. His use of Jung offers some clues. Psychoanalytic systems fade from the trilogy after *Molloy,* but Jung's influence revives in *The Unnamable* in terms of the Tavistock diagram. The Unnamable is a **voice** (qv) speaking from the dark core. SB's writings after *Murphy* dramatized a relentless process of falling under the fascination of that core unconscious content. Successive protagonists become victims of the autonomous activity that "starts from the dark sphere," culminating in the reduction of consciousness to an unstable identification with an unnamable voice compelled to speak. Having reached this core SB shows no concern with the archetypes a Jungian might discover; he has adopted an impoverishment of symbolic content to convey the bare phenomenon of the voice. For SB the unnamable core consists of this compulsion to express. This is ultimately antithetical to Jung's archetypes, which survive only in an intellectual vacuum shielded from the main trends of modern philosophy, ethnology, and psychology. Having used Jungian thought as a crutch to aid his advance, SB came to dominate a modern intellectual landscape in which Jung is an anachronism. [DL]

Juniperus: in *Dream* (98) and "**Echo's Bones**" (7); from **Cooper**'s *Flagellation* (DN, 51), with other like references (**Caterina of Cardona**, Adamite, Evite, **ecce homo**, **Lupercal**), to celebrate the naked bottom, "gymnosophist" meaning "naked sage." Brother Juniperus was a

Franciscan monk persuaded he might assimilate himself to the prelapsarian Adam by nakedness and made his processions thus, "regardless of the contempt and ill-treatment of the public and even his own brethren" (Cooper, 47). **Belacqua** imagines him dreaming of whipping a naughty vestal in a dark room; the detail is mistranscribed, Cooper's point being (DN, 51) that *she,* obliged to wear a dark veil, would be naked.

"jusque dans la caverne ciel et sol": last of twelve *Poèmes 38–39,* published in *Les Temps modernes* (novembre 1946). It is a fitting finale, twelve lines encapsulating a somber sense of one for whom the self is a cavern, **voices** and light fading from afar. The intimation of Proserpine, with the light ("viols") on the *capillaires,* both Maidenhair ferns and the deeper reaches of the human cavern, forcibly integrates the self with the outside world, but the effect is finally an acceptance or allegiance (as Proserpine or **Atropos**) to the world of shadows.

Juvenal: Decimus Junius Juvenalis (ca. 60–127), Roman satirist. SB makes casual use of cliché from the *Satires,* such as "Cacoethes scribendi" (VII.52), the incurable itch for writing, implied of **Joyce** ("best of penmen") in *Dream* (133), or the "rara avis" (VI.165) of *Murphy* (193). His diatribe against women is invoked: "et lassata viris necdum satiata recessit" ("then exhausted by men but unsatisfied she went back" [VI.130]). This is Messalina, wife of Claudius, who took on all comers in a reeking brothel, leaving with passion still raging. The **Syra-Cusa** was "never even lassata, let alone satiata" (*Dream,* 50). SB wrote "lassata sed" on a card to Con **Leventhal** (2 May 1934; Pilling, "Losing One's Classics," 13). Compare the insatiable Miss **Counihan** (*Murphy,* 225).

K

Kakiamouni: *Sakya-Muni* is the Buddhist avatar of forgiveness and gentility. Recast in *Dream* (179) from *caca*, "shit"; the first of many "caca" jokes.

Kampendonck, Heinrich (1889–1957): German artist associated with Marc, **Kandinsky**, and Klee. He participated (1912) in the first Blaue Reiter exhibition. In 1931 the Nazis declared him a degenerate and dismissed him from his teaching post. He moved to Belgium, then Holland, where he worked at the Rijksacadamie. His pastoral subjects, treated with the exaggerated proportions of mosaic and folk art, possess an aura of fantasy to emphasize the metaphysical experience. Mentioned in *Murphy* (196) and "**Lightning Calculation**."

Kandinsky, Wassily (1866–1944): Russian-born painter, active in the Bauhaus and Blaue Reiter movements. His *Punkt und Linie zu Fläche* ("Point and Line to Surface"), 1926, may underpin **Murphy**'s experience of being a point in the passing of line (112). Meeting Kandinsky (1939), SB described him as a "sympathetic old Siberian" (Knowlson, 266). SB translated Kandinsky's preface, "Abstract and Concrete Art," *London Bulletin,* 14 (May 1939): 2, for Peggy **Guggenheim**'s exhibition of May 1939 (F&F, #492C). Whatever his opinion of Kandinsky's affirmation of the spiritual in art, SB admired his mastery of color and form. He read appreciatively a study by Willi Grohmann, former director of Dresden's Zwinger Gallery (Knowlson, 233), recommending it and Kandinsky in "La **Peinture des van Velde**" as an escape from the **feasible**.

Kant, Immanuel (1724–1804): German philosopher and author of *The Critique of Pure Reason* (1781). Much of SB's understanding of Kant was gained through **Schopenhauer**, whose admiration was unstinting but who scrutinized Kant's philosophy closely. Kant spent most of his life in Königsberg, East Prussia, leading a life of such regularity that townsfolk reportedly set their watches by his daily walk. Trained in the philosophy of **Leibniz**, he was influenced by **Rousseau** and **Hume**. The *Critique* established his reputation. Kant tried to prove that though knowledge cannot transcend experience it is nevertheless in part *a priori,* and not inferred deductively from experience. A first distinction was between analytic propositions, in which the predicate is part of the subject, and synthetic propositions, the truth of which cannot be discovered by mere analysis of their concepts. His distinction between empirical and *a priori* propositions shaped the central question of his *Critique:* how are synthetic judgments *a priori* possible?

As Schopenhauer affirms (*WWI,* II, 6), "Kant's greatest merit is the distinction of the phenomenon from the thing in itself," his precursors having affirmed **time** and space, causality and inference as *aeternae veritates*, absolute laws under the guidance of which the riddle of the world must be capable of solution. Schopenhauer's summary must suffice (I.2 #24, 154): "We have learnt from the great Kant that time, space, and causality, with their entire constitution, and the possibility of all their forms, are present in our **consciousness** quite independently of the objects which appear in them, and which constitute their content." They may therefore be termed forms of intuition or perception of the subject, and their **objects** (Kant's term) constitute *phenomena*, distinct from *noumena*, or things-in-themselves. Kant defined twelve *a priori* "categories," in four sets of three: *quantity* (unity, plurality, totality); *quality* (reality, negation, limitation); *relation* (substance and accident, cause and effect, reciprocity); and *modality* (possibility, existence, necessity). His "manifold" defined the sum of the particulars furnished by the senses before being unified by the understanding. He acknowledged the fallacies that arose from applying time or space, or categories, to things that are not experienced, terming such contradictory propositions *antinomies*. The narrator of *Company* (38) summarizes Kant's sense of things beyond experience, then rejects Kant's conclusion: "Pure reason? Beyond experience. **God** is love. Yes or no. No." Contending that moral concepts have their origin *a priori* in the reason, Kant articulated his "categorical imperative," the requirement to act *as if* one's action were to become through one's will a natural law. Schopenhauer, and after him SB, did not follow this path, but both accepted the synthetic unity of **apperception**, the mind's perception of itself as a conscious agent. **Molloy** acknowledges the **hypothetical imperative** (87), which becomes categorical.

To reduce such complexity to a hatful of precepts is an impertinence. *Murphy* includes: a witticism about the antinomies of unmarried love (64); life in the marketplace as an end to means (67); Murphy's punctual return (70); **Celia**'s accosting him in form (15, 90); a critique of pure love (103); and **Cooper**'s *amours* with Miss A and Miss B as a parody of analytic and synthetic reasoning (206). Kant's "manifold" contributes to the third zone of **Murphy's mind** (112), as to **Belacqua**'s, that "marsh" containing no distinction in terms of the logical or empirical categories. Despite notes in German in the **Whoroscope Notebook** (1937?), SB's sense of Kant derived largely from **Windelband**. He cited Kant's dictum, "*Zweckmassigkeit ohne Zweck*" ("purposiveness without purpose"), meaning that we must act as if the manifold embodied some transcendent purpose, although we know it does not. This gives way to Schopenhauer's sense of will-lessness.

In *Watt*, the encounter between **Arsene** and Mr. Ash reflects Kant's description of Westminster Bridge, on which he had never set foot; this is a paradigm for Watt's attempt to comprehend the noumenal reality of Mr. **Knott**, who appears in various phenomenal manifestations. The outcome may be summed up as "*das fruchtbare Bathos der Erfahrung*" ("the fruitful bathos of experience"), as recorded in the Addenda (253), deriving from the "Prolegomena to Any Future Metaphysics," where Kant attacks a reviewer who had misunderstood him. Kant uses "bathos" in its Greek sense of a deep place, in contrast with "High towers, and metaphysically tall men like them, round both of which there is commonly a lot of wind." It can be misread (as SB intended) as the more usual "pathos," or suffering.

Kapp and Peterson: the pipe smoked by Pozzo (*WG*, 23.b), its loss another intimation of attrition. Kapp and Peterson of 35 O'Connell Street were **Dublin**'s best-known tobacconists; their slogan was "The thinking man's pipe." Pozzo says "briar," but **Estragon** "dudeen," a distinction between the bourgeois and peasant worlds.

Karmitz, Mariu: with Jean Ravel and Jean-Marie Serreau, filmmakers with whom SB worked on the film of "**Comédie**" for the Venice Biennale (septembre 1966). It was screened privately with *Film* before its Venice premiere, then lay dormant until reprised at the Musée d'Art Moderne (**Paris**, 2000) and the Anthony Reynolds Gallery (**London**, 2001). Although indebted to Serreau's staging (11 juin 1964), the production was essentially SB's. He told Alan Schneider (11 February 1966): "Making this was exciting and I am pleased with result."

Kassel: on the river Fulda (*Dream*, 69), capital of Hesse-Nassau; hence sardonic references to the "choked channel of Hohenzollern rocaille" on the castle (67) and "the pleasant land of Hesse" (111). Kassel forms the setting of "**Dortmunder**." SB's Aunt Cissie and her Jewish husband "Boss" **Sinclair** had lived there since 1922 (Landgrafenstrasse 15), dealing in

art, until the Nazis made conditions intolerable and they were forced back to **Dublin**. SB visited Kassel to see his cousin Peggy, that fraught relationship shaping the first part of *Dream*, which culminates in a disastrous New Year's Eve in 1929.

Keaton, Buster (1895–1966): comic genius of the **silent movies**, his classics like *The Navigator, The General*, and *Steamboat Bill Jr.* marked by exquisite visual gags and precise timing. His later films flopped, he struggled with alcoholism, his marriage failed, and he barely managed as a gagman. In this depressed condition he was contacted to act **O** in *Film*. Keaton had earlier been offered and had refused the role of **Lucky** in the American premiere of *Waiting for Godot*, which he hadn't understood; he now needed the money and took the **job**. Without a clue about it (he later commented, "That was a wild daydream he had"), he set about filming with professional patience, becoming almost interested despite his conviction that everyone was nuts. Keaton handled the early scenes as directed, excelled with the **cat** and **dog**, and achieved exactly the right "look" as O finally realizes that there is no escape from **E**, from being perceived. For an absorbing account of the filming process, including the meeting between SB and Keaton (the actor barely looking up from his baseball and beer), see Alan **Schneider**'s "On Directing *Film*" (in *Film*, Grove, and Faber, 1969).

Keats, John (1795–1821): English poet whose medical background intensified his awareness of impending death from tuberculosis. SB told **MacGreevy** (July 1930): "I like him best of them all, because he doesn't beat his fists on the table. I like that awful sweetness and thick soft damp green richness." He liked, he said, "that crouching brooding quality." Yet he contrasted **Proust**'s aesthetic detachment with "the terrible panic-stricken stasis of Keats . . . 'drowsed with the fume of poppies' and watching [*sic*] 'the last oozings, hours by hours'" ("To Autumn"). "Take into the air my quiet breath" ("To a Nightingale") is cited in "**Dante and the Lobster**"; alluded to in *Dream* (107); parodied in "**Malacoda**"; invoked in *Murphy* (229), the "panting rhyme to 'breath'"; and echoed in *Watt* (33): "the breath that is never quiet." In *Dream*, the **Smeraldina** (68) is "pale and belle" ("sans Merci"); this in the manuscript is in the "peacock's claws" passage (15) but is omitted in print. She turns on him "like a leopardess" (88), but he has not the smallest inclination to have her ruin him. Compare Praz, *The Romantic Agony* (274), Keats describing a young Anglo-Indian: "Not a Cleopatra, but she is at least a Charmian . . . the Beauty of a leopardess . . . I should like her to ruin me." The **Alba** is "furled in her coils" (174), like a Lamia. In *Watt*, the tubercular postman was once **Shannon**; this became "Severn," one river replacing another (Joseph Severn attended the dying Keats). **Moran** (164) hears that life is a thing of beauty and a joy forever (*Endymion*, 1.1). The **Unnamable** (399) has known windows, "some opened on the sea," like the "magic casements" of "To a Nightingale." **Winnie** remembers the "beechen green" (*Happy Days*, 38). **Krapp** recalls Fanny, a "Bony old ghost

of a whore" (62); the crass might see the specter of Keats's beloved, the ill-named Fanny Brawn.

Kelly, Hugo (1739–77): one of **Johnson**'s friends, a minor **Dublin** dramatist who survived in **London** as a maker of corsets. Reborn in "**Human Wishes**" as the author of *False Delicacy*, a "drunken staymaker . . . dead and damned these five years."

"Le Kid": a pastiche of **Corneille**'s *Le Cid*, out of Charlie Chaplin's *The Kid*, attributed to SB but written by Georges **Pelorson** for performance at the Peacock Theatre (1931) by the **Trinity** Modern Languages Society. Described in the program as "a Cornelian nightmare," it was "clever, avant-garde, and rather **Surrealistic**, but with a mixture of the effete, the pretentious, and the puerile" (Knowlson, 127). SB was the Cid's aged father, Don Diègue. Carrying an alarm clock, he began deliberately but when the clock started ringing went faster, as **Lucky** would later. It was a succès de scandale, **Rudmose-Brown** offended to the point of insult as he left the theater. Unable to face the second night SB got drunk in his room, whence he was extracted for a disastrous performance. The text has not survived, but reviews in *TCD* (26 February 1931) and the *Irish Times* (20 February 1931) praised its exuberance; SB commented to MacGreevy (24 February 1931) that the vulgarization had left him exhausted and disgusted. For his satirical reply to a critical review, see "The **Possessed**."

"Kilcool manuscript": an unpublished fragment of dramatic monologue, dated

"Paris, Dec. 1963" (TCD, MS 4664); a precursor to *Not I* and *That Time* with its image of a woman's head illuminated in the darkness. The story concerns an orphaned girl recalling her journey from **Dublin** to Kilcool, to live with her aunt, traveling to Bray on the **Slow and Easy**, passing the graveyard at "Redford by the Sea" (O'Brien, 106). Kilcoole [*sic*] is a village south along the Wicklow coast from Greystones, where William **Beckett** rented a summer house. The manuscript is discussed in Gontarski's *Intent of Undoing* (141–49) in relation to *Not I*, indicating that the central conflict grew out of the struggle to give shape to recollections, but until he "undid" the material and self from which it emerged SB's creative efforts were unsuccessful. Once the subject was defined and orchestrated musically, by repetition and variation, the process proved fruitful. The struggle challenges any assumption that SB's compositional method is **surrealistic** (even as parody) or the plot incoherent.

Killiecrankie, Dr. Angus: in *Murphy,* Resident Medical Superintendent of the **MMM**. His name connotes, in English, killing the cranky, the mentally ill (G. *krank*, "ill"). The Pass of Killicrankie, near Pitlochry in Tayside, saw a bloody victory by the Highlanders over the English (1689). The doctor is a case study of the type described in the third **Tavistock** lecture, where **Jung** suggested that complexes may form personalities: "They appear as visions, they speak in **voices**." In the **French** *Murphy,* the link between his Outer Hebridean origins, the schizoid voice, and **Ossian** is explicit. The original of Dr. Killiecrankie,

according to Brian Ryder, was the senior assistant physician at the **Bethlem Royal**, one Murdo MacKenzie, originally from Inverness, the **pun** on "murder" ("Killie") being further identification. Ryder also suggests: Dr. John Porter-Phillips, who insisted that suicide could be effected by **apnoea** and whose outside interests, which included golf, meant that he was by no means always present, as the willowy, dapper original of the Coroner in Chapter 12; and Kenneth Cantle, the nurse in charge of the wards, and whose father and uncle founded Bethlem's orchestra (their photo in the waiting room), as the original of **Bom** [Brian Ryder to CA].

Killiney Beach: a long stony bay south of **Dún Laoghaire**, the setting of several scenes in SB's work: the sucking-stones episode of *Molloy,* and his cave (at Whiterock); "**Embers**"; "**Eh Joe**"; and "**My way is in the sand flowing**." Frank Beckett's house, The Shottery, overlooked Killiney Beach.

k'în music: the "k'în" is described in Louis Laloy's *La Musique chinoise* (68–76), SB's source, as an ancient Chinese musical instrument, a lute on a base with five (later seven) silken strings plucked by the right hand while the left controls the length of the strings, each capable of producing fourteen different notes, which do not represent the fixed order of the *liù* (qv). Laloy calls it a delicate instrument, to be played "dans le secret des salles retirées" (70), to be listened to with a pure heart, as the "k'în profané" will not deliver its beauty: "le k'în est sacré" (72). Compare "**Dortmunder**" with its "thin

K'in **music** of the bawd." **Belacqua**'s vision of saved souls (*Dream*, 113–14) is accompanied by "laughter and old K'in music, rising demitonically"; it becomes "keen music." In "**Alba**" this is the "singing silk," the black "areca" or wooden sounding board (Laloy's "faite en bois d'aréquier et vernie en noir" [68]), and the "rain on the bamboos" (Laloy's "la pluie sur les bambous" [75]). This is heard by *Watt* (209); **Neary** after his Chinese meal and lychee is consoled by "a dusk of lute music" (*Murphy,* 117).

kips: the **Dublin** red-light district, the area of Railway, Mecklenburgh, and Montgomery Streets. Becky **Cooper**'s establishment is recalled in "**Sanies II,**" with its incongruous picture from **Dante** on the wall. Also incongruous is the Pro-Cathedral in Marlborough Street, with its pros and cons (*Dream*, 78), all **puns** intended. "**Ding-Dong**" ends with **Belacqua**, his vision of paradise thwarted, heading for Railway Street, beyond the river. **Mercier and Camier**, coming from the mountains, "smell kips" (91).

Klein, Melanie (1882–1960): Austrian child psychologist who studied under **Freud** and practiced in **London**. Wilfred **Bion** recommended to SB *The Psychoanalysis of Children* (Hogarth Press, 1932). Klein used play to understand the mental processes of **children**, games establishing contacts with realities in the external world in accordance with: i. the principle of intelligibility, as governed by rules; ii. the symbolic relation between the game and the outside world; and iii. extrapolation from the one to the other. Intimated in *Murphy* by the "shrouded instruments of recreation" (236) and the **chess** game. Rabaté notes ("Fluxions," 26) in the tearoom scene underpinnings of Klein deriving from Bion in respect of the primitive link between the truth ("Vera") and the "good breast" (milk and mammary organs). Less earnestly, Baker suggests (101–3) that SB's interest in Klein reflects his ambivalent relationship to his **mother**. The *Quatre nouvelles* respond to Kleinian readings that equate the text and the mother's **body**, although SB's fixation was more upon the womb than the breast.

Kleist, Heinrich von (1777–1811): German writer known for his comedy *Der zerbrochne Krug* (1802). SB was affected by his essay "Über das Marionettentheater" (1810), which he read in German and could quote years later to exemplify gesture (see **puppets**). In 1969 SB visited his memorial at the Wannsee, where Kleist had blown out his brains with the words "O Unsterblichkeit—nun bist du ganz meine" ("O immortality, now you are mine").

Klopstock, Friedrich (1724–1803): German poet whose religious epic *Der Messias* (1748–73) was inspired by **Milton**'s *Paradise Lost*. His *Odes* have lasted better. The narrator of *How It Is* (42) refers to "the great shadow he casts towards his native east," his sense of the *Abendland* rather than his birthplace in Quedlinburg, Saxony. To Mary **Manning** (2 January 1959), SB recalled his 1936 visit to **Germany** and a cold afternoon in Ohlsdorf cemetery looking for Klopstock's tomb, "which isn't there." As the **German Diaries** and *How It Is* confirm, he found it in the Christiankirche, Altona.

knife-rest: when **Molloy** evicts himself from **Lousse**'s garden he takes a silver knife-rest, two crosses joined by a bar (63). It reminds him of **Christ** and the **two thieves**. **Moran** plays with his knife-rest (115). Another is included in **Malone**'s inventory of **Macmann**'s possessions (258). The detail suggests the shared identity of the four characters.

knook: admitting that "Beauty, grace, truth of the first water" (*WG*, 22.b) were beyond him, **Pozzo** says, "I took a knook." The usual suggestion is a "knout," a Russian whip used to beat serfs, but Knowlson suggests (349) that **Lucky** is a **knouk**, or a carrier.

Knott, Mr.: master of **Watt**. Like **Cooldrinagh**, his house has fine chimneys, a red-tiled floor, three stories, and the view of a racecourse (**Leopardstown**). Mr. Knott is a good master, in a way (67), but the comma qualifies the relationship. Ending his first period of service, on the ground floor (148), Watt feels aloner, sicker; he has learned nothing of Knott, and knows nothing of him. Nor are his conclusions (203) any more secure. Mr. Knott's habitual tone is one of assurance; Watt is his **witness**, albeit an imperfect one, for Mr. Knott needs the succession of servants that he might be witnessed, and thus not cease to be. This inverts **Berkeley**'s *percipi,* as Watt may not appreciate.

Watt's "ancient error" is to suppose he might comprehend his master's essence by his accidents, which he labors to understand. This is to prove **God** by exhaustion, using **Descartes**'s *Method,* moving from the known by rational enumeration until all is clear and distinct. The consequences are tragic. Reaching the end of the line, and taking a ticket to it, Watt arrives at the **asylum**. The one time he sees his master **face** to face, like Adam (146), Mr. Knott's eyes are closed, and the experience is "as it were in a glass," i.e., darkly. Further complications arise from glimpses of Mr. Knott's figure; these formulate the most complex, and so the most useless, of the logical paradigms (209–11). Watt (or **Sam**) recognizes (77) that the only way to speak of **nothing** is to speak of it as though it were something, just as the only way to speak of God is to speak of him as though he were a man, which, with what is called elsewhere an anthropomorphic insolence, SB does.

Mr. Knott is a God figure and the novel an **allegory** of mankind's quest for salvation, and the frustration of that quest. It is cast in Christian terms, although the manner of Mr. Knott's rising and retiring suggests he is a sun god, a notion not pursued. A related theme is prominent: **Arsene**'s attempt to eff the **ineffable** (62) has failed, and Watt's world becomes unspeakable (85). Arsene describes his employer (57) as "one who neither **comes nor goes**," but rather abides. The sense of Mr. Knott as unchanging, his servants turning about him in tireless devotion, is the traditional one; "sempiternal," implying (as in **Dante**'s *Paradiso*) an eternity with a beginning but no end, is cited in the Addenda (248). His immortality may be relative, however, like that of the decanter to the whisky in *Proust,* or the gardener to the roses in the dream of d'**Alembert** (qv).

Koffka, Kurt (1886–1941): founder of the **Gestalt** school. His *Grundlagen der psychischen Entwicklung* (1921; *The Growth of the Mind*, 1927) stressed interaction between innate capacities and environmental conditions, calling it the convergence factor, and identified how a figure emerges as an organized whole from a homogenous ground. His *Principles of Gestalt Psychology* (1935), a complete theory of behavior, became an immediate classic. **Neary** has written him, wanting to know why Miss **Dwyer**, having made him happy, is now one with the ground against which she had figured so prettily (*Murphy*, 48).

Köhler, Wolfgang (1887–1967): German Gestaltist. *The Mentality of Apes* (1925) reported his studies into simian intelligence at the Prussian Academy Anthropoid Station, Tenerife, 1913–17, where he had been marooned during the war. "**Acte sans paroles** I" (1957) draws directly on Köhler's book for its action and setting. (See **monkeys**.)

"Kottabista": a four-line verse adaptation of **Chamfort**'s *Maxime* ("Hope is a knave") in *Hermathena: A Dublin University Review* 115 (spring 1973): 19. An earlier version (1969) is inscribed on a copy of *Endgame* (**HRHRC** #218). **Dante**'s "All hope abandon" (*Inf.* III.9) should be graven on heaven's door, for happiness is impossible if hope endures. "Kottabista" invokes an ancient Greek drinking game in which wine flung from a drinking cup makes a noise on impact. The "title" is misleading; *Hermathena* 83 (May 1954): 81 (Spanish originals facing, 80), offered under "Kottabistae," SB's translations of

two sonnets by Miguel de Guevara: "I am not moved to love thee, my lord **God**," and "**Time** and account" (F&F, 501.02). These were intended for the *Anthology of Mexican Poetry*.

Kov: "beyond the **gulf**" (*Endgame*, 52); a homophone of "Cobh," near **Cork**.

Kraft, Adam (1455–1509): sculptor of Nuremberg, whose masterpiece is the tabernacle in the Church of St. Laurence. **Belacqua** puns on the Iron Maiden of Nuremberg, with a hint of Krafft-Ebing (*Dream*, 71).

Kram and Krim: in *How It Is*, witness (lamp) and scribe (pen) at the tribunal over the life below. They are **serial**, "generations of scribes keeping the record" (80). The narrator dreams (82) "of the great Kram the Ninth the greatest of us all" (**Beethoven**? **Schubert**?).

Krap, Victor: protagonist of *Eleutheria*, who has chosen to escape the fiasco of existence by seeking **asylum** in his bedroom, whence he occasionally emerges to scavenge from the better-class Parisian dustbins. He rejects the petty Krap and Piouk households, seeking freedom by renouncing **desire** like **Schopenhauer**, whose pessimism he shares. He is the despair of his **father** (Henri) and **mother** (Violette). He abandons his quest for the inner dark after his father dies, yet refuses to enter the outer world. He rejects Dr. Piouk's **suicide** pill, finally turning his back on the audience, and on life.

Krapp's Last Tape: a one-act play written in 1958, translated by SB and Pierre

Leyris as *La Dernière bande.* First production, **London**, at the Royal Court
Theatre (28 October 1958), dir. Donald
McWhinnie and featuring Patrick **Magee**,
for whom it had been written and whose
"banana walk" SB admired. As curtain
raiser to *Endgame* it ran for thirty-eight
performances (ending 29 November
1958). The first U.S. performance was
New York (14 January 1960), dir. Alan
Schneider with Donald Davis. Schneider
directed Hume Cronyn during the
widely seen Samuel Beckett Festival at
the Repertory Theater of Lincoln Center (20 November 1972). It was often
adapted to TV with SB's encouragement.
Approached by West-Deutscher Rundfunk, Cologne, to permit a television
version of his 1969 **Schiller-Theater** *Das
letze Band,* SB wrote a set of "Suggestions
for TV Krapp" (see Zilliacus); it was
broadcast (28 October 1969). The first
BBC TV version was produced by Peter
Luke, featuring Cyril Cusack (13 November 1963), a second for "Thirty
Minute Theatre," dir. McWhinnie with
Patrick Magee (29 November 1972).
Schneider directed Jack **MacGowran** in
an American TV version, produced by
Mark Wright (June 1971), after considerable delay taped (in color) for National Educational Television, New York.
Schneider's request for camera changes
prompted SB's disingenuous reply: "Re
Camera B use it as you deem best. My
notes are no more than suggestions & and
have no pretensions to finality" (Harmon,
256). The Schneider/MacGowran collaboration, never broadcast and long
thought lost, is available from Pennebaker
Hegedus Films. SB directed several stage
performances. First published in *Ever-*

*green **Review*** 2.5 (summer 1958): 13–
24; then in *Krapp's Last Tape and Embers*
(Faber, 1959), and *Krapp's Last Tape and
Other Dramatic Pieces* (Grove, 1960).
A gramophone recording (New York:
Spoken Arts #788, 1960), based on the
original American production, was distributed in Britain by Argo (RG 220),
and by HEAR, Home Educational
Records, London (1964).
    KLT is a model of structural simplic-
ity. Like his near namesake in *Eleutheria,*
Krapp has rejected **love** and a bourgeois
world for higher spiritual ends, the desire to write his magnum opus. Between
his thirty-first (his precise age gets vaguer
as SB revised the play) and sixty-ninth
birthdays, Krapp has dutifully assessed the
year's events, his accomplishments, and
his spiritual development, using a tape
recorder (the play is set in some vague
future to make this less anachronistic). On
his sixty-ninth birthday Krapp prepares to
tape the year by listening to tapes of his
past. Isolated within life's failures, he can
only scoff at his youth, saving a tender,
erotic moment in a punt before his "Farewell to **love**." That moment of decision
Krapp, now near **death** and in penury,
relives (a **Proustian** experience of involuntary **memory** and genuine since it was
not deliberately retrieved).
    As the story is told, a recording of *All
That Fall* (BBC 3, 13 January 1958) suggested the tape recorder in *KLT.* In fact,
Magee's haunting performance of *From
an Abandoned Work* (BBC 3, 14 December 1957) spurred SB's thinking
about the stage possibilities of monologue. He told Alan Schneider (2 February 1958): "I'm working on a short stage
monologue (in English) for Pat Magee

. . . It looks as if it might come off." The play was written quickly, seven distinct stages within three weeks, each heavily revised, all dated March 1958. SB exploited the technical and dramatic potential of the tapes and developed a complex pattern of Cartesian dualities, particularly the black/white **gnostic** imagery that dominates the play. He refined its tone, moving from an early sentimentality to a comic-pathos mix. SB was intrigued by his new character and considered developing variations on him (see Harmon, 57). In 1975, directing Pierre Chabert in **Paris**, SB said: "I thought of writing a play on the opposite situation, with Mrs Krapp, the girl in the punt, nagging away behind him, in which case his failure and his **solitude** would be exactly the same."

The play developed beyond the confines of the dramatic monologue as SB realized the recorder's dramatic possibilities. The "Magee Monologue" version opens with A's searching for a tape, knocking one off the table, and growing angry. He moves the table to steady it and takes it out of "the zone of light." In defiance of **nature** and logic the light follows. Finally, he listens to himself at thirty-one, "in the third decade of the Ram," a tape whose theme, identified in the ledger, is "Passion." Krapp at thirty-one sees himself heroically, as a pioneer, and appeals to "all-merciful Providence" for the strength to drink less and for a more engrossing sexual life. The plan to have him listen to earlier tapes remained, but SB altered the design as he collapsed two tapes into one, creating a third Krapp, an intermediary between young and old who would evaluate the information in the earlier memoir. A single tape could capture several blocks of **time**, multiple levels of **character**, creating a triple exposure: Krapp at sixty-nine listening to Krapp at thirty-nine (earlier thirty-seven) summarizing a tape made ten or fifteen years earlier. The result is a palimpsest of personalities, a layering of **character**. By presenting them simultaneously SB depicted the inability of the self to perceive itself accurately. Krapp-sixty-nine sneers at Krapp-thirty-nine, who laughs at an even younger Krapp. Each sees the fool he was rather than the fool he is.

A second revision concerned Krapp's sexuality. Krapp had longed for a fuller sex life, uttering "intercourse" as he would later relish "Spool." The woman with whom young Krapp lived was first **Alba** (Holograph 2), then **Celia** (TS1), then Furry (nickname of Anne **Rudmose-Brown**). An autograph revision to TS1 alters Krapp's conflict from inadequacy to overindulgence, the inability to control his **desire**, of mind to control body, spirit to control flesh. Krapp's appeal for a "Less exhausting" (TS1), then "Less wearing" (TS2), and finally a "Less engrossing" (TS3) sex life developed a persistent preoccupation//the conflict of intellect and emotions, wisdom and desire, the outer and inner worlds, problems that have consumed his life//They are echoed in the ledger, "Farewell to love," and in his desire to drink less. In **Schopenhauer**'s terms, intelligent contemplation of life can break the power of the Will: "Man is at once impetuous striving of Will (whose focus lies in the reproductive system), and eternal, free, serene subject of pure knowledge (of which the focus is the brain)" (*WWI*,

I.262). TS2 developed Krapp's struggles to shift his attention from reproductive system to brain, from Will to "pure knowledge." Controlling his desire was further dramatized by adding the opening dumb show, a **mime** with keys, bananas, and drink that introduced both a comic tone and a thematic thread, as Krapp locks away one object of desire. In TS3 the banana acquired sexual overtones as SB twice added "caresses banana," altered in TS4 to "strokes banana." The focus became Krapp's appetites, his desire for sensual gratification. When he turns to the tapes, consequently, he begins a selective retrospect, his abiding concerns the dark nurse and the punt. In TS3 SB contemplated making Krapp's advances more overt; he tried to pat her on the bottom, but she threatened to call a **policeman**. The affair in the punt echoes *Dream* (1932), where **Belacqua** dreams of the departed **Smeraldina** (114), of the shining shore where underneath them the keel of their skiff would ground and stay stuck; he cannot expel that face and site from his eye and mind. Behind the image of the woman in the punt remains the memory of SB's first love, Peggy **Sinclair** (the green eyes, the shabby green coat, *Effi Briest*), a memory mingled, Knowlson suggests (398), with SB's recent loss of Ethna **MacCarthy**.

// At sixty-nine Krapp struggles with his sexual appetite, but the interest is biological, his desire for integration, to merge sex and intellect, light and dark, now abandoned // His relations with the whore Fanny are grotesque, a parallel to his name and constipation, part of the libidinal economy. As he strokes the autoerotic bananas and relives two sexual experiences, he achieves limited gratification. Repeatedly listening to the affair in the punt and trying to tape his current tirade, his mood shifts. His last words are, "Lie down across her," his motionless stare suggesting a postcoital or postmasturbatory loneliness. As SB noted for his 1969 Schiller production: "recorder companion of his solitude agent of masturbation." // The ultimate image is again that of failure, at the least to control desire. //

Yet the play as SB shaped it became a study of failure more universal than personal sexual inadequacy. // Krapp has struggled against the cacophony of human character, a beaten man who now curses his younger selves for the decision to abandon love, but he never acquires the self-awareness that might afford a tragic dimension. // His predicament is finally more ironic than tragic; he could not have made a "correct" decision. SB would explore this theme in *That Time,* that the great decisions and epiphanies in one's life finally make little difference. The struggle for control, the battle against desire is now halfhearted; Krapp employs Fanny but locks away his bananas and times the intervals between drinks. He has failed to mingle, to harmonize with nature, to achieve a personal memorable equinox. His desire for an artificially achieved order, the imposition of the human mind onto natural chaos, is waning. The tapes, once neatly catalogued and indexed, are now strewn about the floor, the last incomplete and hypnotically revolving as Krapp winds his way toward **death**.

As recorded in SB's *Regiebuch* (RUL 1396/4/16), Krapp's struggle has been to reconcile spirit and flesh, the light and dark sides of his nature. SB focused on the light/dark imagery in revision, sharpening the contrast in Krapp's face and clothing (black and white). The chiaroscuro was accentuated. Early Krapp sat in "strong light. Rest of stage in shadow"; "shadow" became "darkness." TS2 specified "strong white light" to contrast this. To the dark nurse TS1 added a uniform, "all white and starch." Between TS4 and the printed version SB specified that the black **ball** be given to a white **dog**. He wrote in his *Regiebuch:* "if the giving of the black ball to the white dog represents the sacrifice of sense to spirit the form here too is that of a mingling." Krapp's reservations about the offering were stated late in TS4: "I wish I had kept it." What he wished was that he had kept sense and spirit separate, that he had not committed the Manichaean ethical fault of trying to mingle the two.

Pathos or sentiment failed to dominate. The mime with keys and bananas was added to TS2, as SB began to increase Krapp's isolation. SB also exploited the comic potential of Krapp's forgetting the definition of "viduity." TS2 read: "comes back with volume of the Concise Oxford . . . looks up viduity, reads, closes dictionary." SB added, "or **Johnson**'s dictionary and quotes example." Johnson must have proved disappointing; TS3 noted: "quotes definition if possible." The definition appeared as an autograph emendation to TS4. The play's most overtly comic touch was introduced here: "trousers too short for him," "Surprising pair of white **boots**, size ten, very narrow and pointed," "Pallid face. Purple nose" (a drinker's snout). These revisions SB as **director** found ex-

cessive and increasingly eliminated in production and so from the text.

Autobiography diminished in composition. Early Krapp identified Aries, SB's sign, representing beginning, birth, creativity, these providing an ironic commentary on his failures. SB struggled with this allusion before finally excising it. He used the name "Miss Beamish" (an eccentric woman whom SB had met in **Roussillon**) for Miss McGlome; her excision removed another connection. SB adjusted the tone, simultaneously deepening Krapp's pathos and undercutting it with comedy. In TS4 Krapp's walk became "laborious" and twice he "heaves a great sigh." Krapp's brief outburst of song, his sentimental return to boyhood, a parallel to old Miss McGlome's song, was enfeebled from "raucous" to "quavering" in TS3. The song was somber, used in *Watt* but excised for the **Calder** edition, about the time SB was working on Krapp (American editions ignore the deletion). In TS3 Krapp no longer "feels" for keys; he "fumbles" for them. His pathos was accented as his isolation increased. The winehouse where he drank at thirty-nine was originally peopled with unfamiliar faces; in revision SB excised even these strangers. The park was more populous; TS4 altered "Deserted spot" to "Hardly a soul," to parallel the winehouse atmosphere. In earlier drafts old Krapp "Sat in the park in the middle of the brats and skivvies"; in the final version he notes "Not a soul," as emblematic of his isolation. To Krapp's "Past midnight. Never knew such silence," SB added, "The earth might be uninhabited" (TS3). Krapp's world is finally as desolate and "unreal" as that of **Hamm** or **Winnie**.

Kreuger, Ivar: Swede who made his fortune from matches but shot himself through the heart (1932) after financial irregularities were revealed (DN, 87–88). In "**Love and Lethe**" (103), **Belacqua** comments as he loads the revolver: "Chevaliers d'industrie . . . nearly all blow their brains out. Kreuger proved the rule." **Malone** says (274): "It's the heart's fault, as in the bosom of the match king, Schneider, Schroeder, I forget."

Külpe School: *Murphy* offers (80) a satire of behaviorism, with reference to a school of *Denkpsychologie* prominent before World War I in Würzburg then Bonn. Oswald Külpe (1862–1915), a pupil of Wundt, broke from his master by systematic use of combined introspective and objective methods in studying thought processes. The Würzburg School was called "the School of imageless thought" from its contention that states of awareness have no sensory content, representation, or image. Marbe, Bühler, Watt, and Ach took the introspective method further, examining the *experience* during associative reactions. SB's source for Murphy's experiment is **Woodworth**'s *Contemporary Schools* (1931), notably a passage on page 36 (later omitted) suggesting that in controlled associations more might be reported from the period of preparation than from action or reaction. Murphy follows the method faithfully, expecting confirmation; hence his elaborate preparation and sense of betrayal when Vera responds wrongly. This is SB's only reference to the Külpe School, yet "imageless thought" is reflected in the divisions of "**Ghost Trio**": I Pre-action; II Action; III Re-action.

Murphy names four of Külpe's followers (81):

Marbe: Karl Marbe (1869–1953), Külpe's successor at Würzburg, from whose experiments with judging arose the notion of *Bewusstseinlage,* or "conscious attitude," awareness of hesitancy and doubt in describing experience.

Bühler: Karl Bühler (1879–1963), who repeated Marbe's experiments with more baffling questions, which confirmed Marbe's findings.

Watt: Henry J. Watt (1879–1925), later professor at Glasgow; his was the discovery, cherished by Murphy, that more experience was reported from the period of preparation than of reaction.

Ach: Narziss Kaspar Ach (1871–1946), who worked with Watt on reaction time using introspection. He discovered that the will to react anticipated the stimulus and formed part of its preparation. This "determining tendency" was of importance beyond the Külpe School.

Kulturkampf: the "cultural struggle" of Bismarck, Iron Chancellor of **Germany**, against the Church in support of Catholics who refused to accept the decisions of the Vatican Council of 1870. Marriage and education were declared civil matters, and monastic teaching was placed under state regulation. In *Watt* (188) the word refers to a **horse** that could extract cube roots. This alludes to a hoax in which a horse ("Clever Hans") stamped out answers to simple sums in response to hidden signals. Asked if it was cheating, it stamped out "nine" ("nay").

L

"Là": a rhymed quatrain inscribed "for Jim [Knowlson] / affectionately / from Sam 21.9.87" (written September 17); published (with **"Brief Dream"**) in the inaugural issue of the new series of *JOBS* 1.1 and 2 (1992): 1–2. It includes SB's final corrections. The poem exists in two versions, the earlier (untitled) using "aillers" instead of "là"; this appeared in a "Note" to the text. SB's untitled translation (24 September 1987), in the same note, begins: "go where never before." This "never before" turns out to be "there always." "Là" thus plays on the ambiguity of place, its simultaneous familiarity and strangeness, a theme SB had explored since first turning to **French** in 1946.

Labbé, Louise: correctly, Louise Labé (1520–66), called *La Belle Cordière* since she was daughter of a ropemaker and married Ennemond Perrin, ropemaker of Lyon. Her **love** for Olivier de Magny, friend of **Ronsard**, caused scandal but inspired a volume of Petrarchan sonnets (1555), sensual and pagan. Lawrence Harvey wrote a study of these. Among **Rudmose-Brown**'s favorite poets, she is parodied when the **Polar Bear** speaks to the **Alba** (*Dream*, 165). See also **"Chanson de Toile."**

Labiche, Eugène (1815–88): master of farce and vaudeville under the Second Empire. Mentioned in "Le **Concentrisme**" (from, Pilling suggests, **Bergson**'s *Le Rire*).

Lachesis: the Fate responsible for spinning out the thread of life; invoked by **Watt** (127) "doing his number one" (urinating); the drafts read "chance."

ladder: a joke that has always been a good joke: *Do not come down the ladder, Ifor, I haf taken it away.* This obscure Welsh jest is repeated in *Murphy* (188) and *Watt* (44); the punch line is, "Too late, I'm halfway down already." Edith Kern (*Existential Thought,* 238) quotes **Mauthner**'s *Beiträge* to the effect that whoever wishes to climb the ladder of language must destroy each step as he goes. Rabinovitz (*Development,* 144) quotes **Schopenhauer** (*WWI,* II.1.vii, 256) to similar effect. **Belacqua** confuses Lord Gall of **Wormwood** with this paradox ("**Echo's Bones**," 14). The ladder is a **mystical** commonplace by which the soul ascends; **Descartes** imagined he might climb, by clear and distinct degrees, to truth and the knowledge of **God**. **Inge** (9–10) comments that the *scala perfectionis* has three stages: the first, the purgative life; the second, the illuminative; and the third, the unitive, or state of perfect contemplation. The ascent is mocked by Walter Draffin's "elevated position on Saint **Augustine**'s ladder" ("What a Misfortune," 120). **Arsene** invokes "existence off the ladder": the sense of almost a **mystical** experience, of epistemological change, of something having "slipped" (*Watt,* 44). Mr. **Hackett** has fallen off the ladder (15), and **Clov** (who uses the "steps") senses a subtle change (see **Zeno**). See *The Lost Ones*.

La Fontaine, Jean (1621–95): French poet, author of the *Contes* and *Fables*. SB told MacGreevy (28 August 1934) that he had been looking at an old La Fontaine with engravings by Merseau le Jeune. *Dream* (9, 122) mentions the "catawampus," the tale of "Le **Rat** qui s'est retiré du monde," living inside a Dutch cheese, "gros et gras" but refusing to help the rats against the **cats**, suggesting that they pray for aid. It satirizes the unwillingness of the clergy during the religious wars in Holland; a "catawampus" is a fanciful beast, fierce without referent. The *Fables* debated the Cartesian contention, mentioned in "**Recent Irish Poetry**" (72), that animals were simply **machines**. See La Fontaine's "Discours à Madame de la Sablière" (29–30): "ils disent donc / Que la bête est une machine." The **Sottisier Notebook** indicates the origin of "à bout de songes un bouquin" (qv) as "Le Lièvre et les grenouilles."

Lamartine, Alphonse de (1790–1869): French **romantic** whose *Méditations poétiques* (1820) were dated by the time **Belacqua** longs for their "champaign" land ("Fingal," 24); the "magic land" is **Ronsard**. Lamartine's family estate (Milly) was in Saône et Loire, the **Macon** country. The title of *Le Dépeupleur* derives from Lamartine's "L'Isolement."

"**Landscape**": a prose poem translated by SB from the Italian of Raffaello Franchi; published in *This Quarter* 2.4 (April–May–June 1930): 672. Franchi wrote novellas in a style called *intimismo*. His touch was described by Samuel Putnam, the associate editor, as light, sure, and delicate, his craft flawless. One might demur: impossibly purple ("the sweetness of vision, its wombfruit of mystery"), his work perhaps warned SB how not to use landscape.

Lao-tzu (6th cent. BC): the "Old Philosopher" and legendary founder of Taoism, whose life is little known but whose sayings have been preserved. Giles (*Civilisation of China*, 58–59) reports his doctrine "that of doing **nothing**, by which means, he declared, everything could be done." He is the "old Chinaman" of *That Time* (230), whose **mother** carried him for sixty-two years, so he was born with long white hair. He shapes the figures of "**Ohio Impromptu**" and other late plays. The Tao informs the prose-poem "The **Way**."

larches: an "obsessional" childhood image. **Cooldrinagh** had a small plantation of larches, one of which turned green, then brown, a week before the others (*Watt*, 47). In "**Sanies I**" they are associated with SB's **birth**: "born with a pop with the green of the larches." Likewise in "A **Piece of Monologue**": "Born dead of night. Sun long sunk behind the larches." In *Molloy* (36), Teddy is buried beneath a larch, the only tree Molloy can identify. **Belacqua** cannot tell an oak from an elm, but larches he knows ("**Walking Out**," 102). See also "**Draff**" (183) and "**Serena II**" (23–4).

La Rochefoucauld, François, duc de (1613–80): his *Maximes* (1665) offer cynical views of life, as in "**What a Mis-**

fortune" (118), of a woman from her second passion, endowed with the love of love. This is #471: "Dans les premières passions, les femmes aiment l'amant; et dans les autres, elles aiment l'amour."

larval stage: in the insect's life cycle, the grub, before chrysalis and **imago** (adult). **Dante** is reminded (*Purg.* XV.124–26): "Non v'accorgete voi che noi siam vermi / Nati a formar l'angelica farfalla?" ("Do you not perceive that we are chrysalides, born to form the angelic butterfly?"). **Diderot**'s "Le Rêve de d'**Alembert**" explores evolutionary **consciousness**, "où vous n'étiez qu'une substance molle, filamenteuse, informe, vermiculaire." "Molle" is one root of **Molloy**. **Haeckel**'s *Riddle of the Universe* likens the **embryonic** soul to the development of the insect. At his **birth**, **Murphy** was projected "larval and dark" (183) into being; he tries to regain the lost **coenaesthesis** of the embryonic stage. Sitting in the **rocking chair**, **Celia** intimates the larval experience, consciousness as a peristalsis of light worming into the dark (66–67). In his "**German Letter of 1937**," SB described language as a veil that must be torn apart to get at the **Nothing** behind it, calling it "A Mask"; in German "Eine Larve" (*Disjecta*, 52, 171). **Macmann** in *Malone meurt* is "nu comme ver" (90), a nuance lost in translation (229); *The Unnamable* portrays **Worm**; *Happy Days* depicts **Willie** going back into his hole; and *Comment c'est* determines the phylogeny of "l'homme lavaire" crawling through the mud in a denial of metamorphosis.

"Last Soliloquy": holograph manuscript (RUL 2937/1–3) of an unpublished dramatic fragment, three leaves torn from an exercise book, recording a dialogue between **A** and **B**, perhaps a rehearsed **suicide**. SB specified the manner of delivery: D = declaim, N = normal. It anticipates *Fin de partie* with the phrase "I'll leave you," and two characters in a rehearsed dialogue; indeed, **Hamm** is warming up for his last soliloquy.

Laurencin, Marie (1885–1956): French postimpressionist painter, mistress of **Apollinaire**, known for her misty pastel portraits of young women. **Belacqua** and the **Smeraldina** flog together eggs and tomatoes in a "steaming Marie Laurencin polenta" (*Dream*, 18).

law: an investigation into the legal status of SB's work, and associated issues of authority, authorship, and ownership, of quotation, appropriation, and transformation, is overdue. The legal status of the work is intimately bound up with its cultural status, and whatever SB's opinions and those of his Estate one cannot assume that its value is unassailable. Edward Beckett, SB's nephew and literary executor since the **death** of Jérôme **Lindon**, has legal control over SB's work. He regulates, in part, its cultural filiation, which helps define its reputation. Questions of who uses whose words, whether they do so legitimately and in whose service, lead to the crux of how SB's work *exists,* in the public sphere as literary property and in the public imagination as a literary aesthetics or experience.

Curiously, given SB's uncompromising control of his drama, scholars have failed to investigate the complex **politics** surrounding his continued claim to sole authority over his work. This entry endeavors to expose, with respect to the legal determinacy of the text, some of the assumptions that dog this subject. It will ignore controversial productions such as: JoAnne Akalaitis's 1984 *Endgame;* De Haarlemse Toneelschuur's all-female *Waiting for Godot,* 1988; George **Tabori**'s circus-inspired productions ("das Tabu zu brechen"); Gildas Bourdet's "pink" *Fin de partie* for the *Comédie Française,* 1988; Susan Sontag's radical *Godot* in war-torn Sarajevo, 1993; the Sydney Wayside Theatre's *Godot,* 1994; Deborah Warner's 1994 production of *Footfalls* at the Garrick Theatre, **London**, which caused a heated debate between radicals and traditionalists; and Katie Mitchell's "peripatetic" *Beckett's Shorts* for the Royal Shakespeare (1996), where several productions were shown at once. However controversial, some were approved by SB or the estate; others were rejected. During his lifetime SB assumed an exigent approach, and conflicts over staging are part of the mythology. He was far from consistent in this respect. For all that he believed in authorial control, in practice, when it came to "alternative" productions, "it made a tremendous difference if he liked and respected the persons involved" (Knowlson, 608).

The tussle over staging rights happens at the threshold of the private and public domains, on the cusp of **art** as idea, and as enactment. The artist is torn between preserving a private ideal and maintaining control, and the consequences of requiring the agency of others to disseminate the work. Many changes in the transmission of cultural texts occur for political reasons. The move from private to public spheres is not just a transition but a transformation; the work becomes a social product as others construct and seek to control it, and it is affected by the new discursive spaces it occupies. As a private manuscript becomes a public document the terms of its ownership alter and are contested.

This encounter lies at the heart of the debate over staging rights. The dilemma is not whether alterations can be made to SB's texts, for the reality is that they are, with or without official sanction. The key question is, who has the power to legitimize these changes? The law defines and enforces a particular type of ownership, and the power invested in the Beckett Estate directly impacts on versions of the work to which the public has access. This legal mandate is contested by those who claim different cultural powers and prerogatives. When a private manuscript enters the public domain it becomes a product, a commodity. To be recognized and maintained, it must be legally protectable—but *what* is this "it" that must be protected? How does the law define "it"? Different cultural authorities define the work in markedly different ways, and competing ontologies affect the way we are permitted to read SB's texts. Copyright assumes, and actualizes, a particular ontology for the dramatic text. Its aims are the regulation of a traded commodity and to establish protective norms for the copying and distribution of texts. This protects only a work's expression, not its underlying idea. A work of literature *is,* in the eyes of the law, its words. The ontology that copyright defines is entirely textual, based on what is scripted, fixed to the page, and, in theory, able to be copied exactly for distribution and sale.

Edward Beckett's stance accords with copyright's letter-based approach to textual essence. He has argued: "There are more than fifteen recordings of **Beethoven**'s late string quartets in the catalogue, every interpretation different, one from the next, but they are all based on the same notes, tonalities, dynamic and tempo markings. We feel justified in asking the same measure of respect for Samuel Beckett's plays" (*Guardian,* 24 March 1994, 25). He suggests that since musicians, however freely they may "interpret" a piece of **music**, do not deviate from the composer's notes, why should a director depart from SB's dialogue or directions? Initially, this seems a fair point. A classical musician should not break into a freewheeling jazz riff in the middle of a Beethoven work. Spontaneity has its place—and a quartet is not it. There are dramatic forms that allow extemporization, and others that do not. And if a conductor should follow a score, should not a director obey a playwright's instructions?

A text may be followed in letter or in spirit, and the debate is rife with references to the Beckettian spirit. The estate claims that the best way to preserve that spirit is by strict observation of SB's text. The goal is to reproduce the "spirit" unique to SB's work. At this point Edward Beckett's analogy starts to break down, as to where the line is drawn with the letter of a score or dramatic text. What is iterable? What is copyrighted? The notes? Certainly. Dynamic and tempo *markings*? Indeed. But *actual* dy-

namic and tempo and tonalities? These qualities cannot be repeated, cannot be fixed, cannot always remain the same. This determines how far reproduction can be policed. Authority, as granted by copyright, accords to a letter-based textual ontology: what is written must be obeyed, in drama as in music. But if copyright is limited to the letter, how far may the policing of the drama extend?

The analogy with Beethoven is otherwise problematic. With the quartets not even a conductor mediates between score and musicians, compared to the multiple agency necessitated by the production of a play, where many collaborators vie for influence. No matter how compatible their general aspirations, they inescapably operate as a series of barriers between playwright and performance. A dramatic text, with the Chinese whispers effect that is an integral aspect of its enactment, cannot hope to be contained. Furthermore, classical music *is* tampered with. Music for one medium transferred to another becomes another work of art, secondary to the original but yielding a new satisfaction. Finally, the analogy presupposes that there is but one score, or one dramatic text, and fails to consider the indeterminacy of the text. Ample evidence demonstrates the complexity of SB's texts *even in print*—multiple versions of copyrighted, authorized texts exist. Thus, the estate's role as guardian of the Beckettian text is more complicated, confused, and compromised than is generally acknowledged — even by the estate itself.

George Bornstein points out that copyright law obscures the protean nature of modernist texts by artificially controlling certain versions. The result is to "freeze" texts in the form distributed by authorized publishers, to the loss of earlier forms, so that projects existing in ongoing states of evolution seem to be fixed and stable (*Material Modernism,* 40). SB established long-term relations with **Minuit** in France, **Suhrkamp** in Germany, **Calder** (prose) and **Faber** (drama) in England, and **Grove** in the United States. None of these publishers' codex editions approaches—attempts to approach—any representation of the process of reworking that characterized SB's authorship both as writer (self-translated texts) and **director** (self-directed plays). Instabilities have been institutionalized in print. Consider *Come and Go* and "**Va et vient**," the manuscripts of which demonstrate an interdependence in the genesis of both versions, as drafts of the **French** "translation" resulted in changes to the English "original." Published textual variants exist in French, English, and German, yet little reference is made to these. The instability of the published "text" (that is, texts) has been little acknowledged by critics and publishers.

Textual inconsistencies prove that SB's plays do not exist in a condition of stasis. The Estate endeavors to protect scripted works, yet variant editions of most plays are available. Legally, a director can follow any of these (which raises the conundrum of a hybrid text), yet conflict with SB's recorded intentions. Some early editions of *Krapp's Last Tape* still depict **Krapp** with a **clown**'s nose. Arguments about staging a *Godot* respectful of SB's wishes are frequently based on the assumption that there is a single authoritative script. In the general

editor's preface to the ***Theatrical Notebooks*** (vii), Knowlson notes that "whole sections of the text have *never* been played as printed in the original editions." Gontarski explains (xxv) that "critics and directors were forced into a position of building interpretations and mounting productions of SB's work not so much on corrupt texts such as almost all English versions of *Waiting for Godot,* but on those the author himself found unsatisfactory, unfinished."

The complexity of the Beckettian text renders the legal intention to preserve the spirit of the plays via adherence to the text unsustainable. The ontological status of the text is further complicated when performance is considered, for this opens up new ways a dramatic text might be said to exist. According to the exponents of innovation, the ontology of the drama is rooted in performance, which includes changing directors, contexts, and audiences. The Estate's position with regard to its legal prerogatives requires unraveling, because the criteria by which SB, Lindon, and Edward Beckett have approved certain productions frequently blur the textual boundary that copyright decrees as defining the limits of the Estate's legal authority. This authority is founded on guardianship of the text but, due to the nontextual influence wrought by changes in directors, contexts, and audiences, extends in practice to practical innovations.

The Estate *fixes* meaning by insisting on adherence to SB's conception of his work. However, with the power invested in it by the law, the Estate *creates* meaning in two key ways, so that the work is defined partly by its juridical context.

The first is effected within the theater. The Estate delimits a director's possibilities, not just by faithfully following SB's precedents and approving only what he approved but by permitting certain transformations, usually, and at times unpredictably, justified by what it considers to be in keeping with the Beckettian "spirit." The Estate shapes what the audience sees, not only by closing down potential variations but by admitting certain changes. Thus the Estate predetermines the range of readings and meanings available at any given performance.

The second process by which the Estate assumes a formative role through its guardianship of SB's work originates outside the theater. Controversy and public debate over rights help form the meaning of the work by molding the public's perception of it, affecting SB's reputation and creating expectations that in turn influence directors seeking to produce a performance conversant with contemporary audiences' thinking. This is the process by which the reputation and value of the work are created, and by which it, and SB, are mythologized in the public imagination. Discussions on rights become evaluative assessments of SB's role as creator and master of his text, either as actual director of his work or as virtual director whose intentions dictate from the grave. Such critiques, while nominally exploring the vulnerability of the text to "outside" influences, fetishize the text by focusing on the fictive world as the locus of conflict. The assumption is that fidelity to the script ensures or jeopardizes the value of the work (however that value be defined). Yet this struggle is not ultimately played out on the boards, but in the legal arena, in the media, and in academia. These "outside" forces are influential in giving definition to SB's work.

SB's plays are historically contingent and are constantly being re-created, on the stage and in the public arena, as different parties, both mainstream and avant-garde, situate them within different theatrical traditions. *Producing* Beckett does not mean simply staging his work. Rather, "production" is appropriate in a fuller sense. The "Beckett myth" is constantly being manufactured out of his texts and the legal documents pertaining to them. The work is deeply imbricated in social power plays, and it is in the social world, not simply in the theater, that its cultural status and value are constructed.

SB's dramatic writing, not yet released from the private into the public sphere, is caught in an ongoing struggle between competing cultural authorities. On the contested ground between legal and symbolic ownership a power play takes place that contributes to the social construction of SB's work, and hence to the theoretical and practical conditions of its existence. The Beckett Estate has inherited a material legacy, and enjoys legally sanctioned guardianship of it. In conflict with the Estate are those who regard themselves as inheritors of SB's commitment to artistic innovation. Members of this group employ strategies to align themselves with SB, but against the Estate, and claim more truly to honor the Beckettian "spirit." These strategies and claims constitute a new conception of ownership, which characterizes itself in opposition to the legal definition. [CB]

Lazarus: either the beggar accepted into **Abraham's bosom** (Luke 16:22–26), or, as in *Proust* (33), the dead man raised by **Christ**, the only occasion, according to **Murphy** (180), when He overstepped the mark, a sentiment (from Anatole France) repeated by the **Polar Bear** (*Dream,* 209). At the beginning of *Watt,* "happy as Larry" refers to the night that Larry was born (12), a parody of the ballad "The Night Before Larry was Stretched." "Larry" thus commits the crime of being born. The name denotes the "incontinent native speaker" of *Dream* (222) and "A **Wet Night**" (69).

Leibniz, Gottfried Wilhelm (1646–1716): German mathematician and philosopher, who invented the calculus (1675), in ignorance of Newton's earlier but unpublished work. His service with the House of Hanover began in 1673, and he remained there all his life, dying in relative neglect. Described by SB as "a great cod, but full of splendid little pictures" (SB to TM, 6 December 1933). In 1937 SB visited his house in the Schmeidestrasse, adding a late reference in *Murphy* (162) to the "garret in Hanover." Murphy's room at the **MMM** assumes the attributes of the **monad**.

Leibniz attempted to synthesize the thought of **Descartes** and **Spinoza** with the atoms and the void, which had once charmed his imagination (*Monadology,* 23). His theory of the monad described simple being. Monads are indestructible, uncreated, and inimitable elements, whose essence is activity (**motion**); although they develop they do not effect one another. The world is an infinite set of independent monads, which precludes causation, that being merely coincidence in **time** and space. The mutual accommodation of each monad to every other, effected by **preestablished harmony**, causes each to express all others and so "to be a perpetual living **mirror** of the universe." Hence the cryptic remark (*Dream,* 179): "What would Leibnitz [*sic*] say?" **Lucien** cites (47) a passage where Leibniz "compares matter to a garden of flowers or a pool of fish, and every flower another garden of flowers and every corpuscle of every fish another pool of fish" (*Monadology* #67, a fractal world in a grain of sand). Leibniz asserts an ascent toward perfection from the lowest to the highest monad, culminating in the Supreme Monad. His dictum is cited in "**Dante**" (6): *Deus est monas monadum gignens et in se reflectens adorem* ("**God** is the Monad of monads, engendering and reflecting in Himself His own **love**"). This is from McIntyre's *Giordano **Bruno*** (1903).

In the **Whoroscope Notebook**, SB noted the "Dynamist ethic of **X**. Keep moving the only virtue." Murphy on the job path embodies the monad in motion, his suit "nonporous" in the **atomist** sense of precluding penetration by the Unlimited. It allows no "vapours" to escape, *vapores* being the Cartesian term for animal spirits that commingle in the **conarium** with spiritual essences. Murphy is a **microcosm**, illustrating on the human level the law of the physical universe iterated in the *Monadology* and in the *Physica* (both "Peripatetica" and "Verum") of **Geulincx**: *Mundus est Corpus in Motu* ("the World is a Body in **Motion**"). Tragically, Murphy discovers in his encounter with Mr. **Endon** that his mind is not bodytight.

One of Leibniz's crucial distinctions is that between *virtual* and *actual*. It seems simple, the virtual apparently corresponding to the dark zone of the mind, and the actual to the light. This is not a Neoplatonic distinction between form and formlessness, but rather between that of which one might have mental-and-physical experience (actual) and that of which one has mental experience only (virtual). This has complex roots in Leibniz's concept of virtuality, concerning the paradox of impressions in the monad of the external world, but a monad that (being hermetically closed) is precluded from receiving *those* impressions from *that* world. Leibniz's resolution of the problem is to invest the monad with *perception* and *appetition* (**desire**), then, to depict God as absolute archivist, storing the imprint of the heterogeneous phenomena that constitute the world but programming in advance what will happen in the universe through **time** (the doctrine of preestablished harmony).

SB uses "virtual" and "actual" in the Whoroscope Notebook of **Abraham's bosom**: "Luke XVI: Dives—Lazarus, prayer from virtual to actual in entelechy . . . petites perceptions to apperceived in monad—poem." The term *petites perceptions* is found in Leibniz's doctrine of the monad, as summed up by Baldwin ("Leibniz"): "Activity of the mind is akin to perception. The monodal development implies the clarification of perception, and substance shows degrees of **consciousness**. Even the unconscious is only relatively so, for it is potentially capable of being perceived, just as the totality of countless drops of water is heard as the splash of a wave (**apperception**) although no single drop makes a perceptible sound (petites perceptions)." *Petites perceptions* (impossible to perceive) are virtual but in their totality may become actual (apperceived); both, however, are equally real *and* ideal. In **Windelband**'s summary (424), they are akin to unconscious mental states. In the paradox of **Zeno**, a single grain of millet falls noiselessly to the ground; a bushel poured out makes a great noise. **Descartes**'s mistake (said Leibniz) was that his insistence on the clear and distinct took no account of perceptions not apperceived: "for it treats as non-existent those perceptions of which we are not consciously aware" (*Monadology*, 224).

As Garin Dowd has established, Leibniz's influence continued into *The Unnamable*, in its evocation of a resilient **Worm** at the threshold of reason and consciousness, his very being the embodiment of Leibniz's "monade nue," the naked or degenerate form of the monad at a low level of elevation in the divine hierarchy. Worm is a precursor of "l'homme larvaire" of *Comment c'est*, the **larval** form or **imago** in the **embryonic** development of conscious being. His halting "progress" through the mud does not achieve the synthesis of apperception, despite the three-part thetic structure of that work and the presence of an ancient **voice** apparently from above, offering the promise of transcendence. SB's world remains one where things are ill seen, ill heard, and his monads, rather than mirroring the perfection of a Supreme Monad, remain in the "primeval mud impenetrable dark."

Leixlip: a picturesque village on the upper Liffey near **Lucan**, named for its celebrated "salmon-leap." Hence the "horrid latin" of the *Twilight Herald* (Dublin's *Evening Herald*): "Nicholas **Nemo** saltabat" (*Dream,* 182).

Lemass, Noel: Captain of the Third Battalion of the **Dublin** City Brigade of the IRA, "who died that the Republic might live" (O'Brien, 65–66). Seized by government troops (3 July 1923), his body was discovered on the deserted Glencree peak, where a cross was raised (the plinth remaining) with a tribute from Terence MacSwiney. **Mercier** and **Camier** do not read this (98) but recall a nationalist by name of "Masse, perhaps Massey" who "had done little for the cause" but still has his monument.

Lemuel: a keeper at **St. John of God,** more stupid than malevolent, yet considerably malevolent (*Malone Dies,* 266). On an excursion to the islands he slaughters Maurice and Ernest, the other attendants, then ships out to sea with **Macmann.** The name derives from Proverbs 31. Lemuel is the Christian name of **Swift**'s Gulliver. In **Chaucer**'s *Pardoner's Tale* (l.585) it is curiously accented: "Nat Samuel, but Lamuel, seye I."

Leopardi, Giacomo (1798–1837): Italian poet whom SB studied in his third year at **Trinity** and associated with **Schopenhauer**'s intellectual justification of unhappiness. He admitted to Con **Leventhal** (21 April 1958) that Leopardi "was a strong influence when I was young (his pessimism, not his patriotism)." Leopardi's early thought is grounded in **Vico,** affirming the Greek response to **nature**; but in later works

nature is indifferent or cruel, the stepmother of humanity. In "**Dante**" (17), SB celebrates **Joyce** with "Sopra il monumento di Dante che si preparova in Firenze" ("Concerning the monument to Dante being made in **Florence**"), praising Dante as the only one capable of reaching Homer's height: "colui per lo cui verso—il meonio cantor non è più solo" ("that man through whose **voice** the Homeric bard is no longer alone"). *Proust* has three citations of "A sè stesso" ("To himself"), in which Leopardi declares hope and **desire** to be dead, life an oscillation between desire and delusion. *Proust* (1931) included as epigraph "e fango è il mondo" ("the world is mud"), Joyce approving the consonance of "il mondo" and "immonde" ("immodest"). This inexplicably disappeared in the 1965 **Calder** reprint. Leopardi is invoked to anticipate the tragedy of Marcel and Albertine, and "A sè stesso" adduced as evidence: "In noi di cari inganni / Non che la speme, il desiderio è spento" ("In us has been extinguished not only the hope, but the desire of dear illusions"). The second line is repeated (63), a formula of the ablation of desire.

In *Dream* (18) **Belacqua** reacts to his "rape" by the **Smeraldina** by citing Leopardi's "Le Ricordanze" ("The Recollection"): "alla fioca lucerna poetando" ("composing by the faint light") as "alla fioca lucerna leggendo **Meredith**" ("reading Meredith by the faint light"). Meredith's "married **love**" suggests the change in the relationship. Later (61–62), he declines the darkest passages of Schopenhauer, Vigny, Leopardi et al., citing random phrases from "A sè stesso" (the first changed from future to present tense): "Or posa per sempre . . . stanco mio cor . . . Assai palpitasti" ("Now be forever still . . . weary my heart . . . you have beaten long enough"). **Molloy** (35) cites the earlier line, "Non che la speme, il desiderio," concerning his testicles, from which nothing is to be squeezed. This, the only explicit later allusion to Leopardi, is not present in the **French** text. Yet *How It Is* returns to the world as mud, and Leopardi's ablation of desire casts a faint but discernible light over the later writing.

Leopardstown: deriving from *Baile-na-Lobhar*, or "leperstowne," site of a four-teenth-century lazary. Known for its racecourse, established 1888 on lands owned by monks of St. Bernard (O'Brien, 350), it is visible from the **Foxrock** railway station, indicating to **Watt** (29) that he is "drawing near." The third Addendum to *Watt* celebrates "the Master of the Leopardstown Halflengths" who perished at the railway crossing. *All That Fall* was originally entitled "A Lovely Day for the Races"; Mrs. **Rooney** invokes the white rails and red stands, which are also mentioned in *How It Is* (29). Other stories (*Molloy, Company,* "The **End**") recall the first aviation meeting in **Ireland** (29–30 August 1910). SB saw his first airplane there, an event etched on his mind by his **mother**'s cutting retort that day.

Lessing, Gotthold (1729–81): German dramatist and aesthetician celebrated for his *Laocoön* (1766), which compared the plastic and literary arts, distinguishing (compare *Ulysses,* chapter 3) those unfolding in space from those unfolding in **time**. In 1936, from **Germany**, SB posted home a complete Lessing (Knowlson, 226). Lessing gives the "terms" of a complex jest (*Murphy,* 207). **Neary** crosses his feet like depictions of Sleep on Greek urns; as Rabinovitz notes (*Development,* 102), Lessing mentions (11 n.1) that in antiquity **Death** and Sleep may be represented as twins, their feet crossed. In a later illustrated article, "Wie die Alten den Tod Gebildet" ("How the Ancients Represented Death," 1769), he contends that the crossed feet indicate the unconsciousness of Dream, that Death is but a dream.

Lessness: SB's 1969 translation of *Sans* (completed at the Akademie der Künste); published in the *New Statesman* (1 May 1970): 635, then in John **Calder**'s Signature Series 9 (1970). First American publication in *Evergreen* 80 (July 1970): 35–36, then in *I can't go on, I'll go on,* ed. Richard Seaver (Grove, 1976), 557–61. "Lessness," an oddity for "without," explores the common ground between narrative and theatrical monologue. It was performed for the BBC (7 February 1971; broadcast 25 February) by Donal Donnelly, Leonard Fenton, Patrick **Magee**, Denys Hawthorne, Harold Pinter, and Nicol Williamson, each representing a set of images, A to F (below). Martin Esslin, the producer, submitted it for the Italia Prize in 1971 as a radio play designed for six **voices**. Ruby Cohn calls it a "lyric of fiction," more poetry than prose, but in his BBC introduction Esslin argued that only by hearing *Lessness* do we become fully aware of its structure and meaning, as expressed by its formal pattern (variation within the literary limits of **mathematical** permutations, like

"**Ping**"). In performance the six separate but undifferentiated voices create a fragmented **consciousness**.

Lessness is dominated by formal patterns: 120 sentences, the second 60 repeating the first in a different order, and built around six families of images, as SB outlined them:

> Group A: collapse of refuge. Sign "true refuge"
>
> Group B: outer world. Sign "earth . . . sky" juxtaposed or apart
>
> Group C: body exposed. Sign "little body"
>
> Group D: refuge forgotten. Sign "all gone from mind"
>
> Group E: past and future denied. Sign "never" (except in the last sentence "figment dawn etc.")
>
> Group F: past and future affirmed. Sign: future tense ("He will")

SB combined those images into sixty sentences, each on a separate sheet, and drew them from a container one at a time, recording the result. He repeated the process so that the second set emerged in a different aleatory sequence. Paragraph structure was developed likewise. SB wrote the number 3 on four separate pieces of paper, 4 on six, 5 on four, 6 on six, and 7 on four. These determine the number of sentences in each paragraph. Symmetries of the **French** text are reinforced by the repetition of "*sans*" sixty times; the English offers "less" and "ness." The compositional strategy suggests an experiment with pure chance in what he called a set of variations on disorder, but SB finally determined the words, the arrangement into sentences,

the number of sentences, the paragraph structure, and the motifs around which the fragmented narrative would be arranged. These are then the functions of "writing." The experiment, the only such he conducted, suggests that even when chance or the aleatory intervenes in the creative process the author remains the shaping force.

SB's summary of this "**closed space**" fiction is reflected in his description dictated for the back cover of the Signature edition: "'Lessness' has to do with the collapse of some such refuge as that last attempted in 'Ping' and with the ensuing situation of the refugee. Ruin, exposure, wilderness, mindlessness, past and future denied and affirmed, are the categories, formally distinguishable, through which the writing winds, first in one disorder, then in another." In this ruined refuge, amid the endlessness of earth and sky, the **body** now exposed is the only upright. Its sole function, face to the sky, is (like **Goethe**'s **Prometheus**) to curse **God**. In this series of double exposures, a world of fragments and figments, of refuge and refugee, the figure is both upright and on his back, in the refuge and exposed to the elements, apart from and part of the endlessness. The "blue celeste of poesy" is only imagined happiness, a fleeting dream.

"**Letters on *Endgame***": extracts from fourteen letters by SB to Alan **Schneider**, written between 27 December 1955 and 4 March 1958, published in the *Village Voice* (19 March 1958): 8 and 15, with drawings by Roy Colonna: "A chronicle of the development of *Endgame* from its 'origins in the Marne mud' to its realization on Commerce Street and else-where." Republished in the *Village Voice Reader,* ed. Daniel Wolf and Edwin Fancher (Grove, 1963), 166–69, with several other "voices" on SB. SB consid-ered this a violation of confidence, and wrote to Schneider (9 January 1958) say-ing that he did not like publication of letters (Harmon, 28–29). He sanctioned their reprint in *Disjecta,* however.

Les Lettres nouvelles: a leading **Paris** pe-riodical that published several pieces by SB: "**Trois textes pour rien**" (mai 1953); "**Hommage à Jack B. Yeats**" (avril 1954); *Tous ceux qui tombent* (mars 1957); *La Dernière bande* (mars 1959); "**Cendres:** Pièce radiophonique" (décembre 1959–janvier 1960); "**Comédie**, un acte de Samuel Beckett" (juin–juillet–août 1964); and "L'**Histoire de Watt**" (septembre–octobre 1968): 11–16.

Leventhal, Abraham Jacob (Con) (1896–1979): SB's friend and rival. The *Dublin Magazine* turned down his review of *Ulysses,* so he founded the single issue *Klaxon* (1923) to publish it. When SB resigned from **Trinity**, Leventhal assumed the position. The **friendship** cooled tem-porarily when Leventhal began an affair with Ethna **MacCarthy**, whom he subse-quently married. As assistant editor for *Hermathena,* Leventhal arranged publica-tion of SB's translations of two Spanish sonnets (see "**Kottabista**"). After Ethna's **death** he acted as SB's secretary, dealing with correspondence and shielding him from an intrusive public. He contributed an entertaining memoir to John **Calder**'s *Beckett at 60.* The Leventhal Collection at the **HRHRC** (TXRCOO-A3) is a valu-able archive, with more than 150 letters and postcards and some of SB's poems, with significant variants.

Liebert: in *Dream,* a friend of **Lucien**. Modeled on Georges **Pelorson**. An aes-thete who is turned away (his beautiful plus fours!) from *Die Valkyrie* as inappro-priately dressed, he is described by the exhausted **Belacqua** (48), to whom he gives a pain in the sensitive area, as "a miserable man."

"**Lightning Calculation**": a brief manu-script (RUL 2902), written about Sep-tember 1935, encapsulating details of *Murphy* without their irony. It begins at Mrs. **Frost**'s house, where SB resided. **Quigley** arises to a sky like curdled milk in pale blue tea, the sun pouring down the street, then consults notes on dreams made in the night, concerning his di-lemma, namely, "how to perachieve his book, *The Pathetic Fallacy from Avercamp to Campendonk*" [*sic*]. Hendrik Avercamp (1585–1634) was a Dutch landscape painter, born dumb, who specialized in winter scenes; the link is "camp" (see **Kampendonck**). In a Lyons teashop he replicates Murphy's ploy to get more tea, and calculates that his six biscuits can be arranged in 120 ways if he can overcome his infatuation with the ginger. The story ends in contentment as the permutations help him to know himself.

limbo: the border of hell where those not condemned to torture are deprived of heavenly joy; either the *Limbus Infan-tum,* abode of those unbaptised, or the *Limbus Patrum* or *Sinus Abrahae* ("**Abra-ham's bosom**") of the Old Testament saints liberated by **Christ**'s descent into hell. The term was used by Aquinas and popularized by **Dante** (*Inferno* IV). In *Dream,* it forms the dark annex of **Belacqua**'s mind; in *Eleutheria* (185), Victor **Krap**'s "calm." "**Text** 5" (120) notes of an infant dead in its dead **mother**: "that it may not go to Limbo, sweet thing theology." "**Casket of Pralinen**" includes: "Gloucester's no bimbo / and he's in Limbo."

Lincoln's Inn Fields: a public park, where **Murphy** (79) contemplates lying on the grass beneath the plane trees. The fields of Lincoln's Inn, one of the four **London** Inns of Court, were laid out in 1618 by Inigo Jones and became a dueling ground and place of execution. SB invokes the foul atmosphere of its past, a miasma of laws, with cozeners, cross-biting ("cosenage by whores"), cony-catching ("cosenage by cards"), sacking ("lecherie"), and figging ("cutting of purses, & picking of pockets")—terms taken from Robert **Greene**'s "A Notable Discovery of Coosnage" (1591).

Lindon, Jérôme (1925–2001): Éditions de **Minuit** was formed (1942) by two members of the resistance, Jean Bruller and Pierre de Lescure. The house had published clandestinely during the occupation (hence its name, after curfew) but was bankrupt. Lindon, of Jewish origin, had been with the Combat Cell of the French Maquis; he joined the failing firm in 1946 and bought it two years later. He sought new authors, loosely called the *nouveau romanciers.* His important discovery was SB. Lindon had been running Minuit for two years when Robert Carlier recommended an Irishman writing in **French** who had been rejected by six publishers. Two novels and two plays were soon on his desk. He devoured *Molloy* and from that day, he said, knew he was going to be a *real* publisher ("First Meeting," 17). It was a defining moment. The contract was signed (15 novembre 1950), and the works soon appeared: *Molloy* (15 mars 1951); *Malone meurt* (8 octobre 1951); *En attendant Godot* (17 octobre 1952); and *L'Innommable* (15 juillet 1953). The novels emerged in editions of 3,000, the play 2,500. The printer, a good Catholic, omitted his name. Lindon acquired the world rights to the unsold stock of the French *Murphy* from **Bordas** for almost nothing. Recognition seemed in reach, and SB pursued it, but not without hesitations. He withdrew *Mercier et Camier, First Love,* and *Eleutheria,* and withheld them until circumstances forced his hand.

   In 1972 Lindon formed a semiannual, *Minuit: Revue Périodique.* He was unfailingly faithful to SB, who reciprocated his fealty. Lindon could be stringent and aloof, but also generous and principled; the *Minuit* catalogue reflects his convictions and independence. SB supported tacitly his espousal of independent bookshops and publishers and, openly, his denunciation of torture by the French army in Algeria (see **politics**). *Chez Minuit* assumed innumerable secretarial functions, and when SB won the **Nobel Prize** Lindon accepted it on his behalf (SB was his first laureate; he also published Claude Simon and Elie Wiesel). SB named Lindon his literary executor, a position he exercised assiduously (some might say excessively) until his **death**. This created conflict with scholars (advised to write for permissions in French), producers, and fellow publishers. The bitterest conflict was *l'affaire "Eleutheria"* (see **Grove Press**). He died in Paris (9 April 2001), control of the Estate passing to SB's nephew, Edward Beckett. Jean Echenoz's booklet *Jérôme Lindon* (Minuit, 2001) is an entertaining but fair-minded account of his life.

Lisbon: city of Henry **Fielding**'s death, as prefigured in his *A Voyage to Lisbon*, which SB admired. Shorthand for the great earthquake of 1655, which struck on the Sunday morning of 1 November (All Saints' Day) when many were at church, moving **Voltaire** to write *Candide* to attack **Leibniz**'s doctrine of **preestablished harmony**. In **Diderot**'s *Jacques le fataliste* Père Ange et Frère Jean head to Lisbon to be crushed, swallowed, and burned, "comme il était écrit là-haut" (535). SB refers to "Lisbon's great day" (*Watt*, 43) in "**ainsi a-t-on beau**" and "La **Peinture des van Velde**" (*Disjecta*, 131). In the **Sottisier Notebook** he later noted from "La Dést. de Lisbonne" (a poem by Voltaire): "Tristes calculateurs des misères humaines / Ne me consolez point, vous aigrissez mes peines."

little girl: in *All That Fall* (35) Mrs. **Rooney** recalls a lecture by "one of these new mind doctors," about a little girl treated unsuccessfully for several years. The doctor realized, after she had died, that "she had never really been born." Mrs. Rooney weeps, less for herself than her lost little Minnie. The case was discussed by **Jung** after his third **Tavistock** lecture (2 October 1935), which SB attended with Wilfred **Bion**. A young girl had amazing dreams, which he could not tell her **father** since they contained premonitions of her early **death**; indeed, she died a year later: "She had never been born entirely," Jung concluded. The account made a lasting impression on SB, explaining (he felt) much about his **embryonic** self. In *Murphy,* **Celia** undergoes a "**larval** experience"; in *Not I* the "tiny little girl" is born "before her time," into a "godforsaken **hole**." SB described to Charles Juliet (*Conversations,* 138) his feeling of having inside him somebody that had been murdered; compare "**Rough for Radio II**," where **Fox** intimates this about his fetal twin, a self never properly born. In 1976 in Berlin, SB recalled this Jungian experience to Hildegard Schmahl, who was preparing to act **May** in *Footfalls*. This was in part his explanation for the incompletely developed May who hears (or creates) her **mother**'s voice, or is created by her mother's narrative.

little world: the **microcosm**, as opposed to the "big world" or macrocosm, each reflecting in the other the laws of perfect proportion so that the little world becomes the living **mirror** of the whole, as in the monadology of **Leibniz**. Donne's fifth *Holy Sonnet* begins: "I am a little world made cunningly / Of elements, and an angel sprite." **Schopenhauer** cites (*WWI,* 2.xxii, 18) an obscure verse about one who "feels that he holds a little world / Brooding in his brain," identifying the paradox of the tiny human **consciousness** that alone apprehends the enormous universe. **Goethe**'s Werther turns into himself to find a world but discovers that it is not sustainable. **Murphy** desires to retreat into the little world of the mind, where alone he can be free (see **Geulincx**). The Cartesian disjunction is manifest in *Three Novels,* in the visual **conarium** (characters and setting) of *Endgame,* and in fraught attempts of the protagonists of the minimalist fiction to find a **closed space** (rotunda, cube, or **skull**) that will express the little world within. SB claimed the value of the theater: "One turns out a small world with its own laws, and conducts the action as if on a **chess** board."

liu: Lîng-Liûn went to the Bamboo Valley and made a flute with twelve liù-liú, or notes of the chromatic scale, dividing them into the six male and six female "phoenix," giving each a romantic name (*Dream,* 10–11). As Sean Lawlor discovered, this is from Louis Laloy's *La Musique chinoise* (38–43), "Lîng-Liûn" described (38) as "maître de musique." SB's "Bamboo Valley" is Laloy's "vallée retirée" where he sees "des bambous merveilleux"; the phoenices appear when the note is sounded "sans passion"; and the *liu* are defined as "lois" ("laws"). The tonal difference between "liù" and "liú" is that of the male (*yâng*) as opposed to the female (*yìn*) principle: "Le phénix mâle de la vallée profonde chantait les six *liù,* sa compagne les six *liú*" (Laloy, 43). SB's "Great Liú," "Young Liú," and "Southern Liú" are the wrong sex. His "cubes of jade" (10) are Laloy's "pierres de jade . . . taillées en équerre" (61), struck by Confucius. The narrator hopes that his **characters** might each be a liù, cast for a part in the greater melodic scheme. **Music** reflects social harmony,

the Confucian ideal, each bell rendering "un son determiné" (43). If SB's characters were like that—liù-liú-minded— then a little book could be written that would be purely melodic: "a lovely **Pythagorean** chain-chant solo of cause and effect" (*Dream,* 10); "half-a-dozen Lîng-Liûn phoenices arising as one immortal bird from the ashes of a common pyre" (11). Problems arise with characters like **Nemo** and "our principal boy," who refuse to be condensed into a liu (11), rendering narrative harmony impossible. See **k'în music.**

London: SB lived in London for six weeks (July–August 1932), at 4 Ampton Street, off Gray's Inn Road, renting a room for 17/6 per week from a Mrs. Southon (reassured, he commented, to be so close to the Free Hospital), then from Christmas 1933 to late 1935, scraping a living by occasional reviews and halfheartedly looking for work. He later lived at 48 Paulton's Square, close to Thomas **MacGreevy** at Cheyne Walk Gardens, the two spending much time walking, talking, going to galleries, and reading. In September he stayed with the **Frost** family, 34 Gertrude Street, where he remained fifteen months and where *Murphy* was conceived. "**Text 6**" recollects this "interval," the news in slow letters above Picadilly Circus, and the little tobacconist's in Glasshouse Street (where **Neary** eats a Chinese meal). **Watt** sees the stars he had known "when dying in London" (212); **Malone** (184) also remembers them.

If SB felt in London "the way a slug-ridden cabbage might be expected to be," there were compensations, such as the steamers dipping their funnels to get under the Tower bridge, which he called "Très émouvant" and incorporated into "**Serena I**" and *Murphy*. The poem perambulates from "the grand old British Museum" to Regent's Park Zoo; from Primrose Hill (with its distant view of the **Crystal Palace**) to Ken Wood (Hampstead); and thence to the Thames, the "Bloody Tower," and the Monument. The tone is bleak, SB wishing he were born **Defoe**, to excoriate London. The novel describes the London scene precisely, yet *Murphy* evolved equally out of SB's reading. The **Chelsea** Embankment is invested with elements of **Dante**'s *Purgatory;* Tyburnia suggests Magistrate **Fielding**; Hyde Park invokes a pastoral tradition; and the **Bethlem Royal Hospital** enacts a drama of Bedlam. The "Great Wen" (59) derives from William Cobbett's *Rural Rides* (1822). The depressed **Brewery Road** area, exactly observed, defines a life between **prison** and **shambles**. Murphy applies for a **job** at a chandlery (Thos. Oldfield, 250 Gray's Inn Road). Murphy passes the Royal Free Hospital (founded 1828; moved to Hampstead 1953) and the garden adjacent to it (St. Andrew's Public Garden, once a cemetery, and hence his refusal to lie down) to a Lyons tearoom. In recondite jest (in the 1930s it was **Skinner**'s luncheon room), he uses psychology to defraud a vast commercial operation of 1.8333 . . . cups of tea, and is offered a **job**. London has an air of grubby plausibility, yet much of the detail comes from *Whitaker's Almanack* (1935), which SB used to plot the time-space coordinates of his novel even as **Joyce** had used Thom's *Directory* (1904) for *Ulysses*.

Murphy was conceived as a City Comedy and a decision taken to "Londonize" the novel. This is reflected in familiar echoes of **Shakespeare**, **Marlowe**, and **Jonson**, but also in the Elizabethan and Jacobean quotations in the **Whoroscope Notebook**, many recondite, and ticked off to show they had been used. Some identify specific editions ("*girl* 2 syllables in John Ford" pinpoints the Mermaid); others remain evasive ("Pudenda of the soul" a bashful mystery). There are chunks of **Greene**, **Peele**, and Beaumont and Fletcher; bits of Nashe, **Dekker**, and **Marston**; with a snatch of **Fletcher**'s *Sullen Shepherd*. This is not "casually erudite" (Knowlson, 204) but willfully obscure, an act of Joycean arrogance that pays homage to the literary tradition to which the novel belongs. SB had written for his own delectation, but the example of *Ulysses* could hardly be ignored. He hoped *Murphy* might do for London what *Ulysses* had done for Dublin. It was not to be.

"Long After Chamfort": rhymed gnomic adaptations of six *Maximes* of Sébastien **Chamfort**, written in the early 1970s and previously unpublished, save #6, "Hope is a knave befools us evermore" (see "**Kottabista**"). SB told George **Reavy** (9 August 1972) that he had "disimproved some hours doggerelizing Chamfort's *Maximes*." They appeared in *The Blue Guitar* (Facoltà di Magistero, Università degli Studi di Messina) 1.1 (December 1975): 1–6. Two more ("sleep till death" and "how hollow heart") were written in 1976 to make up "Huit Maximes" ("Long After Chamfort") in *Collected Poems* (1977). The last is not

Chamfort but **Pascal** (*Pensées, #143*). **Wylie**'s comment on the syndrome known as life (*Murphy* 57) originates in Maxim #113, with its sense of a disease from which sleep relieves us, and **death** the only cure. **Murphy** (79) echoes #155: "It is better to be seated than upright, lying down rather than seated, dead than all that"; compare *Malone Dies* (243).

"Long Observation of the Ray": a significant but abandoned prose text that exists in several versions (RUL 2909/1–6), the first stage (four versions) from "27.10.75" and a second stage of two versions roughly a year later, the ultimate draft dated "19.11.76." Conceived as a long piece, in five sections, each to have nine subsections, the text, like *Lessness,* is ordered with **mathematical** precision as SB calculated the sentences to be devoted to each theme, as outlined in the first draft and labeled A–I:

A. Observation
B. Chamber
C. Inlet-outlet
D. Constant intensity
E. Faintness
F. Cross section
G. Constant length
H. Saltatoriality [leaping, from the musical term *Saltando*]
I. Extinction-occulation (duration and frequency) (lantern not quite impermeable).

The light, with occasional extinction and occulation accompanied by faint sound (the open and close of a shutter), develops into an inquisitor, as in **"Play."** As the shape of the chamber in which the ray is observed shifts from cube to sphere, SB considers exit and entrance, as in *The Lost Ones.* The piece links two later preoccupations: cylinders and enclosed places like **"Ping,"** *Lessness,* and *The Lost Ones;* and the dynamics of seeing as in *Film,* "La **Falaise,**" "**Old Earth,**" and *Ill Seen Ill Said.* The second phase of composition, draft 5, develops "observation" into the "eye-mind" relationship, the eye's observation leading to the association of the eye with the ray. What distinguishes "Long Observation" from other **closed space** works featuring the dynamics of seeing, despite the shift to the "eye," is the absence of human agency. Its subject is the **object**, cube or sphere, and then the mind, as the light examining the cube is associated with the eye examining the **skull** or mind. SB traps himself (in a box?) as he pushes these notions to their limits. Can the eye observe itself observing; if so, from what privileged position? The tentative answer is that it can observe itself only from inside itself. The eye explores the outside of self (the ray in the cube) and, as the lids close, the inside of self, as in SB's persistent paradoxes of **apperception**.

The Lost Ones: translation of *Le Dépeupleur,* SB's longest later narrative. Begun 31 October 1965 but abandoned for *Bing* (qv). The concluding paragraph was written just before publication (1970). The **French** title derives from **Lamartine**'s "L'Isolement," but the English moves from **death** ("depopulator") to escape. Published by **Calder** and Boyars and **Grove** (1972); 100 copies signed and bound in half-leather and gilt, anticipated the first British edition. The

New York Times (16 December 1972) printed it on an entire page. A text with **illustrations** by Philippe Weisbecker appeared in *Evergreen Review* 96 (Spring 1973): 41–64 (see *The Lost Ones,* **texts** below). For David **Warrilow**'s astonishing **adaption**, see **Mabou Mines**.

SB's most anthropological work, *The Lost Ones* suggests ancient ruins (compare *Lessness*) and futuristic dystopias. It flirts with **allegory**. The title evokes lost civilizations, their habits and customs recorded by a scientific eye. The opening paragraph establishes the abode, inhabited by 205 people, in which **ladders** (qv) are the only **objects**. These vary in size, the shortest not less than six meters, some with a sliding extension. They are "propped up against the wall without regard to harmony" (203), greatly in demand, yet it takes courage to climb. They "convey the searchers to the niches," **quincunxial** cavities sunk in the wall, whence tunnels may offer an exit. Another possible egress, **religion** of another sect, is through the roof to transcendent celestial harmony. Between the two hopes "Conversion is frequent" (206). Standing "Bolt upright" on the top rung of the great ladder fully extended against the wall, the tallest climbers can touch the ceiling. Planted perpendicular at the center that ladder would enable a climber to explore "the fabulous zone decreed out of reach." Compare **Belacqua**'s image of tearing through the night sky, stretched like a skin, into a quiet zone above the nightmare (*Dream,* 26). But that would entail cooperation, which is lacking. None has succeeded in doing so.

Four classes inhabit this flattened Tower of Babel; 120 are climbers, 60 remain on the floor searching for their lost one(s), 20 are sedentary searchers who have temporarily abandoned the quest. In their Belacqua posture (see **"Sedendo et Quiesc[i]endo"**), these are **still**, in **motion** only when driven "from the coign they have won," or in achieving another coign (a variant of "quoin" or cornerstone, curious in a cylinder). Five of them, four sitting against the wall, are the vanquished. Chief among them is "The **North**," so-called for her fixity (as the Pole Star), from whom others take their bearings. These are likened to the knowing inhabitants of the Inferno who "wrung from **Dante** one of his rare wan smiles." While the principal drive of the inhabitants is an exit, a more attainable freedom is from **desire**: "to feel it no longer is a rare deliverance" (160). The reciprocal need, the search for one's lost one, echoes **Plato**'s *Symposium* where Zeus punishes all three sexes (male, female, and hermaphrodite) by bisection; each yearns for that from which it is severed, for its lost one. The narrator is candid: "Whatever it is they are searching for it is not that" (213).

This **issueless** world is ruled by climatic discomfort, a "twofold storm," fluctuations of temperature and light, the latter emitting a sound like "a faint stridulence as of insects" (214). The temperature oscillates between 25° and 5° C (with occasional drops to 1° C) within four seconds, and so destroys the skin while the oscillations of light lead to blindness. Such an entropic abode, where **nature** seems dead, recalls **Clov**'s dream of order, "A world where all would be silent and still and each thing in its last place" (*Endgame,* 57). The danger is that the expiring system may return, life from a flea, a new day from the old, the vanquished resuming the search. "An intelligence" might be tempted to infer steady decline from climbers to searchers to sedentary searchers to the vanquished, but even in the vanquished the "fevering" may return: "So all is for the best" (216).

The Lost Ones, texts: when David **Warrilow** performed the stage **adaptation** of *The Lost Ones* in **Germany**, he was told that the cylinder's dimensions, "fifty metres round and eighteen high," were incorrect. That is, if the total surface area of the cylinder were 80,000 square centimeters as all book versions, **French** and English, have it on the opening page, then the cylinder would be minuscule. Conversely, if the cylinder's dimensions were correct, then the surface area was off. Warrilow said he would ask SB, who acknowledged "that the figure eighteen was indeed a most regrettable error." When Warrilow made a film version he checked again, and SB confirmed sixteen meters for the height, adding, "After all, you can't play fast and loose with pi." But Warrilow failed to query the impossible surface area.

The only texts to print the cylinder's correct height, sixteen meters, are *Le Dépeupleur* and, surprisingly, a later American version, in **Grove**'s failing *Evergreen Review* (Dell paperback, 1973), which presents the total surface area as "twelve million square cms." The French edition, which has the size of the cylinder correct, gives its surface as "quatre-vingt mille centimètres carrés," as in the American (Grove) and British (**Calder**) editions. Twelve million is correct—eight million for the wall and two million each for ceiling and floor. The narrator confirms these figures in the third paragraph: "Inside a cylinder fifty metres round and sixteen high for the sake of harmony or a total surface of roughly twelve hundred square metres of which eight hundred mural." In all book versions, then, the given surface area is contradicted later. The American, photo-offset from the erroneous British (both have a missing number on page 63), contains another blunder: "The short queue is not necessarily the most rapid and such a one starting fifth may well find himself first before such another starting tenth" (47–48). The figures are transposed. The *Evergreen* edition makes sense: "such a one starting tenth may well find himself first before such another starting fifth" (58). This accords with *Le Dépeupleur* (42). The *Evergreen* version has been largely ignored. It has one aberration, for it drops "two" from "the [two] storms" (56), but until the *Complete Short Prose* (1995) it was the most accurate text.

Louit, Ernest: friend of Arthur, who tells to **Watt** and Mr. **Graves** his tale, a satire of **Trinity College**, the academic enterprise, and the **antiquarians**. Louit's dissertation is *The Mathematical Intuitions of the Visicelts* (compare the Visigoths). His expenses include £5 for colored beads. He reports his hardships: boots sucked off in a bog; the need to drown his faithful bull terrier, to roast and eat him (SB omits the ending: "A pity **O'Connor** isn't here, he'd have loved these bones"); losing his notes in a gentleman's cloakroom on the morn of his return. He produces Mr. **Nackybal**

(qv), who can deduce from six-figure numbers their cube roots (see **mathematics**). Louit is examined, for twenty-two pages, by Messrs. Fitzwein et al., who look at one another exhaustively but allow Mr. Nackybal to demonstrate his skills. The outcome is unknown, as Arthur tires of his story.

Lousse: or Loy, Christian name Sophie; a **mother** figure who takes in **Molloy** after he kills her **dog**, Teddy (**Moran**'s son has a teddy bear). A figure of the *ewige Weib*, in **Jung**'s schema she represents the anima. She digs the hole (35), though Molloy is "the gentleman"; compare the Luddite ditty (1381): "When Adam delved, and Eve span / Who then was the gentleman." A "loy" is a spade for cutting turf. Her garden creates an **allegory** of Paradise; but once Molloy leaves by the wicket gate (compare *Pilgrim's Progress*) he cannot return. She combines *wisdom* and *law* with *lice*, the "eudemonistic slop" (55) of an ethical system based on happiness and rectitude, the "miserable **molys**" (54) that Molloy must reject.

Lovat, Matthew: Venetian shoemaker who in 1806 nailed himself to a cross and by a system of ropes and pulleys hung himself out of a window (*Molloy*, 167).

love: SB's attitude to love tempers ruthless honesty with rare moments of **pity**, as affecting as they are **irrational**. This stems from his concept of **friendship** (qv), **Proust**'s contention that we are "irrémédiablement seuls." Sex and love have little in common, one fulfilling bodily needs, the other a logical impossibility. Instead, *Dream* and *Murphy* analyze **desire** (qv), which, SB insisted in *Proust*, represents the **consciousness** of something lacking: "One only loves that which one does not possess entirely" (*La Prisonnière*). **Belacqua** mocks the **Mandarin**'s sense of love ("authentically and seriously and totally involved in the life of my heart") as using woman as a private convenience (*Dream*, 99–101). The latter replies, "What's wrong . . . with you and **Beatrice** happy in the Mystic Rose at say five o'clock and happy again in No. 69 at say one minute past?" Belacqua can only mutter inchoately that there is no such thing as love.

Murphy is an unusual love story. **Celia** is a prostitute, sympathetic but not a tart with a heart. Her job expresses the demands made on the **body** by the big world, *quid pro quo* reduced to its **fundamental sound**. Murphy distinguishes clinically between sex and love, but cannot reconcile his impulse toward the **little world** with his "deplorable susceptibility" to Celia and ginger biscuits. O'Hara argues that *Murphy* is an **allegory** of **narcissism**. Unable to love Celia because of the depletion of his ego, he turns the capacity for love back into that ego, and loves the inner self at the cost of the outer. Defined by his inability to love, he is found lacking. Reflected in the vacuity of Mr. **Endon**'s eyes, and about to return to Celia (serenade, nocturne, and albada), he meets his Cartesian catastrophe before any incipient love can find expression.

Molloy recalls encounters of dubious satisfaction. He wonders if he has a son, and remembers a little chambermaid, but: "It wasn't true love. The true love was in [*sic*] another." He wonders, "is it true love, in the rectum?"; he would gladly have accepted a **goat**, to know what true love was (57). Love remains a bitter mystery. He has had time to love one or two but "not with true love." Had they met seventy years ago he might have loved the charcoal burner (83), but he never had much love to spare, and that went to the "old men." O'Hara's contention that Molloy, like Murphy, is defined by his inability to love, is belied by the ruthless truth that love has no ultimate value. Like friendship, it is at best a distraction from the **solitude** of self. **Moran** lacks charity, and his wife ("**Ninette**") is barely mentioned. **Malone** sees a couple in silhouette (238), then realizes "they must be loving each other, that must be how it is done." **Macmann**'s interlude with **Moll** is a grotesque mixture of tetty-beshy, **oyster kisses**, and bad poetry, held together by **Augustine**'s notion of love as a lethal glue (*Confessions*, 4.x), as in the "couple and abandon" of *How It Is*. The **Unnamable** claims that love is a carrot that never fails (316; see **Renard**), a lambkin frolicking with a lambkinette gambols before the **shambles**. The "tumefaction of the penis" surprises him (332), but thoughts of Clydesdales and Suffolk stallions leave him "empty-handed."

First Love embodies a self-critique of one unable to love, yet the absence of any moral absolute does not prevent guilt. Either you love or you don't, but since the former is impossible then the latter is inevitable. The narrator turns away from his first love, but cries of pain follow him long after he has gone (the **child**'s tears those he cannot shed). Rejection of love translates into action, but the cost is pain unto himself and others. **Krapp** and Joe are obsessed with a girl in green whom they have "Duly laid" then deserted. Both have abandoned love for something transcendental. Krapp chooses to replay his past and return to dream, but Joe is assailed by a vision of her **suicide**, something he tries to reject but given conscience (or **God**) cannot. Behind both images is the **memory** of Peggy **Sinclair**.

In SB's widely quoted quip, sex without love is like coffee without brandy (in "**Love and Lethe**" this is a Gloria). Peggy **Guggenheim** thought she was the brandy; coffee is rarely taken this way, however. SB's most direct statement of love was "**Cascando**," written during his infatuation with Betty Stockton. The poem invokes the "love love love thud of the old plunger"; and expresses the fear of being terrified again, of not loving, "of loving and not you, / of being loved and not by you." SB had been "in love" with Peggy Sinclair and Ethna **MacCarthy**, but when this overture was rejected he embarked on a torrid affair with Betty's friend Mary **Manning** (qv). Thereafter his love life was not directly expressed in his writing, although "**Play**" suggests the difficulty of sustaining a dichotomy between sex and love when feelings of others are involved.

In *The Lost Ones*, "love" is synonymous with sex. Under harsh conditions, skin like paper, mucus membrane desiccated, copulation persists: "more or less happy penetration in the nearest tube " (220). Love is polarized between ruthless cynicism that places no higher value on it than on any other emotion, and sentimental compassion that is never quite denied. The former finds expression in **Watt**, where Mr. **Hackett**'s seat is still warm from the loving; or "**Text 3**" (110), where the body is assured: "no one's going to love you, don't be alarmed." In *Endgame,* **Hamm**'s "Get out of here and love one other" is offset by the fear that the flea might breed: "Catch him, for the love of God." To Hamm's "You don't love me" **Clov** replies "No"; when Hamm continues, "You loved me once," the reply is nostalgic: "Once!" Texts as various as *Krapp's Last Tape,* "**Eh Joe,**" *Footfalls,* and "**Ghost Trio**" offer complex sentiments of guilt. In "**Words and Music,**" **Croak**'s theme is love, "of all the passions the most powerful passion" (like sloth). Words asks: "to wit this love what is this love"; his song invokes the **face** of the woman "who loved could not be won." W. B. **Yeats**'s theme haunts the late writing: "Does the imagination dwell the most / Upon a woman won or woman lost?" Subtle dissonance of the half-rhyme ("most" and "lost") intimates that the inability to love, however inevitable, forces the imagination to dwell upon the loss.

"**Love and Lethe**": fifth story of *MPTK,* written in early 1933. The Toughs in the equally unromantic Irishtown await **Belacqua.** They drink coffee, Ruby's "gloria," explained with **Fielding**-like omniscience (see **love**). Ruby is past her prime (in Irish idiom "ruby" implies the **residua** in a bottle); she has been disappointed in **love**; her itch for **syzygy** takes refuge in **music** and malt, and she has long suffered from an incurable disorder. She has agreed to a **suicide** pact, her elaborate rationale confounding the narrator's inability to discover Belacqua's resolution (89). Belacqua intends to exit in style. He arrives in "a swagger sports roadster" that embitters Mr. Tough's

cyanosis, with a bottle of "Fifteen year old," Jameson's assuredly, also acquired "on tick"; should he change his mind there may be problems. He has a sign reading "Temporarily sane"; but either the view, the malt, or the "sincerity" of Ruby's legs (compare **Herrick**'s Julia) complicates precedence. The revolver goes off, and a different resolution ensues, from which the narrator discreetly withdraws, his consolation afforded by **Ronsard**'s *Sonnet* LXXVII: "Car l'Amour et la Mort n'est qu'une mesme chose."

Lucan Spa Hotel: in Lucan, near **Leixlip,** whence the drowned **Nemo** is borne "post-haste" (*Dream,* 183). Here, maybe, **Wylie** observed the pneumatic Miss **Counihan** (*Murphy,* 60).

Lucien: based on Jean **Beaufret,** whose "Black diamond of pessimism" (*Dream,* 47) SB admired. A "young aesthetician" (20) and author of an "unpleasant letter" defining what "ce cochon de Marcel" (**Proust**) says about style and **love,** his "**Ce n'est au Pélican**" throws the "demented **Liebert**" toward **Belacqua.** The narrator is tempted to have the **Syra-Cusa** make Lucien a **father,** but this would be "the fruit of a congruence of enormous improbability."

Lucky: servant (or "lackey") of **Pozzo,** the image of suffering inhumanity, first played by Jean **Martin.** When Colin Duckworth asked why the name, if he had found his **Godot,** SB replied, "I suppose he is lucky to have no more expectations" (*Introduction,* lxiii). Or because he gets the bones. SB conceived him as a station porter. His speech, a "word salad," parodies the music-hall demented lecture, with three incoherent premises, one major and two minor, but no logical reconciliation. Endless reiteration ensues in the vain attempt to reach conclusion: *given the existence of a personal God,* outside **time** and without extension, who **loves** us all dearly, with some exceptions (for reasons unknown); *and what is more,* that it is established beyond doubt, despite advances, that man in essence wastes and pines; *and what is more* that the light is fading and the earth an abode of stones. Harold Hobson ("First Night," 26) paid tribute to "Lucky's extraordinary speech, in which all the wisdom and the knowledge of the world are jumbled to the pitiful end of incoherence and madness."

Lucretius: Titus Lucretius Carus (ca. 96–55 BC); Roman poet whose "De rerum natura" expounds in hexameters the teachings of **Epicurus** and **Democritus**. **Malone** (218) quotes "Suave, mari magno" (II.1). SB's source is **Schopenhauer** (*WWI,* I.4, 412): "'tis pleasant, when seas are rough, to stand / And see another's danger, safe on land" (compare **Miranda**). Lucretius does not delight that others are afflicted; rather, it is sweet to see from what evils oneself is exempt. SB often quoted this phrase of the theater, the spectator safely seated while the storm breaks out on stage.

Lucy: in **"Walking Out,"** Belacqua's fiancée. It is, the narrator says, a waste to itemize her; but he persists, describing her jet hair and pale **face**, with its suggestion of the Nobel **Yeats**. She is struck by a Daimler (a hint of Nazi violence) and is crippled for life, two further years

of suffering before she passes, "in a tranquillity of acquiescence" ("What a Misfortune," 114). Their life is spent with the gramophone, **Schubert**'s *An die Musik,* a great favorite. Belacqua is so happily married that he is sorry for himself when she dies. Her features suggest Lucia **Joyce**, but her name owes something to **Wordsworth**'s "Lucy" poems.

Lulu: in *First Love,* the woman met on a bench, on the canal bank, where they engage in conversation ("Shove up, she said"), and **love** (he is "at the mercy of an erection"). Taking refuge in a cowshed, he finds himself "inscribing the letters of Lulu in an old heifer pat" (34). This is not, he concludes, "that intellectual love which drew from me such drivel, in another place" (**Spinoza**, *Murphy,* chapter 6). She becomes "Anna," as if only the narrative **consciousness** (not its **object**) remains constant. Finally she takes him home. Something takes its course: "It was my night of love" (42). Lulu lives (they live) by prostitution, as in Berg's opera (or Wedekind's play). When she becomes pregnant he does not doubt the paternity (despite his "If it's lepping . . . it's not mine") but rejects the **birth** and leaves, ostensibly dismissive ("either you love or you don't"), but haunted thereafter by the cries.

Lupercal: *Dream* says of the **Smeraldina**, "Lupercus a liability" (65); and **Belacqua** fantasizes about "a barren queen . . . bleeding in a Lupercal" (98). **Cooper**'s *Flagellation* (39; DN, 50–51) describes the yearly festivals (15 February) to honor Pan but named for the she-wolf that suckled Romulus and Remus (he places

Lupercal under the Palatine Mount). Two goats and a dog were sacrificed and their skins cut into thongs, with which two youths (*luperci*) would run about the streets, whipping all they met. The lashes were believed to ease the pains of childbirth or relieve barrenness. The festival persisted until 496 AD, when Pope Gelasius ended it.

Lynch family: postulated as necessary for the breeding and care of the famished **dog**. By the time that sufficient conditions have been established, the family has changed from one hypothetical to one that exists: "The name of this fortunate family was Lynch" (*Watt*, 100). All told, five generations, twenty-eight "souls" (including "Bill's boy Sam"), 980 years, but destined not to achieve their millennium, for as they **come and go** the day retreats regularly, that is, irregularly. This parodies Malthusian **mathematics**. In the *Watt* typescript (264) this day, June 26, is that of Watt's entering **Quin**'s service. The "Lynch Twins," perhaps Art and Con, mock the **Rooneys** as they struggle home in *All That Fall.*

M

M: the **thirteenth** letter and SB's favorite (**Murphy, Mercier, Molloy, Malone**). "W" is an inverted "M" (**Watt**, *Waiting for Godot*); "E" one rotated 90 degrees (*Endgame*, "The **Expelled**," "The **End**"). Beginning *L'Innommable*, SB used "M" before choosing "**Mahood**." "M" suggests "Mama," a **fundamental sound**, the first a baby makes. In *Footfalls* it helps identify **May** with her **mother**. In "**Play**," M is the male in an eternal triangle; in "**Bare Room**," one speaker. The narrator in *Company* (59) calls his "hearer" M, and "himself" W. In *How It Is*, language retreats to its roots and names have minimal articulation: **Pim, Bom**, Bem, Pam, "one syllable m at end all that matters" (109).

Mabou Mines: in 1958 Lee Breuer, a UCLA literature major, hitch-hiked to San Francisco to see *Waiting for Godot* performed by the Actors' Workshop, which he joined. What he found appealing in SB's texts was not psychological depth but the multiplicity and fragmentation of **character**, of the modernist ego. Despite an early interest in Stanislavskian method and his directorial focus on "private moments," Breuer rejected illusionistic theater and psychological characterization in favor of Brechtian alienation (but remained interested in the psychological machinery of acting as developed by Stanislavski and Grotowski).

The group Breuer founded (with Ruth Maleczech, JoAnne Akalaitis, Frederick Neumann, and David **Warrilow**) responded to SB's sense of man as motor (see **machine**). Their "**Play**" was characterized by repeated, mechanical behavior. *Come and Go* premiered (May 1971) at the outdoor Brooklyn Bridge festival, three women on a pier with cordless microphones, the audience on another pier amid speakers. In subsequent indoor performances the women, clucking like pigeons, faces veiled, hands crossed symbolically, were situated behind and above the audience, in the balcony, their image reflected to the stage by a huge **mirror** through which the action was viewed. The result was dissociative, distanced, and dehumanized, an assault on perception with **voice** and visual image emanating from opposite ends of the theater, the spectral image allowing one woman to vanish into shimmering darkness while the others discussed her affliction. This was repeated successfully at the Theater for the New City, New York (1975).

Roger Copland noted (*New York Times,* 1 May 1977): "Mabou Mines has always placed words and visual imagery on an equal footing. This is especially evident in their Beckett work—theater pieces based on texts which Beckett never originally intended to be staged." The third work in the ninety-minute "Mabou Mines Performs Samuel Beckett" was an **adaptation** of *The Lost Ones,* which began as a "reading" by David Warrilow. Two hundred and five barely distinguishable creatures, the vanquished, watchers, sedentary searchers, and climbers of **ladders**, live in a "flattened cylinder." Searching for their lost one, they seek an exit through tunnels or ceiling. Warrilow, initially holding the text, demonstrated that world with a miniature cross section of a cylinder and half-inch images of the naked inhabitants, manipulating these with tweezers. Ruby Cohn recounts: "After Warrilow decided to abandon the book, Mabou Mines designer Thom Cathcart, having scraped the paint off 205 toy German railroad dolls, conceived the decisively brilliant idea of seating the live theater audience in a rubber cylinder environment" (*Just Play*, 224). The shoeless audience entering the cylinder to Philip **Glass**'s minimalist sounds (SB's "faint stridulence of insects") spied on the miniature creatures with binoculars. As Bonnie Marranca noted: "Breuer has theatrically conceived *The Lost Ones* with at least four perspectives in mind: that of the narrator; the narrator in the role of a 'lost one'; the model of the cylindrical world; the experience of the audience living through **time** in an environment that approximates the cylinder" (*Soho News Weekly,* 23 October 1975).

Cohn was enthusiastic about the early triptych: "The Beckett evening was to coalesce the three strands of their aesthetics: 1) the Stanislavskian legacy of motivational acting, 2) estrangement-narrative performance deriving from Brecht and Oriental theater, 3) the conceptual formalism of the visual arts of the 1960s" (225). Mabou Mines adopted SB almost as company playwright. Relations were not always harmonious. Akalaitis set "**Cascando**" in a Nova Scotian fisher-

man's cottage, a sixty-minute staging, with Fredrick Neumann (Opener) and David Warrilow (**Voice**). It opened (12 April 1976) with Philip Glass's **music** replacing that of Marcel **Mihalovici**. The cottage was cluttered: photos, a used tire, a goldfish bowl, tortoise shell, polar bear, and rusty kitchenware. Four men and a woman sat around a table, another male in a **rocking chair**. The group represented Voice, speaking sometimes in unison, sometimes separately. Each did something—shaving, knitting, carving wood, playing cards, building card houses, or painting. Visually stunning, the adaptation was chaotic, as stage business distracted from and finally eroded SB's narrative; Akalaitis, however, won an Obie (1976).

Akalaitis independently staged *Endgame* (December 1984) at the American Repertory Theater, New Haven, prompting SB to act to halt the performance. Before opening night lawyers were still negotiating textual alterations. She set her production in a subway station with an abandoned subway car as backdrop, adding music by her ex-husband, Philip Glass. SB further objected to the American practice of colorblind casting, black actors here in two roles. A final compromise let it open but with SB's disclaimer in the playbill: "A complete parody of the play. Anybody who cares for the work couldn't fail to be disgusted." SB, who had allowed the group wide latitude with his prose and radio drama, insisted (again) that his theater pieces were to be performed as written (see **law**). In retrospect, the conflict was inevitable, but Akalaitis felt she had maintained textual integrity since the dialogue remained intact; only the visual imagery—specified in the text—was altered. By moving into a new aesthetic space she altered SB's conception, but whether she enriched or eroded it still divides critics.

Mabou Mines staged many adaptions of SB's prose. In 1979 Neumann set *Mercier and Camier* on high-tech plexiglass, audience separated from actors by a trough (SB's canal). The narrator (David Warrilow, who played **Watt**) appeared on video. Neumann played **Mercier**, and Bill Raymond **Camier**. Music was by Philip Glass, as in every Mabou Mines Beckett production except Warrilow's "**A Piece of Monologue**" (1980). Produced by the New York Shakespeare Festival, it opened at the Public Theater (25 October 1979). Four years later (1983), Neumann (with Honora Ferguson) turned to *Company,* and, disregarding SB's "Keep it simple, Freddie," staged it with lasers, satellite dishes, and video. Mel Gussow's reservation (21 September 1986) defines much of Mabou Mines' later work: "Mr. Neumann was unable to devise a metaphor sizable enough to encompass the various personae within Beckett's single character." Undaunted, Neumann tackled *Worstward Ho* (1986), playing it knee-deep in a grave, with three silent, dimly lit creatures: a solitary woman and a white-haired man and **boy**, who, holding hands, finally walk away on an endless ramp. Ruth Maleczech with Linda Hartinian staged a brief, austere adaptation of *Imagination Dead Imagine,* the protagonist as a catafalque. But Mabou Mines' later work did not capture SB's visual vitality, nor attain the creative balance between his script and their conception evident in their original Beckett evening.

MAC: a limited, *hors commerce* edition from Kickshaws Press (Paris, 1987), a typographical treatment of "passages from *Mercier et Camier* by Samuel Beckett excluded from the English edition, now gleaned, translated and printed, for private circulation only, by John Crombie" (founder, with Sheila Bourne, of the press, printer, bookmaker, and translator). Crombie's attack on **Calder**'s publication of "The **Image**" was published as "The Ill-Made Image" in *JOBS* 4.2 (spring 1995): 15–27. The essay was republished separately by Kickshaws in 1995 for free distribution, then reprinted in 1997 with a curious "Postscript" detailing the history of Crombie's essay and the defeat of his plans to publish his translation of "L'Image" with the original once Edith Fournier's translation appared in *The Complete Short Prose* (1995). Crombie subsequently published a "specially authorized" *Lessness* (2002) in a limited edition of 200, a boxed, "cloverleaf, interactive format," the text spiral bound on all four sides to allow the reader to permutate the sentences, presumably to construct alternate stories.

Macarius, St.: Camier meets **Mercier** on "Monday 15, St Macarius" (13). January 15 is the Day of St. Macarius the Elder, whose name intimates blessedness. He departs with St. Macarius the Younger, performing miracles through abstinence and praying to **God**. Happy in their lives and secure in their faith, they implicitly reproach SB's **pseudocouple**.

MacCarthy, Ethna: SB's contemporary at **Trinity**, where she studied French and Spanish. SB adored her, but their relationship remained platonic, Ethna involved with a married professor. Thus *TCD* (xxx.521 [28 February 1924]: 122): "'Tis good in every case, you know, / To have two strings unto your bow." SB noted to MacGreevy (6 January 1931): "Skeffington affair ended." She became involved with Con **Leventhal**, who married her (1956) after his wife died. In **Dublin**, a respected pediatrician, but in fiction she is the **Alba**, the white **music** of that poem. She is featured in *Dream* (36, 55): "magic name, incantation, abracadabra, two slithers, th, th, dactyl trochee, dactyl trochee"; metrically, *Ethna MacCarthy*. Ethna died of throat cancer in Eastham Memorial Hospital (May 1959). Devastated during her illness, SB wrote to her often during the final months. **Krapp**'s **memories**, based on Peggy **Sinclair**, mingle with this more recent loss (Knowlson, 398).

MacGowran, Jack (1918–1973): Irish actor who achieved brief fame as the Highwayman in *Tom Jones* but lasting acclaim as SB's interpreter for stage, radio, and TV. Or vice versa. Frail and highly charged, MacGowran lived to act. SB met him when BBC 3 did *All That Fall* (1957). He helped prepare MacGowran's "**End of Day**," watching it develop from "a monstrous salad with good moments" (Knowlson, 713) into a fine "entertainment," then into *Beginning to End*, and its audio parallel *MacGowran Speaking Beckett*. SB wrote "**Embers**," "**Eh Joe**," and the discarded "**J. M. Mime**" with him in mind. MacGowran combined with Patrick **Magee** (SB's two "darlings," Jacky and Pat) in *Endgame* (1964), acted **Lucky** in a revival of *Waiting for Godot* (1965), and starred in *Krapp's Last Tape* for PBS TV,

dir. Alan **Schneider** (1971). He read for radio his one-man show and *Imagination Dead Imagine*, and was featured in the BBC *Poems by Samuel Beckett* I and II (1966). SB recommended him, even after he had turned to pills and liquor to stave off the dark moods that sometimes compromised his performances. SB did much to support him, even giving him a favorite painting by Jack **Yeats** (Bair, 617). When MacGowran died (New York, 29 January 1973), a fund was created for his widow, Gloria, and daughter, Tara; SB contributed an unfinished text (see *All Strange Away*) and (from 1965) a manuscript notebook (see **Tara MacGowran Notebook**). For MacGowran's biography, see Jordan R. Young, *The Beckett Actor: Jack MacGowran, Beginning to End* (Moonstone Press, 1989).

MacGowran Speaking Beckett: an audio LP of Jack **MacGowran** reading SB's work, recorded "under the personal supervision of Samuel Beckett" (January 1966) for Claddagh Records (CCT3). Side 1 includes excerpts from *Malone Dies* and *Watt* and the entire *From an Abandoned Work;* side 2, excerpts from "Embers," *Molloy* (2), *Endgame* (2), *The Unnamable,* and *Echo's Bones.* Schubert's D-minor Quartet is played by a Beckett trio: John (harmonium), Edward (flute), and Sam (**gong**). The front cover features a photograph of SB in MacGowran's dressing room, the back a portrait of SB by Avigdor **Arikha**.

MacGreevy, Thomas (1893–1967): long SB's closest confidant. SB's letters to "McGreevy" (as he spelled the name until 1938) offer insights into SB's private world in the 1930s, when SB wrote intimately as he never did to anyone else. Born in Tarbet, County Kerry, MacGreevy worked in **Dublin** and **London** for the British Civil Service, then served in the Royal Field Artillery, was twice wounded, and mentioned in dispatches. The experience fueled his later anti-British sentiments. He read **politics** and history at **Trinity**, and was *lecteur* to the École Normale (1926); when SB arrived (1928), he found MacGreevy still occupying his room. He introduced SB to James **Joyce** and Jack **Yeats**, and contributed an essay to *Our Exagmination* ("The Catholic Element in *Work in Progress*"). Chatto and Windus commissioned studies of **Eliot** (1930) and **Aldington** (1931) for their Dolphin Books; he interested Chatto in a similar work on **Proust** (SB's *Proust*). SB reviewed MacGreevy's only collection of verse, *Poems* (1934) (see "**Humanistic Quietism**").

MacGreevy was a puckish individual, elegant and dapper, irrepressibly witty and a good conversationalist. He was very different from SB—talkative, sartorial, Catholic, and homosexual. SB bowed to his appreciation of poetry, **music, religion**, and **art**, referring to him as a "living encyclopaedia." In 1934, both were in London, MacGreevy scraping a living as a reviewer and occasional lecturer on art history. His love was the Italian Renaissance (SB preferred "the Dutchmen"). He wrote several articles about pictures in the National Gallery, Dublin (he was later appointed its director). MacGreevy was able to arrange reviews for SB (see **Rilke**, "**Schwabenstreich**," and "**Proust in Pieces**"). He appears in *Murphy* as Mr.

Endon, with the inevitable bow tie. Murphy's final monologue (250) imitates a MacGreevy poem. In "**Recent Irish Poetry**" (*Disjecta,* 74), SB considered him an "independent," neither excluding self-perception nor postulating the **object** as inaccessible. His is "the vision without the dip," praised as "probably the most important contribution to post-War Irish poetry." Hardly a dispassionate evaluation, this testifies to SB's admiration of the "unveiling" effect in MacGreevy's verse. He repeated his praise in "**MacGreevy on Yeats**" (1945).

The 300 letters at **Trinity** show how SB's literary identity was forged. Deirdre Bair used them extensively, illuminating a dark period in SB's life, but she was careless in transcription and misdated many, hence the curious accounts of SB's movements. Knowlson corrects her errors and determines the period of those undated. The microfiche sequence is incorrect, #12 and #13 (1931) included among 1930, while #22 is 1930, not 1931. SB sometimes wrote "1935" instead of "1936," another cause of Bair's confusion. The letters touch on much of significance. The first (1930) tells of arriving in **Kassel** and reading **Proust**'s "strangely uneven" first volume. There are references to other reading, comments on his friends, snatches of verse (invaluable for dating certain poems), and hints of work in progress. Two letters (September 1934) criticize the tendency in landscape artists toward "anthropomorphization" (see **Cézanne**). Others recount the genesis of *Murphy:* watching the old men with their kites and determining this as his final image (8 September 1935); complaining that the work was going slowly (8 October); seeking **Geulincx** (9 January 1936); complete, but needing revision (7 May); three copies sent off (27 June); and countering MacGreevy's reservations about the comic bathos of chapter 12 (7 July).

MacGreevy's Catholicism was a foil to SB's agnosticism. SB discusses such works as Jeremy **Taylor**'s *Holy Living and Holy Dying,* H. V. Morton's *In the Steps of the Master,* bought for his mother, and *De Imitatione Christi* (see **Thomas à Kempis**), which encouraged his secular **quietism**. His letters often end "**God** bless." SB later found MacGreevy's ostentatious Catholicism harder to accept, and the correspondence lost this intensive religious center. After World War II the old intimacy was not there. Yet contact was maintained, and the two would meet when SB occasionally came to Dublin, or MacGreevy to **Paris**. For services to French culture MacGreevy was awarded the Croix de Chevalier (1948) and Legion of Honor (1962). His death from cardiac complications following a hernia operation (1967) left SB saddened and with a deeper sense of fragility, for MacGreevy had been one of the few to know him well.

"**MacGreevy on Yeats**": SB's review (*Irish Times* [4 August 1945], 2) of Mac-Greevy's *Jack B. Yeats: An Appreciation and an Interpretation* (Dublin: Victor Waddington, 1945); rpt. in *Disjecta* (95–97). SB wrote at MacGreevy's request, describing it as "the earliest connected account of Mr Yeats's painting." He identifies the quality to be discerned as the relation between the knower and the unknown, MacGreevy lifting the weight of prejudice from the eye, "before *rigor vitae* sets in." Yeats is defined not as a national painter but "with the great of our time," bringing light to "the **issueless** predicament of existence."

machine: animals to **Descartes** were soulless machines; SB, who extended that opinion to mankind, could feel **pity** for a lobster. **Occasionalist** opinion contended that since "I" can have knowledge of mental activity only, the mind is not master of the **body** nor cause of movement in it; thus the "I" is restricted to the act of thinking and does not enter the *res externa,* or world of extension, not even into "my" body, with regard to which "I" am merely the **spectator**. In *Murphy*, the big world is a deterministic machine: "The sun shone, having no alternative, on the **nothing** new." Murphy's **rocking chair** is a machine (30), an extension of his body to take him into his mind. Straps suggest bondage to the physical world, while his nakedness derives from **Geulincx**'s *Ethica* (I.II.ii #8, 33): *Sum igitur nudus speculator hujus machinae* ("I am therefore merely the spectator of this machine"). **Celia** later senses how its **motion** might set the mind free. At the end it becomes an "infernal machine," or anarchist bomb.

Dream begins with **Belacqua** on a **bicycle**. He responds to the clockwork movement of the **Smeraldina**'s arm by controlling the pistons and cylinders of his mind, foiling the "ebullition" (4–5). His **father**'s reading is described (53) as the assembling of cold pipes, turning on the book, and connecting up. **Balzac**'s world is planted with "clockwork cabbages" (119). One such is **Chas**: Belacqua is obliged "to halt and face this machine. It carried butter and loaf" (202). Chas is described as a "clockwork fiend"; in "A **Wet Night**" (50) as "this clockwork Bartlett." SB's dyspraxic characters require mechanical aids because of the failure of the body-mind synchronization.

In *Watt* (21), catching a **tram** depends on "the frigid machinery of a **time**-space relation." The earthball is a machine, the body in bondage to it. Machines range from the **stick** that **Malone** employs to extend his immobilized body to bicycles that creak through the works: in Hugh Kenner's image, man on bicycle, the Cartesian centaur. **Hamm**'s chair enacts the physical part of the **conarium**; outside, the world is running down. "**Act Without Words I**" depicts the simian vulgarity of tools. Mr. Slocum's car in *All That Fall* (18–19) "went like a dream" then went dead, so he chokes her, as she was getting too much air. **Krapp**'s tape recorder is a **memory** machine, the mechanical equivalent of **Proust**'s **vases**. The narrator of *How It Is* ponders a like device, "generations on ebonite" (115). **Mouth**'s attempts in *Not I* to understand the flash are frustrated: "some flaw in the machine . . . disconnected . . . never got the message" (218). Even as the drama retreats into the mind, the Cartesian **dualism** of the earliest works remains unresolved.

MacKenzie, Martin Ignatius: resident of Lourdes ("Ignatius" intimates the crippled Jesuit founder), he writes to Mr. **Spiro** about the **rat** that eats a consecrated wafer (*Watt,* 28). Author of "The Chartered Accountant's Saturday Night," a poem dropped from the drafts, but there headed, "Summo, ergo sum." The

accountant is a figure of respectability, as in "**What a Misfortune**" (118) or in "**Text 12**" (150), when the narrator imagines riding a **bicycle** (to work): "That's the accountants' chorus, opining like a single man." **Malone**, once a "tiny tot" (198), makes his inventory, considering when to "draw the line and make the tot" (181; Ger. *tod,* "dead"). Nearing the end (388), the **Unnamable** insists on doing the summing up.

Macmann: subject of **Malone**'s last "story," **Saposcat** now the Celtic "Son of Man." SB had considered "MacMahon." The name is "legion" in the island (Mark 5:9, the Gadarene swine): sons of Adam sprung from the one illustrious ball (259). Facedown in the mud and perpendicular rain (239) he assumes a **cruciform** position, as if to atone for the sin of living (he is addicted to that chimera). A scapegoat, sent into the wilderness, where "more reptile than bird" he endures. He enacts the Fall, and **Molloy**'s drama, then comes to (255), like Malone, in an **asylum**.

Macon country: Estragon rails against the "Cackon country" (*WG,* 39.b); in the **French** text "Vaucluse" is followed by "Merdecluse." Mâcon [*sic*] is in the département of Saône-et-Loire, and associated with slugs (*Watt,* 28).

MacSwiney, Terence (1879–1920): scholar and revolutionary. He helped form the Irish Volunteers (1913) and became Lord Mayor of **Cork** (1920). Arrested for sedition (August 1920), he began a hunger strike and died (25 October) after seventy-four days, his funeral a day of national mourning. **Malone** attributes his staying power to youth, human and **political** convictions, and sweetened water, all of which he lacks (273).

Madden Prize: a prize bequeathed (1798) by Samuel Madden (1686–1765), philanthropist and divine, to the runner-up in the **Trinity College** Fellowship examination, provided he were of sufficient caliber. **Arsene** would have won this, but for the boil on his bottom (*Watt*, 46); the Addenda (248) mention "the maddened prizeman." This is residua from the drafts, where **Quin**'s man **Erskine**, "pleasantly corrupted into Foreskin," was called "the Maddened Prizeman." **Mercier** and **Camier** (chapter 3) meet an old man whose name is "Madden" and whose theme is fornication; this episode appeared in *Spectrum* (winter 1960), entitled "Madden."

Madeleine: the woman from the café who tends the **Unnamable**; also called **Marguerite**. **Proust**'s madeleine is the tea cake into which Marcel bites, his **consciousness** then suffused with involuntary **memories** of childhood. Mrs. **Rooney** in *All That Fall* is named "Maddy."

Magee, Patrick (1924–82): Irish actor whom SB first heard reading *Molloy* and *From an Abandoned Work* (BBC 3, December 1957), and was impressed and moved by the cracked quality of Magee's distinctly Irish **voice** (Knowlson, 398). SB asked that the tapes be sent to **Paris**, and soon began the "Magee Monologue" (RUL 1227/7/7/1; 20 February 1958). This became *Krapp's Last Tape*. Magee played Krapp, SB enthralled by his performance. They became good friends and formidable drinking partners. Magee read SB's works on radio, notably *Malone Dies* (BBC 3, 18 June 1958). He played **Hamm** to Jack **MacGowran**'s **Clov**, wearing Sean **O'Casey**'s skullcap (Knowlson, 457). He read *The Lost Ones* (1972); recorded *Texts for Nothing*, dir. Martin Esslin (1974); toured the world reading SB (1975); and read *That Time* and "**Rough for Radio II**" (1976), with Harold Pinter and Billie **Whitelaw**. Drinking problems led to his sacking from a Royal Court *Endgame*, but he sobered up to read "**For to End Yet Again**" for BBC 3. His last performance (1982) was *Ill Seen Ill Said*.

Mahaffy, Sir John Pentland (1839–1919): Professor of Ancient History at **Trinity** and author of a study of **Descartes** (1880), which SB used to compile *Whoroscope*. A stalwart of the Georgian Society, Mahaffy opposed the introduction of Irish into TCD and remarked that **Joyce** was a living argument that it was a mistake to establish a separate university for "the aborigines of this island."

Mahood: determined to render "inexistent" his "troop of lunatics," the **Unnamable** finds that **Basil** is becoming important and resolves to call him Mahood, to nominate the **voice** that mingles with his own, and sometimes drowns it (309). He tells Mahood's stories: the **pensum** (310); the "world tour" (318); being stuck in a jar (327). Mahood is a "vice-exister" (315), but the distinction between him and "I" thins until, unable to affirm that man is a higher mammal, he is baptized **Worm** (337). Bair claims (399) that SB intended to call the novel *Mahood*, but in Notebook I SB referred to "**M**" ("je vais donc l'appeler M."), and did not use "Mahood" until June 1949, three months into the writing.

"**Mahood**": an excerpt from *L'Innommable* (*Minuit*, 80–113), in *La Nouvelle revue française* 2 (février 1953): 214–34. One section, the "tumefaction of the penis," was deleted after the proofs were corrected. SB, furious, got a written apology in the next *Revue*, the editors stating that they could have been ruined had they published the offending passage.

"**mais que même dans ces lieux extrêmes donc**": identified by J. C. C. Mays (*JOBS* 6: 137) as an abandoned work beginning thus, two leaves from a quarto notebook, dated 8.11.69 and 10.11.69. Sold for £240 to a private buyer at Sotheby's (4–5 December 1972).

"**Malacoda**": first published in *Echo's Bones* (1934); rpt. in *transition* 24 (June 1936): 8; *Transition Workshop* (1949), 204; *Gedichte* (1959); *Poems in English* (1961); and *Collected Poems* (1977). Alternative titles were "Thrice he came" then "The Undertaker's Man." Responding to the **death** of SB's **father**, the poem images a moment of absurd anguish when, kneeling reverently beside the coffin, the undertaker's assistant delicately breaks wind. SB made casual use of it in "**Draff**" (184–99), where **Belacqua**'s funeral is handled by "Malacoda and Co."

In *Inferno* XX, **Dante** sees Barrators and Peculators plunged into boiling pitch by devils called *malebranche* ("evil claws"). These threaten harm till Virgil

appeases their leader, Malacoda, who restrains Scarmiglione. The canto concludes with Malacoda's reply to the devils gnashing their teeth: *Ed egli avea del cul fatto trombetta* ("And of his arse he made a trumpet"). The modern Malacoda is the undertaker's assistant, in long black tails. He comes *thrice;* to measure, to coffin, to cover. Dante's number informs SB's orchestration, major images and minor phrases reiterated in threes. Death's inevitability echoes the *Muss es sein?* ("Must it be?") motif of **Beethoven**'s last quartet, its coda a musical joke. The son attempts to shield his **mother** from the pain, particularly the final indignity. That pain is most acute at the end of the poem: the impulse to help, yet a wish for decorum; cover him properly, let me hold your **hat**, please don't fart . . . The death ship is about to embark, despite the muted "stay" (Dante's "Posa, posa, Scarmiglione"). An intense moment arises in "mind the **imago** it is he." SB's imago is a butterfly on a flower in the **Huysum** painting, but equally the son's idealized image of the father. Placing flowers on the coffin thus recognizes in art the inevitability of death, an act of devotion (like the poem) from son to father.

The final subversion of "aye aye" by "nay" is less acceptance than a recognition of inevitability. "Evil coda" or not, *it must be.* The lobster's death in "**Dante and the Lobster**" echoes the sentiment: "It had to." **Belacqua** comforts himself with the thought, **God** help us all, that it's a quick death; the text insists: "It is not." In both works easy consolation is withheld, and the keynote is the cruelty of death. Here, the lasting image is an act of irreverence that only the anguished SB can detect, the undertaker's man passing into the air his quiet breath. It is desperately funny, but in the end (as it were) it is not a joke.

Malebranche, Nicolas de (1638–1715): French **Occasionalist**, who affirmed that **body** and mind cannot influence each other; rather, matter forms the *occasion* rather than the *object* of our knowledge, and **God** is first cause of changes in either. Malebranche allegedly died of the excitement induced by metaphysical discussion with **Berkeley** (SB's tutor A. A. Luce studied his influence on Berkeley). Like **Geulincx**, Malebranche propounded the theory of two clocks to explain the body-mind synchronization, each independent but God intervening on occasion to calibrate the two. Hence the sudden movement of the **dog** in *How It Is* (30): "no reference to us it had the same notion at the same instant Malebranche."

Malherbe, François de (1555–1628): French poet at the court of Henri IV, who insisted on classical clarity. Associated with **Racine** (*Dream*, 48) and invoked to sit on the sonnets of Mrs. Blanaid **Salkeld** ("Recent Irish Poetry," 74).

Mallarmé, Stéphane (1842–98): French poet for whom SB felt little enthusiasm, recording (DN, 58), "Un **Baudelaire** coupé en morceaux." SB commented to **MacGreevy** (18 October 1932) that the poetry was "Jesuitical," casting himself as "a dirty low-church P. even in poetry" (compare "**Yellow**"). The problem was less SB's attraction to **Rimbaud** than Mallarmé's toward **symbolism**. Belacqua's family wave a Mallarméan farewell (*Dream,* 12); and the **Smeraldina** (31) does the brave girl in the Mallarmé mode (exaggerated emotion). SB had in mind Mallarmé's poem "Brise marine": "L'adieu suprême des mouchoirs," the "Azure Mist" (31) condensed from his "Azure" (Pilling, *Dream Companion*).

"Malone Dies": an extract from the forthcoming novel, subtitled "From the Author's Translation of *Malone Meurt*"; in *Irish Writing* 34 (spring 1956): 29–35.

Malone Dies: SB's translation of *Malone meurt,* published by **Grove** (1956) as a $1.25 **Evergreen** paperback (E-39), with a limited edition of 500 numbered copies. The trade issue was distributed in Britain by John **Calder**, whose own appeared in 1958. A Penguin issue of 20,000 copies (1962) sold out by 1964. Two extracts had previously appeared: one in *Transition Fifty* 6 (1950): 105–6; another in *Irish Writing* 34 (spring 1956). An excerpt, read by Patrick **Magee** and produced by Donald **McWhinnie**, with music by John Beckett, aired on BBC 3 (18 June 1958). Collected as *Three Novels* by Grove (1958), then by **Olympia Press** in its Traveller's Companion Series, #71 (October 1959), subtitled, without SB's approval, "A **Trilogy**," as it was by Calder (1959). There is no collected French edition.

The title echoes a popular song: "And that was the end of sweet Molly Malone" (compare "**Sanies II**": "alive the live-oh"); also, rhyming slang, "on one's own" (Todd Malone); or, simply, M alone, the novel depicting the isolation and end of **Molloy, Moran**, and Malone. The original title, "L'**Absent**," suggests a narrator sequestered from the world that Molloy and Moran, however feebly, move through. SB's experiments with perspective are similar to but less complex than in *Molloy*. The first-person narrator, approaching paralysis and **death** and confined to a bed in an institution for the indigent, describes his pathetic condition and tells stories, "almost lifeless, like the teller" (180), about an impoverished family and an **asylum**. These mingle with the frame tale of Malone's demise. The novel seems static, at times almost conventional; yet it may be among SB's best parodic efforts, as it travesties literature, the conventions of storytelling. For all his innovation, SB was at heart a parodist, fond of what he called **Sterne**'s "daring zigzagging divagations" (Atik, 57).

The first-person narrator, unnamed until midway through (233), hopes to survive St. **John the Baptist**'s Day and pant on to the **Transfiguration**, perhaps the **Assumption**. Life is regulated by canonical rites; indeed, the narrative will end at Easter. But his life rapidly becomes a series of indecisions and revisions. He discusses his imminent demise and plans for the interim, to tell stories: "four stories, each one on a different theme. One about a man, another about a woman, a third about a thing, and finally one about an animal, a bird probably." The first two can be combined, he thinks, and he cannot die without an inventory. So, "Present state, three stories, inventory, there"; then a new subversion of orderly discourse and dying emerges: "An occasional interlude is to be feared." Interlude is the *mot juste,* a "playing between" moments of note.

The novel itself forms an interlude between *Molloy* and *The Unnamable,* just as *Waiting for Godot* formed an interlude between the agony of finishing *Malone Dies* and that of beginning *The Unnamable.*

"Present state," a set piece (182–86), becomes problematic. He is in a room, apparently his, but how he got there, how long he has been there, and who attends him are mysteries. He seems to be in an asylum of sorts. He surmises like the narrator of "The **Calmative**" that he fainted or received "a blow" and was brought here, but he is not sure he is alive. He mentions an ambulance, perhaps that heard by Molloy. He might be dead, "expiating my sins, or in one of heaven's mansions." Each day the door opens and a hand proffers a dish on a wheeled table, which the bedridden narrator manipulates with a **stick**. The table serves to dispose of his chamber **pot** and so embraces the life cycle: "Dish and pot, dish and pot, these are the poles" (185). Crucially, he is thinking. Immobile, impotent, "prostrate, no supine," immured, "Somewhere in this turmoil thought struggles on." In this only possible Cartesian world, he exists, dead or alive. The section concludes with an orderly restatement: "Such would seem to be my present state."

Story I (186–229) concerns **Saposcat**'s life among the peasants, but with many interruptions (the inventory, Jackson, and the **parrot**), introspective interludes ("I told myself"), narrative commentary ("How plausible all that is"), and **voices** ("one vast continuous buzzing"). Writing provides continuity: "I write about myself with the same pencil and in the same exercise-book as about him" (207). He tells of the **Lamberts**, Sapo's arrival, the kitchen, and the gray **hen**. As the summer draws to a close (210–16), the story focuses on Sapo's exams, burying the mule, the lentils, the white rabbit, and incest. The narrator is in a **skull**, for "these six planes that enclose me are of solid bone" (221). Sapo's departure (217) occasions his transformation to **Macmann** (229–33), whose story includes the interlude of the cab and **horse** (compare "The **Expelled**"). The narrator reflects on his activity: in order not to die, he says, you "must **come and go**, come and go" (232).

Malone, now named, feels "it" coming (233–38), after which it will be "all over" with the "**Murphys**, **Merciers**, Molloys, Morans and Malones [all **M**'s], unless it goes on beyond the grave" (236). Compare SB to **MacGreevy** (30 August 1932): "Desire to write coming. Feel it coming"; writing as a trope of death. Macmann's story resumes with his cruciform image in the rain (238–46), followed by a resumption of the inventory and writing implements, pencil and notebook. Malone in the dark evaluates his possessions, considers using his stick to move his bed (on castors), and desires a turn about the room (246–55); this anticipates *Fin de partie*. The narratives of Malone and Macmann converge. Macmann is a patient in the House of **St. John of God** (255–68), where Malone will die, tended by **Moll**, then by the psychopath **Lemuel**. Moll's "silver **knife-rest**" connects with Molloy's narrative.

Macmann's story concludes in several phases. The first, "the relationship between Macmann and his keeper" (259–60), centers on Moll's two carved crucifixes (earrings) and the "long yellow canine between," a **Christ** between **two thieves**. Her death begins a second phase, its self-mutilations (267–68) anticipating the novel's homicidal end. Macmann receives a visitor whose tightly wound umbrella suggests **Gaber's** visit to Moran (268–74). The grounds are "a little Paradise" (274). Lady **Pedal** arrives for an outing, from **Stillorgan** to Dalkey Island. Four inmates are introduced: "The youth then, the Saxon, the thin one and the giant" (283). The outing continues to its finale, Lemuel's gratuitous slaying of Maurice and Ernest. As Malone dies, as his pencil dwindles, the narrative dissipates, and the five huddled, shrouded inmates with their keeper drift out to sea. The ending is not unlike that of the "Ithaca" chapter of *Ulysses* (Sinbad the Sailor?), but lacking the final **.** of faded **consciousness**. Hence a narrative ambiguity, an ending that is a beginning, a death that is also a **birth**. A novel that began with ironic images of salvation and freedom (John the Baptist and Bastille Day, with a common denominator of decollation) ends at Easter with neither resurrection nor redemption, where, perhaps, *Godot* begins. At best there is the hope of oblivion, invoked in this narrative, but even that is doomed to frustration by the opening tirade of the following novel: "I shall never be silent. Never."

Malone meurt: second of SB's novels in **French** (Minuit, 1951), an issue of 3,000, with fifty deluxe copies. Proof copies were issued to the jury for the 1953 Prix **Goncourt** (it was runner-up).

The autograph manuscript (**HRHRC**) consists of two notebooks, 322 pages, dated intermittently from the outset ("27 Nov. 1947") to the end ("30 May 1948"). The first contains some final sections of *Watt;* both are entitled "L'**Absent**," a toast to the departed, "Absent friends." SB noted on the second: "L'Absent—Original title of *Malone meurt.*" The protagonist is first referred to as "**M.**" The notebooks reflect the process of creation, the sequence of events as in the published text, but they contain additional "narrative" material, notably about **Saposcat** among the peasants. In its place SB developed Malone's comments on his story and his involuntary **memories**, these accentuating the story as play ("interludes") devised to relieve the ennui of waiting and the inevitability of **death**. See *Malone Dies*.

"**Malone s'en conte**": an extract from the forthcoming novel (45–58); published in *84: Nouvelle revue littéraire* 16 (*Minuit*, décembre 1950): 3–10, with some omissions and additions.

Malraux, André (1901–76): French novelist and **politician**. His early writings were influenced by **surrealism**, leading to the conviction of a civilization in crisis and an underlying **absurdity**. His response was the individual attitude of complete lucidity, as in *La Condition humaine* (1933), set in Shanghai. Chapter 9 of *Murphy* adopts an epigraph from this (part 4, 1 April 1927), that it is difficult for one who lives outside the world not to seek his own kind, the words of the terrorist Tchen about to blow up Chang Kai-shek's automobile. It expresses a sense of **solitude** and self ("la

possession complète de soi-même") that only **death** can penetrate. SB stated to **MacGreevy** (16 January 1936) that he could suddenly see *Murphy* as a breakdown between **Geulincx**'s *Ubi nihil vales* and Malraux's *Il est difficile*. Malraux was on the Management Committee of *La Nouvelle revue française* that cut without authorization a passage from *L'Innommable* (see "**Mahood**").

Mal vu mal dit: a prose-poem, 1980–81, translated immediately as *Ill Seen Ill Said* (qv). First published **Minuit** (1981), with a special edition of 114 numbered copies. The drafts indicate how the text was shaped, revised, reduced, and rewritten—SB's typical pattern of building up then cutting down. The holograph notebook (RUL 2903) is inscribed "Mal Vu," but the first page is headed "Soir et Nuit," and a later typescript (RUL 2207/1) is headed "Soit soir soit nuit" before this was deleted. Early drafts have significant differences from the final text and later ones many notes and corrections, but from the outset the woman, white stones, and sepulchre were present.

Mandarin: in *Dream,* **father** of the **Smeraldina**, a portrait based on SB's uncle William "Boss" Sinclair, father of Peggy **Sinclair**. This derives from George Chinnery's *A Portrait of a Mandarin,* in the **Dublin** National Gallery (O'Brien, 150; see *Watt* "**Addenda**" #2); plus the aperitif Mandarin-Curaçao (*Dream,* 37).

mandrake: the mandragora, its bifurcated root resembling a poor forked man, which grows from ejaculations of the hanged and screams when uprooted (*Molloy,* 155). Lord Gall of **Wormwood**, hearing a fearful sound, comments: "There never was such a season for mandrakes" ("Echo's Bones," 6). **Belacqua** replies that, alas, "Gnaeni, the pranic bleb, is far from being a mandrake," reducing the Hindu pantheon to a pustule of Prana, in the presence of a dead cow.

La Manivelle: "The Crank," or barrel organ; a "pièce radiophonique" by Robert **Pinget**, the "texte anglais" by SB (Minuit, 1960). See "The **Old Tune**."

Manning, Mary: the Mannings, Susan and her daughter, Mary, were family friends, but complications arose from SB's depiction of the **Fricas** in *Dream* (not published) and "A **Wet Night**" (which was). Susan Manning's soirees provided the satiric material. In 1936 SB, on the rebound from Betty Stockton (see "**Cascando**"), and Mary, married to Mark de Wolfe Howe of Boston, began an affair. Mary had come to **Ireland** because her play *Youth's the Season . . . ?* was to be produced at the **Gate Theatre**. It was published in *Plays of Changing Ireland,* ed. Curtis Canfield (Macmillan, 1936), 322–404; SB may have suggested some changes (Bair, 235). The affair lasted until Mary returned to Boston in September. SB wrote Mary from **Germany**, 1936–37; those letters (at the **HRHRC**) reveal much that went into *Murphy,* for which Mary tried vainly to find a U.S. publisher. Mary visited SB in **Paris** (1958), and kept in contact until his death. Her daughter Fanny was rumored to have been fathered by SB that summer; this lacks substance, but may

inform the **summerhouse** memories in *Company* and "**Heard in the Dark II**" (see "**To My Daughter**").

mansions: throughout SB's fiction, rooms in an **asylum**. "Mansions of Bedlam" are the cells of Bethlem, visited by **Boswell** and **Johnson** (*Life,* 8 May 1775). SB cited Boswell in his "**Human Wishes**" Notebook (RU 3461/1): "He calls the cell in Bedlam the 'mansions' & the corridors the galleries." From John 14:2: "In my Father's house are many mansions."

Mantegna, Andrea (1431–1506): quattrocento painter. His *Assunta* or *Assumption of the Virgin* (1454–57), a fresco in the Chiesa degli Ermitani, Padua, is referred to in *Proust* and may underlie "**Assumption**." *That Time* may take some of its unusual perspective from his *Foreshortened Christ.*

Manzoni, Alessandro (1785–1873): Italian poet whose ode "Il cinque Maggio" (1822), on Napoleon's **death**, was declared by **Goethe** the greatest of many that mourned that passing. **Belacqua** is studying this ("**Dante and the Lobster**," 16) but prefers **Dante**, dismissing Manzoni as an old woman; that dismissal (*sposi manzoneschi*) is repeated in *Dream* (118). Verdi's *Requiem* was written to honor Manzoni's death.

Marguerite: the woman from the café who tends the **Unnamable**; first called **Madeleine**. Her name suggests the heroine of **Goethe**'s *Faust,* seduced and abandoned but saved at the last. Also, the name of Mme. Piouk in *Eleutheria.*

Marientotenkind: Praz (*Romantic Agony,* 276; DN, 46) tells Heine's tale (*Florentinische Nächte,* 1837) of Maximilian's passion for Mlle. Laurence, called "das Totenkind" ("the dead child") because of her curious **birth**. Her **mother** had been buried, but robbers violating the tomb found her in the pains of childbirth and saved the child (see *Dream,* 72.) **Balzac**'s "Jane la Pâle" (*Dream,* 125) was born in this manner.

Marlowe, Christopher (1564–93): English dramatist, author of *Dr. Faustus* (ca. 1588), to which **Neary**'s "all is dross" (Faustus's love for Helen) alludes (*Murphy,* 5). **Murphy** dreams of Hell, Heaven, Helen, and **Celia** (176). SB recorded in the **Whoroscope Notebook,** "Infinite riches in a little room" (*The Jew of Malta*), ticking it as contributing to **Murphy's mind** (218). He was unimpressed by Marlowe's aspiring mind, as "Dr. Fist" (Ger. *Faust*) suggests (88). Marlowe exemplifies "shortness of poetic sight" (*Dream,* 170); Miss **Counihan** massacres his mighty line (*Hero and Leander,* line 76) about love at first sight (*Murphy,* 221). Consider the "towers circumcised" (topless) of *Eleutheria* (125). The **Unnamable** (341), in extremity, sees the sky streaming into the firmament, as Faustus sees **Christ**'s blood.

Marston, John (1576–1634): English dramatist, author of *The Malcontent* (1604), from which SB noted the well with two buckets (III.iii.60–62), Malevole to Mendoza on Fortune's buffets. This constitutes **equilibrium** in a horse-leeched world (*Murphy,* 58); Marston drew the image from **Shakespeare**'s *Richard II*

(IV.i.184). **Murphy** expostulates that "the entire sublunary world will turn to civet" (138); the sentiment of **Paracelsus** comes via *The Malcontent* (IV.v.110–11). "**Denis Devlin**" rebukes thus the "vile suggestion" that art has anything to do with clarity (*Disjecta,* 94).

Martha: a servant, from John 11:1: "Mary and her sister Martha," emblems of contemplative and active lives ("Echo's Bones," 16). **Moran**'s servant, Martha, serves him shepherd's pie (117).

Martin, Jean: actor recruited to play **Lucky** three weeks before the opening of *En attendant Godot* (3 janvier 1953) when Roger **Blin** undertook **Pozzo.** Martin played a palsied servant who trembled and dripped saliva throughout. He played **Clov** in the premiere of *Fin de partie* (3 avril 1957); was La Voix in "**Cascando**" (13 octobre 1963); and **Krapp** under Jean-Louis Barrault's direction (1970). In his eighties, in a tour de force, he did Lucky's speech at the Royal Court launching of James Knowlson's **biography** (September 1996).

Mary: with Ann, Mr. **Knott**'s increeping and outbouncing maids (*Watt,* 50–55). "Mary Ann" is a generic servant girl, as in "**Draff**" (199): Mary, **mother** of **Christ**; and Ann, mother of Mary. Their existence is conditional on a third person, the mistress or master. This reflects the "Third Man" argument, an onotological "proof" of the existence of **God. Arsene**'s Mary spends her time eating onions and peppermints, a reductio, perhaps, of the dadaist credo of the human figure as a coffee mill: eat, grind, shit, and eat again.

Masaccio: Tommaso di Giovanni di Simone Guidi (1401–28); "sweaty Big Tom" (*Dream,* 216), Italian painter and pioneer of perspective discussed in **Vasari**. In describing the **Frica** as a "gem of ravished Quattrocento" SB alluded, he told Eoin O'Brien, to the central panel of Masaccio's *Madonna and Child* (National Gallery, **London**); but "limy" and "frescosa" (215) intimate the frescoes of the Santa Maria del Carmine, **Florence**.

Masson, André (1896–1987): French painter, influenced by **surrealism**, who from 1947 asserted in landscape a spiritual relation with **nature**. Subject of the second of "**Three Dialogues**," he is one who has enlarged "the statement of a compromise" by remaining "on the plane of the **feasible**." He is contrasted with Bram **van Velde**, who has abandoned that plane and is helpless, incapable of achieving, **desire** and potency dead, yet whose work is on higher level than Masson's "wriggles."

Master of Tired Eyes: in "**Ding-Dong**" (44), an old woman's face is likened to *A Portrait of a Lady* (National Gallery, **Dublin**; purchased 1931). Reproduced by O'Brien (140), who identifies (362) a Flemish painter referred to thus, circa 1540.

mathematics: "**For Future Reference**" (1930) abuses W. N. Tetley, SB's science master at **Portora**, that "red-faced **rat** of a pure mathematician" (the **HRHRC Leventhal** typescript reads "politician"). SB had to take one paper during his first year at **Trinity**, Euclid and algebra; his marks were only average. He did not progress to higher mathematics but achieved competency in the elements, and a mathematical awareness informs his writings. Four categories may be considered:

- **irrationality** in the early writings, notably *Murphy*.
- **seriality**, set theory and logic, with particular reference to *Watt*.
- "Extraordinary how mathematics help you to know yourself": the postwar texts.
- **memory** and measurement: the later prose and drama.

Whoroscope notes that **Descartes** "proves **God** by exhaustion." The phrase is used of a circle with an inscribed polygon: the area of such a figure, be it square or chiliagon, can be calculated. The more complex the polygon, the closer to the circle's area. Yet however exhaustive, the method is approximate only: the infinitesimal gap between God (perfect circle) and reason (*ratio*) remains. Compare the "roundheaded" **Vico**'s "circular progressions" with **Bruno**'s *maxima* and *minima* ("**Dante**," 21); or Bruno's assertion of the identity between "the smallest possible chord and the smallest possible arc" (news to the "arithmomaniac" (*Dream,* 220), who thinks the arc longer than its chord).

Proust declares: "The Proustian equation is never simple" (11). SB accepts regretfully "the sacred ruler and compass of literary geometry," but refuses the "spatial scales" that measure man (12). The root of the equation is the Proustian moment when involuntary memory overcomes the **gulf** separating past and present. Rejected is **Protagoras**'s contention that man is measure of all things; this SB consigns to "la poubelle" in "La **Peinture des van Velde**" (*Disjecta*, 131–32). The artist must shrink from "the nullity of extracircumferential phenomena" (*Proust*, 66); he must withdraw to the impossible center, the "core of the eddy" or "ideal core of the onion."

Dream's mathematical images often derive from **Schopenhauer**. Belacqua gazes at the starfield, an "abstract density of **music**" (16), and invokes the "passional intelligence, when arithmetic abates" that might tunnel through the interstellar **coalsacks** and twist through the stars, "in a network of loci that shall never be coordinate." This reflects the distinction, as old as **Plato**, between arithmetic as that which unfolds in **time** and geometry, the ground of which is extension, or existence in space. Schopenhauer notes (*WWI*, I.1 #12, 70) the need to translate geometry into arithmetic (space into time), as in Cartesian analytic geometry (the "network of loci"). McQueeny invokes his eternity of the present: "the ideal limit which separates the past from the future, the present is as unreal for the senses as a point in mathematics. But if it is inaccessible to empirical **consciousness** it can be seen as the supreme reality for the metaphysical" (133).

Belacqua compares the **Smeraldina** to the **Syra-cusa** as a beautiful **hen** to a drypoint (a needle used in etching), or volume to line. He fails because he cannot establish on base *Aa,* "where *A* is hen and *a* is dry-point," a triangle with the desired apex; he cannot imagine *Aa.* The narrator informs him, unfortunate Belacqua, that he is trying to define beauty by categories (35); his error is using mathematics to go beyond the categories of reason. Better the statistical metaphor of extreme and mean (49), to "work out" the **Alba**. In "**At last I find in my confusèd soul**" (70–71), the single sentence within a binary sonnet form creates an emblem of **syzygy**, One conjoined with the Other and thus with the Infinite. Yet the narrator almost commits the earlier error. He tries to define Belacqua's being, but Belacqua is "a cubic unknown" (which the analytic geometry cannot depict in graphic form), at his simplest trine (120), but his equation cannot be satisfied by three values. He may be a succession of terms, but these cannot be defined: "They tail off vaguely at both ends and the intervals of their series are demented" (124). Belacqua may be described but not circumscribed; his terms may be stated but cannot be summed.

Murphy has such an **irrational heart** that no physician can get to the root of it. At the novel's heart is the *surd,* or irrational number, inexpressible as the ratio of two integers, such as the square root of two, or pi. Such irrationality confounds principles of harmony based on such findings as the musical octave or music of the spheres (see **Apmonia**). Hence **B**'s sense ("**Three Dialogues**," 125) of the rationalist impulse in **art**: "a kind of Pythagorean terror, as though the irrationality of pi were an offence against the deity." As Hesla concludes (7): "The absurd is impervious to the human logos, to human speech and reason." For SB, irrationality is the root of his distrust of the tradition wherein reason is the highest form of consciousness that leads the mind to God. As **Windelband** states

(389), "Rational science is mathematics"; but SB's writings endorse **absurdity**. Hence **Neary**'s anagnorisis (*Murphy*, 217) when he forsakes his rationalism and admits that life is irregular.

Murphy reflects a preoccupation with geometrical shapes, for instance the circle, as in the Round Pond or Murphy's circling the **prison**. The plot is a "**situation circle**" or hexagon, a closed figure disrupted by the algebra of **desire**. Neary is conditioned by his own teaching. Miss Dwyer is his "**tetrakyt**," a Pythagorean figure combining in perfect form all the mystical numbers. He invokes **Pythagoras** and **Hippasos** (47), drowned for betraying the incommensurability of side and diagonal, the existence of pi, and/or the construction of the regular dodecahedron. The dodecahedron was thought to be the largest regular figure to be encompassed within a sphere, thereby assuming the latter's mystical properties (see **Burnet**). Pythagoras discovered that five equilateral triangles meeting at a vertex form a pentagon; each panel consists of a regular pentagon, with three pentagons meeting at a point, that process duplicated until each common point is filled. For a Pythagorean jest about a football (as dodecahedron), see **greatcoat**.

Neary comments (213) that there is no triangle, however obtuse, but some circle passes through its wretched vertices. **Wylie** says: "Our medians . . . meet in Murphy"; Neary adds: "Outside us." **Christ** and the **two thieves** are defined as vertices of a triangle through which the perfect circle of God must pass; any triangle, however "obtuse," may be so circumscribed. This is commonly misunderstood. Ruby Cohn (*Comic Gamut*, 46) considers the meeting point of the medians as the center of its circumscribing circle, and so the circle as a symbol of **solipsism**, Murphy a "seedy solipsist" who pictures his mind a sphere. But *medians* are lines drawn from the vertices of any triangle through the midpoint of the side subtending that angle; they meet at a median point, the center of an *inscribed* circle. Wylie, or Neary, is being obtuse; he has confused medians with perpendiculars drawn from the midpoint of each side of a triangle, the coincidence of which forms the center of the circumscribing circle, but which, for an obtuse triangle (more than 90°), will be "outside" the figure. The trio is trying to enclose Murphy *within* the triangle of their three lives.

At the tearooms Murphy expects a 25 percent to 50 percent return, but does infinitely better. His gain from one cup of tea, which costs nothing, is 1.83' cups "approximately" (84): let x be one cup of tea; he drinks half, splutters, has it filled, and gains half-x. He drinks a third, and has it filled with hot. His sum is therefore $(x + x/2 + x/3)$, or 1.8333333' cups of tea. This is not an irrational number (11/6) but is at best approximate. Little wonder that he squares the circle of his shoulders (92). He arranges his five biscuits in order of edibility (96), the anonymous first and ginger last; the others vary daily. These prepossessions reduce "to a paltry six" the possibilities; could he conquer his prejudice against the anonymous there would be 24; and should he overcome his infatuation with the ginger, 120. The key is simple permutation. The **Whoroscope Notebook** intimates of the biscuits: "indicate that the *outer reality* disappears in fine permutability." The identical problem and its radiant solution is met in "**Lightning Calculation**"; but a vexation arises in "**A Wet Night**" (74), when the sodden Belacqua realizes that of the six ways of being seated only one satisfies his conditions.

The dodecahedron reappears in "Les **Deux besoins**" (1938; *Disjecta*, 55–57), where two needs in this marginal life, "besoin d'avoir besoin" and "besoin dont on a besoin," are likened to the incommensurability of side and diagonal. SB defines the irrational within the enthymemes of art, an argument developed in "**Three Dialogues**" and elsewhere ("La Peinture des van Velde"; "**Peintres de l'empêchement**"). SB comments of the brothers **van Velde** that one paints "l'étendue," the other "la succession": Bram's art is geometrical, but Geer's arithmetical (*Disjecta*, 128).

Provocative conundra, serial themes, and logical exhaustion account for *Watt*'s fascination. When Watt appears, a problem ensues, as Mr. **Nixon** explains (17): "For the past seven years, he said, he owes me five shillings, that is to say, six and ninepence." Watt offers four shillings and fourpence, and Mr. **Hackett** deduces that he owes "two and threepence." This can be "explained": simple interest at 5 percent over seven years improves 5/- to 6/9; were Watt to repay 4/4 he would have paid the accumulated interest, and reduced the principal by 2/7, leaving a debt of 2/5 (2d. forgiven?). During those seven years the only item that Watt apparently buys, from a one-legged man, is a **boot**. Watt requires only one since he has found a shoe: this boot cost

eightpence (219), the precise deficiency. The logic is impeccable but the absurdity remains. Compare averaging the boot (a twelve) and shoe (a ten) to accommodate Watt's feet (eleven); or the end of the novel, when Watt tenders 3/1 for his 1/3 ticket to the end of the line, the round end or the square.

Watt is detained by a **mixed choir**. It sings of the recurrent number formed when the 366 days of a leap year are divided into weeks, then a second verse, with an error, the days of a regular year. Mathematical errors in *Watt* are a vexed subject. Some are intentional, others not, yet others the product of antinomies. The song reflects what Heath Lees (14) calls the "Pythagorean comma," the gap arising in Western music between acoustical reality and the musical octave. The ratios are not quite true, and notes must be tempered to reconcile the anomaly. Three frogs (136–38) croak Krak!, Krek! and Krik! at intervals, respectively, of eight, five, and three, a Fibonacci series in which each interval is the sum of the two preceding ("Krok!" and "Kruk!" would be, presumably, two and one), beginning together but not croaking in unison again until 120 bars. See **serial order**.

Circle and point in the picture raise questions of geometry and perspective but also ontology (130–31). Is the relationship that of man and God? Watt and **Knott**? If so, which is center and which circumference? Is the picture a fixed member of the set of all things pertaining to Mr. Knott, or here today and gone tomorrow, one in a relative series? Watt supposes the latter, and the text says this supposition was "strikingly confirmed"

(131). Yet it appears that the picture was not taken by **Erskine** but, rather, that its significance for Watt diminished with time (208). This confirms only that Watt has changed. The coordinates of the picture are problematic (129–30). Watt wonders how it would look upside down (point west, breach north), or on its right side (point north, breach east), or on its left side (point south, breach west). Spatial relationships (north and west, left and right) determine orientation (consider "**North**" in *The Lost Ones*); but these are disconcerting. Not until left and right (subjectively defined) are understood as the picture's perspective, rather than Watt's, do the directions make sense. This is a **mirror** reflection, disrupting the usual bond between perceiving subject and **object** perceived (the manuscripts attest to this change; early drafts describe the picture from Watt's perspective).

The most exhausting quality of *Watt* is/are the logical paradigms. These are at first manageable; later they become monstrous. This "comedy of an exhaustive enumeration" (*Proust*, 92) is taken to absurdity, reflecting Watt's attempts to comprehend the paradigms that rule his world. They mock Descartes's four rules of the *Méthode*, as stated by **Baillet** (12): "1. De ne rien recevoir pour vrai qu'il ne connût être tel évidemment; 2. De déviser les choses le plus qu'il serait possible pour les mieux résoudre; 3. De conduire ses pensées par ordre en commençant par les objets les plus simples pour monter par degré jusqu'à la connaissance des plus composés; 4. De ne rien omettre dans le dénombrement des choses dont il devait examiner les parties." Watt follows faithfully. He accepts nothing as true that he does not know to be so; he devises things to best resolve them; he orders his thoughts by beginning with the simplest and mounting by degrees to the knowledge of the more complex; and he omits nothing in his numbering of parts. Instead of leading to Knott, the method leads Watt to the **asylum**. The paradigms become more complex as his world disintegrates.

The first paradigm describes **voices** "singing, crying, stating, murmuring" in Watt's ear (29). The sequence exhausts most combinations: {A, B, C, D}; {AB, AC, AD, BC, BD, CD}; {ABC, ABD, BCD}; and {ABCD}. The text comments that "there were others" ({ACD} is missing), and that Watt understood all, much, some, or none (conditions potentially multiplying permissible combinations), but the sequence is satisfying, a model for those that follow. Another paradigm arises from Watt's consideration of Mr. Knott's meals. There are four terms: whether Knott was responsible for the arrangement; whether he knew he was responsible; whether he knew such an arrangement existed; and whether he was content. The possibilities may be displayed as a truth table, A or not-A, B or not-B, C or not-C, and D (as Knott, like the God of Genesis, seems always content; "D" is a constant).

Once logic has insisted that a famished **dog** is necessary (91), the first problem is how the dog and food are brought together. Watt ventures four solutions (94–97), but each (n) is met with (n+1) objections, one solution meeting two objections, two solutions three objections, and so forth. The more solutions, the more objections, one meeting two, two meeting five, three nine, and four four-teen (98). The formula is $n(n+3)/2$, as the **HRHRC** manuscripts reveal (NB3, 96). The reader construes the underlying laws, the discovery thereof apparently confirming a principle of reason of the preestablished arbitrary. The **Lynch** family is created, five generations of twenty-eight souls adding up to 980 years, on the verge of attaining its millennium (104). That figure is derived from the twenty years divided among twenty-eight members, five-sevenths of one year each, if all are spared, which they are not. Thereafter, a simple arithmetical computation assumes increasingly demented dimensions as some die and others are born, each coming and going, changing the variables and setting back the day. The reader is warned that the figures are incorrect (104), so that consequent calculations are doubly erroneous; there is also a *Tristram Shandy*–like element, as figures change more quickly than they can be calculated and so are immediately outdated.

The most outrageous calculations are those of Mr. **Nackybal** (171ff). The explanation (198) of the con is only partial: each number from 0 to 9, cubed, has a unique final digit; in a six-figure number this gives the last digit of the cube root by simple inspection (7 implies 3). For the other digit, it is necessary to learn the cubes from 0 to 9 (0, 1, 8, 27, 64, 125, 216, 343, 512, and 729). If the first three figures lie between, say, 125 and 215, the digit is 5; between 512 and 728, then 8. Provided the figure is a perfect cube of no more than six figures (a cube root of 0 to 99), the answer may be given by inspection: 103,823 gives 47; 778,688

gives 92. Unpleasantness ensues (191–92) when Mr. O'Meldon calls out 519,313, for that number is not a perfect cube. Nor does the trick work in reverse. Mr. Nackybal does (impossibly) well to make only twenty-five mistakes out of the forty-six cubes demanded, compared with four trifling errors out of fifty-three extractions. Compare ". . . **but the clouds** . . .": V when wearied of begging might busy himself with something more rewarding, "cube roots, for example."

As Watt's language regresses, his paradigms become more complex (164–69). For example: "Thus I missed I *suppose* much I *suspect* of great interest touching I *presume* the *first or initial* stage of . . . Watt's stay in Mr. Knott's house." The three terms "suppose," "suspect" and "presume" are distributed as: ABC, ACB, BAC ("CAC" is an error), BCA, CBA, CAB; but since there are eight terms (from "first or initial" to "eighth or final") the sequence must begin again: ABC and ACB. The rules are clear and distinct, but items do not conform to the instructions, and there are deviations from the principles declared.

As the paradigms embrace more terms they assume greater complexity. The drafts devote considerable space to the permutations, the lists both exhaustive and exhausting. At the end Watt tries to understand the essence of Mr. Knott by listing his attributes, to prove him by exhaustion, but fails to comprehend that the gulf between the transcendent and the rational cannot be overcome this way. Watt contemplates Knott's movements (203–4). These involve standing, sitting, kneeling, lying; with respect to the door, window, fire, and bed; seventy-two possibilities of movement in all, beginning with two terms, A to B (window to door) and back again {ABBA}, and ringing up all possible changes on the figures {ABCD}, but limited by the conditions that each must begin where the previous one ended, and that the middle terms must be identical (it is impossible, even for Mr. Knott, to move from where he is not). This is followed by a longer account of Mr. Knott's furniture (204–7), with variables of door, window, fire, and bed; each associated with tallboy, dressing table, nightstool, and washing stand, and the seven days of the week, the restriction being that each location must be occupied by only one piece of furniture on a given day. The permutations become increasingly demented, yet are rigorously logical, again as witnessed in the manuscripts by complete tables, checked to indicate that all combinations have been included. The addition of another term, or the interaction with another series, complicates the possibilities geometrically rather than arithmetically; a few more variables enormously extend the schema. One devastating illustration of this is the "important matter" (209) of Knott's physical appearance, which combines several attributes exhaustively: stature {tall, small, middle-sized}; figure {fat, thin, sturdy}; skin {pale, yellow, flushed}; and hair {dark, fair, ginger}. Out of these simple features (four attributes, each with three variants), eighty-one combinations emerge, precisely tabulated in the manuscripts but presented in apparently random rather than obviously sequential order. The paradigm is complete, but Watt still does not know Mr. Knott through this

"exhaustive" process; his essence is not deducible from his attributes. If other aspects (carriage, expression, shape, size; feet, legs, hands, arms, mouth, nose, eyes, ears) were included, the paradigms would be impossible and Watt no better off. Watt needs reminding of **Augustine**'s dictum, that one cannot know what God is but only what he is not.

Molloy comments, "Extraordinary how mathematics help you to know yourself" (30). The irony goes beyond the *TLS* and its impermeability to farts. Molloy counts these one day, 315 in 19 hours, and concludes: "Not even one fart every four minutes." The arithmetic is shaky. Molloy gets from 315 farts in 19 hours to "Not even one fart every four minutes" not by dividing 19 (1,140 minutes) by 315 but by dividing and rounding off, each stage compounding the error and carrying it forward, so that instead of the accurate figure of one fart every 3.62 minutes he produces the more decorous result. This is perhaps what the Whoroscope Notebook means by "Ars metric." Molloy's **mother** has lost "if not all notion of mensuration, at least the faculty of counting beyond two" (18). Later, Molloy apologizes for excess: "Homo mensura can't do without staffage" (63). The sucking stones sequence (69–74) is carefully charted, as Molloy moves from the obvious {4 x 4} distribution of the stones in his four pockets. This has the disadvantage that the sequence of sucking cannot be controlled, short of his having sixteen pockets, even with shuffling to combat the "diabolical hazard" of chancing always on the same stones. He contemplates other martingales, and finally a {6+5+5+0} arrangement, which guarantees that each stone can be sucked, even if the sequence cannot be guaranteed.

Molloy's other problem is how to get through the forest. Part III of Descartes's *Méthode* advocates being firm and resolute, illustrated by a traveler lost in a forest finding an exit by proceeding in a straight line. Molloy's head being full of useful knowledge (85), he knows the fallacy in this, that one wanting to go in a straight line ends up going round in a circle. He tries instead to describe a circle, hoping thereby to go in a straight line, which meets with limited success in that he did not trace a circle, "and that was something." The method is refined by altering course with every three or four jerks, permitting "if not a circle, at least a great polygon, perfection is not of this world" (90). The day finally comes, by chance or exhaustion, when he reaches the limit, a tangent perhaps, the ditch at the end of the forest.

As **Moran** begins to resemble his quarry, his grasp of matters mathematical deteriorates. He is uncertain (141) how much money he has given his son; a fortnight before he would have calculated "a series of menus asymptotically approaching nutritional zero" (149; compare *Endgame*) but is content to note feebly that he will soon be dead of inanition. He can still distinguish "the sum of countless points of light" (159), but makes no comment (168) on the address of **Youdi**, 8 Acacia Square, which inscribes the rotated symbol for infinity within a simple polygon. He delights in the dance of the **bees** (169) as complicated figures that he can study all his life and never understand.

Three Novels resemble **Murphy's mind**: moving from an outer realm of light (Moran) to a gray zone (Molloy to **Malone**) and an inner dark (the **Unnamable**). Malone intends to make his reckoning, to "draw the line and make the tot" (181), dividing the remaining time into five (182), of what he does not know. He thinks he is an octogenarian but is unsure: "Perhaps I am only a quinquagenarian, or a quadragenarian" (185). Like **Saposcat** he manipulates concrete numbers, practicing mental arithmetic, marshaling figures to throng his mind with colors and forms (187). What tedium. He seeks to discover the forms in which the unchanging seeks relief from its formlessness, a **doctrine of the limit** (197), and has memories of endless counting and dividing by 60 (201–2) to pass the time. His pencil like his life dwindles "little by little," the day approaching when nothing will remain but a fragment too tiny to hold. He imagines **Macmann** lying on the ground and, assuming one extremity to be heavier than the other, rolling along the arc of a gigantic circle, dreaming of a flat land and himself as a cylinder endowed with cognition and volition (246). Malone begins to fade. He begins his inventory, with scant success; his two pots no longer retain their **equilibrium** (252). These are all "pretexts" (276) for "not coming to the point": wonderful **puns** that are enacted in the final pages, until consciousness dwindles to the point of **nothing** and fades out.

The Unnamable begins at a point congruent with the third zone of Murphy's mind. The Unnamable is conceived as a point, not a line (position without extension). SB took extensive notes from **Poincaré**'s *La Valeur de la science*, which outlined a cosmology, by the identification of stars and atoms. The opening pages delineate a cosmos infinitely small, an atom encircled by electrons, yet impossibly large, in which the transit of other bodies may be observed. The Unnamable is uncertain about the distance between center and circumference, or whether he is in **motion**, but chooses finally to think of himself "as fixed and at the centre of this place, whatever its shape and extent may be" (295). This conclusion is in keeping with the paradox of subject and object at the outset of Schopenhauer, the immensity of a universe accessible only by the individual's tiny consciousness.

He acknowledges (298) that he has been taught to count and reason, but he cannot measure **time** (299), which vitiates the calculation of the intervals of orbits or transits about his central figure. As **Mahood**, he makes his way by incremental calculus toward a small rotunda at the center of an enclosure (317), which is never reached (321). Even if it were he would immediately spiral off in an opposite direction, the moment and point of contact indefinable and tangential. Malone's room is a cube, but the Unnamable lives in a universe of curved figures; in *All Strange Away* the cube becomes a rotunda as its dimensions are reduced. Fictions such as Mahood and **Worm**, and those of mathematics, are stripped away, until all that is left is consciousness itself, unadorned, unaccommodated. As the Unnamable says (359): "Enough concessions, to the spirit of geometry." No more calculation, reflections of symmetry, intimations of seriality; only the sense of the end and the mystery of the **voice** (qv), elements that cannot be measured. The last

geometrical shape is a partition, two surfaces and no thickness, a tympanum that feels itself vibrating and will continue until he rattles: "it's mathematical" (383). This is a metaphysical extension of Murphy's sense of himself as a point in the tumult of non-Newtonian motion, not subject to Euclidean principles, a missile without provenance (*Murphy*, 112).

"The **Expelled**" depicts one thrown down the steps, less concerned about that than how many steps there are, because the true figure depends on whether the top and sidewalk should be counted; he arrives at three different figures, uncertain "which of them was right" (46). This parodies the debate as to whether numbers begin with 0 or 1. The dilemma recurs in *Watt* (83) and *All That Fall*, Dan **Rooney** contending irritably that the number of steps must change in the night. In "Text 11" the narrator likens his self to "the square root of minus 1" (145), an imaginary number, represented conventionally as *i* and equivalent (in English) to the noncapitalized form of the first person.

The drama presents "the shape of ideas." *Waiting for Godot* embodies **Pascal**'s famous "bet": if salvation is "an even chance," then the winning strategy is to believe, for the payoff is considerable, and the loss minimal. This is complicated by Gospel accounts of the **crucifixion**, only one in four offering that reasonable chance: the odds diminish logically to one in eight. The "shape of ideas" expresses itself arithmetically and geometrically, the later drama representing an analytical geometry, a spatialization of stage setting, a geometry of the imagination. *Godot* unfolds in da capo form, a repetition in time both symmetrical and asymmetrical (likewise *Happy Days,* "Play," and "Rockaby"), the action shorter and dialogue more ritualized. This is accentuated by the symmetry of the **pseudocouples**, and patterns of **coming and going**, notably the return of **Pozzo** and **Lucky**, or the **boy**. The metaphor of crucifixion is displayed in the **quincunx** of bodies and in the way Pozzo is brought back to his feet by **Vladimir** and **Estragon**, like a Christ between two thieves.

Endgame is set in the **skull**, this assuming the form of the circle, with **Hamm** at its exact center or, rather, concerned lest his chair not be at that metaphysical inexistent point. **Clov**'s kitchen, outside that circle, is "ten feet by ten feet by ten feet," a cube. Hamm and Clov are bound together in the prisoner's dilemma. A key word is "zero," which suggests that the structure is conceived asymptotically, the graph representing the function of their lives and relationship as they approach that unreachable point. The "Second Law of Thermodynamics" implies attrition and homeostasis, and the heap of millet (see **Zeno**) accentuates the sense of life dwindling "little by little." The metaphors are decremental, emblems of the imperceptible fading of the light, the moment when the impossible zero will be reached.

"**Act Without Words I**" plays with cubes and symmetries, exploring the tantalizing "gap" between existence and beyond. The second introduces a brutal permutation: each time the goad provokes A or B they assume new positions relative to the sack, CBA changing to CAB then back again, as they are pushed farther left. The next sequence will presumably push them offstage, into the darkness following a brief interlude in the light. In *Krapp's Last Tape,* the set is reduced to a small circle of light surrounded by darkness, expanding back into time and place as tapes are played. The effect is desolation, as if the circles of the past have contracted into this small point. The psychological setting of *Footfalls* is similar, thought visibly extended into motion by the invariable pattern of pacing.

In "Play," the order of voices in the eternal triangle is unpredictable. It differs from *Come and Go,* which is shaped by mathematical sequence, or ritual movement, until {Flo, Vi, and Ru} becomes {Ru, Vi, and Flo}. *That Time* adopts a similar strategy. SB does not include the pattern adopted, but manuscripts testify to the care with which the sequence of voices was devised, an order imperceptible to reader or audience but which forms an underlying grid. Geometrical structures of light and darkness shape stage settings of "**Ghost trio**," and ". . . but the clouds . . ." In "**Breath**" and *Not I* the light is arithmetical, changing in time. "**Quad**" is ordered geometrically, but the players' movements are defined arithmetically, with absolute precision. The dramaticule offers a metaphor of coincidence, meeting in time and space, and hence the "danger zone" where this might happen. Finally, in "**What Where**" serial order is resumed, Bam, Bem, **Bim**, **Bom** forming bonds that do not quite match the seasons: in the spring, Bom; in the summer, Bim; in the autumn, Bem; but in the winter, Bam alone.

In *How It Is* the narrator reflects: "I always loved arithmetic it has paid me back in full" (37); and: "dear figures when all fails a few figures to wind up with" (47). Manifestations of this love are sometimes curious, such as the **buttocks**: one "twice too big the other twice too small"; and "**Pim**'s though undersized were iso" (37). Plotting his progress (47), the narrator traces his chevrons: straight lines two yards long at 45° from "the old line of march" create alternating right-angled triangles of unit one yard, to generate an irrational length of movement along the hypotenuse, the essential direction: "between two vertices one yard and a half a little less dear figures golden age." The "little less" arises because the square root of two (the sum of the squares on the other two sides) is irrational, 1.41421. . . . In part 2, "with Pim," there will be "no more figures" (51), "vague impressions" only of coordinates, in time or space. He is conscious of the brevity of existence suspended between these two forms, "and hence no more reckoning save possibly algebraical," that is, with terms unknown.

Life is "a slowness of which figures alone however arbitrary can give a feeble idea" (124). Manuscripts confirm SB's obsessive checking of minute detail. The narrator is aware that his number is up (81). In part 3, "after Pim," he calculates his journey as the sum of its halts and stages, an advance of "say forty yards a year" (125). There are thousands of couples linked by identical bonds, "glued two by two," millions or billions, each awaiting his Bom, each approaching his Pim: "it's mathematical" (112). And each with his **Kram and Krim**, **witness** and scribe? It's problematical. The resolution is the self alone. At first this sense

of being "sole elect" is a comfort, but like all else it is rejected. The calculations are "correct," the text insists, but are finally remote from the reality of life in the mud. Reliance on mathematics as a refuge from suffering, or to reach the light, is as illusory as the religious and philosophical myths that the figures have supplanted: they are equally "all balls."

The Lost Ones describes "a flattened cylinder fifty meters round and sixteen high for the sake of harmony," affording some twelve million square centimeters of "total surface." These are the corrected sizes (see *The Lost Ones*, **texts**). Despite SB's dislike of **allegory**, the piece combines **Dante**'s inferno with Borges's library, a cosmos reduced to its elements. The temperature oscillates between hot and cold, moving from one extreme to the other in a manner mathematically defined (215). Niches and tunnels are distributed in quincunxes, "a harmony that might be appreciated by one with a perfect mental image of the entire system" (204). The distribution of various individuals ("One body per square metre") within the three zones is controlled by laws nowhere explicit but which may be inexorably deduced. The definition of "north" is arbitrary in a cylinder that lacks all differentiating criteria.

The late works find the mind turning to measurement as memory fades. *All Strange Away* has a stagelike setting, at first five feet square and six high but as the story proceeds this becomes smaller. It is tightened to three feet square and five high; {a, b, c, d} designates the floor; {e, f, g, h} the ceiling; his body is coordinated accordingly. The ceiling is "down two foot, perfect cube now," then becomes a rotunda, "three foot diameter eighteen inches high supporting a dome" (176). In turn, the rotunda is reduced to three foot diameter and three from ground to vertex, a diminution that entails repositioning the body within. Finally, in "Diagram," it is two feet across and two feet at its highest. In words that define the title, "So little by little all strange away" (178), every accidental eliminated.

Mathematics is finally of dubious value. The protagonist of "**Heard in the Dark II**" consoles himself: "Simple sums you find a help . . . in the timeless dark you find figures a comfort" (250–51). In the **summerhouse**, awaiting the woman, the narrator of *Company* looks at the "rustic hexahedron." The dimensions are identical in both accounts: six feet across, eight from floor to vertex, "Area twenty-four square feet to furtherest decimal." She is late, so he kills time calculating the volume: "Seven yards cubic approximately. This strikes you for some reason as improbable and you set about your sum anew." The figures are curious: a hexagon comprises six equilateral triangles, here of unit three; this equals 27 square feet, not 24; and, assuming a flat ceiling, 216 cubic feet, or eight cubic yards. Another error occurs in the second calculation. The narrator assumes a certain heart rate and reckons "how many thumps a day. A week. A month. A year. And assuming a certain lifetime a lifetime. Till the last thump" (55). Compare *Murphy,* where the reader is invited to make a "simple calculation" of the seconds in one dark night (224); or Krapp: "Seventeen hundred hours, out of the preceding eight thousand, consumed on licensed premises alone. More than 20 per

cent, say 40 per cent of his waking life." In *Company,* the outcome is extravagant: "with hardly more than seventy American billion behind you sit in the summerhouse" (55). This represents 22,000 years; "million" seems more likely. A similar calculation in "**A Piece of Monologue**" (265) gives a different result: "Two and a half billion seconds. Hard to believe so few." Two and a half billion seconds represent eighty years. The speaker reflects on his first night, "Of thirty thousand odd" (268); this matches the estimated eighty years.

A last parable. In "**Enough**" a woman recalls her past with an older man, of taking flight in arithmetic: "Whole ternary numbers we raised in this way to the third power sometimes" (188). Later: "Total milage divided by average daily milage. So many days. Divide. . . . Daily average always up to date. Subtract. Divide" (191). She acknowledges a hundred words a day, "A bare million in all," some thirty years. The figures are futile, a distraction from loneliness, and the story ends with a sentiment that is not mathematical: "Enough my old breasts feel his old hand" (192).

Maupassant, Guy de (1850–93): French writer, master of the short story with the twisted tail. SB alludes to "phylloxera of the spirit" (a greenfly) in "**What a Misfortune**" (140). Maupassant in "Divorce" (1888) invoked "phylloxera des âmes" as the effect of obsessive ideas. The **Unnamable**'s story (406) of the couple in love suggests the *Contes.*

Mauthner, Fritz (1849–1923): author of *Beiträge zu einer Kritik der Sprache*

("Contributions toward a Critique of Language") (1902; 3 vols., Leipzig: F. Meiner, 1923). In his biography of **Joyce** (1959; 661–62), Richard Ellmann claimed that SB was asked to read passages from the *Beiträge*. Linda Ben-Zvi has shown this to be untrue; Ellmann's 1982 revision (648–49) is more circumspect. SB's notes in the **Whoroscope Notebook** are from a later period; many concern "Grenzen der Sprache" (II.506; echoing **Goethe**'s "Grenzen der Menschheit"), the limits of language, as in our deluded sense, like a clever **dog**, that we are free simply because the chain is long (II.532).

Mauthner, like Kafka, was born of German-speaking parents in Czechoslovakia, rejected his Jewish heritage, studied law at Prague, and admired Goethe. He was among the first to investigate systematically the philosophical problems of ordinary language, which names things but must depict an incomplete worldview, and fails to reflect adequately the complexities of the inner world. By subsuming all knowledge under language, then denying its efficacy, Mauthner illustrates how language may interdict itself. His is a Nominalism so radical that it denies the ability of language to represent not only universals but individuals (see **scholasticism**); SB copied verbatim into the Whoroscope Notebook the paragraph (III.615–16) beginning "Der reine und konsequente Nominalismus," a passage underlying the "**German Letter of 1937.**" Influenced by **Kant** and **Schopenhauer**, Mauthner felt they failed to question the premises of their metaphysics, they did not analyze language. Language is a convention, a game (here he anticipates Wittgenstein). Words are inadequate since merely indices of **memories** and no more able to get at true reality than a spider in the corner of a palace can get at the total reality of that palace (III.650; Hesla, 254).

Mauthner's Nominalism leads to skepticism (a "churn of stale words" in "**Cascando**") and a "gottlose Mystik" that might transcend the limits of language. This underlines SB's search in the "German Letter" for a means of boring through language until what is behind it "begins to seep through" (*Disjecta*, 172). Mauthner is a vital station "on the way to this literature of the **unword**" (173). His is the radical conclusion that words are meaningless, "mere ejaculations of air on the part of the human voice" (compare "Aspirate Aitch" of *Company*). Thoughts and words are synonymous but there can be no thinking without words; words are "inane" (*verba inania*), lacking substance or sense, and so our thoughts are inane, empty, never "obviating the void." He is aware (III.634–35) of the **absurdity** of using words to explore the silence but, like **Lucky**, is caught in the net of language. If the meaning of each proposition is explicable only by another, a process of infinite deferral is initiated. That way deconstruction lies, but despair is relieved by the paradox of the absurd, the inexplicable need to express, to leave a "trace." Mauthner rejected the implications of extreme Nominalism, asserting (III.641) that while mankind can despair of ever knowing reality, a quiet despair can "through a denial of self deception" try to make clear the relationship of man to the world (Ben-Zvi, "Limits of Language," 189). He senses in the power of laughter (III.632) a way of breaking the tyranny of words. SB's accentuation of "Nominalist irony" (*Disjecta*, 173) opens the way for an "inane" comedy, a way of rejoicing in the **irrational**, like Moran with his **bees**.

The one explicit reference to Mauthner is in "**Rough for Radio II**" (116): "The least word let fall in **solitude** and thereby in danger, as Mauthner has shown, of being no longer needed, *may be it*." But no word, says Mauthner, can have such transcendent power; however tortured, words cannot reveal truth. Other details owe much to the *Beiträge*. Mauthner's **ladder** of language underlies **Arsene**'s sense of existence "off the ladder" (*Watt*, 44), his inability to utter or "eff" (what is the unword?); **Watt's** problems with the **pot** testify to the incommensurability of word and referent (how then are particulars "real"?). "**Three Dialogues**" scrutinize Mauthner's contention that communication is impossible (why the need to express?). The **Unnamable**'s sense of the "**Not I**" reflects Mauthner's view that the ego is contingent and does not exist apart from language (but whence the **voice**?). SB views with Mauthner a blasted linguistic landscape in which signs are barely interpretable, but that denial is bedeviled by the compulsion to express, so that even as expression is denuded an antic mask may be assumed.

May: protagonist of *Footfalls*, relentlessly, rhythmically pacing, unable to sleep. Said to be in her forties, an isolated daughter caring for a dying **mother**, she is perhaps her older self, recalling her younger self, her upstage **Voice** "revolving it all" in her poor mind. The portrait is based on SB's mother, also "May," who suffered from insomnia and walked about at night. In her "sequel" May tells of Mrs. **Winter** and her daughter **Amy**, in which the mother imagines the daughter (who says she was not there) responding to the blessing at Evensong, a peace that passeth her own understanding.

McCabe, Henry: the "Malahide murderer" in "**Dante and the Lobster**." His petition rejected, he will "get it in the neck," another problematic of **God**'s **pity**. O'Brien outlines the background: on 31 March 1926 a house (*La Mancha*) at Malahide, belonging to a family named McDonnell, was found in flames, and several bodies were recovered. The gardener, Henry McCabe, raised the alarm but inconsistencies in his account led to his arrest. He denied guilt, but his appeal was rejected and he was hanged ("without a hitch") in Mountjoy Prison (9 December 1926). In "A **Wet Night**" (76), the **Frica** patters off like a goose "flying barefoot from McCabe." In "**Draff**," the gardener ravishes "**Mary Ann**," sets the house on fire, then waits in the toolshed (like McCabe) until arrested.

McGillycuddy woman: nominated by Otto **bboggs** ("What a Misfortune," 126) for bridesmaid, although none has heard of her, and she never appears. Mentioned in "**Rough for Radio I**" (110). The MacGillicuddy Reeks are in County Kerry.

McGovern, Barry: Irish actor best known for *I'll Go On*, a monologue composed from *Three Novels*, conceived by

Michael Colgan, director of the **Gate**, with SB's encouragement, and featuring a **greatcoat** lined with the *TLS*. First performed at the Gate on 23 September 1985 directed by Colm Ó Briain. It begins with **Molloy** looking for his **mother**; shades into **Malone**, an old ballocks telling himself tales; then rises in crescendo as the **Unnamable**'s voice pours forth.

McWhinnie, Donald: Assistant Head of BBC Radio Drama, working with Martin Esslin and Barbara **Bray** (then his companion) to produce *All That Fall* (13 January 1957). SB listened from **Paris** and enjoyed it, despite the poor reception, but "didn't think the animals were right" (Knowlson, 389). The audio experiments led to the BBC's Radiophonic Workshop. The animal noises were made by humans rather than with special effects; these and other sounds were processed to eliminate excessive naturalism and to create "the enclosed subjective universe" (Fletcher, 73). McWhinnie directed Patrick **Magee** in readings from *Molloy* and *From an Abandoned Work* (BBC 3, December 1957) and in *Krapp's Last Tape* (1958). He produced "**Embers**" (1959), which SB felt did not succeed. He wrote *The Art of Radio* (Faber, 1959). In 1961 he produced for TV a production of *Waiting for Godot*, which SB watched unhappily, thanking McWhinnie but saying that "it's not right on television" (Knowlson, 435). SB got on well with McWhinnie, the two sharing some "late and lubricated nights" (395). SB's affair with Barbara Bray complicated things, but the working relationship survived, SB helping McWhinnie with *That Time* and "**Ghost Trio**" (1976).

memory: this impossible theme will be treated as a dialogue implicit in much of SB's writing, a **Proustian** critique of the Cartesian position. Memory in the Cartesian paradigm offers an extension of the self into the past (**Vladimir** tries to hold on to his, **Estragon** has let it go); but if **Mauthner** is correct in saying that memory and language are synonymous, the unreliability of the one entails the inevitable failure of the other. Yet elements of unreliability, of forgetting, offer openings for creative invention. Memory is finally a joust between involuntary and creative recollection.

In *Proust* (1931) SB articulates the distinction between voluntary and involuntary memory; the latter restores the past **object** and reveals the real (33). Voluntary memory is rejected (14) as "the application of a concordance to the Old Testament of the individual" (32). Linked with **habit** (qv) as "attributes of the **Time** cancer" (18), it presents the past in monochrome, like "turning the leaves of an album of photographs," with no interest in "the mysterious element of inattention that colours our most commonplace experiences" (32). **Murphy**'s attempt to reconstitute the image of his **father** (251) is an **allegory** of its failings. Involuntary memory is "an unruly magician and will not be importuned" (33–34); **Proust**'s book is a monument to its action. The **madeleine** episode conjures a childhood world that "comes out of a teapot" (34); it offers the only possible "accidental and fugitive salvation" (35). SB calls it a "**mystic** experience," the factor that resolves the Proustian equation. If *by accident* (SB's italics), by "some miracle of analogy" (72), the impression of a past sensation recurs as an immediate stimulus then the total sensation (not its echo or copy) rushes to re-create the experience, and thus overcome the gulf between past and present. Such moments are real without being actual, ideal without being abstract (*Le Temps retrouvé*, III, 872).

SB at first accepted this sense of involuntary memory. His metaphor of the vase (qv) and the paradox of a perfume that is new because already experienced (74) imply a validation of the Proustian experience (see "**Rue de Vaugirard**"). Joyce (who rarely forgot) affirmed the auditory memory as constitutive; Proust found it ephemeral, fleeting, moments of real memory (involuntary) felt as a kind of mystical shock (Piette, 195). SB is disrespectful to both authors, each of whom he admired. In *Dream*, the only unity is involuntary (132); the **hawthorn** (1) and **verbena** (145) irreverently gloss the Proustian moment; and the ending parodies "The Dead." SB's work is marked by an increasing distrust of epiphantic moments, not the psychological experience but its lasting significance. **Arsene** tries to define the mystical sense of something that slips and **Watt** has residual memories of **flowering currant**, but the **ineffable** experience remains fugitive for both. In "**Words and Music**," **Croak** is enthralled by a **face** in the ashes, while texts as distant as "**Enueg II**" and "**Old Earth**" share a motif of the sky suddenly turning to faces, this underlining the persistence of involuntary memory throughout SB's oeuvre.

Watt's memory is impaired and he is incapable of reconstituting a unified self. Of his experiences fragments only remain, and when he leaves incidents (of note) such as the visit of the **Galls** are faded, half-heard, almost forgotten. His world is a place where all is **ill seen**, **ill said**, ill murmured, ill heard. For the composite protagonist of *Three Novels*, memory as a constitutive force is unreliable. **Molloy** does not know (cannot remember) how he reached his **mother**'s room; he has forgotten the name (Edith? **Ruth**? Rose?) of the "little chambermaid" in whom he experienced true **love**. His narrative proper begins with an image of rumination, of cows in the evening silence: "They chew, swallow, then after a short pause effortlessly bring up the next mouthful . . . perhaps I'm remembering things" (8–9). This is **Augustine**'s conceit of memory as the belly of the mind (*Confessions*, X.vii–xxi; DN, 26; *Dream*, 235–36). The saint applauds the vast treasury of images stored, and the mind's capacity to draw on these yet remain detached; this capacity Molloy does not possess. He confuses Bela[c]qua with **Sordello** (10); he cannot remember if **A** or C is going home or the kind of **dog** that followed him (11); he has a curious recollection of how he was born (16); he cannot remember his name (22), nor that of his town (32). He uses the **mythological present** (26) to tell a story he didn't know he knew so well (58). His memories are rooted in some kind of **Jungian** swamp (76), but the sequence that follows, by the sea and in the dark wood, is devoid of memories, until he emerges into a ditch (91) and recalls images of his life, the **corncrakes**, men with clubs, **sheep**, and other scenes.

Moran's discourse provokes echoes of the earlier section (**knife-rest**, **hat**, sheep, bicycles). **Gaber**'s messages exist not in his head but only in his notebook (106). Moran is unable to remember his encounter with the charcoal burner (151), or what caused the violent scene with his son (160). His report, which the reader has just read, is designed to initiate less an allegory than a process of remembering, what Piette (45) terms the **music** of memory. That continues into *Malone Dies*. Malone's memory is unreliable yet his sense of having got there, "In an ambulance perhaps," and the vague recollection of a forest suggest Molloy's experience. All that "belongs to the past" (183). He resolves to write his memoirs, but there are difficulties: "A minimum of memory is indispensable, if one is to live really" (207). Memory is evasive: was "he" in **London**, studying the stars (184)? Is *a* gray **hen** *the* gray hen (203)? Does Jackson's **parrot**, with its **nihil in intellectu** (218), confirm Mauthner's belief that memory is the connection between sensory expression and language? Instead, Malone works with voluntary memories. He makes his "inventory," tells stories, and creates interludes, trying to "invent" (194), to seek relief from formlessness (197). It is "Mortal tedium" (217), or "pretext" (276).

Like Malone, the **Unnamable** is soon at his old aporetics. His namelessness implies non-memory; he insists that past happiness has "clean gone from my memory" (293). Speak he must, "in another present" (306), yet that mythological present cannot *be* without its past, however constituted by erratic memory. Rejecting other **puppets** he devises **Basil**, **Mahood**, and **Worm** as buffers between him and the void. His burden is,

roughly, that he is alive, and this entails a modicum of memory lest he be a parrot (335). The issue is defined as "Feeling nothing, knowing nothing, capable of nothing" (348), until the **voice** intrudes into that "safe place" (or **oubliette**), like a **stick** with a hook (Mauthner's "Häkchen," or pothook of memory [II, 309]) and forces Worm out (358). Memory is "fly-paper" (382), yet the Unnamable admits, "I have memories" (395). He remembers Worm, that is to say he has retained the name, and "the other, what is his name, what was his name, in his jar." The memories, he insists, are invented, they are not of him (396). But that is belied a little later, when he recalls details from the end of "The **Calmative**" (stars, buoys, beacons, the mountain burning) and affirms, "I knew I had memories," only to qualify this immediately, "pity they are not of me" (399). Any sense of self as constituted by memory remains as suspect as ever.

The **Expelled** comments, "Memories are killing" (46). In "**Ascension**," the memory arises of Peggy **Sinclair**, recently dead; "**ainsi a-t-on beau**" recalls the father "mangé sans appétit / par le mauvais temps"; "**Arènes de Lutèce**" depicts the experience of one separated in memory from his "other" self; and in "**Saint-Lô**" the "old mind" sinks, ghost-forsaken, "into its havoc." In *First Love*, the killing memories are of his father, these inhibiting his capacity to love, then of his child, these haunting him for years. The "pretty" blue tie with stars (from SB's mother) is mentioned in "The **End**" and "Text 3" (111) as memory that has "gone out." The narrator of *Texts for Nothing* struggles to reconstitute identity, to "in-corporate" memory. His rheumatism reminds him of his mother's (102); then childhood tales of Joe **Breem** (or Breen, he can't remember which); the "good memory" of Mother **Calvert** (106); and "one last memory" (107), of Piers pricking his oxen o'er the plain, one that initiates, creates, a "far memory" (108). These are as distant voices, of uncertain identity. *Text* 2 intimates the process of memory characteristic of the later works, when the mind turns to the past not to recall but to reshape it, when the received idea that memory is somehow constitutive of its subject is questioned. Memory is equally forgetting, as in the uncertain recollection of Piccadilly Circus ("you don't remember"), or the lightships at night, seen with his father from the bathroom. A shaving **mirror** reflected his father and the harbor behind; then "my father went but the mirror remained" (124). The glass asserts, darkly, continuity between reflections otherwise disparate. Memory, like voice, is finally a "trace" (152).

Waiting for Godot offers less the shaping fictive power of memory (SB's later great theme) than a summa of traditional tropes, whereby memory constitutes identity (unreliable memory, uncertain identity). Estragon remembers maps of the Holy Land and the Dead Sea (8.b), but cannot recall the Gospels nor the story of the **two thieves**. Act II opens on a familiar scene, but Estragon, to Vladimir's "Do you not remember?" (39.a), has forgotten everything—yesterday, the place, the tree, **Pozzo** and **Lucky**, his **boots**. Vladimir is little better. He recalls their time in the **Macon** country, picking grapes for a man called (*he snaps his fingers*), at a place called

("can't think of the name"); the English text accentuates the forgetting (see **Bonnelly**). The boots left overnight should affirm identity, continuity of the external world implied in the persistence of objects, but Estragon says they are not his. This is the paradox of *percipi:* the world exists only in the specious present of consciousness, re-created at every moment and with it partial memories, to provoke an illusion of dubious continuity. One thing only qualifies that assumption, and that is the persistent association of memory with pain (of having been kicked). Vladimir says of Pozzo: "he's thinking of the days when he was happy. (*Pause.*) *Memoria praeteritorum bonorum*—that must be unpleasant" (55.b). For **Dante**'s damned the memory of past happiness is the worst kind of hell, but Vladimir and Estragon are trapped in a present without memory, lacking all differentiation or identity. Pozzo shares that vacuum (56.b); he cannot remember today having met anyone yesterday, and tomorrow he won't remember having met anyone today.

Endgame's funniest (unhappiest) moments are Nell's nostalgic recollections: "Once" . . . "yesterday" . . . "So white." These involuntary flickers of memory fail to redeem the past. **Hamm** assumes a different strategy, one that SB would adopt increasingly henceforth. His memories have mostly gone, so he explores his past by telling his story. *Endgame* marks a transition for SB as the rejection of memory recollected, in tranquility or otherwise, in favor of the shaping power of the imagination, equally dubious though that might be.

Krapp's Last Tape returns to the Proustian "vase" (tapes) to critique any sense of self as a repository of buried memories that might be brought up. Memory on tape constitutes a doubtful encapsulation of a past world. Krapp cannot recall the "memorable equinox" (57); he must look up "viduity," a word he once knew (59); both moments replay in his imagination the set theme of his dying mother. This is a scene he chooses not to dwell on (the voluntary aspect is marked), nor to reconstruct beyond a certain point. His major epiphany concerns the girl in the punt, a recollection that surprises him, so that despite himself he is moved by the power of involuntary memory. SB revisited this theme in "**Eh Joe**," where the mind, the creative imagination, composes and enacts a similar but more complex drama of memory and guilt.

Voluntary memory implies the authentic past of the object and its possible retrieval to the present. In *How It Is* the mind tries to encompass "vast tracts" of time: "unless recordings on ebonite or suchlike a whole life generations on ebonite one can imagine it nothing to prevent one mix it all up change the natural order play about with that" (107). Memory has an archival function, in **Leibniz**'s sense. It is a ventriloquist, throwing past voices into present speech; this personified faculty, memory, becomes dramatic voice (Piette, 81). Memory merges with fiction, and so (Piette argues) the distinction between voluntary and involuntary, triumphantly affirmed in *Le Temps retrouvé* and proclaimed in *Proust,* is eroded. SB's **characters** are left with a profound sense of unreliable memory, of a process of fiction indistinguishable from the act of remembrance. This sentiment, central to SB's later work, is frequently mocked. In "**Rough for Theatre II**," **B** reflects: "Memory . . . memory . . . [*He takes up a sheet*] I quote: 'An elephant's for the eating cares, a sparrow's for the Lydian airs.'" In *Film,* O takes photos of various phases of his life and rips them up. In "**A Piece of Monologue**" photographs, "Pictures of . . . he all but said of loved ones" (266), are ripped from the wall and torn to shreds, as the "rip" word (love) fails to bring about the consummation desired. One apparent exception is *That Time,* which deploys three voices, each an aspect of the past, the narrator's final smile indicative of a fleeting triumph of order over futility, as he finally shapes the fragments of memory into the pattern he has chosen to create. But even here integration is ephemeral, no sooner done than undone.

In *Company,* memory acts as epistemology, almost in parody of Molloy's insistence that there are things "in spite of everything, that impose themselves upon the understanding with the force of axioms, for unknown reasons." Certain memories (father and son, the **diving board, larches**) were, SB insisted, obsessional. The minimalist works record the struggle to remember as the mind threatens to fade, measurement supplanting memory as more tangible, something to be *counted on* (see **mathematics**). Memory as a mode of temporal reintegration is invalid, and characters who reconstitute their worlds will fail, because it is unreliable. Yet something remains. The later works reflect the ethos of Jack **Yeats**, who insisted that the artist did not so much create as "assemble memories";

according to Gilbert Ryle (138–39), Yeats cherished half-memory, "a state where memory was stimulated and transcended by the imagination. He was freed from the past. The new state allowed the memory to develop and fluctuate after it first gripped the mind, to distort the original experience . . . In this way the original experience was translated into a newly created and visionary happening." Themes and images culled from the past might be converted through imagination into poetic complexes, in which the emotion rather than the event becomes the subject of the painting.

Piette concludes (173): "Rhymes, miniature acts of memory, colour the surface of the conscious stream, telling stories of where the stream has flowed before, tiny signals of its countless origins in the complex past of memory, sound, and sense." The lasting, insoluble mystery is thus the power of memory to constitute consciousness and the "earthing" of the musical ear in memory. SB's last works seek to capture the fugitive relationship of sound and sense: "rhythmical and acoustical resources that chime in with a dramatic presentation of a mind remembering or imagining" (18), what Eliot identified as the auditory imagination, acoustical patterns initiating tiny acts of memory. In such a coordination of the acoustic with the conceptual, Piette argues (45), lies the paradox of rhymes as miniature acts of memory, "a mimesis that hears as well as sees the murmurs of the mind, a difficult music of remembered connotations and selves fugitively united." This is the music of memory, a pattern of accumulated rhythms and dramatic emphases. These do not so much constitute an allegory or narrative as initiate a mode of remembering, a way of reading, as in (to return to our beginning) Proust's difficult music. Memory is not the repetition of the past but the miming of the mind seeking to locate its being in the greater mystery of consciousness.

Mendel, Deryk: French dancer, trained at Sadlers Wells, who asked SB for something to perform. SB sent Suzanne to the cabaret "Fontaine des Quatre Saisons"; impressed with his **clown** number, she suggested that SB write a **mime** for him (Knowlson, 377). The outcome was "**Acte sans paroles I**" (avril 1957). Mendel also performed its companion piece (janvier 1960). SB oversaw his world premiere of "**Spiel**," part of *Drei Stücke,* at the Ulmer-Theatre, Ulm Donau (14 June 1963). In his "**Play**" (1964) the characters were too differentiated, and when problems arose with the cast of *Warten auf Godot* (1965) SB went to Berlin to mediate. SB admired Mendel's German TV version of "**Eh Joe**" (1966), with Nancy Illig as **voice**; he remained friends with both actors.

Mens mea Lucia lucescit luce tua: "Lucia, your light enlightens my mind"; the inscription inside the ring ("**Lucy**'s redeemed") that **Belacqua** gives Thelma, his new bride ("What a Misfortune," 140). Cited from **Burton**'s *Anatomy* (III.2.3, 558).

"Mercier and Camier": title of several extracts from the then-unpublished novel. A signed typescript entitled "**In the Train with Madden**" (HRHRC, Lake Collection, #8.8) was sent to David Hayman for *The Texas Quarterly* but did not appear.

a. two extracts, trans. Hugh Kenner and Raymond Federman, in *Spectrum* [Santa Barbara] 4.1 (winter 1960): 3–11; "**Madden**" and "The Umbrella."

b. the eleventh chapter, the bar, in *Annales publiées trimestriellement* [Toulouse]1.3 (novembre 1965), *Littératures XII*: 153–54; with an analysis of the unpublished novel (F&F, #273).

c. extracts in *Le Monde* 7157 (mercredi 17 janvier 1968), "Le Monde des livres": 5.

d. "premier chapitre," in *Le Nouvel Observateur* 282 (27 avril–4 mai 1970): 37–38.

e. in the *Partisan Review* [New Brunswick] 41.3 (1974): 342–61, anticipating the forthcoming English translation.

Mercier et Camier / Mercier and Camier: SB's first novel in French. The autograph manuscript cover (**HRHRC** #365) adds "La Forêt de Bondy" and "Autour du pot / Les **Bosquets de Bondy**." Begun 5 July 1946, completed 3 October 1946, accepted then turned down by **Bordas**, it was shelved as "unpublished and unavailable." Prodded by **Minuit**, SB permitted publication (1970). An English translation on which he had worked intermittently since the 1940s appeared from **Calder** and Boyars (1974; paperback 1976), with a limited signed edition of 100 copies, and **Grove** (1975), paperback and cloth. Six notebooks (RUL 1396/4/17–22) show SB moving from translation toward "reshaping" in English. The novel reads better in **French**, where its colloquial raunchiness has greater impact and the curious idiom is more apparent.

The novel has its admirers. A. Alvarez reviewed it for the **London** *Observer* as "a comedy of high style, terser and, I think, funnier than any of his other novels." SB came to regard it as an apprentice work, useful for attuning him to subtleties of French. It offers vaudeville dialogue, slapstick, and sporadic comic highlights, but the comedy sometimes wearies, the grotesqueries unredeemed by wit. The novel is written in a two-dimensional manner, on flat surfaces, but the sense of going nowhere lacks poignancy. Characters (Mr. **Gall**, Mr. **Graves**, **Watt**, one **Murphy**) who bear little resemblance to their fictive originals seem pointless, even if that is the point (compare the recycled "**Malacoda**" in "**Draff**"). Summaries after every second chapter (English numbering different) do not initiate radical critiques of fictional form. The opening claim that "I" was there, with no further evidence, is an irritant. The problem with the "**pseudocouple**," as the **Unnamable** calls them (297), and perhaps why SB lost interest, is the lack of an interior dimension. The two suggest the derelicts of *Three Novels*, and quite literally cover the same terrain, but they do not inhabit the realm of **consciousness** that constitutes the **Beckett country**.

The title suggests peddling small wares ("Mercier") and **motion** ("Camier" as "camion"). The obvious analogue is **Flaubert**'s *Bouvard et Pécuchet*, with its delight in clichés and truisms; but compare the opening of **Diderot**'s *Jacques le fataliste*: "Comment s'étaient-ils rencontrés? Par hasard, comme tout le monde. Comment s'appelaient-ils? Que vous importe? D'où-venaient-ils? Du lieu le plus prochaine." The two meet to undertake a journey, the point of which is obscure. There are distractions: two **dogs** tightly locked in copulation; a military man named **Saint-Ruth**; an encounter with a ranger ("un gardien"), whom they promote to sergeants then buy off with a bob ("un shilling") before absconding with a **bicycle**. They spend the night at Helen's (see **Ronsard**). They leave next morning and see a gross accident that restores their faith in life. Chapter III begins on the **Slow and Easy**, where they endure an old man named **Madden**. They reach a village (**Foxrock**?) and take a room. Camier is small and fat; Mercier, likened to a capital S, is a big bony hank with a beard. They are thus in the **hardy laurel** tradition. Chapter IV opens in some kind of Potter's Field, brambles and tangles and "Capriciously a **goat**," emblem of the preterit. They look for their bicycle, sack, and umbrella. Camier gets food, four wrapped sandwiches and one unwrapped to give him the strength to bring the others back. En route he encounters Mr. **Conaire**; the obscure **allegory** intimates a Cartesian conundrum. It rains. Chapter V finds the couple in town, back to Helen's, back to a bar. The prose waxes lyrical as life falls away like millet grains (see **Zeno**). Chapter VI is set in a pub, Mercier greeted (as **Vladimir** will **Estragon**): "They didn't beat you?" (82). Mercier has found their bicycle, relieved of wheels, saddle, bell, and carrier, but, in parody of the divine afflatus, the pump is spared (85). Their situation, they agree, is desperate but, back in town, seeking the **kips** (91), they unhand a **policeman**, mortally, with an endocranian blow from his truncheon. Chapter VII celebrates a road still carriageable over the high moorland, bog, and quag,

south of **Dublin**, with a vision of the distant city and **Dún Laoghaire**. There is a giant tree, a "jumble of black boughs" between two branching roads: this is the setting of *Waiting for Godot*, six years in the future but implicit in the making.

The final chapter begins abruptly: "That's it." The **coming and going, body** in bits, mind flayed, **memory** cultivated in vain, waiting for night. To follow? The bill (109). Camier is greeted by a towering figure, Watt. But what Watt? Instead of a mild, milk-drinking innocent, this Watt is large, foul-mouthed, and bibulous, arguing with policemen and badgering those in the pub. In the following uproar our two make their way to the canal, where they observe the black waters and depressing prospects of the Lock Bridge and **Portobello Nursing Home**, as in "**Enueg I**." Camier departs, Mercier is alone, and the sky goes out, leaving (a last **Miltonic** touch) "Dark at its full."

Meredith, George (1828–1909): Victorian novelist, whose prose, "twisted into curl-papers" (Trollope), has an intricacy untypical of his age. The poet, his isolation threatened by the woman, thinks of George Meredith and recovers his calm ("**Assumption**," 6). **Belacqua**, raped by the **Smeraldina**, sits among the **rats**, "alla fioca lucerna leggendo Meredith" (*Dream*, 18). **Leopardi**'s composition by faint light becomes reading Meredith, presumably his sonnet sequence, *Married Love* (1862). *The Egoist* (1879) indelibly shaped *Murphy*. Its willow pattern showed how an intricate comic plot might be handled, and Mr. Willoughby **Kelly** bows to Sir Willoughby Patterne.

Merlin: a **Paris**-based English-language magazine, a "revue trimestrielle," also distributed from Limerick, Maine. Published in the 1950s by a group of expatriates led by Alexander Trocchi and Richard Seaver (editors) and Alice Jane Lougee (publisher), who sought to reestablish the 1920s intellectual climate by reviving little magazines and were deeply engaged by **Sartre** and **Camus** (Knowlson, 356). Seaver asked to publish part of SB's unpublished novel; this led to the **Olympia Press** *Watt* under the imprint of "Éditions Merlin." *Merlin* published extracts from *Watt* 1.3 (winter 1952–53): 118–26; *Molloy* 2.2 (autumn 1953): 88–103; and "The **End**" 2.3 (summer–autumn 1954): 144–59. Its emblem, a blackbird, features on the pen that Mr. **Saposcat** sells to himself (*Malone Dies,* 210).

"Message from the Earth": SB's translation of "Recado terrestre," a fifty-eight-line poem by Gabriela Mistral, for *Goethe: UNESCO's Homage on the Occasion of the Two Hundredth Anniversary of His Birth* (Paris: UNESCO Publication #411), 1949, 75–81, "with the help of a scholar specialized in Spanish" (F&F, #496). SB revised other texts in this volume.

Metropolitan Cattle Market: on Market Road, parallel to **Brewery Road**, Islington. The market was built (1852) to supply meat for **London** but soon offered everything from silver and antiques to chintz and junk. In *Murphy,* it is part of the setting, near the **prison**, its frenzied variety making it an emblem of the big world. There was a tripe shop (J. L.

Hewson, Prop.) at 18 Market Road, opposite the public garden on "Lumpy Hill"; the "little shelter" (a wooden rotunda) was demolished in the 1980s. The prison in 1935 had no clock; SB may have attributed that of the Cattle Market, visible from the garden, to it.

microcosm: man as a **"little world"** (qv), the "imprisoned microcosm" of individual experience (*Proust,* 74), opposed to the macrocosm or big world. The laws regulating the one are reflected in the other, so the microcosm is, said **Leibniz**, a **monad** or living **mirror** of the universe; by understanding the self one becomes conscious of the divine.

Mihalovici, Marcel (1898–1985): Romanian-born composer. SB met him (1956) through Suzanne's friendship with his wife, concert pianist Monique Haas. Mihalovici asked SB (1959) to write a libretto for a small opera; SB offered *La Dernière bande*. He was willing to change his text to accommodate the rhythm and worked with Mihalovici to ensure precise interaction of text and **music**. Mihalovici appreciated the play's "various moods, lyrical, aggressive, cynical or merely contemplative" (*Beckett at 60,* 21). He stressed that SB's musical knowledge was essential to the composition, its cadence, and its tone. Writing *Krapp* took fourteen months. It was published, with a dedication to Monique Haas (1961) as a piano vocal score (Paris: Heugel, 1961) and as a score for baritone, wind, percussion, and strings (Imp. Rolland, Père et Fils, Dépôt légal #658), the instruments including celesta, bass drum, kettledrum, side drum, cymbals, triangle, woodblock, block chinois, glockenspiel, xylophone, and vibraphone. The text became 260 pages of musical score, but performance time is one hour, fifteen minutes more than the stage production.

The opera was designed for the RTF and a German production at the Städtische Bühnen, Bielefeld, but debuted as oratorio at a concert organized by Claude Rostand at the Théâtre National de Chaillot (1960), to lukewarm response. It received its German premiere, and a better reception, at the Théâtre des Nations (**Paris**) by the Bielefeld Opera (25 January 1961), in Elmar **Tophoven**'s German translation, with William Dooley, baritone; produced by Joachim Kleiber and conducted by Bernard Konz. Problems arose from having a voice on tape with a live orchestra, and from vocal discontinuity between the younger **Krapp** and the older man singing live. First broadcast by RTF (15 May 1961), conducted by Serge Baudo. SB attended the Bielefeld production and enjoyed it, but he later admitted that the scoring was too lush. However, he agreed to work on another radio text, "Cascando." Mihalovici received an RTF commission for an original composition (1961) and turned to SB for a radiophonic text. SB responded. The music for "Cascando" was composed a year after the text and the broadcast further delayed until 13 October 1963. Music thereafter was an essential element of SB's writing.

Mildendo: the metropolis of Lilliput (*Gulliver's Travels* I.4), a partial anagram of **London**'s Mile End ("What a Misfortune," 116).

Mildred: a little girl recalled by **Winnie** (*Happy Days,* 55–59). While she was undressing Dolly, a mouse "ran up her little thigh" and Mildred "screamed and screamed and screamed and screamed" till all came running. **Freudian** implications are obvious. Colin Duckworth identifies Mildred Coote, a childhood friend in **Foxrock**, to whom this happened in SB's house (*JOBS* 3 [1978]: 102); presumably the daughter of Mrs. Coote (*Company,* 14), a "small thin sour woman" not unlike Miss Carriage.

Milton, John (1608–74): epic English poet. Captivated by Milton's cosmology, SB explained it to his **father**, in the mountains, "resting against a huge rock looking out to sea" (*From an Abandoned Work,* 158). Milton was anathema to the modernist sensibility. SB's early writings are derogatory: "a case of darkness visible" (*Paradise Lost* I:63) in "A **Wet Night**" (83); Milton House, disinfectant manufacturers, near the Tripe Factory (both real locations) in *Murphy* (73); and dismissal as a "beastly bigot" in "**Ex Cathezra**" (*Disjecta,* 77). **Watt**'s resolve to not "abate one jot" (249) echoes Sonnet XXIII to Cyriac Skinner. The first words penned of *Molloy* ("Cette fois-ci, puis encore une je pense") echo "Lycidas" ("Yet once more, O ye laurels, and once more"), each writer preparing for a major task. *The Unnamable*'s cosmology owes as much to Pandemonium as to **Plato**. Milton was an "old chestnut" to whom SB returned, as in the reference to Proserpine in "**jusque dans la caverne ciel et sol**," or to light in *Company.* The theological incompatibility was treated with respectful irony, as in "Hail, holy light" (*PL*, III.1) in act II of *Happy Days.* In Act I **Winnie** had struggled to remember "Oh fleeting joys . . . oh something [dear bought with] lasting woe" (*PL*, 10.741–42), a curious justification of the ways of **God** to man.

mime: SB's drama contains wholly mimetic works like the two "**Acts Without Words**"; the two mimes singularly linked as "**Quad**"; three jettisoned mimes: "**Mîme du rêveur, A**," "**J. M. Mime**," "**Mongrel Mime for One Old Small (M)**"; and "**Nacht und Traüme.**" *Endgame* and *Krapp's Last Tape* open with mimes. Other works depict mute characters, like **O** in *Film,* Joe in "**Eh Joe**," Listener's **face** in *That Time,* **May** in *Footfalls,* the Male Figure of "**Ghost Trio**," Listener of "**Ohio Impromptu**," **W** of "**Rockaby**," and the Protagonist of "**Catastrophe**." The way silence is embodied underscores the dominance of the visual in SB's theater, often as an element isolated from the flow of words, internalizing action yet retaining the seen. SB's drama is fugal, counterpointing poetry and physical form, an aesthetic principle that emerges through mime. Deryk **Mendel** encouraged SB to try mime, requesting something ("Acte I") for his cabaret act and later claiming that SB wrote *Fin de partie* to accompany it. This is disingenuous, but it suggests SB's ability to write "pour l'occasion" and accounts for the music-hall humor in "**Avant Fin de partie**" (qv).

"**Mime du rêveur, A**": SB's quest for silence led him in the 1950s to **mime**, which opened up possibilities later realized in the drama. Two mimes, written in **French**, saw the lights of stage and page, "**Acte sans paroles**" (I and II). "**Mime du rêveur, A**," never completed and finally discarded, has generic links to these and to *Fin de partie* and *Krapp's Last Tape;* they form, if not a series, then a cluster. When SB began "Mime du rêveur, A" he envisioned another symmetrical structure, two mimes, one embedded in and balanced against the other. The only one drafted displays that pattern of images, action, and latent structure. The **Sam Francis Notebook** (RUL 2926) outlines notes for a mime "for a dreamer," but "Mime du rêveur, A" exists in a single version, at Dartmouth. Typed on four leaves, and revised heavily, it reveals different phases of development. The stage is lit, as for *KLT,* feebly in front, the rest in darkness. The setting suggests a **skull**, like *Fin de partie:* two round windows, one on each side wall, covered with a curtain, "de maniere à se confondre presque avec le mur" (1.1). Beneath each window is a bench. In the center, beside a **rocking chair** and dressed in a bathrobe with two large pockets, a scarf, cap (*Fin de partie's* "calotte"), thick socks, and mittens, stands the dreamer. One short leg suggests deterioration anterior to **Hamm**'s, legs failing but not yet having failed. Action is punctuated by three cuts to a second mime, apparently never written. Two occur within the written mime, but each time Mime B begins it is abruptly interrupted. Its third version occurs at the end, and B is allowed to finish.

The primary mime (A) features a dreamer who searches his pockets for eyeglasses to examine the audience. He sighs, takes off his glasses, loses his equilibrium, wipes his glasses on his robe, and returns them to his pocket. He reflects, then withdraws from his pocket (like O in *Film*) a photo, in an old frame. He cannot see it well so (like **Winnie**) he withdraws a magnifying glass and a box of matches. He kneels, places the photo on the floor, and regards it through the glass, holding a match until it burns his fingers. He looks again, dropping the match before being burned (he is learning). He returns the **objects** to his pocket, looks out the windows, and tries to stop the noise of the wind, there from the outset. When he plugs his ears the noise stops, but it resumes as he withdraws his fingers.

Dreamer returns to his chair, searches anew, withdraws a syringe, retrieves his matches to sterilize the needle, and gives himself a shot "dans la fesse," which projects him forward. He tries to sleep, changes his mind, carries the chair to front right of the stage (clearing it for mime B), and falls asleep. The action shifts to the unwritten mime. SB later no longer recalled his plans, but B complements A, increasing in importance till complete. Its first performance lasts only thirty seconds, when Dreamer awakens. He retrieves a small notebook, scratches a note, apparently recording the dream, and gives himself a second, larger injection to return to his dream. Again, this propels him forward, and he falls asleep as before. His sleep lasts twice as long, one minute, during which B begins again, to be reinterrupted by Dreamer's rewakening. The third phase begins as the dreamer returns to center, where he fumbles through his pockets and pulls out a **mirror** and a box of matches. He twice strikes a match and looks at himself until he burns his fingers. He returns the mirror to his pocket and withdraws a third syringe, the largest, injects himself by sitting on it, falls on his flank, rises, stops the wind with his fingers, staggers to the chair, and falls asleep a third time. Mime B restarts and this time plays through, until B collapses. For ten seconds his breathing is heard, then it abruptly stops: "Silence. Noir sur tout le plateau. Fin" (1.4).

This is a shelter before Hamm's legs failed, before Clov entered his service, when he could look out the window, when there were still **painkillers**. With each version of *Fin de partie,* the deterioration increased; *Endgame* finally begins with "Finished." This early attempt left SB dissatisfied. He made changes before abandoning it, simplifying the action, creating a circular pattern, enfeebling the protagonist. The revision reveals his attention to balance and symmetry, repetition suggesting a helicoidal or Dantean pattern, a tightening gyre. Yet despite attempts to pattern it, "Dreamer's Mime" remains diffuse, a draft whose images never coalesce. Its chief interest now is in how it anticipates the plays to come.

Minuit, Éditions de: a small publishing house, 7, Rue de Bernard-Palissy, **Paris**, acquired (1950) by Jérôme **Lindon** (qv). Its reputation was associated with that of its most celebrated author, SB, whose French works appeared almost exclusively in the small but distinctive Minuit format of white with blue and black lettering.

Miranda: heroine of **Shakespeare**'s *The Tempest* and emblem of the female form divine; as approved by **Belacqua** (*Dream*, 11), of a nurse ("Yellow," 166), and by **Lucky** (*WG*, 28.b). She exemplifies **pity**, as in *Proust* (45): "unlike Miranda, he suffers with her whom he had not seen suffer." Prospero's daughter has seen the ship sink: "O, I have suffer'd / With those I saw suffer" (I.ii.5–6). "**Return to the .Vestry**" is less compassionate. The theme is **Anteros**: "Mumps and an orchid to Fräulein Miranda"—for her Ferdinand and his testicles, sterility engendered by mumps.

mirlitonnades: a *mirliton* is a toy instrument with vibrating parchment reinforcing the **voice**, like a kazoo; "vers de mirliton" denotes words on the spiral bindings of the tube, hence vulgar doggerel. SB's *mirlitonnades* comprise a set of irregular small poems, which SB termed "rimailles," "rhymeries," "versicules," or "gloomy **French** doggerel" (Knowlson, 568). They are written in black ink, pencil and red felt-tip on pieces of card, variously colored scraps of notepaper, diary pages, backs of letters, cheroot packets, a Café Crème cardboard box, a beer mat, the label of a Johnny Walker Black bottle, squared exercise paper, a train timetable, and an airmail envelope. The poems are in a large envelope at the **BIF** (RUL 2460). Some were reworked in the **Sottisier Notebook** (RUL 2901), numbered by SB in approximately the published order. Variously dated from 24.11.76 ("rentrer") to 9.9.81 ("Gone with what"), they were usually composed at a sitting, often at a specific locale. Others were inspired by reading or revisit past concerns. Thirty-five appeared in *Poèmes suivi de mirlitonnades* (Minuit, 1978).

David Wheatley has reconstructed a sequence of composition that differs from the published order, indicating deliberate selection. Several are unpublished, including five in English (1981); the total is about forty-seven, depending on which drafts or jottings are accepted as part of the sequence. The best unpublished may be "par une faille dans l'inexistence" (juillet 1979), a quatrain offering the conceit of miasmata of oxygen infiltrating inexistence through a "fault." For variants and publication details, see Wheatley, "Beckett's *mirlitonnades*."

For all their brevity, the poems are highly crafted, representing in miniature much of SB's earlier work. In the first, "rentrer," the **face** against the window is like the **flies** in "**La Mouche**" or "**Serena I.**" Images are reduced to **fundamental sounds**: light and dark; avoidance of the active verb or pronominal self; life the calculation of seconds ("somme toute"), as in *All Strange Away* and "**Heard in the Dark.**" In "in fond du néant" the fragmented syntax imitates the eyes seeking something, only to conclude, "ce ne fut que dans la tête." The resolution of **L'Innommable** is enacted by "silence tel que ce qui fut," "déchiré" by the murmur of the word, "de ne se taire plus" (the "jamais" that puzzles Wheatley [55] is his "je ne me tairais jamais. Jamais" [8]). **Zeno**'s sorites paradox informs "écoute-les," word upon word halving the impossible heap, steps toward **nothing**: "les pas / aux pas / un à / un." In "lueurs lisières" "pas" is a thread, the self shuttling between light and extinction, an interim not unlike "**Dieppe**": "chez soi sans soi." That moment is accentuated in "imagine si ceci," dated in the Sottisier Notebook as "**Ussy 26.2.77**"; the imagination, one day, one fine day, ceasing, the unimaginable cessation imaged and so imagined. The **body** ("n'importe") is rejected in "D'abord" for the head; the following poem, "flux cause," accepts the **Heraclitean** "all flows" and the need to speak thereof even while doubting its substantiality. The optimistic "fou" is **Thales**, who affirmed water as that from which all flows.

"Samedi répit" offers the "respite" between **crucifixion** and resurrection, as in *Waiting for Godot:* too late to laugh (one has been born), but too soon to cry (one has not yet rattled). Similar sentiments prevail in "chaque jour envie" and in "nuit qui fais tant," which echoes **Baudelaire**'s "Recueillement," as in *Endgame;* while "rien nul" invokes the "mesure pour rien," an interval of **nothing**, as in *Textes pour rien.* Dragging metrical "feet" ("pas") and heavy repetitions of "à peine à bien mené" retrace difficulties with words ("come le veut l'usage"). The next two, "ce qu'ont les yeux" and "ce qu'a de pis," gesture toward "le bien," only to be rejected: "le pis revient / en pire." The "dark sister" of "noire soeur" is **Atropos**, as in "**jusque dans la caverne ciel et sol**"; in *Collected Poems* this is the final *mirlitonnade*. What she awaits is evident in the next three poems: "ne manquez pas à Tanger" is set in the cemetery of Saint-André in memory of Arthur Keyser; "plus loin un autre commémoire" quotes from the inscription in memory of Caroline Hay Taylor, optimist, who died in **Ireland** (August 1932). These were written in Tangier (April–May 1977); their sentiment is echoed in "ne manquez pas à Stuttgart," where the dreary "Rue Neckar" (Neck-

arstrasse, June 1977) induces the sense of living by proxy, a shabby version of "**Arènes de Lutèce**."

A series of short poems follows: "vieile aller" invokes the movement toward stasis, "fous qui disiez" toward silence; "pas à pas" takes "little steps" toward nullity; "rêve" finds no respite ("ni trêve"); the spider "morte parmi" the dead **flies** is rocked by the wind; and the voice "d'où" that says *live* is from another life. The "mots mourant" were originally "mots survivant," but for a moment hold **company**; "fleuves et océans" have left one washed up on the street, living; in "du tiers oeil revenu sur terre" (unpublished) SB uses his "third eye" to efface images of his tomb, before the eyelid closes. "En face" (12.11.77) rhymes "rire" and "pire"; in *Collected Poems* this begins the sequence. Goalless **motion** is sensed in "de pied ferme" and pervades "sitôt sorti de l'ermitage," with its echo of "The Expelled." In "à l'instant de s'entendre dire" the poet laughs at his conceit in imagining that he has no longer long to live; but in "la nuit venue où l'âme allait" he "renders" it an hour earlier. In "pas davantage" he has no more April memories; in "son ombre une nuit" his shadow lengthens, pales, and dissolves. The sequence ends with "**à bout de songes un bouquin**" and "**le nain nonagénaire**." Their place in the series may be a matter of dispute, but the incongruous conjunction of the dwarf longing for a full-size coffin and a light left burning in an empty den suitably concludes a remarkable set of verses.

mirror: a favorite modernist and postmodernist trope, but SB's use of it is limited. The "**Dante**" essay invokes **Leibniz**'s **monad**, the "perpetual living mirror of the universe" (6), the mirror not as convex as that of **Vico**. "Les **Deux besoins**" (*Disjecta*, 55) offers the figure, from *Hamlet* and **Stendhal**, of the mirror going down the road, as if to distinguish between narrative (the monad in **motion**, going **on**) and the stasis of the mind reflecting on its own processes. Yet, particularly in the earlier fiction, there are days when the road reflects better than the mirror. **Murphy**'s experience with Mr. **Endon** is that of seeing himself reflected, unseeingly, in the other's eye, and thus a suggestion (from which he flees in terror) of an endless series of unconsciously reflecting mirrors, the *mise en abyme*. The contrast of **solipsism**, motion, and stasis anticipates crucial changes of emphasis in SB's aesthetics: crudely, **narcissism** (Lacan's mirror stage) gives way to questing (the oedipal stage); then to the **closed place**, stillness (the integrated self). Mirrors deceive; seeming to duplicate they invert laterally the images they present; appearing to restore us to ourselves they dislocate the outer image from the inward sense, distancing our imaged and so imagined selves. Thus **Watt** fails to understand the picture in **Erskine**'s room, a puzzle less puzzling when it is understood that the coordinates (left and right) are those of the **object**, as in a mirror. **Sam** and Watt engage in a mirror-dance, **face** to face (163). Watt's vision, en route to the station, is a fragmented reflection of a self as in a glass darkly, a phrase repeated from part II, to "define" his inability to know Mr. **Knott** or, finally, himself.

The mirror reflects less another virtual or imagined world than the **consciousness** of being trapped within this one. *Three Novels* "mirror" the movement from and to the apprehension of self, **Molloy**'s reflection of himself in the water assuming an integrated pattern for the moment only. **Moran** washes his face (145) and waits for his image to return, trembling in ever increasing likeness before being again fragmented. The two parts of the novel are mirror reflections, needing to be united in an act of imagination. The **Obidil** is a mirror reflection ("Libido") rather than an anagram.

In "**Text 6**," the narrator recalls his **father**'s shaving mirror: he went but it remained (124). **Winnie** has a looking glass in her handbag, but in Act II she says, "it no longer needs me." In *Film*, a mirror "stares" at **O**; he approaches it from the side and covers it with a rug. In "**Ghost Trio**" (qv) the mirror is thematically important. In I, it plays no role, but in II, as F thinks he hears "her," he looks into the mirror, then stands before it with bowed head, **Voice** (**V**) registering surprise. In III there is (Direction 24) "*Cut to close-up of mirror reflecting nothing*"; then (27) a close-up of F's face in the mirror, anticipations of the apparition (or mirage) of the **boy** in the corridor opposite. The play offers an enigmatic suggestion of another dimension, a virtual image the more astonishing for being unexpected, and a curious qualification of SB's usual agnosticism that hints at an inexplicable beyond, seen through a glass, darkly.

Mistinguett: Jeanne Marie Bourgeois (1871–1956), artiste of the French music hall and Folies Bergère, enchanting all with "son air canaille et sa gouaille éternel." Cited in *Dream* (199) and "A Wet Night" (47) as wishing to do away with chalets of necessity.

mixed choir: Watt, resting in the ditch (33–35), is detained by **voices** heard from afar, or at least from without, as in the Addenda (250): "die Merde hat mich wieder." This parodies the moment (I.784) when Faust, about to take poison, hears Easter bells and affirms his allegiance to the Earth: "Die Erde hat mich wieder." In the drafts the **music** of the angelic voices is more detailed, in C major (Watt hears a tone flat), the conductor a principality, and the tempo defined: *Mesto quasi arrabbiato. Marcatissima la misura* ("Sadly, as if enraged. Mark extremely the regularity of the tempo"). Arranged for four voices, it may be sung, but the bass cannot sustain the notes ("Hem! . . . Christ . . . phew! . . . Jesus!"). The first verse invokes days in a leap year divided by seven, to give the weeks. An error has crept into the second verse (introduced in the galleys, it was apparently not noticed): "Fifty-one point . . ." should read "Fifty-two point . . . ," the weeks in a year. "Bun" and "man" imply Happy Families (Mr. Bun the Baker); Lady **Pedal**, discouraged by the poor response to her singing, tells Ernest to hand out the buns (*Malone Dies*, 285). After "**Play**" SB outlines instructions for the chorus and sets out the words in the pattern used for the threne in Watt, the spotlight as conductor. **Mercier** et **Camier** (25) hear a mixed choir, and though it may be a delusion they run. **Molloy** (21) is frustrated in his attempt to listen to distant music. **Malone** (208) hears a distant choir, a mixed choir, unless he is greatly deceived. The narra-

tor of *How It Is* (107) rejects the notion of "these voices meaning a choir" for "**quaqua** meaning on all sides megaphones." For each a distant prospect of salvation is combined with a rejection thereof.

MMM: the Magdalen Mental Mercyseat, hospital for the better-class mentally deranged, where **Murphy** meets his unfortunate end. See **asylum** and **Bethlem Royal Hospital**.

Moll: the female principle reduced to its **fundamental sound**, as in "**Echo's Bones**," Lord **Gall**'s wife, and *Malone Dies*, lover of **Macmann**, ill-favored, with thin yellow arms, thick lips, a tod of hair, two ivory crucifixes as earrings, and a sole tooth carved as a **crucifix**. Moll tends Macmann, engages him in grotesque acts of carnality (tetty-beshy), then is summarily dismissed as "only a female."

Molloy: first of the *Three Novels,* originally published in **French** (Minuit), 10 March 1951, 3,000 copies, with 50 deluxe and 500 signed for "Les Amis des Éditions de Minuit." There were several photographic reprints in runs of 3,000 (1953–67), and a second edition (Club Français du Livre, 1960), a bookclub run of 6,000. Reprinted with "L'**Expulsé**" in a pocketbook edition (Union générale d'éditions, 1963), illustrated with an India ink drawing by **Arikha**. Extracts, with variations, appeared in *Transition* Fifty (octobre 1950): 103–5; *Merlin* (autumn 1953): 88–103; *New World Writing* (April 1954): 316–23; and *Paris Review* (spring 1954): 124–35. Erich Franzen made a German translation (Berlin: Suhrkamp, 1954). The English text, trans. by Patrick **Bowles** in collaboration with SB, was published by the **Olympia Press** (1955) and distributed in England by France Features, **London** (wrappers, some priced in sterling and others in francs indicate that Olympia planned separate editions for France and the UK). The **Grove** edition (**Evergreen**) appeared later that year but the first British edition was not until 1966 (the **Calder** and Boyars "Jupiter" text).

The four manuscript notebooks (**HRHRC**) testify that the writing was done rapidly with little revision. The first paragraph was written last. There is little obvious planning, except diagrams for the sucking stones. *Molloy* was written in six months, the earliest extant draft dated "2 May 1947" and the fourth notebook dated on completion "1 Nov. 1947." Molloy suggests: "you would do better, at least no worse, to obliterate texts than to blacken margins, to fill in the holes of words till all is blank and flat and the whole ghastly business looks like what is, senseless, speechless, **issueless** misery" (13). Rejecting his own prescription, the narrator issues a readable text that both obliterates the tradition of the novel and reinscribes it, subverting and reasserting the structures of narrative. SB's way forward was through a return to the past, displacing the conventions of fiction and simultaneously renewing them, particularly (1) the quest or journey; (2) the detective story or archetype of self-discovery; and (3) the oral fable. Psychologically, to obliterate the novel was to deny one's progenitor; to reiterate it, to give birth to one's self.

Molloy's quest is for his **mother**, which the first page claims has been completed, even as it is narratologically initiated. That quest is overtly oedipal. The narrator says of his mother: "I took her for my mother and she took me for my **father**" (17). The sexual fantasy suggests an autoeroticism since the narrator has "taken her place." This denial of lineage and emphasis on self-creation is a trope for SB's dissociation from modernism, an insistence on separation from his immediate literary past. Molloy's journey, like all oedipal activity, is a quest for sources, origins, true literary parents, and it finally returns him to himself. The circularity is reinforced in both halves, each returning to its origins. The Molloy section opens with Molloy's having completed the journey he is about to embark on, having not so much discovered his mother as replaced her. The **Moran** section opens with the report that Moran begins writing at the end: "It is midnight. The rain is beating on the windows. It was not midnight. It was not raining." His report, which we read as he begins, which we finish as he begins, is a lie, a fiction, as he admits, and so true by virtue of his candid admission. The novel is like the Cretan paradox: the more he undercuts his text, the more he asserts its veracity. Molloy admits, "Perhaps I'm inventing a little, perhaps embellishing" (8). Moran concurs: "it would not surprise me if I deviated, in the pages to follow, from the true and exact succession of events" (133). Such subversion of textual veracity assaults both the tradition of verisimilitude and the aesthetics of **Joyce** and Modernism.

The two halves of this diptych are replete with symmetries. Each features a man in a room writing a report. Each recounts his and its deterioration. Each describes the terrain: Molloy calls it "my region" (65–66, 69, 85–86); Moran calls it the "Molloy country" (131–34, 161). Each receives a visitor on Sundays. Molloy may have a son (7); Moran certainly does (92). Each has bad teeth (54, 103); wears a hat (13–14, 126); has difficulties with his testicles (35–36, 157); needs a **bicycle** (15–16, 144–45), knife (45, 130), and walking **stick** (10, 146–47); and assaults a man (83–85, 150–51). Each has difficulty with tenses (16, 26, 36, 105, 109) and authority figures (9, 20, 173); each encounters a shepherd (28, 158) and a man with a heavy stick (10, 146). Each uses a crutch (12, 89, 147–48, 171), enjoys lying down (120, 165), and enjoys a garden (52, 92). Each shifts to the third person (91, 124, 176) and struggles to conclude his report (89, 174). It is not so much that Moran has become Molloy, or that the second half should precede the first, but that Molloy was always part of Moran, as were **Gaber** and **Youdi**, agents of a superego: "For who could have spoken to me of Molloy if not myself and to whom if not to myself could I have spoken of him" (112). What the Moran section offers, and why it follows the Molloy section (and why the novel is called *Molloy,* not *Moran*), is a fiction written by Molloy of Molloy as Moran encountering Molloy. "Encounter" aligns Moran's discovery of Molloy with Stephen Dedalus's meeting Bloom, to become the self he is ineluctably preconditioned to become.

The quest is not the only culturally coded form reiterated (and subverted). The novel, especially Moran's section, is structured like a detective story, but there is no truth to discover, save that the jour-

ney has been fictive. Oedipus discovers the truth, like Moran's discovery of Molloy, or Molloy's discovery of the Moran who discovers Molloy, that he is himself the criminal he seeks. SB's characters suffer less from the oedipal desire to know, than from the antioedipal **Davus complex** (qv): if sphinges dread Oedipus they might snuggle up to Davus/**Watt**/Molloy/Moran. Molloy takes comfort in the enigma. Contemplating an **object** pilfered from the house of **Lousse**; he rejoices that he "could never understand what possible purpose it could serve" (see **knife-rest**). It is something he can puzzle over without resolving: "For to know **nothing** is nothing, not to want to know anything likewise, but to be beyond knowing anything, to know that you are beyond knowing anything, that is when peace enters in, to the soul of the incurious seeker." When Moran studies the dance of the **bees** he says, with rapture, "Here is something I can study all my life, and never understand" (169).

The novel develops the oedipal paradigm, the Molloy section as maternal (**Jung**), the Moran section paternal (**Freud**). The novel plays the two giants of **psychoanalysis** against each other, Molloy's Jungian quest for [dis]integration critiqued by Moran's enactment of the Freudian drama. When Freud used Sophocles's play to describe psychosexual development, he argued that males (females have the Electra complex) want to destroy competition for sexual favors of the mother and desire the father's death. But the pursuit of the mother is only one element of the oedipal paradigm; what the child learns, says Freud, is the "Reality Principle," to accept limitations on his libido or risk punishment—in Freudian terms, fear of castration forces the son to accept the taboo against sex with the mother. This is acceptance of the law of the father, the prohibitions of society. Moran, projecting the primal scene, says that his son would doubtless and with pleasure have cut his throat, "with that selfsame knife I was putting so placidly in my pocket" (131). His section develops the oedipal model, Moran forcing his son to accept the law of the father, as he has accepted the patriarchal Church. Accepting the law, social restriction, does not destroy the sex drive; it merely represses it. The libidinal, antioedipal, Dionysian element—Molloy, say, with no sense of order—lurks within, as Molloy may lurk within Moran.

Tropologically, the oedipal conflict suggests the artist's tension with literary culture, embodied in a literary father, and the relationship between writing and literary repression. The dominant such force in SB's life was James Joyce. The relationship was, in the Lacanian sense, oedipal: Joyce was the law, transmitter of a cultural/literary heritage, the phallus, the embodiment of language. SB's departure from the language of the father was a means of making room for himself. *Three Novels,* if not overtly an attempt to rewrite modernism in general and Joyce in particular, suggests that after the **war,** after the **death** of Joyce (whose postmortem presence remains potent), SB was free enough of parental control to choose his literary models, not from classical myths like Joyce or **Eliot** but from the popular forms of narrative like the detective story, fairy tale, and vaudeville skit. Finally, SB would triumph where Joyce failed—in the theater.

The third narrative archetype rehearsed is the oral tale, but with as much emphasis on the teller as on the tale. In *Beyond the Pleasure Principle* Freud discusses repeating traumatic events to gain mastery over them. He links this "repetition compulsion" to a new principle, not the pleasure principle but its opposite, *thanatos,* the tendency of animate matter to return to its inorganic state. The goal of life, Freud argued, is cessation, **death,** an end desired by Molloy. It is not strange, then, that the narrative method in *Molloy* is not affirmation but denial, paradox, obliteration. The goal of speaking is to end speaking, of storytelling to end storytelling, of writing to end writing, of life, its termination in death. This is a goal that for the artist must fail, but its pursuit ensures both the production of texts and their failure. The issue of *Molloy,* its issueless inconclusion, continues into *Malone Dies, The Unnamable, Texts for Nothing,* and *How It Is,* a series whose end was SB's own.

"Moly": another title for **"Yoke of Liberty,"** used when SB submitted this poem with three others to *Poetry* (1 November 1934); all four were rejected. Moly is the herb Odysseus used to resist Circe (here, Ethna **MacCarthy**). SB noted it from Victor **Bérard** (DN, 102). **Molloy** resists the "miserable molys" of **Lousse** (54), which might keep him in her earthly paradise.

monad: Gk. *monas,* "unit"; an atom, a **microcosm,** the universe in little. Each monad is a simple, independent percipient and self-acting being whose essence is activity (**motion**); each is a **mirror** of the universe, rising by insensible steps (virtual to actual) from the lowest to the most perfect form. As no monad determines any other, the unity of the aggregate (universe) is possible only through **preestablished harmony** (qv). See **Leibniz**.

"Mongrel Mime for One Old Small (M)": three holograph pages and a heavily revised typescript held in the **HRHRC** Carlton Lake Collection (1.6). The setting is a tight, boxlike area of depth 5 feet and height 5 feet 6 inches; there are side entrances but the effect is enclosure, a **closed space** opening only to the audience. M, "about 5' 9" tall and thus obliged to stoop to avoid contact with the ceiling," is dressed in a shabby black overcoat and battered black **hat**, with "Dishevelled white hair." The light fades up, M enters slowly, stands inert in bowed profile: "Pause. **Voice**." Then, in SB's hand, "aborted mime 1983 *Samuel Beckett*."

monkeys: in *Proust* (63), SB argued that to try to communicate where no communication is possible is a simian vulgarity. He had read in **Woodworth**'s *Contemporary Schools of Psychology* (1931) and **Köhler**'s *Mentality of Apes* (1925) studies of apes, particularly Köhler's experiments at the Prussian Academy Anthropoid Station, Tenerife. Köhler believed that insight into cognition might arise by observing how apes become perplexed in simple situations. Hence **Murphy**'s sneer (5): "Back to Teneriffe and the apes?" Miss **Counihan** is like any other beautiful Irish girl, but more markedly anthropoid (118).

After completing *Murphy,* SB found in the *Daily Sketch* (1 July 1936) photographs of two chimpanzees playing **chess**.

He sent them to his agent, for the cover. George **Reavey** had no intention of displaying them until a contract was signed, the pictures proof of the author's lack of seriousness. They were not even shown to Routledge. SB said he would pass his life "regretting the monkeys." SB's clipping is at the **BIF** (RUL 3000/2); it was used on the covers of *JOBS* 7.1 and 2 (1997) and Chris Ackerley's *Demented Particulars* (1998).

SB returned to Tenerife and the apes in "**Act Without Words I**" (1956). Köhler's experiments form the mimetic action, but despite a prehensile thumb, rudimentary tools, and his mind, the protagonist remains trapped. Compare **Estragon**'s comment that people are "bloody ignorant apes." The narrator of *From an Abandoned Work* (159) is aware of his **voice**, "like a marmoset sitting on my shoulder with its bushy tail, keeping me **company**" (Fr. *marmouset,* colloquially "a grotesque"). A *macaco* (*Dream,* 219) is a black lemur. In *Film,* "O" jostles an elderly couple, the woman holding a pet monkey; as they feel the gaze of "E" (camera, Eye) on them, they assume an expression that SB calls "an agony of perceivedness"; lacking **apperception**, the monkey remains indifferent.

Moore, Thomas (1779–1852): Irish poet, author of the *Irish Melodies.* Moore's bull neck is invoked in *Dream* (200), "**Ding-Dong**" (39), and "A Wet Night" (47). His statue on College Green presides over the underground convenience; in **Dublin** jest, the "meeting of the waters." The **Frica** creates an effect of "throttled gazelle" (*Dream,* 214), as in *Lalla Rookh,* "I never nursed a dear gazelle." SB associated with

"**What Where**" Moore's "Oft, in the Stilly Night," quoting in his Stuttgart Notebook "the light of other days."

Moran: while **Molloy** enacts a **Jungian** quest for integrated self, and encounters his Anima and Shadow, Moran enacts a **Freudian** drama of repression, a patriarchal process that complements Molloy's maternal needs. Molloy is soft and yielding ("mollose"); Moran is hard and fixed, but his outer shell cracks to expose his vulnerability. Moran searches for Molloy, and becomes Molloy, writing of his search. At the outset he enjoys "the Sabbath of the Will" but is set in **motion** to find Molloy, to destroy the "**old man**" within, to bring himself to such abjection that his succadanea of possessions, **religion**, comforts, and family are jettisoned that he might find the real state of himself, unaccommodated man. Moran's ego is defined in fatherhood: his son bears the same name (and *his* teddy bear is **Baby Jack**). He adheres to an authoritarian structure: the Organization, rule of law, church, "**stamp** of the **father**," and renunciation (see "**sollst entbehren**"). He returns a different man: no longer part of a collective enterprise (his **bees** are dead), his identity no longer defined by possessions or authority, and his ego indifferent to the demands of id, superego, or libido.

More Pricks Than Kicks: ten stories (1931–33); published **London:** Chatto and Windus (24 May 1934). SB was offered £25, less 25 percent advance on royalties; 1,500 copies were printed, but only 500 sold. No American publisher could be found, which dissuaded Chatto from accepting SB's other projects. The series probably began with "**Walking Out**" (mid-1931), and "**Dante and the Lobster**" (1932); others were completed by May 1933 ("**Fingal**," "What a Misfortune," "Love and Lethe," and "Yellow"). "**Draff**" came after his father's death (26 June 1933); "**Ding-Dong**" is uncertain; and *Dream* was raided for "A Wet Night" and "The **Smeraldina's Billet-Doux**" in 1933, when the collection was assembled.

The volume was first entitled *Draff,* but Charles **Prentice** requested a livelier title; he preferred the new one, **God's** words to Saul on the road to Damascus (Acts 9:5). *MPTK* omits "**Echo's Bones**," written at Prentice's request and into which SB put all he knew, Prentice seeing that "all" decided against it. SB refused to reprint *MPTK,* calling it a "fiasco," but in 1966 he reluctantly permitted John **Calder** to bring out a "Special edition Hors Commerce for Scholars," a mimeographed typescript. Calder issued a limited edition of 100 copies, signed by SB (1974); then came the Calder and Boyars trade edition and the Picador paperback (1974), and a **Grove Press** issue (1974) based on the 1934 edition. *MPTK* is composite, stories partially interrelated with one character, **Belacqua**, common to each. The sequence follows his amours to beyond the grave but does not constitute a novel. Each story has its own rationale, and while there are echoes SB frustrates accepted notions of unity, even the "involuntary" kind espoused in *Dream* (132), disclaiming interest in such effects as "jigsaw."

Morgante and Morgutte: applied to **Belacqua** and Capper **Quin** ("What a

Misfortune," 141). Morgante is a giant converted by Orlando to Christianity; after many adventures he dies from crab's bite. Best known from Luigi Pulci's *Morgante Maggiore* (1482), a burlesque in *ottava rima* of chivalric romances, he is mentioned in *Don Quixote* and **Rabelais**. His statue by Valerio Cioli sits in the Boboli Gardens, **Florence**. The wedding car is a Morgan, the hint of Morgan-le-Fay adding to the chivalric irony. "Margutte," a giant who died of laughter watching a monkey put on a pair of boots.

Morphy, Paul (1837–84): finest **chess** player of his age. Ernest **Jones**'s "The Problem of Paul Morphy" (1931) examined Morphy's problems finding a **job**, his difficulties with women, his reclusive and sedentary existence, mental illness, and ambiguous **death**. He enters *Murphy* as Mr. **Endon**, and via "the chessy eye" (242): Morphy would barely acknowledge his opponent until he knew the other could not escape defeat, then he would slowly lift his great head and gaze curiously across the board. Looking into Mr. Endon's eyes, Murphy experiences that knowledge of defeat.

morpion: a pubic louse, as in *Dream* (77 and 163) and *Waiting for Godot* (48.b).

"Mort de A.D.": a fifteen-line poem (1949), published in *Cahiers des saisons* 2 (octobre 1955): 115–16; included with "Six poèmes 1947–1949" in *Gedichte* (1959) and *Collected Poems* (1977). It commemorates Dr. Arthur Darley, of **Trinity**, one of SB's colleagues at the Irish Red Cross Hospital at **Saint-Lô**. Darley died of TB aged thirty-five (30

December 1948), "mort hier pendant que je vivais," the poet identifying with his humanity rather than the dying man's prayers and repentance. Knowlson identifies the confict in Darley between his wild behavior when drunk and piety when sober: "dévorant / la vie des saints." Yet the poem challenges the poet: what must he do about his own twilight existence? Forcing himself to grip the board (his table, his cross, even the initials) reflects an awareness of the slow **crucifixion** of **time**. Darley is invoked in *Stirrings Still* (260): "The same place and table as when Darly [*sic*] for example died and left him." SB noted that the error was not his.

Morvan: the realm of **Fingal**, on the northwest coast of Scotland (Gael. *mór,* "great" and *beinn,* "mountain"). In "**Rough for Theatre II**," Morven (**B**), with Bertrand (**A**) is investigating **C**. The two names imply a dialogue between philosophy (Bertrand Russell) and **Ossianic** mystery.

mother: constituted at once by **memories** of May **Beckett** and by generic characteristics of the mother figure in **psychoanalysis**. As with the **father** (qv), the link between personal experience and psychoanalytic theory is not a simple correlation. May Beckett was a difficult and demanding parent, the more so by contrast with William **Beckett**, whose person and **memory** SB cherished. SB's relationship with his mother was fraught and threatening, a source of tension for both. SB's "escape" to France avoided her displeasure, but that freedom generated guilt, particularly during the **war**

when she had Parkinson's disease and his brother, Frank, assumed her care. Long after her **death** (25 August 1950) his guilt was expressed in such works as *Krapp's Last Tape,* with its memories of "the house on the canal" (the Merrion Nursing Home where May Beckett died), and his wishing she were gone (see "**je voudrais que mon amour meure**"). In *From an Abandoned Work* (156), the narrator imagines leaving home, his mother waving from the window, white and thin, "in sad helpless love." This leads to a white rage of repression and the sense of having killed his mother, in the vision of the schimmel, the white **horse**, and white mother. "**Rockaby**" presents a haunting image of a woman not quite dead; *Company* recalls a cutting retort that his mother once made to a childish question; and in *Footfalls* the relentless pacing through corridors of memory echoes the long suffering of SB's mother.

The mother-son dyad threatens to engulf the child in an **irrational** emotional world. SB extricated himself with difficulty. His mother's disappointment when he threw in his lectureship is reflected in **Celia**'s wish to "make a man" out of **Murphy**, by his finding a **job**. The tension drove SB to seek analysis. One stratagem was to turn anxiety and therapy into rhetorical tropes. The neurotic relationship with his mother made his experience of her death more intense, but from that emotional matrix came some of his greatest writing. *Molloy* opens in the mother's room with the familiar rhythms of polymorphous perversity, the child's uninhibited pleasure in the womb. It records such intimate details as May Beckett's **donkey** cart and

Pomeranian and the imperatives of angelus and **gong**. Molloy enacts the Jungian drama of the Great Mother in the idyll chez **Lousse**, followed by the expulsion from an embryonic Eden, a paradise lost that can never be regained. His section concludes with a complex **allegory** of **birth** (the rhyme of womb, room, and tomb).

The paradigm is that of **Jung** (qv). The anima appears as the mother with her all-absorbing world of maternal nurture, the archetypal bondage from which the male can tear himself away only by a traumatic effort. The anima then reprojects itself onto subsequent female partners to integrate the matrix. This characterizes Molloy's various attempts to find "true **love**"; but unlike Jung's integrated male, he (and others for whom he is a paradigm) fails to dominate the feminine qualities of the anima and integrate them into his masculine personality. Sophie Lousse is another projection of the anima, but his relationship with her merely apes the mother-son dyad and represents no progress so he must leave to pursue his quest elsewhere. His mother's image mingles with women he has "loved" (59); this is unendurable, like **crucifixion**. His sterile encounter with **Ruth**/Edith has done nothing to improve his understanding of women; **Macmann** with **Moll** do no better. That failure culminates in *Film*. SB's commented: "This obviously cannot be O's room. It may be supposed it is his mother's room, which he has not visited for many years and is now to occupy momentarily, to look after the pets, until she comes out of hospital" (172). The parallels to Molloy, and to SB's mother, are obvious, and the memory underlying them is intimated in the second photo that O destroys, of SB at a tender age, posed in prayer.

The mother is an absent figure that Molloy must find. She brought him into the world, through the hole in her arse if his memory is correct (16): "First taste of the shit" (**Augustine**'s "inter urinas et faeces nascimur"). Hill explains "Ma, Mag or the Countess Caca" (17): the phonemic distinction between /**m**/ and /**g**/ or /**k**/ as the difference between attraction and repulsion, the mother's kiss and her violence, oral inclusion and anal expulsion (*In Different Words*, 115). The first few months (in the womb) were the only endurable period of Molloy's history. He doesn't think harshly of her (18); she did all she could not to have him, except the one thing; fate left him unstuck for less compassionate sewers. In Molloy's end is his beginning: the forest ends in a ditch (91), and although he longs to retreat into the dark wood his cycle must begin again, either in his mother's room, where he has been (will be) taken by ambulance, or in the narrative to be repeated by **Moran**. Alternatively, he may be reborn as **Malone**, with no recollection of how he got there, save vaguely in an ambulance, but destined to die, to be expelled from the great cunt of existence (283), perhaps to emerge as the **Unnamable**, who despite all intentions could not simply stay in (291).

motion: according to **Windelband** (111), the two characteristics of corporeality are the filling of limited space and the quality of being in motion in the void; and the two categories of corporeal being are

ousia, ever the same with itself, and *genesis,* in process of change (122). The **atomists** (qv) regarded movement in and of the world as mechanical resultants of the motion of atoms, motion itself being causeless, but **Plato** affirmed the ordered motion of the universe, the single principle of all motion, and **Aristotle** believed that matter, as the merely possible or potential, had in itself no principle of motion or generation but required the action of form upon it to impart motion, so ultimately a first mover, itself unmoved. If motion exists, **Epicurus** argued, the void exists: motion exists, ergo, the void exists. **Zeno**'s proofs of the impossibility of motion attack the atomists, particularly their assertion of the void (see **nothing**). **Burton** notes at the outset of the *Anatomy:* "an accidental collision of motes in the sun, all of which **Democritus** held, Epicurus and their master Lucippus of old maintained, and are lately revived by Copernicus, Brunus, and some others." These "others" did not include **Descartes**, who tried to "démontrer l'impossibilité du mouvement sans admettre le vide" (*Baillet,* 247). For Descartes and **Geulincx**, as for **Bacon** and **Galileo**, understanding the physical world (see **physics**) meant understanding the motion of **bodies**.

Such **scholasticism** (qv) underlies much of SB's early writing. The picaresque defines an aesthetics of movement. **Murphy** is the **monad** in motion. "Serena III" ends: "keep on the move / keep on the move." *Dream* and "A Wet Night" end with **Belacqua** urged to "move on." In "Ding-Dong" (36), he gives the Furies the slip by "setting himself in motion." His need to "move constantly" reflects motion as the first law of physics, keep moving the only virtue, "gress" that is neither "pro" nor "re" but "pure blank movement." According to Geulincx (*Metaphysica,* II #11, 176): "Motus enim duas habet partes: *abesse* et *adesse*" ("Motion thus has two parts, *from being* and *to being*"). **Murphy**'s "When he came to, or rather from" (105) is more than a quibble, as it represents this **Occasionalist** conclusion; Murphy affirms that he is coming *from* his mind *to* his body. Thus the **Unnamable** addresses the **dogs** to come: "adeste, adeste, all ye living bastards" (379).

Mercier tries to stay put, then leaves, "feeling the need of a little motion" (8). "**Text 11**" asserts: "But he moved, proof of animation" (147). *First Love* considers "different varieties of motion" (28). **Malone** concludes: "in order not to die you must **come and go**, come and go" (232). The narrator of *From an Abandoned Work* sets out, simply on his way. *How It Is* attempts an art of locomotion. Yet none can move beyond the impasse that "ends" *Three Novels*: "I can't go on, I'll go on"; or that which "concludes" *Waiting for Godot: "They do not move."* SB's major turn in the 1960s was from stories of motion (quests, wilderness journeys, joyous outgoing and sad return, coming and going, home and **asylum**, "**on**" as a goad) to narratives of stillness or imperceptible movement, of **closed space** (qv).

Whoroscope's "That's not moving, that's *moving*" derives from **Mahaffy** (61): "The earth indeed did not move, but it was like a passenger on a vessel, who, though he were stationary, is nevertheless carried along in the motion of the larger system." Geulincx's boat ("Annotata," 16) is an analogy of circum-

scribed freedom (**God** moves the boat, but on it our deliberation is free). Consider *Dream* (134): "he moves forward, like the Cartesian earthball, with the moving ship, and then on his own account to the windy prow"; or *The Unnamable* (336), the ship heading toward the Pillars of Hercules, the galley man crawling toward the rising sun. The earth is at rest relative to a man who moves upon it, as a man might move who yet is carried in a boat. Compare Murphy's "motion in this world depended on rest in the world outside" (110); or *Krapp's Last Tape:* "We lay there without moving. But under us all moved, and moved us, up and down, and from side to side."

The alternative to motion is homeostasis. *Endgame* presents a world running down, as in the vision of two white dwarfs in "**For to end yet again.**" *The Unnamable* locates his self at the still point of a turning world, about which Malone and the others pass, "motionless" (292). Mr. **Knott**'s circular bed offers a cosmic image of ceaseless motion about a still point. In *Happy Days,* **Winnie** presents a *tableau vivant* of the body at rest but the mind in tumult; she is the opposite of the **Alba** (*Dream,* 166): "Alone, unlonely, unconcerned, moored in the seethe of an element in which she had no movement." The contrast is often of the Newtonian universe (a cosmic **billiards** table) and the "ström" of the inner dark (see **Murphy's mind**), where particles are indistinguishable from waves. Winnie restates the Aristotelian premise that "something must move, in the world" (60), but earlier noted as a "curious observation" (36) that one can adapt to changing conditions only if one is at rest. She rejects that to assert that something must happen, in the world, some change, if she is to move again; but mobility is a curse (46) and earth finally is a great extinguisher.

Mott, F. W. (1853–1926): psychologist instrumental in building up the Maudsley Hospital, **London**, and a pioneer of GPI; Dr. **Killiecrankie** is a "devout Mottist" (*Murphy*, 257).

Motte, Madame de la: Jeanne de Saint-Rémy de Valois (1756–91), infamous poisoner; said with a shiver in "**Sanies II.**" From **Cooper**'s *Flagellation* (322–24; DN, 56).

"La Mouche": a ten-line poem, fifth of twelve **Poèmes 38–39,** published in *Les Temps modernes* (novembre 1946). As in "**Serena I,**" a **fly** is trapped against the pane, trying to reach the light to which she is futilely drawn. As the poet is about to crush her, she moves, and the poem ends in tension: the finger "impuissant," but the threat of violent extinction still present.

Mouth: in *Not I,* picked out by a pinpoint of light against a black set, eight feet above the stage, hanging in space. The outpouring is almost unintelligible but a narrative emerges: a **little girl** born before her time; nothing of note until nearly seventy; when on an April morning in **Croker's Acres** a sudden flash of light. At first she thought she was being punished, then perhaps she had something to tell, not knowing what to say. On BBC TV (17 April 1977), Mouth

was introduced as a lifelong deaf-mute who had suddenly acquired speech. Here, reduced to its minima, is **Voice,** compelled to express when there is nothing to express but suddenly the means to do so.

Mozart, Wolfgang Amadeus (1756–91): called the "ultimate *Kunsttreib* of a musical genius"; then the "Kleine Nachtmusik" is dismissed (*Dream,* 48). **Belacqua** anticipates arriving in **Kassel** and ringing the bell, "Così fan tutte with the magic flute" (65). In "**Schwabenstreich**" (qv), SB calls Mozart the "Hexenmeister," because of his Masonic mysteries; in "**Yellow**" (172) Belacqua thinks of the "little Hexenmeister of *Don Giovanni*" (whose premature **death** anticipates his own) as he sees "Fraisse's Ferruginous Ampoules ... Registered Trademark— Mozart." The SJ is bored, he says, as by an infant prodigy, "preferring the chemist Borodine to Mozart" (*Dream,* 210); the **Polar Bear**, nettled, replies that **Christ** was an infant prodigy. "A **Wet Night**" (56) replays this with "the druggist Borodine" and Mozart as "a Hexenmeister in the pilch" (in his nappiee). Una **bboggs** can play from memory any Mozart sonata, but scorns to distinguish the notes that are significant from those that are not ("What a Misfortune," 121). All this would suggest a supercilious attitude, if "Le **Concentrisme**" did not end with an evocation of Mozart's art, "parfaitement intelligible et parfaitement inexplicable," words used at the end of *Proust,* a condition of **music** to which SB's writings aspire.

Mugnone: *il torrente Mugnone,* in the *Valle del Mugnone,* near **Florence** (*Dream,*

51), a tributary of the Arno; "mollecone" implies "soft-shelled," as of a mollusk.

Munch, Edvard (1863–1944): Norwegian expressionist painter and lithographer. The final scream in "**Assumption**" may echo that in his work *The Scream*. SB saw some of Munch's works during his 1936–37 visit to **Germany**. Billie **Whitelaw** commented of SB's direction of *Footfalls* that she felt "like a moving, musical, Edvard Munch painting," constantly drawn in and rubbed out until the image was only faintly there (*JOBS* 3 [1978]: 89).

Murphy: SB's first novel is a rollicking jeu d'esprit in the tradition of philosophical comedy from Cervantes and **Rabelais** to **Fielding** and Joyce. A gigantic joke made up of infinite tiny ones, *Murphy* is the apogee of SB's first decade of writing, the first text he did not consistently reject. It draws on the intense reading of those years yet avoids the earlier arrogance; equally, it is the matrix of his later works, anticipating many of their concerns. A holograph manuscript in six notebooks (unavailable) is dated 20 August 1935. The novel was completed by May 1936, with June devoted to its revision. SB had trouble finding a publisher, with many rejections before Routledge took it. SB corrected the proofs from his hospital bed in **Paris**, following his stabbing (almost a Murphy-like catastrophe). It appeared in green (7 March 1938), 1,500 copies, with a blurb asserting its Irish gusto and the bottom rung of the ladder as an entertaining place for observing people and places.

Reviews were few, and cautious. Dylan **Thomas** enjoyed it, and Kate O'Brien, in

The Spectator (1938), appreciated its wit: "a joke overloaded with the scholarship of great jokes." Hers was the only review SB liked, others acting "Like the **dog**'s hindquarters when the spine is touched in the right place." Sales were poor and most copies (it was rumored) destroyed in the **war** by enemy bombing. F&F note more soberly (21) that about half had sold by 1942, when the rest, 782 copies, were remaindered; their fate is a mystery. Alfred **Péron** helped SB with a **French** translation (Paris: **Bordas** [Collection les imaginaires, #5], 1946), Routledge relinquishing their options. Three thousand copies were printed, but when Jérôme **Lindon** of **Minuit** acquired the rights (June 1948) only ninety-five had sold. The translation is disappointing, many jokes vanishing and a scurrilous element casually introduced. Not until *Waiting for Godot* was there retrospective interest in *Murphy,* **Grove Press** producing photographically (from George **Reavey**'s personal copy) the still-standard American version (1957), followed by John **Calder** (1963), the text reset for Jupiter Books (the template of later British printings). The two texts have minor differences, including a wrong move in the Calder **chess** game.

The plot is intricate, tracing Murphy's fortunes from his days at **Neary**'s Academy, his affections with Miss **Counihan** (to escape which he has gone to London), and his meeting with **Celia**. Complications arise: means must be found, and Providence neglects to provide. Murphy must find a **job**, which means (since work is done by the **body**) betraying his mind. In **Ireland**, the sub-plot is under way, Neary and **Wylie** caught in the machinery of **desire** and needing to find Murphy. Things hobble to the only possible, to a Cartesian catastrophe, and the novel closes elegaically at the Round Pond, Mr. **Kelly**'s kite a final emblem of the separation of body and mind. *Murphy* is that rara avis, a genuine novel of ideas. Its characters inhabit a mechanistic universe, where human qualities assume an element of **absurdity**. The **machinery** of its big world is Cartesian; the inner action concerns Murphy's attempt to attain the **little world** of the mind, where he can (in **Occasionalist** terms) be free, an impulse frustrated by his "deplorable susceptibility" to Celia and ginger biscuits, and, in the **MMM**, by his inability to be a microcosmopolitan. This experience is paralleled by the novel's structure. Chapter 6 moves from Cartesian clarity to **Schopenhauer**'s will-lessness, by means of **Spinoza**'s *Ethics,* **Leibniz**'s *Monadology,* **Geulincx**'s *Ethica,* and **Kant**'s *Critique of Pure Reason.* The ironic edge arises from Murphy's Cartesian goal and the impossibility of its realization in a universe neither clear nor distinct.

The end of *Murphy* is a huge **Democritean** joke, with its insistence upon the soul's dissolution, a would-be Occasionalist universe blown apart by the guffaw of the Abderite, for whom *Nothing is more real than nothing.* The novel is informed by **psychoanalysis**. **Freud** was a major force, his studies of the psychopathology of everyday life confirming SB's intrauterine attraction and psychosomatic problems. Another direct influence was **Jung**. SB attended the third **Tavistock** lecture, at which Jung referred to a diagram of the unconscious that became a model of **Murphy's mind** (qv) and showed how

complexes might appear in visions and speak in **voices** (qv).

Murphy was conceived as a City Comedy, and "Londonized" by echoes of Elizabethan and Jacobean dramatists and eighteenth-century writers (many such citations, some ticked off, are listed in the **Whoroscope Notebook**). Equally contrived is the compositional method, geometric shapes on a flat surface, a deliberate use of echo and repetition, and separate sections structured on precise themes or images. Yet *Murphy* is above all a very funny novel, with some magnificent moments: a Pythagorean academy in **Cork**, Neary battling Cuchulain, the touching little argonautic in the park, the chess game, the postmortem slapstick among them. Irony prevails, and narrative unreliability shapes and deforms the comedy. The combination of particularity and absurdity gives *Murphy*'s world its demented definition, but sheer comic energy creates its eternal delight.

Murphy's mind: SB attempts to depict the mind, not as it really is but as **Belacqua** and **Murphy** picture it to be: a hermetically contained sphere with three zones, light, half-light, and dark. This structure manifests itself in *The Unnamable* and *Endgame* and in circles of darkness in *Krapp's Last Tape*. Parallels may be adduced from classical doctrines of the tripartite soul; divisions of the soul into sensitive, rational, and spiritual components; **Dante**'s *Divine Comedy;* or **Spinoza**'s three levels of knowledge, the third being the identification of the self with the intellectual love of **God**. Also manifest is **Leibniz**'s distinction between virtual and actual, the unconscious realm of confused perception, the conscious realm of relatively clear perception, and the self-conscious realm of **apperception**. **Schopenhauer**'s manifestation of the Will accentuates the three forms of space, time, and causality. The tripartite division is incommensurate with Cartesian **dualism** and thereby critiques the rationalist tradition. In the first zone, "forms with parallel" are perceived by **consciousness** and their refiguration in **Proustian** terms is voluntary. In the second, "forms without parallel" indicate that the constraints of consciousness are relaxed, and activity is involuntary. In the third, the dark zone, the "matrix of surds," the mind experiences total freedom: this is the **atomist** void, the Freudian unconscious, Schopenhauer's will-lessness, or the world of quanta and non-Newtonian **motion**, often imaged as the embryonic state of primal pleasure.

The paradigm is SB's own, as evidenced in *Dream* (120–25). Belacqua at his simplest is trine. Centripetal, centrifugal, and . . . not. Trine. His third being is the dark **gulf**, the glare of will and hammer strokes of the brain expunged; the wombtomb alive with the unanxious spirits of quiet cerebration; its center everywhere and periphery nowhere; an unsurveyed marsh of sloth. There is no authority for supposing this to be the real Belacqua, but emancipation from identity suits his complexion. He is sorry it does not happen more often. If he were free he would take up residence there. But in vain; it is impossible to switch off the inward glare. Which explains why his temper is bad and his complexion saturnine: "He remembers the pleasant gracious bountiful

tunnel, and cannot get back." Here, in the **embryo** of *Dream,* is the **larval stage** of Murphy's mind: "Apollo, **Narcissus** and the anonymous third person" (124).

SB attended with Wilfred **Bion** a lecture at the **Tavistock** Clinic (2 October 1935), where **Jung** (qv) presented a diagram showing the different spheres of the mind and the dark center of the unconscious. SB took notes and added others from **Freud** (qv), defining the id, ego, and superego, with a sketch of the "perceptual conscious," the "pre-conscious," and the "unconscious"; these represent the three zones of Murphy's mind. If Murphy could not have gone into the dark zone without SB's descent into the depths with Bion, equally it could not have been pictured without the aid of Jung and Freud.

music: SB was a proficient pianist, having learned as a child and playing all his life. He had a piano in his **Paris** flat, and another at **Ussy**, a Schimmel, on which he played sonatas from **Haydn**, **Beethoven**, and **Mozart**, or accompanied himself with **Schubert** lieder. Suzanne was musical, and had published a pedagogical work, *Musique Jeux* (Paris and Brussels: Henry Lemoine, 1935). SB did not own a record player but was an avid concertgoer and listened to radio and cassettes. At **Trinity** he attended the **Dublin** Symphony Orchestra. He could be critical, even arrogant, dismissing Horowitz ("the Blue Danube as pièce de résistance"), and finding the Haydn sonatas "unspeakable," although he admired the Brahms intermezzi and a piece of Poulenc (SB to TM, 11 November 1933). His love of music, as of visual **art**, was genuine and informed; music had the same intellectual beauty as **chess**. **Arikha** affirms his passion, noting his favorite pianists ("Yves Not, Cortot, Schnabel, Solomon, Serkin"); his dislike of **Wagner** and Mahler ("less is more"); how they listened to dodecaphonic music (Schoenberg, Berg, Webern); and how SB would return to **romantic** music, an impulse in his writing that he tried to suppress but which persisted. Monique Haas and Marcel **Mihalovici** exposed SB to Debussy, Ravel, Hindemith, Stravinsky, and Bartók, whose third piano concerto he admired. If his loyalty was finally to the traditional it was not unaware of more recent developments. This entry will survey SB's orchestration, from **Proust** and his early (failed) attempt to create a musical structure in *Dream,* to later work that partook, increasingly, of the *lied;* SB always wrote for a **voice** (Bryden, *Music,* 1). His early fiction interrogates Western music, as in *Watt*'s critique of **Pythagoras**, and it responds to the **incoherent continuum**. SB explored the analogies between dramatic composition and musical form: theme and variation; the da capo reprise; changes from major to minor. Of particular interest are the plays ("**Ghost Trio**," "**Words and Music**," "**Nacht und Träume**," and "**What Where**") where the central impulse is musical.

Underlying *Proust* is **Schopenhauer**. SB commented to **MacGreevy** (July 1930): "His chapter in Will & Representation on music is amusing & applies to P., who certainly read it." Schopenhauer insists (*WWI,* I.3 #52, 331ff) that music is independent of the phenomenal world (333). It is the objectification of the Will; other arts "speak only of shadows." SB

responded to ideas such as the deviation from and return to the tonic as indicative of **desire** (336), or the minor as the expression of keenest pain, from which we are delivered by the major (337). He admired Proust as one who integrated Schopenhauer's theory of music to fiction. Music, McQueeny insists, is the catalytic element for Proust, at once the moment of revelation and the means of renewing that revelation (105). It is "perfectly intelligible and perfectly inexplicable" (92), words applied in "Le **Concentrisme**" to Mozart, anticipating SB's sense of art as the arrangement of the inexplicable.

Schopenhauer's claim that music is the Idea, "unaware of the world of phenomena," existing ideally outside the universe, needs clarification. Normally, sense data are organized by the forms of space, time, and causality; but music is a-spatial and a-causal, perceived in and through **time** alone (*WWI,* 344) and so "untouched by the teleological hypothesis" (*Proust,* 92). Its uniqueness arises, Heath Lees indicates (168), because tones make the aesthetic impression as effect, without obliging us to go back to their cause. SB's rejection of opera is based on this: if music is the Idea, then opera becomes a "hideous corruption" because it is distorted by the listener, who being an impure subject insists on incarnating the Idea into an approximate paradigm. The imagination, excited by music, seeks to clothe it in words, so the text is subordinate: "Thus, if music is too closely united to the words . . . it is striving to speak a language which is not its own" (*WWI,* 338). Schopenhauer dismisses Haydn's "Seasons" and "Creation" where external phenomena are imitated: "Such music is entirely to be rejected." This damns *lieder,* but Schopenhauer admits ("On the Metaphysics of Music" [III.xxxix, 231]) that in poetry words are not subordinate, largely undoing his earlier argument. The strife of "Words and Music" informs much of SB's work.

SB attempted to apply this aesthetics in *Dream,* orchestration substituting for literary form, but the task (structure as the musical equivalent of involuntary unity) proved beyond him. Involuntary memory, SB notes, is Proust's *leitmotif,* but *Dream* cannot emulate that nervous structure, "enriched with a strange and necessary incrustation of grace-notes" (*Proust,* 35). *Dream* offers musical motifs and da capo action, reflected symmetries and characters defined in musical terms. One principle derives from Laloy's *La Musique chinoise* (see **liú** and **k'în music**), each bell rendering "un son determiné" (Laloy, 43). Were SB's characters liù-liú-minded, his book could be purely melodic, but they refuse to be condensed into a liu; they remain a "regrettable simultaneity of notes" (*Dream,* 11). The narrator will not bring in the **Syra-Cusa** for the sake of sonata form, "recurrence of themes, key signatures, plagal finale and all" (49). He wants a simple chord, for **Belacqua** is drifting in and out, thickening the tune, the ruined melody, but harmonic composition is impossible (117).

*Dream'*s musical insights anticipate later opinion. The **Smeraldina** is off to Vienna to play the pianoforte (3), caring more than SB did for Bach (the divine sewing **machine**). **Stendhal**'s declaration

that the best music becomes inaudible after a few bars (16) anticipates *Texts for Nothing.* The night firmament is an "abstract density of music" (16). Brahms is "Quatsch" (18). Belacqua is forced to see "the Valkyrie à demi-tarif," but **Liebert** is turned away (37). He appears with a gramophone, turns out the light, and puts on "the Kleine Nachtmusik and then Tristan." The "Winkelmusik" of **Chopin** is dismissed as tubercular, unlike the incoherent continuum of Beethoven, whose Seventh Symphony is a "punctuation of dehiscence" (138). The "**German Letter of 1937**" intuits "the final music" that underlies the All. The music of *Dream,* then, resides less in the "old K'în music rising demitonically" (114), or the **Alba**'s "white music" (193), than in this "music one and indivisible" (138) of Ludwig's bloody labor, an anticipation of *Three Novels,* whose long sonata of the dead enters the incoherent continuum. *Dream* may fail, demitechtonically, but with "the *ut* sharpened, quantified, and sustained" (229), SB would ring hell out of the literary tradition.

Whoroscope abuses **Galileo**'s "consecutive thirds," SB echoing **Mahaffy**'s point (22) that he was the first to assert that major thirds are not, as the Greeks held, discords but concords (**Descartes** to Mersenne, 15 mai 1634). The poem is like a canto, which links it to forms (*Enueg, Alba, Sanies, Serena*) in which the Provençal *son et motz* shapes tone and texture (see "**Ex Cathezra**"). "**Dortmunder**" is marked by thin k'în music, the bawd with her lute, and the "plagal" east (a break in harmonic cadence; and "plagate," streaked). "**Malacoda**" and "**Cascando**" use triadic effects and echoes; "Cascando" is marked by the thud of the metronome and "Malacoda" by an insistent motif of Beethoven's last quartet. "**Spring Song**," written in "the subjunctive minor," concludes: "now the music is over the loud music" (the affair with Peggy **Sinclair**, ending in her death).

Bande et sarabande, the **French** title of *MPTK,* expands "pricksong." "**Ding-Dong**" invokes Ferdinand's dirge in *The Tempest* but equally "Ding Dong Merrily on High"; it parodies celestial harmonies. In "**Love and Lethe**" (95), Belacqua regrets not bringing "Ravel's *Pavane*" (himself the dead Infanta?). "**Yellow**" notes (172) a Registered Trademark for Anaemia as "Mozart." When "A **Wet Night**" was recycled from *Dream,* the **Bovril** sign again danced through its seven phases, "Da capo" (47). There is no Smeraldina, so the resonant phrase from Beethoven's Seventh is omitted. That phrase resounds in "**What a Misfortune**" (141), sharpened, to shadow Belacqua's remarriage with his memory of **Lucy.** Belacqua's happiness with Lucy was defined by Schubert's "An die Musik"; SB copied the song with its music into the **Whoroscope Notebook.**

In *Murphy,* music expresses the theme of attunement and **irrationality** (see **apmonia**). Murphy's "wandering to find home" (4) reflects Schopenhauer's sense of melody as a deviation from the key note of "a thousand capricious wanderings, even to the most painful discord, and then a final return to the keynote which expresses the satisfaction and appeasing of the will" (414). This restates Stephen Dedalus's attempts in *Circe* to reconcile the "fundamental and the dominant," the interval consistent with the ultimate return. This is the **necessary**

journey, toward the self one is ineluctably preconditioned to become. Murphy enjoys his "serenade, nocturne and alba" (74). His explanation is "like difficult music heard for the first time" (40); **Celia** cannot hear the orchestration, Schopenhauer's base to Proust's melody, that would damn a job as *defunctus*. Other musical offerings include: **Ticklepenny**'s sniveling "antiphony" (92); **Neary**'s "low battuta" (116; playing the "spoons"?); **Wylie**'s kiss, "like a breve tied" (117); Murphy's, "in Lydian mode" (141); Haydn on cohabitation as "parallel thirds" (195); **Coleridge-Taylor** (215); a "typographical scream" (236); Celia's pattern of rests (250). Murphy's decision to "face the music" (252) is disrupted before harmony can be restored.

Watt is musically a continuation of *Murphy,* with the protagonist of each having a deficient sense of pitch and with respect to irrationality. Heath Lees has indicated ("*Watt:* Music, Tuning and Tonality") SB's precise deployment of musical detail. He describes Watt's experience in terms of a diminishing response (*diminuendo al niente*) to the musical stimuli around him, things that might have "attuned" his world: his decreasing ability to hear the **mixed choir,** frog song, or final threne; his failure with the **Galls,** that "incident of note"; the collapse of his world as words fail; his difficulty with little "voices" in his head. This constitutes his "untuning." Watt, like the piano, the player, and the tuner, is doomed, not just because attunement is impossible but because of a deficiency in Western music, the "**Pythagorean** comma" (Lees, 174–76). The irrational element arises from the disjunction of mathematical ratios and musical scales, a distortion in the nature of tonality. Lees is excellent on the frog song, its intervals of 3, 5, and 8 corresponding with the first inversion (E, G, and C) in the scale of C major (as SB had noted in the drafts); atonalities arising from the recurrent interval rather than the harmonic note (**seriality**); **Buxtehude** and the **ravanastron**, in terms of the well-tempered clavier and elementary attempts "to resolve the irremediably discordant" (179); precise details of key and pitch in various songs. One might add hymn tunes: "We shall be here all night" (echoing "We love the place, O God") or "Now the day is over" (57). Lees concludes that the quest for Apmonia begun in *Murphy* is doomed in *Watt,* "not just because Watt is what he is, but also because Western music is what it is" (184).

The musical qualities of SB's middle period are defined with difficulty, because earlier effects like involuntary unity and the incoherent continuum are utilized without comment. *Three Novels, Waiting for Godot, Endgame,* and *How It Is* display a musical mastery, the more impressive for being less obvious. SB by his own account *heard* his texts before writing them: "They abound with evocations of aural memories, sounds and their withdrawal, acoustic qualities, rhythms and melodies" (Bryden, 1). The texts can be considered as music, writing as orchestration; indeed, SB encouraged this kind of speculation. "The play is full of echoes," he told the German cast of *Endgame,* "they all answer each other." He described it to Georges **Pelorson** as a cantata for two voices (Brater, 84), and told Roger **Blin** that he regarded it "as a

kind of musical score" (*Blin on Beckett,* 233). *Three Novels* develop according to their self-contained logic as words and rhythm come together to combine and react in a play of sound and semantics. External reference is subordinated to internal harmony, forming a self-sufficient linguistic and musical cosmos. The binary structure of *Molloy* suggests sonata form, as in Molloy's "long sonata of the dead" (31); but this is rejected, as in *Dream.* Inner harmony is rather to be found in the voices and whispers that the protagonists at last begin to hear. **Moran** dislikes music because it gets on his nerves, but he learns to listen. When Molloy hears distant music (21), or **Malone** defines pain as a kind of rhythm, a little tune (198), or the **Unnamable** fears the worst, a soprano (364), the effect seems a local tonality. Yet such effects are developed intricately, notably in Molloy's **forest murmurs**, where Wagner's Siegfried is echoed by Molloy's **bicycle** horn.

SB in *Proust* describes the "beautiful convention" of the da capo (92). *Godot* enacts this: the repeat, to create boredom and tension; two acts not quite identical but symmetrical; stylized rhythm, with differences of tempo and accent. In "**Play**," everyday banality is orchestrated like a musical score: characters responding to the light as to a conductor; stage directions about tempo, volume, and tone; and instructions for a repeat, da capo. The *diminuendo al niente* effect is used in *Texts for Nothing* technically as a *mesure pour rien,* a bar's rest, an interval conveying **nothing** but part of the musical whole. "Text 6" asks, "How are the intervals filled?"; this is answered in "Text 11" with the conceit of playing on the self, adding to the repertory, and being executed, "one dead bar after another" (144).

The later drama is intricately musical. "**Act Without Words I**" (1957) had incidental music by SB's cousin John Beckett ("**Beckett on Film**" sustituted a score by Michael Nyman). SB's **mimes** are like "Songs without Words." In *All That Fall,* "rural sounds" modulate into the mournful refrain of Schubert's "Death and the Maiden." The play's three movements, anabasis, stasis, katabasis, use echoes and repetitions; the *lied* defines that structure. In "**Embers,**" Addie's music master bullies her by beating on the piano case with his **cylindrical ruler** when, in Chopin's fifth waltz in A flat major (SB's suggestion), she plays E instead of F. Henry is unsympathetic: "It was not enough to drag her into the world, now she must play the piano." **Krapp** sings "Now the day is over" and **Winnie** the waltz from *The Merry Widow.* "**Rough for Radio** I" portrays Voice and Music as protagonists. Billie **Whitelaw** said of *Not I* that she had to say the words impossibly fast yet with precise enunciation: "It's like music, a piece of Schoenberg in his head" (*Sunday Times,* 14 January 1973). She described *Footfalls* as "a moving, musical, Edvard **Munch** painting" (Knowlson, 551); the piece is musical in conception, movements measured in terms of pacing, turning, pauses, and chimes. David **Warrilow**, likewise, rehearsed "**Ohio Impromptu**" in terms of tone and tempo (Bryden, 44).

After "Embers" SB asked John Beckett to write the music for a new radio play, and Marcel **Mihalovici** asked SB for a radiophonic text. The outcome was a pair of related radio plays: "Words and Music" in English (December 1961), and "**Cascando**" in French immediately thereafter. "Cascando" is "A radio piece for music and voice," the title meaning diminishing volume and decreasing tempo. The American production featured a musical score by William Kraft, even though the contract specifies Mihalovici's music. "Words and Music" is more intricate, debating which of the two takes precedence, a theme as ancient as song itself. One side claims music as the art to which all others aspire; the other replies that poetry wins since words speak not only to the ear but to the mind. The debate preoccupies the **troubadours**, Wagner's *Die Meistersinger* and *Tannhäuser,* and Strauss's *Capriccio.* Strauss's reconciliation (in opera) was not an obvious solution for SB, yet it answers the dilemma outlined in *Proust* and might justify his love of *lieder:* "Each lives in the other and seeks the other. Music awakens feelings that crave words. In words lies a longing for sound and music."

Music may win the day, but (to dispute SB's opinion) the poetry is such that its work is cut out to match (or catch) the emotion. "Nacht und Träume" and "Ghost Trio" apparently resolve the issue in favor of music. Each is virtually wordless, relying on, respectively, the unspeakable beauty of a Schubert song and a Beethoven trio. "Ghost Trio" (qv) integrates music, gesture, sculptural iconography, and poetry perfectly. "**Quad**" relies on visual sculpture and the geometry of movement closely akin to ballet; SB called it "un fugue statique" (Bryden, 36). Yet ". . . **but the clouds . . .**" invokes the mesmerizing poetry of W. B. **Yeats** at his most beautiful; and in "What

Where" the issue is finely balanced with reference to Schubert's *Winterreise,* where the poetry is inseparable from the music.

Ping has an atonal quality, purged of inflection and coloration, like the "white music" of *Dream. Lessness* has affinities with statistical composition, an impulse SB did not sustain. In the later prose the affinity to Schubert *lieder* and Romantic song is marked: "**Enough**" has twilit scenes, recollections of **love**, sudden focus upon flower or tree, sad sighs, but also emotional honesty and an acoustic awareness. *From an Abandoned Work,* intrinsically a prose piece, was given in concert at the Royal Festival Hall (1960). The late prose reflects the mind listening to itself as it speaks, weighs words, utters, and repeats fragments of dubious comfort. In the words of Adam Piette, this is "a difficult music of memories struggling for tiny life within a formal system of echoes, traces of a remembering voice" (198). Piette is exemplary on "acoustical composition" and "self-audition" in the later works (see **memory**). Unfinished texts like the "**Kilcool manuscript**" testify to the arduous "undoing" required once the subject was defined, to orchestrate it by variation, echo, and repetition.

SB's works have inspired many composers to create musical accompaniments, notably those by Philip **Glass** for **Mabou Mines.** As well as for "Act Without Words I" and "Words and Music" (about which he became diffident), John Beckett supplied music for BBC readings of various works, SB occasionally participating. Humphrey Searle wrote new music for "Words and Music" (1973) and "Cascando" (1984). Morton Feldman was asked by Everett Frost (1987) to supply music for an American "Words and Music"; William Kraft completed his score for "Cascando" after Feldman died. Heinz Holliger set music to *Come and Go* (1977) and "What Where" (1988); he also completed *Not I,* a monodrama for soprano and tape, with Phyllis Bryn-Julson (1981). Wolfgang Fortner set *That Time* to music, with Voice A (baritone) represented by the piano, B (mezzo-soprano) by guitar, and C (female speaker) by harpsichord (Bryden, 141–58).

Others have set SB to music. Mihalovici created the opera of *Krapp's Last Tape,* and set "**que ferais-je dans ce monde**" for solo soprano in the finale of his Fifth Symphony (1972). Feldman's *Neither (Opera in One Act for Soprano)* was performed by the Rome Opera (1977). *For Samuel Beckett* (1987), an orchestral theme, had its UK premiere with the London Sinfonietta (10 November 1995). Earl Kim wrote several multimedia works inspired by SB's texts, such as *Exercises En Route* (1971), for soprano, chamber ensemble, dancers, three actresses, and film; *Narratives* (1979), for woman's voice, high soprano, teleprojected actor, chamber ensemble, television, and lights; a one-act opera, *Footfalls* (1981); and a song cycle of departures and farewells for voice, harp, and double string quartet, *When Grief Slumbers* (1982), inspired by SB's translation of *Le Bateau ivre* ("**Drunken Boat**"). Giacomo Manzoni's *Parole da Beckett* (1976) sets a mishmash of texts for soloists, choir, magnetic tape, amplifiers, instrumental groups, and chamber ensemble (Bryden, 213–32). Roger Reynolds's "A Merciful Coincidence" (1976), for quadrophonic tape and three vocalists, exploits the **serial order** in *Watt,* particularly the frog song; his *Odyssey* (1989–93) uses three poems and "Texte" 9 (Bryden, 195–211). The Hungarian composer György Kurtág, moved by the singer Ildikó Monyók's hesitant recovery of speech after an accident, set to music SB's last text, **"What Is the Word"** (Bryden, 3). See also Bryden's "Select Bibliography" (261–63).

Composers have used SB as a springboard for their own work. Marc Wilkinson, a London-based Australian, created "Voices" from *Waiting for Godot* (Universal Edition, 1960), a miniature score (ten minutes) for contralto, flute, E*b* clarinet, bass clarinet, violoncello, words in English and German ("All the dead voices . . . incapable of keeping silent"). Luciano Berio's *Sinfonia* (1968), for eight voices and orchestra, uses *The Unnamable.* Michael Mantler (1987), a Viennese-born New York composer, recorded *No Answer* (Watts, 18), his accompaniment to *How It Is.* Melanie Daiken has set *Echo's Bones* (1975, thirteen short movements for woodwind, brass, piano, and percussion) and *Quatre poèmes* (1995, for clarinet, viola, and piano). Catherine Laws lists: Bertrand Rands's solo trombone piece, *Memo 2* (1973), from *Not I;* Roger Marsh's *Bits and Scraps,* echoing *How It Is;* Mark-Anthony Turnage's orchestral piece, *Your Rockaby* (1993); and compositions by Richard Barrett (Bryden, 57). Bryden includes Clarence Barlow's extravagant "Textmusic for Piano," based on *Ping* (1971), and Jean-Yves Bosseur's more modest *Bing* (1986), for six performers (voice and instruments), the text prerecorded by solo voice, attempts to accentuate the moments ("bings") when silence is dead but an impulse is gathering pace (the production in Grenoble, 15 May 1975, aroused SB's curiosity).

Given that musical responses are so various, and their quality likewise, Schopenhauer's dilemma, as explored in "Words and Music," is pertinent: speech and song are different phenomena, each capable at best of imitating the other. One does not wish to say with the German pessimist that "Such music is entirely to be rejected," for SB has inspired many, but his works have their own "difficult" music. It is the rare piece that can accommodate that music within a new form.

"musique de l'indifférence": a six-line poem, not translated, sixth of twelve *Poèmes 38–39,* published in *Les Temps modernes* (novembre 1946). The **music** of indifference arises from silence, the erosion of **love**; it muffles the **voices** of others, so he assumes silence. SB sent a copy, entitled "Prière," to **MacGreevy** (31 January 1938).

Musset, Alfred de (1810–57): French poet, who edged **Romanticism** with irony; described in *Proust* (82) as lacking any real cohesion. SB imitated "La Nuit de Mai" in **"Ce n'est au Pélican"** (*Dream,* 21), and cited "Oui, les premiers baisers" from "Souvenir" (189). **Liebert** visits the **Père Lachaise** cemetery to sit by his tomb (49).

mysticism: for all SB's rejection of **religion** (qv) his writing retains a concern with the mysteries of faith and their expression in the Western mystical tradition. He early read **Windelband** on Neoplatonism (219ff) and **Inge**'s *Christian Mysticism,* and late told Charles Juliet that he liked the mystical spirit, the flame that "burns away filthy logic" (*Conversations,* 167). Inge defines mysticism as "dim **consciousness** of the *beyond,* which is part of our nature," arising as we realize "the immanence of the temporal in the eternal, and of the eternal in the temporal" (5). He calls this the voice of **God,** and stresses the medieval doctrine that there is at "the apex of the mind" a spark consubstantial with the deity (7); this is identified with the "Fünkelein" of Meister **Eckehart** (156). Inge insists that mysticism is reason applied above rationalism (21) and that to reject it is to suppose an **irrational** universe. He notes that the **atomists** were "especially odious to the mystics" (22); SB shared their persuasion. **Belacqua** calls himself a dud mystic, a John of the Crossroads, a borderman (*Dream,* 186); **Watt**'s attempts to eff the **ineffable** are disastrous; *Waiting for Godot* and *Endgame* deny redemption; and *How It Is* derides transcendence as "all balls." Yet there remains in SB's thought a contradictory attraction to mystical speculation, manifest in the **voice** and the **Not I.** **Moran** begins and ends his tale with "It is midnight" (*Molloy,* 92, 176), echoing "Faith is midnight" (Inge, 225) of St. **John of the Cross** and the *Dark Night of the Soul.* Consider the **gnosticism** of *Krapp's Last Tape* and the spectral imagery of "**Ghost Trio.**" The "**closed space**" prose reflects the mind's (soul's?) attempt to become entirely passive and receptive, to renounce all self-activity, thought and reflection turning upon itself.

mythological present: as used by **Molloy** (26): "I speak in the present tense, it is so easy to speak in the present tense, when speaking of the past. It is the mythological present, don't mind it." The effect is a double articulation, a story already told, already "minded," as he begins at the beginning, like an old ballocks (8). In *Waiting for Godot,* similarly, all time is present, like **Bergson**'s *durée.* This is the mode of *How It Is,* all reduced to a **voice** (qv) speaking in the eternal present. The speaker's life seems over, even as it begins and/or goes on; he is equally subject and **object,** teller and told; no differentiation of tense secures existence. In Greek this would be the middle voice, one talking to oneself, experiencing in the present past trauma, bearing witness. In *All Strange Away,* the protagonist is "talking to himself in the last person" (169). **Moran** defines the impersonal voice (109) as the "prophetic present": compare the ending of "**Dante and the Lobster**": "It is not"; **Pozzo**'s "They give **birth** astride of a grave"; and **Vladimir**'s "We have **time** to grow old." This voice is neither the **character** speaking nor "without," but eternally now. The mythological present thus anticipates the disembodied, ghostly voices of SB's later fiction and plays.

"My way is in the sand flowing": translation of "**je suis ce cours de sable qui glisse,**" in *Transition Forty-eight* 2 (June 1948): 97, opposite the original. Reprinted in *Poetry Ireland* (April 1949): 8, and in SB's various collected poems.

N

Nabokov, Vladimir (1899–1977): Russian-born writer extraordinaire, whose *Lolita* (1955) shared with *Watt* the dubious distinction of being published by **Olympia Press**, a quag from which each author extricated himself with difficulty. Nabokov described SB as "author of lovely novellas and wretched plays in the Maeterlinck tradition," noting of *Molloy* (his favorite): "Everything is so gray, so uncomfortable, you feel that he is in constant bladder discomfort " (*Strong Opinions,* 172).

"Nacht und Träume": a television play, written in English (mid-1982) for Süddeutscher Rundfunk and broadcast there (19 May 1983) with mimic Helfrid Foron playing both parts. Published in *Collected Shorter Plays* (1984; 303–6). It is a wordless play, the only sound that of a male **voice** first humming, then singing, from the last seven bars of **Schubert**'s *lied* "Nacht und Träume," words by Matthäus Casimir von Collin (1779–1824): "Holde Träume, kehret wieder!" ("Sweet dreams, come back").

The action is simple: in a dark empty room a dreamer (**A**) is seated at a table, the **music** plays, and the light fades until the words of the lied, "Holde Träume," when it fades up on **B**, his dreamt self, sitting on an invisible podium, four feet higher and to the right. A hand ("L") gently rests on B; another ("R") appears with a cup (a chalice?) and gently wipes his brow (the **Veronica**?); B raises his right hand to meet R, and L reappears to rest gently on his head. The dream fades as A awakens, but when the music resumes the sequence is replayed. A strange, haunting beauty arises from the ritualistic movement. Knowlson notes (599) SB's fascination with **Dürer**'s etching of praying hands, which had hung in his room at **Cooldrinagh**, and reports the discussion between SB and Dr. Müller-Freienfels, who directed the SDR production, about the hands, which SB reluctantly conceded had to be "Large but female" (for this "Heil'ge Nacht" intimates the consolation of **Christ**).

Nackybal, Mr.: defending his dissertation (*Watt,* 174), **Louit** produces an old man, Mr. Thomas Nackybal, native of Burren (181). The name is vaguely an anagram of "cannibal," or "Caliban" (the drafts confirm this). He has the gift, claims Louit, not only of extracting from the ancestral half-acre of moraine nourishment for himself and his pig but from four-figure numbers their square roots, and from six-figure sequences their cube roots. Thus, given 389,017, Mr. Nackybal can answer, "Sivinty-thray." This emulation of the idiot savant has possible origins in Vito Mangianele, son of a Sicilian shepherd. Had the story been concluded Arthur's audience might have discovered, as the reader does (198), that Mr. Nackybal's real name is Tisler, and he lives in a room on the canal (Mr. Fitzwein *has* seen that **face** before). For the art of the con, see **mathematics**.

Nagg and Nell: accursed progenitors in *Endgame,* designated "P & M" (Pépé and Mémé, *père* et *mère*) in early drafts. Since losing their legs in a cycling accident in the Ardennes (an echo of World War I), they have been relegated to trash cans and placed in **Hamm**'s reluctant care. Nell remains the **romantic,** but hers is the un-sentimental line: "Nothing is funnier than unhappiness." She dies, a detail explicit in SB's direction, for Clov places the alarm clock on her bin since she will no longer disturb it. Nagg's highlight is the story of the tailor. Nagg suggests the cobra (*naja*), Buddha's guise, as he rises from his bin (compare the lights that rear and swell and hiss in *The Unnamable,* 362); his name, however, features in the genealogy of **Christ:** "Esli, which was the son of Nagge" (Luke 3:25).

"le nain nonagénaire": a rhymed qua-train, first of "**Deux poèmes**" (*Minuit* 33 [mars 1979]: 2): "The ninety-year old dwarf in a last murmur, for **pity**'s sake at least a life-size coffin." David Wheatley (69–70) traces its evolution in the **Sottisier Notebook** to a dwarf who fears being buried before expressing his agony.

Narcissus: beautiful youth of whom the nymph Echo became enamored. Finding him insensible to **love,** she pined away and dwindled to a **voice.** Nemesis caused Narcissus to see his reflection in a foun-tain. Enamored, he too pined away, till nothing was left but a heap of stones (the metaphor of *Echo's Bones,* poems as pre-cipitates) and the flower that bears his name. SB translated Narcissus's long la-ment (DN, 159–60) from **Ovid**'s *Meta-morphoses* (III.395ff). He also noted

Dante's "lo specchio di Narcisso" ("the **mirror** of Narcissus," *Inf.* XXX.128).

Freud sees creativity as neurosis, artists by definition as narcissistic, and **art** the product of self-absorption. *Dream* insists (38) that love condones, nay demands narcissism. The three "terms" of person-ality (see **Murphy's mind**) are Apollo, Narcissus, and an anonymous third. O'Hara (*Hidden Drives,* 56ff) stresses **Murphy**'s retreat from **Celia,** whose de-mands threaten him, toward Mr. **Endon,** whose narcissism renders him immune to Murphy's **love.** O'Hara shows that Murphy's **coming and going** is rooted in SB's knowledge of depth psychology. Murphy cannot submit to an **object** of **desire** outside himself, but this impedes his love of any Other. "**Claude**'s Narcis-sus in Trafalgar Square" (228) depicts the youth seeing his reflection, and Murphy in his encounter with Mr. Endon, O'Hara notes (60), assumes "the pose of Narcis-sus, bent over the stream."

nature: as **Windelband** argues (73), Greek ethics began with a problem that paralleled that of **physics,** the relation-ship between the unchanging order of things and the world of change. He de-fines man's allegiance to an anthropo-morphic principle—man as the measure of all things (see **Protagoras**)—that has shaped a sense of the natural world so intricately that most of Western history and philosophy has assumed it, a pecu-liar suspense between metaphysical mo-nism and ethico-religious **dualism** that "forces together all the thoughts of the time, and condenses them into the most difficult of problems, that of the relation of **God** and the world" (235). SB's philo-

sophical thought embraces a distrust of
and offers a challenge to this tradition of
nature (and hence God) in three ways:

a. his allegiance to a system of
thought, running from **Democritus**
through **Epicurus** and **Lucretius** and ultimately to **Schopenhauer**, which took the
form of pessimistic dissent against the
main vein of Greek and Christian thought.
(See **atomism** and **irrationality**.)

b. increasing suspicion of the un-
qualified relationship between the perceiving subject and the **object** perceived,
a need to rupture "the lines of communication" (*Disjecta,* 70).

c. a theory of **art** that rejected "the
itch to animise" and affirmed instead a
sense of nature incommensurable with
human expression, indifferent to man,
atomistic, mineral, and inorganic. SB felt
landscape as something ultimately unintelligible, and that absence of rapport between himself and the natural world became axiomatic. (See **Cézanne.**)

SB makes ironic use of the pastoral tradition. "**Walking Out**" begins in **Croker**'s
Gallops. Larks are singing, hedges breaking, the sun shining, the sky is Mary's
cloak: "It was one of those Spring evenings
when it is a matter of some difficulty to
keep God out of one's meditations." But
the grass is "spangled with scarlet afterbirths"; the action takes place in "Tom
Wood" (**voyeurism**); Belacqua hears the
cry of the **corncrake** (death); but not the
cuckoo (cuckoldry). The evocation of
spring preludes a story of deviance and
disfigurement and critiques the pastoral,
much as "**What a Misfortune**" subverts
romance.

In *Watt*, SB celebrates the seasons in
Arsene's "short statement": crocuses,
larches, pastures red with uneaten **sheep**'s
placentas, the cuckoo and corncrake,
wasps in the jam, dead leaves, howling
winds, snow, sleet, and slush, "and every
fourth year the February débâcle and the
endless April showers and the crocuses and
then the whole bloody business starting all
over again." This return to the vistas of
"Walking Out" is rendered more ruthless
by adding "uneaten" and interpolating
"an ordure . . . an excrement . . . A cat's
flux" to punctuate the delivery. Watt and
Sam later meet in their unruly arcadia, to
pursue with stones and clods birds of
every kind and grind under their feet larks'
eggs, still warm from the mother's breast.
Their "particular friends" are the **rats**
(155). These they feed with titbits, such
as birds' eggs, frogs, and fledglings, or they
might feed a plump young rat to its
mother or its **father**. On these occasions,
both agree, they come "nearest to God."

Such images of the pitiless process in
which eat or be eaten is the natural order
pervade SB's writing. In "**Serena I**" the
poet turns away in horror from an adder
"broaching" her rat. In "**Enueg I**" his darling's red sputum flecks the "bloodied **rafflesia**," a flower that looks like corrupted
tissue. "**Ooftish**" expresses SB's anger most
vividly, but images of like cruelty are
everywhere: sorrow for the owls enclosed
in **Battersea Park** (*Murphy, The Unnamable*); the lovebird in "**Rough for Theatre II**" (88), left without seed or water
(only a cuttle bone), singing over its dead
mate ("organic waste! All that splendour!"); or "**Rough for Radio II**" (120),
in A's reaction to the embryonic brother:
"No no, such things happen, Nature you
know . . . [*Faint laugh*] Fortunately. A
world without monsters, just imagine."

The ultimate debt to nature is **death**. **Molloy** becomes inseparable from the psychological landscape (shore, swamp, dark wood, and ditch), his journey ending in a painful **birth** that is equally a death. **Moran** becomes like Molloy, returning to find his **hens** and his **bees** dead, his ordered world in a state of entropic decay. When **Malone** thinks of dying (179), he says he will be "natural" at last; his story also culminates in death, expressed as leaving the great cunt of existence (283) in a monstrous breech birth, the head the last to die. The **Unnamable** (293) has lost his natural functions. Unlike **Prometheus**, who "denatured" clay (303), he cares little for his kind, and nature is rejected as a lie (304). **Mahood** finds in disintegration a "natural transition" (330). **Worm** cannot distinguish between nature and the world of man (385). In *How It Is* animal life is reduced to a **dog** (30), "head sunk tail on balls," and the narrator's existence to the chthonic condition of mud.

A wry jest informs every use of "nature." Moran considers it a **superfoetatory** proof of the existence of God (99). Mr. Py states that Jacques Jr. has "naturally" very bad teeth (103). In *Waiting for Godot,* nature is reduced to the tree. This intimates the one Cross, and offers hope of relief from the slow **crucifixion** of living if **Vladimir** and **Estragon** can hang themselves from it. They cannot leave until night, which **Pozzo** describes as "very natural, very natural" (24.a). When **Lucky** is asked to dance first and think afterward, Pozzo concurs: "It's the natural order" (26.b). Lucky's speech on God and nature reduces both to an "abode of stones" (29.b). In the second act the tree sprouts "four or five leaves," but Vladimir's imper-

fect sense of change meets the reply (42.b): "It must be the Spring." When Estragon suggests turning resolutely toward nature (41.b; compare **Darwin**, *Origin of Species,* chapter 5: "Now let us turn to nature"), Vladimir replies, "We've tried that." Nature may prove an inadequate refuge (they cannot hide behind the tree), but it is not quite dead.

Endgame asserts (11), "Nature has forgotten us," and "There's no more nature." Asked what is outside the shelter, **Clov** replies "Zero." One window opens on the earth, the other on the sea; both are desolate. **Hamm** has a vision of arcadia, of somewhere still green beyond the hills ("Flora! Pomona!" [39]), but the rising corn and herring fleet, images of plenitude, turn to ashes (44). When Clov asks if Hamm wants him to leave, Hamm says, "Naturally." As for Mother **Pegg**, "naturally she's extinguished" (42), like the "old doctor" (25), who is dead "naturally." Something is taking its course (32), but the thought of life renewing itself (the flea, the **boy**) is anathema, requiring the powder, the gaff. Hamm longs for the earth to awake in spring, for the rivers and seas to run again with fish, and for manna in heaven for imbeciles like Clov, but he would settle for "a nice natural death in peace and comfort" (53). This is part of his story about a little **child**, which he resumes, wondering if he wants the child to bloom while he is withering (83). This may not be the end. Whatever is taking its course will go on; it's the natural order.

nautch-girl: an East Indian dancing girl (*Dream,* 83, 162). Browning's "Fifine at the Fair" (XXXI) rhymes it with "debauch" (Hesla, 25). In "**Sanies I**" the cyclist describes his love as a "dauntless nautch-girl," then "dauntless daughter of desires," from Crashaw's "The Flaming Heart," used of St. Teresa and applied to the **Alba** (*Dream*, 222).

Näutzsche, Hermione: a remote cousin of **Belacqua**, so invited to his wedding in "**What a Misfortune.**" A "powerfully built nymphomaniac panting in black and mauve" (138), she negates his **nautch-girl**, the **Alba**, in black and flamingo. Her surname mocks **Nietzsche**, and her first *A Winter's Tale,* for like her namesake she finally rises to the occasion.

Neary: philosopher and savant manqué of *Murphy*, his every phrase a parody of literary or philosophical pretension; a comic creation of Falstaffian proportions, **Hardy** to **Wylie**'s Laurel. Neary has a **Pythagorean** Academy in **Cork**, but his passion for Miss **Counihan** undoes him quite and impels the plot by providing motive (and means) to search for Murphy. Neary is a Newtonian (his name an anagram of "yearn"), but the foundations of his universe are subverted by **desire**, his hair turns white, and he affirms that life is irregular. His name echoes Neary's Bar in Chatham Street, **Dublin**, where "the legendary Macran" (Henry S.), an eccentric, tough-talking Hegelian scholar, Professor of Moral Philosphy at **Trinity**, and part of the model for Neary, held court. A Lilly Neary, no obvious relation, arrives at the **Frica**'s party (*Dream*, 218).

necessary journey: an insistent metaphor for SB during the 1930s. **Murphy**'s "wandering to find home" (4) echoes *The*

Witch of Edmonton (Cohn, *Comic Gamut,* 46) but also **Joyce:** Bloom's homecoming and Dedalus's journey to meet the self he is ineluctably predestined to become. Thus **Moran** seeks **Molloy**. During his 1937 visit to **Germany** SB read Walther Bauer's *Die notwendige Reise* ("The Necessary Journey"), and noted in his **German Diaries** (18 January 1937) a critique of that title, based on the figure of Murphy immobile in his **rocking chair**, *Das notwendige Bleiben* ("The necessary Staying Put") (Knowlson, 230). This is the **fundamental unheroic**, to counter the heroism of Joyce.

In the rationalist tradition, the soul seeks **God** by cultivating the highest activity of the mind; in the **mystical** tradition, the seeker confronts an enlightenment not of this world and returns to communicate it to others. For Murphy, the "necessary journey" is into his own dark, where, loving himself, alone he can be free, but a "deplorable susceptibility" to ginger biscuits and **Celia** holds him in the big world and prevents his retreat to the **little world** of the mind. Murphy discovers in his confrontation with Mr. **Endon** that he cannot take the final step into the microcosmopolitan world because the cost would be his sanity. This is a price he is not prepared to pay, for if he can no longer apperceive himself then he no longer exists. This is an irresolvable antinomy, to which SB would return in *Film* (qv).

negative theology: it can be said of **God** only that he has no qualities known to human intelligence—"no name names him" and "we can predicate of God only what he is not" (Windelband, 237, 290).

Watt vainly attempts to exhaust the possibilities of what Mr. **Knott** *is,* but encounters only his attributes and knows nothing of his essence. The deity, thus conceived, is above reason and being; "it has no determination or quality, it is 'Nothing'" (Windelband, 335). Being and knowledge are one, and the God who is and knows creates out of nothing the creatures whose Ideas he knows within himself, for this knowing is his creating. Hence **Spinoza**'s intellectual **love,** by which God loves himself (*Murphy,* 107). This conception passed from Greek thought, through Philo to the **gnostics** and early Christian apologists, including **Augustine,** and informed medieval **scholasticism** in the writings of Duns Scotus, Meister **Eckehart,** Nicolaus Cusanus, and the "extreme theophanism of **William of Champeaux**" (*Murphy,* 81). The *via negativa* of **mysticism** is the **way** by which the soul might know God, and the *docta ignorantia,* the stripping of knowledge so that the deity-as-Nothing might be apprehended as not-knowing, is the first step to nonbeing, to the **Not I.** Rejection of "the loutishness of learning" ("**Gnome**"), stripping the self (*Three Novels*), and the **necessary journey** toward minimalism testify to SB's partial acceptance of "The **Way.**" The *via negativa* retained an attraction, even after SB's most elemental journey and most emphatic utterance (the "all balls" of *How It Is*) had offered a further and apparently final negation of that. See **unword.**

Negro, an Anthology: a book of 856 pages and 500 illustrations, compiled by Nancy **Cunard** (1931–33), dedicated to her "first Negro friend," Henry **Crowder,** and published by Wishart (1934) in an edition of 1,000 copies plus 150 for contributors; reprinted in two special editions. Not a literary anthology but rather "a comprehensive history of the cultural, social, political, and artistic achievements of the black people of the world." SB contributed nineteen translations, 10 percent of the book, receiving £25: Robert Goffin, "The best negro jazz orchestras," 291–93; Ernest Moerman, "Louis Armstrong" (poem), 295; Robert Goffin, "Hot jazz," 378–79; Jenner Bastien, "Summary of the history of Hayti," 459–64; Ludovic Morin Lacombe, "A note on Haytian culture," 470–71; Jacques Boulanger, "The King of Gonaives," 471–73; E. Flavier-Léopold, "The child in Guadeloupe," 497–500; Benjamin Péret, "Black and white in Brazil," 510–14; Georges Sadoul, "Sambo without tears," 570–73; André Breton et al., "Murderous humanitarianism, by the **surrealist** group in Paris," 574–75; Léon Pierre-Quint, "Races and nations," 575–80; René Crevel, "The negress in the brothel," 581–83; J.-J. Rabéarivelo, "A short historical survey of Madagascar," 618–20; Charles Ratton, "The ancient bronzes of Black Africa," 684–86; Henri Lavachery, "Essay on styles in the statuary of the Congo," 687–93; B. P. Feuilloley, "Magic and initiation among the peoples of Ubanghi-Shari," 734–38; Raymond Michelet, "'Primitive' life and mentality," 739–61; E. Steirs, "A negro-Empire: Belgium," 795–801; and Georges Citerne and François Jourdain, "French imperialism at work in Madagascar." (Details from Davis et al., *Calepins de bibliographie,* 1934 D1.) The translations constitute some 63,000 words, and if Alan Friedman, who has edited them in *Beckett in Black and Red* (1999), is wrong to call them SB's "most extensive publication" (some novels are longer), they are certainly "little known and less valued." Friedman overstates SB's tacit commitment to Cunard's crusades, both "black" (racism) and "red" (socialism), yet underlines his early concern for human rights. SB dismissed the "Miserable rubbish" he was doing (SB to TM, 9 October 1931), but as Phil Baker argued in his *TLS* review of Friedman, if some translations are workaday others are extraordinary, displaying such "distinctly Beckettian preoccupations" as a fascination for mouths and **buttocks** in an idiom both surreal and jazzy.

"neither": a prose-poem written (September 1976) to be set to **music** by Morton Feldman. In Feldman's account, SB reluctantly offered "the one theme in his life"; he recited "Neither," which Feldman jotted down on the spot. The work premiered at the Rome Opera (12 June 1977) and was first published in the program. Reprinted in *JOBS* 4 (spring 1979), with one of the eighty-seven words ("neared") omitted from the fourth line. John **Calder** sought to publish it in *Collected Poems* but SB resisted because he considered it prose; it was omitted from the 1984 *Collected Shorter Prose*, then printed in a corrupt version. The date was given as 1962; the title capitalized; and the copy editor's query, "?," retained in place of the previously omitted word, "doors once neared gently closed" becoming "doors once ? gently closed."

The text returns to the old notion of life "evoking nothing more substantial than oscillatory movement" (Laws, 59),

a sense of dislocated "betweenness," a ghostly movement among different gradations of shadow and self ("unself"). The attenuated music concerns the unceasing search for an essential "I," but such absolute presence seems beyond the reach of the shadows: the saying of "I" requires location within the self but the objective existence of this subjectivity cannot be verified other than from without. SB reputedly said that this was his "one" text: unsayable, not located in self or in nonself, but in "neither." The fifty minutes of **music**—lacking story, character, mise-en-scène, decidedly non-theatrical; it hardly qualifies as opera— tries to capture in small incremental differences this single idea without substance or definition, purely and abstractly evocative, music the only compensation for the negation of reference. The piece was recorded (20 February 1990) at Sendesaal Hessischer Rundfunk by the Radio-Sinfonie-Orchester Frankfurt, dir. Zoltán Peskó with Sarah Leonard, soprano. A second edition, including the text, was issued by Hat Hut Records (1998). A new CD version by the Bavarian Radio Symphony on the Col Legno appeared in 2000.

Nelly: Rosie **Dew**'s hot dog in *Murphy*. Also, the subject of a poem from Grehan the poisoner (or solicitor) to Mr. **Hackett** (*Watt*, 11–12). "To Nelly" parodies Cavalier lyric; in draft it was described as lines to Anthea (beloved of Lovelace, hence from **prison**). The author was one "Green," lance corporal and later simple private. References to **Hyde** (qv) and **Byrne** (qv) make the poem more pointed than might first appear.

Nemo: an unnamed nobody in *Dream,* who stands on O'Connell Bridge, not interacting with other characters nor exerting any influence on the action, an emblem of what **Belacqua** cannot be, and, at **Leixlip,** committing **suicide** as Belacqua will not. The *Twilight Herald* reports him as "C. J. Nicholas Nemo" (182); "Nicholas" and the phrase "in amore sapebat" ("[No one] was wise in love") derive from **Burton**'s *Anatomy* ("Preface," 70). He is a verbal construct arising from Burton, leading to the conclusion: "Nicholas Nemo, or Monsieur No-body, shall go free." His fate derives from the *Anatomy* (III.2.2.iv, 541): *Nemo saltat sobrius,* "he is not a sober man that danceth" ("jumps"). Connotations range from Homer's Cyclops to Jules Verne's captain of the *Nautilus* or the mysterious figure in Dickens's *Bleak House;* also the pseudonym of an unknown contemporary who contributed to the *Trinity College Miscellany.* Nemo eludes author and reader: he will not do his dope, will not stand for anything, is not a **liu** (qv); he "simply is not that kind of person" (9). Years later (186), "Mr. Beckett" meets Belacqua and understands, too late, that through Nemo Belacqua came to a little knowledge of himself, and he ("we") to a little knowledge of Belacqua.

Neue Sachlichkeit: a movement in German **art** that reacted against Expressionism by striving for a "new objectivity," as in the paintings of Georg Grosz and Otto Dix or in Brecht's drama. In practice an aggressive realism and politicization of art, suppressed by the Nazis because of its social criticism. The "young thought" of **Belacqua** stocks "a pullulation of Neue Sachlichkeit maggots" (*Dream,* 35). SB commented unsympathetically of Dix's etchings, "a nightmare talent, a Georg Grosz of mutilation" (Knowlson, 221).

New Place: where May **Beckett** moved after her husband's **death;** in Tory Lane, **Foxrock,** a cul-de-sac off the Brighton Road, five minutes from **Cooldrinagh,** which she sold in 1941. "**Text 6**" (124) recalls the **mother** doing her hair with twitching hands; and *From an Abandoned Work,* her death "in a new place soon old" (162). SB began writing *Molloy* (2 May 1947) literally in his mother's room: "I sat down in my mother's little house in **Ireland** and began to write *Molloy*" (Mercier, 161). **Krapp**'s vision occurs on the **Dún Laoghaire** pier amid "great granite rocks the foam flying up in the light of the lighthouse and the wind-gauge spinning like a propeller." SB told James Knowlson (319): "Krapp's vision was on the pier at Dún Laoghaire; mine was in my mother's room. Make that clear once and for all."

New Review: subtitled "An International Notebook for the **Arts** Published from **Paris**" and edited by Samuel Putnam, in which SB published "**Return to the Vestry**" (I.3, August–September–October 1931: 98–99), "**Text**" [poem] (I.4, winter 1931–32: 338–39), and "**Text**" [extract from *Dream*] (II.5, April 1932: 57).

New Writing and Writers: successor to John **Calder**'s *New Writers* series (twelve volumes), *NWW* expanded featured authors from the usual three or four to thirteen in #13 (1976). One was SB, represented by "**For to End Yet Again**" (11–14). "**Heard in the Dark**" appeared in #17 (1980): 11–12, and "**One Evening**" in #20 (1983): 15–16; both originally appeared in the *Journal of Beckett Studies*, then a Calder publication.

New World Writing: a semiannual New York magazine begun (April 1952) in the tradition of Penguin's *New Writing*, associated with the New American Library and subtitled "A New Adventure in Modern Reading." It published the opening of *Molloy* in #5 (April 1954: 316–23), with Niall Montgomery's essay "No Symbols Where None Intended" (324–37), and republished "**Yellow**," with variations, in #10 (November 1956: 108–19).

The New Yorker: an urbane American weekly, generally uncongenial to the avant-garde, which published *Ill Seen Ill Said* (5 October 1981): 48–58 (interspersed with ten cartoons); "**Catastrophe**" (10 January 1983): 27; and "The **Cliff**" (13 May 1996): 84. Two letters by SB appeared under the title "Who Is Godot?" (24 June and 1 July 1996): 136–37. The first is to Michel Polac ([January] 1952), trans. Edith Fournier. Polac was presenting excerpts from *En attendant Godot* on his **Paris** radio show. Declining to be interviewed, SB sent this letter by way of "introduction"; it was read by Roger **Blin**. For details of this "first" performance of *WG*, SB's letter in French, and another translation, see Angela Moorjani, "*En attendant Godot* on Michel Polac's *Entrée des auteurs*." The **French** text (with a variation from

SB's original) appeared in *Le Nouvel observateur* (24 octobre 1996). The second letter was written under similar circumstances to Desmond Smith, who was producing *WG* in Canada. Both assert SB's standard position on interpretation, as to Smith: "I am quite incapable of sitting down and writing out an 'explanation' of the play."

Nidder, Mr.: the lawyer visited by the **Expelled** (54). He plays with a **cylindrical ruler** and hands over a pittance. The word means a base coward or wretch.

Nietzsche, Friedrich (1844–1900): German philosopher greatly influenced by **Schopenhauer** and **Wagner**, before concluding that the latter's vision whitewashed the former's pessimism. Nietzsche suffered mental distress in his last years; his sanity remains problematical. SB shared his interest in the **preSocratics** but took little interest in Nietzsche's thought, the *Wille zur Macht* having no attraction for one to whom the *Ubermensch* was anathema, and to whom the Judeo-Christian tradition was a matter of both fascination and disbelief. SB rejects "the Nietzschean conception that **friendship** must be based on intellectual sympathy," for one is irremediably alone (*Proust*, 66). The post-Cartesian tradition ended for SB with Schopenhauer, rather than continuing with Nietzsche and Heidegger. Yet he knew the basics of Nietzsche, for "**Sanies I**" is "beyond good and evil" (*Jenseits von Gut und Böse*, 1885–86). Hermione **Näutzsche** appears in "**What a Misfortune**," and Hairy **Quin** hardens his heart "to the consistence of an Uebermensch's" (135).

Nietzsche's distinction between Apollonian and Dionysian (*Die Geburt der Tragödie,* 1870–71) constitutes the "Apollo" of Belacqua's mind (*Dream,* 124), but SB's structure is tripartite rather than dual and the other two elements, of **Narcissus** and **limbo,** have no parallels in Nietzsche.

nihil in intellectu: an ancient dictum, "**Nothing** in the mind," which continues, *quod non prius fuerat in sensu,* "that was not first in the senses." See **parrots** and **scholasticism.**

nimis sero: L. "too late" (*Molloy,* 87), echoed by **Moran** (105). This is **Augustine**'s "sero sero te amavi" (*Confessions,* X.27). **Malone** says, "Too soon, too soon" (181); the **Unnamable** (381) repeats: "you came too early, here we'd need latin." M. **Krap** consoles himself (*Eleutheria,* 17): "Nimis sero, imber serotinus" ("too late the summer showers").

Ninette: Moran's wife, mentioned once (173): "Not that I miss Ninette." The name, hinting at the diminutive and childish (*niña*), is not in the manuscript.

Ninus the Assyrian: from Jeremy **Taylor**'s *Holy Dying* (1.i), the tale of Ninus, who had an ocean of riches but "having mingled his wines he threw the rest upon the stones." Once Ninus, a living man, he is now (like **Belacqua**) "nothing but clay" ("Echo's Bones," 7).

Nixon, Mr. and Mrs.: a lady (Tetty) and a gentleman (Goff) present at the outset of *Watt,* who converse with Mr. **Hackett** at the end of the dying day and observe Watt's arrival. "Tetty" was the name Samuel **Johnson** used for his wife, Elizabeth. The Nixons listen as Mr. Hackett recites "To **Nelly,**" then recollect the night that Larry was born. Watt is discussed, in vain. This is the first paradigm of unknowing, and the Nixons depart, leaving Mr. Hackett and the reader quite literally in the dark.

Noailles, Comtesse Anna de (1876-1933): poet whose **Romantic** pantheism earned **Proust**'s approbation but SB's contempt (*Proust,* 82): "Saperlipopette!"

Nobel Prize: in 1969 SB was awarded the Nobel Prize for literature, "for his writing in new forms for the novel and drama in which the destitution of modern man acquires its elevation." The Nobel committee saw behind the pessimism to note that his writing "rises like a *miserere* from all mankind, its muffled minor key sounding liberation to the oppressed and comfort to those in need." SB was in Tunisia, but it was the end to his anonymity. Not wishing the attention, he saw it as a disaster; Suzanne's words after the call confirming an earlier telegram from Jérôme **Lindon**—"despite everything they have given you the Nobel Prize"—were "Quelle catastrophe." Nor did he wish to reject it, so Lindon went to Stockholm to "face the turnips" for him. The Irish ambassador expected to accept it according to protocol, but SB resisted that. The prize was a diploma and a gold medal, plus 375,000 kronor, most of which he gave away, much going to the **Trinity** library. A special issue of *Malone meurt* and *Oh les beaux jours* was published through the Swedish Academy and the Nobel

Foundation (Paris: Éditions Rombaldi, 1971) as part of a series, *Collection des Prix Nobel de Littérature*. It was illustrated by **Arikha**, with a portrait of SB by Michel Cauvet and cover decoration by Picasso; a foreword, "La 'Petite Histoire' de l'attribution du Prix Nobel à Samuel Beckett," by Dr. Kjell Strömberg, former Swedish cultural attaché in Paris; and a study by John Montague, "La Vie et l'oeuvre de Samuel Beckett."

Nohow On: SB's title for his second "**trilogy**" or family triptych. *Company* (1980) features a **father**/son; *Ill Seen Ill Said* (1981) presents a ghostly woman/**mother**; and *Worstward Ho* (1983) portrays a nearly **mystical** union of father and son moving motionlessly. The three appeared independently, then under the collective title (Calder, 1989; Grove, 1996), in which the **aporia** of "how" is **mirrored** by "no" and "**on**." Gontarski's introduction to the **Grove** edition identifies SB's turn in fiction during the 1960s from stories of **motion** to the **closed space** pieces featuring barely perceptible movement (see **character**). The individual entries argue that these works, however "ill seen and ill heard," are not autobiographical, that memories are often indistinguishable from imaginings, and that the attempt to go "On" leads only to the resolution to "Fail better."

Nordau, Max (1849–1923): German eugenicist whose *Degeneration* (1895) was acclaimed but is now despised for its proto-Nazi tendencies. Dedicated to Caesar Lombroso (who identified criminal types by phrenological features), it was quickly translated into English. Dismissed by Praz in *The Romantic Agony* as "discredited by its pseudo-erudition, its grossly positivist point of view, and its insincere moral tone." SB was unimpressed by its lack of tolerance, intimating to **MacGreevy** (1931) that his own was wearing thin. Nordau's moral degeneracy differs from SB's sense of decay yet, curiously, the book was important to him. Nordau gave SB some key words ("**cicisbeo**," "aboulia," "echolalia," "**gigerl**"), used in the early writing (DN, 89–97). The "bloodied **rafflesia** in sombre Sumatra" left its mark on "**Enueg I**" and *The Unnamable*, and odd details persist as images of degeneracy (see **sausage poisoning**). The circle and point in *Watt* (128) is "blue, but blue!" The manuscript reads "almost black," but the change echoes Nordau on Maeterlinck (229): "but blue! blue!"

Inge's *Christian Mysticism* notes Nordau's value for the study of pathological states that counterfeit mystical ones (DN, 91). More important was book III (241–472), "Egomania," an account of the psychology of pathology, including the notion of **coenaesthesis** (qv), that SB documented and developed as a subtle tool. Another crucial idea is the **Not I**, discussed by Nordau at length (257ff) and described by Pilling (DN, 97) as "an extraordinary anticipation" of SB's later play. Nordau's Not I reflects a tripartite theory of ontogeny, owing much to **Haeckel** and **Freud**, in which the three broad phases are the undifferentiated **preconsciousness**, the ego or subjective being, and the Not I or altruistic sense of social entity beyond the self. This is not SB's Not I, the **voice** within or without, but Nordau's survey of the psychological terrain contributed to its mapping. The notion of degeneracy, whatever Nordau's arrogance and pseudoscience, was intriguing to one whose sense of humanity was pessimistic and entropic. Nordau's vision is finally antithetical to that of SB. Toward the end of *Degeneration* (541), having rejected degenerates, aesthetes, reprobates, and neurasthenics, Nordau imagines such shabby beings "in competition with men who rise early, and are not weary before sunset, who have clear heads, solid stomachs and hard muscles: the comparison will excite our laughter." Indeed it does, but for the admirer of SB, it is devoutly or otherwise to be wished, in terms of **Arsene**'s *risus purus* and the guffaw of the Abderite rather than the humorless vision of Nordic regeneration.

The North: a limited edition of 137 numbered copies, with three original etchings by **Arikha**, printed by Will and Sebastian Carter at the Rampant Lions Press, Cambridge, handset on fine paper (London: Enitharmon Press, 1972). The text is the penultimate paragraph of *The Lost Ones,* with variations. "The North" is one of the vanquished, noted for her "greater fixity"; in a featureless cylinder she functions as the Pole Star.

Norwich School: an East Anglian school of landscape painters, founded (1803) around John Crome (1768–1821), referred to as "Crome Yellow esq." (SB to TM, 8 September 1934). The School typically took for its subjects the East Anglian heath and woodland, the River Yare and Norfolk coast. In *Murphy,* the Hindu polyhistor's thesis on the Pathetic Fallacy runs into trouble when he stumbles on the Norwich School (see **Wilenski**).

No's Knife: subtitled *Collected Shorter Prose, 1945–66* (Calder and Boyars, 1967), 3,000 copies, with an advance issue of 200 numbered and signed, bound in calf with gilt edges; reissued 1975. It contains: "The **Expelled**," "The **Calmative**," "The **End**," *Texts for Nothing 1–13, From an Abandoned Work,* "**Enough**," *Imagination Dead Imagine,* and "**Ping**." The latter two appear for the first time in book form. The title derives from an anguished cry in "**Text 13**" (154): "screaming silence of no's knife in yes's wound," the final negation of faint hope and pity in the face of "extinction of this black **nothing**."

Nothing: the **atomist** void or **Schopenhauer**'s contemplation, when the Will is at abeyance; the experience of the *Nichts,* or Nothing, peace beyond reason, calm of spirit, the confidence of serenity. Described by **Belacqua** as going "womb-tomb" (*Dream,* 45). It is *the Nothing than which . . . naught is more real* (*Murphy,* 246), said by SB to be (with the *Ubi nihil* of **Geulincx**) one departure point for his work. This is **Malone**'s region of calm indifference beyond the tumult and commotion of the mind (198); but first his terror (192): "I know those little phrases that seem so innocuous and, once you let them in, pollute the whole of speech. *Nothing is more real than nothing.* They rise up out of the pit and know no rest until they drag you down into its dark. But I am on my guard now."

The sentiment is attributed to **Democritus** but does not appear thus in existing fragments; closest is his opinion that "Naught exists just as much as Aught." **Parmenides** argued for the One by means of such propositions as: "What is nothing cannot be." Democritus asserted that not-Being (the Void) had an equal right with Being to be existent. He distinguished in a curiously **Kant**-like way between "true" and "bastard" knowledge, the latter of the senses (phenomenal) but the former of the atom and the void (real). He asserted that the void (that which Is Not) is as real as the atom that Is; or, in other words, that sensible objects do not truly exist but only the atoms and the void. SB's rendition, with its capitalized "Nothing" set against an antithetical "naught," is a remarkable image of this impossible antinomy. See **Gorgias**.

Schopenhauer accentuated SB's sense of existence as extended suffering, passing into empty nothingness: "No will: no idea, no world" (I.4 #71, 531). In the "**German Letter of 1937**," SB wrote that language seemed increasingly a veil to be torn apart, "to get at the things (or the Nothingness) behind it." He yearned for silence to bore holes in language, until that Nothing seeps through, waiting to hear a whisper of "that final music or that silence that underlies All." That consciousness of Nothing is expressed in *Watt*, particularly the early drafts (Addenda #22), which invoke the Nothingness (sky above, waste below) of **Quin**'s first awareness. This is the primal scene of the novel to be. "Nothing" and "Void" give way, like "**God**," to routine, the nothingness of everyday life, as in "no nothing I said nothing" (*How It Is*, 93), that "almost blank nothing" (104). In

That Time, old tales keep out the void, but "nothing" billows in like a great shroud. In "A **Piece of Monologue**," pictures from the past have been ripped to shreds: nothing there, nothing stirring, nothing to be seen. These lowercase nothings reach their apotheosis, or nadir, in *Texts for Nothing*, particularly in the strangely stirring thirteenth, "the extinction of this black nothing and its impossible shades" (154). This is as close as SB got to the expression of the impossibility to express, when there is nothing to express and no means by which to do so.

"Rien à faire" was SB's comment to **MacGreevy** (31 August 1932) with respect to his **Dublin** situation, and "nothing to be done," from *Dream* (5), resonates through the works. These embrace an ontology of Nothing, with a rhetoric of **aporia** and indifference, which has made them central to the poststructuralist debate, in which "nothing" is less an ontological referent than a linguistic effect. The "subject" implied by an earlier **humanism** fades to a condition of textuality. Perhaps. If in *Waiting for Godot* nothing happens, twice, or in *Endgame* "they" are beginning to mean "something" (the existentialist paradigm having broken down), the condition of **consciousness** resists reduction to a poststructural construct. When **Hamm** says modestly that he has got on with it all the same, not very far but nevertheless better than nothing, **Clov** makes the inevitable response: "Better than nothing! Is it possible?" There is no reply.

Not I: a twenty-minute dramatic monologue written in 1972 (March 20 to April 1), translated as *Pas Moi;* premier at the

"Samuel Beckett Festival," by the Repertory Theater of Lincoln Center, New York (22 November 1972), dir. Alan **Schneider**, with Jessica Tandy (**Mouth**) and Henderson Forsythe (**Auditor**). Hume Cronyn is wrongly listed as Auditor in the **Grove Press** edition. First **London** performance at the Royal Court (16 January 1973), dir. Anthony Page, SB in attendance (production notes, RUL 1227/7/12/11), with Billie **Whitelaw** (Mouth) and Brian Miller (Auditor); reprised (29 January 1975) with Melvyn Hastings (Auditor). The production was videotaped for BBC TV, without Auditor, and broadcast as part of "**Shades**" (17 April 1977). *Pas Moi* opened at the Théâtre d'Orsay (Petite Salle), Paris (8 avril 1975), nominally directed by Jean-Marie Serreau but supervised by SB, who directed it three years later (11 avril 1978) in the Grande Salle. Both featured Madeleine **Renaud**, but SB eliminated Auditor. Published for the British premier (Faber, 1973), and in *First Love and Other Shorts* (Grove, 1974).

Jessica Tandy experienced difficulties in the role. Schneider wrote to SB (3 September 1972): "Because Jessie having great psychological problem with learning lines in *Happy Days* and *Not I* at same time, we have been working with small 'teleprompter,' which has her *Not I* lines printed on roller controlled by stage mgr. She'll be using this until quite sure of lines; this mechanism, of course unseen by audience." Tandy was never quite weaned from the technology and found SB's dictates exasperating. When she complained that the running time of twenty-three minutes rendered the work unintelligible, SB telegraphed back his famous injunction, "I'm not unduly concerned with intelligibility. I want the piece to work on the nerves of the audience." It worked on the nerves of Billie Whitelaw: "*Not I* came through the letter-box. I opened it, read it, and burst into tears, floods of tears. It had a tremendous emotional impact on me. I knew then that it had to go at great speed." "Play" had prepared her for *Not I*, but the experience was nerve-racking. Blindfolded with a hood over her face, she suffered sensory deprivation: "I went to pieces. I felt I had no **body**; I could not relate to where I was; and, going at that speed, I was becoming very dizzy and felt like an astronaut tumbling into space. I swore to **God** I was falling."

Schneider put ten questions to SB (3 September 1972), suggesting his bafflement. SB responded (16 October): "I no more know where she is or why thus than she does. All I know is in the text. 'She' is purely a stage entity, part of a stage image and purveyor of a stage text. The rest is Ibsen." Schneider, Tandy, and audiences were puzzled by the neo**surrealist**, metonymic stage image, a pair of spotlit lips some eight feet above stage level (Mouth), the residua of a body Mouth calls the **machine**, and a silent figure who makes four brief movements "of helpless compassion." The audience experiences twenty-three minutes of linguistic ejaculation. Mouth's speech, SB said, is "purely a buccal phenomenon." She seems possessed by a **voice** that recounts a loveless life for seventy years when inexplicably she blacks out. Conscious and sentient, she thinks she is being punished, but she is not suffering. In addition to the buzzing in her

skull, there is a light, tormenting, as in "Play." She feels no pain, as in life she felt no pleasure. She could perform a scream, but the "she" recognizes that after years of speechlessness words are flowing from her. She recognizes the voice as her own by vowels "she had never heard . . . elsewhere." SB's suggestions for pronunciation (not an Irish accent) were: baby as "babby," any as "anny," either as "eether." She feels she has something to tell but never knows what. In addition to this enigma is the tension between the speaking voice and the "I" of identity or **consciousness**, of unified **character** that Mouth resists despite proddings. To this refusal to acknowledge that she is one with the voice and so might use the first person, Auditor responds with his four gestures. He alone has any apprehension of the text, said SB, the audience sharing Mouth's confusion (Harmon, 283).

"**Not-I**": A. Alvarez suggests (146), "If Beckett had had a coat of arms for his funerary urn, 'Not I' would have served very well as the family motto." "Not-I" is an important theme, notably in the play so entitled. Its etiology is curious. Baker discusses **Schopenhauer**'s "On Human Nature": that the thought of the external world is accompanied by "a constant feeling of *Not I, Not I, Not I*" (174). **Moran** uses the refrain to demarcate himself from others. **Nordau** offers (249–51) a tripartite schema of conscious being: **coenaesthesis** or unconscious organic being; development from this to the conscious "I"; and further growth of the "Not I." In Nordau's account, not incompatible with later psychiatry, the Ego is linked with the **birth** of **consciousness**, but as images of the world advance, the "I" retires behind the "Not-I." When the external world is incorrectly grasped, the "Not-I" will be unsuitably represented in consciousness and the "I" will be preoccupied with the processes taking place in its own organism (256). This for Nordau is a sign of mental disease. SB's turning back to the "I" and assuming the middle ground of self would thus be a sign of degeneracy, whereby "the grown man remains a child all his life" (254).

By turning to the "I," SB went against the grain of psychoanalytic theory. **Molloy**'s quest for integration becomes one of the disintegrated self, unaccommodated man. The **voice** is insistent, yet it must be premised not on the altruistic acceptance of an external world but on the dubious affirmation of the aporetic self, the **Unnamable**'s "I, of whom I know **nothing**" (304), words that initiate that remarkable paragraph, a 110-page "analysis" of the "subject." These issues are further explored in the *Texts for Nothing*, where "I" in the accusative is on trial and its sense of self as both subject and **object** (not I, not me) sustains (if barely) the text (or pretext).

If Nordau is an unexpected source of the "Not I," then its persistence is equally surprising, for voices heard by various protagonists ("Be of good cheer . . . help is on its way") are Pauline in tone. Paul considers scriptural authority, that by which he speaks. Consider 1 Corinthians 15:10: "by the grace of **God** I am what I am . . . yet not I, but the grace of God which was with me." This was echoed in Jakob Böhme's *De signatura rerum,* to those questioning by what authority he spake: "Not I, the I that I am, knows these things, but God knows them in me." For SB, God remained problematical, so the words are less revelation than metaphor. They define a voice not that of the self, whose comings and goings would be a presence (yet mystery) in the works to come.

"**La Notion**": prepublication of the second paragraph, with minor variants, of *Le Dépeupleur*, in *L'Éphémère* 13 (printemps 1970): 20–21.

La Nouvelle revue française: a prestigious Parisian monthly, begun (1909) by André **Gide**, who encouraged a neoclassicism, free from ideology. The *NRF* accepted new writers but unlike *transition* discouraged radical experiment, so had greater respectability. It published part of "**Anna Livie** [*sic*] **Plurabelle**" (#212 [mai 1931]: 633–46). Its integrity in World War II was compromised when it became a collaborationist voice. It was revived (1953) as "La Nouvelle nouvelle revue française," before reclaiming its original title. The restructured *NRF* published "**Mahood**" (#2 [février 1953]: 213–34) and "Samuel Beckett et la peinture" (#54 [juin 1957]: 1125–26). "**Souffle**" appeared in their *Cahiers du Chemin* (15 avril 1971): 21–22.

Nouvelles et textes pour rien: three stories ("L'**Expulsé**," "Le **Calmant**," and "La **Fin**") and thirteen "texts," not named but numbered (**Minuit**, 1955). A second edition (1958) was illustrated by **Arikha**. *Les Nouvelles* date from 1945 and *Textes pour rien* from 1950. Some had appeared before: "**Suite**" (1946), revised as "La Fin" and now presented in full; "L'Expulsé," revised from *Monde nouveau—Paru* (mai 1955); and "**Deux textes pour rien**," I slightly revised, XII unaltered, from *Monde nouveau—Paru* (mai–juin 1955): 144–49.

Nye, Dr.: protagonist of "A **Case in a Thousand**," whose **irrational heart** misfires, so he tries to discover the origins of his melancholy. Chance unites him with Mrs. Bray, his old nanny (see **Bibby**), whose sick **child** (like himself, like **Christ**) he cannot save. Watching water flowing from the shadow beneath the bridge (shades of **psychoanalysis**), he learns of a matter connected to his childhood, "so trivial and intimate that it need not be enlarged on here." It indicates an attachment to her as a **mother** figure, an emotional tie that has inhibited his development. He is one of the sad men, or like the **little girl** who had never really been born. The child, perhaps, continued to live in him, arresting his growth, but it is now laid to rest and he can go, although leaving to carry out a Wassermann test (for syphilis) is an ambiguous validation of his being.

O

O: protagonist of *Film* (1964); "Object" to "E," Eye or camera. For **Schopenhauer**, the object's existence implies a perceiving subject. *Film* details O's efforts to escape being perceived—by the flower seller; **mirror**; window; **cat, dog, parrot**, and goldfish; the eye of **God** looking at him from the wall; photographs. It is in vain, for he finally cannot escape E, self-perception, or **apperception**. As E enters into the angle of perception, the camera at last reveals a frontal vision of O, with the eye patch of the final photograph. As O experiences the "anguish of perceivedness," E's features are finally seen, identical to O, but with an acute *intentness* and a gaze as incessant as **consciousness** itself.

oakum: old tarry rope unpicked by prisoners and used to caulk shipboard seams; the **Smeraldina** considers a husband "oakum in the end" (*Draff*, 184). **Celia** in the cell of her mind teases out the oakum of her history (*Murphy* 149), which the next day is "hackled into tow" (see **Haeckel**). Oakum defines "words ill-heard ill-murmured" (*How It Is*, 134).

Obidil: the mysterious figure behind **Youdi** in *Molloy*, a **Freudian** framing of the **Jungian** drama, a **mirror** reflection of "libido." In one draft (see **Bally**), the Obidil was a Big Landlord, rarely emerging from his mansion but responsible for all the petty regulations in the district.

object: the **Unnamable** ponders, "what is the correct attitude to adopt towards things?" (292). *Molloy* offers one answer: "To restore silence is the role of objects" (13). The relationship of object and subject is a defining element of twentieth-century art, as heretofore recognizable objects are offered through the prism of a creative **consciousness**. *Dream* asserted the need to break from the **desire** to bind "in imperishable relation the object to its representation, the stimulus to the molecular agitation that it sets up" (160). SB in *Proust* defined the relation in terms of a mobile subject before an ideal object, immutable and incorruptible: "The observer infects the observed with his own mobility" (17). Against the "grotesque fallacy of a realistic art" (76), SB posits **Proust**'s "relativism" and "impressionism," his "non-logical statement of phenomena in the order and exactitude of their perception," before they have been distorted into intelligibility (86). Such an infection of object by subject is virtually a summary of **surrealist** aesthetics, which SB contracted as he translated their defining documents for *This Quarter* (1932). Objects are as they appear to consciousness. They are, Husserl argues, "intended," brought into being by consciousness, the exploration of which is SB's pervasive theme. This phenomenology endorses **Berkeley**'s idealism: *esse est percipi*, "to be is to be perceived"; or **Schopenhauer**'s "riddle of the world," the deep **gulf** between the ideal and the real, the object and the subject. Its analogy is man's vain attempt to see God, as through a glass, darkly (Corinthians 13:12).

Knowledge of self is mediated through representation, but the subject that posits that self can itself be known only through representation, and so on, ad infinitum. A paradox of **apperception** displaces the spatial, temporal, and psychological configurations of representation, using the "logical detritus" of paradox, antinomy, and **aporia** as its trope. "**Recent Irish Poetry**" (1934) criticizes the Irish "**antiquarians**" for rupturing of "the lines of communication between subject and object." Unaware of "the acute and increasing anxiety of the relation" (70), they remain provincial, unmodern, mired in prosodoturfey. As the late theater is accessorized by fewer objects, those that remain are disproportionately potent, like the pacing **May**'s tangle of tatters in *Footfalls*, the **rocking chair** in "**Rockaby**," or the Latin Quarter hat of "**Ohio Impromptu**"—the **residua** of an enduring aesthetics. See "**Three Dialogues**" and "**La Falaise**."

Oblomov: Peggy **Guggenheim**'s name for SB in her memoirs *Out of this Century* (1946, 197); from the novel by Ivan Goncharov (1812–91), its protagonist reluctant to rise. George **Reavey** described Geer **van Velde** as "the Oblomov type" (*JOBS* 2 [1977]: 13).

O'Casey, Sean (1880–1964): **Dublin** playwright celebrated for his three **Abbey** plays. See "The **Essential and the Incidental**" and **censorship**.

Occasionalism: from L. *occasio*, "an event"; the theory that matter and mind do not act on each other directly, but that *on occasion* of changes in one **God** intervenes to bring about corresponding changes in the other. **Geulincx** (qv) and **Malebranche** developed the theory to resolve problems arising from the extreme **dualism** of thought and extension, with respect to the interaction of mind and matter in general, **body** and soul in particular, and causation in principle. **Descartes** asserted that all changes of matter in **motion** may be accounted for by extension, and that psychical matters referred to the mind; this did not account for confused ideas (as opposed to those *claire et distincte*), nor the passions and emotions connected with them. Here was an exception, God having arranged in man a coexistence of two substances, so that a disturbance of the "animal spirits" (in the **conarium**) excited in the mind an unclear idea, whether sensation or emotion. This doctrine of *influxus physicus* was so obviously contradictory that post-Cartesians tried to eliminate it.

Geulincx denied any efficient causality by matter, changes but cues on which God effects the real results. Hence the "little miracle" of *How It Is* (35). Malebranche affirmed not only that one substance cannot directly influence the other but that they are so heterogeneous that mind cannot know matter; rather, we "see things in God," matter the occasion rather than the **object** of knowledge. Their reasoning was based on the Cartesian method of doubt, the first knowledge of the self as a thinking thing, and the principle that nothing can be done unless there is knowledge of how it is to be done. Geulincx contended that bodily movement could not be attributed to the self, for (here he departed from the Cartesians) mind or soul is not *cause* of bodily movement. Not only are we unaware of changes in the brain, nerves, and muscles necessary for such movement, but even if we were our knowledge would be *post facto,* based on observation and not on awareness of mental activity. Although we have immediate knowledge of internal activities, we cannot know how movement is initiated in the body, nor how external actions occur (paralysis proving that volition does not lead to movement). Thus, the mind is limited to knowledge of itself and is not master of the body nor cause of movement in it. The implication of this, SB's major debt to Geulincx, is that in the **little world** of the mind alone can one be free.

Geulincx offered two analogies to show that only through God's agency (and His volition) is movement possible. The first is the child, wanting the cradle to rock, and "making" it do so, this possible only because the mother has willed it. The second is the theory of the two clocks, body and mind running independently, with God intervening upon each occasion with a miracle to calibrate them. Many of SB's grotesques are dyspraxic, metaphysically speaking, from a miscalculation in the body-mind synchronization. The Occasionalists deeply affected *Murphy,* which makes Murphy's lack of interest in the partial congruence of his mind and body (*the* great philosophical conundrum of the seventeenth century) even more ironic. The substitution of astrology for the Occasionalist

God is the *non plus ultra* of metaphysical jests. SB's interest in Occasionalism did not so much wane (consider the Occasionalist underpinnings of *Still*) as accommodate itself to complementary theories. Characters in *Three Novels* return "occasionally" to Geulincx, and the **Unnamable** defines his sense of worthlessness in terms of the ethical absolute, *Ubi nihil vales* (qv).

O'Connor, Frank (1903–66): Irish writer, pseudonym of Michael John O'Donovan, born in **Cork** and pupil of Daniel Corkery. He left school at sixteen to join the IRA, fought in the Civil War, and became a teacher of Irish in rural schools and then a librarian in Sligo before being appointed (1935) to the board of the **Abbey Theatre**. SB disliked his writings, noting to **MacGreevy** (15 May 1935) that he "flinched at every 4th page." In revenge, he placed O'Connor in the **asylum** (*Murphy,* 184) and named after him **Louit**'s **dog**.

Octave: the character **Belacqua** assumes, impotent rather than active (*Dream,* 50). **Stendhal**'s first novel, *Armance,* recounts the vicissitudes of Octave of Malivert's love for his cousin, Armance de Zohilof, against (the subtitle) "Quelques scènes d'un salon de **Paris** en 1827"; the comparison with **Valmont** occurs in chapter xxix. Octave conceals his secret, as Stendhal does from the reader, but believing himself dying declares his love; then, unexpectedly cured, he must honor his declaration. He resolves to marry then kill himself, leaving her wealthy and socially advantaged. Like **Byron**, he embarks for Greece, feigning fever until a mixture of opium and digitalis gently delivers him from an agitated life. To **MacGreevy** (8 August 1932) SB recalls a private frisson, when Octave looks at Armance's "curly Moscow coiffure" and makes "un petit mouvement d'admiration passionée" (chapter v). Stendhal to Prosper Mérimée (23 December 1826) outlined the "secret" (impotence), turning futile romance into complex tragedy by "Babilanisme" (see **babylan**). He suggests Armance's complicity, from love or timidity or the satisfaction of receiving "avec la main . . . deux ou trois extases chaque nuit." This answers SB's query to MacGreevy (26 April 1935): "They are married a week before he leaves her to **suicide**. How does he evade the fiasco in that time?"

"Ohio Impromptu": written for a symposium at Ohio State honoring SB's seventy-fifth birthday. Its premier (9 May 1981) was a single performance at the Stadium II Theater, dir. Alan **Schneider,** with David **Warrilow** (Reader) and Rand Mitchell (Listener), before an audience of 400 "crrritics." The production went to the Centre Georges Pompidou, **Paris,** for the Festival d'Automne (14 octobre 1981), which honored SB. Acceptance was delayed. Joseph Papp's plans to stage it at the Public Theater, New York (1982), foundered on Actors' Equity's refusal to let Billie **Whitelaw** perform in the accompanying "**Rockaby**." The Manhattan Theater Club was interested, but the Actors' Equity prohibition held and Warrilow's availability was uncertain. Alan Mandell (of the San Francisco Actors' Workshop) staged the play with "Rockaby" and *Footfalls* at the Los Angeles Actors' Theatre as

"Three by Beckett," with Mandell, Martin Beck, Beatrice Manley, and Bea Silvern (23 February 1982). Schneider's second show was part of "The Beckett Project" at the Goodman Theater, Art Institute of Chicago. Warrilow again played Reader, but Rick Cluchey, of the **San Quentin Drama Workshop** (around whom "The Beckett Project" had been built), replaced Rand Mitchell as Listener (18–30 January 1983). The play was published in *Rockaby and Other Short Pieces* (Grove, 1981) with "Rockaby," *All Strange Away,* and "**A Piece of Monologue**" (also performed at the Ohio Symposium). Schneider's New York debut was at the Harold Clurman Theater, "Ohio Impromptu" presented with "**Catastrophe**" and "**What Where**" in a program of "Samuel Beckett Plays." The triptych ran from 15 June 1983 to 15 April 1984 so successfully that the venue was renamed the Samuel Beckett Theater. The three were published together by Grove in its attempt to revive *Evergreen* (#98 [1984]: 39–51). The manuscripts appeared in foldout facsimile and transcription as an appendix to *Samuel Beckett: Humanistic Perspectives* (Ohio State University Press 1983), generated by the Ohio symposium.

In New York nothing was said about its Ohio origins. Pauline Kael in the *New Yorker* noted the enigmatic title. The origins are hardly enigmatic. S.E. Gontarski suggested to SB that if a new work were available the Ohio State symposium organizers would produce it professionally. SB replied (2 March 1980) that although he was "unfitted" to write at request, he would do his best "to let you have something for your symposium." He invited Gontarski to attend rehearsals of *Endgame* (7–22 May) at the Riverside Studios, London, to discuss a possible production. SB reiterated (20 June 1980) that he would try but was not certain he'd succeed: "I thought I was on to something, but it has petered out. I'll try again." He told Schneider (5 September), "I have not promised anything to Gontarski, except that I wd. do my best. Which in vain so far. I feel drained [and] dry as an old herring bone." He remained pessimistic: "I simply have failed so far to write a piece for you . . . I'll try again," he wrote Gontarski (26 October). He wrote Schneider (20 November 1980): "Shall now try yet again to concoct something for Stan's do in May. Scant hope." Yet Gontarski received the manuscript (1 December 1980). SB wrote Schneider (3 December): "Have offered enclosed playlet to Gontarski for his May days. For you too of course if you deem it worthwhile."

The simple action is dominated by the act of reading. A figure with long white hair and in a long black coat sits at a table in a pool of light and listens (Listener) to the end of a tale read by a ghostly visitor of identical appearance (Reader). On the table sits the "old world Latin Quarter **hat**" of the text. The tale concerns a lost **love** from which the survivor seeks relief in flight to a new abode whose window gives on to an image of parting and reunion, the Seine separating around the artificial Isle of Swans (on which is a replication of the Statue of Liberty). He paces the islet, from where the river divides to where it reunifies, contemplating the "joyous eddies" created by the two arms conflowing. He had been warned by the

spirit of the departed to avoid flight and find comfort instead in her spirit, advice he first ignored. He contemplates undoing his earlier decision and accepting the advice, since he is tormented by insomnia, the white nights of the text. In this torment he is visited by another spirit, emissary of the departed, who offers solace by reading from a text. The narrative echoes (but does not replicate or anticipate) the stage(ed) image. This leads to reconciliation, the image of which is the conflowing Seine. Is this a unity of **body** and spirit, of lover and loved, of themes in the narrative read, of narrative and visual iconography, fiction and theater, or all of these? After the (re)integration, the visitor announces that his presence is no longer necessary, and so the "sad tale," presumably complete, is read one last time, after which Reader and Listener are frozen in "Profounds of mind." Story told, book closed (with a thud), Reader and Listener leave the text and, like the figure in "Catastrophe," raise their partially hidden faces to stare at each other in a perhaps too obvious **mirror** image of reconciliation. Less obvious is the slippage between narration and drama tales, whether the story is that read every night and so repeated in its entirety as the audience has just heard it. Or is this a progressive narrative improved nightly, as an author might work on a story, now completed, and told a final time, "Nothing is left to tell"? Like an author, Listener occasionally calls for the repeat of a phrase, but Reader has his own agency, repeating a phrase unbidden at least once. The play ends (or stops) poised between two possibilities, the circular (read night after night) or linear (now completed), but reconciled by "**neither**."

Oh les beaux jours: SB's translation of *Happy Days*. Previewed at the twenty-second Venice Biennale, Teatro del Ridotto (28 septembre 1963). First **Paris** production at the Odéon-Théâtre (15 novembre 1963), at first in the Petite Salle, dir. Roger **Blin** (SB attending), with Madeleine **Renaud** (**Winnie**) and Jean-Louis Barrault (**Willie**). Published (Minuit, 1963), with 500 "exemplaires" and 4,000 copies. Reprints of 3,000 (1963) and 5,000 (1964) indicate SB's growing **French** readership. Republished in *Avant-scène* 313 (15 juin 1964): 10–19 and sold with a recording (Paris: Disques Adès, 1964), linking passages read by Roger **Blin**; reprinted "suivi de" *Pas moi* (Minuit, 1975).

"**Old earth**": "Fizzle 6" ("Tangier, 29.3.74"); translation of "Foirade IV," "**Vieille terre**." It picks up the sentiment in "**From an Abandoned Work**": "for **love** of this old earth that has carried me so long" (160). About 300 words, in the first person, it tells of one who has outlived his loved ones and anticipates his **death**. Lying beneath a little oak, as if already in the grave, he sees in the sky **faces** of those known. He arises and goes in to examine the sky from a series of windows. The single paragraph trifurcates. It first invokes the "old earth," of which the speaker will soon be part. He addresses it as a loved one, whom he promises to join. This hints at a drama, one suffering for love of a woman unloved, or refused, whom he now desires to be with in death, a tonal metaphor

(compare **Hardy**) for one anticipating his burial. In the second section, an interlude, he contemplates the cockchafers (those the moles don't get) rising from the earth after three years of gestation, **nature** mocking any impulse toward self-**pity**, humanity without metamorphosis from the **larval** state. Finally the **voice** returns to itself, standing at the windows, gazing at the sky, seeing memories and faces suddenly there, "gaze" in each part linking vision and **memory**. Most painful is the fact that some memories were happy. This moves the narrator to apostrophize about loving to the last, but he quickly demurs, the "ah" uncalled for. His injunction to "simply stay still" anticipates "Fizzle 7," *Still*. Echoes of "Old earth" arise elsewhere. **Belacqua** looks astern from the stars to the sea and reflects, "Vieil Océan!" (*Dream*, 137). **Malone** reminisces about lying in bed gazing at the night sky; the image suggests the paintings of Caspar David **Friedrich** (198). **Winnie** comments, "Ah earth you old extinguisher" (*Happy Days*, 28). **Hamm** reaches out his hand and murmurs "Old wall!" (*Endgame*, 104). In *How It Is* the narrator is grateful for the "old cord." Images of lost love, faces in the sky, the clouds, ashes, approaching but never immersing themselves in sentiment, dominate SB's late work.

old man: for **Augustine**, the Old Adam, the inner man unredeemed, as in Romans 6:6: "our old man is **crucified** with him, that the **body** of sin might be destroyed." Used of Murphy's struggle against the part of himself he dislikes, that yearns for **Celia**. **Moran**'s assault on the old man in the forest indicates the emergence of his **Molloy** part, overcoming the Jungian Shadow.

"The Old Tune": a radio play commissioned by the BBC and translated from Robert **Pinget**'s *La Manivelle,* SB turning Pinget's Parisians, Toupin and Pommard, into Dubliners, **Cream** and **Gorman**; in *Watt,* Cream was a lawyer, and here his son is a county judge (Berry is recalled). Broadcast on BBC 3 (23 August 1960), dir. Barbara **Bray** with Jack **MacGowran** (Cream) and Patrick **Magee** (Gorman); rebroadcast September 11. For the unspecified tune played by Gorman on the barrel organ, SB selected "The Bluebells of Scotland," suggested by the bank of bluebells (178). The play was adapted to the stage shortly after publication in *Evergreen Review* 5.17 (March–April 1961): 47–60. First presented off-Broadway at the Royal Playhouse, New York (23 March 1961), dir. Steve Chernak with Sy Travers (Gorman) and Jack Delmonte (Cream). In 1964 it opened at the avant-garde Judson Poets' Theater, New York, dir. Peter Feldman with Jerry Trichter and Sean O'Ceallaigh. Published in *New Writers* 2 (Calder, 1962): 95–127, and in Pinget's *Plays* I (Calder, 1963), 1–17; included in all collected editions of SB's drama, as "An **adaptation**." The British stage version opened (22 November 1964) at the Mercury Theatre, Notting Hill Gate, dir. Alan Simpson, with Godfrey Quigley and Gerry Duggan. *La Manivelle* opened (3 september 1962) at the Théâtre de la Comédie, dir. Georges Peyrou, with Georges Adet and Henry de Livry. The two plays appeared in a bilingual edition (Minuit, 1960), texts on facing pages.

Pinget had asked SB innocently if **Ireland** was the place to perfect his English and was reassured: "on y parle l'anglais du roi." SB suggested he might transpose *La Manivelle* into Ireland, "où les deux vieux parlant l'anglais du roi usent d'expressions anciennes" (Pinget, "Notre Ami," viii). Adapted details include: the "Dee Dyan Button" (De Dion Bouton), a car SB's **father** once owned (O'Brien, 9); Irish names such as "Seymour Bush" (179); and Hibernian phrasing: "wasn't it your father owned" (180), "beyond the beyonds" (181), and "gallous" (184). The play is only loosely compatible with SB's theatrical development. Two elderly Dubliners on a park bench misremembering while a lost **Dublin** is haltingly evoked by an old tune on a barrel organ is hardly theatrical innovation. Calder's reprint in *Beckett Short* #7 (1999) places SB's name alone on the title page; only in the "Postface" is Pinget credited. When Gontarski staged it at the Magic Theatre, San Francisco, an evening of one-acts called "Visions of Beckett" (5 November 1986), SB reminded him (26 September), "Be sure Pinget gets full & visible credit. 'The Old Tune' his vision not mine."

Olympia Press: established 1953 (7, Rue St-Séverin, **Paris** 5) by Maurice Girodias (1919–91), who intended like his father, Jack Kahane, to release books unpublishable in England or America. Kahane's Obelisk Press had published **Joyce**'s *Haveth Childers Everywhere* and works by Lawrence Durrell and Anaïs Nin. He achieved notoriety with Henry Miller's *Tropic of Cancer* (for which Girodias, aged fourteen, designed the cover) and

Frank Harris's *My Life and Loves*. In 1938 Kahane invited SB to translate **Sade**, a commission finally declined. Girodias inherited a tradition of risqué literature, quality and sleaze, and described himself cheerfully as "a second generation Anglo-French pornographer." "Olympia" (retaining Kahane's phallic "O") derived from a painting by Manet, where a nude looks insolently at the viewer. His accent was like that of Barney Rosset, and **Grove** first printed from the Olympia proofs, but Olympia became much tackier. It did not escape the French courts but was treated lightly. Although its obscene books were automatically banned, the six months between publication and prohibition allowed Girodias to sell most of them. While earning an honorable niche in literary history by publishing masterpieces that nobody else would touch, both press and publisher were regarded as scumbags by the very authors they promoted.

Girodias, half Jewish, survived World War II on fake ID by publishing art books (Éditions du Chêne). He turned (1953) to fiction and politics. Insufferable yet magnetic, he began with Miller's *Plexus* and Sade's *Bedroom Philosophers*. He usually printed 5,000 copies, paying a flat fee, which enriched him if one hit the jackpot but created legal entanglements when for copyright reasons he was designated the writer. Among his controversial publications were **Nabokov**'s *Lolita* (1955), Donleavy's *The Ginger Man* (1955), and Burroughs's *Naked Lunch* (1959). Notorious for his "dirty books," which he saw as a duty against the "square world," Girodias was unscrupulous, reluctant to honor royalties, and prone to litigation, especially when authors (SB, Nabokov) fled his stable. Olympia published *Watt* (Collection **Merlin**, 1953), in a dreadful magenta wrapper, and *Molloy* (1955); its Traveller's Companion series featured *Watt* (1958) and *Three Novels* (1959). With liberalized censorship, largely because of *Lolita*, and outmaneuvered by Donleavy (who outbid him for his own company), Girodias and Olympia lost their way, finally offering more porn than provocation. In the 1960s Girodias tried unsuccessfully to establish himself in the United States. He went flamboyantly, dying on radio in a Paris studio while promoting his memoirs.

on: Porter Abbot (*Beckett Writing Beckett,* 33) defines this Victorian trope against three metaphors of progress: the *exhortative,* duty and moral imperative; *linear directionality,* progressive or ascending advance; and *processionality,* the ennobling and arduous process of improvement. The opening word of "**Embers**," it encapsulates "gress," a minimal morpheme of **motion** undone by its **mirror** image, "no" (see *Nohow On*), from the outset of *The Unnamable* ("call that going, call that on") to the end ("I can't go on, I'll go on"). Characters are "getting on," to no avail. Their plight is summed up in the "**Worstward Poems**": "on whence / no sense / but on / to whence / no sense."

onanism: SB's literary interest in "le rhythme par le dactyle," as the **Whoroscope Notebook** puts it (Gk. *daktylos,* "finger"), was stimulated by reading (1931) Pierre **Garnier**'s *Onanisme seul et à deux.* He noted (DN, 60) biblical references to "Onan and Shelah, sons of Judah & Shuah" (see **Tamar**), and Onan's spilling his seed (Genesis 38:9). **Belacqua** is practiced in the rites of that patron of Irish birth control and makes cryptic reference to **Zurbarán**'s Saint-Onan (*Dream,* 72). He adopts (43) "a fraudulent system of Platonic manualisation, chiroplatonism" (Gk. *cheiros,* "hand"), orgasm as the act that unites the **body** with the Idea. Masturbation features in "**Calvary by Night**," Novalis's **blue flower** related to Bloom's "languid floating flower." See **Jalade-Lafonte**. Acts of solitary consolation are infrequent in *Three Novels,* **Moran** deriving little pleasure from it (145), but **Malone** resolving (180) that when the **puppets** have gone he will play with himself. The **Unnamable** arouses a flutter by concentrating on a Clydesdale, a Suffolk stallion (332–33), a passage castrated in a prepublication excerpt.

"**On coming to**": see "**Ceiling.**"

"**One Dead of Night**": a seventeen-line poem (RUL 2901), dated "26.6.77," written in the Park Hotel, Stuttgart; associated with the *mirlitonnades* but different in length and form. The seven uneven sections describe one at dead of night looking up from his book to that other dark and seeing it closed by a hand not his, "for good or for ill—for good or for ill." Compare "**Ohio Impromptu**" and *Stirrings Still.* The poem appeared after SB's **death** in *Poetry Review,* 86.3 (autumn 1996): 9.

"**One Evening**": a prose-poem related to *Ill Seen Ill Said.* Translated from "**Un Soir**" (4 November 1979); published in

JOBS 6 (1980): 7–8, and then *art press* 51 (September 1981): 4; *New Writers and Writing* 20 (Calder, 1983); and *Complete Short Prose* (253–54). A copy with variants and cover note was donated (7 March 1980) to Amnesty International for auction. It tells of one lying on the ground, in a green **greatcoat** with a **hat** near his head, at once on its brim and its crown. The **body** is found by an old woman searching for wild yellow flowers, dressed in the black she assumed when widowed young. The composition forms a *tableau vivant,* a nocturne in **green and yellow.**

"**On My Way**": an "aborted monologue 1983?" (SB's note), untitled, in two holographs (the revised on an envelope) in the **HRHRC** Carleton Lake Collection (1.1). The sole paragraph, heavily repetitious, images the need to write, to play for a song, like a beggar with his bowl, when the truer impulse is not to go **on** but to sit in a quiet corner, head in hands.

"**Ooftish**": a nineteen-line poem published in *transition* 27 (April–May 1938): 33; report in Ruby Cohn's *Comic Gamut* (1962), and in *Collected Poems* (1977). "Auf dem Tisch" in gambling parlance is to front up, to put your money "on the table," contribute to the pot. The poem, an angry critique of Christian piety, offers a relentless catalogue of suffering, cancer, angina, TB, the whole misery: "it all boils down to blood of lamb" (Revelation 7:14). SB's working title was "Whiting," as in the bleaching of linen. A personal **memory**, from 1926, invokes the insoluble problem of suffering. SB accompanied his

father to All Saints Church, Blackrock, to hear Canon Dobbs deliver a sermon about pastoral visits to the sick, the suffering, the dying, and the bereaved. What got him down, the minister said, was pain; all he could say was that the **crucifixion** was only the beginning: "You must contribute to the kitty" (Knowlson, 80). The "kitty" came to represent a senseless accumulation of pain, without moral value. That evil and pain are part of an inscrutable divine plan was an appalling affront to individual suffering. Miss **Counihan** sneers at **Celia**'s pain (*Murphy,* 232) as a contribution to "the post-golgothan kitty." **Moran** is relaxed about the Sabbath, "so long as you go to mass and contribute to the collection" (92); Father **Ambrose** gets his "kit" (100).

"L'Ooneyverse de Samuel Beckett": selections of SB's works broadcast (24 December 1962 to 5 January 1963) on Radio KPFK (L.A.), a program endorsed by SB and coordinated by Raymond Federman (F&F, #504).

opopanax and assafoetida: bad-smelling gum resins used in the perfume industry. From **Burton**'s *Anatomy* (III.2.5.iii), and applied to Una **bboggs** in "**What a Misfortune**" (121).

orange peel: an obscure joke in "**Enueg II,**" *Dream,* and *Murphy,* from Georges **Pelorson**, "J'ai les pieds en marmalade" (Knowlson, 136), shambling and perspiring. SB's favorite marmalade was **Cooper**'s, hence, perhaps, the gait of that individual. SB noted (DN, 15): "Lean on the orange peel / . . . that your soul may arise from its weariness." This combines

Augustine (*Confessions,* 4.xv, 5.i) with "Lemon-sole" (*Dream,* 87; "lemon of lemons," 79) and the jaundiced "lemon of faith" ("A Wet Night," 47).

Ossian: son of Fingal and putative poet of *Fingal: An Ancient Epic Poem in Six Books,* supposedly translated from the Gaelic by James Macpherson (1762). Schiller and **Goethe** joined the chorus of praise; **Johnson** was skeptical but **Boswell** credulous. Asked for his originals, Macpherson fabricated them. "**Fingal**" (qv) critiques **Belacqua**'s doughty deeds. The **French** *Murphy* notes Dr. **Killiecrankie**, conceived in the Shetlands, born in the Orkneys, and weaned in the Hebrides, as an admirer of Ossian and aware of schizoid **voices**. "Ossianic emotions" was **Jung**'s term for wild **romanticism.** "**Recent Irish Poetry**" (70) accuses the **antiquarians** of "delivering with the altitudinous complacency of the Victorian Gael the Ossianic goods."

O'Sullivan, Owen Roe (1748–84): Gaelic poet, called "Owen of the Sweet Mouth" because of his musicality (*Dream,* 217–18; "A Wet Night", 64). [LM]

oubliette: a dungeon with no entrance save at the top, totally dark, into which a prisoner might be precipitated and forgotten (Fr. *oublier,* "to forget"). The **Unnamable** uses the word (369) of the self as constituted by **memory** and destabilized by forgetting.

Our Exagmination Round his Factification for Incamination of Work in Progress: a book of essays initiated by Eugene Jolas, editor of *transition,* to celebrate **Joyce**'s *Work in Progress* [*Finnegans Wake*] (Paris: Shakespeare and Co., 1929). Republished **Faber** (1936), from the same type; then Faber and New Directions (1962), photographic reprint. Joyce's friends made contributions, with "Letters of Protest" from G. V. L. Slingsby (Sylvia Beach) and Vladimir Dixon (JJ: "Dear Mister Germ's Choice"). SB's essay (3–22), his first properly published work, was "**Dante . . . Bruno . Vico . . Joyce**" (qv).

Ovid: Publius Ovidius Naso (43 BC–ca. 17 AD); Augustan poet whose *Amores* and *Ars Amatoria* provoked his banishment to the Black Sea. SB noted from the *Metamorphoses* (DN, 155–60) a long account (Bk. III) of **Narcissus**, the theme for "**Echo's Bones**." Ovid's "multis latebra opportuna" ("many a secret opportunity," III.443), the words of Narcissus to the woods around him, is cited (DN, 158) with the gloss "Bois de Vincennes" and used in *Dream* (13) and *Murphy* (74) of **voyeurism**. Pilling records (DN, 158-59) other bits of the *Metamorphoses* in *Dream:* "Stygian water" (77), from "In Stygia spectabat acqua" ("he inspected himself in Stygian water," III.505); "exiguous" (128), from

"Exigua prohibemur aqua" ("a scanty water prohibits," III.450); and "beating his bosom . . . with marble palms" (227), from "nudaque marmoreis percussit pectora palmis" (III.481). The "city ramparts" that separate lovers ("What a Misfortune," 136) feature in *Molloy* (DN, 159). Ovid's "vellem, quod amamus, abesset," SB's "I would that what I love were absent from me" (III.468, DN 158), initiates **Belacqua**'s "If what I love . . . were only in Australia" ("What a Misfortune," 136) and "**je voudrais que mon amour meure.**" **Arsene** has a "reversed metamorphosis" (*Watt*, 44), as in Daphne's transformation into laurel (I.v.452ff).

oyster kisses: given by the **Smeraldina** to **Belacqua** (*Dream*, 17) and by **Wylie** to Miss **Counihan** (*Murphy*, 117). SB recorded "oyster kisses" from **Burton**'s *Anatomy* (III.2.5.v; DN, 130). **Wilenski** discusses (196–97) a motif in Dutch art (Dirck Hals, Jan Steen), young bloods entertaining their mistresses at tavern "oyster parties," the woman typically sitting on the man's knees and the aphrodisia in evidence. **Moll** offers **Malone** oyster kisses (262) and enquires about the oysters, of which she has hopes.

P

P: protagonist of "**Catastrophe**," who like a speechless **Lucky** suffers mutely but in a final gesture (the "catastrophe," or turning point) asserts his humanity with a defiant, compelling gaze; a late instance of "**Dante**'s rare movements of compassion in Hell" ("Dante and the Lobster," 18). See **Havel**.

painkillers: for SB's creatures, the expedient response to pain (even that of existence or **consciousness**). Belacqua stills "the tempestuous poles of his thorax" by pouring "painkiller on its zones" (*Dream*, 139). **Neary**'s palliation (*Murphy*, 57) derives from **Chamfort**'s Maxim 113, "Vivre est une maladie dont le sommeil nous soulage toutes les seize heures. C'est un palliatif; la mort est le remède." SB's translation jumps to the "remède": **death** "come ease this life disease." "The **Calmative**" denotes a palliative; "The **End**" presents a phial, for relief. **Moran**, receiving the host, feels "like one who, having swallowed a pain-killer, is first astonished, then indignant, on obtaining no relief" (*Molloy*, 102). Moran takes morphine and gives his son sleeping powder in milk. He once had a phial: "Laxatives? Sedatives? I forget. To turn to them for calm and merely obtain a diarrhoea, my, that would be annoying" (255). The **Unnamable** draws freely on painkillers, "without however permitting myself the lethal dose that would have cut short my functions" (320). *Eleutheria* cuts short those "functions." Dr. Piouk purveys poison, a **suicide** machine; producing a tablet, he shouts, "Freedom!" (181). **Hamm**'s cry for painkiller defines codependency; there were lozenges, but **Clov** controlled those. Finally, there are no more painkillers; the little box, once full, is now empty (71), in accordance with the second law of thermodynamics.

In "**Mime du rêveur, A**," the characters inject painkillers. In "**Avant *Fin de partie***" X asks F to fill the syringe quickly: "De morphine. De cocaine. De hachiche. De cyanure." X also asks for a **Bible**. In "**Act Without Words II**," **A** has a chemical breakfast; he takes "a little bottle of pills from his shirt pocket, gets to his feet, broods, swallows a pill" (*CDW*, 209). Both monologues of the "**Petit Odéon fragments**" project painkillers. As Hamm says: "In the morning they brace you up and in the evening they calm you down. Unless it's the other way round" (24). In "**Embers**," Bolton refuses Holloway's plea for an injection, for relief—temporary or permanent. Painkillers, as even SB's creatures recognize, treat the symptoms but not the sources of pain and may be no more efficacious than laxatives. Humanity's recourse is death or "on somehow **on**."

panpygoptosis: duck's disease, crudely, bum too close to the ground, a condition afflicting Miss **Dew** (*Murphy*, 97). Dr. Richard Busby (1606–95), Headmaster of Winchester and a celebrated disciplinarian, laments its lack among males. SB recorded Busby's name (DN, 52) from **Cooper**'s *Flagellation*. The neologism derives from Gk. *pan* and *ptosis*, "all falling," plus *pygos*, "**buttocks**"; thus, "all rump falling." The *Oxford English Dictionary* features this unique reference. Steiss's *Nosonomy* (correctly, *nosology*, a classification of diseases) is invented (Ger. *Steiss*, "buttock"). **Nelly**, the dachshund, is a panpygoptic canine.

"Papini's Dante": SB's review of Giovanni Papini's *Dante vivo*, trans. Eleanor Broadus and Anna Benedetti (London: Lovat Dickson, 1934), in *The Bookman* 87 (Christmas 1934): 14; rpt. in *Disjecta* (80–81). Because Signor Papini is **Florentine**, Catholic, and a poet of sorts, this does not qualify him to understand **Dante** nor justify his reducing the poet "to lovable proportions." SB exposes Papini's confusion in identifying the citizen with the artist and condemns his incomprehension of Dante as literature, whatever the poet's "moral" failings.

Paracelsus: Theophrastus Bombast von Hohenheim (1493–1541), Swiss-born alchemist and physician. His assumed name asserts his superiority over Celsus. **Belacqua** calls **Liebert** "the illegitimate cretin . . . of Mrs Beeton and Philippus Bombastus von Hohenheim" (*Dream*, 48; DN, 101). **Murphy** respects the *Archaeus* (20), or immaterial principle governing **microcosmic** man. The chief archeus was in the stomach, with subordinate archei regulating other organs; simply, Murphy likes eating. See *Mercier and Camier* (109). Murphy's comment about the sublunary excrement turning to civet (138) derives, via **Swift**'s *Tale of*

a Tub (165), from Paracelsus, who tried to make perfume from human excrement; compare the "human civet" in "**What a Misfortune**" (115).

Paris: the crucible in which SB's reading turned to writing. He went to the **École Normale** (1928–30) intending to work on **Jouve** and **Unanimisme**. There Thomas **MacGreevy** introduced him to **Joyce**. SB published his first essays and poems, and a monograph (*Proust*, 1931), and returned a writer. Paris was "a happy land," as "**Sanies II**" (1929) suggests. The narrator, coming from the nearby baths, weaves along the Rue Mouffetard toward an "American Bar" with "red eggs" (pickled eggs? caviar?). Street façades suggest the fairytales of **Perrault** and the Comtesse d'**Aulnoy**. He is a "slouching happy **body**," in his "old stinking suit." Molly Malone's "alive the live-oh" signals a **Dublin** memory, that of being ejected from a brothel (Becky **Cooper**'s) for laughing at its picture of **Dante** and **Beatrice**. Having (like Graves) said "au revoir to all that," he repeats the faux pas. Amid the pimps at **billiards**, he offends the Barfrau and is caned (*fesse à la mode*). Ejected, **expelled** from the American Bar (as from the Dublin brothel), he can but cry for mercy.

SB loved the École's fine old library. He cultivated there his lifelong habit of working closely with reference books and dictionaries, cannibalizing them like Joyce. He read widely in **Descartes**, **Bruno**, **Vico**, and others. He absorbed the **surrealist** atmosphere and literary scene with its private presses and little magazines, theaters and galleries. He worked with the prewar *transition,* which serialized Joyce's *Work in Progress.* For the surrealist number of *This Quarter,* 1932, SB translated poems by André **Breton** and Paul **Éluard.** Edward Titus singled these out for special praise, published "**Dante and the Lobster**" in the following (final) edition, and commissioned a translation of **Rimbaud**'s "**Drunken Boat.**" The Paris years were not without conflict, notably a falling out with Joyce, but SB made a peace offering, an acrostic called "**Home Olga**" (qv). His Éluard translations appeared in *Thorns of Thunder* (Europa Press, 1936). SB "was imbibing a very heady mixture indeed" (Knowlson, 113).

In 1936 SB moved into the Hotel Libéria. After a stabbing incident, he remet Suzanne **Deschevaux-Dumesnil.** In 1937 they moved to a seventh-floor studio at 6 Rue des Favorites, in the 15th arrondissement. They lived there until 1961, when SB moved to his final address, a purpose-built flat in the 14th at 38 Boulevard St. Jacques, near the "Falstaff" and "hygenic anonymity" of the Bar Américain in the Hôtel PLM, where he often met visitors. The 15th arrondissement pervades SB's work. Murphy's mew, in translation, is in the **Impasse de l'Enfant-Jésus,** where Victor **Krap**'s flat is located in *Eleutheria.* A poem is set on the **Rue de Vaugirard.** The **Unnamable**'s world is the Rue Brancion, opposite the former **shambles,** with its statue to the "hippophagist," Émile **Ducroix.**

If particulars of Paris decline in the later work, those that appear are the more salient. "**Text 8**" sees an old man as a surrogate self in La Place de la République, near the Bastille and **Père Lachaise** cemetery. "**Text 11**" leads to the Rue d'Assas (*Guynemer* in French), and a Parisian *pissoir,* a "two-stander" where he remains irremediably alone. In "**Ohio Impromptu**" the dejected lover paces, as SB with Joyce, the Isle of Swans. Paris in 1986 celebrated SB's eightieth birthday, the Centre Pompidou sponsoring a weeklong celebration of his work with lectures, exhibits, discussions, and performances; SB, embarrassed, attended a small reception at La Coupole. Paris had finally claimed him as its own. SB's last resting place, beside his wife Suzanne, was in the Cimetière de Montparnasse, in the heart of the city that had shaped his world as Dublin had, and was now his permanent home.

Paris Review: founded (1953) by Peter Matthiessen and Harold L. Humes, the *Paris Review* preferred original fiction and poetry to "writing about writing." George Plimpton, a Cambridge student, became editor. He solidified its finances by approaching Prince Sadruddin Aga Khan at the 1954 Pamplona running of the bulls; the Aga Khan supported the *Review* until 1975, ensuring its survival. SB published an "Extract from *Molloy,*" the sucking-stones episode, in #5 (spring 1954): 124–35. That issue included poetry by Patrick **Bowles** (75–77), then Paris editor. An excerpt "from *How It Is*" appeared in #28 (summer–fall 1962): 113–16 [Grove, 103–7].

Parmenides (ca. 515 BC): Greek philosopher, native of Elea. **Socrates** in youth met him in age and learned much. SB was introduced to him at the **École**

Normale by Jean **Beaufret**, who was translating *On Nature,* an allegorical poem in hexameters. Parmenides considered the senses illusory and asserted "The One," with **consciousness** and being identical (Windelband, 37). His insistence that we cannot know what *is not* was opposed by **Heraclitus**, for whom all was flux, and by the **atomists** (Leucippus, **Democritus**), for whom **Nothing** (what *is not*) is as real as what *is*. Parmenides asserted **death** as not the end of sensibility but only the cessation of the individual's sensations, a doctrine mocked by Democritus but one that underlies a poignant *mirlitonnade:* "imagine si ceci . . . cessait."

Parmigianino, Girolamo Francesco Maria Mazzuoli (1503–40): Italian painter trained in the tradition of Correggio only to reject Renaissance classicism for mannerist elegance. *La Madonna dal colla longa,* in the Uffizi, and the self-portrait in a convex **mirror**, in the Kunsthistorisches Museum, Vienna, offer graceful elongations of the human figure. Had Parmigianino painted dogs, "he would have painted them like **Nelly**" (*Murphy,* 101).

"Paroles et musique": SB's translation of **"Words and Music."** Subtitled "Pièce radiophonique," it appeared in *Comédie et actes divers* (Minuit, 1966), 61–78.

parrots: emblems of thought and speech, the feathered biped capable of one but not the other. *Whoroscope* invokes Anna Maria **Schurmann**, adversary of **Descartes**, whose formidable intellect was reduced to pieties: "Pale abusive para-

keets in the windows of the mind." This derives from **Mahaffy** (179), Descartes contending that words and signs differentiate us from **machines**, but excluding parrots. **Belacqua**, sick as a parrot, feels them swinging, roosting from his palate (*Dream,* 30); the **Smeraldina** (70) looks like a parrot in a pietà; and **"For Future Reference"** images the snowy floor of the parrot's cage. **Celia** has no more idea of what she has said than a parrot of its profanities (*Murphy,* 39). Such are uttered by **Lousse**'s parrot, "very pretty, all the most approved colours" (*Molloy,* 37), which had belonged to an American sailor ("Fuck the son of a bitch"), and a **French** one ("putain de merde!"). The pink and gray parrot (*Malone Dies,* 218) can utter the **scholastic** dictum *nihil in intellectu,* but without "the celebrated restriction," *quod non prius fuerat in sensu.* **Malone** will not finish his inventory: "a little bird tells me so, the paraclete perhaps, psittaceously named" (249); this echoes Félicité's final vision in **Flaubert**'s "Un Coeur simple." The **Unnamable** recalls the "old sour teachings" he was required to belch: "A parrot, that's what they're up against, a parrot" (335). Finally, in *Film,* a parrot stares at O until its cage is covered with his coat.

Pas: translation of *Footfalls* (Minuit, 1977), 135 numbered copies in an edition of 227; rpt. in *Pas suivi de quatre esquisses* (1978). Premiered at the Théâtre d'Orsay, **Paris**, dir. SB (11 avril 1978), with Delphine Seyrig (**May**) and Madeleine **Renaud** (*voix de maman*).

Pascal, Blaise (1623–62): French **mathematician** and writer. SB admired his

Pensées (1670), as in *Proust* (33). Pascal offered the definition of **God** as all center and no circumference (see **Inge**). Miss **Counihan**'s bust (*Murphy*, 60) owes something to *Pensée* #72, where Pascal remarks of the power of God that our imagination loses itself in that thought, and our little **body** is imperceptible in the *bosom* of the whole. Murphy wrestles with "the demon of gingerbread" (97), as Pascal with the demon of uncertainty inseparable from the spirit of faith (#434). The **Whoroscope Notebook** records Pascal's sense of humanity as a "roseau pensant" (#200); compare the "choux pensant" of "Les **Deux besoins**." The last of **Chamfort**'s *Huit Maximes* derives from the *Pensées* (#143). Pascal defines SB's sense of the **gulf** and **nothing**. The "reasonable chance" of salvation in *Waiting for Godot* reflects the famous *pari*, that it is better to bet on God's existence than against it; the **Unnamable** invokes St. Paul, "to be on the safe side" (301). Jean Anouilh commented that **Estragon** and **Vladimir** resemble Pascal's *Pensées* played by the Fratellini **clowns**; fittingly, Anouilh wrote about *Becket*, and Beckett about **ennui**.

Pas moi: translation of *Not I*, premiered at the Théâtre d'Orsay, **Paris**, 1975, dir. SB, with Madeleine **Renaud** ("Bouche") and Jean-Louis Barrault ("Auditeur"). Published in *Minuit* 12 (janvier, 1975): 2–9; followed by Éditions de Minuit.

Pas suivi de quatre esquisses (Minuit, 1978): first collected French edition of SB's drama, comprising *Pas* (1977) and four sketches: "**Fragment de théâtre I**," "**Fragment de théâtre II**," "**Pochade**

radiophonique," and "**Esquisse radiophonique**."

Pedal, Lady: a grotesque woman of good intent who organizes a trip to the islands at the end of *Malone Dies* but fails to inspire others to join her in joyous song, so (echoing *Watt*, 35: "Thanks . . . And you?") hands out the buns. Her name suggests **onanism**, SB having taken that association (**bicycles**, sewing machines) from **Garnier** (compare the **Frica**).

Peele, George (1556–96): Elizabethan dramatist and lyricist. Educated at Pembroke and Christ Church, he achieved theatrical success, led a dissolute life, and died in distress. Leslie **Daiken**'s notes from **Trinity** reflect his standing: "a master of song-sense, Lyly's earliest follower. Popular pastoralian. Rhyming pentameters. His style must have produced MND. *Poor old pastoral Peele pegged out from pox.*" His song "What Thing Is **Love**," from *The Hunting of Cupid* (1591), shapes **Celia**'s elegy (*Murphy*, 235): "It is a prick, it is a sting / It is a pretty pretty thing."

Pegg, Mother: **Hamm**'s neighbor, but her light and she are extinguished, "naturally." In a draft of *Endgame* she was "Clochard" ("vagabond"); the change accentuates **crucifixion**. She was bonny once, "like a flower of the field"; see Isaiah 40:6: "All flesh is grass, and all the goodliness thereof is as the flower of the field." When she asked for oil for her lamp (Matthew 25:8), Hamm told her to get to hell, so she died "of darkness" (75). Her name supposedly invokes Peggy **Guggenheim**, but the biblical echoes suggest Peggy **Sinclair**.

"Peintres de l'empêchement": SB's critique of Bram and Geer **van Velde**, in *Derrière le mirroir* (juin 1948); rpt. in *Bram van Velde* (1958) and *Disjecta* (133–37). SB translated it for the catalogue of Bram's first New York exhibition (Samuel Kootz Gallery, March 1948). Originally entitled "Le Nouvel objet," it reflects SB's concern with the relation of subject and **object**. This is treated with irony. One can say nothing about such troublesome works, only re-say, but maintaining that restatement can free one from the tiresome obligation of looking at individual paintings. SB identifies three "chemins" an artist might take: work in the old tradition of representation; risk uncertain steps toward the new land ("le pays conquis"); or discover in the absence of rapport a new relation and object ("le nouveau rapport et le nouvel object"). The brothers van Velde exemplify this but the road bifurcates: resistance of the object ("l'empêchement-objet"), that taken by Geer van Velde; and resistance of the eye ("l'empêchement-oeil"), that followed by Bram.

"La Peinture des van Velde, ou: le monde et le pantalon": a critique of the brothers **van Velde**, intelligent and witty. SB's first published work in French, *Cahiers d'art* [Paris] 20–21 (1945–46): 349–56, with six black-and-white reproductions by Bram and nine by Geer; rpt. in *Disjecta* (118–32). It coincided with exhibitions at the Galeries Mai and Maeght respectively by the little-known brothers, unmentioned until halfway through the essay. The subtitle anticipates the joke in *Endgame*, a tailor unable to make a pair of trousers in six months,

whereas **God** made the world in six days: "Mais Monsieur, regardez le monde, et regardez votre pantalon." The argument is rehearsed in "**Three Dialogues**" (qv). SB dramatizes the plight of the amateur, faced by a bewildering display of postures, advice, and verbiage; to such is the "propos" dedicated, its plea being to trust the eye, not the words. Only then does he introduce the brothers van Velde, whose vision is similar but whose expression differs each from the other (like trousers, singular yet twain). He affirms the need for **solitude**, even if the cost is the audience's silence. SB ends with cynical observations on what it means to be human; many stupid things will be said about the brothers van Velde, and he is honored to open the series.

Pellico, Silvio (1788–1854): Italian dramatist who opposed Austrian despotism, for which he was sentenced to **death** and his works suppressed. His prison sufferings are described in *Le mie prigioni* (1832), which **Belacqua** may intend in "**Dante and the Lobster**" (16) when he dismisses Pellico, with **Manzoni** and **Carducci**, as old maids and suffragettes.

Pelorson, Georges (b. 1909): translator, poet, and essayist, who became Georges Belmont. At the **École Normale** he was nominally SB's sole pupil; years later ("Remembering Sam," 111) he described the first meeting, turning up as agreed to find SB asleep. They met next day for lunch, SB apologetically insisting that mornings were impossible. Pelorson was part of the model for **Liebert** in *Dream*, where his enthusiasms (**Wagner**, surrealism) are mocked, not unkindly. He signed the manifesto, "**Poetry is vertical.**" Some of his expressions, such as "J'ai les pieds en **marmalade**" or "Cardiac calculus," entered SB's work (Knowlson, 136). Pelorson later lectured in **French** at **Trinity**, the two often sharing a bottle of Jameson's and talking into the night. Pelorson initiated the MLS production of "Le **Kid**," in which SB participated. His enthusiasm for Marcelle Grahame (O'Connell), an Irish widow whom he married, is translated into Ginette Mac Something, the hem of whose **vidual** virginity **Chas** feels unworthy to lift, let alone hoist thigh-high (*Dream*, 143). Pelorson's departure was "a very real dereliction," as SB was left to his "indolence and mooching" (SB to TM, 9 October 1931). In **Paris** the acquaintanceship was renewed, as indicated by an extensive correspondence from 1951, now at the **HRHRC**; the intimacy was lost, however, Belmont's right-wing politics and his editing the glossy *Jours de France* (European royalty and the jet set) alienating a sympathy that (from *Dream*) had always been qualified. For Belmont's recollections, see his *Souvenirs d'outre-monde* (Paris: Calmann-Lévy, 2001).

pensum: the "task" of living, as defined by **Schopenhauer**'s Doctrine of Suffering (*Parerga und Parapomena* II.xii #157): "Das Leben ist ein Pensum zum Arbeiten: in diesem Sinne is *defunctus* ein schöner Ausdruck" ("life is a task to be worked off: in this sense *defunctus* is a fine expression"). "Pensum" and "defunctus" derive from public-school parlance, a punishment and the completion thereof—fagging, detentions, and small senseless demands that intrude upon **time.** *Proust* ends thus: "the invisible reality that damns the life of the **body** on earth as a pensum and reveals the meaning of the word: 'defunctus.'" **Molloy** laments (32): "all you do is stammer out your lesson, the remnants of a pensum one day got by heart and long forgotten." The **Unnamable** repeats his cry (310–11), defining his relationship to the Master as the need for punishment, fixation, and order. "**Text 7**" (129) invokes a "Terminus," the third-class waiting room of the **Slow and Easy** and the pensum of waiting among the dead, for a train that will never come. Doherty comments (43), "Man needs the fiction of punishment for a crime uncommitted in order that he bear up under the burden of an emptiness and isolation which are unbearable but must be borne." Inseparable from this, as the Unnamable appreciates (311), is the "Strange task, which consists in speaking of oneself"—the obligation to express.

Père Lachaise: site of a Jesuit settlement founded in **Paris** (1626), enlarged by Louis XIV's confessor, Père Lachaise, and set out as a cemetery after the French Revolution (1804). **Liebert** meditates at the tomb of Alfred de **Musset** (*Dream*, 49); in "**Text 8**" (134) the decrepit narrator is aware of its adjacency.

Péron, Alfred (1904–45): graduate of the **École Normale**, where he shared a study with **Sartre**. Péron came to **Trinity** as *lecteur*, 1926–28, reciprocal of SB's later position in **Paris**. Of Jewish descent, dark and slender, witty and intelligent, he was popular within the Modern

Languages Society. Two years older than SB, he became a close friend, often visiting **Cooldrinagh**. Donating his plus fours to **Liebert**, he enters *Dream* as **Belacqua**'s "dear friend, Jean du **Chas**" (140), who meets him at Cobh and tells him of the "tenebrous Ginette" (144) whom he adores in **Racinian** vein. In 1928 Phillippe Soupault asked them to help translate *Work in Progress* (SB probably suggested Péron). A draft was finished by August 1930 and reached the proofs before complications arose (see "**Anna Livia Plurabelle**"), including spelling his name in the Présentation as "Perron." SB described Péron's future wife, Maya Lézine ("Mania"), to **MacGreevy** as Alfy's "subtle Russian sweet" (born in Russia, she had lived in France since childhood). The **friendship** continued in 1938 when SB moved to Paris, Péron teaching at the Lycée Buffon but finding time for Tuesday lunches, followed by tennis, drinks, and translation of the French *Murphy*. Péron translated "**Alba**," also published with his name misspelled.

When **war** broke out Péron went to Brittany as liaison officer to a British ambulance unit, but with the Occupation he was demobilized and resumed teaching. He recruited SB into the Resistance (1 September 1941) after the arrest of Paul Léon. Knowlson offers an enthralling account (278–90): how Jeannine **Picabia** set up the cell called "**Gloria**"; Péron's nickname "Dick" ("Moby") and his role as carrier; SB's typing and translation of scrappy reports to be microfilmed; betrayal by the treacherous priest, Robert **Alesch**; Péron's arrest (16 August 1942); Mania's telegram warning SB and Suzanne to escape: "Alfred arrêté par

Gestapo. Prière faire nécessaire pour corriger l'erreur"; and their difficult days on the run. Péron was taken (February 1943) to Mauthausen where, thanks to the extraordinary care of others, he survived until liberation. Weakened beyond redress, he died on 1 May 1945 and was buried in the cemetery of Samedan near St. Moritz.

SB's concern was for Mania and her twin sons, Aléxis and Michel, with whom he remained in close touch. He engaged Mania in his work, valuing her colloquial French and including her translations in the postwar *Transition*. The French *Murphy* is dedicated to Péron, but the lasting tribute is *Waiting for Godot,* with its images of brutality and inhumanity that invoke if only by absence the **pity** arising from suffering—in the words of the **Nobel Prize** citation, the perception of degradation that is not possible if human values are denied. When pressed to publish after the award SB offered "**Premier Amour**" to *Minuit;* written in late 1946, the autograph includes SB's translation into **French** of two tributes to Péron from the *Irish Times* (Lake, *No Symbols,* #359).

Peron "Godot": the Carlton Lake Collection at the **HRHRC** includes a file labeled "SB to Mania Péron" 1–40, consisting mostly of postcards and letters (1954 to 1983). Described as "Rémy Alfred **Péron** material," letters to Mania Péron (1950 to 1989), the file was acquired September 1999 from Bertram Rota, Ltd., **London**. Placed in file #19 with a card dated 12.6.70 and written to Mania is a one-page typescript that offers a curious commentary on *Waiting for*

Godot. The card discusses "quelques malentendus" that have arisen with "Edith" (Fournier), but it has little to do with the typescript. There is no assurance that the commentary is by SB, as tone and style seem totally at odds with anything that SB might have written; indeed, it would be a unique and unlikely testament. The typescript identifies a **dualism**, an almost **gnostic** element in the play, man as **body** and spirit, an invisible **God** and the **boy** (his messenger) as hope, but hope that is always falsified. Other aspects are discussed in similar terms, including the mind's perception of the "miracle" of the leaves. A paraphrase would render the piece nonsensical. Lois Overbeck has resolved the mystery. The onion-skin paper and the typeface confirm SB's typewriter, but Edith Fournier often borrowed it, and the note is almost certainly by her.

Perrault, Charles (1628–1703): French lawyer and author of fairy tales such as "Sleeping Beauty," "Cinderella," "Puss-in-Boots," and "Tom Thumb." **Rudmose-Brown** called him "father of all fairy stories" (*French Short Stories,* xiii). SB recorded details from his *Contes de ma Mère l'Oie* (DN, 160–62) and made modest use of them in *Dream,* though he preferred the tales of the comtesse d'**Aulnoy**. "Tire la chevilette, la bobinette cherra" ("Pull the bolt, the latch will come off"), said by the Wolf to Red Ridinghood, is echoed by the **Alba** unlatching the gate (*Dream,* 237). "How many pebbles in Tom Thumb's pockets?" (DN 162; *Dream,* 215), anticipates **Molloy**'s sucking stones.

Perugino, Pietro (ca. 1450–1523): Umbrian painter who worked in **Florence**. His best-known works are the Uffizi *Assumption* and the Accademia *Pietà,* which SB saw in 1927. SB's "**Assumption**" ends in a pietà. In "**Love and Lethe**" (87) the reader is directed to the Magdalene of the Perugino *Pietà* in the National Gallery, **Dublin**, for an image of Ruby Tough, but is reminded that Ruby has black hair rather than ginger. This picture of the Magdalene sitting beside Mary, **Christ**'s legs upon her knees, is reproduced by O'Brien (141). SB went several times when it was acquired in 1931. He complained to **MacGreevy** (20 December 1931) about the shining glass but admired the women and the "lovely cheery Xist full of sperm."

"Petit Odéon fragments": an untitled manuscript (RUL 1227/7/16/3), 1967–68, with deletions and corrections, of an unpublished play in **French**, consisting of two monologues. A female **voice** recalls a conversation with a medical specialist, asking about the unpredictable effects of the self-administration of drugs; she reverts to the present and contemplates two liquids to be injected, the red and the green. The second monologue is similar, but involves more calculations about capacities and dosages, the liquids referred to as **A** and **B**, with reflections on their "effets contraires" (see **painkiller**). SB intended the play for Madeleine **Renaud**, then abandoned it.

"Petit sot": "Little fool"; a twenty-four-line poem, untitled, written in French about 1938. The manuscript and typescript were given to Avigdor **Arikha**, and a facsimile is included in Anne **Atik**'s *How It Was* (10). Despite the writing being SB's, and signed by him to Arikha, Jérôme **Lindon** has insisted that it is by Suzanne. Twenty more short poems, as yet unpublished, form a cycle on "Le Petit sot," re-creating the games and fantasies of a little **boy**, simple in vocabulary, syntax, and ideas (Knowlson, 270). They were shown only to a few friends and found among the papers of Bram **van Velde**, with Bram's comment "Poèmes à Beckett" (not "de"), so that, Knowlson concedes (676), some authorial doubt exists, despite their clear relation to the title poem.

Petrarch: Francesco Petrarca (1304–74); **Florentine** poet and humanist, who in the Church of St. Clara, Avignon, first saw Laura (6 April 1327), a married woman whom he celebrated thereafter. SB studied his *Canzoniere* at **Trinity**. Sonnet XII's "I benedico il loco e'il tempo e l'ora" ("And I bless the place and **time** and hour/Laura") is deployed in *Dream* (191), as the **Alba** surrenders to the place and the hour. Lying in the ditch, listening to the frogs, **Watt** wonders "if it was the time and the place and the loved one already" (136).

Petrie, Dr.: invoked in "**Fingal**" (29), as **Belacqua** foolishly asks if the tower is old when patently it is not. O'Brien (233) suggests George Petrie, archaeologist, musician and artist, Fellow of the Royal College of Surgeons, and an authority on **Ireland**'s round towers.

Petrouchka: central figure of a ballet by Igor Stravinsky (1882–1971), set in a fairground of old St. Petersburg during carnival. It premiered in **Paris** (13 January 1911); SB saw two versions of the ballet in **London** (Knowlson, 185). It grew ingeniously from a composition where the piano represents a mischievous **puppet** playing tricks to make the orchestra retaliate. SB likens **Murphy**'s **irrational heart** (3) to Petrouchka in his box.

Phidias and Scopas: classical Greek sculptors; used in *Murphy* (238) as paradigms of fatigue. Phidias represents restraint and repose, Scopas violence and emotionalism; **Neary** contrasts them as Sleep and Insomnia. Phidias (ca. 490–30 BC) created the statue of Athena, a thirty-nine-foot work of ivory and gold commissioned by Pericles for the Parthenon. He may have carved the Elgin marbles. Admired for his taste and learning, he was accused of arrogance and banished from Athens to Elis, where his statue of Zeus, sixty feet high, was a wonder of the world. Scopas, an architect and sculptor of Ephesus (ca. 430 BC), made the mausoleum that Artemisia raised to her husband; this too was reckoned a wonder. His statue of Aphrodite was much admired by the Romans.

Philautia: from Gk. *philo,* "loving," and *auto,* "self"; hence, "self-**love**"; as in **Burton**'s *Anatomy* (I.2.3.xiv, 193). SB noted this (DN, 111) and used it in *Murphy* (216). The word occurs in **Spinoza**'s *Ethica* (III #55; *Brunschvicg,* 209); and in the *Ethica* of **Geulincx**, in opposition to "Ratio" or reason: *Philautia* is the greatest cause of error, because "Amor" is an amphibology ("Annotata," 154). This wrongly read becomes *Amor Concupiscentiae,* concupiscent love that violates the ethical axiom of *Humilitas,* and thus betrays the opening statement and central proposition of the *Ethica: Virtus est rectae Rationis Amor unicus* ("Virtue is uniquely the Love of right Reason").

physics: defined by its **scholastic** opposition to metaphysics (see **Geulincx**) and primarily concerned with laws of **motion** within a classical Newtonian universe, but also with respect to such contemporary advances as splitting the atom, quantum mechanics, relativity, and uncertainty. SB's characters often assume that their universe is a closed system, where laws of **reason** and harmony pertain and **equilibrium** holds sway, a notion found in **Epicurus,** who asserted that the sum of things is forever the same. SB noted from Minchin's *Students' Dynamics* the movement of **billiard** balls as a function of their speed. The stability of this universe is challenged on two complementary fronts: the Greek **atomists** with their sense of Plenum, the Void, and a universe ever changing; and the quantum world of subatomic particles where gravity no longer prevails. **Belacqua** experiences the "dark **gulf**" (*Dream,* 120), akin to the **incoherent continuum** explored by the greatest artists, **Beethoven, Hölderlin, Rembrandt,** and **Rimbaud** (138). The third zone of **Murphy's mind** is likewise "a tumult of non-Newtonian motion" (*Murphy,* 113).

This is, specifically, the "commotion" in the universe of quantum mechanics, where classical laws, as defined by Newton and regulating the **machine** of the big world, do not apply. Entities such as electrons exist as two things simultaneously, matter or energy; electromagnetic radiation behaves as waves and particles ("quanta"). Such contemporary dynamics are applicable to the Occasionalist definition of the **little world** of the mind, where one might be free. **Murphy**'s sensation of being a missile without provenance or target is weighted with the full wantum of quanta; and **Molloy** feels, as identity fades, the "namelessness" of "waves and particles" (31), nameless things, thingless names. Earlier, **A** and **C** acted like particles in an undulating landscape, "which caused the road to be in waves" (9); their meeting is the kind of random coincidence that binds other pairs of characters in the novel, encounters emitting destructive energy. SB recorded in the **Whoroscope Notebook** details from **Poincaré**'s *La Valeur de la science* about the paradoxical similarities of atoms and stars. This image first Rutherford then Bohr had invoked to describe the brave new subatomic world. In *L'Innommable,* forces move around the fixed central figure in a way that suggests both planetary and atomic systems, the immensity of space, and the mirroring of the micro and macro worlds. The activity is a splitting of the atom of self, the Cartesian "I" isolated by this point in the **trilogy**: no longer an indivisible entity, strange new particles within, yet no ultimate understanding reached and the **voice** still a mystery. One "resolution" to that mystery, the voice within yet equally without (the **Not I**), might be in terms of Bohr's complementarity and/or Heisenberg's Uncertainty Principle: it can be heard but not located, or vice versa, but not heard and located simultaneously. The antinomy of the "I" and the "Not I" remains absolute.

Endgame expresses a postnuclear winter, a universe running down to an unimaginable zero in accordance with the laws of thermodynamics. **Clov** notes (13), "Something is taking its course"; the **chess** analogy intimates attrition. The alarm clock suggests Paley's watchmaker, **time** running out. Clov is "Putting things in order," exemplifying the paradox of local increases in entropic order in a universal process of homeostasis: "I love order. It's my dream. A world where all would be silent." Similar sentiments underlie *Waiting for Godot,* with the deterioration between the two acts; *How It Is,* with the certainty that one day movement will no longer be possible; and *Happy Days,* where **Winnie**'s physical predicament, her humdrum activities, and her emptying her handbag suggest the entropic theme, a universe doomed to final extinction.

Picabia, Jeannine: Gabrielle Cécile Martinez Picabia, called Jeannine, daughter of painter Francis Picabia and Gabrielle Buffet-Picabia. SB met her before World War II and probably introduced her to Alfred **Péron**. As a driver for a medical group delivering supplies to French POWs, she could observe German activities. In Cannes, she walked on impulse into the American consulate and told them what she knew; she then returned to **Paris** to collect information for the British (Bair, 320). She contacted Péron, who recruited SB into the "**Gloria SMH**" *réseau,* or cell, which Jeannine ran. Her mother, a respectable sixty-year-old unlikely to attract suspicion, acted as courier, taking microfilms into the unoccupied zone. SB at first acted as a *boîte aux lettres,* then compiled information; Bair wrongly says (311) that he did microphotography. Jeannine avoided capture when the cell was betrayed by Abbé Robert **Alesch**. She was debriefed in **London** in 1943, where SB met her by chance in 1945. For his Resistance work SB was awarded the Croix de Guerre and the Médaille de la Reconnaissance Française, the latter at the recommendation of Jeannine, who wrote the citation (Bair, 320).

Piccarda: in *Paradiso* III, **Dante** meets Piccarda dei Donati, who chose virginity but was forced by her brother Corso to marry the brutal Rossellino della Tosa. She tells Dante that **love** quietens the will and reconciles us to **God**. Mentioned in "**Dante and the Lobster**" (9) and *Dream* (130). See **Constance**.

"A Piece of Monologue": originally titled "Gone," this fifty-minute monologue was begun 2 October 1977 (RUL 2068) and completed 28 April 1979. The minimal stage directions and final title were added at the last. Published in *The Kenyon Review* 1.3 (1979): 1–4, then by **Grove** in *Rockaby and Other Short Pieces* (1981), 67–79, and **Faber** in *Three Occasional Pieces* (1982), 11–15. "Adapté" as *Solo* (qv). The "occasion" was a solicitation (1979) by David **Warrilow** for a play about **death**. Warrilow premiered it in the Annex at La Mama, ETC, New York, 14–31 December 1979; it was so associated with him that performance by another seemed unimaginable. It accompanied the "**Ohio Impromptu**" premiere (9 May 1981). Martin Esslin was also instrumental, since his request for something to revive *The Kenyon Review* had provoked SB to "complete" a trunk manuscript.

A draft begins, "My **birth** was my death," a variation on *First Love*, "What finished me was the birth." Like *Company* and *Film*, this is a **memory** play, as it persists through the creative imagination, featuring "Funerals of . . . he all but said of loved ones" (*CDW*, 425). The white-haired narrator staring front, in white nightgown and socks, recounts the process of dying, which began at birth, two billion seconds earlier. His story is remarkably like that witnessed in performance, a figure in white in dim, unspecified light staring before a window then a wall now blank that formerly held family photographs, since destroyed. The interest rests not in parallels between sight and sound, stage and narrative, but in the slippage between. As the narrator discusses (re-creates) lighting an oil lamp with matches, the audience looks to the lighted (electric) globe stage left as if it were the narrated light. But the narrator is not necessarily the figure in the narrative. To confuse the stage image, the present theatrical moment, with the narrative or fragments of memory is to miss the point. That is, if the narrated figure is the **mirror** image of the narrator, the mirror is cracked, even as the nightly ritual (looking out the western window at sunset, lighting the lamp, examining the photographs on the eastern wall) continues after the photographs are destroyed. The altered perspective of what Gontarski has called "playing against

text" is reinforced in the narrative by treating the funeral scene like a film ("Umbrellas round a grave. Seen from above"), then by foregrounding its theatricality: "Thirty seconds . . . Then fade" (428); or "White foot of pallet edge of frame stage left" (429). The monologue is, as stated, a "piece," a fragment, yet while it remains incomplete something continues, the narrator its testimony. The play belies the closure of "Gone": "Ripped from the wall and torn to shreds" over the years, images of "he all but said loved ones" yet persist, if only in the **consciousness** and in the telling.

Pike Theatre: a short-lived experimental theater in **Dublin**, founded by Alan Simpson and Carolyn Swift, which gave the premiere of Brendan Behan's *The Quare Fellow* (19 November 1954), then the Irish premiere of *Waiting for Godot* (28 October 1955). **London** producers tried to stop the production; Simpson argued, with SB's support, that since **Ireland** had in 1948 left the Commonwealth it was not bound by its rules. In deference to SB, Simpson waited until after the first London run but, as Anthony Roche notes, the almost simultaneous presentation of *Godot* in London and Dublin "stands as an important event in the decolonization of Irish theatre" (46). The Pike production was based on a typescript sent to Simpson before final corrections and revisions for **Grove Press** were made (TCD, 10731). The three English-language premieres of *Godot,* then, each used a different text. The Pike production ran for 100-plus performances over a year, after which it transferred to the **Gate Theatre**, played at the Gas Company Theatre in **Dún Laoghaire**, and went on tour. An avant-garde play in **Paris** and London was accepted as popular theater in Ireland, where less cultural distance separated audience and characters. The Pike survived less well: in 1957, during a production of Tennessee Williams's *The Rose Tattoo*, dropping a condom onstage led to the arrest of Alan Simpson, and public ostracism of his theater.

Pim: in *How It Is*, the "other" (or self-projection), companion to the nameless narrator in the mud. Communication is relayed by "basic stimuli" (69). The narrative is divided into three parts: "before Pim with Pim after Pim." See **Bom**.

Pim, Mrs. Penny-a-hoist: an old "put" (Fr. *putain*, "whore") (*Watt*, 240-41), with winter in her hair but "plenty of spring in her do you follow me"; the manuscript (NB6, 103) reads "mattress." The "something" Mr. Nolan murmurs (242) refers to this jest.

"Ping": translation of *Bing* (1966) into English, the plosive now voiceless (SB tried "Pfft" but quickly revised to the equally onomatopoeic "Ping"). Published in *Encounter* [London] 28.2 (February 1967): 25–26, and *Harper's Bazaar* [New York] 3067 (June 1967): 120, 140, then in *No's Knife* (July 1967). Typescripts and proofs are held by Washington University and the **BIF**, the two exchanging photocopies. Lacking the intensity of the original compositional process (see *Bing*), the translation was arduous, as witness the many revisions and division of the text into a tablature to allow scrutiny of its eighty-six parts. Meters are changed to yards, indicative of a shift of sensibility. The work reacts against *The Lost Ones*, olympian hauteur abandoned for the obsessive repetition of limited sounds.

David Lodge's analysis of this cryptic tale reflects the kind of crisis that SB's late prose poses for the traditional writer: "I suggest that 'Ping' is the rendering of the **consciousness** of a person confined in a small, bare, white room, a person who is evidently under extreme duress, and probably at the last gasp of life." Lodge suggests that "Ping" records "the struggles of an expiring consciousness to find some meaning in a situation which offers no purchase to the mind or to sensation. The consciousness makes repeated, feeble efforts to assert the possibility of colour, movement, sound, **memory**, another person's presence, only to fall back hopelessly into the recognition of colourlessness, paralysis, silence, oblivion, **solitude**." He struggles to situate "Ping" within a realistic frame, deferring narratological questions: Who is the figure to whom all is "known"? By whom is the image "never seen"? To whom is it repeatedly "invisible"? Certainly not the reader to whom these white-on-white images are strikingly visible, for s/he, like the narrator, sees them clearly if fleetingly in the mind's eye through the imaginative construct called fiction. The figure, the narrator hints, is "perhaps not alone," and so others possibly exist, whose perceptions also fail. Although the story lines of the late tales are simple, narratologically they are complex. The reader focuses not only on a figure in a **closed space**, but on another figure and a narrator imagining them. There is not just the psychologically complex image of a self imagining itself, but a self imagining itself imagining itself, often suspecting that it, too, is being imagined.

Pinget, Robert (b. 1919): Swiss-born writer who studied at the École des Beaux Arts, **Paris**, then taught **French** in **London**. After World War II he rejected painting for literature, publishing his first collection of stories, *Entre Fontoine et Agapa* (Laffont, 1951), in the manner of Henri Michaux. He published *Mahu ou le Matériau* (1953), which SB admired, and *Le Renard et la Boussole* (1954), both with Gallimard. When Robbe-Grillet, who had reviewed *Mahu* positively, introduced Pinget to Jérôme **Lindon**, Pinget met SB and befriended him and Suzanne. Pinget said of his experimental prose that the "New Novel" was "a reaction against the traditional novel, which no longer corresponds to the modern writer's way of looking at life or of expressing himself. It is a desire to record the unverifiable, which was born forty years ago with **surrealism** and the phenomenon of automatic writing."

Pinget's drama derives from his fiction. *The Dead Letter* (1959) from *Le Fiston* was produced at the Théâtre Récamier. From *Clope au dossier* Pinget extracted *Clope* (1961) and *La Manivelle* (1960), which opened (3 septembre 1962) at the Théâtre de la Comédie, dir. Georges Peyrou, with Georges Adet—**Nagg** in the Royal Court *Fin de partie*—and Henry de Livry. Pinget has been translated by Barbara Wright, Barbara **Bray**, Donald Watson, and SB (see "The **Old Tune**"). He had earlier worked with SB on *Tous ceux qui*

tombent (1957). The American publication of *The Inquisitory* (Grove, 1966), trans. Donald Watson, boasts SB's blurb: "One of the most important novels of the last ten years." Pinget offered a moving tribute, "Notre ami," in the SB memorial *Revue d'Esthétique* (Paris: Éditions Jean-Michel Place, 1990). This was a reissue of the 1986 volume with new prefaces by Pinget and **Arikha**; hence the odd pagination of Pinget's homage (vii–viii and 1).

Pinget sometimes felt constricted by SB. According to Anne **Atik** (52), he "fought against Beckett's style. He left Paris after this rebellion, saying about Sam 'il est vieux.'" She and Arikha assumed it was to find his own **voice**. SB was nonplussed, because Pinget had been so close. Emerging from SB's shadow was not helped by the inclusion of "The Old Tune," in *CDW* (1986), then in John **Calder**'s *Beckett Shorts #7* (1999), with no mention of him on the title page. Only on the "Postface" to the play, which Calder calls "very much a part of the Beckett theatrical canon" (24), is Pinget even acknowledged.

pity: a comment in **Mahaffy**'s study of **Descartes**, which SB knew well, concerns the Cartesian attitude toward vivisection: "They kicked about their **dogs** and dissected their **cats** without mercy, laughing at any compassion for them, and calling their screams the noise of breaking machinery" (181). Intellectually SB might have agreed, extending the image of the **machine** to the human **body**; emotionally he could not. **Windelband** (620) analyses **Schopenhauer**'s sense of pain in the life of the will: "Compare the pleasure of the beast that devours with the torture of the one that is being devoured—and you will be able to estimate with approximate correctness the proportion of pleasure and pain in the world." Various conclusions follow: that the best lot is never to have been born; that sympathy alone can be an ethical feeling yet this alleviation of the hurt is but a palliative (*Murphy,* 57) for it does not abolish the Will, and with the Will unhappiness remains.

Scattered throughout SB's writings are moments of pity, the more affecting for being rare or unexpected, the more haunting for being seen through apparent unconcern. The cruelties of existence are scrutinized unflinchingly, but a twinge of sympathy arises for the fledgling chicken devoured with gusto by Descartes in *Whoroscope.* "**Dante and the Lobster**" encapsulates **Dante**'s untranslatable "**Qui vive** la pietà quando è ben mortà" (*Inferno* XX.28), the **pun** on "pietà" provoking the wretched **Belacqua** into pondering the relationship between **God**'s *pity* and *piety* in terms of Dante's "rare movements of compassion in Hell" (18). **Cain** is an emblem of one from whom God's pity is withheld, and **McCabe** is his likeness. Much of SB's cruelty is defined in terms of its opposite, such as the callous description of the young girl "triturated" in "**Ding-Dong**" (another martyr for **Ireland**): her fate is the more incongruous given that Dante's *Paradiso* structures the story.

Belacqua seems to lack pity. His treatment of his fair to middling women diminishes any chivalric ideal, noticably in "**Fingal**," where, twice a sad animal, he steals a **bicycle** and rides furiously through the landscape of "Dane **Swift**," whose treatment of women is exemplary.

He is brutally beaten by the Tanzherr in "**Walking Out,**" and his lovely **Lucy** is crippled for life. Yet the marriage is so successful that Belacqua in "**What a Misfortune**" feels sorry for himself when she dies, a narrative strategy unlikely to move the reader but one that asserts "impersonal pity" (114) and anticipates the cruelty to follow, when Thelma née **bboggs**, now Mrs. Shuah, intimates her married fate. In "**Yellow**," the clinical comedy precludes compassion, and in "**Draff**" farce mocks any dignity in **death**.

The cruelest portrait is the **Smeraldina**, whose billet-doux is mocked, and whose description focuses on her flaws, these unredeemed by her birdlike face. She is the more deficient in the white light of the **Alba**. Yet this is the defining relationship in Belacqua's life, as was that with Peggy **Sinclair** for SB, and a curious complexity arises. The cruelty is unforgivable and unforgiven; still, the pain of that first **love** is intense. There arises from the ruthless withholding of pity a strange respect for the honest portrayal, in which the victim is finally Belacqua, who neither seeks sympathy nor permits the reader to grant it.

Reporting to **MacGreevy** on a visit to Jack **Yeats** (3 February 1931), SB wrote that the painter "wanted a definition of cruelty," claiming that you could work back from that to Original Sin. SB's comment was a cryptic "No doubt." He could not isolate cruelty thus. His is the relentless scrutiny of a world in which pity, like **friendship** or any ethical value, lacks a rationale, is negated, yet persists. In his fourth **German Notebook** (18 January 1937), SB said of Käthe Kollwitz, "there is no passion of compassion." With **Celia**, compassion arises unexpectedly and is the more effective for being denied. *Watt* generates a curious sympathy for its ill-fitting protagonist, often indirectly, as with the baited bear (see **Walpole**), or by analogy with **Christ** (see **Veronica**). The novel is a metaphysical farce of cruelty, in which Watt's anguish is offset by the final image of self-satisfied men scratching themselves and proclaiming that "Life ain't such a bad old bugger."

First Love is cast without pity, its ending invoking the desolation of a life without love. A strange pity arises in "The **Expelled**," as the narrator considers that the boys who mocked his hat might have been kind, "like those who make game of the hunchback's big nose" (48). Despite their extremity, SB's moribunds rarely call for pity, and when they do they are usually conscious of the futility of so doing. **Molloy** communicates with his **mother** by knocking on her head; **Moran** with his son by sarcasm; both beat up their alter egos in the dark wood. *Malone Dies* ends grotesquely, as first Maurice then Ernest is dispatched with the hatchet. **Lemuel** then turns to Lady **Pedal**, who moans and groans as if she were the only one "deserving of pity" (287). The **Unnamable** bemoans his fate, his eyes opening and shutting "like the owl cooped up in the grotto in **Battersea Park**, ah misery, will I never stop wanting a life for myself" (361). Compare Job 30:29: "A companion to owls," invoking **Job**'s frequent cries for pity. "**Text 13**" (138) contemplates "this pity" in the air, asking if it's not hope gleaming "evilly among the imaginary

ashes," the faint hope of faint being. Such hope is extinguished in *How It Is,* with the can opener in the **buttocks** and the Molloy-like manner of communicating with one's fellow.

The persistence of hope may be the cruelest delusion of all. In *Waiting for Godot* when **Estragon** approaches the weeping **Lucky**, responding to **Pozzo**'s "Comfort him, since you pity him" (21.b), he gets for his pains a kick on the shin. In Act 2, Estragon cries, "God have pity on me!" (49.b). His plea is repeated by Pozzo (50.a, 53.a). The air is full of cries but none is acted on, if heard. **Hamm** is "the remains of a monster"; his cry for pity is angrily dismissed as an "aside" (77). He speaks without love, with irony: "Perhaps it's compassion . . . A kind of great compassion" (76). When a small **boy** is seen, **Clov** responds: "I'll take the gaff" (78). Again, comic energy reflects a cosmic coldness.

In *All That Fall* (20), as Mrs. **Rooney** gets out of Mr. **Slocum**'s car, her cry of "Pity!" implies giving **birth**, an effect lost when the BBC production substituted "Merde!" Unhappiness prevails, from Mrs. Rooney's painful waddle to the removal of the whole "bag of tricks" from Mr. **Tyler**'s daughter, from the constant pain of Mr. Tully (who beats his wife) to the child who fell out of the carriage. Similar cruelties inform the shorter plays: tantalizing or goading of the mute protagonists in the two "**Act Without Words**"; the pain of **memory** in *Krapp's Last Tape,* "Embers," and "Eh, Joe"; the inhumanity of the crippled to the blind in "**Rough for Theatre I**"; torture in "**Rough for Radio II**," "**Catastrophe**," and "**What Where**" ("Give him the works"); the pain of **mother** and daughter in *Footfalls;* and **Auditor**'s helpless gesture of supplication in *Not I*. The "rare movements" of compassion in hell are translated to the stage, without resolution. Yet in awarding the **Nobel Prize** to SB in 1969 and in recognizing that his writing "rises like a *miserere* from all mankind, its muffled minor key sounding liberation to the oppressed and comfort to those in need" the committee spoke more truly than it knew.

Plato (ca. 428–348 BC): Athenian philosopher whose dialogues immortalize the life and teachings of his master, **Socrates**, and inform the learning of his greatest pupil, **Aristotle**. His effect on Western thought is incalculable, but SB read him with curiosity and skepticism. Intrigued by the theory of forms and tripartite division of the soul, SB yet deeply distrusted Plato's theory of knowledge, its foundation in ethical rationalism, and the doctrine of the soul's immortality. SB found in **Windelband** (122ff) a persuasive account of Plato's "unfortunate thought" of developing his Ideas according to **Pythagorean** number theory, designating the Good as the One and declining from this to the corporeal world. This, Windelband argues, not only asserted an immaterial reality but saw it as arising from the ethical need for knowledge beyond sense perception. Its triumph relegated to historical obscurity the alternative of **atomism** (qv), with which SB aligned himself intellectually.

SB's references to Plato are few and cynical: in *Dream* (234), the **Polar Bear** sneers at him as a "dirty little Borstal Boehme"; and in *Murphy* (85) Tickle-penny refers to "the divine son of Ariston" (Plato's **father**, who died when Plato was young). **Neary**'s Grove is a Platonic academy in **Cork**, and **Celia**'s accosting Murphy "in form" (90) parodies the theory of Ideas. Murphy's **desire** for "the supreme Caress" (109) implies the primacy of the more tangible physical kick. Although he is happy with the beatific idols of his cave (178) the destiny of his "**body**, mind and soul" (275) affronts the immortal soul. Murphy's understanding of **consciousness** (110) takes definition from the three stages of the Platonic ascent to the Good, the **mystical** journey of the soul from darkness to light; however, his quest inverts that pattern as a descent into his inner darkness.

SB's affirmation of the demented particulars of existence as the only straws that the mind might clutch and his rejection of rationalism as the last refuge of animism conceal an attraction to Platonism that could not always be denied. His favorite philosopher, **Schopenhauer**, parlayed pessimism with Platonism, and SB found there a mythos and strategy for exploring the dark. Schopenhauer offers (*WWI* I.2 #31, 221–22) a useful summary of Plato's theory of knowledge: perceived things of this world have no true being, and consequently cannot be **objects** of true knowledge but rather objects of an opinion based on sensation. So long as we are confined to the perception of these we are like men in a dark cave, bound so that they cannot turn their heads. They see only the shadows of real things that pass between them and a fire burning behind, the light of which casts shadows on the wall. The archetypes to which these shadows correspond are the Ideas, the eternal forms of all things, which alone have true being (*ousia*), for they have no "coming into being" (*genesis*) nor passing away. Of these only can there be true knowledge, for the object of such knowledge is that which always is.

Platonism may be considered as the sense of transcendence whereby the Heraclitean process of eternal becoming is sensed as immanence toward something. This is parodied in *Watt* (50–51), by the assertion of a "third person" on whom the existence of Mary and Ann depends, a regression to the Form of forms, but it remains an impulse at the heart of SB's fiction from *The Unnamable* through *Texts for Nothing* to *How It Is*, even if the "something" is ultimately **nothing**, a final Form that is not a perfect sphere but "all balls." *The Unnamable* owes much to Plato's cave (*Republic,* 520.C.1) as the primary archetype of the confined self (compare the **skull**); *Texts for Nothing* seek the silence beyond words; and a primal drama is played out in the mud of *How It Is,* with the rock below and the light above. SB moved little from his early rejection of the **Borstal Boehme**, but Platonism afforded him some of the myths and images with which to scrutinize his being.

"**Play**": a one-act play, written 1962–63, translated into **French** as *Comédie*. The first production was in German, at the Ulmer Theater, Ulm-Donau, 14 June 1963 (see "**Spiel**"). The first American production was at the Cherry Lane Theater, New York, 4 January 1964, dir. Alan **Schneider**, without the da capo structure; reviews were "grim" and SB was not pleased. The first **London** performance was at the Old Vic, 7 April 1964, dir. George Devine, with Rosemary Harris (W1), Billie **Whitelaw** (W2), and Robert Stephens (M), a curtain raiser to Sophocles's *Philoctetes.* The text was published as *Spiel,* in *Theater Heute* (1963); by **Faber** as *Play and Two Short Pieces for Radio* (1964); then by **Grove** in *Cascando and Other Short Dramatic Pieces* (1968) but anticipated by Grove's *Evergreen Review* 34 (December 1964): 43–47, 92. The French text appeared from **Minuit** in *Comédie et actes divers* (1966). The *Evergreen* version is the most accurate, the only text to contain SB's final revisions made in the performances he oversaw or directed; it has never been commercially republished.

SB wrote Herbert Myron (31 May 1962) outlining his "idea for a new act, one hour, three faces (mouths) and lights." The earliest version was written for a woman and two men, Syke and Conk, figures in white boxes. By summer's end it was entitled "Play," with one male and two females in funerary urns indistinguishable from their flesh. The play reflects SB's affair with Barbara **Bray**, with the inevitable guilt arising from the intense banalities of an emotional triangle. Knowlson notes (444) that it is steeped in an English "Home Counties" atmosphere, rather than an Irish one. Its structure is **musical**, with a chorus for three voices, orchestration, stage directions concerning tempo, volume, and tone, and a da capo repeat of the entire action. SB specified either an exact replica, as in the first London production, or certain variations, as in the **Paris** production, the repeat being shorter, more breathless, and the light less strong.

"Play" is an assault on itself, on theater, as *Eleutheria* and **Waiting for Godot** had been a decade earlier, drama playing against itself. If *WG* eliminated "action" from the stage, "Play" virtually eliminated **motion**. If *WG* eliminated intelligible causality, "Play" almost eliminated intelligibility. SB modified "whole movement as rapid as possible" (TS 5) to "Rapid tempo throughout" (147) in response to the National Theatre's literary manager, Kenneth Tynan. As Billie Whitelaw recalls: "Rows between Sir Laurence Olivier and Ken Tynan turning up at rehearsals and saying 'you cannot possibly go as quickly as this' and everyone keeping very quiet, as George Devine had no intention of going any slower—and neither had Beckett." Tynan found SB's presence at rehearsals intrusive, as he noted in an acrimonious exchange with Devine. He argued that before SB arrived "Play" was a work the actors were eager to do, **puppet**like and mechanical but not stripped of emphasis and inflections. SB "changed all that," the lines thereafter "chanted in a breakneck monotone with no inflections." Tynan was producing the play not to satisfy SB but for an audience, to many of whom it would be inaudible. He trusted Devine as director, but not SB as codirector; if the text could be "rehumanized" actors and audience would thank him, "even if Beckett doesn't." Devine retorted that he intended "to perform the play as written," not to "demolish its dramatic purpose and turn it into literature," into something it was not, to please the majority.

Bamber Gascoigne sided with Tynan and complained: "The words are to be gabbled so fast that we can't understand them (we may seem to catch them the second time round but not in such a way as to appreciate them)" (*Observer*, 12 April 1964). Michaël Lonsdale, **M** in Jean-Marie Serreau's French premier, notes of SB's instructions: "Il voulait qu'on parle à une vitesse de mitrailleuse" ("He wanted it spoken with the speed of a machine gun"). SB's instructions for the American premiere were that "Play" was to be "played through twice without interruption and at a very fast pace, each time taking no longer than nine minutes." The producers, Richard Barr, Clinton Wilder, and, surprisingly, Edward Albee, threatened to drop it if Schneider followed SB's instructions. Schneider capitulated, slowed the pace, and eliminated the da capo: "For the first and last time in my long relationship with Sam," he wrote in his autobiography, "I did something I despised myself for doing. I wrote to him, asking if we could try having his text spoken only once, more slowly. Instead of telling me to blast off, Sam offered us his reluctant permission" (not in the Schneider/ Beckett letters).

Admittedly, "Play" was unusual theater in 1963. No more shocking than *WG* a decade earlier, it assaulted another set of theatrical conventions and audience expectations. Its **characters** are postmortem, for one. But "characters" is not the right word. They are **voices**, instruments, or spirits, part of the urns that appear to be swallowing them, only their heads remaining. The girth of the urns and their openings decreased as SB involved himself in productions; movement became all but impossible, and the faces assumed the texture and complexion of the earth-encrusted urns. (The cover of the French text still exhibits unacceptable bulbous urns, protruding heads apparently freshly washed.) The stage image became more like a sculpted triptych. Dialogue disappeared. The figures never speak to one another but respond to a mechanical stimulus, an inquisitorial light like a fourth character (Schneider named it "Sam"). Devine's rehearsal notes describe his strategy: "Rehearse separately to start with to get the idea of cues from the light and not from each other." Billie Whitelaw recalls rehearsing with the stage manager playing the light, pointing a finger, giving a cue. In the first German production the action was repeated twice, but during the Paris rehearsals, and more so in the London production, variations were introduced: a weakening of light and voices in the first repeat, and more so in the second; an abridged second opening; increasing breathlessness; changes in the order of the opening words. SB described these as dramatically more effective, but they intimate an evolution in his conception of the replay, the sense of things gradually running down.

In "Play" SB assaulted literature with a plot remarkable for its banality, language devalued from the opening, "largely unintelligible" chorus, and an attack on the very idea of closure. The da capo structure, even as revised in rehearsals, suggests figures trapped not only in urns but on a Möbius strip of narrative. (SB recast that image visually a decade later in the pacing figure of *Footfalls*.) Circularity and repetition characterized SB's earlier drama, but in "Play" they grew more sinister, more punishing (especially for the performers), the characters less corporeal, more dehumanized. Devine referred to the light as a dental drill; for Billie Whitelaw, "it was an instrument of torture." "Play" suggests that SB had returned to his fiction for stage tropes, most obviously the figure of the **unnamable** in his jar, and the use of monologue. (*Not I* may emerge from the same jar.) The dramatic movement is staccato, incessantly interrupted, a series of short bursts, which in his 1978 rehearsals SB likened to a lawn mower— a burst of energy followed by a pause, a renewed burst followed by yet another pause. The image is built into the play. W2 notes: "I could hear a mower. An old hand mower." M repeats the image: "Some fool was cutting grass. A little rush, then another." In his **Schiller-Theater** notebook for "Spiel," SB describes the voices as: "Broken, breathless—extorted," and quotes M's line: "ein rascher Ruck, dann wieder einer."

After "Play," SB's stage images grew increasingly dehumanized, reified, and metonymic, featuring dismembered or incorporeal creatures. His became a theater of **body** parts and specters, one striving for transparency rather than solidity, trying to undo itself. As plot and character dissipated, the arena grew more delimited, circumscribed, controlled. The proscenium arch is indispensable, framing a playing space. Works after "Play" make little sense on modern thrust stages or in the round. In his program notes, George Devine, clearly echoing SB, sounds prophetic: SB's words are not often used for their intellectual content or emotional impact, and this is especially so in "Play," where story and dialogue are deliberately banal. Words are used as sounds, "dramatic ammunition," to quote SB's own phrase; although they take equal place with the visual action they do not dominate it. Devine implies that the antiliterary nature of the dialogue—or three monologues—in "Play" is characteristic of SB's work, but his comments ill-fit the original texts and productions of the earlier plays. Yet this is precisely the perspective SB was to bring to revising his works. Devine's observation not only presages the theater SB would write after "Play" but anticipates his revisionist need to reconstitute all his theater works through the aesthetics "Play" offered.

"**Pochade radiophonique**": a radio play of the early 1960s, translated as "**Rough for Radio II**." Published in *Minuit* 16 (novembre 1975): 2–12; then as the third of *Quatre esquisses,* in *Pas suivi de quatre esquisses* (Minuit, 1978). A "pochade" is a rough sketch, differing from an "esquisse" by being a finished work, albeit drafted in one sitting.

Poèmes: in 1960 SB resisted John **Calder**'s request to include the French poems with what therefore became *Poems in English* (1961). Jérôme **Lindon** was unhappy about their being in *Gedichte* as SB had said that he did not want an edition of the French poems. However, the **Minuit** edition of eighteen poems appeared in 1968, 762 numbered copies, with "notes et variantes" by John Fletcher. They comprise the twelve

Poèmes 38–39 and the *Six Poèmes 1947–1949;* a 1976 reprint added "**hors crâne seul dedans**." These appeared in 1978 as *Poèmes suivi de mirlitonnades,* the previous text augmented by thirty-five short poems.

Poèmes 38–39: twelve poems written before World War II; published in *Les Temps modernes* 14 (novembre 1946): 288–93, where, curiously, they are numbered I to XIII, with no XI. Collected in *Gedichte* (1959), 53–77, as a section entitled "1937–39," with minor variants. They mark a new direction in SB's expression, less the incoherence he had claimed in his "**German Letter of 1937**" than toward a minimalism that reveals that mind and world are interactive, creating what John Pilling has called "miniature dramas of an interpersonal kind" (*BBG,* 157). Most are occasional, the poet's **voice** aware of another; but the mode is expressive, each element of the verse existing as a self-contained entity, conscious of its own texture. These, the first significant creative works in **French**, are not so much "without style" as sensitive to the acoustic and harmonic possibilities of the new language.

"**Poems by Samuel Beckett**": two readings of SB's poetry on BBC 3. The first, selected by John Fletcher, produced by Martin Esslin with readings by Jack **MacGowran** and Denys Hathorne, was broadcast Wednesday, 9 March 1966: *Whoroscope,* "**Enueg I**," "**Serena II**," "**Alba**," "**Cascando**," "**Saint-Lô**," "**my way is in the sand flowing**," "**what would I do without this world**," and "**I would like my love to die**." When SB remarked that he would have chosen different poems, Esslin suggested a second series, broadcast Thursday, 24 November 1966: "The **Vulture**," "Serena III," "**Echo's Bones**," "Serena I," the first addendum from *Watt*, "**Da tagte es**," "**Sanies I**," and "Who may tell the tale" (also from the *Watt* addenda). Small variations were made of some lines: in "Enueg I" "into a black west" became "into the black west"; in "Serena II" the "sodden packet of Churchman" became "packet of Churchman sodden"; and in "I would like my **love** to die" the final line was changed to "mourning her who thought she loved me" (as in later editions).

Poems in English: Samuel Beckett: published John **Calder**, 1961, with an advance edition of 100 on handmade paper, signed by SB; rpt. (cloth) May 1968, and as a "Calderbook" paperback (1969), with a misleading publishing history on the title page (see *Collected Poems*). The twenty poems comprise: I, *Whoroscope* (1930); II, the **thirteen** poems of *Echo's Bones and Other Precipitates;* III, *Two Poems* ("**Cascando**," "Saint Lô"); and IV, *Quatre poèmes,* including "**Dieppe**" (in the contents only "Dieppe" is listed). Published by **Grove Press** (1963), identical texts but different pagination, followed (1964) by a paperback.

"**Poetry is vertical**": a **surrealist** manifesto published in *transition* 21 (March 1932): 148–49 and signed by Hans Arp, SB, Carl Einstein, Eugene Jolas, Thomas **MacGreevy**, Georges **Pelorson**, Theo Rutra [Jolas], James J. Sweeney, and Ronald Symond, affirming in a world ruled by the hypnosis of positivism the autonomy of the poetic vision and freedom from materialistic conceptions then in vogue. The title derives from Léon-Paul Fargue: "On a été trop horizontal, j'ai envie d'être vertical." **Verticalism** was a "Revolution of the Word" associated with Jolas's *transition.* In the next issue the name was changed to "vertigral," a portmanteau of vertical and Ger. *Graal* ("grail"). SB never seriously entertained the Orphic call for a collectivisim of spirits or "a new mythological reality" (language as a "mantic instrument"), but "the hegemony of the inner life over the outer" might have appealed.

Poincaré, Jules-Henri (1854–1912): French mathematician, known for his popular expositions of science, including *La Valeur de la science: histoire de la physique mathématique* (Paris: 1925), from which SB quoted extensively in his **Whoroscope Notebook**. Poincaré explains the laws of **physics** in the subatomic world, as compared with the bigger universe in which Newtonian principles (the inverse of distance squared) apply. He makes the poetic point: "Ces astres infiniment petits, ce sont les atomes." His discussion of Newtonian gravitation shows that its laws do not apply to the movement of electrons. SB notes the minute size of particles, laws of thermodynamics, conservation of energy, mass and inertia, action and reaction, relativity, Brownian motion, Maxwell's theories of light and electromagnetism, his Demon, Heisenberg's Uncertainty Principle, the speed of light, and the impossibility of attaining absolute zero. Poincaré's point is the subversion of classical physics at the subatomic level. He is mentioned in "Les **Deux besoins**" (*Disjecta,* 56), the "petitions" of science contrasted with the "pets" (farts) of theology. These details inform **Murphy's mind** and the cosmogony of *The Unnamable;* see also **mathematics** and **physics**.

Polar Bear: in *Dream* and "A **Wet Night**," an enormous block of a man, purple-faced, cursing, blaspheming, with a witty or disagreeable word (often "merde") for all. He has altercations with a bus conductor and a Jesuit, and does not entirely prevail. The portrait is based on SB's tutor, Thomas **Rudmose-Brown**, with little of the affection SB normally felt. In a letter to **MacGreevy** (September 1932?), SB commented that Ruddy had been good to him, "and I wish there were no PB in *Dream.*" The breach of the protégé with his mentor would recur with **Joyce**.

policemen: figures of authority who rise up to instruct one, more in sorrow than in anger, to move **on**, and must be greeted in terms of deferential promotion. Thus **Belacqua** to the Dogberry in "A **Wet Night**" (72), though not to the Civic Guard in the analogous passage of *Dream* (226); **Neary** to the "Sergeant" in *Murphy* (44); and **Mercier and Camier** to the ranger (13). In "**Enueg II**," the narrator, forced to keep moving, is "tired of policemen." **Molloy** is detained by one wanting his papers. They represent autocratic authority, as in "The **Expelled**" (51): "Like a bit of Old Testament." One tells the narrator to walk on the sidewalk, another to clear it for others. However nobly proportioned, they are usually rough, gritty men, like the wharfinger and jarveys of

Dream. **Endgame's** joke about the Englishman in the brothel is completed by Ruby Cohn (*JOBS* 1 [1976]: 42): asked if he wants a blond or brunette or redhead, he says he wants a boy. The bawd, outraged, threatens to call a policeman: "O no, they're too gritty."

politics: James Plunkett begins *The Gems She Wore: A Book of Irish Places* with a joke of which, he claims, SB was fond. The nations are gathered and their representatives write an essay on the subject of "The Camel." The Frenchman's was called "The Camel and **Love**," the German's "The Camel and Metaphysics," and the Irishman's "The Camel and the Fight for Irish Freedom." Although SB did not share the national obsession, to conclude that he and his works were fundamentally apolitical is to distort both. The charge is often linked to a nihilism and anti**humanism** in his work or associated with misanthropy. SB was not beyond glibness. Asked to write a paragraph about the Spanish Civil War he offered the ambiguous "¡UPTHEREPUBLIC!" Equally famous is his retort to the question "Are you English?" His "Au contraire" suggests the alterity that the Irish finally embraced as a badge of honor (see Declan Kiberd's *Inventing Ireland* [1995]). Attacks on the Irish poetic tradition in "**Recent Irish Poetry**" were taken up afresh in *First Love,* but his youthful disdain was increasingly leavened by "just plain human convictions." While major artists of his generation were at least flirting with totalitarianism (Lewis, Pound, W. B. **Yeats,** and **Eliot,** to name just a few), SB's commitment to "human convictions" remained unshaken.

SB's oft-cited preference for France at war to **Ireland** (qv) at peace was as much a statement of solidarity with his adopted land as a slur on Irish patriots. "Ireland at peace" is edged, implying criticism of the dubious neutrality in what his countrymen called "The Emergency" (even as Belfast was bombed by the Nazis). If his countrymen could stand by idly during World War II, SB could not. "**Walking Out**" had presented in the Tanzherr and the Daimler a reflection of **Germany** in the 1930s; and SB's translations for Nancy **Cunard**'s *Negro* represented a commitment, however qualified, to a work that flaunted its antiracist and communist agenda long before it was fashionable to do so. After the horror of World War II, his work for **Gloria SMH**, exile in **Roussillon**, and personal losses like the **death** of Alfred **Péron**, SB's political **consciousness**, while never flaunted, never faltered.

Knowlson's discussion of the **German Diaries** of 1936–37 revealed the breadth of SB's sympathy for proscribed artists, especially Jewish ones, those associated with experimental or decadent **art**, outsiders in general. Such sympathy, which **Schopenhauer** saw as the only possible ethical virtue, led to SB's work for the **Resistance**, for which, although he denigrated it as Boy Scout stuff, SB received the Croix de Guerre and the Médaille de la Reconnaissance Française. *Waiting for Godot* reflects this wartime dislocation. After the **war** SB worked as an ambulance driver for the Irish Red Cross in **Saint-Lô** (qv) as a means of returning to his devastated adopted home. The experience produced a poem of that title and another, "**Mort de A.D.**" (a tribute to

Arthur **Darley**, a friend at the hospital who died of TB); and "The **Capital of the Ruins**" (qv).

SB's sympathies for the oppressed continued long after the war. To Charles Juliet SB quoted Mitterrand's "fanaticism is stupidity" as he analyzed the "Troubles" of his homeland: "In Ireland there are not just two branches of fanaticism, but three or four or five, and each of those are [*sic*] being torn apart by other factions" (159). In 1958 the Archbishop of **Dublin**, Dr. Dennis McQuaid, refused a request for a votive Mass to celebrate the Tóstal or Theatre Festival, because the program included O'**Casey**'s *The Drums of Father Ned* and a transcription of *Ulysses;* O'Casey refused to let his plays be staged, and SB withdrew permission for his mimes and *All That Fall.* In 1972 he refused to allow his work to be shown in South Africa before segregated audiences. He signed a letter to *Le Monde* (28 septembre 1967, 5) in defense of Fernando Arrabal. He was one of 100 signatories to a letter in *Le Monde* (4 août 1971, 12) sent to the Brazilian Ambassador on behalf of a group of actors from the Living Theater Company, imprisoned at Belo-Horizonte, Brazil. "**Catastrophe**" (1982) is a tribute to Václav **Havel**, who wrote to SB after his release to say how much this meant to him, and how moved he was by the play. More important than particular political incidents is the general tenor of SB's work and its critique of the tormentor-victim relationship, as in *How It Is* or "**What Where**," where each character is in turn torturer and victim. The play is not simply a failure to understand the what and where of existence, but a critique of totalitarianism, inquisition, and torture.

Pompette: from *pomponner,* "to titivate, to dress up"; the equivalent of "Sucky Molly" (*Malone Dies,* 262) in the **French** text (147): "toujours gaie." Drafts of *Watt* refer to Madame Pompedur, otherwise "Pompette" (see *Watt* "**Addenda**" #4).

Portigliotti, Giuseppe: Italian scholar and author of several studies of the Borgias. The **Frica** is adorned with his *Penumbre Claustrali* (Milan: Treves, 1930) on her concave breast (*Dream,* 179). SB derived his name and book from Praz, *The Romantic Agony* (49), where Portigliotti discusses **Brignole-Sale** (qv).

Portobello Nursing Home: located on the Grand Canal, **Dublin**, near the Portobello Bridge and Lock. "**Enueg I**" has the poet exiting "in a spasm," tired of his darling's "red sputum" (Peggy **Sinclair** was dying of TB, but not there) and seeing in the perilous footbridge and shrieking hoarding images of his own anguish. In "A **Case in a Thousand**" the hospital is not named, but the canal, bridge, lock, and hoarding are mentioned. Despite O'Brien's doubts (369) it is surely the "grim pile" mentioned by **Mercier** to **Camier** as they walk along the Grand Canal (121). Jack **Yeats** died there in 1957.

Portora: after SB left **Earlsfort House**, his schooling continued at Portora Royal School, founded 1618, near Enniskillen, County Fermanagh, Ulster, overlooking Lough Erne. Portora was a Protestant public school, preparatory for **Trinity College**. In SB's time it had about 120 pupils, a mixture of daybugs and boarders. One infamous former pupil was Oscar Wilde, whose name (since restored) had been removed from the Honours Board. SB joined his brother, Frank, there in the Hilary (Easter) term, 1920. The school offered the predictable package of discipline, prayers, bullying, and appalling food, but also a sound education. SB did well, without displaying promise of future brilliance. He developed his literary interests, but it is uncertain if or what he contributed to the *Portora,* the school magazine. Deirdre Bair misattributes an article entitled "Some Home Truths About the Ancients" (31), which SB denied; but he may have composed as "John Peel" a sonnet entitled "To the Toy Symphony" to commemorate the school orchestra's performance of **Haydn**'s work in which SB played "some sort of birdcall" (O'Brien, 119). Called "an effort in mangled metre after hearing the first practice," it concludes: "But human words, though strong, can ne'er express / This unsymphonic clamour's awfulness." This may constitute SB's first published work.

SB played halfback for the rugby team and made the First Eleven (**cricket**) in his first year. He participated in athletics, boxing, and swimming, the latter recalled, with an unfavorable image of his science and **mathematics** master, W. N. Tetley, in "**For Future Reference**" (O'Brien, 116). SB took part in ragging him and other masters; Bair describes (32) his caricatures of Tetley, and Knowlson (45) the devastating manner in which another master, Thomas Tackaberry, was brought to tears ("a convenient piss-pot for the whole school"), suggesting that such incidents shaped SB's sense of human cruelty. SB met Geoffrey **Thompson**, with whom he developed an enduring **friendship** and cultivated the habit of reading poetry as well as playing bridge and **chess**. SB's years there were not unhappy, yet they are recalled through such images as the Master and **pensum** of *The Unnamable*. SB did not retain for Portora the affection he reserved for Trinity, and later overtures for recognition were ignored.

A Portrait of the Artist as a Young Man: James **Joyce**'s account (1916) of his decision to become a writer. In "**Dante** . . . **Bruno** . **Vico** . . **Joyce**," SB refers three times to *Portrait*'s aesthetics: the "detached attitude" of Stephen Dedalus who discusses Epictetus (22); the "incredulous Joshuas" whose fingernails are not yet refined out of existence (27); and the use of "apprehension" as Stephen uses it to Lynch (28). Implicit is the identification of Joyce's aesthetics with Stephen's, and SB's with both—a perspective that changed as SB found his own **voice**, Joyce increasingly a force to resist rather than a model to emulate. As with *Ulysses* (qv), SB's use of *Portrait* is fugitive rather than allusive. The "shrieking paullo-post-Expression" of the Last Supper in *Dream* (77) assumes the excremental sense of the "paulo post futurum" in Dixon's suave analysis of the future perfect (*Portrait*, 230). SB's use of "detained" and "tundish" in *Murphy* (2, 87) intimates Stephen's discussion of the literary tradition and marketplace (*Portrait*, 188). When Murphy gazes at **Celia** (14), the phrasing echoes Stephen's encounter with the wading girl: "Long, long, she suffered his gaze"; one epiph-

any played against another. **Wylie**'s purity at his second communication (51) suggests *Portrait* (47) when Stephen learns that **Napoleon**'s happiest day was that of his first communion. **Neary**'s allusion to the bed wetter (217) recalls the opening page of *Portrait,* and the use of "whined" with **Vermeer** (228) invokes the yellow ivy that whines on Stephen's wall. The drafts of *Watt* contain a burlesque of Joyce's epiphany scene, which did not make the final version (see **Spiro**). *Portrait* does not figure in SB's postwar writings, as its aesthetic concerns and affirmation (however ironic) of the artist as hero had become irrelevant and outdated.

Portrane: the coastal district north of Malahide, the setting of "**Fingal**" and "**Sanies I**," a place "as full of towers as **Dun Laoghaire** of steeples" ("Fingal," 26), notably, those of the Portrane Lunatic **Asylum**, now St. Ita's Hospital. The asylum was built on the Evans demesne between 1886 and 1901 (O'Brien, 233). Opposite the entrance lie the ruins of a church and graveyard and, two fields away, the square "bawnless" tower (lacking outworks) associated with "Dane Swift" ("Fingal," 33).

"The Possessed": a short dramatic satire, unsigned, responding to an unfavorable review of the Modern Languages Society production of "Le **Kid**," published in *TCD: A College Miscellany* 37 (12 March 1931): 138. Reprinted in *TCD* 1307 (14 February 1968): 6, as "A play by Samuel Beckett lost in TCD." The review had dismissed the production as akin to "those grand old parodies" of the Gaiety, forty years earlier and "rather a strain on the digestion." SB mocks its phrases in an incoherent **Dostoyevsky**-like pseudodrama. This was described by the *TCD* editorial subcommittee (4 June 1931, 185) as "a Joycian medley" with "diverting verbal acrobatics," but "too allusive to be generally comprehensible."

pots: elemental **objects** that characters eat out of, excrete into, or inhabit. **Malone** (252) has two, one for soup and another for his bodily needs: one remains full and the other is filling slowly. In "The **End**," a woman brings in a tray and removes the chamber pot. This reflects the dynamics of **equilibrium**, as in *Murphy* (58), the well with two buckets: if one empties and the other fills equilibrium is maintained, but if one remains full while the other fills entropic deterioration has begun. Malone comments (185): "What matters is to eat and excrete. Dish and pot, dish and pot, these are the poles." The Proustian **vase** (qv), that dubious repository of **memory**, is similar.

Problems of identity arise from the relationship of "pot" and pot in *Watt*, concerning the word and the world in which it functions. Watt, whose character is not so curious as to suppose he can know what words really mean (75), nevertheless tries to ascertain the relation of "pot" and pot. The more he reflects on Mr. **Knott**'s pot, the less sure he feels (81): "It resembled a pot, it was almost a pot, but it was not a pot of which one could say, Pot, pot, and be comforted." The **dualism** of *langue* and *parole* cannot be resolved even by pot, that is, the nominal relationship of one word for one thing

only, or, in **Platonic** terms, the identity of the Idea with its representation. This hairsbreadth departure from the nature of a true pot excruciates Watt, for had the approximation been less close he would have been less anguished. If he fails with pot, what hope has he with Knott? Watt's need of "semantic succour" (83) is strong; but he works to no avail. He is equally unhappy with "man," thinking of himself as one, but for all the relief this brings him, "he might just as well have thought of himself as a box, or an urn." Or a pot.

"Pour Avigdor Arikha": a paragraph written by SB for an exhibition of drawings by **Arikha** opening 26 January 1967 (Paris: Galerie Claude Bernard). Published in *Avigdor Arikha: Dessins 1965–1970* (Paris: Centre National d'Art Contemporain, 1970), 3, but earlier translated for *Avigdor Arikha: Drawings 1965/66* (Jerusalem and Tel Aviv: Tarshish Books, 1967), 3. The tribute appeared at other exhibitions of Arikha's work, in **Paris** (8 December 1970 to 18 January 1971), **London** (Victoria and Albert Museum catalogue, February–May 1976), and the United States, and in *Arikha* (Paris: Hermann, 1985), 10. The original and translation are reprinted in *Disjecta* (152); they express SB's sense of art as the siege laid to "the impregnable without," "deep marks" that show the battle of eye and hand with the "unself." Six successive drafts appear in Atik, illustrations 10–12, pp. 26–28, with English translation, illustration 13, p. 29.

"Pour Bram [van Velde]": see "La Falaise."

"Pour finir encore": a short prose text of the mid-70s, included with the *Foirades,* and translated as **"For to end yet again"** (qv). Published in a limited edition of 125 numbered copies (Minuit, 1976), then as first item in the trade edition, *Pour finir encore et autres foirades,* the first collection of SB's shorter prose pieces in French (Minuit, 1976).

Pozzo: in *Waiting for Godot,* Lucky's master. The name may imply It. *pozzo nero,* "a cesspool." In Act I he is bullying and conceited, but in Act II he is blind and cries for **pity,** before giving **voice** to a diatribe against **time** and an impassioned summary of existence: "They give **birth** astride of a grave, the light gleams an instant, then it's night once more." He demands of **Vladimir** and **Estragon** if his name means nothing to them (it was that of the reserve goal keeper in Italy's winning 1938 World Cup side). SB toyed with identifying Pozzo as **Godot,** unaware that those waiting are Vladimir and Estragon: "But the messenger" (Duckworth, lxi). In garb and attitude, Pozzo is the Ascendancy landlord, smoking a **Kapp and Peterson** "briar" (23.b) and deciding that his "half-hunter" has been left at "the manor" (31.a). **"Text 5"** inquires (118): "Why did Pozzo leave home, he had a castle and retainers." Like figures include **Conaire** in *Mercier et Camier;* "a big ruddy farmer" encountered by **Moran** (*Molloy,* 172); and a visitor whom **Malone** imagines, dressed in leggings, riding breeches, and a check cap, with a whip (273).

preestablished harmony: *harmonia praestablia,* the doctrine associated with **Leibniz,** confronting problems inherent in the Cartesian and **Occasionalist** relationship of **body** and mind by proposing that these have been harmonized by **God** for all **time,** so that changes synchronize without influencing one another and without requiring God's incessant intervention. In Leibniz's opinion, a harmony established before creation, whereby **monads** correspond though there is no communication between them, each so prearranged that its changes are accompanied by corresponding changes in others (*Monadology,* 41). He wished to reconcile mechanical and teleological views of the world, to unite scientific and **religious** interests (Windelband, 420). **Voltaire**'s *Candide* mocks the notion that all is for the best in the best of all worlds (since the only possible). **Diderot**'s *Jacques le fataliste* insists, "il était écrit là-haut." In **Swift**'s *Tale of a Tub* (193), Jack consoles himself for bouncing his Head against a Post: "*It was ordained, said he, some few Days before the Creation, that my Nose and this very Post should have a Rencounter; and therefore, Nature thought fit to send us both into the world in the same Age.*"

SB's response was also parodic. In **"Dante and the Lobster"** (10) **Belacqua** assumes that "some niggling curriculum" has been drawn up for his day (compare the **pensum**). In **"Fingal"** (32) the characters are "met together" in **Portrane,** the narrator complacently reflecting that "Surely it is in such little adjustments that the benevolence of the First Cause appears beyond dispute"; **Belacqua,** however, fails to show up at the appointed time. The Hindu polyhistor of *Murphy* has better success (225): he makes a gesture of metaphysical liquidation and springs into a taxi that "was clocking off an inscrutable schedule from all eternity," i.e., happened to be passing when he needed it. *Murphy* is structured on the principle of all things hobbling together for the only possible (227), a maxim derived from classical, biblical, and philosophical precepts. Elements of Leibniz fuse with the **atomist** contention that Necessity ordains all things for all eternity; yet in accordance with Romans 8:28: "And we know that all things work together for good to them that love God, to them that are the called according to his purpose." In **Molloy**'s words (41): "For all things hang together, by the operation of the Holy Ghost, as the saying is." "Hang together" derives from Ger. *Zusammenhang,* used for the historical and systematic relationship of one system to another. The sentiment is repeated (62), the harmony a "sweet **music**," before Molloy's world lapses into filthy circumstance.

In *Watt,* the parable of the famished **dog** is an elaborate instance of the kind of problem that must have beset Mr. **Knott** when he set up his *establishment* (93). It functions smoothly with respect to the various servants who **come and go** while he abides; however, the narrator struggles to articulate the *preestablished arbitrary,* "a chain stretching from the long dead to the far unborn" (134). The existence of a series, or an infinite number of interacting series, does not imply causality: Tom's time on the first floor is not *because* of Harry's service on the ground floor, which is in turn not *because* of Dick's arrival. That kind of excessive order might be finally identical to maximal disorder, an **identified contrary** that

Bruno might approve. See also **serial order**, for the piano tuners and frog song as exempla of this principle, a world with rhyme but little reason.

In "The **Expelled**" (48), when it is time for the narrator to have a **hat**, his **father** says, "Come, son, we are going to buy your hat, as though it had preexisted from time immemorial in a pre-established place." The "Organisation" for **Moran** constitutes an elaborate metaphor of such harmony. In *How It Is,* where movement is "imparted by chance or necessity," a dilemma arises concerning the **coalsacks** (136). If "all the sacks in position like us at the beginning that hypothesis such an acervation [a heaping] of sacks on the track" (137), then there is a logical impasse, with all progress impossible, "frozen in injustice"; alternatively "a **love** who all along the track at the right places according as we need them deposits our sacks" (138) is inconceivable and is rejected (145), just as SB, decades earlier, had dismissed Leibniz for all his splendid little pictures as a "great cod."

Premier amour: bowing to pressure for publication after the **Nobel Prize**, SB produced from his trunk this novella, which he had abandoned in 1946. It was published, to his stated regret, in a first edition of 399 (Minuit, 1970), with 106 numbered copies. The translation, *First Love* (qv), was begun about then, slowly and unwillingly, and not completed until 11 February 1973.

Prentice, Charles: classical scholar and senior partner at Chatto and Windus, who in 1931 encouraged SB to write

Proust for their Dolphin Books series and later accepted *MPTK* (but without "Echo's Bones," which he had asked SB to add). Prentice remained a good friend long after their business dealings were over. He felt that SB had the talent to be a major writer, but his literary tact (which SB respected) and sense of commercial realities made him refuse *Dream* and other works. The failure of *MPTK* discouraged his associates, who refused *Murphy* (hence SB's abuse of "Shatton and Windup"). SB's correspondence with Prentice is held at the **BIF**.

pre-Socratic philosophy: as preparation for writing *Murphy* SB acquainted himself with **Windelband**'s *History of Philosophy,* **Burnet**'s two books on early Greek philosophy, Bailey's *Greek Atomists and Epicurus,* and various studies of **Heraclitus**, **Pythagoras**, and **Democritus**. This led to a rejection of a rationalist tradition, running from Heraclitus and Pythagoras through **Plato** and **Socrates** to the Christian fathers (**Augustine**) and thence to **Descartes**, in favor of the lesser-known **atomists**, from Leucippus and Democritus to **Epicurus** and **Lucretius** and thence to contemporary atomic theory.

At **Neary**'s academy, "The Grove," students would be introduced to the major tenets of pre-Socratic thought. Following Windelband, they might divide Greek philosophy into three periods: cosmological, anthropological, and systematic. They would study these in relation to Pythagoras, who led to Plato. They would consider the primary substance or substrate of the universe, of which other elements were transient forms. This was variously said to be

water (Thales) or fire (Heraclitus), but Anaximenes, followed by **Diogenes of Apollonia**, declared it to be air. Others, such as Anaximander, held that all things came from a different primal substance. Yet others, such as **Empedocles**, said that the essential force was the strife of opposites, in a cosmos based on the four elements, with natural ("physical") extensions to the **microcosm**, or little world of man.

The difficult concept of *to apeiron,* "the Unlimited," would be illustrated from Neary's tractate, *The Doctrine of the Limit,* the problem being to show how the Limit gave form to the Unlimited; in the words of Anaximander, "that becoming might not fail." The relationship between the Limit and the Unlimited, in terms of odd and even numbers, would arouse speculation. Other basic oppositions postulated by the Pythagoreans were: one and many; right and left; male and female; rest and **motion**; straight and curved; light and darkness; good and evil; square and oblong or with unequal sides. Other problems would concern the nature of true being, in terms of what *is* and what *is not,* and the nature of motion, which supposes (most assumed) the preexistence of the void. Anaxagoras insisted on the preeminence of mind (*nous*) in the composition of living things, but this was disputed by the atomists and questioned by Sophists like **Zeno**. An important voice was **Parmenides**, whose sense of "the One" (*to en*) asserts that what *is not* cannot be known; Leucippus would dispute this by insisting that what *is not* is just as real as what *is.* This debate voices itself for Murphy in the guffaw of Democritus (246), that

Nothing is more real than nothing; a contention bound up with the nature of the soul and its survival after **death**. Murphy's opinion (as implicit in his fate) might differ from his master's.

The problem of freedom of the will would be considered, the ethical rationalism of Socrates and Plato critiqued by the determinism of **Stoicism** and the rejection of that by Epicurus, in whose writings the metaphysical conception of freedom arises in terms of the uncaused function of the will (Windelband, 194), something that **Schopenhauer** would later endorse. This reasoning might lead to **Geulincx** and **Leibniz**, the latter's affection for atomist paradoxes acknowledged in the *Monadology*. Murphy might have found anticipations of his desire to retreat into the freedom of the mind and further reasons for his attraction to the Democritean tradition.

A prime area of study would be **mathematics**, as fundamental to physics and aesthetics. The Pythagorean contention that "all things are number" underlies the mystical doctrine that numbers are eternal rather than existing in time—"one" identified with the point, "two" the line, "three" the surface, and "four" the solid. Hence Plato's sense of **God** as a master of geometry. Two thousand years of rationalist speculation, a world revealed to the intelligence rather than to the senses, has its roots in this conjunction of mathematics and **mysticism**. The post-Cartesian rationalist tradition, from Descartes to **Kant**, might be affirmed as natural extensions of Pythagorean thought. Yet the **irrationality** of pi and the incommensurability of side and hypotenuse would continue to affront the

rationalist deity and invite encroachments of the **absurd**. At this point, conscious that Neary could not blend the opposites in an **irrational heart**, Murphy may have departed.

Prince William's Seat: highest point between **Glencullen** and Glencree, in the heart of the **Beckett country**; large flat rocks on a bleak furze-covered summit. The name may derive from the "Coronation Plantation" of William IV (O'Brien, 353). Mr. **Hackett**'s father was breaking stones in a quarry there, presumably at Her Majesty's invitation (*Watt*, 16).

prison: Pentonville Prison, in Islington, on the Caledonian Road, opposite **Brewery Road** and close to the cattle market, shapes the setting of Chapter 5 of *Murphy*. It was opened in 1872 but operative before that; designed to take 520 convicts, with the cessation of transportation it became vastly overcrowded and even in the 1930s was overfull. SB's first flat in **Paris** (6 Rue des Favorites) was near the slaughterhouse; his second, at 38 Boulevard Saint-Jacques, overlooked La Santé prison and, beyond that, the little church of the Val-de-Grâce and the Panthéon. The conjunction of prison and **shambles** sets the scene for *The Unnamable,* in which dungeons, **oubliettes,** and prisons feature, with the sense of being trapped within the "**closed space**" of the self or **skull**.

"Project I": three intended films by SB, Ionesco, and Pinter, instigated by Barney Rosset for **Evergreen** Theater (1964); SB alone produced a text. Ionesco's *Hard-*

Boiled Egg was postponed indefinitely, and Pinter's *The Compartment* was later adapted for TV as *The Basement*. Called "An Untitled Film Script," SB's text is at the **HRHRC** (#309), a mimeographed scenario of *Film*, signed on the title page, with four photocopied pages of "Further notes to Beckett film" laid in.

Prometheus: son of Iapetus and brother of **Atlas** and **Epimetheus**. In the words of the **Unnamable** (303), who trusts he has nothing in common, Prometheus mocked the **gods**, invented fire, denatured clay (animating man and woman with the stolen fire), and domesticated the **horse**. Jupiter ordered Vulcan to carry him to the Caucasus and tie him to a rock, where for 30,000 years a **vulture** would feed upon his liver. He was delivered after thirty years by Hercules, who slew the vulture. SB took these details from Lemprière. The English translation reads (oddly) "after having purged his offence," whereas the **French** says "avant d'avoir purgé sa peine"; SB's marginal calculation arrives at 29,970 years. SB admired **Goethe**'s "Prometheus" and the figure of one who, punished for having revolted against the Gods, will not cease from cursing them (compare *Lessness*, 197).

Protagoras (ca. 485–410 BC): originally from Abdera, he became leader of the Sophists, but was convicted of impiety and, fleeing Athens, met his **death**. Little of his work has been preserved, but his theory of perception influenced **Democritus** and **Plato**. He is best known for the dictum that man is the measure of all things, which marks the beginning of the anthropomorphism to which SB was opposed (see **Cézanne**). Protagoras regarded perception as the only source of knowledge and so denied any knowledge of what *is,* yet he asserted its value as a transient and relative reality and thereby, **Windelband** indicates (104–6), distinguished in a pre-**Kantian** way between two kinds of knowledge, that of perception to a changing actuality (phenomena) and that of thought to a reality absolute and abiding. The rationalistic basis of the Platonic doctrine of knowledge and its allegiance to an immaterial reality, Windelband argues (116–18), is rooted in this theory of perception. SB, having read this passage, was intrigued by its implications.

Proust, Marcel (1871–1922): French novelist, author of *A la recherche du temps perdu,* which SB read (twice) over the summer of 1930, in the "abominable" *Nouvelle revue française* (Gallimard) edition, for his monograph *Proust.* His fifteen volumes, with markings and marginalia, were donated to the **BIF** (Reading). SB found the work "strangely uneven" but with "incomparable passages." It was published in seven volumes between 1913–27, the last three posthumously. The narrator, usually identified as Marcel, tells his life, and the novel celebrates the processes of its own genesis, exploring these with ironic sensitivity and in such detail as to constitute an incomparable fictional autobiography. Proust had to pay for the publication of the first volume, which was full of errors, these exacerbated by his ceaseless revising of proofs and typescripts. He died before the task was done. SB appears to have worked entirely in **French**, ignoring the Scott Moncrieff translation available by 1924 (books I–IV) or 1927 (books V–VII) as *Remembrance of Things Past.*

Du côté de chez Swann (1913) describes Marcel's childhood, and the day when as an adult he tasted a **madeleine** soaked in tea, this arousing ecstasy as he recalled with all attendant sensations the pleasures of Combray. This involuntary **memory** forms the climax of the entire novel—in *Le Temps retrouvé,* the final part—as life, memory, and **art** together achieve their full realization. The madeleine releases memories of landscape and country walks, family and friends, as recounted in *Combray,* volume one of part one. The second volume, *Un amour de Swann,* tells how Swann (whose daughter Gilberte Marcel admires) was partly ruined by the affair with Odette de **Crécy**, whom he eventually married. Part two, *A l'ombre des jeunes filles en fleurs* (1919), deals with Marcel's adolesence: his visit to Balbec; meeting Odette; his acquaintance with the writer Bergotte; his appreciation of the composer Vinteuil; making friends with Saint-Loup, nephew of the duchesse de Geurmantes; his first encounter with Baron Charlus; and his love for Albertine. In Part three, *Le Côté de Guermantes* (1920–21), Marcel makes his way in this society and is invited to dine by the Guermantes; his grandmother dies and Swann is dying; Marcel is uncertain of himself as a writer. Part four, *Sodome et Gomorrhe* (1921–22) reveals Charlus's homosexuality and a suspicion of lesbianism in Albertine's past. He nevertheless brings her back to his **Paris** flat, determined to marry her. Part five, *La Prisonnière,* concerns Marcel's jealous **love**

of Albertine and his quasi-imprisonment of her; this leads into part six, *Albertine disparue* (1925), describing her flight and accidental **death**, and the waning of his jealousy. In Venice, he learns that Saint-Loup is to marry Gilberte, thus unifying the Swann and Guermantes sides of his life (SB's *Proust* erroneously says that she becomes the duchesse de Guermantes). The finale, *Le Temps retrouvé,* describes Paris during the war. Marcel's experience at the *matinée* of the princesse de Guermantes releases a flood of involuntary memories, notably those associated with the madeleine, giving him the confidence to create his work of art, the very book which the reader is concluding as Marcel's life reaches its end.

SB admired Proust's detachment from moral considerations and his sense that, as underlined in his copy of *Jeunes filles* (II.196), we are "irrémédiablement seuls" (see **friendship**). Proust adapted **Schopenhauer**'s theory of **music** to a fictional end, thereby raising the possibility of transcending ordinary perception by involuntary memory. Crucial to Proust's thinking, and thus to SB's response, is the demonstration that memory is ruled by **habit**. **Joyce** and Proust are antithetical in this respect: good memory (Joyce) leading to classical control, but poor memory (Proust) to an art both fugitive and ephemeral. SB defined himself thus in his "non-Joycian" [*sic*] marginalia in his personal copy of Proust. Yet much as he admired the sentiment as a working principle, SB distrusted Proust's notion of salvation through involuntary memory. This is evident in **Arsene**'s "short statement" in *Watt,* where the experience "off the ladder" is acknowledged but its significance denied. SB agreed with Proust that art "explains" nothing, and this conviction of art as the arrangement of the inexplicable would for SB endure.

Sentiments expressed in Proust manifest themselves, sometimes obviously (the **Fricas**'s party parodies the Guermantes's *matinée*) but often fleetingly ("**Yellow**" alludes Bergotte's death). The narrator prays that the only unity of *Dream* will be an involuntary one (132), and uses fleeting images of Proust's **hawthorn** to invoke it. Not until **Belacqua** sits down in approximate silence and *sees* the **Smeraldina** does he have her "truly and totally"; here, the ideal is real, as opposed to "when he . . . er . . . held her in his arms" (25), a Proustian paradox indeed. *Dream* notes "the zone of evaporation between damp and incandescence" (191), adding: "(We stole that one. Guess where.)" "Where" is *Swann* (I.124); "un corps incandescant" refers to the screen between Marcel's consciousness and the **object** it perceives, underlying **Murphy**'s incandescent sense of his self (250). *Murphy* is shaped by the Proustian paradox of **desire**, that one can love only what one cannot possess: thus **Neary** pursues **Miss Counihan** with **cattleyas**, as Swann does Odette (II.26), but his allusion is not comprehended and he is unsuccessful: "pas de cattleyas ce soir." Proust provided many incidental details: Murphy's eyes, green as a gull's (2), are those of Albertine; echoes of the street (2) keep Marcel awake at Combray; Neary's syncopation (56) is that of Marcel's *tante Léonie* (*Swann*, I.242–43), a water lily driven from bank to bank, like **Dante**'s damned; his concept of **friendship** (200) is "curious" because

it denies the condition of irremediable solitude; and **Cooper**'s treatment of his hat (273) imitates Baron Charlus (*Guermantes*, II.219). These trivialities create a Proustian tonality—in Hesla's felicitous summary (41), "a Cartesian cosmos with Proustian inhabitants."

Arsene notes the bony cavity that reminded his dear tutor of Crécy, a sentiment to arouse an involuntary Proustian frisson (*Watt*, 44). **Flowering currant** (*Swann*, I.207) haunts A **Watt** (74 and 80) and the **Unnamable** (305); Hawthorn flowers in "The **Expelled**" (47) and *Molloy* (27). **Moran**'s Sunday walk (128) imitates that of Marcel in *Swann*. References to city and plain are as much Proustian (*Sodome et Gomorrhe*) as biblical: they extend from "**Love and Lethe**" (95) and "**Hell Crane to Starling**" to constitute the very geography of the **Beckett country** in *Molloy* and *Texts for Nothing*. Enticed by smells from the kitchen, **Moran** ventures "à la recherche des oignons" (in the French text only [139]). One **Madeleine** attends the Unnamable's horsemeat café. *Endgame* invokes the Lake Como experience, **Nagg and Nell**'s memory of the bottom: "So white. So clean" (21). Piette contends (82–83) that Proust's presence is pervasive; his "rimes intérieures" articulate the human voice which SB's later work assumes. SB's interest in the paradox of the "self-accompaniment of a **voice** that is not mine" is thus "an extreme development of this Proustian concern." If so, SB's 1931 monograph on Proust is a vade mecum not only for the Beckett country but for the terrain beyond.

Proust: in 1930, through the agency of Thomas **MacGreevy**, Charles **Prentice**, and Richard **Aldington**, SB was offered the opportunity of writing an essay on **Proust**. He read *A la recherche* twice that summer, looking forward, he wrote MacGreevy, to "pulling the balls off the critical and poetical Proustian cock." The essay went to Chatto and Windus in mid-September and appeared as #7 in their Dolphin Books (March 1931). By 1937, 2,600 had sold (at 2/-); 400 were remaindered in 1941. The book was reprinted photographically by **Grove Press** (**Evergreen** E-50, 1957, with a signed edition of 250 copies) and by John **Calder** (1965), who added "**Three Dialogues with Georges Duthuit**" but omitted the epigraph from **Leopardi.** The 1999 reprint misspelled SB's name on the spine as "Samuiel Becket." Dissatisfied, SB told MacGreevy (11 March 1931) that it was too abstract, "a merely critical extension of Proust—like an anus, no sinewy membrane," adding "I don't want to be a professor." He dismissed it as "cheap flashy philosophical jargon" (Bair, 109; from a copy found in a **Dublin** bookstore, presumably sold by SB).

Like the earlier "**Dante**" essay, *Proust* relies on recent critics: Benoît-Méchin, Pierre-Quint, and Firmin-Didot, with **Schopenhauer**'s pessimism filtered through Arnaud **Dandieu**'s *Marcel Proust: sa révélation psychologique* (1930). SB later admitted that he had overstated this element. These authors were available at the **École Normale.** Terence McQueeny has shown that while the method of this essay is similar to "Dante" its impact differs, for SB engages more deeply in dialogue with his sources and himself. Dandieu offered a synthesis of aesthetics and epistemology, but doctrines of pessimism increasingly

defined SB's attitude to **art**. The essay reveals less about Proust than it does about SB, "aspects of myself" that he admitted to MacGreevy alone. Yet, despite its brevity, it engages with its original and offers a remarkable synthesis of sensibility. Although he opposed its being translated into **French** (it appeared after his **death**), SB's dismissals are unwarranted.

The "Proustian equation," SB begins, "is never simple" (11). It centers about **time** ("that double-headed monster of damnation and salvation"). Its beginning is Proust's end, in the Guermantes' library, where Marcel affirms his book in terms of the past regained. Proust cannot ignore *causality;* he must accept "the sacred ruler and compass of literary geometry" (12). Yet his characters are prisoners of time. SB likens that dimension to the vertigo experienced by two-dimensional lower organisms confronted with the mystery of height. Our mystery is "Yesterday": we are not simply more weary because further on the way, but we are other, "no longer what we were before the calamity of yesterday" (13). Aspirations of yesterday were valid for yesterday's ego, not for today's; their attainment, "The identification of the subject with the object of his **desire**" (14), has no lasting validity.

SB introduces voluntary **memory**, rejecting it as providing an image "as far removed from the real as the myth of our imagination or the caricature furnished by direct perception." The individual, he argues, is at the point of "decantation" between the fluid of future and past time, existing in a state of smug optimism (15), broken only by rare moments of desire, which in the case of human intercourse ("two separate and immanent dynamisms related by no system of synchronisation") leads to an insatiable thirst for possession (17), unattainable in time. Wisdom, SB concludes (18), consists not in the satisfaction but the ablation of desire (**Neary**'s rational universe is undone by desire). SB subjects Proust's universe to the searching critique of Schopenhauer's categories that limit perception (the *forms* of space, time, and causality), and to his pessimism. Schopenhauer is mentioned here for the first time, but more openly at the end of the essay.

Habit, SB insists, is "the ballast that chains the **dog** to his vomit" (19), mankind to memory. We are creatures of habit, and that alone separates us from the cruelties and enchantments of reality, "the mystery of a strange sky or a strange room" (20). Marcel cannot sleep in a strange room (22–25). Life oscillates between suffering and boredom, but habit (as **Vladimir** acknowledges) is the great deadener, making existence tolerable but closing the window upon the real (28). This derives from Schopenhauer's discussion of inner being (*WWI*, I.4 #57, 402): "Thus its life swings like a pendulum backwards and forwards between pain and ennui."

Proust had a bad memory (unlike **Joyce**), and voluntary memory was not a key to unlock the past (31). Yet in the inaccessible dungeon of being, at the bottom of the "gouffre interdit à nos sondes" (Baudelaire's "**gulf** forbidden to our sounding"), much is stored and may be retrieved by accident. Through the agency of involuntary memory, the diver into the deep (32) may restore the past

object in its fullness and brightness, as with the "famous episode of the **madeleine** steeped in tea," which would alone, SB insists, justify the book: "The whole of Proust's world comes out of a teacup" (34). The Proustian equation can be simplified: involuntary memory may identify past and present and so overcome the three-headed monster of *time, habit,* and *voluntary memory* (the two-headed monster now trine).

Involuntary memory, that "accidental and fugitive salvation" (35), is Proust's leitmotif. SB identifies (36–38) some instances, with attention to "*Les Intermittences du coeur*" (39–45), and Albertine's "tragedy" (45–67), in terms of the paradox of **love** and desire annunciated earlier: "One only loves that which is not possessed" (consider the pursuit in *Murphy*). Love, SB insists, and Albertine bears **witness**, coexists with dissatisfaction (55). It is a function of man's sadness, as **friendship** of his cowardice. The attempt to communicate is "a simian vulgarity, or horribly comic, like the madness that holds a conversation with the furniture" (63). The conclusions are honest but ruthless: if friendship is but a social expedient, somewhere between fatigue and ennui (65)—in a word, *habit*—then its rejection is a necessity: "**art** is the apotheosis of **solitude**" (64), the assumption of "**Assumption**." Art is detached from all moral considerations (66). Tragedy is unconcerned with justice (67) but is, rather, the expiation of the original sin of having been born. As McQueeny argues (107), SB is rejecting Dandieu, who sees Proust's seclusion as a kind of **suicide** resulting from morbidity, a failure of will; SB instead affirms renunciation as proper to the artistic vocation.

The essay returns to the ending of Proust's novel, the *matinée,* and the implications thereof to the shaping of the work of art. This constitutes, firstly, the victory over time, then, the victory of time, the two (salvation and damnation) intricately bound (69). There follows the analysis of the Proustian experience: the "**vases**" in which experiences are suspended and the identification of immediate with past experience (the "equation"). SB insists (75) that involuntary memory is "at once imaginative and empirical, at once an evocation and a direct perception, real without being merely actual, ideal without being merely abstract, the ideal real, the essential, the extra-temporal" (*Le Temps retrouvé,* II.872–73). The conclusion follows: if this **mystical** experience communicates an extratemporal essence, then the communicant is momentarily an extratemporal being, time less recovered than obliterated (75).

The essay finally considers Proust as artist, for whom the idea is embodied not in **allegory** but in the concrete (79). SB acknowledges the **Romantic** strain in Proust: unable, like the classical artist (Joyce), to seek omniscience and omnipotence (81), he affirms the primacy of perception (83), instinct not vitiated by habit, the "non-logical statement of phenomena" before they have been distorted into intelligibility (86). Thus the concession to causality, at the outset of the essay, is qualified. The essay ends with Schopenhauer's values, or, rather, indifference to value. The flowers shamelessly exposing their genitals (89) derive from *The World as Will and Representa-*

tion, as does the expression of the pure subject "exempt from will" (90), the object "exempt from causality" (90), and the meditation on **music** in terms of "the Idea itself, unaware of the world of phenomena, existing ideally outside the universe, apprehended not in Space but in Time only" (92). The dismissal of opera reflects Schopenhauer's insistence on the subordination of words to music (*WWI* I.3 #52, 338); the acceptance of vaudeville, SB's "comedy of an exhaustive enumeration," improves on his "why the same composition is suitable to many verses" (341); and the celebration of the da capo likewise (342). Music, SB asserts, is the "catalytic element" in Proust, the transcendent or "invisible reality" (93) that damns the life of the body on earth as a **pensum** and reveals the meaning of "defunctus" (*Parerga und Parapomena,* II.12 #157). McQueeny concludes that SB's synthesis of Proust's psychology and aesthetics reveals a profound sympathy for pessimism. Schopenhauer's chapters on suffering, the vanity of existence, and the transcendent qualities of music were formative influences on SB's view of Proust's achievement. He would later doubt less the reality of the Proustian experience as any value that might be attributed to it, but at the end of this essay, Proust's "salvation" (a word SB noted in the margins of his copy, as Marcel listens to the Septour), a musical solution to the difficult equation, is essentially affirmed.

"Proust in Pieces": SB's review of Albert Feuillerat's *Comment Proust a composé son roman;* in the **Spectator** 5, 530 (23 June 1934): 975–76, reprinted in **Disjecta**

(63–65). SB begins dispassionately, discussing Professor Feuillerat's argument to the effect that the process of writing over so many years led to "grave dissonances and incompatibilities," which (based on changes to the galleys) would have been tidied up so as to "remove all discord and dissension." SB attacks that assumption, rejecting "the sweet reasonableness of plane psychology" and asserting that it is "the uncontrollable agency of unconscious **memory**" that constitutes the essence of **Proust**'s originality, the book being the search, with all its clues and blind alleys, rather than the *compte rendu* of a round-trip.

Prout, Father: Francis Sylvester Mahony (1804–66), priest and humorist. Born in **Cork**, the son of a Blarney woolens manufacturer, he became a Jesuit seminarian, was educated then taught at Clongowes, but was expelled from the school and the Order after a late-night escapade. The Jesuits failing to convince him that his calling came not from **God**, he was ordained at Lucca (1832) but soon abandoned the clerical life for one of literary bohemianism. In **London**, he became Father Prout, the kidnapped by-blow of **Swift** and Stella, cruelly abandoned on the bleak summit of Watergrasshill and taken to the Cork Foundling Hospital, whence he escaped in a milk churn to begin his literary career, most famously in the *Reliques,* where he indulged his frivolity and erudition. Bryden notes (*Idea of God,* 50) something of Father Prout in the Jesuit who bests the **Polar Bear** (*Dream,* 209–11). He is remembered for his melodic poem "The Bells of Shandon." He died in **Paris** but was buried in the Church of St. Anne in Shandon, where SB attended his grave en route to **Germany** in 1936, sketching it as the first entry in his **German Diaries** ("Cork 28/9/36"). Here, the one place in Cork reconciling fresh air, privacy, and immunity from assault, Miss **Counihan** rejects **Neary** (*Murphy,* 50).

Provence: see **troubadour poetry. Moran**'s discussion of "Molloy" and "Mollose" (*Molloy,* 112) parodies the philological distinction between southern and northern forms of **French**, based on the word for "yes": "langue d'oui" and "langue d'oc" (Languedoc). **Molloy**'s name "might have been oy as it might have been ose, or one, or even oc."

pseudocouples: pairs of characters pervade SB's terrain like animals in search of an ark. Some wander deserted byways in pursuit of a savior; others go nowhere, doomed to existence in claustrophobic rooms or ashbins. Whatever their predicament, the men and women who make up SB's teetering twosomes are tied to each other, figuratively or, like **Pozzo** and **Lucky**, literally. SB's experimentation with pairs of characters begins early, notably in *Murphy* with the "hardy laurel" pairing of **Neary** and **Wylie** (**Dante**'s *ubi* and *quando* [*Par.* XXIX.12], space and **time**). Rabinovitz suggests that couples complement the symmetry and repetitiveness of the entire novel: two coroners, two homosexuals, two waitresses, two fortune-tellers, two alcoholics, two Hindus, two alumni of Neary's academy, two scholars, two doctors, two men with tiny heads, and two men with large heads. Biblical pairings, such as Jacob and

Esau and the rich man and **Lazarus** (see **Abraham's bosom**), surface throughout the novel, to underscore the motif of repetition. *Watt* further boasts numerous pairs of characters: Watt and **Knott**, **Art and Con**, Rose and Cerise, **Cream** and Berry, Blind Bill and Maimed Matt. On the other hand, **Molloy** and **Moran** enact a psychic drama that is much more complex than mere repetition (see **Jung**).

In SB's minimalist works, populated cities and detailed environments give way to fictional and theatrical settings of vast emptiness, containing the barest essentials. A mere tree and low mound make up the setting of *Waiting for Godot,* while in *Endgame,* the characters move within a sterile gray shelter. Yet SB's fascination with symmetry, with analogies and repetition, grows more intense. Their surroundings evaporate, but couples remain, the more pronounced against the sparsely adorned backdrops. In the 1999 Barbican **Gate** production of *Godot,* for instance, **Vladimir** and **Estragon** shared a single suit, in Act I Didi had the jacket and Gogo the trousers, and in Act 2, vice versa, an innovation SB had developed for his 1975 **Schiller-Theater** production. Michael Billington called this "a perfect symbol of their singularity and indissolubility, and a reminder that everything that happens in the first half is repeated with variations in the second" (*Guardian Weekly,* 16–22 September 1999, 17).

SB's couples are rather, to borrow a term the **Unnamable** uses to describe **Mercier and Camier**, "pseudocouples" (409), halves of a single personality. SB saw them, like the tree on stage, as branches of a single trunk (or as arms to a single human trunk), Didi associated with the air, Gogo with the earth. Martin Esslin suggests the possibility that **Hamm** and **Clov** (both four-letter names) are also "vice-existers," the former symbolizing the instinctual and tyrannical side of the mind and the latter the intellect. Others read SB's couples as critiques of Cartesianism. Murphy and **Celia**, Mercier and Camier, Pozzo and Lucky, Hamm and Clov, Bertrand and **Morvan**, blind men and cripples, symbolize the relationship between mind and body. Murphy is primarily associated with the mind and obsessed with trying to withdraw from the world, but Celia is connected with the physical world as a prostitute and by her bodily measurements. Hamm, blind and immobile, plays the mind by dictating activities of the day, while Clov responds by carrying them out. The constant dysfunction that plagues SB's pairings repudiates rationalist views of mind and body. Clov as body and Hamm as mind are interdependent. Hamm needs Clov to serve him, Clov needs the combination to Hamm's cupboard; Hamm cannot stand, Clov cannot sit: "Every man his speciality" (10).

Pseudocouples serve as literary and theatrical equivalents to Cubist art. Pairs such as Vladimir and Estragon, Hamm and Clov, **Willie** and **Winnie** present audiences with several views of a single figure, much as Picasso's *Grande Tête* constitutes two interlocking profiles. This contrasting nature suggests the self and its other. In later works that inseparable duality is represented by an external **voice** a solo character perceives. In *Company, That Time,* and "Rockaby," for instance, the voice is familiar and alien, the self and other; the interplay offers a late variation on the pseudocouple theme. A further variant, from *How It Is* to "What Where," concerns the complex relationship of tormentor and victim (see **politics**). The term "pseudocouple" contains a fitting Beckettian ambiguity that frustrates such **allegorical** arguments. One might read SB's pairs as pseudocouples not because the characters are one in the same but, on a more literal level, because they are, as human beings, isolated and unable to overcome the distance that separates them. Their shapely form only underlines the imperfection and disorder of their lives, as Rabinovitz explains at the end of his essay on *Murphy*. Most paired characters remain together not because of their harmonious friendships but out of fear, guilt, and, in a **Berkeleyan** echo, the need to be perceived, to be **witnessed** ("Something of this is being heard," Winnie assures an uninterested Willie in *Happy Days;* "Can you see me," asks Nell to a nearly blind **Nagg** in *Endgame*). SB's couples recognize a fundamental principle of the creation story in Genesis: "It is not good for the man to be alone." All linger, alas, just this side of paradise, always taking, despite the appearance of **company**, their solitary way. [PS]

psychoanalysis: SB encountered psychoanalysis through three sources: his two-year analysis; attentive reading of texts and commentaries; and the all-pervasive ethos of the *Freudzeit,* that twentieth-century mythology of loss and psychic displacement. All three converge upon an important structural element in his

work. Critical consensus extends little further, alas, and SB's borrowings from psychology remain disarmingly eclectic, major debts to the ideas of **Freud** (qv) and **Jung** (qv) in particular leaving him short of allegiance to either. The literary role of SB's psychoanalysis begins with a sense of what he encountered, and how, through those three crucial sources.

In *Dream,* jargon such as "anal complex" and "narcissism" dropped "knowingly" into the narrative show SB absorbing psychoanalytic ideas, playing with them as useful tools, yet undercutting them in a not entirely convincing attempt to distance himself ironically from his protagonist's intellectual floundering. Despite the novel's failings, the hyperaesthetized, hystericoreflective, and ultimately claustrophobic context is significant. The birth of psychoanalysis in Vienna was in complex ways the product of its cultural setting. Europe was suffering from a **Romantic** hangover; the aesthete-gentleman had a decadent predilection for heightened consciousness of his own exquisite feelings, analyzing them in pseudointellectual terms. This morbid *Innerlichkeit,* brilliantly portrayed by Arthur Schnitzler and Thomas Mann and not unrelated to **Joyce**'s "paralysis," produced the kind of mental ferment encompassed by enervated stasis that makes **Belacqua** a creature of his time. It was fertile breeding ground for the neuroses that Freud proposed to cure by genuine analysis, reaching beneath the shallow froth and bringing the fundamental content to a healthy realignment with conscious awareness. Yet his cathartic method and terminology could

serve as grist to the mill of decadent intellectualizing, with the bonus of titillat-
ing sexuality. Playboy analysts of the
Vienna circle such as Fritz Wittels and
Wilhelm **Stekel** demonstrated as much.
As Freudian concepts filtered into public
currency they became virtual emblems of
sexuality, a guide to self-**voyeurism**. Was
this trivialization of a profound discovery?
Depth psychology of unconscious mental content may be incoherent despite its
enduring appeal, but that is not at issue
here. Rather, psychoanalysis was a dynamic process fostering intense scrutiny
of the contents of **consciousness**, regardless of whatever depths, spurious or
otherwise, it might have been dredged
from. SB was not a social satirist, and the
"knowing" ethos absorbed into *Dream*
simply nourished the isolated self-
scrutiny that was to become ever more
emphatic in his protagonists with an increasingly extensive and rigorous use of
psychoanalytic procedure.

The theory is familiar. The psychoanalytic mind consists of conscious identity (ego); the unconscious realm of
instinctual drives (id); and the pre-
conscious, a repository of mental content
potentially available to consciousness.
The primitive urges of the id seek satisfaction by pushing up into consciousness
and dominating behavior. But the ego,
having to exist in a civilized world, must
repress or moderate these urges if it is to
remain stable; often it cannot afford to
acknowledge them. The mind's **censorship** mechanism represses any thoughts
deriving from the id's dictates that are incompatible with the ego's integrity or
distorts them into a symbolically related
acceptable form. Repressed material oc-

casionally breaks out, especially in
dreams. A well-adjusted ego maintains
equilibrium, but a maladjusted ego, one
that has not negotiated infantile sexuality, cannot assimilate the id's demands;
it can deal with them only by distorting
them into drastically different forms,
often somatic symptoms and ritualistic
or hysterical complexes. Therapy seeks to
make patients aware of their symptoms'
growth from instinctual urges by helping them to trace the thread of symbols
and thoughts back to its origin in the id,
thus bolstering the ego with cathartic
insight and giving it scientific acceptance
of human nature with which to come to
terms with the id's demands.

SB, suffering from a racing heart, night
sweats, panic, and unhappiness, was prepared to take psychoanalysis seriously. His
knowledge of theory derived from extensive reading during the early 1930s.
Woodworth's *Contemporary Schools* offered an overview; from Ernest **Jones**'s
Papers on Psychoanalysis he took twenty
pages of notes; he read books by **Adler,
Rank, Stephens,** and Stekel; and he paid
due attention to Freud and Jung. He
translated **surrealist** texts with titles such
as "Simulation of general paralysis essayed" or "Simulation of mental debility essayed." Such sources yielded quirky
details, like **Cooper**'s acasthisia, one of
SB's eccentric trifles. His interest centered on narcissism, neuroses, and the
psychopathology of daily life rather than
on the wilder flights of analytic fancy
into the realm of totems and taboos. He
found in these studies, dated as they now
seem, confirmation of his intrauterine
attraction and psychosomatic problems,
insights into the fraught relationship

with his **mother**, and a means of determining his own condition.

SB's experience of analysis at the **Tavistock** Clinic began shortly after Christmas 1933 and lasted nearly two years. His symptoms were too severe to ignore, and he was forced to acknowledge the morbidity of his arrogant superiority and isolation. Wilfred **Bion** took him for thrice-weekly sessions, drawing undogmatically on various schools of psychoanalytic thought and delving into his past and family ties. Free association and dream analysis were the principal techniques. SB's love-hate relationship with his mother was a major nexus; what he called her "savage loving" contributed to his problems. The emphasis was on cathartic insight into the buried etiology of his ailments. He was intensely committed to the therapy and had an intellectual respect for Bion, whom he found personable outside of treatment. The archaeological aspect of the process fascinated him: "I certainly came up with some extraordinary memories of being in the womb. Intrauterine memories" (see **geology**).

Two aspects of this experience left indelible traces on his writing. Childhood memories, often taken from his own life, haunt his characters; a **larch** tree in the garden, stonecutters in the hills at night, images of mother and child, of father and son, surface repeatedly in the destitute monologues of old men who have never properly grown up. These he called "obsessional." He absorbed the psychoanalytic emphasis on development and the importance of childhood, mindful of his own journey back to infancy on Bion's couch. The process of free association entered his narrative style. The compul-

sion to speak, endlessly, breathlessly, reeling through empty phrases, trying not to think about thinking, desperate to say the right thing, to be able to stop, but not knowing what it is, not knowing whether you've already said it, having to go **on**: this becomes the medium of *The Unnamable* and subsequent works (a synthesis, not a product, of free association).

SB acknowledged his therapy, though hardly emphatically: "I think it helped me to control my panic." The chance to share his troubles, banal as that is, probably did benefit him. Whether he emerged convinced of the truth of oedipal theory, mythic archetype, **birth** trauma, or other paraphernalia is a moot point. What certainly did intersect potently with his personal experience was the concept of **narcissism** (qv). His new perspective on his "abject self-referring **quietism**" (qv) had the force of an epiphany. The transformation of his life into secular sainthood owed much to this turning point, but as he turned away from histrionic arrogance in his personal life he began to explore it in his writing with increased distance and insight. Belacqua becomes **Murphy**, the narcissist par excellence but for his "distractions," **Celia** and ginger biscuits.

Critics diverge in their assessment of SB and psychology. What is to be made of **Murphy's mind**? (qv). It is certainly not Freudian, as O'Hara points out at length. It originates in the diagram Jung showed in his Tavistock lecture, which SB witnessed, but that is difficult to reconcile with any psychoanalytic topography. Is it a throwaway indulgence before the real business of dramatizing analytic themes in *Molloy*? Or is it an expression of philosophical interest in the *ubi nihil* maxim and all that entails, as pursued to its logical extreme in *The Unnamable,* for which purpose psychoanalytic motifs, *Molloy* included, are intermediate? The debate is unlikely to be settled, depending as it does on readers' instinctive responses to SB's work. On one side stand those who approach SB through his minimalism, and find in him stoic affirmation or the possibility of some kind of (psychoanalytic?) redemption; the other side consists of those who approach SB through the philosophical tumult of his early prose, emphasize the process of paring down to the unnamable in style and content, and assert the uncompromising nihilism of SB's vision.

Paring down the narrative voice is precisely where psychoanalysis for SB comes into its own. The ego/id topography is a potent mythology offering writers a new way to dramatize mental life, as *Molloy* demonstrates. For SB the *process* of undergoing analysis becomes the vital informing metaphor. After *Molloy,* having reduced the mind's interaction with the external world to an archetypal minimum, he leaves behind theoretical paraphernalia and uses the relentless compulsion of "the talking cure" to descend to unnamable depths. Here the outline of Murphy's mind seems more apposite than byzantine psychoanalytic schemes. It is a simple model, but the fundamental principle of *The Unnamable is* simple; it is a literary metaphor, not an exercise in systemic psychology.

Molloy depicts psychic disintegration; ego, id, libido are dramatized as separate entities interacting under tension. In *The Unnamable* the narrative voice is so prob-lematic that "I" constantly implodes into "he," "they," or "it." The implied analyst has become internalized as a compulsion to speak that is part of yet apart from that "I." Freud's position is clear: "neurosis is the result of a conflict between the ego and its id, whereas psychosis is the analogous outcome of a similar disturbance in the relations between the ego and the external world" ("Neurosis and Psychosis," 149). Psychosis is the extreme example of psychic disintegration, and SB's writing, like that of many modern artists, incorporates aspects of **schizophrenia**. Analysts hold that psychotic fragmentation is caused by a disruption of the ego's unity and indiscriminate thrusting into consciousness of autonomous complexes deriving from primitive sexual or archetypal material. Caution is necessary for those wishing to consider SB in the context of psychology. Psychoanalysis evolved as an explanation of, and treatment for, neurosis; efforts to make it accommodate psychosis remain unconvincing. Schizophrenic symptoms are better accounted for by a disturbance of conscious attentional mechanisms resulting in a pathologically reflexive and pervertedly logical state of mind. This perspective, deriving from cognitive psychology, remains uncommitted regarding the general accuracy of psychoanalytic anatomies of mind. SB arguably *used* psychoanalytic *process* to evoke experiences akin to schizophrenia while remaining similarly uncommitted regarding psychoanalytic theory, and making no attempt to dramatize the dubious psychoanalytic version of psychosis.

SB commented in *Dream* (149): "We shall pack off the pair of them to a thalamus that by day folds up for psychoanalysis," a marriage bed that becomes a couch. His literary concerns were never subordinate to psychoanalysis, but he conducted a critique of it. Freud left much unsaid on the subject; it remained for Lacan to formulate the unconscious *as* language. But SB knew that no matter how deep we delve in the psyche, there will always be a **voice**, whatever that is, and that the fundamentals begin and end with words. [DL]

ptomaine: Gk. *ptoma,* "a corpse"; food poisoning by amino compounds from putrefying animal tissues, as suffered by the **Unnamable**'s family (318), particularly the women as the "menstrues" in the **French** text (52) intimates. See **sausage poisoning**. One child is named "Ptoto," like "Toto," the *gamin* in the *En Route* and *En Marche* texts used in many British schools.

Puget, Pierre (1620–94): native of Marseilles, sculptor, naval decorator, and marine artist; mentioned in *Murphy* (239). In 1656 the Toulon authorities decided to embellish their Town Hall with Puget's design for the facade: two *Atlantes* in the style of Michelangelo, three meters high, supporting the balcony, one representing *Force* and the other *Fatigue.* The model for *Strength* was Bertrand Marquet, a local strongman, but the similarity to *Weariness* explains Murphy's perplexity. Compare **Proust**'s Marcel at Combray (*Swann,* I.121, as marked in SB's copy), where faced with the "Vertues et Vices de Padour" he dislikes their rapport with their **allegorical** subjects, then understands that their beauty arises not from their symbolic force but from the ex-

pression of this as felt. Consider, too, **Estragon**'s outburst (*WG,* 55.a): "We're not caryatids."

pun: Murphy reflects (65), "What but an imperfect sense of humour could have made such a mess of chaos. In the beginning was the pun." This subverts the New Testament Logos, the response of John 1:1 to the Genesis creation myth. The *logos* was equated with **reason**, and its antonym, *alogos,* was used by Euclid to express mathematical irrationality; this was translated into Latin by *surdus* ("deaf"), and hence "absurd." A complex etymology links the word to the Theater of the **Absurd**. As **Schopenhauer** notes (*WWI,* 1.1 #13, 76–80), the cause of laughter is the sudden perception of incongruity between a concept and the **objects** thought through it into some relation. Laughter expresses incongruity: "All laughter then is accompanied by paradox." Yet, he insists, the pun or double entendre is spurious wit, foolish because it brings different concepts by the assistance of accident under one word. This, for **Freud** as much as for SB, was a key insight into wit's relation to the unconscious, an important qualification of Schopenhauer's assumed **gulf** between "real objects" and "words," not easily bridged. The pun, however appalling, is an expression of an absurdist creation structured (or perceived) by language, a syzygy that subverts as it creates. The challenge to the rational universe is thus embodied in the vaudeville nature of language, glossed in *Proust* (92) as the comedy of exhaustion.

puppets: a word SB borrowed from **Rudmose-Brown** for his **Trinity** lectures on **Racine**, when he insisted that the artist and his material were in a state of flux, yet more had to be done to "organise this mess" than simply "make puppets and set them in motion" (Rachel Dobbin). In "**Love and Lethe**" (95), **Belacqua** and Ruby Tough are like "fantoccini controlled by a single wire." **Murphy** differs from other characters (122) as one "who is not a puppet" (the phrase added to the typescript), though his **irrational heart** jumps like "**Petrouchka** in his box" (3). SB used **Valéry**'s phrase: "il avait tué la marionette" (*Monsieur Teste,* 27) in a 1934 review of **Rilke**: "popping up for a gulp of disgust" (*Disjecta,* 66). **Schopenhauer**'s "On Genius" (*WWI,* III.3.xxxi, 152) likens the normal man to "a complex set of wires, by means of which puppets are set in motion," whereas the genius, likened to a living man among the famous puppets of Milan, can master the Will. The narrator in "**Text 8**" (133) feels like "a mere ventriloquist's dummy," his head left in an Irish bar.

These terms would change in response to an essay by Heinrich von **Kleist.** Knowlson recounts (517) SB's admiration for the 1810 essay, in which Kleist compares the human dancer with the marionette, the latter superior since lacking in self-awareness and affectation, which destroy natural grace and charm. "Über das Marionetten-theater" offers three "allegories of the **body**" and a thesis on self-consciousness and **motion** whereby the presence of the one destroys the dynamics of the other, a sentiment compatible with a lack of synchronicity in an **Occasionalist** world. Consider the stiffness of **Molloy** and **Moran** as they move toward awareness. **Malone** tells

how well it went at first (180): "If I said, Now I need a hunchback, immediately one came running, proud as punch." Alone in the dark, the **Unnamable** resolves to scatter such adjuncts (292). The Unnamable is the reductio of Kleist's assertion, and **aporia** his procedural mode.

Knowlson contends that Kleist's essay expressed some of SB's deepest aesthetic aspirations, extending this insight from the lack of self-consciousness of the protagonist in "**Ghost Trio**" before seeing himself in the mirror to the pacing of **May** in *Footfalls,* the puppetlike movements of **Krapp,** and **Winnie**'s gestures in *Happy Days.* During rehearsals at the 1971 **Schiller-Theater** production of *Happy Days,* SB quoted Kleist to instruct Eva-Katharina Schultz in the art of gesture. He did so again to Ronald Pickup and James Knowlson during rehearsals for the BBC production of "**Shades**" (1976), comparing the man in "Ghost Trio" with a fencer who fights a bear, a creature completely without awareness of self and thus able to respond naturally and spontaneously as the fencer cannot. Such a state of grace is impossible for one cursed with **consciousness.**

purgatory: the *Purgatorio* is part II of **Dante**'s *Divina commedia,* that toward which SB felt the greatest affinity. Thence he drew the figure of **Belacqua,** whose meditation on **pity** and piety (It. *pietà*) shapes "**Dante and the Lobster,**" and whose indolence and **embryonal** repose underlie **Murphy**'s **desire** for the unparalleled bliss of contemplation. Purgatory, more than Hell, two "admirable singulars" ("Text 6," 124), defines life on earth, a zone between the hell of existence in the big world and the impossible *Paradiso* of self. Whereas **Eliot**'s purgatorial figures embrace their suffering joyously because they anticipate its remission, no such relief awaits SB's characters, for whom existence is perpetual expiation for the nonvenial sin of being alive. The emphasis is on punishment (see **pensum**), but with no correlative sense of sin: when **Vladimir** suggests repenting, **Estragon** queries, "Our being born?" (*WG*, 8.b). Purgatory is a state rather than a process, and thus SB's vision differs from that of his Italian maestro. As Bryden puts it (*Idea of God*, 157), though the suffering is similar, "the ills which assail humankind are not transactions within a divine economy"—the kind that can be shortened by a godly prayer.

"**Dante**" concludes (33) that Dante's Purgatory is "conical and consequently implies culmination"; whereas **Joyce**'s is "spherical and excludes culmination." In the one there is "progression and a guaranteed consummation"; in the other flux. He asks how Joyce's work can be purgatorial, and answers with "the absolute absence of the Absolute," a continuous purgatorial process. Again, SB says more about himself than about Joyce. This anticipation of living in the caesura, the hyphen, persists in his later work, for instance, in "Text 6" (the interval between apparitions), where **prison** shades close into a little nook where he will be forever. *The Lost Ones* presents a purgatorial world, between hell and hope, with an elaborate if futile arrangement of cylinders and **ladders** suggesting purpose, informed by the ethos of waiting that defines the later texts.

Puvis de Chavannes, Pierre (1824–98): French painter of decorative frescoes, notably those of Ste. Geneviève in the Pantheon, alluded to in "**Sanies II**": "slouching up to Puvis."

Pythagoras (ca. 580–500 BC): Greek philosopher of Samos who established a school at Crotona (529), celebrated for its magnificent garden and rigorous learning. Neophytes were admitted only after a novitiate of five years' silence. The order assumed great authority. Its history is speculative, accentuating metempsychosis, abstention from flesh and beans, and curious prohibitions (such as not to touch a white cock nor let swallows share one's roof). Pythagoras died, perhaps, fleeing a mob, when faced by a field of fava beans. He considered number the first principle, the universe expressing regularity, correspondence, and harmony; hence **Neary**'s jest about the "**Apmonia**" and death of **Hippasos**. The discovery of musical ratios and the famous theorem were probably his own, but most Pythagorean doctrines were those of his followers. He wrote little, but his *Ipse dixit*, "the Master said so," carried authority. His combination of **mathematics** and theology characterized religious philosophy from the Greeks to **Descartes**, the rationalist tradition suggesting that exact reasoning applies to ideal rather than sensible things. **Objects** of thought are thus more real than those of sense perception. Mathematical objects such as numbers or circles, if real, are eternal rather than in **time**, and such eternal objects represent God's thoughts. Pythagoras's **mystical** mathematics thus initiates the tradition against which SB's **absurdity** and **irrationality** must be measured.

Q

"**Quad**": a "Ballet for four people" written for television (1981); produced as "Quadrat 1 + 2" by Süddeutscher Rundfunk (8 October 1981), dir. SB with Walter Asmus, with Helfried Foron, Juerg Hummel, Claudia Knujpfer, and Susanne Rehe as dancers. First English broadcast BBC 2 (16 December 1982), the SDR production. SB's thought of staging geometry dates at least from 1963, with a mime for Jack **MacGowran** (see "**J. M. Mime**"). There two pairs, son and **father**, son and **mother**, describe paths along quarters of a square to arrive back at center, 0. The pattern of composition is toward greater complexity, an impulse not apparent in "Quad," where the triangles are enlarged and rhythm added. The theme is reversed as the center is avoided, not sought. The playing area consists of a square, or quad, ABCD, center **E** (originally **O**), with one fixed camera position, X. The seven-minute "Quad" consists of wordless movements by four identical players, the "course" of each meticulously plotted. The major "problem" is the negotiation of O when any converge. In production the timing proved difficult. SB almost scrapped it, but the actors finally mastered the intricate, rapid movement. When he saw the color production rebroadcast on a black-and-white monitor, SB decided instantly to create "Quad II." He added a black-and-white version, percussion restricted, tempo monorhythmic, the movements half those of "Quad." The variation was

a performative masterstroke, a "repeat" to dramatize the entropy of **motion** (compare **Winnie**: "What a curse mobility"). No printed text acknowledges this change, nor the fuller title; only a short endnote indicates that the ballet was revised to a two-act structure. SB's videotaped German production constitutes the only "final" and accurate text. The fifteen-minute "Quad I and II" may be SB's most formal and symmetrical work. Four figures, each in pastel djellabas, appear to describe a quadrangle to a rapid, polyrhythmic percussion, then depart in sequence. Each describes half the quad, but abruptly avoids the center, turning to the left, like **Dante**'s damned. The action first seems comic, as characters rush toward a central collision, avoided by abrupt turns, but "something terrifying" emerges. The pattern repeats, from one to four participants, then back to one, then none in an oscillation, crescendo, and diminuendo that shatters whatever comic possibilities were anticipated. The effect is of prescribed, determined, enforced motion.

quaquaquaqua: **Lucky**'s repeated utterance (*WG*, 28.b), the root "qua" as *meaning* (or *nonsense*) reduced to its **fundamental sound**. It parodies Quintilian's logical categories, which reduce all propositions to basic components. Compare *Finnegans Wake* (195): "Quoiquoiquoiquoiquoiquoiquoiq!"; or "Quatsch quatsch quatsch" (*Dream,* 36). In "**Em-**

bers" (99), the Music Master shouts "Qua!" and thumps his **cylindrical ruler** when Addie cannot "Eff" (a theological drama in miniature). In *How It Is* "quaqua" is a refrain: "**voice** once without quaqua on all sides then in me" (7). The narrator hears not a **mixed choir** but "quaqua meaning on all sides megaphones" (107).

Quatre esquisses: four theatrical "sketches": "**Fragment de théâtre I**," "**Fragment de théâtre II**," "**Pochade radiophonique**," and "**Esquisse radiophonique**"; in *Pas suivi de Quatres esquisses* (Minuit, 1978).

Quatre nouvelles: a grouping of *Premier amour,* "L'**Éxpulsé**," "Le **Calmant**," and "La **Fin**." SB told George **Reavey** (December 1946) he hoped to have a book of short stories (in **French**) ready by spring, adding that he would probably not write much more in English. **Bordas** dropped *Quatre nouvelles,* which had been announced as forthcoming, and when **Minuit** accepted his creative backlog SB withheld much of the earliest French writing. *Premier amour* waited till 1970, but the other three *nouvelles* appeared from Minuit (1955) and **Grove** (1967), with *Textes pour rien / Texts for Nothing.*

"**Quatre poèmes**": a subgrouping in *Poems in English* (1961) and *Collected Poems* (1977) of four French poems, translations facing: *Trois poèmes* (1948) and "**Dieppe**." Only "Dieppe" is listed in the table of contents. The English versions appeared as "Four Poems" in *The Guinness Book of Poetry, 1960–61* (London: Putnam, 1962), 40–41.

"**que ferais-je sans ce monde**": second of *Trois poèmes: Three Poems* (1948); a fifteen-line verse published in *Transition Forty-Eight*. Translated as "**What would I do without this world**." Nine lines consider this world, where to be lasts but an instant, a world of silence where murmurs die and the sky soars above the dust of existence. Six lines respond: he will wander, looking for another like himself, "sans voix parmi les voix / enfermées avec moi." The poem is remarkable for its incantatory effects and its identification of the "gouffre des murmures," intimating the **voice** that he, voiceless, is hearing within himself. A major theme of *Three Novels* is almost audible.

"**Quel malheur**": an extract from *Malone meurt* in Sartre's *Les Temps modernes* 71 (septembre 1951): 385–416, printed a month before publication by **Minuit** (88–151, with variants; 222–54 in translation). Compare "**che sciagura**"; Malone's "misfortune" is to lose his pencil.

" . . . **que nuages** . . .": Edith Fournier's translation of " . . . **but the clouds** . . ."; in *Quad et autres pièces pour la television* (Minuit, 1992).

quietism: a doctrine of asceticism and devotion, teaching that the chief duty of man is the contemplation of **God** or **Christ**, through independence of outward circumstance. It emerged in the teachings of Miguel Molinos (1640–96) countering the bureaucratic ecclesiasticism of Rome by individual conscience. It distinguishes the **voice** of God from vagaries of imagination by rejecting deliberate thought and will. The first duty of the quietist is to be passive or, in terms familiar to SB from **Schopenhauer**, to renounce the Will. During the early 1930s SB read the *Imitatio Christi* of **Thomas à Kempis** with quiet intensity, attracted to its modesty, and the uncomplaining acceptance of pain. It had a lasting influence. He doubted it might be "twisted into a programme of self-sufficiency" (SB to TM, 10 March 1935), but this was a rejection less of the teaching than of its Christian premises. **Rousseau**'s *Rêveries du promeneur solitaire* offered a secular account of the mode of acceptance mapped by Thomas, a path SB would follow; see "**Humanistic Quietism**" (1934). Yet that title is oxymoronic, questioning the "abject self-referring quietism" of Thomas, but affirming **MacGreevy**'s poetry as prayer. **Murphy**'s encounter with Mr. **Endon** critiques the retreat into the cubicle of the mind: attracted to quietism, SB was not unaware of its consequences. Bryden contends (*Idea of God*, 85) that SB rejects Thomas's assumption that virtue is better acquired in **solitude** than in society, but solitude took precedence over **humanism**. Or rather, from this strife of opposites a more complex *ethics* was forged, reflected equally in the *aesthetics* that SB stated to Charles Juliet (1977): "Negation is no more possible than affirmation. . . . It is impossible to protest, and equally impossible to assent" (*Conversations*, 165). Such quietism underlies the "**fundamental unheroic**." It allowed SB to accommodate the ethics of Thomas and **Geulincx** within a **contingent** world, to escape **Joyce**'s language, and to write "without style."

Compare "**bon bon il est un pays**," a plea to be left in the realm of the mind, in solitude, seeking its "calme," that "**nothing**" experienced by Murphy (246) and sought by **Malone** (198), beyond the tumult a great calm. This echoes Thomas's "post tempestatum, magna serenitas," serenity beyond the mind's commotion. SB would spend much time exploring that region.

Quigley, Mr.: a deus ex machina providing the pittance to support **Murphy**. He lives in Holland, necessarily, as a *Dutch uncle,* one to whom the smallest appeal will meet with severe rebuke. The name suggests Oscar Quigley, a **Dublin** chess player; he was earlier the protagonist of "**Lightning Calculation**."

Quin: early protagonist of *Watt*. His father, Alexander Quin, married "Leda, née Swan, demi-mondaine," who passed away after the death of her fourth Willy, her married life (Appendix #1) "one long drawsheet," an infinite process of giving birth. The name implies "quin" or "quî ne" ("that by it not"), negative intentionality. It suggests actor James Quin (1693–1766). Traces remain: Quin's Hotel (*Watt*, 20); his "happy expressions" ("Echo's Bones," 21); his name (*Mercier and Camier,* 119; Camier comments, "That must be someone who does not exist"); his "flannel" (*Malone Dies,* 251). The Saxon tells **Lemuel** that he has "Dreamt all night of that bloody man Quin again" (282); in *Malone meurt* (206) this appears in English.

Quin, "Hairy" Capper: Belacqua's best man and, after his death, in "**Draff**," the man in the gap, helping the **Smeraldina** organize the funeral and doing what "darling Bel would wish." He is *glabrous* (bald), but "Hairy" suggests potency (Blazes Boylan is a "hairy" man); "Capper" echoes *Cappoquin,* a Trappist monastery in Münster.

quincunx: the corners and center of a square, as the mural cavities (*The Lost Ones,* 204) or St. Andrew's cross (*How It Is,* 58); intimating the five wounds of **Christ**. In *Mercier et Camier,* the Place **Saint-Ruth** features quincunxes. The abandoned "**J. M. Mime**" is staged on a "quink," a design restored in "**Quad**."

qui vive: the sentry's cry in *Murphy* (71) and *Watt* (122). The French "who lives" modulates into Italian "where lives," as in "Qui vive la pièta quando è ben mortà" (*Inferno* XX.28; see "**Dante and the Lobster**"), repeated in *Dream* (148). Lady **Pedal** is on the *qui vive*

(*Malone Dies,* 285). The phrase resonates in *The **Unnamable*** (345), ***Happy Days*** (22), and *The **Lost Ones*** (219) as the mind's vigilance on the frontiers of **consciousness**.

"Quoi où": original of "**What Where**" (Minuit, 1983), a special edition of ninety-nine numbered copies; added to *Catastrophe et autres dramaticules* (1982). A revised text was prepared for Pierre Chabert, Théâtre de rond-point, **Paris** (22 mars 1986), six performances, with David **Warrilow** as **Bam**. The changes, described by Gontarski (*JOBS* 2.1 [1992]: 22–24) and Brater (*Beyond Minimalism,* 163–64), include: elimination of Bam's "interventions" and the mime ("Je recommence" became "Ici Bam"); the megaphone replaced by an artificial circle of orange light; no full human figures but three heads suspended in space; a faster tempo; and an irony rendering the **political** implications less overt.

R

Rabelais, François (ca. 1483–1553): French satirist, author of *Gargantua and Pantagruel,* a compendium of irreverent learning, a quest for the Holy Bottle. Attracted by its sense of carnival, SB read the Génie de France edition in 1935, taking extensive notes (Knowlson, 205); yet *Murphy* refers to Rabelais only to describe **Cooper**'s thirst: "Pantagruel had him by the throat" (120). Rabelais provided **scholastic** tags to pepper the text: "Deus det" (58), "gambadoes" (85), and things that hobble toward the only possible (227). On his deathbed Rabelais set out to investigate "le grand peut-être"; the narrator of "Text 8" pants toward "the grand **apnoea**" (134).

Racine, Jean (1639–99): French classical tragedian studied and taught by SB at **Trinity**. In *Dream* (144) **Belacqua** laments the post-Racinian decline of preterits and past subjunctives, citing a half line from *Phèdre* (I.iii.254), which **Chas** caps: "Vous mourûtes aux bords où vous fûtes laissée" ("You were believed to have died on the shore where you were thought to have been left"). *Phèdre* illustrates Marcel's sense of "the ever-wakeful Gods" who [seduce] the hearts of feeble mortals (II.v.279–82; *Proust,* 59); SB nodded, using "réduire" for Phèdre's "séduire." *Murphy* imitates Racine's **situation circle** of **desire**, as events and characters are brought to a pre-established ending, and in the conflict between the structural **machinery** and the characters'

impulses. Leslie **Daiken**, citing SB's lectures, notes Racine's "replacing the mediaeval preoccupation with predestination as being an exterior force responsible for doom and the phenomena of **consciousness** of sin" with the promptings of interior being (in the **Whoroscope Notebook** SB mentions "Racinian lighting"). Ludovic Janvier described *Murphy* as "*Andromaque* jouée par les Marx Brothers." In 1956 SB reread Racine for the possibilities of monologue, with virtually immobile characters in a **closed space**. Reading Racine, Knowlson concludes (383), pointed SB toward *Happy Days,* "Play," and the shorter monologues.

rafflesia: of the family Rafflesiaceae, named after Sir Stamford Raffles, six species found only in Malaya and Sumatra, and parasitical on vine roots, only the gigantic scarlet flower visible above ground. *R. arnoldi,* discovered (1818) by Joseph Arnold in West Sumatra, is the largest flower known, Arnold's original described as a yard across, five petals attached to a huge nectary over which swarms of carrion flies hover to pollinate it and giving off the smell of decaying flesh. SB recorded "bloodied rafflesia in sombre Sumatra" (DN, 94). **Nordau**'s *Degeneration* (192) describes "the wondrous rafflesia" that "illumines the sombre forests of Sumatra with the wild magnificence of its blood-red colour. **Wagner**'s poems have in them something of the carrion stench and uncanny beauty of this plant of rapine and corruption." In "**Enueg I**," the "still flagrant rafflesia" of Sumatra breaks with sudden color, its "blood-red" splendor ("the banner of meat bleeding") a reminder of his darling's "red sputum" (Peggy **Sinclair**'s TB). Degeneracy and "rafflesia stinking of carrion" recur in *The Unnamable* (317), as **Mahood**, one leg left somewhere off the coast of Java (in French, "Sumatra"), hobbles home to find his family dead of **sausage poisoning**.

Rahab: the harlot saved when Jericho was destroyed (Joshua 2:1–6); in *Whoroscope* she is compared to Queen **Christina** of Sweden; in *Dream* (53) to **Yang Kuei-fei**; and in "**From the Only Poet to a Shining Whore**" and "**To Be Sung Loud**" to **Beatrice**. Writing to MacGreevy (July 1930) SB dismissed "the Rahab tomfoolery."

Rank, Otto (1884–1939): German psychologist and associate of **Freud**. SB found in his *The Trauma of Birth* (1929) compelling accounts that explained, he felt, his problems with his **mother** (qv) and intrauterine attraction. In Rank's conclusion, "the real Unconscious consists only in the libidinal relation of the **embryo** to the womb" (195). Similar sentiments underlie **Belacqua**'s preference for embryonic repose, **Murphy** for his inner dark, **Watt** for the **asylum**, and **Molloy** for his mother's room.

Rasima: the **Smeraldina**'s eyes have "a Rasima look" (*Dream*, 5). SB noted: "**Job** chastises his wife (Rasima)" (DN, 54); the **Bible** does not name her. **Cooper** tells how the tempter appeared as a bald

crone and asked for Rasima's locks in return for prosperity; he showed them to Job to prove her dishonor, and Job swore to chastise her (*Flagellation*, 376).

rats: in Toulouse, in the Basilica Saint-Sernin, a low capitol in the crypt is carved to represent a rat gnawing into a globe (*Dream*, 9). SB links this to **La Fontaine**'s fable of the rat who retired from the world and into a large Dutch cheese. Rats represent the animal world reduced to its **fundamental sound**, as in "**Serena I**," where the adder broaches its rat. They slither behind the wallpaper of the blue Hof (*Dream*, 15). **Murphy** cannot sleep (110) because he knows the rat is behind the wall; the rat cannot move because it knows he is awake. "**Draff**" celebrates the magic hour when subliminal rats come abroad on their rounds (184). **Molloy**, imagining himself hunted by terriers, notes that each man "counts his rats" in the afternoon (67). The **Unnamable** imagines himself gnawed to death by an old satiated rat (303), and later (314) compares himself with a dying turkey hen, spied on by the rats, like **Moran**'s gray **hen** (128). **Watt** welcomes being abandoned by his last rats, left to face the lonely silence without "the gnawing, the scurrying, the little cries" (84). **Clov** has half-exterminated one: "If I don't kill that rat he'll die" (*Endgame*, 68). The denatured environment of *How It Is* (18) is expressed in the cry "rats no no rats this time"; in *That Time*, a dead rat is caught in the reeds. The narrator of "**The End**" (96) has a soft spot for rats but must contend with the water rats, lean and ferocious. **Sam** and Watt like those that dwell by the stream, long and black (155–56). They bring them titbits and, seizing a plump young rat, "resting in our bosom after its repast," feed it to some less-fortunate relative: on these occasions, they agree, they come "nearest to **God**."

ravanastron: identified by Heath Lees (178) as an ancient Indian instrument of the banjo family, with a long neck, tuning peg, and rounded sounding board. One hangs from the wall of the **music** room (*Watt*, 71). In the drafts it is gray-green, hanging from a red nail; the comparison with a **cruciform** plover was added later. Its association with **Buxtehude**, Lees suggests, accentuates acoustical discord.

Reavey, George (1907–76): Russian-born English poet, translator, and publisher; SB's agent and friend. They met in **Paris** through Thomas **MacGreevy**. Reavey ran the Europa Press (corner of the Rues Bonaparte and Beaux-Arts), which brought out (at SB's expense) *Echo's Bones* (1935). He published SB's translations of Paul **Éluard**'s poems in *Thorns of Thunder* (1936) and Denis **Devlin**'s *Intercessions* (1937), which SB reviewed. He placed *Murphy* with Routledge (1937) but was unsuccessful with *Watt*. A memorial tribute was published in *JOBS* 2 (1977). SB chose four of Reavey's poems, including "Green and Blue," dedicated to him. He added a personal farewell (5 February 1977): "Adieu George, to whom I owed so much, with whom I shared so much, for whom I cared so much."

"Recent Irish Poetry": a provocative article in *The Bookman* 86.515 (August 1934): 235–44, under the pseudonym "Andrew **Belis**"; rpt. in *The Lace Curtain* [Dublin] 4 (1971): 58–63, and in *Disjecta* (70–76). AB/SB proposes as his principle of individuation the degree to which Irish writers are aware of "the breakdown of the **object**." He accuses the "**antiquarians**" of "delivering with the altitudinous complacency of the Victorian Gaels the **Ossianic** goods," and condemns the "iridescence of themes" from such as George **Russell**, James Stephens, Austin **Clarke**, and Frederick **Higgins** (see **Ireland**). **Denis Devlin** is approved as one of the few who is "aware of the vacuum which exists between the perceiver and the thing perceived"; and Thomas **MacGreevy** is praised for his clear elucidations, "the vision without the dip." The response to W. B. **Yeats** is mixed. The essay reflects SB's attitude to the **Dublin** literary scene shortly before he would leave it.

red and gray: in *Watt* (Part 1) the ashes in the grate "redden" and "greyen" until they are extinguished. Watt's scant hair is "red-grey" (37). In *Murphy*, "greyen" is used of the "dayspring" (275), and "dayspring" of the zodiac (78), as in "il Zodiacal rubecchio" ("the reddened zodiac") of the *Purgatorio*. The **Unnamable** (301) recalls the cockatoo, gray shot with rose, as the dim light surrounds him. Nudity in *The Lost Ones* loses its charm "as pink turns grey and transforms into a rustling of nettles the natural succulence of flesh against flesh" (220). See **green and yellow** and **blue and white**.

Regiebuch: for his German productions SB kept a director's notebook, similar to

Brecht's *Modellbücher* but more personal, tentative, and exploratory. Although the basis for SB's revised acting texts, the *Regiebücher* were never designed as production models. They are the record of self-collaboration, the artist in dialogue with himself, replete with insights into the plays and suggestions for staging. They have been published, with SB's Revised Texts, in facsimile, transcription, translation, and annotated, in the *Theatrical Notebooks* (qv).

Reinhold, K. L. (1758–1823): reshaper of **Kant**, his teachings at Jena (1788–94) offering a systematic exposition that became that of the "Kantians" (Windelband, 570). He asserts that neither subject nor **object** is knowable but only the **consciousness** (the "ideational faculty"), which hovers between. Dismissed in *First Love* (32) as a "**syncretist**" (qv).

religion: a photograph of SB, recalled in *Film* (173), shows a child kneeling on the veranda amidst the **verbena**, hands clasped in prayer. In *How It Is* (15–16) the narrator recalls this moment, and his **mother**'s eyes burning down on him when he looked up. Intimate memories of bedtime prayers in "**Serena II**," *Dream*, and *Company* testify to religion as part of everyday life. Like **Belacqua** in "**Yellow**" (172), SB was "a dirty low-down Low Church Protestant high-brow," whose attendance at church and Sunday school left an indelible mark on his character and writings long after he had lost, or failed to find, his faith. SB told Tom Driver (1961) that he had no religious feeling: "Once I had a religious emotion. It was at my first com-

munion. No more." Its efficacy at times of crisis was, he suggested, that of an old school tie. In *Dream* (185), Belacqua reports that his first communion had come and gone, leaving in his breast "a void place and a spacious **nothing**." **Krapp** recalls going to Vespers in his short trousers, falling asleep then off the pew (63). Yet SB's deep agnosticism did not preclude an intense interest in religious matters, and his works make intricate reference to Christian symbols and rituals. At his uncle's trial (1937), asked if he were Christian, Jew, or atheist, he replied, "None of the above." When asked by Charles Juliet (1977) if he had rid himself of the influence of religion, SB replied that outwardly, perhaps, but "pour la reste. . . ." Notes from **Augustine**, close readings of the **Bible** and Christian **mysticism** (qv), and a curiosity about the theological impasses into which the seventeenth-century rationalists fell bear witness to his obsession with the paradoxes of faith, if not the affirmation of any belief. He preferred the King James Bible, yet held an inheritance both Catholic and catholic, verses, tags, images, and symbols that constituted if not a living at least not a "wholly dying" tradition (see Jeremy **Taylor**).

SB's early confidant was Thomas **MacGreevy**, whose poetry he likened to prayer but whose faith he could not share. Yet MacGreevy's Catholicism contributed to the evolution of the arrogant, **narcissistic** young man of the 1930s into one noted for his kindness, courtesy, and good works. SB's letters, signed "God bless," tell of sending his mother Morton's *In the Steps of the Master*, comment on the second lesson at church that evening, and expound **Geulincx**'s conviction that the *sub specie aeternitatis* vision is the only excuse for remaining alive. In a remarkable letter (10 March 1935), SB responds to MacGreevy's recommendation that he should find comfort in **Thomas à Kempis** (qv) but doubted this could be twisted into "a programme of self-sufficiency." Thomas had served only to reinforce his deliberate immersion in self, and any "**Christlike imitative pentimenti**" could not redeem a composition invalid from the word go.

SB cherished religious inanities. *Whoroscope* parodies **scholastic** absurdities; "**Text**" (poem) those of the Old Testament; and six biscuits in *Murphy* (81) generate speculations about the theophanism of **William of Champeaux**. *Watt* is full of oddities such as the **eels of Como**, or the **rat** that ate of the consecrated wafer, or dogmatic prescriptions such as Mr. **Spiro**'s *Podex non destra sed sinistra* (27–28), which hand one should use to wipe the bum. Considerable ingenuity went into such detail. The manuscripts reveal the effort of rearranging the fifteen letters of the Holy Family into: *Has J. Jurms a po? Yes.* **Moran** amuses himself (137) with the thought that women have souls that they may be damned, and is preoccupied (166–68) with "questions of a theological nature" (again, which hand should absterge the podex), such as #13, "What was God doing with himself before the creation?" (see Augustine's *Confessions,* 11.x–xii; DN, 27). **Vladimir** similarly wants to know why of the four Evangelists only one speaks of a thief being saved.

SB shared **Schopenhauer**'s pessimism, his sense of a universe without redemp-

tion. "**Dante and the Lobster**" ponders the paradox of **pity** and piety; "**Malacoda**" dramatizes the futility of resenting the enormity of his **father**'s **death**; "Yellow" burlesques his own. Peggy **Sinclair**'s death was another futility, her "red sputum" marking the bleak landscape of "**Enueg I**" and her **face** recalled in "**Enueg II**." In "**Ascension**," religious festivity is belied by thoughts of her that rise in mockery. "**Ooftish**" catalogues suffering, cancer, angina, TB, and misery, boiled down to "blood of lamb." Biblical echoes are invariably bleak or satirical, yet the relentless scrutiny of eschatology and SB's obsessive return to the same images and themes, like a **dog** to its vomit, inform some of the most powerful religious literature in the Western tradition. This is a paradox SB might have resented but not one he could escape. Whatever his disbelief, he is a major religious writer.

Attracted to detachment, SB inverted the structure of mystical experience to explore the darkness within (see **Murphy's mind**). This suggests a powerful religious sensibility coexisting with **absurdity** and skepticism, most obviously in the postwar period. *Watt* is predicated on the most basic question—What?—with the implied answer, Not (knot?): the Augustinian paradox, that we cannot know what God *is* but only what he *is not*. It concerns the relationship of servant and master but assumes an unexpected **Berkeley**-like twist: if God is not **witnessed** then how can he exist? The novel adopts **Descartes**'s *Method,* but Watt's attempts to move from the clear and distinct unto the mystery of Mr. **Knott** lead not to rational understanding but to the **asylum**. In the *Three Novels,* the organizing principle is the **cogito** but, again, the attempt to move beyond **consciousness** of the self toward God meets with an impasse. The mind cannot know more than itself, and even that is dubious: the "I, of whom I know nothing" (304) is finally the "**Not I**" (qv).

SB scorned those who saw *Godot* as an allegory of Christian salvation, or assumed that **Godot** might come tomorrow. Still, many overlook the presence of "God" in the title, however obscured by the original **French** and mocking diminutive. At its heart, in the story the **two thieves**, is the mystery of salvation. This may be a cruel joke, for worse than an atheistic universe is one in which hope, though *almost* certainly delusory, is never quite snuffed. That theme is presented more ruthlessly in *Endgame,* with its inexorable vision of a world running down, Paley's clock abandoned by its maker. In *Happy Days,* **Winnie**'s incurable optimism is belied by her physical experience, and in *How It Is* life in the light is finally negated. Yet not least of SB's achievements in the century following **Darwin** is to have given **voice** and dramatic image to the agonies and absurdities of religious uncertainty for those to whom God is no longer an option but remains a significant absence ("The bastard! He doesn't exist").

Rembrandt: Rembrandt Harmensz van Rijn (1606-69); greatest painter of the Dutch school, one in whom SB discerned a dehiscence, "a disfaction, a désuni, an Ungebund," the **incoherent continuum** or "corrosive ground-swell of Art" (*Dream,* 138). **Wilenski** gave SB a lasting appreciation of the **Caravaggio-Honthorst** tradition of spotlight paint-ing and "twilight effects" leading to Rembrandt, whose affection for aged idiosyncracies contributed to SB's art of disintegration. The **Dublin** National Gallery's Rembrandts made an early impression, notably *Rest on the Flight into Egypt.* **Molloy** thinks of "flight and bivouac" in an Egypt without bounds, and *Watt* mentions "One resting on the flight" (48). Those in *Dream* are from the Louvre: **Lucien** is described in terms of "Rembrandt's portrait of his brother"; this is echoed (138) and placed beside "the Selbstbildnis" (self-portrait) in toque and golden chain; and "the cute little Saint Matthew angel"—a reference to *The Evangelist Matthew Inspired by the Angel* that underlies the reference in *Murphy* (215) to "Luke's portrait of Matthew" and the **Unnamable**'s inability to write (301). Spotlight painting dominates the late drama. *Krapp's Last Tape* visually echoes *The Money Changer,* which, as SB noted in his **German Diaries** (III, 5 January 1937), is in the Kaiser-Wilhelm-Friedrich Museum, Berlin: "very early *Geldwechster* (1627), apparently influenced by Honthorst. One aspect of Rembrandt is nothing but a development of Honthorst."

Renard, Jules (1864–1910): French man of letters and diarist, wary and unsentimental. SB in 1931 read his *Journal intime* (1927), fascinated by the total honesty of Renard's self-scrutiny, something he would eventually realize in his own writing. He copied "odd things" (DN, 30–34): the virgin's "attendez que je mouille" in "**être là sans mâchoires sans dents**"; the greater obscenity of "carrot plucked from tin of grease" ("Draff,"

180; DN 31, "Le chien se retira de la chienne"); and "rapid as a zebra's thought," in *Dream* (184), "**Echo's Bones**" (12), and *Murphy* (42). Murphy's "plaisir de rompre" (48) echoes Renard's play (1897). In "**Ex Cathezra**," SB cites Renard's "bien dumaficélée" ("artfully arranged") (31 août 1901; DN, 34). One passage became an elaborate jest. Renard describes how, unable to get to the chamber pot, he sat on the bed's edge, watching urine trickle down his leg; **Neary**'s leaking hotwater bottle causes a like effect (*Murphy,* 208–13). This is the final entry (6 avril 1910). His influence is felt in *Film,* as **O** tears up photographs of his younger self. As Renard noted, many want to kill themselves but remain content with tearing up their photographs.

Renaud, Madeleine (1900–94): actress who left *la Comédie française* and founded with her husband, Jean-Louis Barrault, *la Compagnie Renaud-Barrault* at the Théâtre Marigny. She became the definitive French **Winnie**, as Billie **Whitelaw** was the English. Her tribute to SB (*Beckett at 60,* 81–83) is warm and uncritical, expressing her admiration for him as a man ("he is very handsome") and **director**. She thought *Oh les beaux jours* "a marvellous **love** poem" (82), partly directed to her, for SB had said he could not imagine it without her.

"**Rentrer**": an eight-line poem (1976), on the inside front cover of the **Sottisier Notebook** (Reading), acknowledging in a final parenthesis "Hans Meyer." Meyer (1760–1832), art historian and theorist, was a friend of **Goethe**. The poem depicts one in a lighted room who returns to hear and see the night seeing his **face** (its face?) pressed to the window.

Residua: a trilingual gathering of four prose pieces in English, French, and German (the latter translated by Elmar **Tophoven** with SB), published in Frankfurt: Suhrkamp, 1970: *Schussjezt-Assez-Enough; Ausgeträumt Träumen-Imagination morte imaginez-**Imagination Dead Imagine**; Bing-Bing-Ping; and Lösigkeit-Sans-Lessness.*

"**Return to the Vestry**": a forty-six-line poem published in *The New Review* 1.3 (1931): 98–99; omitted from later collections. In 1926, SB and Charles Clarke visited the grave of Pierre **Ronsard** at the Prieuré de Saint-Cosmé near Tours. The chapel had become a stable and SB was saddened by the neglect. This feeling he disguises as burlesque ("the deaf conceited lecherous laypriest"), the poem riddled with allusions to Ronsard's life and writings, but especially to "Magie, ou delivrance d'amour." The verse enacts a ritual of **Anteros**, or rejection of amour in favor of solitary exclusion.

Reynolds' News: a Sunday tabloid, founded (1850) by George Reynolds, combining socialism with sensationalism. Its name changed (1925) to *Reynolds's Illustrated News,* then the *Sunday Citizen,* ceasing publication in 1967. **Willie** might read titbits to **Winnie** (*Happy Days,* 46), the pun perhaps intentional.

Richilda: relict of Albert, Earl of Ebersberg, mentioned in "**Echo's Bones**" (10), **Belacqua** bruised in spirit as she in **body**, i.e., fatally. In Jeremy **Taylor**'s *Holy Dying* (1.2), the widow entreats Henry III to restore her lands, but "the chamber-floor suddenly fell under them, and Richilda, falling upon the edge of a bathing-vessel, was bruised to **death**."

Rilke, Rainer Maria (1875–1926): German poet best known for his *Duino Elegies* and *Sonnets to Orpheus* (1922). His lyrical writing is colored by **mysticism**. SB published an initialed but untitled review of his *Poems* (trans. J. B. Leishmann, Hogarth Press, 1934) in *The Criterion* 13.53 (July 1934): 705–7; rpt. *Disjecta* (66–67). He criticized Rilke's failure to make **solitude** his element, always "popping up for the gulp of disgust that will rehabilitate the *Ichgott*." He noted a "breathless petulance," seeing in Rilke's relation to **God** a "turmoil of self-deception" and "a childishness to which German writers seem specially prone." **Eliot** was unimpressed, and further commissions were not forthcoming.

Rima: the **Smeraldina**-Rima of *Dream*, like W. H. Hudson's wild girl of the Brazilian jungle in *Green Mansions* (1904). Her statue in **Hyde Park**, by Jacob **Epstein**, is being cleaned in *Murphy* (96). The cenotaph depicts a girl and a flock of ascending birds; it was occasionally tarred and feathered or defiled with green paint (not permanganate).

Rimbaud, Arthur (1854–91): French poet and adventurer, whose life as a vagabond, soldier, deserter, circus hand, thief, and trader in gold and ivory in Ethiopia creates a fascinating saga. He represents the **incoherent continuum** (*Dream*, 102),

"the Infernal One, the Ailing Seer" (137), whose symbolist language distrusts its very medium. His poetry, written when he was young and later rejected, ended in silence. Teaching Rimbaud's poetry at **Trinity**, SB could not explain the mystery of "eye-**suicide**" to his "foul senior sophisticers" (SB to TM, 11 March 1931), who guffawed at "pissante" in the phrase "averse glapissante." Pilling ("Itch to Make," 20) identifies "Les Poètes de sept ans," and explains "eye-suicide" as "ego-suicide," as in "JE est un autre" (letter to Paul Demeny, 15 mai 1871). **Wylie**'s way of looking and **Murphy**'s (90) differ as a *voyeur*'s from a *voyant*'s; compare the letter to Demeny, in which Rimbaud determines to be not just a poet but a visionary. His *Le Bateau ivre* was sent to Paul Verlaine, who immediately saw its genius. It became a flagship of **symbolism**. Translated by SB "pat into English" (*Dream*, 137), it constitutes a significant apprentice piece (see "**Drunken Boat**"). Rimbaud destroyed Verlaine's family life and provoked Verlaine into shooting him. Rimbaud's *Une Saison en enfer* (1873) depicts that extravagant relationship; in 1875 he disappeared.

Believing him dead, Verlaine published Rimbard's poems as *Les Illuminations* (1886). "**Enueg I**" concludes with a translation from "Barbare": "Le pavillon en viande saignante sur las soie des mers et des fleurs arctiques; (elles n'existent pas)." The arctic flowers reappear in *Mercier and Camier* (119). **Belacqua** lowers himself onto a rosewood toilet seat with Rimbaud's refrain of "Douceurs!" (*Dream*, 145). The **Alba**'s peignoir is "like a Rimbaud Illumination, barbarous and royal" (172). In 1891, a tumor in his leg forced Rimbaud to leave Harrar and return to France; the gangrenous limb was amputated, but he died grotesquely in Marseilles, away from his **mother**'s farm. The **Unnamable** returns from his world tour (317), one leg left in Java, like a decrepit Rimbaud. The letter to Demeny, invoking "les choses inouïes et **innommables**," intimates the novel's title as well as its procession of decrepitudes, those "horribles travailleurs; ils commenceront par les horizons où l'autre s'est affaissé." See also "**What where**." [Details from DL]

Ringelnatz, Joachim (1883–1934): pseudonym of Hans Bötticher, a harmless water snake, suited to a satirist and jongleur. After running away to sea then becoming a librarian, cabaret singer, and pilot, Ringelnatz made a career singing his comic pieces and nonsense verse. SB accepted an invitation (1936) to translate his poems for **Faber**, but did not do so. The project was suggested by Axel Kaun. Its lasting legacy is the "**German Letter**" (9 July 1937) in which SB qualifies his sense of a man of extraordinary interest by **Juvenal**'s "Kakoethes," or *cacoethes scribendi* (VII.52), Ringelnatz's incurable itch for writing that manifested itself as "Verswut," or futile rhyming (*Disjecta*, 52, 171).

Rio Santo: the incomparable marquis, **byronic** hero of Paul Féval's *Les Mystères de Londres* (1844). Described by Praz (*The Romantic Agony*, 79) as "puissant pour le mal comme l'ange déchu," a "highly sweetened Satan" with an "oeil rêveur," he is linked to **Gilles de Rais** (*Dream*, 79).

Robinson: Plessis-Robinson, a suburb of **Paris**, with a café set in a chestnut tree, as in Johann Wyss's *The Swiss Family Robinson* (1812). Mentioned in *Eleutheria* (45).

"**Rockaby**": a one-act play, written in English (1980) and translated as "**Berceuse**." First published in *Rockaby and Other Short Pieces* (Grove, 1981) and *Three Occasional Pieces* (Faber, 1982; SB's suggested title); rpt. in *Collected Shorter Plays* and *Complete Dramatic Works*. These represent four versions. Two lines added in production—"one other living soul" and "down the steep stair"—appear only in Grove. *CSP* and *CDW*, set from the Faber text, exclude these lines and print "where **mother** rocked" for Grove's "where mother sat." *CDW* additionally confuses the opening, as the compositor mistook the second for the first "for another" and dropped the intervening eight lines. The "occasion" refers to the conference for which "Rockaby" was written, at the Center for Theater Research, Buffalo (8 April 1981), dir. Alan **Schneider**, with Billie **Whitelaw** replacing Irene Worth. The first London performance, a reprise of the Buffalo premiere, was at the Cottesloe (December 1982). The American production, rehearsals, conference scenes, and performance, was filmed in cinema verité style, and is available commercially from Pennebaker Hegedus Films. "Rockaby" was televised by BBC 2 (15 December 1982).

The fifteen-minute action is deceptively simple. It features a "prematurely old" woman, **W**, in a chair apparently rocking of its own accord, since her feet are visible on its footrest. The **motion** creates a ghostly atmosphere. W listens to a **voice,** presumably hers, recount the story of a lonely life, which has contracted from the "going to and fro" of her earlier years, in search of another, to sitting beside the upstairs window in search of another **face** behind glass, to her current to and fro, her life and search unfulfilled. The voice is a poignant poem of **solitude,** its rhythms punctuated by the metronomic beat of the chair, which stops as *it* stops. Dressed like her mother in her "best black," she seems (like Molloy) to be replacing (becoming) her dead mother, "Mother rocker," and simultaneously becoming "her own other," the **object** of her yearning. On four occasions when live and recorded voice coincide, W interacts with that other. The recorded voice carries the action, against which the live performance plays. W's repetitious inner voice suggests that the pattern of narrative has been honed to an essential, minimalist poem, to which W's live repetition creates a duet—for **death,** perhaps. Pain, loneliness, and isolation are exquisitely aestheticized, the action punctuated by the sequined glitter of W's dress as it moves in and out of the light. As W entreats the voice four times with a whispered "More," she suggests that she has become another to her own voice, mother to her inner being (W has no offspring). As her live voice and the illumination fade with each segment, W rocks toward her demise, an echo of her mother's, but not without some understanding of the nature of being and identity suggested by her live interaction with her recorded voice. Less gentle than the

quiet demise and gentle rocking suggested by the lullaby title is the final insight: "Fuck life."

rocking chair: a **machine** that gives **Murphy**'s **body** pleasure, then sets him free in his mind. It is his one possession, and when he returns from the **MMM** to fetch it **Celia** knows he has chosen his mind over her. The chair asserts the **pun** "off his rocker." It reappears in "**Mime de rêveur, A**" and "**Rockaby,**" the protagonists passing from **motion** to **equilibrium** and thence to **death.** T.. chair in *Endgame* is in direct line of de :ent, casters replacing the rockers but lir ited **motion** still possible. **Martha** has ins ted that hers be kept in the kitchen (*Mc 'loy,* 108). The room in *Film* contains a rock-ing chair with a carved headrest, whic when "**O**" sits back, frames his head. I: rocking matches his emotions as he gazes at various images of his self and when "**E**" finally violates the angle of immunity. The central issues of *Film* are linked to their origins in *Murphy* by this mechanism.

Rodin, Auguste (1840–1917): French sculptor. References to his work (hands, thinking) tend to be implicit, as with the Musée Rodin of "**What a Misfortune**" (141). **Moran**'s allusion to "a burgess of Calais" (129) invokes Rodin's *The Burghers of Calais* (1886, erected 1895), in Calais, with a replica in **London**'s Victoria Tower Gardens (1913).

Rolland, Romain (1866–1944): French novelist, playwright, biographer, **Nobel** laureate (1915), and musicologist, once professor of **art** history at the **École**

Normale. His *Vie de Beethoven* (1903) offered the image of **Beethoven** smoking his pipe and dreaming of the "unsterbliche Geliebte" (*Dream,* 138) and the motif of the "unbuttoned symphony" (DN, 157).

Romains, Jules (1885–1972): pen name of Louis Fariguole, French poet and novelist, who graduated in philosophy from the **École Normale** (1909) to become the principal exponent of **Unanimisme** (see **Jouve**). SB knew Romains's poetry, *La vie unanime* (1908), his first novel, *Mort de quelqu'un* (1911), and his farcical *Les Copains* (1913). *Murphy* could be described as "the **death** of a nobody," with elements of farce. SB appreciated the simplicity of Romains's expression and the ease with which he moved from reality to the **irrational** domain. While his faith in a movement compelled by psychic phenomena could not persist, he claimed in "**Ex Cathezra**" (1934) that "Romains *is* Unanimism, and a poet of importance."

Romanticism: despite dismissing the "ineluctable gangrene of Romanticism" (*Proust,* 80), an opinion indebted to **Huysmans**, and a determination not to move back to the elegant skepticism and Marmorean modes of Laforgue and **Mallarmé** (**Eliot**'s way of disciplining his romantic temperament), SB shared with **Proust** a strain that neither quite lost. While SB shared the modernist suspicion of Romantic excess, throttled the lyric impulse, and trampled the **blue flower** of beauty, he retained an attraction to the **mystical**, a recognition of the need to express, the **voice** within too strong ultimately to be denied.

Stephen Dedalus was both example and warning. He experiences the appropriate infatuations with **Shelley** and Dumas, and heroically refuses to abandon **Byron** when bullied to admit the "right" answer, **Tennyson**. His villanelle is conceived by the seraph Gabriel in the womb of the imagination; *Portrait* ends with his resolve to "forge" in the smithy of his soul the uncreated conscience of his nation. This is the portrait of the artist *as a young man,* and in *Ulysses* Stephen's aesthetics assumes the classical temper. The classical artist, SB asserted (with Joyce in mind), assumes omniscience and omnipotence, but his way lay in impotence and ignorance. Unlike **Neary**, who retains "something of **Hugo**" (*Murphy,* 201), SB refused to attribute value to his sufferings (see the **fundamental unheroic**). More devastating is his rejection of the epiphany (the modernist legacy of the Romantic aesthetics of transcendence). SB did not so much deny the phenomenon or lament its transitory nature as reject the possibility of *any* value, transcendental or otherwise, in such moments (consider **Arsene**'s "**ineffable**" moment in the sun).

SB's reading in the early 1930s included Mario Praz, *The Romantic Agony* (1930; trans. 1933), from which he took many details (DN, 36–46). A study of decadence, and remarkable for its unexpected insight, it fueled SB's antipathy. Praz saw **Sade**, if not a "surromantique" (x), at least as "a sinister force" in Romanticism. He described the cult of "Medusan" beauty, the sexual pathology of decadence, and the satanic hero. Yet even as SB noted such oddities as "treaclemoon" (Praz, 71; Byron's honeymoon) and avoided the Byronic overtones of sin and heroism in **Cain**, he responded to Praz's sense of the Romantic agony as the withdrawal from outer to inner experience.

"**Recent Irish Poetry**" (1934) castigates the Irish **antiquarians** as unwilling or unable to respond to "the breakdown of the **object**," delivering instead the "**Ossianic** goods." *Dream* embodies a complex aesthetics, far removed from **Coleridge**'s organic form. *Murphy* parodies the pastoral, mocking the worthy **Wordsworth** ("fields of sheep/sleep") and W. B. **Yeats** ("turn their broody heads"). The **Expelled** recollects emotion "with the celebrated advantage of tranquility" (58). Shelley's moon, pale for weariness, casts its cold enchantment in vain from *Dream* (65; a continental third-class insomnia) to *Waiting for Godot* (34.b; **Estragon** was once a poet). The "cackle of a nightingale" in *Murphy* (240) echoes the "terrible panic-stricken stasis of **Keats**," indicative of the "collapse of the will" typifying the Romantics from **Spenser** to **Giorgione** (*Proust*, 90).

Molloy is a classic case of romantic agony. He asserts the "killing of the Aegean," thirsting for heat and light, i.e., he rejects the rational prurit. Nevertheless, he is ruled by emotion for, throughout his journey, his account curiously refuses to admit feeling, "no, I won't say it." His anger often builds to lyricism, then is undercut, deliberately, with a "Pah" or scatology or a cliché sadly abused. But, occasionally, the pull of the moon is too strong, emotion prevails, is recollected, and must be rejected that the "tranquility of decomposition" be restored in the

"anguish of return." His condition is essentially that of SB himself, mockery qualified by an undercurrent of **German** Romanticism, in literature (**Hölderlin**), music (**Schubert**), and art (Caspar David Friedrich). Not least of this, as in the art of Jack **Yeats**, was the sense of isolation, the insignificant human figure in an indifferent world, far from Wordsworth's pantheistic belief but at the heart of the *Winterreise*. This **love** is manifest more obviously in the later drama, where SB is less fearful of deciduous beauty. A good study of the Romantic impulse in SB's writings, revealing unexpected insights into a tradition vehemently rejected but never quite denied, is currently lacking. [Details from Penny Bond].

Ronsard, Pierre de (1524–85): French sonneteer and "prince of poets," his life spent in service until his diplomatic career was curtailed by deafness, which rendered his pursuit of the fair to middling Hélène de Surgères more literary and Platonic than he might have wished. His poems deserve a better fate than they received from her. "**Return to the Vestry**" and "**It is high time lover**" recall SB's 1926 pilgrimage to Ronsard's grave. They invoke "Magie, ou delivrance d'amour," in *Dream* (68) "the liquorish laypriest's Magic Ode." **Anteros** earlier delivers **Belaqua** from the magic of the evening (28). The **Alba** calls Ronsard "a comic old lecher" (175). In "**Fingal**," the landscape is described as "a magic land" (24). SB's unpublished "Epître à Ronsard" (January 1938; now at TCD) identifies Ronsard as a poet of "esprit," as compared to himself, a poet of "corps." "**Love and Lethe**" ends with a line from

Sonnets pour Hélène LXXVII: "Car l'Amour et la Mort n'est qu'une mesme chose." "S'abuser en amour n'est pas mauvais chose" lacks Ronsard's intended sense, but is no worse than the consolation **Mercier** and **Camier** find with their "Hélène."

Rooney, Mr. and Mrs.: protagonists of *All That Fall* (1956), Dan blind and Maddy unable to walk easily. Earlier named "Kennedy," after a **Foxrock** family (Knowlson, 701). Maddy's unmarried name was "Dunne," that of a local butcher. She resembles Ida, one of the **Elsner sisters** who sometimes fell from her **bicycle** and flopped "like a big fat jelly" in the road (Knowlson, 44). No **madeleine** for Maddy. She hints at something "Done long ago and ill done," connected with "Little Minnie!" (14). She recalls the mind doctor's story of the **little girl** who had never really been born; finally, she hears why the train has arrived late. O'Hara concludes that both are mentally ill and diagnoses Dan as one "unable to fend off the idea that he has pushed a child under the wheels of a car" (*Hidden Drives,* 86), a critique based on **Freud**'s *The Question of Lay Analysis* (1926).

La Roquette: mentioned in *En attendant Godot* (6) but not in the English text; *La Petite Roquette* (**Paris**) was "a kind of Borstal for *jeunes détenus*" (Duckworth, 95).

Rosa mundi, non rosa munda: the rose of the world, not the rose that is pure. The tag derives from Praz, *Romantic Agony* (218; DN, 46), said of the lovely

Rosamond, concubine to Henry II and a type of tainted beauty. She was poisoned by Elinor and buried in "an house of nunnes" with these verses on her tomb: *Hic jacet in tumba Rosa mundi, non Rosa munda, / Non redolet, sed olet, quae redol'ere solet* ("Here Rose the graced not Rose the chaste reposes, / The smell that rises is no smell of roses") (Brewer). *Dream* (105–6) echoes the "**veronica** mundi / veronica munda" of "**Enueg II.**"

Roscellinus (1050–1125): Roscellinus Compendiensis of Amorica, French Nominalist theologian whose sole surviving work is a letter to Abelard arguing that universals are merely verbal constructs and that the truly real is the individual thing, and that alone (Windelband, 296). Mentioned in "**être là sans mâchoires sans dents.**"

Rose Marie: in "**A Wet Night**" (78), but not in *Dream,* the **Alba** makes everyone move up "Like the totem chorus" in *Rose Marie*. This is not the sentimental Nelson Eddy / Jeanette MacDonald movie about the Mountie who gets his woman (1936), but either the stage musical (score by Rudolf Friml, text by Harbach and Hammerstein), which SB could have seen in **Paris**, or the little-known 1928 movie starring Joan Crawford and James Murray.

Rosencrantz and Guildenstern Are Dead: Tom Stoppard's first major comedy, its fringe success at the Edinburgh Festival (1966) leading to the National Theatre (11 April 1967). Explicitly indebted to *Waiting for Godot,* it features two individuals on a lonely stage, "passing the **time** in a place without any visible character" in pointless routines (the coin tossing redefines "an even chance"). There is a sense of theatricality, of being **witnessed**, of life constrained by **death**. Stoppard described to Ronald Hayman (12 June 1974) the "Godotesque" element, and "a Beckett joke which is the funniest joke in the world," confident statement followed by immediate refutation, a process of "elaborate structure and sudden—and total—dismantlement."

Rosset, Barney: see **Grove Press.**

Rouault, Georges (1871–1958): French painter, associated with Les Fauves, of **clowns**, prostitutes, and outcasts, who from 1940 devoted himself to **religious** themes. In **"Peintres de l'empêchement"** (*Disjecta,* 135), SB admires his **Christs** as clowns, and the quality called *la choseté* ("thingness," or tangibility).

"Rough for Radio I": originally "**Esquisse radiophonique**" (1961); published in *Minuit* 5 (septembre 1973): 31–35, where it is dated "*vers 1962-3?*" First English publication as "Sketch for Radio Play" in *Stereo Headphones* 7 (spring 1976), then under its current title in *Ends and Odds* (Grove, 1976; Faber, 1977). Anticipating "**Cascando**" and "**Words and Music**," which surpass it, "Rough" attempts to control sound by manipulating "two knobs" of a radio set. A character, He, is joined by She, to listen to **Voice** and **Music**, but these are faint and "not together"; She leaves and He rings the doctor concerning the plight of Voice and Music. He is promised "confinement" by noon; but

Voice and Music are feeble and fading fast.

"Rough for Radio II": a radio play, originally *Pochade radiophonique* and published in *Minuit* 16 (novembre 1975): 2–12, where it is dated "*années 60s?*" Translated into English just before its broadcast on BBC 3 (13 April 1976), dir. Martin Esslin, with Harold Pinter, Billie **Whitelaw**, and Patrick **Magee**. Published in *Ends and Odds* (Grove, 1976; Faber, 1977). As an exercise in torture it anticipates "**What Where**." "Animator" with his **cylindrical ruler** is accompanied by Stenographer and a mute named "Dick," who wields a bull's pizzle. The victim, bound, gagged, blindfolded, ears plugged, and hooded, is "**Fox**," a fricative removed from "Vox," or **voice**. The session begins, like *Endgame,* with an unveiling—of the "ravishing" F/Vox, who is prodded to speech. To date all dicta have been "inacceptable" (see **Mauthner** for the word that may be "it," that will end this torment). After torture, off the record, Fox utters a fragment. His life surrounded by stones, he lived, but confesses to embodying another, a brother, within him, like voices embedded within narrative. With the potential br(other) Fox mentions a woman, the "fecundated" Tennysonian Maud, and sheds a tear, "the human trait." To urge more sentiment, Animator urges Stenographer to "Kiss it white," after which Fox faints. He forces a maudlin emendation to Stenographer's account, and has Maud speak "between two kisses." With confession and artful revision Fox's (or a) story may have been told and the participants released from their obligations.

Thereupon the play ends. It remains a sketch, compelling a story from voice, and so expressing SB's lifelong exploration of the voice as a literary entity, the source of creativity.

"Rough for Theatre I": a one-act theatrical sketch, written in the late 1950s as *Fragment de théâtre* and published in *Minuit* 8 (mars 1974): 65–72, dated "*anées 60s.*" Published in English in *Ends and Odds* (Grove, 1976; Faber, 1977). Staged as **"Fragment for Theater I"** at the Magic Theater, San Francisco (September 1986) by S. E. Gontarski, with Tom Luce (**B**) and Robert Wagner (**A**), in an evening of one-acters called *The Beckett Vision*. An earlier version was entitled "The **Gloaming**" (qv). A crippled vagrant, B, drawn to the violin melodies of a blind beggar, A, offers to join forces "till death ensue," his sight complementing the other's mobility. Things turn sadistic as B threatens to take A's fiddle, and A seizes B's pole, the sketch ending in a tableau of A about to strike B with his own weapon. Despite the resemblance to W. B. **Yeats**'s *The Cat and the Moon,* where a blind man and a cripple form a symbiotic relationship, the theme was developed more artfully in *Fin de partie.*

"Rough for Theatre II": a one-act sketch, written in the late 1950s as **"Fragment de théâtre II"**; published in *Ends and Odds* (Grove, 1976, and Faber, 1977). Despite some similarity to **"Rough for Radio II,"** the drama is restricted to little more than a recalcitrant light source. It is, justifiably, among the least performed of SB's works. Two men, **A** (Bertrand) and **B** (**Morvan**), assess **C**, who stands motionless and unspeaking, back to the audience, apparently ready to jump from the window, his "literary aspirations incompletely stifled," a letter to an "admiratrix" unsent. The investigators, working pro bono, offer an inventory adding up to not much (like **Malone**'s), apparently to help put C over the edge. They note his morbid sensitivity to the opinion of others—rather offensively, given their prying. A refers to "Our Lady of [Perpetual] Succour" whose feast is June 27, the next full moon and the anticipated date of **suicide** of C, for whom that succor would be appropriate. The unctuous A once belonged to the Band of Hope, a youth temperance movement. They hear a "lovebird" singing, like **Hardy**'s darkling thrush, its mate dead, and in the cage only an old cuttle bone (a squid skeleton). They decide that C has no prospects ("black future, an unpardonable past") and condemn him to jump, only to discover something inexplicable: an enigmatic smile that links this piece to **"Eh Joe,"** *Catastrophe,* and *That Time.*

Rouletabille: the reporter-detective in Gaston Leroux's *Le Mystère de la chambre jaune* (1907), whose manner of closing his eyes and thinking is invoked in *Dream* (68).

"Roundelay": a thirteen-line poem, published in *Modern Drama* [Toronto] 19 (September 1976): 223; an issue devoted to SB, including three essays on his plays, a checklist of criticism, and Breon Mitchell's revised *Come and Go.* It was added to *Collected Poems* (1977). It retraces the steps of "**Dieppe**," but the circular roundelay, a "ring" poem with a refrain ("on all that strand / at end of day"), prescribes turning back "towards the lights of old" even as it debates the impulse to "stay" or "go."

Rousseau, Jean-Jacques (1712–78): Genevese philosopher and writer. He describes his early life in the *Confessions* (1764–70), recounting such escapades as the stolen ribbon (he let a servant girl be blamed), his love for Mme. de **Warens**, quarrels with the philosophes, his bizarre affair with Thérèse Levasseur, and placing their five children in a foundlings' home. In 1749, en route to visit **Diderot** in prison, he experienced a vision that turned his vagrant writings into a speculative theory of human history as a decline from a solitary state of **nature** through degenerating states of society. This is eloquently expressed in: *Du contrat social* (1762); *Émile* (1762); and *Julie, ou la Nouvelle Héloïse* (1761). SB admired Rousseau's final work, *Rêveries du promeneur solitaire,* a complement to the *Confessions.*

SB cites "le baiser saporito de St Preux" (the "tasty kiss"), of Letter XIV of *Julie,* invoked as "Saint-Preux and the baci saporiti" (DN, 47; *Dream,* 45). This moment binds Saint-Preux to his pupil Julie forever, and seals their love (Rousseau has "ce baiser mortel"; SB's Italian derives from act 2 of Guarini's *Il Pastor Fido* [Pilling, *Dream Companion*]. In "**Fingal**" (24) **Belacqua** alludes to Mme. de Warens, Rousseau's "maman" and lover. He imagines himself "like Jean-Jacques sprawling in a bed of saxifrages" (31), during the idyllic period at Les Charmettes (*Confessions,* I.6), where the lovers tend their alpine plants. The tone is mocking, but to **MacGreevy** (16 September 1934) SB celebrated Rousseau as champion of the right to be alone, an authentic tragic failure as he was denied enjoyment of that right: "not easy in a society that considered **solitude** a vice." He qualified his praise of the "promeneur solitaire" by observing Rousseau's "infantile aspect," his fear "of the dark of his own constitution." SB notes that Rousseau always fell for a show of tenderness, his misfortune being always "de ne pouvoir résister aux caresses" (*Confessions* I.1); compare **Murphy**'s "Kick" and "Caress."

Roussel dummy: when **Celia** meets **Murphy** (14), she rotates "like the Roussel dummy in Regent Street." The window of J. Maison Roussel (173–77 Regent Street, **London** W1), elastic belt makers, retailers of trusses, corsetry, and intimate apparel, featured a dummy with outstretched arms, the figure their logo.

Roussillon: a town in the Vaucluse, thirty miles from Avignon, in unoccupied France, where SB and Suzanne took refuge from October 1942 until early 1945. SB worked occasionally in the vineyard of M. **Bonnelly**, who features in *En attendant Godot,* and with a family named Aude, whose farm suggested **Saposcat**'s life among the peasants. Friends made there included Anna Beamish, an idiosyncratic Irish woman; Yvonne and Marcel Lob, whose books SB borrowed; Henri and Josette **Hayden**, with whom he discussed **art** and writing; and Eugène and Edith Fournier, Edith later his translator. Much of the time was spent waiting, an ennui that made its way, like the red soil, into *Godot* and *Watt*. Writing the latter, especially the long pointless permutations, was a means of coping with an attenuated existence. For details of this excruciating period, see Knowlson's biography (chapter 13), "Refuge in Roussillon," which was excerpted by the *Sunday Times* (August 1996) to illustrate the forthcoming *Life*.

Roxane: heroine of *Cyrano de Bergerac* (1897) by Edmond Rostand (1868–1918), won by words penned by another; the **Alba** alludes (*Dream*, 173) to mutes at her beck (not "call").

Rudmose-Brown, Thomas: Professor of French at **Trinity**, under whom SB developed his love of literature and language and who passed on to SB his witty irreverence toward the texts he taught. His courses combined the canon with the contemporary; compare SB's use of the "**Alba**," "**Enueg**," and "**Serena**," Provençal forms taught by R-B. A large man, red-faced and with a shock of white hair, "Ruddy" lived with his wife, Anne ("Furry"), in Malahide, but had rooms in **Dublin** where he might give parties for his students. He cultivated an eccentric image, swearing and castigating in epigraphs both witty and obscene. SB eventually found these tedious, and to MacGreevy (5 October 1930) he complained of "the enduring and unendurable QUIP . . . he quipificates." R-B recommended SB as *lecteur* at the **École Normale** and, unhappily, for a teaching **job** at **Campbell House**. His scholarship consisted of essays on French poets, some anthologies of French poetry and prose,

and a slim volume of verse (*Walled Gardens*, 1918). R-B was never elected a Fellow, and was treated badly by such as John **Mahaffy**. He appears as the **Polar Bear** in *Dream*. SB regretted the portrayal, which R-B read when *Dream* was recycled into "A **Wet Night**." R-B's unpublished memoirs fail to mention his most illustrious student.

"Rue de Vaugirard": a five-line poem, tenth of the twelve *Poèmes 38–39*, published in *Les Temps modernes* II.14 (novembre 1946). It is deceptively simple: on his **bicycle**, on the Rue de Vaugirard (near SB's Rue des Favorites), the poet brakes, caught by the moment and exposed like a photographic plate to the play of light and shadow, before carrying on his way, with a lasting negative of the experience.

Russell, George (1867–1935): Irish poet and theosophist, otherwise "AE" (aeon), one who "enters his heart's desire with such precipitation as positively to protrude into the void" ("Recent Irish Poetry," 71). In *Murphy* (155), Miss **Carriage** returns to *The Candle of Vision* (1918), where Russell peers through the windows of his soul to see images of the divine imagination and relate his vision of the far-off Many-Coloured Land to seers and writers of the sacred books. It is as bad as that sounds. In translation, SB unveiled "*Roses de Décembre*, par Madame Rosa Caroline Mackworth Praed." Mr. Case (*Watt*, 228) reads *Songs by the Way* "by George Russell (A.E.)" (1894); otherwise *Homeward*. What he reads is uncertain but one draft indicates (NB6, 53) that

SB, presumably without the *Songs* handy, intended a "(Quotation)" [*sic*], then preferred the lacuna.

Ruth: Molloy admits that his true **love** was not a little chambermaid but "in another" (7). She against whom he has rubbed is (he thinks) Ruth, or Edith (56). His confusion is logical: "Ruth" is a "peaceful name" (56), but "Edith" means "glory in battle." She becomes "Rose" (83). Peggy **Sinclair**, SB's first love, was christened Ruth Margaret.

Ruysdael, Salomon van (1602–70): Dutch landscape painter, native of Haarlem. SB admired *The Halt* (National Gallery, **Dublin**) and could recall such intimate details as the small boy piddling against the wall (Knowlson, 72). Despite SB's love of *Entrance to the Forest,* Ruysdael epitomized an impasse, an emotion no longer authentic. To **MacGreevy** SB noted (8 September 1934) that there was no entrance anymore, no commerce with the forest: "its dimensions are its secret & it has no communications to make." He found in **Cézanne** (qv) an indifference of **nature** and absence of rapport better to express the incommensurability of man and the dark wood within.

S

Saadi: Muslih-uddin (1184–1291), Persian poet. The pathos of his *Diwan,* or collection of lyrical poetry, places him among the pessimists (*Dream,* 62). See **Hafiz.**

Sade, Donatien-Alphonse-François, Marquis de (1740–1814): French writer who, found guilty of unnatural offenses and poisoning, was committed to the Bastille (1778), then to the Charenton **Asylum** (1789). *Dream* refers (27) to *Justine* and *Juliette;* this derives from Mario Praz, *The Romantic Agony.* Praz notes (ix–x) that Sade was admired by the **surrealists** but warns against the "fashionable" adulation of him. The casual error of the *Hundred Days* (*Dream,* 179) is corrected in "A Wet Night" (50): "120 days." In 1938 SB was asked by Jack Kahane to translate *Les 120 jours de Sodome,* which SB admired for its rigor ("It fills me with a kind of metaphysical ecstasy," he told **MacGreevy,** 21 February 1938). SB accepted the commission, 150 francs per thousand words, but fearing it might affect his "future freedom of literary action" he withdrew (Knowlson, 269, 676). He later admired Peter Brook's Royal Shakespearean production of the Peter Weiss *Marat/Sade.*

Saint-Bridget the Rose: an Irish saint, "Mary of the Irish." Her feast is February 1 (Imbolg), the quarter day marking spring. Invoked in *Dream* (97). SB's confused source is **Cooper,** *Flagellation* (11; DN, 48), where a "bunch of keys" belongs to "one very devotional lady," the "besom" (birch rod) to Father Dominic, and there is no **goat** (or Rose). Pilling notes (*Dream Companion*) that the white goat is from **Musset**'s *La Confession d'un enfant du siècle* (part 3) where it belongs to one Brigitte Pierson.

St. John of God (1495–1550): of Portugal, patron of hospitals, nurses, and the sick. His feast is May 16. In **Ireland,** patron of alcoholics. St. John of God's is an **asylum** near **Foxrock,** housing the docile rather than the criminally insane; mocked in *Dream* (183) as the "**Stillorgan** Sunshine Home." **Wylie** informs the Guard (*Murphy,* 43) that **Neary** is from Stillorgan, not Dundrum, i.e., that he is harmless. Part III of *Watt* is set there, and the narrator of "The **End**" leaves from it. **Malone** dies there, in Room 166; the French text reads "numéro cent soixante seize" (i.e. 176). The description of the "Pleasure Grounds" (the surrounding park) and the high wall encompassing them about is both literal and Edenic. Malone calls it a "little Paradise" (277), adds an underground stream (as in **Coleridge**'s "Kubla Khan"), then loses patience: "to hell with all this fucking scenery." The inmates' outing with Lady **Pedal** takes the recognizable route from Stillorgan to **Dalkey** Island.

Saint-Lô: a Normandy town of 13,000 on the river Vire, an operational center for German forces that had been heavily bombed at the end of World War II. The Irish Red Cross set up a field hospital with 100 beds, replacing the ruined hospital (see Eoin O'Brien, *The Beckett Country*, chapter 10). SB at the invitation of Alan Thompson volunteered for the job of quartermaster-interpreter, arriving August 1945 to scenes of total devastation. Most of the town was destroyed, and it was a sea of mud, some 3,000 citizens surviving (see "The **Capital of the Ruins**"). SB acted as interpreter and driver, and ran the hospital store, from August 1945 until early 1946, when he returned to **Paris**. The horror shaped *Endgame*.

"Saint-Lô": a five-line poem published in *The Irish Times* (24 June 1946, 5); revised for *Poems in English* (1961): "ghost-abandoned" is modified to "ghost-forsaken" and attached to line 3, making four lines. An idiosyncratic printing appeared in *Rhinozeros* 2 (1960). SB's first creative post**war** work, it invokes the river Vire, which winds (Fr. *virer*) through the town, an image of the mind, "ghost-forsaken," coming to terms with the recent havoc. The poem moves from a mellifluous evocation of landscape to apocalyptic introspection. "Vire" suggests a crossbow bolt, winding through the shadows.

St. Nicolas, Church of: **Belacqua** anticipates bringing his bride, Thelma, to this Galway church to invoke "the spirits of Crusoe and Columbus, who had knelt there before him" ("What a Misfortune," 125). **Defoe** does not mention the Collegiate Church of Saint Nicholas [*sic*] of

Myra, 1320, but local legend insists that Christopher Columbus prayed there in 1492, before "committing his indiscretion" (SB to TM, 8 October 1932).

Saint-Roch (1295–1327): born in Montpellier with a red cross on his breast; patron of the plagued. Being smitten, he was fed by a **dog** that brought him bread as he was perishing in a forest. Returning home, disfigured, he was taken for a spy and died in **prison**. His festival is August 16. **Moran**, reduced to eating mosses, wonders if the saint refused suck on Wednesdays and Fridays (*Molloy*, 167).

Saint-Ruth: Mercier meets **Camier** (10) in a "place" (square) featuring a copper beech with a sign saying it was planted by "a Field-Marshal of France peacefully named Saint-Ruth" (*Ruth* means "peace" in Hebrew), who was immediately struck by a cannonball. O'Brien identifies (353) the Marquis de St. Ruth, sent by Louis XIV to support Patrick **Sarsfield**. He fought at the battle of Aughrim Hill (12 July 1691), dying for **Ireland** as Sarsfield did for **France**. There is no such monument in **Dublin**; "St. **Macarius**" (13) implicates St. Macaire (as in the French), near Bordeaux.

Saint-Sulpice: the **Alba**, listening to Jean du **Chas**, "Je hais les tours de Saint-Sulpice," is hugely amused (*Dream*, 233). Pilling notes (*Dream Companion*) that this is the first line of a squib by Raoul Ponchon, which continues, "Quand je les rencontre / Je pisse / Contre." Du Chas refers to an eighteenth-century neoclassical masterpiece, Giovanni Niccolò

Servandoni's *église* St-Sulpice, with its asymmetrical towers, but the Alba assumes a restaurant in that *faubourg,* with a notorious *toilette à la turc* that had to be flushed as one retreated quickly; *ingénus* emerged deluged, to the delight of those awaiting (**Belacqua** has just entered the casa **Frica** soaked). Omitted from "A **Wet Night.**"

Salkeld, Mrs. Blanaid (1880–1959): poet whose "Hello Eternity" (1933) is rendered blue in the face by the sonnet form ("Recent Irish Poetry," 74; see O'Brien, 377).

Sallust: Gaius Sallustius Crispus (ca. 86–35 BC), Roman historian whose experience of the depravity of his age led to elegant descriptions thereof, except (according to Lemprière) his portrait of Cicero, whose ex-wife he married. Hence, perhaps, the "dreadful hash" (*Dream,* 126).

Sam: in part III of *Watt,* and here alone, the narrative **voice** is identified as Sam's, and an account is offered of how the narrative has been composed. If we foolishly thought to know Watt, the impediments are greater now. Yet to assume that Sam is responsible for everything is dubious. He was introduced late, and the opening scenes only hint at his presence, through self-conscious footnotes (8); textual lacunae (29); ironic authoritative comments (37); and curious commas ("he appeared again, to Watt," 63). But these need not imply a mediating **voice,** one without. The narrative **rats** become more insistent as part II gresses: Watt's "mouthpiece" (69); "me" (79); "I" (125);

that "I" knew nothing save what Watt had told "me" (125); the description of how "I" took notes (126). In part III, the entire novel purports to be recounted by Watt to Sam, on rare occasions (the wind high, the sun bright) when they met, coaxed from their **mansions** into the garden. Watt's deterioration is suggested by his backward **motion,** his resemblance to the scourged **Christ** (159), probable blindness, and degenerate language. His discourse undergoes (164–69) inversions of sentences within the period, words within the sentence, letters within the word; thus Sam misses (he presumes) much (he supposes) of Watt's account of his stay in **Knott**'s house. In the end (he says) he gets used to the sounds, but the narrative is at best an impetuous murmur ill heard, misunderstood, with much lost forever.

Sam Francis Notebook: a soft-covered brown exercise book (RUL 2926) from the late 1950s. It contains notes for a translation of Georges **Duthuit**'s essay on Sam Francis (1923–94), an American abstract expressionist who studied in **Paris** and was influenced by Japanese abstraction and Oriental notions of negative space. There are preliminaries to *Fin de partie.* One, a ten-leaf holograph, is dated 15 September 1950, shortly after SB's return from **Ireland** and his **mother**'s funeral. Two characters, **A** and **B,** discuss the uncertain (possibly divine) presence of an invisible third ("**Avant** *Fin de partie*" uses X and F). Other notes are on Mexican poets and vocabulary items for use in SB's *Anthology of Mexican Poetry;* a letter to Alexander Trocchi (several drafts); and a loose page with some lines of an unfinished poem beginning "Caught among eyelashes."

A Samuel Beckett Reader: a selection of SB's works, ed. John **Calder** (1967); published simultaneously with the New English Library paperback. Pan published an expanded *Reader* as a Picador original (1983). Compare *I can't go on, I'll go on,* edited with an "Introduction" by Richard Seaver (Grove, 1974).

Samuel Beckett Society: founded by S. E. Gontarski and Calvin Israel at the 1976 MLA in Chicago. The society had no institutional support so the gesture might have seemed hollow. However, Barney Rosset of **Grove Press** agreed to host a social gathering (December 1977), which created the semblance of an organization. To ensure an international character, Gontarski and Israel invited papers for the inaugural session from James Knowlson, newly named editor of *JOBS* and curator of the fledgling archive at Reading, John Pilling, and John Fletcher (guest commentator). John **Calder**, who had recently begun publishing *JOBS,* attended as a special guest. The response encouraged Gontarski to approach Ohio State for support. The university offered a publication grant from the John Galvin Foundation, and in spring 1978 volume 1.1 of *The Beckett Circle: Newsletter of the Samuel Beckett Society* appeared. The foundation's assistance supported such activities as SBS-sponsored social hours at the New York University Beckett Festival (October 1978) and at the Ohio State symposium "Samuel Beckett: Hu-

manistic Perspectives" (May 1981), where "**Ohio Impromptu**" premiered. The goals of the SBS outlined in the first issue of the *Newsletter* have changed little: "In addition to the general purpose of encouraging scholarly study of and critical attention to the work and career of Samuel Beckett, the Society is designed to encourage contact and communication among scholars, critics, teachers, and students of Beckett's work." Honorary trustees currently include Edward Beckett, Ruby Cohn, Raymond Federman, James Knowlson, John Calder, and Barney Rosset.

Samuel Beckett Today/Aujourd'hui: founded (1991) by Marius Buning (Amsterdam) and Sjef Houppermans (Leiden), chief editors, anticipating the Second International Beckett Symposium, "Beckett in the 1990s" (The Hague, spring 1992). An annual bilingual journal, it is open to contributions in English or French, by new and established critics, "provided they meet equally the tests of sound scholarship and a high degree of readability, and avoid academic fustiness and learned obfuscation," as the first editorial put it. Published by Rodopi in Amsterdam and New York.

A dozen issues have appeared [2003]: I, *Samuel Beckett 1970–89* [1992]; II, *Beckett in the 1990s* (Second International Beckett Symposium, The Hague, 1992) [1993]; III, *Intertexts in Beckett's Work* [1994]; IV, *The Savage Eye* (film and TV) [1995]; V, *Beckett and Psychoanalysis* [1996]; VI, *Crossroads and Borderlines,* ed. Emmanuel Jacquart (Strasbourg Symposium, 1996) [1997]; VII,

Beckett versus Beckett [1998]; VIII, *Poetry and Other Prose* [2000]; IX, *Beckett and Religion / Beckett / Aesthetics / Politics*, ed. Mary Bryden and Lance St. John (religion; Stirling Conference, September 1999), and Peter Boxall (aesthetics/politics) [2000]; X, *L'Affect dans l'oeuvre beckettienne*, ed. Michèle Touret and Yann Mével (Rennes Conference, December 1999) [2001]; XI, *Endlessness in the Year 2000*, ed. Angela Mooranji (Beckett in Berlin, 2000) [2001]; XII, "Pastiches, Parodies, and Other Imitations" [2002]. Issues in preparation at the time of writing will feature the 2003 Sydney symposium and SB's notebooks. Each is composed around one perspective, but unsolicited articles are accepted; #8 published Bruce Arnold's controversial article, alleging that Anthony Cronin's *The Last Modernist* took unauthorized material from a proof copy of James Knowlson's **biography**. *SBT/A* has become a useful forum, a European complement to *JOBS*. Ideally, there could be another publication, a SB literary supplement (as in **Joyce** studies) devoted to keeping up with the numerous studies appearing each year.

"Sanies I": in *Echo's Bones*, a fifty-two-line poem, set in the spring of 1933, depicting the poet on his **bicycle** speeding north of **Dublin**, to **Portrane**, then through Donabate, passing the domain of Turvey with its sad swans, the village of Swords, and back to Dublin. Originally entitled "Weg du Einzige" ("Away, you only one," echoing **Hölderlin**'s "O du Einzige! vergib, vergib . . . Meine Liebe, tränenvoll und trüb" ["An Lyda"]). Said by Knowlson (162) to have been inspired by a ride on Easter Saturday 1933 and a chance meeting with Ethna **MacCarthy**, but a letter to **MacGreevy** (23 December 1932) describes a bike ride to Portrane "last Saturday." It retraces the route taken by **Belacqua** in "**Fingal**"; some material derives from the unpublished "**Spring Song**." A signed copy, in the **HRHRC** (#42), notes: "Exitus Redditus this evening Montparnasse 1957," suggesting (five pentades later) the joyous outgoing and sad homecoming of **Thomas à Kempis**.

"Sanies" is a "morbid discharge," a seropurulent emission from an infected ulcer or wound (DN, 145); in "**Yellow**" (167) **Belacqua** likens the dribble of **time** to sanies into a bucket. The tone belies that sentiment, on this day of sweet showers (**Chaucer**), no deep care (**Horace**'s *atra cura*), "all heaven in the sphincter," tired indeed, but potwalloping along nicely. Pessimism arises as he thinks of his parents' marriage ("seven pentades past") and his birth in terms of "Spy Wedsday" [*sic*], when Judas betrayed **Christ** (Matthew 26:3–5): "ah to be back in the caul now with no trusts" (14). Pain alternates with euphoria, the motif "tired now" becoming more dominant; "**Botticelli** from the fork down" means "his legs felt heavy." The poem reaches its main verb (43), when the poet sees "her whom alone in the accusative / I have dismounted to **love**," gliding toward him like the splendor of **God** on the waters. The encounter does not meet the success his euphoria might have assumed. The poem ends in anger, his "**nautch-girl**" going back to her cob (male swan) in Holles Street (the maternity hospital turns his anger into that of being born), and the smile on the face of this tiger, coming back from his ride, a little wry.

"Sanies II": a second such poem in *Echo's Bones;* on a signed copy, now in the **HRHRC** (#42), SB noted "**École Normale** Paris 1929." Referred to by SB as "The Happy Land," it begins lightly. Although his **body** is clean he delights in his dirty mind: the "red eggs" in the American Bar are "henorrhoids" (caviar, or perhaps pickled eggs). He toys with **Dante** and blissful **Beatrice** being there, "prior to Vita Nuova," as back in **Dublin** in Becky **Cooper**'s establishment. SB is blending two experiences, one in **Paris**, the other back home, when he was thrown out for laughing at the incongruity (Knowlson, 139). And everybody happy: "gobble-gobble / suck is not suck that alters." Those present are enchanted: "Gracieuse," "Percinet," and "Belle-Belle," from the fairy tales of the Comtesse d'**Aulnoy**, Marie Catherine de la Motte. But the tone changes, as in the "Circe" chapter of *Ulysses;* the Barfrau with the mighty bottom becomes Madame de la **Motte**, infamous poisoner, and the saloon assumes a terrible hush. He has done something untoward (his laughing misunderstood by the booted Percinet?), and, in a mélange of mumbo and parody of Plautus (*Asonaria,* I.i: "dead bullocks, that make incursions upon living [wo]men," "vivos homines" here "vivas puellas"), he must plead for mercy: "call off thine adders Becky." The poem ends in broken supplication (compare **Eliot**, "The Hollow Men") but of dubious efficacy, as he imagines being whipped. The final lines seem ambivalently poised between suffering and a curious delight in chastisement, more jest than pain, the two not incompatible. The detail is drawn from **Cooper**'s *Flagellation:* a "cavaletto" is a marble flogging block; "supplejacks" are rattan canes; "bastinado" caning on the soles; the "**cang**" a Chinese instrument of correction; "fessade" a regular whipping (DN, 47–57). Their presence in the fairy tale makes for a poem much wittier than is generally appreciated, however heartfelt the last line might be.

San Quentin Drama Workshop: a company headed by Rick Cluchey, former inmate at San Quentin **Prison**, that specialized in productions of SB's work under SB's supervision. Cluchey encountered SB's work (19 November 1957) when the San Francisco Actor's Workshop brought *Waiting for Godot,* produced by Alan Mandell and directed by Herbert Blau, into San Quentin and presented it to an unusual audience, 1,400 convicts. The impact has become legendary. Cluchey asked Mandell to coach a group of untrained convicts in a drama workshop. The group eventually staged productions of *Godot,* *Endgame,* and *Krapp's Last Tape.* Members frequently changed and only Cluchey had San Quentin roots, but those plays became their repertory. Cluchey accounts for SB's appeal to the inmates by suggesting that convicts have an acute sensitivity to human suffering and face uncertain waiting. In 1965, a year before he was pardoned, Cluchey wrote a play called *The Cage.* In 1973, in **London** performing it, Cluchey wrote to SB for permission to perform his prison repertory professionally. With SB's enthusiastic support

Cluchey opened *Endgame* at the Traverse Theatre, Edinburgh, before the 1974 Festival. The production was held over for the Festival, then moved to Berlin's Forum Theatre and the American Cultural Center, **Paris**. In 1975 Cluchey prepared to direct Genet's *Deathwatch* at the Forum Theater, Berlin, as SB was directing *Godot* at the **Schiller-Theater**, Cluchey acting as his assistant. This allowed him to study SB as **director**. In 1977 he was back in Berlin as artist in residence at DAAD, and SB directed him in *Krapp's Last Tape* at the Akademie der Künst Festwochen. In May 1980 SB agreed to direct the group in *Endgame* at the Riverside Studios, London, and in May 1984 he again worked with them to refresh their *Godot,* also at the Riverside Studios. Those three productions, the original San Quentin repertory, were filmed by the group under the slightly misleading title of *Beckett Directs Beckett,* a coproduction of the Visual Press at the University of Maryland and the Smithsonian Institution Press.

Sans: a short prose text, translated by SB as *Lessness* (qv). Published in *Quinzaine littéraire* 82 (1 novembre 1969): 3–4, with a sketch of SB (16 juillet 1968) by **Arikha;** the first edition of 742 numbered copies appeared two weeks later (Minuit, 1969). *Sans* was added to *Têtesmortes* (Minuit, 1972).

Santa Maria del Fiore: the duomo in **Florence;** designed (1298) by Arnolfo di Cambio, completed by Brunelleschi, and consecrated (1436). Nearby stand Giotto's campanile and the baptistery with Ghiberti's bronze doors. Depicted in Isidoro Del Lungo's edition of the *Commedia divina* (Florence: Le Monnier, 1926), as noted in *Dream* (51).

Saposcat: protagonist of **Malone**'s first narrative, from L. *sapere,* "to know," and Gk. *skatos,* "dung"; hence, knowledge as waste. He becomes **Macmann.** Sapo's family has few redeeming qualities, their lives a petit bourgeois parody of **Balzac**'s *Comédie humaine.* Sapo's time among the peasants reflects SB's long exile in **Roussillon.** His story was originally much longer; considerable chunks were excised and replaced by comments such as "Quel ennui" (20), "Quelle misère" (27), or "Ça avance" (31). These break up the narrative, convey boredom, and create "interludes."

saprophile: one who loves "to get rotten," as in "**A Wet Night**" (65); replacing the macaco (lemur) "the worse for drink" of *Dream* (219).

Sarsfield, Patrick (1655–93): Earl of Lucan, Irish Jacobite, and soldier, who returned to **Ireland** to fight at the Boyne (1690), Aughrim, (1691) and Limerick (1691), becoming a popular hero. When the Jacobite cause failed, he entered French service in the Irish Brigade and died in the Netherlands. In *Mercier and Camier* (13), the ranger emulates "the great Sarsfield," risking himself for territory that means nothing to him.

Sartre, Jean-Paul (1905–80): French **existentialist** philosopher who was SB's near contemporary at the **École Normale.** Sartre shared a study with Alfred **Péron,** who was as charming as Sartre was disagreeable (Knowlson, 79). SB read *La Nausée* on publication (Mai 1938) and admired it. An early supporter of **surrealism**, Sartre later published "The Situation of the Writer in 1945," which outlined his political approach to literature in the post-Auschwitz era. His commitment to a literature of engagement put him on a course different from that of SB. Complications arose (1946) with the publication of "**Suite**" in Sartre's *Les Temps modernes,* and the two later treated each other with distant politesse. In 1962, asked by Sartre to petition against the Algerian war, SB refused (Bair, 544). Sartre was awarded the **Nobel Prize** (1964) but pointedly rejected it. SB described the refusal as "inelegant," but a Beckettian touch followed, when Sartre later requested and was denied the money. A great **gulf** exists between Sartre's existentialism and SB's condition of doubt, as in the **Unnamable**'s "all their balls about being and existing" (348), or the impasse of *Waiting for Godot* where no meaningful choice is possible but only waiting. *Endgame,* unlike *Huis clos,* offers neither **stoicism** nor endurance, yet as **Hamm** rests his hand against the wall he comments, "Au-delà c'est . . . l'autre enfer," echoing Sartre's celebrated *mauvais mot:* "l'enfer, c'est les autres."

sausage poisoning: the *Watt* notebooks record Willy, son of Leda née Swann and brother of James **Quin**, who died of sausage poisoning (*Watt,* "Addenda" #1). The **Unnamable** returns from his world tour (317–18), from jungles red with **rafflesia**, "stinking of carrion," to find his family, all ten or eleven of them (the number of Quin's siblings), "carried off by sausage poisoning" (L. *botulus,* "a sausage"; the "bacillus botulinus," 322). The jest is more than etymological, for SB would have read in **Nordau**'s *Degeneration,* in the final diatribe against a diseased society, references to poisoned sausage (552). The **French** text does not make this connection, its fatal effect wrought by "conserves avariées" ("spoilt preserves" [canned beef]). In the second version of the extermination, the English sausage becomes "the fatal corned-beef" (324), the change made because of the following cabbage; the French text has "du fatal corned beef" (62) and a child "trouvé dans un chou."

Savonarola, Girolamo (1452–98): Dominican priest and reformer who established a republic in **Florence** (1494), with stringent laws against vice and frivolity that led to the "bonfire of the vanities." His denunciations of clerical abuse and Pope Alexander VI brought charges of heresy, excommunication, and public burning in the Piazza della Signoria. Hence the deferential jests in *Dream* (202) and "A **Wet Night**" (49).

Savory: Moran's lawyer (*Molloy,* 120 and 175). One D. L. Savory edited introductory French texts used in SB's day; **Rudmose-Brown** published his *French Short Stories* (Oxford, 1925) in the series.

Schiller-Theater Werkstatt: the Berlin theater closely associated with SB's work. He **directed** there many of his own plays (1967–78), each undergoing rigorous revision in the process (see *Regiebuch* and *Theatrical Notebooks*). SB's relationship with Berlin began on 8 September 1953, when *Warten auf Godot* premiered at the Schlosspark-Theater, almost two years before the English premiere. Boleslaw Barlog, head of the Berlin theater, stressed his good fortune in discovering SB, and German critics were enthusiastic. Although SB was not entirely happy with it, the production was performed forty-five times in Berlin before touring to other cities in **Germany.**

Endspiel opened at the *Schlosspark-Theater* (30 September 1957) less than six months after the world premiere and a year before the first English production. Unlike *Godot,* it was not a critical success. In 1959 Albert Bessler negotiated the German rights of *Krapp's Last Tape* for the Schiller-Theater. SB's drama was now popular in Germany. The play was in a double bill with Edward Albee's *The Zoo Story* as the opening production of the Schiller-Theater Werkstatt (28 September 1959), well before the French and American premieres. The critical reaction was positive, the novelty of SB's dramatic style gradually replaced by a deeper understanding of his work. In June 1961 Bessler asked SB to supply program notes for the German premiere of *Happy Days,* which he declined. This did not sour his relationship with the theater, as *Glückliche Tage* premiered at the Werkstatt (30 September 1961) as part of the Berlin *Festwochen,* two weeks after the world premiere in New York and a year before the English or French openings. SB's affinity with the Schiller-Theater grew out of discussions with Barlog and Bessler concerning the staging of these plays. A personal friendship developed from the working relationship. Critical reaction varied but the initial popularity of *Godot* in Germany was a vital factor in establishing SB's reputation beyond the avant-garde French theater. His appreciation of this early acceptance was reflected in his loyalty to the Schiller-Theater thereafter.

SB attended Deryk **Mendel**'s Berlin *Godot* in 1965, responding to a request from Albert Bessler to amend an unhappy production. He stayed in the Akademie der Künste, of which he grew fond (part of *Footfalls* was written there), and got to know Berlin and the German art scene intimately. The German element in his career became distinct. He established a rapport with a young Israeli woman, Mira Averech, which led to a relationship. As a result of these affinities, SB directed seven of his stage plays at the Schiller-Theater between 1967 and 1978. Although he claimed these productions were not intended to be definitive, they have assumed a major role in the interpretation of his drama.

SB's directorial work began (1967) with *Endspiel,* which formed part of the Berlin *Festwochen* and was described by many critics as the festival highlight. He found it a curious experience, with the Irish voices of Pat **Magee** and Jacky **MacGowran** echoing in his head (Knowlson, 488), but SB's initial foray into directing was successful. The linguistic playfulness of the French text was reflected in the revised German translation and transferred to the stage in patterns of physical action detailed in his *Regiebuch.* SB returned to Berlin (1969) to direct *Das letzte Band,* again concentrating on patterns of verbal and gestural repetition. This production became a focus of the *Festwochen,* the tenth anniversary of the Werkstatt. It was a resounding success and, following his *Endspiel,* consolidated SB's reputation in the German theater as a meticulous director.

SB returned to the Werkstatt (1971) to direct *Glückliche Tage* as part of the *Festwochen,* claiming it was the only way he could get his plays performed exactly as he wanted. This time critical opinion turned against him. Although he succeeded in focusing attention on the lack of action, many found this rigidity too oppressive. During rehearsals, SB was invited to direct a German-language *Godot.* Despite his dissatisfaction with the 1953 German premiere, he had avoided assuming full directorial control of the play in any language. By 1975 conditions seemed amenable for him to create his own version of his best-known work. SB's *Godot* marked the pinnacle of his directorial work in Berlin. Audiences agreed, as more than 100,000 people saw the Schiller-Theater *Godot,* prompting comparisons with Brecht about SB's influence on contemporary German theater.

Autumn 1976 found SB back in Berlin to direct a double bill of *Damals* (*That Time*) and *Tritte* (*Footfalls*), again as part of the *Festwochen.* Critical opinion on this hourlong evening was divided. These short, stark pieces proved too radical for many. Despite a mixed critical reception, the Schiller-Theater invited him to direct a double bill composed of "**Play**" and *Come and Go* as part of the 1978 *Festwochen.* SB agreed to direct "Spiel," but handed over *Kommen und Gehen* to Walter Asmus.

Unfortunately, the critics' enthusiasm for SB's directorial work did not extend to these later, fragmentary pieces, which proved equally demanding for audiences.

SB's Berlin productions reflect considerable changes to tone and texture, a consequence of their stage redefinition. Some scholars have felt that he moved away from his original intentions; others argue that they represent his final and therefore lasting word. All agree, however, that Beckett directing Beckett at the Schiller-Theater was a unique theatrical experience. [JG]

schizophrenia: mental alienation par excellence. **Psychoanalysis** has never been at its most convincing when dealing with schizophrenia, which is fundamentally pathological, but the assertion that much modern literature has affinities with the condition is a commonplace. SB's fascination with mental fragmentation takes him on a parallel course, without constituting an outright synthesis of the disease. Thus, consideration of actual schizophrenia serves as a legitimate point of orientation for reading his works and clarifies his use of psychoanalytic theory as a structural device rather than a psychological given.

SB recalled a hospitalized schizophrenic who was "like a hunk of meat. There was no one there. He was absent" (Knowlson, 198). Mr. **Endon**, possessed of "a psychosis so limpid and imperturbable that **Murphy** felt drawn to it as **Narcissus** to his fountain" (*Murphy,* 186), represents the hermetic existence in the **little world** of the mind that Murphy aspires to but is denied by his fundamental sanity. SB's fascination with aberrations of the inner **voice** is indicated by Dr. **Killiecrankie**, who "had some experience of the schizoid voice" (185). SB had in mind the third **Tavistock** lecture, when **Jung** described complexes as breaking from conscious control and forming personalities and voices of their own. **Watt**'s psychic disintegration is heralded early, as "there came, with great distinctness, from afar, from without, yes, really it seemed from without, the voices, indifferent in quality, of a **mixed choir**" (33).

Schizophrenia as a literary motif can be elucidated by a sketch of the illness. A brain disease affecting attentional mechanisms, it disrupts the ability to integrate perception and behavior in a coherent narrative. Familiar features become drained of secure meaning; trivia seem uncannily significant; the world undergoes a sinister, infinitesimal slip into unreality. It is akin to the common experience of derealization whereby prolonged fixation renders a word or **object** "peculiar" (*unheimlich*). These phenomena indicate an inward focus of attention, albeit not consciously undertaken, upon cognition itself until **consciousness**, not designed for such hyperreflexivity, becomes lost in a mental **mirror** world and begins to fragment. Typical of such confusion is the inability to distinguish between external voices and one's own inner voice; the latter may be objectified into the "voices" of schizophrenic hallucination. The resulting "madness" raises problems, in that psychotic reason cannot be equated with **irrationality** or incoherence. Bizarre as schizophrenic behavior can seem, it rarely lacks logic. Rather, reasoning is no longer grounded in the

implicit framework of practical orientations and shared cognitive skills maintained by social existence. Schizophrenics often try to mitigate the instability of their subjective worlds by holding fast to very *explicit* principles and reasoning from them inflexibly until reason itself becomes a path to "insane" beliefs. Watt is a case in point.

SB was intrigued by the consciousness that tries to objectify and scrutinize itself; as Victor says in *Eleutheria*, "I want to enjoy my **death**. That's where liberty lies: to see oneself dead" (150). "It's schizophrenia," diagnoses Dr. Piouk (165), flippantly but ominously. Watt strives to retain normal cognizance of the outside world but fails through the very strain of his efforts. Desperate attempts to make the incident of the **Galls** yield meaning leave Watt baffled as it "gradually lost, in the nice processes of its light, its sound, its impacts and its rhythm, all meaning, even the most literal" (73). This is one of Watt's many perceptual fluxes. His relentless scrutiny of experience has effects like those of the reflexive focus of schizophrenia, although genuine psychosis sets in at a level of cognition prior to conscious intentionality. Watt's horror at this chaos drives him to more rigorous applications of logical scrutiny, which lead to such absurdities as the famished **dog**. As schizophrenia frequently demonstrates, logical reasoning divorced from the implicit scaffolding of "normal" socialized orientation is itself the surest path to insanity.

SB's satire is directed at the Cartesian method of systematic inquiry. The Cartesian conception of a mind that has direct and privileged access to its own contents underlies the urge to reify and objectively examine the subjective "self" and its experiences. If this urge is taken to extremes, it becomes apparent that the mind is not so designed and will tend to short-circuit. The Cartesian epistemological project is erected upon a model of the human mind more akin to pathology than normality. When Watt rounds off his disintegration with a reference to **Hölderlin** (239), the inference is clear. But SB's concern goes beyond satire to the ultimate experiential consequences of such crisis. The **cogito** buckles under the strain: "I think, therefore I am" is not a clear and distinct idea. A normal healthy mind takes the "I" for granted and puts no pressure on it, but for schizophrenics identity can become distorted. They may experience a bizarre conjunction of virtual **solipsism** and a terrifying loss of self; thoughts may seem to emanate from some external source, or the world seem appallingly dependent on one's mental concentration. As Watt, having left Mr. **Knott**'s house, gazes entranced at a spectral figure with a gait strangely like his own (225–28), he is moving into territory where "self" is uncertain. In this sense the novel is a bridge toward SB's direct encounter with the problem of the voice.

This encounter takes place in *The Unnamable*, where SB's structural use of psychoanalysis impinges on the motif of schizophrenia. He simulates free association to convey a compulsive reflexive turn that does not yield insight because it cuts itself loose from the framework of cognitive skills that integrates mental content into a coherent self. It is effectively a simulation of an essential quality of schizophrenic alienation, with comparable effects upon the identity of the voice, "as if he were I" (403). The procession of **Basil**, **Mahood**, and **Worm** accords with psychoanalytic theories of primitive complexes thrusting rudely to the shattered surface of consciousness. However, this traditional psychoanalytic version of psychosis is fraught with problems. It posits a loss of self-awareness with a selfless abandonment to concrete immediacy and a profound regression to prelogical thinking. This is at odds with the introspection and logical inflexibility observed by clinicians, and is fundamentally irreconcilable with the insights of cognitive psychology. While SB is interested in pursuing the voice back through what he envisages as its progressively more **embryonic** states to the depths of the unconscious, *The Unnamable* patently does not enact a surrender to archetypes. The text is more in tune with a view of schizophrenia not as a withdrawal from the higher levels of cognition but as a condition in which these faculties operate in pathological overdrive and turn inward on thought processes themselves until they assume an objective reality that usurps the physical world. The outcome is perhaps the most acute analysis of schizophrenic alienation in Western literature, but the reader is made to respond to a literary process and not simply to react to a psychological given. [DL]

Schneider, Alan (1917–84): a rarity among American **directors,** the Russian-born Schneider worked with equal facility in professional and in academic theater. A committed teacher at Catholic University (1941–47, 1949–52), Boston University (1972–79), the Julliard Theater Center (1975–79), and the University of California, San Diego (1979–84), he made his theatrical reputation on and off Broadway, and in regional theater, particularly the Arena Theater, Washington, DC. He staged premieres of major playwrights like SB, Edward Albee, Harold Pinter, and Edward Bond, in all some 175 productions at professional and university theaters, from his first undergraduate production of Valentin Katayev's *Squaring the Circle* (1939) to a remarkable series of SB's one-act plays at the Harold Clurman Theater (1983–84) just before his **death**.

In 1956 he was selected to stage the American debut of an unknown Franco-Irish playwright, SB. The venue, Miami's Coconut Grove Playhouse, was unfortunate, for the audience expected lighter fare than was being offered with the existential enigma of *Waiting for Godot*. What might have been a career-ending fiasco began a lifelong association with a playwright who cultivated failure. Schneider went on to stage the premiere of *Endgame* at the Cherry Lane Theater, New York, two years later. In 1960 at the Provincetown Playhouse he staged the American premiere of *Krapp's Last Tape* with Albee's *The Zoo Story,* then the world premiere of *Happy Days,* and Albee's *Who's Afraid of Virginia Woolf?* He became principal American director for Albee (six more premieres) as well as for SB. In 1972, after a hiatus of twenty years, Schneider accepted a professorship at Boston University. He staged two world premieres on college campuses at festivals celebrating SB's seventy-fifth birthday (1981): "**Rockaby**" at SUNY Buffalo (8 April), produced by Daniel La Beille, and "**Ohio Impromptu**" at Ohio State (8 May), produced by S. E. Gontarski.

What endeared him to the playwrights he served was his invisiblity. Schneider advocated a transparency that made manifest the author's literary text and the actors' skills. He was both praised and blamed, he complained, for serving the text, but that concept of the director's role brought him some of the best new plays. He often sounded remarkably like SB: "in the theater as in all **art**, the only thing that counts is the work itself, the need to go on with that work at the highest possible level—not to be distracted or disturbed by success or failure, by praise or blame, by surface or show, analysis or abstraction, self-criticism or the criticism of others. This is especially important with work of Beckett's magnitude, possessed of his sublimity, his degree of compassion, his eloquent understanding of the potentialities both of the stage and of human frailty." Schneider was finally a playwright's director.

In London to direct *The War Home* by James Duff, Schneider was hit by a motorcycle after posting a letter to SB. He died in the Royal Free Hospital (3 May 1984), two weeks after delivering the manuscript of the first volume of his autobiography to Viking Press (published as *Entrances: An American Director's Journey,* 1986). In his obituary (4 May 1984), *New York Times* theater critic Mel Gussow called Schneider "one of the most important American directors of contemporary theater." Thirty years of correspondence with SB, *No Author Better Served,* ed. Maurice Harmon, was published by Harvard University Press (1998).

scholasticism: a tradition of medieval learning and speculation rooted in the Platonic doctrine of Ideas and Aristotelian logic and centered about the "schools" that gave instruction in the seven liberal arts that constituted the educational curriculum from the ninth to the fifteenth centuries, from Erigena to Occam. Early scholasticism was championed by **Roscellinus,** Anselm, **William of Champeaux,** and Abélard, and the later by Albertus Magnus, Thomas Aquinas, and Duns Scotus, who wrought the rigid codification that brought it into disrepute. The powerful *Analytics* of **Aristotle,** emphasizing the syllogism and categorical forms, dominated Greek science and ruled logical thought until the close of the Middle Ages, and beyond. Scholasticism was shaped by that tradition of logic, by Neoplatonic speculation and mysticism, and by the impulse to reformulate the dicta of Aristotle in accordance with the precepts of Christian theology; it was characterized by speculative reason, in turn subordinate to prescriptive authority and revealed truth.

The great question concerned the metaphysical significance of logical genera (Windelband, 271), or how universals relate to reality. *Realists* maintained the independent (Platonic) existence of genera and species; *Nominalists* saw in universals only designations that apply commonly. SB was fascinated by the paradoxes and impasses implicit in such speculation and by the legacy of curious learning that persisted in **Bacon** and **Descartes,** despite their ambition to destroy the edifice of scholastic learning and institute a new epistemology. He accepted **Schopenhauer's** criticisms of "the schoolmen" as privileging rational knowledge as abstract cognition, thereby losing the character of *perceptio* (*WWI,* I.i. #7, 34), agreeing that Descartes was essentially scholastic, claiming to "throw off all the early implanted opinions belonging to his age and nation," but doing so only apparently, "to assume them again immediately and hold them all the more firmly; and so it is with all his successors down to **Kant**" (II.13). See **Occasionalism.**

Whoroscope depicts Descartes's dispute with scholastic tradition, culminating (56–65) in the "Eucharistic sophistry" whereby he reconciles his doctrine of transubstantiation by aligning himself with Aristotle against the theologians who believe that "accidents réels" can exist without the substance to which they are normally attached. Orthodoxy held that the *substance* of the bread and wine changed into the body and blood of **Christ,** but the *accidents* remained; Descartes's theory of matter denied that an *accident* could remain when its habitual substance had been removed, hence, a contradiction. In reply to the Jansenist Antoine Arnauld, who maintained that Descartes was unorthodox because of this theory of matter, the speaker contends that the *superficiae* only of the bread and wine remain the same, but their substance is changed since **God** may "jig" infinitely close to those surfaces, hence, no contradiction. The accidents are not so much real as perceived as real. While SB invokes Bacon as one who will not swallow cave phantoms, his demonstration conforms (as he is aware) to scholastic reasoning. His point is the ease with which it is done, another "hen-and-a-half" one, or simple conundrum: if a hen-and-a-half lays an egg-and-a-half in a day-and-a-half, how long will it take one hen to lay one egg. The correct answer, a day-and-a-half, still perplexes the imperceptive.

In *Dream,* the **Smeraldina** and the **Syra-Cusa** are compared in terms of their physical accidents, the process mocked as the essence of beauty is predicateless, transcending categories, just as "all **mystics**, independent of creed and colour and sex, are transelemented into the creedless, colourless, sexless Christ" (35). This is followed (38–43) by an elaborate use of scholastic logic to define the Smeraldina as bride of **Belacqua**'s soul, one and indivisible, until the **Beatrice** lurking in every brothel divides him and makes her fade away, and so, like **Dante** (43), he concedes defeat at the point of attaining paradise. In **"Echo's Bones"** (17), Belacqua asks if there is more of God in an elephant than in an oyster, to which Lord Gall replies, "Exactly the same amount." This derives from two citations from **Augustine** (DN, 13): "God's being not bulk; for the infinite bulk contains parts lesser than its infinitude; so not wholly everywhere" (III.7); and "More God in an elephant than in a sparrow (Sophistry of spatial divinity)" (VII.1). In **"Ding-Dong"** (39) Belacqua's immobility is likened to **Buridan's ass.** In *Dream* (208) the **Alba's** decisiveness is similarly couched: "Is she,

who *knows,* to be equilibrated in Buridan's marasmus?" ("who *knows*" intimating Aristotle, *maestro di color che sanno*). In **Mercier and Camier,** the **pseudocouple** and giant barman look at each other (82), three versions of self creating nine images; this is described (96) as "Mercier's contribution to the controversy of the universals." That sentiment underlies, doubtless, the exchange of glances in *Watt* between Mr. Fitzwein and the other examiners.

Celia's love for **Murphy**, and vice versa, is explained as the condition of their walking away, as shown "in Barbara, Baccardi and Baroko, though never in Bramantip" (16). This alludes to the system of mnemonics deriving from Aristotelian logic, required for the **Trinity** examinations in scholastic logic, used to determine the condition and mood of syllogisms and test their validity. Each name contains three vowels, which define one of four categories (universal or nonuniversal, affirmative or negative); their conjunction gives the *form* or *mood* of the syllogism, *Barbara,* for example, naming the first mood of the first figure, as in the simple instance: "Murphy is a man; all men love Celia; therefore Murphy loves Celia." With the exception of "Baccardi" (a rum variant of "Bokardo"), the terms are authentic.

Wylie is galvanized by Miss **Counihan's** bust: "All centre and no circumference" (60), as in the scholastic definition of God as an eternal sphere whose center is everywhere and circumference nowhere, which SB had recorded (DN, 97) with a cryptic "St. Bonaventura." It reflects the idea of God as a **monad,** complete in every part of himself, so that in every moment and every place he constitutes the center of all moments and all places. Murphy orders his biscuits in terms of the "extreme theophany" of William of Champeaux, the revelation of himself that God makes through his works, leading to the logical-realist conclusion that since the universal is res, then it is essentially present in all particulars: Murphy's preference for the ginger is **irrational** as God is equally in them all. Murphy in his **greatcoat** (72) forms the image of peripatetic **motion**, monad as nomad. The coat's composition and qualities are the very materials of scholastic disputation: that it feels like "felt" and much "size" has entered into its composition suggest the visible world as extension and the sensory agents that permit its perception. Murphy is a **microcosm** or, in a sartorial saw deriving from another parody of scholasticism, Swift's *Tale of a Tub* (78), "a Microcoat." His fate takes a scholastic turn: when Neary says "An accident" (262), this may be the only time that he has used this word in the tradition of the marketplace rather than in its metaphysical sense (the coroner is uncertain whether a joke has been made). **Mahaffy** (101) tells of the furor provoked when a Cartesian proposed that "man, as being composed of two heterogeneous elements, thinking and extension, was not a substance *per se*, but a substance *per accidens*"; SB may have elaborated the jest.

In SB's "**German Letter of 1937**," movement toward "the literature of the **unword**" is described in terms of Nominalism ("in the sense of the Scholastics") and Realism, the issue requiring "some form of Nominalist irony" (*Disjecta*, 173). This reflects the scholastic opinion of universals as names only, expressing the qualities of a reality posterior to things. It defines an essential skepticism. Not the least of ironies concerning SB is that his postmodernist **aporia** is rooted in scholastic disagreements about the reality of language and its metaphysical relationship to the world. His insistence (*Proust*, 75) upon the "real without being merely actual, ideal without being merely abstract," crucial to **Proust**'s involuntary memory, assumes a nominalist irony, as does Murphy's distinction (108–9) between "the kick *in intellectu* and the kick *in res*," let alone the supreme Caress.

The manuscript of *Watt* begins with Quintilian's rhetorical categories; the traditional *memoria technica* by which any subject may be divided into its parts for analysis, these reduced to the **fundamental sound** of **Quin**. The thesis of the novel finds Watt trying to understand the *essence* of Mr. **Knott** by his *accidents,* an "ancient error" replicating that of Descartes in the *Méthode* where he assaults the godhead by reason. Many details invite a scholastic gloss. Watt's confusion (128–30) before the picture of the circle and (its?) center is a variant on the theme of *Deus est spaera cujus centrum ubique;* such incidents of note as the piano tuners (72) and frog song (137) critique **preestablished harmony**; Watt is unable to reconcile the nominalist anomaly between "**Pot**" and pot (81); and his use of syllogism, truth table, and logical exhaustion satirizes Aristotelian procedure. The most outrageous scholastic parody derives from the simple premise that if a **dog**'s dish is put outside at evening full, and is brought in the next morning empty, then someone or something must have wrought that change of state. A dog. A famished dog. A dog kept famished so that it will eat the food. A family that owns the dog. A family that (necessarily) must breed dogs so that a famished dog is always at hand. And so on until, from the statement that "it was necessary" (91) that a dog call at the house, and a series of conditional propositions, there comes into being (112) a declaration in the indicative that the name of this dog "was" Kate and that of the family necessary for her being "was" Lynch (100). The reification is purely linguistic, Nominalist, but Watt has made to comfort himself "a pillow of old words," and the image of Kate eating from her dish with the dwarfs standing by *is* substantive (117).

As later works shed their accidents to assume their essence, explicit references to scholasticism are refined out of existence. Nevertheless, **Lucky**'s speech draws on scholasticism, and *How It Is* and "The Lost Ones" have their roots in its rationalist legacy. One dictum determined much of SB's thinking: in his "Dante" essay (24), he argues that poetry is "the antithesis of Metaphysics," the one cultivating the disembodiment of the spiritual and concerned with universals, the other animating the inanimate and concerned with particulars. He cites (from Croce) the scholastics' axiom: "niente è nell'intelletto che prima non sia nel senso." In Latin: *nihil in intellectu, quod non prius fuerat in sensu* ("nothing in the mind that was not first in the senses"). The dictum is found in **Burton**, **Leibniz**, and Schopenhauer. SB cited it in his

Whoroscope Notebook, adding the response of Leibniz to Locke: *nisi intellectus ipse,* "except the mind itself" (Windelband, 464). The axiom is parodied in *Malone Dies* (218) by Jackson's pink and gray **parrot**: "He used to try and teach it to say, Nihil in intellectu, etc. These first three words the bird managed well enough, but the celebrated restriction was too much for it, all you heard was a series of squawks." This seems a suitable *punctilio* on which to conclude.

Schopenhauer, Arthur (1788–1860): heir to **Kant** and forerunner of **Nietzsche** in the tradition of German counter-rationalism from Fichte and Schelling to Nietzsche and Heidegger. Born in Danzig, he was brought up in Hamburg and **Paris**, learning to admire the Greek and distrust the Hebraic element in Western thought and, through Schlegel, becoming aware of Indian philosophy. At Göttingen (1809) he became an admirer of Kant. In 1819 he was appointed *Privatdozent* at the University of Berlin, where he foolishly set his lectures against those of **Hegel**. The consequent failure to attract students or attention was a lasting irritation ("stupid Hegel" is a recurrent sentiment). His principal work, *Die Welt als Wille und Vorstellung,* had appeared in 1818, but it was virtually ignored. He retired to Frankfurt and settled to a bachelor existence with a poodle named Atma, imitating Kant in every manner save early rising. In 1844 he persuaded a publisher to bring out a second edition of *The World as Will and Idea* (the title of the Haldane and Kemp translation that SB read; hereafter *WWI*), and finally received the recognition he craved. His work has dubious standing among philosophers, who note stridency, inconsistency, and shallow thought. His lasting influence, apart from that on Nietzsche and **Wagner**, is on literature, **Proust**, Mann, Borges, and SB not alone in their attraction to his lucidity and the fine metaphors through which his ideas are expressed.

SB commented: "his intellectual justification of unhappiness—the greatest that has ever been attempted—is worth the examination" (SB to TM, July 1930). He added, with reference to his own essay, *Proust*, "Schopenhauer says 'defunctus' is a beautiful word—as long as one does not **suicide**." Ill with gastric influenza, SB found that the only thing he could read was Schopenhauer: "It was very curious. Like suddenly a window opened on a fug. I always knew he was one of the ones that mattered most to me, and it is a pleasure more real than any pleasure for a long time [compare **Murphy** in his chair] to begin to understand now why it is so. And it is a pleasure also to find a philosopher that can be read like a poet" (Knowlson, 248). Schopenhauer underwrote SB's view that suffering is the norm, that Will represents an unwelcome intrusion, and that real **consciousness** lies beyond human understanding.

WWI manifests itself in three volumes. The first consists of four books, considering: (1) the world as idea—that the entire world is only **object** in relation to subject, to perception; that is, *phenomenon*, or *idea*, subjectively perceived, no object without its subject; (2) the equal and contradictory truth, the world as Will, which Schopenhauer identifies with the Kantian *Ding-an-sich*, one vast force in **nature**, which Schopenhauer does not equate with a pantheistic **God**; (3) the world as Idea, in the **Platonic** sense, by means of which ideas become objects of knowledge, and the importance of aesthetic contemplation with respect to architecture, **art**, poetry and **music**; and (4) the assertion and denial of the Will, whereby that blind incessant force is considered in relation to the state of **nothing** from which things are born and to which they return, with no fixed end or purpose, but only suffering and extinction. These certainties may be palliated by attaining the state of will-lessness, surrender or abnegation of the will. The second volume contains a long appendix, a critique of Kant's philosophy. The rest of it and the entirety of the third book consist of supplements to volume 1, expounding such matters as a priori knowledge, the ludicrous, methods of **mathematics**, genius, and madness, the metaphysics of music, and the vanity and suffering of life, to identify but a few that SB would draw on (his images and insights are taken from these chapters as well as from the main argument).

According to Schopenhauer, in every act of perception the mind treats sense data as effect and tries to explain cause by ordering the data within a spatiotemporal framework. Space, **time**, and causality are the three forms of perception without which sense data would remain undifferentiated; in Kantian terms, "time, space, and causality do not belong to the thing-in-itself, but only to its phenomena, of which they are the form" (*WWI*, 39). The world is thus "idea": sense data perceived under the forms. But the world is also Will: an implacable driving force working within the individual, forcing one to survive, to propogate, to seek pleasure and avoid pain. In O'Hara's words, "It manifests itself in all its phenomena, and it uses the human intellect in order to see itself in its representations, in the **mirror** of phenomenal existence" (*Hidden Drives,* 17). The doctrine is pessimistic, asserting the impossibility of true knowledge and lack of ultimate purpose: as **Estragon** says to **Vladimir:** "We are happy. (*Silence.*) What do we do now, now that we are happy?" Schopenhauer suggests that limited transcendence may be attained through aesthetic contemplation. Some of SB's dramatic moments are rooted in this paradox, in his acceptance of the experience, as at the end of *Proust* or Nell's **memory** of the sand, "So white" (*Endgame* 21), but also his distrust of its value, as in **Arsene**'s "short statement."

McQueeny notes Schopenhauer's refutation of Kant's position that for human cognition there is no existence, essence, or reality *except in time,* by the doctrine of the eternity of the present: "As the ideal limit which separates the past from the future the present is as unreal for the senses as a point in mathematics. But if it is inaccessible to empirical consciousness it can be seen as the superior reality for the metaphysician" (McQueeny, 133). This informs SB's *Proust,* as the French writer is scrutinized through a lens of pessimism, an element SB later admitted he might have overstated. The debt to Schopenhauer is real but not overwhelming, as SB suggests, and in this respect the essay reveals more

of SB's thought. The paradigm of pessimism is apparent in the image of present consciousness as decantation from the fluid of future time to that of the past (*Proust,* 15); this may draw on Schopenhauer's image of the poet as chemist (*WWI,* 313).

Proust first mentions Schopenhauer with reference to the world as a projection of individual consciousness, "an objectivation of the individual's will, Schopenhauer would say" (19), but his presence is marked in the final section. Here the artist's role is considered in terms primarily derived from Schopenhauer, with Proust's **romanticism**, relativism, and impressionism having their roots in the doctrine of pessimism. This leads to a definition of the artistic procedure as "the contemplation of the world independently of the principle of reason" (87), based on three key principles. First, the indifference of nature to moral values, as in the sentiment, "Flower and plant have no conscious will. They are shameless, exposing their genitals." The image arises directly out of *WWI* (I.2 #28, 204), and is mocked in *Dream* (13), where the Dunkelbrau gals lie on the roof and bronze their bottoms and impudenda. Second, the definition of Proust as the subject of pure will, but exemplifying no collapse of the will: "The Proustian stasis is contemplative, a pure act of understanding, willless, the 'amabilis insania' and the 'holder Wahnsinn'" (91). These terms, referring to **Horace** and Wieland, are taken directly from Schopenhauer (*WWI,* 246). Third, music: "The influence of Schopenhauer on this aspect of the Proustian demonstration is unquestionable" (*Proust,* 91). Music is "the Idea itself, unaware of the world of phenomena, existing ideally outside the universe, apprehended not in Space but in Time only." However, it is distorted by the listener who, being an impure subject, unable to apprehend the *Ding-an-sich,* insists on incarnating this Idea into "what he conceives to be an appropriate paradigm."

The philosophical structure of *Murphy* might be defined as a Proustian critique of a Cartesian universe, shaped by the thought of Schopenhauer. Murphy attempts to attain the freedom of the little world of the mind, and although this is defined in terms of the **Occasionalist** sense of the **microcosm**, its condition may be defined in Schopenhauer's terms as the transition from Will to Contemplation. In *WWI* (III.xxv, 67–69), he articulates his paradox: the world, and all in it, is an aimless and incomprehensible play of external necessity, an inscrutable and inexorable *Ananke.* In one aspect it is phenomenon (or idea), and in another Will, "and indeed absolutely *free will,* for necessity only arises through the forms which belong entirely to the phenomenon" (67). But if the idea is conditioned by necessity, and the Will alone is free, how then is freedom possible? One has the choice of seeing the world as "a mere **machine** which runs on of necessity" (68) or of recognizing a free will as its inner being. This riddle, he suggests, can be resolved only "by placing the whole *necessity* in the *acting and doing* (*Operari*), and the whole *freedom* in the *being and nature* (*Esse*)" (68). In Schopenhauer's words: "To save freedom from fate and chance, it had to be transferred from the action to the ex-

istence" (69). The key to freedom is thus the knowledge of the Will in one's self-consciousness by **apperception**; this allows SB to move between the phenomenal worlds of Kant and Schopenhauer and consciousness of and in the little worlds of **Descartes** and **Geulincx**.

Schopenhauer contends (*WWI,* III.xxv, 74–75) that consciousness belongs to the phenomenal, as opposed to the inner nature: "In this root of existence the difference of beings ceases, like that of radii of a sphere in the centre; and as in the sphere the surface is produced by the radii ending and breaking off, so consciousness is only possible where the true inner being runs out into the phenomenon, through whose forms the separate individuality becomes possible upon which consciousness depends, which is just on that account confined to phenomena. Therefore all that is distinct and thoroughly comprehensible in our consciousness always lies without, upon this surface of the sphere. Whenever, on the contrary, we withdraw entirely from this, consciousness forsakes us." He suggests that the will as *Ding-an-sich* is undivided, "as the centre is an integral part of every radius" (75). This splendid image of the sphere with an outer surface of consciousness and a core of inner being may have allowed SB to move from **Leibniz**'s **monad** into Murphy's inner darkness.

In Chapter 6 of *Murphy,* "will-lessness" derives explicitly from Schopenhauer, whose dualistic view of the world as will and idea forms the final critique of the various philosophies that have contributed to **Murphy's mind**. Murphy's three zones correspond to Schopenhauer's manifestations of the Will in accordance with the three forms of space, time, and causality. The outer zone mirrors or reflects representations of the world as interpreted by the intellect in accordance with the forms (in SB's terms, "actual"); removal of the causal brings about the contemplative status (Ideas) of the second zone (SB's "virtual"); but the third zone expresses the paradox of Will: that of not being free yet existing as a mote in the dark of absolute freedom. This is possible through the abnegation of the Will, or withdrawal into the realm of pure contemplation. Murphy favors such cosmic freedom of the third zone over the limited personal freedom of the first two; *Three Novels* assumes as its tripartite paradigm a movement toward that realm.

Schopenhauer's chapter "On the Vanity and Suffering of Life" (*WWI,* III.xlvi, 382–401) fundamentally affected SB's understanding of his world. **Pozzo**'s lament that we give **birth** astride of a grave intimates that pervasive sense of ephemeral existence, in a world in which everything lingers only for the moment and then hurries on to **death**. SB found the *principium individuationis* compelling: that the individual is limited in what it can know to its own body and the few ideas that the individual subject can apprehend as immediate "objects of knowing," aspects of the object necessarily different from the noumena and Ideas that lie beyond the representations. These convictions shape SB's philosophy of doubt and dubiously validate its emphasis upon particulars, demented or otherwise, though O'Hara is right to suggest (*Hidden Drives,* 21) that it took SB some time to overcome the hope for disinterested truths

(which Schopenhauer found in aesthetic contemplation and Eastern nirvana), such as are implied at the end of his essay on Proust.

Schopenhauer's writings formed a wonderful grab bag from which SB might draw unexpected oddities, some of them copied into the **Whoroscope Notebook**. The phrase "tat twam asi" (Sanskrit, "this thou art") appears there and underlies **Belacqua**'s "I am what I am" in "**Yellow**" (160); **Quigley**'s protest to his sweetheart in "**Lightning Calculation**"; and **Celia**'s "I am what I do" (*Murphy,* 37). As O'Hara points out (19), the phrase is used by Schopenhauer of the saintly person who, although limited by the *principium individuationis,* has merged his self with the phenomenal world. **Calderón**'s quotation (*Proust,* 67) about the sin of being born derives from *WWI,* where it is repeated several times. In *Murphy,* **Neary**'s vague fear about his terminals not being connected arises from the image in *WWI* (II.x, 304) of the voltaic pile as an expression of the illogical syllogism, its "terms" transposed. Details of Mr. **Endon** derive from Schopenhauer's discussion of the fine line between madness and genius (*WWI,* III.xxxi and xxxii, 138–72), his indifference closely resembling the state of aesthetic contemplation. The confusion over Murphy's "will" may constitute an elaborate jest on the frustration of Schopenhauer's impulse, in particular, of the refusal to countenance **suicide**, this seen as an expression of the Will rather than its abnegation.

The Addenda of *Watt* (#21) record: "*zitto! zitto! dass nur das Publikum nichts merke!*" ("Hush, hush, so that the public may notice nothing"). This derives from Schopenhauer's "Concerning the Four-fold Roots of the Statement of Sufficient Ground," a tirade against German academics. **Malone** appears to be quoting **Lucretius** (II.1) with his "Suave mari magno" (218), but the source is probably *WWI* (I.4, 412), with its cynical reflection (compare the divine **Miranda**) that this aspect of the will to live, the sufferings of others, affords satisfaction and pleasure. The **Unnamable** invokes Schopenhauer more directly with his memory of the Master. This emphasis on punishment is drawn from book four of *WWI* and the corresponding essays on the doctrine of suffering in the world in volume three of *WWI*, and in the *Parerga* 11 and 12 (see **pensum**).

One tenet is articulated from the beginning of *WWI* (38), that the principle "no object without a subject" renders materialism impossible, annihilates the visible world. Schopenhauer contends that the existence of the phenomenal world is dependent upon the first eye that opened: "For such an eye is a necessary condition of the possibility of knowledge, and the whole world exists only in and for knowledge, and without it is not even thinkable." This antinomy, and its expression as the (all)-seeing eye, pervades SB's writing from the Judas hole in the monadlike cells in *Murphy*, to the inability of "O" in *Film* to escape being perceived. Even more pervasive is Schopenhauer's belief that it would have been better had the universe never come into being: the lost paradise of nonexistence, as in Malone's sense that once having lived there is no recovery from that, or **Worm**'s belated realization that he

should have killed his mother before being born. But once the stain has been left on the silence it cannot be wiped clean.

Schubert, Franz (1797–1828): son of a Viennese schoolmaster, contemporary of **Beethoven**, and composer in the nineteenth-century German **Romantic** tradition of deep melancholy and lyricism, the influence of which SB never escaped. Although he wrote nine symphonies and much choral and chamber music, Schubert is revered as the composer of more than 600 *lieder*, some of inexpressible beauty. He died in poverty from complications of syphilis as his genius was coming into full flower, the *Winterreise* eloquent testimony to that loss. Schubert was, unequivocally, SB's favorite composer. That admiration came early and stayed late. SB discussed a concert in which a Beethoven quartet was dismissed as a waste of time, a Mendelssohn piece described as "bloody," but the Schubert quintet approved: "I don't know any chamber music that *works* so skillfully" (SB to TM, 24 February 1931). He might sing *lieder* to his own accompaniment, and in his final years was heard to remark, "I think that the opening of Schubert's Quartet in A minor [Deutsch 804] is more nearly pure spirit than any other **music**" (Bryden, *Music*, 42).

SB's writings make few direct references to Schubert. "**Ding-Dong**" (42) notes a "great major symphony," often assumed to be Beethoven's seventh in A major, but the "fulcrate" middle C suggests Schubert's Ninth, the "Great" in C major, where "wearisome tactics of gress and dud Beethoven would be done away with." At the end of "**Walking Out**," **Belacqua** marries his **Lucy** and they sit up to all hours playing the gramophone, "An die Musik" a great favorite. SB copied the words and music of this early lied (D.547b, Opus 88–4 [1817]) into the **Whoroscope Notebook**: in the gray hours that so constrict life, music, "du holde Kunst" ("thou sweet **art**,") will afford his heart a deeper **love** and lead him to "eine bessre Welt" ("a better world.") The ironies are obvious yet the simple beauty offered an ideal, even as SB was unable to accept such comfort. The likeness of the late prose to *lieder*, the intricate fusion of words and **music**, lyrical and melancholy, testifies to Schubert's lasting influence. In "**Words and Music**," although his name is not mentioned, the theme arises from the oft-debated question about the *lieder*, whether the magic resides most in the melody or in the song.

Act I of *Eleutheria* ends with M. **Krap** listening, with increasing agitation, to Schubert's Quartet in A flat, by the Kopek Quartet. This is probably the Quartet in A minor, D.804, the "Rosamunde" theme. Since he dies that night it is a moot point whether the music has done Monsieur any good (60). *All That Fall* depicts Mrs. **Rooney** dragging herself along the country road, hearing faint music on the way: "Death and the Maiden." This is Schubert's String Quartet #14 in D minor, D.810, a late work tinged with the composer's sense of approaching death. The piece offers fierce opening triplets and dramatic silences, but its slow movement is based on a poem by Matthias Claudius and Schubert's

song of that title written seven years earlier, telling of a girl frightened by **Death** who suavely pleads his **friendship**: "Be not afraid! I am not fierce, you shall sleep softly in my arms." In 1960 SB told Anne **Atik** that he was "learning Matthias Claudius by heart! 'Friend Death.'" The theme introduced and concluded Jack **MacGowran**'s recorded readings (1966), SB playing a **gong** to mark the transition of one piece to another (Knowlson, 479). SB indicated that **Krapp** looks over his shoulder lest Death await him in the darkness. The harmony is haunting, underscoring the slowing heartbeat of the girl and belying the facile optimism apparently residing in the major triad. SB's "comedy" likewise becomes chilling. Maddy draws attention to the music: "Poor woman. All alone in that ruinous old house." She is never seen, but the music intimates the tragedy that follows and expresses Maddy's loss of "little Minnie." The theme is heard again at the end and triggers Dan Rooney's tears as it brings to his mind the little **child** who "fell" out of the carriage.

SB's acknowledged debt to Schubert is "**Nacht und Träume**" (qv), a wordless piece first entitled *Nachtstück* ("Nightpiece"), written for Suddeutscher Rundfunk (1982). It is set to the last seven bars of Schubert's late *lied* "Nacht und Träume" ("Night and Dreams"; D.827, Op.43–2), words by Mattäus Casimir von Collin. Only the last lines are invoked: "Kehre wieder, holde Nacht! Holde Träume, kehret wieder!" ("Come back, sweet night; sweet dreams, come back"), with a particular emphasis upon the "kehret wieder" of the last three bars. Action is minimal, a controlled reaction to the music as it is repeated ritualistically, with the strange haunting beauty that SB made his own.

Knowlson entitles his last chapter "Winter Journey" and describes how SB adored the Fischer-Dieskau / Gerald Moore recording of *Winterreise* (D.911, Opus 89; to the verse of Wilhelm Müller), which he regarded as Schubert's masterpiece. Echoes of the cycle are heard in "**Texts**" 2 and 12 with their winter journeys. It is present in SB's final stage composition, "**What Where**," written for the 1983 Autumn Festival in Graz, where Schubert once stayed, in the sense of cold, love-lost journeys and a structure based on the cycle of the seasons. The play ends with the voice of Bam alone, perhaps from beyond the grave, certainly at journey's end: "It is winter. Without journey. Time passes. That is all."

Schurmann, Anna Maria: as noted in *Whoroscope,* "the Dutch blue-stocking, a pious pupil of Voët, the adversary of **Descartes**." Harvey (28–30) tells how Voetius tried to ruin Descartes's reputation at Utrecht and prevailed on "this marvel of a girl" to engage in dispute. **Baillet** (II, 60–62) lauds her scholarship, piety, and modesty, citing her motto: *Amor meus crucifixus est.* She is one who entered too far into theological intricacies and lost contact with the world. The abusive parakeet in the window is from **Mahaffy** (179).

"**Schwabenstreich**": SB's review of Eduard Mörike's *Mozart on the Way to Prague* (Blackwell, 1934); in the *Spectator* 5, 517 (23 March 1934): 472; rpt. in *Disjecta* (61–62). SB commends the shortness of its attempt to "exhaust the inessential," renders some instances, then concludes by wishing that Herr Mörike had been restrained from presenting the *Hexenmeister* as "a compound of Horace Skimpole and **Wagner** in half-hose." The title means "tomfoolery," buffoonery typical of those from Mörike's Swabia.

"**A Seaside Reminiscence**": an extract from *Molloy* in *Advanced Level French Course, Book II,* by W. T. John and M. A. Crowther (London: Thomas Nelson and Sons, 1963), #9 among passages for "Translation into English"; a shortened and incorrectly copied extract from "Il y a des gens à qui la mer ne réussit pas" to "je n'entends pas grincer sur la grève la frêle carène" (F&F, #257.002). See "**Getting One's Money's Worth**."

"**Seats of Honour**": the **Leventhal** "Poems by Samuel Beckett" (**HRHRC**) include an unknown one by this title, as in "she waggled her seat of honour" in *Dream* (97). This echoes **Cooper**'s "a claque on the seat of honour" (*Flagellation,* 25; DN, 50).

"**Sedendo et Quiesc[i]endo**": a phrase originating in **Aristotle**'s *De anima,* as recorded in Paget Toynbee's *Dictionary* of *Dante* (74; DN, 44). It means "Seated and in quiet," and continues *anima effictur sapiens,* "the soul becomes wise." SB associated the sentiment with **Belacqua** (qv), and **Thomas à Kempis**, whose *De Imitatione Christi* expressed a mode of **quietism** he would make increasingly his own. The phrase was used by SB (with an extra "i") for an extract from *Dream,* written in 1931 and published in *transition* 21 (March 1932): 13–20. Eugene Jolas called it an "anamyth" (reflecting preconscious relationships) or "psychograph" (projecting hallucinations and phantoms). SB showed it to Charles **Prentice**, saying "it stinks of **Joyce**" (15 August 1931), but Prentice was dubious. It depicts the arrival of Belacqua in Vienna and corresponds to "TWO" (64–74) of the published novel, with minor changes of detail, paragraphing, and emphasis. The most significant are: the change of narrative voice from "I" to "we"; of "Mr. John Kissmearse" to "Pope John Kissmine"; and toning down chromatic obscurities by muting "the long fever of the midos and the dolas in a scorching a piacere" (*CSP*, 13). Reprinted in Gontarski, *Complete Short Prose* (8–16).

Séjour: first paragraph from *Le Dépeupleur*, with minor variants, and with five engravings by Louis Maccard (see **illustrations**). A limited issue of 175 copies (150 numbered) on *grand vélin de Rives,* loose sheets within original wrappers, uncut, in publisher's folding box, printed in 20-point Caslon Old Face by Foquet et Baudier.

Semiramide (ca. 800 BC): an Assyrian princess renowned for her sexual excesses; mentioned in **Dante**'s *Inferno* (V.58). A prototype of the **Syra-Cusa** (*Dream,* 50).

"**Serena I**": the serena is a **Provençal** song of evening, wherein the lover laments his unhappiness during the day and longs for night to unite him with his beloved. "Serena I" is set in **London**. The poet exits from the British Museum, where he has been reading **Thales** ("all things full of gods") and the **Aretino** (*Sonetti lussuriosi di Pietro Aretino* [Roma, 1525], with sixteen erotic engravings by Marcantonio Raimondi), out into the hostile world of the city, in a series of flights from different images of suffering, until he finds refuge, alone. The details, SB told Lawrence Harvey, derive from a walk taken one evening. The scarlet phlox in Regent's Park gives way to brutal images of cages from the nearby zoo. The trapped animals are imagined staring out across the hills toward home, and he recalls "**Ireland**." The light promises illusory relief, the images culminating in lasting horror, an adder "broaching" its white **rat**. There follows a muted prayer, which is yet a cruel reminder of **death**: "ah **father** father that art in heaven" (the poem was drafted October 1932; William **Beckett** died on 26 June 1933, but the line would have subsumed this pathos by the time it was collected and revised for *Echo's Bones*). From Primrose Hill, north of Regent's Park, he can see the **Crystal Palace**, which he calls the Blessed Isles (usually the Canaries but here suggesting thoughts of home). His impulse is to retreat into the deepest thickets where only the "most quarried" lovers might find him, in Ken Wood, north of Hampstead, a seventy-six-acre estate bought by Lord Iveagh of Guinness fame (again, the connection with home). Images of **prison** embrace all London, from the Tower to the gray hold of the ambulance, from the guttersnipe wanting the *Mirror* (is *he* self-absorbed?) to the platform of "Wren's giant bully," the Monument designed by Sir Christopher

Wren to commemorate the great fire of 1666 (Pope's *Moral Essays,* Epistle III, 340: "Like a tall bully"). He curses not having been born **Defoe**, that he might excoriate the city. The poem ends with the closely observed image of his brother, the **fly**. This section was written some months later in **Dublin**. It takes up "Ireland," but instead of relief there is a different futility, the poet trapped like a fly upon the windowpane, like those of "La Mouche," *Watt* (236–37) or "**Text 6**" (123). Alienated from the human zoo and jobless, too, he serves neither "typhoid" nor "mammon." Even if he has escaped London, he remains trapped.

An early draft of the poem attached to a letter to **MacGreevy** (8 October 1932) expresses clearly the feeling from which the poem arose, a fourteen-line grumble more like the **Enueg** than a Serena: "I put pen to this / vague carmen." As the listing of SB's poems in the **Leventhal** collection (**HRHRC**) indicates, the three Serenas were indexed by their opening lines, then called "**Cri de coeur**" (1, 2, and 3). This suggests that they are related in content and tone but that the generic **Provençal** term may have been an afterthought. The rejected lines have a Pound-like tonality and freedom of form, but constitute what Pound called work of a second intensity, and their deletion is little loss.

"**Serena II**": in *Echo's Bones,* another song of evening, written in the late summer of 1932. The theme announced by the opening line, "this clonic earth," is separated from the rest of the poem. The convulsions are, immediately, those of the **dog**, SB's Kerry Blue bitch, trembling in her sleep as she redreams her life, but also those of the **birth** that brought him into being. The aging bitch, fat, half-dead, with ashen pelt, in her dreams hounds harlots out of the ferns and tears her prey in the brake. She trembles her way back to the West of **Ireland** (Kerry, Galway, Mayo), whence her breed derives. References to the Pins, Clew Bay, **Croagh Patrick**, and Blacksod Bay are set in the fading light. He imagines her dropping her litter in a bog, an act of shame.

The finale reverts to the Wicklow mountains. Man and dog look on County Meath beyond the **Dublin** hills and the steeples and harbor of **Dún Laoghaire**, its twin piers (as in *Murphy,* 259) like a woman covering her breasts in shame. At a cairn, muzzled with a sodden packet of Churchman tobacco, he experiences spasmic panic, the earth about him ("this clonic earth") shuddering and reeling in broken chords. The poem ends with the imagined childhood ritual of going to bed, prayers before byebye, lamps singing behind the **larches**, but the tone is less tranquility than incipient terror (toads, bones) at the dying of the light.

"**Serena III**": in *Echo's Bones,* the third song of evening; sent to **MacGreevy** in October 1933, but written nearer Peggy **Sinclair**'s **death** in May. Like "**Enueg I**" and "**Sanies I**" it moves swiftly through the **Dublin** environs. The poet flees the choice **love** offers in the opening lines: to "fix" the pothook of beauty upon his palette (Hogarth's eulogy of the sigmoid line in his *Analysis of Beauty,* 1753 [Harvey, 151]) or to leave her in a virginal paradise ("plush hymens on your eyeballs"). The route taken is to the southeast, through a landscape of sexual insistence: Butt Bridge, "mammae," "cock up thy moon," Venus, the phallic gasometer on Misery Hill, the (male) Bull lighthouse and the (female) Pool Beg ("little pool") that will never meet. The "something heart of Mary" is the Church of the Immaculate Heart of Mary on City Quay (O'Brien, 222), another longing "not in this world." The tone becomes frantic as he darts over Victoria Bridge, down Ringsend Road, through Irishtown and Sandymount (where the ruin of the Hell Fire Club might be visible), past the Merrion Flats and marsh of Booterstown. He chooses not to hide "in the Rock," the cave near Whiterock, where **Molloy** takes refuge (68), the echo of "Rock of Ages" barely heard as he urges himself **on**: "keep on the move / keep on the move."

serial order: SB's early writings toy with intimations of a serial universe, one in which the perceived order of existence is subject to other orders, perhaps unperceived. Consider *Proust* (21): "The mortal **microcosm** cannot forgive the relative immortality of the macrocosm. The whisky bears a grudge against the decanter"; or "**Draff**" (191), the words of the rose to the rose: "No gardener has died, comma, within rosaceous memory" (see d'**Alembert** and **Fontenelle**). *Watt* depicts a physical universe in which crocuses flower then fade, the **larches** turn green then brown, and the whole bloody business of renewal begins again. In **Arsene**'s "short statement" the theme appears in the biblical terms of servants who **come and go**, into the ground floor,

up to the first floor, then out of the house, a sequence that began with those unknown, through Walter, Vincent, Arsene, **Erskine**, Watt, Arthur, and Micks to others as yet unknown. Their coming and going is of a different order to the seasons, but it has a sequential logic, so that eventually Watt who came, served on the ground floor, then moved to the first floor must go. During that time, and in recorded **memory**, the famished **dog** has been a constant although the individual dogs, from Kate to Cis, that make up the series have changed. Even the pictures, Watt concludes, are but terms in a series, here today and gone tomorrow, like the dogs, the servants, or centuries that fall from the pod of eternity (131). Such **motion** contrasts with the stasis of Mr. **Knott**, "who neither comes nor goes" but rather "abides" (57). Like the whisky decanter or gardener he seems immortal, perhaps because he is **witnessed** from a different serial perspective. Hence two significant notes in the addenda. The first (250–51) describes another picture in **Erskine**'s room, of a gentleman seated at the piano, said in the manuscripts to be Mr. Knott's **father**. In the second (251–53), Arthur encounters an old man who worked for Knott's father. This argues against the God of **Spinoza**, as rehearsed in "Le Rêve de d'Alembert" (317), for if He is immanent then He too must grow old and die. The serial theme in *Watt*, as the manuscripts confirm, came surprisingly late, given its importance, not only with respect to the serial or sempiternal nature of Mr. Knott but equally the problems of permutation, perception, witnessing, and order.

Watt's routine is disturbed by the **Galls**, father and son, come to "choon" the piano (70–72), to find only nine dampers remaining and an equal number of hammers, but corresponding in one instance only. The incident parodies harmony and correspondence and intimates an **irrational** universe. A clearer pattern is seen in the celebrated frog song, where three frogs, croaking respectively at intervals of 8, 5, and 3, begin on a common chord and, a combined 360 intervals later, end on another (see **mathematics**). After **Olympia Press** mangled the proofs, SB pointed out that the three voices worked at different intervals, representing seconds: "Entre deux k̲r̲a̲k̲ 7 secondes, entre deux k̲r̲e̲k̲ 4 secondes, entre deux k̲r̲i̲k̲ 2 secondes. Il faut soulinger ce deroulement par groupes de trois voix au moyen d'une interligue après chaque groupe." But (to echo Arsene) to conclude from this that the universe is harmonious would, I think, be rash. The song forms a parable of periodicity: when two or more independent series operate in a given universe, coincidence is a mathematical inevitability, and the observance of it, with the consequent attribution of significance to 360, says more about the mind that clings to such meaning than about the phenomenon itself. The incessant logic creates a cosmos in which coincidence is an accidental function of the arbitrary, a riposte to notions of synchronicity (**Jung**) and **preestablished harmony** (**Leibniz**). One terrifying difference between SB and **Joyce** and **Proust** is reflected in SB's rejection of the epiphany or the Proustian moment, less the experience than the attribution of value to it. The theme runs

throughout the musings of voice "C" in *That Time:* "turning point that was a great word with you . . . always having turning points" (230). Not least of SB's nihilism is to deny ultimate significance even to the signifying quality of the mind.

serotine: a small reddish bat (*How It Is*, 89) that comes out *late* (see "**nimis sero**"). Serotonin is a vasoconstrictor in brain tissue and blood platelets; hence, "I'm the brain."

"Se voir": the eighth "**Foirade**"; published thus in *Minuit* 4 (mai 1973): 72, but known also as "**Endroit clos**." Translated by SB as "**Closed place**."

"Shades": SB's title for a TV program on BBC 2, *The Lively Arts* (17 April 1977), consisting of *Not I*, "**Ghost Trio**," and the premiere of ". . . but the clouds . . ."; produced by Tristram Powell and introduced by Melvin Bragg, with the first directed by Anthony Page and the others by Donald **McWhinnie**. Parts were read by Ronald Pickup and Billie **Whitelaw**. The program included an interview with Martin Esslin. John **Calder** (*JOBS* 2 [1977]: 117–21) explained the thematic and autobiographical aspects of the works, concluding that "the lively arts" might be a misnomer but that the BBC had offered a memorable fifty minutes.

Shakespeare, William (1564–1616): SB's allusions to Shakespeare range from clarion calls to distant echoes. Like his **biblical** motifs, they are ostentatiously manifest in the early works, are assimilated into the texture of the great works, then used sparingly in the minimalist drama and later prose fiction. Their presence is more marked in the English texts and translations, yet even in some of the French originals Shakespeare's bleak compassion for the poor forked creature is an important point of reference.

Irreverence is evident in "**Casket of Pralinen**," in "Gloucester's no bimbo / and he's in Limbo" (68), or "the gorgonzola cheese of human kindness" (70; *Macbeth* I.v.14). **Belacqua** imagines in "**Dante and the Lobster**" "smiting the sledded Polacks on the ice" (13; *Hamlet*, I.i.63), and "suck is not suck that alters" in "**Sanies II**" or *Dream* (108; Sonnet CXVI). Knowlson (69) notes the impact of Professor W. F. Trench's course on Shakespeare at **Trinity**, citing Ariel's dirge in "**Ding-Dong**" (*The Tempest*, I.ii.403); the funeral meats and marriage tables in "**Fingal**" (*Hamlet*, I.ii.181); and the livery of death and its pale flag in "**Draff**" (185) and *Happy Days*. Some echoes are explicit, such as "Dogberry" in "**A Wet Night**" (72), or two footnotes in "**Echo's Bones**" (4). The first is to "Titania and the ass" (*MSND*), which SB had noted from **Gaultier** as an image of reason undone by desire (see *Dream*, 160, and *Murphy*, 49). The second cites "Richard III" as "a very nervous subject," afraid of his shadow, which in the *au-delà* Belacqua no longer has as he waits (27) till perdition catch him (*Othello* III.iii.91), Others are more intricate, such as the "beyond recall in the abyss" (*The Tempest*, I.ii.49), the "divine" **Miranda** (qv) in "**Yellow**" (170, 173), or the "labours lost" of **Lucky**'s speech (*WG*, 28.b).

The "gentle peace" of "the immortal Shakespeare" in "A Wet Night" (72), like "the usual pale cast" in "**Love and Lethe**" (95), is that of Hamlet contemplating **suicide** (III.i.85). The poem "**Echo's Bones**" invokes Prospero's "revels" from *The Tempest*, a phrase assuming greater irony in *Endgame* (56), as **Hamm** rounds off his little life with a sleep.

Dream is riddled with Shakespearean allusions, including references to Miranda (11); Dunsinane (27); a springe to catch woodcocks (*Hamlet*, V.ii.298); Hamlet rolling his belly (68), the ancient crux of "fat" (V.ii.279); Titania's bottle of moss (51); "Corporal Banquo" (68); "Keycold Lucrece" (71); Ophelia (82); and the intricate statement of silence (197): "She was white and still and Hermioned all of a sudden," as in *A Winter's Tale*. *Murphy* offers the **Phidias** of Fatigue as "nature's soft nurse" (239; *2 Henry* IV.i.4), and Scopas, to "knit up the sleave" of sleep (*Macbeth* II.ii.37). The **horoscope** is framed with Romeo's defiance of the stars (32–33; *R&J*, V.i.24); Murphy has a vague recollection of **Ticklepenny** at a **Gate Theatre** production (86), which SB described as "all wrong" (SB to TM, 21 November 1932). Murphy encounters **Celia** on Midsummer's Eve and his fortunes assume the complexities of poet, lunatic, and lover. Two buckets, an image of **equilibrium**, reach down to *Richard II* (IV.i.84). Portia's quality of mercy and the gentle rain (62; *Merchant of Venice* IV.i.179–81) suggest Murphy's "surgical quality" and Miss **Counihan**'s wish to get her pound of flesh, **quid pro quo**, in the mercantile Gehenna. The **green and yellow** melancholy of *Twelfth*

Night (II.iv.116) is picked up in *Mercier and Camier* (109): "The pretty colours, expiring greens and yellows . . . will they die, yes, they will." That novel describes the falling rain as fine, "and no doubt gentle."

SB's great Shakespearean theme is unaccommodated man, rehearsed in *Watt* for full play in the *Three Novels*. **Arsene** states that "**nature** is so exceedingly accom[m]odating" (41). About to leave the house and go out into the wilderness, he informs Watt indirectly of the elements of the play, from Lear's angry "**Nothing** will come of nothing" (I.i.87) to his growing insight into the dark, the sense that man is no more than a poor, bare, forked animal, his life as cheap as beasts' (see **betîse**). "Bugger these buttons" is a gloriously banal echo of Lear's "Pray you undo this button" (V.iii.309). That total futility is pursued in the fiction to follow: old men telling tales to pass the **time**; outcasts in a wilderness, accompanied by fools; stripping until literally naked, divested of **greatcoat**, **hat**, and **boots**, Lear's "lendings." **Molloy** may not diffuse the perfumes of Araby (19; *Macbeth*, V.i.49); and **Malone** may joke about carnal **love** as the be-all and end-all (261; *Macbeth*, I.vii.5); but the **Unnamable**'s "I of whom I know nothing," the unaccommodated **voice**, all that remains from the process of disintegration in the former two novels, is in direct descent from Lear. *Lear* stayed with SB to the end. In 1983 he reread it, declaring it "Unstageable; wild; scenes and words impossible to stage." He used "The worst is not; so long as we can say, "This is the worst" (IV.i.27) as the "very

important" preoccupation of *Worstward Ho*. And "vile jelly" (III.vii.82) appears in *Ill Seen Ill Said* (81).

In *Endgame*, other motifs constitute a reminder of the play as play: **Hamm** as Player King (if not Hamlet); his "kingdom for a nightman" (*Richard III* V.iv.7); **Clov**'s lament that he can speak only what Hamm has taught him, as Caliban to Prospero; the sense of the revels ended. Yet, again, underlying all is *Lear*, as Peter Brook recognized. His *King Lear* (1971) was influenced by Jan Kott's *Shakespeare Our Contemporary* (1964), which brings it to *Endgame* in the common theme, "When we are born we cry that we are come / to this great stage of fools." Emphasizing the grotesque as crueler than tragedy could be, Brook omitted vital bits of Shakespeare to make his play more like SB's, with such great moments as the blinded Gloucester sitting cross-legged on the bare stage and hearing afar the sounds of chaos. Paul Schofield's opening "Know" blends with SB's "no" and Shakespeare's "never" to create a compelling nothing. SB made *King Lear* the play for his time, as **Joyce** made *Hamlet* speak for an earlier generation. Shakespeare's Lear and SB's grotesques are emblems of the promised end, twinned images of that horror.

Later texts encapsulate major motifs in minimalist works. "**Bare Room**" intimates "No longer mourn for me when I am dead" (Sonnet LXXI). *Krapp's Last Tape* singles out (60) "chrysolite," as in *Othello* (V.ii.144–46): "If heaven would make me such another world / Of one entire and perfect chrysolite / I'd not have sold her for it" (SB wrote these lines on one draft). "**Embers**" tells of a "naughty world" (104; *M of V*, V.i.90–91): "So shines a good deed in a naughty world." *Come and Go* begins (194): "When did we three last meet?" as in *Macbeth* (I.i.1): "When shall we three meet again?" "**Rough for Radio II**" offers "Crabbed youth" (117) for *The Passionate Pilgrim*'s "crabbed age"; and "**Rough for Theatre I**" insists on the rhyme of "wind" and "unkind," as in *As You Like It* (II.vii.174–75): "Blow, blow, thou winter wind, / Thou art not so unkind / As man's ingratitude." "**Ohio Impromptu**" reworks *A Winter's Tale,* a play SB appreciated in later life. In *Happy Days,* **Winnie** consoles herself with rags and tags of Shakespeare: "woe woe is me . . . to see what I see" (11), from Ophelia's "O, woe is me / I have seen what I have seen, see what I see" (*Hamlet,* III.i.160–61); "Ensign crimson . . . Pale flag" (14; *R & J,* V.iii.94–96): "beauty's ensign yet / Is crimson in thy lips and in thy cheeks, / And death's pale flag is not advanced there"; "Fear no more the heat o' the sun" (21; *Cymbeline,* IV.ii.258); "bird of dawning" (31; *Hamlet,* I.i.158–60); and "no damask" (39), as in "[She] let concealment, like a worm i' the bud, / Feed on her damask cheek" (*Twelfth Night,* II.iv.113–15). Optimistic, yet consumed with irony, her remaining "classics" link Winnie to SB's great fiction, as another who draws breath in a world of pain to tell her story.

shambles: a slaughterhouse. **Molloy**'s **mother** lives near the shambles (22) and the **Unnamable** (like SB) in a quiet street "near the shambles" (327); the bluebottles "naturally abounding" (328) suggested *Othello* (IV.ii.66): "as summer flies are in the shambles."

Shannon, Bill: original of the **Foxrock** postman (*Dream,* 146; *Watt,* 47), who rides up to the house whistling "The Roses are Blooming in Picardy," the tune foreshadowing his death from consumption. His name is anglicized to "Severn" (69), as Joseph Severn, **Keats**'s physician. The manuscripts (NB5, 7) originally read "Shannon."

Shaw, George Bernard (1856–1950): **Dublin**-born playwright, socialist, and **Nobel Prize** winner. SB was lukewarm: "You can keep your George Bernard Pygmalion" (*Dream,* 78–79), and commenting to **MacGreevy** (25 August 1930) that Shaw "might be considered as called rather than chosen." **Leibert** is described as "The perfect Wagnerite" (*Dream,* 37) the title of Shaw's 1898 study (Pilling, *Dream Companion*). Asked (1956) for an appreciation of Shaw, SB responded in negatives, that he wouldn't say he wasn't a great playwright, whatever that was, but that he would give "the whole unupsettable apple-cart for a sup at the Hawk's Well [W. B. **Yeats**], or the Saints [**Synge**] or a whiff of Juno [**O'Casey**], to go no further" (Knowlson, *Frescoes,* 259).

sheep: one fateful spring **Belacqua** pauses to observe the scene, with its "legions" (Mark 5:9: "for we are many") of sheep and lambs springing into the world, the grass spangled with scarlet afterbirths ("Walking Out," 101). In **Arsene**'s "short statement" (*Watt,* 47), the word "uneaten" is added late to the typescript (175). This land of breeders and bleeders is repeated in *Company* (48) and "Heard in the Dark I" (247). The horror is missing from **Murphy**'s "touching little argonautic" in the park (100). The narrator of *First Love* sits in the necessary house, staring dully at an almanac, "with its chromo of a bearded stripling in the midst of sheep, Jesus no doubt" (28). For **Christ**'s separation of the sheep from the **goats**, see Matthew 25:31–46. At the end of act I of *Waiting for Godot*, one **boy** looks after the goats, and his brother the sheep (31.b). **Molloy** awakens (28–29) to find a shepherd watching over his sleep. This Good Shepherd (John 10:11–16) saves his sheep, only to send them to the **shambles** (I Corinthians 10:25: "Whatsoever is sold in the shambles, that eat"). Molloy considers himself "a black sheep entangled in the brambles," as in Abraham's sacrifice of Isaac (Genesis 22:13). In **Moran**'s similar scene (158), the flock is black. Compare "the lamb black with the world's sins" (*How It Is*, 70), as in John 1:29: "Behold the Lamb of **God**, which taketh away the sin of the world"; or the "ecce" and "pickthank agnus" of "**Home Olga**" (Genesis 22:7: "Behold the fire and wood: but where is the lamb?"). Abraham's faith is an *exempli gratia*, an emblem of grace and thanks; but both are lacking in SB's outrage in "**Ooftish**," where suffering and sickness "all boils down to blood of lamb" (Revelation 7:14). **Mercier** and **Camier** find a pub full of butchers, "whom the blood of the lamb had made rather intolerant" (116). SB was unable to accept the sacramental significance of the sacrifice of the Lamb.

Shekinah: "that which dwells," specifically the presence of **God** within the tabernacle, a glimpse of the holy in the midst of the profane; as vociferated by Hairy **Quin** in "**What a Misfortune**" (132): "Fornication . . . before the Shekinah." The word is associated with the **Alba**: Walter Draffin has a vision of the "mercy seat al fresco and Shekinah" (146). Used of a certain Fräulein Furtwängler in a house of ill fame (229): "The true Shekinah," said Belacqua, "is Woman" (*Dream*, 105); and later (187) to describe **Belacqua** and the Alba: "the Shekinah has fizzled out." SB took the word from **Carlyle**'s *On Heroes and Hero-Worship* (247): "The true Shekinah is Man" (DN, 41).

Shelley, Percy Bysshe (1792–1822): English poet drawn on when **romantic** cliché is needed. **Nemo**'s foaming spit is scattered by the Wild West Wind (*Dream*, 55); the **Alba** intones from *Prometheus Unbound* ("A Wet Night," 69); **Neary**'s heart, pressed to the thorn, pants and bleeds (*Murphy*, 49); and the **Unnamable** (393) murmurs Shelley (Prometheus on the thorns of life?). The tragedy of Shelley's first wife, Harriet, who inconsiderately drowned herself in the Serpentine, forms the staffage of *Murphy* (99). **Cooper** is likened to Frankenstein's daemon (124). SB often cites "To the Moon": arriving in Vienna, **Belacqua** is "pale from weariness" (the "frosty Caucasus" suggests *Prometheus Unbound*); **Celia** climbs the stairs like Shelley's moon (*Murphy*, 155). Estragon, once a poet, quotes the lines: "Pale for weariness / Of climbing heaven and gazing on the earth" (*WG*, 34.b).

Shepherds' Gate: built into the town's walls in "The **Calmative**" (64), as the "Sheep Gate" into the south wall of Jerusalem (Nehemiah 12:39). The "Shepherd" (*Proust,* 17) is Le Berger, an *apéritif anise.*

Sheridan, Richard Brinsley (1751–1816): Dublin-born dramatist of *The Rivals* (1775) and *School for Scandal* (1777). The **Whoroscope Notebook** notes "Don't rip up old stories," from *A Trip to Scarborough* (1777), recycled in "**Echo's Bones**" (13) and *Murphy* (18): to obtain the good opinion of a woman one should not recount stories of her past.

Sholto: the young doctor, a pale dark man with a brow, who turns up in "**Fingal**" and offers **Belacqua** an excuse to forsake **Winnie**. He has a "pleasantly appointed sanctum" within the **Portrane Asylum**. Despite his decorous behavior, his name derives from John Sholto Douglas, eighth marquis of Queensberry, father of Lord Alfred, and a notorious bully.

Signorelli, Luca (1441–1523): Italian artist whose figures are round and muscular. **Lucy**'s legs "would have done credit to a Signorelli page" ("Walking Out," 106).

Silence to Silence: an eighty-minute documentary, with French subtitles ("D'un silence l'autre"), produced by Radio Telefis Éirann. It opened at the Edinburgh Festival (19 August 1984), was broadcast on RTE (25 October), and screened at the twenty-eighth London Film Festival, National Film Theater (29 November). It went to festivals in Cork, Belfast, Antwerp, and Los Angeles. Directed by Seán Ó Mórdha, narrated by Tony Doyle, with commentary by Richard Ellmann and Declan Kiberd. The credits acknowledge a veritable who's who of SB's interpreters, friends, and critics. The profile of SB's life is flecked with fragments of his poetry (read by David **Warrilow**), extracts from his work, and lyrical moments of **Schubert** *lieder.* Sometimes errant in its chronology, and occasionally wrong in specifics (SB's "revelation" on the **Dún Laoghaire** pier), it is a remarkable evocation of SB's life, authentic footage of the places he lived, and images (photographic and literary) of the **Beckett country**, moving in their simplicity and profound in their (often mute) eloquence.

silent movies: SB developed a technical interest in montage and wrote to Eisenstein asking to be taken on at the Moscow State Institute of Cinematography. There was, he reported, "No word from Eisenstein" (SB to TM, 9 April 1936). He told Pudovkin that he wanted to revive the two-dimensional silent film, which he felt had died unjustly (Bair, 204–5). The interest is reflected in the early poetry, which Coughlan describes (71–72) as "exceptionally close" to Eisenstein's classic conception of sequence as a succession of disruptions, or montage. The music hall is the spoken equivalent of the silent screen, and its traditions infiltrate *Dream*, such as the "Charlie Chaplin" song parodied in *The Waste Land* (79). Cinematic technique is specified when **Ticklepenny** is "as though thrown on the silent screen by **Griffith** in midshot soft-focus" (*Murphy,* 191); in the **hardy laurel** pairing of **Wylie** and **Neary**; and in **Cooper**'s destitute walk. SB defended the "postmortem burlesque" of the ending, including the Keystone Kops scene of the crowded doorway (259), which he repeated in *All That Fall* as Miss Fitt and Mrs. **Rooney** get stuck at the top of the stairs. Ludovic Janvier rightly described *Murphy* as "Andromache played by the Marx Brothers."

Peter Hall thought of **Vladimir** and **Estragon** as tramps, but SB's conception of them was as **clowns**. Harold Hobson noted the circuslike scenario: **Pozzo** cracking his whip like a ringmaster, the play unfolding in a series of routines, cross talk, gags, quick-fire exchanges, and comic misunderstandings (Bert Lahr's mistake was trying to be top banana). The play is imaged in black and white; the bowlers are a tribute to Chaplin; and the hat-swapping routine is stolen from *Duck Soup.* The ending achieves existential anguish by incongruity, with a botched hanging and a broken rope so that Estragon's trousers fall in comic confusion.

All That Fall's early title, "A Lovely Day for the Races," echoes the Marx Brothers' *A Day at the Races.* Mrs. Rooney's getting in and out of the car or up the stairs is directly in that slapstick tradition. "**Rough for Theatre I**" features a light that goes on and off, a gag that "has gone on long enough"; and a shaggy-dog story about a man called Smith ("Never knew anyone by that name"), who is about to put his head in the oven when he hears that his wife has been run over by an ambulance. Compare the story about the tailor in *Endgame,* or the dialogue: "Our hearing hasn't failed . . . Our what?" *Krapp's Last Tape* offers slapstick, a "banana walk," and simian vulgarities. In early versions Krapp appeared as a **clown**, his white **face** and empurpled nose a comic grotesquerie that SB later removed, as he did the red faces in *Endgame.* In one of his last ventures, SB returned to the black-and-white tradition, refilming "**Quad**" (qv).

Film is silent save for one verbal gag, an audible "sssh" in the opening sequence. Its success depends on treating philosophical themes (**Berkeley**'s *esse est percipi*) in a suitably comic mode. O should invite laughter by his way of moving, his "comic founded precipitancy." Buster **Keaton** may not have appreciated the arcane depths, but he rose to the occasion with their comic rendition, notably in the silly scene with the **cat** and the **dog** but also in the examination of the photographs, a scene that evokes the silent screen, which, for all its slapstick, is unsurpassed as the medium of mute and silent pathos.

Silver Strand: a beach south of Wicklow, County Wicklow (Jack's Hole, which **Belacqua** prefers to call the Silver Strand, is a cove farther south). The **Alba** takes out her scissors and file to beautify his nails (*Dream,* 187), which she describes as those of a bodysnatcher. Belacqua compares it, to the belittlement of the earlier occasion, with a trip a year ago to Venice with the **Smeraldina**. Although it breaks in no **love** storm (198), the episode is seen (1) unusually for SB as having further value, and (2) of confirming the choice of life on the margin. This may inform the memories of Voice **B** in *That Time*.

Sinclair, Peggy: Ruth Margaret Sinclair, SB's cousin (born 9 March 1911), daughter of his Aunt Cissie and William "Boss" Sinclair, a Jewish dealer in **art** and antiques who had lived in Howth before moving to **Kassel** in the early 1920s. SB met Peggy in the summer of 1928 in **Dublin**, when she was seventeen, staying with Harry Sinclair, her father's twin brother. He was captivated by her charm, her laughter, and the way she dressed in green. Her English was comically corrupted by German calques. He drove her to the mountains and beaches, and fell in **love** with her green eyes and little "cameo of a birdface," qualities attributed to the **Smeraldina** (*Dream*, 15). Their relationship constituted SB's first love. Its trauma and uncertainties underlie much of the early poetry, so that "green" invariably invokes her **memory**. SB visited Peggy at the Schule Hellerau-Laxenburg near Vienna (September 1928), staying there a month before returning to the **École Normale**. He often revisited Kassel, getting on well with the family, even after the "calamitous Silvester" of 1929 brought the affair to an "insanitary" end (228)

The relationship was doomed, partly because of SB's inability to come to terms with his emotional contradictions about love and sex and partly because the two were intellectually far apart, Peggy unable to be persuaded that illiteracy was not a crime (SB to TM, 24 August 1929); and finally because Peggy was under sentence of **death**. She acquired a fiancé named Heiner Starcke (the

"mec" of "**Ascension**"), yet remained on good terms with SB, who felt recurrently what he called "the German fever." The Sinclairs' plight in 1932 became desperate. They were forced to sell "for a song" the piano and pictures later worth a fortune, the Nazis making conditions for a Jewish family increasingly impossible. They were forced back to **Ireland**, but without Peggy, who had contracted TB and died (3 May 1933), "quite peacefully after a fit of coughing in a sleeping-draught sleep" (SB to TM, 13 May 1933), as SB was being operated on for the cyst on his neck.

Peggy's illness informs "**Enueg I**" ("my darling's red sputum"). Cronin's suggestion (189) that SB was not deeply moved by her death is belied by the tone and feeling of SB's writing, then and later. The inclusion in MPTK of "The **Smeraldina's Billet-Doux**," based on Peggy's letters to him—though SB regretted the pain it caused her parents—is part of the flagellation that **Belacqua** directs against himself, perhaps miscalculated but not callous mockery. In "**What a Misfortune**" Belacqua becomes emotional at the mention of "Sage-green," and quotes Florine's words as she awaits the lover who will not return. Images of Peggy, invariably associated with green eyes or a green coat, recur in "les grands yeux verts" of the dying girl in "Ascension" and the eyes in "**Text 6**." **Krapp** recalls "A girl in a shabby green coat, on a railway-station platform" (58), into whose eyes he had gazed and almost given himself: "Scalded the eyes out of me reading *Effie* again." He "Could have been happy with her, up there on the Baltic" (62). "**Eh Joe**" recalls the girl who didn't do all right: "The green one." **Voice** reminds Joe how her eyes opened (as in *Knapp's Last Tape*), his telling her, echoing Browning's "Rabbi Ben Ezra," that "the best's to come" as he leaves her, fumbling with the big horn buttons of her coat: "She went young" (205).

Sisyphus: the **Whoroscope Notebook** records (from the *Britannica*) the myth of Sisyphus, King of Corinth, who promoted navigation and commerce but was fraudulent, avaricious, and deceitful. In Hades, he had to roll uphill a huge marble block that always rolled back, because he had attacked travelers, killing them with a large boulder, or because he had betrayed the gods. The porter in *Watt* (26), wheeling milk cans from one end of the platform to the other, imitates Sisyphus: "perhaps it is a punishment for disobedience, or some neglect of duty." Moran comments sardonically on **Camus**'s 1942 essay "Le Mythe de Sisyphe": "But I do not think even Sisyphus is required to scratch himself, or to groan, or to rejoice, as the fashion is now" (*Molloy*, 133).

situation circle: a phrase SB used in his **Trinity** lectures on **Racine** (qv): "A loves B, and B loves C, and C loves D. The great pagan tiger of desire chasing its tail" (see Rachel **Dobbin**). In *Murphy* (5), a hexagon:

Miss Dwyer: the circuit of **love** unrequited ("missed wire"). Loved by **Neary**, she loves:

Flight Lieutenant Elliman: an embrocation (*The Unnamable,* 320). He loves:

Miss Farren: Mary Farren, housemaid at **Cooldrinagh** (Knowlson, 245). *Ring-*sakiddy* is "Ringaskiddy," on the Lee estuary, **Cork**. She loves:

Father Fitt: of Ballin[a]clashet ("town of the trench"), Oysterhaven, Kinsdale, Cork. (Consider Miss Fitt, of *All That Fall*.) He acknowledges a certain vocation for:

Mrs. West: of Passage (West), a small port on the Lee estuary. She loves Neary.

Six Poèmes 1947–1949: "Trois poèmes: Three poems" (1948) and "Trois poèmes" (1955), as collected in *Gedichte* (1959), *Poems in English* (1961), and *Collected Poems* (1977). They are: "bon bon il est un pays"; "Mort de A.D."; "vive morte ma seule saison"; "je suis ce cours de sable qui glisse"; "que ferais-je sans ce monde"; and "je voudrais que mon amour meure." They represent a new beginning, after the war, a consolidation of earlier themes in a more lyrical vein, accentuating the enduring **dualism** of the inner and outer worlds.

Six Residua: a gathering of shorter prose (**Calder**, 1978): *From an Abandoned Work;* "Enough"; *Imagination Dead Imagine;* "Ping"; *Lessness;* and *The Lost Ones.*

Skeat, Walter (1835–1912): English philologist and Cambridge professor of Anglo-Saxon, whose works include a six-volume **Chaucer** (1894–95), from which SB borrowed (from his frontispiece) the features of **Chas** ("A Wet Night," 49).

Sketch for Radio Play: in *Stereo Headphones* 7 (spring 1976): 3–7; an issue dedicated to SB, with an **Arikha** sketch on the inside front cover, John Christie's montage, "Molloy's solution to the 16 stones," on the back, and a "Tribute Text to Samuel Beckett" by the editor, Nicholas Zurbrugg. Collected as "**Radio I**" in *Ends and Odds* (Grove, 1976; Faber, 1977).

Skinner, B. F. (1904–90): American behaviorist, heir to Watson and Pavlov. He invented the Skinner box, to facilitate observations. **Murphy** experiments with the **Külpe school** in a Lyons tearoom; the **London** equivalent was Skinner's Luncheon and Tea Rooms (84 Gray's Inn Road), which disappeared during the **war**. The main ward at the **MMM** is Skinner's House (modeled on Tyson House at the **Bethlem Royal Hospital**).

skull: an image that pervades *Quatre nouvelles* and *Three Novels*, as SB moved from the fiction of **motion** to that of the **closed place**. **Molloy** asserts the distinction between the without and the within, "all that inner space one never sees, the brain and heart and other caverns where thought and feeling dance their sabbath" (10). In *Malone Dies*, this becomes an emblem of enclosure within a "little space"; it seems that he is "in a head and that these eight, no, six, these six planes that enclose me are of solid bone" (221). The floor of his room whitens, with a "gleaming and shimmering as of bones" (223), then becomes a foul little den, "dirty white and vaulted" (compare Matthew 23:27, the whited sepulchre, also implicit in **Moll**'s tooth, hollow and rotten). The **Unnamable** experiences the terror yet longing of being in a head, "surrounded on all sides by massive bone" (350). These intimations are ex-

plicit in "The **Calmative**," where the narrator has no wish to contemplate the antinomies, "for we are needless to say in a skull" (70). This becomes in "**Text 2**" "perhaps we're in a head, . . . ivory dungeon" (106); in **French**, "**oubliette**." The narrator of *How It Is* has a sense of "the **voice quaqua** on all sides then within the little vault empty closed eight planes bone-white" (128); this becomes "the little chamber all bone-white" (134), with the **oakum** of words ill heard ill murmured.

Lucky's speech moves toward the world as an abode of stones, fading into "the skull the skull the skull the skull in Connemara." Compare *Ill Seen Ill Said* (84): "at the place of the skull" (Golgotha). *Endgame*, with its "two small windows," is set within the skull, its initial action a Cartesian wakening into **consciousness**. The cube of *All Strange Away* and the rotunda of *Imagination Dead Imagine* are white vaults, topographical transformations of the whited sepulchre. The white rotunda is diminished until effectively "a ring as in the imagination the ring of bone" (182), combining Vaughan's image of eternity with **Eliot** and Webster, the skull beneath the skin. "**For to end yet again**" begins with the "skull alone in a dark place" (243), mingling with the dust to which it must return, the reductio of existence to sepulchral whiteness. These fictions are internalized, told from within, but "La Falaise" adopts the external perspective. Here, perception unites the viewer with the view, the subject with the **object** of his perception, gazing at the cliff until "A whole skull emerges"—until the eye flies to the whiteness about and the vision fades.

Skyrm, James: a "moot Struldbrug" ("What a Misfortune," 128), who represents the groom at **Belacqua**'s wedding. "Scrim" is a scanty fabric that supports cheap wallpaper; a *skrimshanker* is one who shirks work or duty.

Mr. Slocum: "Old Cissy Slocum," racecourse clerk in *All That Fall*, a figure based on Fred Clarke, who had that position at **Leopardstown** (O'Brien, 40), and the family name of John Beckett's wife (Knowlson, 386). An old admirer of Mrs. **Rooney**, he offers her a lift, but getting her in and out of the car is traumatic, like giving **birth** (note the **pun** in his name). Metaphors of life as death are further enacted by the failure of his car to restart, until it is choked ("too much air"), and by the death of a **hen**, run over in the road.

Slow and Easy: as **Mercier** notes to **Camier** (39): "Woe is us . . . we're in the slow and easy." The Southern and Eastern railway ran from **Harcourt Street Station** (the "round end," or turntable) via Dundrum, **Stillorgan**, **Leopardstown**, and **Foxrock** to Shankill, where it joined the **Dublin** to Wexford line to Bray (the "square end," or siding); this was SB's usual way in and out of the city. **Watt** travels from Harcourt Street to Foxrock. The Foxrock stationmaster was Mr. Farrell, the Mr. **Barrell** of *All That Fall*, where the town becomes **Boghill**. The waiting room, in which he spends a traumatic night, measures the Foxrock station by the golden rectangle, the manu-

scripts illustrating those proportions. The line opened in February 1859 and was last active on 31 December 1958, to SB's regret, as recorded in *That Time* (231): "all closed down and boarded up Doric terminus of the Great Southern and Eastern all closed down."

Smeraldina: the "little emerald," or green-eyed heroine of *Dream,* a portrait based on SB's cousin Peggy **Sinclair** (qv). The name derives from **Dante**'s *Purgatorio* XXXI.116–17: "li smeraldi / ond' Amor già ti trasse le sue armi" ("the emeralds from which Love once shot his darts at you"). She is sometimes called the Smeraldina-**Rima**, after W. H. Hudson's wild Brazilian girl in *Green Mansions.* In "**Draff**," she is **Belacqua**'s last wife (the only sail in sight). He falls in love with her "pale firm cameo of a birdface" (*Dream,* 15), not recognizing that it comes accompanied with a body that is all wrong. Then, she rapes him (18), wrenching him out of his precious world of **art** and **Platonic** ecstasies and into "a gehenna of sweats and fiascos and tears" (19). Her physicality nauseates him ("collops of pork gone greasy" [111]), and he turns to the **Syra-Cusa** (briefly) and the **Alba** (hopelessly), before returning to **Germany** for the "calamitous Silvester" (228), which brings the affair to a tearful end. The portrait is cruel, but the object of scorn is less the Smeraldina than Belacqua himself, whose emotional inadequacies are equally to blame for everything going "kaputt" (18).

"The Smeraldina's Billet-Doux": a **love** letter in poor English corrupted by German calques, from the **Smeraldina** to her

"Darling Bel"; it was written for and finally published in *Dream* (55–61), but earlier added to *MPTK*. A presumably faithful rendering of one of Peggy's letters, "sentimentality, lust and misspelling exploited for comic effect" (Cohn, *Comic Gamut,* 20), it distressed SB's Aunt Cissie by mocking her daughter, Peggy **Sinclair** (qv). The two versions have points of difference: the "soft white **body** naked" of *Dream* becomes the "soft white body Nagelnackt" of *MPTK;* "Herr Geheimrat Johann Wolfgang **Goethes** Faust" becomes the less pretentious "Goethes Faust"; and Herr **Arschlochweh**'s travels to the Schweiz move forward one paragraph. Other variants are trivial. SB regretted the hurt, but he let it be republished in *Zero Anthology* 8 (1956: 59–61) and in *Vogue* (May 1970): 114–15, anticipating the reprinting of *MPTK* that year.

Socrates (ca. 470–399 BC): Athenian philosopher who was put to **death** at age seventy on charges of impiety and corrupting the young. His last days, as recounted by **Plato** in the *Phaedo* and *Apology,* were his greatest glory. He treated the accusations with contempt, and had the right under Athenian law to suggest an alternative penalty to the death sentence imposed. Imprisonment, a substantial fine, or exile would have been acceptable, but, in the spirit of the gadfly to which he likened himself, Socrates argued that since he had served the state without self-interest he should be given free meals in the Prytaneion, then modified this to a derisive fine of one mina of silver. This was considered an act of contempt, and the death sentence was affirmed by a larger majority than had originally voted for it. The absence of the sacred ship sent yearly to Delos delayed his execution for a month. Socrates refused to escape and instead engaged in philosophical discussion about the survival of the soul beyond death. He drank the hemlock without flinching, his death the lasting emblem of the truth to which his life had been dedicated.

However admirable, Socrates exemplified for SB the Greek tradition that affirmed the immortality of the soul and contributed, through Plato and **Aristotle**, to the mainstream of Christian thought, leading in turn to **Descartes** and rationalism. His insistence that death is but separation of the soul from the **body** was something SB could not accept. The end of *Murphy* rejects this tradition, affirming instead **Democritus,** who asserted that when the atoms that make up the soul are dispersed, the soul must share their dissolution.

In *Dream,* **Belacqua** says that he will arrive in **Kassel** "like Socrates," with only the rags he is wearing; SB had recorded from **Burton**, "Socrates was as cold as January" (DN, 136; the *Anatomy* reads "Sophocles"). The unpublished story **"Echo's Bones"** alludes to Socrates turning up the tail of his "abolla" (ts. p. 14), a detail repeated in *Murphy* (200); it refers to Socrates observing the call of nature, even as his life is most in danger, by lifting his robe and exposing his **buttocks**. When Celia first meets him (15), Murphy is standing in Stadium Street like Socrates in one of his ecstatic trances. He utters "maieutic saws" (71): Phaenarete, mother of Socrates, was a midwife, and Socrates said that he was incapable of giving birth to wisdom, but was an excellent man-midwife, skilled in the art of bringing thought to birth. In the *Watt* mss. (NB1, 3; "4/2/44"), SB listed the Aristotelian categories, noting: "Socrates is a man [who], 70 years old [what], wise [how, mental], teacher of Plato [who to whom], at evening [when], in prison [how, physical], sitting on his bed [where], reaching for his cup [by what means]." This generates SB's protagonist of the next forty years: "X is a man, 70 years old, ignorant, alone, at evening, in his room, in bed, having pains, listening, remembering."

Two parallels bind Socrates and SB, both of which SB might have disowned. The first is SB's espousal of ignorance and impotence (but only after years of intense study) and the reluctant recognition by Socrates that perhaps he knew more than others for, unlike them, he knew he knew **nothing**. The other is more intricate. Socrates was a man of deep piety and **mystical** temperament; his life was regulated, he claimed, by an inner **voice**, neither that of conscience nor a mental disorder but an interior **auditor**. SB believed in neither the immortality of the soul nor providential order, but to the three certainties of having been born, existing, and knowing he would die he added a fourth, as inexplicable as it was imperative: the need to express, a need driven by an inner voice that he might never understand but to which he listened and tried to identify during the course of his life.

solipsism: the theory that self-existence is the only certainty; or, more strongly, the doctrine of extreme idealism, the contention that the world is but a projection of one's individual **consciousness**, to vanish on the instant if the mind but change its theme. **Schopenhauer** terms this "theoretical egoism" and, conscious of his initial insistence that **objects** exist only as perceived by the subject (the world as idea), is at pains to absolve himself of the charge (*WWI*, I.2 #19, 135–36). **Belacqua** "enlivened the last phase of his solipsism" before he toed the line and began to relish the world, with the belief that the best thing to do was to move constantly from place to place ("Ding-Dong," 36). **Murphy** is described (82) as "a seedy solipsist." This anticipates his encounter with Mr. **Endon**, wherein he finds that the cost of total retreat into the fortress of the mind is the loss of **apperception**, a price he is not prepared to pay. See **Berkeley** and **Kant**.

solitude: SB in *Proust* asserts (64) that art is the apotheosis of solitude. Book I.xx of *Imitatione Christi* by **Thomas à Kempis**, "Of the Love of Silence and Solitude," was a favorite part of the meditation, an affirmation of **quietism** and the life of the "solitary sparrow" that SB would make so much his own. Another favorite dictum was "**Sedendo et quiescendo** anima efficitur prudens" ("seated and in quiet the soul becomes wise"). The cost could be terrible loneliness (see **friendship**) and a danger of lapsing into **solipsism** as he retreated into the **little world** of the mind (Thomas's cubicle), where a kind of freedom might be possible and the mysterious **voice** might better be heard. SB felt his solitude acutely but cultivated it deliberately, aware that something was happening within him as he collected knowledge eclectically (Knowlson, 191). The writings of the 1940s and '50s are the apotheosis of the earlier years. The impulse manifested itself in the later prose works in one lovely word, "**still.**" Solitude is implicit in every aspect of SB's life, from **art** to **chess** to **music**. By accepting the truth of the early statement "We are alone" (*Proust,* 66), and acting on it all his life, he has made others aware of the "irremediable solitude" to which all are condemned but, equally, has shown that they are not the only ones to share this fate.

"**sollst entbehren**": "You must renounce!"; the words of **Goethe**'s Faust (I.1549), before he makes his pact with Mephistopheles, to the world's demand that he live without **desire** and be satisfied with conventional life. **Moran** celebrates the "Magic words" (*Molloy,* 110), accepting the restraints that Faust laments and using them to justify the harsh treatment of his son. The phrase underlies the narrator's dream in *How It Is* (56): "I too will renounce I will have no more desires."

Solo: translation of *A Piece of Monologue,* first published in *Solo suivi de Catastrophe* (Minuit, 1982), with a special edition of ninety-nine numbered copies. SB changed "traduit de l'anglais" to "d'après l'anglais." Carlton Lake (to whom SB sent the signed typescript) notes that it reveals SB's mode of "translating": a literal rendering into **French**, with perhaps three choices of phrasing within parentheses or underlined, then further reducing the

text by deletion, so rather than being a strict translation it becomes an adaptation of the original (*No Symbols,* #411). David **Warrilow**, who first performed the piece, reported SB's comment when he sent the play, "this text will never be in French," because of the plosive nature of "birth" and difficulties of sound formation with the mouth, lips, and tongue. The adapted French text is significantly shorter in order to avoid these phonic problems.

"**Some Sayings of Bram van Velde**": several "Paroles de Bram van Velde" (13), translated by SB, followed *Three Dialogues* in *Transition forty-nine* 5 (104). Although unattributed, the translation is clearly by SB: "I do not know what I do. What I put into a picture is not the result of any act of will. I do not know myself what it means."

"**Something there**": a poem of twenty-six short lines, a free translation of "**hors crâne seul dedans.**" Published in a special issue of *New Departures* 7/8 and 9/10 (August 1975): 27; then in *Collected Poems* (1977). The title summarizes the theme: tentative half-questioning, half-asserting that out there ("outside / what / the head what else") may be something ("not life / necessarily"). **Bocca** is eliminated in this spare reworking. To Michael Horowitz, editor of *New Departures,* SB noted "three hearts over two," an invitational raise in bridge parlance. The typescript, with SB's note, appears in *Samuel Beckett Today* 8 (205).

"**Song**": the poem "Words" finally produces in "**Words and Music.**" Included in *Collected Poems* (1984), although the second part, "Then down a little way," was not.

Sordello (ca. 1200–69): a troubadour born near Mantua but who wrote in **Provençal** and so linked the poetry of Provence to Italy; he is subject of a difficult poem by Browning. In "**What a Misfortune**" (136), **Belacqua**'s inability to sleep is likened to the tossing of Sordello's **Florence** (*Inf.* VI.148–51). The **Smeraldina**, huddled on the bed, is described as "Posta sola soletta, like the leonine spirit of the troubadour of great renown, tutta a se romita" ("seated all alone . . . all in himself recluse" [*Purg.* VI.58–59, 72]) (*Dream*, 23). This is **Dante**'s Sordello, like a crouching lion, casually associated in *Dream* (24 and 187) with Belacqua, who was earlier described (IV.101) as sitting behind a great boulder (IV.133). Hence, perhaps, **Molloy**'s confusion (10), watching as **A** and **C** go by, crouching in the shadow of a rock, "like Bela[c]qua, or Sordello, I forget."

Sottisier Notebook: a tiny hardcover notebook now at the **BIF** (RUL 2901), containing several "Rimailles (Rhymeries versicules)," drafts, in **French** and English, of some of the *mirlitonnades*. Other jottings and comments are dated from between 1976 and 1982: from **Job**, Pope, **Johnson**, **Swift**, Parnell, **Schopenhauer**, and **Mallarmé**, with Sidney's advice: "look in thine arse and write." The final pages ("16.1.76") also contain notes for *Company*. **Flaubert** kept a *Sottisier*, or catalogue, or solles.

Soubresautes: the French text of *Stirrings Still*, written in tandem with the English;

first published as a *texte bref* (Minuit, 1989). The title, meaning "starts" or "jolts," might seem to lack the subtle tension of "stirring" and "still"; however, compare **Baudelaire**'s prefatory letter to his *Petits poèmes en prose:* the dream of a poetical prose, "musicale sans rythme et sans rime, assez souple et assez heurtée pour s'adapter aux mouvements lyriques de l'âme, aux ondulations de la rêverie, aux soubresautes de la conscience."

"**Souffle**": translation of "**Breath**," published with the subtitle "Intermède" in *Les Cahiers du Chemin* 12 (15 avril 1971): 21–22, and then in *Comédie et actes divers* (Minuit, 1972).

"**Sounds**": a prose piece, published with "**Still 3**" in *Essays in Criticism* 28.2 (April 1978): 156–57; rpt. in *Complete Short Prose* (267–68). It begins where *Still* leaves off, evening given way to night, the narrator listening for "some sound of some kind here where none come none pass." The setting is the **summerhouse** of other "Still" pieces, from which it differs by acknowledging an objective world rather than the primacy of the subjective experience. There is a sudden movement as the narrator catches up the torch, and "must up suddenly out of the chair," along the path to a tree, which he stands beneath or embraces. Then, back to the chair, "quite still as before," the echo of the earlier text explicit in the description of the head in hand, again listening "for no such thing as a sound."

Spagnoletto: José Ribera (1591–1652), the "Little Spaniard"; baroque painter at the viceroy's court at Naples, praised for his somber tones and dramatic use of light. Mr. **Kelly**'s bones at the end of *Murphy* are described in the typescript as standing out "like a Spagnoletto hermit's." The deletion conceals the artistry.

Spectator: "le commisaire du peuple," as he describes himself, who descends from a box to the stage in Act III of *Eleutheria* (qv), remonstrating with the actors for not delivering the drama that right-thinking people want. He likens the action to a tenth-rate game of **chess**, then feels some of the impulses toward inertia of the others onstage. In Michael Brodsky's translation he is called "An Audience member." The device, never again used by SB, has affinities to the Sphinx in **Cocteau**'s *La Machine infernale.*

The Spectator: since 1828 a weekly devoted to the arts and politics. In 1934 SB visited its literary editor, Derek Verschoyle, who had been "disguised as a student at TCD when I was still functioning" (SB to TM, 18 August 1932). SB reviewed Eduard Mörike's *Mozart on the way to Prague* ("**Schwabenstreich**") and Albert Feuillerat's *Comment Proust a composé son roman* ("**Proust in Pieces**"). Reviewing **Murphy**'s in the *Spectator* (1938), Kate O'Brien was one of the few to appreciate its wit. **Miss Counihan** (195) takes a room directly opposite their office, at 99 Gower Street.

Spenser, Edmund (1552–99): English poet whose term in **Ireland** as the Lord Deputy's secretary smeared his reputation with lasting odium. SB attended

Rudmose-Brown's lectures on "Colin Clout" and *The Faerie Queene,* retaining for the poet a respect the more surprising given what Spenser stood for. In *Proust* (79), after commenting that "Spenser's **allegory** collapses after a few cantos," SB qualifies this by arguing that allegory must always fail in the hands of a poet, the point being that Spenser, like **Dante**, is a poet. SB admitted in 1932 to experimenting with "obscene Spenserian stanzas" (Knowlson, 132). References to Spenser include: Una in "**What a Misfortune**," with the requisite chastity; **Belacqua**'s gift to Hairy of his *Hypothalamion* (124), a *Prothalamion* in skivers (split sheepskin leather); and Mr. **Endon**'s pad as a bower of bliss (*Murphy,* 181). This image continues into *Molloy,* where a disreputable Sir Guyon resists the temptation to remain in **Lousse**'s garden. In "**Text 2**" (107), the Red Cross Knight is conflated with Piers the Plowman: "Piers pricking his oxen o'er the plain." In "**Rough for Theatre II**" (84), **A** contemplates the sky: "And to think all that is nuclear combustion! All that faerie."

"**Spiel**": German translation of "**Play**" by Elmar and Erika **Tophoven**, with SB's help; published in *Theater Heute* [Hanover] 4 (July 1963): II-IV: 58–60. First produced (before the **French** and English premieres) at the Ulmer-Theater, Ulm-Donau (14 June 1963), dir. Deryk **Mendel**, with Nancy Illig (W1), Sigfrid Pfeiffer (W2), and Gerhard Winter (M). It ran six performances, Mendel playing *Spiel ohne Worte I und II* on the same bill. Production notes for SB's "Spiel" for the **Schiller-Theater Werk-**

statt (October 1978) are contained in two manuscript notebooks. The red one (RUL 1976), which contains entries for *Damals* and *Tritte,* offers the text of "Spiel," with textual variations, revisions, detailed notes in German and English on structures and symmetries, and a résumé of "events"; the brown notebook (RUL 1730) contains directorial notes, queries, references, **mathematical** arrangements, and diagrams all of which offer insights into SB's thoughts and practice as a **director**. The notebooks in facsimile, transcription, translation, and with notes are published, with SB's revisions to the German text, in *Theatrical Notebooks* IV (1999).

Spinoza, Benedict de (1632–77): Hebrew prename Baruch; Dutch lens grinder who turned to philosophy to consider how best he might live. A Portuguese Jew, he could not retain that faith. He was rejected by the orthodox, Jew and Christian alike, but was admired and loved by the few who knew him. He believed his own doctrines, and practiced them, meeting his **death**, from phthisis, with courtesy. Heir to **Descartes**, he based his metaphysics on a monistic parallelism rather than on interactionism or **dualism**, considering the human **body** and mind as two aspects of the same reality, **God**. He differs from **Leibniz**, for whom there is an infinity of possible worlds, with the real world contingent upon a **preestablished harmony**. For Spinoza, the world compounded with God is the only possible, and humanity believes itself free only through ignorance of the causes of its acts. SB noted his "Omnis determinatio est negatio" in the

Whoroscope Notebook, from **Inge**'s *Christian Mysticism* (121).

Spinoza's *Ethica* begins with definitions and proceeds to numbered propositions followed by "QED" to affirm his conviction that the order and connection of ideas is as the order and connection of things (I #7). This is the geometrical method, the essence of which is demonstration (Windelband, 396, notes the naïveté of Spinoza's assumptions of the unassailable validity of the definitions and axioms). Two sections discuss the nature and origin of the mind, leading to the proposition that it has an adequate knowledge of the eternal and infinite essence of God, but, as part III contends, the passions distract and obscure our intellectual vision. Book IV, entitled "Of Human Bondage, or the Strength of the Emotions," suggests the image of **Murphy** in his chair and asserts that we are in bondage in proportion to what happens to us as determined by outside causes and free in as much as we are self-determined. Book V concerns human freedom, in the Cartesian perspective but with an insistence on three ways of knowing, the third being that of the mind as it knows itself (V #31), from which arises the intellectual **love** of God (V #32). This is discussed in Brunschvicg's *Spinoza et ses contemporains* (1923), which SB owned.

Chapter 6 of *Murphy* bears the epigraph, *Amor intellectualis quo Murphy se ipsum amat* ("the intellectual love with which Murphy loves himself"). This subverts Spinoza's *Ethica* (V #35), in which is affirmed: "Deus se ipsum amore intellectuali infinito amat" ("God loves himself with an infinite intellectual love"), such intellectual love consisting in the understanding of his perfections and rejoicing therein, with the implication that the more the human mind understands the divine love the less it will be subject to emotion. SB follows not Spinoza's original but **Windelband**'s rephrasing (410): *amor intellectualis quo deus se ipsum amat.* In **Diderot**'s neat formulation, "cette espèce de Dieu" is defined as "La seule qui se conçoive" ("Le Rêve de d'**Alembert**," 317). This implies the recognition of God as first cause; hence Murphy's intellectual love of *himself* implies that his world takes meaning from himself, and this, with all its ironies, becomes a warrant for freeing himself from contingency. Spinoza thus subverted is a convenient formulation for the rejection of the rationalist tradition that informs the chapter to follow, indeed the whole novel. A variation of this theme occurs in *First Love,* where the narrator concludes that his feeling for **Lulu** is not "that intellectual love which drew from me such drivel, in another place": he is in fact defined, despite his dismissal of the principle, by his failure to love.

Spiro: in *Watt,* editor of *Crux,* the popular Catholic monthly. First name Dum, he is so bright and cheerful that the tag is "Dum spiro spero" ("While I breathe I hope"); indeed, a dumb sentiment. Mr. Spiro encounters Watt in the train en route to Mr. **Knott** and expounds some knotty points, from the "devout twist" of rearranging the fifteen letters of the Holy Family to form a question and answer (winning entry: *Has J. Jurms a po? Yes*) to what he knows of the adjuration

of the **eels of Como** and the theological problem arising when a **rat** eats of a consecrated wafer. In the drafts this last is expounded in a comic and irreverent passage that was excluded from the final text. This is the *Mus Eventratus McGilligani,* and the dissertation of Matthew David McGilligan, then a priest. He earns an unorthodox passage to Rome for inquiring what happens to the Sacred Body after the rat, "afther what he's bane an—afther what he's bane—bane an done his doolies." There he pursues his vocation until one day, in the Doria Gallery, his eyes fall upon an **object** that opens them, "the celebrated painting by Gerald of the Nights [see **Honthorst**] of a girl in her nightdress catching a flea by candlelight." No less than Stephen Dedalus (in an outrageous parody of the wading girl scene in *Portrait*), he becomes an artist and master of **Leopardstown** Halflengths. See the Addenda to *Watt* (247). The painting that initiates this epiphany, *Donna che si spulcia,* is in the Galleria Doria Pamphilj, where SB presumably saw it.

Mr. Spiro cites several medieval theologians and authorities:

Saint Bonaventura (ca. 1217–74): John of Fidanza, Franciscan theologian, known as Doctor Seraphicus, canonized in 1482 by Sixtus IV, and ranked sixth among the Doctors of the Church by Sixtus V (1587).

Peter Lombard (ca. 1095–1160): bishop of **Paris** and *Magister sententiarum,* whose four books of *Sententiae* were written between 1145–50.

Alexander of Hales (1175–1245): Doctor Irrefragibilis, English scholar and theologian who included John of Rochelle, Bonaventura, and Roger Bacon among his pupils. His *Summa Universae Theologiae* correlated Augustinianism with the philosophy of **Aristotle** and the Arabs.

Sanchez: François Sanchez (1562–1632), a Portuguese who taught at Toulouse; author of the *Tractatus de multum nobili et prima universali scientia quod nihil scitur* (Lyons, 1581), each chapter concluding with a resounding "Quid?" (Windelband, 362).

Suarez: Francisco Suarez (1548–1617); Spanish theologian and Jesuit, considered the last exponent of **scholasticism**, who sought to reconcile Realism and Nominalism and the **quietism** of Luis Molina with orthodox doctrines of election.

Henno: identified by Bryden (*Idea of God,* 79) as Franciscus Henno (d. 1720), a little-known Franciscan theologian.

Soto, Dominic (1494–1560): Dominican theologian whose *Summulae* (1529) secured a triumph of Realism over the errors of Nominalism. Professor of theology at Salamanca, and later imperial theologian to the Council of Trent and confessor to Charles V.

Diana, Antonino (1586–1663): moral theologian of Palermo. His *Resolutiones Morales* met with wide approbation; its frontispiece was a cross with the legend *non ferro sed ligno.* Consultor of the Holy Office of the kingdom of Sicily.

Concina, Daniello (1657–1756): Dominican theologian at Venice, whose *Theologia Christiana* (twelve volumes, 1749–51) attacked the Jesuits. An authority on the Lenten fast.

Dens: Peter Dens (1690–1775), theologian of Louvain and the seminary of Mechlin, and part author of a fourteen-volume work called *Theologia ad usum seminariorum* (1777).

"Spring Song": a poem sent to Charles **Prentice** (1932), written in the spring of that year; copies were given to Con **Leventhal** and Georges **Belmont**, the latter with significant revisions probably made in 1935. When SB made the final selection for *Echo's Bones,* this was omitted. Pilling calls the poem an outbreak of "the German fever" (SB's feeling for Peggy **Sinclair**), the musical idiom of "**Dortmunder**" returning in "the subjunctive minor" for eighty lines of sexual images that form "a kind of magic-lantern show." The poem forms "a high red cacklebelch": Clytemnestra and Agamemnon, Hamlet and Ophelia, **Cain** toiling in the firmament; these are less literary than imbued with fatigue and disgust. Only **death** (Thanatos "flaming down the couloir") can kill the "white **music**" (compare "**Alba**") of the speaker's **desire**.

Sproule: "a lately axed jobber [broker] to a firm in the City" ("What a Misfortune," 130), recruited by Capper **Quin** to buy the bouquets for **Belacqua**'s wedding. He displays wit ("**Superfoetation**," no need for one bloom upon another) and firmness (he weakens the florist's resistance), earning the modest commission he spends on gin and peppermint.

stamps: SB and his brother collected stamps, Frank later concentrating on Trinidad and Tobago and **Ireland**, with a specialist interest in the British overprints of the 1922 Provisional Government and Free State (Knowlson, 624).

SB's interest did not last, but his first album still exists, a table inside the back cover noting that on 24 October 1915 he had only seventy-one stamps, but by 10 April 1917 he owned 574 (Knowlson, 37). The descent into darkness (*Dream*, 181) is described as "tête-bêche," a technical term for stamps printed top to tail (**Moll** considers [*Malone Dies,* 262) that "tetty-beshy" is well worth persevering with). Sorrow is described as "a thing you can keep on adding to all your life long, is it not, like a stamp or egg collection" (*Watt,* 50). The action of the sower (*How It Is,* 11) is that depicted on the most common French stamp from 1902 to 1920. Jacques Jr. has two albums, one for his collection and one for duplicates (104). He wishes to bring them on the journey and is permitted the latter, but when he is caught transferring his rare and valuable stamps to the duplicate album (109), **Moran** orders him to leave both albums at home. The episode exemplifies not only Moran's anal retentiveness but his authority as a **father** figure in a destructive oedipal relationship.

Three stamps are mentioned in *Molloy:* Timor, five reis orange (1895); Togo, one mark carmine "with the pretty boat"; and Nyassa, ten reis green and black (1901), showing "a giraffe grazing off the top of a palm-tree" (121). The Togo is one of the "Yacht" key types (1900), a rarity used but only moderately valuable mint. The Nyassa was issued by the Nyassa Company of northern Mozambique, not the British protectorate of Nyasaland; it is relatively common. The Timor five reis was probably not worth the florin Moran paid for it, being only moderately rare, but SB's choice was directed by the **pun** on "*timor*," meaning "fear." The figure on the stamp (King Carlos of Portugal) has an uncanny resemblance to SB's father as well as to Moran, and the motif of the mustache affirms the father's authority and rule of law (**Gaber** has one). In the manuscripts at this point a space is left for selection of a suitable stamp. As Phil Baker reveals in "The Stamp of the Father in *Molloy*" (*Psycho-analysis,* 37–47), this becomes an emblem of the book's oedipal structure. Molloy bears the stamp of his **mother** (112; not in the French text), and Jacques Jr. that of his father: an icon of the patriarchy and hierarchy descending from **Youdi.**

Staunton, Howard (1810–74): leading **chess** player in the 1840s, although his avoidance of **Morphy** qualifies that claim. A raconteur and mimic, an expert on Elizabethan and Shakespearean drama, Staunton was widely admired and equally disliked. From 1845 he conducted an influential column in the *Illustrated London News,* and in 1847 he published the *Chess-Player's Handbook,* which went through twenty-two editions and taught thousands to play; the newsagent Evans uses it to play games between masters (*Watt,* 26). In it, Staunton famously remarked that after 1. e4 e5 Black's game is embarrassed, a comment SB parodies in his analysis in *Murphy.* Staunton chessmen, the standard pattern approved by Fédération Internationale des Échecs for world play, were designed (1835) by Nathaniel Cook (the knight inspired by the Parthenon frieze). SB owned a set, originally his **father**'s, which was stolen from **Ussy.**

Stekel, Wilhelm (1868–1940): German psychologist interested in dreams. SB read his *Psychoanalysis and Suggestion Therapy* (1923) in the 1930s, taking detailed notes. **Cooper**'s *acasthisia,* or inability to sit down (*Murphy,* 119), is "deep-seated and of long standing," a citation now in the OED. Stekel uses it (23) of a patient with peculiar posterior problems, arguing that psychoanalysis gives deeper insight into the mechanisms of neurosis than is possible by any other method. SB's rejection of the "complacent conceptualism" that makes contact with outer reality the index of mental well-being (*Murphy,* 176–77) is couched in the language of Stekel.

Stendhal: pseudonym of Marie-Henri Beyle (1783–1842); French writer, master of ironic realism, and plaything of amour, who wished to feel like **Rousseau** but write like Montesquieu, for the "happy few." He wrote several fine novels, an autobiography, *Vie de Henry Brulard* (1835), and numerous pieces on **music**, **art**, and travel. A comic element filters his precisely cynical view of contemporary life. SB's acquaintance was intimate rather than extensive, as reflected by *Armance* (1827), the character of **Octave** (qv) entering into **Belacqua** as **babylan** (qv), and *Le Rouge et le noir* (1830), a celebrated novel of adultery from which SB copied a few details (DN, 127–28) in late 1931 (SB's "sparsely annotated" copy [Garnier Frères, 1925] is now at the **BIF**). **Belacqua** when intimidated is described as rude beyond measure, not "timidly insolent like Stendhal's Comte de Thaler" (*Dream,* 203). At the Hotel de la Môle (II.4) the unfortunate comte is described by M. de Croisenois as having a timid insolence. Stendhal is

cited to the effect that the best **music** is that which becomes inaudible after a few bars (*Dream,* 12); and Belacqua's mind is described (44) as a "chapelle ardente," perhaps that of *Le Rouge et le noir* (I.18). SB admitted to **MacGreevy** (September 1934) his attraction to Stendhal's thesis that the world had lost its energy. He asserts his rejection of mimetic art in "Les **Deux besoins**" (*Disjecta,* 55): "Il y a des jours, surtout en Europe, où la route réflète mieux que le miroir," the allusion being to Stendhal's image from *Le Rouge et le noir* (chapter 49) of the novel as a **mirror** strolling along a highway.

Stephen, Karin [Costelloe] (1889–1953): German psychologist, wife of Adrian Stephen (Virginia **Woolf**'s brother), and author of *The Wish to Fall Ill* (1933), describing the relation between neuroses and mental abnormalities. Stephen recommended that the patient transfer "microcosmic fantasies" onto the analytical relationship to free him from his unconscious delusions and gain contact with the real world. This is one source of the battle in *Murphy* (165) between the psychotic and psychiatric perspectives, those who consider patients curable against those who see them as dysfunctional. Neuroses are associated with abnormalities such as morbid anxiety, depression, phobias, and obsession, as the products of repression (and thus treatable), whereas psychoses lead to insanity (pathological and, presumably, incurable). This distinction was accentuated by **Jung** in his fifth **Tavistock** lecture (167), when he defined a neurosis as a dissociation of personality due to the existence of complexes, which all possess; he then argued that if the split reaches the organic structure the dissociation becomes a psychosis, a **schizophrenic** condition wherein the complex lives an existence of its own. SB took detailed notes from Stephen's book and used them, if not to critique his own troubles then at least to dramatize Murphy's.

Sterne, Laurence (1713–68): British novelist, author of *Tristram Shandy* (1759–67) and *A Sentimental Journey* (1768). SB preferred **Diderot**. He might occasionally refer to them, as with Thelma's present to **Belacqua** of the grandfather clock ("What a Misfortune," 129) or the reference in "The **End**" (94) to Maria's sentiment, "God tempers the wind to the shorn lamb." *Tristram Shandy* irritated him, "in spite of its qualities" (Knowlson, 271), but in "**Rough for Radio II**" (119–20) "A" asks "S" if she knows the works of Sterne. The angel catching a tear alludes to VI.8, when Uncle Toby, provoked, has his oath blotted out by the tear of the Recording Angel. Preferring the word to the spirit, A misses the **pity** of which this incident is a touchstone.

stick: the problem of the stick is that of the **body**, the dilemma of self-extension. If the body is known in immediate relation to the self, as **Schopenhauer** affirms, does the stick exist in the same way or in an intermediate relation, to either self or body? When stick becomes stone, that is, a missile, how does the self occupy the space through which it moves? The **unnamable** wonders where his kingdom ends, within the body or as far as the eye can see? Might the self be extended by

using a **machine**? He craves a stick, or a stone but, having "neither **voice** nor other missile" (361), is abandoned to his solitary resources, like **Köhler**'s anthropoid apes or the protagonist of "**Act Without Words I**," unable to make use of the tools that might extend his being. **Molloy** has his crutch and **Malone**, naked in his bed, has a long stick to rummage in his possessions. His debt to sticks is so great (185) that he almost forgets the blows they have given him. When he loses it (254) and realizes what he has lost, he reaches an understanding of Stick, "shorn of all its accidents." Archimedes and the **monkey** scratching its fleas with the key that opens its cage underline the inevitable restriction of self that will be his lot. His pencil, short and pointed at both ends, a stick that extends the self (or voice) in writing, will see him out (209), but it too slips from his fingers (222). His last words testify that with his pencil or stick he will never never anything there any more, but our very reading of his words bears **witness** to his self-extension (and so that of SB) into our space.

Still: a prose piece written in 1972–73; printed in a limited edition of 160, 30 numbered, folio, loose in sheets with green and white decorative wrappers, uncut, in matching slipcase; with original etchings signed in pencil by Stanley William Hayter (Milano: M'Arte Edizioni [1974]), and with an Italian translation by Luigi Majno, and a facsimile reproduction of the manuscript signed by SB. It appeared as a special edition (Calder & Boyars, 1975 [Signature Anthology, #20]), then in *For to*

End Yet Again and Other Fizzles (Calder, 1976), the second of the sequence, but was placed as "Fizzle 7" in the **Grove Press** *Fizzles* (1976). *Still* was translated as *Immobile* and included as the second *Foirade*.

The immediate setting of "Still" (and of the related "**Sounds**" and "**Still 3**") is the **summerhouse**. This fades imperceptibly into **Cooldrinagh**, the bay windows of the room in which SB first saw the light of day implicitly the scene of the narrator's vision of the dying of that light. The eye adapts itself to the darkness, but "stillness," or the ultimate homeostasis, is impossible to achieve as the mind yet moves and the **body** cannot quite cease its activity, the hands trembling and the breast faintly rising and falling. Yet a condition of tranquility is approached, if not attained, the delicate prose rhythms ("So quite still again then all quite quiet") imitating the failing light and growing stillness—when "suddenly" (splendid hyperbole!) something happens: the right hand, and with it the forearm complete with elbow, slowly rises. This movement of the arm constitutes a return to the concerns of **Geulincx** and the **Occasionalists**, as in the dictum *Ego non facio id, quad quomodo fiat nescia* ("I do not do that which I do not know how to do"), illustrated by this very act: if "I" do not know how that movement is initiated, then "I" do not cause the arm to rise. Yet the miracle of **motion** has occurred, and ended, and now all is "still once more." In this sense *Still* is analogous to "**Breath**," in which **coming and going** into the faint light is reduced to its most **fundamental sound**, that of movement in the silence.

Stillorgan: a **Dublin** suburb near SB's **Foxrock** home, an irresistible **pun** if one wishes he had never been born, as **Neary** does (*Murphy,* 44). **St. John of God's** is there, the **asylum** that is **Watt**'s final destination and forms the setting of *Malone Dies.* The "Stillorgan Sunshine Home" (*Dream,* 183) was next door to the kindergarten run by the **Elsner sisters** in Leopardstown Road (O'Brien, 369).

"**Still 3**": a short prose piece, published with "**Sounds**" in *Essays in Criticism* 28.2 (April 1978): 156–57; rpt. in *Complete Short Prose* (269–70). It continues where *Still* and "Sounds" left off, which they never did, back in the chair before the window, "still listening again in vain," that one phrase encapsulating the other two pieces. Identical images are recapitulated: head in hand, night birds, the ghosts of questions; but with incipient dawn there comes in imagination "stills" of dead **faces**: "no expression marble still so long then out." If this is the apotheosis of darkness and **solitude**, as awaited in the three short pieces, then the experience may be real but its significance unread.

Stirrings Still: SB's last independent prose work, dedicated to Barney Rosset and written in English and **French** (see *Soubresautes*) between 1983 and 1987. It appeared in *The Guardian* (3 March 1989: 5), and in the *Manchester Guardian* (19 March 1989: 29, with a review by Frank Kermode entitled "Miserable Splendour"), then was given a public reading by Barry **McGovern** at the American Irish Historical Society, New York (2 February 1989) before being published: New York: Blue Moon Books ($2,000) and **London**: Calder (£1,000), in a special boxed edition (25 pages) with nine **illustrations** by Louis le Brocquy, limited to 226 copies, each signed by the author and illustrator, and appearing on SB's eighty-third birthday. It was reprinted, New York: North Star Line, 1993; included in *Collected Shorter Prose* (259–65). Rosset, SB's publisher, had fallen on hard times, and his plight stimulated SB into writing something for him (see **Grove Press** for details). SB sent a typescript called "**Fragments**," the first section of the present text, and the other two paragraphs by the end of 1987. Rosset used the text to launch his new venture, Blue Moon Books.

The title is from *Company:* "Pangs of faint light and stirrings still. Unformulable gropings of the mind. Unstillable" (16). The three short passages convey a sense of farewell, a **consciousness** still exploring a self ("so-called") and facing the uncertainties of its own existence. The first presents the image, familiar from *Still,* "**Mort de A.D.**" and "**Nacht und Träume**," of one at the table, head on hands, imagining his self (or a configuration) rising and going, only to reappear at another place or **time**, seeking a way out. "Darly" (Rosset's error) is remembered, and he sees himself in the "Same **hat** and coat as of old." A clock strikes from afar, "Then the lull again," as he finds himself waiting for the "one true end to time and grief and self." The second interlude assumes that he is "in his right mind" (for if not how could he wonder if he were?). He emerges from it "he knew not how into the outer world," to find himself in a field of grass without a fence or "bourne" (the *Hamlet* echo intimates **death**), nor even a stone on which to sit "like **Walther**" to meditate; but he hears the strokes and cries "now clear." This time the imagined experience is sustained, for the mental traveler does not return to "his right mind." The third piece assumes the same posture. The endeavor is not to travel but to "catch" the word, "faint from deep within," that might "end" (but he says "end and so on") the narrative tension between "**on**" and "stayed," implicit in the "stirrings still" that will not be resolved until he can "stir no more," and there is an end to "Time and grief and self so-called. Oh all to end." As Brian Finney concludes in his review essay, "Still Stirring to be Still" (134), this is familiar territory, but what is new is SB's summation of his life's work within a single piece, with a protagonist kept alive on the life-support system of words still.

stoicism: a philosophical movement contemporaneous with Epicureanism, beginning in the third century BC, founded on the teachings of Zeno of Citium, and attaining its influential expression in the writings of Seneca in the first century AD and the *Meditations* of Marcus Aurelius in the second. More Roman than Greek, it accepted the teleology of **Plato** and **Aristotle**, in common opposition to **Epicurus**. The stoics admired **Socrates** and saw in his **death** a perfect exemplum of their teaching, but they were impatient with metaphysical subtleties, valuing virtue but regarding other goods as of little account. Fortitude and an uncomplaining acceptance of the vicissitudes of fortune were the defining features of stoicism, its ethics teaching that happiness can be attained only through freedom from passions and emotions (*apatheia*) and inward peace (*ataraxia*). The doctrine (not unlike **quietism**) might have commended itself to SB, but like its twentieth-century equivalent, **existentialism**, there were things he could not accept, from its acceptance of the soul's immortality to its reliance upon **reason** to elevate the mind above misfortune and its affirmation of the moral value of human action. There is little positive about the "stoic love" of *How It Is* (62), and Kenner's sense of SB as a "stoic comedian" is misleading. A sustained critique of the doctrine concludes Book I of **Schopenhauer**'s *WWI,* and SB accepted his sense of an inherent contradiction in ethics that in the elevation of suffering asserted the dignity of man.

"Stones": the sucking stones "**Extract from *Molloy,***" trans. Patrick **Bowles** for *The Paris Review* 2.1 (spring 1954): 124–35; retitled "Stones" and reprinted in *Best Short Stories from the Paris Review,* ed. William Styron (Dutton, 1959). As "Sixteen Stones" it entered *The Mathematical Magpie,* ed. Clifton Fadiman (Simon and Schuster, 1962), 179–85.

Stories and Texts for Nothing: first English edition of *Nouvelles et textes pour rien* (Grove, 1967; Evergreen E-460): "The **Expelled**," "The **Calmative**," "The **End**," and *Texts for Nothing* I–XIII; with reproductions of the six drawings by **Arikha** used in the second **French** edition (1958). The dust jacket offered a portrait of SB, also by Arikha.

stout porter: Murphy asks (139), "Why did the barmaid champagne? . . . Because the stout porter bitter." The bite is associated with *Origin of the Milky Way* (see **Tintoretto**), but not in the **French** version, since it cannot be translated. When **Belacqua** tells it in "**Echo's Bones**" (12), Lord **Gall** gives the right answer, impatiently. The jest improves in *Watt* (197), where the bitter stout porter is named Power (an Irish whiskey).

Stürmer: in soccer, a striker, but used by SB in the sense of a hooligan, an apache, as in *Dream* (219); in "**A Wet Night**" (66); and in "**Sanies I**." SB freely translated **Diderot**'s *Rameau's Nephew:* "A regular stürmer of the **Paris** pavement" (DN, 83).

Stützenwechsel: an architectural style of lower Saxony, with alternating wings and arches; the "Saxon Stützenwechsel" fails to charm ("The **Calmative**," 68).

sudarium: see **veronica**.

Suhrkamp Verlag: SB's German publishing house originated in an agreement made between Peter Suhrkamp (1898–1959) and Bermann Fischer of the S. Fischer Verlag (2 May 1950). Of Fischer's forty-eight authors, thirty-three stayed with the combined imprint, among them Hesse and Brecht. Suhrkamp Verlag was founded (1 July 1950) with Peter Suhrkamp at its head, intending to focus on contemporary German and foreign literature. Having completed a doctorate on Hesse, the young Siegfried Unseld (28 September 1924 to 26 October 2002) joined the fledgling firm (January 1952) with the responsibility for locating the vital new German literature as well as for sales and advertising. Unseld became a full partner in the company (1 January 1958), and then took over when Peter Suhrkamp died (31 March 1959). He published important and innovative German writers such as Max Frisch, Peter Handke, Peter Weiss, and **Günter Eich**, as well as major foreign authors like Octavio Paz, Paul Celan, and SB, with whom he forged a close friendship. An established author himself, Unseld has edited collections by Brecht, Hesse, **Rilke**, and **Goethe**. He celebrated his fiftieth year at Suhrkamp in 2002. [JG]

suicide: to MacGreevy (July 1930), SB commented that **Schopenhauer**'s "intellectual justification of unhappiness—the greatest that has ever been attempted—is worth the examination." He later added, referring to the end of *Proust*, "Schopenhauer says 'defunctus' is a beautiful word—as long as one does not suicide." SB did not deviate from these opinions: acknowledging unhappiness but rejecting suicide as an option (whatever Jean de **Chas** may have stated in his *Discours de la sortie;* see "Le **Concentrisme**"). As *Dream* asserts (123), "The will and nill cannot suicide, they are not free to suicide"; **Belacqua**'s wretchedness stems from his failure to understand this imperative. **Nemo**'s **death** (182–84) is significant, for Belacqua refuses to accept the verdict of "Felo-de-se from Natural Causes" (183), nor the "simple" (*irremissible fortes peccatorum*) assumption that it was motivated by despair (184); the "Will" forbids this option. The reason-

ing is similar to the contention (27, 228) that suicides jump from a bridge and not a bank, as does Herr Sauerwein. "**Love and Lethe**" parodies these concerns. Though "Temporarily Sane" (97), Belacqua cannot "connive" at suicide alone, so must prime another, with reasons pertinent and **absurd** (90): "Greek and Roman reasons, Sturm und Drang reasons [Werther], reasons metaphysical, aesthetic, erotic, anterotic and chemical, **Empedocles** of Agrigentum [who threw himself into Mt. Etna] and **John of the Cross** reasons" (suicides are buried at crossroads). Ruby Tough agrees to the pact, since she suffers from an incurable disorder, is past her prime, and has the chance to end with a bang.

In *Murphy,* the Old Boy cuts his throat for a necessary reason: it is a cutthroat razor. His *felo de se* violates the **solitude** of the **monad**; the effect on Celia is devastating. Murphy's death (262) is "A classical case of misadventure," a verdict, similar to the Scots "non-proven," suggesting that the circumstances are not satisfactory but no legal conclusion can be reached. Was it suicide, accident, or otherwise? The last will and testament (269) suggests the former, and its sentiment is Murphy's (who else would know the **Brewery Road** address?), but it is undated and the laborious capitals (Murphy would never call Celia "Mrs Murphy") render it suspect. Moreover, suicide is at odds with what is known of Murphy (admittedly, not much); it is contrary to Schopenhauer's Will (the note is a complex **pun** to that effect), and frustrates the decision (252) to return to Celia and face the **music**. Accident? Then why the will? And who turned on the gas? Rabinovitz has suggested that Murphy was murdered, and he chooses **Cooper** as the villain, but his account is preposterous, even in a chapter entitled "Unreliable Narrative" (*Development,* 113–18). Authorial carelessness or (the postmodernist prurit) the **aporia** of paradox evades the issue. The Cartesian structure invites a reasoned response, in the Sherlock Holmes manner, which leads to the only possible conclusion that Murphy was murdered but by **Ticklepenny**, the only one with motive (resentment), opportunity, and inside knowledge. This interpretation is **absurd**, but pi is pervasive. As Chesterton once observed, the problem with our universe is that it is neither reasonable nor unreasonable but that it is almost reasonable but not quite. Murphy's "suicide" is a case in point.

"The **Calmative**" tells how the narrator climbed a spiral staircase to a projecting gallery and cynical parapet (68), there to encounter a wild-eyed man who (one surmises) may have wished to jump. He later meets a man with a big black bag, "full of glittering phials" (73). The narrator obtains one and carries on his way. In "The **End**" he sets out in a boat, having pierced a hole in the floorboards and swallowed his calmative. Although **Moran** has his morphine, suicide is not seriously an issue in the *Three Novels,* the sentiment of which is that one must go **on**. See **painkiller**.

The tree in *Waiting for Godot* offers a dubious salvation: "What about hanging ourselves?" The slapstick comedy critiques **stoicism** or **existentialism**, in particular, the validation of suicide as an authentic or self-defining act, a choice of ending. This is a play that does not end, twice, and these are not stoic comedians. They will be back tomorrow (as will the actors, playing their parts). Even a good bit of rope cannot suppress the anguished response that is SB's final critique of their suffering, the mute scream of the **fundamental unheroic** as **Estragon**'s plaintive cry, "I can't go on like this," meets **Vladimir**'s impassible reply: "That's what you think."

"**Suite**": a story, published in *Les Temps modernes* 10 (July 1946): 107–19; revised and republished as "La **Fin**" in *Nouvelles et textes pour rien* (1955). SB began in English (17 February 1946) but reverted to French, entitling it "Suite et fin." The first part only was published in **Sartre**'s journal, because Simone de Beauvoir had not appreciated that it was in two parts, disliked the obscenity of "Fin," and thought SB had misled her. She was unmoved, despite a plaintive letter from SB protesting its "mutilation," insisting that it was not "une chose achevée" but "une prémisse majeure," and pleading with her not to cut off his **voice** before it had time to mean something. See "The **End**."

summerhouse: a little hexagonal log house, of larch and fir, at **Cooldrinagh**, featured in SB's late prose as a place of **memory** and **desire**. In "**As the Story Was Told**," seeing a hut in a grove the narrator recalls a summerhouse, where he sat in a wicker chair, looking out at the orange light. This is the setting of *Still,* "**Sounds**," and "**Still 3**." In "**Heard in the Dark II**," the narrator awaits a woman to join him. He recalls how his **father** would retire there on Sundays with his copy of *Punch* and chuckle as he turned the pages. The image threatens the anticipated encounter, his father's unbuttoned waistband linked to her big breasts and abdomen, suggesting the fear of pregnancy (she is "late"). The story as retold in *Company* (53–59) embraces memories of SB's affair with Mary **Manning**.

"sup of foul draft from work in regress": identified by J. C. C. Mays (*JOBS* 6: 136) as a five-page fragment in **French**, dated 14 December 1971, acquired (July 1976) for the Theater Collection at Harvard University.

Super Conquérant Notebook: a small softcovered spiral-bound notebook now at the **BIF** (RUL 2934), from 1984–86, containing a dramatic fragment, "**Bare Room**," drafts of *Stirrings Still* in English and **French**, and a short poem, "**Brief Dream**."

superfoetation: a further fertilization in one already pregnant, but applied in *Proust* (13) to **body** and mind. In "**Tristesse Janale**," Beauty is "superfétatoire," with generative power. Bridie **bboggs** may not understand Sproule's compliment in "**What a Misfortune**" (130), but the jest is improved by **Moran**, who sees in plants "a superfetatory proof of the existence of **God**" (*Molloy*, 99).

surrealism: a revolutionary literary and political movement that arose in **Paris**, partly in response to the carnage and futility of World War I. Surrealist poetry took up themes such as the city, the quest, and the night, accentuating such elements as the *merveilleux,* coincidence, chance encounters, the *femme fée,* and personal liberty, and disturbing the sense of the real and unreal in **music**, literature, and **art**. A reaction against positivism, realism, reason, logic, and progress, it was associated with dada until André **Breton**'s 1924 *Manifeste de surréalisme* defined its creative potential. Breton affirmed lyricism, **Freud**, automatic writing, and dreams as ways of exploring the subconscious. He accentuated the disturbing blend of the real and the unreal and the arbitrary juxtaposition of dissociated phenomena, such as a sewing machine and an umbrella. The 1924 manifesto advocated "Automisme psychique pur par lequel on se propose d'exprimer, soit verbalement, soit par l'écrit, soit de toute autre manière, le fonctionnement réel de la pensée, en l'absence de tout contrôle exercé par la raison, en dehors de toute préoccupation esthétique ou morale." His second *Manifeste* (1929) identified the point in the mind where dream and reality fuse, and opposites are integrated, a doctrine blended into the ending of *Murphy* (280), as Mr. **Kelly** tries to determine the meeting point between the seen and unseen.

SB contributed several translations from **Breton** and Paul **Éluard** to a special surrealist number (5.1) of *This Quarter* (1932), and to Nancy **Cunard**'s *Negro* (1934). These alerted him to rhythm and syncopation and the relationship between jazz and surrealist expression. SB's early poetry and works like "**Assumption**" reflect the impulse. Fletcher (25) defines the lasting influence of surrealism: "metrical anarchy, the precedence of the image over the sense, lines of greatly varying length within the same stanza, and a tendency to construct poems on the basis not of syntactical coherence but of associated imagery, the association usually existing only in the mind of the poet." These would remain pervasive elements of SB's art and style as late as *Happy Days,* the setting of which may have been suggested by the final frame of the Salvador Dalí–Luis Buñuel *Un chien andalou* (1928). The final frames of *Film* depict **O** staring at **E** in a manner reminiscent of the famous early scene of that film, an eyeball severed by a razor blade. The late plays bear traces of surrealism, particularly "Play," *Not I, That Time,* and *Footfalls.*

Although he signed "**Poetry Is Vertical**," a quasi-surrealist manifesto (1932), and was later friendly with artists such as **Duchamp** and **Giacometti**, SB cannot be identified as a surrealist writer. The reasons were partly **political**, the surrealists' attraction to Communism an inexplicable incongruity (even by their standards); partly philosophical, questions such as "Le **suicide**, est-il une solution?" having little attraction; but also, finally, aesthetic. **Joyce**'s *Work in Progress* was taken by *transition* as a flagship of the avant-garde, yet SB could not be unaware of the discrepancy between the surrealist sense of freedom from the constraints of **time** and space, as in Joyce's world of dreams, and Joyce's boast that he could justify every syllable of it. He was fond of the story of Joyce's meeting with René Crevel. Presented with the second Surrealist Manifesto, Joyce asked, "'*Pouvez vous justifier chaque mot?*' Silence. Then, '*Car moi, je peux justifier chaque syllable*'" (Atik, 85). While *Dream* rejoices in its freedom from outmoded formal constraints, literary or musical, the young thought of **Belacqua** is likened to "a pullulation of **Neue Sachlichkeit** maggots" (35). He is tempted (117) to "organise a collision," but that would be "the fruit of a congruence of enormous improbability," a comment that indicates the narrator's sense of being caught between opposite modes of expression. As his occasional writings reveal, SB's work is preoccupied by questions of chaos and form, the challenge being that of finding the form that might constrain the chaos. Harvey notes (249) SB's fervent rejection of surrealism on these grounds, which reveals the persistence of a curious **Platonic** weave in his aesthetics that he never quite relinquished: "Being *has* a form. Someone will find it someday. Perhaps I won't but someone will. It is a form that has been abandoned, left behind, a proxy in its place." That said, there is a haunting similarity between the heuristic openings of Breton's *Nadja* ("Who am I?") and *The Unnamable* ("Where now? Who now? When now?"). SB toyed with the possibilities of the aleatory in "**Lessness**" (qv). Fond as he was of pleading ignorance about his texts, however, abandoning the agency of authorship was finally anathema to him.

Swift, Jonathan (1667–1745): Dean of St. Patrick's, poet, and madman, lover of Stella (Esther Johnson) and Vanessa (Esther Vanhombrigh). With him SB felt "a temperamental affinity that goes beyond mere approval" (Fletcher, 85). SB reread Swift intensively in 1933. His presence is explicit in "**Fingal**" (qv), the anecdote about the "motte" placing

Belacqua's treatment of **Winnie** within the tradition of the "sad and serious" (24). Despite the old man's assurance, and whatever the local legend about Stella, for whom the tower is named and whose country place had once been **Portrane** (O'Brien, 373), the tone suggests Vanessa, who on small encouragement had moved to **Ireland** (1714) to be near Swift. The Dean, for whom this was not entirely convenient, kept her at a distance but would occasionally visit her. Vanessa died in frustration (1723); hence references (*Dream*, 27, 34) to the land of sanctuary, where much had been suffered secretly, the "last ditch" before madness, as the nearby **asylum** intimates. W. B. **Yeats**'s *Words upon the Windowpane* invokes the torrid feelings involved. "Little fat Presto" walking out to see Stella (35) may be SB's intrusion, without historical foundation, for the old man's account as recorded by SB to **MacGreevy** (5 June 1933) does not include this. Swift used "Presto" (It. "swift") of himself in the *Journal to Stella* (the foreign-born duchess of Shrewsbury could not remember the English word). Belacqua moves "prestly" ("Dante and the Lobster," 18); "walk like camomile" ("Fingal," 34) also derives from the *Journal*.

"**What a Misfortune**" is like an extended *Table Talk*, replete with ancient Struldbrug [*sic*] (128) and Swift's rebuke of Dublin women for their neglect of Shank's mare, that is, having fat legs because they did not walk. Cycling is an alternative: the narrator of "**Sanies I**" mounts a proud *Swift*, a pun implicit in "Fingal," varied in "**Draff**" (179) when the parson pedals away like a weaver's shuttle, i.e., "swiftly" (Job 7:6). The

Frica's indignation is "Not saeva, fabricated" (*Dream*, 216), as in Swift's epigraph in St. Patrick's Cathedral, "ubi seva indignatio ulterius cor lacerare nequit" ("where savage indignation can lacerate his heart no more"). This is omitted in "**A Wet Night**," but the **Alba**'s comment about going through the world like sunbeams through cracks (*Dream*, 223) adds in the short story (69) "in cucumbers," which turns a phrase from Giles (*Civilisation of China*, 146; DN, 77) into an allusion to part III of *Gulliver's Travels*. In "A Wet Night" (80), but not in *Dream*, Belacqua does "the King of Brobdingnag in a quick dumb crambo"; that is, he concludes the natives to be a pernicious race of odious little vermin, like the king (II.6). These additions suggest that SB reread *Gulliver* before revising *Dream* for *MPTK*.

Swift contributes to *Murphy*. Minor details include **Celia**, to accentuate her bodily functions; "suspicioning the Nasty" (32) from Swift's "Meditation on a Broomstick"; the "clapper from the bell" (117) from "A Letter of Advice to a Young Poet" (via Austin **Clarke**); "**Gilmigrim** [*sic*] jokes" (139), from *Gulliver's Travels* (I.5); Mr. Thomas ("Bim") **Clinch** (156), from "Clever Tom Clinch, Going to be Hanged"; "a race of people," as used by Gulliver of the Brobdingnagians (169); an allusion to *The Drapier Letters* (1722) and **Wood's halfpenny** (170); "Polite Conversation" and platitudes of Chapter X; and the "Description of a City Shower" (1710) as Murphy's ashes are swept into the gutter (275). Conspicuous is *A Tale of a Tub*, written for "the Universal improvement of Mankind," which SB read in the Clarendon Press edition (1920) and to which he likened *Dream*. Murphy in his **greatcoat** is a **monad** in **motion**, a **microcosm** that yet alludes to that splendid puff of clothes and appearances over inner essences: "a Microcoat" (*Tub*, 78). Other details include the "divine flatus" (89; *Tub*, 151); being "turned off" (118; *Tub*, 61–62); the sublunary excrement turning to civet (138; *Tub*, 165); and "illuminati" (177; *Tub*, 186). Consider Swift's contentions: that happiness is the possession of being well deceived ("Echo's Bones," 4); and its ancillary, the division of humanity into fools and knaves (*Murphy*, 170; *Tub*, 174). These are so evident in the **asylum** scenes of *Murphy* that their presence is a given, not merely a reference. Direct allusions to Swift largely disappear after *Murphy*, but SB's later writing suggests that he found no reason to disagree with either sentiment. See Smith, *Eighteenth Century*, 32–45, for the indirect influence of Swift into *Malone Dies* (writing from his bed) and *Watt* (madness and a fractured literary structure): "Deen did tub?" (166).

symbolism: *Watt* proclaims a final credo: no symbols where none intended (see **allegory**). Yet modernism has such intellectual roots in the French avant-garde that the debt cannot be ignored. When SB is contextualized within modernism, this rarely extends back past **Joyce**. The early modernists embraced language with confidence in its synthetic powers: for Pound and **Apollinaire**, **Rilke** and Valéry, **Yeats** and **Eliot**, whatever their tribulations, there is a fundamental optimism, embodied in the figure of Joyce who could make language do whatever he wanted. But some aspects of **Mallarmé**'s revolution were not a universal literary inheritance. With Verlaine, Mallarmé in his darker phases, and **Rimbaud** (qv), whose career ended in silence, there is radical unease, undermining the integrity of language, something that troubled the symbolists more than it did their immediate successors. SB responded to this darker side with the sense (see "**Recent Irish Poetry**") of a new crisis, a "rupture in the lines of communication" (*Disjecta*, 70). Rimbaud is a resonant figure in his imagination, and aspects of SB's work may be amplified by reading them in the wider context of symbolist aesthetics. *Three Novels* (and most of the subsequent fiction) exemplify the impulse toward inwardness, works that develop according to their own self-contained logic as words come together, combine, and react in a play of sound and semantics. External reference is subordinated to internal harmony; the resulting work of **art** is a self-sufficient linguistic universe. The "Univers spirituel" (to use Mallarmé's term), then, is the poet's mind; but with Mallarmé there is little sense that this is radically problematic (see **Murphy's mind**). However, in Rimbaud there arises the sense of the divided mind, most famously in his comment, "JE est un autre" (letter to Demeny, 15 mai 1871), the conscious "I" bearing witness to the dissociated process of thought. Rimbaud fell silent because an aesthetics of failure was beyond his reach; SB, however, inherited the legacy of failure and made it his own. [DL]

syncretism: a term describing how elements of one **religion** are assimilated into another with fundamental changes to both. **Murphy** calls this the **apmonia**; but call it what he might he fails to achieve syncretist harmony. **Gnosticism** incorporated Oriental, Judaic, Christian, and Greek concepts during the Hellenic period (300 BC to AD 300). Orthodox Christians and Jews rejected syncretistic movements, but Manichaeism combined Christianity, Zoroastrianism, and Buddhism. The narrator of *First Love* goes "all syncretist, à la **Reinhold**. What **equilibrium!**" Such equilibrium may have been Krapp's goal, for *Krapp's Last Tape* (qv) approaches light and darkness in Manichaen terms.

Synge, John Millington (1871–1909): **Abbey** dramatist. Like SB, Synge was from a Dublin Protestant background but rejected its values and credo. He went to **Trinity**, then spent time in **Paris**, where he met **Joyce**. Trained in **music**, he had a deep love of writers such as **Villon**, **Petrarch**, **Leopardi**, and **Dante** as well as European and Elizabethan playwrights. Unlike SB and Joyce, he was curious about Irish antiquities, conceiving Irish nationalism and a European **consciousness** as a necessary **dualism**, the **romantic** impulses of the one filtered through the classical and contemporary constraints of the other. SB mentioned Synge rarely, but his countryman's polished craft, aesthetic integrity, and mastery of tragicomedy significantly influenced his writing. Responding to a bold question about such influence, SB referred specifically to Synge (Knowlson and Pilling, *Frescoes*, 260). Although he had little sympathy for Synge's celebration of the peasant ethos, and hence the **Alba**'s sneer at the mists rollin' *up* and *down* the glen (*Dream*,

197), SB saw his plays at the Abbey and admired their imaginative power, lack of overt didacticism, and the poisonous pinpricks that had riled their audiences. *Murphy* jabs (106) with a "drift" of pale uneasy shapes, the word that triggered the 1907 *Playboy* riots. Synge's landscape is recognizably the **Beckett country**. **Belacqua**, planning his felo-de-se in the Dublin mountains, thinks of Synge and recovers his spirits ("Love and Lethe," 95); "**Yellow**" is set in the Elpis Nursing Home, where **Synge** died. SB's characters resemble Synge's in the way they walk the roads and in their poetic expression. *Waiting for Godot* links explicitly with Synge's world, from **Christy** Mahon's problems with his boots to ditches and turnips. SB shares with Synge the ability to turn the local and trivial into the significant and momentous, a tonality that works by oblique allusion and asymmetrical repetition with variation. His too is a drama that (in Synge's words) has the poetic feeling for ordinary life yet strives to avoid definition.

Syra-Cusa: in *Dream,* "her body more perfect than dream creek" (33) but her head, alas, null. She contrasts with the **Smeraldina**, whose face is lovely but body all wrong. She has a "lech" for **Belacqua** (50), as had Lucia **Joyce** for SB. The end comes when she leaves in a bar a precious copy of **Dante** (Lucia did this), although she makes a brief reappearance (Lucia would not get out of SB's life). The narrator is tempted to have her make **Lucien** a father, but that would be to violate the involuntary unity of his tale. The name derives from "Syracuse," the inhabitants of which (according to Lemprière) were most excellent when virtuous, but wicked and depraved otherwise. The identification with Lucia Joyce is confirmed by the legend of St. Lucia of Syracuse, renowned for her beautiful eyes. Pressed by a nobleman for her hand, she tore them out and presented them to her suitor, crying "Now let me live in **God**." Belacqua's farewell to the Syra-Cusa (179) is that she might have sent him at least *one* of her eyes in a dish. Hence, too, the conjunction of "Lucie" and "opticienne" in the poem, "**Ce n'est au Pélican**."

syzygy: in **Windelband** (244), used of the pairing of male and female deities. Ruby Tough mocks an "itch for syzygy" by suggesting **music** and malt as an efficacious remedy ("Love and Lethe," 88). In **astronomy**, syzygy arises when two bodies as seen from the perspective of a third are aligned; **Murphy** (93) is struck by the "sudden syzygy" in Pandit **Suk**'s delineations of lunatic and custodian. Compare the couplet of SB's sonnet "**At last I find in my confusèd soul**": "Like syzygetic stars, supernly bright, / Conjoined in the One and in the Infinite!" The **pun** is a syzygetic device, bringing **identified contraries** into conjunction. There are metrical meanings, two feet combined in a single prosodic unit (as "-ed in the One"), and **mathematical** ones, the tendency of a diminishing series (e.g., $1/2 + 1/4 + 1/8 + 1/16 + 1/32$) to converge at an infinite point. The narrator despairs in *Dream* (24) when he is unable to sum the terms that constitute **Belacqua**: variables are aligned but "tail off vaguely at both ends and the intervals of their series are demented."

T

Tabori, George (b. 1914): itinerant the-atrical director of Hungarian and Jewish descent, who created radical and often controversial productions in an effort to find the concrete and intelligible expression of SB's images; in his words: "The task is not to reproduce the external form, but to find the subtext" (see Anat Feinberg-Jütte's article, *JOBS* 1.1 and 2 [1992]: 95–115). His search for the subtext assumed surprising forms in a series of "dangerous theatre." "Beckett Evening I" (1980) opened in the Atlas-Circus, Munich, with circus artists and animals denoting capture, whips and whistles suggesting the Holocaust. "**Breath**" was recited stage directions and all; *Not I* presented a young actress tied to a wooden wall with knives fixed about her by a knife thrower, Listener an elephant on which the woman, freed by the elecutionary act, rode triumphantly from the arena. "**Play**" depicted the three actors walking about, seeking the lime-light to tell their story.

SB was restrained. When Tabori staged *Le Dépeupleur* he wished him "the best of agonies" but did not restrict a bizarre interpretation that combined Auschwitz with being improperly born, naked bodies, black plastic pipes, a carp in an aquarium, and the subtext of the human condition in a scorched land-scape bereft of love. Tabori's *Waiting for Godot* (1984) was acclaimed, but reports horrified SB. The characters were refu-gees, intellectuals, the subtext SB's Re-sistance activities during the **war**. *Happy Days* (1986) replaced **Winnie**'s mound by a bed, the "woman about fifty" acted by the attractive young Ursula Höpfner, in plunging décolletage. The subtext was to imbue the metaphysical with concrete human experience, that of a tense rela-tionship, but casting the handicapped Peter Radtke as **Willie** and incorporat-ing Karl Böhm's rehearsal comments about *Tristan und Iseult* with the whistles of whales was not a happy mix. Tabori was sincere in his belief that SB's writ-ing is concrete and intelligible, but his presenting "a simple and accessible Beckett" located in the images of the subtext has left some wondering how "sub" a text can be without common sense being buried.

Tal Coat, René Pierre (1905–85): pseud-onym of Pierre Jacob (Breton "tal coat" meaning "forehead of wood"); one of the "Forces nouvelles" group. Cited in the first *Dialogue* with Georges **Duthuit**. His "Franciscan orgies" (102) have "prodi-gious value," but cognate with that "al-ready accumulated," for however they may have enlarged it they still exist on the plane of the **feasible**, he is merely "thrusting towards a more adequate ex-pression of natural experience." Duthuit's query as to what other plane there can be provokes SB's celebrated "nothing to ex-press" outburst. When told by "D" that such an extreme and personal point of view is of no help in the matter of Tal

Coat, "**B**" is reduced to eloquent (and comic) silence. See *Three Dialogues*.

Tamar: widow of Onan's brother, Er (Genesis 38:2–10). Onan, son of Shuah, withdrew his obligation to his brother's widow (see **onanism**), wherefore the Lord slew him. **Belacqua** is married in the fictional St. Tamar's Church, "pointed almost to the point of indecency" ("What a Misfortune,"137).

Tantalus: the "all-wretched." Having divulged the confidences of the gods and hidden the golden **dog** of his father, Zeus (as in the **Whoroscope Notebook**), he was hurled to Tartarus and afflicted with a raging thirst and hunger. He was placed in a lake the waters of which lowered as he bent to drink; above his head fruit receded as he reached. Hence **Cooper**'s frustration (*Murphy*, 121) when the gin palace closes. *Proust* comments (13) that we are in the position of Tantalus, but tantalized by the possibility of escaping from **time**. In "**Act Without Words I**," the mute actor reaches for the receding carafe thus.

Tara MacGowran Notebook: a ninety-seven-leaf holograph notebook given to Jack **MacGowran**'s daughter, inscribed "For / Tara MacGowran / with **love** from Sam / **Paris** June 1965"; now at Ohio State University. On the cover SB wrote out a partial contents list: an early version of *Fin de partie*, *From an Abandoned Work*, a fragment from *Molloy*, other fragments. The notebook was offered at Sotheby's (July 1973) and described in its catalogue (Gontarski, *Intent of Undoing*, 43). The first seventeen

leaves contain a draft of a French story that begins "Ici on ne vient jamais" (15 mars 1952), the only date in the notebook. This is a draft of a typescript at the **BIF** (Reading), "Ici, personne ne vient jamais," and part of a sequence begun immediately after *Textes pour rien*, the **HRHRC** notebooks for which contain three other stories. See Cohn, *A Beckett Canon* (206–7).

Leaves 18 to 48 contain two early drafts of *Fin de partie*. The play is now (1955?) in a single act even though the characters are still **A** and **B**. It is written on both verso and recto in a clear hand only lightly revised. This allows no room for revision and suggests that SB is copying from notes or an earlier draft, probably a two-act version. The first version ends on the verso of 37 (loose, but taped back into the notebook) with the word "Rideau." Several leaves have here been torn away. The second draft begins at mid-play, as **Hamm** threatens to depart on a raft. This version, 38 to 47, is more typically written on the rectos with room for revision on the versos. Gontarski (*Intent*, 45) lists this notebook as stage nine in the composition of *Fin de partie*, when the two acts became one (May 1955).

The verso of leaf 48 contains the *end* of a draft of *From an Abandoned Work*, which continues to 70 where the story begins (counting from the back of the book *FaAW* runs from verso of 28 to recto of 50). On the recto of 70, also upside down, *FaAW* begins with "Up bright and early that day, I was young at the time." The verso of 71 is the end of what appears to be one of the *Foirades* (this story, also upside down, begins on 76). The verso of 77, right side up, contains an early English translation of *Molloy*, which runs to the verso of 85, "And now my progress"—the end of part I of *Molloy*. Some of this "**Extract from *Molloy***" appeared in *Transition* 50.6 (October 1950): 103–5. The recto of 86 contains a draft of a letter about the translation saying, "I can make nothing of it." The covers contain drafts of letters in French to unidentified recipients. Leaves 87 to 96 are blank. The last leaf, 97, includes seven lines of dialogue for *En attendant Godot*.

tarwater: with reference to *A Chain of Philosophical Reflexions and Inquiries Concerning the Virtues of Tarwater* (1744), Bishop **Berkeley**'s nostrum for ills of the material **body**. SB had been fascinated and horrified by the account in *A Voyage to Lisbon* of how **Fielding**, dying of the dropsy, had turned to tarwater and gained immediate relief but no lasting cure. The elixir is alluded to in *Murphy* (108).

Tavistock Clinic: a center for the diagnosis and treatment of neurotic and personality disorders, the Tavistock Clinic was established (1920) by Hugh Crichton-Miller, its founding medical director, as a clinic to provide therapy informed by **psychoanalysis** to outpatients (especially shell-shocked survivors of the Great War) unable to afford private fees. It emphasized neuroses as illuminated by the "new psychology" originating in Vienna and Zürich (see **Freud** and **Jung**). The fourfold aim was *understanding and treatment*, the furthering of *research* into causation, the hope of finding rational means of *prevention*

in mental hygiene, and *teaching* emerging skills and concepts to future specialists concerned (Dicks, *Fifty Years of the Tavistock Clinic*, 1). The Clinic's revenues derived from sympathetic guarantors and donors, public subscriptions, and such small fees as patients could afford; the medical staff often gave their services free or for minimal honoraria. While psychodynamic, the clinic had no fixed doctrine but favored flexible methods and various techniques and viewpoints. It did not grant diplomas or degrees.

The Clinic took its name from its original location in Tavistock Square, but in 1932 moved to larger premises in Malet Place, near University College. It briefly became the Institute of Mental Psychology before reverting to the original name. Direction passed to J. R. Rees in 1934, by which time Wilfred **Bion** had joined the staff. The Clinic evacuated to Hampstead at the outbreak of World **War** II, before the Malet Street Building was bombed. After the war it was integrated with the National Health Service, giving birth to the Tavistock Institute of Human Relations, separate from but linked to the Clinic. Both institutions were located at 2 Beaumont Street until the Institute acquired a house at 3 Devonshire Street in 1959. A new building in Belsize Lane, Fitzjohns Avenue, was opened in 1967 and has been the location of the Tavistock since.

The Clinic's concepts and methods derived from the French School of Charcot as represented by Freud, Adler, Déjérine, and Janet (later, **Klein** and Laing), with some of Jung. The staff viewed personality as developing from the viccisitudes of childhood with impulses formed and disrupted by inherited traits and complicated by an imperfect relationship with society. Therapy varied with the needs of the case and predilections of the doctor, but is summed up by Dicks (29) as analytic counseling with liberal doses of persuasion. The Clinic was anxious to dispel the image of neurotics as either *malades imaginaires* or useless dregs of society. A major focus of sympathy was "the educated poor," the person who had the intelligence and insight to understand the essentials of psychoneurosis and the willingness to examine themselves (Dicks, 17). SB was ideal. He was an outpatient for almost two years, undergoing therapy from Bion and attending in 1935 a lecture by Jung, which radically affected the nature of his writing thereafter.

Taylor, Jeremy (1613–67): English prelate; Christian apologist and once Chaplain to Charles I; author of *Rules and Exercises of Holy Living* and ditto of *Holy Dying* (1650 and 1651). SB asked **MacGreevy** (6 December 1933): "Why two books, Holy Living and Holy Dying, when one would have done the trick. Surely the classical example of literary tautology." SB drew on Taylor for sundry images, such as Miss **Counihan** as a Christian Soldier, Bible in one hand and poker in the other (*Murphy*, 226), or the pun "wholly dying" (see "**Fancy Dying**"). Details entered "**Echo's Bones**" (see **Aeschylus**, **Ninus**, and **Richilda**). Dr. **Johnson** admired Taylor, and in SB's "**Human Wishes**," Miss Carmichael is reading a book, eventually disclosed as "Taylor"; she quotes (not quite accurately) from *Holy Dying* (304) on unexpected **death**, the various means including the curious "by a hair or a raisin."

TCD: A College Miscellany: the undergraduate weekly at **Trinity**, to which SB contributed "**Che Sciagura**" (XXXVI, 14 November 1929: 42) and "**The Possessed**" (XXXVII, 12 March 1931, 138).

Tchoutchi: a Chinese torturer in *Eleutheria*, a grinning comic-book cliché. He extracts from Victor **Krap** ("It won't be the truth") a statement of "negative anthropology" (162), of what his life is not, "pure of all ideation" (165). Compare **Malraux**'s terrorist Chen.

Telephus: son of Heracles and king of Mysia, who assisted Priam against the Greeks and was wounded by Achilles. An oracle proclaimed that only he who had inflicted the wound could cure it; so Ulysses prevailed upon Achilles to scrape the rust from the sword. From this sprang milfoil (*Achillea millefolium*), which was applied to the wound. The relief was immediate and Telephus joined the Greeks. The sword exemplifies the "Proustian equation" (*Proust*, 11): the "double-headed" nature of **time** —damnation and salvation, creation and destruction. In "**Tristesse Janale**" the "flèches de Télèphe" (equally the arrows of Eros) have a similar duality.

Tellus: ancient earth mother, a woman with many breasts distended by the milk of fecundity. Imagining his next "vice-exister" as an inverted **Billy in the bowl**, the **Unnamable** plumps him down on "thousand-breasted Tellus, it'll be softer for him" (315).

Tempe: a valley in Thessaly between Mounts Olympus and Ossa, renowned for its beauty and pleasant climate and sacred to Apollo. SB alludes to it in "**Text 6**" (123), the **flies** at the window trapped by their desire for the warmth of the sun.

Les Temps modernes: an avant-garde **Paris** monthly, founded by Jean-Paul **Sartre** after World War II as an attempt to construct a left-wing ideology compatible with Marxism and contemporary history. Some of SB's works appeared there: "**Suite**" (July 1946; later republished as "La **Fin**"); "**Poèmes 38–39**" (November 1946); and "**Quel malheur**" (September 1951). SB's relationship with "Sartre's canard" was complicated in 1946 when Simone de Beauvoir would not publish the continuation of "Suite"; despite this "resounding difference of opinion," the journal accepted **thirteen** prewar poems for a later issue.

tempus edax [rerum]: "time devours [all things]"; from **Ovid**'s *Metamorphoses* XV.234. Cited ironically in "**Walking Out**" (113). Compare "**ainsi a-t-on beau**": "mangé sans appétit / par le mauvais temps"; and *Malone Dies* (202): "I was **time**, I devoured the world." In a letter to Mania **Péron** (6 December 1952) SB cited **Swift** to **Sheridan** on the *tempus edax* theme: "All devouring, all destroying, / Never tiring, never cloying, / Never finding full repast / Till he eats the world at last."

Tennyson, Alfred, Lord (1809–92): Victorian poet. SB recorded (DN, 167–68) a few details from diverse poems, some from his "Dream of Fair Women," that title implicit in SB's *Dream*. He noted a few lines from "The Poet's Mind," deploying some ("Clear and bright . . .") in *Dream* (87) and "**Echo's Bones**" (24), and alluding to the "purple mountains" in "**Draff**" (190). **Lucien** describes **Belacqua**'s face as "tennysonienne" (*Dream*, 20). Other references are casual: **Celia** climbing the stairs in the dark (*Murphy*, 153), as in *In Memoriam* (55); **Neary**'s "idle" tears (223), the first words of *The Princess* (*Dream*, 149); and "Crossing the Bar" (236), anticipating **Murphy**'s demise.

tertius gaudens: a third who rejoices, profiting from the quarrel of others, as the **Unnamable** postulates his self (338), bathing in a smile between **Mahood** and **Worm**.

Têtes-mortes: a gathering of short prose (Minuit, 1967), each previously published separately in small editions: *D'un ouvrage abandonné, Assez, Imagination morte imaginez,* and *Bing;* 3,000 copies were printed 21 février 1967, with a further 4,000 on 23 octobre 1968. A 1972 reprinting added *Sans.* A "tête de mort" is a death's-head.

tetrakyt: a figure **Neary** uses (*Murphy,* 5) to express his perfect love for Miss **Dwyer**; more correctly, "tetraktys," as in SB's source, **Burnet**'s *Early Greek Philosophy* (102): ten points in four lines that form "the tetrality of the dekade," or an equilateral triangle made up of {1+2+3+4}, combining all the **mystical** numbers. For the **Pythagoreans**, a figure of fire, without dross and perfectly formed. Neary in misnaming it invokes another closed figure, the kite.

"Text": a sixty-nine-line poem, published in *The European Caravan* (1931), 478–80; then, with one misprint ("by" in line 57), in the *New Review* 1.4 (winter 1931–32): 338–39. SB did not include it in later collections. Harvey offers a useful critique with the text (288–96). The **Leventhal** papers (1.i) at the **HRHRC** include a revised typescript, entitled "Text 3." Like other early poems ("**Ooftish**," "A **Casket of Pralinen**"), "Text" confronts the problem of suffering and is pregnant with intricate allusion. Ostentation is redeemed by wit, and the poem displays the demented brilliance SB would demonstrate in later works.

The poem offers six fitts, each taking as "text" a literary character or situation, which it critiques with black humor. The first (1–10) is from **Proust**, the scene in *Swann's Way* when Françoise the cook is overcome by news of the suffering in China but is unable to feel in her colon, her ilium ("in her bowels"), any **pity** for the pregnant maid, about to be delivered of a stillborn child. The second vignette (11–19) derives from **Apollinaire**'s *Les Mamelles de Tirésias,* a grotesque scene of the prophet in female form giving suck to a starving father in prison. The third (20–30) cites **Job**, troubled with the behemoth and not in the least reconciled to his suffering. His problems are addressed in the fourth section (31–36) by **Dante**, who replies to Job's "Shall I cease to lament" with "Not quite," and tells of the peacock: "he stinks eternal." This is Boccaccio's account of Dante's dream, which compares the *Commedia* to the peacock. In the fifth section (37–53), the text is Dante's rare movements of compassion in hell (*Inferno* XX.21, 25), ap-

plied to **Tiresias** ("the bitch she's blinded me"). In the final section (54–69), the tone changes from burlesque to meditation, the text being from *Inferno* XX.28: "**Qui vive** la pietà quand è ben morta." The setting is the eighth circle of Hell, into which falls the invocation "Lo-Ruhamah Lo-Ruhamah," God's prophecy to Hosea that he will have no more mercy on the house of Israel. The overall effect is chilling; the poem is one of SB's finest early works.

"Text": a short fragment from *Dream,* first published (with errors) in the *New Review* 2.5 (April 1932): 57; later rpt. (corrections, new errors) in Ruby Cohn's *The Comic Gamut* (340), and (corrected) in the *Complete Short Prose* (17). There is a typescript ("Text 1") among the **Leventhal** papers (1.i) at the **HRHRC**. It corresponds (with variants) to page 83 of the novel, as **Belacqua**'s silent parody (speaking as a cad) of the **Smeraldina**'s overtures and her criticism of his dialogue, when her own, he feels, is spoke so bad. The lover, because of her "week of redness," must suspend lovemaking yet cries for her "cony" to come and "cull" her. "Text" is considered SB's most "**Joycean**" piece, but as John Pilling has shown ("A Mermaid Made Over," 212) it features less the "multi-puns" of *Work in Progress* than the "weaving" (L. *textile,* "a fabric") of material derived from the plays of John **Ford**, in the Mermaid edition. Of its 200 words, some twenty derive from Ford. These include: "quab" (an unfledged bird) from *The Lover's Melancholy* (III.iii); "gallimaufry" ("all that gallimaufry that is stuffed / In thy corrupted bastard-bearing womb!"), "cony" ("what ferret it was that haunted your cony-berry"), and "lust-belepered," from *'Tis Pity She's a Whore* (IV.iii); "springal" (youth), "cull" (embrace), and "the newest news" from *The Broken Heart* (II.i); "puckfisted" (boaster, puffball) (II.i), "coxcomb" (III.ii), "clapdish" (a wooden vessel carried by "diseased or infectious wretches"), "foreshop" (front of shop) (III.i), "potystick" (a rod for cutting plaits and cuffs after starching), and "cornuted" (cuckolded) (IV.i) from *Love's Sacrifice,* also the source of "singly . . . to bed" (Ford's "Thus singly [one garment] I venture to bed" [II.iv]), and "goldy veins" (Ford's "dig for gold in a coal-pit" [III.ii]); and "twingle-twangle" (Gaelic harp) (III.ii) and "landloper" (wanderer) (V.iii, note) from *Perkin Warbeck.*

"Texte pour Bram van Velde": see "La Falaise."

"Textes critiques": two small appreciations of Bram **van Velde**, written much earlier, included in *Bram van Velde: Edité à l'occasion de la rétrospective Bram van Velde* (Paris: Musée National d'Art Moderne [1970]).

Textes pour rien: thirteen short prose pieces, written mostly in 1951, first published in *Nouvelles et textes pour rien* (Minuit, 1955); a second edition (1958) contained six line drawings by **Arikha**; the third edition (1965) omitted the drawings. The **BIF** (Reading) possesses a two-leaf typescript of "Texte 13," with light corrections (RUL 2916), and drafts of post–*Textes pour rien* prose. The major manuscript (HRHRC #181) is signed 1950–51, and consists of 230 pages, in-cluding abandoned texts, in two quarto spiral-bound notebooks, with numerous deletions, additions, and doodles. The choice of **thirteen** may have been predetermined, but the manuscript shows that they were composed in sequential order and confirms that they represent a unified work. See also: **"Deux textes pour rien"** (1, 12); **"Encore un pour rien"** (4); and **"Trois textes pour rien"** (3, 6, 10). Three *Textes* (4, 8, 13) appeared with short introductions in *Monologues de Minuit,* ed. Ruby Cohn and Lily Parker (New York: Macmillan, 1965), 117–32. See *Texts for Nothing.*

The first NB contains eight *textes:*

1. "Brusquement, non, à force, à force"; begun Christmas Eve 1950.
2. "Là-haut, c'est la lumière"; begun 4 février, completed 6 février 1951.
3. "Laisse"; begun 27 février, completed 5 mars 1951.
4. "Où irais-je, si je pouvais aller"; begun 10 mars, completed 12 mars 1951.
5. "Je tiens la greffe"; begun 19 mars, completed 24 mars 1951.
6. "Entre ces apparitions"; begun 24 mars, completed (Ussy) 28 avril 1951.
7. "Ai-je tout essayé"; begun (Paris) 5 mai, completed 21 mai 1951.
8. "Seul les mots pompent le silence"; begun (Paris) 25 juin, completed 10 juillet 1951.

The second NB contains five, with diagrams, charts, and mathematical calculations:

1. "Si je disais, Là il y a une issue"; begun (Ussy) 14 juillet, completed 6 août 1951.

2. "Abandonner, mais c'est tout abandonné"; begun 8 août, completed 18 août 1951.
3. "Quand je pense, non, ça ne va pas"; begun 20 août, completed (Ussy) 4 septembre 1951.
4. "Elle faiblit encore"; begun (Paris) 7 novembre, completed 23 novembre 1951 (ts. at BIF).
5. "C'est une nuit d'hiver"; completed 20 décembre 1951.

The "abandoned work" in the second NB (described thus by SB in a later note on the cover), an eighty-two-page fragment begun 2 décembre 1951, follows the last *texte*, which suggests an aborted attempt to move into a longer work on completion of the shorter pieces (see F&F, #617). The prose is heavily revised with deletions, insertions, doodles, and diagrams on the versos. Admussen notes, "Beckett's handwriting is here at its worst, and this text may well remain impenetrable" (108). Three of these largely illegible stories, however, exist in incomplete but revised typescripts at Reading **BIF**, misidentified in the catalogue as "four variant drafts of *Textes pour rien*" (182). Called after their first lines they are: "Au bout de ces années perdues" (9 leaves, RUL 1656/1), dated 22 décembre 1951 in the HRHRC manuscript, undated in the BIF typescript; "Hourah je me suis repris" (11 leaves, RUL 1656/2), dated 1 février 1952 in ms. but undated in typescript.; "On le tortura bien" (16 leaves, RUL 1656/3), the story with an unlikely trio of characters, Emmanuel, Matt, Popol, whose names are revised to "Mat et Nat et Pat" in ts., dated février 1951 in ms. but undated in ts. A fourth story, ap-parently part of this sequence since SB numbered the tss. 1–4, "Ici personne ne vient jamais" (13 leaves, RUL 1656/4), exists in an incomplete ts.; a draft appears in the **Tara MacGowran Notebook**, dated 15 mars 1952. Though in a different notebook, "Ici personne ne vient jamais" is related to "On le tortura bien" by the trio of characters, "Mat et Nat et Pat, vieux maniaques," who are joined in the fourth story by "**Quin** et **Watt** . . . et tous les autres immortels." Summaries of all four typescripts are offered by Ruby Cohn in *A Beckett Canon* (202–7).

Texts for Nothing: SB's translations of *Textes pour rien*, begun on completion of the originals (December 1951), and continued over the next year. Some appeared independently: I, *Evergreen Review* 3.9 (summer 1959): 21–24; III, trans. Anthony Bonner and SB, in *Great French Short Stories,* ed. Germaine Brée (Dell, 1960), 313–17; VI, *London Magazine* n.s.7.5 (August 1967); XII, *Transatlantic Review* 24 (spring 1967). They came out collectively in *No's Knife* (Calder and Boyars, 1967) and *Stories and Texts for Nothing* (Grove, 1967), with the six line drawings by **Arikha** from the second **French** edition and his portrait of SB on the back cover. They were published separately (Calder and Boyars, 1974 [Signature Series, #21]), the only such edition of these texts. German translation by Elmar **Tophoven**, *Erzählungen und Texte um Nichts* (Suhrkamp, 1962), predated English publication, "Text 1" preceding that: "Das erste der 'Textes pour Rien,'" *Texte und Zeichen: Eine literarische Zeitschrift* 3.14 (1957). Delicate yet difficult, they represent SB's attempt to move from the impasse of *The Unnamable,* "to get out of the attitude of disintegration" (SB to Israel Shenker, 1956). They point the way to *How It Is.*

The title derives from the musical term *mesure pour rien,* a silent measure at the beginning of a performance, a soundless interval conveying nothing but setting the tempo and so an essential part of the musical whole. It is arguable that the great dramas of the 1950s are derivative of things done earlier, and that SB's original work, the mind-breaking innovations of thought and expression as he came to terms with the complexities of disintegration, resides in the prose. Even so, these difficult texts have received little critical attention, the best accounts being John Pilling's discussion in *Frescoes of the Skull* (1979), which examines them by an aesthetics of failure; and Susan Brienza's *Samuel Beckett's New Worlds* (1987), which elaborates that theme. Gontarski's foreword to *The Complete Short Prose* sets them against *Quatre nouvelles* and sees them as performing "a leap from Modernism to Post-Modernism, from interior **voices** to exterior voices, from internality to externality" (xxv), shards and aperçus of continuously unfolding narrative that can never be complete or completed as the coherent entity of "**character**" is disbursed amidst a plurality of disembodied voices and echoes. Others have noted the impulse toward minimalism, and the instability of "I" as the distinction between the self as subject and **object** ("Not I" and "not me") is blurred. In an unpublished honors thesis (Otago, 1999), Clare Beach argues that the texture of disintegration constitutes a background, a relief, against

which the narrator struggles in vain to reconstitute a sense of identity through **memory**, and that through elusive and allusive details SB locates the narrative in his private world. That theme is further explored here.

"**Text 1**" does not so much "begin" as emerge from the empty pages preceding it, without any "signs" of character, plot, or resolution but with seemingly meaningless statements of negation ("Suddenly, no") and impasse ("I could have stayed . . . I couldn't"), which offer few concessions to understanding. The effect is unnerving, yet there is a pattern of counterpoint, a disintegrating narrative marked against yet held together by details with a biographical basis, words as stepping-stones through the quag of the unsaid. The tone is gentle, repetition creating cadence, sustained with a lilting rhythm that signals the slow entropic decline of one caught between telling and listening, the life sentence of one unable to make for himself a place in the grammatical sentence. Pilling suggests (45) that the narrator is concerned with preserving an integrated self; another emphasis might sense his holding on to an integrated narrative, however fictitious that might be. "Text 1" initiates a difficult journey, across a landscape abstract and universal yet sharply particularized, the **Beckett country** of *Molloy* and *Waiting for Godot,* and, precisely, that of chapter VII in *Mercier and Camier.* Yet the place, like the **body**, is "unimportant," and descriptions annihilate themselves: "Glorious prospect, but for the mist." An exact sense of place is paradoxically the nowhere of a story that moves away from external "description" toward a narrative about narrating. There are moments of rare beauty: the distant sea as hammered lead, the night sky open over the mountain, the final image of **father** and son; yet the tone is pessimistic. Metaphors and intertextual references delineate the process: the body as a "foundered" old hack, as at the end of "**Dante and the Lobster**"; the haggard vulture face, as in "The **Vulture**"; the biblical (**Proustian**) city and plain, as in *Molloy* (91); the **pun** about being "attached" to his **hat**; the phrase (in English only) *stultior stultissimo,* invoking **Thomas à Kempis** and his "fool for Christ," as in "**Echo's Bones**" (20); and retelling the story of Joe **Breem** or Breen, the lighthouse keeper's son, as in "The **Calmative**" (64). This fable shapes SB's text intriguingly. It fills the emptiness and offers the comfort of closure, our narrator finally able to compose himself for sleep. This will prove a false solace, a deceptive victory, for the fight on the linguistic battlefield of the self is barely engaged, and the narrator has taken refuge in a story of another, a story for **children**, rather than narrate himself into the story as it is told.

"**Text 2**" begins with a descriptive passage of night and day and the image of Mother **Calvet**. The plain telling is subverted by the double articulation of words like "endurable" (lasting, having to be endured), which creates metaphysical uncertainty and unreliability, prompting the narrator to wonder if he is better off "here," now that he "knows"; knows, that is, the horror of the light. The sense that he is somehow better off is fleeting, and he is forced to admit that he is in a head, an "ivory dungeon" (in

French, an "**oubliette**"), with a fear of coming to the last, like a **crucified** Jesus. Details are recalled (Mr. **Joly**, the verger), or misremembered (Piers pricking over the plain [see **Spenser**]), journeys, **coming and going**, an **equilibrium** sustained between negations and affirmations, and then a final image of **Schubert**'s *Winterreise* (and the **Graves** brothers) marking the futility of hope. The narrator has tried to assert a sense of connection and familiarity by remembering "above," but (unlike "Text 1") there is no comforting closure, and memory "here" will not constitute a unified self.

"**Text 3**" treats these themes intently, the differing articulation of "I am alone" and "I alone am" revealing a profound metaphysical **solitude**. There will be a departure, and he starts (not suddenly) by stirring, "there must be a body . . . I'll say it's me." This is "I" in the accusative, object rather than subject, which undercuts the effort to imagine himself into existence, as a man, an "old tot." "Text 3" introduces the body according to the criteria of **Descartes** and **Schopenhauer**, as immediate object to the self in a way that the rest of the world is not, but the narrator strains vainly toward corporeality, until he concludes, "There is no flesh anywhere, nor any way to die." Before reaching [that] conclusion, he surveys several aspects of his self: the Nanny fantasy (in English, **Bibby**, and St. Stephen's Green), which reveals him in limbo between childhood and old age; the dark blue tie with yellow stars (which SB's **mother** had given him); the desire for a crony, a fellow, to whom he can listen and tell improbable tales of war and the Easter Rising, familiarized narratives of heroism. As "Text 2" exhausted memory, "Text 3" tires imagination. Having survived, there is old age to "look forward" to: sitting and spitting; getting into the Incurables (the Mater Hospital); the "sere and yellow" (*Macbeth*); unreliable memories (Hohenzollerns); going literally and figuratively to the **dogs**; or ending up like "Vincent" (**van Gogh**), brought home for burial in the rain. He wants to "cut a caper," to be "bedded in that flesh," to move through the *carnival* of life, but in accordance with the dictum of **Thomas à Kempis**, the joyous setting out and sorrowful coming home, the story ends in a sad stasis, the jaded admission that it is all in vain, that nothing has stirred and no one has spoken.

"Text 4" asks, where would he go, if he could go; who would he be, if he could be; what would he say, if he had a voice. Simple questions are complicated by the sense of himself as stranger, the earlier "it's me" generating "for whom alone accusative I exist" (which will in turn generate the metaphor of trial in "Text 5"). A kind of **schizophrenia** ensues, between the nominative ("he" and "I") and the accusative ("him" and "me"), as pronouns vie for supremacy, the struggle generating such forms as "me who am everything." Syntax breaks down as speechlessness is intuited, the voice that cannot be his—for it is there that he would go, if he could go; it is that who he'd be, if he could be. At the end of "Text 4" he finds himself "almost restored to the **feasible**": this, in the interviews with Georges **Duthuit** (103), signifies the realm of quotidian life, from which **art** must break. In the tension between the two realms, the narrator lives out the perennial difficulty of relating life to art.

"**Text 5**" anticipates *How It Is* with the imagery of the trial, the narrator defining himself as clerk and scribe, playing the major roles in this tribunal of reason and peopling the "court" with many voices, the narrative gliding in and out of these, prosecutor, **witness**, judge, and accused. This is an "obscure assize where to be is to be guilty" (117); the crime is that of having been born, the penalty a life sentence. No manner of representation can mitigate this, but equally on trial is the language through which identity is asserted, the sentence sentenced. "Text 5" marks the disintegration of the fundamental ordering units of language, punctuation losing its power, "I" denoting the third person, and definite and indefinite articles interchangeable. The body too disintegrates, ears straining "for a voice not from without" (118), were it only to tell another lie. He is aware of the great **gulf** between himself and others present. He says: "I say it as I hear it"; this theme will dominate *How It Is*, reflecting an inability to determine (or to trust) that authoritative voice. The session ends, not entirely one of sweet silent thought, and phantoms of memory come back; weariness sets in, the quill falls (Hamlet's "special providence in the fall of a sparrow" [V.ii.233]), and though the "minutes" are incomplete "it's noted."

"**Text 6**" sustains the imagery of "Text 5" by noting the "keepers" of his **prison** and wondering how the "intervals" (the "rests" of the title) might be filled. The answer is: by memory, past "apparitions" conjured up in such a way (he imagines fleetingly) that if he cannot live again in the world the world might exist in him again, "a little resolution" being all that is needed to come and go again under the changing sky. Such "high hopes" are condemned to futility; he will fail to find the words to fill the intervals or tell a story, not because he has failed to "hit on the right ones" but because the enterprise is doomed from the start. Yet out of that "farrago of silence" intimate images arise. He recalls standing in Picadilly Circus on Glasshouse Street, and the clatter of bones and castanets (see *Murphy,* 115–16). The famous **ant** is here to memory what it was there to vision; dead **flies** that appeared in "**Serena I**," "La **Mouche**," and *Watt* are obsessional images of futility and dream; the "eyes" (of Peggy **Sinclair**) that he must have believed in for an instant will open poignantly in *Krapp's Last Tape.* These remind him of his father's shaving **mirror** that remained when his father went, and his mother doing her hair in it in her **New Place.** The butterfly refuses to be an emblem of the soul surviving **death,** and the dust remains slime despite all efforts of the Eternal and his son. The "apparitions," however fragmented, are counterpointed against the pattern of textual disintegration (tears are a "crystalline humour," and like Mercutio he jests, "I'll be grave"), so as to offer, if not high hopes, the possibility of a little story told or heard, a way of filling the interval; he gives us his word.

"Text 7" dashes such hopes, with its despairing query, "Did I try everything?" The **purgatory** of waiting is imaged in the "Terminus" where he sits in memory, as so often in the past, in the third-class waiting room of **Harcourt Street Station** whence trains departed for **Foxrock.** He recalls when he could move, but **motion** has slowed and the narrative loses momentum. He compares himself with **X,** "that paradigm of human kind, moving at will," a carcass in God's image with wife and brats, and tries (in vain?) to distance himself from such a likeness. The station turntable parodies the *Paradiso,* the universe rotating about God; the sense of waiting at the Terminus and the vision of Eternity are transposed into the remarkable image of the balance wheel of the station clock, which effects the transition from timelessness to time passing. Although **time** has slowed, and this text has been a static interval, tentative conclusions are reached, but not in haste, "not so fast": that to search for himself elsewhere would be a "loss of time"; that there is no time to lose; that the time has come for him to begin. This seventh text, the midpoint of **thirteen,** is the balance wheel of the sequence.

"**Text 8**" reverts to the silence, broken only by words and tears, assuming its place on the continuum of decline and reflecting a deep pessimism directed at both the inevitability of aging and his "stupid old threne." Continuing the imagery of imprisonment he imagines himself thrown out by the past, or having burrowed his way out, for the moment free of memories. But what is an old lag to do? He does not understand whom he can have offended to have been punished this way, and he repeats the old cry: "It's not me, it can't be me." A bifurcation takes place, one self as a ventriloquist's dummy in the image of a head left behind, in **Ireland,** perhaps, "that other who is me," while to his "certain knowledge" (the irony is unstated) he is somewhere in Europe. While the sense of living by proxy is manifest, and the "right aggregate" unlikely, he cannot but see himself as in imagination he might be, with a white stick and ear trumpet, at the Place de la République adjacent to the **Père Lachaise**, begging for alms without any concession to self-respect (a "previous song"), yet simultaneously aware that this was not him, not his real self.

"**Text 9**" suggests a way out, an image more powerful in French where "issue" generates a sense of the **issueless** predicament of existence, Molloy's "senseless, speechless, issueless misery." Yet **Dante**'s image of the beauties of the skies and stars, at the moment of emergence from the *Inferno,* is powerful in both languages. This is how "Text 9" concludes, and so the narrative vibrates between these two polarities, the predicament less resolved than contemplated. As befits his textual history, the narrator has "convictions," but these pass, and he feels himself instead buried beneath an avalanche of "wordshit," unable to dig himself out, his alternative to the prison the graveyard, emphatically *there* ("là"), as the "way out" is not. But *something* is struggling to emerge, which he can't quite grasp, and although everything is in the conditional ("if I could say") and there's a "minor" difficulty about the body, Dante's great image has revived (if only momentarily) the "high hopes" of "Text 6."

"**Text 10**" knocks such nonsense on the head. Time to give up, the heart's not in it anymore, the appetite not what it

was. There is uttering, agreed, but the image of the mouth as anus of the head defines the worth of what is expelled. This is a pessimistic little text, sentences connected by "and" and "or" in a vain attempt at meaningful concatenation, and with a **Malone**-like lapse: "This is awful, awful, at least there's that to be thankful for." The prospect is unredeemed misery, with the barest gesture toward "a voice of silence" (143), the theme of what follows. "Text 10" closes with the narrator's attempts to sleep, but the closure possible at the end of "Text 1" is here reduced to a verbal wish, less than an act, as befitting one not really there.

"**Text 11**" struggles to begin, when all sense of the self is "scattered by the everlasting words" (a pun on "winds"), where nothing is namable. One possibility is the musical turn, adding "him" to the repertory, executing him "as I execute me," one dead bar after the other, the puns giving a double articulation of movement and death. The outcome is vaguely successful, like a patch of sea under the passing lighthouse beam, a comforting reminder of the closure in "Text 1." He knows the triumph is delusory, vile words to make him believe he's here, but he can affirm he's getting **on**, getting on, though the repetition makes the assertion less convincing. The theme he is trying to utter begins: "when come those who knew me"; but its first articulation failed and the second is "premature" (the imagery of birthing sustained). Striking images of his condition are executed: the square root of minus one, an imaginary number rendered symbolically as i (something less than "I"); a student's face covered with ink and jam, the phrase *caput mortuum* implying "worthless residue" but meaning literally "dead head"; then as an old clot (French "con") alone in the two-stander urinal on the corner of the Rue d'Assas (in French, "dans la vespasienne à deux places rue Guynemer"), rending the air with painful ejaculations (physical and religious), Jesus, Jesus. These, and especially the last, are moving and compelling images of the humanities he insists he has terminated; through these he is able to overcome, if only temporarily, the disjunction between the "I" and the "he" and move to the third utterance of the failed theme. This time it's going to work: "when comes the hour of those who knew me . . . it's as though I were among them," in their "**company**." Thus, "he" *is*. For all its insistence on failure, this is a text carefully structured to build to this triumph, dubious as it must be.

"**Text 12**" returns to the *Winterreise,* a journey toward death. Picking up the theme of identity ("so long as the others are there"), he sets aside "believing in me," or the need for a voice and the power to move as *witness* of his existence, of his being "on earth." He sees his body as a "veteran" (Napoleon's retreat from Moscow may be implied), the "me" in "him" remembering, forgetting. Although (changing the metaphor) he is trapped in the dungeons of this moribund, this represents his "last chance to have been," to listen to the voices that are everywhere, and again to ask, Who's speaking? This composite sense of being, the "me" in "him" and the awareness that sees the disjunction (the "I"), is described

as "a pretty three in one," a Trinity of sorts (in French, "un joli trio"), but the hypostasis is insubstantial, "one" being equally "no one." Finally, he is back to a point of departure, "the long silent guffaw of the knowing nonexister," **Democritus**, for whom **Nothing** is more real than nothing. The hard-won victory of "Text 11" must be set aside, for to accept it as reality would be like joining the accountants' chorus, "opining like a single man," that is, accepting unquestioningly the existence of the body ("riding a **bicycle**") and the need for a god as ultimate witness, whereas the reality is, as it was and ever shall be, "nothing ever but nothing and never, nothing ever but lifeless words." The *Winterreise,* if it has not moved beyond this point of departure, has negated any other option.

"**Text 13**" is an elegy to the dying voice, the "weak old voice that tried in vain to make me," which has foundered (like the old hack of "Text 1") on the nothingness of being. Still, it "embodies" the unnamable indefinable incomprehensible impossible urge to express, to leave a "trace" of its passing, of the life that has passed. This text reaches an equilibrium between the forces that have shaped the others, a kind of peace as the "I" of self is absorbed into the "it" of voice, a *diminuendo al niente* that is also an affirmation, the authoritative voice at last assuming its role as subject of the narrative. For the narrator, now almost absent, this is the end of the farce of making, of the silencing of silence, of the wish to know, an acceptance of death and of the inevitable failure of his attempt to create himself, a startling reminder of which yet breaks out in the extraordinary metaphor of "no's knife in yes's wound," a scream that stains the silence to which the text aspires, a "trace" of its author's passing. In the final sentence the narrator takes his farewell of the light, the verbal tense moving from the subjunctive ("were there one day to be") and conditional ("all would be silent") to the **mythological present**: "it murmurs." Against the odds, despite all, "a coda worthy of the rest" has emerged, a poetical apotheosis of the impossible paradox of being and not-being.

Thales: of Miletus (ca. 625–547 BC), Greek philosopher famous for his practical wisdom. He predicted an eclipse, discovered the right angle in a semicircle, and determined the height of a pyramid by measuring its shadow. He believed that water was the primary element, and his doctrine of the One and the Many informed Greek thought until **Plato**. He is mentioned in "**Serena I**," the poet emerging from the British Museum (where SB in 1932 read the **pre-Socratics**), and citing the sentiment that **Aristotle** in *De Anima* attributed to Thales: "all things full of gods," only to sense its irony in a brutal world, and alluded to later in the poem: "I surprise me moved by the many." Thales created the emblem of **Time** as an old man, bald save for one lock on the forehead (*Murphy*, 114).

That Time: a one-act play, written between 8 June 1974 and August 1975; translated as *Cette fois* and into German (by Elmar **Tophoven**) as *Damals*. First **London** production at the Royal Court, 20 May 1976, dir. Donald **McWhinnie**, with Patrick **Magee** as Listener, celebrating SB's seventieth birthday. The first American production followed that December, dir. Alan **Schneider**, at the Arena Stage, Kreeger Theater, Washington, DC, with Donald Davis. Published by Faber (1976) for the British premiere. First American printing in *I Can't Go On, I'll Go On*, ed. Richard Seaver (Grove, 1976), then collected into *Ends and Odds* (Grove, 1976; Faber, 1977; Grove "enlarged edition," 1981). SB directed it in Berlin at the **Schiller-Theater Werkstatt** (October 1976), with Klaus Herm, revising the translation in the process. The French text was published by Minuit (1978) and collected in *Catastrophe et autre dramaticules* (1982).

SB wrote to George **Reavey** (1 September 1974): "Have written a short piece (theatre): *That Time. Not I* family." The emphasis was to be on listening, not speaking; in *Not I*, he said, "she talks"; in *That Time* "he listens." Because the later play was "cut out of the same texture" as *Not I*, he did not want the two on a double bill (Brater, 37). The stunning, mannerist theatrical device is Listener's face, slightly off center, a disembodied head ten feet above the stage, listening to three **voices** (recorded, not performed) coming from the dark as aspects of his past. The stage image is an exercise in perspective, the head with hair flared as if seen from above, the audience presumably below the feet like the illusionistic *di sotto in sù* technique in Andrea **Mantegna**'s *Foreshortened Christ*. Stunning as it is, SB had "serious misgivings over disproportion between image (listening face) and speech," of accepting its remoteness and stillness "as essential to the piece & dramatically of value" (Harmon, 324). In the **theatrical notebooks** for his 1976 Berlin production he stated the problem in terms of minimalist aesthetics: "To the objection that visual component too small, out of all proportion with aural, answer: make it smaller, on the principle less is more." The aural component is richly textured, as if **Krapp**'s different selves are manifest in a staging of "**What Where**," taunting Listener's emotions and **memories**. The voices take on an interrogative function, repeatedly asking, "When was that," or "Was that the time or was that another time," three seconds into which Listener's eyes close in retreat or defense, a withdrawal that ceases only after the voices stop in the two ten-second pauses that punctuate this text and in the final longer pause.

The title combines **Wordsworth**'s "Immortality Ode": "That time is past," with **Shakespeare**'s Sonnet LXXIII: "That time of year thou mayst in me behold." Its text is taken from Proverbs 26:11: "As a **dog** returneth to his vomit, so a fool returneth to his folly." The folly is first a structure, as O'Brien notes (350), called "Barrington's Tower" in the first manuscript (RUL 1477/1), then changed alliteratively in the final text to **Foley's Folly**, a childhood **memory**. A recalls an old man wanting to return to the ruin where he hid as a child. He hoped to take the number 11 **tram** to the end of the line at Clonskeagh and go "on from there" (SB told O'Brien that this was a route his father often took, although it does not go directly to Foxrock), but "the truth began to dawn"; there is "no getting out to it that way,"

for the trams no longer run, their "old rails" are left to rust. He goes to the **Harcourt Street** terminal for the **Slow and Easy**, but that is closed and boarded up. For the child, the ruined Folly provided refuge, a place to read and create **company** into the night, while the family searched for him. A's physical return fails, but on the stone doorstep waiting for the night ferry (clutching his night bag, drooling, long white hair pouring from under the **hat**) he finds himself "at it again," re-creating the childhood experience (like the author, perhaps), making up stories, one voice and then another, drooling, eyes closed, an object of derision to those who pass by.

B recalls a youthful, celibate **love** ("no pawing in the manner of flesh and blood") at the moment of its demise through separation, the "one thing could ever bring tears." Its re-creation, with images of the sun, the sand (see **Silver Strand**), golden wheat, "stone like millstone," **Lao-tzu**, and a drowned **rat**, keeps "the void from pouring in on top of you the shroud." When words fail and the void billows in, "little or nothing the worse."

C is a broken man, last of his family, taking refuge from the rain in the **London** National Portrait Gallery, where he experiences the shock of a ghostlike **face** emerging from an oil black with age. The face reflected might be his own, that of the guard coming to put him out, or a composite of both overlain on the portrait beneath the glass; "never the same after that." Such a "turning point" was a "common occurrence" for C in his "lifelong mess," his attempts to determine "whose **skull** you were clapped up in." One significant turning point was **birth**, "when they lugged you out." Two others pertain, one in the Post Office (Trafalgar Square, opposite the National Portrait Gallery?), where the failure of *percipe,* no one paying attention to him, suggests nonbeing, and one in the Library where C perceives "nothing only dust." There is fear in a handful of dust, since it suggests **God**'s admonition of Adam, "dust thou art; unto dust shalt thou return" (Genesis 3:19). This image of **death** also speaks: the **comings and goings** of a lifetime have "come and gone." The three sequences, each distinct, are woven into an intricate pattern of echo and repetition: faces; **greatcoats**; figures sitting on stones; biblical allusions, such as the parable of the Good Samaritan ("the passers pausing to gape"), closing of eyes, and human folly, in love as in life. The play is as metatheatrical as anything SB has written, Listener audience to his own narrative as he echoes the theater audience's piecing together fragments of a ruined past into a comprehensible narrative, a life.

The narrative segments were clearly worked out before their fragmented patterns, the manuscript outlining the structure and shape of ideas: characters A, B, and C. The duration of each speech was planned in advance (3 x 5' of speech, with silence after 5', 10'). One manuscript is divided into three vertical columns, A, B, and C, into which SB put each burst of speech in the correct order, the sections separated by "Silence 10 seconds. Breath audible. After 3 seconds eyes open." The pattern of narrative and voice before the first pause is ACB ACB ACB CAB; the next CBA CBA CBA BCA; and the third is BAC BAC BAC BAC. There is no instance of ABC, but the regularity of the third pattern generates a sense of order and hence serenity, the consolation in art for ruin in **time** and the folly of existence, and so the final toothless smile. Or like the revised ending of "**Eh Joe**," the closing smile may suggest an end to or a suppression of, at least for a time, the interrogating voices, since the final silence is extended from ten to at least **thirteen** seconds. Whatever its provocation, the final smile is the most startling image of the play.

Théâtre I: a hardback assemblage (Minuit, 1971), capitalizing on SB's **Nobel Prize** (1969). The volume has no dust jacket but was published with a yellow sheet announcing the prize. It includes: *En attendant Godot, Fin de partie,* and "**Actes sans paroles**" (I and II).

Theatrical Notebooks: a series of edited director's notebooks and revised acting texts of the major plays, under the general editorship of James Knowlson, issued jointly by **Grove Press** and **Faber** in a series entitled *The Theatrical Notebooks of Samuel Beckett.* Based on SB's notebooks, which are reproduced in facsimile and transcription, they offer a remarkable record of SB's involvement with the production of his texts, practical problems of staging, the way that he envisaged his own plays, notes and annotations from his copies of the plays, and changes in his conception of the major works. They comprise:

I. *Waiting for Godot,* ed. James Knowlson and Dougald McMillan (1994)

II. *Endgame,* ed. S. E. Gontarski (1992)
III. *Krapp's Last Tape,* ed. James Knowlson (1992)
IV. *The Shorter Plays,* ed. S. E. Gontarski (1999): "**Play**"; *Footfalls; Come and Go;* "**What Where**"; *That Time;* "**Eh Joe**"; and *Not I*

A prototype *"Happy Days": Samuel Beckett's Production Notebooks,* ed. James Knowlson, was published by Faber and Grove (1985) in a different format.

Thérèse Philosophe: described by Praz (*Romantic Agony,* 98) as "a coarse piece of pornographic fiction" (1748) by Darles de Montigny, and invoked as such in *Dream* (80). Thérèse was **Sade**'s heroine, before she became Justine. Montigny's novel improves on the Marquis's cynical view (that virtue leads to misery, vice to prosperity) by accepting that the passions implanted by **nature** are the will of **God**. Thérèse abandons herself to wantonness, to her profit and satisfaction.

thirteen: neither superstitious nor afflicted with **Joyce**'s *triskaidekaphobia,* SB toyed with this number. His fascination with "**M**" may reflect its being the thirteenth letter of the alphabet; the thirteen poems that form *Echo's Bones* suggest Joyce's *Pomes Penyeach* (1927), twelve and a tilly. *Murphy* from the outset would have thirteen chapters; there are thirteen *Texts for Nothing;* and the narrator of *How It Is* complains: "damn it I'm the thirteenth generation" (83). Good Friday fell/will fall on April 13 (SB's birthday) in 1759, 1770, 1781, 1827, 1838, 1900, 1906, 1979, 1990, 2001, 2063, 2074, 2085, and 2096, a **series** of erratic hendecacolia.

This Quarter: like *transition,* which in some regards it imitated, *This Quarter* was a small, avant-garde literary magazine, edited from Milan initially by Ernest Walsh and Ethel Morehead then, with #3, from Monaco by Ms. Morehead alone after Walsh passed away. Edward W. Titus took it over with volume 2 (1929). Along with running a rare bookshop, at the sign of the Black Manikin (4 Rue Delambre), Titus published limited editions of several expatriates, in particular Anaïs Nin and the memoirs of Kiki de Montparnasse, subsidized initially by his estranged wife, cosmetic magnate Helena Rubinstein. Volume II.4 (1930) included a "Miniature Anthology of Contemporary Italian Literature," edited by Samuel Putnam, to which SB contributed translations of Eugenio Montale's "**Delta**," Rafaello Franchi's "**Landscape**," and Giovanni Comisso's "The **Home-Coming**." André **Breton** guest-edited the celebrated "Surrealist Number" V.1 (September 1932). It was a coup for Titus, Breton accepting on the understanding that the issue would be devoted to surrealist work. Titus gave Breton carte blanche, then deleted "politics and such topics" if not "in honeyed accord with Anglo-American censorship usages"; Breton's happiness, he said, was "not complete" (Lake, *No Symbols,* #23).

Breton spoke no English so the translation of his material was a major obstacle. In his editorial, Titus paid tribute to those involved, but singled SB out for special praise: "His rendering of the Eluard and Breton poems in particular is characterizable only in superlatives" (6). Titus had paid some 700 francs for SB's translation of **Rimbaud**'s "**Drunken Boat**," but it never appeared as *This Quarter* ceased publication after volume 5.2 (October/December 1932), which included "**Dante and the Lobster**."

SB's contributions to the "Surrealist Number" of *This Quarter:*

André Breton: "The Free Union" (1931): 72–73; "Lethal relief" (1932, from *The Whitehaired Revolver*): 74–75; "Factory" (1921, from *The Magnetic Fields*): 75; "Soluble Fish" (prose, 1924): 75.

Paul Éluard: "Lady love": 86; "Out of sight in the direction of my **body**": 86–87; "Scarcely disfigured": 87; "The invention": 87–88; "What is the role of the root?": 88; "The art of living" (prose): 89; "Yet I have never found" (prose, from *The Rehearsal,* 1922): 89; "Definition" (prose): 89; "The Queen of Diamonds" (prose): 89–90; "Do thou sleep" (prose, 1930): 90–91; "Second nature" (from *Love and Poetry,* 1929): 92; "Scene": 92–93; "All proof" (from *The Immaculate Life,* 1932): 94–98.

Breton and Éluard: "The possessions" (prose): 119–20; "Simulation of mental debility essayed" (prose): 121–22; "Simulation of general paralysis essayed" (prose): 123–25; "Simulation of the delirium of interpretation essayed" (prose): 126–28.

René Crevel: "Everyone thinks himself phoenix . . ." (prose, from *Diderot's Harpsichord*): 158–65.

"**thither**": a poem of seventeen short lines, included in *Collected Poems in English and French* (1977), 36, where it is dated 1976. The poem is a muted lament "for one / so little"; it utilizes the cliché "a far cry" and hints at **Herrick**'s "fair daffodils," which haste away so soon, to make the contrast of "then there" and "then thence."

Thomas à Kempis (1379–1471): born Thomas Hamerken near Düsseldorf in Kempken, whence his name, and trained in a tradition of mystical theology and practical benevolence. When conviction of sin and visions of **God**'s grace came to him in a dream he decided to join the Augustinians and was sent to Zwolle, in the Netherlands, to the convent of Mount St. Agnes; he was received in 1399, professed the vows in 1407, received priest's orders in 1413, and became subprior in 1425. He is described (in the 1929 *Britannica*) as the most placid and uneventful of all men who ever wrote a book or scribbled letters. He left several chronicles, mostly relating to convent life (the only one he knew), three collections of sermons, letters and hymns, and the *De Imitatione Christi*. He died there on 8 August 1471, in the odor of sanctity, assuredly.

The *Imitation* is a masterpiece of Christian **mysticism** that has moved the hearts of many as an expression of the inward life. In the early 1930s, at the instigation of Thomas **MacGreevy**, SB read it in the earliest English translation, edited by John K. Ingram from a manuscript at **Trinity** (once belonging to John Madden, founder of the **Madden Prize**). Six pages of entries in the **Dream Notebook** show that SB read books I to III in what Ingram calls the old version and book IV in the translation by Lady Margaret, mother of Henry VII, frequently paraphrasing rather than copying; but several Latin citations indicate that he had an unidentified original at hand. Ingram's archaic flavor and idiosyncratic expression attracted SB. **Belacqua** likens **Lucien**'s appropriation of the "Black diamond of pessimism" (from Gérard de Nerval) to "the little sparkle hid in ashes, the precious margaret" (III.lx; Ingram, 140; *Dream,* 47–48). Belacqua claims that in **D'Annunzio** "You couldn't experience a margarita" (the biblical pearl of great price), because he denies the pebbles and flints that reveal it, as compared with, say, **Racine** and **Malherbe**, pitted and sprigged with sparkles. He concludes with prescience: "they write without style, do they not, they give you the phrase, the sparkle, the precious margaret. Perhaps only the **French** can do it. Perhaps only the French language can give you the thing you want" (48).

Incorporation of phrases from the *Imitation* into the early prose reflects a delight more recondite than reverent. The borrowings are identified by Pilling in the DN (some deployed several times). They include: Belacqua's "prods of compunction" (I.i; Ingram, 2); the **Alba**'s "humiliter, simpliciter, fideliter" (I.v; Ingram, 7); "hurting of conscience" (I.x; Ingram, 11); Doyle's tattooed tum-tum, "Stultum propter Christum" ("a fool for **Christ**") (L.xvii; Ingram, 19), in "**Echo's Bones**" (20); and "internus homo" (II.v; "Ding-Dong" 38), the "inward man" of *Dream* (63). Gide's dismissal as "swine's draff" (*Dream,* 46) reflects Ingram's "I sawe hem delite in swynes draf" (III.xv; Ingram 83), referring to the "shreudenes" or depravity of fallen angels. SB delights

in the empty husks of grain, lees left after brewing, fit only for feeding to swine, devoid of all goodness; he had wanted to use "**Draff**" as the title of the entire volume that became *More Pricks Than Kicks.*

Such echoes are not confined to the early works. One enduring motif is the "Laetus exitus tristem" theme, that a merry outgoing brings forth a sad homecoming (I.xx; Ingram, 25). SB cites this in the DN (83); uses it in *Dream* (16, 129); and redeploys it in "Ding-Dong" (37): "It was very nearly the reverse of the author of the Imitation's 'glad going out and sad coming in.'" "**Sanies I**" is structured on the *laetus exitus* theme, all heaven in the sphincter (going out), but disillusionment (coming home). SB used the phrase in a letter to MacGreevy (see below) and in *Murphy* (103) to describe Rosie **Dew**'s sad return from the park. After he bought from Jack **Yeats** a Sligo skyscape called *Morning,* SB described his elation to MacGreevy (May 7, 1935) as "always morning, and a setting out without the coming home." Consider the increeping and outbouncing house and parlor maids of *Watt* (50). **Moran**'s "setting out" (*Molloy,* 98) anticipates his sad return; but in *From an Abandoned Work* the narrator's life is ordered by the daily journey and return, "in the morning out from home and in the evening back again" (159), the precept of joy and sorrow defining his unhappiness at home. In "**Text 1**" the voice defines itself as "stultior stultissimo, never an imprecation, not such a fool" (103), a distant rattle of "Echo's Bones" and the fool for Christ. Other writings conceal the "pretiosa margarita, a mul tis abscondita";

in SB's rendering, "a precious margaret & hid from many" (III.xxxvii; Ingram, 108), one of Thomas's loveliest lines. The protagonist of *How It Is* hopes for "a pearl" (25), "a little pearl of forlorn solace" (43), and offers "marguerites from the latin pearl" (77). Such echoes are few but precious, the "little sparkle hidden in ashes" testifying quietly to something that has endured, the movement toward the "Internus homo" or "inward man," whose acquaintance SB would increasingly cultivate.

SB responded (10 March 1935) to MacGreevy's recommendation that he should find comfort in *De Imitatione Christi* by defining himself as one who never had the least facility for the supernatural, and so had attempted to replace the terms used by Thomas with others: "I mean that I replaced the plenitude that he calls 'God', not by 'goodness' but by a pleroma [a totality of divine attributes] only to be sought among my own feathers and entrails." He doubted he was now any more capable of approaching the hypostasies and analogies "meekly, simply & truly" (I.v; Ingram 7) than when he first "twisted them into a programme of self-sufficiency." The chief problem with the *Imitation* was that if certain forms of conduct are commended by the way, "it is very much by the way," and incidental and secondary to the fundamental contact for Thomas with God, so that any attempt to read "goodness & disinterestedness" every time for "God" would be to assert the accidental for the essential, to mince the text to allow for the skeptical position, and to replace a principle of faith, "absolute & final," by one "personal & finite of fact." He could

not see how "goodness" could be a foundation or beginning of anything, or that "disinterestedness" would relieve in any way "the sweats & shudders & panics & rages" of the **irrational heart**, simply because his motives are unselfish and the welfare of others his concern: "Or is there some way of devolving pain & monstrosity & incapacitations to the service of a deserving cause? Is one to insist upon a **crucifixion** for which there is no demand?" For years, SB claimed, he was unhappy, "consciously and deliberately," and he linked his symptoms with feelings of arrogance that had characterized his dealings with others. He would have continued thus were it not for his "old internal combustion heart," which brought him to an awareness of mortality by putting the fear of death into him, even though **Bion** had told him that it was only the "least important" symptom of a diseased condition beginning in his prehistory, "a bubble in the puddle." His treasuring of "fatuous torments" and sense of being the "superior man" were part of the same pathology, and he could not see how this allowed of any "philosophical or ethical or Christlike imitative pentimenti" [the remergence of a design painted over], nor how these might redeem a composition that was invalid from the word go and had to be broken up altogether.

This implies a rejection of Thomas, and Mary Bryden (*Idea of God,* 29) accordingly accentuates SB's rejection of "an abject and self-referring **quietism**" in favor of the "**Humanistic Quietism**" promoted in SB's 1934 review of MacGreevy's *Poems.* She considers that for SB the asceticism of Thomas à

Kempis amounted to "an unhelpful path to isolationism" (34). Yet this is less a rejection of the *Imitation* than of its dogma. SB's ethics remains more self-referential (or isolationist) than **humanist** as he acknowledges the heart, which might yet receive consolation "from the waste that splutters most when the bath is nearly empty." He is discussing his irrational heart in its physical and metaphorical manifestations, and with skepticism. What emerges from this detailed response to the *Imitation* is an almost reluctant acceptance of the **way**, that of the solitary sparrow, mapped out by Thomas. That he could not believe in it (*impossibile est*) is no more of a paradox than his feelings for the seventeenth-century philosophers he loved but in whom he could no longer have faith. Having denied the efficacy of the *Imitation* as solace, and turning again toward himself, SB nevertheless shows how much the text influenced him, the ostensible denial of its ethics negated by his recognition of the change in his innermost being.

SB reconciled Thomas à Kempis and Arnold **Geulincx** (whom he was reading at this time) in their renunciation of the will and affirmation of humility, there being a striking similarity between Thomas's "in cubilibus vestris compungimini" (I.xx; translated by SB as "Be ye sorry in your chambers") and Geulincx's retreat into the **little world** of the mind, where freedom is possible. SB's letter to MacGreevy offers many phrases from I.xx of the *Imitation,* "Of the Love of Silence and Solitude," for SB its most enduring part, while the "solitary bird" (IV.xii; Ingram 276) he uses as summary

is for Thomas the image of one enclosed in his chamber. Thomas's retreat to his "celle wel continued" where "In silence & quiete profiteth the deuote soule" (I.xx; Ingram 25) has an affinity to both "**Sedendo et Quiescendo**" and Murphy's rejection of **desire** as he enters his innermost mind.

Where SB parts company from Thomas, as from **Augustine**, **Descartes,** and Geulincx, is at the point of transcendental validation. Yet that departure is not simple. Throughout the later works the quietism of Thomas à Kempis is implicit not only in the unflinching acceptance of "the ingenuous fibres that suffer honestly" ("A **Casket of Pralinen**") but in the enduring impulse toward the cubicle, where Thomas in silence and in quiet could profit his soul, his withdrawal from "seculer noyce" permitting God to "nye unto him" (I.xx; Ingram 25). For SB this was not an option, yet the very impulse toward the realm of calm is thwarted by "this meaningless **voice** which prevents you from being **nothing**" (*The Unnamable,* 370), the indistinct but insistent presence of "an ancient voice in me not mine" (*How It Is,* 7). The theme that preoccupies the later works rises out of the quietism and **solitude** of the early years.

Thomas, Dylan (1914–53): Welsh poet, whose **romantic** impulses and celebration of the processes of life and death set him at odds with SB, but with whose lyrical intensity and witty observation of detail SB has much in common. *All That Fall* on its first broadcast was compared in *The Listener* with *Under Milk Wood* as a "radio classic." Thomas reviewed

Murphy on its first appearance ("Recent Novels," *New English Weekly,* 17 March 1938, 454–55), appreciating its "energy, hilarity, irony and comic invention," but dismissing its wit as "Sodom and begorrah" and decrying the influence of Joyce and "those who have made *transition* their permanent resting place." An echo of Thomas ("Do Not Go Gentle") may be present in *The End,* with the narrator's recollection of being with his **father** at evening "on a height," like Thomas's father "there on the sad height."

Thompson, Geoffrey (1904–76): SB's friend at **Portora**, the two "kindred spirits" in their shared sense of humor, interest in literature (Conan Doyle, Stephen Leacock, **Keats**), as opening batsmen for the First Eleven (see **cricket**), and in their refusal to join the Officers' Training Corps (Knowlson, 54). At **Trinity**, they often went to the **Abbey**, notably during the riots at **O'Casey**'s *The Plough and the Stars* (February 1926). Thompson studied medicine and was a physician at the Rotunda Hospital, **Dublin**, when in July 1933, after the **death** of his father, SB sought help for his "**irrational heart**." Thompson saw the root of the problem in SB's relationship with his **mother**, and suggested **psychoanalysis**. SB went to **London** and began an intensive course of psychotherapy at the **Tavistock Clinic**. "**A Case in a Thousand**" (qv) is based on a story told by Thompson about a woman who attended her sick son and, after he died, kept vigil on the canal towpath (Knowlson, 175). Thompson went to London in February 1935, "sumptu-

ously installed" as Senior House Physician at the **Bethlem Royal Hospital**, where SB visited him, to talk and play **chess**. One visit (3 September 1935) culminated in a tour of the wards. SB made extensive notes in the **Whoroscope Notebook**, turning the experience into the **asylum** scenes of *Murphy*. When Thompson married Ursula Stenhouse (2 November 1935), in West Lulworth, Dorset, SB found himself "booked for the misfortunes of Hairy" (SB to TM, October 1935), to act as best man. Thompson set up in private practice as a London analyst; SB suggested to **Joyce** that Lucia might consult him, but nothing came of this. SB often made contact when he was in London, and Thompson contributed to an RTE program on SB (April 1976), only a month or two before his unexpected death from a massive heart attack left SB saddened and feeling his own vulnerability.

Three Dialogues: Samuel Beckett and Georges Duthuit: three conversations about **art** and criticism between SB and Georges **Duthuit** (art historian and son-in-law of Matisse) about **Tal Coat**, André **Masson**, and Bram **van Velde**. Published in *Transition Forty-Nine* 5 (December 1949): 97–103, and signed "Samuel Beckett and Georges Duthuit"; republished with *Proust* by John **Calder** (1965), under the cover title, "3 dialogues with Georges Duthuit"; included in Martin Esslin's, *Samuel Beckett: A Collection of Critical Essays* (1965); then in *Disjecta* (138–45), where the title was inadvertently shortened to "Three Dialogues." That oversight set a pattern, replicated by Calder, who in his "Beckett

Shorts" #2, *Dramatic Works and Dialogues* (1999), reprinted them as a work by SB, calling them "The Duthuit Dialogues" only on the back cover. The **French** translation is simply called *Trois dialogues* (Minuit, 1998; for the largely specious argument about proper attribution of authorship, see **Duthuit**).

SB's dialogues are very much with Georges Duthuit but equally with the issue of *Transition* in which they appear. Stylized as they are, they are drawn from actual conversations that were reworked and published at Duthuit's insistence that SB make his views better known. They reflect the fourth of SB's certainties: that we were born, we exist, we will die—and the one that is absurd, that subverts the others, "The expression that there is nothing to express, nothing with which to express, **nothing** from which to express, no power to express, no **desire** to express, together with the obligation to express." In this self-deprecating piece, SB exploited the performative and travestied aesthetic debate and the philosophical dialogue favored by **Plato**. The tradition included George Berkeley's decidedly undramatic *Three Dialogues between Hylas and Philonous* (see **Berkeley**), echoes of which persist into *Fin de partie,* which SB began writing shortly thereafter. The *Dialogues* may owe something to W. B. **Yeats**'s dialogic poems. Also unappreciated is the tone: the piece is cast as a music-hall turn, with "D" as prompt and "**B**" as an intellectual **clown**. By all rational rules of debate, D is the winner; it follows, therefore, that B has succeeded in failing.

The "obligation to express" is found in the first dialogue. B contends that al-though the "Franciscan orgies" of Tal Coat have prodigious value, they nonetheless represent a "certain order on the plane of the **feasible**." Asked what other plane there can be, B replies that logically there is none, but art must do more than the same old thing, "going a little further along a dreary road." The second dialogue continues the first, B contending that the problems Masson set himself in the past have lost their legitimacy, and that he is "skewered on the ferocious dilemma of expression." D cannot disagree with the assessment of Masson's gifts, his technical variety, and an art that "endures and gives increase," so B, with nothing to say and no means of saying it, must "Exit weeping."

The duel is resumed in III: "Frenchman, fire first." Here B invokes (and D acknowledges) an art of a different order, of one (Bram van Velde) obliged to paint, helpless to paint, an art that (B admits, a fortnight later) is inexpressive. As such, he would say, it is of a higher order than Masson's "wriggles" or the "every man his own wife" experiments of "the spiritual **Kandinsky**." The debate climaxes in B's longest utterance, where Bram is celebrated as the first to admit that to be an artist is to fail, as no other dare fail. But B will not affirm that, in bringing this "horrible matter" to conclusion, he (or Bram) is in any way making an expressive act, even of the impossibility of such obligation. This perspective is endorsed in a letter to Duthuit (9 mars 1949), in which SB discusses the importance of "rapport"—not only that between the artist and the world outside, but also of the impulses within him; the painting of Bram, he contends, is the first to reject "rapport" in all its forms. His painting instead offers "refus et refus d'accepter son refus . . . Pour ma parte, c'est le *granrifuto* [the great refusal] qui m'intéresse" (see **Celestine**).

Critics too often ignore the context of these dialogues, their place within the particular issue and among the particular issues of *Transition Forty-nine* #5. The dialogues grew out of letters and café conversations not about SB's latent aesthetics in the abstract but about particular artists, essays, and issues in this issue. The *Dialogues* follow André du Bouchet's essay, "Three Exhibitions: Masson—Tal Coat—Miró." SB may have substituted van Velde for Miró because the piece that follows the *Dialogues* is "Some Sayings of Bram van Velde," in which van Velde's impoverished aesthetics sounds very Beckettian: "I have nothing in my pockets, nothing in my hands. Where shall I find what I need" (104). One section called "Documents," an assessment of aesthetics in the postwar era, contains Masson's attack on the "aloof" Modernist aesthetics of art for art's sake. For Masson such prewar work is merely decoration, "with nothing to decorate." He calls, like **Sartre**, for art in the post—World War II era to contribute "to the liberation of man, to the transmutation of all values, to the denunciation of the ruling class responsible for the imperialist and fascist regression." SB's response to such "wriggles" is the aesthetics of failure.

The impact of these *Dialogues* has been considerable, both on SB's work, which from the ***Three Novels*** to the end of his career is implicated in the art of failure, and in terms of the critical dialogue with SB's work. Peter Murphy is skeptical on this point, arguing that Martin Esslin in particular has privileged the sense of an author trying to shape an **existentialist** nothing, and that the tremendous outpouring of formalist readings of SB's work disregards other aspects of his achievement. *Three Dialogues* has chimed with poststructuralist aesthetics in such a way as to encourage interpretations of SB's work that are governed by a pessimism concerning the expressive powers of language: de-centering the discourse, deconstructing it, acknowledging vanishing structures, and seeking transient traces. Another thesis to emerge from the *Dialogues,* more Modernist than Post-, is to see them as exemplifying the impossible and problematical in modern art, but with self-conscious mockery. The danger of this approach is of reducing SB's radical irony to a further "statement of a compromise," itself an enlargement of the plane of the feasible. If so, one might agree with Hesla (4), and with an admission implicit in SB's later interview with Tom Driver (23), that the *Dialogues* are not really as revolutionary as might first appear. Rather, they have achieved in and of themselves and for their subject what artists everywhere have sought—that having admitted the mess, the task of the artist is now (as ever) to find a form to accommodate it.

Three Novels: SB's preference for what is often called *The Trilogy:* the English translations of the three French novels, ***Molloy, Malone meurt,*** and *L'Innommable,* written in an intense burst from May 1947 until early 1950, the sequence interrupted before the last by *En attendant Godot*. Unusually, the writing entailed little revision, and the manuscripts reflect a white-hot outpouring, with minor changes only (a few jests and some specifics were added later). The pages are dated, indicating the place and time of writing, an invaluable record of SB's mode of composition, which indicates a correlation between the writing process and the manuscript, with admissions of fatigue evidenced by a different pen the next day and, curiously, a tailoring of *L'Innommable* to finish on the last page of its second notebook. The three were conceived as two but the need for the third became apparent during writing; hence some anomalies at the outset of the French *Molloy*, which SB "corrected" only in translation. They were published in one volume by **Olympia Press** (1959; Traveller's Companion #71), **Grove Press** (1959), and John **Calder** (1960). The first paperback appeared from Grove (1965), the British slow to follow. No collected French edition was published. As Ruby Cohn contends (*Comic Gamut*, 114), the three might well have been named "L'**Expulsé**," "Le **Calmant**," and "La **Fin**." SB told Gabriel d'Aubarède how the sequence began: "J'ai conçu Molloy et le suite le jour où j'ai pris conscience de ma **bêtise**. Alors, je me suis mis à écrire les chose que je sens." Like others, the two authors of this study are divided as to whether the novels are best considered as separate pieces or as parts of a greater whole, but would agree that the three explore the common theme of the search for the self through the gradual elimination of the world of men, of bodily functions, and of the writer writing, until there remains the **voice** alone, attempting the impossible articulation of the "**Not I**."

Three Occasional Pieces: writing to Barney Rosset (31 December 1980), SB included the typescript to "**Ohio Impromptu**" and suggested that it be published with "**Rockaby**" and "A **Piece of Monologue**" as *Three Occasional Pieces*. Rosset wanted to include "**Enough**," but SB objected: "I don't feel that 'Enough' belongs here" (it had already been published by **Grove** in *First Love and Other Shorts* [1974]). Grove published them as *Rockaby and Other Short Pieces* (1981), substituting ***All Strange Away*** for "Enough." **Faber** followed SB's wishes and published the three under his suggested title (1982).

"**Three poems**": English versions only of "**Trois poèmes: Three poems**"; reprinted without variant in *Poetry Ireland* [Cork] 5 (April 1949): 8.

Ticklepenny, Austin: Pot Poet of *Murphy*. The name suggests one who "tickles pennies" as another might trout (**Sheridan**'s brother-in-law was Tickell, a poetaster and minor dramatist), writing doggerel and flattery for small recompense; here, £1.6.8 a month plus the fancy of **Bim**, not far short of **love**. That fails to inure him to abuse from the mentally deranged in his role as male nurse at the **MMM**. The portrait is SB's revenge on Austin **Clarke** for slights real or imagined. Ticklepenny, dismissed as the merest pawn in the game (85), may (or may not) exact his revenge (see **suicide**).

Tiepolo, Giovanni Battista (1696–1770): Italian master of the fresco, unsurpassed in his mastery of grandeur, rich and glowing color, and decorative art. He worked in Venice until 1750, when he was called to Würzburg by the Prince Archbishop to decorate the Kaisersaal and grand staircase of the Residenz, his masterpieces. SB visited Würzburg in 1937 and gives his memories to **Malone** (235): "Tiepolo's ceiling at Würzburg, what a tourist I must have been, I even remember the diaeresis." The jest is recondite: in the manuscript SB had written "Wurzburg" with neither diaeresis nor comment.

time: in his unpublished dissertation on SB's early work, Terence McQueeny notes (133) **Schopenhauer**'s refutation of **Kant**'s position that human cognition retains no existence, essence, or reality *except in time,* by means of his doctrine of the eternity of the present: "As the ideal limit which separates the past from the future the present is as unreal for the senses as a point in **mathematics**. But if it is inaccessible to empirical **consciousness** it can be seen as the supreme reality for the metaphysical." This insight encapsulates SB's sense of the inexplicable paradox of time. *Whoroscope* won a competition by the **Hours Press** for the best poem on time. Its delineation of existence *ab ovo* to the final starless inscrutable hour (see "**Assumption**") anticipates the enigma that would haunt SB's writing from its beginning to the inevitable end.

Proust opens by examining "that double-headed monster of damnation and salvation—Time." Proust's "crea-tures," SB states (12), are the victims and prisoners of time, with no escape from the hours and days (the essay rejects the Kantian time/space paradigms, time expressed as "literary geography," in the language of extension). Yesterday is a "calamity" (13), because the eternity of the present means that there is no escape save by **memory** (qv). **Habit** (qv) deadens the suffering of being only *temporarily,* that is, in time. Time, Habit and Memory (even the Proustian "solution" of *involuntary* memory) constitute a "Janal, trinal, agile monster or Divinity," from whose jaws there is at best "accidental and fugitive salvation" (35).

This is **tempus edax** (qv), time devouring all, a sentiment expressed in the "mauvais temps" of "**ainsi a-t-on beau,**" and in *Malone Dies:* "I was time, I devoured the world" (202). "**Arènes de Lutèce**" dramatizes the *unheimlich* dislocation in time, the experience of alterity. **Belacqua** likens the dribble of **time** to **sanies** into a bucket ("Yellow,"167). The time-space continuum is annihilated when **Murphy** meets **Celia** "at the usual at the usual" (8). *Murphy* is a novel in which the narrative (that which unfolds in time) is plotted (that which extends in space) obsessively, SB using **Whitaker** to determine the grid. The dark zone of **Murphy's mind** is a locus, yet a tumult of non-Newtonian **motion** in which the normative space-time laws are suspended, until, that is, he comes *from* (113, 105). The **Unnamable** cannot measure time, "which in itself is sufficient to vitiate all calculation" (299). **Watt** is moved, he knows not why ("Watt knew nothing about **physics**"), by the circle and its center, "in boundless space, in endless time" (129). His split between inner and outer experience becomes disjunctive, as the Kantian sense of time, not measurement but inner form, a category structuring the consciousness of being, breaks down. This disjunction within the **microcosm** is reflected in the big world, through the problem of the individual in a **serial** universe. As Richard Coe puts it, either Tom is temporal, in which case his being is determined by his place in the series; or else he is a-temporal (a-spatial) and independent of the series. He cannot logically be both. And yet, says SB, this is precisely what he is. Human existence is a logical impossibility, for it belongs to yet evades the series; it is at once in and out of time.

The impact of time cannot be dismissed by such sophistry. In *Waiting for Godot*, the waiting is real and immediate, **Godot** imponderable, **ineffable**. Life is slow **crucifixion**; habit and routine help pass the time that would have passed anyway but not so rapidly (**Proust** in pieces, basic Bergson). When **Vladimir** suggests that time has stopped (24.b), Pozzo replies: "Don't you believe it, Sir, don't you believe it . . . Whatever you like, but not that." Act II is shorter than Act I, but it does not seem so. Things have changed since "yesterday" (that Proustian imponderable). Time has wreaked its effect, for **Pozzo** is blind and **Lucky** is mute. Pozzo insists that the blind have no notion of time, that the "things of time" are hidden from them too (55.b); when Vladimir persists, he explodes: "Have you not done tormenting me with your accursed time" (57.b). One day Lucky went dumb, one day he went blind, one day we'll go deaf, one day we were born, one day we shall die: "the same day, the same second, is that not enough for you?"

The sense of the world running down, time running out, drives much of the later work. *Endgame* iterates the motif of "little by little," time broken into incremental elements that may or may not "mount up to a life" (see **Zeno**). As **Hamm** says: "But we breathe, we change! We lose our hair, our teeth! Our bloom! Our ideals!" (11). Something *is* taking its course. Disintegration is temporal, yet rendered spatially, a moment as a bit of grit in the middle of the steppe (36), the clock wound up as the world winds down. Yet the movement toward homeostasis, in a world of asymptotic time, does not correspond to the reality endured by the individual. The everyday routine and the sense of time passing intimate no change, for when **Clov** asks what time it is, he is told, "The same as usual" (4). It is a day like any other (45), but perhaps, just maybe, this could be the day, *the* extraordinary day, when something has "slipped."

Or it may be "busy-ness" as usual, as in "**Act Without Words II**," in a world that varies little from day to day. The narrator of *From an Abandoned Work* desires "a long unbroken time without before or after" (163); *How It Is* intimates vast tracts of time, endless wastes before and after. Yet the sense of an enduring present is identical: "the space of a moment the passing moment that's all my past little **rat** at my heels the rest false" (*How It Is*, 16). The ambiguous syntax ("that's all / my past" or "that's all my past") ensures that the present formulation is not so neatly disposed of, for even in this attenuated world, memory disrupts the conviction of the eternity of the present.

This is the experience of **Krapp** and of the narrator of *That Time*, both of whom attempt vainly to fix some part of their life in time. They remain starkly representative of SB's narrative figures whose journey through life has culminated in vague regrets, a sense of nostalgia or loss because they have tried to retain something of their identity and being in time. The impulse does not go, but in the late **closed space** writing such portraits give way to a form of still life. *Stirrings Still* plays off the impulse to arise and go with that to sit still, and culminating in the stilling of "Time and grief and self so-called" (265). "A **Piece of Monologue**" (265) translates a life into "Two and a half billion seconds [some eighty years]. Hard to believe so few." The narrator is acutely aware of the "ghosts" of those dead. *Company* (29) offers an improbable "seventy American billion" (22,400 years). This response is complex, a counterpoint of stillness and contracted space ("Imagine closer"), of place and time, the one fixed, still, but the other ephemeral, the span of a life. The same sentiment is expressed in the image of the narrator spending the night watching the second hand of his watch going round and round, following or preceding the shadow it makes on the dial. A central image of *Ill Seen Ill Said* (76–77) is the "Close-up of a dial," a stopwatch with "sixty black dots," advancing by fits and starts, leaping from dot to dot with "so lightning a leap but for its new position it has not stirred," each second set to a compass point. In the last stories ("**As the Story Was Told**," *Stirrings Still*, "**neither**," "**La Falaise**," and the "**Variations on a 'Still' Point**") time has apparently slowed and space contracted, so that minimal **motion** takes place in maximal time to bring about a creative homeostasis. These works represent the final shadowing of a life SB first outlined in his early essay on Proust; and confirm the implicit promise made there, that "In Time creative and destructive [SB] discovers himself as an artist" (78).

Tintoretto: Jacopo Robusti (ca. 1518–94); Italian painter, known as Tintoretto ("little dyer") because his father was a *tintore*. After struggling for recognition, he became a great of the Venetian school, celebrated for his mastery of color and depictions of the human form. *Origin of the Milky Way* (1580), in the National Gallery, **London**, depicts Jupiter's attempt to guarantee the immortality of his son by the mortal Alcmene by raising the infant Hercules to drink from the sleeping Juno, who, waking suddenly, spills her milk in two streams, one falling to form lilies on the ground and the other creating the Milky Way. Seeing the countless distant points of light, **Moran** thinks of "Juno's milk" (*Molloy*, 159); compare the comment in Lemprière (**Democritus**) that "the milky way was occasioned by a confused light arising from a multitude of stars." In **Murphy**'s less than reverent response, the look on Juno's face and the stars emerging from the nipple like a cartoon depiction of pain suggest that the goddess has been awoken by a painful nip on the nipple.

Tiresias: prophet of Thebes, who in his youth tried to separate two copulating serpents and was punished by being changed into a woman; seven years later he repeated the offense and was changed back again. This qualified him as arbiter in the dispute between Zeus and Hera as to which sex experiences more pleasure in love. Siding with Zeus, he was blinded by Hera, but in compensation Zeus gave him the power of prophecy. His steps were guided by his daughter Manto when they fled Thebes after its fall. Tiresias died after drinking the icy waters of the fountain Telphoussa, which froze his blood. His story is told in "Text" (51–53): "the bitch she's blinded me! / Manto me dear / an iced sherbert and me blood's a solid." After **Moran** has left his little paradise by the wicket gate, he passes down the lane that skirts the graveyard wall and soon is "faring below the dead" (*Molloy*, 135); the analogy is that of Tiresias leaving Thebes.

"To Be Sung Loud": an unpublished twenty-line poem among the **Leventhal** papers (1.i) at the **HRHRC**; a reworking of "**From the Only Poet to a Shining Whore**," with differences of phrasing and an unattended **Nabokovian** "spears of pale fire."

Toffana: wife of **Mercier** and mother of his children: "Like fucking a quag" (84). *Aqua tofana* is a poison containing arsenic, the "Wine of the Borgias" from which Pope Alexander VI died in 1503. Named after a Sicilian woman strangled for murdering hundreds of men and used by young wives wanting to get rid of their husbands.

tohu-bohu: an image of chaos in the first **biblical** creation myth, transliterated from Heb. *tohu-wa-bhohu* in the King James version as "without form, and void" (Genesis 1:2). SB invokes it in *How It Is,* "shat into the incredible tohu-bohu" (42), the scatology returning in the subsequent reference to "YOUR LIFE HERE BEFORE ME utter confusion" (73–74).

Tolomea: a division of Cocytus, the fourth river of Hell in **Dante**'s *Inferno* XXXIII.124, in which are punished those who murdered guests and friends, as did Ptolemy XII, King of Egypt (51–47 BC), after whom it was named. Mentioned in *Proust* (56) and echoed in "**Ding-Dong**" (45): "her tiresome Ptolemy."

"To My Daughter": an unpublished poem among the **Leventhal** papers (HRHRC). The fifteen lines vary "**Hell Crane To Starling**," but without the wit. Yet compare *Company* and "**Heard in the Dark II**," the **memory** of waiting for the woman (see Mary **Manning**) perhaps pregnant with the daughter SB did not have: "never will you see that glabrous cod [Belacqua] / flaunting a Babylonian belt." That is, called from afar (Mary had returned to Boston), as in Ezekiel 23:14–16, where the whore Aholiba sees on the wall the Chaldeans "pourtrayed with vermilion," and, doting, "sent messages unto them into Chaldea." Instead, this Aholiba will remain content with her comely donkey and fed ass (Mary had returned to her husband), for, as the poem finally states: "what more do you want."

Tophoven, Elmar (1923–89): born in Straelen on 6 March 1923. Although he translated many famous authors, including Alain Robbe-Grillet, Claude Simon, and Nathalie Sarraute, "Top" is best known for definitive German translations of most of SB's drama, poetry, and prose. He became the first postwar *Lektor* at the Sorbonne (1949) and later succeeded Paul Celan as *lecteur* at the **École Normale**. Through Arthur Adamov he was introduced to SB in the early 1950s. His role as SB's translator began with *En attendant Godot*. Erika Schöningh, later to become his wife, became involved with *All That Fall* in 1957, as Tophoven had no formal training in English. Many later texts, particularly those translated from an English original, are credited to both Elmar and Erika. SB and Tophoven collaborated in revising SB's dramatic texts for his Berlin productions. Their efforts resulted in a text that "makes its own statement in translation just as it does in English" (Tophoven, "Translating Beckett," 324). The German translations sometimes appeared before SB's English or **French** versions, and SB's translations often reflected his work on the German texts. When revising the German SB tended to bring it into line with the English versions, which he increasingly preferred (his revisions are detailed in the *Theatrical Notebooks*). The German text often provided significant linguistic and stylistic insights and thus acted as a parallel version alongside SB's original. In 1978 Tophoven founded the Europäisches Übersetzer-Kollegium in Straelen as a center for translation studies. His **friendship** and translation with SB continued until his **death** (23 April 1989). [JG]

Tous ceux qui tombent: subtitled "pièce radiophonique"; the translation by Robert **Pinget**, with SB (whose name does not appear), of *All That Fall*. Published in *Les Lettres nouvelles* 5.47 (mars 1957): 321–51; anticipating the paperback (Minuit, 1957). The play was broadcast on French radio (19 décembre 1963) but made less of an impression than the RTF television version (25 janvier 1963), with which SB was not happy.

Toussaint l'Ouverture: François-Dominique Toussaint (ca. 1743–1803); liberator of Haiti, who claimed descent from an African chief and changed his name from "Breda" to "l'Ouverture" to recognize his valor in causing a gap in the ranks of his enemies. In 1796, having raised an army of blacks, he made himself master of the country, renounced the authority of France, and announced himself as the Bonaparte of Santo Domingo. Captured by the French he died in prison in Besançon (27 avril 1803). SB's translations for *Negro* include Jenner Bastien's "Summary of the history of Hayti" and Ludovic Morin Lacombe's "A note on Haytian culture." Caught in a squall (*Dream*, 31), **Belacqua** envies Toussaint-l'Ouverture, either because of the tropical climate or because he resents customs officers. Seeking his independent **voice**, the **Unnamable** despairs that he is no longer **Worm** but "a kind of tenth-rate Toussaint L'Ouverture" [*sic*] (349); compare Wordsworth's sonnet, "22nd September 1802," from which SB earlier quoted, "Most unhappy Man of Men."

tram: combining **motion** with inevitability, like the author in *Dream* (150). The

Polar Bear describes it as an "accursed bolide," or meteor (158). **Watt** first appears, to the reader, when a tram stops short of the station and the conductor's voice is raised in anger. No explanation is forthcoming, and the incident of the faculative stop anticipates other imponderables. Similar mysteries persist in the works of Puncher (conductor) and Wattmann (driver), as invoked by **Lucky**. In *That Time* the voice of **A** recalls the disappointment of returning to **Dublin**: "no no trams then all gone long ago . . . not a tram left in the place only the old rails"; buses had completely replaced trams by 1949 (O'Brien, 367). The more poignant, then, SB's favorite limerick:

> There was a young man who said,
> "Damn!
> I suddenly see what I am,
>   A creature that moves
>   In predestined grooves—
> In fact, not a bus but a tram.

Transfiguration: **Christ** took Peter, James, and John up into an high mountain, "And was transfigured before them" (Matthew 17:2). This is Christ as Messiah, revealed in his glory but as Suffering Servant. The festival is August 6; **Malone** hopes to pant on till then (179).

transition: an avant-garde literary magazine subtitled "An International Quarterly for Creative Experiment"; founded in **Paris** by American-born Eugène Jolas and his wife Maria, to promote a "Revolution of the Word." In 1924 Jolas was hired by the Paris edition of the *Chicago Tribune* as literary editor, replacing Ford Madox Ford. His weekly column, "Rambles Through Literary Paris," later served him well as editor and founder of *transition,* the first issue of which appeared in April 1927. The journal ran for twenty-seven sporadic issues until 1938. Its contributors represented the antibourgeois tradition of European art and literature, including German Expressionists, Dadaists, and **Surrealists**. Its primary intention was to form a bridge between European experimentalism (loosely, Modernism, although Jolas saw it as another mode of **Romanticism**) and emerging currents in American art. As Jolas said in his introduction to the first issue, "*transition* wishes to offer American writers the opportunity to express themselves freely, to experiment, if they are so minded, and to avail themselves of a ready, alert and critical audience." Its most famous contributor was James **Joyce**, whose *Work in Progress* appeared in issues 1 to 8, then in 11–13, 15, 18, 21–23, 26–27—eighteen fragments in ten years. Issues that did not contain Joyce's work usually contained an essay about it. SB was delighted to be associated with *transition,* and published in issue 16/17 (1929) his essay "**Dante . . . Bruno . Vico . . Joyce**" and his first short story, "**Assumption**." Issue 19/20 included "**For Future Reference**"; #21 "**Sedendo et Quiesciendo**" [*sic*]; #24 "**Malacoda**," "**Enueg II**," and "**Dortmunder**"; and the journal's final issue, #27, "**Ooftish**" and a commentary on "**Denis Devlin**." Jolas's "**Poetry Is Vertical**" (qv) manifesto appeared in #21; SB was an unconverted signatory. See Dougald McMillan's history of the era, *Transition 1927–1938* (1976).

By 1938 **war** seemed inevitable, and the aesthetic, orphic magazine was out of step with the times. Jolas ceased publication, but after the war he edited *Transition Workshop: An anthology of work published in transition 1927–38* (New York: Vanguard Press, 1949). This included "Assumption" (41–44) and "Malacoda" (204), the former more carefully proofread. After the war, Georges **Duthuit** sought to develop a new journal to introduce French literature to the English-speaking world, but paper was rationed and denied to new publications. Jolas offered Duthuit the name of the defunct *transition* and accepted a title as advisory editor for *Transition Forty-Eight,* the title capitalized and the year forming part of it. In addition to several unsigned translations that SB did for the new *Transition,* including a story called "F——" by his wife Suzanne, he contributed "**Trois poèmes: Three poems**" (1948); "**Three Dialogues**" (1949); and "**Two Fragments**" (1950).

SB's translations (mostly unsigned) for the postwar *Transition* include (F&F, 97–99): "Apoem 4," by Henri Pichette; 2 (June 1948): 24–43 (French text on the left) "F——," by Suzanne **Dumesnil**; 4 (January 1949): 19–21 "**Some Sayings of Bram van Velde**"; 5 (December 1949): 104 "Armand, Last Chapter," by "Emmanuel Bove"; 6 (October 1950): 99–102 "**Zone,**" by Guillaume **Apollinaire**; 6 (October 1950): 126–31 Parts of Duthuit's article, "**Sartre's Last Class**"; 1–4 and 6 (1948–50); precise sections unknown "The Revenge of a Russian Orphan," by Henri Rousseau, trans. Jack T. Nile [SB probably only checked this]; 3 (October 1948): 41–46.

trilogy: *Three Novels* may have been conceived as a duo, for the first begins (after a paragraph written later): "Cette fois-ci, puis encore une je crois." In English this became: "This time, then once more I think, then perhaps a last time." The first novel was probably conceived in two parts (**Molloy**'s and **Moran**'s), with another to follow, so that a tripartite structure would have been implicit. SB resisted "trilogy" in relation to these *Three Novels,* and equally of the later three works that constitute the "second trilogy" of *Nohow On* (*Company, Ill Seen Ill Said,* and *Worstward Ho*). When John **Calder** asked (29 December 1957) to use "Trilogy" on the jacket with the three books listed beneath, SB replied (6 January 1958): "Not 'Trilogy,' I beseech you, just the three titles and nothing else." He later reiterated (19 December 1958): "TRINITY would not do. It seems to me the three separate titles should be enough." He took a similar line with **Grove Press**, telling Barney Rosset (5 May 1969) that he couldn't bear the thought of "trilogy." He would consistently refer to the "so-called trilogy." The Picador reprint authorized by Calder (1979) is entitled *The Beckett Trilogy,* and the British edition of *Nohow On* refers to the three later works as a trilogy, for which Calder was suitably taken to task by John Banville (*NYRB,* 13 August 1992, 20). Yet "trilogy" or not, the three novels in each sequence form a cohesive and extended exploration of the imaginative **consciousness**. In the first, the "disintegration" and "dying" of the old self in *Molloy* and *Malone Dies* are essential precursors to the expression of the **Not I** in *The*

Unnamable, just as the "devising" and **aporia** of *Company* and *Ill Seen Ill Said* suggest the inevitable impasse in the ineluctable aesthetic march "worstward."

trim: a possible prototype of **Molloy** was "Stoney Pockets," an eccentric who walked round Dublin with a tilt, using stones to straighten himself (O'Brien, 95). Concerned for his **equilibrium** (71), Molloy invokes "the principle of trim . . . like a verse of Isaiah, or of Jeremiah." The reference is Jeremiah 2:33: "Why trimmest thou thy way to seek **love**." Thus **Moran** trims his lamp, an emblem of **Christ** watching over those who sleep (he cannot). The **Unnamable**, having lost his appendages, finds himself "in sorry trim" (327). In **"Act Without Words I"** and *Happy Days* (20), the protagonists trim their nails.

Trinity College: Elizabethan University of **Dublin** and intellectual center of the Anglo-Irish Ascendancy, TCD was the alma mater of **Swift, Berkeley, Sheridan,** Burke, and **Synge,** the bastion of a proud tradition of scholarship, and the repository of vast learning. The College was predominantly Protestant, Catholics until recently forbidden to enter unless granted a special dispensation by the Archbishop of Dublin (O'Brien, 120). SB came to Trinity as a scruffy student in October 1923 to study Arts and Modern Languages; he graduated with a BA in 1927, even scruffier but with a fine record of scholarship, a training of the mind, and a love of literature that would thereafter underlie what he would later dismiss (see **"Gnome"**) as "the loutishness of learning." The received idea that the

creative SB somehow had to reject the scholarly SB is simply untrue; rather, SB's reading during his Trinity years and those following formed the foundation of his later writing; never again would he read so widely, or so intensely.

SB's passion for literature developed under the influence of his professor of French, Thomas **Rudmose-Brown.** "Ruddy's" affections combined an unusual respect for the canon with a relish for what was happening in the world: a mixture of the traditional (**Villon, Rabelais, Ronsard, Racine, Corneille,** Molière), the recent (**Rimbaud, Baudelaire, Mallarmé, Valéry, Hugo**), and the contemporary (**Proust,** Vielé-Griffin, Fargue, Le Cardonnel, Larbaud, Jammes, **Malraux, Gide**). This integration of past and present, long before SB had heard of **Eliot's** "Tradition and the Individual Talent," would henceforth characterize his way of reading. The Trinity syllabus was demanding and thorough (see Smith, *Eighteenth Century,* and Pilling, *Beckett before Godot*). The system encouraged wide reading: not just *Andromaque* but all Racine; not just the *Drapier Letters* but all of Swift. SB's love of **Dante** (a third-year course) grew under the external guidance of Bianca **Esposito,** but he absorbed **Petrarch, D'Annunzio,** Machiavelli, **Leopardi,** and Ariosto. He took courses in English: **Spenser, Shakespeare, Donne, Milton,** More, **Bacon,** Pope, and Swift. Like many of his time, he rejected the Victorians and the "ineluctable gangrene of **Romanticism**" (*Proust,* 80), excepting always **Keats.** Like **Joyce** before him, he reacted against the Twilighters, saving only W. B. **Yeats** (O'Casey and **Synge** were separate loves). He read widely in the eighteenth century, both in English and French. SB gained not so much a degree in literature as an opening to the mind of western Europe, with German (**Hölderlin, Goethe**) and Spanish (**Calderón**, Cervantes) natural extensions, as were the Greek thinkers, Latin poets, and post-Cartesian philosophers he would later study. Trinity was not so much an education as a cornerstone of knowledge. SB's next decade would build upon that, the love remaining even as the skeptical distrust of its value grew.

SB entered Trinity at seventeen, living for two undergraduate years at home then moving in to #39 New Square, as in *Dream* (72); when he returned as a lecturer he occupied #40. His tutor was A. A. Luce, an authority on **Descartes** and **Berkeley** and with whom he sustained a distant but friendly relationship. For two years he took a variety of courses, including **mathematics**, Latin, and English literature. By his third year he moved into modern languages, with French and Italian as Honours subjects, and his academic record improved dramatically. He attained fourth in his class and was elected to a Foundation Scholarship in Modern Languages (1926). Among his distinctions were first of First Class Honours in Italian, and First Class in French, English literature, and modern literature, a French Term Composition Prize, a Senior Exhibition, and a First Class "Little Go" (Bair, 40, citing the *Irish Times* of 1 June 1926). His final year was marked by equal success: first of First Class in modern literature in the 1927 autumn exams, and first place in French and Italian in the Finals, a Gold Medal and a £50 prize. In March

1927, he was nominated for the Trinity College exchange lecturer to the **École Normale Supérieure, Paris**. His appointment was delayed for a year because of a misunderstanding over the tenure of his predecessor, Thomas **MacGreevy**. He spent nine months teaching at **Campbell House** before taking it up in October 1928.

The Trinity years were crucial for other reasons. SB started going to the theater, seeing premieres of O'Casey's *Juno and the Paycock* and *The Plough and the Stars* and revivals of Synge (a partial list, ticked off by SB, is included in the **BIF** archives). The **silent movies** would leave indelible marks on his later work. He developed an abiding affection for the old masters, with a special love of the seventeenth-century Dutch tradition. He fell in love, with Ethna **MacCarthy** and then with his cousin Peggy **Sinclair**. He reduced his golf handicap to 6 or 7 on the nearby Carrickmines course, and in his third year won his "pink" by representing Trinity in **cricket**. He played **chess** and **billiards** as well as joining the University Motor Cycle Club to race his AJS. And he traveled abroad, touring the Loire valley in the late summer of 1926 and **Florence** in 1927. These were busy and stimulating years. SB was shy and retiring and during his fourth year began to reveal signs of introspection, but they were not unsociable ones.

Returning to Trinity, SB accepted a three-year appointment as Lecturer in French, at a salary of £200, with annual increments to £350. In Paris, he had intended to work on **Jouve** and **Romains** and aspects of "**Unanimisme**"; according to Knowlson (87) he probably completed a research essay before going, as a condition of the award. However, his writing now assumed different directions. He had launched his literary career with *Whoroscope* and an essay on Joyce; *Proust* would soon follow. During his absence, *TCD,* the College Miscellany, had published "Che Sciagura," and shortly after his return he gave a talk to the Modern Language Society, by the invented poet Jean du **Chas**, and took part in "Le **Kid**." He lectured on Racine, de **Vigny**, de **Mussett**, **Balzac**, **Stendhal**, **Flaubert**, and **Bergson**; read intensively among the **pre-Socratics** and medieval lyricists, **Schopenhauer** and **Kant**; and came to an appreciation of English novelists, particularly **Fielding**. The scrupulous honesty of Jules **Renard** was a major discovery. Yet he did not feel comfortable in his new role. His European experience made him unhappy with the insularity of Dublin, and tensions at home led him again to take rooms at the college. Friendship with Georges **Pelorson** and Alfred **Péron** helped, as did the acquaintance of Jack B. **Yeats**, but he felt isolated, and teaching, he claimed, was like exhibiting himself—how could he teach others what he did not know himself? Bair caricatures his method (123), but his students remembered him kindly, and the notes of Rachel Burrows [**Dobbin**], now at Trinity (MIC 60), and those of Leslie **Daiken**, at the **BIF**, testify to the soundness of what he said (notably, some fine comments on Racine). But he was not suited to teaching, describing it to MacGreevy as "the horseshow"; the thought of going back to it was "paralyz-

ing." The relationship with Peggy Sinclair had become fraught, and his physical health was poor, the "**irrational heart**" and black depression, perhaps of a psychosomatic nature, rendering him incapable of work. At the end of 1931, having gained his MA and taken flight to **Kassel**, SB wired his resignation. Con **Leventhal** was appointed in his place. It was not an easy decision. SB regretted having let down his family and having lost, he felt, the best, but it was a necessary move in a process of intellectual growth, the pattern of which he might intuit but could not yet clearly discern, let alone justify.

The Trinity years were crucial to SB, the smithy in which his soul was forged, even as it took Paris to temper it. He published more critical writing than many "successful" academics do in a lifetime; he made many literary contacts and lasting friendships; and he lived through experiences that would enter directly into his writings. Several fine poems ("**Enueg II**," "**Gnome**") rose from the bleakness, while *Dream* and the stories of *MPTK* expressed in fictional form his experiences. The summary of this first decade as a writer, yet bringing it to a close, was *Murphy*, its philosophical and literary allusiveness both a tribute and a farewell to the learning he had imbibed and (r)ejected.

Echoes of Trinity haunt the later works. In "**Dante and the Lobster**," **Belacqua** likes his toast hard and black, not softly buttered like Senior Fellows with nothing but false teeth in their heads (12). "A **Wet Night**" (82) quotes the December rainfall "as cooked in the

Dublin University Fellows' Garden," there being since 1904 a climatological station there. In "**Draff**" (180), Hairy asks to see Belacqua's body, whispering "like a priest asking for a book in the Trinity College Library," a crack at its Protestant orientation. **Neary** is based upon Professor H. S. Macran, and named for the bar where he held court. When Neary's hair suddenly turns white (224), he is said to look like a Junior Fellow already, one elected, usually when quite young, after having passed the fellowship examinations and provided evidence of distinction. This is the "sweated sinecure" that **Wylie** mentions (58), won by arduous examination but the successful candidates were assured of free college rooms and commons (dining privileges) for life. In *Watt* (46), **Arsene** has failed that examination because of the boil on his bottom and is thus a "maddened prizeman" (the **Madden Prize** was awarded to the runner-up in the Fellowship Examination). The story of **Louit** is a sustained satire on the academic process of research, scholarship, and examination, the latter taking place in what is recognizably the Trinity Examination Hall, with its elevated dais and round windows. SB later recalled his graduation day with ambivalence: "Academic gown. Mortar-board under arm. On a platform, receiving scroll from Rector. Smiling." Royalties from *Krapp's Last Tape* were presented to the college.

SB never lost his affection for Trinity. Despite an understandable diffidence, he returned to the library in 1933 to read **Heraclitus** and the **atomists**, and

in 1936 to read **Geulincx** in the Long Room. During the Paris years, he welcomed news of and acquaintances from the college. In 1959, he was asked if he would accept from Trinity an honorary Doctor of Letters. Despite his dislike of such tributes, he agreed, Knowlson suggests (416), because it seemed like a gesture of forgiveness from the institute he had walked out on so long ago. Although he dreaded the ceremony, it passed off most pleasantly, and he renewed contact with old friends. Following the award of the **Nobel Prize** (1969), SB gave a considerable sum to the TCD Library, which has since augmented its small but significant holding of Beckett manuscripts (the invaluable items being the twenty years of intimate correspondence with **MacGreevy** and the letters of Barbara **Bray**). Trinity has named the Samuel Beckett Theatre for him. Following SB's death in 1989, the Beckett estate has gradually disposed of the manuscripts in accordance with his intentions, many going to the **BIF** (Reading) but others bequeathed to TCD, notably SB's notes on philosophy and psychoanalysis which, appropriately, will become an important center of Beckett studies.

"**Tristesse Janale**": an unpublished fifteen-line poem, of uncertain early date. The original title, "Lamentation Janale," is crossed out in the index of SB's poems in the **Leventhal** papers (HRHRC). The title embraces the sadness of looking back (or forward), Janus being the two-faced Roman deity. The poem addresses Beauty in terms of the **Kantian** *Ding-an-sich* yet as an "icone bilitique" (see **Bilitis**), a mute enigma that has cut his distress into conical sections and sets against his **desire** "un trait antithétique." Such antinomies are suggested by the "flêches de Télèphe," the arrows of Eros having the double-headed nature of the spear of **Telephus**. Other oppositions include "abîme" and "sonde"; "le greffé et la greffe" (subject, **object**); "**superfétatoire**" and "frêle furibonde" (creation, disintegration); the divergent impulses of **Mallarmé** and **Michelangelo**; "extases farouche" and the "crispations de fange" (crazy ecstasies, shrivelings of mud). These culminate in "lacustre conifère," the poet conceiving himself in littoral terms as a pine on the margin of forest and sea, to resolve "tes tensions ambigues de crête et de cratère."

Trois Dialogues: Edith Fournier's translation (Minuit, 1998) of "**Three Dialogues**," published nine years after SB's **death** as if to confute his opinion that they should remain in English only. For a qualification of Fournier's claim in her preface that SB alone wrote these dialogues, see **Duthuit**.

"**Trois poèmes: Three poems**": [1] in *Transition Forty-eight* 2 (June 1948), French (96) and English facing (97). The three are: "**je suis ce cours de sable qui glisse / my way is in the sand flowing**"; "**que ferais-je sans ce monde / what would I do without this world**"; and "**je voudrais que mon amour meure / I would like my love to die**." They enter *Six poèmes 1947–1949*, in *Gedichte* (1959), 86–91, and *Collected Poems* (1977). Unaccompanied English

versions were published in *Poetry Ireland* (April 1949): 8; *Stand* V.1 (1961): 2–3, the first printing in England; and *Poems in English* (1961), 46–53.

"**Trois poèmes**": [2] in *Les Cahiers des saisons* 2 (octobre 1955): 115–16. The three poems, printed for the first time, are: "**Accul**"; "**Mort de A.D.**"; and "**vive mort ma seule saison**." Reprinted in *Gedichte* (1959) as three of *Six poèmes 1947–1949*, unchanged save that the title "Accul" was omitted, and in *Collected Poems* (1977).

"**Trois textes pour rien**": three prose passages in *Les Lettres nouvelles* 1.3 (mai 1953): 267–77; revised and republished as *Textes* III ("Laisse"), VI ("Entre ces apparitions"), and X ("Abandonner, c'est tout abandonné") in *Nouvelles et textes pour rien* (1955).

troubadour poetry: many poems in *Echo's Bones* are imitations of **Provençal** forms: the "Alba," the "Enueg," the "Serena," the two "**Sanies**" poems as a kind of *planh*, and "**Da tagte es**" as imitation of a poem by **Walther** von der Vogelweide. SB cites details from Jean Beck's *La Musique des troubadours* (1910), including a list of verse forms (DN, 72–73). He felt an affinity for the *trobar clus* mode of intricate **musical** complexity, and for its central tensions of sacred and profane **love**, eros and agape, piety and **pity**. These feelings were doubtless intensified by the fact that his **Alba**, Ethna **MacCarthy**, was attracted to the Provençal forms, delivering the lectures on them that SB might have given had he not resigned from **Trinity** to assume the life of a jongleur. SB helped her prepare these from *Lou Tresor d'ou Felibrige* (Mistral's Provençal-French dictionary, 1878–86), commenting to **MacGreevy** (29 January 19[36]) that Arnaud [Daniel] seemed the best of them. The emotions behind his poems, such as the loss associated with the **deaths** of Peggy **Sinclair** and his **father**, the theme of exile, and the paradoxes of love, are essentially *trobar* in nature, Beck indicating (70–71) how the public act of poetry ("qui se dérobe si jalousement aux regards de la foule") might retain the personal touch. SB's poems imitate the forms of their originals, vexations turned into "complaint" by a complex orchestration that is both musical and verbal, self-conscious though the artistry might be. SB took "plagal finale" from Beck (77), translated it as "off the tonic" (DN, 72), and used it in "**Dortmunder**" to resolve "the long night phrase," that phrase illustrating Beck's principle of emphasizing "l'avant-dernière note." *Dream* uses the words (49, 111), again of the Alba, and mentions the "**Chanson de Toile**" and the nostalgia of Doon for his "belle Doette" (165); this is Beck on the art of harmonic modulation.

"**Tryst**": an early title for "**Ghost Trio**," the name persisting in the drafts until almost the final copy (see *Beckett at Reading*, 44–45).

tucutucu: a South American burrowing rodent, *Ctenomys brasiliensis,* resembling a small squirrel ("What a Misfortune," 133). In Chapter 14 of *The Origin of Species,* **Darwin** discusses "complex and little-known laws of variation," the way that varieties entering a given zone may develop or dis-use certain forms: "we look at the burrowing tucutucu, which is occasionally blind, and then at certain moles, which are habitually blind and have their eyes covered with skin." The "tuco tuco" [*sic*] is discussed in Chapter 5 of the *Origin.*

tulips: tokens of incongruous beauty, as the green tulips of the evening in "**Enueg II.**" The image occurs in *Dream* (28), expanded (137) as a metaphor of slick writing. SB noted "tulipomania" (DN, 152), the hysteria that swept the Netherlands in the early 1700s when the flower was introduced. He associated tulips with Geer **van Velde**, commenting of his birth, "Ce fut l'instant des tulipes."

Turdy: Moran's home (134, 173); the **French** equivalent is "Shit." In proximate relation to **Hole**, in the **Molloy** Country. While the name intimates Moran's anal fixations, the black madonna reflects traditions of a Black Virgin brought to southern France by Mary Magdalene and associated with St. Sara, patron saint of gypsies. See **Bally**.

"**Two fragments**": published in *Transition Fifty* 6 (October 1950): 103–6; the first an extract from *Molloy*, the second, the opening of *Malone Dies* (English translations preceding the **French** originals). This issue contains two unsigned translations by SB: the last chapter of *Armand,* by Emmanuel Bove, and "**Zone**," **Apollinaire**'s poem from *Alcools* (1913).

two thieves: at the **crucifixion** of **Christ**, the repentant thief (Dysmas) was saved but the unrepentant one (Gestas) damned. SB recorded a curious detail from **Burton**'s *Anatomy* (III.4.2.iii, 717; DN, 139): "That night two shall be in a bed—one received and the other left." The **Whoroscope Notebook** records: "Never despair (1 thief saved) / nor presume (only 1 saved)." These are early anticipations of SB's most celebrated theme, best known from his comment to Harold Hobson in 1956: "I take no sides. I am interested in the shape of ideas. There is a wonderful sentence in **Augustine**: 'Do not despair, one of the thieves was saved. Do not presume, one of the thieves was damned.' That sentence has a wonderful shape. It is the shape that matters." The origin of this sentiment is not in Augustine but in "The Repentance of Robert **Greene**," the Elizabethan writer's recantation of his wicked ways, which includes several notions echoed by SB: a diatribe against his having ever been born; a cry to Dives to "haue one drop of water" for his tongue; admitting his faults as "red as skarlet"; but falling like the **dog** to his old vomit; despairing that his soul could find favor in the sight of its maker, yet hoping that "as his iudgements are inscrutable, so are his mercies incomprehensible." The essay concludes with the sentiment that so appealed to SB that he made it his own: "To this doth that golden sentence of S. *Augustine* allude, which hee speaketh of the theefe, hanging on the Crosse. *There was* (saith hee) *one theef saued and no more, therefore presume not; and there was one saued, and therefore despaire not.*"

Neary comments: "do not despair. Remember there is no triangle, however obtuse, but the circumference of some circle passes through its wretched vertices. Remember also one thief was saved" (*Murphy,* 213). The perfect circle, which is **God**, must pass through each vertex of the triangle comprising the thief who is saved, Christ, and the thief who is damned. References to the Two Thieves appear in the *Trilogy:* Molloy's **knife-rest,** two crosses joined at their points of intersection by a bar (63); **Malone**'s needle stuck into two corks: "like a—no, it is like nothing" (247); his hope: "one of the thieves was saved, that is a generous percentage" (255); and **Moll**'s two earrings (thieves) and her tooth between them, carved to represent "the celebrated sacrifice" (264). The **French** text uses "larrons," whereas the English (41) simply refers to **A** and **C.** In *How It Is* (43), the reference is more oblique: "joy and sorrow those two their sum divided by two and luke" [*sic*].

The theme is most famously rehearsed in *Waiting for Godot,* as an image of uncertain salvation, "Didi" and "Gogo" echoing Dysmas and Gestas. In a 1961 interview with Tom Driver, SB mentioned the two thieves, one saved and one damned, and asked: "Have you pondered the dramatic qualities of this theology?" If there were only darkness, all would be clear; but because there is light the situation becomes inexplicable. He gave as example the dramatic possibilities in Augustine's doctrine of grace (the two thieves), compared with the destiny of Phèdre, which is sealed from the outset. She may be illuminated but she unquestionably moves into the dark. Neither Greek nor Jansenist, SB lacked such clarity: "The question would also be removed if we believed in the contrary— total salvation. But where we have light and dark we also have the inexplicable. The key word in my plays is 'perhaps.'"

When **Vladimir** asks **Estragon** how his foot is, the latter replies, "Swelling visibly." Vladimir comments, "Ah yes, the two thieves." The link is Golgotha, that swollen mound. Of the four Evangelists "thereabouts," only one speaks of a thief being saved. This is Luke (23:39–43); Matthew (27:38) and Mark (15:27) simply mention the thieves, Matthew (27:44) adding that they abused Christ; while John (19:18) refers to "two others with him, on either side one." Vladimir is wrong to state that "two don't mention any thieves at all"; the Gospels do not altogether fail to agree but Luke is the only one to mention their salvation. Even so, since only one in four says that one of the two was saved, the chance of salvation is logically reduced from fifty-fifty to one in eight. Estragon is little help: "Saved from what?"; but Vladimir persists in his folly: "Why believe him rather than the others?" Told that everybody does, Estragon replies: "People are bloody ignorant apes," the **Darwinian** overtones brutalizing the French: "Les gens sont des cons." This initiates the motif: "It's an even chance," which applies to everything from the ability of the tree to bear their weight to the possibility of Godot coming or the chance of Estragon's **boots** fitting. SB supposedly remarked that one of the feet was saved. The two thieves are not mentioned again, but the tree remains as emblem of the Cross, casting a shadow of theological uncertainty over the play. Other images enforce the theme: when Vladimir and Estragon attempt to "raise" Lucky and Pozzo in Act II, they fall into a cruciform heap; and when they help Pozzo to arise, he sags between them, arms around their necks, an icon of the crucified Christ between two malefactors, whose only crime is to have been born.

Tyler: a figure from SB's youth, described in *Malone Dies* (269–70) as a market gardener with only one eye and side whiskers. He had a small farm at Tyler's Gate, near **Foxrock**, a location graven on SB's childhood memory by his **mother**'s cutting remark when he asked how far away the sky was (see *Company*). Tyler was known as "Watt," after the leader of the Peasants' Revolt (1381). In *Watt* (48), **Arsene** asks for a name: "Mr—? I beg your pardon. Like Tyler?" His name is given to the retired bill broker of *All That Fall*, who pulls up on his **bicycle**, only to curse the wet Saturday afternoon of his conception as he finds the back tire has gone down again; this suggests a faulty condom.

U

Ubi nihil vales, ibi nihil velis: L. "where you are worth **nothing,** there you should want nothing"; the central axiom of the *Ethica* of Arnold **Geulincx** (qv). The *Ethica* is a book of the cardinal virtues, virtue assuming for Geulincx the **love** of right reason that leads directly to **God** and, as such, contrasted with **Philautia,** or love of the self. The virtues Geulincx defines as cardinal are *Diligentia,* listening to the **voice** of reason; *Obedienta,* compliance with the dictates of reason; *Justitia,* to will no more nor less than reason dictates; and *Humilitas,* the sense of the lack of one's worth before God. This last is the core of his ethical teaching. It has two parts, both deriving from the *Ipse te nosce* ("know thyself") of the Greeks: *inspectio sui,* looking into the self; and *despectio sui,* contempt of the self. The two are discussed in terms of the ethical axiom: *Ubi nihil vales,* by looking into oneself, one realizes one's essential lack of worth, *ibi nihil velis;* by so doing one is led to despise and hence not **desire** the material world (which having inspected, one sets at naught). The axiom is expounded fully in a footnote to the "Annotata" (III, 222–23). The further consequence (225) that, as a result of self-inspection and the discovery that one is worth nothing, one has no value until dead (*"ex Derelectione me"*) underlies the value system in SB's writings of the many derelicts who have this precise metaphysical definition of their being.

Uccello, Paolo (1397–1475): **Florentine** painter whose night scene *The Hunt* (Ashmolean Museum) suggests the "swarthy Uccello" of "**Draff**" (182). In "**Echo's Bones**" (11), a genuine Uccello flies out the window.

Ulysses: SB's debt to *Ulysses* is not easily defined, but as the major literary achievement of the century it was something to both emulate and resist. References, accordingly, are both manifold and insignificant. Five instances will suffice: (1) the Purefoy triplets are among the bridesmaids of Thelma **bboggs** in "**What a Misfortune**"; (2) **Murphy**'s "surgical quality" (62) echoes the "operative surgical quality" of Bloom's hand as he makes cocoa (*U,* 627); (3) the **Cox** swallows 110 aspirins (*Murphy,* 272) in defiance of Bloom's "POST 110 PILLS"; (4) *Watt* (213) describes the smoke from the different pavilions as at the end of "Scylla and Charybdis" (and so of *Cymbeline*), as if to suggest reconciliation and sundering; and (5) "below sea level" and the old woman in *Ill Seen Ill Said* suggest the Dead Sea and the gray sunken cunt of "Calypso." Such references are trivial, less allusion (plagiarism, literary allegiance, intertextuality, or the anxiety of influence) than an act of homage and intricate self-delight. The echoes are evasive, *diminuendo al niente,* but are discussed in the following entries: **Aristotle; Aulnoy; Belacqua; Bible; biography; Byrne; "Calvary by Night"; Cathleen ni**

Hennessy; censorship; the **Cox**; **Dante**; "Dante . . . Bruno. Vico . . Joyce"; dog; *Dream;* Dún Laoghaire; *Eleutheria; European Caravan;* French; Freud; fundamental unheroic; Gogarty; "Home Olga"; Joyce; Lessing; London; Mac-Greevy; Mary; memory; *Molloy; More Pricks Than Kicks; Murphy;* necessary journey; "The **Old Tune**"; onanism; Paris; *Portrait;* Proust; *Proust;* Renan; Romanticism; "Sanies II"; "Sedendo et Quiesc[i]endo"; Synge; the Syra-Cusa; "Text"; Thomas à Kempis; *transition;* Trinity College; voice; *Watt; Whitaker's Almanack;* Whoroscope Notebook; Woolf; Wordsworth; and Wynn's Hotel.

Unanimisme: the expression of "la vie unanime et collective," in the words of its founder, Jules **Romains**, who with Pierre-Jean **Jouve** and the Abbaye poets established a movement asserting the writer's intense awareness of belonging to a collective existence that gives point to private experience, a "composite **consciousness**" influenced by **Bergson**. The narrator might say of a unanimist, "that he imposed his personality on a group" ("**Assumption**," 4). SB became aware of the movement at **Trinity**, through **Rudmose-Brown**, and pursued it in a long research essay (a "scrappy work," now lost) before he went to **Paris**.

The Unnamable: translation of *L'Innommable,* first published as an **Evergreen** Original paperback (Grove, 1958), with a special edition of 100 numbered copies, another 26 lettered from "A" to "Z." The third of the post**war** French novels, it was collected under SB's suggested title *Three Novels* by **Grove Press** (1958) and **Olympia** (1959) in its Traveller's Companion series, #71 (subtitled, without consultation, "A **Trilogy**"), as in the **Calder** and Boyars edition (1960). Extracts appeared in: *Texas Quarterly* 2 (spring 1958): 127–31; *Chicago Review* 12 (summer 1958): 82–86; and *Spectrum* 2.1 (winter 1958): 3–7. Extracts were recorded for BBC 3 (19 January 1959), read by Patrick **Magee**, produced by Donald **McWhinnie**, music composed by John Beckett and conducted by Bernard Keefe.

The Unnamable is the most overtly liminal of SB's texts, as it assesses (and finds wanting) earlier narratives and anticipates much of the later writing. Earlier work is dismissed as "clumsily done, you could see the ventriloquist" (348). This story would have no ventriloquist, no namable being, perhaps no phenomenal being at all. An interrogatory, heuristic opening suggests the ubiquitous process of deferral, as in the opening "Where now? Who now? When now?" Such questions return periodically to move forward what action there is, outlining the epistemological and ontological cruxes in terms that resist denotation. SB described his task to Avigdor **Arikha** (11 November 1958): "To try to tell one more time what it is to have been" (Atik, 39). But being is more easily signified than realized. Moreover, the report of this **witness** is undercut by its being told by a series of discontinuous, contradictory, often unidentifiable voices, the sources and reliability of each, its grounding in actual events or coherent being, at issue throughout.

The novel's premises are relatively simple, its methods borrowed from

Descartes. If human existence were reduced to its elemental function, **consciousness**, and if spirit, in Locke's metaphor, is a tabula rasa, then being (or identity) is the sequence of sensory impressions recorded on consciousness and stored on the *tabula* of **memory**. *Nihil in intellectu:* "There is nothing in the mind"; continuing, *quod non prius fuerat in sensu*, "which was not first in the senses." But **Leibniz** retorted to Locke, as SB noted in his **Whoroscope Notebook** (from Windelband, 464): *nisi intellectus ipse,* "except the mind itself." Human consciousness is the ideal core of our onion. If not existence itself, then it is human existence (capable of, or plagued by, **apperception**). Its agent is sensory impression; that is, our understanding of what goes on around us, of how we connect to it, is accomplished by how we understand our body's perception. **Time** and space, two terms implicated in the opening questions, are understood through consciousness; perception within a context constitutes our understanding of space, perception within a sequence of contexts our understanding of time. Our comprehension of the world reaches us through our **body** (qv) but, even functioning properly, the body does not perceive the world directly. It acts though intermediaries, light striking the retina, sound waves the tympanum, a nervous system that cannot finally differentiate internal from external stimuli. As a subject, consciousness (and being) can be explored only from within (as **Krapp** discovers on the jetty in the howling wind). The story of *The Unnamable* as that of the Unnamable is the story of such intermediaries.

Consciousness of self entails a second set of filters and a fundamental contradiction. Trying to tell "what it is to have been," SB critiques "the double nature" of being outlined by **Schopenhauer**, particularly the impossibility of "self-existing unity." If this existed, "it would be possible for us to be conscious of ourselves in ourselves, and independent of the objects of knowledge and will. Now this is by no means possible, for as soon as *we turn into ourselves* to make the attempt, and seek for once to know ourselves fully by means of retrospective reflection, we are lost in the bottomless void; we find ourselves like the hollow glass globe, from out of which a **voice** speaks whose cause is not to be found in it, and whereas we desired to comprehend ourselves, we find, with a shudder, nothing but a vanishing spectre" (*WWI,* I.4 #54, 358n.). If self is the **object** of perception what then is perceiving it? Or if self is that which is doing the perceiving then what, in self-perception, is being perceived? Something other than self? Even if the mind can know no more than itself, how can it be conscious of or know even that? The Unnamable's critique of being dismantles the last of Cartesian essentialism, and throws into relief the fundamental tautology of the **cogito**, that Descartes has already assumed what he sets out to prove when he speaks the "I" of "I think." What self exists may be at best a nominal self or self as function of performance, self in narrative, in language, say, expressed by a voice from out of a hollow globe whose source can be named only as a series of "vice-existers." That is, the report, the telling of "what it is to have been," entails another filter, language. But language is not phenomenal (see "**German Letter of 1937**," **Mauthner**, and **unword**). Stating the pronominal "I" is not an act of ontology, and certainly not a telos, that which might put an end to the question. At best language can signify, a process that leads to a chain of signifiers, the signified for which is perpetually elusive, deferred. If it "all boils down to a question of words" (335), as the Unnamable claims, being is deferred along a similar chain of signifiers.

Such focus on consciousness allows for the exploration of what lies below the familiar surface of existence, including the nature of language, perception, truth, and the phenomenal world, perhaps, that which ordinarily escapes notice. Action is eliminated, reduced to the report or translation of voices. Rather than **coming and going** as in the earlier work, the Unnamable one day "simply stayed in" (291). But the perceiver of voices in *The Unnamable* is immaterial, or at least less material than his immediate predecessors, **Molloy**, **Moran**, and Malone, a groundless (if not bodiless) voice. *The Unnamable* offers its readers a vivid image of how we understand the actual, which is based on the stories we hear; yet the phenomenal world, the actual, is all but eliminated. As a report, *The Unnamable* offers a counternarrative to the grand totalizing cultural narrative of the self. Actuality is replaced by language, by narrative; action ("Keep going, going **on**") exists in the naming ("[let us] call that going, [let us] call that on"). The theme is more directly stated in "**Closed Place**": "There is **nothing** but what is said" (236). But what is said is

built on what is said, one story on another. Voice is reporting voice, interceding within voice; voice a voice telling a story of a voice telling a story told by a voice (see "**Echo's Bones**"). Whatever grounding narrative (and so being and actuality) has had traditionally in literature is here eroded, as the phenomenal being to which a voice is usually attached is dissolved, or at least is reduced to its function in performance. Consciousness is explored but it is consciousness without ground, as idea, self itself mere language, constructed by language, an extreme Nominalism (see **scholasticism**).

The unnamable's teleological hope is expressed in terms of the desire for silence, denied by his interrogators until the right word is spoken. That word unknown to him is the authentic "I" of being. To state the "I" completely and so merge with it in a unity, a totality (of voices, of signified and signifier), entails simultaneously the disappearance of the "I," and so silence or nothingness. But such a merger with the voice of the other, or even with the other of language itself, is the fate of the appropriated, the colonized, self become or replaced by an other who speaks through you. Such assimilation is an act of violence. But the "I" can never be identical with language, and so the Unnamable resists the stability of meaning. Resisting the appropriation by the other, through language, he asserts his independence, his otherness, by resisting the discourse of appropriation—leading to silence—he asserts the counterdiscourse of incoherence, a perpetually evasive language. If *The Unnamable* is a narrative of existence reduced to **fundamental sounds**, those sounds are themselves discordant.

The "vice-existers" of the novel are antithetical: the exfoliation of **Basil**, **Mahood**, and **Worm** may echo the earlier **Belacqua**, **Murphy**, and **Watt**; as Molloy had Moran, Mahood has his "anti-Mahood." His first story is a journey home in spirals around the earth, on the model of Molloy, say. It is told both by Mahood and by the Unnamable as Mahood, on the model of Molloy and Moran, say. On his return he finds destroyed by **sausage poisoning** his family, through whose remains he treads. In his second story the one-armed, one-legged Mahood is reduced to a trunk, a head, and his useless "virile" member, in a jar outside a restaurant on the Rue Brancion in the 15th Arrondissement, opposite a monument to the "hippophagist" Emile **Ducroix** (340), near SB's Rue des Favorites. He is tended by **Marguerite** or **Madeleine**, who loses faith in him as she fails to acknowledge him. That failure of perception leads to his disappearance, his ceasing to exist. He is replaced by Worm, who is little more than pure protoplasm, the naked **monad**, life without being: "I'm Worm, no, if I were Worm I wouldn't know it" (347). The Unnamable reverberates or oscillates between the antitheses, *neither* one nor the other but the space between: "I'm in the middle, I'm the partition, I've two surfaces and no thickness . . . I'm the tympanum, on the one hand the mind, on the other the world I don't belong to either" (383).

The plot is easily outlined. An entity (a being, a sentient, conscious creature) perceives a voice (from within or without is very much the question), and tries to determine what it hears and the relation of heard to hearer. If the voice is other it must have a being associated with it, hence the series of projected "vice-existers." Complications arise as perception is turned inward, toward the self, as attempts are made to express its processes. Part I (291–304) constitutes a "preamble"; its seventeen paragraphs include the story of one of the Unnamable's named interrogators, Basil (298–300). For details of its cosmology, **atomist** structure as an analogue of the universe, with suggestions of **Plato**'s cave, Leibniz's monad, and **Milton**'s Pandemonium, see **physics**. Part II is the Unnamable's "Statement," one long paragraph (304–414), a magnificent tour de force. It tells of himself and his satellites, the master and the **pensum**, the obligation to speak (304–14). It moves to Mahood's first story, the world traveler (315–24), and a second story (326–34, 340–45, 373–74), a being in a jar (**Proust**'s **vase**, Schopenhauer's globe). There are interludes, but Mahood changes to Worm (337), and the voice begins its apodosis (the clause of a conditional sentence that gives result or effect), but interwoven with Worm's story. Like those of *Malone Dies,* the embedded narratives of *The Unnamable,* all told in the reporting voice, suggest a series of narrative parodies or fantasies that rely on the credulous reader's suspending more and more disbelief. Such a dialectic within the monologue, between the Unnamable and his others, is fundamentally dialogic or performative, as implicit in the opening heuristic.

Through *The Unnamable,* then, SB developed the dialogic monologue, a variation of **schizophrenic** internal voices, the disintegrating voice as remnant of the earlier two novels, that which is sought, or heard, by Molloy and Moran, that which is "born" when Malone "dies." In terms of SB's transition to drama, he folded the sense of an audience into a new form of dramatic monologue: "the audience, well well, so there's an audience, it's a public show . . . he's only preluding, clearing his throat, alone in his dressing-room, he'll appear any moment, he'll begin any moment, or it's the stage-manager, giving his instructions, his last recommendations, before the curtain rises, that's the show, waiting for the show" (381–82). That comment suggests the propinquity between the work for theater and the prose narratives, a distinction that will all but disappear later (although *That Time* and *Company* contain figures that resist identification with the voice of others). In *The Unnamable,* SB develops the dialogic monologue through Schopenhauer's image of the voice in the globe. The sentient entity that hears a voice, tries to determine what it hears, what its source is, and what relation the heard has to the perceiver thus not only offers a summa of SB's previous work and the paradigm for *The Unnamable* but is also the evangelist for much of the post-*Unnamable* work, a mode wherein theater and fiction are finally indistinguishable.

"The Unnamable": two prepublications by this title:

a. *Texas Quarterly* 1.2 (spring 1958): 129–31; introduced by David Hayman (127–8). Some variations; revised before publication. Earlier entitled "Extract from *The Unnamable.*"

b. *Spectrum* [Santa Barbara] 2.1 (winter 1958): 3–7; the opening pages, translated by SB.

"Un Soir": a short prose poem, translated as "One Evening." Imaginatively coherent, it constitutes an early draft leading to *Mal vu mal dit.* First printed in *Minuit* 37 (janvier 1980).

unword: in his "German Letter of 1937" to Axel Kaun (9 July), SB used the phrase "Literatur des Unworts," of the need to avoid the method of Joyce, the verticalists, and others attempting the apotheosis of the word (172). He sees this "in the sense of the Scholastics" as a kind of realism (maintaining the ideal existence of genera and species), and suggests the need for some form of Nominalist irony (the doctrine that universals have no corresponding reality either in or out of the mind). A "literature of the unword" would constitute an erasure of verbal being through which (negation as cancellation rather than denial) the unsayable or unspeakable might yet be heard. This is the countersign of SB's statement in "Three Dialogues" that there is nothing to express, together with the obligation to express. It leads to what Carla Locatelli has memorably called "unwording," the *via negativa* that begins precisely because the escape from language is felt as compelling, and yet the "unwording" proves that escape impossible. Just as the tropes of negative theology are structured on negative predication and characterized by a rhetoric of aporia, evasion, and denial, SB's linguistic processes of erasure and erosion have a perlocutionary effect, which Locatelli calls an "impotence potential," offering an "inanity challenge." That is, SB unveils the efficacy of demented particulars and **fundamental sounds** so as to constitute from the **love** of them an "inane" (or "antic") dynamic that is far from nihilism or **surrealism** but is grounded in the attempt to work through language to something beyond language, a mode Gontarski has called "the intent of undoing." Examples may be selected at will: **Moran**'s "It is midnight. The rain is beating on the windows. It was not midnight. It was not raining" (176); the **Unnamable**'s "I shall have to speak of things of which I cannot speak" (291); his use of "Inexistent" (304); his final "I can't go on, I'll go **on**" (414); or the voice "in me not mine" of *How It Is* (7). Yet the question abides as to what kind of virtual reality is created through this nominalistic irony of negation and aporia; whether any "presence" exists behind the denials of being (surely no ontological referent); and whether, in the words of the "German Letter of 1937," it is something or **nothing** that begins to seep through. A thousand years "**on**," and the Nominalist-Realist debate is as unresolved as ever.

Ussy: a village sixty kilometers east of **Paris**, where SB after the **war** sometimes rented a house called the Maison Barbier. He used his **mother**'s legacy to have built a little house, "banal, austere, and aesthetically dull" (Knowlson, 351). He retreated there to write and to escape the pressures of fame, calling it his "hole in the Marne mud" (Harmon, 6), into which he might "crawl" to take refuge in **solitude** and contemplation, amidst the snows and the crows, planting trees (see "The **Gloaming**"), building a stone wall, and combating the moles making mountains of his lawn (the "fodient rodents" of "**Rough for Radio II**"). He kept there a radio, a gramophone, a little German piano (a "Schimmel"), and books, including a 1911 *Britannica* and volumes on **chess**. Many later pieces, notably *Comment c'est*, found their inspiration in or are dated from Ussy. Despite an acrimonious dispute with the local council (1954), a bizarre accident in which he walked into a deep garage pit and cracked two ribs (1967), and occasional burglaries (he lost his **Staunton** chessboard), SB regarded the cottage as the one place where he might be truly alone.

V

V: a signifier of **voice** (qv) and "**charac-ter**" in several later plays: *Footfalls;* "**Ghost Trio**"; "**What Where**," ". . . but the clouds . . . ," and "**Rockaby**." In "**Cascando**" and "**Eh Joe**" the role of Voice is fully articulated; in *Not I* it is audible before and after **Mouth** can be seen.

"**Va et vient**": SB's translation of *Come and Go,* the two written in tandem. The **French** text, subtitled a "dramaticule," was published first in *Comédie et actes divers* (Minuit, 1966), 38–44. The French drafts reflect a process of compo-sition almost as arduous as the original. SB at one point (RUL 1532/1) noted the three words "miséricorde," "malheur," and "misère" to be worked into the text in an operatic manner. He directed the work at the *Petite Salle* of the Odéon-Théâtre de France (28 février 1966) in a "Spectacle Beckett, **Pinget**, Ionesco," with Annie Bertin as Flo, Madeleine **Renaud** as Vi, and Simone Valère as Ru.

vagitus: the cry of the newborn baby as it takes its first breath, a protest of grief and pain as it is "**expelled**" from the warmth and security of the womb, as in *Not I,* when **Mouth** recalls the cry that got her going. In *Murphy* (23), a meta-phor of **birth**; the infant Murphy's alone off-key (71). The text notes cynically that his rattle will make amends, but **Malone** is skeptical (249): "To have vagitated and not be bloody well able to rattle." The

Unnamable hears a feeble cry, after long silence (296), but it is stifled outright. In "**Breath**" the instructions include, "Faint brief cry . . . cry as before." In his notes SB comments: "Instant of re-corded vagitus. Important that the two cries be identical."

Valéry, Paul (1871–1945): French **sym-bolist** poet who experienced a Cartesian crisis of the divided self in 1892 ("la nuit de Gênes"), leading to a twenty-year "si-lence" before he returned to poetry. SB admired *La Soirée avec Monsieur Teste* (1896), the testament of one who mini-mizes outward circumstances, a "mys-tique sans Dieu" who is "hors de ce monde" (his name is an ancient form of "tête"), a mind observing its own opera-tions and composing from them a way of life. As such, he is a prototype of **Murphy**, a denizen of the head and mind, one who has killed the **puppet**, a phrase SB used in his 1934 review of **Rilke**, and whose life is essentially *facultatif.* Like Edmond Teste, Murphy (189) has got rid of his books and pictures. He is equally the lit-erary ancestor of **Watt**. As Bryden sug-gests (*Idea of God,* 26), M. Teste's sense of life as something that passes from one zero to another is present in SB's work as a *via purgativa* that does not lead to the *via unitiva.*

Valmont: seducer in *Les Liaisons dangeureuses* (1782) by Choderlos de Laclos. Preferring the impotent **Octave**,

Belacqua wishes on the **Syra-Cusa** a chesty version of Valmont, in crimson sweater, tweed casquette, and **bicycle** clips (*Dream,* 50).

van Gogh, Vincent (1853–90): Dutch painter admired by SB for his mastery of detail and physical desolation, his world a canvas abandoned by **God**. Consider "the remains of Vincent arriving in sheets of rain," his head swathed in a bloody clout ("**Text 3,**" 112); or the "pair of brown **boots** lacerated and gaping" of "Text 8," an evocation of *Boots with Laces* (1885), implicit in the placing of **Estragon**'s boots on stage ("we're not tied"). Brater suggests (175–76) van Gogh's *La Berceuse,* his portrait of Madame Augustin Roulin, in the composition of "**Rockaby.**" Juliet reports SB saying, "When you think he never sold a single canvas" (*Conversations,* 160), emphasizing how much van Gogh had meant to him.

van Velde, Bram and Geer: two Dutch brothers, artists whom SB much admired and promoted in his rare critical writings: "**Geer van Velde**" (1938); "La **Peinture des van Velde, ou: Le monde et le pantalon**" (1945–46); "**Peintres de l'empêchement**" (1948); "**Three Dialogues**" (1949). In the *Pantalon* essay SB sums up their beginnings: "A. van Velde est né à La Haye en octobre 1895. Ce fut l'instant des brumes. G. van Velde est né près de Leyde, en avril 1897. Ce fut l'instant des **tulipes.**" He defined them as two men walking toward the same horizon, with different goals: "A. van Velde peint l'étendue. G. van Velde peint la succession." SB met

Geer through George **Reavey** in 1936 and was initially more interested in him. They remained friends, Geer asking to see SB on his deathbed (1977). The closer friendship was with Bram. Geer was the more philosophical; Bram lived on the edge, with "a kind of wild desperation." Their sister Jacoba (1903–85), who wrote under the name of Toni Clerkx, translated some of SB's minor works and acted as his unofficial literary agent. SB may have had a brief liaison with her.

The meeting of SB and Bram proved momentous for both, the painter finding for the first time someone who understood his silent struggle and obstinate determination, and who perhaps saved him from despair after the **death** of his wife, Lilly Klöker, and the misery of the **war** years. SB held Bram in high esteem, admired his integrity, and talked about him with affection and fervor. In 1937, scarcely able to afford it, he bought from Bram a piece "Without Title" (otherwise *Composition 1937*), which he hung opposite his desk, fascinated by its abstract masks and eyes (Juliet, 15; frontispiece to his *Conversations*). Bram told Juliet (47–48) that in reading *Fin de partie* he recognized the tone and odd fragments of their conversations. They shared a self-imposed exile and the sense that their best works were driven by an inner force that had nothing to do with the will. SB wrote a few short introductions for exhibitions of Bram's work, celebrating him as the first to admit that to be an artist was to fail, "as no other dare fail" ("Three Dialogues," 125). "La **Falaise,**" written "Pour Bram," attempts in words what Bram had done in **art**.

"Variation on a 'Still' Point": the gathering of "**Sounds**" and "**Still 3**" in *Essays in Criticism* 28.2 (April 1978): 156–57; Rpt. in *The Complete Short Prose* (1995).

Vasari, Giorgio (1511–74): Italian architect responsible for the Uffizi, but best known for his *Lives of the Most Eminent Italian Architects, Painters and Sculptors* (1550). SB acquired a copy (now in private hands) before he went to **Florence** (1927), but in *Dream* (76–77) **Belacqua** uses it to avoid having to "promenade" the **Smeraldina**.

vase: a recurrent image of **memory**. In *Proust* (15), the individual is the seat of "a constant process of decantation," from the vessel containing the fluid of future time, "sluggish, pale and monochrome," to that containing the fluid of past time, "agitated and multicoloured by the phenomena of its hours." For **Proust**, SB contends, the most trivial experience is crystalline, the potential occasion of involuntary memory, the past imprisoned in a vase filled with perfume and "suspended along the height of our years" (73). The purity of their content is guaranteed by forgetfulness, but when the imprisoned **microcosm** is besieged, "we are flooded by a new air and a new perfume (new precisely because already experienced), and we breathe the true air of Paradise, of the only Paradise that is not the dream of a madman, the Paradise that has been lost." This metaphor is translated into images, such as **Belacqua**'s "exuviae as preserved in an urn" ("Echo's Bones," 1). **Molloy** refers to "that sealed jar to which I owed my being so well pre-

served" (49), but a wall has given way and he is full of roots and stems, "stakes long since dead." L'Innommable imagines himself "entouré, dans un capharnaüm" (9) at a bazaar. This Ali Baba image has in English (292) the sense of being smothered in a throng, a bargain sale, but that crush and bustle gives way to the stasis of the urn, the "great traveller" (327) stuck like a sheaf of flowers in a deep jar. **Nagg and Nell** are in their ashcans; **Hamm** asks, "Are they bottled yet?" (24). The three characters of "**Play**," each in an urn, are trapped in their past and in their selves. In *Krapp's Last Tape* the vases become spools, images of yesterday captured on celluloid, another paradise lost.

Vega: a star in the constellation Lyra, brightest in the northern hemisphere. In "**Assumption**" (7) and *Dream* (16, 70) it is associated with the **mystical** experience of the **blue flower** of Novalis, **God**, and the "birdless cloudless colourless skies." **Belacqua** calls the **Smeraldina** his "Fünkelein," the little spark in his Lyre (*Dream*, 17). **Henry** in *Embers* recalls the night that Bolton met Holloway: "Vega in the Lyre very green" (95).

Venerilla: the **Alba**'s maid, her name implying venery. SB picked it up from **Burton**'s *Anatomy* (III.2.3, 565): "she is his idol, lady, mistress, venerilla, queen" (DN, 123).

Venus Callipyge: Venus of the beautiful **buttocks**; a late Greek statue (not clearly of Aphrodite) in the Museo Nazionale, Naples. *Dream*, 97.

Verbatim: SB's projected title for *Company*. See "The **Voice**."

verbena: an "obsessional" image, like **Proust**'s **flowering currant**. A lemon verbena flowered near the porch at **Cooldrinagh**; **Belacqua** returns home and plunges his head into it (*Dream*, 128). **Moran** inhales the scent of his lemon verbena (93). In *How It Is* (15), the speaker recalls his mother's **face** as he kneels on that veranda "smothered in verbena"; that childhood photograph, reproduced by **Bair** (114), is among those in *Film* that **O** tears up.

Vermeer, Jan (1632–75): Dutch painter of Delft, his output limited but exquisite. The lemon of Miss Carriage's walls whines "like Vermeer's" (*Murphy*, 228). This is the *View of Delft* (Mauritshuis, The Hague), specifically, **Proust**'s *La Prisonnière* (I.255), where the dying Bergotte drags himself from his death-bed to see once more the "petit pan de mur jaune." **Joyce** had a reproduction in his **Paris** flat (Ellmann, 592). One of the last things **Belacqua** sees in "**Yellow**" (167) is "the grand old yaller wall" outside the hospital. *View of Delft* is referred to in "La **Peinture des van Velde**," and shapes "the warm bright wall" of **Arsene**'s almost-mystical moment (*Watt*, 42) and "declining sun" on the white wall (*Molloy*, 25). Knowlson notes (236) SB's description of "Kupplerin" in Dresden as "indescribably lovely," and suggests (525) that Vermeer's fascination with frozen gestures, as in *The Geographer* or *The Astronomer*, may underlie those of *Still*.

veronica: the cloth with which St. Veronica wiped **Christ**'s brow, and which retained the imprint of His face; the false etymology of "true icon." "**Enueg II**"

invokes the *via dolorosa*, without one wipe ("for the love of Jesus") from the *veronica mundi* ("of the world"), let alone the *veronica munda* ("pure"). **Belacqua**'s buttonhole in "**What a Misfortune**" is a veronica, more *mundi* than *munda*, for it falls to the ground and is trodden underfoot. **Watt** carries in his pocket a "little red sudarium" (literally, a cloth for wiping sweat, technically the veronica), which he uses to stanch blood as he moves from the station (the late addition of "sudarium" developed the latent potential of "stations of the cross"). In the beginning of *Endgame*, as at the end, **Hamm**'s face is covered with a large bloodstained handkerchief, his "Old stancher!" A photograph of Hamm with the bloody stancher was long used on the cover of the **Grove Press** edition of the play. In Alan **Schneider**'s *Endgame*, the bloodstains suggested a **skull**, but SB's 1969 production removed the stains. More delicate is "**Nacht und Träume**," when hand R with a cloth wipes gently B's brow.

Verticalism/Vertigralism: like impressionism, cubism, **surrealism**, dadaism, and imagism, "verticalism" was one of the stars in Modernism's constellation, although among the least bright of them since much of it was more derivative of James **Joyce**'s book of the night, *Work in Progress*, or Carl **Jung**'s theories of the **subconscious** than anything like what it professed to be, a "Revolution of the Word," the name given to Verticalism's earlier incarnation. Much of the manifesto, in fact, was developed incrementally in Jolas's essays and editorials in almost every issue. It was, however, the only one of the Modern period's "isms" that SB linked his name to directly, if less than wholeheartedly, his signature as much to appease **MacGreevy**, another signatory, and to be associated with the *transition* crowd (especially Joyce) than from any personal commitment. It was associated exclusively with Eugene Jolas's *transition* (qv) magazine in which SB was publishing regularly. Its manifesto, "Poetry Is Vertical," appeared in No. 21(1932): 148–9 (for the whole of the manifesto and an excellent critique see Macmillan, *Transition 1927–38*, 62–75). In the subsequent issue, the name was changed to 'vertigral," a portmanteau of verticality and the German word for grail, "Graal." SB would have found its rejection of positivism and the proclamation of "the autonomy of the poetic vision, the hegemony of the inner life over the outer life" compatible with his own thinking, but the celebration of "orphic forces," "The transcendental 'I,'" language as a "mantic instrument," and art that moves "upward toward the illumination of a collective reality and a totalistic universe," with implications of divinity and Modernist teleology, must have given him pause. Ironically, his own story, "**Assumption**," may, at least in part, parody just such thinking, although it appeared in *transition* 16/17, in 1929 where Jolas's movement was still called the "Revolution of the Word." For SB's views on such Nominalist ironies see also "**German Letter of 1937**."

Vico, Giambattista (1688–1744): Italian philosopher and jurist, whose sense of the circular nature of culture and history is expressed in his *Scienza nuova*

(1725), and 215 years later in *Finnegans Wake*. In SB's "**Dante**" essay, the "round-headed Neapolitan" preoccupies half the space. Most of the Viconian detail derives from **Croce**'s *La filosofia di Giambattista Vico* (1911), but SB disputes Croce's view of Vico as mystic or speculative. He differentiates between Vico's "convex **mirror**" and Joyce's "direct expression." Vico could never be a sympathetic source (the identifications are too neat; individuation for SB was never the concretion of universality), but the Vichian schema survives into *How It Is*, as the speaker clings to fragments of the theocratic, heroic, and human and looks back to a golden age.

viduity: looked up by **Krapp** in an enormous dictionary (in draft, **Johnson**'s), a word he once knew but no longer does: "State—or condition—of being—or remaining—a widow— or widower." This is from the OED or *Shorter Oxford*, Krapp adding the pauses and the last two words. He is puzzled by "being—or remaining," but is distracted by "Deep weeds of viduity" and an image he relishes: "The vidua-bird!" Neither the quotation nor the bird is in the OED. SB had referred to the vidual virginity (*Dream*, 143) of Ginette Mac Something (see Georges **Pelorson**) and described the **Frica** as a "vidual virgin" (216). There may be a private jest: SB had noted from **Garnier** (DN, 60) the word "vidual," of the consolations of **onanism** among the elderly and the widowed.

"Vieille terre": "**Foirade** IV"; in *Minuit* 4 (mai 1973): 71, dated "*années 50*," and translated as "**Old earth**"; *Fizzle* 6 in the Grove edition.

Vigny, Alfred de (1797–1863): French author and tragic poet occupied with the dilemma of the creative artist deprived of the consolations of faith; set among the melancholy poets (*Dream,* 62).

Villon, François (1431–63?): French *poète maudit,* whose elegant *Lais* and virtuoso *Grand testament* sound the note of repentance subverted by irony and, in a virtuoso weaving of **voice** and allusion, dramatize the *ubi sunt* themes: the contrast of youth and age, beauty and ugliness, **death** and dissolution. His "Ballade des pendus" is invoked by **Molloy** (19), who like Villon has "all shame drunk"; in the original (24), "toute honte bue."

Vimy Light: in "**Assumption**" (3), the apogee of a parabola commanding undeserved attention because of its brilliance. Correctly, the Very Light, a distress flare (1877) named after Edward W. Very (1847–1910), U.S. admiral and inventor. The Vimy Ridge above Arras was the scene during World War I of an offensive (April 1917) in which many Canadian troops were slaughtered. SB is either confused or ironic (consider "bombshell perfection" [4]).

"**The Vision of Mirza**": by Joseph Addison (1672–1719), in *Spectator* #159; described by SB as "good **allegory** because it is flat writing" (*Proust,* 80). Mirza has a vision of human life as a bridge with three score and ten arches, over which multitudes pass, some dropping through concealed trapdoors into the flood beneath.

Vitrac, Roger (1899–1952): **surrealist** playwright whose disordered fantasies broke down the barrier between the everyday and the unconscious. His *Victor ou les Enfants au pouvoir* (1928), a spoof on drawing-room comedy, may have helped SB's *Eleutheria.*

"**vive morte ma seule saison**": a five-line poem (1947), published in *Cahiers des saisons* 2 (octobre 1955): 116; included with *Six poèmes 1947–1949* in *Gedichte* (1959) and *Collected Poems* (1977). It begins with the paradox "vive mort," and in several **natural** oppositions (lilies and chrysanthemums; abandoned nests; leaves turning to mud; fine days grayed with rime) SB images his life as one long autumn. The phrase is repeated in *How It Is* (24–25), as the clink of a tin revives the narrator and (62) an illusion of progress offers respite.

Vladimir: one of the two tramps keeping their appointment in *Waiting for Godot,* Laurel to **Estragon**'s **Hardy.** Vladimir is the more resilient, with a tendency to intellectualize ("Didi" = "dire"?), as opposed to Estragon's more instinctive behavior ("Gogo" = "go"?). SB associated him with the sky, the air, and Gogo with the ground. For reasons unknown, he is addressed by the **boy** as "Mister Albert."

voice: the mystery of the voice is the paradox that drives SB's supreme fiction, then manifests itself powerfully if ambiguously in the drama that follows. It may be, finally, SB's most profound literary creation. The mystery consists of where the voice is located, without or within ("La voix . . . Ma voix"), and its authenticity, whether transcendent or delusional, a marker of discrete, essential identity or a cultural echo. These questions drew SB's work beyond the delineation of literary **character**, but the origin of voice remained irresolute, part of the enigma, the paradox of being and the mystery of creativity. SB's exploration took a variety of amorphous forms: an early fascination with echo, then with the schizophrenic voice; his desire expressed in the "**German Letter of 1937**" for a kind of Nominalist irony en route to the **unword**; his attempt in fiction from *Three Novels, The Unnamable* in particular, to *Company* to determine the nature and location of that impossible imperative, the need to express; and finally his representations in the theater of a dramatic monologue beyond the unity of interior monologue, beyond the coherence of ego and character, difficulties that dominate the late fiction as well.

Beyond such psychological and ontological enigmas, SB reflects one of the century's technological signatures, the recording and broadcast of the human voice. The past century was the first to confront the separation of voice from its sources, then to record it. **Music** and the performing voice could be listened to at will, drama presented without the presence of actors. As Eugene Jolas noted in "Towards a New Form" (*transition* 19/20 [June 1930]: 104): "The development of the talking film and radio will doubtless have a revolutionary influence on the drama, among other things. And since sound seems to be the basis of the hearplay [radio play] and the cinema-drama, it is safe to say that the problem of the new form will be the word." A voice (word, and perhaps image) from the dark would provide SB with a compelling metaphor for his art of **aporetics**, fragmentation, and disintegration.

"**Assumption**" concerns the poet's need to "whisper" the turmoil down, to dam the stream of whispers before "it" happens, and a great storm of inchoate sound overwhelms all. SB had reservations about the orphic authenticity of "**Verticalism**," the plunge to the depths of the artistic soul through which the artist ascends to divine heights and achieves communion. His story, rather than affirming Jolas's "New **Romanticism**" and the "Revolution of the Word," asserts the failure of the poet to find his personal voice. That search assumed classical proportions in *Echo's Bones* (1935), with the myth of **Narcissus** (qv) and Echo, and the poems as calcified and petrified remnants of what once was, of a voice that is no more. *Dream* mocks the voice of "the little poet" (26) but acknowledges **Augustine**'s sense (*Confessions* 11:6) of that voice which "passed by and passed away, began and ended" (105, 137). SB recorded this (DN, 27) and used it in "**Echo's Bones**" (6) and *First Love* (37); it is his first but lasting statement of the disjunction between the eternal and the noneternal voices.

In *Murphy* casual ironies delineate this disjunction. **Ticklepenny** refers to "the vocal stream issuing from the soul through the lips" (85); **Plato** is mocked, but the source of the voice cannot be as easily dismissed. Rosie **Dew** uses the Ouija board to access voices from *au-delà* (98); the fakery is obvious, yet the phenomena persist. The patients in the MMM (167–68) offer written and verbatim reports of their inner voices; they are paranoid, but their problem remains. Dr. **Killicrankie**, admirer of **Ossian**, has experience of the schizoid voice: "It was not like a real voice, one minute it said one thing and the next minute something quite different" (185). Underlying the nonsense is a critical juncture, SB's visit with Wilfred **Bion** (2 October 1935) to the **Tavistock Clinic** to hear **Jung** (qv) describe how complexes may appear in visions and speak in voices, assuming identities of their own. Jung argued that unity of **consciousness** was an illusion, because complexes could emancipate themselves from conscious control and become visible and audible. SB's determination of the authentic voice would henceforth be compelling and problematic.

Watt is a classic case of the schizoid voice (see **schizophrenia**). He hears nothing of Mr. **Spiro** (29), because of "other voices, singing, crying, stating, murmuring, things intelligible, in his ear." He hears a **mixed choir**, "from without, yes really it seemed from without" (33); it offers the **irrationality** of pi ("Fifty-two point two eight five seven one four"). At Mr. **Knott**'s house he experiences many "incidents of note," the force of which is to dislocate his sense of reality and complicate the relationship of his inner and outer worlds. Abandoned by its inner **rats** (84), his world becomes increasingly "unspeakable" (85). He hears "a little voice" (91) saying that Mr. Knott is shy of **dogs**, but knows not what to make of "this particular little voice." At the station (239), knocked to the ground, he distinguishes fragments of **Hölderlin**, the schizoid poet. The consequences of his illness are seen in his disintegrating discourse with **Sam**, the

Cartesian *méthode* having succumbed under the weight of the trust placed in it. Derrida in "La voix et le phénomène" calls the voice listening to itself "the major instance of illusory self-transcendence"; the voice in *Watt* constitutes a warning of the fate awaiting one who tries too hard to eff the **ineffable**.

Yet the attempt to deconstruct, to decompose, to hear, and to identify the voice is the incessant concern of *Three Novels*. That concern is anticipated in the "German Letter of 1937" where SB expressed his post-**Mauthner** distrust of language and sought a means of boring holes in the silence, seeking not the Joycean "apotheosis of the word" but something on the way to "the literature of the unword" (*Disjecta*, 171–73). What he thought desirable, a necessary stage, was "some form of Nominalist irony," as the basis for an irrational **art**. "Irony" is important. **Windelband** (296) notes the consequences of assuming that universals cannot be substances (the Realist position), and asks what they then might be. Boethius had defined a word ("vox") as a "motion of air produced by the tongue." With this the elements of an extreme Nominalism were given (compare the "extreme Realism" of **William of Champeaux**, *Murphy* 294): universals as collective names and sounds that serve as signs for a multiplicity of substances or their accidents. Nominalism thus formulated (that is, lacking irony) was propounded and defended with some of the intensity of recent poststructuralists, whose assumption of extreme Nominalism accounts for much in SB's writing, but not the ironic "something" seeping through. As Windelband notes (296), the *metaphysics of individualism* that accompanies such a theory of knowledge asserts that only particulars can be regarded as truly real (he invokes **Roscellinus**), and this is a position that SB accepted. The form of Nominalist irony required is thus one that acknowledges the immediacy of "demented particulars." Such **scholasticism** constitutes the background from which the voice emerges in the great writing of the middle period.

The poem "**bon bon il est un pays**" (1947) dramatizes the mind as a place, a location, to which the poet retreats to seek "le calme le calme"—that realm sought by **Malone** (198), beyond the tumult. The voice disturbs that peaceful prospect, because it constitutes a different imperative. **Molloy**'s quest for the self is equally a quest for the voice. He cries out (25), "this time, then another time perhaps, then perhaps a last time." This is the outer voice, not the inner, but it serves to focus the theme. Molloy intuits the inner voice when he hears that of a world collapsing endlessly (40). He chooses not to listen to the whisper, but it is not a sound like other sounds; "it" stops when "it" chooses, and he will hear it always, though it does not suit him to speak of it now. The Unnamable will speak of nothing else. But Molloy soon hears "the small voice" (59) telling him to take his crutches and go; and he obeys. He hears it again (65), telling him his region is vast, and he acknowledges (86) that he is subject to imperatives, **hypothetical** or categorical. The voice that tells him to leave the forest manifests itself as a murmur, "something gone wrong with the silence" (88); at the critical moment (91) he hears a reassuring voice: "Don't fret Molloy, we're coming." This suggests Matthew 14:27 or Acts 23:11, the voice of the Lord saying "Be of good cheer"; it anticipates the Pauline voice heard by the Unnamable.

Moran undergoes a like experience. He recognizes the silence "beyond the fatuous clamour" (121), and tells of the voice that needs no **Gaber** to make it heard, one *within*, ambiguous and not easy to follow, one he is just beginning to know but one he will follow "from this day forth, no matter what it commands" (132). When it ceases he will wait for it to come back. Tomorrow, he adds, he may be of a different mind; indeed, he later recounts (169–70) how he first heard that voice (giving orders, a voice *without*) but paid it no attention. In the final paragraph he returns to that voice, he is getting to know "it" better now, beginning to understand what "it" wants. It tells him to write "this report" (ambiguous and not easy to follow), at once that which has just concluded and the next volumes that relentlessly go **on**.

Malone presents a different aspect of the voice, that of the author who tells stories to pass the **time** and creates **puppets** through which he may be heard. This compulsion for identity will be stripped away in the endeavor to isolate the voice itself. Stories, inventories, **objects**: he must divest himself of these, little by little, in order to fail, to reach the great calm (198). He hears "noises" (206) but has lost the faculty of "decomposing" them. The voice manifests itself in this text less directly than in those flanking it, but Malone's sense (233) that "it's coming" (**death**, the voice), like the images of St. **John**, cry the way of one to come.

The search for the voice is the great theme of *The Unnamable*. The French and English texts vary their beginnings, but their first paragraphs conclude the same way: "Je ne me tairai jamais. Jamais" ("I shall never be silent. Never"). The tone is a composite biblical one. Like John (14:10) he must speak of things of which he cannot speak; like Paul (1 Corinthians 15:10) he invokes an authority not his own, **not** I (qv), but "the grace of God which was with me"; like **Job** (7:11) he speaks in the anguish of his spirit; and like Jeremiah (later said by SB to be the voice behind *Company*) he utters his lamentations. A distinction is drawn between the self that "utters" and the "not I," which cannot so easily be identified. This is implicit in "These things I say" (301), which echoes John 5:34: "these things I say, that ye might be saved"; in imagining "a without" (305; the Calder text omits "a"); and in the paradox of "this voice that is not mine, but can only be mine," and must continue to utter, in order "not to peter out" (307), or go silent (310). This is the drama of *Not I.*

Mahood tells his tale, then is silent, "that is to say his voice continues, but is no longer renewed" (325). The narrator is surrounded by murmurs, vociferations, the "burden" (refrain, **pensum**) of which is "roughly" that he is alive (335). But all this "business about voices" requires to be "revised" (336); he speaks of voices ("Let them come") but the problem remains that of "Assumption": "if I could only find a voice of my own, in all this babble" (348). Mahood and

Murphy sometimes spoke, "but it was clumsily done, you could see the ventriloquist" (348). Yet there is another sound that never stops (349), which forces the recognition that he is in a head, a **skull**, assailed with "noises signifying **nothing**" (351), a voice that has "denatured" him. He considers going deaf (354), invokes the conceit of a head growing out of the ear (356), a kind of transformer, the aural equivalent of the eye, of *percipi,* the paradox of no voice without a listener. If only the voice would stop (364), what could be worse (a soprano perhaps), he's in a dungeon (369), an **oubliette**, with a voice that never stops, he wishes it would stop, this blind voice, "this meaningless voice which prevents you from being nothing" (370), he is the tympanum, vibrating (383).

These agonies culminate in a remarkable passage, accentuating the contrast between "My voice" and "The voice" (393–94), the euphony in French (177) between "Ma" and "La" rendering the difference poignant. The Unnamable hears the voice failing, fears he is going silent, listens hard, intimates the real silence, then as he pauses for air listens for his voice in the silence. It returns ("elle revient"), and with renewed breath he moves to the end. This passage is not in the second manuscript notebook, but two additional leaves containing it are pasted into the flyleaf of the first and were reworked into the novel. Internal evidence reveals that this material predates that around it, and is probably the earliest part. This passage may well be "text" for the entire novel, the nucleus, a point of departure that in turn forms the conclusion. Yet the nature and location of the voice at the end are as much a mystery as in the beginning. This is implicit in the subatomic imagery that governs the novel (see **physics**), the old stable ego of self split to reveal a quantum world of non-Newtonian **motion**, in which the voice may be heard but not located, or located but not heard, and in which the very attempt to "id-entify" it is doomed to frustration. Such uncertainty (in Heisenberg's sense) suggests why the novel must end in an impasse.

Yet the voice in need of an **auditor**, a **spectator**, an audience, say, the paradox of *percipi* (no voice without a listener) dramatically turns in the novel, and anticipates the structure of the dialogic within the monologue, an audience folded into the discourse, that informs much of SB's later drama. The unnamable invokes his audience, waiting for the show to begin, a free show, perhaps compulsory, "it takes time, you hear a voice, perhaps it's a recitation, that's the show" (381). Much of the later drama, like "A **Piece of Monologue**," is virtually indistinguishable from the late prose fiction, which is why so many theater professionals staged the haunting, monologic short prose where the source of the voice is uncertain, its role as a marker of being increasingly dubious. *From an Abandoned Work* was initially published as a theater piece (Faber, 1958), after it was performed on BBC 3 by Patrick **Magee** (14 December 1957). With it the separation of prose fiction from stage drama dissolved as SB explored the sources and authenticity of voices. Yet it was some time before he would trust drama for direct expression of his major theme; until the mid-1960s he explored it first in the fiction.

Following *Three Novels* SB tried still to move (the paradox implicit in this phrasing) beyond the impasse, to locate the voice within that is equally the voice without. *Texts for Nothing* pursue this goal, unsuccessfully (SB considered them failures), rehearsing the "old aporetics." "Text 2" accepts that "it must be in the head" (106), "Text 3" that the voices are "only lies" (109), that they "have no life in them" (113). "Text 4" asks, "what would I say, if I had a voice," only to conclude, "this voice cannot be mine." "Text 5" strains for a voice "not from without," but fears it might be "the voice of reason" (118), different from "all these voices, like a rattling of chains in my head" (120). The awareness of "that other who is me" in "Text 8" makes it difficult to accept "this voice as mine" (133); "Text 10" seeks "a voice of silence, the voice of my silence" (the disjunction between "la voix" and "ma voix"). The "vile words" of "Text 11" make him believe he's here, "a head with a voice belonging to it" (145), and that "a voice speaks that can be none but mine" (146). Yet in "Text 12" it's "not me" ("Not I" in the accusative), and the final text begins by affirming, "Weaker still the weak old voice that tried in vain to make me." The old paradox remains: "No voice ever but in my life"; the impersonal phrasing, "it murmurs"; and the partial resolution, "nothing but a voice murmuring a trace" (152). The image of the "trace" is poignant and ephemeral, a flurry of dust disturbed by movement in the air, evidence of the voice that was but cannot endure, leaving no trace against the "black nothing" (154), the voice that cannot speak yet cannot cease. The "impasse" has not been broken but the voice goes on.

The issue is unresolved yet again in *How It Is*. The novel introduces the voice that was "once without" and then "in me," "an ancient voice in me not mine." This restates the thesis of *The Unnamable*, the need to express as obligation or pensum. Before **Pim**, the voice is "afar" (13); "changeable" (15); "once **quaqua** then in me" (20); "barely audible" (23); yet "not mine" (40). With Pim, attention moves to the voice of the other. Pim's voice is "extorted" (21), but his is not that ancient voice the narrator seeks, and there is no telling whether Pim has heard it (74). Again, the distinction is between the voice that utters and the "first voice." Whatever the status of the latter, "above" or "without" (79), there is "only one voice my voice never any other" (87) that he hears and murmurs, though it be folly. It leaves, it comes back (95), like that of the unnamable, in **Mauthner**'s terms asserting the unity of word and thought and being. Part 2 ends with the restatement of the voice "in me that was without quaqua," but introduces the notion of "the voice of us all" (99), to be examined in Part 3. This notion constitutes the difference between the narrator as sole elect or the sense of universal experience. By a rigorous process of logic when the voice comes "back at last" (106), the universal (a choir, megaphones, "the voice of us all") manifests itself as that of the self alone, just as the possibility of the many is ruthlessly reduced to knowledge of the one (108–28). The given is the **solitude** (129), and

the voice that recounts it is the sole means of living it; "a past a present and a future" have been joined by the fourth inevitability, the voice. His life comprises "bits and scraps strung together" (133) by "an ancient voice ill-spoken ill-heard," the modality of both **witness** and scribe in doubt. His only conclusion (134) is that "my life" is constituted by "a voice without" (ill spoken, ill heard), which is now "in me in the vault bone-white" (ill heard, ill murmured). This is not an advance on *The Unnamable*, nor even on the opening of this novel, because no advance is possible beyond the deductive logic (139) that reduces "this anonymous voice self-styled quaqua the voice of us all" to the "single voice" within: "this voice quaqua yes all balls yes only one voice here yes mine yes" (144–45). The echo of the end of *Ulysses* mocks univocality, but (when the panting stops) there is finally "only me yes alone yes with my voice" (146), for that is how it is.

In *Company* the voice returns, but mostly as **memory**, as the old themes are rehearsed once more. SB considered calling the piece "**Verbatim**" or "Voice" but came to think of it as a text to "keep going (company)" (Knowlson, 574). Like other **closed space** tales, *Company* is neither memoir nor autobiography but an interplay of voices, a fugue between one imagining himself into existence and an external voice addressing the hearer as "you." A voice (not "the voice") comes from the dark (3). It is company but not enough (5); it comes from first one quarter then another (9); like that of Augustine it ebbs and flows (11), **comes and goes**. Its goal is "To have the hearer have a past and acknowledge it" (24), or to create "an addition to company" (41). But the images are ill seen, and the voices often false, fictions, or figments whose role is that of aesthetic play, or devising company, for one who at the end as in the beginning finds himself as he always was: alone.

Yet that voice, the enigmatic disembodied sound that swells out of the darkness like a radio transmission, for all its paradoxes and ambiguities, for all its irresolutions, is SB's most profound, original, and complex literary creation. At once seducer and assailant, comforter and adversary, it has been stageable since its dramatic appearance in *Molloy,* where it was imprisoned on the page. It made its escape, its liberation in *plein air,* as the voice of **Krapp** (1958) and thereafter moved freely from page to stage, as the line dividing SB's prose monologues from his stage monologues grew fainter and as he began to explore the theatrical possibilities of the voice as thoroughly as he had explored the fictive. Liberated from the page, the voice would never again sit mute.

SB returned to the structural idea of echo that dominated his early poetry to provide the foundation of pastiche in *Fin de partie.* In his 1967 staging he told the cast, "The play is full of echoes, they all answer each other." The echoes of *Endgame* are less bodiless voices than bodies with voices not their own, voices with indeterminate sources. **Clov**'s opening monologue is already an echo, a repetition, the voice heard when one character echoes another. This becomes a central structural and thematic element of the play. His "Finished, it's finished, nearly finished, it must be nearly fin-

ished" not only announces the end of the play barely begun, a paradox played throughout the drama; it is equally an echo of **Christ**'s Parthian shaft, His final words on the cross, as recorded in John 19:30. Among the play's play of echoes, **Hamm** reiterates these words near the play's end to announce his own, his giving up the ghost, but his echo of Christ is thus an anticipation of Clov's opening remarks. Like Caliban, Clov has no language, no voice of his own; he is a replica, a re-presentation, an echo. He snaps at Hamm, "I use the words you taught me. If they don't mean anything any more, teach me others. Or let me be silent" (44). If Clov had a language of his own he might offer his version of life in the shelter; instead, he can speak only by appropriating another's voice, he can only re-play Hamm's set piece. The ontological enigma in *Endgame* might be summed: can a multiplicity of voices make up an identity, a life?

All That Fall began SB's infatuation with broadcast technology and allowed him to push the exploration of voice into unforeseen areas, the drama of pure voice. His first radio play was fairly conventional, relying on a bevy of semirealistic sound effects and a plot that ends as the beginning of what may be a murder mystery. Hearing the BBC recording, SB incorporated the recorded voice into *Krapp's Last Tape.* As Krapp prepares for his annual birthday ritual, he listens to past tapes and the voice of memory is reified in those weighing heavy on his desk as memories lie heavy on his mind. The voices he hears are as strange to him as if they were another's. They must be *his* tapes, a record of *his* life, but whether or not they represent his being, his identity, his essence, is one expression of the paradox of voice.

The success of *All That Fall* prompted "**Embers**" (1957), which SB withheld until 1959. He spoke about its structure to P. L. Mignon, and in so doing restated the paradox of voice. The play rests "sur une ambiguité: le personnage a-t-il une hallucination ou est-il en présence de la réalité?" (Zilliacus, 83). Like *Endgame,* "Embers" is set on the margins of land and sea, with Henry speaking at first to his drowned **father,** whose death has haunted him, then to Ada about their daughter, Addie; the scenes are replayed against the incessant sounds of the sea. Ada tells Henry that he will soon be quite alone with his voice, that there will be no other voice in the world but his. Whether the voices represent physical presences or are the product of Henry's mind, recurrent echoes of his past, remains irresolute, but such ambiguity substantially advances SB's manipulation of the medium. It prompted a flurry of pieces, two abandoned in the 1960s and resurrected in the 1970s ("**Rough for Radio I and II**"), and two that were **mirror** images of each other ("**Cascando**" and "**Words and Music**"). The metaphor for "Rough I" is two knobs on a radio, but the work remains a weaker version of the theme treated masterfully in "Cascando" and "Words and Music," the attempt to bring if not harmony between two forms of the voice, words and music, at least peace.

With "Rough for Radio II" SB began to explore torture as a metaphor for creativity. As such the radio play anticipates "**What Where.**" The victim, bound, blindfolded, gagged, ears plugged, hooded, is "**Fox,**" the voiceless form of "Vox," or voice. The session begins with an unveiling of the "ravishing" F/Vox, whom the "same old team" prods to speech or confession. The difficulty is access to the voice and its veracity once tapped, but the too-obvious links between voice and repressed memory may account for SB's decision to jettison the work. In 1964 the voice took a dramatic turn toward the ethereal, the ghostly. All that remained of the characters were their voices, the echo of their lives. "**Play**" features three postmortem characters—voices, instruments, part of the funeral urns that have swallowed all but their heads. Side by side, the figures never speak to one another but respond only to a mechanical stimulus, the inquisitorial light that forces them to speak.

In "**Eh Joe,**" the voice is aggressive, antagonistic, an assailant, as it insinuates itself into Joe's consciousness to torment him over a suicidal lover. This echoes the Unnamable's "I can't stop it, I can't prevent it, from tearing me, racking me, assailing me" (307). Joe struggles to suppress it as he has suppressed the voices of his family. The voice is "Mental thuggee," and the final smile, added to SB's production of the play, suggests that Joe is temporarily successful at suppressing it. This voice, that of a former lover, appears to emanate from "that penny farthing hell" he calls his mind, but it is not just memory of a dead past. She rehearses details of a suicide that neither she nor Joe could know firsthand and that the dead lover could not report. Yet SB insisted on the concrete reality of the assailing voice, insisting to Siegfried

Melchinger, "She really whispers in him. He hears her. Only if she lives can he have the wish to kill her. She is dead, but in him she lives. That is his passion: to kill the voices, which he cannot kill" (Kalb, 103). She is both person and figment, internal and external; the broader problem of where the voice is located is unresolved.

SB's tour de force of the staged voice is a pair of plays written just before his seventieth birthday, and performed in that honor. *That Time* and *Footfalls* opened at the Royal Court (May 1976), the latter directed by SB and starring Billie **Whitelaw**. In *That Time,* Listener, a floating head some ten feet above stage level, listens to three voices, **A, B,** and **C,** recite what are apparently memories of his past. The voices come from both sides of the theater and above. Only the face of Listener is seen, hair spread out so that the audience may be looking down on a figure in bed, perhaps. The rest of the stage is dark, which focuses attention on the face, but the face is off center, suggesting that although it is the only physical representation on stage it is not the sole focus of attention. The three voices that speak continuously (save two pauses and the last twenty-three seconds) are thus "central." Like Krapp's tapes, they represent the same person at different stages in his life: A in middle age trying to remember his childhood, B in childhood, and C in old age. Yet the stories are alien, voices of another, Listener barely responding until the end appears, not suggesting success in stilling the voices but in having arranged their succession in an artful pattern.

Written to accompany *That Time, Footfalls,* featuring an aged, pacing woman in tattered nightwear, is divided into four parts, each separated by chimes, which grow fainter in each sounding. In part I the pacing **May** addresses the voice of her dying **mother,** whom May is apparently attending at her last, the mother in her nineties, May in her forties. In part II Woman's Voice (the Mother, apparently) observes and narrates her daughter's obsessive pacing as the daughter tries to confirm her existence with the material sounds of her footsteps and the dragging of her nightwear. The "Sequel" begins part III, May's story. May, who herself may be narrated, narrates herself (in both senses), a semblance of what the audience thinks it sees on stage. Her anagrammatic other, **Amy,** is represented in dialogue with *her* mother, Mrs. **Winter,** concerning the former's attendance at Evensong: "I saw nothing, heard nothing, of any kind. I was not there." SB took pains to suggest the coda's thematic significance, emphasizing that the thought-tormented body is not there, or rather that it exists only within the embedded narratives of the play, constructed by the interplay of bodiless voices. The final ten seconds with "No trace of May" is a crucial reminder that May was always "not there," or there only as a "trace," a voice. Such dramatic absence, bodiless presence, anticipates the ghostly works for television, where being is twice removed, and the late plays, **"Ohio Impromptu," "Rockaby,"** and "What Where."

In "What Where," a dimly lit megaphone (in the original, unrevised text) announces images of the last five beings, "In the present as were we still." The apparently authoritative voice of Bam, as bodiless megaphone or (later) shimmery light or hologram, is already a voice from beyond the grave, according to SB. Four characters, Bam, **Bom**, **Bim**, and Bem (a fifth unseen is being "worked over" as the play opens), nearly identical in appearance, their names differentiated by a vowel (see **Rimbaud**), are represented as if they existed. Bam's voice (V) controls the action, switching light (of memory, imagination) on and off the playing area, or the space of memory, to initiate action. Recasting the play for television, SB altered the visual imagery and simplified dialogue and action, trimming the false starts, revising away much of the metatheatrical revisions of the original. In Stuttgart the speaking voice became a huge, distorted face of Bam, refracted, diffuse, and dominating half the television screen. In his Stuttgart notebook SB wrote that "S (Stimme [Voice]) = **mirror** reflection of Bam's face." This deathmask replaced the suspended "small megaphone at head level" of the original publication; as SB noted, "Loudspeaker out."

The image that now intrigued him was the hooded statue of John **Donne**, the Dean of St. Paul's, spectral in his sculptured rendering. The two staged Bams, however, two stage or video representations and their corresponding voices, are not the same entity, not two versions of the same body or character. In the Stuttgart TV production the difference was achieved mechanically. "There was a slightly higher frequency in [the voice] of the younger Bam, and a lower, deeper effect in the older Bam," according to cameraman Jim Lewis (Fehsenfeld, 237). In both French and English stage productions that followed

SB's revised text, the vocal difference was achieved by recording and altering V to create, as Walter Asmus suggests, "the ghost Bam, dead Bam, distorted image of a face in a grave, somewhere not in this world any longer, imagining that he comes back to life in the world, dreaming and seeing himself as a little face on the screen" (Fehsenfeld, 238). In the Stuttgart notebook SB wrote, "S's voice prerecorded. Bam's, but changed." He added, "Bam's voice in dialogue with some colour. S colourless." Instead of players in long gray gowns, their corporeality suspect, the four figures of the revised "What Where" appeared as floating faces dissolving in and out of the TV screen, which became the field of memory to replace the lighted rectangle of the stage, in a dialectic of "disappearance and manifestation." Neither representation of Bam is corporeal, SB representing instead a specter and its mirror reflection. The rest of the figures are also ghosts, the more so as they are re-presented by the patterns of dots on the TV screen. Whatever characters or bodies finally exist in "What Where" are created by voice, less absent presences than present absences. Such a treatment of dramatic figures simultaneously effaces and reinscribes the body in the body of SB's drama.

"What Where" was SB's last dramatic work, and being is finally represented by voice. SB said he could spend hours sitting quietly, doing nothing but listen to his inner voice and observe his inner life. That comment could gloss his creative output, coupled as it inevitably is with the disappearance of the body, its literary representation both as character and as self. To Charles Juliet he noted that he had eliminated self increasingly: "In the end you don't know who is speaking any more. The subject disappears completely. That's the end result of the identity crisis" (*Conversations,* 7). As the subject disappears so does its literary emblem, the **body**. What remains is its echo, its recording, its trace, its footfalls, its voice.

"The Voice" [Verbatim]: unpublished manuscript (RUL 2910) of a prose text ("Paris, Jan. 1977") with affinities to *Company* in its references to Ballyorgan Road, **Croker's Acres**, a **father**'s shade, and topcoat green and stiff with dirt and age. It asserts an intimate relationship between **Voice** and Hearer, dramatized as if to be spoken: "Why die I not? My life is mud. I shall not be. O that I were. Perish the day. Let me be (same flat tone)." Then, breathless, faint, and fading away.

Voltaire: pseudonym of François-Marie Arouet (1694–1778), French writer and universal genius of the Enlightenment, whose attacks upon the ancien régime and abuses of clerical and **political** power twice led to his incarceration in the Bastille, and to exile. SB appreciated the wit of *Candide*'s attack on **Leibniz**'s doctrine of **preestablished harmony** and affirmation of the best of all possible worlds (the "celebrated conviction" articulated by **Arsene** in *Watt,* 41). He used its image of the 1755 **Lisbon** earthquake as an emblem of the arbitrary, and deployed "**Che Sciagura**" many times. Miss **Counihan** suggests Candide's beloved Counégonde. In 1937 SB visited the Palace of Sans-Souci, Potsdam,

and wrote of Voltaire's room there with its ambience of exile and loneliness (Knowlson, 229), describing it to **MacGreevy** (18 January) as "charming and comic." Yet, like **Johnson**, SB had deep-rooted objections to Voltaire, particularly his Deism and belief in progress. He offers **Lucky**'s critique in *Waiting for Godot,* that man was born to waste and pine. This is anticipated in *Dream* (197), the "withered pontiffs" reflecting **Carlyle**'s opinion of Voltaire (DN, 41) and **Belacqua** preferring **Racine**'s twilight to the "chiarinoscurissimo" of the Enlightenment.

voyeurism: an unhealthy minor motif resonant through the early fiction, most clearly in "**Walking Out**" when **Lucy** wonders if her **Belacqua** could be "a creepy-crawly" (108). Indeed he could: Belacqua's delight in finding that Lucy has spied upon him anticipates his solitary pleasures observing copulating couples, in [Peeping] "Tom's Wood." Watching the young German girl and her **Harold's Cross** Tanzherr, he is perceived and soundly thrashed. In *Dream* (72) Belacqua is called a "hedgecreeper," similarly disposed.

The Schule Dunkelbrau is on a park, "more beautiful and tangled far than the Bois de Boulogne or any other multis latebra opportuna that it is possible to imagine" (13); this gives Viennese "swells" the chance to watch the Evites bronzing their impudenda. "Lurking holes of opportunity for many" derives from **Ovid** (*Metamorphoses* III.443), the words of **Narcissus** to the woods about him (compare "Bois de Vincennes," DN, 158). The phrase is repeated in *Murphy*

(74), with similar intonations, to distinguish between a voyeur and a *voyant* (90), mocking **Rimbaud**'s desire to be a seer. **Wylie** has worshiped Miss **Counihan** afar, "through Zeiss glasses, at a watering place" (60). Miss **Carriage** has hopes frustrated watching through the keyhole as **Cooper** prepares for bed (256). **Moran**'s son instinctively imitates his **father** by spying on him (94).

Dream asserts (207) that the author or reader peeps and creeps on the characters, particularly when they are dressing. In later works, themes of perception persist. **Clov** looks out the windows with his telescope for any signs of life. In *How It Is* the narrator recalls another: "I watched him after my fashion from afar through my spy-glass sidelong in **mirrors** through windows at night" (9). The "shuttered judas" in the cells at the **MMM** (*Murphy*, 181) permits the custodian to observe the lunatic. In *Film,* the protagonist **O** is the **object** of E, the camera eye. This is identical to the sense that many characters have, that they are **witnessed**. M in "**Play**" suggests the central dramatic and ontological problem in that play when he asks, "Am I as much as being seen?" Theater is inherently a voyeuristic medium, the audience from the safety of the dark spying on the "life in the light."

"**The Vulture**": first poem in *Echo's Bones,* which in six succinct lines defines the poet's despair. In a signed copy, now in the **HRHRC** (#42), SB noted: "not without reference to **Goethe**'s Dem Geier gleich, etc" (the first stanza of "Harzreise im Winter"). "Der Geier," was used in *Lyrik in Limes Verlag* (1961), a publicity booklet for *Gedichte.* Goethe's sensibility, like a hovering vulture, seeks its prey for it hungers to create, but SB's is encompassed within the cranium "shell." It swoops like a vulture on the hope of **death** ("the prone"), but is mocked by living tissue that, like the palsied man cured by **Christ** (Matthew 9:6), insists on living and will not "serve": an insatiable hunger that can be appeased only by its own death, when "earth and sky" will equally be offal. The image returns in "**Text 1**": "Eye ravening patient in the haggard vulture face, perhaps it's carrion time." Peter Murphy in *Reconstructing Beckett* sees the poem as embodying an aesthetics of Orphic creation "re-written" in the later works, mocking yet enacting the integration of language, self, and world.

W

W: woman, as in "**Play**" (W1 and W2) or "**Rockaby**." In *Company* (59), having decided to call the hearer M, the narrator calls himself W, but concludes that "W too is creature. Figment" (63). This echoes the **Unnamable**'s transformation from **Mahood** to **Worm**.

Miss Wade's: a "select school for young ladies" (O'Brien, 357), run by the Misses G. and E. Wade at 78 Morehampton Road. SB's cousins Sheila and Molly Roe and also Mary **Manning** attended. In *Come and Go*, Vi, Ru, and Flo sit as "in the playground at Miss Wade's."

Wagner, Richard (1813–83): German composer who celebrated the heroic ethos. SB did not admire his music, as antithetical to his sense that less is more (Knowlson, 443). In *Dream* (28) and "Enueg I," Chapelizod is reduced to "the snug chez Isolde" and a "perturbation of sweaty heroes" from Kilmainham. A reluctant **Belacqua** is dragged along by **Liebert** to *Die Walküre* (Georges **Pelorson** was a confirmed Wagnerite), only to be turned away because the latter's beautiful plus fours are unacceptable (*Dream*, 37). Wagner is, Belacqua opines (citing **Burton**), "a roaring meg" against melancholy (38). Liebert appears one night (48) and insists on playing *Tristan* with the light out. A sustained Wagnerian parody concludes **Molloy**'s narrative: unable to hear the celebrated **forest murmurs** (qv) he replies to a dis-tant **gong** like Siegfried, but with his **bicycle** horn, an exquisite burlesque intimating a greater awareness of the *Ring* than SB might usually admit.

Waiting for Godot: SB's translation of *En attendant Godot,* subtitled (in English only) "a tragicomedy in two acts." First published by **Grove Press** (1954), $4.75 in hardcover but in a $1.00 trade paperback, which delighted SB, pages numbered oddly on the verso only (corrected only in Grove's 2001 reprint). A version, with photos from the first New York and London productions, appeared in *Theatre Arts* 40.8 (August 1956): 36–61, mispaginated. The **Faber** edition did not appear until 1956, nor in paperback until 1959, and then in a bowdlerized form (see **censorship**). An acting edition, with details of the first production, a stage diagram, properties, and lighting effects, was published (London: Samuel French [Acting Editions #510], 1957), with significant variants. The first English and American editions differ significantly. Faber printed the text of the Criterion production, but hundreds of variants exist between it and Grove. Faber "corrected" its *Godot* (1965) to what it called the "complete and unexpurgated text . . . authorized by Mr Beckett as definitive" (but see *Complete Dramatic Works*). The most accurate text is in *Theatrical Notebooks* I, ed. Dougald McMillan and James Knowlson (Faber, and Grove, 1993). It is based on SB's revisions for his **Schiller-Theater** production (1975) and the London **San Quentin Drama Workshop**, based on the Schiller production but revised further at the Riverside Studios (March 1984). Two limited editions have appeared. One, forty copies (seven signed by SB), was printed with fourteen original etchings by Dallas Henke (May 1977 to July 1979). A Folio Society edition (London and New York, 2000), preface by Edward Beckett and illustrated by Tom Phillips, uses the 1965 Faber text.

The first English performance was in the New Arts Theatre, London (3 August 1955 to 3 September, thirty-one performances), dir. Peter Hall, with Peter Woodthorpe (**Estragon**), Paul Daneman (**Vladimir**), Timothy Bateson (**Lucky**), and Peter Bull (**Pozzo**). It was transferred to the Criterion Theatre, Picadilly (12 September to 24 March 1956, a further 226 performances); it used what SB called Faber's "mutilated" version (the Gozzo family with warts, rather than the clap, no unbuttoned flies or erections). A **Dublin** performance followed (28 October 1955) at the **Pike Theatre**, dir. Alan Simpson, with Austin Byrne (Estragon), Dermot Kelly (Vladimir), Nigel FitzGerald (Pozzo), and Donal Donnelly (Lucky). A popular success, it moved to the **Gate**, went on tour, and ran for more than a hundred performances. This was possible as, no longer in the Commonwealth, **Ireland** was not bound to observe English copyright law.

The first American performance, dir. Alan **Schneider**, was a comic fiasco. *Godot* ran at the Coconut Grove Playhouse in Miami Beach (3 January 1956 to 14 January 1956), with Bert Lahr (Estragon), Tom Ewell (Vladimir), Charles Weichman (Lucky), and J. Scott Smart (Pozzo). Audiences and cast were bemused. Billed as "the laugh hit of two continents," it left vacationing heliophiles unamused. Tours in Washington, Boston, and Philadelphia, and the planned transfer to the Music Box theater, New York (16 February), were canceled. The debacle (which left SB "cold as camphor") did little for his faith in America. With a new director (Herbert Berghoff) and, save Lahr, a new cast—E. G. Marshall (Didi), Alvin Epstein (Lucky), and Kurt Kasznar (Pozzo)—the play opened at the John Golden Theater (19 April 1956). Producer Michael Meyerberg appealed in the *New York Times* for seventy thousand "intellectuals" to support the play, which ran for ten weeks, a respectful New York debut. It was recorded for Columbia Records (02L-238, High Fidelity), SB finding it quite good and Pozzo remarkable. Myerberg proposed another production, and SB wrote to Rosset, "I mentioned to him that I thought *Godot* by an all Negro cast would be interesting." The new *Godot* opened at the Ethel Barrymore Theater with Mantan Moreland (Gogo), Earle Hyman (Didi), Geoffrey Holder (Lucky), and Rex Ingram (Pozzo). SB's loyalties remained with Schneider. Fired after the Miami fiasco, Schneider staged the premiere of *Endgame* (28 January 1958) to become SB's preferred American director.

America was the scene of an amazingly apposite early performance. The Actor's Workshop of San Francisco took Herbert Blau's production (selected because of its all-male cast) into

San Quentin prison (November 1957). While New York "intellectuals" puzzled over the meaning of Godot—God? Happiness? Eternal Life? Christian salvation? The future (by definition never *present*)?—the "captive" audience at San Quentin, inmates "sentenced to life," understood the play immediately, viscerally. They might not comprehend critical theory, **surrealist** or Dadaist manifestos, existential philosophy, or phenomenological aesthetics, but they knew the waiting game—waiting for change in their condition, for the mail, for appeals, for pardons. Waiting with **nothing** happening, doing **time**. As the inmate reviewer wrote for the *San Quentin News* (28 November 1957): "We're still waiting for Godot, and shall continue to wait. When the scenery gets too drab and the action too slow, we'll call each other names and swear to part forever—but then there's no place to go." The Actor's Workshop production was chosen by the State Department to represent the United States at the 1958 World's Fair, Brussels.

SB generally refused permission for filmed versions of *Godot* ("I will not consent to a film being made of *Godot*"). He rejected lucrative offers from Bert Lahr ("I do not wish *Godot* or any other of my works to be made into a film," SB to Grove [17 March 1959]), and by Tyrone Guthrie, the latter to be directed by Igmar Bergman ("Continue not to want *Godot* 'turned' into a film, even by Ingmar Bergman," SB to Grove [8 December 1959]), but he finally accepted television. A version was filmed at the BBC (26 June 1961), dir. Donald **McWhinnie**, with Peter Woodthorpe (Estragon), Jack **MacGowran** (Vladimir), Felix Fenton (Pozzo), and Timothy Bateson (Lucky). A production for NTA followed, dir. Alan Schneider, and finally filmed in New York (3–8 April 1961) with Zero Mostel (Estragon), Burgess Meredith (Vladimir), Kurt Kasznar (Pozzo), and Alvin Epstein (Lucky), commercially available from Applause Books. The San Quentin Drama Workshop production, based on SB's Schiller-Theater staging of 1975 and revised at the Riverside Studios, London (March 1984), is available on videotape in the "Beckett Directs Beckett" series, from the University of Maryland Visual Press and the Smithsonian Institution Press, with Lawrence Held (Estragon), Bud Thorpe (Vladimir), Alan Mandel (Lucky), and Rick Cluchey (Pozzo). Cluchey, an inmate at San Quentin (1957), later founded the San Quentin acting group.

Godot revolutionized Western theater. In the words of Harold Hobson, "It renewed the English theatre in a single night"—like the tree in Act 2, perhaps. Jean Anouilh described it as "a music-hall sketch of Pascal's *Pensées* as played by the Fraterlini clowns." William Saroyan, in the liner notes to the Columbia recording, noted, "It is an important play, perhaps one of the most important of all, of all times." So unexpected a play, yet in retrospect inevitable. Its nearly bare stage and disconnected dialogue captured a sense of emptiness, desolation, uncertainty, a post**war** malaise, an angst that had never been staged before. Small but significant differences separate the **French** and English texts. Some, like Vladimir's inability (40.a) to remember the farmer's name (**Bonnelly**), show how the translation became more indefinite, attrition and loss of **memory** more pronounced. Vladimir's "He said Saturday. (*Pause*) I think," is less assured than "Samedi soir et suivants." The French text does not include Vladimir's half-allusion to Proverbs 13:12, the heartache of hope deferred (8.a), which gives the English extra poignancy. Estragon's "Les gens sont des cons" lacks the **Darwinian** implications of "people are bloody ignorant apes" (9.b). Lucky's dance, "The Scapegoat's Agony" (27.a), is a curious echo of Leviticus 16:7–10, intensifying the religious anguish, the image of the preterit. Above all, the difference between a tree "couvert de feuilles" and one with "four or five leaves" diminishes the hope of Christian renewal, as in **Dante**'s *Purgatorio* (XXXII.59–60): "s'innovò la pianta / che prima avea le ramora sì sole" ("the tree was renewed that first had its branches so bare"). To rephrase Estragon's lament (34.b), the English text crucifies more slowly.

There was nothing really new about the play. For SB, it revisited familiar themes rather than reflecting ideas he was exploring in the fiction (notably the **voice**). Its elements have been part of Judeo-Christian culture for thousands of years. As Vladimir says, "Hope deferred maketh the something sick, who said that?" (8.a). This is Proverbs 13:12: "Hope deferred maketh the heart sick; but when **desire** cometh, it is a tree of life." On stage the tree of life looks suspiciously like the tree of **death**. Yet it sprouts overnight and represents minimal vitality in an otherwise arid world. Where leaves sprout, when life changes, when time passes, then hope remains; yet

the very presence of such hope, the fact that it cannot be quite extinguished, may be the cruelest joke of all. Lamentations 3:26 states: "It is good that man should both hope and quietly wait for the salvation of the Lord." In Romans 8:24-25 salvation and hope remain out of reach: "We are saved by hope: but hope that is seen is not hope; for what a man seeth, why doth he yet hope for? But if we hope for that we see not, then do we with patience wait for it." **Moran** calls this "hellish hope." Such concerns are as old as the **Bible**. To Vladimir's "Time has stopped," Pozzo replies brutally, "Don't you believe it, Sir, don't you believe it. . . . Whatever you like, but not that." As SB suggested in *Proust*, time is "a double headed monster of damnation and salvation." Its passing fuels hope, but in that passing humanity deteriorates, "wastes and pines." The rock on which the hope of the world might flourish is a wasteland, the earth an "abode of stones."

What is to be made of these waiters, finally? Are they **irrational**, foolish, **absurd**, maintaining hope despite overwhelming evidence to the contrary? Or are they the epitome of faith and so of Christianity, the imagery of which permeates the play, like **Job**? To such questions SB might answer "perhaps"—the most important word, he told one interviewer. Vladimir refers to Luke 23:39–43 when he suggests that one of the **two thieves** (qv) was saved: "It's a reasonable percentage." Yet the more reflection Vladimir gives the matter, the worse the odds grow. Only one of the four Gospels mentions the saved thief, but all four Apostles were there, or (in Vladimir's devastating qualification) thereabouts. The even chance diminishes to one in eight, as the absurd relationship of **mathematics** and **irrationality** is highlighted. Even when salvation appears possible its dispensation seems arbitrary. SB said, only half jokingly, that one of Estragon's feet is saved. And if one thief is saved, why? In Matthew 25:32–33, the **sheep** are saved, the **goats** are punished. SB's reversal ("He beats my brother, sir") accentuates the arbitrary nature of a religious system of rewards and punishment, of salvation and damnation, and so of human existence, possibility, dignity. Were Godot to arrive, would he be predictable? Which of the two would be saved?

"And if we dropped him?" Estragon asks. "He'd punish us," Vladimir replies. "And if he comes?" (E), then "We'll be saved" (V). Saved from what? When Vladimir suggests that they might repent, the question is repent what: "Our being born?" But it is too late for that. **Existential** pessimism is not peculiar to modern man's alienation and angst, but this restates the traditional Christian view of the world as a place of suffering, a vale of tears, a *via dolorosa.* Yet *Godot* is not somber tragedy. SB called it a tragicomedy, and its sources are the tradition of harlequin in tears, *Il Pagliacci,* Charlie Chaplin's sad **clowns**. This is the view of **Schopenhauer**, who states (*WWI,* I.iv #58, 415–16) that the life of every individual is really a tragedy, but in detail it has the character of a comedy: "Thus, as if fate would add derision to the misery of our existence, our life must contain all the woes of tragedy, and yet we cannot even assert the dignity of tragic characters, but in the broad detail of life must

inevitably be the foolish characters of a comedy." The play ends without tragic dignity, without any sense of suffering ennobled by man's **stoic** endurance. When the two in despair decide to try to end physical existence by hanging themselves the cord breaks and Estragon's trousers fall about his ankles, an image of bathos and absurdity. Like the audience, they may resolve to come back tomorrow, but if, in the famous **aporia**, nothing has happened, twice, at best they can expect the same again, a spiritual and physical impasse, hope still deferred.

"Walking Out": sixth story of *MPTK,* but probably the first composed (August 1931), as echoes of "**Sedendo et Quiesc[i]endo**" intimate; "A hedge-creeper! A peeping Tom in bicycle-clips" (15) indicates that **voyeurism** was central to its concern (the action takes place in "Tom's Wood"). The title is an Irish expression for courting, yet **Belacqua** walks out *on* his fiancée before a celibate marriage. The story begins one "fateful fine Spring evening" in **Croker**'s Gallops, the locale of **Arsene**'s celebration of the seasons, and of *Not I.* Only the cuckoo is wanting, this anticipating Belacqua's hopes, not quite to be realized, of cuckoldry. But when all is said, what a splendid thing to be young and vigorous. Ironies abide.

Belacqua is at best a dubious hero, but any residual sympathy the reader might have for him is rendered impossible, if not by his casual treatment of **Lucy** then by his activities as a voyeur. Yet sympathy, **pity**, is what the story challenges. What Belacqua finds charming in Lucy is not her entrancing figure or **face** but that she climbed onto the roof to spy on him (see 2 Samuel 18:24), curiously asserting the dictum that to be is to be perceived. The truth about his solitary promenades (see **Rousseau**) strikes her, and she wonders how this young man of good family, "so spiritual, a Varsity man too, could be such a creepy-crawly." Before she can reconcile her doubts Lucy is casually run over by a "superb silent limousine, a Daimler no doubt" (110), which renders her crippled for life. Meanwhile, Belacqua receives the kicks he richly deserves from the so-called Tanzherr (Harold's Cross is a tough Dublin suburb), a hint of the political brutality of **Germany**. The ending is ironic: unlike **Wordsworth**, Belacqua laments not his Lucy but his celebration of their life together in terms of **Schubert**'s "An die Musik" mocks sentimental *Dichtung*. That he is so happily married to the crippled Lucy as to be sorry for himself when she dies ("What a Misfortune," 114) is a dubious endorsement of such pleasure.

Wallenstein: the beer (Brauerei Cheb, Pilsen) **Moran** offers **Gaber** (97). "Wallensteins Lager" ("camp") (1798) is the first part of Schiller's trilogy on the life of Count Albrecht von Wallenstein, who led the Imperial armies during the Thirty Years' War. The lager's label depicts Wallenstein's camp.

Walpole, Hugh (1884–1941): English novelist whose *Judith Paris* (1931) SB read in **Roussillon**, taking from it for *Watt* (31) the detail of bears that turn their heads when baited (Knowlson, 297–98). This generates **pity**: "He was a very old bear, who had been travelling for

an infinity of years; he was very weary and did not understand why things were as they were" (*Judith Paris*, 71). The bear represents dignity in suffering and, by lifting its head, becomes finer than his tormenters, like the protagonist of "**Catastrophe**," baited and humiliated.

Walther: in "The **Calmative**" (71) the narrator sits on a stone seat and crosses his legs "like Walther," an image repeated in *Molloy* (125) and *Stirrings Still* (263). This is Walther von der Vogelweide (ca. 1170–1230), greatest of the medieval German *minnesänger* (see "**Da tagte es**"). The posture derives from Walther's *Spruch* beginning: "Ich saz ûf eime steine / und dahte bein mit beine" ("I sat on a stone and crossed my legs").

war: latent in much of SB's work, as subtext, the unstated, the absent. One interpretation sees *Waiting for Godot* as an autobiographical account of the flight of SB and Suzanne from **Paris** to the Vaucluse, tired and hungry. Yet the play is about stasis, not an arduous journey. Some of the dialogue and stress may have been borrowed from the escape to unoccupied France and the strains of hiding from the Nazis, but the core of the play—the uncertainty, emptiness, waiting—is different. Despite his fluent **French** SB would easily have been identified as an alien because of his Irish accent. Hitler had violated his agreement with the Vichy government to protect his southern flank, ordering the seizure of unoccupied France (10 November 1942). Until the Americans entered **Roussillon** (24 August 1944) SB was in danger. John **Calder** has suggested that the threat of German patrols sent him and Suzanne (or Henri **Hayden**, a Polish Jew) to hide in the forest and wait, sometimes for days, for word to return. When someone approached they could not tell whether it would be a Nazi patrol or friendly villagers. This personal, **political** situation underlies much of SB's post–World War II literature.

Despite little direct reference to it, *Godot* grew out of the war, one of the formative experiences in SB's life. It became another example of the human predicament, an emblem of a ruined humanity. A similar composite of experience underlies *Fin de partie*. The war background is not indispensable precisely because of SB's successful transformation of his material, his undoing of his creative origins. "**Avant Fin de partie**" (qv) is replete with war detail. It is set in Picardy, the devastation of which was familiar to SB, the World War I setting deflecting the play from his World War II experiences there (see **Saint-Lô**). "Dieppe," while not directly connected with the war, is set close to Picardy. It invokes an ending, "the last ebb." The narrator stands on a beach between ocean and city. He seems to have chosen life over **death**, as he moves toward the lights. *Fin de partie* is set between land and sea; one window opens to each. **Hamm**, some fifteen years after "Dieppe," longs for the oblivion that high tide promises: "If I could drag myself down to the sea! I'd make a pillow of the sand for my head and the tide would come" (see also "**Eh Joe**"). That choice is no longer possible. Not only is he paralyzed but, Clov informs him, "There's no more tide."

"**Saint-Lô**" focuses on desolation and death; "the old mind ghost-forsaken" can "sink into its havoc." (See also "**Mort de A.D.**") After returning to Paris SB was recalled to drive matron Mary Crowley on a snowy Christmas Eve in an open Red Cross jeep from Dieppe to Saint-Lô, around bomb craters and through minefields. They arrived at the bombed-out cathedral in time for midnight Mass, at which she worshiped and SB watched. Matron Crowley found a serious problem with **rats**. No poison was available locally, so SB was asked to find it in Paris, which he did. Much of the desolation, the bombed buildings, ironies of religious devotion, shortages of food, **painkillers**, and rats roaming the city were reworked into *Fin de partie*.

Happy Days has some of its roots in a technological travesty, SB suggesting that it was part of a technological world gone awry, even originally calling his set a "battlefield." **Winnie** is buried up to her waist in Act I, to her neck in Act II. The final play offers no explanation of her plight, but earlier she and **Willie** were war survivors: "Rocket strikes Pomona, seven hundred thousand missing . . . Rocket strikes Man, one female lavatory attendant spared . . . Aberrant rocket strikes Erin, eighty three priests survive."

Warens, Mme. de: Louise-Éléonore, a pretty young widow of Chambéry. From 1732 to 1738 she accepted **Rousseau** as substitute son ("Petit" and "Maman") and *amant en titre,* or domestic lover, diverting herself with chemistry, **music**, and him. For complex reasons of health and amour Rousseau left her service, and when he returned (1742) another had taken his place. She is remembered fondly in his *Rêveries.* Mentioned in "**Fingal**" (24).

Warrilow, David (1934–95): English actor of Irish extraction, who studied at Reading with James Knowlson and edited in **Paris** a magazine called *Réalités,* before joining **Mabou Mines** (1970). One of the finest interpreters of SB's works, his astonishing performance in Lee Breuer and Thom Cathcart's **adaptation** of *The Lost Ones* (1973) came to SB's attention, the two meeting in Berlin (1976). In 1977 Warrilow asked for a solo piece to perform, something with a man standing on a stage lit from above and talking about **death**. SB's reply began "My **birth** was my death," and the outcome was "A **Piece of Monologue**," first performed in New York (December 1979), Warrilow directing and acting. He was Reader in the premiere in Columbus, Ohio, of "**Ohio Impromptu**" (1981), introducing it to audiences in New York (La Mama), Edinburgh, **London**, and Paris. He was remarkable as the voiceless Protagonist in "**Catastrophe**" (1983), his eyes glowing like coals and the "look" making Alan **Schneider** recoil in terror (Harmon, 454). He was a memorable **Krapp** with Antoni Libera (described by SB as "my ambassador in Eastern Europe") in London (1989–90), a casting suggested by SB. The first production after SB's death, it was faithful to his later intentions, eliminating much of the slapstick, incorporating his modifications, and presenting a "tragic mask" when Krapp "suddenly fixes the fourth wall of audience with an expression that seems to be clawing back into **time**, into memory" (Eric Prince). For the "Beckett Festival of Radio Plays" Warrilow played Dan Rooney in *All That Fall* and Words in "**Words and Music**." SB was impressed by Warrilow's ability to perform equally in **French**, regarded him as one of the definitive performers of his work, and trusted him sufficiently to let him make a film of *The Lost Ones* (1984): "No such request from you will ever be refused by me" (Knowlson, 608).

Warten auf Godot: first German publication of the play, translated from the French by Elmar **Tophoven** (Suhrkamp, 1953). The first collected German edition appeared in *Dramatische Dichtungen in drei Sprachen,* two volumes, 1963 and 1964; rpt. in one volume (1981). SB used and revised these for his 1975 **Schiller-Theater** production; details in the *Theatrical Notebooks* I (423–65). This includes a text based on SB's changes for the Schiller production and for the English production based on it by the **San Quentin Drama Workshop**; this SB revised at the Riverside Studios, **London**, in March 1984 (9–85).

Watt: SB's "ugly duckling," written (he said) to occupy himself through the **war**, and later disparaged as "just an exercise," or "unsatisfactory book," a paradigm of waiting. But, he told George **Reavey** (14 May 1947), "it has its place in the series, as will perhaps appear in time." It was begun in **Paris,** mostly written in **Roussillon**, and completed in 1948. SB had the usual difficulties of publication. **Routledge** was unable to feel "the same whole-hearted enthusiasm" that it had for *Murphy.* SB placed *Watt* with the **London** literary agency A. P. Watt, but the symmetry did not work. Attempts in America were equally fruitless. After the success of *Waiting for Godot,* Richard

Seaver of *Merlin* wrote to SB for a text and was given the manuscript. An excerpt was published, and contact was made with Maurice Girodias of **Olympia Press**, who agreed to take the novel, advertising it on a leaflet with the Marquis de **Sade** and Henry Miller. The novel was published by Olympia, Collections Merlin (31 August 1953). SB disliked the magenta wrappers and typographical errors; Barney **Rosset** was horrified by the scruffy text but was keen to print it. The first American edition was published by **Grove Press** (1959; **Evergreen** Books, E-152), and distributed in the UK by John **Calder**, whose edition waited until 1963, Jupiter Books with the Olympia Press, with a simultaneous paperback. The original, uncorrected, reappeared (1958) in Olympia's Traveller's Companion series, with an extract printed in *The Olympia Reader* (Grove, 1965), 213–20. A **French** translation, by "Ludovic et Agnès Janvier en collaboration avec l'auteur" appeared in "1968" (Minuit, 1969). It is unsatisfactory, as the novel does not easily adapt to French.

The Olympia edition is riddled with errors. SB's copy, now at the **BIF**, records spelling mistakes, punctuation glitches, words left out, and an omitted line ("That depends where he got on, said Mr. **Nixon**" [19]). SB intended a more accurate text for Grove, which used the Olympia plates, but only half his corrections were made, errors remaining in the Grove reprintings to this day, though later editions have made some changes. There remain such oddities as "vitamens" (52); "it's" for "its" (70); "excema" (103); "As is was" (115); "trouser's" (127); "xenia"

for "xenium" (132); "medullars" (173); and "sphinxes" for "sphynges" (251). Grove cut one page, in which **Arsene** recites a poem about his East India runner duck ("Eamon"), and digresses on the "little rascal," before commenting, "But I am worse than Mr Ash" (45). This line is heavily indented, the elision made without realignment; hence a discrepancy between the two editions (until 67). In the Grove text (80), Watt often "wondered what had become of the duck"; this is explicable only through the textual history. Such matters are not trivial, for in a text that challenges logic, as *Watt* does, discrepancies might set deliberate puzzles. What is the status, for instance, of "yellowist" (148), which SB did not correct? The Grove text is unreliable, nor is the British text entirely accurate. SB marked in his personal Grove copy (at the BIF) some fifty errors he wanted Calder to correct. Changes were made, but Calder introduced new errors, such as the final omission of the threne heard by Watt. Despite its greater accuracy, the Calder text is unsatisfactory in other ways. A better edition is needed, even if a definitive one is impossible.

The manuscripts of *Watt* are at the **HRHRC**, but Washington University, St. Louis, holds the galleys. *Watt* is the white whale of Beckett studies, a mass of documentation that defies attempts to make sense of it. The nucleus of the Austin collection constitutes six notebooks (#157), 945 pages of autograph manuscript, changes, deletions, doodles, sketches, calculations, truth tables, rhyming schemes, and drawings. The first contains a later insert: "Begun evening of Tuesday 11/2/41"; #2 is dated "3/12/41"; #3 notes

"5/5/42"; #4 is marked "Poor Johnny Watt Roussillon" and dated "October 4th 1943"; #5 is marked "Watt V / Suite et fin / 18/2/45 / Paris / Et début de *L'Absent* / Novembre-Janvier 47/48"; and in #6, the final note is dated "Dec. 28th 1944 / End." It underwent considerable revision.

The metaphor of evolution accounts for the survival (in the Addenda) of textual curiosities. Early drafts began with the **scholastic** categories, *Quis? quid? ubi quibus auxiliis? cur? quomodo quando?* ("Who? what? where? by what means? why? in what way? when?"), by which any proposition could be reduced to basic elements. These become **Quin** (qv), whose trace remained long after his hypostasis into Watt and Knott. Other aspects to survive include: the theme of one not properly born; the episode of the piano tuners; Hunchy **Hackett**; Arsene's monologue; and the talk with Arthur in the Addenda. NB3 establishes the method of relentless enumeration and exhaustive logic. Recognizable details include: the **Lynch** family (a long history); the famished **dog** (a longer pedigree); **Erskine**'s bell; the painting with center and circumference; and "Johnny Watt." NB4 has a gardener called Gomez (later **Graves**); the tale of Mr. **Nackybal**; and a revised "short statement." In NB5 Watt is more distinctly the heart of the action, the text resembling the published novel, in blocks if not in the final order. SB's aphasic narration, his reversal of figure and ground, and his dwelling on the trivial while ignoring the significant parodies **Descartes**'s method of making "enumerations so complete and reviews so general" as to be sure of omitting nothing (see **Whoroscope:** "He proves **God** by exhaustion").

If "Watt" is the question, then "Knott" is the answer, as in the formulation of **Spinoza** in the **Whoroscope Notebook**: *Determinatio negatio est* ("Determination is negation"). The novel is a metaphysical quest, or parody thereof, whereby Watt, applying logic and reason in accordance with the Cartesian "Method," finds that rational attempts to understand his master through his accidents leads not to substantive knowledge but to the **asylum**. Compare the **Augustinian** precept that we cannot know God, but only what he is not: "For the only way one can speak of **nothing** is to speak of it as though it were something, just as the only way one can speak of God is to speak of him as though he were a man, which to be sure he was, in a sense, for a time" (77). There is a further twist to the perception of "God" (subject and object genitive), whereby if his servants need the **witness** of Mr. Knott to know that they exist, then equally Mr. Knott needs to be witnessed, lest he not exist. That way madness lies.

The novel could sustain infinite exegesis, but a "short statement" must suffice. It begins indirectly, with Mr. Hackett and the **Nixons** conversing about this strange creature, Watt, until the angry outburst (21): "I tell you nothing is known." The opening encapsulates the greater theme: if nothing can be known of Watt, then how can Watt know anything of Knott? The question is rhetorical. Watt arrives, by **tram**, to what in SB's world was the **Harcourt Street Station**, where he will take a train to what etc. is **Foxrock**. En route he encounters Mr. **Spiro**, editor of

Crux, who expounds to him knotty points of **religion**, of which Watt hears nothing (29). He makes his way to Mr. Knott's house in a "headlong tardigrade" (30), a sigmoidal movement not unlike that of a reptile. After a short interval in the ditch, where he hears a **mixed choir**, Watt arrives at Knott's house, the model for which is **Cooldrinagh**. He never knows how he got into it; if he cannot comprehend such minor matters, what chance has he of understanding more complex ones? Part I ends with Arsene's "short statement," a critique of the **Proustian** moment, or epiphany, when something "slipped." Arsene insists it was not an illusion, although he is buggered if he can understand how it could have been anything else. This should warn Watt of the futility of his quest, but it does not.

Part II, the first year of Watt's employment, consists of several episodes, but in no strict order. The compositional principle is the set piece, and within that logical disjunction, with the heavy use of the qualifying comma: "Mr Knott was a good master, in a way" (67). It details the daily routine, such as emptying the slops. The first "incident of note" is the visit of the **Galls**, father and son, come to choon the piano. The episode irritates Watt, at first, for it frustrates his inquiry into what such incidents "might be induced to mean" (75). The narrator, in his first intrusion, is scathing of such vexations (77): "One wonders sometimes where Watt thought he was. In a culture-park?" Another semantic misadventure concerns the **pot** (81–84), the tragedy being that as **object** it resists the linguistic formulation "pot," if only by a hairsbreadth. At this point, the text insists (85), Watt's

words and thus his world have not yet failed him. He copes with routine, such as preparing the weekly "poss" (87–88), yet simple tasks generate complexities beyond his understanding.

More frustrating is the following parable, the satire on **preestablished harmony** and proofs of the existence of God from cause, the story of the Lynch family and their famished dog (90–117). This demented scenario is the excrescence of scholastic logic working from the simple premise that if the dog's dish is put outside at evening full, and is brought in the next morning empty, then something has caused that change of state (see **scholasticism**). Watt is preoccupied by **seriality** (qv), the preestablished arbitrary (134) imaged in the comings and goings of servants. Even if a series is established, the sequence of elements is not necessarily *because* they are related (design need not imply cause), and so Watt, "having opened this tin with his blowlamp, found it empty" (136). Seriality gives way to periodicity, as in the frog song, Krak!, Krek! and Krik! croaked at intervals, respectively, of eight, five, and three, a Fibonacci sequence, beginning but not croaking again in unison for 120 bars. Olympia made a ballocks of this, but SB insisted they get it right. Thereafter the text concerns itself with less philosophical matters; the amours of Watt and the fishwoman (138–42); conversations with Mr. Graves (142–45); and Watt's occasional glimpses of Mr. Knott (145–47). The chapter ends, in Watt's frustration. What had he learned? Nothing. What did he know of Mr. Knott? Nothing. Of his anxiety to improve, understand, get well, what remained? Nothing. "But was not that something?" Might not this be a first step to wisdom? But all that happens is that one morning, on arising, he finds Erskine gone, and a strange man in the kitchen. Arthur. A new point in the series has been reached.

Part III is set in an asylum, metaphorically at the end of the line. The sequence violates logical order, and the explanation vouchsafed (215) is barely satisfactory: "Two, one, four, three." Heroic quatrains are *not* thus elaborated, nor has this narrative followed that sequence. The narrative assumes suitably **irrational** form, and the reader's security within this dislocated world is undermined. Despite impediments to communication (the weather, Watt's deterioration, the hole in the fence), **Sam** is able to talk with Watt, to construe an imperfect narrative (which the book purports to be). Watt's language undergoes several inversions (164–69). These affect sentence order, letters of the words, and sentences in the paragraph in orders of increasing complexity until the "sense" is unintelligible (Cohn offers a "translation," *Comic Gamut* 309–10). The particulars are demented, but (Sam insists) it is to such conversations that the narrative is indebted, including the problems of the impotent Mr. Graves (see **Bando**) and the interminable story of **Louit** (171–98).

The ending of part III differs in complexity only from that of part II: "Of the nature of Mr. Knott himself Watt remained in particular ignorance" (199). That simple statement derives from a listing of the attributes of Mr. Knott: his dress (200–1); his furniture (203–7); and

the "important matter" of his physical appearance (209–11). The lists get longer and more complex. In the manuscripts SB created exhaustive truth tables, ticking off each permutation so as to cover every possibility. Earlier the number of variables was small and the combinations limited; as the variables increase their combinatory total expands factorially. The intent is not simply to frustrate the dedicated reader but equally to parody the complete enumeration of Cartesian methodology, in particular, the theological impasse that arises from attempting to derive (by exhaustion) the essential from its accidents.

Part IV is the shortest, dealing with Watt's departure. Inevitably, Watt comes down one evening to find Micks in the kitchen and knows he must go. He puts on his **greatcoat** and **hat**, his shoe and **boot**. The night is of unusual splendor, but on his way to the station (223) Watt feels on his nape the cold air: an intimation, imperfectly understood, of the Dream of **Descartes**, which fails to confirm him in the path he must take. Watt prevails on Mr. **Case** to stay the night, despite a problem with the keys. Watt is admitted to the waiting room and droops sigmoidally (235). He spends the night in darkness, until it lightens, and he can distinguish a chair, a print of a **horse**, Joss, and **flies**, of skeletal thinness, pressed against the window, as in "**Serena** I" and "La **Mouche**." When Mr. Nolan arrives, he unlocks the door so vigorously that Watt is knocked unconscious. He is revived with the contents of the muck bucket (239). Watt distinguishes fragments of **Hölderlin**'s *Hyperions Schicksalslied* as the slime engulfs him. The process is like an obscene **birth**, excruciating because Watt's vulnerability renders him an object of **pity**, a sentiment alien to those on the platform, to whom he remains an object of derision. The train arrives, and although not a single passenger is taken up Watt without further comment is gone. The novel ends in the early morning light. In Doherty's words (*Beckett*, 20), a metaphysical farce of cruelty is taking place in the midst of an unconcerned and smugly self-satisfied Irish world, which can claim on its penultimate page that "Life isn't such a bad old bugger."

"Watt": a prepublication extract, with variants, from the French *Watt*, with "Desins inédits, 1968" by Bram **van Velde**, in *L'Éphémère* 6 (mars 1968): 81–89.

Watt: a character in *Mercier et Camier*, one of several reincarnations of earlier figures, but "quite unrecognizable" (111). Old and unwashed, he invites the **pseudocouple** to have one on him (the earlier Watt drank milk only), shouting for three doubles. He has, he says, "sought" but has come to terms with that. He crackles with vehemence, "Bugger life," and slams his stick on a table, bawling out, "Fuck life." This is not obviously the man who sought to comprehend the mysteries of Mr. **Knott**.

Watt, **"Addenda"**: the thirty-seven addenda represent, according to SB, precious and illuminating material, and only fatigue and disgust prevented their incorporation. As enigmatic fossil records they bear witness to earlier states of creation, and, like all records

of the rocks, pose problems for creationists. Much of the detail comes from the **HRHRC** notebooks.

1. *her married life one long drawsheet:* "Leda, née Swan, demi-mondaine, of Enniskillen"; **mother** of James **Quin** (original of Mr. **Knott**), and wife to Alexander; a faded and dejected woman who passes away after the death of her fourth Willy, her last born, who has died of **sausage poisoning**, "half-heartedly pressing a crucifix of bog-oak to what was left of her bosom." A *drawsheet*, on the natal bed, is one that can be drawn without disturbing the patient (see *Footfalls*). Of Mrs. Quin's eleven children (Willy, Willy, little Leda, Willy, Agnes, Lawrence, Prisca, Zoe, Perpetua, Willy), James is the sole survivor.

2. *Art Conn O'Connery:* forebear of Art and Con, and painter of the second picture in **Erskine's** room (see #26). His premature death at eighty-one from heart failure brought on by the downfall of Parnell or a surfeit of corned beef and cabbage was a loss to Rathgar. "Black velvet" is a backdrop to a portrait but also a mixture of stout and champagne. George Chinnery (1774–1852) painted landscapes and portraits, the **Dublin** National Gallery acquiring (1918) his *A Portrait of a Mandarin*. John Joseph Slattery was a portraitist active in Dublin (1846–58). O'Brien suggests (148–50) that the composite portrait may include the landscape painter James Arthur O'Connor (1792–1841) and Jan "Velvet" **Brueghel** (1568–1625), both in the National Gallery.

3. *Master of the Leopardstown Halflengths:* Matthew David McGilligan,

priest and artist, for whose dissertation on the *Mus Exenteratu McGilligani* (the **rat** that swallowed the consecrated host) see **Spiro**. O'Brien (364) identifies the sixteenth-century Flemish "Master of Female Half-Lengths."

4. *who may tell the tale:* attributed to the author's executrix, Madame Pompedur de Videlay-Chémoy ("**Pompette**"), 69ter Rue de Vieux Port, Cette; a form formerly divine, recalling, in age and **solitude**, the old has-been who might-have-been. SB noted "Isaiah 40:12": "Who hath measured the waters in the hollow of his hand, and meted out heaven with a span?" The final lines echo Isaiah 40:17: "All nations before him are as nothing, and they are counted to him less than nothing, and vanity."

5. *judicious Hooker's heat-pimples:* in early drafts, "we" (the narrator) meets **Arsene** and Eamon at the foot of the stairs (see #37). Arsene comments: "You said that what warmed you to Hooker was his heat-pimples." Izaak Walton's *Life of Mr. Richard Hooker* (London, 1675), having sung the praises of "Judicious Hooker," suggests that visitors to the parsonage of Bourne might find "an obscure, harmless man, a man in poor Cloaths . . . his Body being worn out, not with Age, but Study, and Holy Mortification; and his Face full of Heat-pimples, begot by his unactivity and sedentary life."

6. *limits to part's equality with whole:* the conversation takes a **mathematical** turn, the point being that the relationship between life, experience, and the lamentable tale of error, folly, waste, and ruin works for 0 and 1 but for nothing

else, but thereby confounds the Euclidean axiom that the whole is greater than the part.

7. *dead calm . . . to naught gone:* the talk turns to "the unconscious mind! What a subject for a short story," and the attempt to go "deep down in those palaeozoic profounds, midst mammoth Old Red Sandstone phalli and Carboniferous pudenda . . . into the pre-uterine . . . the agar-agar . . . impossible to describe . . . anguish . . . close eyes, all close, great improvement, pronounced improvement" (see **geology**).

8. *Bid us sigh:* from James Thomson's "To Fortune," anticipating the paean to the seasons (*Watt*, 47). Dropping the question mark makes the quatrain an imperative.

9. *Watt learned to accept:* i.e., **nothing** (see p. 80). The final page of NB5 lists details to be included in the novel. None was, directly, but several (#9–#13) entered the addenda.

10. *Note that Arsene's declaration gradually came back to Watt:* SB's instruction to himself at the end of NB5. It marks the decision to tell the tale erratically through Watt, a perspective not originally present.

11. *One night Watt goes on roof:* the drafts describe Quin's house: "There was a ground floor, a first floor, and a second floor. And access to the roof was provided by a skylight in its midst, for those who wished to go on the roof." Compare *Dream* (26–27), and *The Lost Ones*, for the impulse to rip into the quiet zone above the nightmare.

12. *Watt snites:* Anglo-Saxon *snÿtan*, to blow the nose. SB recorded: "Part IV.

Watt snites in his toilet paper." The word is eliminated from Watt's nasal masturbation (234–35).

13. *Meals:* the drafts comment: "Quin changed his seat at each repast. He even carried this disposition so far, on days of ill-humour, as to change his seat between courses." His erratic ways anticipate the mysterious moves of Mr. Knott.

14. *the maddened prizeman:* Arsene, but for the boil on his bottom (46), might have received the **Madden Prize**. Quin's servants, Arthur and Erskine, were maddened prizemen.

15. *the sheet of dark water:* in early drafts, there is a silence as Quin and his valet, Arthur, try to locate the lavatories (compare *Watt,* 203). Quin, about to descend the stairs and meet a strange man (**Hackett**), listens to the echo of his words and the nothing behind them.

16. *never been properly born:* an early impulse behind the novel, Quin's sense of the nothingness of his being: "The plain fact of the matter seems to be, that Quin had never been properly born. / The five dead little brothers support this view, as do the five dead little sisters. / His relatively great age, and comparative freedom from grave bodily disease, confirm this conception. / For all the good that frequent departures out of **Ireland** had done him, he might as well have stayed there." The sentiment echoes SB's sense of the unborn embryonic self, that *être manqué,* and his fascination with **Jung**'s comment after the Tavistock lecture (1935) about the **little girl** who "had never been born entirely."

17. *the foetal soul is full grown:* the draft continues: "The feeling of nothingness,

born in Quin with the first beat of his heart, if not before, died in him with the last, and not before. And between these acts it waned not, neither did it wax . . . The foetal soul is full grown (Cp. Cangiamila's *Sacred Embryology* and the *De Synodo Diocesana,* Bk. 7, Chap. 4, Section 6, of Pope Benedict XIV)." Francesco Emanuele Cangiamila (1702–63), Sicilian theologian, wrote *L'Embriologia sacra* (1745). It concerns Caesarian birth and the problems of salvation in difficult circumstances, teachings noted approvingly by Benedict. SB's learned reference is wrong, for Benedict's *De Synodo diocesana libri tredecim* (1748), a summa of ecclesiastical traditions from the 1725 Synod, discusses Cangiamila and the problem of uterine baptism at XL.vii.xiii and VII.v.iv (compare the Messrs. de la Sorbonne, *Tristram Shandy* [I.xx]). This excessive pedantry illustrates the danger of demented details leading into blind alleys— precisely the experience of Watt.

18. *sempiternal penumbra:* darkness having beginning but no end. Compare the "rosa sempiterna" (*Par.* XXX.124) or the light of Paradise (I.76). Here, Quin's coal hole.

19. *for all the good:* see #16, above.

20. *a round wooden table:* this mahogany table, described extensively in the drafts, is like Quin's round bed, which survives into the novel (207), first in the bed and later under the table, "Quin began the fatal journey towards the light of day."

21. *zitto! zitto! dass nur das Publikum nichts merke!:* "Hush, hush, so that the public may notice nothing." From **Schopenhauer**'s *Über die vierfache Wur-*

zel des Satzes vom zureichenden Grunde ("Concerning the four-fold root of the Principle of Sufficient Ground"), a tirade against German academics.

22. *on the waste, beneath the sky:* the sense of Nothingness (the sky above, the waste below) that was Quin's first awareness; the primal scene of the novel to be.

23. *Watt will not / abate one jot:* the typescript is identical save for initial capitalization, "Johnny" instead of "Watt," and "Naught's habitat" ("Knott" had not yet materialized). The narrator, then called Johnny, visits Quin's establishment and converses with Arsene. This meeting would be published in *A Clean Old Man,* destined to become Book of the Week in 2080, the praises of which are sung in the leap-year song, "Fifty two point two eight . . ." (34–35). Compare **Milton**'s second sonnet to Cyriack Skinner: "Yet I argue not / Against Heaven's hand or will, nor bate a jot / Of heart and hope."

24. *die Merde hat mich wieder:* compare **Goethe**'s "die Erde hat mich wieder" ("the earth has me again"), as Faust listens to the choirs of angels and disciples, and hears their summons to life (Line 784). "Merde" appears in the **Whoroscope Notebook,** dated 2/10/36, but not in the *Watt* drafts, although its link to ditches and **mixed choirs** is manifest.

25. *pereant qui ante nos nostra dixerunt:* "let those who used our words before us perish," attributed to St. Jerome (his commentary on *Ecclesiastes*), via Aelius Donatus (a fourth-century grammarian), who took it from Terence (see **Bartlett**). In the Whoroscope Notebook but not in the drafts of *Watt.*

26. *Second picture in Erskine's room:* Alexander Quin, father of James (see #2). Lees shows how the manuscript change from the first inversion of C major to the second creates the effect of "faint cacophony of remote harmonics stealing over dying accord" (22). Quin/Knott, like all around him, may equally be **serial** (see #29). The movement of the painting from Quin's drawing room to Erskine's bedroom contradicts the observation (128) that the only object of note therein is the picture of the circle and dot.

27. *like a thicket flower unrecorded:* this echo of Gray's *Elegy,* "Full many a flower is born to blush unseen," was part of a discussion about the mating of Irish Setters and Palestine Retrievers to produce the right kind of famished **dog**, only to conclude of the spectacle: "Did it, as age succeeded age, and misery changed name, die only to revive, revive only to die . . . like a thicket flower unrecorded?"

28. *Watt's **Davus complex** (morbid dread of sphinxes):* in Terence's *Andria* (194), a slave quips: "Dáuos sum, non Oédipus" ("I am Davus, not Oedipus"), as he feigns ignorance of amorous matters. Not in the drafts of *Watt.*

29. *One night Arthur came to Watt's room:* an encounter, present in all early drafts, between Quin and an old man. A revised typescript adds a reference to the Knott family and its serial nature. The passage anticipates Watt's encounter with Knott in the garden (145), permitting the joke about the passing shrub, or bush (see **hardy laurel**), a further arabesque on the theme of relative immortality, as in the whisky's grudge against

the decanter (*Proust,* 22) or the words of the rose to the rose ("Draff," 191).

30. *Watt looking as though nearing end of course of injections of sterile pus:* not in the manuscripts, but compare the inoculation of anthropoid apes (*Murphy,* 50).

31. *das fruchtbare Bathos der Erfahrung:* "the fruitful bathos of experience." From Kant's *Prolegomena zu einer jeden künfigen Metaphysik die als Wissenschaft wird auftreten können* ("Prolegomena to Any Future Metaphysics that Will Be Able to Present Itself as a Science"), in which **Kant** attacks a reviewer who had misunderstood his earlier work.

32. *faede hunc mundum intravii:* "in filth I entered this world, anxious I lived, troubled I go out of it, cause of causes have mercy on me." In Lemprière, said to be the dying words of **Aristotle**; the mistranscription ("faede" for "fœde") is SB's own.

33. *change all the names:* the manuscript instructs: "Walterize selon p. 81," i.e., change all the names, e.g., from "Walter" to "Vincent" (162 in the HRHRC foliation, SB numbering versos only). In the following passage SB does so. The note encapsulates a moment of metamorphosis in the textual history.

34. *descant heard by Watt on way to station (IV):* no mention of a descant appears in the novel. Originally attributed to a "Distant Mixed Fifth-rate Choir," heard by those waiting in Quin's passage for anything "of note." In the drafts, SB plays with a version in **French**.

35. *parole non ci appulcro:* "I will add no words to embellish it," This derives from Dante (*Inf.* VII.60), where Virgil, describing the corruption of avaricious cardinals, is unable to remain silent. The phrase appeared near a song sung by Erskine and Watt (Johnny) after they have prepared the poss of Mr. Knott. The words so bravely sung are from *Candide* (see "**Che Sciagura**").

36. *Threne heard by Watt:* one of the few addenda directly related to the final text: "(1) What, it may be enquired, was the **music** of this threne? What at least, it may be demanded, did the soprano sing?" (31). As Lees notes (7), some editions (Olympia, Grove, Italian) give the sentence with the music; others (Calder, Swedish, Spanish) retain the sentence but omit the music; yet others (Minuit, German) omit both; and the Norwegian translation retains both but "corrects" mistakes of key and time signature. No music appears in the galleys.

37. *no symbols where none intended:* Watt thinks about Arsene (80) and wonders what has become of the duck, the only mention of this bird. This is a magnificent fossil, in perfect preservation, but one that disappeared (at SB's instigation) from the **Calder** edition. The manuscripts depict an encounter between Johnny Watt (or "we") and two bipeds: a featherless maddened prizeman named Arsene and a feathered India Runner Duck named Eamon (see #5-#8). In Quin's dark hallway a long conversation concludes thus, "Each in his own way, all are in the dark." A match is struck, and burns bravely, until its fire reaches the fingers and it is dropped, whereupon "it continued for a little while bravely to burn, till it could burn no longer, bravely or otherwise. Then it went out." In that brief light, much is

revealed. It is too easy: a little light in the big dark; feathered and featherless bipeds; a dark passage; purgatorial stairs; hints of the Eucharist in distant bells. But "we" remains in the dark. In a context insistently demanding symbolic interpretation, in the presence of details often used to translate consciousness into meaning, all Watt can say is: "no symbols where none intended." That phrase, by a strange synecdoche, stands for the entire novel.

Watteau, Antoine (1684–1721): French painter who created a "Parisian" style. SB responded to the ultrasophisticated depictions of the pastoral that yet reveal a tinge of melancholy and a hint of decadence. **Malone** alludes (237) to *L'Embarquement pour l'ile de Cythère* (1717, Louvre), as SB does to **MacGreevy** (8 September 1934), "the Débarquement" illustrating landscape "part-anthropomorphised." In the **German Diaries** SB uses "Watteau" as shorthand for this trend, describing Sans-Souci as not in the least "Watteauesque," or the conscious artificiality of **Mozart**'s *Marriage of Figaro* (which he enjoyed) as a "more puerile world than Watteau's," one that had moved from "fête champêtre" to decadence. He praised Jack **Yeats** for getting so well, but "not tragically like Watteau," **nature**'s heterogenity and the "unalterable loneliness" of its human denizens (Knowlson, 229, 235, 247). In his 1945 book on Yeats, MacGreevy recorded SB's curious comment on the former: "He grows Watteauer and Watteauer" (O'Brien, 284). Knowlson (670) defines this as the movement toward the inor-

ganic or mineral (see **geology**), which SB recognized in Watteau and admired in Yeats and which expressed an enduring value beneath the artificial surface.

Watts, George Frederic (1817–1904): Victorian painter and sculptor. His *Physical Energy,* an equestrian statue in Kensington Gardens, is a twelve-foot replica of part of the Rhodes Memorial on Table Mountain, Cape Town, mentioned as **Celia** is feeling most languid (*Murphy,* 152). SB's phrasing, identical to that on the statue, was presumably copied from it. **Watt** (20) lacks the energy to turn the other cheek.

"The Way": an unpublished and enigmatic prose-poem, the first of several manuscripts dated "Ussy 14.5.81" (HRHRC #433). It offers a *paysage symbolisé,* featuring "the way": journey six miles, time six hours, foot to peak two miles (SB's note). The route circumscribes an 8, symbol of infinity, from foot to peak then down again, one way only, **on** is back and back is on, crossways at the halfway point, thorns hemming the way (once "giant thistles"), the half-light, the loose sand underfoot: "so no sign of remaining no sign that none before. Not one ever before so—" A marginal "Gideon" suggests the "sign" (Judges 6:17) of one talking to the Lord, but the route as much as the title implies the Tao (see **Lao-tzu**), the Chinese character for which contains such a radical. It retraces (more soberly) a path taken fifty years earlier in *Dream* (226), where **Belacqua** following "the way he had chosen" finds that the line of the drink graph loops back on itself "like an eight"; if "you" did not end up where you started, coming down you met yourself going up. Carlton Lake stresses SB's meticulous rewriting, concluding (*No Symbols,* #434): "here, in one short piece— 'The Way'—is the distillation of all the journeys made by all of Beckett's eternal wanderers."

Weekly Irish Times: Saturday Supplement of the *Irish Times,* "**Ireland**'s Picture Paper," with sports and features of the gossipy kind. Dismissed in *Murphy* (216).

"**A Wet Night**": fourth and longest story in *MPTK,* written in late 1933 when SB, having given up hope for the publication of *Dream,* was looking to complete his short stories. It duplicates much of *Dream* (199–241), the parody of the Guermantes's *matinée* in **Proust**. It expands the original by accretion of details rather than new material; these are legion, but minor. Major changes are: the portrait of the **Frica**; omission of the **Smeraldina**; and a more deliberate parody of "The **Dead**." The ending is ambiguous, *Dream* not allowing **Belacqua** to stay with the **Alba** but the story leaving this open to speculation. The soirée casa Frica is the focus of the action. This parodies the social evenings given by the **Mannings** (qv), Susan and her daughter Mary. The portrayal is cruel, only partly excused as an elaborate literary exercise in the grotesque, but the President of the Immortals would exact an exquisite revenge a little later when SB engaged in an affair with Mary.

The story begins in the season of festivity and goodwill, neither much in evidence. Belacqua emerges from the underground urinal in College Green to contemplate the **Bovril** sign and seek direction. He is accosted by **Chas**, cliché incarnate, and then the Homespun Poet, whom he evades. He has been invited to the casa Frica, his only reason for going being that the Alba will be there, in her scarlet dress that buttons down the back. The text orchestrates the dressing tables and movements of characters soon to coincide in time and place: the Alba; the **Polar Bear**, engaged en route in Jesuitical disputation; Chas and his Shetland Shawly; the Homespun Poet rehearsing "**Calvary by Night**"; the Frica creating her effect of throttled gazelle; her cronemother and the Countess of Parabimbi. First to arrive is the Student, a foul little brute, followed by the Poet and a gaggle of nondescripts, the Polar Bear, a somewhat **Chaucerian** Man of Law, various tarts and would-be literati. Belacqua's absence is noted but not regretted; polite conversation assumes **Swiftian** niceties as the Professor of Bullskrit and the arithmomaniac compete against the ruins of Ravenna and the immortal **Byron**. The Bel-dam sits like a weary old **Norn**. The satire scintillates until, with the arrival of the Alba (65), a biblical reverence ensues. The rising strumpet studies how the effect is achieved, and Larry, the Gaelic native speaker, is stretched for words.

The scene changes back to Belacqua, discomfited by his encounter with a Civic Guard (71), over whose **boots** he cats copiously. He is obliged to "wipe them boots" before moving on. By the time he reached the casa Frica he is soaked through, an object of contempt to all but the Alba who, having routed her admirers, in a moment of misericord takes **pity** upon him. She asks Belacqua to see her home, the two making their escape, as Belacqua says in the Frica's hearing, "before it starts." To his unspoken awe and delight he is invited in where there is a fire and a bottle. When Belacqua emerges it is darkness visible. The ending consists of further pains in his feet (he throws away his boots) and belly (he doubles up in agony). He hears another **voice**, more in sorrow than in anger, enjoining him to move on, "which, the pain being so much better, he was only too happy to do." The climax defies easy analysis, neither triumph nor defeat, **romanticism** nor parody, epiphany nor pathos: *das fruchtbare Bathos der Erfahrnung,* perhaps (*Watt,* 253). A moment of *misère* arises from the complex orchestration of human folly that has preceded it, yet it is redeemed, dubiously, by a *jubilate* that the images of desolation cannot quite deny.

Weulles: described in SB's notes to *Whoroscope* as "a Peripatetic Dutch physician at the Swedish court, and an enemy of **Descartes**." "Peripatetic" implies a follower of Aristotle. Weakened by fever, Descartes agreed to the act ("Oh Weulles spare the blood of a Frank") that ensured his **death**. SB derived his phrasing from the last pages of **Mahaffy**.

"What a Misfortune": seventh story of *MPTK,* which despite affinities to **"Walking Out"** was written later (early 1933), when SB was reading **Swift** intensively. The misfortune in question derives from **Voltaire**'s *Candide,* the words of the eunuch confronted with the beau-

tiful Counégonde: "**che sciagura** d'essere senza coglioni" ("What a misfortune to be without balls"). The narrative is simple but the narrative voice is not, almost a parody of **Meredith**, before it settles down. Following the death of **Lucy**, Belacqua feels sorry for himself, but he wakes up one fine afternoon "madly in **love** with a girl of substance" (116). Narrative delicacies to the contrary ("Olympian fancies for a fairly young person with expectations"), his interest in Thelma **bboggs** (qv) is more substance than love. She does not match his other women, and he gives his prospective father-in-law a "Beltschmerz"; but nor is she a brood mare, and amicable arrangements lead to the nuptial day. The wedding is to take place at the Church of Saint **Tamar** (qv). The guests are all friends and relations of the bride, the groom apparently lacking either, save only his best man, "Hairy" Capper **Quin**. The bridesmaids include **Alba** Perdue, "the nice little girl in *A Wet Night*" (127); among the motley guests are a couple of Struldbrugs, Hermione **Näutzsche**, and James ("Jimmy the Duck") **Skyrm**, who will act for Belacqua.

The day arrives. Belacqua arises at midday, the solemnization takes place with a mystical radiance that Joseph Smith (a hint of polygamy) finds touching, and Thelma is adorned with **Lucy**'s ring and its inappropriate inscription. This sounds a musical phrase (140) that will be repeated (151), a **Beethoven** pause, a fragment of the Seventh Symphony, before the ström as the **memory** of Lucy enters the movement; her presence in the interval will ruin the marital companionship that Bel can offer Thelma. This *moment musical* strikes a tragic intonation into the comic **absurdity**. The wedding degenerates from farce to shambles, then tragedy. Belacqua is arrested by the Civic Guard; Thelma refuses to cut the cake; Walter gives a contorted speech, and Belacqua a white reply. A frantic **Caudine** exit creates such indignity that Belacqua dates from then a loss of interest in himself, as in "a grape beyond his grasp" (150). Finally, in the Morgan (Arthurian imagery runs through the story), Lucy's presence manifests itself again. She is "atra cura" in the dicky (151), that is, Belacqua is accompanied from behind by **Horace**'s "black care" on the way to Galway. He finally asks Thelma if she has ever heard of a **babylan**. The story ends with Belacqua's vision of impotence, a **beaver** on a mired mule, flogging it with a wooden sword, and the **veronica** "gone west," literally and figuratively. The tone is complex, accentuating the note sounded at the beginning, an unexpected tenderness entering into Belacqua's feelings for his lost Lucy, but at a most insensitive moment. It is no surprise to learn in "**Draff**" (175) that Thelma has perished of sunset and honeymoon on that trip to Connemara, abode of stones.

"**What Is the Word**": SB's translation of "**Comment dire**," a fifty-three-line poem that constitutes his last original work. Written in the Hôpital Pâsteur (July 1988); translated in the rest home, *Le Tiers Temps;* and printed off Barbara **Bray**'s computer (SB's unique instance of "word-processing"). The poem, an elegiac meditation on language, begins with "Folly," usually taken as SB's last word. It was first published in SB's obituary (*Sunday Correspondent,* 31 December 1989). For some years it was most readily available in *The School Bag* (Faber, 1997), an anthology compiled by Seamus Heaney and Ted Hughes, which said, erroneously, that the poem would be "included in [the nonexistent] *Collected Poems 1930–1989* by Samuel Beckett." It finally appeared in *Poems 1930–1989* (Calder, 2002).

"**What Where**": in the summer of 1982 SB was invited to write something for the 1983 Steirischer Herbst in Graz, Austria. Between February and March (1983) he wrote a short play, "**Quoi où**," which he translated as "What Where," for an evening of three one-acts (with "**Catastrophe**" and "**Ohio Impromptu**") staged by Alan **Schneider** at the Harold Clurman Theater (15 June 1983). In December SB prepared to go to Stuttgart to direct "Was Wo" for television, but the project, scheduled for spring 1984, was postponed because of his illness. When he came to the studios of Süddeutscher Rundfunk, the outcome was a dramatic distillation and transformation of the original, effectively a re-creation. A photocopy of "Was Wo" (RUL 3097/1), trans. Elmar and Jonas **Tophoven** and published in *Theater Heute,* was heavily annotated before and during the filming (18–25 June 1985). That version ("What Where II") SB thereafter considered more desirable for the theater; it premiered at the Théâtre de rond-point, **Paris**, dir. Pierre Chabert (22 March 1986). An American revised version premiered at the Magic Theater, San Francisco, dir. S. E. Gontarski (November 1986), and a film of the stage production was released by Global Village as *Peephole Art: Beckett for Television* (1992). Publication of "Quoi où" was scheduled in conjunction with the stage premiere, however, the text added to **Minuit**'s "Catastrophe" was not the version staged but SB's original. Except for the text in *JOBS* 2.1 (1992): 1–25, and The *Theatrical Notebooks* IV (408–414), SB's revised "What Where" remains unpublished in any language.

The original play featured a downstage megaphone, SB's most recent stage icon for the inner **voice** of the artist, and a separate lighted playing area 3m x 2m, which SB called the experimental field of **memory** and on which all is remembered as from a distant past. Hence the distinction between the voice of Bam and other remembered figures, including Bam himself. The setting alludes obliquely to Thomas **Moore**'s "Oft, in the Stilly Night," a poem SB could quote from memory (although he had forgotten the title), emphasizing the shift from "Fond memory . . ." to "Sad memory brings the light of other days around me." The dimly lit megaphone speaks first, announcing: "In the present as were we still." It is a voice from beyond the grave. Four characters, Bam, **Bom**, **Bim**, and Bem (the fifth player [Bum?] is being "worked over" as the play opens), are identical in appearance, differentiated by a single central vowel. (See James Joyce, *Finnegans Wake* [341]: "Binbambombumb.") SB wrote in his Stuttgart Notebook that the characters of "**What Where**" should be "differentiated by colour": BAm—black; BEm—white; BIm—red; and BOm—blue. This was suggested by **Rimbaud**'s sonnet "Voyelles," where each vowel is color-

coded; the idea was dropped in rehearsal. Bam's voice (V) controls the action, switching light (memory and imagination) on and off the playing area to initiate action. The original version opened with a **mime**, "First without words," which V deems a false start since Bom is already present with Bam. A second version follows with Bam alone, this one as regular as the passing of the seasons, a pattern that underlies the play: Bam alone; Bom joins Bam; Bim leads Bom away; Bim enters alone followed by Bem; Bem leads Bom away; Bem joins Bam, and he too is led away by Bam; Bam enters alone, "head bowed." After the circle is closed, Bam alone, V restages the scene with words. When a failed Bem appears, Bam leads him away, presumably to "give him the works." At last Bam appears to himself: "I am alone. In the present as were I still." It is winter, Bam's end, since, in an echo of **Schubert**'s *Winterreise,* there are no more journeys for Bam. The cycle is completed and V entreats the audience to "Make sense who may. I switch off."

Each episode is characterized by a false start, a revision by the Voice of Bam, but as SB revised the work for TV he removed these *faux départs*. The first figure to join Bam is interrogated about whether another has confessed (in this first perception of a cycle, the tormented is evidently the fifth figure of V's opening). The object of the confession remains indeterminate: "He didn't say anything?" "He didn't say it?" Each player appears bowed in failure and claims to have been unsuccessful eliciting information, despite torture and Bam's accusation of mendacity. A third with head "haught" joins the two and is asked to give the failed player "the works." The **politics** sounded in *Catastrophe* echo in the interrogatories, "What Where," the plot suggestive of repetitive, mindless torture. SB briefly entertained making each character wear a tarboosh, fezlike headgear associated with Armenians.

Revising for television, SB drastically simplified the visual imagery, dialogue, and action, trimming all the false starts. The speaking voice was now a huge, refracted, diffuse face of Bam dominating half the television screen. Instead of gowned players, they now appeared as floating faces dissolving in and out as the TV screen itself became the field of memory. Rather than facing one another around three sides of a rectangle, the three players were aligned side-by-side, facing the camera. The original play had a substantial emphasis on eliciting "where" from the victims, even where the victim said "where." As SB revised the work for TV, he eliminated that potentially confusing repetition, substituting a balanced "He didn't say what?" "He didn't say where?" into each encounter. The emphasis on "where" was decreased, many changed to "it," and each "where" followed a "what." For the post-television **French** stage production, a ring of diffuse light the size of a human head, upstage right, replaced the oversized refracted face of Bam. In place of cowl-covered heads that created the impression of floating faces, SB substituted shaved **skulls**. The field of memory was now implicit, neither a lit rectangle onstage nor the glowing TV screen. On the stage the players appeared unrealistically high, standing on a concealed two-foot platform, their heads aligned with the pulsing light that echoed the TV tube. The symmetrical dialogue of the television version was retained, but the opening mime was cut entirely so that the play lasted some eight minutes, half the television length. Yet this new stage version still did not please SB fully, still seemed unfinished. Although he had attended rehearsals and "approved" it, he admitted that he had reservations; it could come still closer visually and rhythmically to the television version, he advised his American director: cowl-covered heads replacing the skulls, the light somehow taking on the image of Bam (but not, he emphasized, televised), the mime reintroduced. **Directing** "What Where" for German TV thus led to a new work, "What Where II," and such revision is a powerful argument for the influence of television on SB's late drama.

"what would I do without this world": SB's translation (1948) of the second of **"Quatre poèmes,"** retaining the broken "sonnet" of the original. See **"que ferais-je sans ce monde."**

whirligig: an ancient instrument of punishment, in which the prisoner was spun in a wooden cage. Cited by **Belacqua** of his moment of marriage in **"What a Misfortune"** (148), "this instant of whirligig"; from **Burton**'s *Anatomy of Melancholy* (III.2.1.i, 491): "*ludus amoris tu es,* thou art Cupid's whirligig," Juno's words to Jupiter.

Whitaker's Almanack: a **London**-based annual, with details of the calendar year, public places and happenings, and an astrological bias. SB used the 1935 edition extensively in writing *Murphy,* the *Almanack* providing him, as Thom's *Directory* (1904) had *Ulysses,* a means of plotting the **time**-space coordinates of his fictional world, anchoring the comic action to an exact realistic grid. *Whitaker* provided details of the stars and moon, the astrological significance thereof, and accurate information about time and tides and weather. Minor inconsistencies have led commentators (Rabinovitz, Kennedy) to assume deliberate error rather than careless transcription, but this seems unlikely.

Whitelaw, Billie: SB's favorite actress, almost at times his muse. Her roles in "**Play**" (1963–65), *Not I* (1973–75), *Footfalls* (1976), "**Rough for Radio, II**" (1976), "**Ghost Trio**," ". . . **but the clouds . . .**" (TV, 1977; see "**Shades**"), *Happy Days* (1979), "**Rockaby**" (1981–84), and "**Eh Joe**" (1989) have become the standard by which other performances are measured. Her autobiography, *Billie Whitelaw: Who He* (1996), tells of her Coventry childhood, coping with the boy's name given on her **father**'s whim, marriage to Paul Miller, the broad outline of her career, and her retirement in the Stour Valley. She is reticent about her private life. Half the book deals with SB, for working with him was the defining period of her career. Otherwise, she said, "Nobody would have been remotely interested in my autobiography." She was introduced to SB when preparing for the National Theatre production (1963) of "Play" (with Robert Stephen and Rosemary Harris) at the Old Vic,

dir. George Devine. She did not understand the play, she admits, but was moved by it and instinctively trusted SB "at first sight." She presents an image of SB in a raincoat, quiet, thoughtful, and describes the Light as a dentist's drill, "an instrument of torture."

In 1973, she appeared in *Not I.* When she read the script she burst into tears, finding it incredibly moving. She knew that it had to go fast, even if doing so produced sensory deprivation and a tension that made her feel that the top of her head would blow off. She broke down in rehearsal, leading SB to say, "Oh, Billie, what have I done to you?" The performance was marked by a determination that became her hallmark: "If it is necessary, I will walk through brick walls . . . Later, I will collapse with broken bones, but if I've got to do it I will do it." This was not entirely hyperbole, as her efforts led to a damaged spine and a back "like a corkscrew." She commented: "I felt as though I was a medium, and very much part of his creative process." SB's insistence sometimes caused stress, or pervasive but minor changes to the text difficulty when she had committed to memory the original lines, but SB was, she said (1989), the only director with whom she felt "unafraid and safe." She offered in return her trust and desire to get it exactly right, arguing that to do so gives "a marvelous freedom, because within his meticulous framework and I suppose surrounded by this feeling of compassion and safety, there is freedom to experiment . . . you can expand."

The trust was reciprocated. In *Footfalls* (1976), SB wanted her to accentuate the similarity between **mother** and

Whitelaw, Billie

daughter. Her performance was informed by the recent **suicide** of a young niece. Her approach was instinctive, her job at times, she felt, to "bore them to death." She thought in pictures, and *Footfalls* felt to her like a painting by Edvard **Munch**. SB wrote "Rockaby" for her, but her tour de force was *Happy Days* (1979). The rehearsals were so frustrating that SB had to withdraw. The performance was a triumph, and it was filmed for BBC television by Tristram Powell, who had also filmed "Shades." When Actors Equity prevented her playing the role in New York (1982), SB protested, Equity finally reversing its decision (1983). Her last performance under SB's guidance (but directed by Walter Asmus) was "**Eh Joe**" (1989); she remarked that she had suddenly felt the identity between the girl and the one in *Krapp's Last Tape*. After SB's **death** she chose not to appear in his plays but let herself be interviewed and spoke about her association with the dramatist who had given her life definition, and with whom she appreciated working in a context of **love** and compassion, "the most fertile thing in the world."

Whoroscope: SB's first separately published work, a poem of ninety-eight lines with seventeen notes, based on the life of **Descartes** and published by the **Hours Press** (Paris: August 1930), in an edition of 100 signed copies and 200 unsigned. Nancy **Cunard** had offered a £10 prize for the best poem under 100 lines on **time**, to be judged by Richard **Aldington**. SB entered at the last moment, writing on paper from the Hotel Bristol,

Carcassonne, and dropping it into her box at dawn. His entry mystified the sponsors sufficiently to win the prize. At their suggestion he added two pages of "explanatory" notes; these have since been regarded as part of the poem. *Whoroscope* is admired as a distillation of deep erudition reflecting SB's immersion in **Baillet**'s *La Vie de Monsieur Des-cartes* (1691) and the twelve-volume *Oeuvres de Descartes* by Charles Adam and Paul Tannery (1897–1910). However, in 1992 Francis Doherty showed that the poem is derived from **Mahaffy**'s *Descartes* (1880; hereafter "M"), the source of almost all its enigmatic phrases. The composition is thus like that of the early "**Dante**" essay, SB working extensively from unacknowledged sources.

While not a dramatic monologue *Whoroscope* has affinities with that genre. Descartes is talking to his valet, **Gillot**, demanding his egg not fresh but hatched some eight to ten days. The passage of time is measured from the outset (the egg fresh) through the different stages of incubation. As SB explains, the shuttle of the ripening egg combs the warp of days, the interwoven fitts dramatizing key events, acquaintances, and discoveries in Descartes's life, until the tone rises in a crescendo as he anticipates his own **death**. The title reflects Descartes's reluctance to note his birthday, "because it exercised idle people in superstitions about his horoscope" (M, 9). The egg is a hermetic mystery, a minor problem to pass to Gillot. The reference to the Brothers **Boot** (M, 147) sets the tone for a comic refutation of **scholasticism**. Lines 5-10 address **Galileo**, confused with his musical father (M, 35), and confront the paradox of **motion**, as resolved by Descartes: the image of a sailor or horseman, stationary in relation to what carries him, as the earthball is carried through the heavens. "[L]ead-swinging" refers to Galileo's pendulum, yet it was Descartes who spent mornings in bed, "swinging the lead," rather than his adversary Voët whom he described as the "son of a sutler, brought up among harlots and camp-followers" (M, 105).

Lines 11–16 return to the egg, the "lashed ovaries" indicative of sterility; again, "Give it to Gillot" (M, 79; details of the omelet from M, 138). There follow enigmatic references to Faulhaber, **Beeckman**, and Peter the Red (17–20): great minds casually dismissed ("hen-and-a-half") as Descartes notes how easily his work on **mathematics**, optics, thunderstorms, and parhelia ousted theirs (M, 32). He thinks of his life (21–26): his crude brother who swindled him (but not of the "coppers" won as a soldier), and the celebrated *poêle,* 1619, when he conceived the grand scheme of repiling the foundations of philosophy. His fame is such (27–28) that Franz Hals can wait (his portrait of Descartes is frontispiece to Mahaffy's study). He thinks of the little girl with a squint who was his childhood playmate (M, 10), and hence of his daughter, Francine, who died of scarlatina (M, 62). This leads to his appreciation of **Harvey**'s discovery of the circulation of the blood (37–40), and to thoughts of death, as of Henry IV, whose heart was sent to Descartes's college, La Flèche (41).

Back to the egg (42–44); not yet ready, so doubt (45–56), then triumph (57–65): the wind as a malignant spirit; problems of faith; a flirtation with the Rosicrucians. Then the overthrow of the Jansenist Antoine Arnauld, who had challenged him to reconcile his doctrine of matter with transubstantiation, which he did by arguing that the *superficie* of the bread and wine remain the same even as their substance is changed into the **body** and blood of **Christ**. He calls on **Bacon** (66–67) as a kindred spirit, opposed to systematic philosophy and aware of the "phantoms" that lead men into error. Yet Descartes broke the hermetic egg of mind and **body** so completely that they couldn't be put together again.

Still the egg is not ready. He thinks (68–71) of Anna Maria **Schurmann**, the bluestocking, atrophied by her excessive faith (the **parrot** is from Mahaffy, 73). He recalls **Augustine**'s "Fallor, ergo sum" in anticipation of his own **cogito**; he, too, is a chip off **God**'s block, thereby reconciling his sense of self with an acceptance of God as creator: "He proves God by exhaustion," by the logic of the *Method.* Mahaffy notes (97) that attempting to establish the existence of the deity by **consciousness**, and the authority of consciousness by the existence of the deity, is to reason in a circle.

At last the egg is ready (84–89) but it intimates death ("ripeness is all"). He predicts his fate (90–98) at the hands of "**Christina** the ripper," who will force him to rise at five in the morning, to catch his death of cold. After **Weulles** has bled him, he will cry out in agony: "Messieurs, épargnez le sang français!" (M, 136). The poem ends in a **pun**, the Seigneur du *Perron* mounting the bitter *steps* as if to execution, and with a phrase that SB varied in his sonnet "**At last I behold**," of the starless, inscrutable hour. Descartes's death, an ultimate separation of mind from body, acts as an emblem of the end of consciousness.

Whoroscope Notebook: a red-covered notebook, 17 x 11 cm, at the **BIF** (RUL 3000/1), which SB used from 1932 to 1937; so-called because "Whoroscope" appears on the inside cover and because many of the earliest notes, mostly from the *Britannica,* concern matters astrological. Since its greater significance is as a guide to SB's reading and work habits in the 1930s, particularly as they affected the writing of *Murphy,* it might equally be called the "Murphy Notebook." The dating of entries is imprecise. The notebook contains a variety of materials in many languages. There are thirty-four numbered paragraphs, not easily deciphered, specifically related to *Murphy,* moving from astrological details through the topography of **Dante**'s **Purgatory**, toward the first writing of the final novel. These are augmented by other notes, preliminary sketches (a Dantean schema), and essential ideas ("keep moving the only virtue"); also, following a visit by SB to the **Bethlem Royal Hospital**, a fascinating piece of original composition dealing with the postmortem scene and indicating how the text moved from recorded details to comic **absurdity**. At the end of the book, several quotations from minor Elizabethan and Jacobean playwrights are noted "for interpolation," many ticked to confirm their inclusion. Some form enigmatic fragments in *Murphy,* reflecting SB's deliberate attempt to cultivate mystery in

the Joycean manner, as well as a conscious decision to "**Londonize**" the work in progress. Other bits would be used in *Watt* and later texts.

The rest of the book is both a treasure trove and a midden, full of notes, quotations, and epigraphs. These include: a list of books "sent home" from Germany; the publishers who had turned down *Murphy;* bars of music and a libretto, Cherubino's aria from *The Marriage of Figaro;* entries in **French** and English on classical figures like Ixion, **Pythagoras**, **Hippasos**, **Tantalus**, **Sisyphus**, and the labors of Hercules (including the thirteenth and most arduous, deflowering in one night forty-nine of the fifty daughters of King Thespius); notes on **physics** from **Poincaré**'s *La Valeur de la science;* citations from **Kant**, **Aristotle**, **Spinoza**, and **Leibniz**; extracts from **Mauthner**; a summary of ancient Greece; a **geological** table; passages from **Burton**; quotations from **Johnson** anticipating "**Human Wishes**"; and, scattered throughout, quips and curiosities of the kind that would continue to entrance SB long after the itch to work in the **Joycean** mode had ceased.

Wilenski, R. H. (1887–1975): **art** historian, whose *An Introduction to Dutch Art* (Faber & Gwyer, 1929) SB purchased (1932) on advice from Thomas MacGreevy. Details appear in the early fiction. In *Murphy,* Miss **Counihan** sharing "**oyster kisses**" (117) is modeled on Wilenski's description of "oyster parties" in the paintings of Dirck Hals and Jan Steen. The Hindu polyhistor's thesis on "The Pathetic Fallacy from Avercamp to **Kampendonck**" and his interest in the

Norwich school derives from Wilenski's "Postscript" to *Dutch Art*. There are similarities between Murphy's death and Wilenski's description (255) of that of Carel Fabritius, killed in the explosion of a powder magazine in Delft (12 October 1654), aged about thirty. Most significant is Wilenski's discussion (50–54) of "the **Caravaggio**-Honthorst tradition" of spotlight effects, particularly in the painting of Gerrit van **Honthorst** (qv).

William of Champeaux (1070–1121): French logician and theologian. Abelard studied under him in **Paris**, and esteemed his abilities. A logical realist, he contended that the universe was a thing, or *res*, essentially common to all its singulars, individuals distinguished only by their accidents and forms; this is his "extreme theophanism," the revelation of Himself that **God** makes through His works, so that the world may be seen as the theophany of the divine. Abelard objected that according to this theory contradictory accidents would have to be ascribed to the same substance (Windelband, 294), and obliged William to restate the doctrine less extremely. The logic of his position for **Murphy** (81) is that each biscuit is essentially the same, so his preference for the ginger is **irrational**.

William the Silent (1533–84): Count of Nassau and Prince of Orange during the Netherlands wars for independence. So-called because when Henry II of France, thinking him an accomplice, revealed a plan to massacre Protestants, William did not betray his horror. Nominally Catholic, William risked his position and fortune for the nationalist cause. He helped form the Seven United Provinces (Holland), which eventuated after his assassination in Delft at the instigation of Philip II, whose sovereignty he overthrew. The **Unnamable** (366) invokes him, urging **Worm** not to lose heart, but finds he is "going silent" (393).

Willie: male foil in *Happy Days* (qv). One of SB's less rewarding parts, even when played by Jean-Louis Barrault and Hume Cronyn, each to his wife's **Winnie**.

Wincarnis: a full-bodied English aperitif, which, like the ditto theater sister of "**Yellow**" (168), improves on acquaintance. The label displays a full-bodied course.

Windelband, Wilhelm (1848–1915): Professor of Philosophy at the University of Strassburg and authority on the ancients. His *Geschichte der Philosophie* (Freiburg, 1892 and 1900), trans. James H. Tufts (1893 and 1901) as *A History of Philosophy,* offers a comprehensive guide to Western thought, remarkable for insight and clarity in relation to the origin and development of the categories of cognition. SB took extensive notes from him, notably with respect to the **preSocratics**, **scholasticism**, and **Leibniz**.

Winnie: [1] sole female character of *Happy Days* (qv). One of the great female roles in SB's theater, having been played by Madeleine **Renaud**, Jessica Tandy, Dame Peggy Ashcroft, Irene Worth, and, most notably, under SB's direction, Billie **Whitelaw**.

Winnie: [2] the girl **Belacqua** takes into the country in "**Fingal,**" later named "Miss Coates" (31), pretty, hot, and witty. They make **love,** twice, and admire the view, several times, before Belacqua, a sad animal, forsakes her for a **bicycle.** As she awaits him, a local yokel tells her about a nearby tower and "Dane **Swift**" who "kep a motte in it." The "motte" was Stella, but the tragedy of Vanessa, loved then forsaken by Swift, better mirrors Winnie's fate.

Winter, Mrs.: in the "sequel" related by May in *Footfalls,* **mother** of Amy, an anagram of "May," which links May's fiction to her restlessness. The name invokes *Ill Seen Ill Said* with its "endless winter" and "**What Where**" with its "winter. / Without journey." The name echoes **Schubert**'s *Winterreise.*

wistiti: the ouistiti, *Happale jacchus,* or marmoset, whose little cry almost stirs the **Unnamable** to **pity** (348). The narrator of *From an Abandoned Work* (159) hears a **voice,** not his, like a marmoset sitting on his shoulder, keeping him **company.**

witness: SB invariably uses "witness" in the biblical sense, as in Romans 1:9: "**God** is my witness, whom I serve," reflecting the orthodox opinion that we are set upon this earth to bear witness to His glory. But God, it is observed (*Watt,* 9), is a witness that cannot be sworn (a line added late to the manuscript). SB's interest in **Berkeley** shapes itself in *Watt* into a sustained conceit: that **God** could not exist were He not perceived, and so He must be witnessed, "Not that he

might know, no, but that he might not cease" (*Watt,* 203). This paradox is sustained in the *Three Novels,* particularly *The Unnamable,* where **Mahood**'s **voice** continues to "testify," as though woven into his own and so "preventing me from saying who I was" (309). "Witness," "testify," and "utter" are activities that need another, a reader, a listener, that they might be. The unnamable decides (375) that he doesn't believe in the eye, its evolution or function: "a world without **spectator,** and vice versa, brrr! No spectator then, and better still no spectacle." The dilemma assumes dramatic form in *Waiting for Godot,* which SB thought might best be played in an empty theater. The players need to be witnessed that they might exist, that their performance might be reified; but the play is like Berkeley's tree, existing only insofar as it is perceived, with no "eye of God" to save it from inexistence. This is articulated variously: the suspicion in *Endgame* that perhaps they are beginning to *mean* something; **Krapp** bearing witness to his past self, perhaps the last of SB's creations able to do so; and **Winnie** in *Happy Days* needing a witness, or auditor. She creates "Shower" and "Cooker," from the Ger. *schauenkucken,* "to look," and has a constant sense that somebody is looking at her (God? the audience?), giving her the impression that she exists. In "**Play**" this is manifest as inquisitorial light, as M suggests, mere eye: "Just looking. At my face. On and off." He wonders, "Am I as much as . . . being seen?" (317). In *Not I,* the **Auditor** is indispensable because s/he, like Listener in "**Ohio Impromptu,**" witnesses.

"**Text 5**" presents the self "in the accusative" as clerk and scribe, "judge and party, witness and advocate" at an "obscure assize where to be is to be guilty." This sets up the possibility of providence in the fall of a sparrow, or a quill: "it's noted"; but such "high hopes" are doomed: "grave, I'll be grave"; there is no "way out." "Text 12" concludes that no matter how many "billions" might opine otherwise, to make sense of anything "you'd need a god, unwitnessed witness of witnesses, what a blessing it's all down the drain." The voice of "Text 13" wants to "leave a trace", but if the air should tremble the flurry of dust will soon be settled, as "written" in Genesis 3:19: "for dust thou art, and unto dust shalt thou return."

The narrator of *How It Is* cries out for "a witness I'd need a witness" (18). Such a witness would "need good eyes" (44), or a good lamp (**Christ** as the Light of the World?). He needs to bear witness to the unspeakable (in the biblical sense of that word), to privilege the life above so that the life below might be justified, or rehabilitated in accordance with that light, to which he bears witness. In part 2 the witness is named **Kram**, and the scribe Krim; they are entrusted with "keeping the record" (80), but the record finally testifies only to YOUR LIFE HERE, and the irrefutable truth: DIE ONE DAY (96). The voice persists into part 3; the bottom line is "martyring and being martyred" (127), literally, rather than in the etymological sense (Gk. *martyros*, "a witness"). The theological terms are *grounded*, rendered into **fundamental sounds**, the "piss of being" (132; 2 Kings 18:27). Kram is needed, "otherwise desert flower" (138), blooming unseen, a mute inglorious **Milton**. The record itself is nothing, given the "vast tracts" (of **time**, writing) that must pass into oblivion. This is SB's fourth certainty, with **birth**, existence, and **death**: the need to express, sans *foi,* sans conviction, but in response to the irrational need to testify even while knowing the futility of doing so. Billions have kept their appointments, but the record is largely blank; SB exists as he is perceived through these inscriptions that bear witness to his having been.

Woburn: a figure in "**Cascando**," of uncertain identity since the construct of **Voice**, who, having failed to tell the right tale "thousands and one" times, resumes the story. Woburn gets up, knees first, same old coat, goes down to the sea. He is like "**O**" in *Film,* in running to evade definition. His name intimates a stream of woe, making its uncertain way to the shore. The narrative assumes immediacy ("he's down"): the large figure of Woburn struggles up, falls down, sees a **face** in the sand, goes **on,** in the dark, through the stones, knee deep in the sand, to a boat on the shore that he pushes out, face in the bilge, into the oblivion of the sea (compare "The **End**," or *Malone Dies*). Words and **Music** struggle with Voice to tell the story that will end the "obligation to express," but the closure is incomplete, Woburn clinging, not letting go, as the story approaches its ending, Words, Music, and Opener still urging it to completion ("come on . . . come on"), as the words die away in the decrescendo of the title.

Wood's halfpenny: since Charles II the right to mint copper coins in **Ireland** had been farmed out to individuals.

The Irish government petitioned Parliament to introduce coins of guaranteed value, but a patent was granted to William Wood, a hardware merchant (12 July 1722), who bribed the King's mistress, the Duchess of Kendal. Irish indignation flared and was fanned by four vicious letters from **Swift**, published under the name M. B. Drapier. Irish parties united against Wood and Walpole, and Swift was hero of the hour, particularly when (27 October) £300 was offered for the apprehension of the anonymous writer, and he claimed the award. SB studied the *Drapier Letters* at **Trinity**, 1926; see *Murphy* (170).

Woodworth, Robert (1869–1962): American psychologist whose *Contemporary Schools of Psychology* (1931) was a "help" for *Murphy*. The detail about **Gestalt psychology** is lifted directly from Woodworth, who contributed to the tearooms scene, with its parody of the **Külpe** school. Later versions deleted most of the detail cited by SB from the first edition.

Woolf, Virginia (1882–1941): English member of the Bloomsbury group, whose snobbery SB despised; hence the *canaille* (*Murphy*, 224). He thought little of her work, and less of the Hogarth Press, which rejected *Ulysses* and *Murphy*. He referred to "the Hogarth Private Lunatic **Asylum**," and, when Leonard Woolf failed to return his typescript, he wondered if it was his turn in the bin.

"Words and Music": a radio play (November–December 1961), dramatizing an interchange between two arts: Words ("Joe") and Music ("Bob"). SB's return to radio drama arose from evenings spent with Marcel **Mihalovici** on the opera of *Krapp's Last Tape*, working "to adjust the words to the musical phrases and vice versa" (Knowlson, 443). Recorded and broadcast on BBC 3 (13 November 1962); repeated (7 December 1962 and 8 May 1963); produced by Michael Bakewell, **music** composed and conducted by John Beckett; with Patrick **Magee** (Words) and Felix Felton (**Croak**). An American production, part of "The Beckett Festival of Radio Plays," was broadcast by National Public Radio (April 1989), with David **Warrilow** (Words) and Alvin Epstein (Croak); original music by Morton **Feldman**. (See Everett Frost, "Recording Samuel Beckett's Radio Plays.") The play appeared in *Evergreen Review* 6.27 (November–December 1962): 34–43, and was reprinted in *Cascando and Other Short Dramatic Pieces* (Grove, 1968). The first British publication was in *Play and Two Short Pieces for Radio* (Faber, 1964). Translated as "**Paroles et Musique**" and published in *Comédie et actes divers* (Minuit, 1972). Words's final poem appeared as "**Song**" in *Collected Poems* (1984) but without the second part, "Then down a little way."

Creative tensions between the two characters (and arts) are mediated by an old man, Croak, who calls them "My comforts!" and "**Dogs!**" and wants them to be "friends." Croak arrives late, having been contemplating "The **face** . . . On the stairs" of one later called Lily (compare **Joyce**'s "The Dead"), and he implores his servants to develop the theme of "**love**." Words begins disingenuously by adapting the phrasing he had been applying to "sloth," an overblown set of repetitions and clichés. But he grows introspective and begins to doubt whether he has been describing love at all: "Is love the word?" Prompted by Croak and Music, Words adjusts his rhythms to the tempo set by Music and eventually produces an extraordinary poem, "Song" ("Age is when to a man"), and its extension, "Then down a little way." The meditation on love lost is as poignant and erotic as the lyric scene in the punt that haunts the aged **Krapp**: "She comes in the ashes / Who loved could not be won / Or won not loved / Or some other trouble." The second poem continues an inspection of the loved one's **body**, from "the great white rise and fall of the breasts . . . to their natural . . . aperture": "Down a little way / To whence one glimpse / Of that wellhead," or "Jusqu'au noir d'où / La source s'entrevoit," in SB's translation. Croak is left speechless. Overcome by overt emotion, he drops his club and wanders off as Words shouts after him, then after "Bob." Rather than a poetic triumph, the play ends in failure as Music makes a "*brief rude retort.*" Music then, the least referential of the arts, wins the day. As SB acknowledged to Katherine Worth, "music always wins." He reportedly told Adorno that the play "ends unequivocally with the victory of the music." The challenge of any composer approaching this piece is to construct a musical score capable of transcending the erotic libretto of Words. Whether any has done so is a matter of debate. "**Cascando**," written in **French** a month later, may have been, in part, an attempt to overcome this inherent problem.

Wordsworth, William (1770–1850): English poet of the pastoral. SB's one serious use of his work is the name "**Lucy**" in "**Walking Out**," where her death rebukes an idle theme. Elsewhere he is treated irreverently, emotion recollected in tranquillity echoed in *Dream* (185) and "The **Expelled**" (58). **Molloy**'s confusion is recalled in "the tranquillity of decomposition" (25). "A **Casket of Pralinen**" invokes "Willy the idiot boy" and his "transcendental horse-power." The mockery of "that most excellent man" continues into *Murphy* (100), with the celebrated crux in the "Immortality Ode" (line 28), whereby "fields of sleep" became "fields of **sheep**" (compare "Casket of Pralinen"). Other echoes include **Neary**'s "Since heaven lay about you as a bedwetter" (217), also from the "Immortality Ode": "Heaven lies about us in our infancy" (with a hint of **Joyce**'s *Portrait*); "the still, sad music of humanity" (219); and the "**chessy** eye" (242), as in "Daffodils," the "inward eye / That is the bliss of **solitude**."

World's End: in "**Rough for Theatre II**," A remembers "Smith," a big fat redhair, "Always to be seen hanging round World's End" (87). This is the locale of **Murphy**'s mew, "World's End Place" and "World's End Passage" just across the King's Road, near Gertrude Street. Keir Elam, missing SB's one direct reference, relates this topography to SB's cloacal cysts, his preoccupation with **buttocks**, **Turdy**, and other godforsaken holes.

Worm: the final identity assumed by the **Unnamable** before he is alone, the last "old buffer" between him and his self, whatever that is, enlisted to tell his story and suffer his pains. Just as **Basil** became **Mahood** (309), so Mahood, unable to affirm that Man is a higher mammal, gives way to Worm (the "BMW" pattern of **Belacqua**, **Murphy**, and **Watt** in miniature). Worm is the final stage of unaccommodated man, "creature" reduced to its **fundamental sound**, squirming at the end of the line, swallowing three hooks and still hungry (338). This is **Leibniz**'s "monade nue," the naked degenerate monad at the lowest level, furtherest from **God**; humanity at the **larval stage** of embryonic **coenaesthesis**; the lowly prototype of *l'homme lavaire* who will crawl through the mud of *How It Is.* However "inexpungable" (347), Worm is not "subject" (343). He is at best "prehistory" (357), unable to set himself in **motion** even if dragged out of his **hole** with a long hooked **stick** (358), and so must be rejected as the Unnamable seeks the **voice** more truly his own.

Wormwood, Lord Gall of: wormwood is the bitter shrub (*Artemisia absinthium*) that sprang up along the writhing track of the serpent driven from Paradise; it is commonly associated with gall (Lamentations 3:18). The touch of Wormwood Scrubs does little for his Lordship (first name "Haemo"). Childless and impotent despite his hundred thousand golf balls, his Eden of Wormwood may fall into the hands of Baron **Extravas**, and can be saved only if a male heir is produced (for the outcome, see **"Echo's Bones"**). Lord Gall's problems continue into *Murphy.* He has enlisted the help of Rosie **Dew**'s Ouija board for testamentary pentimenti

from the *au-delà* (99); but the protector is a man of iron and will not bar.

Worstward Ho: a short prose piece, written 9 August 1981 to 17 March '82 (RUL 2602/1–3); published 1983, the third of SB's second threesome, the others being *Company* (1980) and *Ill Seen Ill Said* (1982). The title derives from Webster and **Dekker**'s *Westward Hoe* (1607) and Kingsley's *Westward Ho!* (1885). Published independently (Calder, 1983; Grove, 1983, dust jacket illustrated by **Giacometti**); then in *Nohow On* (Calder, 1989; Grove, 1996). First broadcast on BBC 3 (4 August 1983), dir. Ronald Mason, with Norman Rodway. Translated after SB's **death** by Edith Fournier as *Cap au pire* (Minuit, 1991), a title she had discussed with SB, who had deemed the work untranslatable.

In *Worstward Ho* SB's aesthetics of failure coalesce into pursuit of the worst. If language by definition fails, paring it down to the "meremost minimum" may result in better failures, as in SB's working title, "Better worse." The starting point was *King Lear,* most notably, "The worst is not so long as one can say, This is the worst." The images are iller seen, iller said, as we move worstward, still trapped in "the madhouse of the **skull**." In addition to the "pained body" and "combined image of man and child," there is "The perceiving head or skull. 'Germ of All.'" But "All" contains a paradox that threatens to become a narratological impasse: can the skull be "Germ of All," even of itself: "If of all of it too?" (18). Can it perceive itself if there is, to adapt Jacques Derrida, no outside the skull. From what perspective, from what grounding could such perception take place? If "All" happens inside the skull is the skull inside the skull as well? Such paradoxes shift the focus to language and its complicity in the act of representation. The pivotal word, "the rip word," is "gone": "Gnawing to be gone. Less no good. Worse no good. Only one good. Gone. Gone for good. Till then gnaw on. All gnaw on. To be gone" (41–42). Denial reinvokes, reconstitutes the image or the world, the gone always a going. That is, writing about absence reifies that absence, makes of it a presence, as writing about the impossibility of writing about absence is not the creation of silences but its representation. SB's silences have always been wordy. As the image shifts in *Worstward Ho* from the skull, "Germ of all," to the language representing it, the narrator tries to imagine the end of words, for which he substitutes the word "blanks"—still, however, a word—then a dash, "—." But the dash as representation recalls outmoded conventions of proper names in fiction. The closer to emptying the void, of man, boy, woman, skull, the closer void comes to an entity imagined in language. The desire to worsen language and its images generates an expansion of imaginative activity in its attempt to order experience. The drive worstward is, thus, doomed to failure; all an artist can do, as SB reiterates, is "Try again. Fail again. Fail better" (7).

"Worstward Poems": two rough poems (1981–82) written on the verso (f18) of an original draft of *Worstward Ho*

(RUL 2602/1). The first, "ashes burning," is a single three-line draft; the second, "on where," exists in two drafts, of six and ten lines, respectively. Their themes are summarized in their opening words.

Wu, the Empress (ca. 694 BC): mentioned in *Dream* (111), the details from H. A. Giles, *Civilisation of China* (82–83; DN, 75). The Empress, suffering from midsummer madness, sat among her ministers wearing a false beard. She styled herself Divine Empress, then **God** Almighty, and insisted that none could say that the Empress was fair as a lily or lovely as a rose, but that these were as lovely as she. She commanded peonies to bloom and, when they did not instantly obey, had them pulled up, burned, and prohibited (SB's "Bloom, bloom blast you"). The parable implies the powers a narrator can exercise, the **lius** not always obedient.

Wylie: tall and thin ("Needle"), Laurel to **Neary's Hardy**, **time** to his space, and straight man to the comic banana. He rescues Neary from Cuchulain and consoles Miss **Counihan**.

Wynn's Hotel: 35–36 Lower Abbey Street, **Dublin**. In *Murphy* (54) it will always find Miss **Counihan**, who is later discovered on **Wylie's** knees (117), *not* in Wynn's Hotel lest an action for libel should lie. Largely destroyed in Easter 1916, it was rebuilt (1926). Mentioned in *Ulysses* (687), the proprietor (1904) one D. J. Murphy. *Malone meurt* originally read "Hôtel Wynne" instead of "Bellevue" (91).

X

X: the algebraic unknown. *Murphy* was conceived as an engagement between H, **horoscope**, and X as protagonist. In "**Text 7**" (128), X is "that paradigm of human kind . . . a carcass in **God**'s image." In "**Avant** *Fin de partie*," X is the central character, a prototype of **Hamm**, in consort with F, his factotum.

X: A Quarterly Review: a London literary journal that first published "*L'Image*" (I.1 [novembre 1959]: 35–37); part of *Comment c'est* (Minuit, 1961, 33–38), with numerous variants, mostly in the layout, an unbroken block without the "verse" divisions.

xenia: Watt (132) is pleased with his "tenth rate xenia" (corrected by SB to "xenium" for the **Calder** text) about the **serial** nature of existence. "Explanation" (NB5, 81) is crossed out and "xenia" substituted. It suggests a "flower of thought," a curious cross-fertilization. "**Gnome**" imitates **Goethe**'s "Xenien" (1796), satirical epigrams written as a classical distich, hexameter and pentameter, to denounce the platitudinous intellectual world. The title, borrowed from Martial, means presents made to departing guests.

Xerxes (ca. 519–465 BC): King of Persia, who invaded Greece but was defeated at Salamis. He threw two bridges across the Hellespont; hence "whipping the Hellespont" from **Burton**'s *Anatomy* (preface, 41; DN, 106). Compare *Proust* (58).

Y

Yang Kuei-fei: concubine of the T'ang Emperor Hsüan-Tsung (712–56), who took her from his son and neglected his duties. Her adopted son and lover, An Lu-shan, rebelled against the emperor, who fled south, but was forced to order the eunuch Kao Li-shih to strangle her (she was hanged upon a pear tree). Her fate became the stuff of poetry, as in Po Chü-i's "Everlasting Remorse." SB recorded (DN, 75): "Yang Kuei-fei, famous concubine, strangled by eunuch, breaking with her hands the yellow gold in the Isles of the Blest, dividing the enamel, crying over the spray of peach bloom." His source is Giles, *Civilisation of China* (85–87), the "bloom" pear rather than peach, the "gold" a hairpin, and the "enamel" a brooch, broken by the concubine in the afterworld to send to the emperor, keeping half herself. Invoked in *Dream* (52–53), as **Belacqua** looks at "the tattered flowers of the evening"; and in *Murphy* (117), as **Neary** mutters with his chopsticks against the perfidy of the fair sex.

Yeats, Jack B. (1871–1957): Irish painter, younger brother of W. B. **Yeats**, who studied art in London and was a cartoonist and illustrator before returning to Ireland. He often worked in black and white (see his illustrations to **Synge**'s *Aran Islands*), but his characteristic work is in oils, bold in concept and color, with a love of the fantastic and a feeling for the Irish peasantry. He also wrote for adults and children, his works experimental in structure and style. His enigmatic plays at the Peacock Theatre attracted attention in the 1930s.

SB met Yeats (November 1930) through Thomas **MacGreevy**. He sometimes went to his Thursday "at homes" in Fitzwilliam Square, where Yeats would offer Madeira with a twist of lemon and conversation on **art** and literature. SB preferred to see Yeats alone, without his English-born wife, Cottie ("Madam"), whose chatter he found a distraction. They might walk together, and Yeats (with Joseph Hone) visited **Cooldrinagh** to meet SB's **mother** and see her **donkey**, of which he was curiously fond (Knowlson, 670).

The first visit and the sight of so many fine pictures was staggering. A few years later in London, SB picked up for 30/- one of Yeats's watercolors: "Probably the fish market in Sligo," Yeats said vaguely when SB showed it to him (Bair, 201). He owned reproductions of *Low Tide* and *Boy and Horse* (Knowlson, 670), but his most important purchase was *Morning*, described to MacGreevy (29 January 19[36]) as "almost a skyscape, wide street leading into Sligo looking west as usual, with boy on a horse. 30 pounds." It might have been thirty million. SB offered to pay for it over time, and borrowed from his brother Frank and mother, but it was acquired at terrible cost, with an emotional debt to his mother and numerous self-deprivations as he struggled to pay for the work. It was, he told MacGreevy (7 May 1936), echoing **Thomas à Kempis**, "always morning, and a setting out without the coming home"; that is, an eternal joy. See Bair (617) for the curious story, not mentioned in Knowlson, of how casually SB gave it to Jack **MacGowran** in 1971.

Not having read *Murphy,* Yeats commended it to T. M. Ragg, describing SB's writing as "the real thing" (Knowlson, 268). Yeats acted as referee for a job in the National Gallery, London, and an academic appointment in Capetown. Nothing came of either, but SB appreciated his support. The debt was partly repaid by public homage. SB offered the *Dublin Magazine* (1936) a review of *The Amaranthers* (see "An **Imaginative Work**"). In "**Recent Irish Poetry**" he linked Yeats's art with *The Waste Land* as notable statements of the no-man's-land between the self and world, Yeats aware of the breakdown between subject and **object**, and thus to be distinguished from the **antiquarians**. After the **war** SB published in the *Irish Times* a review entitled "**MacGreevy on Yeats**," affirming Yeats as one of the greats of our time, "because he brings light, as only the great dare to bring light, to the **issueless** predicament of existence" (*Disjecta,* 97). In the 1946 "Pantalon" essay (*Disjecta,* 118), he likened Yeats to **Watteau**.

When Cottie died (1947) SB went to her funeral, and on that visit bought *Regatta Evening* (Knowlson, 333). Having written "**Hommage à Jack B. Yeats**" for a 1954 exhibition at the Wildenstein Gallery, something he called "real torture," SB went to the exhibition many times. Yeats died (28 March 1957) at the

Portobello Nursing Home, but SB was unable to attend the funeral. He sent two paintings to an exhibition of Yeats's paintings in Venice (May 1962). He continued to pay tribute to the work, emphasizing that Yeats was his own man, impervious to influence, and noting the artist's comment that all painting must have some "ginger of life." The greater debt may be incalculable, if Knowlson is correct (342) in accounting Yeats's *The Two Travellers* and *Men of the Plain* among the influences on *Waiting for Godot,* or O'Brien in suggesting (285) the impact of Yeats's refusal to compromise his art by painting what others would like him to have seen.

SB was attracted to Yeats's lonely figures set against an alien landscape, hints of cruel humor, and the theme of man's isolation from **nature**, which he identified with **Cézanne**'s landscape as indifferent to man. He admired the way that Yeats in a few deft strokes could capture compelling particulars, and that he was not part of any movement. Having suggested an affinity between Yeats and Constable, he later stressed a difference, Constable's art as romanticized and humanized as Turner's, but as Cézanne's was not. Yeats's painting, he asserted, stressed the "ultimate *inorganism* of everything" (SB to TM, 14 August 1937). In his book on Yeats, MacGreevy recorded SB's comment on Yeats's recent work: "He grows Watteauer and Watteauer"; and expressed his surprise, given the "exquisitely pencilled quality" of the one and the "extraordinarily telling" brushwork of the other (O'Brien, 284). He missed SB's point that Watteau was painting "pure inorganic juxtapositions," his people "mineral" (see **geology**). SB saw in Yeats "loneliness in **solitude**, the impassable immensity between the solitude that cannot quicken to loneliness and the loneliness that cannot lapse into solitude" (14 August 1937). This marks the beginnings of *Watt*, a lonely figure set between the sky above and the waste below, and the setting of *Godot*.

The older man's artistic integrity afforded a fine model, even if Yeats was unimpressed with SB's work, finding it "amoral" (Pyle, 146). His admiration is curious. Yeats's painting invokes the emptiness of waste and sky, lonely individuals on lonely roads, but it also offers a **romantic** view of peasants and fishermen, with an optimism and Celticism SB chose not to see, denying the "**allegory**" and affirming instead ironies and discontinuities. Yeats was an emblem of one whose art had found the means to express such matters, values that SB, for all his outspoken rejection of them, could never quite deny.

Yeats, William Butler (1865–1939): elder brother of Jack B. **Yeats**, poet, Irish Senator, **Nobel** laureate (1923), and the most celebrated literary figure of his day. SB's response was ambivalent. The relationship has been variously assessed, most seeing little influence on SB until later, but Harrington arguing for a closer awareness. Bair contends (121) that SB avoided Yeats, regarding him as pompous and posturing, and states that the two met only once, at **Killiney**, SB disgusted with the way Yeats simpered over his wife and children. Cronin (63) states that the two never met, but Roche (15) qualifies Bair's account of the Killiney

meeting by telling how SB was taken aback when Yeats praised *Whoroscope*.

SB distrusted much that Yeats stood for: Irish nationalism; the Celtic twilight; aristocracy; Neoplatonic speculation; occult belief; and ornate rhetoric. Early references are sardonic: in "**Walking Out**" (106), **Lucy** looks like "the Nobel Yeats" (Jack B. Yeats's portrait, in the National Gallery, **Dublin**). In *Dream* (129), a butterfly on "the eternal toilet-roll" is said to "pern [*sic*] in a gyre," as in "Sailing to Byzantium." **Neary**'s assault on Cuchulain's "deathless rump" mocks the "sacrifice" (*Murphy*, 42) of "Easter 1916," as does the Civic Guard's meditation on a theme near to his heart (45). Miss **Counihan** and **Cathleen na Hennessy** as Cathleen ni Houlihan invoke *The Countess Cathleen;* "consume away" (19) echoes "Sailing to Byzantium"; and the **sheep** that turn "their broody heads aside" (100) offer an emetic to "Who Will Go with Fergus" and **love**'s bitter mystery.

SB may have compiled "A Review of the Works of W. B. Yeats" (1934); this cannot be traced (F&F, 105). "**Recent Irish Poetry**" (1936) numbers Yeats among the **antiquarians** (*Disjecta*, 70). He does not fare well, as witness the mockery directed against the "last **romantics**" who chose for theme "Traditional sanctity and loveliness" ("Coole Park and Ballylee, 1931"). Yeats has woven "the best embroideries" (71), but this cutting of the cloths of heaven is a dubious compliment. Finally, SB mocks the "hardship borne and chosen out of pride" (72) that forms the Irish writer's theme. These serrated comments make it difficult to agree with Knowlson (181) that SB is not attacking the poet but high-lighting the subtle Yeats; or that SB's quarrel is less with Yeats than with the Celtic Twilight and poets spawned by the Irish literary revival. Ruby Cohn cites "Hommage à Jack B. Yeats" (1954): "L'artiste qui joue son être est de nulle part. Et il n'a pas de frères," seeing this as "a backhanded slap" at Ireland and W. B. Yeats (*Comic Gamut*, 2, 313).

That attitude changed as SB began to appreciate Yeats, particularly as a drama-tist. He was not uncritical. He saw *Res-urrection* and *The King of the Great Clock Tower* (August 1934), describing them as unbearably dull: "Balbus building his wall would be more dramatic" (Knowlson, 181). Nor was he averse to parody: Winnie's "when I was young and foolish" (*Happy Days*, 27) echoes "Down by the Salley Gardens"; and Words's "Arise then and go now" mangles "The Lake Isle of Innisfree" ("Words and Music," 128). SB disliked Yeats's Noh drama but admired the minimalism of *Purgatory* and *At the Hawk's Well*. Yeats as a playwright was avant-garde in ways he could never be as a poet, "an isolated creator continuing his dramatic experiments for almost forty years in the teeth of personal hostility and indifference" (Roche, 29). By fol-lowing his example SB embraced a the-ater of failure.

In later years SB was fond of citing Yeats as one who did his best work at the end of his life. In the 1960s he read Yeats deliberately, and echoes appear with more affection than irony: the blind man and the cripple in "Rough for Theatre I"; in *Happy Days*, the opening line of *At the Hawk's Well*, "I call to the eye of the mind," words copied into the Produc-tion Notebook; the echo of "Words for Music Perhaps" in the title of "Words and Music"; the image of the woman "Who loved could not be won" from "The Tower": "Does the imagination dwell the most / Upon a woman won or woman lost?" SB's most poignant trib-ute is the 1976 television play ". . . but the clouds . . . ," a title taken from the final lines of "The Tower," when the aging poet decides it is time to "make" his soul, as SB perhaps made his peace with Yeats.

"Yellow": the penultimate story of *MPTK* (1934), written after SB's first (December 1932) or second (May 1933) operation for the boil on his neck, revenant "since the dépucelage" (SB to TM, 22 June 1933). It was republished, with variants, in *New World Writing* 10 (November 1956): 108–19. The setting, SB informed Eoin O'Brien (156), is the Elpis Nursing Home, 17–21 Lower Mount Street, where Synge died (SB was in the Merrion Nursing Home, 28 Upper Merrion Street). The story an-ticipates *Murphy* in its orchestration, one bad joke made up of countless smaller ones; it remained SB's favorite. The title suggests Belacqua's fear, but also the scene in *Proust* where Bergotte drags himself from his deathbed to see again the beauty of the "petit pan du mur jaune" of Vermeer's *View of Delft;* before the operation Belacqua sees sunlight on "the grand old yaller wall outside." The six hours before the ordeal are a terrifying prospect, to which he finds two responses: Heraclitus, the weeping philosopher, or Democritus, the laughing one. Affirming the latter, he finds the hospital and nurses objects of hilarity; leaves the **cat** his toe; tells of the clergyman shot during amateur theatricals ("By **Christ!**"); and sees a box of Ferruginous Ampoules for the treatment of anemia, trademark "**Mozart.**" Comic assurance works. Belacqua swaggers through the antechamber, but the last laugh is on him: the surgeon's invaluable hands have been at a wedding where the champagne flowed freely, the mixture is too rich, Belacqua experiences terrible yellow yerks, and dies under the anaesthetic.

Casual allusion creates dramatic irony. **Hardy's** *Tess* (158) invokes fatalism; the family's Huguenot guts (159), the St. Bartholemew's Day massacre; and, plucky or not, a game-cock (161) is inauspicious. The "Delian diver" (164) does not return to the surface; Aschenputtel (166) is no Cinderella; and Sherlock Holmes (167) will not return. The theater sister is called a "**châteaubriant**" (168), an echo of *Mémoires d'outre-tombe* ("Posthumous memories"). **Julian of Norwich's** "all will be well" (171) is mocked by "a truly military **evacuation**"; and a last cigarette (172) is ominous. These details support such obvious ironies as the death of Bergotte, the suffering of a divine **Miranda**, the parson's tale, and a Mozart who died ingloriously young.

Yellow House: a Rathfarnham pub, in the **Dublin** mountains (O'Brien, 373). The homespun Poet of "A **Wet Night**" (59) in *Dream* (213) prefers the Hill of Allen.

Yerkes, Robert M.: American psychologist (Harvard), discussed in **Woodworth**, who followed **Köhler** on how apes might learn a language of gesture; his major work was *The Mental Life of Monkeys and Apes: A Study in Ideational Behavior.* Traces of his name are left in "**Yellow**" (174): "terrible yellow yerks in his skull." **Moran** discusses the "Yerk affair": he found Yerk on the third day, but it took three months to conclude, and was over when he took Yerk's tiepin and destroyed it (136). Consider the song "O let us howle" in Webster's *Duchess of Malfi,* the masque of madmen before the Duchess's murder (IV.ii): "Till yerksome noyce, have cloy'd your ears / and corasiv'd your hearts." The drafts reveal that "the **London** affair" became "the York affair," and thence "the Yerk affair."

"Yoke of Liberty": a thirteen-line poem (August 1931), published in *The European Caravan* (1931), 480. It was rejected by the *Dublin Magazine* because the editor assumed that the opening lines ("The lips of her desire are grey") referred to the female genitalia. SB retained his liking for the poem (also called "**Moly**") but withheld it from later collections. The title derives from **Dante's** *De monarchia* (II.1), as hinted at in SB's "Dante" (7), a Necessity that is not Fate, a Liberty that is not Chance. Dante's yoke is here the lure of the erotic. The poem was written for Ethna **MacCarthy** and captures the poet's attraction yet wariness: those lips are gray; she preys on sensitive wild things. Caughlin (193) writes of "antithetical impulses towards detachment and attachment." Like **Ronsard** with his Hélène (or **Eliot's** "Portrait of a Lady"), the poet imagines her dead and her snare tendered so patiently will "break and hang / in a pitiful descent." The sense is delicate, with regret; as SB told Lawrence Harvey: "he will not be caught in this trap but not to be caught is a burden."

Youdi: in *Molloy,* the one who runs the "Organisation" in which **Gaber** and **Moran** are messenger and agent, in turn subject to the mysterious **Obidil**. Youdi's name, "Dieu" transposed into pig-Latin, derives from "Jehovah" or "Yahweh," the authoritarian **God**, or French argot for "Jew." The original read "le directeur." Gaber inveighs against him (94), but Moran knows he must obey, or be punished.

Young, Edward (1683–1765): English poet, whose *Night Thoughts* (1742–45) instituted the school of graveyard poetry, the sleepless poet lamenting and meditating on mortality. SB liked Young's settings (illustrated by **Blake**) but not his orthodoxy; "night's young thoughts," repeated from *Murphy* (73) in "**Text 8**" is a casual quip, despite the adjacent graveyard.

Z

Zaborovna: otherwise the *Privet* (a surgical instrument for probing a wound); a "tasty" temptress in "**Echo's Bones.**" Concerned about **Belacqua**'s lack of shadow, she invites him home for a repast of garlic and white Cuban rum and thoroughly ravishes him.

Zeno (ca. 495–430 BC): Zeno of Elea, Greek philosopher, a **Pythagorean** then a Sophist, master of dialectic. He would take his adversaries' axioms and draw from them contradictory conclusions. Best known for his paradoxes of **motion**, by which he "proves" (1) that motion is impossible; (2) that Achilles cannot ever catch the tortoise; (3) that an arrow can never reach its mark; and (4) that bodies moving toward one another cannot pass. These challenge the **atomist** assumption that **time** and space consist of indivisible minima.

At the outset of *Endgame,* **Clov** comments: "Grain upon grain." **Hamm** later refers to "that old Greek." Most assume an allusion to Zeno the Eleatic, and in Berlin SB spoke of "Zeno's grains, a logical jest." The paradox is that of the part and the whole: at what point do one grain and other separate grains make up a unit called a heap? Hamm restates the paradox in human terms: at what point do separate moments of existence make up a life: "all life long you wait for that to mount up to a life" (70). SB told O'Brien that the allusion was not to Zeno but to a philosopher he no longer recalled; **Windelband** (89) indicates Eubulides of Miletus, dialectitian of Megara, to whom is attributed a series of "little catches," retraceable to Zeno: "Which kernel of grain by being added makes the heap? Which hair falling out makes the bald head?" Hence, perhaps, the *millet,* despite SB's later denial that this was intended.

The philosopher is less important than the paradox. As SB put it in his Riverside Notebook: "C perplexed. All seemingly in order, yet a change. Fatal grain added to form impossible heap. Ratio ruentis acetvi." **Horace** in the *Epistle* to Augustus (II.i, 47) uses the logical puzzle called *sorites* or "heap" (*acervus*) to consider how long it takes for a poet to be considered an "ancient" and hence great: "*dum cadat elusus ratione ruentis acervi*" ("till after the fashion of the falling heap he is baffled and thrown down"). Clov senses the almost imperceptible change, the single extra grain "needed to make the heap—the last straw," according to SB. That sense of change provides the impetus for his own.

Mercier and Camier (77), a decade earlier, refers casually to "every millet grain that falls"; every day brings **death** a little closer. **Malone** (225) tells of his "fun and games with the cones and cylinders, the millet grains beloved of birds and other panics." Big Lambert's wife (214) has on her table a heap of lentils, which she sorts into two heaps, the big one getting smaller and the smaller bigger, until she sweeps them together, "annihilating thus in less than a second the work of two or three minutes." In *Watt* (43), **Arsene**'s semi**mystical** moment is likened to a great alp of sand in which, "in tiny packets of two or three millions the grains slip"; this is his **Proustian** moment, the sudden sense of existence off the **ladder**, a change hymeneal yet imperceptible, of kind and not degree (he trusts he makes himself clear). **Louit** comments (194), "Little by little the bird"; the typescript (241) continues, "builds its nest," but the aposiopesis suggests impossibility. In "The **Expelled**" and *How It Is* "little by little" describes "progress" through memories and mud. The **machinery** of motion derives from yet is ultimately confounded by the logical paradoxes of Zeno.

Zero Anthology: an expatriate **Paris** anthology, ed. Themistocles Hoetis for the Zero Press, New York, which published "The **Smeraldina's Billet-Doux**" in issue #8 (1956), 59–61.

"**Zone**": SB's translation of **Apollinaire**'s poem, the first in *Alcools* (1913), on the theme of sudden incandescence of beauty in a ravaged world, the contrast making him sick at heart. *Dream* (171) depicts "the ravaged zone." The translation, made much earlier, appeared in *Transition fifty* 6 (October 1950). SB gave his only copy to Liam Miller for the Dolmen Press, **Dublin**; this appeared (1972) in an edition of 250 copies, signed and leather-bound. The poem and translation are included in *Collected Poems*.

zoomorphism: if SB's portrayals of human beings warrant accusations of cruelty and aggrandizement, his depictions of animals are less contentious, though no less nuanced. **Belacqua**'s recoil from the doomed lobster (and the parallels with capital punishment) implies objections to anthropocentrism. Animals prompt ineffable narratorial responses; consider the apparitional white **horse** in *From an Abandoned Work* and the **goat** in "The **Calmative**." **Clov** is associated with **Hamm**'s "**dog**"; **Croak** calls Words and **Music** "dogs"; **Malone** identifies with "old dogs" (191) whose masters contemplate putting them to **death**—he even finds consolation in the thought. When not calling **Lucky** a pig, **Pozzo** says, "Old dogs have more dignity" (*WG*, 21.b). Zoomorphism characterizes **Murphy** (5) and Mr. **Kelly** (11), **Molloy** (28–29), **Moran** (165–67), **Saposcat** (192), and **Macmann** (244). **Lousse**'s parrot (*Molloy*, 37–38) and that of Jackson (*Malone Dies*, 218), fixated on obscenity or collapsing into cacophony, imitate the seizures of language of SB's human narrators. Zoomorphism is a kind of convenience, a "calmative" for comfort and reassurance. Belacqua's resigned attitude to the lobster's fate (22)—"it's a quick death, **God** help us all"—is contradicted by the celestial assertion, "It is not." This discrepancy between the empathic and the actual attests to a basic ungraspability. Human and animal being may share fundamental conditions of penury, but the latter is not "knowable" enough to become part of human dominion, to submit to the "mastery" underwritten by human orthodoxy.

The question arises as to how "knowable" the human being is. Pozzo seems comfortable outside the species: "I am not particularly human, but who cares?" (*WG*, 19.b). The serial selves of *Three Novels* make intermittent reflections on "humanness." Any relationship with their species is provisional and under constant renegotiation. "Human nature. Marvellous thing," ruminates Molloy (35), later adding, hesitantly, "But I am human, I fancy" (78). For Moran, "being only human" (138) is a locution for the reassurances he seeks that tally with "the all too human feeling." Malone assigns "human" to Macmann (232), Lemuel (268), an assailant (269), his exercise book (270), and the Lord Mayor of Cork (273). But he has not quite disowned it. As he prepares to depart not just from life but from the species to which he has maintained an uneasy relationship, he muses that "you begin to fancy yourself the last of human kind" (253). The need to identify with one's species is dropped by the Unnamable. In a place where "there are no human creatures" (296), one voice identifies itself as "the little murmur of unconsenting man, to murmur what it is their humanity stifles" (325). Another entity, with a permanently weeping eye, is in danger of "getting humanized" (360). If animal being is unbridgeably remote from human being, by the end of the *Trilogy* the latter is as surely dispossessed of itself. See humanism. [PS]

Zulu: the Aberdeen terrier belonging in life to the Elsner sisters, the fictionalized neighbors of Moran. In a draft of *Fin de partie,* a detail deleted, Hamm's dog reminds him of "Zoulou."

Zurbarán, Francisco de (1598–1664): Spanish painter in the Caravaggio tradition, known for his devotional pictures, monks, and virgin martyrs. Hence Belacqua's comment (*Dream,* 72): "Livid rapture of the Zurbaran Saint-Onan." Zurbarán depicted St. Lucia with her eyes in a dish, a legend alluded to later (179).

Bibliography

A. Samuel Beckett

"Abandonée." Paris: Éditions Georges Visat, 1972.

"Assumption." *transition* 16/17 (spring–summer 1929): 268–71. Rpt. in *Samuel Beckett: the Complete Short Prose*, ed. S. E. Gontarski, 3–7.

"As the Story Was Told." *Günter Eich zum Gedächtnis*. Frankfurt: Suhrkamp Verlag, 1975.

As the Story Was Told. Uncollected and Late Prose. New York: Riverrun Press, 1990.

Beckett's Dream Notebook, ed. and annotated with an introductory essay by John Pilling. Reading: Beckett International Foundation, 1999.

"Cascando" [poem]. *Dublin Magazine* XL.4 (October–December 1936): 3–4.

Cascando and Other Short Dramatic Pieces. New York: Grove Press, 1968.

"A Case in a Thousand." *Bookman* LXXXVI (August 1934): 241–42; rpt. in *Samuel Beckett: The Complete Short Prose*, ed. S. E. Gontarski, 18–24.

"Che Sciagura." *TCD: A College Miscellany* XXXVI (November 14, 1929): 42.

Collected Poems in English and French. London: John Calder, 1977.

Collected Poems 1930–1978. London: John Calder, 1984.

Collected Shorter Plays. New York: Grove Press, 1984.

Comment c'est. Paris: Éditions de Minuit, 1961.

Compagnie. Paris: Éditions de Minuit, 1985.

Company. London: John Calder, 1980.

"Dante . . . Bruno . Vico . . Joyce." *transition* 16/17 (spring–summer 1929): 242–53. Rpt. in *Our Exagmination Round his Factification for Incamination of Work in Progress*. London: Faber and Faber, 1929, 3–22.

Le Dépeupleur. Paris: Éditions de Minuit, 1970.

Le Dernière bande. Paris: Éditions de Minuit, 1959.

Disjecta: Miscellaneous Writings and a Dramatic Fragment by Samuel Beckett, ed. Ruby Cohn. London: John Calder; New York: Grove Press, 1983.

Dream of Fair to middling Women, ed. Eoin O'Brien and Edith Fournier. Dublin: Black Cat Press, 1992; New York: Arcade Publishing, 1993.

"Echo's Bones" [unpublished ts]. Baker Library, Dartmouth College.

Echo's Bones and Other Precipitates. Paris: Europa Press, 1935.

Eleutheria. Paris: Editions de Minuit, 1995.

Eleutheria, trans. Michael Brodsky. New York: Foxrock, 1995.

Eleutheria, trans. Barbara Wright. London: Faber, 1996.

En Attendant Godot. Paris: Éditions de Minuit, 1952.

Endgame: A Play in One Act Followed by Act Without Words: A Mime for One Player. New York: Grove Press, 1958.

"La Falaise." In *Celui qui ne se peut servivir de mots.* Montpellier: Fata Morgana, 1975.

Film: New York: Grove Press, 1969.

Fin de partie suivi de Acte sans paroles I. Paris: Éditions de Minuit, 1957.

First Love and Other Novellas, edited and with an introduction and notes by Gerry Dukes. London: Penguin, 2000. [Replaces *The Expelled and Other Novellas,* 1980.]

"German Diaries" [6 notebooks]. Samuel Beckett Archives, University of Reading [RUL number unassigned at time of writing].

Happy Days. New York: Grove Press, 1961.

How It Is. New York: Grove Press, 1964.

"Human Wishes" [3 notebooks]. Samuel Beckett Archives, University of Reading [RUL MS 3461/1–3].

L'Innommable. Paris: Éditions de Minuit, 1952.

Krapp's Last Tape and Other Dramatic Pieces. New York: Grove Press, 1960.

Letters to Mary Hope Manning [Mary Manning Howe]. Harry Ransom Center, University of Texas at Austin.

Letters to Thomas MacGreevy. Samuel Beckett Archives, Trinity College, Dublin.

"Lightning Calculation" [unpublished ts]. Samuel Beckett Archives, University of Reading [RUL MS 2902].

Malone Dies. New York: Grove Press, 1956; rpt. in *Three Novels,* 1959, 177–288.

Malone meurt. Paris: Éditions de Minuit, 1951.

Mal vu mal dit. Paris: Éditions de Minuit, 1981.

Mercier and Camier. New York: Grove Press, 1974.

Mercier et Camier. Paris: Éditions de Minuit, 1970.

Molloy. Paris: Éditions de Minuit, 1950.

Molloy. New York: Grove Press, 1955; rpt. in *Three Novels,* 1959, 7–176.

More Pricks Than Kicks. New York: Grove Press, 1970.

Murphy. London: Routledge, 1938.

———. New York: Grove Press, 1957.

———. 1938 [Jupiter Books]; London: John Calder, 1963.

Murphy [French translation]. Paris: Bordas, 1947.

"Murphy" [carbon copy of the ts]. Harry Ransom Humanities Research Center, University of Texas at Austin [Samuel Beckett Collection, #75].

Negro: An Anthology, ed. Nancy Cunard. London: Wishart and Co., 1934. [Includes several translations by SB; see Davis et al., *Calepins de bibliographie;* 1934.]

Nouvelles et textes pour rien. Paris: Éditions de Minuit, 1958.

Oh les beaux jours. Paris: Editions de Minuit, 1963.

Pas suivi de quatre esquisses. Paris: Éditions de Minuit, 1978.

Premier amour. Paris: Éditions de Minuit, 1970.

Proust. London: Chatto and Windus, 1931; rpt. New York: Grove Press, n.d. [1957].

"Recent Irish Poetry" [pseud. "Andrew Belis"]. *Bookman* LXXXVI (August 1934): 235–44; rpt. in *Disjecta,* ed. Ruby Cohn, 70–76.

Samuel Beckett's "Company" / "Compagnie" and "A Piece of Monologue" / "Solo": A Bilingual Variorum Edition, ed. Charles Krance. [Garland Reference Library of the Humanities, vol. 1400]. New York: Garland Publishing, 1993.

Samuel Beckett's "Mal Vu Mal Dit" / "Ill Seen Ill Said": A Bilingual, Evolutionary, and Synoptic Variorum Edition, ed. Charles Krance. [Garland Reference Library of the Humanities, vol. 1266]. New York: Garland Publishing, 1996.

Samuel Beckett: The Complete Short Prose, 1929–1989, ed. S. E. Gontarski. New York: Grove Press, 1995.

"Sedendo et Quiesc[i]endo." *transition* 21 (March 1932): 13–20.

Se voir, Pour finir encore et autres foirades. Paris: Éditions de Minuit, 1976.

Stirrings Still, with illustrations by Louis le Brocquy. New York: Blue Moon; London: John Calder, 1988. [Collector's edition; limited to 200 copies.]

Stirrings Still. New York: North Star Line, 1993. [Trade edition, including le Brocquy illustrations.]

This Quarter (September 1932), édité par André Breton. [Includes several translations by SB; see Davis et al., *Calepins de bibliographie;* 1932].

Three Novels by Samuel Beckett: Molloy; Malone Dies; The Unnamable. New York: Grove Press, 1959.

Tous ceux qui tombent. Paris: Editions de Minuit, 1957.

The Unnamable. New York: Grove Press, 1958; rpt. in *Three Novels,* 1959, 289–414.

Waiting for Godot. New York: Grove Press, 1954.

"Waiting for Godot." *Theatre Arts* XL.8 (August 1956): 36–61.

Watt. Paris: Olympia Press, 1953.

Watt. New York: Grove Press, 1959.

Watt. Paris: Éditions de Minuit, 1968.

Whoroscope. Paris: The Hours Press, 1930.

Whoroscope Notebook. Samuel Beckett Archives, University of Reading [RUL MS 3000/1].

B. Critical Studies Relevant to Samuel Beckett

Acheson, James. "Beckett, Proust, and Schopenhauer." *Contemporary Literature* 19 (1978): 165–79.

———. "Murphy's Metaphysics." *JOBS* 5 (autumn 1979): 9–24.

———. *Samuel Beckett's Artistic Theory and Practice: Criticism, Drama and Early Fiction.* London: Macmillan, 1997.

———. "A Note on the Ladder Joke in *Watt.*" *JOBS* 2.1 (autumn 1992): 115–16.

Ackerley, C. J. "'In the Beginning Was the Pun': Samuel Beckett's *Murphy*." *AUMLA* 55 (1981): 15–22.

———. "The Unnamable's First Voice." *JOBS* 2.2 (spring 1993): 53–58.

———. "Beckett's 'Malacoda': or, Dante's Devil Plays Beethoven." *JOBS* 3.1 (autumn 1993): 59–65.

———. "Fatigue and Disgust: The Addenda to *Watt*." In *Samuel Beckett Today / Aujourd'hui* 2 (1993): 175–88.

———. "'Do Not Despair': Samuel Beckett and Robert Greene." *JOBS* 6.1 (autumn 1996): 119–24.

———. "The Rat which Ate of the Consecrated Wafer: A Theological Crux in Samuel Beckett's *Watt*." In *Word and Stage: Essays for Colin Gibson*. Otago Studies in English 6. Dunedin: Department of English, University of Otago, 1998, 233–41.

———. *Demented Particulars: The Annotated* Murphy. Tallahassee, Fla: Journal of Beckett Studies Books, 1998.

———. "Forest Murmurs: Beckett, Molloy and Siegfried." *JOBS* 8.2 (spring 1999): 73–75.

———. "Samuel Beckett and the Bible: A Guide." *JOBS* 9.1 (autumn 1999): 53–125.

———. "Samuel Beckett and Thomas à Kempis: The Roots of Quietism." *Samuel Beckett Today / Aujourd'hui* 9 (2000): 81–92.

———. "Lassata Sed: Samuel Beckett's Portraits of his Fair to Middling Women." *Samuel Beckett Today / Aujourd'hui* 12 (2002): 55–70.

Admussen, Richard. *The Samuel Beckett Manuscripts: A Study*. Boston: G. K. Hall, 1979.

Adorno, Theodor. "Trying to Understand *Endgame*," trans. Samuel Weber. In Bell-Chevigny, ed., *Twentieth Century Interpretations of Endgame*. Englewood Cliffs, N.J.: Prentice-Hall, 1969, 82–114.

Alvarez, A. *Beckett* (2nd ed). London: Fontana, 1992.

Anzieu, Didier. "Beckett et Bion." In *Revue de Psychothérapie* 5–6 (Paris, 1968): 21–30.

Arikha, Avigdor. "Un point pour le grand souffle." *Revue d'Esthétique* [numéro hors-série] (1990): 3–5.

Armstrong, Gordon S. *Samuel Beckett, W. B. Yeats, and Jack Yeats*. Lewisburg, Penn.: Bucknell University Press, 1990.

Asmus, Walter A. "Practical Aspects of Theatre, Radio and Television: Rehearsal Notes for the German Premiere of Beckett's 'That Time' and 'Footfalls' at the Schiller-Theater Werkstatt, Berlin (Directed by Beckett)." Trans. Helen Watanabe. *JOBS* 2 (summer 1977): 82–95.

Atik, Anne. "Beckett as Reader." *American Poetry Review* 28.5 (September–October 1999): 33–38.

———. *How It Was: A Memoir of Samuel Beckett*. London: Faber, 2001.

Bair, Deirdre. *Samuel Beckett: A Biography.* London: Jonathan Cape, 1978.

Baker, Phil. *Beckett and the Mythology of Psychoanalysis.* Basingstoke: Macmillan, 1997.

Barale, Michèle Aina and Rubin Rabinovitz. *A KWIC Concordance to Samuel Beckett's Murphy* (2 vols). New York and London: Garland, 1990.

———. *A KWIC Concordance to Samuel Beckett's Trilogy: Molloy, Malone Dies, and The Unnamable* (2 vols). New York and London: Garland, 1988.

Bataille, Georges. "Review of *Molloy*" [1951]; rpt. in Graver and Federman, *Critical Heritage,* 55–63.

Beach, Clare. "Silencing the Silence: A Text by Text Analysis of Samuel Beckett's *Texts for Nothing.*" BA hons. diss., University of Otago, 1999.

Begam, Richard. *Samuel Beckett and the End of Modernity.* Stanford: Stanford University Press, 1996.

Belmont, Georges and John Calder. "Remembering Sam." In *Beckett in Dublin,* ed. S. E. Wilmer. Dublin: Lilliput Press, 1992, 111–29.

Ben-Zvi, Linda. *Samuel Beckett.* Boston: Twayne, 1986.

———. "Samuel Beckett, Fritz Mauthner, and the Limits of Language." *PMLA* 2.95 (March 1980): 183–200.

———. "Fritz Mauthner for Company." *JOBS* 9 (spring 1983): 65–88.

Bersani, Leo and Ulysse Dutoit. *Arts of Impoverishment: Beckett, Rothko, Resnais.* Cambridge, Mass.: Harvard University Press, 1993.

Birkett, Jennifer and Kate Ince. *Samuel Beckett.* New York and London: Longman [Longman Critical Readers], 2000.

Blanchot, Maurice. "Review of *The Unnamable*" [1953]; rpt. in Graver and Federman, *Critical Heritage,* 116–21.

———. "Où maintenant? Qui maintenant?" *Nouvelle Revue française* 2 (octobre 1953): 678–86.

Bowles, Patrick. "How Samuel Beckett Sees the Universe." *The Listener* LIX.1525 (19 June 1958): 1011–12.

———. "How to Fail: Notes on Talks with Samuel Beckett." *Poetry Nation Review* (*PNR*) XX.4 (March-April 1994): 24–38.

Brater, Enoch. *Beyond Minimalism: Beckett's Late Style in the Theater.* New York: Oxford University Press, 1987.

Breuer, Rolf and Werner Huber (Hrsg.). *A Checklist of Beckett Criticism in German.* Paderborn: Ferdinand Schöning, 1996.

Bryden, Mary. *Women in Samuel Beckett's Prose and Drama: Her Own Other.* Basingstoke and London: Macmillan, 1993.

———. *Samuel Beckett and Music.* Oxford: Clarendon Press, 1998.

———. *Beckett and the Idea of God.* Basingstoke: Macmillan, 1998.

———, Julian Garforth, and Peter Mills, eds. *Beckett at Reading: Catalogue of the Beckett Manuscript Collection at the University of Reading.* Reading: Whiteknights Press and the Beckett International Foundation, University of Reading, 1998.

Butler, Lance St. John. *Samuel Beckett and the Meaning of Being: A Study in Onto-logical Parable.* New York: St. Martin's Press, 1984.

—— and Robin Davis, eds. *Rethinking Beckett: A Collection of Critical Essays.* Basingstoke: Macmillan, 1990.

Büttner, Gottfried. *Samuel Beckett's Novel Watt,* trans. Joseph P. Dolan. Philadelphia: University of Pennsylvania Press, 1984.

Calder, John, ed. *Beckett at 60: A Festschrift.* London: Calder and Boyars, 1967.

——, ed. *A Samuel Beckett Reader.* London: Calder and Boyars, 1967.

——, ed. *"As No Other Dare Fail": For Samuel Beckett on His 80th Birthday by His Friends and Admirers.* London: John Calder and Riverrun Press, 1986.

Caselli, Daniela. "Looking it up in My Big Dante: A Note on 'Sedendo et Quiesc[i]endo.'" *JOBS* 6.2 (spring 1997): 85–93.

——. "Beckett's Intertextual Modalities: The Case of Leopardi." *JOBS* 6.1 (autumn 1996): 1–24.

Coe, Richard N. *Samuel Beckett.* New York: Grove Press, 1967.

——. "Beckett's English." In *Samuel Beckett: Humanistic Perspectives,* ed. Morris Beja, S. E. Gontarski, and Pierre Astier. Colombus: Ohio State University Press, 1983, 36–57.

Coetzee, J. M. "The English Fiction of Samuel Beckett: An Essay in Style and Analysis." Ph.D. diss., University of Texas at Austin, 1969.

——. "The Manuscript Revisions of Beckett's *Watt." Journal of Modern Literature* 2 (1972): 472–80.

Cohen, David. "'For This Relief Much Thanks': Leopold Bloom and Beckett's Use of Allusion." In Phyllis Carey and Ed Jewinski, eds. *Re: Joyce'n Beckett.* New York: Fordham University Press, 1992, 43–49.

Cohn, Ruby. "Samuel Beckett Self-translator." *PMLA* lxxvi (December 1961): 613–21.

——. "Philosophical Fragments in Works of Samuel Beckett." *Criticism* 6.1 (winter 1964): 33–43; rpt. in Martin Esslin, ed., *Samuel Beckett: A Collection of Critical Essays.* Englewood Cliffs, N.J.: Prentice-Hall, 1965, 169–77.

——. *Samuel Beckett: The Comic Gamut.* New Brunswick, N.J.: Rutgers University Press, 1962.

——. *Just Play: Beckett's Theater.* Princeton: Princeton University Press, 1980.

——. "Mabou Mines Translations of Becket." In *Beckett Translating / Translating Beckett,* ed. Allen Warren Friedman et al. University Park: Pennsylvania State University Press, 1987.

——. "The 'F—' Story." *Samuel Beckett Today / Aujourd'hui* 7 (1998): 41–45.

——. *A Beckett Canon.* Ann Arbor: University of Michigan Press, 2001.

Colleran, Jeanne. "Beckett Festival, Gate Theatre; Dublin, October 1–20, 1991." *JOBS* 2.1 (autumn 1992): 145–47.

Connor, Steven. *Samuel Beckett: Repetition, Theory, and Text.* Oxford: Basil Blackwell, 1988.

Coughlan, Patricia. "'The Poetry Is Another Pair of Sleeves': Beckett, Ireland and Modernist Lyric Poetry." In Patricia Coughlan and Alex Davis, eds., *Modernism and Ireland: The Poetry of the 1930s.* Cork: Cork University Press, 1995; rpt. in Birkett and Ince, eds., *Samuel Beckett,* 65–82.

Cousineau, Thomas. "Anti-Oedipal Tendencies in *The Trilogy.*" In *Beckett and Beyond,* ed. Bruce Stewart, 70–77.

Crombie, John. "The Ill-Made Image." *JOBS* 4.2 (spring 1995): 15–27.

Cronin, Anthony. *Samuel Beckett: The Last Modernist.* London: HarperCollins, 1997.

Culik, Hugh. "Mindful of the Body: Medical Allusions in Beckett's *Murphy.*" *Eire-Ireland* 14.1 (spring 1979): 84–91.

———. "Entropic Order: Beckett's *Mercier and Camier.*" *Eire-Ireland* 17.1 (spring 1982): 91–106.

Davies, Paul. *The Ideal Real: Beckett's Fiction and Imagination.* London and Toronto: Associated University Presses, 1994.

Davis, R. J., J. R. Bryer, M. J. Friedman, and P. C. Hoy, eds. *Samuel Beckett: calepins de bibliographie,* no. 2. Paris: Lettres modernes Minard, 1972.

———. *Samuel Beckett: Checklist and Index of his Published Works 1967–1976.* Published from the Library, University of Stirling, 1979.

———. "Beckett Bibliography after Federman and Fletcher." *JOBS* 2 (summer 1977): 63–69.

Dettmar, Kevin J. H. "The Joyce that Beckett Built." *James Joyce Quarterly* 35.4 and 36.1 (summer/fall, 1998): 605–19.

Dobbin, Rachel [Burrows]. Notes from Beckett's lectures [unpublished ms]. Trinity College, Dublin [MIC 60].

———. "Interview with Rachel Burrows, Dublin, Bloomsday, 1982." Interviewers: S. E. Gontarski, Martha Fehsenfeld, Dougald McMillan. *JOBS* 11 and 12 (1989): 6–15.

Doherty, Francis. *Samuel Beckett.* London: Hutchinson, 1971.

———. "Mahaffy's Whoroscope." *JOBS* 2.1 (autumn 1992): 27–46.

Dowd, Garin. "Nomadology: Reading the Beckettian Baroque." *JOBS* 8.1 (autumn 1998): 15–49.

———. "Mud as Plane of Immanence in *How It Is.*" *JOBS* 8.2 (spring 1999): 1–28.

Driver, Tom. "Beckett by the Madeleine." *Columbia University Forum* IV (summer 1961): 21–25.

Duckworth, Colin, ed. "Introduction" to *En attendant Godot.* London: George Harrap, 1966, xvii–cxxxv.

Dukes, Gerry. "Beckett's Synge-song: The Revised *Godot* Revisited." *JOBS* 4.2 (spring 1995): 103–12.

———. *Samuel Beckett.* London: Penguin Books, 2001.

Eade, J. C. "The Seventh Scarf: A Note on *Murphy.*" *JOBS* 7 (spring 1982): 115–17.

Earnest, Steve. "*Texts for Nothing.* Directed by Joe Chaikin. Seven Stages, Atlanta, Georgia. April 16, 2000." *JOBS* 9.1 (autumn 1999): 141–43.

Elam, Keir. "World's End, West Brompton, Turdy and Other Godforsaken Holes." *Samuel Beckett Today / Aujourd'hui* 6 (1997): 165–80.

Ellis, Rueben J. "'Matrix of Surds': Heisenberg's Algebra in Beckett's *Murphy.*" *Papers on Language and Literature* (winter 1989): 120–23; rpt. in Lance St. John Butler, ed., *Critical Essays on Samuel Beckett.* Aldershot, Hants.: Scolar Press, 1993, 362–65.

Esslin, Martin. "Dionysos' Dianoetic Laughter." In John Calder, ed., *As No Other Dare Fail,* 15–23.

———. "Samuel Beckett's Poems." In John Calder, ed., *Beckett at 60,* 55–60.

———. "Samuel Beckett." In John Cruikshank, ed., *The Novelist as Philosopher: Studies in French Fiction 1935–1960.* London: Oxford University Press, 1962, 128–46.

Farrow, Anthony. *Early Beckett: Art and Illusion in More Pricks Than Kicks and Murphy.* Troy, N.Y.: Whitston, 1991.

Federman, Raymond. *Journey to Chaos: Samuel Beckett's Early Fiction.* Berkeley & Los Angeles: University of California Press, 1965.

——— and John Fletcher. *Samuel Beckett: His Works and His Critics: An Essay in Biography.* Berkeley and Los Angeles: University of California Press, 1970.

Feinberg-Jütte, Anat. "'The Task Is Not to Reproduce the External Form, but to Find the Subtext': George Tabori's Productions of Samuel Beckett's Texts." *JOBS* 1.1 and 2 (summer 1992): 95–115.

Fletcher, Beryl S. et al. *A Student's Guide to the Plays of Samuel Beckett.* London: Faber, 1973.

Fletcher, John. *The Novels of Samuel Beckett.* London: Chatto and Windus, 1964.

———. "Modernism and Samuel Beckett." In Janet Gorton, ed., *Facets of European Modernism: Essays in Honor of James McFarlane (presented to him on his 65th birthday, 12 December 1985).* Norwich: University of East Anglia, 1985, 199–217.

Foucault, Michel. "What Is an Author?" [1969], trans. Joseph V. Harari. In David Lodge, ed., *Modern Criticism and Theory.* London and New York: Longman, 1988, 197–210.

Friedman, Alan Warren, ed. *Beckett in Black and Red: The Translations for Nancy Cunard's Negro (1934).* Lexington: University Press of Kentucky, 2000.

Frost, Everett. "Fundamental Sounds: Recording Samuel Beckett's Radio Plays." *Theatre Journal* 43.3 (October 1991): 361–76.

Garforth, Julian. "'Beckett, unser Hausheiliger?': Changing Critical Reactions to Beckett's Directorial Work in Berlin." *Samuel Beckett Today / Aujourd'hui* 9 (2000): 309–29.

Gibson, Andrew. *Reading Narrative Discourse: Studies in the Novel from Cervantes to Beckett.* Basingstoke: Macmillan, 1990.

Gluck, Barbara Reich. *Beckett and Joyce: Friendship and Fiction.* Lewisburg, Penn.: Bucknell University Press, 1979.

Gontarski, S. E. *Beckett's "Happy Days": A Manuscript Study.* Columbus: The Ohio State University Library Publications, 1977.

———. *The Intent of Undoing in Samuel Beckett's Dramatic Texts.* Bloomington: Indiana University Press, 1985.

———, ed. *On Beckett: Essays and Criticism.* New York: Grove Press, 1986.

———. "Working Through Beckett." In Steve Wilmer, ed., *Beckett in Dublin.* Dublin: Lilliput Press, 1992, 33–52.

———, ed. *The Theatrical Notebooks of Samuel Beckett,* vol. II, *Endgame.* London: Faber and Faber; New York: Grove Press, 1993.

———, ed. *The Beckett Studies Reader.* Gainesville: University Press of Florida, 1993.

———. "Editing Beckett." *Twentieth Century Literature* 41.2 (summer 1995): 190–207.

———. "Revising Himself: Performance as Text in Samuel Beckett's Theater." *Journal of Modern Literature* 22.1 (fall 1998): 131–145.

———, ed. *The Theatrical Notebooks of Samuel Beckett,* vol. IV, The Shorter Plays. London: Faber and Faber; New York: Grove Press, 1999.

———. "A Hat Is Not a Shoe: *The Theatrical Notebooks of Samuel Beckett* and Postmodern Theories of Texts and Textuality." In *Beckett and Beyond,* ed. Bruce Stewart, 129–44.

——— and Annamaria Cascetta, eds. *Beckett in scena: Interpretazione memorabili nel mondo* (*Drammaturgia* 9). Roma: Salerno Editrice, 2002.

Graver, Lawrence and Raymond Federman. *Samuel Beckett: The Critical Heritage.* London: Routledge and Kegan Paul, 1979.

Griffiths, Eric. "All That Fond Trash: German Romantic Music and the Acoustics of Beckett's Writing." *TLS* (15 May 1998): 3.

Hansford, James. "'Imaginative transactions' in 'La Falaise.'" *JOBS* 10 (autumn 1983); rpt. in *The Beckett Studies Reader,* ed. S. E. Gontarski, 203–13.

Harmon, Maurice, ed. *No Author Better Served: The Correspondence of Samuel Beckett and Alan Schneider.* Cambridge, Mass.: Harvard University Press, 1998.

Harrington, John P. *The Irish Beckett.* Syracuse, N.Y.: Syracuse University Press, 1991.

Harrison, Robert. *Samuel Beckett's Murphy: A Critical Excursion.* Athens: University of Georgia Press, 1968.

Harvey, Lawrence. *Samuel Beckett, Poet and Critic.* Princeton, N.J.: Princeton University Press, 1970.

Henning, Sylvie Debevic. *Beckett's Critical Complicity: Carnival, Contestation, and Tradition.* Lexington: University of Kentucky Press, 1988.

———. "The Guffaw of the Abderite: *Murphy* and the Democritean Universe." *JOBS* 10 (1985): 5–20.

Hesla, David. *The Shape of Chaos: An Interpretation of the Art of Samuel Beckett.* Minneapolis: University of Minnesota Press, 1971.

————. "Being, Thinking, Telling and Loving." In *Samuel Beckett: The Art of Rhetoric,* ed. Edouard Morot-Sir, 11–23.

Hill, Leslie. *Beckett's Fiction: In Different Words.* Cambridge: Cambridge University Press, 1990.

Hobson, Harold. "Samuel Beckett, Dramatist of the Year." In *International Theatre Annual,* no. 1. New York: Citadel Press, 153–55.

————. "The First Night of *Waiting for Godot.*" In *Beckett at 60,* ed. John Calder, 25–28.

Hoefer, Jacqueline. "*Watt.*" *Perspective* 11 (1959): 166–82.

Horowitz, Arthur. "Beckett's *Endgame* and Henley's *Invictus.*" *JOBS* 2.1 (autumn 1992): 119–20.

Hutchings, William. "Abated Drama: Samuel Beckett's Unbated 'Breath.'" *Ariel* 17:1 (January 1986): 86–94.

Janvier, Ludovic. *Pour Samuel Beckett.* Paris: Minuit, 1966.

Jones, Anthony. "The French *Murphy:* from 'Rare Bird' to 'Cancre.'" *JOBS* 6 (autumn 1980): 37–50.

Juliet, Charles. *Conversations with Samuel Beckett and Bram van Velde,* trans. Janey Tucker. Leiden: Academic Press, 1995. [Originally published separately as *Rencontre avec Bram van Velde* (Montpelleir: Fata Morgana, 1973; rev. ed., 1978); and *Rencontre avec Samuel Beckett* (Fata Morgana, 1986).]

Kennedy, Sighle. *Murphy's Bed: A Study of Real Sources and Sur-Real Associations in Samuel Beckett's First Novel.* Lewisburg, Pa.: Bucknell University Press, 1971.

Kenner, Hugh. *Samuel Beckett: A Critical Study.* New York: Grove Press, 1961.

————. *A Reader's Guide to Samuel Beckett.* New York: Farrar, Straus, and Giroux, 1973.

Kern, Edith. *Existential Thought and Fictional Technique: Kierkegaard, Sartre, Beckett.* New Haven, Conn.: Yale University Press, 1970.

Kiely, Declan D. "'The Termination of This Solitaire': A Textual Error in *Murphy.*" *JOBS* 6.1 (autumn 1996): 135–36.

Knowlson, James. *Damned to Fame: The Life of Samuel Beckett.* New York: Simon and Schuster, 1996.

————. *Lightness and Darkness in the Theatre of Samuel Beckett.* London: Turret Books, 1972.

————. "Good Heavens." *Gambit: International Theatre Review* 7.28 (1976): 101–08.

————. "Practical Aspects of Theatre, Radio and Television" [Extracts from an unscripted interview with Billie Whitelaw by James Knowlson. A television recording made on 1 February 1977 for the University of London Audio-Visual Centre]. *JOBS* 3 (summer 1978): 86–90.

———— and John Pilling. *Frescoes of the Skull: The Later Prose and Drama of Samuel Beckett.* New York: Grove Press, 1980.

————, ed. *Happy Days: Samuel Beckett's Production Notebooks.* London: Faber and Faber; New York: Grove Press, 1985.

————, ed. *The Theatrical Notebooks of Samuel Beckett,* vol. III, *Krapp's Last Tape.* London: Faber and Faber; New York: Grove Press, 1993.

———— and Dougald McMillan, eds. *The Theatrical Notebooks of Samuel Beckett,* vol. I, *Waiting for Godot.* London: Faber and Faber; New York: Grove Press, 1995.

————. "'My Texts Are in a Terrible Mess.'" In *Beckett and Beyond,* ed. Bruce Stewart, 176–86.

————. "*Krapp's Last Tape,* Beckett regista allo Schiller-Teatro." A cura di S. E. Gontarski e Annamaria Cascetta, *Beckett in scena: Interpretazione memorabili nel mondo* (*Drammaturgia* 9). Roma: Salerno Editrice, 2002.

Kroll, Jeri L. "The Surd as Inadmissible Evidence: The Case of Attorney-General v Henry McCabe." *JOBS* 2 (summer 1977): 47–58

————. "Belacqua as Artist and Lover: 'What a Misfortune'." *JOBS* 3 (summer 1978): 10–39.

Lake, Carlton, ed. *No Symbols Where None Intended: A Catalogue of Books, Manuscripts, and Other Materials Relating to Samuel Beckett in the Collections of the Humanities Research Center.* Austin: Harry Ransom Humanities Research Center (University of Texas), 1984.

Lawley, Paul. "'Embers': An Interpretation." *JOBS* 6 (autumn 1980): 9–36.

Laws, Catherine. "Music and Language in the Work of Samuel Beckett." Ph.D. Diss. Phil. University of York, 1996.

————. "Morton Feldman's *Neither:* A Musical Translation of Beckett's Text." In Mary Bryden, ed., *Samuel Beckett and Music,* 57–85.

Lees, Heath. "*Watt:* Music Tuning and Tonality." *JOBS* 9 (spring 1983): 5–24; rpt. in *The Beckett Studies Reader,* ed. S. E. Gontarski, 167–85.

Leventhal, A. J. "The Thirties." In *Beckett at 60,* ed. John Calder, 7–13.

Levy, Alan. "The Long Wait for Godot." *Theatre Arts* XL.8 (August 1956): 33–35, 96.

Lindon, Jérôme. "First Meeting with Samuel Beckett." In *Beckett at 60,* ed. John Calder, 17–19.

Little, Roger. "Beckett's Mentor, Rudmose-Brown: Sketch for a Portrait." *Irish Literary Review* 14.1 (spring 1984): 34–41.

Locatelli, Carla. *Unwording the World: Samuel Beckett's Prose Works after the Nobel Prize.* Philadelphia: University of Pennsylvania Press, 1990.

————. "Beckett's 'Obligation to Express': from a Mythology of Demystification to the Utterance of Better Failures." In *Beckett and Beyond,* ed. Bruce Stewart, 193–204.

————. "Beckett's *Stirrings Still.*" *American Poetry Review* 28.5 (September–October 1999): 39–44.

Marculescu, Ileana. "Beckett and the Temptation of Solipsism: 'Esse est aut percipere aut percipi'." *JOBS* 11 and 12 (December 1989): 53–64; rpt. in *The Beckett Studies Reader,* ed. S. E. Gontarski, 214–25.

Mays, J. C. C. "Mythologized Presences: *Murphy* in its Time." In Joseph Ronsley, ed., *Myth and Reality in Irish Literature*. Waterloo, Ont.: Wilfrid Laurier University Press, 1977, 197–218.

———. "Beckett Bibliography: A Revised Edition of Federman and Fletcher, or Not?," *The Beckett Circle / Le cercle de Beckett: Newsletter of the Samuel Beckett Society* 1.2 (fall 1978): 1.

———. "Undertaking Murphy and the Question of Apmonia." *Gaéliana* 4 (1982): 159–78.

———. "Young Beckett's Irish Roots." *Irish University Review* 14.1 (spring 1984): 18–33.

———. "How Is MacGreevy a Modernist?" In Patricia Coughlan and Alex Davis, eds., *Modernism and Ireland: The Poetry of the 1930s*. Cork: Cork University Press, 1995, 125–26.

McCarthy, Patrick A., ed. *Critical Essays on Samuel Beckett*. Boston: G. K. Hall, 1986.

McCormack, W. J. "Samuel Beckett and the *Negro Anthology*." *Hermathena: A Trinity College Review* (1992): 73–92.

McMillan, Dougald. "*Echo's Bones:* Starting Points for Beckett." In Eduard Morot-Sir et al., eds., *Samuel Beckett,* Chapel Hill: University of North Carolina Press, 1976.

——— and Martha Fehsenfeld, eds. *Beckett in the Theater: The Author as Practical Playwright and Director*. New York: Riverrun Press, 1988.

McQueeny, Terence. "Beckett as a Critic of Joyce and Proust." Ph.D. Diss., University of North Carolina, 1977.

Menzies, Janet. "Beckett's Bicycles." *JOBS* 6 (autumn 1980): 97–105.

Mercier, Vivien. *Beckett/Beckett*. New York: Oxford University Press, 1977.

Mihalovici, Marcel. "My Collaboration with Samuel Beckett." In *Beckett at 60,* ed. John Calder, 20–22.

Mintz, Samuel. "Beckett's *Murphy:* A Cartesian Novel." *Perspective* 11.3 (autumn 1959): 156–65.

Mitchell, Breon. "Art in Microcosm: The Manuscript Stages of Beckett's *Come and Go*." *Modern Drama* 19.3 (1976): 245–54.

Mood, John J. "'The Personal System': Samuel Beckett's *Watt*." *PMLA* 86 (1971): 255–65.

Mooney, Michael. "Presocratic Skepticism: Samuel Beckett's *Murphy* Reconsidered." *EHL* 49.1 (spring 1982): 214–34.

Moorjani, Angela. *Abysmal Games in the Novels of Samuel Beckett*. Chapel Hill: University of North Carolina Press, 1982.

———. "*En attendant Godot* on Michel Polac's *Entrée des Auteurs*." *Samuel Beckett Today / Aujourd'hui* 7 (1998): 47–56.

Morot-Sir, Edouard. "Samuel Beckett and Cartesian Emblems." In *Samuel Beckett: The Art of Rhetoric,* ed. Edouard Morot-Sir, Howard Harper and Dougald McMillan III [North Carolina Studies in the Romance Languages and Literature, #5]. Chapel Hill: University of North Carolina Press, 1976, 25–103.

Murphy, P. J. *Reconstructing Beckett: Language and Being in Samuel Beckett's Fiction.* Toronto: University of Toronto Press, 1992.

———. "Beckett and the Philosophers." In *The Cambridge Companion to Beckett,* ed. John Pilling, 222–40.

———, Werner Huber, Rolf Breuer and Konrad Schoell. *Critique of Beckett Criticism.* Columbia, S.C.: Camden House, 1994.

O'Brien, Eoin. *The Beckett Country: Samuel Beckett's Ireland.* Dublin: Black Cat Press, 1986.

O'Brien, Kate. "Fiction." *The Spectator* (March 25, 1938): 546.

O'Hara, J. D. "Freud and the Narrative of 'Moran.'" *JOBS* 2.1 (autumn 1992): 47–63.

———. "Beckett Backs Down: From Home to Murphy via Valèry." *JOBS* 3.2 (spring 1994): 37–55.

———. *Samuel Beckett's Hidden Drives: Structural Uses of Depth Psychology.* Gainesville: University Press of Florida, 1997.

Page, Malcolm. "The Perils of Bibliography." *JOBS* 3 (summer 1978): 91–96.

Piette, Adam. *Remembering and the Sound of Words: Mallarmé, Proust, Joyce, Beckett.* Oxford: Clarendon Press, 1996.

Pilling, John. *Samuel Beckett.* London: Routledge and Kegan Paul, 1979.

———. "Beckett's Proust." *JOBS* 1 (winter 1976): 8–29.

———. "From a (W)horoscope to *Murphy.*" In *The Ideal Core of the Onion: Reading Beckett Archives,* ed. John Pilling and Mary Bryden. Reading: Beckett International Foundation, 1992, 1–20.

———, ed. *The Cambridge Companion to Beckett.* Cambridge: Cambridge University Press, 1994.

———. "Losing One's Classics: Beckett's Small Latin, and Less Greek." *JOBS* 4.2 (spring 1995): 5–14.

———. *Beckett before Godot.* Cambridge, Eng.: Cambridge University Press, 1998.

———. "Guesses and Recesses: Notes on, in and towards *Dream of Fair to Middling Women.*" *Samuel Beckett Today / Aujourd'hui* 7 (1998): 13–23.

———. "A Mermaid Made Over: Beckett's 'Text' and John Ford." In *Beckett and Beyond,* ed. Bruce Stewart, 221–16.

———. "Beckett and the 'Itch to Make': The Early Poems in English." *Samuel Beckett Today / Aujourd'hui* 8 (1999): 15–25.

———. *A Companion to Dream of Fair to Middling Women.* Tallahassee, F.: Journal of Beckett Studies Books, 2004.

Pinget, Robert. "Notre Ami." *Revue d'Esthétique* [numéro hors-série] (1990): vii–1.

Prince, Eric. "'I Just Want to Make the Space Mine': An Interview with David Warrilow." *JOBS* 1.1 and 2 (summer 1992): 117–28.

Putnam, Samuel. *The European Caravan,* part 1. New York: Brewer, Warren and Putnam, 1931.

Rabaté, Jean-Michel, ed. *Beckett avant Beckett: Essais sur le jeune Beckett.* Paris: Presses de l'École Normale Supérieure, 1984.

———. *Beckett et le psychoanalyste.* Paris: Mentha, 1992.

———. "Beckett's Ghosts and Fluxions." In *Beckett and la Psychoanalyse / and Psychoanalysis,* ed. Sjef Houppermanns. Amsterdam: Rodopi, 1996, 23–42.

———. *The Ghosts of Modernity.* Gainesville: University Press of Florida, 1996.

Rabinovitz, Rubin. "Unreliable Narrative in Murphy." In *Samuel Beckett: Humanistic Perspectives,* ed. Morris Beja, S. E. Gontarski, and Pierre Astier. Columbus: Ohio State University Press, 1983, 58–70.

———. *The Development of Samuel Beckett's Fiction.* Urbana: University of Illinois Press, 1984.

———. *Innovation in Samuel Beckett's Fiction.* Urbana: University of Illinois Press, 1992.

Rathjen, Friedhelm, ed. *In Principle, Beckett Is Joyce.* Edinburgh: Split Pea Press [1999].

Renaud, Madeleine. "Beckett the Magnificent." In *Beckett at 60,* ed. John Calder, 81–83.

Revue d'Esthétique [numéro hors-série]. *Samuel Beckett.* Paris: Jean-Michel Place, 1990.

Robbe-Grillet, Alain. "Samuel Beckett, or 'Presence' on the Stage (1953, 1957)." In *For a New Novel: Essays on Fiction,* trans. Richard Howard. New York: Grove Press, 1965, 111–25.

Robinson, Michael. *The Long Sonata of the Dead: A Study of Samuel Beckett.* London: Rupert Hart-Davis, 1969.

Ross, Charles. *Beckett in Black and Red.* Lexington: University of Kentucky Press, 1999.

Schneider, Alan. "Waiting for Beckett." In *Beckett at 60,* ed. John Calder, 34–52.

Segrè, Elisabeth Bregman. "Style and Structure in Beckett's 'Ping': That Something Itself." *Journal of Modern Literature* 6.1 (1977): 127–47.

Senneff, Susan. "Song and Music in Beckett's *Watt.*" *Modern Fiction Studies* 10 (1964): 144.

Shenker, Israel. "Moody Man of Letters." *New York Times* (5 May 1956); rpt. in *Samuel Beckett: The Critical Heritage,* ed. Graver and Federman, 146–49.

Smith, Anna. "Proceeding by Aporia." *JOBS* 3.1 (autumn 1993): 21–37.

Smith, Frederik N. "'A Land of Sanctuary': Allusions to the Pastoral in Beckett's Fiction." In *Beckett Translating / Translating Beckett,* ed. Alan Warren Friedman, Charles Rossman, and Dina Sherzer. University Park and London: Pennsylvania State University Press, 1987, 128–39.

———. "Dating the Whoroscope Notebook." *JOBS* 3.1 (autumn 1993): 65–70.

———. "*Godot* and the Manuscripts of *Watt.*" *JOBS* 11.1 (spring 2001): 38–53.

———. *Beckett's Eighteenth Century.* New York: St. Martin's Press, 2002.

Stevenson, Kay Gilliland. "Belacqua in the Moon: Beckett's Revisions of 'Dante and the Lobster.'" In *Critical Essays on Samuel Beckett,* ed. Patrick A. McCarthy. Boston: G. K. Hall, 1986, 36–46.

Stewart, Bruce, ed. *Beckett and Beyond* [Princess Grace Irish Library, 9]. Gerrards Cross: Colin Smythe, 1999.

Tanner, James and J. Don Vann. *Samuel Beckett: A Checklist of Criticism.* Kent, Ohio: Kent State University Press, 1969.

Tophoven, Elmar. "Translating Beckett." In Dougald McMillan and Martha Fehsenfeld, eds., *Beckett in the Theatre.* London: John Calder, 1988, pp. 317–24.

Toynbee, Philip. "Review of *Molloy*" [1955]. In Graver and Federman, *Critical Heritage,* 73–76.

Trezise, Thomas. *Into the Breach: Samuel Beckett and the Ends of Literature.* Princeton, N.J.: Princeton University Press, 1990.

Tynan, Kenneth. "Review of *Endgame*" [1957]. In Graver and Federman, *Critical Heritage,* 164–66.

Uhlmann, Anthony. *Beckett and Poststructuralism.* Cambridge: Cambridge University Press, 1999.

Verdicchio, Massimo. "Exagmination round the Fictification of Vico and Joyce." *James Joyce Quarterly* 26.4 (summer 1989): 531–39.

Watson, David. *Paradox and Desire in Beckett's Fiction.* Basingstoke: Macmillan, 1991.

Webb, Eugene. *Samuel Beckett: A Study of His Novels.* Seattle and London: University of Washington Press, 1971.

Weisberg, David. *Chronicles of Disorder: Samuel Beckett and the Cultural Politics of the Modern Novel.* Albany: State University of New York Press, 2000.

Wheatley, David. "Beckett's *mirlitonnades:* A Manuscript Study." *JOBS* 4.2 (spring 1995): 47–75.

Wood, Rupert. "*Murphy,* Beckett, Geulincx, God." *JOBS* 2.2 (spring 1993): 27–51.

Worth, Katharine. *Samuel Beckett's Theater: Life Journeys.* Oxford, Eng.: Oxford University Press, 1999.

———. "Words for Music Perhaps." In Mary Bryden, ed., *Samuel Beckett and Music,* 9–20.

Wulf, Catharina. *The Imperative of Narration: Beckett, Bernhard, Schopenhauer, Lacan.* Brighton: Sussex University Press, 1997.

Zilliacus, Claus. *Beckett and Broadcasting: A Study of the Works of Samuel Beckett for and in Radio and Television.* Abo, Finland: Abo Akadamie, 1976.

Zurbrugg, Nicholas. "Beckett, Proust, and Dream of Fair to Middling Women." *JOBS* 9 (spring 1983): 25–41.

———. *Beckett and Proust.* Gerrards Cross: Colin Smythe, 1988.

C. General Studies Used in This Work

Aldington, Richard. *Life for Life's Sake: A Book of Reminiscences.* 1941; rpt. London: Cassell, 1968.

Arikha. Paris: Hermann; London: Thames and Hudson, 1985.

Aslan, Odette. *Roger Blin and Twentieth Century Playwrights,* trans. Ruby Cohn. London: Cambridge University Press, 1988.

Augustine, St. *Confessions,* trans. William Watts [Loeb Classical Library] 2 vols. London: Heinemann, 1922.

————. *The Confessions of St. Augustine,* trans. E. B. Pusey [Everyman]. London: Dent, 1907.

Bacon, Sir Francis. *Novum Organum,* ed. Thomas Fowler. 2nd ed., corrected and revised; Oxford: Clarendon Press, 1889.

Bailey, Cyril. *The Greek Atomists and Epicurus.* Oxford: Clarendon Press, 1928.

Baillet, Adrien. *La Vie de Monsieur Des-cartes.* 2 tomes; Paris: Daniel Horthemels, 1691.

Baudrillard, Jean. *The Infinite Conversation,* trans. by Susan Hanson. Minneapolis: University of Minnesota Press, 1993.

Beare, John I. *Greek Theories of Elementary Cognition.* Oxford: Clarendon Press, 1906.

Beck, Jean. *La Musique des troubadours.* Paris: Henri Laurens, 1910.

Bérard, Victor. *L'Odyssé: Poesie Homérique.* Texte établi et traduit par Victor Bérard. 3 tomes. Paris: Société d'Édition "Les Belles Lettres," 1924.

Bergson, Henri. *Creative Evolution,* trans. Arthur Mitchell. New York: Modern Library, 1944.

Bion, W. R. *Experiences in Groups and Other Papers.* London: Tavistock Publications, 1961.

Bléandou, Gérard. *Wilfred Bion: His Life and Works 1897–1979.* London: Free Association Books, 1994.

Boccaccio, Giovanni. *Trattatello in laude di Dante,* ed. Pier Giorgio Ricci. In *Tutte le opere di Giovanni Boccaccio,* ed. Vittore Branca, vol. III. Milan: Mondadori, 1974.

Bornstein, George. *Material Modernism.* Cambridge: Cambridge University Press, 2000.

Boswell, James. *Life of Johnson, Including Their Tour to the Hebrides,* ed. J.W. Croker. London: John Murray, 1847.

Brett, George Sidney. *A History of Psychology, Ancient and Patristic.* London: Allan and Unwin, 1912.

Brunschvig, Léon. *Spinoza et ses contemporains* [1894]. 3 ième édition, révue et augmentée; Paris: Félix Alcan, 1923.

Burnet, John. *Early Greek Philosophy.* 1892; 3rd ed., revised, London: A. and C. Black, 1920.

————. *Greek Philosophy: Thales to Plato*. 1914; rpt. London: Macmillan, 1950.

Burton, Robert. *The Anatomy of Melancholy, what it is, with all the kinds, course, symptoms, prognostics, and several cures of it. In three partitions; with their several sections, members and subsections, philosophically, medically, historically opened and cut up. By Democritus Junior* [Robert Burton], *with a satyrical preface, conducing to the following discourse* [1621]. London: Chatto and Windus, 1881.

Carlyle, Thomas. *On Heroes and Hero-Worship*. London: Dent, 1908.

Cary, Henry Francis. *The Vision: or, Hell, Purgatory, and Paradise, of Dante Alighieri,* trans. the Rev. Henry Francis Cary, M.A. London: Bell and Daldy, 1869.

Chamfort [Sébastien Roch Nicolas]. *Oeuvres principales, comprenant de nombreux textes réprimés pour la première fois*. Paris: Pauvert, 1960.

Cooper, the Rev. William M. [pseud. of James Glass Bertram]. *Flagellation and the Flagellants: A History of the Rod in all Countries from the Earliest Period to the Present Time*. London: John Camden Hotten, 1869.

Critchley, Simon. *Very Little . . . Almost Nothing: Death, Philosophy, Literature*. London: Routledge, 1997.

Croce, Benedetto. *The Poetry of Dante,* trans. Douglas Ainslie. London: Allen and Unwin, 1922.

Cunard, Nancy. *Negro: An Anthology*. London: Wishart, 1934.

————. *These Were the Hours: Memories of My Hours Press,* ed. Hugh D. Ford. Carbondale: Southern Illinois University Press, 1969.

Daiken, Leslie. Unpublished notes from courses at Trinity College, Dublin, 1928–31. Samuel Beckett Archives, University of Reading [RUL number unassigned at time of writing].

Dandieu, Arnaud. *Marcel Proust: sa révélation psychologique*. Paris: Firmin-Didot, 1930.

Dante Alighieri. *Tutte le opere di Dante Alighieri,* nuovamente rivedute nel testo dal Dr. E. Moore, con indice dei nomi propri e delle cose notabili compilato dal Dr. Paget Toynbee. Terza edizione, riveduta; Oxford: nella stamperia dell'università, 1904.

————. *La Divina commedia,* ed. G.A. Scartazzini, Eighth edition, largely revised by G. Vandelli with an improved rhyming dictionary by L. Polacco. Third run, revised and corrected, Milan: Hoepli, 1922.

————. *Divina commedia,* ed. Isidoro del Lungo. Florence: Le Monnier, 1926.

————. *The Divine Comedy,* trans., with a commentary, by Charles S. Singleton [Bollingen Series LXXX]. 6 vols., 1970; rpt. Princeton, N.J.: Princeton University Press, 1977.

Darwin, Charles. *On the Origin of Species*. London: John Murray, 1859.

Deleuze, Gilles. *Essays Critical and Clinical,* trans. Daniel W. Smith and Michael A. Greco. Minneapolis: University of Minnesota Press, 1997.

Derrida, Jacques. *Acts of Literature,* ed. Derek Attridge. New York and London: Routledge, 1992.

de Sanctis, Francesco. *Storia della letteratura Italiana*. Turin: Contini, 1868.

Descartes, René. *Oeuvres choisis de Descartes*. Nouvelle édition, Paris: Garnier Frères [n.d.]

———. *A Discourse on Method, Meditations and Principles,* trans. John Veitch and intr. A. D. Lindsay [Everyman]. London: Dent, 1912.

Dicks, H. V. *Fifty Years of the Tavistock Clinic*. London: Routledge and Kegan Paul, 1970.

Diderot, Denis. "Entretien entre d'Alembert et Diderot: Le Rêve de d'Alembert: Suite de l'entretien." In *Oeuvres philosophiques de Diderot,* édition de Paul Vernière. Paris: Garnier Frères, 1964, 247–385.

———. *Jacques le fataliste*. In *Ouvres romanesques,* édition de Henri Bénac. Paris: Garnier Frères [n.d.], 493–780.

———. *Le Neveu de Rameau*. In *Ouvres romanesques,* édition de Henri Bénac. Paris: Garnier Frères [n.d.], 395–492.

Ellmann, Richard. *James Joyce*. London: Oxford University Press, 1959; 2nd ed., revised, New York, Oxford, Toronto: Oxford University Press, 1982.

Esslin, Martin. *The Theatre of the Absurd*. Garden City, N.Y.: Anchor Books, 1961.

Evans, E. P. *The Criminal Prosecution and Capital Punishment of Animals*. London: Heinemann, 1906.

Freud, Sigmund. *The Standard Edition of the Complete Psychological Works of Sigmund Freud,* ed. James Strachey, in collaboration with Anna Freud. 24 vols; London: Hogarth Press and the Institute of Psychoanalysis, 1953–74. In particular: "Heredity and the Aetiology of the Neurosis" [1896], III, 141–56; *The Psychopathology of Everyday Life* [1901], VI; *Jokes and the Relation to the Unconscious* [1905], VIII; "Five Lectures on Psycho-Analysis" [1909], XI, 1–55; "On Narcissism: an Introduction" [1914], XVI, 73–102; "The Unconscious" [1915], XVI, 166–215; *General Theory of the Neuroses* [1917], XIV; "The Ego and the Id" [1923], XIX, 1–59; "Neurosis and Psychosis" [1922], XIX, 149–53.

Garnier, Pierre. *Onanisme seul et à deux*. Paris: Garnier Frères [n.d.].

Gautier, Théophile. *Histoire de Romantisme*. Paris: Fasquelle, 1927.

Geulincx, Arnoldus. *Opera Philosophica,* recongnivit J. P. N. Land. 3 vols; Hague Comitum: Martinum Nijhoff, 1891–93.

Giles, H. A. *Chinese Literature*. London: Heinemann, 1901.

———. *The Civilization of China*. London: Williams and Norgate, [1911].

Guggenheim, Marguerite. *Out of This Century: The Informal Memoirs of Peggy Guggenheim*. New York: Dial Press, 1946.

———. *Confessions of an Art Addict*. New York: Macmillan; and London: André Deutsch, 1960.

Hayman, Ronald. *Tom Stoppard.* London: Heinemann [Contemporary Playwrights], 1977.

Hooper, David and Kenneth Whyld, eds. *The Oxford Companion to Chess*. 1984; revised and rpt. Oxford: Oxford University Press, 1988.

Horace. *Satires. Epistles. Ars Poetica,* trans. H. Rushton Fairclough [Loeb Classical Library]. London: Heinemann, 1926.

Inge, William Ralph. *Christian Mysticism.* 1899; 2nd ed., London: Methuen, 1912.

Jeans, Sir James. *The Universe Around Us.* Cambridge, Eng.: Cambridge University Press, 1929.

Johnson, Samuel. *A Dictionary of the English Language, in which words are deduced from their originals and illustrated in their different significations by examples from the best writers.* 10th ed., 2 vols; London, 1810.

———. *Johnsonian Miscellanies,* ed. George Birkbeck Hill. 2 vols; London: Constable, 1897.

Jones, Ernest. *Papers on Psycho-Analysis.* London: Ballière, Tindall and Cox, 1920.

———. "The Problem with Paul Morphy." *International Journal of Psychoanalysis* 12.1 (Jan. 1931): 1–23.

Jung, Carl. "The Tavistock Lectures" [1935]. In *The Collected Works,* XVIII, *The Symbolic Life: Miscellaneous Writings,* trans. R. F. C. Hull. London and Henley: Routledge and Kegan Paul, 1977, 5–182.

Juvenal. *Juvenal and Persius,* trans. G. G. Ramsay [Loeb Classical Library]. London: Heinemann, 1918.

Kant, Immanuel. *Immanuel Kant's Critique of Pure Reason* [1781], trans. Norman Kemp Smith. 1929; rpt. London: Macmillan, 1933.

Kershaw, Alistair and Fréderic-Jacques Temple, eds. *Richard Aldington: An Intimate Portrait.* Carbondale and Edwardsville: Southern Illinois University Press, 1965 [tribute from SB, 3].

Klein, Melanie. *The Psychoanalysis of Children.* London: Hogarth Press, 1932.

Koffka, Kurt. *The Growth of the Mind,* trans. R. M. Ogden. 1924; 2nd ed., rev., London: Kegan Paul, Trench, Trubner and Co, 1931.

———. *Principles of Gestalt Psychology.* New York: Harcourt, Brace and World, 1935.

Köhler, Wolfgang. *The Mentality of Apes,* trans. Ella Winter. 1917; 2nd ed., rev., London: Kegan Paul, Trench, Trubner and Co., 1925.

Laloy, Louis. *La Musique chinoise.* Paris: Librairie Renouard (Henri Laurens), [1900?].

Leibniz, Gottfried. *The Monadology and Other Philosopical Writings,* trans. and ed. Robert Latta. London: Oxford University Press, 1898.

Lemprière's Classical Dictionary. 1865; rpt. London: Bracken Books, 1984.

MacGreevy, Thomas. *The Collected Poems of Thomas MacGreevy,* ed. Susan Schreibman. Dublin: Anna Livia Press, 1991.

Mahaffy, J. P. *Descartes.* Edinburgh and London: William Blackwood, 1880.

Malebranche, Nicholas. *Dialogues on Metaphysics and Religion,* trans. Morris Ginsberg. New York: Macmillan, 1923.

Malraux, André. *La Condition humaine.* Paris: Gallimard, 1933.

Marlowe, Christopher. *Plays,* ed. Havelock Ellis [Mermaid]. London: Vizetelly and Co., 1887.

Marston, John. *The Works of John Marston*. 3 vols; ed. A. H. Bullen. London: John C. Nimmer, 1887.

Mauthner, Fritz. *Beiträge zu einer Kritik der Sprache*. 3 Bände; Leipzig: F. Meiner, 1923.

McHugh, Roger, ed. *Jack B. Yeats: A Centenary Gathering*. Dublin: Dolmen Press, 1971.

McIntyre, J. Lewis. *Giordano Bruno*. London: Macmillan, 1903.

McMillan, Dougald. *"transition": The History of a Literary Era*. London: Calder and Boyarc, 1976.

Nordau, Max. *Degeneration*. 1895; rpt. London: Heinemann, 1913.

Oxford Companion to Irish Literature, ed. Robert Welch. Oxford: Clarendon Press, 1996.

Pierre-Quint, Léon. *Marcel Proust: sa vie, son oeuvre*. Paris: Éditions de Sagittaire, 1925.

Portirelli, Luigi. *La Divina commedia di Dante Alighieri*, illustrated with notes by Luigi Portirelli. Milan: Dalla Società Tipografica de' Classici Italiani, 1804.

Praz, Mario. *The Romantic Agony* [1930], trans. Angus Davidson. 1933; 2nd ed., London, New York, Toronto: Oxford University Press, 1951.

Proust, Marcel. *A la recherche du temps perdu* [Édition de la *Nouvelle revue française*]. 16 vols.; Paris: Gallimard, 1919–27. [SB's copy, annotated, one volume missing, in the Samuel Beckett Archive, University of Reading]. Individual texts cited by short title: *Swann; Jeunes filles; Guermantes; Sodome et Gomorrhe; La Prisonnière; Albertine disparue; Le Temps retrouvé.*

———. *A la recherche du temps perdu*, ed. Pierre Clarac et André Ferré. 3 vols; Paris: Gallimard [Bibliothéque de la Pléïäde], 1968–69.

———. *Remembrance of Things Past*, trans. C. K. Scott Moncrieff [Books 1–6] and Frederick A. Blossom [Bk. 7]. 2 vols; 1924 and 1927; rpt. New York: Random House, 1934.

Pyle, Hilary. *Jack B. Yeats: A Biography*. 1970; 2nd ed., rev., London: Andre Deutsch, 1989.

Rabelais, Francis. *François Rabelais: tout ce qui existe de ses oeuvres: Gargantua— Pantagruel*, édité par Louis Moland. Paris: Garnier frères [n.d.].

———. *The Works of Mr. Francis Rabelais, Doctor in Physick. Containing Five Books of the Lives, Heroic Deeds and Sayings of Gargantua and His Sonne Pantagruel*, trans. Sir Thomas Urquhart [Books 1–3] and Peter Motteux [Books 4–5]; illustrated by W. Heath Robinson. London: The Navarre Society, 1931.

Racine, Jean. *Théâtre complet*, édité par Felix Lemaistre. Paris: Garnier, n.d.

Rank, Otto. *The Trauma of Birth*. London: Kegan Paul, Trench, Trubner and Co., 1929.

Renard, Jules. *Journal*. Paris: Gallimard, 1935.

Redshaw, Thomas Dillon. *Thomas MacGreevy: Collected Poems*. Dublin: New Writers Press, 1971.

Rimbaud, Arthur. *Oeuvres de Arthur Rimbaud, vers et proses,* préface de Paul Claudel. Paris: Mercure de France, n.d.

Roche, Anthony. *Contemporary Irish Drama: From Beckett to McGuinness.* New York: St. Martin's Press, 1995.

Rolland, Romain. *Vie de Beethoven.* 1903; rpt. Paris: Librairie Hachette, 1927.

Rousseau, Jean Jacques. *Émile, ou, de l'éducation* [1762]. Paris: Garnier, 1919.

———. *Les Rêveries du promeneur solitaire* [1782]. Genève: Librairie Droz, 1948.

Rudmose-Brown, T. B., ed. *French Short Stories.* Oxford: Clarendon Press, 1925.

Russell, Bertrand. *History of Western Philosophy.* 1946; 2nd ed., rpt. London: Routledge, 1991.

Sartre, Jean-Paul. *Being and Nothingness.* London: Routledge, 1969.

Schopenhauer, Arthur. *On the Fourfold Root of the Principle of Sufficient Reason* and *On the Will in Nature,* trans. Mme. Karl Hillebrand. 1887; rev. ed., London: George Bell, 1915.

———. *Parega and Paralipomena: Short Philosophical Essays,* trans. E. F. J. Payne. 2 vols.; Oxford: Clarendon Press, 1974.

———. *The World as Will and Idea,* trans. R. B. Haldane and J. Kemp. 1883; 3 vols; rpt. London: Kegan Paul, Trench, Trübner and Co., 1896.

Spinoza, Baruch. *Ethica.* In *The Chief Works of Benedict de Spinoza,* vol. 2; trans. and ed. R. H. M. Elwes. London: George Bell, 1909.

Stekel, Wilhelm. *Psychoanalysis and Suggestion Therapy: Their Technique, Applications, Results, Limits, Dangers.* London: Kegan Paul, Trench, Trubner and Co., 1923.

Stendhal [Henri Beyle]. *Le Rouge et le noir.* Paris: Garnier [n.d.].

———. *Armance.* Paris: Garnier, 1926.

Stephen, Karin. *Psychoanalysis and Medicine: A Study of the Wish to fall Ill.* Cambridge, Eng.: Cambridge University Press, 1933.

Stoppard, Tom. *Rosencrantz and Guildenstern Are Dead.* New York: Grove Press, 1968.

Swift, Jonathan. *The Works of the Rev. Jonathan Swift, D.D.,* ed. D. Laing Purves. Edinburgh: William P. Nimmo and Co., 1880. In particular: *Gulliver's Travels,* 110–216; *Journal to Stella,* 226–403; "A Letter of Advice to a Young Poet," 498–505.

———. *The Poems of Jonathan Swift, D. D.* 2 vols; ed. William Ernst Browning. London: George Bell, 1910.

———. *Polite Conversation, in Three Dialogs,* ed. George Sainstbury. London: Charles Whittingham and Co. at the Chiswick Press, 1892.

———. *A Tale of a Tub, to which is added The Battle of the Books and The Mechanical Operation of the Spirit* [1704], ed. A. C. Guthkelch and D. Nicol Smith. Oxford: Clarendon Press, 1920.

Taylor, Jeremy. *Holy Living and Dying, together with Prayers Containing the Whole Duty of a Christian and the Parts of Devotion Fitted to All Occasions, and Furnished for All Necessities.* London: Henry G. Bohn, 1851.

TCD: A College Miscellany. Dublin: Trinity College, 1923–30 [various issues].

Thomas à Kempis. *De Imitatione Christi: Libri Quatuor.* Paris: Librairie Tross, 1868.

———. *The Earliest English Translation of De Imitatione Christi, Now First Printed from a Ms. in the Library of Trinity College, Dublin, with various Readings from a Ms. in the University Library, Cambridge,* ed. John K. Ingram [Early English Text Society]. London: Kegan Paul, Trench, Trubner and Co., 1893.

Titus, Edward W., ed. *This Quarter* V.1 (September 1932); rpt. New York: Arno and *The New York Times,* 1969.

Toynbee, Paget. *Concise Dictionary of Proper Names and Notable Matters in the Works of Dante.* Oxford: Clarendon Press, 1914.

Walpole, Hugh. *Judith Paris.* London: Macmillan, 1931.

Welch, Robert, ed. *The Oxford Companion to Irish Literature.* Oxford: Clarendon Press, 1996.

Whitaker, Joseph. *An Almanack for the Year of Our Lord 1935.* London: Whitaker, 1934. [Also consulted: volumes for the years 1931 to 1937.]

Whitelaw, Billie. *Billie Whitelaw . . . Who He?* New York: St. Martin's Press, 1996.

Wilenski, R. H. *An Introduction to Dutch Art.* London: Faber and Gwyer, 1929.

Windelband, Dr. Wilhelm. *A History of Philosophy, with special reference to the formation and development of its problems and conceptions,* trans. James H. Tufts. 2nd ed., revised and enlarged, London: Macmillan, 1914.

Woodworth, Robert. *Contemporary Schools of Psychology.* New York: The Ronald Press, 1931.